Number One

The Corrie Herring Hooks Series

THE BIRD LIFE OF TEXAS

upper left: Scissor-tailed Flycatcher, *Muscivora forficata*, perched on mesquite (*Prosopis*)
lower: Painted Bunting, *Linaria ciris*

The Bird Life of Texas

By Harry C. Oberholser

Paintings by Louis Agassiz Fuertes

Edited, with distribution maps and additional material, by
Edgar B. Kincaid, Jr.

With the assistance of Suzanne Winckler and John L. Rowlett

VOLUME TWO

UNIVERSITY OF TEXAS PRESS, AUSTIN & LONDON

International Standard Book Number 0-292-70711-8
Library of Congress Catalog Card Number 73-21216
Copyright © 1974 by University of Texas Press
All Rights Reserved
Printed in the United States of America
Composition by G&S Typesetters, Austin, Texas
Text printed by The TJM Corporation, Baton Rouge, Louisiana
Color separations by Hart Graphics, Inc., Austin, Texas
Color plates printed by Steck-Warlick Company, Dallas, Texas
Binding by Universal Bookbindery, Inc., San Antonio, Texas

NAT
R

CONTENTS

ILLUSTRATIONS

THE BIRD LIFE OF TEXAS

Cotingas: Cotingidae

ROSE-THROATED BECARD, *Platypsaris aglaiae* (Lafresnaye)

SPECIES ACCOUNT

Arizona race formerly known as Xantus' Becard. A big-headed, flycatcherlike bird with a large, stout, slightly hooked bill. *Texas male*: dark gray (paler below) with black cap and nape and a rose throatpatch. *Texas female*: brown above with blackish cap and cinnamon tail; buffy collar (extending almost around nape) and under parts. *Arizona birds*: paler on back; almost whitish below. Length, 6¾ in.

RANGE: S.e. Arizona, s.w. New Mexico, and extreme s. Texas, south at low and moderate altitudes through Mexico to n. Costa Rica. Northern races winter chiefly in Mexico.

TEXAS: (See map.) *Breeding*: Early Apr. to late July (3 nests located, 13 mi. southwest of Harlingen, late Apr. and early May, 1943, L. I. Davis; pair tending 1 young, Santa Ana Nat. Wildlife Refuge area, June 27, 1943, L. I. Davis; nest building, Mission, Apr. 19, 1953, H. J. Bock; pair tending 3 or 4 fledglings, Anzalduas, July 5, 1972, J. C. Arvin) from near sea level to about 100 ft. Rare in Rio Grande delta, where found nesting in Hidalgo and Cameron cos. *Vagrant*: Accidental at Galveston (1 female sighted, May 1, 1955, Lawrence Tabony, S. G. Williams). *Winter*: Oct. 8 to Mar. 27. Rare, local, and irregular in Hidalgo and Cameron cos. One report from Zapata Co. (female, Oct. 8, 1972, Mr. and Mrs. O. C. Bone).

HAUNTS AND HABITS: Cotingas form a remarkable neotropical family of ninety species; most either exhibit highly ornamental plumage or build magnificent nests. The Rose-throated Becard, northernmost ranging of the Cotingidae, is in the splendid weaver category, but the male does have one vivid spot—his rose-colored throat.

In the more arid parts of its range, as in the southern tip of Texas and throughout lowland Tamaulipas, this becard is chiefly confined to trees growing along rivers. In Mexico it and many other tropical birds gather in strangler figs (*Ficus*) to eat the fruit; the present bird also gleans bugs from leaves and catches flying insects in the manner of tyrannids. The female, aided considerably by the male, suspends her globular nest from the tip of a long, drooping branch, often one that is

growing over water. Montezuma baldcypress (*Taxodium mucronatum*), black willow (*Salix nigra*), and American Sycamore (*Platanus occidentalis*) are some trees commonly used for nest support.

Most frequently heard vocalization of the Rosethroated Becard is a thin, slurred whistle which has been spelled *seeoo* by L. Irby Davis; the whistle is sometimes preceded by a low chatter. Becards are heard chiefly from early April to late July.

DETAILED ACCOUNT: ONE SUBSPECIES

TAMAULIPAS ROSE-THROATED BECARD, *Platypsaris aglaiae gravis* van Rossem

DESCRIPTION: *Adult male, nuptial plumage*: Acquired by wear from winter plumage. Pileum and nape glossy black, more brownish anteriorly; remainder of upper surface, including wing-coverts, deep mouse gray, some feathers of back and scapulars with concealed pure white basal spots; tail dark hair brown; wing-quills (second primary from outermost very short) dark hair brown or chaetura drab; sides of head rather brownish deep mouse gray; sides of neck rather deep mouse gray; chin rather brownish light mouse gray; sides rather darker and more in-

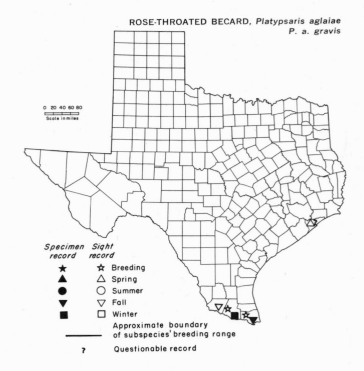

ROSE-THROATED BECARD, *Platypsaris aglaiae*
P. a. gravis

0 20 40 60 80
Scale in miles

Specimen record	Sight record	
★	☆	Breeding
▲	△	Spring
●	○	Summer
▼	▽	Fall
■	□	Winter

—— Approximate boundary of subspecies' breeding range

? Questionable record

clining to brownish neutral gray; breast light mouse gray; crissum and middle of abdomen rather brownish light mouse gray; middle of throat rose red; lining of wing and axillars brownish gray. Maxilla black or blackish plumbeous, tip paler; mandible and rictus plumbeous blue, edge of commissure dull white; inside of mouth orange; iris umber brown; legs and feet dull bluish gray or plumbeous blue. *Adult male, winter*: Acquired by complete postnuptial molt. Similar to nuptial adult male. *Adult female, nuptial (brown phase)*: Acquired by wear from winter. Second primary not short. Pileum and hindneck dull brownish slate color, rather paler on forehead, where sometimes tinged with buff; hindneck dull cinnamon buff, forming narrow collar; back, scapulars, and lesser wing-coverts raw umber, broccoli brown, or dull rufescent hair brown; tail buffy brown, somewhat grayish on middle feathers, and tending toward cinnamon on base of inner webs; wing-quills fuscous, edged exteriorly with buffy brown and anteriorly with dull cinnamon; greater and median wing-coverts similar to back but broadly edged with dull cinnamon; ear-coverts and most of sides of neck light clay color; lower parts pale clay color or dull cinnamon buff; whitish on chin and middle of abdomen; lining of wing clay color. *Adult female, nuptial (gray phase)*: Similar to brown phase, but pileum and hindneck neutral gray instead of dull brown. *Adult female, winter*: Acquired by complete postnuptial molt. Like corresponding phase of nuptial adult female. *Male, third winter*: Acquired by complete postnuptial molt. Like adult in winter. *Male, second nuptial*: Acquired by wear from second winter. Similar to nuptial adult male, but many lower surface much suffused with brown or olive; tail feathers terminally mottled or edged with cinnamon; pink of throat usually more restricted. *Male, second winter*: Acquired by complete postnuptial molt. Similar to second nuptial male. *Male, first nuptial*: Acquired by partial prenuptial molt and wear from first winter. Differs from nuptial adult male much as does juvenal male, including lack of very short second primary which instead is similar in length to adjoining quills. *Male, first winter*: Acquired by partial postjuvenal molt. Similar to nuptial adult female, but top of head black; upper surface darker and more grayish brown; lower surface lighter and more grayish buff; throat often light salmon pink. *Male, juvenal*: Acquired by complete postnatal molt. Similar to nuptial adult male, but pileum duller and darker; upper parts wholly or partly light russet or cinnamon rufous; tail, wing-coverts, and outer edges of wing-quills light russet or hazel; lower parts similar to those of adult female, but middle of throat with patch of light rose color. Maxilla blackish brown; mandible flesh color tinged with brown or lilac. *Female, juvenal*: Acquired by complete postnatal molt. Similar to adult female, but pileum duller and more overlaid with cinnamon; upper surface mostly bright cinnamon rufous or ochraceous tawny; back

rather duller; wings and tail as in juvenal male; lower parts more deeply cinnamon buff or ochraceous than in adult female. *Natal*: White.

MEASUREMENTS: *Adult male*: Wing, 89.9–97.1 (average, 93.7) mm.; tail, 67.6–75.9 (71.9); bill (exposed culmen), 16.0–17.5 (16.5); tarsus, 21.1–22.1 (21.4); middle toe without claw, 13.0–14.5 (13.7). *Adult female*: Wing, 89.9–98.1 (93.7); tail, 68.1–75.4 (72.4); bill, 15.0–18.0 (16.5); tarsus, 21.6–23.1 (22.4); middle toe, 14.0–15.5 (14.7).

RANGE: Extreme s. Texas, south to w. Nuevo León and e. Tamaulipas.

TEXAS: *Breeding*: See species account. *Winter*: Four specimens: Hidalgo Co., 6 mi. south of McAllen (2 on Dec. 29, 1 on Dec. 30, 1948, G. M. Sutton); Cameron Co., Brownsville (Oct. 30, 1891, F. B. Armstrong).

NESTING: *Nest*: In forests on lower tropical mountain slopes or bottomlands (subtropics into Tropics); at or near end of branch of tree or bush; hanging globular nest, approximately 15 × 8 in., with entrance at side near bottom; made of grass, strips of bark, weed stalks, Spanishmoss and tendrils, usually with streamers of grass or Spanishmoss hanging from lower parts. *Eggs*: 2–4; oval; white, cream white, or pale pinkish buff; with small spots and scratches of pale reddish brown and dark gray and markings of pinkish red at larger end; average size, 24.1 × 17.8 mm.

[JAMAICAN BECARD, *Platypsaris niger* (Gmelin)

Profile much like that of an American flycatcher. Has big head, thick bill, and short tail. *Male*: glossy black above; sooty black below; in flight, shows small white wing-patch. *Female*: rufescent above, grayish on back; cinnamon on sides of head and throat, becoming grayish white on breast. Length, 8 in.

RANGE: Jamaica.

TEXAS: *Hypothetical*: One sighting, first for North America: Galveston Co., middle part of Galveston Island (1 adult female studied at close range, Sept. 23, 1951, G. G. Williams, S. G. Williams, Mr. and Mrs. C. W. Hamilton). Hurricane had crossed Jamaica and gone inland in Tamaulipas and Veracruz, Mexico, three weeks previous, perhaps accounting for sighting.]

Tyrant Flycatchers: Tyrannidae

EASTERN KINGBIRD, *Tyrannus tyrannus* (Linnaeus)

SPECIES ACCOUNT   *See colorplate 18*

A large tyrant (American) flycatcher. Has broad, slightly hooked bill with bristlelike feathers at base. Blackish head (orange-red crown-streak seldom visible) and upper parts; broad white terminal band on black, rounded tail; white under parts. Length, 8½ in.; wingspan, 14¾; weight, 1¼ oz.

RANGE: N. British Columbia to Nova Scotia, south to extreme n.e. California, n.e. New Mexico, c. Texas, Gulf coast, and s. Florida. Winters mainly in Peru and Bolivia.

TEXAS: (See map.) *Breeding*: Late Apr. to early Aug. (eggs, May 2 to June 22; young in nest to July 31) from near sea level to 4,000 ft. Common to uncommon in much of northern Panhandle, north central Texas (south to Waco), and eastern third; scarce and local in central portions, south rarely to San Antonio and central coast (formerly regular). *Migration*: Late Mar. or early Apr. to mid-May; mid-Aug. to early Oct. (extremes: Feb. 23, June 1; Aug. 1, Nov. 17). Very common (sometimes abundant) to fairly common through most of eastern two-thirds and northern Panhandle; scarce in southern Panhandle and western Edwards Plateau; rare through eastern Trans-Pecos; casual in western Trans-Pecos. *Winter*: No specimen, but a few sightings from late Dec. to late Jan. along coast and in Rio Grande delta; inland sightings from Harrison (no details) and Bexar cos.

HAUNTS AND HABITS: Nomenclaturally, the Eastern Kingbird could be termed the most typical of the world's 365 species of tyrant flycatchers. From its technical name, *Tyrannus tyrannus*, naturalists erected the family name Tyrannidae. With birds instead of words, however, the Eastern is more typical of kingbirds than of flycatchers in general: The species wears a golden crown, it lives mostly in open country, and it rules its domain like a tyrant by chasing off hawks and crows.

The Eastern Kingbird occurs in various open and semiopen habitats. It frequents prairies, pastures, fields, and trees along streams; it is also found in clearings in pine woods and on woodland edges. Along roadsides the Eastern perches on telephone wires and barbed wire fences. Another favored vantage is atop a tall weed stalk or bush that offers an unobstructed view

and from which the bird guards its territory or looks for insect prey. It is seen for the most part singly or in pairs, but during migration, flocks up to seventy-five or more birds are occasionally noted.

In flight, the Eastern Kingbird can be swift, especially when pursuing prey. Ordinary flight is rather slow and hovering; at times the bird glides on motionless wings. To take a bath it flies down into the water, flaps its wings therein, and then returns to a perch to dry its feathers. More frequently this flycatcher flies upward to catch a passing beetle, wasp, bee, fly, or dragonfly. The Eastern, like most tyrannids, typically captures its prey by dashing into the air from its lookout perch, then returning to the same or a nearby perch. This and other large flycatchers eat fruits of hackberry, dogwood, elderberry, etc., by flying out and vigorously snatching them from twigs as if the berries were insects on the verge of taking flight. During territory-courtship display, the male flies rather low with rapid, very short wing-beats and with tail spread, simultaneously calling in a peculiar tone.

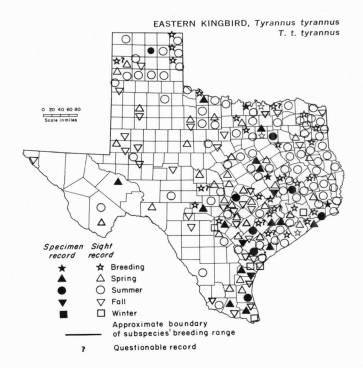

EASTERN KINGBIRD, *Tyrannus tyrannus*
T. t. tyrannus

0 20 40 60 80
Scale in miles

Specimen record	Sight record	
★	☆	Breeding
▲	△	Spring
●	○	Summer
▼	▽	Fall
■	□	Winter

——— Approximate boundary of subspecies' breeding range

? Questionable record

At most times a noisy bird, the Eastern utters its sharp, harsh calls both on the wing and while perching. One is a *dzee* several times repeated. Another is something like *kit-kit-kitter-kitter*. A nasal *dzeeb* is also sounded. The Eastern Kingbird, like most flycatchers, has a song which it sings at or just before dawn and seldom at any other time. This song has been described as *i-i-i-i, ee, tweea*; in common with almost all vocalizations of *Tyrannus tyrannus*, it is squeaky and very high pitched for such a large bird. Singing is mainly from early April to mid-July. (Note: In the following flycatcher write-ups, dawn songs are mentioned chiefly when they are of substantial aid in identifying the species.)

DETAILED ACCOUNT: TWO SUBSPECIES

EASTERN EASTERN KINGBIRD, *Tyrannus tyrannus tyrannus* (Linnaeus)

No races recognized by A.O.U. check-list, 1957 (see Appendix A).

DESCRIPTION: *Adult male, nuptial plumage*: Acquired by partial prenuptial molt. Top and sides of head dull black; crown with concealed patch of orange or orange-red and white; remainder of upper surface, including exposed surface of lesser wing-coverts, slate color or blackish slate; upper tail-coverts dull black; tail black with broad white tip, outer feathers more brownish, and outermost with narrow white edge; wing-quills dark hair brown or chaetura drab, slightly darker at tips, and secondaries with narrow white edgings on external webs; greater and median wing-coverts chaetura drab or chaetura black, very narrowly edged with brownish white; lower surface white, breast washed with pale smoke gray; lining of wing hair brown mixed with white. Bill black but slightly brownish at base of mandible; iris dark brown; legs and feet grayish black or brownish black; claws black. *Adult male, winter*: Acquired by complete postnuptial molt. Practically identical with nuptial adult male. *Adult female, nuptial*: Acquired by partial prenuptial molt. Similar to nuptial adult male, but tips of outermost primaries less abruptly narrowed; orange crown-patch smaller. *Adult female, winter*: Acquired by complete postnuptial molt. Like nuptial adult female. *Male, first nuptial*: Acquired by partial prenuptial molt. Like nuptial adult male. *Male, first winter*: Acquired by complete postjuvenal molt. Similar to first nuptial male, but colored crown-patch smaller and of paler yellow. *Female, first nuptial*: Acquired by partial prenuptial molt. Like nuptial adult female. *Female, first winter*: Acquired by complete postjuvenal molt. Similar to first nuptial female, but yellow of crown-patch paler and less extensive. *Juvenal*: Acquired by complete postnatal molt. Similar to nuptial adults, but tips of two outer pairs of primaries not emarginate; upper surface paler and duller, fuscous or brownish slate gray with narrow bars of paler brown, particularly on pileum and rump; crown without concealed patch of orange and white; wing-quills and upper coverts duller and lighter fuscous or dark hair brown; wing-coverts conspicuously edged with buffy white or pale buff, wing-quills tipped with same; outer margins of secondaries more broadly white; white tip of tail narrower and tinged with pale brown. Bill, legs, and feet black; iris dark brown. *Natal*: Pileum pale pinkish buff, dull pinkish buff, cartridge buff, or dull white; rump buffy white.

MEASUREMENTS: *Adult male*: Wing, 113.0–121.9 (average, 117.3) mm.; tail, 83.6–90.9 (85.9); bill (exposed culmen), 15.5–18.5 (16.8); tarsus, 17.5–20.1 (18.8); middle toe without claw, 13.0–14.7 (14.2); white tip of middle tail feather, 6.1–13.0 (9.1). *Adult female*: Wing, 109.0–117.1 (112.8); tail, 77.0–84.1 (80.5); bill, 15.0–18.5 (16.3); tarsus, 18.0–19.0 (18.5); middle toe, 13.0–14.5 (13.7); white tip, 5.8–13.0 (10.2).

RANGE: N. Ontario to Nova Scotia, south to s.e. Texas and s. Florida. Winters from Costa Rica through n.w. South America to s. Bolivia.

TEXAS: *Breeding*: Collected north to Hutchinson, east to Cooke (eggs) and Jefferson, south to Refugio, west to Kerr cos. *Migration*: Collected outside breeding range west to Pecos Co. Common.

NESTING: *Nest*: In open country, upland or bottomland, often near rivers or other bodies of water, in meadows, borders of marshes, or cultivated lands; in bush, tree, on stump, fence post, or rail, not very high above ground or even on the ground; rude bowl though neatly lined; made of twigs, roots, weed stalks, hair, twine, and vegetable down; lined with moss, wool, feathers, horsehair, fine vegetable fibers, fine grass, and vegetable down. *Eggs*: 2–5, usually 3–4; short ovate to elongate ovate; cream white; irregularly spotted with reddish brown and dull heliotrope or lavender gray, but sometimes unmarked; average size, 24.1 × 18.3 mm.

WESTERN EASTERN KINGBIRD, *Tyrannus tyrannus hespericola* Oberholser

No races recognized by A.O.U. check-list, 1957 (see Appendix A).

DESCRIPTION: *Adult male and female, nuptial plumage*: Similar to *T. t. tyrannus*, but wing, tail, and tarsus longer; white tip of tail decidedly broader; upper surface with less black or slate mixture, thus more uniform and rather lighter.

MEASUREMENTS: *Adult male*: Wing, 119.1–127.0 (average, 121.7) mm.; tail, 81.0–90.9 (87.6); bill (exposed culmen), 15.0–18.5 (16.8); tarsus, 20.1–22.6 (21.4); middle toe without claw, 11.9–13.5 (13.0); white tip of middle tail feather, 9.9–14.5 (12.2). *Adult female*: Wing, 111.0–119.4 (115.8); tail, 78.0–86.6 (81.8); bill, 15.0–17.0 (16.3); tarsus, 18.5–22.1 (20.6); middle toe, 11.9–14.5 (13.2); white tip, 10.9–13.0 (12.2).

RANGE: S. Mackenzie, south to s.w. California and n. New Mexico. Winters probably in South America.

TEXAS: *Migration*: One specimen: Calhoun Co., s.w. Matagorda Island (Apr. 7, 1937, A. R. Hines).

[GRAY KINGBIRD, *Tyrannus dominicensis* (Gmelin)

Resembles Eastern Kingbird, but bigger; has much larger bill, giving bird a bull-headed or top-heavy look; pale gray (not blackish) upper parts; blackish ear-coverts; notched (not rounded) tail without terminal white band. Length, 9¼ in.; wingspan, 14¾.

RANGE: Coasts of s.e. South Carolina (rarely), Georgia (rarely), Florida, West Indies, and offshore islands and n. mainland of Venezuela. Winters from Hispaniola to Colombia, Venezuela, and Guianas, rarely to coast of Yucatán Peninsula.

TEXAS: *Hypothetical*: Two sightings: Harris Co., La Porte (Oct. 25, 1958, Clinton Snyder, Linda Snyder); Aransas Co., Rockport (1 observed in wake of hurricane, Aug. 31, 1951, Connie Hagar, G. G. Williams, S. G. Williams).]

THICK-BILLED KINGBIRD, *Tyrannus crassirostris* Swainson

SPECIES ACCOUNT

Distinguished from similar *Tyrannus* species (Tropical, Western, and Cassin's) by largely whitish under parts—i.e., bright white throat, grayish white breast, and pale yellow (sometimes almost white) belly. The large thick bill gives bird a bull-headed look. Length, 9 in.

RANGE: U.S.-Mexico border (n. Sonora, s.e. Arizona, s.w. New Mexico), south along Pacific slope of w. and s. Mexico to n.w. Chiapas. Apparently winters south of Sonora to Guatemala (one record).

TEXAS: *Casual*: Two records, both from Brewster Co., Big Bend Nat. Park: Chisos Mts. Basin, 4,900–5,100 ft. (1 seen, June 21, 1967, initially by Michel and Mr. and Mrs. O. R. Henderson, later by R. H. Wauer, R. C. Nelson; photographed by Mr. Henderson; details of occurrence and black-and-white photograph subsequently published by Wauer, 1967, *Southwestern Naturalist* 12: 485–486); mesquite floodplain of Rio Grande in eastern part of park (1 seen on Audubon Christmas Bird Count, Dec. 23, 1970, Wauer).

HAUNTS AND HABITS: The few nesting Thick-billed Kingbirds in the United States have been found in riparian situations in southwestern deserts, especially in sycamores. In Mexico, *T. crassirostris* frequents patches of tall semiarid brush or edges of woodlands from sea level to five thousand feet. From rather high perches (30–50 ft.) in open trees it makes vigorous sallies—wings quivering and crest erect—for insects.

Distinctive calls of the Thickbill are a loud vibrato, *weeerr* or *kiterreer*, and a sharply accented *chweet* or *cut-a-reep* inflected upward toward the end. The dawn song, heard at the first of the nesting season, is a series of phrases, each described as *wit wu-wu-wu-wuwuah wit-wuah wu-weeea-yah* (L. I. Davis).

CHANGES: The Thick-billed Kingbird is one of several tropical species of dry semiopen terrain that has moved northward since the middle of the twentieth century. *T. crassirostris* was first taken in the United States in Guadalupe Canyon, junction of southeastern Arizona and southwestern New Mexico, June 4, 1958, by Seymour Levy. Since 1962 a small colony has resided in summer along Sonoita Creek near Patagonia, Arizona. The next jump was to the Texas Big Bend, three hundred miles east of its southwestern New Mexico nesting ground. The June 21, 1967, Texas individual exhibited aggressive behavior toward other birds as if it were trying to establish a nesting territory. However, through 1971 there was no firm evidence of nesting in the Lone Star State.

Causes of the northward movement remain obscure but are likely connected with the massive dam and irrigation projects that have taken place in recent years in Mexico, especially in Sonora and Sinaloa. Impoundments inundate scarce riparian nesting trees, such as may have escaped being chopped down by dam construction workers. Pesticides foul up insect fauna of irrigated regions. Some of these kingbirds apparently wander far in an attempt to locate less poisoned and less cutover terrain.

NOTE: The Texas individuals probably belong to *T. c. pompalis*, the only race known to range north of the Tropic of Cancer, but field observation and photographs usually cannot be used for subspecific identification.

TROPICAL KINGBIRD, *Tyrannus melancholicus* Vieillot

SPECIES ACCOUNT

Olive-backed Kingbird and Fork-tailed Kingbird of various writers. Texas race is sometimes regarded as a separate species; it is then called Couch's Kingbird or Thornbrush Kingbird, *Tyrannus couchii*. A yellow-bellied kingbird with no white in its well-notched, dusky brown tail. Gray head (orange streak on crown usually concealed) with blackish mask through eye; olive upper parts; whitish chin, throat; yellowish (not gray) breast usually washed with olive. Length, 9¼ in.; wingspan, 15¾.

RANGE: S.e. Arizona and s. Texas, south at low and moderate altitudes through Mexico and Central America to c. Argentina. Winters from Sinaloa and s. Texas southward, though northeastern race often largely retreats south of Tropic of Cancer.

TEXAS: (See map.) *Breeding*: Early or mid-Apr. to late June (eggs, May 5 to June 2) from near sea level to 400 ft. Common to fairly common in Rio Grande delta north irregularly to Zapata and Jim Hogg cos.; increasingly scarce north to Alice and Sinton, probably to Laredo and possibly to Beeville vicinities, where rare. *Vagrant*: Wanders, chiefly during nonbreeding season, north along Rio Grande to Big Bend Nat. Park and El Paso, where casual, and north along coast to Bolivar Peninsula, where casual. Accidental in Kerr Co. (see detailed account). *Winter*: Late Dec. to late Mar.

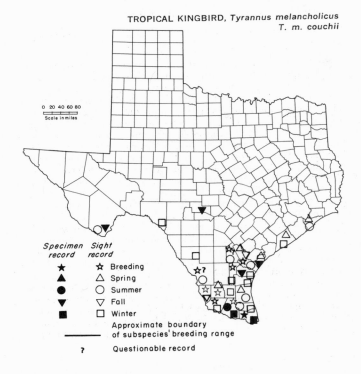

TROPICAL KINGBIRD, *Tyrannus melancholicus*
T. m. couchii

0 20 40 60 80
Scale in miles

Specimen record	Sight record	
★	☆	Breeding
▲	△	Spring
●	○	Summer
▼	▽	Fall
■	□	Winter

——— Approximate boundary of subspecies' breeding range

? Questionable record

Irregularly fairly common to scarce in Rio Grande delta; scarce north to Falfurrias, rarely to Alice; increasingly rare north to Del Rio, Corpus Christi, and Rockport, where casual.

HAUNTS AND HABITS: As is expected of hot country birds, the Tropical Kingbird is a bit brighter of plumage and less migratory of habit than others of its genus. In south Texas, this species lives in groves and trees beside lakes, ponds, resacas, and the Rio Grande. It also inhabits mesquite (*Prosopis glandulosa*) trees—such as have so far escaped bulldozers—some distance from water. It is one of the relatively few subtropical birds which comes freely to cities and towns. Here it perches on wires, fences, houses, and upper branches of ornamental shrubs and trees. Frequently it mounts to the tops of sizable native trees—tepeguaje or great lead-tree (*Leucaena pulverulenta*), Texas ebony (*Pithecellobium flexicaule*), and others—where it calls, bickers, and makes quick round trips to snap up flying insects. Less solitary than some of the small flycatchers, it gathers, particularly during the nonbreeding season, into loose companies.

Flight and behavior of the Tropical Kingbird are very much like the Eastern's; its wing-beats are rapid, and flight ordinarily not prolonged or very swift, but often more or less hesitant and hovering. It is generally not shy and may be approached within a reasonable distance.

Calls of the Tropical include a nasal *queer* and *chiqueer*, like freakishly high-pitched Cassin's Kingbird notes. A long, fast, breezy *bereeeeer* seems to be characteristic only of *T. m. couchii*, the south Texas–northeastern Mexico race. This bird is heard along the Rio Grande chiefly from late March to early August.

DETAILED ACCOUNT: ONE SUBSPECIES

COUCH'S TROPICAL KINGBIRD, *Tyrannus melancholicus couchii* Baird

DESCRIPTION: *Adult male, nuptial plumage*: Acquired by partial prenuptial molt. Pileum and sides of head neutral gray; ear-coverts and lores rather darker; central part of crown serpentine green with concealed patch of orange chrome and yellow mixed with white; back, scapulars, and rump serpentine green; upper tail-coverts and tail between fuscous and buffy brown, edges slightly paler; wing-quills of same color, secondaries broadly edged on outer webs with yellowish white, tertials with brownish white; wing-coverts rather lighter than wing-quills with broad pale brownish or grayish margins but forming no distinct wing-band; chin and throat grayish white; remainder of lower surface dull lemon chrome, paling to penard yellow or picric yellow on crissum and shaded with olive across breast and jugulum; lining of wing citrine yellow. Bill black or brownish black; base of mandible more brownish, iris dark brown; legs and feet black or brownish black. *Adult male, winter*: Acquired by complete postnuptial molt. Similar to nuptial adult male but rather more deeply colored. *Adult female, nuptial*: Acquired by partial prenuptial molt. Similar to nuptial adult male, but tips of primaries much less abruptly narrowed and tips themselves much less sharply pointed; orange crown-patch usually smaller. *Adult female, winter*: Acquired by complete postnuptial molt. Similar to nuptial adult female but coloration somewhat richer. *Male, first nuptial*: Acquired by partial prenuptial molt. Similar to nuptial adult male but usually with some retained juvenal wing-quills. *Male, first winter*: Acquired by partial postjuvenal molt. Similar to first nuptial male, but without concealed patch of orange or yellow on crown and with all juvenal tail feathers and wing-quills retained. *Female, first nuptial*: Acquired by partial prenuptial molt. Similar to first nuptial male, but differs as does nuptial adult female from nuptial adult male. *Female, first winter*: Acquired by partial postjuvenal molt. Similar to first nuptial female but without yellow crown-patch and with wing-quills and tail feathers of juvenal. *Juvenal*: Acquired by complete postnatal molt. Similar to nuptial adults, but upper parts much duller and more brownish, pileum and hindneck brownish gray, back similar but more tinged with olive green; crown without concealed orange or yellow spot; upper tail-coverts tipped with tawny or russet; tail feathers of more rufescent brown, edgings tawny or ochraceous tawny, tips dull pale cinnamon; upper wing-coverts conspicuously margined and tipped with cinnamon or pale buff; lower parts duller. Bill blackish brown. *Natal*: Pale pinkish buff to slightly buffy white; down feathers whitish at base.

MEASUREMENTS: *Adult male*: Wing, 124.0–131.0 (average, 126.7) mm.; tail, 101.1–108.0 (104.4); bill (exposed culmen), 21.1–24.4 (22.4); tarsus, 18.0–20.1 (19.3); middle toe without claw, 14.5–16.0 (15.2). *Adult female*: Wing, 115.6–122.5 (119.4); tail, 89.4–102.1 (94.7); bill, 20.1–23.1 (21.9); tarsus, 18.0–21.1 (19.3); middle toe, 14.0–15.5 (14.7).

RANGE: S. Texas, south to Puebla and n. Veracruz.

TEXAS: *Breeding*: Collected in Cameron and Hidalgo cos. *Vagrant*: Two specimens: Brewster Co., Big Bend Nat. Park, Cottonwood Campground (1 immature, Sept. 2, 1968, R. H. Wauer; identified by A. R. Phillips); Kerr Co., Turtle Creek (Sept. 11, 1908, H. Lacey). *Winter*: Taken in Aransas (Sept. 11), Cameron, and Hidalgo cos.

NESTING: *Nest*: In woodlands, brush, on marshy or bushy margins of lakes, and in cultivated areas; in tree or bush, usually not high above ground; bowl composed of twigs, Spanishmoss, weed stalks, and leaves; lined with rootlets and sometimes Spanishmoss. *Eggs*: 3–5; ovate or elongate ovate; cream color or rich buff; spotted with dark brown and lilac over most of surface; average size, 24.4 × 18.5 mm.

WESTERN KINGBIRD, *Tyrannus verticalis* Say

SPECIES ACCOUNT   *See colorplate 19*

Also known as Arkansas Kingbird. A yellow-bellied kingbird; has a white line along each side of its black, square-tipped tail. Pale gray head (orange streak on crown usually concealed) and breast; olive gray upper parts; whitish chin, throat. Length, 8¾ in.; wingspan, 15½; weight, 1¾ oz.

RANGE: S. interior British Columbia to s. Manitoba, south through w. United States and Great Plains to n. Baja California, Sonora, Chihuahua, and s. Texas. Winters mainly from s.w. and s. Mexico to n. Nicaragua; also along s.e. U.S. coast (a few).

TEXAS: (See map.) *Breeding*: Late Apr. to late July (eggs, May 16 to July 12) from near sea level to 4,800 ft. Very common to uncommon in most of western two-thirds (maximum densities from northwestern Panhandle to El Paso), east locally and somewhat irregularly to 96th meridian; uncommon and local in south Texas brush country; rare on upper coast. *Migration*: Mid- or late Apr. to late May; mid-Aug. to late Oct. (extremes: Mar. 5, June 7; July 15, Dec. 1). Very common to fairly common through most of western two-thirds; uncommon to scarce through eastern third and along central coast. *Winter*: No specimen, but a scattering of sightings from late Dec. into early Jan. along Rio Grande and Gulf coast.

HAUNTS AND HABITS: Open flatlands of the West with a few scattered trees—typically cottonwoods—furnish prime habitat for the Western, the most widespread of North American yellow-bellied kingbirds. It usually occurs singly or in pairs, although loose aggregations sometimes appear where the bird is common. In Texas, Westerns are generally seen perched on or flycatching near an exposed tree limb, utility pole or wire, or fence.

In flight and behavior this kingbird closely resembles its relative the Eastern. The Western, however, is not quite so pugnacious toward either its own kind or other species. It appears somewhat less aggressive toward larger birds, particularly hawks, but will drive off ravens or crows intruding in the vicinity of its nest. Also it is not uncommon for several nesting pairs of Western Kingbirds to occupy the same tree or share a small grove.

A common note of *Tyrannus verticalis* is a sharp *whit*. It also has a variety of bickering calls and twitters; many of these are similar to those of the Eastern, although lower pitched. Dawn song and other vocalizations are most frequent from late April to late July.

CHANGES: During the 1950's, the Western Kingbird expanded as a regular breeder eastward to Austin and southward to Eagle Pass and Cotulla; in the late 1960's, it became established locally as a nester in the Rio Grande delta. Probably man's constant opening up of mesquite woodlands, his irrigating activities, and his

stringing of more and more wires—used as lookout perches by this and related birds—have been factors in this spread.

DETAILED ACCOUNT: NO SUBSPECIES

DESCRIPTION: *Adult male, nuptial plumage*: Acquired by partial prenuptial molt. Four outer primaries sinuate on inner webs and much narrowed at tips, outermost very narrow and attenuate. Top and sides of head, except malar region, and hindneck brownish neutral gray; ear-coverts rather darker; middle of crown washed with olive green and with concealed patch of orange chrome or orpiment orange mixed with white and yellow; back and rump similar to hindneck but washed with olive green; upper tail-coverts dull black, shorter feathers fuscous black or fuscous, edged with olive gray; tail black, very narrow tip pale brownish, outer web of outermost feather pure white; wing-quills and coverts rather rufescent hair brown, all feathers with rather paler margins, secondaries with brownish white edgings on terminal portion; lining of wing light yellowish olive; throat and jugulum brownish pale neutral gray; remainder of lower surface canary yellow, crissum paler, near primrose yellow; chin dull rather brownish pallid neutral gray, sometimes dull white. Bill black, bluish black, or dark brown; iris dark brown or hazel; legs and feet bluish black, dark slate color, or dark brown; claws dull black. *Adult male, winter*: Acquired by complete postnuptial molt. Similar to nuptial adult male, but head and lower parts rather more deeply colored. *Adult female, nuptial*: Acquired by partial prenuptial molt. Similar to nuptial adult male, but tips of outermost primaries much less abruptly narrowed and not so sharply pointed at tips, only three at all narrowed; orange-red crown-spot smaller. *Adult female, winter*: Acquired by complete postnuptial molt. Similar to nuptial adult female, but rather more richly colored. *Male, first nuptial*: Acquired by partial prenuptial molt. Similar to nuptial adult male, but with wings and tail retained from juvenal. *Male, first winter*: Acquired by partial postjuvenal molt. Very similar to first nuptial male. *Female, first nuptial*: Acquired by partial prenuptial molt. Similar to first nuptial male, but yellow crown-patch smaller; tips of outer primaries only slightly narrowed. *Female, first winter*: Acquired by partial postjuvenal molt. Similar to first nuptial female. *Juvenal*: Acquired by complete postnatal molt. Similar to nuptial adults, but outer primaries little narrowed at tips, only outermost noticeably so. Coloration paler, duller, and much more brownish on upper surface, latter grayish olive on back, paler and more grayish on head, crown without concealed orange or yellow spot; rump and upper tail-coverts with pale brownish edgings; upper wing-coverts conspicuously edged with pale buff; outer secondaries with broader whitish edgings; lower parts duller and paler; gray of breast more brownish and entirely overlaid with dull pale grayish buff. Bill smaller and dull brown. *Natal*: Cream white to very pale tilleul buff.

MEASUREMENTS: *Adult male*: Wing, 125.0–134.6 (average, 130.3) mm.; tail, 87.1–97.6 (93.5); bill (exposed culmen), 16.0–21.1 (18.8); tarsus, 16.5–20.1 (18.8); middle toe without claw, 12.4–15.0 (13.7). *Adult female*: Wing, 118.6–129.5 (122.2); tail, 81.5–94.0 (86.9); bill, 16.5–19.6 (18.3); tarsus, 18.0–19.6 (18.5); middle toe, 13.5–14.5 (13.7).

TEXAS: *Breeding*: Collected north to Dallam and Wheeler, east to Kaufman (eggs), south to Hidalgo and Webb, west to Presidio and Culberson cos. *Migration*: Collected north to Oldham, east to Dallas, south to Aransas and Cameron, west to Brewster cos.

NESTING: *Nest*: In open country on lower parts of mountains, on plains and mesas in timber along streams, and even in clumps of trees in deserts; on tree, bush, or utility pole, usually not high above ground, but sometimes up to 50 ft., occasionally on rocky ledge or in nest of some other bird; bulky bowl of grass, weed stalks, leaves, string, paper, rags, and similar materials; lined with cotton, wool, and finer materials of nest. *Eggs*: 3–6,

WESTERN KINGBIRD, *Tyrannus verticalis*

0 20 40 60 80
Scale in miles

Specimen record / Sight record

★ / ☆ Breeding
▲ / △ Spring
● / ○ Summer
▼ / ▽ Fall
■ / □ Winter

——— Approximate boundary of subspecies' breeding range

? Questionable record

usually 4; short ovate or rounded ovate to elongate ovate; light cream color; blotched with lavender and brownish purple, usually near larger end; average size, 23.6 × 17.5 mm.

CASSIN'S KINGBIRD, *Tyrannus vociferans* Swainson

Species Account

Closely resembles Western Kingbird, but darker gray of head, back, and breast contrasts abruptly with white chin; blackish tail lacks white edgings on sides but sometimes has whitish tip. Length, 9 in.; wingspan, 16; weight, 1¾ oz.

range: C. California to s.e. Montana and extreme n.w. Oklahoma, south through highlands to c. Mexico. Winters mainly from s. California, s. Arizona, and n. Mexico to Guatemala.

texas: (See map.) *Breeding*: Probably mid-May to late July (young in nest near Alpine, June 9, 1935, Lovie Whitaker; nest found in Guadalupe Mts., F. R. Gehlbach) from about 4,000 to 7,000 ft. Very common to uncommon in Culberson, Jeff Davis, and northern Brewster cos.; scarce in southern Brewster Co. *Migration*: Early Apr. to late May; mid-Aug. to early Oct. (extremes: Mar. 9, June 4; July 31, Oct. 16). Very common to uncommon through much of Trans-Pecos; rare in remainder of western third from western Panhandle to Pecos River Valley and Del Rio region; casual along coast. *Winter*: Late Dec. to early Mar. No specimen, but casual in western third. Sightings in flat mesquite country at Norias, Kenedy Co. (Dec. 22, 1965, Feb. 27, and Mar. 1, 1966, E. B. Kincaid, Jr., J. L. Rowlett).

haunts and habits: Cassin's Kingbird is one of the characteristic sights and sounds of grassy pinyon-juni-

per-oak uplands of the West. Apparently, conditions are exactly suited for it in the Davis Mountains of the Trans-Pecos since it is a numerous summer resident there. During the nesting season, its low-pitched, husky voice sounds all day long and even into the night about camp grounds where lanterns and flashlights are especially bright. The few individuals which winter in Texas sometimes select a flat mesquite area near the coast, very different from their summer highland home. While generally observed singly and in pairs, this fly-catcher also appears throughout its range in scattered companies like other kingbirds.

Although the Cassin's and Western kingbirds are similar in appearance, there are some differences in behavior; the Western is typically noisier, more active, and appears more "nervous," while Cassin's is "calmer" and generally quieter. Like the Western, it perches on an exposed tree limb, telephone wire, or fence where it waits for bees, wasps, and other winged insects; especially during fall and winter, it also eats wild fruits, often in surprisingly large quantities.

Cassin's vocalizations are lower and more nasal than those of the Western. Common notes are heavy *queer*'s, *chi-queer*'s, and *chi-bew*'s. The bird also utters a clamoring *ki-dear ki-dear, ki-dear*, etc.; this raucous outburst often begins in predawn hours during the breeding season. The species is noisy from April through July.

Detailed Account: One Subspecies

COMMON CASSIN'S KINGBIRD, *Tyrannus vociferans vociferans* Swainson

description: *Adult male, nuptial plumage*: Acquired by partial prenuptial molt. Five outer primaries emarginate on inner webs, tips very narrow and attenuate. Top and sides of head and of hindneck, except malar region, brownish rather deep neutral gray, center of crown with concealed spot of orange chrome mixed with white and yellow; back, scapulars, rump, and shorter upper tail-coverts brownish neutral gray, mixed with dull olive green; longest upper tail-coverts and tail fuscous black, broad tip pale brown or light drab, outer edge of outermost tail feather similar; wing-quills and upper wing-coverts dark drab or light hair brown, quills with brownish white or greenish white edgings on outer webs except terminal portions of primaries; wing-coverts broadly tipped and lesser and median series edged on outer webs with brownish white; chin and malar stripe grayish white; throat and jugulum brownish neutral gray; posterior lower parts amber yellow, but sides and flanks strongly tinged with olivaceous; lining of wing straw yellow. Bill black, base of mandible dull brown; iris dark brown; legs and feet black or brownish black. *Adult male, winter*: Acquired by complete postnuptial molt. Like nuptial adult male, but colors somewhat deeper. *Adult female, nuptial*: Acquired by partial prenuptial molt. Similar to nuptial adult male, but tips of outermost primaries less abruptly narrowed, tips themselves broader and less sharply pointed; orange-red crown-patch usually less extensive. *Adult female, winter*: Acquired by complete postnuptial molt. Similar to nuptial adult female but colors somewhat deeper. *Male, first nuptial*: Acquired by partial prenuptial molt. Very similar to nuptial adult male. *Male, first winter*: Acquired by partial postjuvenal molt. Similar to adult male in winter, but wing-quills and tail feathers retained from juvenal. *Female, first nuptial*: Acquired by partial prenuptial molt. Similar to nuptial adult female. *Female, first winter*: Acquired by partial postjuvenal molt. Similar to adult female in

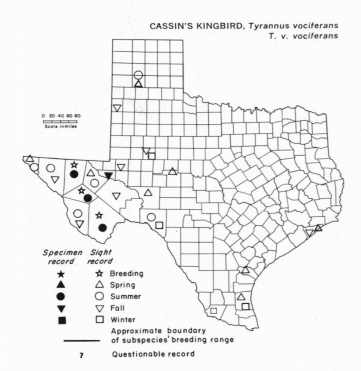

CASSIN'S KINGBIRD, *Tyrannus vociferans*
T. v. vociferans

0 20 40 60 80
Scale in miles

Specimen record	Sight record	
★	☆	Breeding
▲	△	Spring
●	○	Summer
▼	▽	Fall
■	□	Winter

——— Approximate boundary of subspecies' breeding range

? Questionable record

winter, but differs in retention of wing-quills and tail feathers from juvenal. *Juvenal*: Acquired by complete postnatal molt. Similar to nuptial adults, but tips of outer primaries very little narrowed, this noticeable in male on only three, in female on only two; crown and hindneck much more brownish, nearly hair brown; crown without any concealed orange spot; back and scapulars more brownish; rump and upper tail-coverts tipped with russet or cinnamon; tip of tail dull russet; secondaries and primaries more broadly edged with greenish white, buffy white, or pale buff; wing-coverts conspicuously tipped or edged with cinnamon buff or pale cinnamon buff; lower parts paler and duller, anteriorly somewhat more brownish; base of mandible of paler brown. *Natal*: Pale pinkish cinnamon, pale pinkish buff, cartridge buff, or buffy white.

MEASUREMENTS: *Adult male*: Wing, 130.0–136.9 (average, 132.8) mm.; tail, 89.9–96.0 (92.7); bill (exposed culmen), 18.0–21.6 (19.8); tarsus, 18.5–20.1 (19.3); middle toe without claw, 13.5–15.0 (14.2). *Adult female*: Wing, 120.9–131.5 (126.2); tail, 86.1–91.9 (89.2); bill, 18.5–22.1 (19.8); tarsus, 18.0–20.6 (19.3); middle toe, 13.5–16.0 (14.7).

RANGE: Identical with that of species with exception of Guerrero, Mexico. Winters from c. California through w. Mexico to Guatemala.

TEXAS: *Breeding*: Collected in Culberson, Jeff Davis, and Brewster cos. *Migration*: Collected outside breeding range in Ward Co. *Winter*: See species account.

NESTING: *Nest*: On mountains, in valleys, and canyons, in trees, forests; often near end of branch, well hidden; large and bulky; bowl composed of weed stalks, twigs, roots, plant fibers, wool, hair, string, paper, and plant down; lined with similar materials. *Eggs*: 2–5, usually 3–4; short ovate to elongate ovate; pale cream color; blotched and spotted with dull lavender and brownish purple; average size, 23.6 × 17.5 mm.

FORK-TAILED FLYCATCHER, *Muscivora tyrannus* (Linnaeus)

SPECIES ACCOUNT

Also called Swallow-tailed Flycatcher. A medium-sized flycatcher with long (8–10 in.), black, forked tail, which is very pliant (not stiff like Scissortail's). Black top, sides, and back of head; yellow crown-patch (usually concealed); pale gray back; blackish wings; white under parts. Length (including tail), 16 in.; weight, 1½ oz.

RANGE: Veracruz, Chiapas, Tabasco, and Quintana Roo, south through Central America and South America to c. Argentina. Tropical races resident, but birds from s. South America migrate northward, reaching Trinidad, Tobago, and Lesser Antilles. Accidental in Cuba and in widely scattered localities in United States.

TEXAS: *Casual*: Five records, all from south Texas: Uvalde Co., north of Uvalde (1 seen, Aug. 10, 1946, S. G. Williams); s.e. Cameron Co. (1 seen, Nov. 19, 1946, Mr. and Mrs. C. T. Gill, later identified, probably by H. C. Oberholser, from careful sketch made by Mr. Gill during sighting); Refugio Co., in open field a few miles from entrance to Aransas Nat. Wildlife Refuge (1 studied, Oct. 8, 1958, Maurine McFarland; bird photographed by Edith Wilson, photo identified by E. B. Kincaid, Jr., and F. S. Webster, Jr.); Rio Grande delta, exact location not given (Mar. 20, 1959, Mr. and Mrs. E. D. Swedenborg); Hidalgo Co., 18 mi. north-north-

east of Edinburg (1 female collected, Feb. 4, 1961, David Blankinship and Pauline James; specimen subsequently identified as *M. t. tyrannus* by Thomas D. Burleigh at U.S. Nat. Museum; skin deposited in Museum of Zoology, Louisiana State University; see P. James, 1963, *Auk* 80: 85).

HAUNTS AND HABITS: The Fork-tailed Flycatcher, crisply black and white, is the neotropical counterpart of the softly white, salmon-sided Scissor-tailed Flycatcher. Long tail streaming, *Muscivora tyrannus* fly-catches over dry or wet savannahs and marshlands with scattered trees and bushes. As W. H. Hudson described, the Forktail's tail floats behind the bird "like a pair of black ribbons." It is notably different from the stiff tail of *M. forficata*.

The nest of this flycatcher is a shallow cup of soft materials, such as thistle down, cemented with a gummy substance. The species is frequently parasitized by cowbirds. The Forktail is usually solitary, but during migration individuals may gather in flocks and share night roosts. Also, especially at sunset, birds congregate to perform wild aerial flights. All the time loudly chirping, they ascend in the air, then descend rapidly, almost crashing to the ground. As is standard with its family, the Forktail eats insects, which it catches generally in dashes from an exposed vantage atop a bush (sometimes a very low one) or small tree (up to about 25 ft.). Perching posture is quite erect. Birds also consume berries and other small fruits.

Vocalizations include hard, percussive chirpings and twitterings, also noises reminiscent of clapping castanets.

DETAILED ACCOUNT: ONE (?) SUBSPECIES

NOTE: Oberholser believed that stray Fork-tailed Flycatchers sighted in Texas probably belong to the northern race, *M. t. monachus*. However, the only Texas specimen was identified by T. D. Burleigh as *M. t. tyrannus*, a highly similar race of e. South America. Following description, measurements, and range apply to *M. t. monachus* (Hartlaub).

DESCRIPTION: *Adult male, nuptial plumage*: Acquired by partial prenuptial molt, first from second winter plumage, later from winter adult. Three outer primaries deeply emarginate and attenuated at tips; pileum and sides of head to below eyes black; large crown-patch lemon chrome, sometimes light cadmium centrally, bases of these feathers white; upper tail-coverts brownish black, tipped with brownish gray or gray of back; remainder of upper parts dull light to pale neutral gray; tail brownish black, basal half of outer web of outermost rectrix white; wings fuscous to fuscous black, upper wing-coverts edged and tipped with mouse gray, excepting lesser coverts which are tipped with gray of back, primaries and secondaries narrowly margined on outer webs with mouse gray, tertials with brownish white, and inner webs of all wing-quills basally edged with white to brownish white; lining of wing white, edge of wing below mixed with mouse gray; entire lower surface white. *Adult male, winter*: Acquired by complete postnuptial molt. Practically identical with nuptial adult male. *Adult female, nuptial*: Acquired by partial prenuptial molt. Like nuptial adult male but smaller, particularly wing and tail; three outer primaries less deeply emarginate and less attenuated at tips; yellow crown-patch averaging smaller. *Adult female, winter*: Acquired by complete postnuptial molt. Like adult female in winter. *Male and female, second winter*: Acquired by complete molt from first nuptial. Similar to adults in winter, but gray of upper parts duller, more or less tinged with olivaceous; sides of body and lining of wings washed with sulphur yellow. *Male and female, first nuptial*: Acquired by partial prenuptial molt from first winter. Similar to second winter, but three outer primaries without either emargination or attenuation; tail much shorter; pileum olive brown, with no yellow or white; sides of head and narrow nuchal collar blackish brown; back duller, somewhat more brownish; upper wing-coverts tipped and margined with avellaneous or dull buff. *Male and female, first winter*: Acquired by complete postjuvenal molt. Resembling first nuptial, but margins of upper wing-coverts broader, more rufescent—dull cinnamon buff to sayal brown; wing-quills more broadly edged with yellowish white or buffy white. *Juvenal*: Acquired by complete postnatal molt. Similar to first winter, but brown of pileum darker; upper surface duller, more brownish, rump and upper tail-coverts broadly barred with bister to cinnamon brown; inner tail feathers tipped and somewhat margined with same colors; superior wing-coverts more broadly edged and tipped with tawny to cinnamon rufous.

MEASUREMENTS: *Adult male*: Wing, 104.1–119.9 (average, 110.0) mm.; tail, 230.1–303.0 (264.9); bill (exposed culmen), 14.0–17.0 (15.5); tarsus, 16.0–18.5 (17.3); middle toe without claw, 11.4–14.5 (12.7). *Adult female*: Wing, 100.1–106.9 (103.4); tail, 173.0–220.5 (201.7); bill, 15.0–16.5 (15.7); tarsus, 16.0–17.5 (17.0); middle toe, 10.9–13.0 (12.4).

RANGE: S.e. Mexico, south through Central America to n. Brazil.

TEXAS: *Casual*: See species account.

SCISSOR-TAILED FLYCATCHER, *Muscivora forficata* (Gmelin)

SPECIES ACCOUNT   *See frontispiece, vol. 2*

A handsome, trim flycatcher. *Male*: extremely long, black-and-white tail (deeply forked, but usually seen closed); pale gray upper parts with blackish wings; whitish below with salmon pink sides and wing-linings; crown-spot (usually concealed) and patch on

SCISSOR-TAILED FLYCATCHER, *Muscivora forficata*

0 20 40 60 80
Scale in miles

Specimen   Sight
record   record
★   ☆ Breeding
▲   △ Spring
●   ○ Summer
▼   ▽ Fall
■   □ Winter
────   Approximate boundary
               of subspecies' breeding range
?   Questionable record

each side of breast orange-red. *Female*: tail about one-third shorter than male's; colors somewhat duller. Length, 13¼ in. (male), 11¼ (female); wingspan, 14¾; weight, 1¼ oz.

RANGE: S.e. Colorado, s. Nebraska, and w. Arkansas, south to s. Texas. Winters mainly from s. Mexico to Panama; also s. Florida.

TEXAS: (See map.) *Breeding*: Late Mar. to late Aug. (eggs, Mar. 31 to Aug. 10) from near sea level to 4,000 ft. Very common to fairly common in most of state east of Pecos River Valley, though somewhat local in extreme east and far south Texas; scarce in northwestern Panhandle, central Trans-Pecos (northern Culberson to northern Brewster cos.), and Rio Grande delta. One record from El Paso Co., Fabens (pair nesting, May 22, 1959, Roy Fisk, et al.). *Migration*: Mid- or late Mar. to late May; early or mid-Aug. to late Oct. or early Nov. (extremes: Feb. 20, June 22; mid-July, Dec. 7). Abundant (some years) to common through most of state; fairly common to uncommon in much of Trans-Pecos; scarce in northwestern Panhandle and El Paso region. *Winter*: Mid-Dec. to mid-Feb. (extremes: Dec. 1, Feb. 22). Rare along coast and in Rio Grande delta; casual inland, where sighted in Tarrant (Jan. 24, 1967, Bruce Mack), Van Zandt (Dec. 18, 1970, Micky Robinson), Travis (Dec. 28, 1957, F. S. Webster, Jr.), Medina (Feb. 14, 1965, Mr. and Mrs. M. E. Isleib), Bexar, and Brooks (Jan. 22, 1965, A. W. O'Neil) cos.

HAUNTS AND HABITS: The Scissortail is a great favorite among Texans. Its colors are beautifully blended and its movements graceful; from the viewpoint of farmers and ranchers, it is one of the "good guys" because it downs a lot of big, harmful insects and, like kingbirds, chases away hawks. A bird of semiopen country, this flycatcher is found throughout Texas on plains, prairies, mesas, and flats, and about pastures, clearings, ranches, and farms; it is conspicuous along roads and highways where wires furnish excellent lookout perches. Although the Scissortail does most of its feeding in the usual flycatcher manner, it descends to the ground surprisingly often to pick up grasshoppers, beetles, and caterpillars. Here it is careful to lift its long tail well above the dirt. Just before and during migration, Scissortails assemble into flocks, often of considerable size; also at this time they frequently roost in large groups of fifty or more individuals.

Flight is swift and powerful, especially when the Scissortail is in pursuit of a hawk or crow intruding in its territory. Movement from tree to tree is often slow and fluttering. During the breeding season, the male engages in vigorous flight displays. Mounting one hundred feet in the air, he plunges downward, then alternately bursts upward, accompanying these mid-air zigzags with high-pitched cackling; in the final descent he often appears to somersault backward several times.

The Scissor-tailed Flycatcher, in addition to many kingbirdlike bickerings, utters a harsh *keck* or *kew* note. Another vocalization is a rapidly repeated *kaleep*. Dawn song, heard in the breeding season, has been described as a series (usually one to six) of loud, stuttered *pup*'s concluded with an emphatic *perlep* or *peroo*. Scissortails are most vocal from late March to mid-August, but assembled individuals use their simple notes even in winter.

DETAILED ACCOUNT: NO SUBSPECIES

DESCRIPTION: *Adult male, nuptial plumage*: Acquired by partial prenuptial molt. Top and upper sides of head, with sides of neck and hindneck, pallid neutral gray, lores with spot of concealed gray, crown with concealed spot of orange-red surrounded by white; back and scapulars brownish pale neutral gray, washed with testaceous or vinaceous tawny; rump fuscous; upper tail-coverts fuscous, broadly margined with mouse gray, longer upper tail-coverts black, very narrowly edged with pale brownish white; tail white (faintly tinged with light cinnamon orange or bittersweet pink), the feathers broadly tipped with black; wing-quills and coverts hair brown or light chaetura drab, wing-quills broadly edged with pale pink or dull white on basal portion of inner webs, tips rather darker, outer webs of secondaries rather broadly edged with brownish white or pinkish white, all wing-coverts edged with pale drab or brownish white; lower surface white or grayish white; conspicuous patch on each side of breast scarlet red; lining of wing, sides, flanks, and crissum light salmon or bittersweet pink. Bill dark brown, lighter at base, particularly on mandible; iris dark brown; legs and feet dull brown; claws black or brownish black. *Adult male, winter*: Acquired by complete postnuptial molt. Like nuptial adult male. *Adult female, nuptial*: Acquired by partial prenuptial molt. Similar to adult male, but outer tail feathers much shorter; general coloration rather duller, particularly sides, flanks, and crissum which are sometimes pale orange buff; red patch on side of breast smaller and usually less intensely scarlet red, but more orange; concealed orange spot on crown absent or very small; third tail feather from outside more intensely black. *Adult female, winter*: Acquired by complete postnuptial molt. Similar to nuptial adult female. *Male, first nuptial*: Acquired by partial prenuptial molt. Similar to nuptial adult male. *Male, first winter*: Acquired by complete postjuvenal molt. Very similar to nuptial adult female. *Female, first nuptial*: Acquired by partial prenuptial molt. Similar to nuptial adult female. *Female, first winter*: Acquired by complete postjuvenal molt. Similar to nuptial adult female. *Juvenal*: Acquired by complete postnatal molt. Similar to nuptial adult female, but tail still shorter; upper parts paler or darker and duller, more brownish, particularly on back, hindneck, and head; crown without trace of concealed spot of white and orange; wings and tail more brownish; lining of wing, sides, flanks, crissum, and abdomen pale cream buff; no orange or red patch on side of breast. *Natal*: Pale tilleul buff to buffy white.

MEASUREMENTS: *Adult male*: Wing, 120.9–129.0 (average, 124.5) mm.; tail, 199.9–256.0 (225.6); bill (exposed culmen), 17.0–19.0 (17.8); tarsus, 17.5–19.0 (18.3); middle toe without claw, 13.0–14.5 (14.0). *Adult female*: Wing, 111.5–119.6 (115.8); tail, 125.5–182.1 (159.8); bill, 16.0–18.0 (17.3); tarsus, 18.0–19.0 (18.3); middle toe, 13.0–14.5 (13.7).

TEXAS: *Breeding*: Collected north to Hutchinson, east to Bowie and Chambers, south to Cameron, west to Brewster cos. *Migration*: Collected north to Clay, east to Galveston, south to Cameron, west to Culberson cos. *Winter*: Two specimens: Cameron Co., Rio Grande (Jan. 27, 28, 1886, F. B. Armstrong).

NESTING: *Nest*: In open country or scattered woodlands, on prairies, often near human dwellings, or in cultivated areas; in tree, usually not very high above ground, on horizontal limb or fork, on gate post, telephone pole, or similar structure; cup composed of twigs, weed stalks, roots, paper, string, rags, grass, and other vegetable fibers; lined with hair, cotton, wool, rootlets, plant fibers, and feathers. *Eggs*: 3–6, usually 4–5; ovate to rounded ovate; white or cream white, with a few blotches and spots of reddish brown, dark brown, lilac, and gray, chiefly about larger end, but occasionally unspotted; average size, 22.6 × 17.0 mm.

KISKADEE FLYCATCHER, *Pitangus sulphuratus* (Linnaeus)

SPECIES ACCOUNT

Also known as Derby Flycatcher. Raucous *kis-ka-dee* call. A very large, bull-headed flycatcher with striking yellow under parts; rufous wings and tail; bold black-and-white head pattern. Brownish olive back; yellow crown-patch; heavy black bill. Length, 10¾ in.; wingspan, 16½.

RANGE: Extreme s. Sonora and s. Texas, south through lowland Mexico and Central America (very local in Panama) to c. Argentina. Naturalized in Bermuda.

TEXAS: (See map.) *Resident*: Breeds, early Mar. to late July—occasionally to early Sept. (eggs, May 5 to June 23; nest building as early as Mar. 9; fully fledged young being fed, Sept. 3) from near sea level to 400 ft. Common to fairly common in Rio Grande delta upriver to Laredo, where somewhat irregular; uncommon and irregular north of delta to Falfurrias and Norias (Kenedy Co.). *Vagrant*: Sept. 6 to May 21. Individuals irregularly wander north, chiefly during nonbreeding season, to Alice, where scarce, and to Live Oak, San Patricio, and Aransas cos., where rare; rare north of Laredo upriver to Eagle Pass; casual in Val Verde Co. (see detailed account) and Big Bend Nat. Park (Boquillas, May 21, 1964, R. H. Wauer). Casual in summer at Aransas Nat. Wildlife Refuge (pair throughout summer of 1948, Connie Hagar).

HAUNTS AND HABITS: No part of Texas is truly tropical (i.e., frost proof), but three big, raucous, boldly patterned, and colorful neotropical passerines do range regularly to the state's southern tip: Kiskadee Flycatcher, Green Jay, and Lichtenstein's Oriole. The Kiskadee,

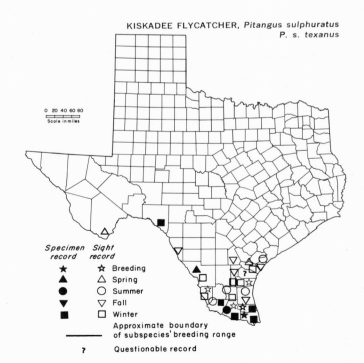

KISKADEE FLYCATCHER, *Pitangus sulphuratus*
P. s. texanus

0 20 40 60 80
Scale in miles

Specimen record	Sight record	
★	☆	Breeding
▲	△	Spring
●	○	Summer
▼	▽	Fall
■	□	Winter

——— Approximate boundary of subspecies' breeding range

? Questionable record

often billed as the largest and most aggressive of the world's 365 species of tyrant flycatchers, is actually equaled in bulk by some of its South American relatives and exceeded in length by Texas' own Scissortailed Flycatcher and several of its long-tailed tropical kin.

In the senior editor's experience, the aggressiveness of this bird is greatly overrated. Beside Olmito resaca in the Rio Grande delta, he once picked up a young Kiskadee just out of the nest. The baby gave its distress squeak; yet an adult, apparently one of its parents, remained inert only a few yards away. In a similar situation, a Cactus Wren, Mockingbird, or even a Rufous-crowned Sparrow would have darted at him until he had released the baby.

In addition to the usual big-flycatcher diet of large insects and hackberries, the Kiskadee catches many tadpoles, frogs, and minnows. Unlike kingfishers, this species makes only shallow dashes that barely break the water's surface. Sometimes the bird swoops down to water, apparently to wet its belly feathers or clean its feet. Because of its greater than academic interest in aquatic life, the Kiskadee characteristically perches on a low branch overhanging a pond or river. Within its Texas range, waterside trees that this flycatcher commonly uses as lookout stations are Montezuma baldcypress (*Taxodium mucronatum*), black willow (*Salix nigra*), huisache (*Acacia farnesiana*), and retama (*Parkinsonia aculeata*).

Kiskadee vocalizations are vigorous and abrupt. Probably the most frequent call sounds like a human baby trying to cry *whank!* A harsh *ick!* is much less frequent. The name-call resembles *kis-ka-dee!*, *get-a-hear!*, or *git-ter-heck!*, depending on what the listener is trying to hear. Call notes sound all year long, but the *kis-ka-dee* is rare during cold weather.

DETAILED ACCOUNT: ONE SUBSPECIES

TEXAS KISKADEE FLYCATCHER, *Pitangus sulphuratus texanus* van Rossem

DESCRIPTION: *Adults, nuptial plumage*: Acquired by partial prenuptial molt. Forehead and superciliary stripe, continuous with collar on hindneck, white; middle of crown and occiput black or dull black with more or less concealed large central spot of lemon chrome or light cadmium yellow; broad stripe from lores to eye, passing across side of head, black or brownish black; back, scapulars, and rump light brownish olive; upper tail-coverts and tail light olive brown, margined with tawny, russet, or hazel, greater part of basal portion of inner webs of tail feathers tawny or russet; wing-quills and upper wing-coverts rather light olive brown, inner webs of quills basally, outer webs of primaries basally, and outer vanes of secondaries, except at tips, tawny or russet; wing-coverts edged broadly with same; chin and upper throat, extending in band onto side of neck, white; remainder of lower surface, including lining of wing, lemon chrome. Bill black, lower part of mandible somewhat brownish; iris hazel; legs and feet brownish black. *Adults, winter*: Acquired by complete postnuptial molt. Like nuptial adults. *First nuptial*: Acquired by partial prenuptial molt. Similar to nuptial adults, but wing-quills and tail feathers retained from juvenal. *First winter*: Acquired by partial postjuvenal molt. Practically identical with first nuptial male and female. *Juvenal*: Acquired by complete postnatal molt. Similar to adults but with-

out yellow on crown and with much broader tawny or russet margins on outer webs of wing-quills and wing-coverts. *Natal*: Unknown.

MEASUREMENTS: *Adult male*: Wing, 120.9–126.5 (average, 123.5) mm.; tail, 90.9–100.1 (95.2); bill (exposed culmen), 27.2–29.9 (28.7); width of bill at anterior part of nostril, 9.9–11.4 (10.7); tarsus, 26.4–29.9 (27.9); middle toe without claw, 17.5–19.3 (18.3). *Adult female*: Wing, 117.1–123.0 (119.9); tail, 90.9–97.1 (93.7); bill, 26.4–29.9 (28.7); width of bill, 9.7–10.4 (9.9); tarsus, 26.4–28.9 (27.2); middle toe, 18.0–18.5 (18.3).

RANGE: Extreme s. Texas, south to Nuevo León, Tamaulipas, and c. Veracruz.

TEXAS: *Resident*: Collected in Willacy, Cameron, Hidalgo, Starr, and Webb cos. *Vagrant*: One specimen: Val Verde Co., Pecan Springs, on Devils River near Juno (Jan. 20, 1888, J. A. Loomis).

NESTING: *Nest*: In brush, low woods, along lagoons and streams or in cultivated areas; in bush or tree, usually not over 30 ft. above ground; large, football-shaped nest with side entrance; composed of weeds, grass, Spanishmoss, twigs, straw, and lichens; lined with finer similar materials, also with hair, feathers, and plant down. *Eggs*: 3–6, usually 4–5; short ovate to elongate ovate; cream white; dotted with reddish brown, dark brown, and lilac or grayish lavender; average size, 29.4 × 21.4 mm.

[SULPHUR-BELLIED FLYCATCHER, *Myiodynastes luteiventris* Sclater

Only U.S. flycatcher streaked above and below. Heavily streaked with brownish, olive, and buff above, except for rufous rump and tail; blackish gray stroke through eye; white streak over eye and on jaw; whitish throat, speckled finely with blackish; pale yellow below, streaked with blackish gray on breast, sides, and flanks. Length, 7½–8½ in.

RANGE: S. Arizona, Chihuahua, Nuevo León, and c. Tamaulipas, south through Mexico and Central America to Costa Rica. Winters in Peru and Bolivia.

TEXAS: *Hypothetical*: Most plausible sighting: Brewster Co., Rio Grande Village in Big Bend Nat. Park (1 observed, May 11, 1969, J. A. Tucker, Doug Eddleman, R. H. Wauer). Another bird reported in Davis Mts., Jeff Davis Co., but Wauer questions record because individual was incubating on an open nest, whereas Sulphurbelly nests in woodpecker holes in tree trunks. Also seen in Rio Grande delta (ca. 1940, A. T. Hale) and southern Big Bend (ca. 1950, Peter Koch), but details lacking.]

GREAT CRESTED FLYCATCHER, *Myiarchus crinitus* (Linnaeus)

SPECIES ACCOUNT   *See colorplate 20*

Also known as Crested Flycatcher. See habitat and voice discussions. A large, somewhat bushy-crested flycatcher with rufous in wings (primaries) and in longish tail. Brownish olive head, upper parts; gray throat and breast contrasting with yellow belly and crissum;

dull white wing-bars; brownish lower mandible. Length, 8¾ in.; wingspan, 13; weight, 1¼ oz.

RANGE: S.e. Saskatchewan to New Brunswick, south through c. and e. United States to c. Texas, Gulf coast, and s. Florida. Winters mainly from e. and s. Mexico through Central America to Colombia; also s. Florida.

TEXAS: (See map.) *Breeding*: Early Apr. to early July (eggs, Apr. 30 to June 8; young in nest, Apr. 18 to June 26) from near sea level to 3,500 ft. Common to fairly common in most of eastern two-thirds west to northeastern Panhandle and Edwards Plateau, and south to San Antonio, Beeville, and Victoria; uncommon and irregular south locally to Frio Co., Falfurrias, and Rockport. *Migration*: Late Mar. or early Apr. to mid-May; late July or early Aug. to late Sept. (extremes: Mar. 9, June 15; June 26, Nov. 5). Common to fairly common through eastern two-thirds west to northeastern Panhandle, San Angelo, and Del Rio; scarce in remainder of Panhandle; rare and local in Trans-Pecos (recorded in Midland vicinity, Jeff Davis Co., and Big Bend Nat. Park). *Winter*: Early Dec. to late Jan.; no Feb. records. Rare along coast and lower Rio Grande (upriver to Del Rio); sightings from Walker and Travis cos., where casual.

HAUNTS AND HABITS: In Texas and throughout temperate eastern North America, shady deciduous and mixed woodlands and their edges furnish summer habitat for Great Crested Flycatchers. Migrating birds in this state scatter as well onto mesquite savannahs and plains dotted with isolated groves. This secretive flycatcher rarely, if ever, assembles in flocks; generally it moves singly or in pairs, and is more often heard than seen.

Flight, although swift for brief intervals, is seldom

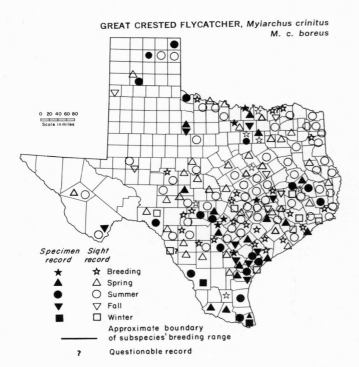

GREAT CRESTED FLYCATCHER, *Myiarchus crinitus*
M. c. boreus

0 20 40 60 80
Scale in miles

Specimen   Sight
record   record
★   ☆ Breeding
▲   △ Spring
●   ○ Summer
▼   ▽ Fall
■   □ Winter
━━━━━ Approximate boundary
       of subspecies' breeding range
?   Questionable record

sustained except during migration. Within woodlands, the Great Crested sails somewhat jaylike from tree to tree, but as it pursues flying insects its motions are quick, erratic, and dashing. When establishing breeding territory, rivals—tumbling in midair and sometimes on the ground—pull, peck, and claw at one another's breast and tail feathers. Once a pair mates, the male carefully guards the territory, especially against intrusions of small birds, but the Great Crested, unlike kingbirds and the Scissor-tailed Flycatcher, is not aggressive toward large birds, such as hawks and crows.

A loud, clear whistled *wheep!* or *whirp!* (with steeply rising inflection) typically betrays the presence of the Great Crested Flycatcher. The bird also utters a raucous, rolling *prrrrreet!* Dawn song has been described by Francis H. Allen as a very leisurely sung *coodle, queedle, coodle, queedle, coodle, queedle,* etc. All vocalizations of this flycatcher are heard in Texas chiefly from late March or April into July.

DETAILED ACCOUNT: TWO SUBSPECIES

SOUTHERN GREAT CRESTED FLYCATCHER, *Myiarchus crinitus crinitus* (Linnaeus)

DESCRIPTION: *Adults, nuptial plumage*: Similar to *M. c. boreus* (see below), but smaller, except bill which is larger; upper parts darker, more greenish (less brownish).

MEASUREMENTS: *Adult male*: Wing, 99.1–106.4 (average, 102.4) mm.; tail, 86.1–92.5 (90.2); bill (exposed culmen), 20.6–23.1 (21.6); tarsus, 20.1–21.6 (20.9); middle toe without claw, 11.9–14.0 (13.0). *Adult female*: Wing, 97.6–101.6 (99.8); tail, 84.6–86.6 (85.6); bill, 21.1–22.1 (21.6); tarsus, 20.1–21.6 (20.9); middle toe, 12.4–13.0 (12.7).

RANGE: S.e. Louisiana to c. South Carolina, south to s. Florida. Winters from s.e. South Carolina (rarely) to s. Florida, and from Honduras to w. Panama; rarely in Bahamas, Cuba.

TEXAS: *Migration*: Three specimens: Cameron Co., Brownsville (Mar. 31, Apr. 27, 1909, Sept. 30, 1911, A. P. Smith). *Winter*: One specimen: Cameron Co., Brownsville (Jan. 24, 1911, A. P. Smith).

NORTHERN GREAT CRESTED FLYCATCHER, *Myiarchus crinitus boreus* Bangs

DESCRIPTION: *Adults, nuptial plumage*: Acquired by partial prenuptial molt. Upper surface rather dark citrine drab, but top of head rather more brownish, lower tail-coverts tipped with dull russet; tail light russet, outer webs of all feathers and both webs of middle pair light olive brown, this color not extending across tip of outermost rectrices; wing-quills and wing-coverts dark hair brown, basal portion of all but outermost primaries edged on outer webs with light russet, this also including outer webs of outermost secondaries, but inner secondaries and tertials edged on outer webs with yellowish white, all wing-quills basally on inner webs pale cinnamon buff; lesser wing-coverts margined with color of back, greater and median series tipped with pale grayish olivaceous or olivaceous white; lores, sides of head, neck, chin, and throat brownish light neutral gray; lining of wing and remainder of lower parts citrine yellow or amber yellow; crissum and lining of wing rather paler. Bill seal brown or slate black, but base of mandible ecru drab; iris vandyke brown; legs and feet slate black or brownish black. *Adults, winter*: Acquired by complete postnuptial molt. Similar to nuptial adults, but coloration somewhat darker and richer. *First nuptial*: Acquired by partial prenuptial molt and wear from first winter. Very similar to nuptial adults. *First winter*: Acquired by complete postjuvenal molt. Very similar to first nuptial male and female. *Juvenal*: Acquired by complete postnatal molt. Similar to nuptial adults, but upper surface much less olivaceous, almost fuscous; wing-coverts conspicuously edged with cinnamon buff, cinnamon, or pale buff; lower surface duller and paler; upper tail-coverts broadly tipped with tawny or cinnamon; outer webs of tail feathers edged with light russet; russet edgings of primaries broader. Bill black; iris dark brown; feet slate black or sepia. *Natal*: Pileum dark hair brown; back between hair brown and mouse gray.

MEASUREMENTS: *Adult male*: Wing, 101.1–109.5 (average, 105.6) mm.; tail, 86.1–96.0 (91.7); bill (exposed culmen), 19.6–20.6 (20.1); tarsus, 19.6–21.6 (20.9); middle toe without claw, 11.4–14.0 (13.0). *Adult female*: Wing, 95.0–101.1 (98.1); tail, 81.0–86.6 (84.3); bill, 18.0–20.1 (19.3); tarsus, 19.6–21.6 (20.3); middle toe, 11.9–13.5 (12.7).

RANGE: S.e. Saskatchewan to New Brunswick, south to c. Texas and North Carolina. Winters from e. and s. Mexico through Central America to w. Colombia.

TEXAS: *Breeding*: Collected north to Lipscomb, east to Cooke and Hardin, south to Bee, west to Kerr cos. *Migration*: Collected north to Cooke, east to Galveston, south to Cameron, west to Val Verde (Aug. 29) cos. Three specimens, all immatures, from Brewster Co., Big Bend Nat. Park probably of this race (Sept. 28, 1968, Sept. 15, 1969, Sept. 16, 1970, R. H. Wauer). *Winter*: Two specimens: Webb Co., Laredo (Jan. 25, 1886, F. B. Armstrong); Cameron Co., Brownsville (Jan. 24, 1911, A. P. Smith).

NESTING: *Nest*: In woodlands, often along streams, orchards (unsprayed), or other cultivated lands; in cavity of tree, post, bird box, or similar place; usually low, but sometimes up to 60 ft. above ground; bottom of nest hole floored with small twigs, moss, hair, grass, leaves, fur, feathers, and snake skins; further lined with moss, hair, fur, and strips of bark. *Eggs*: 4–8, usually 5–6; ovate to short ovate to elongate ovate; cream white to vinaceous buff, with scratches, lines, spots, and blotches of black, purplish brown, and lavender gray over most of surface but somewhat concentrated at larger end; average size, 22.6 × 17.5 mm.

WIED'S CRESTED FLYCATCHER, *Myiarchus tyrannulus* (Müller)

SPECIES ACCOUNT

Also known as Brown-crested Flycatcher, Mexican Crested Flycatcher, Rusty-tailed Flycatcher, and Arizona Crested Flycatcher. See habitat and voice discussions. Resembles Great Crested, but has paler under parts (especially on throat, breast); entirely blackish bill. Closely resembles Ash-throated, but larger and usually somewhat grayer on breast; yellower on belly; longer, thicker, wider bill. Length, 8¾ in.; wingspan, 12¾.

RANGE: Extreme s. Nevada, c. Arizona, s.w. New Mexico, and s. Texas, south through Mexico and Central America to n. Argentina; also Lesser Antilles, Dutch West Indies, Tobago, and Trinidad. Winters chiefly south of Tropic of Cancer.

TEXAS: (See map.) *Breeding*: Late Mar. to late July (eggs, Apr. 3 to July 7) from near sea level to 1,000 ft., possibly higher. Common to fairly common (local north of Rio Grande delta) from Laredo, Crystal City, Pearsall, Karnes City, Beeville, and Refugio (irregular) south through Rio Grande delta; scarce and irregular north along watercourses to Brackettville and San Antonio. Summer birds recorded from Mar. 3 to Sept. 14. Vagrant at Big Bend Nat. Park, where recorded from

Apr. 26 to Sept. 13. *Winter*: Mid-Nov. to late Jan.; no Feb. records. Rare and irregular in Rio Grande delta; very rare on central coast; casual on upper coast.

HAUNTS AND HABITS: Wied's Crested Flycatcher is the subtropical and tropical version of the Great Crested Flycatcher. Flight, migration habit, and other behavior of the two species are highly similar. In fact, the only strong differences are distribution, habitat, and voice; even in these departments there is some overlap.

South of San Antonio through the south Texas brush country, trees—large mesquites, hackberries, ashes—along rivers, especially the Rio Grande and Nueces and their tributaries, are inhabited by Wied's Crested Flycatchers; low mesquite brush and cactus between these rivers is largely left to that desert *Myiarchus*, the Ash-throated Flycatcher. In more northerly parts of the brush country, some eastern type trees—especially baldcypress, live oak, black willow, eastern cottonwood, and pecan—grow south along well-watered floodplains; also in towns many pecan trees are planted for shade and nuts. Here in these detached pieces of eastern woodlands, Great Crested Flycatchers nest. In the vicinity of some towns, notably Beeville, where this eastern, western, and southern woody vegetation comes together, all three common species of Texas *Myiarchus* breed. Sometimes the balance between eastern and southern ecological conditions is delicate; thus, during the 1960's at Frio County Park near Pearsall, the same live oak grove was claimed one year by a pair of Wied's and the next by a pair of Great Cresteds.

Voice of the Wied's Crested Flycatcher is its most important field mark. A short *whit* is a common note. Most distinctive call is a short *wirrp* or *weerrp*, delivered without rise in pitch. In spring and summer a

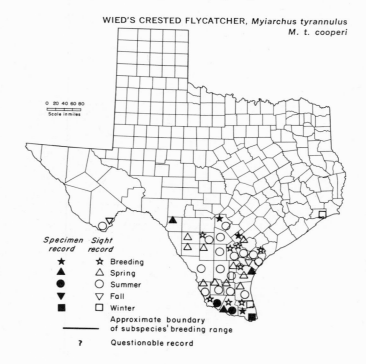

WIED'S CRESTED FLYCATCHER, *Myiarchus tyrannulus*
M. t. cooperi

0 20 40 60 80
Scale in miles

Specimen record / Sight record

★ ☆ Breeding
▲ △ Spring
● ○ Summer
▼ ▽ Fall
■ □ Winter

———— Approximate boundary of subspecies' breeding range

? Questionable record

rolling, throaty *purreeer* is also frequent. Dawn song is an alternately repeated *whit-will-do* and *three-for-you*, according to L. Irby Davis, who has made a special study of dawn songs of many tyrannids. Singing lasts from about mid-March to early July.

DETAILED ACCOUNT: ONE SUBSPECIES

MEXICAN WIED'S CRESTED FLYCATCHER, *Myiarchus tyrannulus cooperi* Baird

DESCRIPTION: *Adults, nuptial plumage:* Acquired by partial prenuptial molt. Pileum light brownish olive, centers of feathers darker; remainder of upper surface rather dark buffy olive, nape washed with dull gray, outer tail-coverts light brownish olive edged with lighter; tail light russet, middle tail feathers, outer webs, and shaft stripe on inner webs of all remaining feathers olive brown; wing-quills olive brown, basal portion of inner webs of primaries and most of inner webs of inner primaries and secondaries, dull pale cinnamon buff, but primaries basally edged on outer webs with cinnamon or tawny, outer secondaries edged with same, inner secondaries and tertials with dull yellowish or brownish white; upper wing-coverts hair brown, lesser series broadly margined with color of back; lesser and median series edged with brownish or olivaceous white, forming rather well marked wing-bars; lores and ear-coverts brownish mouse gray; chin, throat, and jugulum rather brownish pallid neutral gray; lining of wing, lower breast, abdomen, and crissum straw yellow; sides slightly washed with olivaceous. Bill brownish black, but base of mandible more brownish; iris dark brown; legs and feet brownish black. *Adults, winter:* Acquired by complete postnuptial molt. Similar to nuptial adults but coloration richer. *First nuptial:* Acquired by partial prenuptial molt. Practically like nuptial adults. *First winter:* Acquired by complete postjuvenal molt. Practically identical with adults in winter. *Juvenal:* Acquired by complete postnatal molt. Similar to nuptial adults, but upper surface much more rufescent brown, upper tail-coverts nearly all cinnamon or tawny, back with scarcely a tinge of olivaceous; middle tail feathers mostly russet; dark brown areas of other rectrices much reduced and replaced by light russet; superior wing-coverts edged with dull cinnamon buff, and outer webs of primaries and secondaries much more

broadly margined with tawny or russet, all wing-quills tipped with this color; lower surface duller and paler. *Natal:* Upper parts anteriorly dull wood brown or drab; posteriorly light drab.

MEASUREMENTS: *Adult male:* Wing, 99.1–106.4 (average, 102.4) mm.; tail, 89.4–97.6 (93.2); bill (exposed culmen), 20.6–22.6 (21.6); tarsus, 21.6–23.9 (23.1); middle toe without claw, 13.5–15.5 (14.2). *Adult female:* Wing, 96.0–103.1 (99.8); tail, 85.1–93.5 (89.7); bill, 20.1–21.1 (20.9); tarsus, 22.1–23.9 (22.9); middle toe, 13.5–15.0 (14.2).

RANGE: N.e. Coahuila and s. Texas, south through e. Mexico to Honduras.

TEXAS: *Breeding:* Collected north to Bexar (eggs), east to Karnes (nest and eggs), south to Nueces and Cameron, west to Kinney cos. *Winter:* One specimen: Cameron Co., Brownsville (Jan. 9, 1890, F. B. Armstrong).

NESTING: *Nest:* In open woods or brush, usually near streams; in woodpecker or other hole in tree, stump, pole, or post, or in birdhouse, mostly not over 20 ft. above ground; bottom of nest hole lined with leaves, strips of bark, hair, wool, and sometimes bits of snake skin. *Eggs:* 4–6, usually 5; ovate to short ovate; cream white to cream buff, spotted, blotched, and lined with purplish brown and lavender gray; average size, 22.4 × 17.5 mm.

ASH-THROATED FLYCATCHER, *Myiarchus cinerascens* (Lawrence)

SPECIES ACCOUNT

See habitat and voice discussions. A small pale *Myiarchus* (see Wied's Crested) with a white or whitish throat, and small slender bill. Brownish head, upper parts; pale gray breast; yellowish belly; rufous in wings and tail; white wing-bars. Length, 8½ in.; wingspan, 12½, weight, 1 oz.

RANGE: S. Oregon and e. Washington to s.w. Wyoming, w. Oklahoma, and c. Texas, south to s. Baja California, Guerrero, Puebla, s.w. Tamaulipas, and n. Coahuila. Winters mainly from U.S.-Mexico border (local) to El Salvador.

TEXAS: (See map.) *Breeding:* Early Apr. to late July (eggs, Apr. 12 to June 17; young in nest to July 14) from near sea level to about 7,000 ft. Common to fairly common in most of southwestern half (excluding coast, delta) north to southern Panhandle, east to Austin and Beeville; uncommon and local in northern and middle Panhandle; scarce and irregular to central coast and Kenedy Co.; rare in Rio Grande delta. Vague report of breeding in Fannin Co. lacks substantiation. *Migration:* Late Mar. to early May; early Aug. to mid-Sept.— occasionally a few to mid-Nov. (extremes: Mar. 9, May 3; July 17, Dec. 5). Common to fairly common through regular breeding range; scarce from Refugio south along coast to Rio Grande delta; rare east to Waco, Victoria; casual to Dallas, upper coast. *Winter:* Late Dec. to late Feb. Uncommon to scarce along Rio Grande from Big Bend to Laredo; rare north to Pecos Co.; casual in Palo Pinto, Harris, and Chambers cos.

HAUNTS AND HABITS: Mesquite-acacia-cactus deserts and open juniper-oak woodlands of the West furnish habitat for the Ash-throated Flycatcher. Favorite haunts in Texas are thorn scrub and brushy groves on flats, valleys, mesas, canyons, gulches, and slopes of

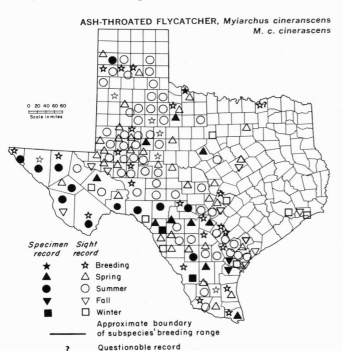

ASH-THROATED FLYCATCHER, *Myiarchus cineranscens*
M. c. cinerascens

0 20 40 60 80
Scale in miles

Specimen record	Sight record	
★	☆	Breeding
▲	△	Spring
●	○	Summer
▼	▽	Fall
■	□	Winter

——— Approximate boundary of subspecies' breeding range

? Questionable record

hills and mountains. Often the bird is found along fence rows and on telephone wires. For the most part, it is seen singly or in pairs.

The Ashthroat, aridland counterpart of the Great Crested Flycatcher, resembles its relative in habits and appearance. In feeding operations, the Ashthroat appears to confine itself less to a restricted area than do most other flycatchers; instead it tends to range widely over its brushlands in search of bees, wasps, ants, beetles, caterpillars, and other insects. Most prey is taken on the wing, but the bird will readily pluck a sedentary insect off a leaf; some wild fruit is consumed when animal matter is scarce.

Notes of the Ash-throated Flycatcher are somewhat more subdued than those of the Wied's Crested Flycatcher and much softer than the calls of the Great Crested. Two common utterances of the Ashthroat are *pwit* and *prrit*; diagnostic are *ka-brick, ha-whip* and *ka-wheer.* Dawn song is a series of rapid *tea fo you's,* with occasional insertions of a soft roll, *r-r-r* (L. I. Davis). All vocalizations are heard mainly between early April and mid-July.

DETAILED ACCOUNT: ONE SUBSPECIES

NORTHERN ASH-THROATED FLYCATCHER, *Myiarchus cinerascens cinerascens* (Lawrence)

DESCRIPTION: *Adult male, nuptial plumage:* Acquired by partial prenuptial molt. Similar to Mexican Wied's Crested Flycatcher, *Myiarchus tyrannulus cooperi,* but centers of feathers of pileum rather darker, forehead inclining to dull gray; remainder of upper surface rather dark buffy olive, sometimes lighter, and always somewhat more grayish on hindneck, longer upper tail-coverts rather light olive brown, edged with dull cinnamon; tail light russet, middle pair of feathers and outer webs of remaining feathers, as well as entire tips of feathers on both inner and outer webs, rather light olive brown; lores and ear-coverts brownish neutral gray; wings and lower parts same as those of *M. t. cooperi.* Bill black or brownish black, but mandible of lighter brown or dull flesh color at base; iris dark coffee brown or hazel; legs and feet black or brownish black. *Adult male, winter:* Acquired by complete postnuptial molt. Similar to nuptial adult male, but coloration darker. *Adult female, nuptial:* Acquired by partial prenuptial molt. Similar to nuptial adult male, but dark brown terminal or subterminal area on inner web of lateral tail feathers smaller, usually not occupying entire part of web, and sometimes not even outer half, outer part of inner web cinnamon or cinnamon rufous, like most of remainder of inner web. *Adult female, winter:* Acquired by complete postnuptial molt. Similar to nuptial adult female, but coloration somewhat darker. *Male and female, first nuptial:* Acquired by partial prenuptial molt. Similar to corresponding sex of nuptial adults. *Male and female, first winter:* Acquired by complete postjuvenal molt. Similar to corresponding sex of adults in winter. *Juvenal:* Acquired by complete postnatal molt. Similar to corresponding sex of nuptial adults, but upper parts paler and more brownish, pileum cinnamon brown or wood brown, upper tail-coverts and tail dull cinnamon rufous, except for narrow shaft streaks of dull brown on some of rectrices; edgings of primaries and secondaries more broadly cinnamon rufous; superior wing-coverts tipped and edged with pale buff or cinnamon buff; lower surface paler and duller. *Natal:* Drab.

MEASUREMENTS: *Adult male:* Wing, 98.6–104.1 (average, 100.8) mm.; tail, 88.4–97.1 (92.5); bill (exposed culmen), 18.0–20.1 (19.3); tarsus, 21.6–23.9 (22.9); middle toe without claw, 11.9–13.5 (12.7). *Adult female:* Wing, 91.9–100.6 (95.5); tail, 84.1–91.9 (87.4); bill, 17.0–19.0 (18.8); tarsus, 22.1–23.6 (22.9); middle toe, 12.4–13.5 (12.7).

RANGE: S. Washington and w. Texas, south to n. Baja California and s. Tamaulipas. Winters mainly from Colima and Guerrero to Guatemala.

TEXAS: *Breeding:* Collected north to Oldham, east to Wilbarger, south to Bexar and Cameron, west to Brewster and El Paso cos. *Winter:* Two specimens: Kinney Co., Fort Clark (Feb. 22, 1893, E. A. Mearns); Webb Co., Laredo (Jan. 30, 1886, F. B. Armstrong).

NESTING: *Nest:* On arid mesas, slopes, canyons, and in semiarid, flat, open country, in brush or sparse vegetation along washes; in natural cavity of tree or stump, old woodpecker hole, or even Cactus Wren nest; cavity lined with dry grass, roots, weed stalks, fur, cattle and other hair, and sometimes snake skins. *Eggs:* 3–7, usually 4; ovate to elliptical ovate; light cream color to pinkish buff, with longitudinal lines, streaks, and spots of dark purplish brown, dark brown, and grayish lavender; average size, 22.4 × 16.5 mm.

OLIVACEOUS FLYCATCHER, *Myiarchus tuberculifer* (D'Orbigny and Lafresnaye)

SPECIES ACCOUNT

Dusky-capped Flycatcher of various writers. Voice is a plaintive whistled *wheeeeyou,* slurring downward. Resembles Ashthroat, but noticeably smaller, with gray, rather than white, throat; more olivaceous above with much less rufous on wings and tail; duller wing-bars. Most individuals are deeper yellow on belly than the Ashthroat. Length, 7½ in.; wingspan, 10½.

RANGE: Mountains of s.e. Arizona, s.w. New Mexico, c. Nuevo León, and c. Tamaulipas, south through Mexico and Central America to n. Argentina and s.e. Brazil. Winters (often at lower elevations) from s. Sonora and c. Tamaulipas south.

TEXAS: *Migration:* Apr. 2 to June 17; July 7 to Oct. 23. Rare through Big Bend Nat. Park; casual in spring at El Paso.

HAUNTS AND HABITS: In montane pine-oak forests of southeastern Arizona and through Mexico, the Olivaceous is just as ubiquitous as the Coues' Flycatcher and, in some places, it is even more numerous. In winter, individuals of both species descend to warm and even tropical woods. At this season, the Olivaceous usually continues giving its mournful call, while its cousin ceases its whistle. Not at all gregarious, it is found singly and in pairs and is of retiring habits. It is inclined to move southward soon after the young—which have been raised inside a hole in a tree trunk—are strong on the wing. Favorite perches of the Olivaceous are branches of bushes or trees from where it dashes out to catch insects in mid-air.

The whistled *wheeeeyou* call is heard in Mexico throughout the year; in Texas it is not to be expected at any time due to bird's extreme scarcity in the state.

DETAILED ACCOUNT: ONE SUBSPECIES

NORTHERN OLIVACEOUS FLYCATCHER, *Myiarchus tuberculifer olivascens* Ridgway

DESCRIPTION: *Adults, nuptial plumage:* Acquired by partial prenuptial molt. Upper parts rather dark buffy olive; pileum rather darker and more brownish with still darker centers of feathers; upper tail-coverts rather light olive brown edged with tawny; entire tail rather light olive brown, but basal portion of feathers edged on outer webs with cinnamon or tawny; wing-quills and wing-coverts hair brown, quills edged basally on inner webs with very pale cinnamon buff, and on outer webs, except at tips of primaries, with tawny or russet, outer webs of tertials margined with dull yellowish or greenish white, lesser wing-coverts margined with color of back, others with dull brownish olive buff; lores, cheeks, chin, throat, and jugulum rather brownish pale neutral gray; lining of wing and remainder of lower parts citrine yellow. Maxilla blackish brown or brownish black; mandible similar but paler at base; iris dark brown; legs and feet brownish black or blackish brown. *Adults, winter*: Acquired by complete postnuptial molt. Similar to nuptial adults but coloration darker. *First nuptial*: Acquired by partial prenuptial molt. Practically identical with nuptial adults. *First winter*: Acquired by complete postjuvenal molt. Like first nuptial male and female. *Juvenal*: Acquired by complete postnatal molt. Similar to nuptial adults, but upper parts much more brownish; lores olivaceous; upper tail-coverts mostly tawny or russet; tail broadly edged on both webs with light russet; wing-quills more broadly edged on outer webs with tawny, and on inner webs with deeper cinnamon buff; wing-coverts broadly edged and tipped with cinnamon and tawny; lower parts duller and rather paler.

MEASUREMENTS: *Adult male*: Wing, 74.9–85.1 (average, 81.3) mm.; tail, 70.1–81.0 (76.2); bill (exposed culmen), 16.0–18.5 (17.8); tarsus, 18.0–19.6 (18.8); middle toe without claw, 8.9–10.4 (9.7). *Adult female*: Wing, 74.4–79.0 (76.2); tail, 67.6–76.5 (71.4); bill, 16.0–18.5 (17.3); tarsus, 16.0–19.0 (17.8); middle toe, 8.9–10.4 (9.4).

RANGE: S. Arizona and s.w. New Mexico, south to Nayarit. Winters from Sonora to Oaxaca. Rare to casual in Trans-Pecos Texas.

TEXAS: *Migration*: Three specimens: El Paso Co., El Paso (2 on May 11, 1891, F. Stephens); Brewster Co., 9 mi. southeast of Glenn Springs (June 17, 1932, E. C. Jacot).

EASTERN PHOEBE, *Sayornis phoebe* (Latham)

SPECIES ACCOUNT   *See colorplate 21*

A medium-sized flycatcher given to wagging its longish tail downward; lacks eye-ring and conspicuous wing-bars; entire bill black. Grayish brown head, upper parts; whitish or yellowish under parts with olive wash on breast and sides. Length, 6¾ in.; wingspan, 10¾; weight, ¾ oz.

RANGE: C. Mackenzie to New Brunswick, south (east of Rockies) to c. Texas, n. Mississippi, c. Alabama, n. Georgia, and North Carolina. Winters mainly from s.e. United States through c. and e. Mexico to Oaxaca and Quintana Roo.

TEXAS: (See map.) *Breeding*: Mid-Feb. to late July (eggs, Mar. 17 to June 27; nest just completed, July 8) from 200—rarely lower—to about 2,500 ft. Fairly common to scarce in central portions from Red River to San Antonio; increasingly scarce and local west of 101st meridian to central Trans-Pecos, where rare; rare and extremely local in eastern third. *Winter*: Early Oct. to late Mar.—often well into Apr. (extremes: July 9, May 28). Very common (usually along coast) to uncommon in most of state; scarce in southern Panhandle; rare in northwestern Trans-Pecos. Absent from northern and middle Panhandle, where normally an uncommon to scarce transient.

HAUNTS AND HABITS: In the breeding season, the familiar Eastern Phoebe seeks fresh water and some leafy shade in humid, cool situations. This solitary but unshy bird is conspicuous along streams, roadsides, about cultivated fields, and, more than most U.S. tyrannids, in farmyards and gardens of towns.

Flight of the Eastern is light and butterflylike. Midair flycatching for wasps, bees, flies, beetles, and other insects involves easy turns, dives, and tumbles; often the phoebe swoops down over a stream to snap up a dragonfly or other winged insect near the water's surface or it will hover before a tree or bush to snatch an insect or berry from the foliage. When perching, the Eastern typically wags or sways its tail downward, recoiling it to one side or the other; this gesture is not a twitch but a sweeping motion, as if the tail were being gently blown by the wind.

Note of the Eastern is a sharp *chip*. Its song is a clearly enunciated *fi-bee* or *fi-bree*, sometimes with a repetition of the second syllable; in the breeding season this is persistently sung in early morning and rather infrequently throughout the day. In spring, the Eastern Phoebe also sings from the air, here trilling the *bee* to a series of *bee-bee-bee*'s. Song season is mainly from February into July.

DETAILED ACCOUNT: NO SUBSPECIES

DESCRIPTION: *Adults, nuptial plumage*: Acquired by wear from winter plumage. Pileum and sides of head dark olive brown; remainder of upper surface including lesser wing-coverts grayish olive; tail hair brown, outermost feather on each side narrowly margined with yellowish or brownish white on outer web, except at tip; wing-quills and greater and lesser wing-coverts dark hair brown, secondaries broadly margined on outer webs with yellowish or brownish white, and more broadly on inner webs at base with dull buff or brownish white; edges of

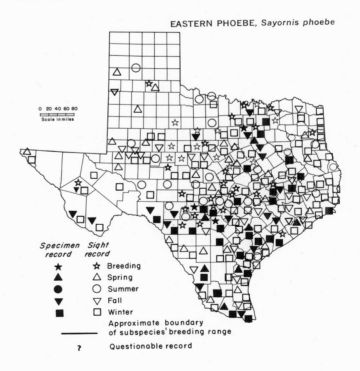

EASTERN PHOEBE, *Sayornis phoebe*

0 20 40 60 80
Scale in miles

Specimen   Sight
record   record
★   ☆ Breeding
▲   △ Spring
●   ○ Summer
▼   ▽ Fall
■   □ Winter

――― Approximate boundary
     of subspecies' breeding range

?   Questionable record

median coverts slightly paler than coverts; lower parts yellowish white, breast shaded on sides with grayish olive of upper surface, and sides and flanks washed with same; lining of wing very pale yellow or yellowish white, outer coverts with hair brown or drab centers. Bill essentially black, slightly paler below; legs and feet black; iris vandyke brown. *Adults, winter*: Acquired by complete postnuptial molt. Similar to nuptial adults, but white portions of lower surface primrose yellow; back and posterior upper surface more decidedly olivaceous (less grayish); pale edgings of wings more yellowish. *First nuptial*: Acquired by wear from first winter. Like first nuptial male and female, except for wing-quills and tail retained from juvenal. *First winter*: Acquired by partial postjuvenal molt. Very similar in coloration to adults in winter, but wing-quills and tail feathers retained from juvenal. *Juvenal*: Acquired by complete postnatal molt. Similar to nuptial adults, but upper parts more brownish with faintly barred appearance, upper tail-coverts broadly edged with dull buffy brown, median and greater series of wing-coverts forming two conspicuous wing-bars broadly margined with cinnamon or cinnamon buff; lower surface, particularly anteriorly, somewhat duller. Bill black, blackish slate, or raw umber; iris dark brown; feet clove brown or black. *Natal*: Mouse gray or drab.

MEASUREMENTS: *Adult male*: Wing, 81.0–90.4 (average, 87.4) mm.; tail, 67.1–77.5 (72.4); bill (exposed culmen), 13.5–16.0 (14.5); tarsus, 17.5–19.6 (18.3); middle toe without claw, 9.9–10.9 (10.7). *Adult female*: Wing, 77.0–89.4 (83.3); tail, 63.0–74.9 (69.3); bill, 13.5–15.0 (14.2); tarsus, 16.5–19.0 (17.8); middle toe, 9.9–10.9 (10.4).

TEXAS: *Breeding*: Collected north to Cooke (Sept. 4), southeast to Brazoria, west to Bexar (eggs) and Kerr (eggs) cos. *Winter*: Taken north to Collin, east to Jefferson, south to Cameron, west to Jeff Davis (Oct. 12) cos.

NESTING: *Nest*: On hills or lowlands, along streams, on cliffs, in forests, open country, or cultivated areas; bulky cup placed in crevice of bank, cave, bridge, or building (even in towns), sometimes on upturned roots of fallen tree, or even brake-beam of freight car; composed of mud, moss, dead leaves, and a little vegetable down; lined with grass, moss, roots, and feathers. *Eggs*: 3–8, usually 5; ovate; moderately glossy; pure white, unmarked, or with a few scattered reddish brown or black dots; average size, 19.0 × 14.5 mm.

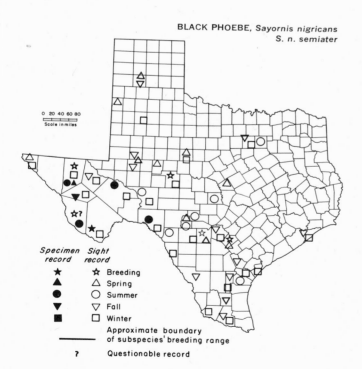

BLACK PHOEBE, *Sayornis nigricans*
S. n. semiater

0 20 40 60 80
Scale in miles

Specimen   Sight
record   record

★   ☆ Breeding
▲   △ Spring
●   ○ Summer
▼   ▽ Fall
■   □ Winter

——— Approximate boundary of subspecies' breeding range

?   Questionable record

BLACK PHOEBE, *Sayornis nigricans* (Swainson)

SPECIES ACCOUNT

Black or blackish head and upper parts, breast, and sides contrast sharply with white belly and crissum. Length, 7¼ in.; wingspan, 11¼; weight, ¾ oz.

RANGE: California to w. Texas, south through n. and highland Mexico and mountains of Central and South America to n. Argentina. In winter individuals of northern race wander slightly.

TEXAS: (See map.) *Breeding*: Late Feb. to early July (eggs, Mar. 30 to May 9; young in nest to June 28) from about 1,000 to 7,000 ft. Fairly common in much of Trans-Pecos east locally to southwestern Edwards Plateau; rare and local on remainder of western Plateau. Nest under construction at Floresville (elevation, 390 ft.), Wilson Co., in late Feb., 1963 (Mrs. W. A. Smith); nest and one bird observed at site, Mar. 23 (Elisabeth R. Blount, Betty Roberts); nest subsequently abandoned (fide C. R. Bender). *Winter*: Mid-Oct. to mid-Mar. (extremes: Aug. 6, May 14). Common to fairly common throughout breeding range; rare north to Panhandle; increasingly rare east to Dallas, Gulf coast, and Rio Grande delta, where casual.

HAUNTS AND HABITS: The handsome Black Phoebe is attracted to water and light shade in dry country. On its range in the southwestern United States, it typically seeks cottonwoods, willows, and sycamores skirting the lower reaches of a rocky mountain stream. The Black Phoebe and Vermilion Flycatcher are the only widespread U.S. tyrannids which are essentially nonmigratory throughout most of their range.

Flight, normally not protracted, is rather slow and mothlike, although mid-air insect chases are swifter. Avoiding treetops, the Black is usually seen wagging its longish tail while perched on a rock, fence, or branch in the lower part of a tree.

The Black Phoebe's call is a crisp *tsip*. Song is a thin, often repetitious *fi-bee, fi-bee*, the first *fi-bee* rising, the second dropping in pitch. In Texas, the bird begins singing late in February and may continue into July.

DETAILED ACCOUNT: ONE SUBSPECIES

NORTHERN BLACK PHOEBE, *Sayornis nigricans semiater* (Vigors)

Sayornis nigricans semiatra of A.O.U. check-list, 1957.

DESCRIPTION: *Adults, nuptial plumage*: Acquired by wear from winter plumage. Pileum chaetura black, remainder of upper surface, including wings, tail, chin, throat, and breast, chaetura drab, paling to hair brown on shorter upper tail-coverts; secondaries and tertials margined on outer webs with dull white; median and greater wing-coverts tipped with hair brown or dull drab, forming two rather conspicuous wing-bars; outer web of outermost tail feathers dull white; lining of wing, abdomen, and crissum white, the last sometimes with very narrow central shaft streaks of chaetura drab. Bill black, but base of mandible somewhat brownish; inside of mouth and rictus yellow; iris dark brown; legs and feet black or brownish black. *Adults, winter*: Acquired by complete postnuptial molt. Like nuptial adults but darker. *First nuptial*: Acquired by wear from first winter. Like nuptial adults, except worn wing-quills and tail feathers re-

Black Phoebe, *Sayornis nigricans*

tained from juvenal. *First winter*: Acquired by partial postjuvenal molt. Like adults in winter, except for retained wing-quills and tail feathers of juvenal. *Juvenal*: Acquired by complete postnatal molt. Similar to nuptial adults, but upper and lower parts duller and more brownish; scapulars and rump tipped with dull cinnamon or hair brown; tertials terminally washed with cinnamon; wing-coverts, particularly greater and median series, tipped with dull cinnamon; anterior lower parts duller and more brownish. *Natal*: Light drab.

MEASUREMENTS: *Adult male*: Wing, 84.1–96.0 (average, 91.4) mm.; tail, 71.1–84.1 (79.7); bill (exposed culmen), 14.0–16.5 (15.5); tarsus, 17.5–19.6 (18.3); middle toe without claw, 9.4–10.9 (10.4). *Adult female*: Wing, 81.0–93.5 (86.6); tail, 68.1–80.0 (74.7); bill, 14.0–16.0 (14.7); tarsus, 15.5–18.0 (17.3); middle toe, 9.4–10.9 (10.2).

RANGE: N. California to w. Texas, south to Baja California and Sinaloa. Wanders slightly in winter.

TEXAS: *Breeding*: Collected in Culberson, Jeff Davis, Pecos, Val Verde, Brewster, and Presidio cos. *Winter*: See species account.

NESTING: *Nest*: In rocky canyons, on mesas, lowlands, and hills, wooded or sometimes more open country; rocky ledge, in shallow cave, under bridge, in well, or nook about building, usually not far from water; rarely even in a low tree; bulky cup composed of mud, weeds, grass, hair, moss, and feathers; lined with fine roots, strips of bark, tops of grass, wool, hair, fine wood fibers, and a few feathers. *Eggs*: 3–6, usually 4–5; ovate; white, unmarked, or with a very few dots of reddish brown; average size, 18.8 × 14.5 mm.

SAY'S PHOEBE, *Sayornis sayus* (Bonaparte)

SPECIES ACCOUNT

Sayornis saya of A.O.U. check-list, 1957 (see Appendix A). A large, pale phoebe with orange-brown belly and crissum. Grayish brown above; buffy gray throat, breast; black tail. Length, 7¾ in.; wingspan, 13; weight, 1 oz.

RANGE: C. Alaska to s.w. Manitoba, south to n. Baja

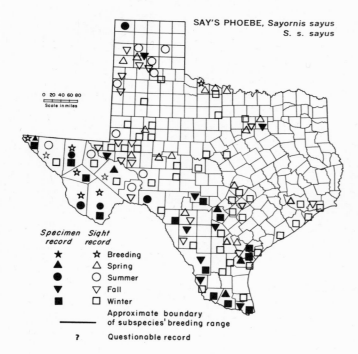

SAY'S PHOEBE, *Sayornis sayus*
S. s. *sayus*

0 20 40 60 80
Scale in miles

Specimen   Sight
record   record

★   ☆ Breeding
▲   △ Spring
●   ○ Summer
▼   ▽ Fall
■   □ Winter

——— Approximate boundary of subspecies' breeding range

?   Questionable record

California and c. mainland Mexico. Winters mainly from California, n. Arizona, c. New Mexico, and s.w. Texas to s. Baja California, Puebla, and Veracruz.

TEXAS: (See map.) *Breeding*: Late Mar. to late Aug. (eggs, Apr. 7 to June 27; parents tending nearly grown young, Aug. 25) from 1,000 to about 6,000 ft. Common to uncommon in most of Trans-Pecos; uncommon in summer in Panhandle, apparently nesting locally (closest definite record: Wilbarger Co., Vernon, nest and 5 eggs taken, May 29, 1932, R. L. More). *Winter*: Early Nov.—often late Sept.—to mid-Mar.—often late Apr. (extremes: Aug. 28, May 19). Common to fairly common in Trans-Pecos; fairly common to uncommon in remainder of western half south of 32nd parallel and in Rio Grande delta; scarce north to middle Panhandle, east to Dallas, Bastrop, and central coast; rare and local on upper coast.

HAUNTS AND HABITS: The Say's Phoebe inhabits open, arid regions of western North America. In Texas, the species is as typical in the vicinity of ranches as the Eastern Phoebe is about farms. Particularly during winter, Say's moves into groves along streams or on prairies but seldom if ever into heavily wooded situations. This bird is another solitary flycatcher; rarely are more than two seen together.

Flight for short distances is jerky and usually zigzag but capable of being long sustained during migrations. Say's insect-catching sallies are typical of its family. In perching it sits much like the Eastern but pumps its tail less frequently.

The note of the Say's is a soft, melancholy sounding *pee-ur* (described also as *phee-eur*) or *pee-ee*; the bird sometimes twitches its tail and raises its crest as it vocalizes. Another call, which probably serves as song, is heard chiefly during breeding season but occasionally in winter; it is a swift *pit-tsee-ar*, sometimes followed by a trilling note. Song is most frequent from March well into July.

DETAILED ACCOUNT: TWO SUBSPECIES

ROCKY MOUNTAIN SAY'S PHOEBE, *Sayornis sayus sayus* (Bonaparte)

DESCRIPTION: *Adults, nuptial plumage*: Acquired by wear from winter plumage. Upper surface hair brown; pileum darker, back and rump paler and more rufescent, verging somewhat toward mouse gray; upper tail-coverts and tail chaetura black, outer feathers rather lighter; wing-quills hair brown, inner margins at base rather paler, tips of primaries rather darker; wing-coverts hair brown, edges rather lighter; tips of greater coverts brownish white or light dull drab, forming inconspicuous wingbar; outer edges of secondaries and tertials rather paler; sides of head and neck hair brown; lores chaetura black or chaetura drab; chin and throat light brownish gray, slightly washed with cinnamon; remainder of lower parts cinnamon; lining of wing dull pinkish buff. Bill black or dark brown, mandible sometimes chaetura black or paler; iris bister or hazel; legs and feet plumbeous black or dark brown; claws black. *Adults, winter*: Acquired by complete postnuptial molt. Similar to nuptial adults but darker both above and below. *First nuptial*: Acquired by wear from first winter. Like nuptial adults, but wing-quills and rectrices retained from juvenal. *First winter*: Acquired by partial postjuvenal molt. Like adults in winter, except for retained juvenal wing-quills and tail feathers. *Juvenal*: Acquired by complete postnatal molt. Similar to nuptial adults but duller, rather lighter, and more brownish above, particularly on back, shorter upper tail-coverts tipped with dull cinnamon; all wing-coverts broadly edged with dull cinnamon, outer edges of tertials also dull cinnamon; anterior lower parts rather duller. *Natal:* Brownish gray.

MEASUREMENTS: *Adult male:* Wing, 100.1–108.5 (average, 104.6) mm.; tail, 79.0–85.6 (82.3); bill (exposed culmen), 14.0–15.0 (14.2); tarsus, 20.1–22.1 (21.4); middle toe without claw, 10.9–12.4 (11.7). *Adult female:* Wing, 96.0–103.1 (99.6); tail, 74.9–81.0 (78.2); bill, 12.4–15.0 (13.7); tarsus, 19.6–21.6 (20.3); middle toe, 10.9–11.9 (11.4).

RANGE: E. Oregon to s.w. Manitoba, south to n.w. Durango and n. Coahuila. Winters from n. California and n. Texas to Veracruz.

TEXAS: *Breeding:* Collected in Wilbarger (nest and eggs), Brewster, Presidio, Culberson, and El Paso cos. One summer specimen from Panhandle: Dallam Co., Texline (Aug. 7, 1903, A. H. Howell). *Winter:* Taken northeast to Dallas (Nov. 13), south to Refugio and Cameron, west to El Paso cos. Fairly common.

NESTING: *Nest:* On mesas, in canyons, hollows, cliffs, or cultivated areas; on rock ledge, under bridge, in old mine shaft, old well, cave, or about barn, even in old nest of Cliff Swallow, or in burrow of Bank Swallow, or in Robin's nest in a bush; compactly built though rather flat cup; with little or no mud, composed mostly of moss, weeds, grass, and other vegetable fibers, feathers, hair, and wool; lined with wool, hair, or feathers. *Eggs:* 3–6, usually 4–5; ovate to short ovate; white, unmarked; average size, 19.6 × 15.0 mm.

YUKON SAY'S PHOEBE, *Sayornis sayus yukonensis* Bishop

DESCRIPTION: *Adults, nuptial plumage:* Similar to *S. s. sayus* but darker above and below; upper surface more clearly grayish; wings and tail somewhat shorter. *Juvenal:* Differs from juvenal of *S. s. sayus* as does adult, but differences more pronounced; upper parts much less rufescent and anterior lower parts darker.

MEASUREMENTS: *Adult male:* Wing, 99.1–109.0 (average, 104.4) mm.; tail, 74.9–87.1 (81.3); bill (exposed culmen), 11.9–14.5 (13.2); tarsus, 20.1–22.9 (21.1); middle toe without claw, 10.9–12.4 (11.7). *Adult female:* Wing, 95.0–104.9 (99.8); tail, 74.9–82.0 (78.2); bill, 11.9–14.0 (12.7); tarsus, 19.6–22.1 (20.3); middle toe, 10.9–12.4 (11.4).

RANGE: C. Alaska to n.w. Mackenzie, south to c. California. Winters from n. California to c. Baja California, Texas, and Tamaulipas.

TEXAS: *Winter:* Taken northwest to El Paso, east to Kerr and Nueces, south to Cameron (Mar. 20) cos. Uncommon.

YELLOW-BELLIED FLYCATCHER, *Empidonax flaviventris* (Baird and Baird)

SPECIES ACCOUNT

The yellowest below of the U.S. look-alike *Empidonax* flycatchers. Members of this genus have whitish or yellowish eye-rings, wing-bars (2 per wing), and lower mandibles; all species except Gray (see below), jerk or twitch tail up, then down. *Empidonax* wings are much shorter than those of phoebes or wood pewees. Voice, range, and breeding habitat are only reliable field aids in identification of most. See voice discussion. *E. flaviventris:* olive above; dull yellow below (from chin to crissum) with olive wash on breast and sides; yellowish eye-ring, wing-bars. Length, 5½ in.; wingspan, 8½; weight, ½ oz.

RANGE: N. British Columbia to Newfoundland, south to n. North Dakota, n. Great Lakes region, and s. New Hampshire, and in Appalachians to n.e. Pennsylvania. Winters mainly from e. and s. Mexico to Panama.

TEXAS: (See map.) *Migration:* Late Apr. to late May; early Aug. to early Oct. (extremes: Feb. 21, June 2; July 23, Nov. 12). Common to fairly common along coast; fairly common to scarce in remainder of eastern half; casual in Trans-Pecos. *Winter:* No specimen, but two sight records, both from Cameron Co.: Harlingen (2 seen, Dec. 27, 1947, Ruby Sandmeyer); Brownsville (1 seen, Dec. 31, 1971, Rose Ann Rowlett, Suzanne Winckler).

HAUNTS AND HABITS: Among the many notoriously similar *Empidonax* flycatchers, the Yellow-bellied is the species most attracted to cool, swampy, northern thickets. It summers in dense shade of coniferous forests in Canada and northern United States where it sinks its nest in a cavity of moss usually among upturned roots of a tree. When migrating through eastern Texas, it frequents similar dense situations: timber and brush along streams, woodland undergrowth, and thickets bordering fields. It is seldom found in companies but is usually scattered singly.

In flight it is rather weak except for quick bursts into the air after insects. The Yellow-bellied Flycatcher also eats spiders—in larger quantities than do other tyrannids—and occasionally wild fruits. Shy and retiring, the bird keeps ordinarily within cover of protective vegetation.

On the breeding territory, the Yellow-bellied Flycatcher's voice is a key factor in identifying the species. There is some disagreement about which notes are songs and which are calls or alarms; however, the common vocalization is a simple, plaintive *chu-wee* or *perwhee* rising on the second syllable; this is somewhat

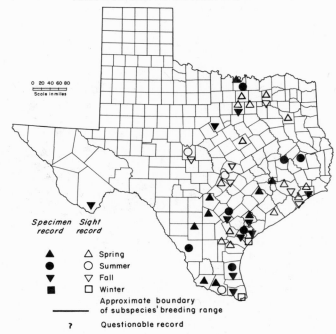

YELLOW-BELLIED FLYCATCHER, *Empidonax flaviventris*

0 20 40 60 80
Scale in miles

Specimen | Sight
record | record

▲ | △ Spring
● | ○ Summer
▼ | ▽ Fall
■ | □ Winter
—— Approximate boundary of subspecies' breeding range
? Questionable record

suggestive of the call of the Semipalmated Plover. Also heard is a *killic*, often given while the bird is on the wing. During migration, it utters a soft *pea-pea-pea* which is often muffled by dense vegetation. This flycatcher, however, seldom calls and almost never sings during its migrations through Texas.

DETAILED ACCOUNT: NO SUBSPECIES

DESCRIPTION: *Adults, nuptial plumage*: Acquired by partial prenuptial molt. Upper parts dull olive green, feathers of pileum with fuscous centers; tail hair brown, exterior web of outermost rectrix a little paler, but remainder of rectrices with outer margins narrowly edged with dull olive green; wing-quills and wing-coverts rather dark hair brown or chaetura drab, inner margins at base paler or yellowish white; primaries edged on outer webs basally with dull olive green, secondaries with greenish or yellowish white; lesser wing-coverts margined with dull olive green; greater and median coverts broadly tipped with pale yellowish white or naphthalene yellow, forming two conspicuous wing-bars; sides of head and of neck dull olive green, lores paler, and conspicuous eye-ring white or pale yellow; chin and upper throat dull primrose yellow, tinged on sides with dull grayish olive green; jugulum and upper breast rather grayish light yellowish olive; remainder of lower surface dull citrine yellow, but sides and flanks washed with olivaceous; lining of wing primrose yellow. Bill black, slate black, blackish slate, or clove brown, mandible deep chrome or buffy yellow; iris dark brown; legs and feet slate color, clove brown, olive brown, or hair brown. *Adults, winter*: Acquired by complete, but protracted postnuptial molt. Like nuptial adults. *First nuptial*: Acquired by complete prenuptial molt. Like nuptial adults. *First winter*: Acquired by partial postjuvenal molt. Similar to adults in winter, except for retention of wing-quills and tail feathers from juvenal. *Juvenal*: Acquired by complete postnatal molt. Similar to nuptial adults, but upper parts duller, rather lighter, and more brownish or yellowish; light wing-bars chamois or cream buff; anterior lower surface duller, rather more brownish. Bill slate color, but mandible flesh color; feet slate color or brownish flesh color.

MEASUREMENTS: *Adult male*: Wing, 65.0–70.1 (average,

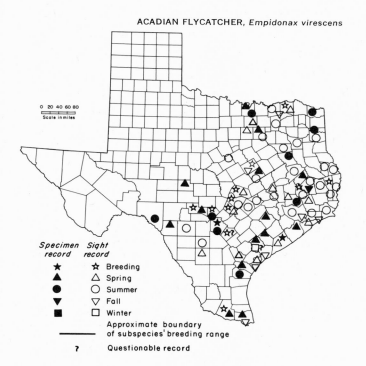

ACADIAN FLYCATCHER, *Empidonax virescens*

0 20 40 60 80
Scale in miles

Specimen   Sight
record   record

★   ☆ Breeding
▲   △ Spring
●   ○ Summer
▼   ▽ Fall
■   □ Winter

——— Approximate boundary of subspecies' breeding range

?   Questionable record

67.8) mm.; tail, 49.5–55.6 (52.8); bill (exposed culmen), 10.9–11.4 (11.2); tarsus, 15.5–17.0 (16.5); middle toe without claw, 8.6–9.4 (8.9). *Adult female*: Wing, 62.5–65.0 (63.8); tail, 47.0–52.1 (50.0); bill, 10.9–11.4 (11.2); tarsus, 16.0–17.0 (16.8); middle toe, 8.1–8.9 (8.6).

TEXAS: *Migration*: Collected north to Cooke, east to Polk (Aug. 28) and Chambers, south to Cameron, west to Webb (Aug. 25), Bexar, and Erath cos.; two specimens from Brewster Co., Big Bend Nat. Park (Sept. 3, 1968, Sept. 1, 1969, R. H. Wauer).

ACADIAN FLYCATCHER, *Empidonax virescens* (Vieillot)

SPECIES ACCOUNT

Only member of its genus that normally breeds in central and east Texas. A nondescript eastern *Empidonax*, greener above than most. See voice discussion. Greenish above; whitish or yellowish (especially in fall) below with olive wash on breast and sides; whitish or yellowish eye-ring, wing-bars. Length, 5¾ in.; wingspan, 9; weight, ½ oz.

RANGE: S.e. South Dakota to extreme s. New England, south to c. and s.e. Texas, Gulf coast, and c. Florida. Winters from s. Mexico (a few) through Central America to Ecuador and w. Venezuela.

TEXAS: (See map.) *Breeding*: Early May to late July (eggs, May 9 to July 11) from near sea level to about 2,000 ft. Fairly common to uncommon in eastern third west locally to Gainesville, Waco, and Austin, south to vicinity of Houston (formerly to Matagorda Co.), and locally on southern and eastern Edwards Plateau. Casual in Rio Grande delta: area of Santa Ana Nat. Wildlife Refuge (nest and eggs located, July 1, 1940, L. I. Davis). *Migration*: Mid-Apr. to mid-May; early Aug. to mid-Sept.—occasionally mid-Oct. (extremes: Mar. 17, May 22; July 15, Dec. 8). Common to uncommon through eastern half west to Edwards Plateau.

HAUNTS AND HABITS: The Acadian is so exasperatingly similar to the Traill's, Least, and fall-plumaged Yellow-bellied flycatchers that only by its nesting habits and voice can it be identified in the field with any degree of certainty. Although it breeds from South Dakota and New England southward, the Acadian is characteristically a bird of the South. A typical breeding ground is a baldcypress swamp south of the Mason-Dixon line. In Texas—where it is the only *Empidonax* which nests in central (except for one 19th century report of a Traill's breeding in Concho Co.) and eastern portions of the state—it also seeks oak woodlands along a creek or in a valley. Good habitat for the present species is still rather widespread in the eastern third of Texas, especially in the famed Big Thicket region.

Like others in its genus, the Acadian is weak and fluttery on the wing except when it darts into the air for a fly, moth, wasp, bee, or beetle. A bird of the lower parts of the woods, it usually perches inconspicuously in deep shade where it sometimes flicks its tail as it calls. In spring, as the Acadian is nest building, it gath-

PLATE 18: Eastern Kingbird, *Tyrannus tyrannus*

ers gossamers of the webworm which the bird uses extensively to swathe the supporting crotch of its nest, thus strengthening the rather flimsy appearing structure.

The common note of this flycatcher is a simple *peet*. The retiring Acadian is generally first betrayed by an explosive *spit-chee*, labeled as the bird's song, or by its hiccup note, *wicky-up*. The *spit-chee* is heard in Texas generally from April to mid-July.

DETAILED ACCOUNT: NO SUBSPECIES

DESCRIPTION: *Adults, nuptial plumage*: Acquired by partial prenuptial molt. Upper parts grayish olive green, rather darker and more brownish on pileum, where feathers have obvious fuscous brown centers; tail hair brown, outer web of outermost pair of feathers barely paler than remainder of tail; wings rather dark hair brown; primaries and secondaries edged on inner webs, except at tips, with brownish white; secondaries and tertials margined on outer webs with yellowish white; lesser wing-coverts broadly margined with grayish olive green like back, median and greater series broadly tipped with dull dark olive buff or yellowish white, forming two conspicuous wing-bars; sides of head and of neck grayish olive green, but eyelids pale sulphur yellow or yellowish white, forming conspicuous eye-ring; chin and throat yellowish white; jugulum pale grayish olive washed with olive green; posterior lower parts primrose or pale sulphur yellow, sometimes whitish on middle of abdomen, sides washed with olivaceous; lining of wing pale sulphur or primrose yellow. Bill slate black or dark brown, mandible light yellow or dull white with faint tinge of flesh color; iris seal brown; legs and feet plumbeous. *Adults, winter*: Acquired by complete postnuptial molt. Practically identical with nuptial adults, except flanks and abdomen often more deeply yellow. *First nuptial*: Acquired by complete prenuptial molt. Like nuptial adults. *First winter*: Acquired by partial postjuvenal molt. Like adults in winter, except for retained wing-quills and tail feathers from juvenal; also much more yellowish, sometimes lower parts almost uniformly sulphur yellow. In this plumage often closely resembles Yellow-bellied Flycatcher, *E. flaviventris*.

Juvenal: Acquired by complete postnatal molt. Similar to nuptial adults, but upper parts duller and more brownish, feathers tipped with pale dull buff; wing-coverts, particularly two light wing-bars, cinnamon buff or pale dull buff; lower parts duller and anteriorly more yellowish. Bill black, but mandible pinkish buff; feet sepia. *Natal*: White, slightly buffy.

MEASUREMENTS: *Adult male*: Wing, 71.1–80.5 (average, 74.2) mm.; tail, 55.1–61.5 (59.2); bill (exposed culmen), 11.4–13.0 (12.4); tarsus, 14.5–16.0 (15.5); middle toe without claw, 8.1–9.9 (8.6). *Adult female*: Wing, 67.6–75.4 (70.4); tail, 54.1–61.0 (56.1); bill, 10.9–12.4 (11.9); tarsus, 14.5–15.5 (14.7); middle toe, 8.1–8.9 (8.6).

TEXAS: *Breeding*: Collected north to Cooke, east to Bowie, south to Montgomery and Bexar, west to Kerr cos.; formerly south to Matagorda Co., taken in summer in Val Verde Co. (nesting unconfirmed). *Migration*: Collected north to Cooke, east to Polk, south to Cameron and Hidalgo, west to Kinney and Menard cos.

NESTING: *Nest*: In shady forests, thickets, usually damp, or open woodlands, along streams, or on slopes of valleys; in bush or low tree, often on horizontal fork near end of branch; cup that appears very carelessly built, often looking much like handful of drift left by high water; composed of grass, moss, weed stems, and roots, decorated with blossoms and catkins; little or no lining. *Eggs*: 2–4, usually 3; ovate to elliptical ovate; cream white to buff; very sparsely dotted with dark brown or reddish brown, mostly at larger end; average size, 18.3 × 13.5 mm.

TRAILL'S FLYCATCHER, *Empidonax trailii* (Audubon)

SPECIES ACCOUNT

Alder Flycatcher of many authors. A nondescript *Empidonax*, browner above than most, whiter on throat. See voice discussion. Dark olive brown upper parts; white throat contrasting with olive wash on breast and sides; whitish eye-ring, wing-bars. Length, 5¾ in.; wingspan, 8¾; weight, ½ oz.

RANGE: C. Alaska to Newfoundland, south to s.w. California, s. Arizona, s. New Mexico, Trans-Pecos Texas (rarely), n. Oklahoma (locally), s. Illinois, and Maryland. Winters mainly from Guatemala to Bolivia and n. Argentina.

TEXAS: (See map.) *Breeding*: Has nested (19th century) in Brewster and Concho cos.; also nested in New Mexico near El Paso Country Club (1944, Lena G. Mc-Bee). May still breed rarely in Big Bend Nat. Park, where recorded from May 12 to Aug. 26 (R. H. Wauer). Recently reported breeding in Davis Mts. (Pansy Espy). *Migration*: Late Apr. to late May; early Aug. to mid-Sept. (extremes: Mar. 27, June 18; July 18, Oct. 11). Common to uncommon through eastern two-thirds; uncommon to scarce in western third. *Winter*: No specimen, but 2 birds sighted at Welder Wildlife Refuge, San Patricio Co. (winter of 1958–59, Clarence Cottam); 1 seen and heard at Corpus Christi (Dec. 26, 1968, Beth Payne, Emilie Payne).

HAUNTS AND HABITS: Breeding widely in the United States, except in the South, the Traill's Flycatcher nests in willow, cottonwood, and mesquite groves lining western creeks, as well as in dense damp thickets of alder, elderberry, sumac, and dogwood bordering northeastern streams and bogs. It has the reputation

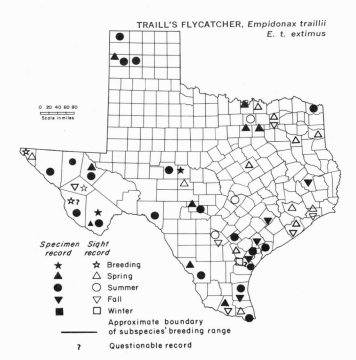

TRAILL'S FLYCATCHER, *Empidonax traillii*
E. t. extimus

0 20 40 60 80
Scale in miles

Specimen record	Sight record	
★	☆	Breeding
▲	△	Spring
●	○	Summer
▼	▽	Fall
■	□	Winter

───── Approximate boundary of subspecies' breeding range

? Questionable record

of being the only *Empidonax* which will set up breeding territories along wooded desert streams. In the nineteenth century, *E. t. extimus*, the southwestern race, apparently bred very locally in the Trans-Pecos and Edwards Plateau of Texas where it found favorable habitat; twentieth century nesting in the Trans-Pecos is possible. Migrants in the state visit open country, cultivated fields, deciduous and mixed woodlands, and swampy thickets. It is a solitary species which remains inconspicuous at low levels in shadowy woods and brush.

Flight of the Traill's is somewhat stronger than that of other small flycatchers and at times the bird makes long, swift passages through the woods. Its mid-air sallies after winged insects are quick and snappy. As do others of its genus, it sits erectly on a perch with tail straight down.

Notes of the Traill's Flycatcher are a low *pep* or *pit* and a sharp *whit*. Its song varies in different localities: In some places it is a hoarse *fee-be-o* accented on the middle syllable; in other localities this sounds more like a wheezy *fitz-bew* or *witch-brew*. Neither song type is heard much in Texas; as a matter of fact, knowledge of which sections of the state are favored by *fee-be-o*'s and which by *fitz-bew*'s seems to be nonexistent.

DETAILED ACCOUNT: FIVE SUBSPECIES

EASTERN TRAILL'S FLYCATCHER, *Empidonax traillii traillii* (Audubon)

DESCRIPTION: *Adults, nuptial plumage (olive green—normal—phase)*: Acquired by partial prenuptial molt. Upper parts rather grayish deep olive; pileum somewhat paler and more brownish or grayish, often with fuscous centers of feathers; upper tail-coverts lighter and somewhat more brownish; tail hair brown, edge of outer web of outermost tail feather slightly paler, particularly at base; wing-quills dark hair brown, inner webs edged with yellowish or brownish white, except at tips, secondaries margined with rather light grayish olive green on middle or terminal portions of outer webs and slightly tipped with same color; tertials with similar but broader edgings; wing-coverts hair brown like quills, lesser series like back, median and greater series broadly tipped with dull yellowish or grayish olive buff, paler olive buff, or yellowish white, forming two conspicuous wing-bars; sides of head and of neck like upper surface, lores dull white with chaetura black spot in front of eye, and eyelids yellowish white forming well-marked eye-ring; lower parts yellowish white or primrose yellow, jugulum, upper breast, and sides washed with dull grayish olive; lining of wing colonial buff. Bill dark brown or blackish brown, mandible dull brownish yellow, except at tip; iris dark brown; legs and feet black or brownish black. *Adults, nuptial (brown phase)*: Similar to olive green phase, but upper surface decidedly brownish, particularly on back. *Adults, winter*: Acquired by complete postnuptial molt. Like nuptial adults in corresponding phase. *First nuptial*: Acquired by complete prenuptial molt. Like nuptial adults. *First winter*: Acquired by partial postjuvenal molt. Very similar to adults in winter, except for wing-quills and tail feathers retained from juvenal. *Juvenal*: Acquired by complete postnatal molt. Similar to nuptial adults, but upper parts duller, more brownish, and edgings of wing-coverts, particularly light wing-bars, dull cinnamon buff or chamois; olive gray breast and sides somewhat more brownish. Bill black, but mandible pinkish buff; feet sepia. *Natal* (this plumage of this race not seen in Texas): Pale olive brown.

MEASUREMENTS: *Adult male*: Wing, 64.5–78.0 (average, 71.7) mm.; tail, 54.1–62.5 (58.2); bill (exposed culmen), 10.9–13.0 (11.9); tarsus, 15.5–17.5 (16.8); middle toe without claw, 8.9–10.4 (9.4). *Adult female*: Wing, 64.5–74.9 (68.3); tail, 51.6–61.5 (55.3); bill, 9.9–12.4 (11.7); tarsus, 14.5–17.5 (16.0); middle toe, 8.6–9.9 (9.1).

RANGE: W. Alaska to Newfoundland, south to n. British Columbia, c. Manitoba, and s.w. Virginia. Winters from Yucatán through Central America to n. Argentina.

TEXAS: *Migration*: Collected northeast to Polk, south to Cameron (Aug. 29), west to Kerr and Brewster cos. Uncommon.

PLAINS TRAILL'S FLYCATCHER, *Empidonax traillii campestris* Aldrich

Race not in A.O.U. check-list, 1957 (see Appendix A).

DESCRIPTION: *Adults, nuptial plumage*: Similar to *E. t. traillii*, but upper parts decidedly paler.

MEASUREMENTS: *Adult male*: Wing, 69.0–75.0 (average, 71.3) mm.; tail, 55.0–59.0 (57.5); bill (exposed culmen), 10.0–12.0 (11.3); tarsus, 15.0–18.5 (16.5); middle toe without claw, 9.0–10.5 (9.5). *Adult female*: Wing, 66.0–68.0 (66.8); tail, 52.0–56.5 (54.5); bill, 10.0–11.0 (10.8); tarsus, 14.5–16.0 (15.5); middle toe, 8.7–10.0 (9.5).

RANGE: Extreme s. Mackenzie, south to n.e. Oklahoma and e. Ohio. Winters from Nicaragua, probably into South America.

TEXAS: *Migration*: Collected north to Oldham (June 6), east to Tarrant, south to Hidalgo, west to Presidio (Aug. 7) and Hudspeth (June 18) cos. Uncommon.

LITTLE TRAILL'S FLYCATCHER, *Empidonax traillii extimus* Phillips

Race not in A.O.U. check-list, 1957 (see Appendix A).

DESCRIPTION: *Adults, nuptial plumage*: Similar to *E. t. traillii*, but bill larger; outermost primary not distinctly longer than sixth; wing-bars darker, duller, and much more brownish; upper parts decidedly paler and more brownish or grayish above. Maxilla black; mandible pale brown or lilaceous brown, somewhat yellowish at base; inside of mouth orange-yellow; iris dark brown; legs and feet black. *Natal*: Probably similar to *E. t. traillii*.

MEASUREMENTS: *Adult male*: Wing, 68.6–72.9 (average, 70.4) mm.; tail, 56.9–66.0 (60.2); bill (exposed culmen), 12.4–13.5 (13.0); tarsus, 15.5–18.3 (16.8); middle toe, 8.9–10.4 (9.7). *Adult female*: Wing, 63.0–67.3 (65.3); tail, 52.1–63.5 (58.2); bill, 11.9–13.0 (12.2); tarsus, 15.5–17.5 (16.3); middle toe, 8.9–10.7 (9.7).

RANGE: C. California to n.e. Texas, south to Durango. Winters from Guerrero through Central America to n.w. Venezuela and n. Argentina.

TEXAS: *Breeding*: Two (?) specimens (19th century): Concho Co. (young taken, 1884–1886, exact date(s) unknown, W. Lloyd); Brewster Co., 15 mi. northwest of Alpine (nest and female parent, July 26, 1890, W. Lloyd). One summer specimen (20th century): Brewster Co., 9 mi. southeast of Glenn Springs (June 17, 1932, E. C. Jacot). (See species account.) *Migration*: Collected north to Dallam (Aug. 3), east to Bowie (July 4), south to Cameron (Aug. 24), west to Culberson (June 9) cos. Fairly common.

NESTING: *Nest*: In sparsely or well-wooded country; usually in brush along rivers, streams, groves, or woodland edges; in bush or tree, usually in upright crotch; compact small cup composed of plant fibers, twine, rags, pieces of newspaper, and plant down; lined with bark fibers, feathers, tops of grass, or horsehair. *Eggs*: 2–4, usually 3–4; ovate, pale cream white to pale buff; marked with a few large and numerous small reddish brown spots, chiefly at larger end; average size, 17.8 × 13.5 mm.

MOUNTAIN TRAILL'S FLYCATCHER, *Empidonax traillii adastus* Oberholser

Race not in A.O.U. check-list, 1957 (see Appendix A).

DESCRIPTION: *Adults, nuptial plumage*: Similar to *E. t. extimus*, but upper surface darker, more grayish or greenish (less yellowish or rufescent) brown. Similar to *E. t. traillii*, but with larger bill; paler, more brownish upper parts; more brownish wing-bars; outermost primary not distinctly longer than sixth.

MEASUREMENTS: *Adult male*: Wing, 69.6–73.7 (average, 71.7) mm.; tail, 58.9–62.0 (60.7); bill (exposed culmen), 10.9–12.7 (12.2); tarsus, 17.0–18.0 (17.3); middle toe without claw, 9.1–10.9 (9.9). *Adult female*: Wing, 65.3–71.9 (67.8); tail, 55.6–61.0 (58.2); bill, 11.2–12.7 (12.2); tarsus, 16.0–18.0 (17.0); middle toe, 9.1–10.4 (9.9).

RANGE: E. British Columbia and w. Alberta, south to n.e. California and n. Utah. Winters from Nicaragua to n. Colombia.

TEXAS: *Migration*: Collected north to Oldham, southeast to Kerr and Refugio (Aug. 14), south to Webb, west to Reeves cos. Fairly common.

NORTHWESTERN TRAILL'S FLYCATCHER, *Empidonax traillii brewsteri* Oberholser

DESCRIPTION: *Adults, nuptial plumage*: Similar to *E. t. extimus* but smaller; darker, more brownish (less grayish) above; breast also darker.

MEASUREMENTS: *Adult male*: Wing, 66.0–71.8 (average, 68.5) mm.; tail, 55.0–62.0 (58.7); bill (exposed culmen), 11.0–13.0 (11.7); tarsus, 16.0–17.8 (17.0); middle toe without claw, 9.0–10.0 (9.6). *Adult female*: Wing, 60.5–68.0 (65.6); tail, 53.5–59.0 (56.3); bill, 11.0–12.0 (11.7); tarsus, 15.5–17.5 (16.4); middle toe, 8.5–10.0 (9.2).

RANGE: S.w. British Columbia, south to s.w. California. Winters from Central America to Colombia.

TEXAS: *Migration*: Two specimens: Reeves Co., Pecos City (Aug. 28, 1902, M. Cary); Calhoun Co., 10 mi. south of Port Lavaca (Aug. 5, 1955, D. E. Dallas, Jr.).

LEAST FLYCATCHER, *Empidonax minimus* (Baird and Baird)

SPECIES ACCOUNT

A nondescript eastern *Empidonax*. See voice discussion. Grayish olive above; whitish below; white eye-ring, wing-bars; brownish lower mandible. Length, 5¼ in.; wingspan, 8; weight, ½ oz.

RANGE: S. Yukon and c. Mackenzie to c. Quebec and Nova Scotia, south chiefly east of Rockies to n. Wyoming, s.w. South Dakota, s.w. Missouri, Ohio River Valley, n. Georgia, and e. Pennsylvania. Winters mainly from Mexico to Panama.

TEXAS: (See map.) *Migration*: Late Apr. to late May; early Aug. to mid-Oct. (extremes: Mar. 18, June 16; July 19, Nov. 27). Common to fairly common through eastern two-thirds; fairly common to uncommon west of 100th meridian to Randall, Reeves, Jeff Davis, and Presidio cos. *Winter*: Dec. 26 to Feb. 7. Casual in Rio Grande delta upriver to Zapata Co. *Empidonax* believed to be Least sighted on Galveston Island (Dec. 31, 1957, fide C. E. Hall).

HAUNTS AND HABITS: In spring and early summer, the Least Flycatcher *che-beck*s incessantly within patches of woods in northeastern United States northward into open deciduous and mixed woodlands of Canada. Here it braces a compact, deep-cupped nest against upright forks of small twigs on a horizontal limb of a tree—apple (unsprayed) being especially favored in New England, but willow, oak, alder, elm, and others are used as well. Bird watchers in Texas cannot rely on the Least's distinctive call, for the bird is typically quiet and retiring as it migrates and infrequently winters in this state. As it passes through, it ranges shade trees, timber, and brush along streams, mesquite thickets, and borders of fields.

Its flight, quick although irregular and fluttering, is ordinarily confined to short excursions after insects from a perch on a bare twig or atop a tall dead weed stalk. In addition to flycatching, the Least works creeperlike on tree trunks for ants, beetles, other insects, and an occasional spider.

The usual note of the Least Flycatcher is *whit*. Its song, energetically uttered early in the morning and again toward evening, is an emphatic *che-beck* strongly accented on the last syllable and accompanied with an upward jerk of the head and flick of the tail. In Texas the bird jerks out a few *che-beck*'s in April and May, but otherwise it is little heard in the Lone Star State.

DETAILED ACCOUNT: NO SUBSPECIES

DESCRIPTION: *Adults, nuptial plumage (gray phase)*: Acquired by partial prenuptial molt. Upper parts dull, rather greenish, deep grayish olive, pileum darker and with fuscous or chaetura drab centers of feathers; upper tail-coverts rather lighter and somewhat more brownish than back; tail hair brown, outermost feathers slightly paler on outer webs; wing-quills rather dark hair brown, inner edge of inner webs paler, on secondaries dull white or yellowish white, inner secondaries and tertials edged except at base with yellowish white on outer webs, this broadest on tertials; upper wing-coverts dark hair brown, lesser series broadly edged with grayish olive of back, median and greater coverts broadly tipped with yellowish or brownish white; sides of head and neck deep grayish olive, lores dull white, and eye-ring grayish or yellowish white; anterior lower parts grayish white, somewhat tinged with olive grayish on sides of throat and

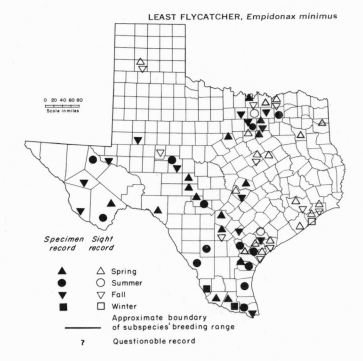

LEAST FLYCATCHER, *Empidonax minimus*

0 20 40 60 80
Scale in miles

Specimen   Sight
record   record

▲   △ Spring
●   ○ Summer
▼   ▽ Fall
■   □ Winter

Approximate boundary
of subspecies' breeding range

?   Questionable record

jugulum; sides of breast grayish olive, breast, sides, and flanks washed with same color; middle of breast, abdomen, and lower tail-coverts marguerite yellow or yellowish white; lining of wing cartridge buff, somewhat mixed with hair brown. Bill brownish black, slate black, blackish slate, slate color, or brownish slate, but mandible dull deep chrome, pinkish buff, buff yellow, dark fawn color, ecru drab, or brownish flesh color, and tip dark brown; iris prout brown or bister; gape and tongue buff yellow; legs and feet olive brown, black, or slate color. *Adults, nuptial (brown phase)*: Similar to gray phase, but upper surface much more brownish—light brownish olive. *Adults, nuptial (green phase)*: Similar to gray phase, but upper surface much more greenish—greenish buffy olive. *Adults, winter*: Acquired by complete postnuptial molt. Similar to corresponding phase of nuptial adults, but upper surface darker and much more brownish or greenish (less grayish); breast and jugulum more brownish or yellowish; posterior lower parts much more deeply yellow —about primrose yellow or straw yellow. *First nuptial*: Acquired by partial prenuptial molt. Like corresponding phase of nuptial adults. *First winter*: Acquired by partial postjuvenal molt. Very similar to first nuptial male and female in corresponding phase, except for retained wing-quills and tail feathers of juvenal. *Juvenal*: Acquired by complete postnatal molt. Similar to adults in winter, but upper surface darker and more sooty; wing-bars and other edgings of wing-coverts much more deeply buff or cinnamon buff; anterior lower surface darker and more brownish; posterior lower surface paler, less deeply yellowish. Bill slate color or dull black, but mandible pinkish buff; iris very dark brown; feet cinereous or sepia.

MEASUREMENTS: *Adult male*: Wing, 58.9–67.1 (average, 64.3) mm.; tail, 50.5–57.9 (54.3); bill (exposed culmen), 9.9–11.4 (10.7); tarsus, 15.0–17.0 (16.3); middle toe without claw, 7.6–8.6 (8.4). *Adult female*: Wing, 59.4–64.5 (60.7); tail, 51.1–56.4 (52.6); bill, 9.9–10.9 (10.4); tarsus, 15.5–17.0 (16.0); middle toe, 7.6–8.9 (8.4).

TEXAS: *Migration*: Collected north to Cooke and Hunt (July 26), south to Victoria and Cameron, west to Val Verde, Presidio, and Jeff Davis cos. *Winter*: Two specimens: Zapata Co., San Ygnacio (Dec. 26, 1948, G. M. Sutton); Hidalgo Co., Lomita Ranch (Feb. 7, 1880, M. A. Frazar).

HAMMOND'S FLYCATCHER, *Empidonax hammondii* (Xántus)

SPECIES ACCOUNT

A nondescript western *Empidonax*. See voice discussion. Olive gray upper parts; whitish throat and grayish breast contrasting more or less with pale yellow belly; whitish eye-ring, wing-bars. Length, 5½ in.; wingspan, 9½; weight, ½ oz.

RANGE: S.e. Alaska and s. Yukon, south through mountains of w. North America to c. California, n. Utah, Colorado, and n. New Mexico. Winters chiefly from n. Sinaloa, c. Nuevo León, and c. Tamaulipas through Mexican mountains to Nicaragua.

TEXAS: (See map.) *Migration*: Mar. 24 to May 31; Aug. 1 to Oct. 9. Fairly common to uncommon through Trans-Pecos; rare in remainder of western third. (See detailed account for specimen evidence.)

HAUNTS AND HABITS: The Hammond's Flycatcher tends to summer at higher altitudes than do other *Empidonaces*. Prime habitat is an open forest of firs, spruces, or pines, although the bird occasionally frequents deciduous trees growing near evergreens. Its neat nest of bark and moss is most often saddled on a horizontal forked branch, usually of a conifer. As a migrant through Trans-Pecos Texas, it seeks, as does its "twin" the Dusky Flycatcher, coniferous trees, mixed woods, and thickets along canyons, streams, gulches, slopes, mountains, and hills.

Although not as active as others in the genus, this flycatcher's flight style is much the same. Most activity involves dashes out from its perch to catch winged insects; it flycatches usually from high branches of trees where it is more at home than other *Empidonaces*.

Typically quieter than its relatives, the Hammond's gives a soft *pit* or *quip* call; occasionally it delivers a single sharp *peep*. To the consternation of *Empidonax* watchers the present bird's thin, colorless song is quite easily confused with those of the Dusky and Gray. Descriptions vary, but common renditions of Hammond's song are *se-lip, twur, tree-ip* or *se-put, tsur-r-r-p, tseep*. Ralph Hoffmann, who had a good ear for bird vocalization, believed the inclusion of a low *twur* or *tsurp* note in the song to be diagnostic. The Hammond's almost never utters anything distinctive when migrating through Texas.

DETAILED ACCOUNT: NO SUBSPECIES

DESCRIPTION: *Adults, nuptial plumage (white-bellied phase)*: Acquired by partial prenuptial molt. Upper surface deep grayish olive, pileum darker; back slightly more greenish; upper tail-coverts lighter and rather more brownish; tail hair brown, outer web of outermost feather slightly paler; wings rather dark hair brown, inner margins of quills, except at tips, of paler brown or yellowish white, middle portion of secondaries and terminal part of tertials edged on outer webs with yellowish white; lesser wing-coverts broadly margined with color of back, median and greater series broadly tipped with dull brownish white; sides of head and neck like upper parts, but lores somewhat paler with rather dark spot in front of eye; anterior lower parts rather pale

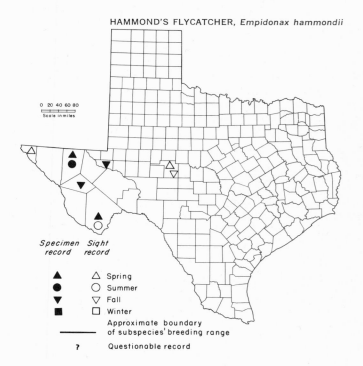

HAMMOND'S FLYCATCHER, *Empidonax hammondii*

0 20 40 60 80
Scale in miles

Specimen   Sight
record   record

▲ △ Spring
● ○ Summer
▼ ▽ Fall
■ □ Winter

——— Approximate boundary of subspecies' breeding range

? Questionable record

light grayish olive; center of throat dull white or yellowish white; posterior lower surface dull marguerite yellow or yellowish white, sides washed with light grayish olive; lining of wing colonial buff or marguerite yellow. Bill black above, mandible light brown or reddish brown; corner of mouth orange-yellow; iris dark bister; legs and feet black. *Adults, nuptial (yellow-bellied phase)*: Similar to white-bellied phase, but upper surface more olivaceous, brownish, or greenish; breast and jugulum much more yellowish or greenish; abdomen much more deeply yellow. *Adults, winter*: Acquired by complete postnuptial molt. Similar to nuptial adults, but upper parts much more greenish or brownish; lower surface, particularly posteriorly, much more deeply yellow or much more strongly suffused with this color. *First nuptial*: Acquired by partial prenuptial molt. Very similar to corresponding phase of nuptial adults, except for wing-quills retained from juvenal. *First winter*: Acquired by partial post-juvenal molt. Similar to corresponding phase of first nuptial male and female. *Juvenal*: Acquired by complete postnatal molt. Similar to nuptial adults, but upper surface darker and much more brownish (less greenish or yellowish), wing-bars much less clearly yellow (more brownish or buff); lower surface duller, anteriorly much more mixed with grayish, posteriorly duller.

MEASUREMENTS: *Adult male*: Wing, 68.1–73.9 (average, 71.4) mm.; tail, 55.1–61.0 (57.7); bill (exposed culmen), 9.9–10.9 (10.7); tarsus, 15.0–17.5 (16.3); middle toe without claw, 8.9–9.9 (9.1). *Adult female*: Wing, 64.5–70.1 (67.8); tail, 52.6–56.9 (55.3); bill, 9.4–10.9 (10.2); tarsus, 15.0–17.0 (15.7); middle toe, 8.6–9.4 (8.9).

TEXAS: *Migration*: *Empidonax hammondii* personally identified by H. C. Oberholser include specimens from the following localities: Culberson Co., McKittrick Canyon (Oct. 9, 1938, T. D. Burleigh); Ward Co., Monahans (Sept. 22, 1902, M. Cary); Jeff Davis Co., Limpia Canyon (Sept. 25, 26, Oct. 3, 1916, A. P. Smith); Brewster Co., Boot Spring (May 6, 1932, J. Van Tyne).

DUSKY FLYCATCHER, *Empidonax oberholseri* Phillips

SPECIES ACCOUNT

Empidonax wrightii of *Distributional Check-list of the Birds of Mexico*, pt. 2, 1957; Wright's Flycatcher of many authors. See voice discussion. Closely resembles Hammond's, but grayer (less olive) above; paler and less yellow below; more distinctly whitish throat; larger bill; slightly longer, brownish tail contrasts somewhat with olive gray of back. Length, 5¾ in.; wingspan, 8¾; weight, ½ oz.

RANGE: S. Yukon to s.w. Saskatchewan and Wyoming, south in mountains to s. California and n. New Mexico. Winters from s. Arizona, c. Nuevo León, and c. Tamaulipas through Mexican mountains and plateaus to Guatemala.

TEXAS: (See map.) *Summer*: Two specimens: Culberson Co., Upper Dog Canyon, 6,650 ft. (2 females collected, largest ovarian follicles of each measured 2 mm., June 20, 24, 1972, G. A. Newman; original nos., 308, 327). Nesting very likely in major canyons on western side of Guadalupe Mts., fide Newman. *Migration*: Apr. 13 to June 6; Aug. 5 to Oct. 4. Fairly common to uncommon through Trans-Pecos; rare in remainder of western third. (See detailed account for specimen evidence of migrants.) *Winter*: Rare and sporadic in Big Bend Nat. Park, Santa Elena Canyon (1 collected

from group of 5, Dec. 30, 1968, at least 1 bird remained through Feb. 8, 1969, R. H. Wauer).

HAUNTS AND HABITS: In western mountains of North America the Dusky Flycatcher nests in open clumps of deciduous woods and thickets on foothills and slopes, leaving conifers at higher altitudes to its look-alike the Hammond's. In a willow, alder, or similar small tree or bush, the Dusky builds a compact bark and moss nest on a low, horizontal branch; the three or four eggs are dull white and usually unmarked. In Arizona this flycatcher is said to migrate more commonly in mountains than in valleys, but in Texas it seems to move at the same altitudes as other members of its genus. However, virtually nothing is known about this species in the Lone Star State since here it is almost impossible to identify with certainty in the field.

Flight and behavior are standard for *Empidonax*.

The present bird's *whit* alarm call seems to be common to practically all members of its group. Male territorial song is reported to be more vigorous and varied than that of Hammond's Flycatcher. A few weak *whit*'s are about all the Dusky utters in Texas.

DETAILED ACCOUNT: TWO SUBSPECIES

OBERHOLSER'S DUSKY FLYCATCHER, *Empidonax oberholseri oberholseri* Phillips

No races recognized by A.O.U. check-list, 1957 (see Appendix A).

DESCRIPTION: *Adults, nuptial plumage (white-bellied phase)*: Acquired by partial prenuptial molt. Upper parts rather greenish hair brown, but pileum darker, central portions of feathers fuscous; rump and upper tail-coverts lighter, somewhat more greenish; tail hair brown, outer web of outermost tail feather distinctly paler, often dull white; wings brown, all but tips of inner webs with inner margin paler, mostly brownish white or yellowish white; outer webs of middle portion of secondaries and outer

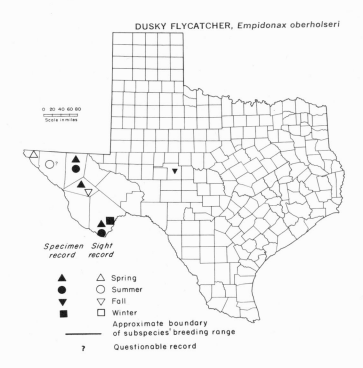

DUSKY FLYCATCHER, *Empidonax oberholseri*

0 20 40 60 80
Scale in miles

Specimen Sight
record   record

▲ △ Spring
● ○ Summer
▼ ▽ Fall
■ □ Winter

——— Approximate boundary
of subspecies' breeding range

? Questionable record

webs of terminal portions of tertials margined with yellowish white; lesser wing-coverts edged with color of back; median and greater series broadly tipped with pale brown, brownish white, or yellowish white, these edgings forming two conspicuous wing-bars; sides of head and neck like upper surface, but lores grayish white and more or less well defined eye-ring yellowish white; middle of chin and upper throat grayish or yellowish white; remainder of lower surface dull white or yellowish white, but breast, sides, and flanks tinged with olive gray, this most conspicuous on sides of breast and jugulum; lining of wing pale colonial buff. Bill black or brownish black, paler basally, mandible brownish white, drab, deep purplish brown, or reddish brown, darker at tip; inside of mouth lemon or orange-yellow; iris dark sepia or vandyke brown; legs and feet black. *Adults, nuptial (yellow-bellied phase)*: Similar to white-bellied phase, but upper parts more brownish or olivaceous; breast more ochraceous; posterior lower parts more deeply yellow. *Adults, winter*: Acquired by complete postnuptial molt. Similar to corresponding phase of nuptial adults, but upper parts more yellowish or olivaceous; posterior lower surface much more deeply yellow. *First nuptial*: Acquired by partial prenuptial molt. Practically identical with corresponding phase of nuptial adults. *First winter*: Acquired probably by partial postjuvenal molt. Very similar to first nuptial male and female. *Juvenal*: Acquired by complete postnatal molt. Similar to nuptial adults, but upper parts duller and more brownish, upper tail-coverts, and particularly edgings of wing-coverts, pale buff or dull cinnamon buff; anterior lower surface duller, more mixed with brownish ochraceous and gray; posterior lower surface distinctly buff instead of yellow. Bill black, basal two-thirds of mandible lilaceous white or pale pinkish flesh color; iris dark sepia; legs and feet plumbeous black.

MEASUREMENTS: *Adult male*: Wing, 64.5–72.4 (average, 69.1) mm.; tail, 59.4–67.6 (63.8); bill (exposed culmen), 9.9–11.9 (11.2); tarsus, 18.0–19.6 (18.8); middle toe without claw, 8.9–10.4 (9.7). *Adult female*: Wing, 64.0–71.1 (66.3); tail, 56.4–67.1 (61.2); bill, 9.9–11.4 (10.7); tarsus, 16.0–19.0 (17.8); middle toe, 8.6–10.2 (9.7).

RANGE: S.e. Idaho to n.w. South Dakota, south to s.w. California and c. New Mexico. Winters from n. Chihuahua and c. Nuevo León to Guatemala.

TEXAS: *Migration*: E. o. oberholseri personally identified by H. C. Oberholser include specimens from the following localities: Culberson Co., head of Dog Canyon (Aug. 23, 1901, V. Bailey); Presidio Co., DuBois Canyon (May 12, 1905, E. F. Prade); Brewster Co., Boot Spring (May 7, 9, 15, 1932, M. M. Peet); Brewster Co., 4 mi. south of Marathon (May 5, 1933, G. M. Sutton); Tom Green Co., San Angelo (2 specimens, fall 1884, W. Lloyd). Fairly common.

IDAHO DUSKY FLYCATCHER, Empidonax oberholseri
spodius Oberholser, new subspecies (see Appendix A)

DESCRIPTION: *Adults, nuptial plumage*: Similar to E. o. oberholseri, but wing longer; olive of upper parts more grayish or greenish (less brownish, ochraceous, or yellowish); yellow or ochraceous of lower parts averaging somewhat paler.

MEASUREMENTS: *Adult male*: Wing, 67.1–73.9 (average, 70.9) mm.; tail, 58.4–67.8 (63.2); bill (exposed culmen), 10.4–11.9 (11.2); tarsus, 16.5–19.6 (18.3); middle toe without claw, 8.9–9.9 (9.7). *Adult female*: Wing, 65.0–71.9 (67.1); tail, 59.9–66.0 (62.0); bill, 9.9–11.4 (10.7); tarsus, 17.0–18.5 (17.8); middle toe, 9.1–10.4 (9.7).

TYPE: Adult male, no. 397487, U.S. National Museum; Gray, Bonneville Co., Idaho; June 15, 1949; T. D. Burleigh, original no., 12142.

RANGE: N.w. British Columbia to s.w. Saskatchewan, south to s. Oregon. Winters from Durango to Guatemala.

TEXAS: *Migration*: E. o. spodius personally identified by H. C. Oberholser include specimens from the following localities: Culberson Co., Bear Canyon, Pine Springs Canyon (May 2, 3, 1939, T. D. Burleigh); Culberson Co., 16 mi. southeast of Van Horn (Aug. 5, 1940, B. E. Ludeman); Jeff Davis Co., Limpia Creek near Fort Davis, and Limpia Canyon 6 mi. east of Mt. Liver-

more (Apr. 24, May 5, 1937, J. Van Tyne); Brewster Co., Boot Spring (May 5, 1932, E. C. Jacot); Brewster Co., Pine Canyon (May 11, 1933, G. M. Sutton, May 13, 1933, A. C. Lloyd). Uncommon.

GRAY FLYCATCHER, Empidonax obscurus
(Swainson)

SPECIES ACCOUNT

Empidonax wrightii of A.O.U. check-list, 1957 (see Appendix A); *Empidonax griseus* of *Distributional Check-list of the Birds of Mexico, pt. 2,* 1957. Gray dips tail down evenly like a slow Phoebe; other *Empidonaces* jerk or twitch tail up, then down. Grayest western *Empidonax*. See voice discussion. Gray above (with very pale olive wash); whitish or grayish below; whitish eye-ring, wing-bars; base of lower mandible flesh color. Length, 6 in.; wingspan, 9.

RANGE: E. Oregon to s.w. Wyoming and w. Colorado, south mainly within Great Basin to e. California, s. Nevada, and w. New Mexico. Winters from s. California, s. Arizona, c. Chihuahua, s. Coahuila, and s. Tamaulipas to c. Mexico.

TEXAS: (See map.) *Migration*: Apr. 3 to June 6. Uncommon through Trans-Pecos. One fall record: Big Bend Nat. Park (1 seen, Aug. 29, 1970, J. A. Tucker, et al.). (See detailed account for specimen evidence.)

HAUNTS AND HABITS: The Gray Flycatcher, characteristic *Empidonax* of the Great Basin region, inhabits more open and arid land than do its close western relatives the Hammond's and Dusky. Good breeding haunts include sagebrush plains and brushy hills grown with scattered juniper or pinyon; here it conceals a bulky, ragged nest in debris at the base of a

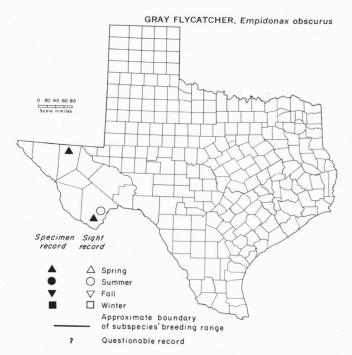

GRAY FLYCATCHER, *Empidonax obscurus*

0 20 40 60 80
Scale in miles

Specimen record
Sight record

▲ △ Spring
● ○ Summer
▼ ▽ Fall
■ □ Winter

Approximate boundary of subspecies' breeding range

? Questionable record

dead sage bush or on the fork of a juniper limb. In Trans-Pecos Texas it can easily be confused with other *Empidonax* migrants. Migrating Grays in the Huachuca Mountains of Arizona move across oak scrub of foothills and largely avoid the canyons and mountain slopes favored by *E. hammondii* and *E. oberholseri*. This habitat preference, however, is not to be relied on heavily in field identification. Currently (1971), the claim is advanced that the Gray is the only *Empidonax* that moves its tail slowly downward instead of jerking it. Time is unlikely to prove this mannerism infallibly diagnostic, especially since wind can dip any bird's tail down.

Flight and behavior of the Gray are characteristic of the genus. It frequently perches atop a bush or low tree from where it flycatches; if startled, it dives swiftly into the brush.

Most frequently heard vocalization is the standard *whit*. Song on the breeding territory is a vigorous *chi-wip*, followed by a faint, high-pitched *cheep*. An occasional *whit* or *pit* is usually all that is heard in Texas.

DETAILED ACCOUNT: NO SUBSPECIES

DESCRIPTION: Similar to Dusky Flycatcher, *E. oberholseri*, but bill longer and relatively narrower; wing longer; tail shorter; upper parts more grayish and usually paler. *Adults, nuptial plumage (gray—normal—phase)*: Acquired by partial prenuptial molt. Upper parts, including sides of head and of neck, between mouse gray and deep olive gray, pileum nearer mouse gray; wings and tail hair brown, outermost tail feather with outer web white; tertials and secondaries conspicuously tipped and margined with grayish white; wing-coverts, except primary coverts, also conspicuously tipped with grayish or brownish white, forming two conspicuous whitish wing-bars; basal portion of inner webs of secondaries yellowish white; eye-ring grayish white; lores and sometimes extreme forehead mixed with grayish white; lower parts grayish white, breast more shaded with brownish gray, slightly or not at all tinged with pale primrose yellow or ivory yellow, particularly on posterior portion; lining of wing pale primrose yellow, somewhat spotted exteriorly with light hair brown or drab. Bill brownish black or blackish brown, base of mandible flesh color; iris dark brown; legs and feet blackish brown or brownish black. *Adults, nuptial (yellowish phase)*: Similar to gray phase, but upper parts grayish olive; lower surface posteriorly primrose yellow. *Adults, nuptial (brown phase)*: Similar to gray phase, but upper parts much more brownish—between hair brown and light brownish olive. *Adults, winter*: Acquired by complete postnuptial molt. Similar to nuptial adults in corresponding phase, but both upper and lower parts very slightly more yellowish. *First nuptial*: Acquired by partial prenuptial molt. Practically identical with corresponding phase of nuptial adults. *First winter*: Acquired probably by partial postjuvenal molt. Similar to first nuptial male and female. *Juvenal*: Acquired by complete postnatal molt. Similar to nuptial adults, but lower parts white; jugulum brownish gray; wing-bars pale buff; upper tail-coverts pale buffy brown.
MEASUREMENTS: *Adult male*: Wing, 68.6–76.5 (average, 72.7) mm.; tail, 57.4–64.0 (60.7); bill (exposed culmen), 11.9–13.5 (12.7); tarsus, 17.0–20.6 (18.3); middle toe without claw, 8.4–9.9 (9.4). *Adult female*: Wing, 66.0–74.4 (69.3); tail, 56.4–62.0 (58.7); bill, 10.4–13.0 (12.2); tarsus, 16.5–19.0 (17.8); middle toe, 8.4–9.4 (8.9).
TEXAS: *Migration*: *Empidonax obscurus* personally identified by H. C. Oberholser include specimens from the following localities: Culberson Co., Pine Springs Canyon in Guadalupe Mts. (May 1, 1939, T. D. Burleigh); Brewster Co., 4 mi. south of Marathon (May 2, 3, 1933, G. M. Sutton); Brewster Co., Pine Canyon (May 11, 1933, G. M. Sutton).

WESTERN FLYCATCHER, *Empidonax difficilis* Baird

SPECIES ACCOUNT

Western counterpart of Yellow-bellied. Only *Empidonax* that breeds regularly in Trans-Pecos. See voice discussion. Brownish olive upper parts; pale yellow throat, under parts; whitish eye-ring; buffy or dull whitish wing-bars. Length, 5¾ in.; wingspan, 8¾.
RANGE: S.e. Alaska and s. British Columbia to s.w. South Dakota, south through w. United States and highland Mexico (lowlands in Sinaloa) to s. Baja California, Guerrero, and Oaxaca; also mountains to Chiapas, Guatemala, and Honduras. Northern races winter mainly in Mexico.
TEXAS: (See map.) *Breeding*: Late May to late July (eggs, June 10; young just out of nest, July 19) from 6,000 to about 8,500 ft. Fairly common but local in Trans-Pecos mts. (Guadalupes, Chisos). *Migration*: Mid-Apr. to mid-May; late Aug. to mid-Sept. (extremes: Apr. 8, May 14; Aug. 26, Sept. 17). Common to fairly common through much of Trans-Pecos. *Winter*: No specimen, but single sighting at Big Bend Nat. Park (Dec. 21, 1966, R. H. Wauer).
HAUNTS AND HABITS: The Western Flycatcher, lookalike of the eastern-ranging Yellow-bellied, seeks woodland shade at fairly high and moderate altitudes, chiefly from the Rocky Mountains westward. In Trans-Pecos Texas, where the Western is the only regular breeding *Empidonax*, it maintains territory in Arizona cypress (*Cupressus arizonica*), western yellow pine (*Pinus ponderosa*), Douglasfir (*Pseudotsuga mucronata*), bigtooth maple (*Acer sinuosum*), and other trees

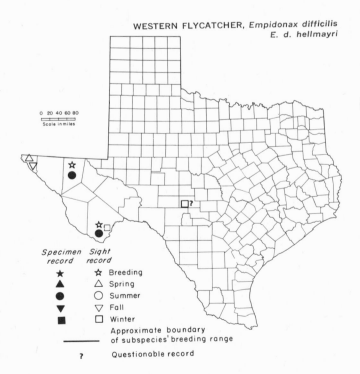

growing along or near canyon streams of the Guadalupe or Chisos mountains.

Flight and habits of the Western are typical of the *Empidonax* group. It flits unobtrusively through shady openings beneath the tree canopy where it snaps up winged insects from the air and plucks caterpillars from tree trunks.

Migrating Western Flycatchers utter the usual *whit*. From the Chisos Mountains, June 9–14, 1901, H. C. Oberholser interpreted one vocalization as a "quaintly emphatic *ter-chip*." Song of Texas birds has apparently not been recorded, but it is probably fairly similar to the song in Arizona as described by Roger Tory Peterson: *bzeek-trit-seet!* Song season in Texas appears to be from May into July.

DETAILED ACCOUNT: ONE SUBSPECIES

CHISOS WESTERN FLYCATCHER, *Empidonax difficilis hellmayri* Brodkorb

DESCRIPTION: Similar to Pacific Western Flycatcher, *E. d. difficilis*, but larger; bill slightly broader and lateral outlines of bill somewhat more convex; wing-bars and light edgings of wing-quills darker, less yellowish (more brownish or grayish) olive green. *Adults, nuptial plumage*: Acquired by partial prenuptial molt. Upper surface yellowish olive, pileum darker and somewhat more brownish, with central portion of feathers fuscous; tail hair brown, basal part of feathers edged narrowly on outer webs with yellowish olive; wings hair brown, coverts rather darker, wing-quills margined on inner webs, except at tips, with pale buff or buffy white, primaries narrowly edged on outer webs with olivaceous, secondaries on outer webs with grayish olive; broad tips of greater and middle wing-coverts isabella color, forming two conspicuous wing-bars; sides of head and neck yellowish olive; lores paler except for dark spot in front of eye; conspicuous eye-ring pale yellow or yellowish white; middle of chin and upper throat dull straw yellow; sides of throat like sides of head; jugulum light buffy olive; sides of body light yellowish olive; middle of breast, abdomen, and crissum straw yellow, deepest on abdomen; lining of wing colonial buff or chamois. Bill black or dark brown, mandible pale dull yellowish or lilac white; iris dark brown; legs and feet brownish black or dark brown. *Adults, winter*: Acquired by partial prenuptial molt. Similar to nuptial adults but more richly colored; above decidedly more yellowish or greenish (less grayish or brownish); yellow of lower parts deeper; jugulum more yellowish or ochraceous (less grayish). *First nuptial*: Acquired by partial prenuptial molt. Like nuptial adults. *First winter*: Acquired probably by partial postjuvenal molt. Practically same as first nuptial male and female. *Juvenal*: Acquired by complete postnatal molt. Similar to nuptial adults, but upper parts much more brownish (less greenish); edgings of wing-coverts cinnamon buff or brownish buff; lower surface duller, yellow portions more buffy, and sometimes paler than in adult, olive areas more brownish or ochraceous. *Natal*: Rather dull wood brown or yellowish gray.

MEASUREMENTS: *Adult male*: Wing, 66.0–72.4 (average, 69.6) mm.; tail, 56.4–63.5 (61.2); bill (exposed culmen), 10.4–12.4 (11.2); width of bill at posterior end of nostril, 6.1–6.9 (6.4); tarsus, 16.8–18.0 (17.3); middle toe without claw, 8.9–9.9 (9.1). *Adult female*: Wing, 65.0–67.6 (66.3); tail, 56.6–62.0 (59.2); bill, 10.2–11.9 (10.9); width of bill, 6.1–6.9 (6.4); tarsus, 16.5–18.0 (17.3); middle toe, 8.6–9.1 (8.9).

RANGE: N. Montana and s.w. South Dakota, south to n.e. Arizona and n. Coahuila. Winters from Sinaloa and Durango to Oaxaca.

TEXAS: *Breeding*: Collected in Culberson and Brewster cos.

NESTING: *Nest*: In mountains; forests of slopes and canyons, usually not far from water; sites and materials used probably

similar to those of *E. d. difficilis*, which are as follows: in cavity in bank along creek, among roots of fallen tree, natural hole in tree, or old woodpecker excavation, or even in corner of rail fence, cavity in rocks, or nook about building; depression matted with plant stems, roots, dead leaves, fine grass, and various other vegetable fibers, cobwebs, vegetable down, and moss; lined with fine grasses, a few feathers, bark strips, rootlets, and horsehair. *Eggs*: 3–5, usually 3 or 4; ovate to short ovate or rounded ovate; cream white or white; spotted finely and coarsely with reddish brown and cinnamon, black, light chestnut, and purplish brown, sometimes well distributed over entire surface, at other times more confluent toward larger end, and forming well-defined ring; average size, 16.5 × 13.2 mm.

[BUFF-BREASTED FLYCATCHER, *Empidonax fulvifrons* (Giraud)

A tiny *Empidonax* with cinnamon buff on breast. Also identified by its dull *pt* note, and its breeding habitat—open pine or streamside groves, usually at lower altitudes than those preferred by Western Flycatcher. Length, 5 in.

RANGE: Sierras of s.e. (formerly c.) Arizona and s.w. New Mexico, south through w. Mexico to El Salvador and Honduras.

TEXAS: *Hypothetical*: The nominate race, *E. f. fulvifrons*, was accredited to Texas by the original describer, J. P. Giraud, Jr. (1841, *A Description of Sixteen New Species of North American Birds . . .*, pl. 4, fig. 2); however, the unique type specimen probably actually came from some part of Mexico. A bird which appeared to be the Arizona race, *E. f. pygmaeus*, was seen in Big Bend Nat. Park, near Chisos Remuda in the Basin (Aug. 12, 1969, Dr. and Mrs. R. C. Smith).]

COUES' FLYCATCHER, *Syrichta pertinax* (Cabanis and Heine)

SPECIES ACCOUNT

Contopus pertinax of A.O.U. check-list, 1957 (see Appendix A). Also known as Greater Pewee and José María. Song is a whistled *ho-say, ree-ah*. Resembles Olive-sided (see below), but under parts more uniformly gray (lacking whitish area on mid-breast), throat grayer; lower mandible dull yellow; tail longer; lacks white tufts at lower back; often shows short, pointed crest. Length, 8 in.; wingspan, 13¼.

RANGE: C. and s.e. Arizona, s.w. New Mexico, s. Coahuila, c. Nuevo León, and c. Tamaulipas, south chiefly through highlands to n. Nicaragua. Winters from s. Sonora, s. Chihuahua, and San Luis Potosí south.

TEXAS: *Summer*: One sighted and heard calling at Big Bend Nat. Park (June 8, 1968, R. H. Wauer). *Migration*: One specimen (juvenal plumage): Jeff Davis Co., Limpia Canyon, 6,000 ft. (Sept. 12, 1916, A. P. Smith). Five sightings: Chambers Co., Cove (Oct. 4, 1959, James Easter, A. K. McKay); Galveston Co., Galveston (Apr. 2, 1964, Mr. and Mrs. J. O. Ellis); Jeff Davis Co., Davis Mts. (Nov. 9, 1963, W. J. Graber

III); Brewster Co., Big Bend Nat. Park (South Rim, Sept. 3, 1966, R. H. Wauer; above Juniper Flat, May 29, 1971, Ted Parker, Harold Morrin).

HAUNTS AND HABITS: The Coues' Flycatcher is a sweet-voiced bird of highland southern Arizona, Mexico, and Central America, ranging at times up to ten thousand feet; in winter many individuals descend from the sierras to warm foothills and even tropic lowlands. Its occurrence throughout Texas is most irregular and rare. The bird breeds in pine-oak situations in canyons, on slopes and ridges, and in timber along streams where it saddles a moss and lichen cup moderately high (15 to 25 feet) on a limb of a coniferous or deciduous tree. The territory of a nesting pair is of considerable size and is carefully defended. Coues' is not gregarious, but during migration and in winter it sometimes associates with companies of nuthatches, warblers, tanagers, and other small forest-roaming species.

In flight it is very similar to its look-alike the Olive-sided Flycatcher. The Coues', like the Olive-sided, often perches on the tip-top of a tree where it calls and darts into the air to capture winged insects.

Usual call of the Coues' Flycatcher is a subdued *beep-beep*. Oddly enough, as noted by Mabel Deshayes, this vocalization sounds similar to a call of the Hooded Grosbeak, *Hesperiphona abeillei*, which lives near the flycatcher in the mountains of Mexico and Guatemala. The distinctive song of the Coues' is a haunting whistle, *ho-say, re-ah* or *ho-say, ma-re-ah*, thus the species' Mexican name, José María. The bird is too infrequent in Texas for its song to be heard much, but through montane forests of Mexico, the Coues' whistle sounds usually from late March to late August.

DETAILED ACCOUNT: ONE SUBSPECIES

NORTHERN COUES' FLYCATCHER, *Syrichta pertinax pallidiventris* (Chapman)

DESCRIPTION: *Adults, nuptial plumage*: Acquired by wear from winter plumage. Upper parts rather brownish, deep grayish olive, but pileum darker, centers of feathers fuscous; wings and tail dark hair brown; secondaries narrowly edged with brownish white, lesser wing-coverts like back, median and greater wing-coverts dark hair brown tipped with dull drab, forming two evident wing-bars; sides of head and neck like back; lores mixed with grayish white or brownish white; chin and upper throat yellowish white or very pale grayish buff; breast and jugulum between light grayish olive and light drab, somewhat washed with pale dull yellow; middle of abdomen and crissum pale buff or yellowish white; lining of wing dark olive buff or dull chamois. Maxilla dark brown or brownish black; mandible dull yellow or dull orange, but tip dark brown; iris dark brown; legs and feet dark brown or brownish black. In worn summer plumage, colors both above and below much more grayish or brownish (less greenish or yellowish) than in fresh nuptial; chin, throat, and abdomen much more whitish (less yellowish). *Adults, winter*: Acquired by complete postnuptial molt. Similar to nuptial adults, but colors of upper and lower parts' darker—upper parts more olivaceous, lower surface more strongly tinged with buff. *First nuptial*: Acquired by wear from first winter, with which it is practically identical. *First winter*: Acquired probably by complete postjuvenal molt. Similar to adults in winter, but lower parts more deeply ochraceous. *Juvenal*: Acquired by complete postnatal molt. Similar to nuptial adults, but upper parts more

brownish; scapulars, rump, and upper tail-coverts broadly edged with cinnamon or dull buff; tail tipped with cinnamon buff; all upper wing-coverts broadly tipped with cinnamon or cinnamon buff; anterior lower parts darker, duller, and more tinged with gray, and on breast and crissum more deeply tinged with buff, nearly as deep as cinnamon buff; mandible and inside of mouth orange-yellow.

MEASUREMENTS: *Adult male*: Wing, 101.1–111.0 (average, 107.2) mm.; tail, 83.6–90.4 (86.6); bill (exposed culmen), 17.0–20.1 (18.8); tarsus, 16.5–17.0 (16.8); middle toe without claw, 9.9–10.9 (10.7). *Adult female*: Wing, 97.6–101.1 (99.3); tail, 76.5–82.0 (78.7); bill, 16.0–18.5 (17.8); tarsus, 15.5–17.0 (16.3); middle toe, 9.9–10.4 (10.2).

RANGE: C. Arizona and s.w. New Mexico, south to Nayarit and s. Tamaulipas. Winters from s. Sonora and c. Tamaulipas to Guatemala.

TEXAS: *Migration*: One specimen (see species account).

EASTERN WOOD PEWEE, *Contopus virens* (Linnaeus)

SPECIES ACCOUNT

Song is a *pee-wee, pee-ah-weee*. Wings long, extending halfway down tail. Dark olive brown above; whitish below (breast and sides washed with pale grayish olive); whitish wing-bars; dull yellow under wing-coverts; yellowish lower mandible. Could be confused with an *Empidonax* but lacks eye-ring. Length, 6¼ in.; wingspan, 10¼; weight, ½ oz.

RANGE: S. Manitoba to Nova Scotia, south mainly east of Great Plains to c. and s.e. Texas, Gulf coast, and c. Florida. Winters chiefly from Costa Rica to Peru and Venezuela; casually as far north as U.S. Gulf coast.

TEXAS: (See map.) *Breeding*: Late Apr. to late July (eggs, May 15 to July 10) from 50—perhaps somewhat lower—to about 3,700 ft. Common (some years) to

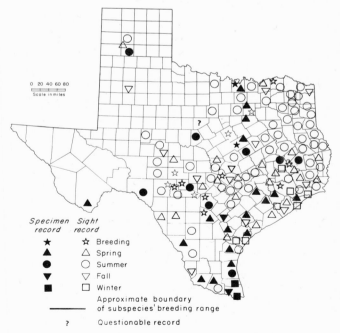

EASTERN WOOD PEWEE, *Contopus virens*

0 20 40 60 80
Scale in miles

Specimen record   Sight record

★ ☆ Breeding
▲ △ Spring
● ○ Summer
▼ ▽ Fall
■ □ Winter

—— Approximate boundary of subspecies' breeding range

? Questionable record

fairly common in eastern third south to northern Harris Co.; locally fairly common to uncommon in rest of eastern half and on much of Edwards Plateau south to San Antonio (formerly Atascosa Co.) and Victoria. Probably nests occasionally in northern Panhandle. May have bred formerly at Brownsville (Apr. 20, 1876, J. C. Merrill; 1911, A. P. Smith), but no specific nesting evidence accompanied vague reports. *Migration*: Mid-Apr. to late May; early Aug. to mid-Oct. (extremes: Mar. 4, June 12; July 3, Dec. 1). Abundant to fairly common throughout eastern two-thirds; scarce in Panhandle and on northwestern Edwards Plateau; casual in Trans-Pecos. *Winter*: Dec. 7 to Feb. 23. Very scarce along coast and in Rio Grande delta; one sighting from Walker Co., Huntsville (Dec. 10, 1936, D. W. Lay).

HAUNTS AND HABITS: A late and leisurely migrant, the Eastern Wood Pewee usually waits until spring is well underway and its favored woodlands are green and lush before returning to its breeding grounds. In eastern Texas and generously wooded portions of the Edwards Plateau, the species nests in more open deciduous and mixed woods; migrants also seclude themselves high in shade trees of yards and gardens in towns and about country dwellings.

Flight is fluttering and ordinarily slow. As it flycatches, the Eastern dashes from its perch—usually an exposed, dead branch; it works from this vantage often for long periods, perching in a noticeably vertical posture in between sallies. It also ventures from woodland margins to feed in clearings over fields. To supplement its mid-air catches, the bird, hovering before a tree, snatches an insect from a leaf or twig. Occasionally it descends to the ground to pick up bugs or grasshoppers; less frequently it forages for fruits of pokeberry, blackberry, dogwood, and elderberry.

During the day while feeding, the Eastern Wood Pewee utters a *chip* note and a downward slurred *pee-ur*. The bird often whistles its sweet plaintive *pee-wee, pee-ah-weee* song off and on throughout the day, sometimes for spells of thirty or forty-five minutes.

DETAILED ACCOUNT: NO SUBSPECIES

DESCRIPTION: *Adults, nuptial plumage (white-bellied phase)*: Acquired by wear from winter plumage. Upper surface deep grayish olive, but pileum darker, more brownish, centers of feathers fuscous or fuscous black; wings and tail chaetura drab, outer web of outermost tail feather barely paler than rest; inner margins of wing-quills paler toward bases, outer webs of secondaries narrowly, tertials broadly, margined with brownish white; wing-coverts chaetura drab, lesser coverts broadly margined with deep grayish olive of back, median series tipped with dull brownish olive gray, lesser series tipped with pale grayish drab, forming two rather well marked wing-bars; sides of head and neck like back, but lores mixed with grayish white and spot in front of eye slightly darker; lower surface grayish or yellowish white; breast and jugulum shaded with pale grayish olive, sides slightly washed with same color; lining of wing dull yellowish white, slightly mixed with hair brown. Bill clove brown, black, or slate black, but mandible deep chrome or dull pale yellow at base; iris dark brown; legs and feet slate black, black, or clove brown. *Adults, nuptial (yellow-bellied phase)*: Similar to white-bellied phase, but under wing-coverts somewhat duller and more

buffy; lower parts of body much more strongly tinged with primrose yellow. *Adults, winter*: Acquired by complete postnuptial molt. Similar to nuptial adults. *First nuptial*: Acquired by wear from first winter. Practically same as nuptial adults. *First winter*: Acquired by partial postjuvenal molt. Like first nuptial male and female. *Juvenal*: Acquired by complete postnatal molt. Similar to nuptial adults, but upper surface more brownish, especially posteriorly, feathers of rump and upper tail-coverts broadly tipped with dull cinnamon; all upper wing-coverts broadly and conspicuously tipped with pale buff or pale cinnamon; lower surface more yellowish anteriorly; lining of wing more buffy. Bill black or slate black, but mandible at least basally pale yellow, chrome yellow, wood brown, or brownish slate; iris dark brown or black; legs and feet sepia, black, or slate black. *Natal*: Light drab, but bases of down feathers dull buffy white.

MEASUREMENTS: *Adult male*: Wing, 81.5–90.4 (average, 85.3) mm.; tail, 62.0–70.1 (65.3); bill (exposed culmen), 12.4–14.5 (13.2); tarsus, 12.4–14.5 (13.7); middle toe without claw, 8.1–8.9 (8.4). *Adult female*: Wing, 77.5–83.6 (80.5); tail, 57.4–63.0 (61.2); bill, 12.4–14.5 (13.2); tarsus, 12.4–14.0 (13.2); middle toe, 7.1–8.9 (8.1).

TEXAS: *Breeding*: Collected north to Cooke, east to Polk, south to Bexar, west to Val Verde cos. *Migration*: Collected north to Randall (Aug. 11), east to Cooke and Galveston, south to Cameron, west to Brewster cos. *Winter*: Three specimens: Willacy Co., El Sauz (Dec. 7, 1921, T. G. Pearson); Cameron Co. (Jan. 30, 1886, Feb. 2, 1897, F. B. Armstrong).

NESTING: *Nest*: In hills, valleys, or lowlands, usually forests, edges of woods, open woodlands, orchards, or shade trees about dwellings, or in towns; on horizontal branch, sometimes rather high above ground; well-built, saucer-shaped, usually shallow, rather thin structure, saddled on top of limb, appearing as knot; composed of rootlets, bark, fine grass, and other plant fibers; covered on outside with lichens; lined with finer bits of same materials, also plant down and horsehair. *Eggs*: 2–4, usually 3; ovate to short ovate; white to cream color; blotched and spotted with various shades of brown, heliotrope, grayish purple, and grayish lavender, usually in wreath about larger end; average size, 18.3 × 13.7 mm.

WESTERN WOOD PEWEE, *Contopus sordidulus* Sclater

SPECIES ACCOUNT

Song is a nasal *peeer*. Closely resembles its eastern counterpart, but breast, sides, under wing-coverts, and lower mandible usually darker. Length, 6¼ in.; wingspan, 10¼.

RANGE: C. Alaska and s. Yukon to c. Manitoba, south through w. United States and Mexican highlands to mountains of w. Panama. Winters mainly from Colombia and Venezuela to Peru and Bolivia.

TEXAS: (See map.) *Breeding*: Mid-May to late Aug. (eggs, June 5 to Aug. 18) from about 1,900 to 8,500 ft. Common to fairly common locally in Trans-Pecos mts.; rare and local on Edwards Plateau east to Middle Bosque River, Bosque Co. (nest located, May, 1967, F. R. Gehlbach). *Migration*: Mid-Apr. to late May; late Aug. to mid-Oct. (extremes: Mar. 3, June 4; Aug. 20, Nov. 9). Common to fairly common through Trans-Pecos; uncommon in western Panhandle; scarce to rare from Edwards Plateau south to Rio Grande delta; casual on upper coast. *Winter*: No specimen, but single sighting in Rio Grande delta: Hidalgo Co., Bentsen–Rio Grande Valley State Park (Dec. 23, 1965, Edward Dearing).

HAUNTS AND HABITS: In the western United States, including Trans-Pecos Texas, the Western Wood Pewee is mostly a bird of pine-oak mountains and canyons. In the few scattered places where it occurs on the Edwards Plateau, it seeks sycamore, cottonwood, and oak groves along or near lakes, rivers, and streams. Fortunately, since most of the west is arid, this bird will accept drier and more open woods than those inhabited by the Eastern Wood Pewee.

In general, flight and behavior of the Western are indistinguishable from the mannerisms of its relative. Like the Eastern, it is generally observed perching erectly on an exposed, dead branch of a tree.

A common note of the Western Wood Pewee, uttered on the wing, is a rapid chattering *pit, pit, pit,* etc. Song is the key difference between the pewees. The Western, apparently quieter during daylight than is the Eastern, sounds its buzzy, nasal *peeer* (sometimes preceded by *pee-yee*) generally at sunset, singing louder as the sky darkens.

DETAILED ACCOUNT: ONE SUBSPECIES

COMMON WESTERN WOOD PEWEE, *Contopus sordidulus veliei* Coues

DESCRIPTION: *Adults, nuptial plumage*: Acquired by wear from winter plumage. Similar to Eastern Wood Pewee, *Contopus virens*, but upper surface more grayish (less greenish) and rather paler; lower parts, particularly breast and jugulum, more extensively and usually more deeply grayish (less yellowish or greenish); lining of wing dull dark olive buff instead of yellow. Maxilla black; mandible light brown, base dull yellow; interior of mouth deep orange-yellow; iris dark brown; legs and feet black. *Adults, winter*: Acquired by complete postnuptial molt. Practically identical with nuptial adults. *First nuptial*: Acquired by wear from first winter. Similar to nuptial adults. *First winter*: Acquired by partial postjuvenal molt. Very similar to first nuptial

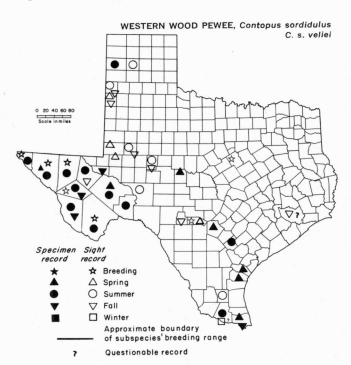

WESTERN WOOD PEWEE, *Contopus sordidulus*
C. s. *veliei*

0 20 40 60 80
Scale in miles

Specimen / Sight record / record

★	☆ Breeding
▲	△ Spring
●	○ Summer
▼	▽ Fall
■	□ Winter

—— Approximate boundary of subspecies' breeding range

? Questionable record

male and female. *Juvenal*: Acquired by complete postnatal molt. Similar to nuptial adults, but pileum darker—clove brown or fuscous black—feathers edged with pale dull brown; remainder of upper surface with paler edgings; rump and upper tail-coverts more brownish, broadly tipped with dull buff or dull brownish buff; wing-coverts widely tipped with dull buff or buffy white or cinnamon; lower parts much more brownish, yellowish, or olivaceous, particularly on breast and jugulum. Bill black, mandible pale yellow except at tip; inside of mouth yellow; iris sepia; legs and feet black. *Natal*: Buffy white.

MEASUREMENTS: *Adult male*: Wing, 86.1–90.9 (average, 88.9) mm.; tail, 62.0–71.1 (66.8); bill (exposed culmen), 11.4–13.0 (12.2); tarsus, 13.0–14.0 (13.7); middle toe without claw, 8.1–9.4 (8.6). *Adult female*: Wing, 78.0–86.6 (82.0); tail, 59.4–66.5 (62.7); bill, 10.9–12.4 (11.7); tarsus, 12.2–14.0 (13.2); middle toe, 7.6–8.6 (8.1).

RANGE: C. Alaska to s. Manitoba, south through w. United States to Durango and Tamaulipas. Winters from w. Venezuela to n. Bolivia; also possibly in Guerrero.

TEXAS: *Breeding*: Collected in El Paso, Hudspeth, Culberson, Jeff Davis, and Brewster cos. *Migration*: Collected north to Oldham (June 4), southeast to Concho, Karnes (Aug. 31), and Cameron, west to Culberson cos.

NESTING: *Nest*: In forests and open woodlands of mountains, slopes, and canyons, open country with scattered trees, orchards, or other cultivated areas; in bush or tree, usually only moderately high above ground, against upright twigs, or saddled on bare limb, one nest even in brush heap; well-constructed saucer of weeds, strips of bark, other plant fibers, grass, and vegetable down, lined with fine grass, vegetable down, plant fibers, and occasionally a few feathers. *Eggs*: 2–4, usually 3; ovate to short ovate or rounded ovate; cream white, with spots of chestnut, umber, and lilac gray, usually forming a wreath at larger end or in middle; average size, 18.0 × 13.7 mm.

OLIVE-SIDED FLYCATCHER, *Nuttallornis borealis* (Swainson)

SPECIES ACCOUNT

Similar to the smaller wood pewees, but has much larger bill and head; white on throat and middle of breast (becoming yellowish on belly) contrasting with dark olive side-patches; a white tuft which may appear from beneath wing at lower back. Length, 7½ in.; wingspan, 13.

RANGE: C. Alaska to Newfoundland, south to n. Baja California, c. Nevada, c. Arizona, n. Trans-Pecos Texas, n.e. North Dakota, Great Lakes region, and Massachusetts, and in Appalachians to North Carolina. Winters chiefly from Colombia and Venezuela to Peru.

TEXAS: (See map.) *Breeding*: Probably late May to late July (no egg dates available, but nest located at about 8,000 ft. in Guadalupe Mts. by F. R. Gehlbach). Uncommon and irregular in The Bowl, Guadalupe Mts. *Migration*: Late Apr. to late May; mid-Aug. to late Sept. (extremes: Mar. 3, June 15; July 4, Nov. 27). Common to fairly common in fall through much of Trans-Pecos, along coast, and in Rio Grande delta; fairly common to uncommon through remainder of state. Fairly common (some years) to scarce in spring through most parts. *Winter*: Dec. 1 to Jan. 31. Casual along coast and in Rio Grande delta; inland sightings from Bexar and Walker cos.

HAUNTS AND HABITS: The Olive-sided Flycatcher

seeks forest solitudes. In Canada and the northern United States, it finds ideal breeding grounds in cool conifers near water. Southward its numbers wane until nesting stops where mountains become critically warm and dry near the U.S.-Mexico border. In the Guadalupe Mountains, it nests in pines, Douglasfirs, and oaks, but during migration the species spreads into lowlands and is commonly observed in deciduous as well as evergreen trees.

Flight, while capable of being long sustained, is not particularly swift, and is very flycatcherlike. The solitary Oliveside prefers a lofty perch in a tall tree, generally on a dead branch; from here it calls between and during sallies for winged insects—largely ants, wasps, and bees—which comprise 99 percent of its diet. Even in migration, this flycatcher seeks the highest arboreal vantage point available; the tip-top of a vertical bare branch protruding from the crown of a large tree is the place to look for this bird.

The call of the Olive-sided Flycatcher is a brisk *pep-pep-pep*. Males are persistent and loud singers on the breeding grounds, where their whistled *whip-whee-peeoo*'s (sometimes described as *quick-three-beer*'s) are heard from sunup to sundown; the first syllable of this song is short, sharp, and not so loud as the latter two, the middle note is highest, and the last slurs down. Migrating Olivesides are usually silent; the few which defend breeding territories in the Guadalupes generally sing from early April to early July.

DETAILED ACCOUNT: TWO SUBSPECIES

WESTERN OLIVE-SIDED FLYCATCHER, *Nuttallornis borealis borealis* (Swainson)

No races recognized by A.O.U. check-list, 1957 (see Appendix A).

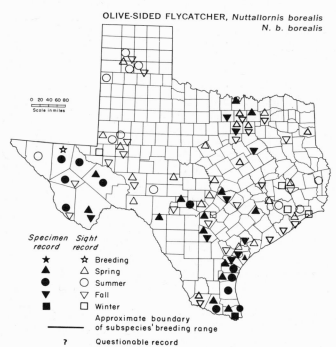

OLIVE-SIDED FLYCATCHER, *Nuttallornis borealis*
N. b. borealis

0 20 40 60 80
Scale in miles

Specimen   Sight
record   record
★   ☆   Breeding
▲   △   Spring
●   ○   Summer
▼   ▽   Fall
■   □   Winter
            —— Approximate boundary
                of subspecies' breeding range
?   Questionable record

DESCRIPTION: *Adults, nuptial plumage (gray phase)*: Acquired by wear from winter plumage. Upper surface between dark grayish olive and chaetura drab, but pileum more brownish, feathers centrally fuscous; wings and tail fuscous black; tertials and inner secondaries edged terminally with brownish white; lesser wing-coverts like back, others with barely paler margins, forming scarcely evident wing-bars; sides of head and neck like upper parts, lores with some admixture of grayish white; lower parts white or yellowish white; sides of throat, of breast, and of body brownish mouse gray or grayish hair brown, feathers with darker shaft markings; crissum with centers of feathers of same color but usually mostly white; lining of wing light hair brown, feathers edged with yellowish white. Maxilla black, blackish slate, or fuscous; mandible slate gray or wood brown, middle portion deep chrome or dull yellow except at tip; inside of mouth orange-yellow; iris olive brown; legs and feet sepia, clove brown, fuscous, or black. *Adults, nuptial (yellowish phase)*: Similar to gray phase, but upper parts more yellowish or greenish (less grayish); light portions of under surface straw yellow or naples yellow. *Adults, winter*: Acquired by complete postnuptial molt. Practically identical with nuptial adults. *First nuptial*: Acquired by wear from first winter, also possibly by partial prenuptial molt. Practically identical with nuptial adults. *First winter*: Acquired by complete postjuvenal molt. Practically identical with adults in winter. *Juvenal*: Acquired by complete postnatal molt. Similar to nuptial adults, but upper surface much more brownish, feathers of rump and upper tail-coverts narrowly tipped with paler dull brown; wing-coverts tipped with saccardo umber or dull cinnamon; lower parts duller; sides of breast and of body more brownish (less grayish); secondaries and primaries narrowly tipped with brownish white or yellowish white. Maxilla black; mandible yellow, tip dark brown; iris sepia; legs and feet olive gray, light brown, or dark plumbeous. *Natal*: Unknown.

MEASUREMENTS: *Adult male*: Wing, 106.9–116.6 (average, 111.3) mm.; tail, 70.1–77.0 (72.7); bill (exposed culmen), 18.0–20.1 (18.8); tarsus, 14.5–15.0 (14.7); middle toe without claw, 11.4–12.4 (11.9). *Adult female*: Wing, 100.6–109.0 (104.6); tail, 66.0–73.9 (68.8); bill, 16.5–18.5 (17.3); tarsus, 13.5–15.0 (14.2); middle toe, 10.9–11.9 (11.4).

RANGE: C. Alaska to Minnesota, south to n. Baja California, c. New Mexico, and n. Trans-Pecos Texas. Winters from Venezuela to n. Peru.

TEXAS: *Breeding*: Four specimens: Culberson Co., The Bowl (May 20, 1938, G. H. Lowery, Jr.; June 14, 1939, W. B. Davis; May 18, 1938, June 11, 1939, T. D. Burleigh). *Migration*: Collected north to Cooke, east to Colorado, south to Cameron (Aug. 8), west to Jeff Davis (Aug. 23) cos. Fairly common.

NESTING: Similar to that of *N. b. cooperi* (see below).

EASTERN OLIVE-SIDED FLYCATCHER, *Nuttallornis borealis cooperi* (Nuttall)

No races recognized by A.O.U. check-list, 1957 (see Appendix A).

DESCRIPTION: *Adults, nuptial plumage*: Similar to *N. b. borealis* but smaller, particularly wings, tail, and bill.

MEASUREMENTS: *Adult male*: Wing, 103.1–109.0 (average, 105.6) mm.; tail, 64.0–70.1 (67.6); bill (exposed culmen), 16.0–18.0 (17.0); tarsus, 13.5–15.0 (14.2); middle toe without claw, 11.4–12.4 (11.9). *Adult female*: Wing, 96.0–102.9 (99.3); tail, 61.0–67.1 (64.3); bill, 16.0–17.5 (16.8); tarsus, 13.5–14.5 (14.0); middle toe, 10.9–11.9 (11.4).

RANGE: N. Ontario to Newfoundland, south to e. Tennessee and s.w. North Carolina. Winters from s. Tamaulipas through Central America to Peru; casually in s. Texas.

TEXAS: *Migration*: Collected north to Cooke, east to Navarro, south to Aransas and Cameron, west to Brewster and Culberson (Aug. 24) cos. Fairly common. *Winter*: Two specimens: Cameron Co., Brownsville (Dec. 24, 1888, and Jan. 4, 1889, J. A. Singley).

NESTING: (This race does not nest in Texas.) *Nest*: On mountains, their slopes, in valleys and canyons, in lowlands, occasionally even in an orchard, usually in more open parts of woods near clearings; saddled on horizontal limb, generally of a conifer, often high from ground; rather small bowl composed of small twigs, roots, and moss; lined with moss and rootlets. *Eggs*: 3–5, usually 3; ovate; cream to pinkish white; blotched and spotted with various shades of chestnut, grayish purple, and dull lavender, often in wreath about larger end; average size, 21.6 × 16.0 mm.

VERMILION FLYCATCHER, *Pyrocephalus rubinus* (Boddaert)

SPECIES ACCOUNT   *See colorplate 22*

Male: scarlet crown (often appears round crested) and under parts; blackish mask, upper parts, tail. *Female*: grayish brown above (darker on wings, tail); dusky-streaked whitish below becoming yellowish or pinkish posteriorly. Length, 6 in.; wingspan, 10¼; weight, ½ oz.

RANGE: S.e. California to s.w. Utah and c. Texas, south through Mexico to Honduras; Colombia and Venezuela, south to c. Chile and s. Argentina; also Galápagos Islands. Northern races winter chiefly from U.S.-Mexico border south into Mexico, but some individuals remain well within U.S. breeding ranges or move slightly north, and a few wander east mainly through Gulf states to n.w. Florida.

TEXAS: (See map.) *Breeding*: Mid-Mar. to mid-July (eggs, Mar. 25 to June 23) from near sea level to 5,000 ft. Common locally (some years) to fairly common in central and southern Trans-Pecos, on most of Edwards Plateau (east to Coleman, Burnet, Austin, and San Antonio), and in much of south Texas brush country (avoids humid parts); scarce and local in extreme

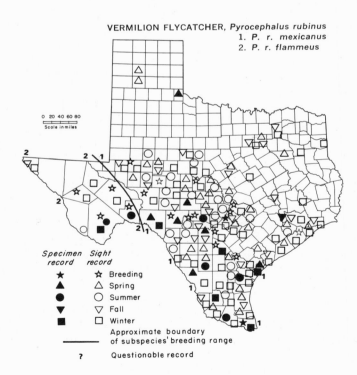

VERMILION FLYCATCHER, *Pyrocephalus rubinus*
1. *P. r. mexicanus*
2. *P. r. flammeus*

0 20 40 60 80
Scale in miles

Specimen | Sight
record | record

★   ☆ Breeding
▲   △ Spring
●   ○ Summer
▼   ▽ Fall
■   □ Winter

Approximate boundary
——— of subspecies' breeding range
?   Questionable record

southern Panhandle and along coast. *Winter*: Late Sept. to early Apr. (extremes: Sept. 12, May 15). Common to fairly common along Rio Grande, on western Edwards Plateau, in south Texas brush country, and along coast; uncommon to scarce in extreme southern Panhandle and eastern Edwards Plateau; rare in northern Panhandle and north central and eastern sections.

HAUNTS AND HABITS: The fiery Vermilion Flycatcher, in brilliant contrast to its desert or semiarid habitat, haunts the vicinity of cottonwood, willow, oak, mesquite, and sycamore-lined streams, lakes, and ponds. In Texas, good summer habitat—widely spaced junipers and oaks—is at present widespread on the Edwards Plateau. In winter, mesquite and huisache shelter numerous individuals. The species usually, but not invariably, lives close to fresh water. Seldom does this bird venture into canyons, nor does it live at very high altitudes. Not gregarious, it is usually seen singly or in pairs; even in winter it does not associate with other birds.

Flight is not strong or swift, although this does not hinder the Vermilion's mid-air flycatching abilities. The bird flits from perch to perch on the outer portions of low trees, bushes, and tall weed stalks; rather frequently it flies to the ground to pick up a beetle or small grasshopper.

Both sexes of the Vermilion Flycatcher give a *pisk* note; perched males call *p-p-pit-zeee* or *pit-a-zee*. The male's flight song is an elaboration of the call notes. One observer William Beebe has rendered it *ching-tink-a-le-tink*. Often this song sounds like a repetition of ten or more *pit-a-zee*'s. From a perch on a weed stalk or dead tree branch, the male flies up with flaming crest erect, breast fluffed, and tail lifted; in the air from ten to forty feet above the ground he hovers on butterflylike wings, pouring out his soft, tinkling song before slowly fluttering down to territory. Surprisingly for a flycatcher, the Vermilion sometimes sings its regular daytime song at various times of the night during spring. Hover singing lasts usually from mid-March to early July.

CHANGES: Since 1933, wholesale clearing of woody vegetation from ranches in central and south Texas has created much scattered-tree or parklike landscape. During this same period, dozens of rivers and hundreds of streams and arroyos were dammed, chiefly to make water holes for cattle. Thus, most of the 24,000,000 acres of the Edwards Plateau and the 20,000,000 of the south Texas brush country were made more suitable for Vermilion Flycatchers. Their population has not increased greatly, but nesting pairs are more widespread.

DETAILED ACCOUNT: TWO SUBSPECIES

EASTERN VERMILION FLYCATCHER, *Pyrocephalus rubinus mexicanus* Sclater

DESCRIPTION: *Adult male, nuptial plumage*: Acquired by partial prenuptial molt. Pileum and short crest scarlet vermilion; remainder of upper surface, including lesser wing-coverts, olive brown or warm fuscous; upper tail-coverts clove brown; tail dark fuscous, outermost pair fuscous, outer webs paler, sometimes whitish at base; wings fuscous, greater and median coverts and outer webs of secondaries narrowly margined with paler wood brown or grayish brown, forming two very inconspicuous wing-bars; inner margins of quills somewhat paler at base; lower parts scarlet, sometimes slightly mixed with orange; lores and broad stripe through eye to neck brown like upper surface; lining of wing hair brown, feathers tipped with scarlet. Bill brownish black; iris dark brown; legs and feet black or brownish black. *Adult male, winter*: Acquired by complete postnuptial molt. Similar to nuptial adult male, but coloration of upper parts somewhat darker. *Adult female, nuptial*: Acquired by partial prenuptial molt. Upper parts hair brown or drab; pileum with darker shaft streaks but without red; tail fuscous or chaetura drab, outermost feather narrowly margined with brownish white; wings hair brown or dark drab; tertials margined on outer webs with brownish white; greater and median wing-coverts edged with brownish white, forming two conspicuous wing-bars; sides of head like back, but lores, superciliary stripe, and cheeks much mixed with grayish white; chin and upper throat white; jugulum and breast dull brownish white, broadly streaked with drab or light hair brown; middle of abdomen yellowish or buffy white; remainder, with crissum, peach red, rose doree, and strawberry pink; lining of wing dull white mixed with drab or light brown, sometimes slightly tinged with pink. *Adult female, winter*: Acquired by complete postnuptial molt. Like nuptial adult female, but coloration of upper parts somewhat darker. *Male, third winter*: Acquired by complete postnuptial molt. Like adult male in winter. *Male, second nuptial*: Acquired by partial prenuptial molt. Similar to nuptial adult male, but red of lower surface not so uniform and paler, somewhat more yellowish; red feathers of pileum sometimes with fuscous tips. *Male, second winter*: Acquired by complete postnuptial molt. Similar to second nuptial male. *Male, first nuptial*: Acquired by partial prenuptial molt. Similar to second nuptial male but somewhat paler above; red feathers of pileum with larger and more numerous fuscous tips; lower surface less uniformly red and much mixed, particularly on breast, with white or pale gray, though throat mostly red. *Male, first winter*: Acquired by complete postjuvenal molt. Similar to first nuptial male, but upper surface paler; red of pileum mostly concealed by fuscous; lower surface paler and less extensively red; throat mostly white or grayish white; breast and jugulum often largely so. Similar to adult female, but upper parts darker, crown with large more or less concealed patch of peach red or pale scarlet; posterior lower parts more extensively and usually more deeply red—strawberry pink or pale scarlet—and sometimes with a few red feathers on throat. *Female, second winter*: Acquired by complete postnuptial molt. Like adult female in winter. *Female, first nuptial*: Acquired by partial prenuptial molt. Similar to nuptial adult female, but posterior lower parts not pink, instead light yellow, orange buff, light salmon, or dull orange. *Female, first winter*: Acquired by complete postjuvenal molt. Practically identical with first nuptial female. *Juvenal*: Acquired by complete postnatal molt. Upper parts dull brown, between hair brown and wood brown, all feathers tipped with dull buff, light dull brown, or buffy white; upper tail-coverts somewhat more buffy; wings and tail similar to those of adult female, except for more conspicuous tips of feathers and buffy edgings of tertials and of outer webs and buffy tips of secondaries; lower parts white, but jugulum, breast, and sides with short streaks of drab or light hair brown; abdomen and crissum often washed with lemon yellow; crissum with narrow shaft streaks of drab or light hair brown. *Natal*: Buffy white to pale tilleul buff.

MEASUREMENTS: *Adult male*: Wing, 80.0–87.1 (average, 82.8) mm.; tail, 56.9–65.0 (59.7); bill (exposed culmen), 11.4–13.0 (12.2); tarsus, 15.0–17.8 (16.8); middle toe without claw, 8.9–10.2 (9.7). *Adult female*: Wing, 77.5–85.1 (80.7); tail, 55.6–62.5 (59.7); bill, 10.9–12.7 (11.7); tarsus, 15.5–17.5 (16.8); middle toe, 8.9–9.9 (9.4).

RANGE: S. Texas, south to Jalisco and Veracruz. Winters from s. Louisiana (a few) throughout breeding range.

TEXAS: *Breeding*: Altitudinal range, near sea level to 2,000 ft.

Collected north to Kimball, east to Comal, south to Cameron, west to Val Verde cos. Fairly common. *Winter*: Taken northwest to Val Verde, east to Atascosa and Aransas, south to Cameron cos. Fairly common.

NESTING: *Nest*: In rather level open country, valleys, on mesas, hills, and lower parts of mountains; in timber or scattered trees along watercourses; usually on horizontal branch of bush or tree; small, shallow, rather poorly built saucer; composed of twigs, plant fibers, weed tops, cocoons, plant down, spider webs, with occasionally a few lichens on the rim; lined with wool, plant down, fur, cattle hair, horsehair, and feathers. *Eggs*: 2–4, usually 3; short ovate to rounded ovate; cream white to buff; blotched with dark brown and grayish lavender, mostly in wreath at larger end or at middle; average size, 17.5 × 13.0 mm.

WESTERN VERMILION FLYCATCHER, *Pyrocephalus rubinus flammeus* van Rossem

DESCRIPTION: *Adult male and female, nuptial plumage*: Similar to *P. r. mexicanus* but smaller. Male with upper parts except head averaging somewhat paler; red of lower surface lighter, of more orange tint. Female with under surface less heavily streaked.

MEASUREMENTS: *Adult male*: Wing, 76.5–82.0 (average, 79.5) mm.; tail, 55.9–61.0 (58.4); bill (exposed culmen), 10.9–13.0 (11.7); tarsus, 15.0–17.0 (16.3); middle toe without claw, 8.9–10.4 (9.7). *Adult female*: Wing, 74.9–81.0 (78.7); tail, 55.1–61.0 (57.4); bill, 10.9–11.9 (11.7); tarsus, 15.0–17.0 (16.3); middle toe, 9.1–10.2 (9.7).

RANGE: S. California to Trans-Pecos Texas, south to s. Baja California and Nayarit. Winters from c. California (casually) throughout breeding range.

TEXAS: *Breeding*: Altitudinal range, 1,800 to 5,000 ft. Collected in Jeff Davis and Brewster cos. Locally fairly common.

NESTING: Similar to that of *P. r. mexicanus*, but average egg size, 18.0 × 13.5 mm.

BEARDLESS FLYCATCHER, *Camptostoma imberbis* Sclater

SPECIES ACCOUNT

Camptostoma imberbe of A.O.U. check-list, 1957 (see Appendix A). A tiny, very plain flycatcher with a short, dark "Roman nose" (lower mandible lighter in color) and small head; olive gray above; whitish below; indistinct eye-ring; buffy wing-bars. Length, 4½ in.; wingspan, 7.

RANGE: S. Arizona and extreme s. Texas, south at low and moderate altitudes through Mexico to n.w. Costa Rica. Winters chiefly from s. Sonora, c. Nuevo León, and s. Tamaulipas (a few), south.

TEXAS: (See map.) *Breeding*: Late Apr. to late July (nest and eggs, Harlingen, June 15, 1940, L. I. Davis; young just out of nest, Bentsen–Rio Grande Valley State Park, June 15, 1958, E. B. Kincaid, Jr., Don Woodard) from near sea level to perhaps 250 ft. Uncommon to scarce in Rio Grande delta, irregularly north to southern Kenedy Co. *Winter*: Late Nov. to late Mar. Rare and erratic in delta.

HAUNTS AND HABITS: The tiny and plain Beardless Flycatcher—so called because it lacks the usual copious flycatcher bristles about the base of its bill—suggests an immature Verdin, kinglet, or warbler more than it does a tyrannid. This bird of subhumid Tropics is attracted in Texas to mesquite woodlands. Near the Rio Grande it also frequents cottonwood, willow, elm, and tepeguaje (great leadtree). This bird's favorite mesquites are good habitat as well for the Verdin, the immature of which is the closest of this species' various look-alikes. Since appearance and habitat are so similar, at least in Texas, observers should know that the upper mandible of the Beardless curves like a vireo's bill; the Verdin's two mandibles go straight to a point as does a siskin's. Also, voice of the Beardless Flycatcher (see last paragraph of section) is unique among U.S. birds.

When it behaves like a flycatcher—chiefly in summer—this usually inconspicuous bird perches on the top branch of a tree from where it makes short aerial sorties after flying insects. However, during much of the year it also inspects lower branches of trees and bushes in the manner of a vireo; here it gleans scale insects, caterpillars, butterfly larvae, ants, and occasionally small berries and seeds.

The Beardless Flycatcher's loud and far-reaching voice is its best field mark. The usual call is a *pee-yerp*. Song, starting high and thin, is a descending series of three to five whistled *eee*'s; each *eee* trails evenly downward in pitch. Males have the habit of singing from atop a tree early in the morning. Song season usually lasts from late March to early July.

BEARDLESS FLYCATCHER, *Camptostoma imberbis*
C. i. imberbis

0 20 40 60 80
Scale in miles

Specimen | Sight
record | record

★ | ☆ Breeding
▲ | △ Spring
● | ○ Summer
▼ | ▽ Fall
■ | □ Winter

———— Approximate boundary
of subspecies' breeding range

? Questionable record

CHANGES: Populations of this species in the Rio Grande delta have probably always been somewhat erratic. Since 1951, however, summers in which Beardless Flycatchers were in good numbers have been few and far between. Of late years it has been very rare in winter; apparently the last winter specimen was collected February 15, 1916, by A. P. Smith.

DETAILED ACCOUNT: ONE SUBSPECIES

EASTERN BEARDLESS FLYCATCHER, *Camptostoma imberbis imberbis* Sclater

DESCRIPTION: *Adults, nuptial plumage (olive phase)*: Acquired by partial prenuptial molt. Upper parts grayish olive, darker and more brownish on pileum; paler on upper tail-coverts and lower rump where feathers have silky white concealed subterminal areas; wings and tail hair brown, inner margins of tail feathers rather paler, outer margins narrowly grayish olive; inner edges of wing-quills, except at tips, brownish or grayish white, secondaries and tertials edged on outer webs with brownish or olivaceous white, lesser wing-coverts like back, longer lesser wing-coverts, median coverts, and greater coverts broadly tipped with dull olive buff; sides of head and neck like back; lores mixed with dull white, malar region rather paler; chin grayish white slightly washed with yellow; remainder of lower surface naphthalene yellow or yellowish white, breast washed with light grayish olive; lining of wing naphthalene yellow. Bill dark brown, mandible lighter brown, base flesh color tinged with orange; iris dark brown; legs and feet dark brown, blackish brown, or plumbeous. *Adults, nuptial (gray phase)*: Similar to olive phase, but upper parts more grayish (less olivaceous); crown little, if any, darker than back, often practically concolor. *Adults, winter*: Acquired by complete postnuptial molt. Similar to nuptial adults, but upper parts more greenish (less brownish or grayish); lower parts more strongly tinged with yellow. *First nuptial*: Acquired by partial prenuptial molt. Like nuptial adults. *First winter*: Acquired by complete postjuvenal molt. Similar to adults in winter. *Juvenal*: Acquired by complete postnatal molt. Similar to nuptial adults, but upper parts more brownish (less greenish); pileum not distinctly different from remainder of upper surface; edgings of upper tail-coverts, of wing-coverts, and of wing-quills, also tips of tail feathers, cinnamon or wood brown. *Natal*: Unknown.

MEASUREMENTS: *Adult male*: Wing, 50.5–58.4 (average, 54.1) mm.; tail, 37.6–48.5 (42.9); bill (exposed culmen), 8.1–8.9 (8.4); tarsus, 13.5–15.0 (14.2); middle toe without claw, 7.6–8.9 (8.4). *Adult female*: Wing, 48.5–55.1 (51.3); tail, 37.1–43.9 (39.6); bill, 8.1–8.6 (8.4); tarsus, 13.0–15.5 (14.2); middle toe, 8.1–8.6 (8.4).

RANGE: Extreme s. Texas (irregularly), south through n.e., e., and s. Mexico to n.w. Costa Rica. Winters chiefly from Nuevo León and s. Tamaulipas (a few), south.

TEXAS: *Breeding*: Collected in Kenedy, Hidalgo, and Cameron cos. *Winter*: Two specimens: Cameron Co., Arroyo Colorado near Harlingen (Jan. 22, Feb. 15, 1916, A. P. Smith).

NESTING: *Nest*: In flat, sandy lowlands, edges of groves, or scattered trees; in bush or tree, usually near ground; globular 4 in. nest with entrance at side; composed of palm fibers, weed stems, or other vegetable materials; lined with cottonlike and weed fibers. *Eggs*: 2; white; spotted with dark brown, reddish brown, and lilac, markings sometimes forming ring about larger end; average size, 17.0 × 12.2 mm.

Larks: Alaudidae

HORNED LARK, *Eremophila alpestris* (Linnaeus)

SPECIES ACCOUNT

A small, pale, terrestrial bird of open country; elongated hind claws; walks rather than hops; often sings in flight, high above ground. Brownish above with bold black markings on head; two small black "horns" (often inconspicuous); white or yellow face, throat; blackish tail with white outer feathers; whitish or yellowish below with black breast-band. Length, 6¾ in.; wingspan, 12½; weight, 1¼ oz.

RANGE: Holarctic; in Old World, south locally to n. Africa; in North America, south to s. Baja California, Isthmus of Tehuantepec, s. Texas, s.w. Louisiana (a few), n. Georgia and North Carolina; also Bogotá Savannah of Colombia. Retreats from excessively cold regions in winter; in Western Hemisphere, northern races winter from s. Canada into n. Mexico, Texas, southern parts of Gulf states (irregularly), and Florida (rarely).

TEXAS: (See map.) *Breeding*: Mid-Feb. to mid-July (eggs, Feb. 20 to June 26) from near sea level to 5,500

ft. Very common in northern Panhandle; common to fairly common locally in remainder of Panhandle, north central portion (east irregularly to Tyler), and along coast from Galveston Bay to mouth of the Rio Grande (inland to Columbus, Beeville, and Alice); scarce and local in Trans-Pecos, on western Edwards Plateau, and in central portions (casually south to La Salle Co.). *Winter*: Early Nov. to late Mar. (extremes: Aug. 22, Apr. 28). Abundant locally to uncommon in most regions, but scarce on much of Edwards Plateau and in forested southeastern portion.

HAUNTS AND HABITS: The Horned Lark is the only member of the 75-species Alaudidae native to the Western Hemisphere. It is one of the very few songbirds which seeks for its feeding habitat not woodlands, not brushlands, not grasslands, but *bare* ground. In England this species is rather closely confined to shores and is therefore called Shore Lark; in America, where competition from other larks is lacking, the Horned occupies open country from damp seashore to waterless desert. Other situations this bird inhabits are plains, prairies, plowed fields, airports, golf courses, and even barren alkali flats. Breeding races in Texas are conspicuous on Panhandle plains and the Gulf coast. Gregarious in winter, Horned Larks gather on the ground to forage in irregular, loose flocks. A startled group of these larks forms a shimmering burst of white as the light-bellied individuals, each trailing its black tail, fly up and away to safety.

Flight is noticeably undulating; periods of rapid, regular strokes interrupted by short spells on tightly closed wings create this choppy effect. In a crouching and mouselike manner, the Horned walks rapidly, taking long steps for such a short-legged bird. On the bare ground or in short grass and stubble, it searches for grasshoppers and other insects, spiders, seeds (those of smartweed, pigweed, amaranth, purslane, others), and occasionally waste grain. Rarely does it perch on anything higher than a rock, clod, stone wall, or low stump.

Usual note of the Horned Lark is a clear *tsee-ee* or *tsee-titi*, often given in flight like a goldfinch. When flushed, the bird sometimes utters a high-pitched, mournful *zu-weet*; *zur-reet, zeet-eet-it*; or *zeet-it-a-weet*. The male's territorial song is sung either from a clod of dirt on the ground or at "heaven's gate" in the

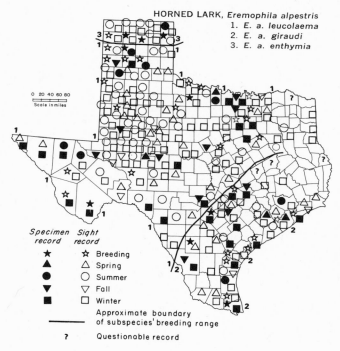

HORNED LARK, *Eremophila alpestris*

1. *E. a. leucolaema*
2. *E. a. giraudi*
3. *E. a. enthymia*

0 20 40 60 80
Scale in miles

Specimen record	Sight record	
★	☆	Breeding
▲	△	Spring
●	○	Summer
▼	▽	Fall
■	□	Winter

——— Approximate boundary of subspecies' breeding range

? Questionable record

Horned Lark, *Eremophila alpestris*

manner of a European Skylark. In the latter instance, the bird silently climbs one hundred feet or more to its "platform" in the sky, where it sings while flying in large circles and arcs; then—once again silent—it plunges headlong toward earth on closed wings. This song is an irregular, metallic tinkling described as sounding like distant sleigh bells intermingled with old gate squeaks. The senior editor especially remembers a Horned Lark drifting his tinkling "sleigh bells" down from the sky in front of two great Mexican volcanoes—Iztaccihuatl and Popocatepetl—whose snowy crests seemed to float high above the clouds. The Texas Horned Lark, _E. a. giraudi_, sings from early January, occasionally late December, to late June. Other races breeding in the state have rather similar song periods.

DETAILED ACCOUNT: SEVEN SUBSPECIES

DESERT HORNED LARK, _Eremophila alpestris leucolaema_ Coues

DESCRIPTION: _Adult male, nuptial plumage_: Acquired by wear from winter plumage. Back, wings, and middle pair of tail feathers fuscous, edged with buff; remainder of tail brownish black, outer pair of feathers margined with white; occiput, cervix, bend of wing, and upper tail-coverts pinkish cinnamon; fore part of crown, hornlike tuft of feathers on each side of head, lores, cheeks, and jugulum black; superciliary stripe, forehead, and auriculars white, the last somewhat grayish; throat yellowish white; remainder of lower surface white, lining of wing, sides, and flanks tinted with cinnamon. Bill black, blackish slate, slate color, or dark brown, but basal half or two-thirds of mandible solid white, pearl gray, light bluish gray, bluish white, plumbeous, or dull yellow; iris dark sepia, burnt umber, hazel, or black; legs and feet black, brownish black, purplish black, slate black, blackish slate, purplish cinereous, reddish sepia, or drab, but soles of toes yellow; claws black. _Adult male, winter_: Acquired by complete postnuptial molt. Similar to nuptial adult male, but upper surface more blended and more uniform due to broad buff or gray edgings; cinnamon areas—including upper tail-coverts and bend of wing—more pinkish, this color on occiput and cervix almost hidden by grayish or buffy tips of feathers; upper tail-coverts more broadly tipped with pale buff; superciliary stripe dull light yellow; throat more deeply yellow; black areas and white forehead obscured by pale gray or buff tips of feathers; breast somewhat spotted with gray or drab; sides and flanks more deeply colored. _Adult female, nuptial_: Acquired by wear from winter. Similar to nuptial adult male, but cervix, bend of wing, and upper tail-coverts cinnamon, without pinkish tinge, first narrowly streaked with dull brown; black of head replaced by brown and buff; tail more brownish; superciliary stripe and auriculars buff; sides and flanks with dull brown streaks. Bill bluish slate color, but base of mandible dull yellow or light blue; iris brown; legs and feet dull black or dark slate color. _Adult female, winter_: Acquired by complete postnuptial molt. Like nuptial adult female, but upper surface lighter, more uniform, and more blended due to very broad buff or gray edgings of feathers which obscure dark centers, also cinnamon of upper tail-coverts and bend of wing, with nape, more pinkish than in nuptial; breast more strongly tinged with brown or buff, spotted obscurely with pale brown, brownish gray, or light drab; also black crescent on jugulum veiled with gray or buff; throat usually more deeply yellow. _Male, first nuptial_: Acquired by wear from first winter. Similar to nuptial adult. _Male, first winter_: Acquired by complete postjuvenal molt. Similar to adult male in winter, but breast more buffy and more heavily spotted with gray or drab, these spots larger. _Female, first nuptial_: Acquired by wear from first winter. Similar to nuptial adult female. Feet slate brown. _Female, first winter_: Acquired by com-

plete postjuvenal molt. Similar to adult female in winter, but upper parts usually more deeply buff, jugulum usually more deeply brown or buff, more heavily spotted with dull brown. Feet brownish black. _Juvenal_: Acquired by complete postnatal molt. Upper parts dull brownish ochraceous, each feather with subterminal bar of sepia and terminal spot or bar of white or buff; wings and tail fuscous, margined with buff and ochraceous; superciliary stripe buff; sides of head grayish brown, spotted with buffy white; throat white, marked with dull brown; jugulum buffy ochraceous, spotted with dull dark brown; sides and flanks buff, marked with dull brown; remainder of lower surface white. Bill black, slate color, or dark plumbeous above, basal portion of mandible dull white or light bluish gray; iris dark brown; legs and feet dull flesh color, slate gray, or dull black. _Natal_: Cartridge buff. Bill pinkish buff, darker at tips; feet raw umber.

MEASUREMENTS: _Adult male_: Wing, 101.1–110.0 (average, 105.6) mm.; tail, 68.1–77.0 (71.7); bill (exposed culmen), 9.9–13.0 (11.4); tarsus, 20.6–23.1 (21.9); middle toe without claw, 10.9–11.9 (11.7). _Adult female_: Wing, 95.0–102.1 (98.8); tail, 57.9–67.1 (64.0); bill, 9.4–11.4 (10.4); tarsus, 20.1–22.1 (21.4); middle toe, 10.4–11.9 (11.2).

RANGE: S. Alberta, south to Trans-Pecos and c. Texas. Winters from s. Idaho and Nebraska to n. Baja California and s. Texas.

TEXAS: _Resident_: Altitudinal breeding range, about 400 to 5,500 ft. Collected north to Potter, east to Clay and Dallas, southwest to Concho, Brewster, and Hudspeth cos. Common. Taken in winter outside breeding range east to Lee (Nov. 3), south to Webb, west to Kinney cos.

NESTING: _Nest_: On plains, prairies, or in cultivated lands (cornfields, hayfields, similar places); depression in ground a little below surface, usually under tuft of grass; sometimes well built, at other times slightly constructed; sometimes well concealed; composed of grasses, grass fibers, fine hair, roots, pieces of willow and other bark; lined with horse and deer hair, old cocoons, bits of grass, and remains of flowers and feathers. _Eggs_: 3–4, usually 3; ovate or sometimes elongate ovate; olive buff, drab gray, grayish or greenish white, thickly marked with small spots of drab and lavender and blotched and spotted with different shades of light brown, olive brown, and gray; average size, 21.9 × 15.7 mm.

PRAIRIE HORNED LARK, _Eremophila alpestris praticola_ (Henshaw)

DESCRIPTION: _Adult male and female, nuptial plumage_: Similar to _E. a. leucolaema_ but much darker, more brownish (less ochraceous) above; superciliary stripe usually without yellow. _Juvenal_: Acquired by complete postnatal molt. Similar to _E. a. leucolaema_ but usually much darker and less buffy.

MEASUREMENTS: _Adult male_: Wing, 100.1–108.0 (average, 104.4) mm.; tail, 67.1–72.9 (69.6); bill (exposed culmen), 9.9–11.9 (11.2); tarsus, 20.6–22.6 (21.9); middle toe without claw, 10.9–11.9 (11.7). _Adult female_: Wing, 95.0–100.6 (96.8); tail, 58.9–66.0 (61.7); bill, 9.9–11.4 (10.7); tarsus, 20.1–23.1 (21.6); middle toe, 10.9–12.4 (11.7).

RANGE: S. Manitoba to s. Quebec, south to n.e. Oklahoma and c. North Carolina. Winters from n. Minnesota to c. Texas, c. Arkansas, and s. Florida.

TEXAS: _Winter_: Taken north to Cooke, east to Ellis and Lee, southwest to Bexar and Kendall cos. Fairly common.

TEXAS HORNED LARK, _Eremophila alpestris giraudi_ (Henshaw)

DESCRIPTION: _Adult male and female, nuptial plumage_: Similar to _E. a. praticola_ but smaller; upper parts much more grayish; yellow of throat deeper and suffusing superciliary stripe. Differs from _E. a. leucolaema_ and _E. a. enthymia_ (see below) in smaller size, darker and more grayish upper surface. _Adult male, winter_: Acquired by complete postnuptial molt. Similar to same plumage of _E. a. praticola_, but dark brown streaks on breast heavier.

MEASUREMENTS: *Adult male*: Wing, 91.9–102.1 (average, 96.8) mm.; tail, 56.4–66.0 (62.2); bill (exposed culmen), 9.4–10.9 (10.4); tarsus, 20.6–22.6 (21.9); middle toe without claw, 10.4–11.9 (11.2). *Adult female*: Wing, 87.1–93.5 (90.2); tail, 52.6–58.9 (55.6); bill, 9.9–10.9 (10.2); tarsus, 20.6–22.6 (21.4); middle toe, 9.9–11.9 (10.7).

RANGE: Texas Gulf coast and extreme n.e. Tamaulipas.

TEXAS: *Resident*: Altitudinal breeding range, near sea level to about 200 ft. Collected northeast to Harris and Galveston, southwest to Cameron cos.; taken inland in Bexar (eggs) and La Salle (eggs) cos. Common on coast.

NESTING: *Nest*: In salt marshes, coastal prairie, and other grassy areas; on ground in shallow depression, top of nest even with surface of ground; constructed, rather more substantially than nest of other races, of tamarisk, twigs, coarse dry grass, and similar vegetable materials; lined with moss, thistle down, and a few feathers. *Eggs*: 3–4; ovate, less often elongate ovate; ground color whitish, with pale lavender suffusion, irregularly blotched and marked with lavender gray, drab, and various shades of brown; average size, 21.9 × 15.5 mm.

MONTEZUMA HORNED LARK, *Eremophila alpestris occidentalis* (McCall)

DESCRIPTION: *Adult male and female, nuptial plumage*: Similar to *E. a. leucolaema* and *E. a. enthymia* (see below), but upper parts somewhat darker and much more cinnamomeous or ochraceous, particularly on cervix and bend of wing.

MEASUREMENTS: *Adult male*: Wing, 103.6–110.5 (average, 106.1) mm.; tail, 67.1–74.9 (71.4); bill (exposed culmen), 9.9–13.0 (11.2); tarsus, 20.1–23.1 (21.9); middle toe without claw, 10.4–12.4 (11.7). *Adult female*: Wing, 95.0–103.1 (98.8); tail, 62.0–66.0 (63.8); bill, 9.4–11.9 (10.2); tarsus, 19.0–22.1 (21.1); middle toe, 9.9–11.9 (11.2).

RANGE: N. Arizona to c. New Mexico. Winters from Arizona and n.w. Texas to n. Sonora and s. Texas.

TEXAS: *Winter*: Taken north to Armstrong (Aug. 22), south to Webb, west to Presidio, Hudspeth, and El Paso cos. Uncommon and local.

CHIHUAHUA HORNED LARK, *Eremophila alpestris aphrasta* (Oberholser)

Race not in A.O.U. check-list, 1957 (see Appendix A).

DESCRIPTION: *Adult male and female, nuptial plumage*: Similar to *E. a. occidentalis* but smaller and somewhat less deeply colored. Similar to *E. a. leucolaema* but smaller; more uniform and more cinnamomeous above.

MEASUREMENTS: *Adult male*: Wing, 99.1–104.6 (average, 102.1) mm.; tail, 64.0–71.9 (68.6); bill (exposed culmen), 10.4–11.9 (11.2); tarsus, 20.6–22.6 (21.4); middle toe without claw, 9.9–11.9 (11.2). *Adult female*: Wing, 91.4–99.1 (95.2);

tail, 57.4–65.5 (61.0); bill, 9.4–11.9 (10.7); tarsus, 18.5–22.1 (20.6); middle toe, 9.4–11.4 (10.7).

RANGE: S.e. Arizona and s.w. New Mexico, south to s. Durango and s.e. Coahuila; casual in winter in Trans-Pecos Texas.

TEXAS: *Winter*: One specimen: Hudspeth Co., Sierra Blanca (Dec. 26, 1889, V. Bailey).

SASKATCHEWAN HORNED LARK, *Eremophila alpestris enthymia* (Oberholser)

DESCRIPTION: *Adult male and female, nuptial plumage*: Similar to *E. a. leucolaema* but more grayish (less ochraceous) above; bend of wing and upper tail-coverts more pinkish (less cinnamomeous); eyebrow less yellowish, often white. *Juvenal*: Acquired by complete postnatal molt. Variable, but averaging more grayish than juvenal of *E. a. leucolaema*. *Natal*: Cartridge buff.

MEASUREMENTS: *Adult male*: Wing, 101.1–107.4 (average, 104.6) mm.; tail, 67.1–74.9 (70.4); bill (exposed culmen), 10.4–12.4 (11.2); tarsus, 21.1–23.1 (21.9); middle toe without claw, 11.4–13.0 (12.2). *Adult female*: Wing, 93.5–101.1 (97.8); tail, 58.9–66.0 (62.2); bill, 8.9–10.9 (10.2); tarsus, 20.1–22.1 (21.4); middle toe, 10.4–11.9 (11.4).

RANGE: C. and e. Saskatchewan, south to n.w. Texas and c. Oklahoma. Winters from s. Idaho and South Dakota to s. California and s. Texas.

TEXAS: *Breeding*: Altitudinal range, 2,300 to 3,700 ft. Collected in Moore (eggs), Hutchinson (eggs), Hemphill (eggs), and Lipscomb cos. Common. *Winter*: Taken north to Randall, east to Cooke (Nov. 6), south to Kendall and Webb, west to Presidio and Culberson cos. Uncommon.

NESTING: Similar to that of *E. a. leucolaema*.

OREGON HORNED LARK, *Eremophila alpestris lamprochroma* (Oberholser)

DESCRIPTION: *Adult male and female, nuptial plumage*: Similar to *E. a. leucolaema* but smaller; central areas of feathers on upper parts posterior to hindneck darker and more blackish; rest of plumage on these parts more grayish (less ochraceous); nape and rump more pinkish (less ochraceous cinnamon).

MEASUREMENTS: *Adult male*: Wing, 101.1–105.9 (average, 102.9) mm.; tail, 61.0–69.1 (66.5); bill (exposed culmen), 10.4–12.4 (11.7); tarsus, 20.1–23.1 (21.9); middle toe without claw, 9.9–11.9 (11.2). *Adult female*: Wing, 91.9–98.1 (94.7); tail, 55.9–62.5 (58.7); bill, 9.9–12.4 (11.2); tarsus, 18.5–22.1 (20.9); middle toe, 9.9–11.9 (10.7).

RANGE: C. Oregon, south to e. California and w. Nevada. Winters from Oregon and n. Utah to s. California; casual in n.w. Texas.

TEXAS: *Winter*: One specimen: Randall Co., 10 mi. east of Canyon (Feb. 9, 1936, J. O. Stevenson).

Swallows: Hirundinidae

VIOLET-GREEN SWALLOW, *Tachycineta*
thalassina (Swainson)

SPECIES ACCOUNT

Resembles Tree Swallow (see below), but greener above with purple gloss; has a large white patch on each side of rump; extensive white on face almost encircles eyes. Length, 5 in.; wingspan, 11¾; weight, ½ oz.

RANGE: C. Alaska and s.w. Yukon to s.w. Alberta and s.w. South Dakota, south to s. Baja California, Oaxaca, and Trans-Pecos Texas. Winters chiefly in Mexico and Central America; also c. coastal and s. California.

TEXAS: (See map.) *Breeding*: Probably mid-May to mid-Aug. (no egg dates available, but nest located in Guadalupe Mts. by F. R. Gehlbach) from about 6,000 to 8,700 ft. Common to fairly common in Guadalupe Mts.; uncommon in Davis and Chisos mts. *Migration*: Mid-Mar. to mid-May; early Sept. to early Oct. (extremes: Feb. 24, June 3; Sept. 1, Oct. 24). Common to fairly common in much of Trans-Pecos; rare to casual in remainder of western third, along coast, and in Rio Grande delta; accidental at Dallas (Sept. 26, 1970, Hazel Nichols, et al.). *Winter*: Late Dec. Casual at Big Bend Nat. Park.

HAUNTS AND HABITS: The seventy-five members of Hirundinidae are small, lithe, very aerial birds. Eight species course regularly, especially during summer, in Texas skies. Tiny feet allow swallows to perch, but barely can they walk. The pretty Violet-green, distinct westerner among North American swallows, sails lightly over streams and rivers of canyons and nests in open coniferous and mixed forests of mountains; but the species is also seen on clear days circling high over fields and it comes freely to the vicinity of human dwellings. As is true of many western insect-eating birds, this swallow makes a shorter journey to its winter quarters than do its far-tripping eastern relatives. Quite gregarious, these birds gather in flocks, especially just prior to migration; groups often perch in a long row on a telephone wire or in the top of a leafless tree.

Flight of the Violet-green, like other swallows, is graceful, swift, and powerful; in comparison to. the Tree Swallow, the present species soars less and its wing-beats are more rapid. In mid-air, the bird deftly changes direction as it darts about catching mosqui-

toes, flies, wasps, and bees. It often swoops down to a pond or stream, skims along the surface, and drinks without touching wings or body to water.

The ordinary note of the Violet-green is a series of thin *chip*'s delivered at various speeds; this is somewhat similar to its song but not so shrill or rapid. During the breeding season, male Violet-green Swallows, each more or less within his nesting territory, indulge in twittering early morning flight songs; these rapid, shrill *tsip tseet tsip*'s, uttered with a few musical notes heard only during the nuptial period, begin in predawn darkness and grow fainter as the stars dim. In the Guadalupes, these morning flight choruses last from March or early April until late June.

DETAILED ACCOUNT: ONE SUBSPECIES

NORTHERN VIOLET-GREEN SWALLOW, *Tachycineta*
thalassina lepida Mearns

DESCRIPTION: *Adult male, nuptial plumage*: Acquired by wear from winter plumage. Pileum and cervix rich velvety dark dull yellowish green, cervix in some individuals dark livid purple, sometimes forming narrow collar; back and scapulars dark

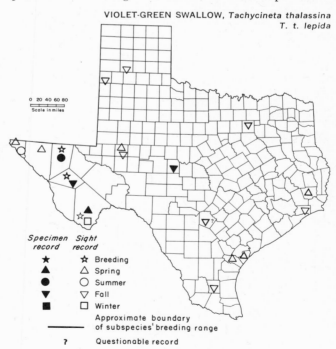

VIOLET-GREEN SWALLOW, *Tachycineta thalassina*
T. t. *lepida*

0 20 40 60 80
Scale in miles

Specimen Sight
record   record

★   ☆   Breeding
▲   △   Spring
●   ○   Summer
▼   ▽   Fall
■   □   Winter

————   Approximate boundary of subspecies' breeding range

?   Questionable record

dull yellowish green or danube green, not infrequently overlaid by purple of cervix; rump and upper tail-coverts dark bluish green to deep violet purple or deep blue; wings and tail chaetura black, paler on inner margins of feathers, and their exposed surface glossed with metallic dark green or purple, lesser coverts purplish or green like back, but margins of outer feathers brighter dark green; lores chaetura black mixed with white; under wing-coverts light hair brown, margined with paler brown or dull white; axillars white, partly tinged with drab; remainder of lower surface, including sides of head and patch on each side of rump, white. Bill black; inside of mouth light yellow; iris burnt umber; legs and feet dark sepia, brownish black, or drab. *Adult male, winter*: Acquired by complete postnuptial molt. Similar to nuptial adult male, but tertials conspicuously tipped with pure white. *Adult female, nuptial*: Acquired by wear from adult female in winter. Similar to nuptial adult male but much duller; pileum and cervix dull olive brown with faint greenish sheen or with purplish tinge; remainder of under surface similar to that of adult male but duller; sides of head brown like pileum but paler and somewhat mixed with dull gray; anterior lower parts duller, more grayish white. Bill black; interior of mouth pale naples yellow; iris dark sepia; legs and feet light purplish sepia or black. *Adult female, winter*: Acquired by complete postnuptial molt. Similar to nuptial adult female, but tertials conspicuously tipped with pure white. *Male and female, first nuptial*: Acquired by wear from first winter. Similar to corresponding sex of nuptial adult. *Male and female, first winter*: Acquired by complete postjuvenal molt. Similar to corresponding sex of adult in winter. *Juvenal*: Acquired by complete postnatal molt. Upper surface rather dark purplish fuscous; wings and tail somewhat lighter; sides of head light fuscous, sometimes slightly mixed with light gray; chin and crissum dull white; white patch on each side of rump as in adults; remainder of lower surface dull smoke gray; lining of wing hair brown; inside of mouth cream white. *Natal*: Drab gray to cream color.

MEASUREMENTS: *Adult male*: Wing, 108.0–119.9 (average, 115.3) mm.; tail, 43.9–51.1 (46.0); bill (exposed culmen), 4.5–5.6 (5.3); tarsus, 9.9–10.9 (10.7); middle toe without claw, 8.9–10.9 (10.2). *Adult female*: Wing, 108.0–115.1 (109.7); tail, 41.9–46.0 (43.7); bill, 5.1–5.6 (5.3); tarsus, 9.9–10.9 (10.7); middle toe, 9.4–10.9 (10.2).

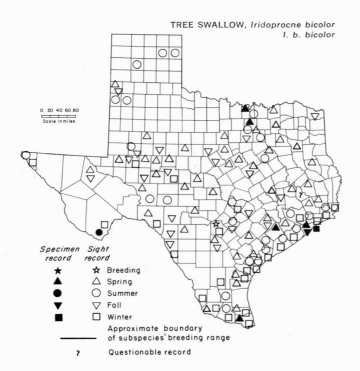

TREE SWALLOW, *Iridoprocne bicolor*
I. b. bicolor

0 20 40 60 80
Scale in miles

Specimen / Sight record

Specimen record	Sight record	
★	☆	Breeding
▲	△	Spring
●	○	Summer
▼	▽	Fall
■	□	Winter

——— Approximate boundary of subspecies' breeding range

? Questionable record

RANGE: C. Alaska to w. South Dakota, south to n. Baja California and n. Durango. Winters from s. California and s.w. New Mexico through Mexico to Costa Rica.

TEXAS: *Breeding*: Collected in Guadalupe Mts., Culberson Co. *Migration*: Collected in Jeff Davis, Brewster, and Concho cos.

NESTING: *Nest*: In cliffs along streams, on edges of woodlands, or in cultivated areas; in hole in tree, not so frequently in bank or under eaves of building, sometimes deserted woodpecker hole; cavity floored with dry grasses, straw, small sticks, and feathers; lined with thick mass of feathers. *Eggs*: 4–5; elliptical ovate; pure white with little or no gloss and unmarked; average size, 18.5 × 12.7 mm.

TREE SWALLOW, *Iridoprocne bicolor* (Vieillot)

SPECIES ACCOUNT

Streamlined body; long, pointed wings; slightly forked tail; short bill with wide gape. Iridescent green-black or blue-black above; immaculate white below. Length, 5¾ in.; wingspan, 12½; weight, ¾ oz.

RANGE: C. Alaska to Newfoundland, south to s. California, Idaho, Colorado, s. North Dakota, e. Nebraska, n.w. Tennessee, and Virginia; casually to southern states. Winters chiefly from c. California, extreme s. United States, and s.e. Virginia through Mexico to Honduras and Nicaragua; also Cuba.

TEXAS: (See map.) *Breeding*: Three records, all from Bexar Co.: Mitchell Lake (nest with 6 eggs and several nests with young located, June 1, 1913, Ridley Holleman, R. W. Quillin); 8 mi. west of San Antonio (nest with young, June 11, 1916, F. B. Eastman); Mitchell Lake (nest with 2 nearly grown young, June 6, 1920, Quillin). *Migration*: Mid-Mar. to mid-May; early Aug. to mid-Nov. (extremes: Feb. 19, June 18; July 4, Dec. 5). Abundant (some years) to fairly common over most parts; normally uncommon in Trans-Pecos. *Winter*: Late Nov. to early Mar. Common locally (some years, usually on upper coast) to scarce along coast and over open water in southern third; rare as far north as El Paso, Midland, and Austin.

HAUNTS AND HABITS: A hardy swallow, the Tree is typically the first of its family to arrive on the breeding grounds in Canada and the northern United States. This earliness demands that the bird be more of a vegetarian than other swallows, and often it must subsist on seeds—smartweed, rice cutgrass (*Zizaniopsis*), others—gleaned from iced-over ponds and frozen earth. At times, particularly in fall, it eats prodigious quantities of berries for a swallow; fruits of wax-myrtle, Virginia creeper, dogwood, and redcedar are favored.

Only very casually does the Tree nest as far south as Texas, but it is a conspicuous migrant throughout much of the state, especially on the Gulf coast where large flocks, often with Barn Swallows, roost in coastal marshes. It is seen also on prairies, in canyons of hills, meadows bordering lakes and river valleys, and around cultivated areas, farms, and ranches. During a few winters, large flocks feed over Texas lakes, such as Falcon Reservoir, but most years the Tampico marshes on the coast of Tamaulipas, Mexico, are the closest point to Texas where the species winters in astronomical numbers.

In flight this swallow is swift and strong but appears less steady than does the Barn due to its quick and flickering, but less powerful wing-beats. More given to sailing than most other swallows, it glides often in circles with hunched back and lowered wing-tips. Because of the triangular shape of its wings, it resembles a Purple Martin in mid-air. Particularly in late afternoon and early evening, Tree Swallows skim a field, lake, or stream in search of insect prey. As well as fly-catching, they often forage on the ground for bugs, beetles, and an occasional spider.

The note of the Tree Swallow is a *cheet* or *chi-veet*; also uttered is a gentle, liquid twitter. Its song, often given in early morning concerts near the bird's nest, is a *weet, trit, weet*, repeated with variations. Song season has not been established in Texas, since it is such a rare and erratic breeder in the state.

Detailed Account: One Subspecies

EASTERN TREE SWALLOW, *Iridoprocne bicolor bicolor* (Vieillot)

No races recognized by A.O.U. check-list, 1957 (see Appendix A).

DESCRIPTION: *Adult male, nuptial plumage (blue phase):* Acquired by wear from winter plumage. Upper surface, including sides of head and of neck, metallic glossy gobelin blue or juvenile blue; wings and tail fuscous black or chaetura black, paler on inner margins of feathers, exposed surface of wing-quills and rectrices glossed with metallic dark green; lesser wing-coverts like back; middle wing-coverts broadly margined with color of back; lores velvety black; lower surface white; lining of wing light hair brown, edges of feathers paler. Bill black or blackish slate above, sometimes with base of mandible orange buff; iris dark brown; legs and feet broccoli brown, chocolate, grayish brown, or drab gray, feet sometimes clove brown; claws black. *Adult male, nuptial (green phase):* Similar to blue phase, but upper surface metallic french green or bronzy green. *Adult female, nuptial (blue phase):* Acquired by wear from winter. Similar to blue phase of nuptial adult male, but with extreme anterior part of forehead dull dark brown or blackish brown; upper parts often duller than in male. Bill black; interior of mouth very pale flesh color; iris dark brown; feet dark sepia or broccoli brown; soles of toes with pinkish tinge. *Adult female, nuptial (green phase):* Similar to blue phase female, but upper surface metallic french green or bronzy green. Bill black; iris dark brown; legs and feet brown or light drab. *Adult male and female, winter:* Acquired by complete postnuptial molt. Similar to corresponding sex and phase of nuptial adults, but tertials broadly tipped with pure white. *Male and female, first nuptial:* Acquired by wear from first winter. Practically same as corresponding sex and phase of nuptial adults. *Male and female, first winter:* Acquired by complete postjuvenal molt. Similar to corresponding sex and phase of adults in winter. *Juvenal:* Acquired by complete postnatal molt. Upper parts rather purplish fuscous; wings and tail fuscous, tertials and inner secondaries slightly margined with pale gray, as are upper tail-coverts; lower parts white, slightly shaded across breast with pale fuscous, white of throat sharply defined against fuscous sides of head; lining of wing hair brown mixed on outer edge with white. Bill dull black; interior of mouth yellow; iris dark brown; feet dark sepia, broccoli brown, or pinkish buff. Differs from juvenal of Northern Violet-green Swallow, *Tachycineta thalassina lepida,* in having chin and throat usually more

clearly white; white of side of throat more clearly defined from brown of pileum, with always some whitish feathers about hind part of eye (absent in *T. t. lepida*); region below eye more or less mixed with dull white (not solidly brown); lacking white patch on each side of rump. *Natal:* Pale smoke gray.

MEASUREMENTS: *Adult male:* Wing, 115.1–124.5 (average, 119.4) mm.; tail, 53.1–57.9 (55.6); bill (exposed culmen), 6.1–7.4 (6.6); tarsus, 11.9–13.0 (12.4); middle toe without claw, 10.9–11.9 (11.7). *Adult female:* Wing, 110.0–119.9 (115.3); tail, 53.1–57.9 (55.1); bill, 6.1–7.1 (6.6); tarsus, 10.9–12.4 (11.9); middle toe, 9.9–12.2 (11.2).

RANGE: C. Alaska to s.e. Labrador, south to n. Arizona and Virginia; casually to Texas and s. U.S. Winters from n. Chihuahua, occasionally along Atlantic and Gulf coasts from Massachusetts, through Mexico to Nicaragua; also Cuba.

TEXAS: *Breeding:* See species account. *Migration:* Collected north to Cooke, east to Galveston, south to Cameron, west to Brewster (Aug. 1) cos. *Winter:* One specimen: Galveston Co., High Island (Feb. 23, 1907, A. H. Howell).

NESTING: *Nest:* On edges of swamps, streams, or other water, often near seashore, or in cultivated areas, even about human habitations on outskirts of towns, as well as in the country; in woodpecker or other hole in tree or stump, crevice about bridge or building, even in hollow fence rail, or man-made nesting box; rather loosely constructed mass of materials in nesting cavity, consisting of dry grass, straw, leaves, and other similar materials; lined with fine grasses and leaves, down, feathers, and other soft materials. *Eggs:* 3–10, usually 4–6; ovate or elliptical ovate; plain white, unspotted; average size, 19.3 × 13.2 mm.

BANK SWALLOW, *Riparia riparia* (Linnaeus)

Species Account

Sand Martin of British authors. Places nest in bank burrow; colonial. Erratic flight. Brown above; white below with brown breast-band. Length, 5¼ in.; wingspan, 10¾; weight, ½ oz.

RANGE: Widespread in Northern Hemisphere; in

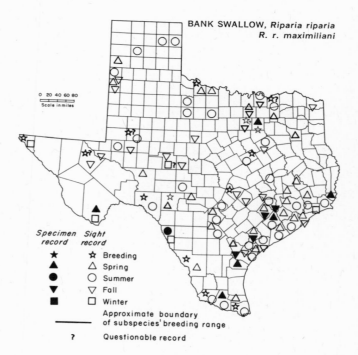

BANK SWALLOW, *Riparia riparia*
R. r. maximiliani

0 20 40 60 80
Scale in miles

Specimen record / Sight record
★ / ☆ Breeding
▲ / △ Spring
● / ○ Summer
▼ / ▽ Fall
■ / □ Winter

——— Approximate boundary of subspecies' breeding range

? Questionable record

North America from arctic region, south locally to s. United States. Winters in South America, e. and s. Africa, and s. Asia.

TEXAS: (See map.) *Breeding*: Mid-Apr. to late June (eggs, June 6) from near sea level to about 3,800 ft. Colonies scarce and extremely local over most of state; rare as far south as Rio Grande delta. *Migration*: Late Mar. to early May; mid-Aug. to mid-Oct. (extremes: Feb. 20, May 30; Aug. 5, Nov. 15). Very common to uncommon through most parts. *Winter*: No specimen, but a handful of sightings along Rio Grande and on upper coast.

HAUNTS AND HABITS: The Bank Swallow—one of the very few cosmopolitan songbirds—breeds in the New World from the Arctic throughout most of North America, but as a nester its colonies dwindle in Texas and other southern states. Its primary habitat requirement is a sand, clay, or gravel bank or bluff skirting a river, stream, lake, or bay where it can excavate a nest burrow; the bird is numerous in parts of the country where glacial deposits abound. Unlike other swallows which have adapted to man-made structures—bird boxes, bridges, eaves of buildings, etc.—the Bank maintains its riparian nesting habits.

Riparia riparia does, however, readily accept banks scraped out by bulldozers. A striking example of this—also of the advantage of its migratory habit in finding newly created breeding habitat—was demonstrated recently in eastern Uvalde County, Texas. In 1965, excavation began on a gravel pit along the upper floodplain of the Sabinal River, two miles north of Sabinal and one hundred yards from the Kincaid Shelter, noted for its 12,000-year-old Ice Age mammal bones and associated human artifacts. No Bank Swallows had been recorded in the area for thirty years prior to the digging of the pit; however, by 1969, when sufficient vertical walls had been created, one hundred birds appeared "out of nowhere" and began digging their nest tunnels. In 1970, at least one thousand Bank Swallows nested here with roaring bulldozers still enlarging a different part of the pit (Edgar Bryan Kincaid, Sr.). Apparently some migrants, on their way either to or from South America, had located the new sand-clay-gravel bank; somehow the scouts communicated their find to the breeding pairs.

When the young are reared, Bank Swallows, always gregarious, gather, often with other swallow species, in large premigration flocks. These flocks sleep in tall-grass marshes, trees, or bushes; birds occasionally venture to cities to roost with Purple Martins in trees.

Flight is swift, graceful, and fluttering like a butterfly's. In mid-air, the Bank is distinguished from the Tree Swallow as it sails with wings held close to its sides. When foraging, the bird dashes about high in the air and at moderate heights, especially over fields, or it skims over water. While maintaining normal flight speed, it sweeps winged insects—beetles, weevils, flies—into its mouth. Near and on the ground it also eats moths, termites, ants, and spiders. The burrowing habit

of this swallow has some drawbacks. The nest is vulnerable to egg-eating predators, particularly badgers, skunks, and rats, which dig their way into the holes; also, House Sparrows and Starlings, where numerous, often confiscate the Bank Swallow's burrow for their own uses. Additional and greater dangers are burrow cave-ins, bank collapses, and flooding.

The voice of this swallow is a rapid series of gritty buzzes or rattles—*brrt* or *bzzht*.

DETAILED ACCOUNT: ONE SUBSPECIES

AMERICAN BANK SWALLOW, *Riparia riparia maximiliani* (Stejneger)

Split from *R. r. riparia* of A.O.U. check-list, 1957 (see Appendix A).

DESCRIPTION: *Adults, nuptial plumage*: Acquired by wear from winter plumage. Upper parts light grayish olive brown; rather darker on head, but paler on rump, feathers usually with obscure paler margins; wings and tail darker than upper surface, except for tertials, tail with numerous narrow very obscure darker bars; forehead and superciliary region of paler brownish gray; lores of darker brown; sides of head like crown; chin, throat, breast, abdomen, and crissum white, but sides and broad band across jugulum brown and rather lighter than upper parts; lining of wing like back, outer coverts with pale brownish gray margins. Bill black, blackish slate, or brownish black; iris dark brown; legs and feet dark brown, chocolate, drab gray, or drab; claws dark brown or black. *Adults, winter*: Attained by complete postnuptial molt. Practically identical with nuptial, except for darker coloration above. *First nuptial*: Acquired by wear from first winter. Similar to nuptial adults, but shadowy bars on tail less appreciable, particularly on outer feathers, and, though observable, sometimes nearly absent. *First winter*: Acquired by complete postjuvenal molt. Similar to first nuptial male and female. *Juvenal*: Acquired by complete postnatal molt. Similar to nuptial adults, but feathers of tertials, rump, and upper tail-coverts broadly tipped with light cinnamon buff, pale wood brown, or dull white; upper wing-coverts more narrowly margined with same color; tail entirely without narrow obscure darker bars; brown jugular collar often edged with warm buff; chin and throat slightly washed with buff and usually finely spotted with grayish brown or drab. Bill dark brown; feet flesh color; claws dull yellow. *Natal*: Light drab, pale drab gray, or mouse gray.

MEASUREMENTS: *Adult male*: Wing, 95.5–103.6 (average, 99.1) mm.; tail, 45.0–50.5 (48.0); bill (exposed culmen), 6.1–7.1 (6.4); tarsus, 9.9–11.4 (10.9); middle toe without claw, 8.9–10.4 (9.4). *Adult female*: Wing, 95.5–104.1 (99.1); tail, 45.0–52.1 (48.3); bill, 5.6–6.6 (6.1); tarsus, 9.9–11.4 (10.9); middle toe, 8.9–10.4 (9.4).

RANGE: N. Alaska to s.w. Newfoundland, south to s.w. California, Texas, and c. Alabama. Winters in South America to Bolivia; also Puerto Rico.

TEXAS: *Breeding*: Nesting colonies observed north to Wilbarger (1915), east to Dallas, south to Cameron (1891), west to Webb (1900), Uvalde (1969, 1970), and El Paso (1949; eggs examined, 1922) cos. *Migration*: Collected north to Dallas, east to Orange, south to Hidalgo, west to Brewster cos.

NESTING: *Nest*: Usually in colonies, along streams, by seaside (but not in Texas where there are no sea cliffs); in railroad cuts, along highways, or in sand and gravel quarries; hole dug by male and female (using bill and feet) in more or less vertical sand or clay banks, sometimes near top of bank, at other times lower; burrow commonly 1½–2 in. in diameter and 1½–3 ft. in length; nest chamber floored with grasses, straw, and feathers; lined with similar materials. *Eggs*: 3–7, usually 4–5; ovate to elliptical ovate; pure white, unmarked; average size, 18.3 × 12.7 mm.

ROUGH-WINGED SWALLOW, *Stelgidopteryx ruficollis* (Vieillot)

SPECIES ACCOUNT

Places nest in bank burrow or other available cavity; normally breeds in solitary pairs. Direct flight. Brown above; whitish below becoming pale smudgy brown on breast. Length, 5½ in.; wingspan, 11¾; weight, ½ oz.

RANGE: S. Canada, south somewhat locally over most of North America, Mexico, and Central America to Argentina and Paraguay. Migratory races winter chiefly from extreme s. United States (a few) southward.

TEXAS: (See map.) *Breeding*: Late Mar. to early July (eggs, Apr. 11 to June 21) from near sea level to 3,800 ft. Locally common to uncommon over much of state; summers very occasionally along coast and from Laredo to Rio Grande delta, but actual nesting here unconfirmed. *Migration*: Mid-Mar. to early May; early Aug. to late Oct. (extremes: Feb. 15, May 24; July 11, Nov. 25). Very common to fairly common through most parts. *Winter*: Late Dec. to mid-Feb. Fairly common (some years) to rare from Big Bend Nat. Park, Austin, and upper coast, south to Rio Grande delta.

HAUNTS AND HABITS: The Rough-winged Swallow is named for the roughened leading edge of its spread wing. The species is nearly as widespread in the Western Hemisphere as is the Bank in the Northern Hemisphere. It is unusual for a songbird to nest in both temperate and tropical zones; however, the Roughwing is not restricted by climate—as is apparent in Texas—but by suitable nesting sites. Like the Bank Swallow, it seeks a sand and clay bluff on a river, road cut, or gravel pit in which to burrow its nest tunnel. But un-

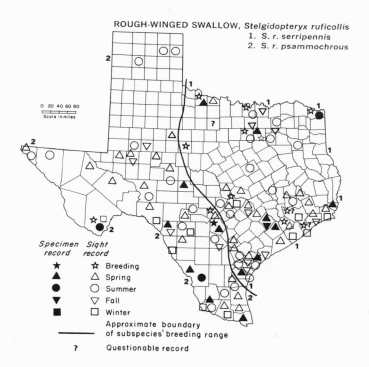

ROUGH-WINGED SWALLOW, *Stelgidopteryx ruficollis*
1. *S. r. serripennis*
2. *S. r. psammochrous*

0 20 40 60 80
Scale in miles

Specimen record / Sight record

★ / ☆ Breeding
▲ / △ Spring
● / ○ Summer
▼ / ▽ Fall
■ / ▢ Winter

——— Approximate boundary of subspecies' breeding range

? Questionable record

like its close relative, the Roughwing has adapted its nest also to man-made structures, such as bridges, drain pipes, and holes and chinks in adobe or brick buildings. In identifying the nests of these two burrowing swallows, it is generally observed that the Roughwing's entrance hole tends to be larger, more elliptical, and less carefully excavated. More solitary than other swallows, the Roughwing is not a colonial nester—another way to distinguish it from the Bank—nor does it gather in such large, closely knit premigration flocks.

Flight of this bird is light and graceful, and the stroke of its wing tends to be higher than that of other swallows. In comparison to the Bank, it is less rapid but more direct. It does not sail as much as other members of its family, especially the Tree, nor does it spend as much time in the air. When feeding, it skims over fields or water, sifting the air for insects in the typical swallow manner.

In general, the Rough-winged Swallow is a quiet bird. On the wing or when perched, it twitters a rasping but rather weak *trrit, trrit*, often repeated in a series. It appears to have no song.

DETAILED ACCOUNT: THREE SUBSPECIES

EASTERN ROUGH-WINGED SWALLOW, *Stelgidopteryx ruficollis serripennis* (Audubon)

DESCRIPTION: *Adults, nuptial plumage*: Acquired by wear from adult winter plumage. Upper parts, including sides of head and neck, between buffy brown and hair brown, head slightly darker; wings and tail conspicuously so, most feathers of upper parts, including wing-coverts and tertials, with obscurely paler brown margins; anterior lower parts, sides, and flanks pale grayish hair brown, without buffy tinge; remainder of lower surface white; lining of wing hair brown, outer coverts tipped with grayish white. Bill dark brown or black; iris bister; legs and feet dark sepia or black; claws black. *Adults, winter*: Acquired by complete postnuptial molt. Similar to nuptial adults, but upper surface much darker, more sooty (less brownish)—chaetura drab to light chaetura drab; tertials more broadly and distinctly tipped with white; throat, particularly chin, slightly washed with buff; brown of jugulum more grayish (less buffy). *First nuptial*: Acquired by wear from first winter. Similar to nuptial adults, but chin and throat with decided buffy tinge. *First winter*: Acquired by complete postjuvenal molt. Similar to first nuptial male and female, but upper parts very much darker, more sooty (less brownish)—chaetura drab to light chaetura drab; tips of tertials much more broadly and distinctly white; throat strongly tinged with buff; upper parts and jugulum more grayish (less buffy) brown. This plumage becomes rapidly more brownish, particularly by spring. Similar to that of adults in winter, but chin and throat much more buffy. *Juvenal*: Acquired by complete postnatal molt. Similar to nuptial adults, but upper parts washed with fawn or cinnamon; wing-coverts, tertials, and outer webs of terminal portion of inner secondaries broadly margined with fawn or cinnamon; anterior lower parts more or less tinged with same color. Similar to juvenal of American Bank Swallow, *Riparia riparia maximiliani*, but wing and tail much longer; rump and upper tail-coverts not conspicuously barred with buff; tips of tertials and greater coverts much broader and darker (cinnamon to dull pecan brown, instead of buff); chin, throat, and jugulum duller, much more buffy or cinnamomeous—throat not so nearly clear white, jugulum not so dark or so well defined, and more rufescent (less grayish) brown, though sometimes there is a fairly well defined jugular band. *Natal*: Pallid mouse gray or pale drab gray. Bill and feet brownish flesh color.

MEASUREMENTS: *Adult male*: Wing, 101.6–112.5 (average,

107.7) mm.; tail, 46.0–50.5 (48.8); bill (exposed culmen), 6.1–
7.1 (6.6); tarsus, 9.9–11.9 (11.2); middle toe without claw, 8.9–
10.4 (9.7). *Adult female*: Wing, 97.1–104.9 (101.9); tail,
46.0–48.0 (46.8); bill, 6.1–6.9 (6.6); tarsus, 10.9–11.9 (11.2);
middle toe, 9.4–9.9 (9.7).

RANGE: C. Alberta to New Hampshire, south to s.e. Texas and
e. Florida. Winters from s.e. Texas (casually) and s.e. South
Carolina through Mexico to Panama.

TEXAS: *Breeding*: Altitudinal range, near sea level to 2,400 ft.
Collected in Wilbarger and Bowie cos. (see species account).
Fairly common. *Migration*: Collected north to Dallas, east to
Orange, south to Cameron, west to Menard cos. Fairly common.

NESTING: *Nest*: Along rivers and streams, in more or less open
country, along edges of forests, or even in cities; usually not in
colonies; in hole in embankment, crevice in cliff, about bridge or
building, even occasionally in a hole in a tree, in a drain pipe, or
kingfisher's hole; when in sand bank or other similar situation,
it has a chamber several inches in diameter at end; nest material a mass of dry grass, straw, feathers, leaves, and weed
stalks; lined with fine dry grass, rootlets, bits of dead leaves, and
feathers. *Eggs*: 3–8, usually 6; elliptical ovate; pure white,
slightly glossy, unmarked; average size, 18.5 × 13.2 mm.

WESTERN ROUGH-WINGED SWALLOW, *Stelgidopteryx ruficollis aphractus* Oberholser

Race not in A.O.U. check-list, 1957 (see Appendix A).

DESCRIPTION: *Adults, nuptial plumage*: Similar to S. *r. serripennis* but larger; lower parts paler, middle of abdomen more
clearly white, less tinged with gray; upper parts averaging more
sooty (less rufescent).

MEASUREMENTS: *Adult male*: Wing, 108.0–115.1 (average,
111.3) mm.; tail, 48.0–52.1 (50.3); bill (exposed culmen),
5.6–7.1 (6.4); tarsus, 10.4–12.4 (11.7); middle toe without
claw, 8.9–10.4 (9.7). *Adult female*: Wing, 100.6–110.0 (105.1);
tail, 45.5–50.0 (48.0); bill, 6.4–7.1 (6.9); tarsus, 10.9–12.4
(11.7); middle toe, 9.1–9.9 (9.7).

RANGE: C. British Columbia to w. Montana, south to w. California and n. New Mexico. Winters from Nuevo León to e.
Honduras.

TEXAS: *Migration*: Two specimens: Wilbarger Co., Vernon
(May 1, 1894, J. A. Loring); Dallas Co., 6 mi. east of Dallas
(Apr. 21, 1939, W. A. Mayer).

SONORA ROUGH-WINGED SWALLOW, *Stelgidopteryx ruficollis psammochrous* Griscom

S. *r. psammochroa* of A.O.U. check-list, 1957.

DESCRIPTION: *Adults, nuptial plumage*: Similar to S. *r. aphractus* and to S. *r. serripennis* but decidedly paler on upper parts
and somewhat paler on anterior lower surface; in size like
former.

MEASUREMENTS: *Adult male*: Wing, 104.1–117.1 (average,
110.5) mm.; tail, 43.9–52.6 (49.5); bill (exposed culmen), 6.1–
8.1 (6.9); tarsus, 9.9–11.9 (11.2); middle toe without claw, 8.6–
9.9 (9.7). *Adult female*: Wing, 99.1–103.6 (102.1); tail,
46.0–47.5 (46.8); bill, 6.6–7.1 (6.9); tarsus, (10.9); middle toe,
8.6–10.4 (9.7).

RANGE: S. California to c. Texas, south through w. Mexico to
Jalisco. Winters from s. Arizona (probably) and w. Tamaulipas
to Michoacán.

TEXAS: *Breeding*: Altitudinal range, 500 to 3,800 ft. Collected
in Brewster and Bexar cos. Fairly common. *Migration*: Collected
in Brewster, Kinney, Webb, and Starr cos. Fairly common.

NESTING: Similar to that of S. *r. serripennis*.

BARN SWALLOW, *Hirundo rustica* Linnaeus

SPECIES ACCOUNT   *See colorplate 23*

Places cup-shaped nest of mud on beam of building

or under culvert; somewhat colonial. A sleek swallow
with deeply forked tail. Metallic blue-black above;
chestnut forehead, throat; cinnamon buff breast and
belly; white tail-spots. Length, 6¾ in.; wingspan, 12½;
weight, ¾ oz.

RANGE: Widespread in Northern Hemisphere. Winters chiefly in Africa, s. Asia, and South America.

TEXAS: (See map.) *Breeding*: Late Mar. to mid-Aug.
(eggs, Apr. 8 to Aug. 1) from near sea level to 5,100 ft.
Common to uncommon in much of western half south
to Laredo, but scarce in middle and southern Panhandle and on Edwards Plateau; uncommon to scarce and
local in eastern half south to Corpus Christi, where
rare. *Migration*: Late Mar. to mid-May; mid-Aug. to
late Oct. (extremes: Feb. 8, June 3; July 9, Dec. 7).
Abundant to fairly common through most parts. *Winter*: Dec. 13 to Jan. 12. No specimen, but a few scattered sightings along coast and in Rio Grande delta.

HAUNTS AND HABITS: The Barn Swallow, only U.S.
swallow with the classical "swallow tail," usually
places its nest on the inside of barns; those Cliff Swallows which use barns generally build on the outside.
In Texas, perhaps more so than in other states, Barn
Swallows also often nest with Cliff Swallows on the
under side of concrete highway bridges. Ever since the
white man began building barns and bridges in North
America, *Hirundo rustica* has appropriated these facili-
ties for its nests, but in wilder places the bird still nests
where it did previously—in rocky, shallow caves or on
shelves of projecting rocks. The present species is
widespread in Texas but tends to avoid both heavy
woods that restrict its flycatching and exceptionally
arid land where it cannot obtain mud for its nests. The
bird is a one-pair or semicolonial nester. At other times
of the year, it is exceedingly gregarious, particularly in

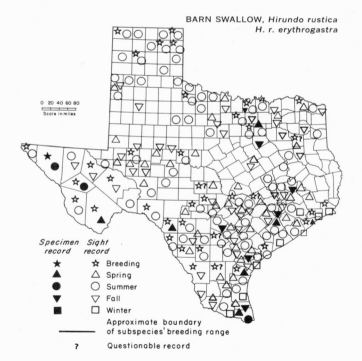

BARN SWALLOW, *Hirundo rustica*
H. r. erythrogastra

0 20 40 60 80
Scale in miles

Specimen record	Sight record	
★	☆	Breeding
▲	△	Spring
●	○	Summer
▼	▽	Fall
■	□	Winter

——— Approximate boundary
of subspecies' breeding range

? Questionable record

autumn when large flocks gather with Tree and Cliff swallows to roost at night in marshes or thickets or perch in long rows on telephone and power lines.

Flight of the Barn is swift, direct, and especially graceful due to its deeply forked tail and its habit of pulling back the wing-tips at the end of each stroke. The bird generally flies close to the ground, rarely as high as the Tree Swallow, and does not glide much. This bird habitually sweeps over grassy meadows and fields where it snaps up low-flying grasshoppers and other insects. It often follows the farmer's plow, taking advantage of insects that are stirred up; for the same reason it frequently forages amid grazing cattle.

The note of the Barn Swallow is a soft but energetic *kvit-kvit, wit, wit,* or simply *wit.* The song, uttered by individuals or in chorus, is a brisk musical twitter interspersed with rattling gutturals. April, May, and June are the chief singing months.

DETAILED ACCOUNT: ONE SUBSPECIES

AMERICAN BARN SWALLOW, *Hirundo rustica erythrogastra* Boddaert

H. r. erythrogaster of A.O.U. check-list, 1957 (see Appendix A).

DESCRIPTION: *Adult male, nuptial plumage:* Acquired by wear from winter plumage. Forehead chestnut; remainder of upper surface metallic indigo blue, sometimes slightly more purplish blue; wings chaetura black, paling to chaetura drab or fuscous on inner webs of wing-quills, exposed surface with metallic green sheen, except lesser coverts which are like back; tail chaetura black glossed with metallic green, all feathers, except middle pair, with conspicuous large white or buffy white spot on inner web, these largest and oblong on outer pair; lores and cheeks fuscous or fuscous black; sides of neck like crown; chin, throat, and jugulum chestnut to cinnamon rufous, separated from remainder of lower parts by incomplete jugular band of dull metallic blue or green feathers; remainder of lower parts, including lining of wing, varying from chestnut to pale pinkish buff. Bill black; iris vandyke brown or black; legs and feet clove brown, seal brown, or light seal brown. *Adult female, nuptial:* Acquired by wear from winter. Similar to nuptial adult male but averaging slightly smaller, with much less deeply forked tail; upper parts slightly more greenish and lower parts averaging a little paler. *Adults, winter:* Acquired by complete postnuptial molt. Like nuptial adults. *Male, first nuptial:* Acquired by wear from first winter. Like nuptial adult male, but outermost tail feathers decidedly shorter; light spots on tail feathers somewhat tinged with pinkish buff. *Male, first winter:* Acquired by complete postjuvenal molt. Like first nuptial male. *Female, first nuptial:* Acquired by wear from first winter. Like nuptial adult female, but tail shorter and forehead paler. *Female, first winter:* Acquired by complete postjuvenal molt. Similar to first nuptial female. *Juvenal:* Acquired by complete postnatal molt. Similar in general appearance to nuptial adults, but tail very slightly forked; colors much duller; pileum and cervix fuscous black or chaetura black with faint metallic greenish sheen, remainder of upper parts much duller, sheen more greenish; forehead brownish buff or fawn color; chin and throat vinaceous cinnamon, blackish jugular band much mixed with this color; light spots of tail smaller and strongly tinged with buff. Bill black or slate black; iris dark brown or black; legs and feet dark reddish brown. *Natal:* Light drab or smoke gray. Maxilla dull brown; mandible dull pink.

MEASUREMENTS: *Adult male:* Wing, 115.1–127.0 (average, 121.4) mm.; tail, 88.9–106.9 (97.1); bill (exposed culmen), 7.1–8.9 (7.9); tarsus, 10.4–11.4 (10.9); middle toe without claw, 11.4–13.0 (11.9). *Adult female:* Wing, 111.0–120.4

(114.8); tail, 69.6–82.0 (76.5); bill, 7.1–8.6 (7.9); tarsus, 10.4–10.9 (10.7); middle toe, 10.9–11.9 (11.7).

RANGE: N.w. Alaska to Newfoundland, south to n. Baja California and n. Florida, and through Mexico to Puebla. Winters from s. Mexico through Central America to Argentina; irregularly from s.e. California to s.e. South Carolina.

TEXAS: *Breeding:* Collected in Hudspeth and Jeff Davis cos. (see species account). *Migration:* Collected north to Cooke, east to Galveston, south to Cameron, west to Brewster cos.

NESTING: *Nest:* In more or less open country, wild or cultivated; in shallow cave or crevice in cliff or rocks, old mine, under bridge, wharf, or even in cavity in seawall, but usually in barn, shed, or other outbuilding when available, often not far from water. When about buildings, normally inside, though sometimes outside, attached to rafters or other similar support, often plastered against side, as well as resting on support at bottom, but sometimes without support underneath; cup-shaped and composed of pellets of mud, with hair, straw, grass, and small sticks; lined profusely with fine grass, feathers, hair, and other soft materials. *Eggs:* 3–6, usually 4 or 5; ovate to elliptical ovate, somewhat variable; creamy white or rather pinkish white, slightly glossy, and with small spots and dots of reddish brown, dark brown, purplish brown, and cinnamon, also sparingly marked with lilac, lavender, and vinaceous gray; average size, 19.6 × 13.7 mm.

CLIFF SWALLOW, *Petrochelidon pyrrhonota* (Vieillot)

SPECIES ACCOUNT   *See colorplate 23*

Places jug-shaped nest of mud under cliff overhang, bridge, eaves; colonial. A square-tailed swallow that soars frequently. Buffy white (most races) forehead; blue-black crown, back (streaked with dull white); rich buffy rump; chestnut throat (with black patch), cheek; brownish collar; whitish belly. Length, 5¾ in.; wingspan, 12; weight, ¾ oz.

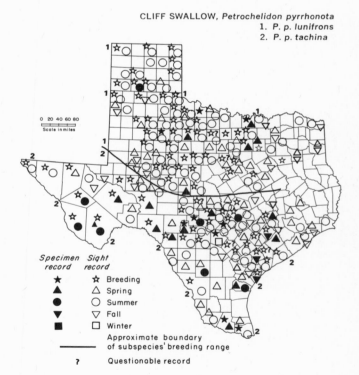

CLIFF SWALLOW, *Petrochelidon pyrrhonota*
1. *P. p. lunifrons*
2. *P. p. tachina*

0 20 40 60 80
Scale in miles

Specimen record	Sight record	
★	☆	Breeding
▲	△	Spring
●	○	Summer
▼	▽	Fall
■	□	Winter

—— Approximate boundary of subspecies' breeding range

? Questionable record

RANGE: C. Alaska to s. Quebec and Nova Scotia, south to n. Baja California, Nayarit, Tamaulipas, Texas, extreme n. Alabama, w. North Carolina, and Delaware, and over Central Plateau of Mexico to Oaxaca. Winters chiefly from c. Brazil to c. Chile and c. Argentina.

TEXAS: (See map.) *Breeding*: Late Mar. to early Aug.—rarely later (eggs, Apr. 1 to July 30; also Sept. 21)—from near sea level to 5,100 ft. Very common to fairly common in much of western three-quarters south to Uvalde, San Antonio, and Victoria; local in south Texas brush country. Breeding lately discovered in east Texas: Henderson Co., at bridge and spillway of Cedar Creek Reservoir (spring of 1973, fide C. D. Fisher). May occasionally summer on upper coast, but no good evidence of nesting. *Migration*: Mid-Mar. to mid-May; early Aug. to late Oct. (extremes: Feb. 24, June 10; July 2, Dec. 6). Abundant (some years) to fairly common through western three-quarters and on upper coast; uncommon to scarce over much of wooded eastern quarter.

HAUNTS AND HABITS: The Cliff Swallow requires a rocky bluff, sheer cliff, or facsimile thereof for its nest. Colonies of Cliffs frequently attempt nesting on or under bridges, sides of dams, eaves of barns and outbuildings, and crevices and ledges of buildings, but the birds are usually more successful in wilderness regions. Civilization's structures have not greatly expanded the geographical range of the Cliff Swallow, but they have allowed the bird to nest on cliffless flatlands. In Texas, the species is found on plains, prairies, and broken country away from heavy woodlands, and generally near streams, lakes, or ponds that provide mud for its jug-shaped nest. In autumn, Cliffs are especially conspicuous when they gather, often with Tree, Bank, and Barn swallows, in large flocks prior to their long migration to South America.

Flight of this swallow is erratic in speed, but rather steady in direction; it is characteristic of the Cliff to move through the air as if on a roller coaster, flying upward on rapid wing-beats then descending in a glide. It feeds, like all hirundinids, on insects and occasional spiders, taken almost exclusively on the wing. A colony of nest-building Cliff Swallows is a spectacle of animation and industry as the birds go about their work. Chattering individuals gather around a puddle or wet stream bank; while picking up mouthfuls of mud, most individuals elevate their tails and quiver their wings butterflylike high above their backs. Each glob of mud they shape and temper in their mouths; then they fly to the site of their masonry work to deposit the pellet.

Cliff Swallows nesting in or near towns face problems: Boys delight in breaking up colonies with sticks, rocks, and bottles; House Sparrows take possession of nests; and/or streets are paved, thus eliminating swallow mud. One such street-paving calamity happened at the Texas State Capitol. A colony of many years standing was extirpated when the main thoroughfare leading to the building, Congress Avenue, was paved.

The note of the Cliff Swallow is a low *chur*, sometimes sounding like *chieu*. Its unmusical song is a creaking twitter followed by guttural gratings. Song is heard chiefly from the air about the nesting colonies in April, May, and June.

DETAILED ACCOUNT: SIX SUBSPECIES

NORTHERN CLIFF SWALLOW, *Petrochelidon pyrrhonota albifrons* (Rafinesque)

Race not in A.O.U. check-list, 1957 (see Appendix A).

DESCRIPTION: *Adults, nuptial plumage*: Acquired by wear from winter plumage. Forehead cream white to very pale wood brown; lores dull black, their lower part somewhat mixed with dull buff or tawny; pileum and back metallic bluish black or greenish slate black, back with a few narrow streaks of dull white formed by edges of feathers; cervix dull hair brown, anteriorly more or less tinged with chestnut, this sometimes forming almost complete narrow collar; rump tawny to pinkish buff; upper tail-coverts dull hair brown, margined at tips with grayish white; wings and tail chaetura drab on exposed surfaces with slight metallic greenish sheen; lesser wing-coverts slightly more metallic, chaetura drab or fuscous, lighter on inner webs; tertials and inner secondaries very narrowly tipped with brownish white; chin, throat, and sides of neck chestnut, paler posteriorly; center of throat metallic greenish slate black; jugulum dull light drab, more or less washed with buff or ochraceous; rest of lower parts dull white, central portions of longer lower tail-coverts hair brown; lining of wing dull drab washed with chestnut. Bill black; interior of mouth dull pink; iris dark claret brown or vandyke brown; legs dark reddish brown or dull pinkish vinaceous; feet dull pinkish vinaceous, plumbeous, or seal brown; claws black or seal brown. *Adults, winter*: Acquired by complete postnuptial molt. Similar to nuptial adults, but feathers of back and scapulars with narrow brownish gray edgings, dulling color of upper surface; upper tail-coverts broadly tipped with buff, brownish white, or buffy white; all upper wing-coverts narrowly tipped with brownish white or light brownish gray; tertials and inner secondaries rather conspicuously tipped with white or brownish white. *Adults, first nuptial*: Acquired by wear from first winter, with which it is practically identical. *First winter*: Acquired by complete postjuvenal molt. Like adults in winter. *Juvenal*: Acquired by complete postnatal molt. Similar to nuptial adults but very much duller, without distinctly metallic plumage everywhere; upper parts fuscous black, hindneck pale dull fuscous; forehead dull russet, feathers of back and scapulars edged narrowly with buffy white or dull buff, upper tail-coverts and tertials tipped broadly with same colors; chin, throat, and sides of neck light tawny mixed with fuscous, much paler and duller than in adults; breast and sides between hair brown and drab and washed with buff. Bill dull black; legs and feet dull sepia. *Natal* (this plumage of this race not seen in Texas): Dull grayish white tinged with pale drab. Bill clove brown, basal portion of mandible pale yellow; iris dark brown; feet broccoli brown.

MEASUREMENTS: *Adult male*: Wing, 108.0–109.0 (average, 108.5) mm.; tail, 49.0–50.0 (49.5); bill (exposed culmen), (7.1); tarsus, 11.9–13.0 (12.4); middle toe without claw, 9.9–10.2 (10.0). *Adult female*: Wing, 101.1–108.5 (105.6); tail, 47.0–51.1 (48.8); bill, 6.6–7.6 (7.4); tarsus, 11.9–13.0 (12.4); middle toe, 10.9–12.4 (11.4).

RANGE: N.w. Manitoba to c. Ontario, south to Missouri and Tennessee. Winters from Brazil to Argentina.

TEXAS: *Migration*: One specimen: Kinney Co., Fort Clark (Apr. 28, 1898, E. A. Mearns).

GREAT PLAINS CLIFF SWALLOW, *Petrochelidon pyrrhonota lunifrons* (Say)

Race not in A.O.U. check-list, 1957 (see Appendix A).

DESCRIPTION: *Adults, nuptial plumage*: Similar to *P. p. albi-*

frons, but middle toe shorter; rump somewhat paler; brownish gray of hindneck lighter; forehead averaging slightly paler, more whitish; lower parts, particularly breast and jugulum, lighter, more grayish (less buffy or ochraceous). *Natal*: Probably similar to *P. p. albifrons*.

MEASUREMENTS: *Adult male*: Wing, 105.4–108.5 (average, 106.7) mm.; tail, 48.0–51.1 (49.3); bill (exposed culmen), 7.1–7.6 (7.1); tarsus, 11.9–13.5 (12.7); middle toe without claw, 10.4–11.9 (10.9). *Adult female*: Wing, 102.6–108.0 (105.6); tail, 47.0–52.6 (49.3); bill, 7.1–8.1 (7.4); tarsus, 11.9–13.5 (12.4); middle toe, 9.4–11.7 (10.7).

RANGE: North Dakota, south to c. New Mexico and n. Texas. Winters in s. Brazil.

TEXAS: *Breeding*: Altitudinal range, 400 to 4,700 ft. Collected in Kent (eggs), Wilbarger (eggs), Cooke (eggs), and Dallas cos. Nesting activity observed north to Lipscomb (June 19–July 10, 1903, A. H. Howell), east to McLennan (July 10, 1931, T. F. Smith), west to Tom Green (May 4, July 20, 1886, W. Lloyd) and Deaf Smith (June 1, 15, 1920, A. J. Kirn) cos. Locally common. *Migration*: Collected north to Dallas, east to Wharton, south to Nueces, west to Presidio (June 10) cos. Common.

NESTING: Similar to that of *P. p. tachina*, but average egg size, 20.1 × 13.7 mm.

CANADIAN CLIFF SWALLOW, *Petrochelidon pyrrhonota hypopolia* Oberholser

DESCRIPTION: *Adults, nuptial plumage*: Resembling *P. p. albifrons*, but wing and middle toe longer; lower parts lighter, less rufescent (more grayish); forehead more whitish.

MEASUREMENTS: *Adult male*: Wing, 110.0–115.1 (average, 112.0) mm.; tail, 49.0–52.1 (50.8); bill (exposed culmen), 6.1–8.1 (7.4); tarsus, 10.9–13.0 (12.2); middle toe without claw, 10.4–11.9 (11.2). *Adult female*: Wing, 108.0–111.5 (110.2); tail, 49.5–51.6 (50.8); bill, 6.9–7.4 (7.1); tarsus, 10.9–13.0 (12.2); middle toe, 11.9–12.4 (12.2).

RANGE: C. Alaska to e. Mackenzie, south to British Columbia and Alberta. Winters probably in South America.

TEXAS: *Migration*: Two specimens: Travis Co., Austin (Apr. 25, 1893, J. A. Singley); Aransas Co. (Sept. 9, 1912, J. M. Priour).

OREGON CLIFF SWALLOW, *Petrochelidon pyrrhonota aprophata* Oberholser

Race not in A.O.U. check-list, 1957 (see Appendix A).

DESCRIPTION: *Adults, nuptial plumage*: Like *P. p. hypopolia*, but lower surface lighter; forehead more buffy (less clearly white).

MEASUREMENTS: *Adult male*: Wing, 109.0–113.3 (average, 111.3) mm.; tail, 49.0–52.6 (50.3); bill (exposed culmen), 7.1–8.1 (7.4); tarsus, 12.2–14.0 (13.2); middle toe without claw, 10.9–12.7 (11.9). *Adult female*: Wing, 108.0–112.0 (109.7); tail, 48.5–50.0 (49.3); bill, 7.1–8.1 (7.6); tarsus, 11.9–14.0 (13.0); middle toe, 10.7–12.4 (11.7).

RANGE: S. and probably e. Oregon, south to n.e. California and n.w. Nevada. Winters probably in South America.

TEXAS: *Migration*: One specimen: Brewster Co., 12 mi. south of Marathon (May 4, 1933, A. C. Lloyd).

LESSER CLIFF SWALLOW, *Petrochelidon pyrrhonota tachina* Oberholser

DESCRIPTION: *Adults, nuptial plumage*: Similar to *P. p. albifrons* but smaller; forehead darker (dull cinnamon, fawn color, or wood brown); lower parts rather more rufescent. *Natal*: Probably similar to *P. p. albifrons*.

MEASUREMENTS: *Adult male*: Wing, 98.1–107.4 (average, 102.9) mm.; tail, 43.4–49.5 (46.0); bill (exposed culmen), 7.1–8.4 (7.6); tarsus, 11.9–13.2 (12.7); middle toe without claw, 10.2–10.9 (10.7). *Adult female*: Wing, 101.6–106.9 (104.4);

tail, 45.0–51.1 (47.8); bill, 7.1–7.9 (7.4); tarsus, 11.9–13.5 (12.7); middle toe, 9.4–11.4 (10.4).

RANGE: S. Arizona to c. and s. Texas. Winters probably in s. South America.

TEXAS: *Breeding*: Altitudinal range, near sea level to 5,100 ft. Collected northwest to Presidio, Jeff Davis, Brewster, and Pecos, east to Travis and Washington, south to Nueces and Hidalgo cos. Locally common.

NESTING: *Nest*: Mostly about ledges or rocky cliffs, along streams, under bridges, on dams, in eaves or similar crevice of building, even on terrace or ledge of tall building several hundred feet above ground, occasionally on bill boards; in colonies; retort shape, like nests of other Cliff Swallows, with entrance at side or bottom; composed of pellets of mud, securely cemented together and to supporting surface, inside composed of straw, grasses, leaves, and bits of trash, with a few feathers, apparently less quantity of material than in some other races; lined with a few feathers, sometimes only two or three. *Eggs*: 3–6, usually 5; ovate; white or creamy white, with dots, spots, and small blotches of reddish brown, chiefly near larger end; average size, 20.3 × 13.7 mm.

SONORA CLIFF SWALLOW, *Petrochelidon pyrrhonota minima* van Rossem

DESCRIPTION: *Adults, nuptial plumage*: Resembling *P. p. tachina*, but forehead much darker, chestnut to cinnamon rufous, rather than pale cinnamon or fawn color.

MEASUREMENTS: *Adult male*: Wing, 100.1–108.0 (average, 103.1) mm.; tail, 43.9–50.0 (46.5); bill (exposed culmen), 6.1–7.1 (6.9); tarsus, 10.9–13.0 (11.9); middle toe without claw, 10.9–11.9 (11.4). *Adult female*: Wing, 102.1–105.9 (103.9); tail, 43.9–50.0 (47.3); bill, 6.6–7.9 (7.4); tarsus, 11.9–13.5 (12.7); middle toe, 9.9–11.4 (10.7).

RANGE: Chihuahua, south to Michoacán, Oaxaca, and Veracruz. Casual in summer in Trans-Pecos Texas. Winters probably in South America.

TEXAS: *Summer*: Collected in Jeff Davis (2 specimens) and Brewster (3) cos. Casual.

CAVE SWALLOW, *Petrochelidon fulva* (Vieillot)

SPECIES ACCOUNT

Nests in rocky caves. Closely resembles Cliff Swallow, but throat and cheeks buffy (rather than chestnut); forehead chestnut (rather than whitish as in most races of Cliff). In the Cave Swallow the blackish throat-patch is almost or completely lacking, and the white back-stripes are prominent. Length, 5¾ in.

RANGE: Locally in s.e. New Mexico (Carlsbad Caverns region, Eddy Co.), s.w. Texas, n.e. Mexico, Chiapas, n. Yucatán, and Greater Antilles. Winter range imperfectly known; presumed migrants reported from Chiapas and s.w. Costa Rica.

TEXAS: (See map.) *Breeding*: Late Feb. to early Sept. (eggs, Apr. 5 to Aug. 15; active nests to Sept. 8) from 600 to 3,000 ft., perhaps somewhat higher. Very locally common to uncommon in Trans-Pecos (Dillahunty Swallow Cave in Culberson Co.; near Fort Stockton, Pecos Co.; and Mariscal Mt., Brewster Co.) and on southwestern portion of Edwards Plateau. As of 1970, recorded in 32 caves within the following cos.: Culberson (1), Brewster (2), Sutton (2), Mason (1), Val Verde (2), Edwards (9), Kerr (10), Uvalde (2), and Kinney (3) cos. In 1973, species was discovered nesting in culverts in Val Verde, Kinney, Uvalde, Real, Medina, Maverick, Zavala, and Frio cos. (600+ clutches under observation, Apr. 7 to Sept. 15, 1973, R. F. Martin, M. R. Lewis); the last three counties represent a significant southern extension of the species' range in Texas. Culvert-nesting Cave Swallows also discovered in Pecos Co., vicinity of Fort Stockton (9 birds banded and 1 nestling collected, June 25, 1973, K. A. Arnold). *Migration*: Mid-Feb. to mid-Apr.; mid-Aug. to late Sept. (extremes: Feb. 6, Apr. 18; Aug. 11, Oct. 5). Fairly common but local through breeding range. Sighted outside nesting areas during spring migration only in Brewster Co. (Castolon and Rio Grande Village, both in Big Bend Park); during fall in Reeves (Balmorhea), Pecos (Fort Stockton), Brewster (Big Bend Park), Kinney (Fort Clark, Brackettville), and Uvalde (Uvalde Fish Hatchery, also 4 mi. north of Sabinal) cos. Apparently casual at San Antonio.

HAUNTS AND HABITS: Breeding habits of the Cave Swallow are unlike those of any other North American bird: It is the only one which nests in colonies within deep caves and sinkholes. However, in 1973, a U.S. first occurred: The species was discovered nesting in manmade highway culverts in close association with Barn Swallows. Also, there is apparently limited association with Cliff Swallows. One active Cliff Swallow nest was found in a culvert in Uvalde County in addition to the nests of Cave and Barn Swallows (R. F. Martin); also, in Pecos County, Cliff and Cave swallows were observed nesting in culverts of a highway bridge (K. A. Arnold).

In Texas, the Cave Swallow nests within caves which meet rigid specifications. First of all, the hole used apparently must be located in an area where the average annual rainfall is between fifteen and thirty-one inches; an altitude in the range of approximately six hundred to three thousand feet above sea level also seems to be required. The recently discovered nest culverts in southwestern Texas also meet these altitude and rainfall requirements. Breeding swallows select walls that are dry so as not to dissolve their mud nests; however, a source of mud or wet guano has to be present either at the site or within three miles flying distance of the colony.

Normally, Cave Swallows construct their open-topped mud pellet nests only within a twilight zone—ideally provided by caves and subterranean chambers. A few minutes of direct sunlight can kill young swallows; however, the adult birds cannot feed their nestlings in total darkness, as can the South American Oil Bird, *Steatornis caripensis.*

The Cave Swallow is a skillful flier, perhaps even more so than others of its strong-winged family. An excellent place to observe its skill was at the Devil's Sinkhole—now closed to the public—in Edwards County. Here, Edgar Kincaid, Jr., senior editor of the present work, often watched the swallow colony during the 1950's.

A typical day progressed thus: About half an hour after the last bats had flopped into the monstrous old hole (said to be 60 feet in diameter at the flush-to-the-ground opening and 407 feet deep), roosting swallows one hundred feet below awoke with loud *weet*'s. After several more *weet*'s, individuals and groups of swallows began winding themselves out of the sink by flying in wide ascending spirals, *weet*ing as they flew. When all the groups had exited the sinkhole, they gathered into a loose flock of perhaps five hundred, which circled high above the hole, then drifted and dispersed, mostly in an easterly direction.

After an hour, more or less, of catching beetles, winged ants, and flies, groups of swallows returned to their cave. A few feet above the opening, each swallow in its turn would close its wings and drop headfirst into the pit. About two-thirds of its way down, the descending bird half-spread its wings and zigzagged from side to side. Just above the deepest hanging rock formation visible to a topside observer, the individual straightened out, spread its wings a little more, and glided with wonderful smoothness into the twilight depths to its resting niche or nest. When adults were busy feeding young, some were entering and leaving virtually all day long. At other stages during the breeding cycle, sometimes an hour or more would pass without any swallow being seen about the sink.

Once during a freak May cold snap that grounded insects and swallows for three days, the editor found a dead Cave Swallow just back from the rim of the Devil's Sinkhole. The bird's shrunken stomach contained a rock the size of a small marble—very large for so small a bird. Had extreme hunger forced this bird of the air down to the ground to eat this hard lifeless substance?

Usual note of the Cave Swallow is a *weet!*, but an individual in a disturbed flock will utter from one to

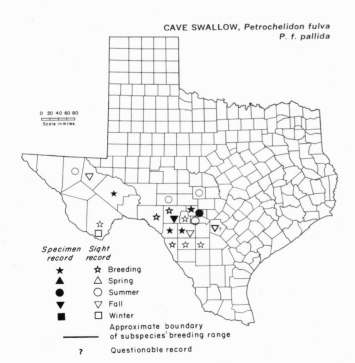

CAVE SWALLOW, *Petrochelidon fulva*
P. f. pallida

0 20 40 60 80
Scale in miles

Specimen   Sight
record   record

★   ☆ Breeding
▲   △ Spring
●   ○ Summer
▼   ▽ Fall
■   □ Winter

Approximate boundary
of subspecies' breeding range

?   Questionable record

four *che* or *chu* calls. Song consists of squeaks which merge into a melodic warble. All vocalizations are given most frequently in flight. Song season is chiefly from early March into July.

CHANGES: Before 1915, *P. fulva* was not known to breed anywhere in the United States. From 1915 until 1957, the species, according to the American Ornithologists' Union check-lists and other literature, was officially believed to nest within this nation only in Kerr County, Texas. From the 1950's through 1970, the intermittent and various explorations of J. K. Baker, Don Davis, E. B. Kincaid, Jr., Richard Prasil, J. R. Reddell, R. K. Selander, Sandy Sprunt, and R. H. Wauer have resulted in the accumulation of much additional data, especially regarding the species' distribution in caves and sinkholes in the state. The recently discovered (1973) culvert-nesting activities and the long-range results of interspecific relationships of Cave Swallows with other hirundinids are currently being studied by R. F. Martin, curator of vertebrates of the Texas Memorial Museum at Austin. Pertinent information is summarized and incorporated into the species' map and above text. For more details on variation, distribution, and ecology of the Cave Swallow on the Edwards Plateau, see Selander and Baker, 1957, *Condor* 59: 345–363.

DETAILED ACCOUNT: ONE SUBSPECIES

COAHUILA CAVE SWALLOW, *Petrochelidon fulva pallida* Nelson

Formerly known as Coahuila Cliff Swallow.

DESCRIPTION: *Adults, nuptial plumage*: Acquired by wear from winter plumage. Forehead russet, chestnut, or tawny; lores and orbital ring dull black, sometimes slightly mixed with tawny; pileum and back metallic greenish slate black, former duller, latter with a few grayish white streaks formed by edges of feathers; narrow collar on hindneck between ochraceous orange and tawny; rump tawny to cinnamon rufous; upper tail-coverts fuscous; wings and tail chaetura drab, slightly glossed with dull metallic green, but inner webs of quills light fuscous; outer tail feathers margined on inner webs terminally with white; tertials tipped narrowly with pale brownish white; lesser wing-coverts with slightly more metallic sheen; sides of head below eyes and sides of neck between ochraceous orange and tawny; throat buffy cinnamon; lower breast and abdomen dull brownish white or buffy white; sides and flanks light hair brown washed with cinnamon; lower tail-coverts white, longer ones hair brown centrally and all tinged with cinnamon buff or pale orange cinnamon; lining of wing dull light hair brown or drab washed with buff; exterior coverts hair brown centrally with buffy white edges. Bill dull black; iris dark brown; legs and feet dull light brown. *Adults, winter*: Acquired by complete postnuptial molt. Like nuptial adults. *First nuptial*: Acquired by wear from first winter. Not essentially different from nuptial adults. *First winter*: Acquired by complete postjuvenal molt. Similar to first nuptial male and female. *Juvenal*: Acquired by complete postnatal molt. Generally similar to nuptial adults but much duller in color with very little metallic sheen on upper parts; pileum dark fuscous; back fuscous black with a few whitish streaks formed by edges of feathers, and on lower back inconspicuous bars formed by buffy white or dull buff tips of feathers; russet forehead duller, lighter, and narrower, cinnamon collar about hindneck paler and duller; tertials and upper tail-coverts broadly, scapulars and wing-coverts narrowly, tipped with dull buff, cinnamon, or white; ear-coverts fuscous; chin and throat much paler and duller, sometimes with small fuscous

spots; breast darker, more grayish, dull brownish cinnamon, washed and sometimes spotted with fuscous; sides of body and flanks duller and darker. *Natal*: Buffy white.

MEASUREMENTS: *Adult male*: Wing, 106.9–110.5 (average, 109.0) mm.; tail, 48.0–50.0 (48.8); bill (exposed culmen), 7.1–8.4 (7.9); tarsus, 12.4–13.5 (13.0); middle toe without claw, 10.9–11.9 (11.4). *Adult female*: Wing, 106.4–113.5 (108.7); tail, 45.5–51.6 (48.8); bill, 6.6–8.4 (7.4); tarsus, 11.9–12.4 (12.2); middle toe, 11.4–12.4 (11.9).

RANGE: S.e. New Mexico, s.w. Texas, Coahuila, and highland Tamaulipas. Exact winter range unknown; reported during migration in Chiapas and s.w. Costa Rica.

TEXAS: *Breeding*: Collected in Pecos, Edwards, Kerr, Kinney, and Uvalde cos.

NESTING: *Nest*: In rocky caves or sinkholes (lately, also in culverts) in semiarid, hilly terrain; in colonies; in holes in ceiling or on ledges of sides of caves; an open-topped, thick-walled bracket constructed of mud or guano pellets, lined with cotton-like plant fibers, thin strips of bark, grasses, and feathers. *Eggs*: 3–5, usually 4; elliptical ovate, rather more elongated than those of Lesser Cliff Swallow, *P. pyrrhonota tachina*; white, everywhere with fine spots of light brown and dark brown, sometimes with a few shell markings of lilac and dull purple; average size, 19.6 × 14.0 mm.

PURPLE MARTIN, *Progne subis* (Linnaeus)

SPECIES ACCOUNT

Largest U.S. swallow. *Male*: uniformly glossy blue-black above and below. *Female*: dull blue-black above; grayish forehead, throat, breast; whitish belly; brownish collar (usually) on hindneck. Length, 8 in.; wingspan, 16¼; weight, 1¾ oz.

RANGE: S.w. British Columbia, south (west of Cascades and Sierra Nevada) to Baja California, Sonora, and Arizona, and locally through highland Mexico to Michoacán; also n.e. British Columbia to Nova Scotia, south (east of Rockies) to Texas Gulf coast, and s. Florida. Winters in South America to Brazil.

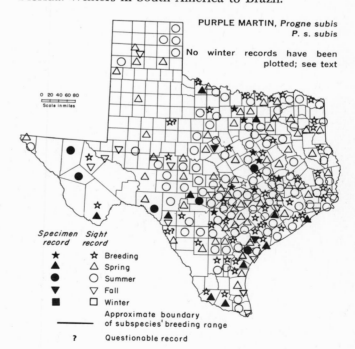

PURPLE MARTIN, *Progne subis*
P. s. subis

No winter records have been plotted; see text

0 20 40 60 80
Scale in miles

Specimen record   Sight record
★   ☆ Breeding
▲   △ Spring
●   ○ Summer
▼   ▽ Fall
■   □ Winter

———— Approximate boundary of subspecies' breeding range

?   Questionable record

TEXAS: (See map.) *Breeding*: Early Mar. to late July —occasionally to mid-Aug. (eggs, Apr. 13 to June 18; young in nest to Aug. 7)—from near sea level to 5,000 ft.—possibly 8,000 ft. Locally common to fairly common in most of eastern two-thirds south to Beeville and Corpus Christi; uncommon and irregular south to 27th parallel and west to western Edwards Plateau; scarce and local west to Reeves, Culberson (breeding suspected), and northern Brewster cos. Last reported breeding colony in Rio Grande delta: Starr Co., Rio Grande City (June 5–10, 1891, W. Lloyd). *Migration*: Mid-Feb. to mid-Apr.; early July to early Sept.—a few to late Oct. (extremes: Jan. 8, May 20; June 10, Dec. 23). Abundant to fairly common through most parts; uncommon to scarce in Trans-Pecos.

HAUNTS AND HABITS: The Purple Martin, ranging through most of the United States, except the Cascade, Sierra Nevada, and Rocky mountains, is probably the number one birdhouse species in the country; certainly it is the prime, and virtually only, apartment house dweller among native North American birds. Few birds are more generally accepted and less persecuted by man than is this big blue-black swallow. It breeds locally in most of Texas except within deep woods, on waterless deserts, and in hot subtropical brush. For nesting sites it depends largely on bird boxes in yards and gardens of farms and ranches and in cities and towns. Highly sociable, the birds nest in colonies and gather, as do most swallows, in large postbreeding flocks which roost at night in trees, thickets, or shrubs in woodlands or towns.

A very early but leisurely spring migrant, the species, normally with glossy black old males in the lead, begins arriving in February—occasionally even in January—and continues on into April. The Purple Martin is noteworthy as being the only North–to–South American migrant which begins returning in force to Texas in late winter. When enough of these swallows have arrived to form colonies, their predawn singing is impressive. From high in the black sky their gurgling chorus drifts down. Just as the martin announces spring to Texans by returning in late winter so it announces morning by singing in the late night.

Flight of the Purple Martin exhibits its swallow gracefulness. Typically, the bird flies with rapid wing-beats, then glides for a period either in a sweeping arc or straight line; it also spreads its tail more than do other swallows. Martins dash, dive, and wheel erratically in the air as they glean winged insects. Occasionally, they forage on the ground for terrestrial bugs, beetles, ants, and spiders. Often the bird skims over water, swooping down for a drink or dipping its hind parts for a quick on-the-wing bath. Like all swallows, this bird's perching posture is very erect.

The voice of the Purple Martin, not musical but quite pleasing to the human ear, is one reason why the bird is welcome about man's dwellings. Its common notes include a series of throaty *tchew-wew*'s and a *pew, pew*, sometimes described as *peuo, peuo*. The song is a medley of gurgling notes interspersed with rich gutturals. Song, especially the night song, is heard chiefly during March, April, May, and June.

DETAILED ACCOUNT: ONE SUBSPECIES

AMERICAN PURPLE MARTIN, *Progne subis subis* (Linnaeus)

DESCRIPTION: *Adult male, nuptial plumage*: Acquired by wear from winter plumage. Above and below metallic dusky violet blue or indulin blue, bases of feathers dark hair brown, deep mouse gray, or blackish mouse gray, small concealed tuft of white feathers on each side of rump and another larger tuft of white on each side of body; wings and tail fuscous black, inner webs fuscous with slight metallic greenish gloss; lesser and median wing-coverts like upper parts, remaining wing-coverts like rest of wing; lining of wing chaetura black with metallic blue sheen. Bill deep black or deep brownish black; iris dark brown; legs, toes, and claws black or brownish black. *Adult male, winter*: Acquired by complete postnuptial molt. Similar to nuptial adult male. *Adult female, nuptial*: Acquired by wear from winter. Upper surface similar to that of nuptial adult male but much duller and less uniform, more of gray bases of feathers visible; forehead and fore part of crown hair brown, mixed with metallic blue, sometimes becoming grayish white on forehead; narrow light hair brown collar on hindneck; breast hair brown or dark mouse gray with dull white or grayish white edgings of feathers, which give plumage a scalelike appearance; throat and sides of head and of neck similar but paler, with only ear-coverts showing entirely metallic blue; lores dull black; sides and flanks like breast; middle of posterior lower parts white; lining of wing hair brown, coverts edged with white. *Adult female, winter*: Acquired by complete postnuptial molt. Like nuptial adult female. *Male, second winter*: Acquired by complete postnuptial molt. Similar to adult male in winter. *Male, first nuptial*: Acquired by wear from first winter. Similar to nuptial adult female, but below posteriorly more extensively white, also sometimes with a few metallic and dull blue feathers on anterior lower parts. *Male, first winter*: Acquired by complete postjuvenal molt. Like first nuptial adult male. *Female, second winter*: Acquired by complete postnuptial molt. Like adult female in winter. *Female, first nuptial*: Acquired by wear from first winter. Similar to nuptial adult female, but upper parts with much less of metallic blue, all but pileum and scapulars with little or none, and this color more greenish; remainder of upper parts between chaetura drab and hair brown; feathers of anterior lower surface usually more broadly margined with dull white, also posterior lower parts more uniformly and extensively white. *Female, first winter*: Acquired by complete postjuvenal molt. Similar to first nuptial female. *Juvenal*: Acquired by complete postnatal molt. Similar to first nuptial female, but upper parts more uniform, with more brownish (less gray) cervical collar; forehead duller and somewhat darker; throat and jugulum somewhat more uniform and tinged with buff; down underneath this plumage between mouse gray and deep mouse gray. Bill, legs, and feet brownish black. *Natal*: Unknown.

MEASUREMENTS: *Adult male*: Wing, 138.9–152.9 (average, 146.3) mm.; tail, 68.6–78.0 (73.7); bill (exposed culmen), 10.4–12.4 (11.7); tarsus, 14.0–16.5 (15.2); middle toe without claw, 15.0–17.0 (15.7). *Adult female*: Wing, 135.9–147.1 (142.2); tail, 68.1–74.9 (70.9); bill, 9.9–13.0 (11.7); tarsus, 14.5–16.0 (15.2); middle toe, 15.0–17.0 (16.3).

RANGE: Identical with that of species with exception of Baja California, lowlands of Sonora and s. Arizona, and w. slope of Sierra Madre Occidental in s.w. Chihuahua and n. Nayarit.

TEXAS: *Breeding*: Collected north to Wilbarger, east to Dallas, south to Nueces (prior to 1900, to Hidalgo and Starr), west to Kerr, Brewster, and Culberson (nesting suspected) cos. Nesting activity observed east to Jefferson Co., Port Arthur (55 nesting pairs, 1921; young banded, July 26, 1927, Bessie Reid).

NESTING: *Nest*: Ordinarily in open country, often not far from water; in abandoned woodpecker nest or other hole in tree, cavity in cliff or under boulders, crevice about building on farm or ranch, and in Purple Martin birdhouse or gourd; usually in colonies; carelessly built nest in cavity, made of weeds, weed stems, grass, twigs, leaves, straw, bits of string, paper, and rags, sometimes with a little mud as foundation; lined with feathers or other soft materials. *Eggs:* 3–6, usually 4 or 5; elliptical ovate; glossy; white, unmarked; average size, 24.9 × 18.5 mm.

GRAY-BREASTED MARTIN, *Progne chalybea* (Gmelin)

SPECIES ACCOUNT

Both sexes resemble female Purple Martin, but are noticeably (in direct comparison) smaller; have darker, blackish foreheads; lack grayish collar around necks; usually more distinctly white-bellied. Length, 6¾ in.

RANGE: Tropical Mexico, south through Central America to Peru, Bolivia, c. Argentina, and Uruguay. In fall migrates from n.e. Mexico and other northern parts of its range.

TEXAS: *Casual*: Two specimens from Rio Grande delta: Starr Co., Rio Grande City (male, Apr. 25, 1880, M. A. Frazer); Hidalgo Co., Hidalgo (female, May 18, 1889, J. A. Singley). Many unsubstantiated 20th-century sightings in various parts of state; most of these reports are probably based on mated immature Purple Martins. Genuine Gray-breasted Martins have bred at Brownsville, according to egg collector F. Nyc.

HAUNTS AND HABITS: In its normal haunts in continental tropical America, the Gray-breasted Martin is as much attracted to man's habitations as is the Purple Martin in the United States. Only extremely rarely does this bird wander north to the Rio Grande delta of Texas; during the 1950's, the closest big colonies were at Valles, San Luis Potosí, Mexico, a day's journey by automobile south of Brownsville. It lives most abundantly about farms and in cities and towns where it nests in a bird box or any available nook or eaves of a building. It is found as well about wharves on waterways, bridges, in fields, clearings, at woodland edges, and in more open forests. The bird ranges up to about four thousand feet, perhaps at times higher. The species is highly gregarious. After the breeding season, flocks can often be seen circling high in the air; just before sunset they gather, sometimes in huge numbers, evidently as they prepare to roost. At such times this species often associates with other swallows, such as the Mangrove Swallow, *Iridoprocne albilinea*.

Flight and behavior of the Graybreast are practically identical with that of its relative, the Purple. When perching it uses either trees, bushes, or roofs of buildings. Courtship of *Progne chalybea* includes many aerial evolutions by the male. The Gray-breasted Martin—like the Sulphur-bellied Flycatcher and Yellow-green Vireo—is one of the few highly migratory tropical birds. It ordinarily returns to its nesting locality in late winter as does the temperate-zone–nesting Purple Martin.

The Graybreast's vocalizations closely resemble those of the Purple, although they are not so loud nor quite so rich. Birds can be heard at all hours of the day during the breeding season.

DETAILED ACCOUNT: ONE SUBSPECIES

COMMON GRAY-BREASTED MARTIN, *Progne chalybea chalybea* (Gmelin)

DESCRIPTION: *Adult male, nuptial plumage*: Acquired by wear from winter plumage. Upper parts metallic dusky blue, forehead duller, inclining to fuscous or dull black; wings and tail chaetura black with metallic bluish sheen, inner webs of wings fuscous, lesser and median coverts metallic blue like back, outer edges of greater coverts somewhat glossed with same metallic color; sides of neck similar to back but rather duller; sides of head, with chin, throat, and jugulum, between hair brown and fuscous, middle of chin and of throat paler, inclining to drab; feathers of throat and jugulum tipped with dull white; sides of jugulum often with metallic blue feathers; remainder of lower surface white, longest lower tail-coverts sometimes with grayish shaft lines; sides and flanks like breast but with some admixture of metallic blue feathers; lining of wing chaetura drab with slightly paler edgings and a little metallic bluish sheen. Bill black; iris dark brown; legs and feet dull brown or blackish brown. *Adult male, winter*: Acquired by complete postnuptial molt. Like nuptial adult male. *Adult female, nuptial*: Acquired by wear from winter. Similar to nuptial adult male, but upper parts duller, often more greenish, and pileum much more extensively brown, this color extending to occiput, sometimes even to nape; chin and throat paler, sometimes whitish. *Adult female, winter*: Acquired by complete postnuptial molt. Like nuptial adult female. *Male, second winter*: Acquired by complete postnuptial molt. Like adult male in winter. *Male, first nuptial*: Acquired by wear from winter. Similar to nuptial adult female, but upper parts brighter, more metallic, and more purplish (less greenish). *Male, first winter*: Acquired by complete postjuvenal molt. Like first nuptial male. *Female, first nuptial*: Acquired by wear from first winter. Like nuptial adult female. *Female, first winter*: Acquired by complete postjuvenal molt. Like first nuptial female. *Juvenal*: Acquired by complete postnatal molt. Similar to nuptial adult female but much duller, upper parts fuscous or chaetura black with little or no metallic sheen, this decidedly greenish instead of violet or bluish; under surface more uniform, gray or buffy gray of anterior portions passing more gradually into white of posterior lower surface; sides and flanks sometimes washed with buff or pale brown; male usually with more metallic sheen on upper surface. *Natal*: Mouse gray.

MEASUREMENTS: *Adult male*: Wing, 128.0–141.0 (average, 133.9) mm.; tail, 59.9–73.9 (66.5); bill (exposed culmen), 8.9–11.9 (10.7); tarsus, 11.9–15.0 (13.5); middle toe without claw, 13.5–15.5 (14.7). *Adult female*: Wing, 128.0–136.9 (133.4); tail, 54.1–69.1 (64.3); bill, 9.9–11.4 (10.4); tarsus, 13.0–14.0 (13.7); middle toe, 14.0–16.0 (14.7).

RANGE: Nayarit and n.e. Coahuila to w. Tamaulipas, south through lowland Mexico and Central America to Peru and Brazil. Winters in warmer parts of breeding range, but migrates from n.e. Mexico and other cool parts of its range.

TEXAS: *Casual*: Two specimens (see species account).

NESTING: *Nest*: Mostly in towns or about human habitations in country, but sometimes on woodland edges; in hole in tree, nook about eaves, and elsewhere about building (old or inhabited), under tiles of house, in bird box, even in hood of electric street lamp, or in angle between two beams of a steamship deck; often in colonies; entrance sometimes more or less closed with mud and straw; nest chamber floored with dry grass, sticks, straw, hair, lichens, string, bits of cloth, and similar materials; lined with feathers. *Eggs:* 3–5; ovate; white, slightly glossy, unmarked; average size, 23.9 × 16.8 mm.

PLATE 19: Western Kingbird, *Tyrannus verticalis*, perched on mullein (*Verbascum*)

PLATE 20: Great Crested Flycatcher, *Myiarchus crinitus*

Jays and Crows: Corvidae

BLUE JAY, *Cyanocitta cristata* (Linnaeus)

SPECIES ACCOUNT

A raucous bird with a crest; strong, longish bill; ample, rounded tail; short, rounded wings. Bright blue above with white spots and black bars on wings and tail; black collar around throat and base of head; white face and throat; whitish under parts. Length, 11¼ in.; wingspan, 16¼; weight, 3¼ oz.

RANGE: C. Alberta to Newfoundland, south (east of Rockies) to c. and s.e. Texas, Gulf coast, and s. Florida; particularly during fall, flocks wander about essentially within breeding range, but in Texas spill over irregularly into w. and s. portions.

TEXAS: (See map.) *Resident:* Breeds, early Feb. to late July (eggs, Feb. 27 to June 15) from near sea level to 3,200 ft., possibly somewhat higher. Very common to fairly common through most of northeastern two-thirds, west to Amarillo (irregular), Lubbock, and eastern Edwards Plateau, south to San Antonio (highly irregular breeder) and Victoria; has bred in Refugio Co., Refugio (female incubating eggs, May 6, 1968, T. C. Meitzen). Common (some falls) to scarce straggler and winter visitor west to western Panhandle, Midland, western Edwards Plateau, Uvalde, and Corpus Christi; rare and erratic south to Rio Grande City and Brownsville; casual at Big Bend Nat. Park and in Davis Mts.

HAUNTS AND HABITS: In the more heavily urbanized portions of the eastern United States, the Blue Jay is the chief representative of the Corvidae, a cosmopolitan family of one hundred species. The Blue Jay was originally a bird of pine, oak, and mixed woodlands, and their edges. However, with settlement of the land many individuals have followed man into towns, cities, and suburbs. This exuberant bird, with its bold blue, black, and white markings, is one of the most striking species in yards, gardens, and parks of east and central Texas. In wilder places it still frequents timber along streams, groves on prairies, and woods on hills.

Flight of the Blue Jay is steady, direct, and deliberate but not particularly swift. With full, regular, and quick flaps of the wings, it moves easily through the trees. Seldom does it fly across open country except during its erratic migrations or wanderings which in Texas are most likely to take place in October. Although very active, groups of Blue Jays do not appear as hurried or anxious as do their smaller relatives, the chickadees. Except during the breeding season, they troop noisily through woodlands and parks in loose companies, gleaning a variety of insects, some spiders, acorns, wild fruits and berries, and picnic scraps; some individuals also flycatch a bit or help themselves to the contents of nests they come upon. Resident birds, in addition to their normal foraging operations, store—in the ground and elsewhere—acorns and nuts for winter use. Some of these buried seeds grow to trees when the jays forget to retrieve them.

This bird is one of those that makes a habit of sunning itself; with breast facing the sun, it raises its wings to expose under plumage to the rays, or it lies breast down on the ground, wings spread, to warm its back and rump. Blue Jays, like other passerines, at times excitedly rub ants over their feathers. Another habit, frequently observed in rural areas, is that of mobbing predatory birds. A flock of jays surrounds a heron, owl, hawk, or crow; screaming loud *jay*'s and

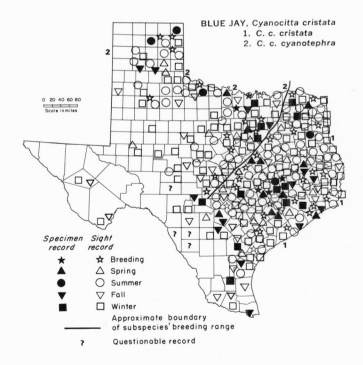

BLUE JAY, *Cyanocitta cristata*
1. *C. c. cristata*
2. *C. c. cyanotephra*

0 20 40 60 80
Scale in miles

Specimen record	Sight record	
★	☆	Breeding
▲	△	Spring
●	○	Summer
▼	▽	Fall
■	□	Winter

———— Approximate boundary of subspecies' breeding range

? Questionable record

jeer's, a few individuals even dart at the head of the pestered one. Owls, from the size of the Screech on up, seem to release the Blue Jay's ganging-up response most often. The jays are usually careful to do their hectoring in broad daylight when the owl can't properly see to defend itself!

The Blue Jay has various notes, the most common one being a loud, harsh *jay*, sometimes slurred to sound more like *jeer* or *peer*. Usually in spring the bird whistles a pleasing *teekle, teekle* that is often joined with a *whee-oodle*, the latter commonly called its creaking wheelbarrow note. Members of foraging groups, particularly in autumn, converse with a chuckling *kuk*. This bird's *teearr* cry sounds like that of the Redshouldered Hawk; the similarity of the screams is apparently more coincidental than imitative. Another call is a low throat rattle. What qualifies as Blue Jay song is a series of its notes considerably keyed down to low, sweet whistles, lispings, and chipperings. Usually the bird performs this jumble while concealed in tangled vegetation or on interior branches of a tree. This song is heard infrequently from March into June.

DETAILED ACCOUNT: THREE SUBSPECIES

FLORIDA BLUE JAY, *Cyanocitta cristata cristata* (Linnaeus)

Also called Southern Blue Jay.

DESCRIPTION: *Adults, nuptial plumage*: Acquired by wear from winter plumage. Crown and occipital crest deep plumbeous blue; nasal plumes grayish white, slightly tinged with blue; narrow line across forehead, lores, and rather narrow collar around entire neck black; back, scapulars, and sides of neck between madder blue and deep dutch blue; rump and upper tail-coverts similar but somewhat less purplish; tail blue—from brownish porcelain blue to gobelin blue, inner margins of all but middle pair of rectrices basally dark mouse gray; middle tail feathers regularly and numerously barred with black; remaining rectrices also thus barred on outer webs, except basally and on outermost pair of feathers, these bars becoming duller toward outer feathers, and all but middle pair of tail feathers broadly tipped with white; wing-quills and tertials dark mouse gray, inner margins somewhat lighter and more brownish, tips of primaries washed with blue, outer edges of primaries deep alice blue, chiefly basally, tertials and outer margins of secondaries indigo blue, but middle part of outer webs of tertials paler blue, tertials and outer webs of secondaries barred with black; lesser and median coverts like back; greater coverts partly china blue, partly indigo blue, and partly black, greater coverts rather broadly, secondaries and tertials very broadly, tipped with white; superciliary stripe, cheeks, auriculars, with chin and throat anterior to black collar, pale grayish white, sometimes washed with pale purplish blue; breast light drab, sometimes washed with pale purplish blue; sides and flanks drab gray; rest of lower parts dull white; lining of wing fuscous black, axillars and edge of wing washed with dull blue. Bill black, slate black, or brownish black, but tip sometimes whitish; tongue lavender gray; inside of mouth slate gray; iris dark vandyke brown; legs, toes, and claws black or slate black. *Adults, winter*: Acquired by complete postnuptial molt. Practically identical with nuptial adults. *First nuptial*: Acquired by wear from first winter. Very much like nuptial adults, but primaries and secondaries, as well as tail, retained from juvenal; black markings on wings and tail not so well defined as in adult. *First winter*: Acquired by partial postjuvenal molt. Similar to first nuptial male and female, but blue of upper surface is rather deeper and richer; white edgings of wings and tail somewhat broader. *Juvenal*: Acquired by postnatal growth. Wings and tail similar to those of adult,

but white tips of wings and tail duller, sometimes slightly buffy, bars on wings and tail much less numerous, narrower, and fainter; black markings of head and neck much duller, more brownish, and less well defined; crest much shorter; pileum brownish neutral gray with blue wash; back hair brown; breast dull drab gray; remainder of lower surface dull white, sometimes tinged with buff. Bill black or brownish black, but tip of maxilla dull white; legs and feet black. *Natal*: None. Bird hatched unfeathered. Bill brownish black; legs and feet raw umber.

MEASUREMENTS: *Adult male*: Wing, 119.6–135.1 (average, 126.0) mm.; tail, 114.6–126.5 (119.9); bill (exposed culmen), 23.1–25.9 (24.4); tarsus, 32.5–35.1 (33.5); middle toe without claw, 18.0–23.1 (20.1). *Adult female*: Wing, 117.6–127.0 (122.5); tail, 108.5–117.6 (113.5); bill, 23.1–25.1 (24.4); tarsus, 32.0–34.5 (33.5); middle toe, 17.5–19.6 (18.8).

RANGE: S. Missouri to Maryland, south to c. Texas and c. Florida.

TEXAS: *Resident*: Altitudinal breeding range, near sea level to 600 ft. Collected north to Titus, south to Chambers and Wharton, west to Travis cos. Taken outside regular breeding range, southwest to Atascosa and Bexar cos. Common.

NESTING: *Nest*: In open woodlands, groves of evergreen or deciduous trees, sometimes in open country, along roadsides, in orchards, cemeteries, or parks; usually well concealed in bush, thicket, or tree—ornamental, orchard, or native (e.g., oaks, elms, hickories, pines, others), sometimes in crotch, close to main trunk of tree, or even at extremity of horizontal limb, 5–50 ft. above ground; bulky, roughly but compactly built bowl, sometimes partly cemented with mud, otherwise composed of twigs, roots, bark, moss, lichens, paper, string, wool, dry grasses, leaves, rags, and similar materials; lined with strips of cedar and other bark, rootlets, leaves, grass, and feathers. *Eggs*: 2–7, usually 4; ordinarily ovate, sometimes elliptical ovate; slightly glossy; exceedingly variable in ground color: greenish or brownish buff, olive green, olive buff, pea green, vinaceous buff, pale bluish green or grayish green, olive brown or olive drab; spotted with olive and other shades of brown, sometimes with small black dots and shell markings of lavender and drab; average egg size, 27.1 × 20.4 mm. (A. C. Bent).

PALE BLUE JAY, *Cyanocitta cristata cyanotephra* Sutton

DESCRIPTION: *Adults, nuptial plumage*: Similar to *C. c. cristata* but larger; upper parts paler and more bluish, white areas on wings and tail more extensive. Similar to *C. c. bromia* (see below), but smaller; much paler and usually somewhat more purplish above, particularly on pileum.

MEASUREMENTS: *Adult male*: Wing, 127.0–139.4 (average, 132.6) mm.; tail, 122.5–136.9 (129.0); bill (exposed culmen), 22.9–28.9 (26.2); height of bill at base, 9.9–11.4 (10.7); tarsus, 34.5–38.1 (35.8); middle toe without claw, 17.5–20.3 (19.3). *Adult female*: Wing, 120.9–138.4 (129.8); tail, 120.9–135.1 (127.8); bill, 24.4–26.7 (25.1); height of bill, 9.4–11.2 (10.2); tarsus, 34.0–38.1 (35.8); middle toe, 17.5–20.1 (19.0).

RANGE: C. Colorado to n.w. Kansas, south to n. Texas.

TEXAS: *Resident*: Altitudinal breeding range, 400 to 3,200 ft. Collected northwest to Randall and Lipscomb, southeast to Cooke, Ellis, and McLennan cos. Common. Taken outside breeding range east to Trinity and Brazoria, south to Nueces, west to Kerr cos.

NESTING: Similar to that of *C. c. cristata*, but average egg size, 27.4 × 19.8 mm.

NORTHERN BLUE JAY, *Cyanocitta cristata bromia* Oberholser

DESCRIPTION: *Adults, nuptial plumage*: Similar to *C. c. cristata* but much larger; upper parts more bluish (less purplish); white tips of greater coverts, tertials, secondaries, and tail feathers larger.

MEASUREMENTS: *Adult male*: Wing, 132.6–148.1 (average, 139.7) mm.; tail, 121.9–147.6 (133.6); bill (exposed culmen), 23.1–29.9 (26.9); tarsus, 35.6–37.1 (36.3); middle toe without claw, 20.6–23.6 (21.9). *Adult female*: Wing, 128.3–138.9 (132.1); tail, 122.5–130.0 (127.0); bill, 23.1–26.4 (24.1); tarsus, 31.8–36.1 (33.8); middle toe, 18.5–21.1 (19.6).

RANGE: N. Alberta to Newfoundland, south to n.e. Kansas and w. North Carolina. Winters from s. Manitoba and Nova Scotia to Texas and c. South Carolina.

TEXAS: *Winter*: Taken north to Lamar, east to Chambers (Nov. 6), south to Cameron, west to Travis cos. Uncommon.

STELLER'S JAY, *Cyanocitta stelleri* (Gmelin)

SPECIES ACCOUNT

A very dark jay with a long black crest. Blackish foreparts; deep blue hindparts (wings and tail narrowly barred with black); fine whitish streaks on forehead and chin; short white line above eye. Length, 12 in.; wingspan, 17½; weight, 3 oz.

RANGE: S. Alaska, south through much of w. North America (chiefly in mountains) to highlands of Nicaragua.

TEXAS: (See map.) *Resident*: Breeds, probably late Apr. to mid-July (no egg dates available, but nest located at about 8,000 ft. in Guadalupe Mts. by F. R. Gehlbach). Common in The Bowl, Guadalupe Mts.; uncommon to scarce above 6,000 ft. in remainder of Guadalupes and in Davis Mts.; rare in northwestern Brewster Co. (nesting doubtful). Scarce and irregular winter visitor to El Paso region; casual in northern Panhandle, on Edwards Plateau, and in southern Brewster Co. (first recorded in Big Bend Nat. Park, winter of 1972–73). One coastal sighting: Rockport (May 23, 1940, Connie Hagar).

HAUNTS AND HABITS: The darkly handsome Steller's Jay prefers coniferous mountain forests and the fringes thereof, but also resides locally in mixed pine-oak woodlands. In Texas, its chief home is in western yellow pine (*Pinus ponderosa*) and Douglasfir (*Pseudotsuga mucronata*) high in the Guadalupes. Particularly during cooler months, birds wander to lower altitudes within foothills and valleys; also they scout out camping areas and the vicinity of human habitations where they pick up table scraps and edible trash. Small, noisy groups range the forest together except during the breeding season when the birds become quiet, secretive, and nongregarious.

Flight of the Steller's, like that of the Blue Jay, is strong and deliberate but is seldom sustained across open country. With great vigor, the bird bounds from branch to branch through a tree, frequently moving up successive limbs as if ascending a spiral staircase. Here it feeds on insects, acorns, nuts, pine seeds, wild fruits, and an occasional egg. While foraging, this active bird often flicks its wings and tail or whacks its bill on a branch. Members of a group sometimes bicker amongst themselves. Where the species comes about human dwellings it tends to be rather tame, but in remote forests it is shier and more difficult to observe.

Of the various Steller's Jay notes, the most common are a loud, rasping *shaack-shaack-shaack*, a softer but still raucous *shook-shook-shook*, and a rapid *wheeck-wek-wek-wek-wek*. The very soft song, difficult to hear because the bird becomes shy and retreats to a high perch, is a series of warbles said to resemble somewhat the song of the Ruby-crowned Kinglet. Singing apparently occurs mostly from late March to mid-June.

DETAILED ACCOUNT: TWO SUBSPECIES

ARIZONA STELLER'S JAY, *Cyanocitta stelleri browni* Phillips

Race not in A.O.U. check-list, 1957 (see Appendix A).

DESCRIPTION: *Adult male, nuptial plumage*: Acquired by wear from winter plumage. Pileum, including crest, dull black or blackish mouse gray; forehead and crown streaked narrowly with pale bluish white; back brownish deep mouse gray; rump between glaucous blue and alice blue to near orient blue; middle tail feathers dusky blue to indigo blue; remainder of tail deep orient blue to greenish orient blue, tips darker—inclining more to indigo blue, inner margins fuscous or chaetura drab, and all tail feathers more or less distinctly barred with black on outer webs, middle pair barred on both webs; wings fuscous, but outer margins of primaries deep orient blue to greenish orient blue, outer margins of tertials and secondaries dusky blue to indigo blue, former conspicuously barred with black; greater wing-coverts similar and also barred with black; remaining wing-coverts similar to blue edgings of primaries except lesser wing-coverts decidedly more greenish; sides of head like crown but with long white spot over eye; chin blackish mouse gray, streaked with grayish white or pale gray; throat deep mouse gray; remainder of lower surface between glaucous blue and alice blue to orient blue; lining of wing hair brown or chaetura drab, outer edge blue like under parts. Bill, legs, toes, and claws deep black; iris bister or vandyke brown. *Adult male, winter*: Acquired by complete postnuptial molt. Practically identical with nuptial adult male. *Adult female, nuptial*: Acquired by wear from winter. Similar to nuptial adult male but often with bars on wings and tail narrower and less distinct. *Adult female, winter*: Acquired by complete postnuptial molt. Like nuptial adult female. *Male, first nuptial*: Acquired by wear from first winter. Practically identical with nuptial adult male.

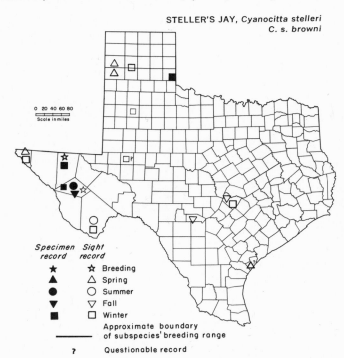

STELLER'S JAY, *Cyanocitta stelleri*
C. s. *browni*

0 20 40 60 80
Scale in miles

Specimen record | *Sight record*
★ | ☆ Breeding
▲ | △ Spring
● | ○ Summer
▼ | ▽ Fall
■ | □ Winter

—— Approximate boundary of subspecies' breeding range

? Questionable record

Male, first winter: Acquired by partial postjuvenal molt. Similar to first nuptial male. *Female, first nuptial*: Acquired by wear from first winter. Like nuptial adult female. *Female, first winter*: Acquired by partial postjuvenal molt. Like first nuptial female. *Juvenal*: Acquired by postnatal growth. Similar to nuptial adult female, but bill and crest shorter; black of head decidedly brownish, pileum fuscous black or chaetura black; back fuscous or chaetura drab; forehead sometimes with a few dull gray spots; lower parts entirely without blue, anterior portion deep mouse gray, posterior part brownish neutral gray, chin with a few dull pale gray spots. *Natal*: None. Bird hatched unfeathered.

MEASUREMENTS: *Adult male*: Wing, 141.7–151.5 (average, 148.0) mm.; tail, 125.2–140.7 (134.0); bill (exposed culmen), 26.4–29.9 (28.2); height of bill at base, 10.4–11.9 (11.2); tarsus, 41.9–46.5 (44.2); middle toe without claw, 20.6–23.1 (21.6). *Adult female*: Wing, 141.3–146.0 (142.7); tail, 127.7–133.5 (130.7); bill, 25.4–28.4 (27.2); height of bill, 9.9–10.7 (10.4); tarsus, 40.9–45.0 (43.2); middle toe, 19.0–21.6 (20.6).

RANGE: N. Arizona to c. New Mexico, south to n. Sonora and Trans-Pecos Texas.

TEXAS: *Resident*: Collected in Culberson and Jeff Davis cos.

NESTING: *Nest*: In mountain forests, on slopes, or in canyons, sometimes more open country; in small or large pine or other tree, 8–15 ft., or more, above ground; rather more bulky nest than that of the Blue Jay, usually not well concealed though sometimes difficult to find; rough bowl of large sticks, smaller twigs, mud, moss, dry grass, and similar materials; lined with fine rootlets, horsehair, grass, and pine needles. *Eggs*: 3–6, usually 4–5; ovate to elongate ovate; greenish blue, spotted with various shades of brown and lavender, most thickly about larger end; average size, 31.8 × 21.9 mm.

COLORADO STELLER'S JAY, *Cyanocitta stelleri macrolopha* Baird

DESCRIPTION: Similar to *C. s. browni* but darker, particularly on under parts.

MEASUREMENTS: *Adult male*: Wing, 149.0–158.0 (average, 153.2) mm.; tail, 135.0–158.5 (142.5). *Adult female*: Wing, 144.2–150.3 (147.3); tail, 131.8–141.4 (136.6).

RANGE: N. Utah and Colorado, south to s. Nevada and n.w. New Mexico. Winters from breeding range to Sonora and w. Texas.

TEXAS: *Winter*: Three specimens: Collingsworth Co., Parker Creek (2 on Jan. 21, 1915, R. L. More); Culberson Co., The Bowl (Jan. 1, 1939, T. D. Burleigh).

SCRUB JAY, *Aphelocoma coerulescens* (Bosc)

SPECIES ACCOUNT

Calls: a raspy *kwesh* or a series of harsh *tschuck*'s. A crestless blue jay. Blue above with pale brownish back; narrow white eye-streak; blackish ear-patch; grayish below with white or whitish throat, faintly streaked on jugulum with gray or bluish; blue breastband (often incomplete). Length, 11¾ in.; wingspan, 12½; weight, 2¾ oz.

RANGE: S.w. Washington to s.w. Wyoming, Colorado, and c. Texas, south through s.w. United States to s. Baja California and Oaxaca; also c. Florida.

TEXAS: (See map.) *Resident*: Breeds, early Mar. to late June (eggs, Mar. 14 to May 30) from about 800 to 8,000 ft. Common to fairly common in mountain scrub of Trans-Pecos—though usually absent from Chisos Mts.—and on western Edwards Plateau; irregularly fairly common to uncommon and local on most of eastern Edwards Plateau; fairly common (some winters) to scarce in canyons of northern Panhandle (breeding unconfirmed). *Winter*: Fairly common to uncommon visitor to El Paso region and broken country north of Edwards Plateau as far as Midland, Big Spring, and Abilene; scarce to rare farther north in Panhandle to Terry and Bailey cos.

HAUNTS AND HABITS: Shy and elusive, at least in the Texas part of its range, the Scrub Jay appears most often as a blue-gray streak flashing through brush. It is found in pinyon, juniper, and oak scrub of Trans-Pecos hills and canyons, leaving somewhat humid coniferous forests to the Steller's Jay in the Guadalupe Mountains and dry conifer woods to the Mexican Jay in the Chisos. On the Edwards Plateau it lives in thickets of Lacey's Oak (*Quercus laceyi*), Spanish oak (*Q. texana*), other oaks, and junipers; individual birds sometime winter along willow-lined streams of Panhandle canyons. It is usually seen singly or in pairs, occasionally in small flocks, but the species is somewhat less gregarious than other jays.

Flight is strong and regular when sustained, while bursts through the brush are short and dashing. The Scrub keeps much to lower levels of trees, although it frequently uses bushtop lookout perches in the manner of a Mockingbird. Occasionally the jay descends to the ground, where it feeds on insects, acorns, pinyon nuts, wild fruits, and berries; also it raids nests of small birds, such as flycatchers and vireos, for their eggs and young. Though largely resident, the species wanders in fall and winter, frequently into the vicinity of country dwellings to pick up waste grain and scraps. A typical and often observed action of the Scrub Jay is a swift and graceful dive from a high vantage point into a thicket.

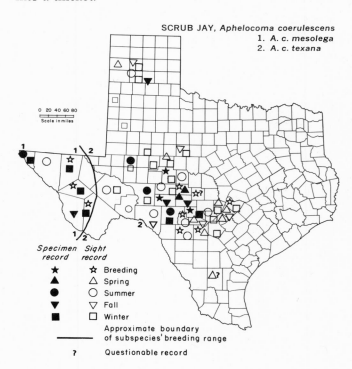

SCRUB JAY, *Aphelocoma coerulescens*
1. *A. c. mesolega*
2. *A. c. texana*

0 20 40 60 80
Scale in miles

Specimen record / Sight record
★ / ☆ Breeding
▲ / △ Spring
● / ○ Summer
▼ / ▽ Fall
■ / □ Winter

—— Approximate boundary of subspecies' breeding range
? Questionable record

The common calls of this jay are a rasping *kwesh—kwesh* and a series of harsh *tschuck*'s. A frequently heard vocalization on the Edwards Plateau is a noise like a sudden ripping of a piece of canvas. Feeding groups often converse in odd chuckles as do Blue Jays, but flocks of Scrubs are seldom so boisterous. Occasionally it delivers the low throat rattle which appears to be common to all Texas jays. In spring a well-hidden Scrub Jay, though difficult to hear, sings a soft, whispery, cooing song. The infrequent singing lasts from March to about June.

CHANGES: Prior to 1950, the Scrub Jay was unknown on extreme eastern portions of the Edwards Plateau. It seemed odd that this western bird should stop at Kerrville while its scrubby juniper-oak habitat continued one hundred miles eastward to Austin. However, in 1950 the bird was first sighted in this vicinity and since has become locally fairly common in the cedar brakes west of Austin. Scrub Jays in this state do not appear to flourish as do those in California.

What caused this supposedly static bird to occupy a new range? Texas Scrub Jays seem almost as tied to juniper (cedar) on rough ground as is the Golden-cheeked Warbler. In the 1940's and 1950's, ranchers on the central and western parts of the Plateau, with the aid of a U.S. government subsidy, removed most of the cedar from their land. In addition, the drought of 1950 to 1957 killed many of the remaining junipers on the western Edwards Plateau. Extensive growths of cedar, however, were left near Austin where land was being held for housing developments. Apparently, a goodly number of Scrub Jays sought out and colonized the best extant cedar brakes.

DETAILED ACCOUNT: THREE SUBSPECIES

WOODHOUSE'S SCRUB JAY, *Aphelocoma coerulescens woodhousii* (Baird)

A. c. woodhouseii of A.O.U. check-list, 1957 (see Appendix A).

DESCRIPTION: *Adults, nuptial plumage*: Similar to *A. c. mesolega* (see below), but bill larger; back darker with somewhat more of blue wash; jugulum and breast with more blue; under tail-coverts usually of darker blue, not white; breast and abdomen darker, less whitish, light streaks of throat and jugulum less whitish (more grayish).

MEASUREMENTS: *Adult male*: Wing, 129.5–135.6 (average, 133.1) mm.; tail, 138.9–147.6 (143.0); bill (exposed culmen), 26.4–28.9 (28.4); tarsus, 39.9–41.9 (40.9); middle toe without claw, 20.6–23.1 (22.1). *Adult female*: Wing, 120.4–130.5 (126.5); tail, 128.5–140.0 (135.6); bill, 24.4–27.9 (25.9); tarsus, 37.1–41.4 (39.6); middle toe, 19.6–21.1 (20.6).

RANGE: S.e. Oregon to n.w. Oklahoma, south to s.e. California and n.w. Chihuahua. Winters from breeding range to Trans-Pecos Texas (rarely).

TEXAS: *Winter*: Three specimens: Armstrong Co., Dripping Springs near Claude (Sept. 24, 1938, J. O. Stevenson); El Paso Co., Ascarate Lake (Aug. 27, 1944, A. E. Eynon); Culberson Co., Bear Canyon (Jan. 6, 1939, G. H. Lowery, Jr.).

NESTING: (This race does not nest in Texas.) *Nest*: Along streams, in canyons, on hill or mountain slopes; in more or less open woodlands; in pinyon, juniper, oak, or similar tree, usually scrubby or low, often near water, usually well concealed; rather roughly constructed bowl of twigs, roots, weed stalks, horsehair, and similar materials, with thick lining of rootlets and horse-hair. *Eggs*: 3–6, usually 4–5; ovate or short ovate to elongate ovate; dull bluish green, dull pea green, or light sage green; sparingly spotted and irregularly marked with burnt umber, tawny, and other shades of reddish brown, with shell markings of lilac, gray, and lavender; average size, 27.7 × 20.1 mm.

PECOS SCRUB JAY, *Aphelocoma coerulescens mesolega* Oberholser, new subspecies (see Appendix A)

DESCRIPTION: *Adults, nuptial plumage*: Similar to *A. c. texana* (see below), but bill and middle toe shorter; upper parts lighter; lower parts darker; breast and jugulum with more blue; crissum more bluish, usually almost wholly blue. Like *A. c. woodhousii*, but bill and middle toe smaller; back lighter with rather less blue tinge; breast and jugulum with less blue; lower tail-coverts usually of lighter blue; breast and abdomen lighter, more whitish, light streaks of throat and jugulum more whitish (less grayish). *Natal*: Probably similar to *A. c. texana* (see below).

MEASUREMENTS: *Adult male*: Wing, 127.5–134.1 (average, 130.0) mm.; tail, 134.1–146.0 (141.5); bill (exposed culmen), 23.9–27.4 (24.9); height of bill at base, 9.4–11.9 (10.4); tarsus, 38.6–42.4 (40.6); middle toe without claw, 19.0–22.6 (20.3). *Adult female*: Wing, 120.9–128.0 (124.2); tail, 129.5–137.9 (133.9); bill, 22.1–26.4 (24.6); height of bill, 8.6–10.9 (9.9); tarsus, 38.1–41.4 (39.6); middle toe, 18.0–22.6 (19.6).

TYPE: Adult female, no. 139592, U.S. National Museum, Biological Surveys collections; Fort Davis, Texas; Jan. 11, 1890; Vernon Bailey.

RANGE: S.e. New Mexico and Trans-Pecos Texas.

TEXAS: *Resident*: Altitudinal breeding range, 1,800 to 8,000 ft. Collected in El Paso, Culberson, Jeff Davis, and Brewster cos. Fairly common.

NESTING: Similar to that of *A. c. woodhousii*, but average egg size, 28.2 × 20.6 mm.

TEXAS SCRUB JAY, *Aphelocoma coerulescens texana* Ridgway

DESCRIPTION: *Adults, nuptial plumage*: Acquired by wear from winter plumage. Pileum and hindneck deep cadet blue to indigo blue, with slight metallic sheen; nasal tufts fuscous black washed with blue; back and scapulars dark hair brown; rump dull vanderpoel blue; wings and tail indigo blue to dark tyrian blue, inner edges of all but middle pair of tail feathers fuscous; wings fuscous, except on exposed surface; sides of head fuscous, slightly washed with blue, sides of throat and cheeks more clearly blue, narrow superciliary stripe white; sides of neck like crown; lower surface smoke gray, rather whitish on chin and throat, abdomen and crissum usually white, jugulum streaked with darker gray and slightly with dull blue; lining of wing dull mouse gray washed with blue. Bill, tarsus, and toes deep black; iris chestnut to hazel. *Adults, winter*: Acquired by complete postnuptial molt from first nuptial, later from nuptial adults. Similar to nuptial adults, but colors darker and richer. *First nuptial*: Acquired by wear from first winter. Nearly identical with nuptial adults, but wing-quills, rectrices, and many of wing-coverts retained in dull worn condition from juvenal; wing-coverts with dull brown tips; tips of rectrices and outer primaries more pointed; wing and tail averaging shorter; tail less strongly rounded. *First winter*: Acquired by partial post-juvenal molt. Like first nuptial male and female. *Juvenal*: Acquired by postnatal growth. Resembling nuptial adults, but wing and tail averaging shorter; outer primaries and rectrices more pointed at tips; tail averaging less strongly rounded; pileum blackish brown washed with dull blue; back rufescent hair brown; wings and tail much like those of adult, but greater and primary coverts more or less edged with brown of back, and lesser coverts mostly brown like back; superciliary stripe very indistinct or practically nonexistent; lower parts anteriorly dull light brownish drab, sometimes with buffy tinge, darker on upper breast and jugulum, paler—even whitish—on abdomen, and without decided streaks. Bill and feet black; iris dark brown. *Natal*: None. Bird hatched unfeathered.

MEASUREMENTS: *Adult male*: Wing, 125.0–135.4 (average,

130.0) mm.; tail, 134.6–147.1 (141.2); bill (exposed culmen), 24.9–27.9 (26.2); height of bill at base, 10.4–10.9 (10.7); tarsus, 38.1–41.9 (40.1); middle toe without claw, 20.6–23.9 (22.1). *Adult female*: Wing, 118.1–130.0 (124.2); tail, 126.5–141.0 (131.8); bill, 24.4–26.9 (26.2); height of bill, 9.4–10.9 (10.2); tarsus, 37.6–40.9 (38.9); middle toe, 19.0–23.1 (21.4).

RANGE: Edwards Plateau region of Texas.

TEXAS: *Resident*: Altitudinal breeding range, 800 to 2,200 ft. Collected in Midland (1904, breeding doubtful), Tom Green (eggs), Crockett, Sutton (eggs), Kimble, Menard, Edwards, and Kerr cos. Locally fairly common.

NESTING: Similar to that of *A. c. woodhousii.*

MEXICAN JAY, *Aphelocoma ultramarina* (Bonaparte)

SPECIES ACCOUNT

Gray-breasted Jay of various writers. Call is typically a querulous *jink*. A plain, crestless, pale blue jay (dull blue in Arizona, bright blue in Texas); gregarious. Resembles Scrub, but somewhat paler above, with grayish, rather than brownish, back; more uniformly grayish below; lacks white eye-streak, bluish breast-band, and streaks on throat; voice is very different. Length, 11½ in.; weight, 3½ oz.

RANGE: C. Arizona, s.w. New Mexico, and s. Trans-Pecos Texas, south through Sierra Madre Occidental and Sierra Madre Oriental to mountains of c. Mexico.

TEXAS: (See map.) *Resident*: Breeds, mid-Apr. to late June (eggs, Apr. 27 to June 13) from about 5,000 to 7,800 ft. Common in Chisos Mts., Big Bend Nat. Park; casual visitor (nonbreeder) in remainder of southern Trans-Pecos.

HAUNTS AND HABITS: In the juniper-pine-oak woods of the Chisos Mountains, garrulous bands of Mexican

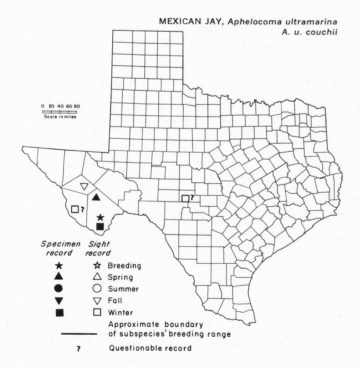

MEXICAN JAY, *Aphelocoma ultramarina*
A. u. couchii

0 20 40 60 80
Scale in miles

Specimen Sight
record record
★ ☆ Breeding
▲ △ Spring
● ○ Summer
▼ ▽ Fall
■ □ Winter
—— Approximate boundary of subspecies' breeding range
? Questionable record

Jays can hardly be ignored as they *jink* through the trees. In short flights they often leapfrog from tree to tree, one or several birds in the rear flank advancing to the front only until displaced members of the group regain the lead. Wary but inquisitive, they generally respond excitedly to a bird watcher's squeaks. These birds are gregarious throughout the year; even nesting pairs are frequently visited by other flock members, which sometimes assist in nest building or cooperate in feeding fledglings.

Flight is strong, darting, and seldom sustained; Mexican Jays prefer protection of trees and typically move through, rather than over, forests, even when crossing a canyon. Seldom on the ground, the birds work instead through low undergrowth to uppermost branches of tall trees where they feed on cicadas, grasshoppers, other insects, acorns, nuts, seeds, and wild fruits; also occasionally eggs or young of small birds. In the Chisos Mountains, Mexican Jays frequently eat insects on, and flower parts of, century plants (*Agave*); they also drink nectar and other plant juices from the blossoms. There are few more colorful sights than a bright blue Couch's Mexican Jay probing intensely yellow agave blossoms on a big flowering stalk. Eggs of the two U.S. races of the Mexican Jay are dissimilar; the Couch's, *A. u. couchii*, are spotted, while those of *A. u. arizonae* are unmarked. It is extraordinary for a difference of this nature to be found within a species.

The call note of the Mexican Jay, heard throughout the year, is a rough fretful *jink*, which sometimes sounds like *jenk* or *drenk*. The apparent lack of territorial song is probably a consequence of the species' year-round flocking habit.

DETAILED ACCOUNT: ONE SUBSPECIES

COUCH'S MEXICAN JAY, *Aphelocoma ultramarina couchii* (Baird)

DESCRIPTION: *Adults, nuptial plumage*: Acquired by wear from winter plumage. Pileum, hindneck, and sides of head orient blue to deep orient blue, lores blackish, ear-coverts sometimes slightly brownish; upper tail-coverts of same blue; back dull hair brown or smoke gray overlaid with delft blue; tail similar to pileum but rather darker and more grayish, margins of inner webs fuscous or chaetura drab; wings fuscous or chaetura drab, exposed surfaces like tail; breast dull light mouse gray, sometimes slightly washed with buff; throat grayish white with narrow shaft streaks of pale gray; middle of abdomen and crissum white; lining of wing neutral gray, washed with blue of upper parts. Bill normally black, sometimes irregularly suffused with dull white; legs and feet black; iris dark brown. *Adults, winter*: Acquired by complete postnuptial molt. Similar to nuptial adults. *First nuptial*: Acquired by wear from first winter. Resembling nuptial adults, but wing-quills, rectrices, and many of wing-coverts retained in more or less worn condition from juvenal; tips of rectrices and outer primaries more pointed; wing and tail averaging shorter; tail less strongly rounded. *First winter*: Acquired by partial postjuvenal molt. Similar to first nuptial male and female. *Juvenal*: Acquired by postnatal growth. Similar to nuptial adults, but wing and tail averaging shorter; rectrices and outer primaries more pointed at tips; tail averaging less strongly rounded; upper parts duller, more brownish, with little or no blue; pileum rather deep neutral gray, between neutral gray and deep neutral gray, slightly washed with dull dark blue; remainder of upper surface rufescent hair brown, but upper tail-coverts hair brown; wings and tail chaetura drab, but tail, primaries, and secondaries edged with dull blue on exposed surfaces, wing-coverts mostly brown like back, except greater and primary coverts which are tipped with blue; sides of head like upper parts, but lores dull black and auriculars fuscous or chaetura drab; sides of neck like crown; jugulum and breast dull light drab or rather light mouse gray; chin and throat grayish white; middle of abdomen and crissum cream white; thighs like jugulum. Bill partly brownish black, most of mandible and cutting edges of maxilla dull flesh color. *Natal:* None. Bird hatched unfeathered.

MEASUREMENTS: *Adult male:* Wing, 146.0–157.5 (average, 153.2) mm.; tail, 127.0–138.9 (132.6); bill (exposed culmen), 24.9–28.4 (26.9); height of bill at base, 10.9–12.4 (11.7); tarsus, 40.4–42.9 (41.4); middle toe without claw, 21.6–23.6 (22.9). *Adult female:* Wing, 143.5–155.9 (151.1); tail, 126.0–138.9 (131.8); bill, 24.9–27.7 (26.4); height of bill, 10.7–11.9 (11.2); tarsus, 37.1–42.9 (40.4); middle toe, 20.1–23.9 (22.6).

RANGE: S. Trans-Pecos Texas, south to c. San Luis Potosí and s.w. Tamaulipas.

TEXAS: *Resident:* Collected in Chisos Mts., Brewster Co. One specimen from n. Brewster Co., 5 mi. south of Alpine, 5,300 ft. (Mar. 25, 1935, J. Van Tyne).

NESTING: *Nest:* On slopes, mountain tops, and in canyons; low woodlands of pinyon, pine, oak, or other tree; bulky bowl, usually compactly, sometimes loosely, constructed; composed of coarse twigs of pinyon, juniper, and similar trees; lined with rootlets or horsehair. *Eggs:* 3–4; ovate to rounded ovate; pale nile blue; sparingly speckled and blotched with pale brown, markings sometimes concentrated at larger end, even in wreath; average size, 29.9 × 22.1 mm.

GREEN JAY, *Xanthoura yncas* (Boddaert)

SPECIES ACCOUNT

Cyanocorax yncas of A.O.U. check-list, 1957 (see Appendix A). Brilliant green above; blue head; whitish forehead; extensive black throat-patch; yellow undertail and outer tail feathers; yellow-green below (amount of yellow varies with race); eyes dark brown (Texas) or yellow (races from s. Mexico south). South American birds are heavier bodied; have blue frontal crests. Length, 11½ in.; wingspan, 15.

RANGE: Extreme s. Texas, south through e. and s. Mexico to n. Honduras, and along Pacific slope of Mexico from s. Durango (locally) and Nayarit southward. Also in n.w. South America from Colombia and n. Venezuela through e. Ecuador and Peru to n. Bolivia.

TEXAS: (See map.) *Resident:* Breeds, late Mar. to mid-July (eggs, Apr. 2 to June 29) from near sea level to about 400 ft. Common locally to uncommon in south Texas from Laredo, Falfurrias, Armstrong, and Norias south to the Rio Grande; somewhat irregular along northern limits; rare winter visitor north to Alice and central coast; casual at San Antonio.

HAUNTS AND HABITS: The Green Jay is everything a tropical bird should be: colorful, lively, and raucous. This dazzling corvid, found in the United States only in south Texas, is the bird whose green, yellow, and blue plumage blends so beautifully with patches of sunlight and leaf-shadow inside its favored woods and thickets. The Green Jay is most numerous in willow

trees and tall brush along the lower Rio Grande and its tributaries; but it is also at home, especially during summer, in mesquite (*Prosopis glandulosa*) woodlands at a distance from water. In cooler months when mesquite leaves are sparse, many individuals retreat to concealment of their favorite evergreen trees and shrubs—huisache (*Acacia farnesiana*), Texas ebony (*Pithecellobium flexicaule*), and anaqua (*Ehretia anacua*). In localities where native evergreens have been cleared—just about everywhere nowadays—troops of Green Jays bound and flit through citrus groves. As spring approaches, the noisy flocks partially disband and pairs search out remaining thickets in which to breed; these jays, like most of their relatives, are notably quiet near their nests.

Flight is strong and steady but rarely sustained. This jay is skillful at keeping itself concealed when stalked, but if the stalker turns to walk away, several birds are quite likely to set up an outcry; some may even come to the edge of the brush to look the intruder over. In common with most members of the Corvidae, the Green Jay is omnivorous; large insects are a favored source of protein. Many early-day (ca. 1870–1951) settlers in the Rio Grande delta claimed that the present jay's diet consisted almost wholly of corn and eggs of chickens and White-winged Doves. Since the freeze of 1951, however, these supposedly essential food items have been practically eliminated without any visible effect on the Green Jay population. During the 1960's, picnic tables and garbage cans were installed along U.S. Highway 77, sole public road through the King Ranch in Kenedy County. Those tables and cans placed beside live oak (*Quercus virginiana*) mottes have attracted groups of Green Jays in the southern half of the county. The birds reside in

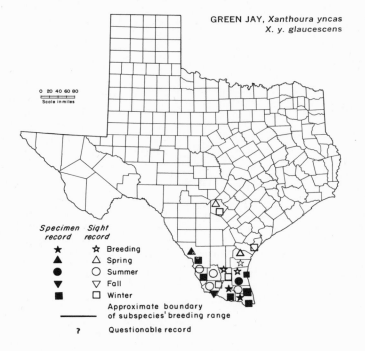

GREEN JAY, *Xanthoura yncas*
X. y. glaucescens

0 20 40 60 80
Scale in miles

Specimen record / Sight record

★ / ☆ Breeding
▲ / △ Spring
● / ○ Summer
▼ / ▽ Fall
■ / □ Winter

Approximate boundary of subspecies' breeding range

? Questionable record

the evergreen oaks and troop out to pick up bits of hamburger, french fries, etc., as soon as people abandon them. Surely these birds rank among the most gorgeous of all garbage collectors!

Frequent Green Jay calls are a rapid, vigorous *cheh-cheh-cheh-cheh* (sometimes sounding more like *ick-ick-ick-ick*) and a slower *cleep, cleep, cleep, cleep* (varies to *toot, toot, toot, toot*); there is also a dry throaty rattle which sounds somewhat like the cry of a cricket frog, but even more like the throat rattles of the Blue and Scrub jays. These calls are given year-round, but perhaps the rattle is more frequent in spring.

DETAILED ACCOUNT: ONE SUBSPECIES

RIO GRANDE GREEN JAY, *Xanthoura yncas glaucescens* Ridgway

Race not in A.O.U. check-list, 1957 (see Appendix A).

DESCRIPTION: *Adults, nuptial plumage*: Acquired by wear from winter plumage. Nasal tufts, extreme forehead, crown, and hindneck gentian blue to deep cadet blue, fore part of crown paler, even whitish; back sage green to chromium green, often with distinct wash of blue; rump and upper tail-coverts deep chrysolite green; four middle tail feathers cress green at base, shading to dusky greenish blue at tip, inner webs of second middle pair margined on inner webs with fuscous; remainder of tail naples yellow to straw yellow, unmarked; exposed upper surface of wings deep glaucous green, but lesser coverts like back; wing-quills hair brown or light chaetura drab, inner edgings of secondaries and of primaries at base straw yellow or pale straw yellow; lores and anterior subocular region, broad superciliary stripe, postocular stripe, and sides of neck black, continuous with black of chin and throat; longitudinal spot above eye and rest of malar area blue like hindneck; remainder of lower parts naples yellow—all but lining of wing and thighs more or less overlaid with turtle green. Bill black; iris dark brown; legs and feet black or plumbeous. *Adults, winter*: Acquired by partial postjuvenal molt. Similar to nuptial adults but somewhat darker. *First nuptial*: Acquired by wear from first winter. Similar to nuptial adults but somewhat duller, wing-quills and tail feathers retained from juvenal. *First winter*: Acquired by partial postjuvenal molt. Practically same as first nuptial. Like adults in winter but colors somewhat duller. *Juvenal*: Acquired by postnatal growth. Similar to nuptial adults, but pileum and cheek-spot as well as hindneck motmot blue, hind part of forehead, subocular and superciliary spot paler; nasal tufts duller; black of sides of head, chin, and throat duller and more brownish; lower parts very much paler, posterior portion pale straw yellow. *Natal*: Bird hatched unfeathered.

MEASUREMENTS: *Adult male*: Wing, 110.0–117.6 (average, 113.0) mm.; tail, 118.1–131.0 (126.0); bill (exposed culmen), 23.1–25.4 (24.9); tarsus, 35.6–38.6 (37.6); middle toe without claw, 20.1–22.1 (21.1). *Adult female*: Wing, 104.1–116.6 (112.0); tail, 121.9–131.5 (127.5); bill, 23.9–25.4 (24.4); tarsus, 34.0–39.6 (37.6); middle toe, 19.6–22.6 (20.1).

RANGE: Extreme s. Texas, south to w. Nuevo León and e. Tamaulipas.

TEXAS: *Resident*: Collected northwest to Webb, east to Kenedy, south to Cameron and Hidalgo cos.

NESTING: *Nest*: In timber along streams, brush, scrub, or more or less heavily wooded country, usually woodlands or thickets; in low bush, such as retama, condalia (Brazil wood), hackberry, or in tree, ordinarily 5–10 ft. above ground, rarely higher; rather slight bowl, sometimes a little bulky; composed of twigs, weeds, moss, plant stems, and similar materials; lined with rootlets, small pieces of vine, bits of Spanishmoss, occasionally dry grass, leaves, and hair. *Eggs*: 3–5, usually 4; ovate to short ovate; greenish buff or white, sometimes greenish white; spotted with various shades of brown, gray, and lavender, mostly near larger end; average size, 27.4 × 20.3 mm.

[**PLAIN-TAILED BROWN JAY,** *Psilorhinus morio* (Wagler)

Also called Northern Brown Jay and simply Brown Jay. A big, floppy-flighted, crowlike jay. Sooty brown, except for grayish white belly and crissum; bill yellow (young bird), black (old bird), or patchwork of the two colors. Loud explosive *aw!*, *kee-ow!*, and *pow!* calls in combination with popping of throat pouch (a partially hidden air sac connected with lungs) are distinctive and account for its Mexican name *Papán*; sometimes the bird pops the pouch without calling. Length, 16–18 in.

RANGE: Lowlands of e. Mexico from c. Nuevo León and Tamaulipas, south to n.e. Chiapas. White-tipped Brown Jay, *P. mexicanus*, often regarded as conspecific, ranges from c. Veracruz to n.w. Panama.

TEXAS: *Hypothetical*: Two recent plausible sightings, both from same locality: Starr Co., along Rio Grande below Falcon Dam, in mesquites between Southmost Girl Scout Camp and Chapeño (2 birds seen well, Apr. 28, 1969, L. B. Cooper, Paul Schulze; 2 individuals again carefully observed, June 15, 1972, Wally Sumner). It is rather likely that a Brown Jay or two will be photographed or collected within the United States in the near future. The species occurs more or less regularly at China, Nuevo León, which locality is on the Río San Juan, a tributary of the Rio Grande, some 60 mi. southwest of the Texas locality where *P. morio* was sighted. The mesquites along the San Juan and lower Rio Grande are similar.]

BLACK-BILLED MAGPIE, *Pica pica* (Linnaeus)

SPECIES ACCOUNT

A slim corvid, larger than a grackle; very long (longer than body), wedge-shaped tail; short rounded wings. Black-and-white body; iridescent greenish black (may appear green, bluish, or purplish) tail and wings; large white wing-patches; black bill. Length, 19 in.; wingspan, 24; weight, 6 oz.

RANGE: Widespread in temperate Eurasia, reaching n.w. Africa; in w. North America, from s. Alaska to w. Manitoba, south to n.e. California, n. New Mexico, n.w. Oklahoma, and w. Kansas. North American race wanders erratically south to near U.S.-Mexico border and east to Mississippi River.

TEXAS: *Vagrant*: Casual visitor to northern Panhandle, Trans-Pecos, and Tarrant Co.; accidental in southwestern Uvalde Co. (2 birds sighted, early Nov., 1849, G. A. McCall). Fossil from Pleistocene (see detailed account). Records of escaped cage birds or pets fairly numerous.

HAUNTS AND HABITS: The handsome Black-billed Magpie—a bird with long trim tail and flashing white wings—is one of the few perching birds common to both North America and northern Eurasia. Ancestors of the American race must have come from northeastern Asia because the U.S. bird thrives only in a Siberian-type climate—blazingly hot in summer and fiendishly cold in winter with humidity generally low. Our Blackbill, unlike European races, has not been able to colonize humid areas, such as eastern Canada, or warm regions, like the southwestern United States. The fact that a Pleistocene fossil of this species has been discovered in the state hints that the Black-billed Magpie was probably common in Texas during the last Ice Age.

Shunning dense forests and high peaks, this magpie lives chiefly in foothills and on elevated plains in mountainous regions; within this terrain it favors canyons and streamsides with thickets and scattered trees. In small loose colonies, the birds build bulky domed nests in sturdy thorn bushes or in cottonwood, aspen, alder, hawthorn, or other trees. Even more gregarious after the breeding season, they feed and roost together in rather large groups and also go in foraging parties to camping areas and the vicinity of ranches and farms. Thus far, the species has adapted well to human encroachments in its habitat by making trash and scraps of cultivated areas another source of nesting material and food.

Flight of the Blackbill, usually from tree to tree or bush to bush, is slow, wavering, and at times even cumbersome due to its long magpie tail. The bird often feeds on the ground where it jerkily walks about twitching its slightly uplifted tail. Here it eats predominantly insects, also carrion, and small mammals, resorting to vegetable food only when animal matter is scarce. Being poor fliers, these shy and wary birds seldom stray very far from brush and thickets which they seek for protection should any danger arise.

The common notes of the Black-billed Magpie are a rapid, high-keyed *cheg cheg cheg cheg* and a whiny *maag?* or *maa-maa?* Although the species is not particularly noisy, its notes are sounded rather frequently through the year. In captivity, some Blackbills become fairly good at imitating human words and phrases; the species probably ranks first in this ability among native U.S. birds.

Detailed Account: One Subspecies

AMERICAN BLACK-BILLED MAGPIE, *Pica pica hudsonia* (Sabine)

DESCRIPTION: *Adults, nuptial plumage*: Acquired by wear from winter plumage. Head, neck, back, upper tail-coverts, throat, breast, and lining of wing black, feathers of middle of throat with large but mostly concealed white spots, pileum with metallic bronzy green sheen; remaining plumage with more or less bluish, purplish, or greenish gloss; scapulars, sides, flanks, lower breast, and upper abdomen white; lower back and upper rump greenish white; abdomen and crissum black; tail variegated with glossy metallic chromium green, danube green, indigo blue, and dark hyssop violet, last mostly toward ends of feathers; under surface of tail chaetura black or fuscous black; primaries mostly white but tips and outer webs chaetura black, becoming metallic green on inner feathers; secondaries chaetura black to fuscous black, their exposed surfaces metallic bluish green to marine blue—on tertials, tips of sec-

ondaries, and basal portion of outer webs of inner primaries becoming metallic nickel green. Bill black or slate black, unfeathered area above eye black or grayish; iris black or very dark brown with bluish gray outer ring; legs, toes, and claws black, but soles of toes gray. *Adults, winter*: Acquired by complete postnuptial molt. Similar to nuptial adults, but colors somewhat brighter. *First nuptial*: Acquired by wear from first winter. Similar to nuptial adults, but wings and tail duller, more brownish, particularly primaries and primary coverts. *First winter*: Acquired by partial postjuvenal molt. Similar to first nuptial, but colors rather brighter; wing-quills and tail retained from juvenal. *Juvenal*: Acquired by postnatal growth. Similar to nuptial adults but duller, all black portions of adult replaced by fuscous to clove brown or brownish black, white scapulars tinged and spotted with fuscous or mixed with drab, as are sometimes center of abdomen and anterior part of white area on lower parts; sides also more or less brownish, grayish white band on rump indistinct or practically absent; wings somewhat more brownish; white concealed spots on throat much larger and more exposed but not so purely white, appearing very large and wedge-shaped on brown feathers of jugulum and upper breast. Bill and feet black; bare space below eye larger than in adult; iris black.

MEASUREMENTS: *Adult male*: Wing, 181.6–211.6 (average, 202.9) mm.; tail, 235.0–302.5 (268.0); bill (exposed culmen), 33.0–39.6 (36.6); tarsus, 45.0–50.0 (48.0); middle toe without claw, 23.6–27.9 (25.9). *Adult female*: Wing, 190.0–206.0 (197.6); tail, 231.6–283.4 (259.6); bill, 31.0–36.6 (34.5); tarsus, 42.9–48.5 (46.0); middle toe, 22.6–27.9 (24.9).

RANGE: S.w. Alaska to c. British Columbia and c. Manitoba, south to c. California and s.w. Kansas.

TEXAS: *Vagrant*: No skin collected, but the fossil discovered in early Pleistocene of Texas (fide A.O.U. check-list, 1957) is probably of this subspecies or its direct ancestor.

COMMON RAVEN, *Corvus corax* Linnaeus

Species Account

Call is typically a low hoarse croak. Considerably larger than Common Crow; heavy bill with curved culmen produces "Roman nose" effect; ample, wedge-shaped tail; alternately flaps and sails. Entirely glossy black (may appear purplish, greenish); shaggy throat-feathers (visible at close range). Length, 24 in.; wing-span, 4 ft.; weight, 2 lbs.

RANGE: Widespread in Eurasia, n. Africa; in Western Hemisphere from Alaska, Canada, and Greenland, south through w. United States and Mexico to Nicaragua, also south in e. United States to n. Great Lakes region, Maine, and locally in Appalachians.

TEXAS: (See map.) *Resident*: Breeds, mid-Apr. to late June (eggs, Apr. 25 to June 1) from 1,000 to 8,000 ft., possibly higher. Fairly common in southern Trans-Pecos and on roughest portions of western Edwards Plateau; uncommon and irregular in Davis Mts. and on remainder of Plateau east to 99th meridian (scarce to Llano, Boerne) and north to Abilene; rare in remainder of Trans-Pecos and in broken country north from Abilene to northern Panhandle. Said to have bred in Lavaca Co. (1861–1864, J. D. Mitchell). Nonbreeders casual at San Antonio; accidental east to central coast (1 killed in Refugio Co., ca. 1900) and Galveston.

HAUNTS AND HABITS: The Common Raven is often listed as the largest passerine bird; however, the much longer Superb Lyrebird, *Menura superba*, of Australia, may measure up to forty inches in length. *Corvus corax* inhabits mountains, canyons, and cliffs. Few if any other land birds pay less attention to climate or altitude. Provided only that terrain is rough and not too civilized, the species is at home from the Arctic to Central America and from near the tops of highest mountains to sea cliffs, stacks, and rocks. In southern Trans-Pecos Texas and more rugged parts of the Edwards Plateau it ranges through wooded and open country and cliffs and canyons of high hills. Omnivorous and a crafty scavenger, it roams singly, in pairs, or occasionally in small groups, searching for carrion, rabbits, small rodents, frogs, lizards, snakes, insects, and some vegetable matter. While shy and suspicious, this raven cautiously ventures to the vicinity of farms and ranches and outskirts of towns to pick up meat scraps and bread crumbs.

Majestic in flight, the Common Raven soars like a large hawk, alternating measured flaps with glides on flat wings. It also hovers in the air Sparrow Hawk fashion. During springtime courtship and when harassing or being harassed by other birds, it performs spectacular mid-air dives, tumbles, twists, and somersaults. On the ground it walks about in a seemingly composed and dignified manner.

The unforgettable voice of the Common is a hoarse croaking *cr-r-uck*, *prruk*, or *tok*, which is lower pitched and more throaty than that of the White-necked Raven. Some croaks from old male Common Ravens are extremely low pitched, almost like *wook* or *woek*. *Corvus corax* apparently has no territorial song, but in late summer, individuals within a group sometimes emit a few gargling warbles.

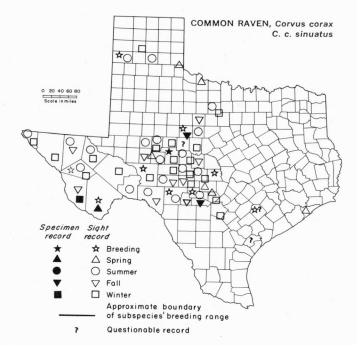

COMMON RAVEN, *Corvus corax*
C. c. *sinuatus*

0 20 40 60 80
Scale in miles

Specimen | Sight
record | record
★ | ☆ Breeding
▲ | △ Spring
● | ○ Summer
▼ | ▽ Fall
■ | □ Winter
——— | Approximate boundary of subspecies' breeding range
? | Questionable record

DETAILED ACCOUNT: ONE SUBSPECIES

WESTERN COMMON RAVEN, *Corvus corax sinuatus* Wagler

DESCRIPTION: *Adults, nuptial plumage*: Acquired by wear from winter plumage. Upper and lower parts glossy black, inner edges of primaries and secondaries, at least basally, fuscous or fuscous black, feathers of chin and throat pointed instead of rounded; upper parts, except hindneck and a few outer primaries, with metallic sheen of dark slate violet, this also on lining of wing, throat, and jugulum; chin and remaining lower parts, as well as outer primaries, with metallic gloss of greenish black or blue; bases of feathers of neck dull hair brown to chaetura drab; feathers of upper parts with more or less invisible darker tips which in some lights produce decided squamate effect; similar effect produced on feathers of breast and abdomen by metallic tips of feathers, remaining portions being dull black with little or no gloss. Bill, legs, toes, and claws black; interior of mouth deep violet black, shading to dull flesh color posteriorly; iris deep vandyke brown or black. *Adults, winter*: Acquired by complete postnuptial molt, at first from first nuptial. Similar to nuptial adults. *First nuptial*: Acquired by wear from first winter. Similar to nuptial adults but averaging smaller; everywhere somewhat duller, more brownish; wing-quills and tail feathers more brownish and worn (retained from juvenal), also more pointed or rounded; tail less strongly rounded. *First winter*: Acquired by partial postjuvenal molt. Similar to first nuptial, but wing-quills and tail retained from juvenal. *Juvenal*: Acquired by complete postnatal molt. Similar to adult, but upper parts of body duller, general color fuscous to fuscous black with slight or no metallic gloss on wings and tail, which are practically as in adult; lower parts of still duller fuscous or fuscous black with little or no metallic sheen except anteriorly. *Natal*: Hair brown.

MEASUREMENTS: *Adult male*: Wing, 396.2–459.7 (average, 430.8) mm.; tail, 218.2–254.0 (236.7); bill (exposed culmen), 66.0–80.0 (74.2); height of bill at nostril, 24.1–27.9 (25.4); tarsus, 64.8–73.7 (69.8); middle toe without claw, 39.6–58.2 (48.3). *Adult female*: Wing, 386.3–431.8 (408.7); tail, 208.3–251.5 (228.9); bill, 64.8–76.2 (69.8); height of bill at nostril, 23.1–27.4 (24.9); tarsus, 63.5–73.2 (66.8); middle toe, 40.1–47.0 (41.7).

RANGE: S. Mackenzie, south through w. United States and w. Mexico to Honduras.

TEXAS: *Resident*: Collected north to Taylor, south to Bandera, west to Brewster and Presidio cos.

NESTING: *Nest*: Usually in wild, rather open country, on mountains, slopes, and mesas; ledge of high cliff, top of tall tree, and on cliff of canyon; large platform, well put together, sometimes very bulky; foundation of sticks, some of large size, well interlaced; thickly lined with small sticks or twigs, inner bark of cottonwood and other trees, grass, cattle hair, wool, or goat hair. *Eggs*: 4–7, usually 5; ovate, elongate ovate, or cylindrical ovate; pale pea green, drab, or greenish olive, light greenish blue, or even dark green; blotched with umber and other shades of dark brown, with similar shell markings of drab, lavender, and dull purple; average size, 49.5 × 32.8 mm.

WHITE-NECKED RAVEN, *Corvus cryptoleucus* Couch

SPECIES ACCOUNT

Ravenlike croak similar to Common's, but flatter and usually higher pitched. A crow-sized raven of arid, flat, open country; gregarious. Resembles Common, but feathers of neck and breast, when ruffled, reveal white bases; tail slightly wedge-shaped. Length, 19¾ in.; wingspan, 3½ ft.; weight, 1¼ lbs.

RANGE: Arid regions from s.e. Arizona, New Mexico,

s.e. Colorado, s. Nebraska, and w. Kansas, south to c. Mexico. Some seasonal movement noticeable though normally within general breeding range; may largely withdraw from northern limits in winter.

TEXAS: (See map.) *Breeding*: Mid-Feb. to late Aug. (eggs, Mar. 11 to July 3) from near sea level (scarce) to about 5,500 ft. Very common to uncommon through western third (locally in northern Panhandle) east to Wichita Falls, Brown Co., northwestern Edwards Plateau (irregularly), and southwestern portions of south Texas brush country downriver to western Hidalgo Co. (scarce to Brownsville); casual (no recent nesting record) east to Tarrant (eggs examined, Mar. 11, 1911, J. B. Litsey, Jr.), Kerr (nest located, Mar. 22, 1883, H. Lacey), and Kenedy (eggs taken, May 4, 1922, G. H. Stuart III) cos. *Winter*: Mid-Sept. to late May (extremes: Aug. 25, June 25). Abundant locally to uncommon through most of regular breeding range, but largely retreats from northern Panhandle; irregularly abundant to fairly common in southernmost parts of Rio Grande delta; scarce in northeastern portion of delta north to central coast, where very rare; casual in central portions and on upper coast.

HAUNTS AND HABITS: Seeking flatter, less rugged country than the Common Raven, the White-necked Raven ranges arid regions of western and southern Texas where there are scattered yucca, mesquite, and cactus. Noted flockers, even more so than the Common Crow, these birds are often seen in immense numbers streaming to and from their roost at dusk and dawn and circling vulturelike high in the sky on midday thermals.

Although similar to the Common Crow in social behavior and size, the Whiteneck exhibits its raven abilities in the air. Flight is strong and well sustained. Courtship performances involve elaborate mid-air displays, and often when groups are flying together they indulge in playful aerial evolutions, turning, somersaulting, even sailing short distances on their backs. This bird, generally less suspicious than the Common Raven, is bolder in its scavenging raids near human habitations and garbage dumps. In addition to edible trash, scraps, and waste grain of cultivated crops, individuals forage for a variety of insects, carrion, and small reptiles and rodents; fruit of cacti is an important source of food and water in the bird's desert haunts, especially during dry summer months.

As does the Turkey Vulture, this raven patrols west Texas highways in order to feast on flesh of jack rabbits and other animals smashed by automobiles. Another adaptation to the white man's technology is the building of wire nests. In western Texas and eastern New Mexico where sticks are rare, many White-necked Ravens, especially since 1940, have taken up the habit of constructing their nests partially or wholly of wire scraps. In the Texas Memorial Museum at Austin there is a display of such nests built by Whitenecks; Glen Evans, formerly of the Museum staff, gathered the material for this exhibit near Portales, New Mexico.

This raven's call is a hoarse *kraak*, similar to that of the Common Raven but flatter and usually higher pitched. It is quite different from the *caw*, *cah*, or *car* of the Common Crow, but astonishingly many west Texas ranch people still refer to their Whitenecks as crows. *Kraak*'s are heard throughout the year, but less frequently in winter.

DETAILED ACCOUNT: NO SUBSPECIES

DESCRIPTION: *Adults, nuptial plumage*: Acquired by wear from winter plumage. Feathers of chin and throat more or less pointed; upper and lower parts black, the former, as well as throat and jugulum, glossed, except on hindneck and outer primaries, with metallic heliotrope slate, inner webs of wing-quills fuscous black except at tips, feathers of neck all around with pure white bases; feathers of upper parts posterior to hindneck with invisible darker tips that in some lights give in part a squamate effect; outer webs of primaries, chin, posterior lower parts, outer primaries, and lining of wing with metallic gloss of dull bluish or greenish black, the last with invisible darker squamate tips of feathers as in upper parts. Bill, legs, feet, and claws black; iris dark brown. *Adults, winter*: Acquired by complete postnuptial molt, at first from first nuptial. Similar to nuptial adults. *First nuptial*: Acquired by wear from first winter. Similar to nuptial adults but averaging smaller, somewhat duller, more brownish; wing-quills and tail feathers more brownish and worn (retained from juvenal), also more pointed or rounded at tips; tail less strongly rounded. *First winter*: Acquired by partial postjuvenal molt. Similar to first nuptial. *Juvenal*: Acquired by postnatal growth. Wings and tail similar to those of nuptial adults, but bill smaller; upper parts dull fuscous black with slight metallic bluish or greenish sheen; rump fuscous; lower parts anteriorly fuscous black with slight greenish sheen; posterior lower parts fuscous; bases of feathers of neck all around dull white. *Natal*: Plumage scanty; pale vinaceous fawn or dull buffy white to light tilleul buff.

MEASUREMENTS: *Adult male*: Wing, 337.1–379.0 (average,

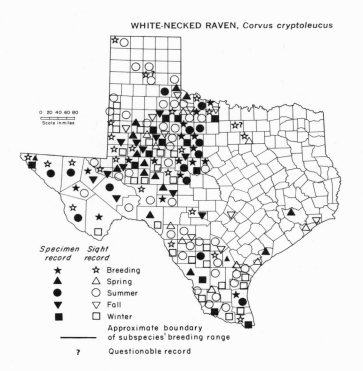

WHITE-NECKED RAVEN, *Corvus cryptoleucus*

0 20 40 60 80
Scale in miles

Specimen record   *Sight record*

★ ☆ Breeding
▲ △ Spring
● ○ Summer
▼ ▽ Fall
■ □ Winter

—— Approximate boundary of subspecies' breeding range

? Questionable record

355.6) mm.; tail, 193.0–214.1 (199.2); bill (exposed culmen), 52.1–58.9 (56.9); height of bill at nostril, 19.8–22.6 (21.1); tarsus, 57.9–68.6 (62.0); middle toe without claw, 37.6–43.4 (40.4). *Adult female*: Wing, 327.4–360.4 (347.5); tail, 181.6–211.2 (198.1); bill, 49.5–57.9 (53.1); height of bill at nostril, 17.8–20.3 (19.6); tarsus, 55.6–64.0 (58.9); middle toe, 35.1–42.4 (38.1).

TEXAS: *Breeding*: Collected north to Hall and Wichita (eggs), southeast to Cameron, west to Brewster (eggs) and El Paso cos. Records outside breeding range: Harris Co., west shore of Galveston Bay (several birds shot, May, 1890, W. E. Grover); Calhoun Co., southwest end of Matagorda Island (2 specimens, Apr. 2, 9, 1937, A. R. Hines). *Winter*: Taken north to Dickens and Archer, southeast to Cameron, west to Webb and El Paso cos.

NESTING: *Nest*: In rolling or level, more or less open country, often along streams, in cedar or other low scrubby woods, but preferably in mesquite or other thornbrush plants, such as acacia (catclaw), ash, or desert willow, usually 7–20 ft. above ground; ordinarily not well constructed, but somewhat larger than nest of the Common Crow. Commonly composed of sticks, thorny twigs, grass, often clods of earth and grass, occasionally—and in some localities often—of fence wire; lined with leaves, grapevine and other bark, grass, yucca fibers, hair of deer, goat, or cattle, hog bristles, wool, rabbit fur, or even rabbit skin. *Eggs*: 3–8, usually 5; mostly ovate or elongate ovate; pale bluish green to grayish green; sparingly spotted and scrawled with sepia, deep grayish olive, other shades of brown, and dark moss green, streaked and blotched with various shades of lilac, lavender gray, and drab; average size, 44.2 × 30.2 mm.

COMMON CROW, *Corvus brachyrhynchos* Brehm

SPECIES ACCOUNT

Also known as American Crow. Call is typically a loud raucous *caw*, often given in series. Large, chunky; gregarious. Entirely glossy black (may appear greenish, purplish); square-tipped tail. Length, 18 in.; wingspan, 35¾; weight, 1 lb.

RANGE: British Columbia and s.w. Mackenzie to Newfoundland, south to n. Baja California, c. Arizona, c. New Mexico, Colorado, Texas, Gulf states, and s. Florida. Winters from s. Canada to Baja California and extreme s. United States.

TEXAS: (See map.) *Breeding*: Early Feb. to June (eggs, Feb. 23 to May 15; young in nest as late as June 5) from near sea level to 2,500 ft. Common to fairly common in most of northern half east of 101st meridian and in eastern half south to counties along 29th parallel; uncommon and local in remainder of northern Panhandle and on Edwards Plateau; rare along northern limits of south Texas brush country. Formerly bred south along central coast to Kleberg Co. (May 26 to June 2, 1921, A. R. Cahn). *Winter*: Sept. to Mar. (extremes: Aug. 21, May 25). Abundant to fairly common through northern and eastern parts irregularly west to western Panhandle, Midland, and El Paso, where normally rare, and irregularly south to Uvalde, San Antonio, and Welder Wildlife Refuge, where normally rare.

HAUNTS AND HABITS: Leaving mountains and arid country largely to the ravens, the Common Crow is the glossy black corvid distributed generally through central and east Texas pine or oak woodlands. Like its cousin, the Blue Jay, it avoids, for the most part, areas where mesquites and cacti predominate. Only in the Panhandle does it enter much into big ranches. Here Common Crows reside in cottonwoods along rivers, while White-necked Ravens croak over dry rangelands between watercourses. Exceedingly gregarious during the nonbreeding season, these birds, often numbering in the hundreds, share common roosts in patches of woods, high bushes, or cattails. During the day, loose flocks scatter to feed along fence rows, in shelter belts, farmland, and not too dense thickets and groves of rivers and streams.

Flight of the Common Crow is direct, steady, though not swift, and usually performed with moderately rapid wing-beats. It is capable of being long sustained, although movement is typically from tree to tree or bush to bush. The crow is wary and suspicious at all times; when a flock is feeding or resting, sentinel birds are posted to warn the group of any danger. Very adaptive and resourceful, as are most jays and crows, the omnivorous Common eats what the season and locality provide; its diet including insects, crustaceans, snails, reptiles, small mammals, carrion, grain, and edible trash discarded by humans; also eggs and young of wild birds. Often on the ground, the bird walks deliberately; when running it uses its wings to aid in accelerating.

This unmusical bird displays its versatility in the use of various notes and calls, many of which seem to be important in flock communications. The well-known note of the Common Crow is its loud, easily imitated

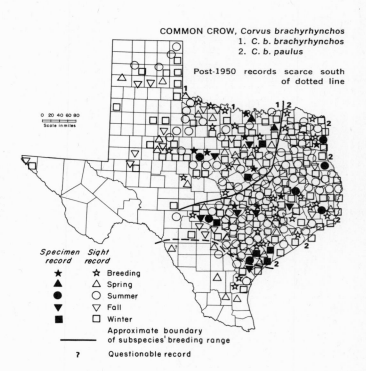

COMMON CROW, *Corvus brachyrhynchos*
1. *C. b. brachyrhynchos*
2. *C. b. paulus*

Post-1950 records scarce south of dotted line

0 20 40 60 80
Scale in miles

Specimen record / Sight record

★ / ☆ Breeding
▲ / △ Spring
● / ○ Summer
▼ / ▽ Fall
■ / □ Winter

—— Approximate boundary of subspecies' breeding range

? Questionable record

caw; variants are *cah* and *car*. Some captive birds can be taught to say a few words.

DETAILED ACCOUNT: THREE SUBSPECIES

EASTERN COMMON CROW, *Corvus brachyrhynchos brachyrhynchos* Brehm

DESCRIPTION: *Adults, nuptial plumage*: Acquired by wear from winter plumage. Feathers of chin and throat rounded at tips; entire plumage glossy black, pileum with slight greenish sheen; remainder of upper parts, except hindneck and outer primaries, glossed with metallic dark slate violet or dusky slate violet, feathers of outer webs of outer primaries, chin, outer tail feathers, and remainder of lower parts with dull greenish or bluish gloss; bases of feathers of neck between mouse gray and neutral gray; inner webs of secondaries and bases of inner webs of primaries mostly fuscous black; feathers of upper parts posterior to hindneck with invisible darker terminal edges imparting squamate effect to plumage in certain lights, this effect to a lesser degree seen on breast and abdomen. Bill, legs, feet, and claws black; interior of mouth dark flesh color; iris deep vandyke brown, hazel, or black. *Adults, winter*: Acquired by complete postnuptial molt, at first from first nuptial. Like nuptial adults. *First nuptial*: Acquired by wear from first winter. Much like nuptial adults, but length of wing averaging less; metallic gloss of upper parts more brownish and less distinct, particularly on wings and tail; tail less strongly rounded; shafts of wing-quills more whitish to tips; primaries and rectrices retained from juvenal more worn, their tips also more pointed or rounded (less square); lower surface duller, somewhat more brownish, posteriorly with somewhat grayish or slaty tinge. *First winter*: Acquired by partial postjuvenal molt. Similar to first nuptial. *Juvenal*: Acquired by complete postnatal molt. Similar to first winter male and female, but bill smaller; plumage still duller, upper parts dull fuscous black with but slight metallic bluish or violet sheen; lower parts fuscous black, chaetura black, fuscous, or chaetura drab to clove brown with little or no metallic sheen; wings and tail duller. Bill dull black or slate color, but tip somewhat lighter, more brownish, base lavender; inside of mouth lavender; iris brown or slate gray; legs and feet dull black, slate gray, or dark brown, but hind part of tarsus and soles of toes dull white or yellowish white. *Natal*: Grayish clove brown. Bill and feet grayish black.
MEASUREMENTS: *Adult male*: Wing, 305.1–337.1 (average, 321.1) mm.; tail, 167.6–195.6 (182.1); bill (exposed culmen), 48.0–53.8 (51.6); height of bill at nostril, 17.5–20.6 (19.6); tarsus, 59.9–65.5 (62.0); middle toe without claw, 35.6–39.9 (38.1). *Adult female*: Wing, 281.9–326.7 (305.1); tail, 172.7–198.1 (177.0); bill, 45.5–50.0 (48.0); height of bill, 17.0–19.6 (18.0); tarsus, 55.1–61.0 (57.4); middle toe, 32.5–36.6 (35.1).
RANGE: N.w. Mackenzie to s.e. Newfoundland, south through w. Minnesota to n. Texas and New Jersey. Winters from s. Manitoba and s.e. Newfoundland to c. Texas and s. South Carolina.
TEXAS: *Breeding*: Altitudinal range, 350 to 2,500 ft. Collected north to Cooke, south to McLennan, west to Callahan cos. Fairly common. *Winter*: Taken outside breeding range south to Victoria and Refugio (Aug. 27), west to Kendall cos. Common.
NESTING: *Nest*: In level or rolling country, usually not near human habitations, in open cultivated lands, sometimes more open wild country, or in forests or along streams, along fence rows, or even in open fields; in various trees, such as pines and oaks, or in bushes, 6–50 ft. above ground; bulky platform, usually well built of sticks, weed stalks, corn husks, grass, bits of earth, strips of bark, dead leaves, roots, moss, and similar materials; lined with rootlets, strips of grapevine, cedar (juniper) or other bark, leaves, straw, moss, rags, wool, hair, bits of vines, pine needles, plant fibers, hog bristles, hair of skunks or other animals. *Eggs*: 3–9, usually 5; short ovate or rounded ovate to elongate ovate, variable in shape; bluish or greenish white to pale bluish green, olive green, or malachite green, even olive buff, and light to dark green of various shades; sparingly or densely spotted

and blotched with different shades of brown, lilac, and gray; average size, 41.9 × 29.2 mm.

SOUTHERN COMMON CROW, *Corvus brachyrhynchos paulus* Howell

DESCRIPTION: *Adults, nuptial plumage*: Similar to *C. b. brachyrhynchos* but decidedly smaller; bill much more slender.
MEASUREMENTS: *Adult male*: Wing, 285.0–318.0 (average, 295.1) mm.; tail, 166.1–192.0 (174.8); bill (exposed culmen), 46.0–55.1 (50.3); height of bill at nostril, 17.0–18.0 (17.5); tarsus, 55.9–67.1 (60.7); middle toe without claw, 31.0–37.6 (34.0). *Adult female*: Wing, 270.0–305.1 (290.8); tail, 154.9–186.2 (172.7); bill, 42.9–50.0 (46.8); height of bill, 16.0–17.5 (16.8); tarsus, 54.1–62.0 (59.2); middle toe, 32.0–36.1 (33.8).
RANGE: E. Oklahoma to Maryland, south to e. Texas and e. South Carolina.
TEXAS: *Resident*: Altitudinal breeding range, near sea level to 1,800 ft. Collected north to Marion, south to Hardin, southwest to Refugio, west to Kerr cos. Fairly common.
NESTING: Similar to that of *C. b. brachyrhynchos*.

WESTERN COMMON CROW, *Corvus brachyrhynchos hesperis* Ridgway

DESCRIPTION: *Adults, nuptial plumage*: Similar to *C. b. brachyrhynchos* but smaller, with much more slender bill. Similar to *C. b. paulus*, but wing longer; bill and tarsus shorter; bill slightly more slender.
MEASUREMENTS: *Adult male*: Wing, 281.9–325.1 (average, 302.5) mm.; tail, 159.0–190.0 (170.9); bill (exposed culmen), 45.5–50.5 (47.5); height of bill at nostril, 15.0–17.5 (16.5); tarsus, 54.6–58.4 (57.4); middle toe without claw, 33.0–38.1 (35.6). *Adult female*: Wing, 278.1–300.0 (294.9); tail, 160.5–183.1 (169.4); bill, 42.9–48.0 (45.5); height of bill, 15.0–16.5 (16.0); tarsus, 53.1–58.9 (55.6); middle toe, 30.5–37.6 (34.0).
RANGE: N. British Columbia to n.w. Wisconsin, south to w. California and Colorado. Winters from s. British Columbia and s. Manitoba to n. Baja California and c. Texas.
TEXAS: *Winter*: Collected north to Tarrant (Nov. 1), south to Calhoun, west to Kerr (Nov. 25) and Eastland (Oct. 21) cos. Uncommon.

FISH CROW, *Corvus ossifragus* Wilson

SPECIES ACCOUNT

Call is typically a high explosive *bah!* Closely resembles Common Crow, but most individuals somewhat smaller and thinner billed; plumage more uniformly glossy. Length, 15¾ in.; wingspan, 32½; weight, 14¾ oz.
RANGE: Atlantic seaboard from Rhode Island to Florida (virtually entire state), west along Gulf coast to extreme s.e. Texas, and inland along major river systems (local and irregular beyond tidal limits). Winters chiefly within breeding range, moving into contiguous areas occasionally; may withdraw somewhat from northern limits during coldest months.
TEXAS: (See map.) *Breeding*: Mar. to June (eggs, May 4) near sea level, perhaps higher. Common in Orange Co.; fairly common to uncommon (breeding suspected) in Jefferson, Chambers, and Liberty cos. Lately observed in summer (breeding suspected) in northeastern corner (Caddo Lake–Big Cypress Bayou area, 8–10 birds, June 14, 1973; Lake Texarkana spill-

way, flock of 4, June 15; Bowie Co. on Red River flood-plain, total of 13 birds, June 16, C. D. Fisher, Suzanne Winckler). *Winter*: Mid.-Nov. to Mar. (extremes: Oct. 9, May 12). Common in Orange Co.; fairly common to uncommon in suspected breeding range; scarce and local visitor in remainder of southeastern corner west to Huntsville, Houston, and Freeport and north along Sabine River to Shelby Co.; apparently rarely to Tyler and Marshall.

HAUNTS AND HABITS: The Fish Crow inhabits Atlantic and Gulf tidewaters and lower reaches of large rivers. Where trees meet salt water, as at Biloxi, Mississippi, this crow is a beach scavenger, but in Orange County, Texas, only locality in the state where the species greatly flourishes, it appears to stick to freshwater situations. In and about the city of Orange it is a familiar sight and sound as it *bahs* along the baldcypress-lined bayous and swamps. In the eastern states the bird frequents bays, inlets, and lagoons but lives also in lowland woods, both coniferous and deciduous. Where numerous, it accumulates in large flocks, the biggest gatherings being at wintertime roosts. During the breeding season, in contrast to the Common Crow, individuals form nesting colonies.

Flight and behavior are similar to that of the Common Crow, although the Fish beats its wings faster; it also appears more buoyant because it sails more, taking advantage of sea breezes. When feeding, it often hovers gull fashion in mid-air, then swoops down over the water to pick up a bit of floating food. Fish Crows forage for aquatic animals, insects, carrion, edible garbage, wild berries and fruits; they also raid eggs and young from nests in rookeries of herons, egrets, ibises, and other water birds.

Usual notes of the Fish Crow are an explosive *bah!*, *car!*, or *ca-ha!*; all of these are higher pitched, more

nasal, and more abrupt than the adult Common Crow's *caw*, *car*, or *cah*. There appears to be no record of song in the Fish Crow or of its learning to talk.

DETAILED ACCOUNT: NO SUBSPECIES

DESCRIPTION: *Adults, nuptial plumage*: Acquired by wear from winter plumage. Glossy black above and below; anterior upper surface with metallic bluish black sheen; back, posterior upper parts, and tertials with dull violet black sheen; outer webs of secondaries and of inner primaries metallic dusky violet blue or dusky slate violet, edges of alula and outer webs of primaries metallic dull greenish black; feathers of body with little or no shadowy darker tips, plumage thus without conspicuous squamate appearance; lower parts with metallic greenish slate black sheen; bases of feathers of neck all around mouse gray or rather light mouse gray; lining of wing chaetura black or fuscous black, glossed with dull violet black or bluish black. Bill, legs, toes, and claws black; iris seal brown. *Adults, winter*: Acquired by wear from first winter. Similar to nuptial adults but duller, somewhat more brownish, particularly wings and tail, these retained from juvenal; tips of tail feathers more rounded (not so square). *First winter*: Acquired by partial postjuvenal molt. Similar to first nuptial male and female; wings and tail somewhat more brownish (less glossy) than adults in winter. *Juvenal*: Acquired by complete postnatal molt. Similar to nuptial adults but—excepting wings and tail—much duller, pileum and back deep chaetura black glossed with dull metallic green or blue; rump chaetura drab; lower parts chaetura drab to chaetura black with slight dull greenish gloss. Bill and feet brownish black or blackish brown. *Natal*: Pileum light drab; back and rump drab.

MEASUREMENTS: *Adult male*: Wing, 263.9–300.0 (average, 278.1) mm.; tail, 148.1–176.5 (158.5); bill (exposed culmen), 40.4–45.0 (42.9); height of bill at nostril, 14.5–15.4 (14.9); tarsus, 45.5–50.0 (48.0); middle toe without claw, 33.5–39.9 (35.6). *Adult female*: Wing, 264.4–282.4 (271.5); tail, 137.4–165.1 (151.9); bill, 39.1–41.9 (40.4); height of bill, 13.5–15.0 (14.0); tarsus, 44.4–47.0 (46.0); middle toe, 32.5–38.6 (34.0).

TEXAS: *Breeding*: No skin, but evidence of nesting in Orange Co. (5 fresh eggs collected, May 4, 1886, R. E. Rachford). *Winter*: Three specimens, taken same place and day: Jefferson Co., mouth of Neches River, 5 mi. north of Port Arthur (all males, Nov. 25, 1972, C. D. Fisher; 2 specimens in Stephen F. Austin State University collection, nos. 1597, 1598; 1 in Texas A&M University collection, no. 9046).

NESTING: *Nest*: In level or rolling country, often near bayous or streams, in forests or isolated trees; in pine, baldcypress, cedar, or other tree, usually 20–50 ft. above ground; bulky, though rather compact, platform of sticks, coarse grass, seaweed, moss, and other similar materials; lined with strips of baldcypress, cedar, and other bark, pine needles, sometimes Spanishmoss, dry leaves, eelgrass, horse and cattle hair. *Eggs*: 4–6, usually 5; short ovate to elongate ovate; bluish or greenish white or various shades of light green, occasionally olive buff or even light blue with slight greenish tinge; blotched and spotted with light or dark brown, with shell markings of lilac and gray; average size, 37.1 × 26.9 mm.

TAMAULIPAS MEXICAN CROW, *Corvus imparatus* Peters

SPECIES ACCOUNT

Diagnostic call is a low, burry, froglike *owwwk*. A gregarious tiny crow, smallest of its genus in Texas-Tamaulipas region. Black (glossed with violet above, greenish blue below); bases of neck feathers gray (not white as in *C. cryptoleucus*); has short, square-tipped tail. Length, 14–15 in.

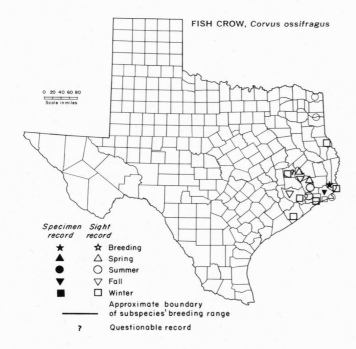

FISH CROW, *Corvus ossifragus*

0 20 40 60 80
Scale in miles

Specimen   Sight
record   record

★   ☆ Breeding
▲   △ Spring
●   ○ Summer
▼   ▽ Fall
■   □ Winter

———   Approximate boundary of subspecies' breeding range

?   Questionable record

RANGE: Lowlands of extreme s. Texas (no nesting evidence, as of summer 1972), e. Nuevo León, Tamaulipas, San Luis Potosí, and n. Veracruz.

TEXAS: (See map.) *Newcomer*: First certified in state in 1968. *Winter* (chiefly): Seasonal occurrence still erratic. In 1968, appeared Aug. 2, when 3 birds were verified 3½ mi. inland from Boca Chica. By Sept. 1, at least 200 birds were feeding in goat-cattle pens on Lerma Ranch off Boca Chica Road. About Nov. 25, most birds had disappeared, but 1 crippled individual lingered until mid-May, 1969, at Port Isabel garbage dump (J. C. Arvin). In 1969, first individual of fall season appeared in Cameron Co. in Nov. Thousands of crows visited Laguna Atascosa Nat. Wildlife Refuge for a day or two in late Jan., 1970 (M. C. LeFever). "Last of winter" was 1 bird near Laguna Atascosa, July 30, 1970 (fide C. L. Ryan). On Dec. 29, 1970, an Audubon Christmas Bird Count at Brownsville, including the dump, revealed no crows. Next positive report of *C. imparatus* was 480 at Brownsville dump, Oct. 14, 1971 (H. H. Axtell). The Dec. 31, 1971, Brownsville Christmas Count reported 284 crows amid the garbage (David Simon, et al.). By Mar. 27, 1972, the number had dwindled to 9 (Guy McCaskie, et al.). No crows were at the dump on June 11, 1972 (Mr. and Mrs. P. A. Buckley), but on July 27, 1972, at least 30 crows were counted there (John and Susanne Luther, Rose Ann Rowlett). The Dec. 29, 1972, Brownsville Christmas Count reported 243 birds (E. B. Kincaid, Jr., Suzanne Winckler). All the above localities are in Cameron Co., same county wherein the only U.S. specimens of the species have been collected. By mid-1972 a few sightings had been made up the Rio Grande to Starr Co., Fronton (1 on Falcon Dam Christmas Count, Dec. 28, 1971, G. F. Oatman, Jr., R. A. Rowlett, S. Winckler);

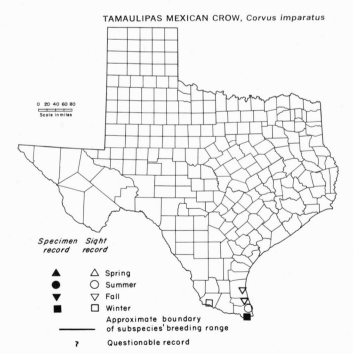

TAMAULIPAS MEXICAN CROW, *Corvus imparatus*

0 20 40 60 80
Scale in miles

Specimen Sight
record record

▲ △ Spring
● ○ Summer
▼ ▽ Fall
■ □ Winter

——— Approximate boundary of subspecies' breeding range

? Questionable record

and upcoast through Willacy Co. to s. Kenedy Co., Rudolph on King Ranch (30 in flock, Sept. 4, 1968, B. A. Fall), with one unauthenticated report of a flock in Victoria Co. In a letter postmarked Aug. 28, 1972, Arvin, of Port Isabel, stated, "I am 99 percent sure that they [Mexican Crows] have never nested in the U.S." Ryan, of Laguna Atascosa Nat. Wildlife Refuge, reported no evidence that the species has ever nested in Texas, as of Aug. 31, 1972.

HAUNTS AND HABITS: The little Tamaulipas Mexican Crow appears to be unique on two counts: (1) It is the exact duplicate in size and color of the Sinaloa Mexican Crow, *Corvus sinaloae* Davis, yet its vocalizations are utterly different, even uncrowlike; and (2) it is the only lowland Mexican endemic bird known to have started a massive invasion of the U.S.A. during the historic period. (The Thick-billed Parrot, *Rhynchopsitta pachyrhyncha*, which flocked into Arizona during World War I, 1914–1918, has always been a high-mountain species.)

Unlike the Fish Crow, *C. ossifragus*, the Tamaulipas Mexican Crow is not normally a beachcomber. It inhabits semiarid brushland, riparian vegetation, native villages, corrals, ranches, farmland, and garbage dumps; these habitats occur throughout the low subtropical portions of Tamaulipas, and the Tamaulipas Crow accordingly abounds in this Mexican state. This crow is gregarious at all seasons, and flocks as dense as those of small blackbirds, such as Brewer's, are commonly seen perched on palm- or yucca-thatched huts, cactus or stick fences, and on the ground; in Texas, so far, the longest used perch has been amid the trash, bushes, and low mesquite trees of the Brownsville Municipal Garbage Dump.

The Tamaulipas Crow usually flies in flocks, but sometimes in odd numbers of three or one; there is seldom any indication of pairing within a group such as occurs commonly with parrots. Flight is usually low (seldom more than 50 ft. high) over the ground or brush, and wing-beats are quick and steady, ordinarily uninterrupted by glides. The White-necked Raven, the only other *Corvus* which occurs regularly in the same habitat, spends much of its life soaring above 100 feet.

The U.S. Bureau of Biological Survey, forerunner of the U.S. Fish and Wildlife Service, collected many hundreds of bird stomachs in the early years of the twentieth century with the purpose of scientifically studying the diets of numerous species. One team from the bureau, that of E. H. Nelson and E. A. Goldman, collected birds by the hundreds in Mexico, 1892–1906, but they largely ignored the stomach contents; it was felt that only the food habits of temperate North American birds would be of interest to U.S. farmers. In those days nobody dreamed that a neotropical crow would ever venture into the United States. As a consequence of the old idea that only U.S. birds are important, the diet of *Corvus imparatus* is poorly known. However, a few observations have lately been made in Cameron County, Texas. The stomachs of the two birds taken north of the border (Laguna Atascosa Nat. Wildlife Refuge, Jan. 30, 1970) were not closely examined but they contained seeds and berries (M. C. LeFever). One crow was picking meat scraps from the hide of a flattened opossum on a road at Olmito, October 25, 1968 (E. B. Kincaid, Jr.). Birds at the Brownsville dump seemed to be foraging for edible garbage and table scraps (many observers). LeFever reported 2,300 Mexican Crows apparently feeding on grasshoppers and other insects in the gunnery range portion of Laguna Atascosa in late January, 1970.

The unique voice of the Tamaulipas Crow is the only sure field mark. The call is a low-pitched, low-volumed, burry, burpy, slightly rattling, froglike note. Some interpretations are: *owwwk, buurrr, buhrrr, gurrr, durrr, carrk, boys, whow, gurick,* and *gar-lic.* At no time does it utter any noise even remotely resembling the loud, high-pitched, Brown Jay–like *pow* or *ceow* of the Sinaloa Crow or the abrupt explosive *bah!* or *car!* of the Fish Crow. Only a deaf person would be justified in merging these three crows at the species level, yet this very lumping has been performed many times in the past! Perched or in flight, *Corvus imparatus* calls almost incessantly through the year. During delivery, a stationary bird bows slightly, puffs out its chin, and flips the ends of its wings.

CHANGES: Mass invasion of the United States by a tropical bird unassisted by man's transport is a rare event. Within the historic period it has happened only once via the Texas route. (The Cattle Egret arrived by way of Florida.) Official start of the history-making *Corvus imparatus* invasion was August 2, 1968, but first the stage needs to be set for the coming of this tiny "toy" crow.

Throughout the years prior to 1960, the Tamaulipas Mexican Crow and the Brown Jay, *Psilorhinus morio,* were famous as being the first non-U.S. species that southbound bird watchers from Brownsville, Texas, were likely to see. The crow was usually sighted a few kilometers farther north since it, unlike the jay, is not especially partial to riverside trees—very sparse in this dry land. Strangely, *C. imparatus* seemed to avoid the flat part of the Rio Grande delta, which is some sixty miles wide near the coast in Mexico. It usually put in its appearance among the first tree yucca (*Yucca australis*) and ceniza (*Leucophyllum frutescens*) growing on the gravelly hills seventy miles south of the border. But on December 28, 1960, this strange anti-levelland bias was observed to be breached. On that day, three Tamaulipas Crows were heard and seen well at Moquetito, far into the delta and only thirty-five miles southwest of Brownsville (Elizabeth Henze, Maggie Schwartz, E. B. Kincaid, Jr., G. F. Oatman, Jr., J. L. Rowlett, Rose Ann Rowlett).

As the 1960's progressed, there were occasional rumors that *C. imparatus* had crossed over to *El Otro Lado* (the Other Side), as border Mexicans call the Colossus of the North. Plausible in retrospect is the story by a Volkswagen salesman in Brownsville that a flock of crows had stayed in the northwest part of town for several weeks in the fall of 1967. However, Brownsville's numerous White-necked Ravens and Great-tailed Grackles are very frequently misidentified as Mexican Crows. Verification of the species as a U.S. visitor finally came when J. C. Arvin, highly experienced birder in Texas and Mexico, found birds north of the Rio Grande on August 2, 1968.

Other milestones in the epic coming of the Mexican Crows were: First still photographs (on record) on U.S. soil—Port Isabel, Cameron County, a small group photographed in color about February, 1969, on and near his bird bath by Malcolm Riess; first listing of the species on the annual (since 1900) nationwide U.S. Audubon Christmas Bird Counts—Port Mansfield, Willacy County, three birds heard and seen at close range on December 27, 1969, by E. B. Kincaid, Jr.; first motion pictures in the United States—Port Isabel, a flock of three hundred filmed in color on January 8, 1970, by Arvin; first painting by a wildlife artist—a realistic watercolor of three birds perched on pricklypear cactus (*Opuntia*) near Port Mansfield, painted in early 1971, by Nancy McGowan with the help of habitat photos taken by James Pruitt.

The three major incursions of the Tamaulipas Mexican Crow into south Texas can be summarized as follows: (1) August 2, 1968, to November 25, 1968—several hundred birds appeared; (2) November, 1969, through January, 1970—thousands of birds flocked in; (3) October 14, 1971, to March 27, 1972—480 crows at Brownsville dump on first date had dwindled to 9 on latter date.

Causes of the range extension are obscure, but there may have been a food failure in Tamaulipas. During World War II (1939–1945), many square kilometers of land in northeastern Mexico were brought under cultivation. Cotton, sorghum, and corn furnished seeds and grasshoppers for Tamaulipas Crows. However, increasing alkalinity of the soil in the irrigated districts plus rising immunity of many insects to DDT precipitated a steep farming decline by 1968. The agriculturally inflated crow population suddenly found itself with little to eat except poison-carrying insects. This apparently triggered flocks into jumping out of the Tamaulipas frying pan into the Cameron County fire. Perhaps in addition, the birds' erratic behavior was stimulated by pesticide residues in their brains.

DETAILED ACCOUNT: NO SUBSPECIES

DESCRIPTION: (From Robert Ridgway, 1904, *Bull. U.S. Nat. Mus.,* no. 50, pt. 3, p. 275.) Somewhat like *C. ossifragus,* but decidedly smaller and plumage much more lustrous. *Adults (sexes alike):* Pileum, hindneck, wing-coverts, and secondaries lustrous dark violet; sides of neck, back, scapulars, rump, upper tail-coverts, and primary coverts lustrous dark violet blue; alula, primaries, and tail dark steel blue, the middle rectrices tinged with violet and the outermost primaries more greenish blue; sides of head and under parts lustrous dark steel blue or greenish steel blue, becoming more decidedly greenish posteriorly, the anterior portions sometimes inclining to violet. Bill, legs, and feet black; iris brown.

MEASUREMENTS: (Ibid.) *Adult male:* Length (skins), 362.0–

388.5 (average, 370.5) mm.; wing, 246.5–259.0 (250.5); tail, 146.5–158.0 (155.5); bill (exposed culmen), 40.0–42.0 (41.0); depth of bill at nostrils, 13.0–14.5 (14.0); tarsus, 38.5–42.5 (41.0); middle toe, 28.0–31.5 (30.0). *Adult female*: Length (skins), 338.0–355.5 (344.0); wing, 231.0–241.5 (236.0); tail, 143.5–158.5 (148.0); bill, 37.5–40.5 (38.5); depth of bill, 12.5–13.0 (13.0); tarsus, 38.0–41.0 (39.0); middle toe, 27.5–29.0 (28.0).

TEXAS: *Winter*: Two specimens: Cameron Co., gunnery range (Unit 7) of Laguna Atascosa Nat. Wildlife Refuge, mesquite brushland–yucca coastal prairie habitat (2 females taken from flock of 2,300, Jan. 30, 1970, G. A. Unland, M. C. LeFever; U.S. National Museum collection, nos. 532726, 532727). One bird was adult, ovary 8 × 5 mm., with light body fat; the other was first year, ovary 9 × 5, with medium body fat.

PINYON JAY, *Gymnorhinus cyanocephalus* Wied

SPECIES ACCOUNT

Also spelled Piñon Jay. Suggests a small blue crow in appearance and habits; long, spikelike bill; short tail; gregarious. *Adult*: uniformly grayish blue above, somewhat paler below; whitish throat streaked with blue. *Immature*: gray. Length, 11 in.; wingspan, 18.

RANGE: C. Oregon to c. Montana and w. South Dakota, south through interior w. United States to n. Baja California, c. Nevada, Arizona, New Mexico, and extreme n.w. Oklahoma. Wanders widely during nonbreeding season irregularly north to s. Canada, east to Great Plains, south to n. mainland Mexico (Chihuahua), and west to California coast.

TEXAS: (See map.) *Vagrant*: Highly erratic (Aug. 20 to early June); wanders in large flocks. Common to scarce in Guadalupe Mts. region; scarce and irregular wanderer in remainder of Trans-Pecos and in northern Panhandle; flocks rare to casual in southern Panhandle, on western Edwards Plateau, and in Del Rio region.

HAUNTS AND HABITS: Flocks of Pinyon Jays—appearing and behaving like tiny blue crows—range through the pinyon, juniper, scrub oak, and sagebrush foothills and low mountains of the Cascades, Sierra Nevadas, and Rockies. During fall and winter, nomadic groups scatter erratically into adjacent areas in search of food; those that wander to western Texas seek out a similar pinyon, juniper, scrub oak habitat. On the breeding territory, the birds, often in loose companies, nest low in trees, building a bulky but well-camouflaged bowl of twigs, bark, roots, and vegetable fibers. Where common, Pinyon Jays are extremely gregarious. A roving "cloud" of these nomads, with or without the Grand Canyon as a backdrop, is an impressive sight. Frequently, gray young—some tinted with lavender or ash—are mixed in with blue adults. Members of the flock keep up curious incessant mewings which resemble sounds that might issue from weird hybrids between crows and gulls.

Flight is crowlike, though swifter, and usually confined to movements from one feeding area to another. Pinyon Jays, advancing leapfrog fashion through trees and scrub or on the ground, search for their favored food—pinyon nuts—but also eat other pine seeds, wild fruits, grasshoppers, beetles, waste grain, and infrequently the eggs and young of smaller birds. On the ground the bird appears quite dignified as it walks or runs with body erect and head high.

Notes of the Pinyon include many jaylike chatterings, chuckles, and caws, but the common call is a nasal, mewing *kaa-eh, karn-eh*, uttered with a descending inflection. Territorial song seems to be absent as one would expect in this colonial species.

CHANGES: The Pinyon Jay is perhaps not absolutely dependent upon the pinyon pine (*Pinus cembroides* and closely related forms) for food, shelter, and nest sites; nevertheless, destruction of pinyons on many acres is almost certain to have some effect on this jay's population. During the 1940's, 1950's, and 1960's, there was a great deal of pinyon, juniper, and scrub oak clearing, aided by U.S. government subsidy, on ranches in the Southwest, particularly Arizona, New Mexico, and western Texas. Pinyon Jay habitat is protected inside Grand Canyon National Park, a favorite haunt of this species, but the park alone is not large enough to maintain a viable population. Pinyons do not bear nuts in the same locality every year; therefore, the jays sometimes have to wander over hundreds of square miles in search of a good crop. It would seem that thousands of square miles of pinyon country would be necessary to insure enough local nut crops to keep the Pinyon Jay flourishing. A study of the effect of range clearing, subsidized or not, should be started immediately; however, Texas would not enter heavily into the study since the few Pinyon Jays we get are obviously overflow from states to the west and northwest.

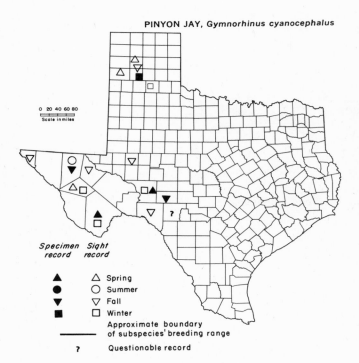

PINYON JAY, *Gymnorhinus cyanocephalus*

0 20 40 60 80
Scale in miles

Specimen Sight
record record

▲ △ Spring
● ○ Summer
▼ ▽ Fall
■ □ Winter

Approximate boundary
of subspecies' breeding range

? Questionable record

Clark's Nutcracker, *Nucifraga columbiana*

DETAILED ACCOUNT: ONE SUBSPECIES

SOUTHEASTERN PINYON JAY, *Gymnorhinus cyanocephalus cassinii* (McCall)

No races recognized by A.O.U. check-list, 1957 (see Appendix A).

DESCRIPTION: *Adult male, nuptial plumage*: Acquired by wear from winter plumage. Pileum deep slate blue; back and rump greenish blue slate; exposed surface of wings somewhat paler; inner webs of quills chaetura black, shading to chaetura drab or hair brown on inner edges, except at tips of primaries; upper tail-coverts somewhat more bluish than back; exposed surface of tail similar to back, inner edges of inner webs, except middle pair, mostly chaetura drab or fuscous; lores mixed dark gray and light gray; postocular region like pileum; malar region and auriculars paler—between tyrian blue and olympic blue; sides of neck like back; lower surface similar to back but lighter and more brightly bluish; chin and throat dull grayish white streaked with color of lower parts; middle of jugulum streaked with grayish white; anal region very pale bluish gray or grayish white; lining of wing hair brown, washed with blue of lower parts. Bill black; iris dark sepia; legs, toes, and claws black, spaces between scales of toes pale gray. *Adult female, nuptial*: Acquired by wear from winter. Like nuptial adult male but much smaller and coloration somewhat duller. *Adult male and female, winter*: Acquired by complete postnuptial molt. Like corresponding sex of nuptial adults but somewhat darker. *Male and female, second winter*: Acquired by complete postnuptial molt. Like corresponding adult in winter. *Male and female, first nuptial*: Acquired by wear from first winter, with which it is practically identical. *Male and female, first winter*: Acquired by partial postjuvenal molt, which does not involve wing-quills or tail. Similar to nuptial adults but decidedly lighter and more grayish; forehead yale blue; pileum slate blue; back brownish slate gray; rump and upper tail-coverts deep or dark gull gray; wing-quills fuscous, but inner edges of quills hair brown, exposed surface similar to back; greater and median upper wing-coverts and tertials somewhat more brownish; lower parts dark gull gray, paler posteriorly. *Juvenal*: Acquired by complete postnatal molt. Very much duller than even first nuptial or first winter male and female with little or no bluish except on wings and tail; above dark hair brown to mouse gray, almost uniform. Bill smaller and paler; paler and whitish on anal region and on chin; wings and tail even more grayish or brownish, particularly on wing-coverts; lining of wing with little or no bluish tinge.

MEASUREMENTS: *Adult male*: Wing, 146.0–160.5 (average, 152.9) mm.; tail, 103.6–117.1 (111.3); bill (exposed culmen), 33.0–37.1 (35.3); tarsus, 37.1–40.9 (38.6); middle toe without claw, 20.1–22.4 (21.1). *Adult female*: Wing, 140.5–148.1 (144.5); tail, 103.6–109.0 (106.1); bill, 29.9–36.1 (32.8); tarsus, 34.0–38.6 (37.1); middle toe, 18.0–21.1 (19.3).

RANGE: E. Nevada to extreme n.w. Oklahoma, south to c. Arizona and c. New Mexico; nonbreeders wander irregularly in Oklahoma and Texas.

TEXAS: *Vagrant*: Collected in Randall, Sutton, Crockett (not assigned to race), Brewster, and Culberson cos.

CLARK'S NUTCRACKER, *Nucifraga columbiana* (Wilson)

SPECIES ACCOUNT

Also called Clark's Crow. A crowlike bird of western mountains. Whitish face; gray head and body; large white patches in black wings and tail. Length, 12½ in.; wingspan, 22.

RANGE: C. British Columbia, south through mountains to highest parts of n. Baja California, Arizona, and New Mexico. Wanders erratically north to c. Alaska, south to Sonora, Texas, and Nuevo León (Cerro Potosí).

TEXAS: (See map.) *Vagrant*: Highly irregular (mostly fall and winter) in Panhandle and Trans-Pecos (2 summer specimens from Guadalupe Mts., see detailed account). During the fall, winter, and spring of 1972–73, an unprecedented massive visitation of this species occurred within the state, sweeping from the northern Panhandle to extreme southern Trans-Pecos. Sightings were made in the following counties: Moore, Hemphill, Potter, Randall, Wichita, Terry (as late as Apr. 30), Dawson, Midland, El Paso, Jeff Davis, and Brewster (Alpine to Terlingua); two specimens were collected in the Trans-Pecos (see detailed account). *Accidental*: Liberty Co., near Cedar Bayou (1 seen, Nov. 7, 1958, A. K. McKay, Clinton Snyder, Drew Snyder, Linda Snyder); Aransas Co., Rockport (1 present, Sept. 28–Oct. 1, 1969, Elizabeth Henze, et al.).

HAUNTS AND HABITS: The holarctic nutcrackers fill an unusual habitat niche. Unlike most other cold-country species, they are mountaineers. These birds do not inhabit flatlands—at least not for long—even if the temperature and vegetation are suitable. The present species was named by Alexander Wilson for William Clark, of the famous Lewis and Clark Expedition to the wild upper drainage of the Missouri River at the dawn of the nineteenth century.

During summer, Clark's Nutcracker seems to be most at home in cold-stunted, wind-twisted Englemann spruce, subalpine fir, limber pine, bristlecone pine, and willows of the Hudsonian Zone—so named because of its resemblance in temperature and plants to the shores of Hudson Bay (although this bay is too near sea level for Clark's Crow). At other seasons, *N. columbiana* lives mostly on the edges of lodgepole pine and quaking as-

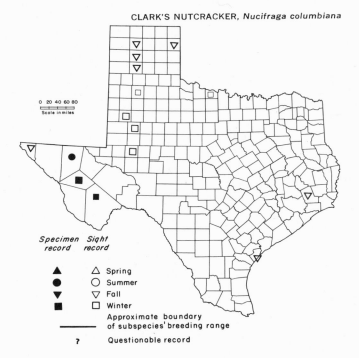

CLARK'S NUTCRACKER, *Nucifraga columbiana*

0 20 40 60 80
Scale in miles

Specimen record / Sight record

▲ / △ Spring
● / ○ Summer
▼ / ▽ Fall
■ / □ Winter

―― Approximate boundary of subspecies' breeding range

? Questionable record

pen woodlands of the Canadian Zone; a few birds, especially in winter, fly downmountain to the widely spaced ponderosa pines of the Transition Zone, or to scrubby pinyons of Upper Sonoran foothills. In extremely unusual autumns, this bird will even visit plains.

The nutcracker places its nest, like itself, usually in a conifer. The bowl of sticks and twigs—large, compact, and snug—is built to withstand the sharp cold of late winter and early spring when this species nests.

Flight of Clark's Nutcracker when passing from tree to tree is rather sweeping and undulating; however, when the bird travels from one mountain peak to another, flight is direct, moderately rapid, and performed with firm wing-beats. At times, particularly in canyons, the bird performs aerial dives with great speed. It perches freely on trees, snags, rocks, or on the ground, at which latter level it either hops like a jay or walks like a crow. Favorite foods of *N. columbiana* are seeds of various species of pine, including pinyon; juniper berries and acorns are also consumed in quantity. Grasshoppers, cicadas, crickets, beetles, ants, caterpillars and many other insects are taken, as well as some spiders, ticks, and meadow mice. It also snatches any meat scraps, fish, or garbage that campers leave unattended. Because of this habit it is often called "big camp robber." The Gray Jay, *Perisoreus canadensis*, which operates in the same manner, is dubbed simply "camp robber." In Rocky Mountain National Park, Colorado, and many other parts of the mountainous west, it is a bit disconcerting to watch these two wilderness species fly toward a hiker in the expectation of getting a handout of peanuts, popcorn, potato chips, or corn chips.

The flat caw of the Clark's Nutcracker is variously rendered as *chaarr*, *khaaa*, and *khraa*.

DETAILED ACCOUNT: NO SUBSPECIES

DESCRIPTION: *Adults, nuptial plumage*: Acquired by wear from winter plumage. Nasal tufts, anterior portion of forehead, eye-ring, cheeks, and anterior part of chin white, usually more or less soiled; rest of head, hindneck, back, and scapulars smoke gray to brownish neutral gray, head somewhat paler; rump dark mouse gray or blackish mouse gray; upper tail-coverts blackish mouse gray or chaetura black; middle tail feathers dull black with faint metallic greenish sheen; remainder of tail feathers white, except for fifth pair, which has most of inner webs and basal portion of outer webs like middle pair; wings black, exposed portions with greenish metallic sheen; secondaries broadly tipped with white; lower tail-coverts white; remainder of lower surface like upper parts but rather paler; lining of wing chaetura black, some of feathers with dull white edgings. Bill black or brownish black; iris dark brown, umber brown, or black; legs, feet, and claws black or brownish black. *Adults, winter*: Acquired by complete postnuptial molt. Like nuptial adults. *First nuptial*: Acquired by wear from first winter. Practically identical with nuptial adults. *First winter*: Acquired by complete postjuvenal molt. Practically identical with first nuptial male and female and adults in winter. *Juvenal*: Acquired by complete postnatal molt. Similar to nuptial adults, but bill smaller; upper parts rather paler and more brownish—drab to very pale drab or drab gray, palest anteriorly; upper tail-coverts fuscous; lower parts similar but somewhat paler; lesser wing-coverts fuscous; wings and dark portion of tail fuscous or fuscous black, with little metallic gloss.

MEASUREMENTS: *Adult male*: Wing, 190.5–198.7 (average, 194.6) mm.; tail, 114.0–118.6 (116.6); bill (exposed culmen), 37.6–45.5 (41.9); tarsus, 35.1–38.1 (36.6); middle toe without claw, 23.1–24.9 (23.6). *Adult female*: Wing, 187.5–192.5 (189.5); tail, 111.0–118.6 (114.0); bill, 37.1–39.6 (38.1); tarsus, 32.5–36.1 (35.1); middle toe, 20.6–24.9 (22.6).

TEXAS: *Vagrant*: Two summer specimens: Culberson Co., Guadalupe Mts., The Bowl (1 male, 1 female, June 1, 1969, G. A. Newman, original nos. 161, 162; skins in Texas A&M University collection). Two specimens collected during 1972–73 invasion: Jeff Davis Co., Ft. Davis (late Jan., 1973, J. C. Henderson; skin designated for Texas A&M collection); Brewster Co., Alpine (1 collected from flock of 7, Dec. 29, 1972, J. F. Scudday, Sul Ross State University collection).

Tits: Paridae

BLACK-CAPPED CHICKADEE, *Parus atricapillus* Linnaeus

SPECIES ACCOUNT

Song typically has two notes. Closely resembles Carolina Chickadee (see below), but noticeably (in direct comparison) larger; wings appear frosted due to white secondary edgings; posterior border of bib less sharply defined. Length, 5¼ in.; wingspan, 8; weight, ½ oz.

RANGE: C. Alaska to Newfoundland, south through Canada and n. United States to n.w. California, n. New Mexico, n. Kansas, Ohio, and n. New Jersey, and in Appalachians to e. Tennessee and w. North Carolina. Winters throughout breeding range; a few south irregularly into s. United States.

TEXAS: (See map.) *Winter*: Sept. 5 to May 19. Casual and erratic visitor to northern half. See detailed account for specimen evidence.

HAUNTS AND HABITS: The Black-capped Chickadee is the most widespread American representative of the tits, Paridae. This family is usually considered to have sixty-four members—fourteen species in the New World, and fifty in the Old. Like most European tits, the Blackcap prefers colder climates than Texas'. In its northern home, its usual nest site is a natural cavity in a decaying tree or stump, which the birds further excavate, then line with bark strips, moss, fur, and fine hair. This bird seeks woodlands, occasionally venturing onto a prairie, if scattered trees and thickets are present. Particularly in fall the species moves into gardens and ornamental shrubbery of parks and houses in towns and cities. Small, loose companies of Blackcaps gather in winter—although this is not to be expected in Texas due to the bird's extreme rarity here. These bands, often joining other small woodland birds, rove woods and thickets in search of insects, their larvae and eggs, spiders, also a few seeds and berries.

Flight is quick, light, and fluttering, usually from bush to bush or tree to tree, and accompanied often with flirts of tail and wings. When foraging, the Blackcap performs its characteristic chickadee acrobatics mostly in lower parts of the forest, in thickets and bushes, but frequently it moves to the very tops of trees or descends to the ground. Notably unshy, the bird is ordinarily easy to approach and observe.

A common note of the Blackcap is a *chicka-dee-dee*, the *chicka*'s and *dee*'s often varying in number; an abbreviated version is simply *dee-dee-dee*. The typical two-note song is a sharp, clear whistled *fee-bee*, which is sometimes misidentified as that of the Eastern Phoebe, although the latter bird's notes are more emphatic.

DETAILED ACCOUNT: ONE SUBSPECIES

LONG-TAILED BLACK-CAPPED CHICKADEE, *Parus atricapillus septentrionalis* Harris

DESCRIPTION: *Adults, nuptial plumage*: Acquired by wear from winter plumage. Pileum black; rest of upper parts between mouse gray and light grayish olive; rump tinged with pale buff; anterior portion next to hindneck paler, sometimes whitish; wings hair brown, greater wing-coverts, tertials, and inner secondaries broadly margined with dull white, remainder of wing-quills and upper wing-coverts edged with color of back or with dull white; tail dark mouse gray, outer margins of feathers pale grayish white, these on outermost feathers broad and conspicuous; sides of head and of neck white, sometimes slightly washed with buff; chin and throat black, feathers of posterior part of throat with whitish edgings; rest of lower parts dull

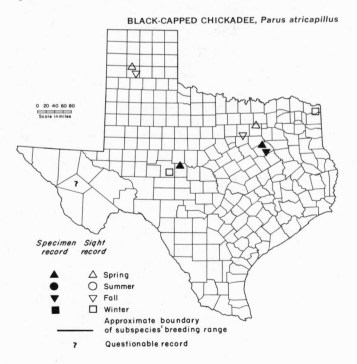

BLACK-CAPPED CHICKADEE, *Parus atricapillus*

0 20 40 60 80
Scale in miles

Specimen   Sight
record   record

▲   △   Spring
●   ○   Summer
▼   ▽   Fall
■   □   Winter

—————— Approximate boundary of subspecies' breeding range

?   Questionable record

white, but sides, flanks, and crissum cartridge buff or pale pinkish buff; lining of wing white washed with buff. Bill black, brownish black, or slate black; tongue white but gray at tip; iris dark brown or black; legs and feet slate color, slate black, plumbeous, or brownish slate. *Adults, winter*: Acquired by complete postnuptial molt. Similar to nuptial adults, but gray of upper parts more buffy—mouse gray strongly washed with cinnamon buff; white edgings of wings and tail broader; sides, flanks, and crissum more deeply colored—dull cinnamon buff or pinkish buff. *First nuptial*: Acquired by wear from first winter. Similar to nuptial adults. *First winter*: Acquired by partial postjuvenal molt. Similar to adults in winter. *Juvenal*: Acquired by complete postnatal molt. Similar to nuptial adults, but pileum duller and more brownish; remainder of upper surface of much darker gray, duller and more brownish; black of throat duller and more brownish. Bill slate black, but slightly paler at base of mandible; iris dark brown; legs and feet slate color or plumbeous; claws brownish black.

MEASUREMENTS: *Adult male*: Wing, 65.5–72.9 (average, 69.8) mm.; tail, 63.5–71.1 (67.8); bill (exposed culmen), 8.9–10.9 (9.7); tarsus, 16.5–18.5 (17.3); middle toe without claw, 9.4–11.4 (10.4). *Adult female*: Wing, 63.5–68.6 (66.5); tail, 61.0–67.1 (64.3); bill, 8.6–9.9 (9.4); tarsus, 15.0–18.0 (16.8); middle toe, 8.6–10.9 (9.7).

RANGE: E. Idaho to n. North Dakota, south to n.w. New Mexico and w. Missouri; casual in winter into Texas.

TEXAS: *Winter*: Four specimens: Concho Co. (Apr. 17, 1883, W. Lloyd); Navarro Co., Rice (Mar., 1880, and Sept. 23, 28, 1880, J. D. Ogilby).

CAROLINA CHICKADEE, *Parus carolinensis* Audubon

SPECIES ACCOUNT

Song typically has four or six notes. A very small, plump, short-billed bird; tame, acrobatic. Gray above with black cap and bib, white cheeks; white below with buffy wash on flanks. Length, 4¾ in.; wingspan, 7½; weight, ¼ oz.

RANGE: S.e. Kansas to c. New Jersey, south to c. Texas, U.S. Gulf coast, and c. Florida.

TEXAS: (See map.) *Resident*: Breeds, mid-Feb. to late June (eggs, Mar. 2 to June 4) from near sea level to 2,800 ft. Common to fairly common through most of eastern half south to vicinity of 29th parallel, and in northeastern Panhandle; uncommon and local on central Edwards Plateau; scarce and irregular along central coast (breeding locally) south to Welder Wildlife Refuge near Sinton; rare winter visitor to Corpus Christi.

HAUNTS AND HABITS: The Blackcap's southern lookalike is the Carolina Chickadee. Swamps on coastal plains of the southeastern United States comprise typical but by no means the only habitat for the present species. In Texas, on the western fringe of its range, it inhabits less damp woodlands as well. Live oaks (*Quercus virginiana*), other oaks, elms, and junipers seem to be especially attractive. The Carolina frequents woodlands, edges of clearings, and brush along streams. It often visits cultivated areas and comes freely to dwellings in country and town, particularly if feeder and suet are present. In fall and winter, nonbreeders gather into small bands. These groups also frequently join forces with the Tufted Titmouse,

Brown-headed and White-breasted nuthatches, and other small woodland birds. On the Edwards Plateau it often forages near the Black-crested Titmouse.

Flight is quick and flitting, usually from bush to bush or tree to tree. Only rarely does the Carolina descend to the ground. In thickets and trees where it gleans insects, their larvae and eggs, seeds, and a few berries, it works rapidly and in a variety of positions, being particularly active on terminal foliage.

Carolina vocalizations are quite similar to the Blackcap's. Common notes are a higher, more rapid *chicka-dee-dee-dee* or a shortened *dee-dee-dee*. Its ordinary song, rather weaker but more mellow than that of the Blackcap, is a four-note whistle: *fee-bee, fee-bay*; sometimes the latter two notes are repeated. Song period usually begins in January, if the weather is mild, and continues into June.

DETAILED ACCOUNT: THREE SUBSPECIES

LOUISIANA CAROLINA CHICKADEE, *Parus carolinensis guilloti* (Oberholser)

Race not in A.O.U. check-list, 1957 (see Appendix A).

DESCRIPTION: *Adults, nuptial plumage*: Acquired by wear from winter plumage. Pileum and hindneck dull black; remainder of upper parts gray, between deep olive and mouse gray, rump somewhat paler and sometimes slightly buffy; wings and tail dark hair brown, margined on outer webs with color of back, this becoming whitish on exterior margins of tertials and inner secondaries; sides of head and neck dull white; chin and throat black, posterior edge sharply defined against white of remaining lower surface; sides, flanks, and crissum washed with light buff; lining of wing white. Bill black or bluish black; iris dark brown; legs and feet bluish gray or black. *Adults, winter*: Acquired by complete postnuptial molt. Similar to nuptial adults, but gray of upper surface more tinged with buff; sides, flanks, and crissum more deeply buff. *First nuptial*: Acquired by wear from first winter. Similar to nuptial adults. *First winter*:

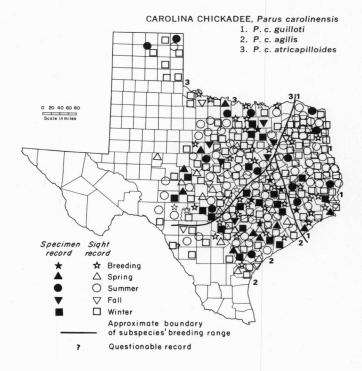

CAROLINA CHICKADEE, *Parus carolinensis*
1. *P. c. guilloti*
2. *P. c. agilis*
3. *P. c. atricapilloides*

0 20 40 60 80
Scale in miles

Specimen record / Sight record

★ / ☆ Breeding
▲ / △ Spring
● / ○ Summer
▼ / ▽ Fall
■ / □ Winter

—— Approximate boundary of subspecies' breeding range

? Questionable record

Acquired by partial postjuvenal molt. Very much like adults in winter. *Juvenal*: Acquired by complete postnatal molt. Similar to nuptial adults, but black of pileum and throat duller and more brownish; gray of back darker, duller, and more brownish —between hair brown and dark grayish olive. *Natal*: Light drab. Bill and feet dull pinkish buff.

MEASUREMENTS: *Adult male*: Wing, 56.9–61.0 (average, 58.9) mm.; tail, 48.0–54.3 (50.5); bill (exposed culmen), 6.9–7.6 (7.1); tarsus, 16.0–16.5 (16.3); middle toe without claw, 9.4–10.9 (9.9). *Adult female*: Wing, 53.1–58.9 (56.4); tail, 46.5–52.1 (48.5); bill, 6.6–7.6 (7.4); tarsus, 15.0–16.5 (15.5); middle toe, 8.9–9.9 (9.7).

RANGE: E. Oklahoma to s.w. Kentucky, south to s.e. Texas and c. Alabama.

TEXAS: *Resident*: Altitudinal breeding range, near sea level to 550 ft. Collected north to Bowie, south to Jefferson and Galveston, west to Harris cos. Fairly common. Taken in winter outside breeding range in Collin (1 specimen, Sept. 3), Dallas (1), and Matagorda (1) cos.

NESTING: Similar to that of *P. c. agilis* (see below).

PLUMBEOUS CAROLINA CHICKADEE, *Parus carolinensis agilis* Sennett

DESCRIPTION: *Adults, nuptial plumage*: Similar to *P. c. guilloti* but larger; much paler on upper surface.

MEASUREMENTS: *Adult male*: Wing, 59.9–64.3 (average, 62.5) mm.; tail, 52.6–58.4 (54.6); bill (exposed culmen), 7.6–8.9 (8.1); tarsus, 16.0–17.5 (16.5); middle toe without claw, 9.4–10.9 (9.9). *Adult female*: Wing, 57.4–61.0 (59.9); tail, 48.0–55.1 (51.3); bill, 7.6–8.6 (8.1); tarsus, 15.0–17.0 (16.0); middle toe, 8.9–9.9 (9.7).

RANGE: C. Texas.

TEXAS: *Resident*: Altitudinal breeding range, near sea level to 1,130 ft. Collected north to Brazos, south to Wharton and Refugio, west to Bexar cos. Fairly common. Two specimens outside breeding range: Trinity Co., Trinity (Dec. 15, 16, 1936, P. D. Goodrum).

NESTING: *Nest*: On uplands and bottomlands; slopes, or level country, in more or less open woodlands or cultivated areas, such as orchards and ornamental grounds; in hole in tree, stub, stump—usually decayed and further excavated by the bird, or in natural cavity, old woodpecker hole, Purple Martin or other bird box, 2–15 ft. above ground; nest chamber floored with grasses, moss, fur; lined with fine grasses, feathers, also rabbit or other fur. *Eggs*: 3–8, usually 6; rounded oval; white, dotted with cinnamon rufous and dark reddish brown; average size, 15.5 × 11.9 mm.

NORTHWESTERN CAROLINA CHICKADEE, *Parus carolinensis atricapilloides* Lunk

DESCRIPTION: Similar to *P. c. agilis* but larger; buff of sides and flanks somewhat darker; light outer margins of wing-quills more evident.

MEASUREMENTS: *Adult male*: Wing, 62.0–69.0 (average, 65.2) mm.; tail, 54.0–63.0 (57.9); bill (exposed culmen), 8.5–9.5 (9.0); tarsus, 15.5–16.5 (16.0); middle toe without claw, 9.5–10.5 (10.0). *Adult female*: Wing, 59.0–66.0 (62.8); tail, 51.0–62.0 (56.9); bill, (8.5); tarsus, (14.0); middle toe, (9.0);

RANGE: S.e. Kansas, south to n.e. 'and n. Texas.

TEXAS: *Resident*: Altitudinal breeding range, 380 to 2,800 ft. Collected north to Lipscomb, east to Cooke and Navarro, south to Kendall, west to Sutton cos. Fairly common.

NESTING: Similar to that of *P. c. agilis*.

MOUNTAIN CHICKADEE, *Parus gambeli* Ridgway

SPECIES ACCOUNT

Resembles Blackcap, but has prominent white stripe over each eye; gray, rather than buffy flanks; lacks white edgings on wing feathers. Length, 5¼ in.; wingspan, 8¼; weight, ¼ oz.

RANGE: N.w. British Columbia to s.w. Alberta, south through Coast Ranges, Sierra Nevadas, and Rockies to n. Baja California, s.e. Arizona (except Chiricahua Mts., which are occupied by Mexican Chickadee), s. New Mexico (excluding San Luis and Animas mts., also occupied by Mexican Chickadee), and n. Trans-Pecos Texas. Winters at lower altitudes.

TEXAS: (See map.) *Breeding*: Probably late Apr. to late July (no egg dates available, but adults with fledglings located by F. R. Gehlbach) from about 7,000 to 8,500 ft. Fairly common in Guadalupe Mts.; scarce and irregular in Davis Mts. (occasional nesting suspected). *Winter*: Sept. 2 to Apr. 14. Common (some years) to fairly common in Guadalupe Mts.; uncommon to scarce and highly erratic in western Panhandle, El Paso region, and Davis Mts.

HAUNTS AND HABITS: The Mountain Chickadee prefers healthy, instead of desiccated, coniferous mountain forests; thus, in Trans-Pecos Texas it breeds almost exclusively in the Guadalupes. In winter, however, the bird drops to lower altitudes where it meets other small woodland species in streamside willows and cottonwoods.

Its flight and mannerisms are typical of the acrobatic parids. Ordinarily, the Mountain forages for insects and their larvae and eggs on lower parts of trees, even in bushes, but at times it works tops of tall trees and infrequently descends to the ground, here feeding on a few seeds and wild fruit. Active and industrious, the bird hunts in all kinds of positions, even upside down, on branches and about foliage. Sometimes it takes a

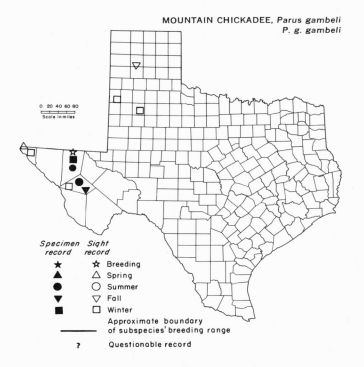

MOUNTAIN CHICKADEE, *Parus gambeli*
P. g. *gambeli*

0 20 40 60 80
Scale in miles

Specimen record	Sight record	
★	☆	Breeding
▲	△	Spring
●	○	Summer
▼	▽	Fall
■	□	Winter
	———	Approximate boundary of subspecies' breeding range
?		Questionable record

seed to a limb and hammers it open much as would a jay or nuthatch.

The common call of the Mountain Chickadee, huskier than the Blackcap's, sounds very much like *chuck-a-zee-zee-zee*. Its whistling song is a three-note *fee-bee-bee* or *fee-bee-bay*, often uttered in a strongly descending scale. Song in the Guadalupe Mountains usually extends from March into July.

CHANGES: In common with many other birds which nest in cool forests, the Mountain Chickadee retreated northward during the first half of the twentieth century with increasing warmth and aridity of the climate. In the Davis Mountains, H. C. Oberholser collected specimens on July 10, and 12, 1901; he considered the species abundant above 7,000 feet in these mountains from July 10 to 15, 1901. By September 2 to October 16, 1916, the collector A. P. Smith termed the status of this bird in the Davis range, "rather common resident in the pine areas." Between the late 1920's and 1970, E. B. Kincaid, Jr., observed birds in the Davis Mountains many times without seeing even one Mountain Chickadee.

DETAILED ACCOUNT: ONE SUBSPECIES

GAMBEL'S MOUNTAIN CHICKADEE, *Parus gambeli gambeli* Ridgway

DESCRIPTION: *Adults, nuptial plumage*: Acquired by wear from winter plumage. Forehead and superciliary stripe white; crown and hindneck black; upper parts deep grayish olive or mouse gray; wings and tail hair brown edged with color of back; cheeks and sides of head and neck dull white washed with brown or buff posteriorly; chin, throat, and jugulum black; remainder of lower surface dull white; sides, flanks, and lower tail-coverts smoke gray or between smoke gray and light drab; lining of wing dull white. Bill black or dark plumbeous; iris dark claret brown, fuscous black, or burnt sienna; legs and feet dark plumbeous, plumbeous, slate black, or blackish slate. *Adults, winter*: Acquired by complete postnuptial molt. Similar to nuptial adults, but upper parts more brownish—between light grayish olive and hair brown; sides and flanks more buffy; white of forehead and superciliary stripe more extensive. *First nuptial*: Acquired by wear from first winter. Practically identical with nuptial adults. *First winter*: Acquired by partial postjuvenal molt. Similar to adults in winter. *Juvenal*: Acquired by complete postnatal molt. Similar to nuptial adults, but bill shorter, top of head and hindneck duller, more brownish; white superciliary stripe less distinct; edgings of greater wing-coverts and tertials somewhat buffy; mantle duller and darker. *Natal*: Grayish white, very pale smoke gray, or between smoke gray and drab gray.

MEASUREMENTS: *Adult male*: Wing, 68.6–72.4 (average, 70.4) mm.; tail, 59.4–65.5 (62.2); bill (exposed culmen), 9.4–11.4 (10.2); tarsus, 16.5–20.1 (18.3); middle toe without claw, 8.9–10.2 (9.7). *Adult female*: Wing, 65.5–71.9 (68.6); tail, 58.4–64.0 (60.2); bill, 8.6–10.9 (9.9); tarsus, 17.5–20.1 (18.3); middle toe, 8.9–10.4 (9.7).

RANGE: W. Idaho and c. Montana, south to s.e. Arizona and Trans-Pecos Texas.

TEXAS: *Breeding*: Collected in Culberson Co.; also in summer in Jeff Davis Co. *Winter*: One specimen: Culberson Co., The Bowl (Jan. 1, 1939, T. D. Burleigh).

NESTING: *Nest*: On mountains or mesas, in canyons and more open country, cultivated areas, vicinity of dwellings; in hole of tree—aspen, pine, or similar species—2–20 ft. above ground, nesting cavity excavated by the bird or adapted from natural cavity, abandoned woodpecker hole, or bird box; nest materials placed in bottom of cavity, consisting of grasses, roots, cattle or wild animal hair, and sometimes moss; lined with fine grasses, rabbit or other fur, and feathers. *Eggs*: 5–9, usually 7; elliptical ovate; pure white, faintly marked with reddish brown; average size, 16.0 × 12.2 mm.

TUFTED TITMOUSE, *Baeolophus bicolor* (Linnaeus)

SPECIES ACCOUNT

Parus bicolor of A.O.U. check-list, 1957 (see Appendix A). A gray tit with a slender crest. Gray above (including crest) with black spot on forehead just above bill; whitish below with rusty orange wash on flanks. Length, 6¼ in.; wingspan, 9½.

RANGE: S.e. Nebraska to s. Ontario and s. New England, south to e. Texas, Gulf coast, and c. Florida. Hybridizes along southwestern limits with Blackcrest.

TEXAS: (See map.) *Resident*: Breeds, late Feb. to late June (eggs, Mar. 3 to May 26; young in nest to June 26) from near sea level to about 750 ft., formerly higher. Common to fairly common throughout eastern third, west to Gainesville, Fort Worth, Waco, Bastrop, and Refugio; uncommon west along Red River to Clay Co.—formerly to Wilbarger Co., and locally along eastern border of northern Panhandle; highly irregular winter visitor west to Coleman and San Patricio cos., where rare. Formerly west to San Angelo and San Antonio, and south to Corpus Christi.

HAUNTS AND HABITS: Bold and lively, the Tufted Titmouse is, by a slight margin, the largest of New World Paridae. In east Texas, it is conspicuous in oak groves and other woodlands, about edges of prairies, forest margins, their clearings and deadenings, and in open,

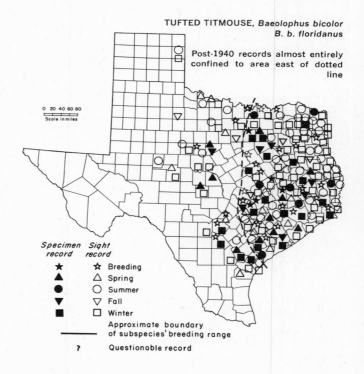

TUFTED TITMOUSE, *Baeolophus bicolor*
B. b. floridanus

Post-1940 records almost entirely confined to area east of dotted line

0 20 40 60 80
Scale in miles

Specimen record	Sight record	
★	☆	Breeding
▲	△	Spring
●	○	Summer
▼	▽	Fall
■	□	Winter
	———	Approximate boundary of subspecies' breeding range
	?	Questionable record

brushy, or sparsely wooded pastures as well as stream-side thickets and timber. Especially in fall and winter, it visits cultivated areas, shrubbery and trees about country dwellings, even shade trees and feeding stations of houses in towns and cities. It is found usually singly or in pairs, although during the nonbreeding season, small companies gather, often joining Downy Woodpeckers, Carolina Chickadees, Brown Creepers, and kinglets.

Flight of the Tufted, ordinarily from bush to bush or tree to tree, is bounding, quick, irregular, and accompanied often by spreading of the tail. It ranges through the woods and frequently descends to the ground as it hunts insects, especially caterpillars and wasps, their larvae and eggs, also seeds and wild fruit. The Tufted flits restlessly about trees and bushes, clinging at times chickadeelike to terminal ends of branches. Very inquisitive and unshy, the bird is readily attracted by a bird watcher's squeaks and imitations of its whistle. Particularly aggressive during the breeding season, it fiercely guards its territory, and when nest building often collects fur and hair from live animals, not excluding any human beings who might be present. At night or during storms, the bird roosts in unoccupied woodpecker holes and cavities in trees.

Often heard before seen, the noisy Tufted Titmouse has a repertoire of notes, one being a harsh *day* several times repeated; another, *tsee-eep*. Its common song is well represented by the syllables *peter, peter, peter*. This bird has a long singing season which usually extends from December into August.

CHANGES: The Tufted Titmouse has been retreating eastward during the first half of the twentieth century. In the late 1800's and early 1900's, it occurred, and was probably resident, west to San Angelo, San Antonio, and Corpus Christi. By 1940, it lived almost entirely east of a line beginning on the Red River near Gainesville and continuing southward to Fort Worth, Waco, Bastrop, Goliad, Refugio, Victoria, and Port Lavaca. The species' eastward trek has coincided with thinning of woodlands by drought and by man; during this period the Black-crested Titmouse, better adapted to arid conditions, has been invading the Tufted's original range from the southwest.

DETAILED ACCOUNT: ONE SUBSPECIES

FLORIDA TUFTED TITMOUSE, *Baeolophus bicolor floridanus* (Bangs)

No races recognized by A.O.U. check-list, 1957 (see Appendix A).

DESCRIPTION: *Adults, nuptial plumage*: Acquired by wear from winter plumage. Forehead black or brownish black, margined narrowly posteriorly with clove brown; remainder of upper surface dark neutral gray, slightly paler posteriorly; wings chaetura drab, wing-coverts and edgings of quills like back; tail dark mouse gray, edged with color of back; lores grayish white; sides of head and of neck anteriorly dull grayish white; posteriorly very pale buffy gray; lower parts grayish or buffy white, including lining of wing; sides and flanks orange cinnamon or

cinnamon rufous. Bill slate color, slate black, or black, base of mandible plumbeous or french gray; iris chocolate, hazel, or black; legs and feet plumbeous. *Adults, winter*: Acquired by complete postnuptial molt. Similar to nuptial adults, but gray of upper surface somewhat lighter, back usually washed with olive brown. *First nuptial*: Acquired by wear from first winter. Very similar to nuptial adults. *First winter*: Acquired by partial post-juvenal molt. Practically identical with adults in winter. *Juvenal*: Acquired by complete postnatal molt. Similar to nuptial adults but darker, more brownish above—hair brown to brownish neutral gray; black of forehead absent or of less extent and duller, more brownish—fuscous or fuscous black; lower parts anteriorly more grayish or more buffy; sides of paler cinnamon orange or pinkish cinnamon. Bill brownish black, paler below, maxilla slate or slate gray, mandible plumbeous; iris dark brown; legs and feet plumbeous. *Natal*: Drab gray; legs and feet dull pinkish buff.

MEASUREMENTS: *Adult male*: Wing, 77.0–81.0 (average, 79.2) mm.; tail, 68.1–73.4 (70.4); bill (exposed culmen), 9.9–11.9 (11.2); tarsus, 20.6–22.1 (21.4); middle toe without claw, 12.4–14.0 (13.2). *Adult female*: Wing, 71.1–77.0 (74.4); tail, 62.5–68.6 (65.3); bill, 10.9–11.9 (11.7); tarsus, 19.6–22.1 (20.3); middle toe, 11.9–13.5 (12.7).

RANGE: N. Texas to Georgia, south to c. Texas and c. Florida.

TEXAS: *Resident*: Collected north to Cooke, east to Bowie and Jefferson, south to Refugio, west to McLennan; prior to 1940, west to Eastland, Bexar, and Atascosa cos.

NESTING: *Nest*: In swamps or uplands, woodlands and margins of forests or cultivated areas; natural cavity in living tree, or dead tree or stub, old excavation of woodpecker, or bird box, ordinarily 2–30 ft. above ground, sometimes as high as 110 ft.; nest chamber floored with grass, leaves, moss, bark, various soft vegetable substances, wool, fur, bits of cornstalks, hair of cattle and other mammals, and feathers; lined with bark fibers, leaves, cattle hair, fur, fine cottonlike vegetable substances. *Eggs*: 4–8, usually 6; ovate; white, cream white, or buff; much dotted with reddish brown, with some lavender shell markings, most numerous at larger end, where often confluent; average size, 18.5 × 13.7 mm.

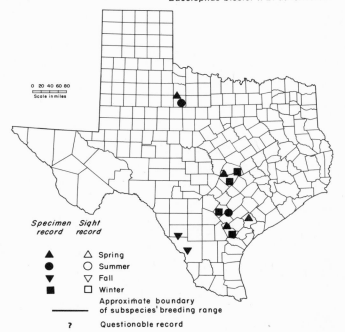

TUFTED TITMOUSE x BLACK-CRESTED TITMOUSE
Baeolophus bicolor x B. atricristatus

0 20 40 60 80
Scale in miles

Specimen   Sight
record   record

▲ △ Spring
● ○ Summer
▼ ▽ Fall
■ □ Winter

——— Approximate boundary of subspecies' breeding range

?   Questionable record

BLACK-CRESTED TITMOUSE, *Baeolophus atricristatus* (Cassin)

SPECIES ACCOUNT

Parus atricristatus of A.O.U. check-list, 1957 (see Appendix A). Resembles Tufted, with which it interbreeds, but has whitish forehead (usually), black or blackish crest; some individuals occurring in and near zone of range overlap (roughly between 97th and 98th meridians) have brownish foreheads. Most hybrids have rich brown foreheads, dark gray crests. Length, 6 in.; wingspan, 9¼; weight, ¾ oz.

RANGE: Extreme s.w. Oklahoma, w. Texas, and n.e. Mexico. Hybridizes along northeastern limits with Tufted.

TEXAS: (See map.) *Resident*: Breeds mid-Feb. to late June (eggs, Feb. 24 to June 11) from near sea level to 7,000 ft., perhaps higher. Common to fairly common in central and southern Trans-Pecos, on Edwards Plateau and its hilly outcroppings, and in south Texas brush country; uncommon and local north of Plateau (chiefly avoiding middle and southern Panhandle) to canyons of northern Panhandle, where again fairly common; increasingly rare and irregular east of 97th meridian to Tarrant, Ellis, Limestone, Grimes, and Lavaca cos. One sighting in Harris Co.: Houston, Hermann Park (Jan. 25, 1931, Roy Bedichek).

HAUNTS AND HABITS: The Black-crested Titmouse inhabits timber and mesquite along streams as well as *Sabal* palms, live oak mottes of semiopen country, and juniper-oak ravines, gullies, and canyons among hills. The bird also comes about dwellings in country and city, particularly if oak trees or tall shrubbery are present. During the breeding season it moves singly and in pairs, but in winter it occurs in small companies, roaming often with other small tree-dwelling birds.

Like the Tufted, it is quick and jerky as it flits amid brush and trees; when moving farther, it is still erratic, although flight is stronger, faster, and sometimes high in the air. Active and inquisitive, the Blackcrest works from the very tops of trees to brush, sometimes even on the ground, in search of insects, a few nuts, and occasionally wild fruit and berries. While foraging, the bird hammers and pecks on the bark to dislodge prey; sometimes it will brace a pecan on a branch and crack it open much like a woodpecker.

The Blackcrest's raspy *eck-eck* is one of a variety of notes, many of which are similar to the Tufted's. The usual song, an abbreviation of that of its eastern relative, is a loud, clear *pete, pete, pete, pete*. Also given is a *peter, peter, peter, peter*; these *peter*'s are almost identical with those of the Tufted, but are usually a bit louder. Its song is heard chiefly from January to June.

CHANGES: The Black-crested Titmouse, adapted to widely spaced trees and brush of hot semiarid northeastern Mexico and southwestern Texas, has encroached upon the humid woodland range of the Tufted Titmouse. Between 1886 and 1940, during a period of warming and drying climate and extensive thinning of woodlands by man, the present species occupied all of the Edwards Plateau and the south Texas brush country; prior to this the Tufted had lived in the eastern portions of these two major natural regions. About 1940, the Blackcrest appeared to halt its advance, although climate continued to warm and desiccate until at least 1957. From 1950 into the 1970's, man's bulldozers have continued to break up woodlands at an accelerating rate, yet the line of contact and interbreeding between the two tits has remained about the same, at least in central Texas, according to the observations of E. B. Kincaid, Jr., and others. This status is in marked contrast to that of two grackles: Man's clearing and "civilizing" activities have resulted in still-continuing (as of early 1970's), large distribution gains by the Great-tailed Grackle at the expense of the Bronzed Common Grackle.

Readers interested in details of the history, status, and hybridization of the Blackcrest and Tufted may consult Keith L. Dixon's well-researched *An Ecological Analysis of the Interbreeding of the Crested Titmice in Texas* (1955, University of California Publications in Zoology, vol. 54, no. 3, pp. 125–206).

DETAILED ACCOUNT: FOUR SUBSPECIES

RIO GRANDE BLACK-CRESTED TITMOUSE, *Baeolophus atricristatus atricristatus* (Cassin)

DESCRIPTION: *Adult male, nuptial plumage*: Acquired by wear from winter plumage. Forehead and lores dull white, often tinged with buff; crown, including crest, dull black, sometimes brownish; remainder of upper surface between deep grayish olive and neutral gray, but rump somewhat paler and often slightly tinged with buff; wings fuscous or dark hair brown, upper wing-coverts and outer margins of primaries gray like back; tail between deep mouse gray and hair brown, narrowly edged, particularly on middle feathers, with color of back; malar region white, grayish white, or buffy white, gradually passing

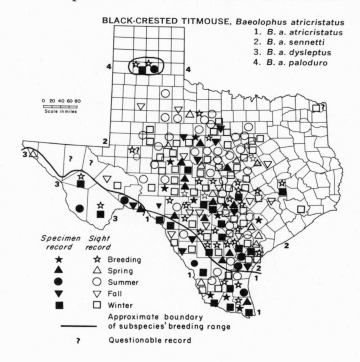

BLACK-CRESTED TITMOUSE, *Baeolophus atricristatus*

1. *B. a. atricristatus*
2. *B. a. sennetti*
3. *B. a. dysleptus*
4. *B. a. paloduro*

0 20 40 60 80
Scale in miles

Specimen record | Sight record
★ | ☆ Breeding
▲ | △ Spring
● | ○ Summer
▼ | ▽ Fall
■ | □ Winter

—— Approximate boundary of subspecies' breeding range

? Questionable record

into pale grayish buff on sides of head and to deep grayish olive on sides of neck; lower parts dull grayish white or buffy white, but sides and flanks cinnamon to cinnamon rufous, crissum and lining of wing tinged with same color. Bill blackish plumbeous; iris dark brown; legs and feet plumbeous. *Adult female, nuptial*: Acquired by wear from winter. Similar to nuptial adult male but smaller; black of pileum averaging slightly more brownish—fuscous black to dull slightly brownish black. *Adult male and female, winter*: Acquired by complete postnuptial molt. Similar to corresponding sex of nuptial adults, but upper parts lighter, more olivaceous (less purely gray)—between grayish olive and neutral gray. *Male and female, first nuptial*: Acquired by wear from first winter. Similar to corresponding sex of nuptial adults, but pileum duller, more brownish; black areas often less extensive; wings, tail, and other upper parts averaging more brownish (less clearly gray). *Male and female, first winter*: Acquired by partial postjuvenal molt, which does not involve wing-quills or tail. Similar to corresponding sex of first nuptial but duller, more brownish; black of pileum veiled and tipped with dull gray; feathers of upper parts tipped with dull brown. *Juvenal*: Acquired by complete postnatal molt. Similar to nuptial adult female but duller and more brownish; crest and forehead light chaetura drab; upper parts lighter, more olive brown than adult—between grayish olive or deep grayish olive and mouse gray; back sometimes more brownish; lower parts duller and more grayish or buffy; sides of paler dull cinnamon buff. *Natal*: Drab gray.

MEASUREMENTS: *Adult male*: Wing, 67.6–73.9 (average, 71.4) mm.; tail, 56.4–66.0 (61.5); bill (exposed culmen), 8.9–10.4 (9.1); tarsus, 18.0–20.6 (19.8); middle toe without claw, 11.4–13.0 (12.2). *Adult female*: Wing, 65.5–71.7 (69.1); tail, 55.6–63.5 (59.7); bill, 8.9–9.9 (9.1); tarsus, 18.0–19.6 (18.8); middle toe, 11.4–13.0 (11.7).

RANGE: S. Texas, south to San Luis Potosí and c. Veracruz.

TEXAS: *Resident*: Altitudinal breeding range, near sea level to 1,000 ft. Collected northwest to Val Verde, southeast to Kenedy and Cameron, west to Webb cos. Fairly common.

NESTING: *Nest*: On uplands or lowlands, in woodlands or more open country, as well as vicinity of habitations; natural cavity in tree, deserted woodpecker hole, usually 4–12 ft. above ground; nest chamber filled with grasses, inner bark of trees, moss, wool, feathers, and usually pieces of snake skin. *Eggs*: 5–7, usually 6; rounded ovate; pure white, sparingly dotted or spotted with reddish or purplish brown and fawn color; average size, 17.0 × 13.7 mm.

SENNETT'S BLACK-CRESTED TITMOUSE, *Baeolophus atricristatus sennetti* Ridgway

DESCRIPTION: *Adult male and female, nuptial plumage*: Similar to *B. a. atricristatus* but larger; upper parts paler and rather more clearly gray (less brownish), particularly in winter; in female, black crest more frequently and extensively tipped with gray.

MEASUREMENTS: *Adult male*: Wing, 74.9–79.5 (average, 77.2) mm.; tail, 64.5–68.6 (66.8); bill (exposed culmen), 9.9–11.4 (10.7); tarsus, 19.6–21.1 (20.6); middle toe without claw, 12.4–14.0 (13.2). *Adult female*: Wing, 70.1–75.9 (72.7); tail, 61.0–69.1 (64.5); bill, 9.4–10.9 (10.2); tarsus, 18.5–20.1 (19.6); middle toe, 11.9–13.0 (12.4).

RANGE: Extreme s.w. Oklahoma, south to c. Texas.

TEXAS: *Resident*: Altitudinal breeding range, near sea level to 2,800 ft. Collected north to Palo Pinto, east to Grimes, south to Aransas and Duval, west to Val Verde cos. Common.

NESTING: Similar to that of *B. a. atricristatus*, but eggs occasionally, though rarely, number as many as 12.

PECOS BLACK-CRESTED TITMOUSE, *Baeolophus atricristatus dysleptus* (Van Tyne)

DESCRIPTION: *Adult male and female, nuptial plumage*: Similar to *B. a. atricristatus* but decidedly larger. Resembling *B. a. sennetti*, but wing, and especially middle toe, shorter; darker and more grayish on upper surface.

MEASUREMENTS: *Adult male*: Wing, 72.7–78.5 (average, 75.2) mm.; tail, 63.0–69.1 (66.3); bill (exposed culmen), 9.4–11.4 (10.7); tarsus, 19.6–21.9 (20.9); middle toe without claw, 9.9–13.0 (11.7). *Adult female*: Wing, 66.0–73.9 (71.7); tail, 58.4–64.0 (62.2); bill, 9.7–11.4 (10.7); tarsus, 18.5–21.1 (19.8); middle toe, 10.9–12.4 (11.7).

RANGE: N. Chihuahua and c. and s. Trans-Pecos Texas, south to c. Coahuila.

TEXAS: *Resident*: Altitudinal breeding range, 1,000 to 7,000 ft. Collected in Jeff Davis, Presidio, Brewster, Terrell, and Val Verde cos. Fairly common.

NESTING: Similar to that of *B. a. atricristatus*.

CANYON BLACK-CRESTED TITMOUSE, *Baeolophus atricristatus paloduro* Stevenson

DESCRIPTION: *Adult male and female, nuptial plumage*: Similar to *B. a. sennetti*, but tail and tarsus longer; middle toe shorter; upper parts somewhat darker, in winter less tinged with brown or ochraceous. Similar to *B. a. dysleptus*, but tail decidedly longer; coloration of upper surface somewhat lighter; flanks averaging darker.

MEASUREMENTS: *Adult male*: Wing, 72.4–78.5 (average, 75.7) mm.; tail, 66.0–71.1 (69.1); bill (exposed culmen), 9.9–11.7 (10.7); tarsus, 20.1–22.1 (21.6); middle toe without claw, 11.2–11.9 (11.7). *Adult female*: Wing, 68.6–80.0 (74.7); tail, 61.5–71.9 (67.8); bill, 9.4–9.9 (9.7); tarsus, 19.6–22.4 (20.3); middle toe, 10.9–12.4 (11.7).

RANGE: Canyons of Panhandle Texas.

TEXAS: *Resident*: Altitudinal breeding range, 2,500 to 3,500 ft. Collected in Randall and Armstrong cos. Uncommon and local.

NESTING: Similar to that of *B. a. atricristatus*.

PLAIN TITMOUSE, *Baeolophus inornatus* (Gambel)

SPECIES ACCOUNT

Parus inornatus of A.O.U. check-list, 1957 (see Appendix A). A very plain, gray titmouse. Resembles Blackcrest, but has shorter, uniform gray crest and grayer under parts; lacks rusty orange wash on flanks. Virtually inseparable from young Blackcrest. Length, 5½ in.; wingspan, 8¾.

RANGE: S. Oregon to s.w. Wyoming, south to n.w. Baja California, s. Nevada, s.e. Arizona, extreme n.e. Sonora, and s.w. and c. New Mexico, and n. Trans-Pecos Texas (first discovered, 1973); also in mountains of s. Baja California. Largely resident, but winters irregularly into Trans-Pecos Texas.

TEXAS: (See map.) *Breeding*: Species has been widely reported in literature to breed in Texas, but actual nesting only lately discovered: Culberson Co., Guadalupe Mts., near Frijole Ranger station (family found in nest cavity in dead pear tree, June 6, 1973, G. A. Newman; young birds well feathered at time of discovery; 1 adult female collected, original no., 405). *Winter*: Sept. to mid-Mar. (extremes: Aug. 10, Mar. 22). Uncommon to scarce in Guadalupe Mts.; rare and irregular at El Paso. One sighting in Davis Mts., Fort Davis (Sept. 1, 2, 1934, K. D. Carlander).

HAUNTS AND HABITS: The Plain Titmouse compensates for its somber gray dullness by displaying all the lively, topsy-turvy acrobatics of the Paridae. Western relative of the Tufted, *B. inornatus* inhabits deciduous or mixed woodlands, where it nests in old woodpecker holes or natural cavities in decaying trunks or limbs of trees. The few which winter in Texas occur in Trans-Pecos mountains—almost exclusively the Guadalupes and higher peaks in the vicinity of El Paso. Here they seek junipers, pinyons, pines, and oaks. The Plain Titmouse is frequently reported by bird watchers in the Davis and Chisos Mountains and on the Edwards Plateau. These sightings are based 99—maybe 100—percent on young of the Black-crested Titmouse, which have short, gray crests and are otherwise practically identical with all ages of the Plain.

Flight and behavior of this bird is very Tufted-like. While foraging, it ranges both low in bushes and thickets and moderately high in trees and occasionally on the ground at the bases of trees. Unlike other tits, this species eats more vegetable than animal matter, consuming particularly acorns, wild fruits, leaf galls, and weed seeds; however, the bird rarely overlooks butterflies, moths, beetles, scale insects, ants, and spiders.

Common calls of the Plain Titmouse include *tsee-day-day*, *tchick-a-dee-dee*, and *tsick-a-dear*. A melodious whistle, heard chiefly in spring, is a *weety-weety* or *tee-wit, tee-wit*. A variation of the Tufted's *peter, peter, peter* song is the Plain's whistled *peto, peto, peto*.

DETAILED ACCOUNT: ONE SUBSPECIES

GRAY PLAIN TITMOUSE, *Baeolophus inornatus griseus* (Ridgway)

Parus inornatus ridgwayi of A.O.U. check-list, 1957 (see Appendix A).

DESCRIPTION: *Adults, nuptial plumage*: Acquired by wear from winter plumage. Upper parts between mouse gray and neutral gray or between mouse gray and grayish olive; forehead usually paler, even somewhat mixed with dull white; wings and tail dark hair brown, wing-coverts, wing-quills, and rectrices edged with color of back; sides of head decidedly paler, mixed with grayish white on auriculars; lower parts dull

buffy smoke gray; lining of wing grayish white. Bill dull brown above, laterally light gray; iris dark brown; feet dull bluish gray. *Adults, winter*: Acquired by complete postnuptial molt. Similar to nuptial adults. *First nuptial*: Acquired by wear from first winter. Like nuptial adults. *First winter*: Acquired by partial postjuvenal molt. Not essentially different from first nuptial male and female. *Juvenal*: Acquired by complete postnatal molt. Similar to nuptial adults, but upper surface more strongly olive brown; forehead darker, less or not at all mixed with grayish white, upper wing-coverts rather paler and greater coverts with distinctly dull buffy tips; lower parts duller, more grayish, somewhat darker. *Natal*: Dull tilleul buff.

MEASUREMENTS: *Adult male*: Wing, 70.1–74.9 (average, 72.2) mm.; tail, 54.6–63.0 (59.7); bill (exposed culmen), 10.9–14.0 (12.7); tarsus, 20.6–22.6 (21.6); middle toe without claw, 10.9–13.0 (12.2). *Adult female*: Wing, 67.8–73.4 (70.4); tail, 55.6–63.5 (59.7); bill, 9.9–13.5 (11.9); tarsus, 19.6–21.6 (20.9); middle toe, 10.9–12.4 (11.7).

RANGE: C. Utah to s.w. Wyoming, south to s.e. California and c. New Mexico; irregularly to Trans-Pecos Texas.

TEXAS: *Breeding*: Racial status as yet not assigned to 1973 specimen taken in Guadalupe Mts. (see species account). *Winter*: Taken (5 specimens) in Guadalupe Mts., Culberson Co.

NESTING: *Nest*: In more or less open woodland, along streams, in more open country, on mesas, in stream valleys, as well as cultivated areas, about human habitations; in natural cavity in tree or stump, or in fence post or old building; nest composed of various kinds of grass, soft felted materials, and feathers. *Eggs*: 5–8; elliptical oval; slightly glossy; white, ordinarily spotted with light brown; average size, 18.3 × 13.2 mm.

[BRIDLED TITMOUSE, *Baeolophus wollweberi* (Bonaparte)

Parus wollweberi of A.O.U. check-list, 1957. Similar in profile and general coloration to other American crested tits, but easily distinguished by black edging on crest, black "bridle" markings on white face, and black bib on throat. Length, 5 in.

RANGE: Mountains of c. and s.e. Arizona and s.w. New Mexico, south through Mexican highlands of Sonora and Chihuahua to Guerrero and Oaxaca.

TEXAS: *Hypothetical*: A specimen collected by John Woodhouse Audubon prior to 1850 supposedly on the Rio Grande in Texas may have actually come from some part of Mexico. Two careful sightings, both in Brewster Co.: Texas side of Rio Grande near Santa Elena Canyon (1 seen, May 6, 1937, Bertha M. Dobie, Henrietta Randall); Chisos Mts. (ca. 1937, Lovie M. Whitaker).]

VERDIN, *Auriparus flaviceps* (Sundevall)

SPECIES ACCOUNT

A very small tit with yellow head; short, pointed bill (straight upper mandible); brownish gray above with chestnut shoulder-patch (sometimes concealed); pale gray below. Young appear brownish gray. Length, 4½ in.; wingspan, 6¾.

RANGE: S.e. California, s. Nevada, and s.w. Utah to s.w. Texas, south to s. Baja California, c. Sinaloa, Jalisco, Hidalgo, and Tamaulipas.

TEXAS: (See map.) *Resident*: Breeds, early Mar. to Aug.—occasionally late Sept. (eggs, Mar. 25 to Sept.

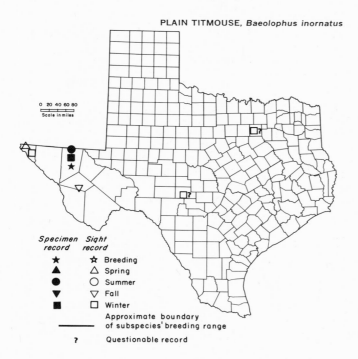

PLAIN TITMOUSE, *Baeolophus inornatus*

0 20 40 60 80
Scale in miles

Specimen record / Sight record
★ ☆ Breeding
▲ △ Spring
● ○ Summer
▼ ▽ Fall
■ □ Winter

——— Approximate boundary of subspecies' breeding range

? Questionable record

Plain Titmouse, *Baeolophus inornatus*

15) from near sea level to about 6,000 ft. Common to fairly common in most of southwestern half, north to Lubbock, Knox, Young, and Palo Pinto, east to Travis and Aransas cos., where uncommon and somewhat irregular. Rare visitor to Amarillo and Vernon (actual nesting unsubstantiated); casual on upper coast.

HAUNTS AND HABITS: The Verdin is a sprightly but elusive bird of thorny scrub in southwestern cactus desert regions. In Texas, it inhabits arid hills and arroyos in the Trans-Pecos, but it is equally at home in brushy gulches and valleys of the western Edwards Plateau and on mesquite-clad flatlands from San Antonio to the Gulf of Mexico. The bird secludes itself in thickets, sometimes along streams or about springs, but also in brush far from water. In fact, water appears to be unnecessary in the life of this bird, although it will drink during the rare occasions when a puddle is available within its territory.

Flight, usually not long continued, is light and jerky, and at times swift. *Auriparus flaviceps* is bushtitlike in size, proportions (except for its shorter tail), and behavior, but is less gregarious, moving usually singly, in pairs, or in loose family groups. Shier than other tits, particularly during the breeding season, the Verdin is more often heard than seen in its thickety habitat. The bird, often completely concealed, moves through the brush searching for caterpillars, weevils, ants, moths, butterflies, and spiders, also some wild fruits and berries, those of agarita (*Berberis trifoliolata*) being especially favored. Like its neighbor the Cactus Wren, the Verdin constructs a roosting nest where it resorts at night, especially during the colder winter months. The usually larger breeding nest is very snugly built and softly lined. Eggs in this nest are

thus extraordinarily well protected; these eggs, even in pre-DDT days, were extraordinarily fragile. Why not double protection—strong eggs in a strong nest? Apparently nature, like most people, only does what it has to do and no more!

Vocalizations are remarkably loud and insistent considering the Verdin's size. Heard frequently during the day and throughout the year as individuals feed in bushes is a rapid *chip-chip-chip-chip*, etc., all on the same pitch and usually not speeding or slowing within the series. On breeding territory, adults repeat, ordinarily from a low branch, a slow *see-lip* or *cee-ip*. The rather seldom heard song, also given from a low branch, is *tsee, seesee*. Late March to early June are the chief *see-lip* and song months.

DETAILED ACCOUNT: ONE SUBSPECIES

EASTERN VERDIN, *Auriparus flaviceps ornatus* (Lawrence)

DESCRIPTION: *Adult male, nuptial plumage*: Acquired by wear from winter plumage. Top and sides of head, together with chin and middle of throat, gamboge yellow or wax yellow, pileum more or less obscured by dark gray; upper parts hair brown or between hair brown and mouse gray; wings and tail chaetura drab, edged with color of back, bend of wing with large patch of bay or burnt sienna; lower parts pale brownish gray, buffy gray, or light grayish drab, palest on middle of abdomen; lining of wing grayish white. Bill black or plumbeous; iris dark brown; legs and feet plumbeous. *Adult female, nuptial*: Acquired by wear from winter. Similar to nuptial adult male, but yellow of head and throat decidedly duller. *Adult male and female, winter*: Acquired by complete postnuptial molt. Similar to corresponding sex of nuptial adult. *Male and female, first nuptial*: Acquired by wear from first winter. Practically identical with nuptial adults. *Male and female, first winter*: Acquired by partial postjuvenal molt. Like adults in winter. *Juvenal*: Acquired by postnatal growth. Similar to nuptial adults but without trace of yellow on head or throat and lacking reddish brown patch on bend of wing; entire upper surface, including wings and tail, nearly uniform, decidedly more brownish than in adults—between buffy brown and hair brown or between drab and buffy brown. *Natal*: None. Bird unfeathered when hatched.

MEASUREMENTS: *Adult male*: Wing, 52.1–55.6 (average, 53.8) mm.; tail, 46.5–50.0 (48.5); bill (exposed culmen), 8.1–8.9 (8.6); tarsus, 15.0–16.0 (15.5); middle toe without claw, 8.9–9.9 (9.7). *Adult female*: Wing, 49.5–54.1 (51.8); tail, 44.4–49.0 (46.8); bill, 8.1–9.4 (8.6); tarsus, 14.5–16.0 (15.2); middle toe, 8.9–9.9 (9.1).

RANGE: S.e. Arizona to s.w. Texas, south to c. Durango and s. Tamaulipas.

TEXAS: *Resident*: Collected northwest to El Paso, east to Menard and Guadalupe, south to Cameron, west to Brewster and Presidio cos.

NESTING: *Nest*: Chiefly on mesas and in desert country; in thorny thickets; brush, such as mesquite, catclaw, allthorn, other shrubs, and cactus; usually not more than 10 ft. above ground; large globular or flask-shaped structure; entrance, a short tunnel, opening on one side or low at one end; composed of interlaced twigs, weeds, and small thorny stalks, coarse grass, weed stems, leaves, and similar materials, very compactly built, thorny on outside and looking very much like an elongated coconut; abundantly lined with plant down, fur, and feathers. *Eggs*: 3–6; ovate; without gloss; pale greenish blue, pale greenish white, or pea green; dotted with reddish brown, chiefly about larger end, where markings are confluent and often form well-defined cap; average size, 15.0 × 10.9 mm.

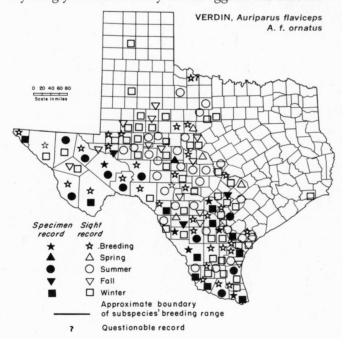

VERDIN, *Auriparus flaviceps*
A. f. ornatus

0 20 40 60 80
Scale in miles

Specimen   Sight
record   record

★   ☆   Breeding
▲   △   Spring
●   ○   Summer
▼   ▽   Fall
■   □   Winter

————   Approximate boundary
of subspecies' breeding range

?   Questionable record

Bushtits: Psaltriparidae

LEAD-COLORED BUSHTIT, *Psaltriparus plumbeus*
(Baird)

SPECIES ACCOUNT

Merged into Common Bushtit, *Psaltriparus minimus*,
by A.O.U. check-list, 1957 (see Appendix A). A tiny,
slim, long-tailed bird with a very short bill. Nondescript; gray above, rather brownish on crown and tail;
brownish cheeks (Rocky Mt. birds); pale grayish
white below. Male has blackish eyes; yellowish in female. Length, 4½ in.; wingspan, 6; weight, ¼ oz.

RANGE: S.e. Oregon to s.w. Wyoming and extreme
n.w. Oklahoma, south to n.e. California, and through
Rockies and Great Basin to n. Sonora and Trans-Pecos
and c. Texas.

TEXAS: (See map.) *Resident*: Breeds, mid-Mar. to
late June (eggs, Mar. 26 to June 13) from 550 to about
8,500 ft. Common to fairly common in mountains of
Trans-Pecos; irregularly fairly common to uncommon
on Edwards Plateau, east rarely to Bosque and Travis
cos.; fairly common (usually in winter) to uncommon
and local in northern Panhandle. Wanders erratically,
chiefly during nonbreeding season, over much of western third, east rarely to Waco, casually to Dallas.

HAUNTS AND HABITS: In Texas, roving choruses of
Lead-colored Bushtits, constantly *tsit*ing to one another, are found in pinyons, pines, junipers, oaks, and
madrones (*Arbutus texana*) of Trans-Pecos mountains,
but the species also scatters out into scrub oak and
cedar brush on the Edwards Plateau and in Panhandle
canyons. Rarely crossing open spaces, flocks pattern
their courses through trees and bushes, where they forage for moths, caterpillars, scale insects, bugs, weevils,
and in winter an occasional seed.

Flight is weak and fitful and when sustained is
noticeably undulating. Mannerisms of the Leadcolor
are as lively and agile as a chickadee's; in fact, a bushtit often appears even more nimble in trees due to the
longer tail which offers added support and balance.
The species is very gregarious except for a brief period
during the breeding season after which individuals
reband. Groups of bushtits are quite fearless of people
or at least so absorbed in foraging operations that
they generally ignore any observers.

The *tsit*—sometimes it sounds more like *clenk*—call
of the Lead-colored Bushtit is a conversational note

used by members of a flock to keep in touch; speed and
volume of it seem to be determined by the pace at
which a group is moving through the scrub. Occasionally, a shrill, quavering *sre-e-e-e* is interspersed in
the *tsit*'s, apparently when the flock is traveling fast
and not feeding; this is drawn out to a *sre-e-e-e-e-e*
that serves as an alarm note. Notes of bushtits are
heard year-round.

DETAILED ACCOUNT: ONE SUBSPECIES

ROCKY MOUNTAIN LEAD-COLORED BUSHTIT,
Psaltriparus plumbeus plumbeus (Baird)

DESCRIPTION: *Adults, nuptial plumage*: Acquired by wear
from winter plumage. Pileum rather dark somewhat brownish
neutral gray, sometimes with narrow darker collar on hindneck;
remainder of upper surface somewhat brownish mouse gray;
wings and tail rather dark hair brown, margined with color of
back; sides of head, sometimes including narrow frontlet, light
broccoli brown; posterior lower surface light drab; anterior
lower parts and under wing-coverts paler and more whitish.
Bill black or blackish slate, base of mandible sometimes light
plumbeous or dull white; iris of male dark bister; iris of female
white, yellowish white, or light straw yellow; legs and feet

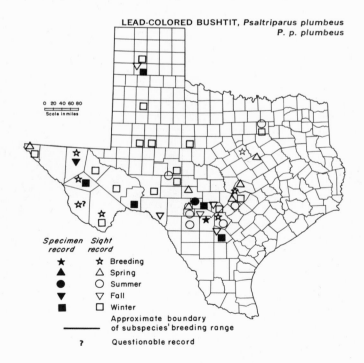

LEAD-COLORED BUSHTIT, *Psaltriparus plumbeus*
P. p. plumbeus

0 20 40 60 80
Scale in miles

Specimen   Sight
record   record

★   ☆ Breeding
▲   △ Spring
●   ○ Summer
▼   ▽ Fall
■   □ Winter

——— Approximate boundary
     of subspecies' breeding range

?   Questionable record

Black-eared Bushtit, *Psaltriparus melanotis*
male (top), female (center), young (bottom)

PLATE 21: Eastern Phoebe, *Sayornis phoebe*

PLATE 22: Vermilion Flycatcher, *Pyrocephalus rubinus*
female (left), male (right)

brownish black. *Adults, winter*: Acquired by complete post-nuptial molt. Like nuptial adults. *First nuptial*: Acquired by wear from first winter. Little, if any, different from nuptial adults. *First winter*: Acquired by partial postjuvenal molt. Like first nuptial. *Juvenal*: Acquired by postnatal growth. Similar to adults, but wings and tail more brownish—dark hair brown—with middle rectrices darker than others; sides of head and forehead paler and more grayish (less distinctly brown); lower parts paler, rather more buffy than drab. *Natal*: None. Bird hatched unfeathered.

MEASUREMENTS: *Adult male*: Wing, 48.5–53.6 (average, 51.1) mm.; tail, 54.6–62.0 (56.6); bill (exposed culmen), 6.6–7.6 (7.1); tarsus, 15.5–16.5 (16.3); middle toe without claw, 7.6–8.6 (8.4). *Adult female*: Wing, 49.0–53.6 (50.8); tail, 51.1–58.4 (55.6); bill, 6.6–7.6 (7.1); tarsus, 15.0–16.5 (15.7); middle toe, 8.1–8.6 (8.4).

RANGE: S.e. Oregon to s.w. Wyoming and extreme n.w. Oklahoma, south to n.e. Sonora and Trans-Pecos and c. Texas.

TEXAS: *Resident*: Collected northwest to Culberson, southeast to Kerr, west to Brewster cos. Two specimens outside regular breeding range: Randall Co., Elkins Ranch (Dec. 26, 1936, T. F. Smith); Atascosa Co., 6 mi. southeast of Lytle (Jan. 22, 1932, A. J. Kirn).

NESTING: *Nest*: On mountains, hills, slopes, and in canyons, woodlands or more open country; 5–20 ft. above ground, in bush or tree, such as pinyon, juniper, oak, and cottonwood, or occasionally suspended from bunch of mistletoe growing on tree or bush; long pensile bag suspended from twig, though often supported other than at top, entrance at side near top; composed of various vegetable fibers, moss, lichens, grasses, ferns, dried and curled leaves of white sage, plant down, oak and other flowers, catkins, cocoon silk, spider webs, and even material from hummingbird's nest; lined with wool and/or feathers. *Eggs*: 4–6, usually 5; ovate; white, unmarked; average size, 13.5 × 10.2 mm.

BLACK-EARED BUSHTIT, *Psaltriparus melanotis* (Hartlaub)

SPECIES ACCOUNT

Many authors merge *P. melanotis* into *P. minimus*, considering the former a color phase (see Appendix A). *Male*: resembles Lead-colored Bushtit, but has black or black-speckled cheek-patch; olive gray back; vinaceous wash on sides, flanks. *Female*: closely resembles Leadcolor, but may have grayer (occasionally blackish) cheeks; pale vinaceous wash on sides, flanks. Length, 4½ in.; wingspan, 6¼; weight, ¼ oz.

RANGE: Extreme s.w. New Mexico and Trans-Pecos and Edwards Plateau Texas, south through highland Mexico to Guatemala.

TEXAS: (See map.) *Resident*: Breeds, early Apr. to early July (eggs, Apr. 11 to June 21) from 1,600—perhaps lower on Edwards Plateau—to 8,000 ft. Fairly common in Davis Mts. and higher mountains of Brewster Co.; uncommon and highly irregular in Guadalupe Mts. and on Edwards Plateau (recorded during all seasons, but no good evidence of nesting).

HAUNTS AND HABITS: Somehow the idea got started that the Black-eared Bushtit in western Texas prefers higher altitudes than does the Lead-colored form. Perhaps observers who had noticed Blackears flourishing in lush pine-oak forests at ten thousand feet in Mexico's Sierra Madres first spread the rumor. In actual fact,

however, *Psaltriparus melanotis* lives with *P. plumbeus* at all elevations that grow juniper-oak scrub in the Trans-Pecos and on the Edwards Plateau. V. L. Emanuel, E. B. Kincaid, Jr., Mary Anne McClendon, G. F. Oatman, Jr., J. L. Rowlett, Rose Ann Rowlett, and others, have all seen bushtits with black ears at various times of the year on a very low part of the Edwards Plateau (near Austin at about 600 feet). Most of these people, plus many other veteran bird watchers, including Anne LeSassier and Frances Williams, have observed Black-eared Bushtits near the tops of the Chisos and Davis mountains many times.

Flight and behavior of this bushtit is identical with that of the Leadcolor. Restless bands flit through vegetation close to the ground, rarely ascending high in trees. These excursions generally include a few individuals who straggle behind and out from the group; hence, bushtit flocks never appear tightly organized.

The Blackear's *tsit* or *clenk* note, like that of the Leadcolor, is used to keep flock members in touch and is heard at all times of the year.

DETAILED ACCOUNT: ONE SUBSPECIES

LLOYD'S BLACK-EARED BUSHTIT, *Psaltriparus melanotis lloydi* Sennett

DESCRIPTION: *Adult male, nuptial plumage*: Acquired by wear from winter plumage. Pileum brownish neutral gray, lighter on forehead; remainder of upper surface between mouse gray and deep olive gray; wings and tail hair brown or rather dark hair brown edged with color of back, wing-coverts broadly, wing-quills and tail feathers narrowly, margined; sides of head and neck black, extending sometimes around hindneck in form of very narrow collar partly obscured by brownish gray feathers of back or hindneck; chin dull black; throat dull white with wash of drab; remainder of lower parts dull white tinged with vinaceous or buff; flanks and sides strongly tinged with vi-

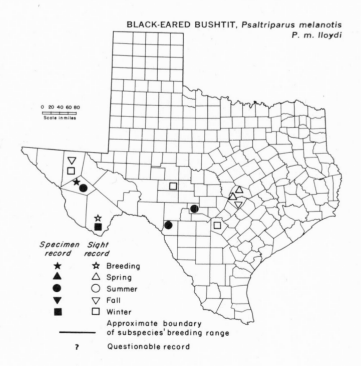

BLACK-EARED BUSHTIT, *Psaltriparus melanotis*
P. m. *lloydi*

0 20 40 60 80
Scale in miles

Specimen record — Sight record
★ — ☆ Breeding
▲ — △ Spring
● — ○ Summer
▼ — ▽ Fall
■ — □ Winter
—— Approximate boundary of subspecies' breeding range
? Questionable record

naceous; lining of wing dull vinaceous white. Bill and feet black; iris dark brown. *Adult male, winter*: Acquired by complete postnuptial molt. Virtually identical with nuptial adult male. *Adult female, nuptial*: Acquired by wear from winter. Similar to adult male but slightly smaller; sides of head broccoli brown or drab, instead of black; upper parts more uniform; chin dull white or drab gray, instead of black; flanks less strongly vinaceous. Iris yellowish white or pale yellow. *Adult female, winter*: Acquired by complete postnuptail molt. Like nuptial adult female. *Male, first nuptial*: Acquired by wear from first winter. Similar to nuptial adult male, but sides of head more brownish or mixed with dark brown; flanks less vinaceous. *Male, first winter*: Acquired by partial postjuvenal molt. Like first nuptial male. *Female, first nuptial*: Acquired by wear from first winter. Practically identical with nuptial adult female. *Female, first winter*: Acquired by partial postjuvenal molt. Like first nuptial female. *Male, juvenal*: Acquired by postnatal growth. Similar to adult female, but sides of head darker brown, sometimes mixed with black; lower parts more vinaceous. Differs from Lead-colored Bushtit, *P. plumbeus plumbeus*, in having auriculars more deeply brown or blackish and flanks often tinged with vinaceous. *Female, juvenal*: Acquired by postnatal growth. Similar to adult female, but pileum paler; upper parts more uniform and duller; wings and tail somewhat paler, more brownish; wing-coverts edged with dull buff; flanks and remainder of lower parts more or less washed with dull buff. *Natal*: None. Bird unfeathered when hatched.

MEASUREMENTS: *Adult male*: Wing, 47.0–52.6 (average, 49.8) mm.; tail, 48.5–58.4 (53.3); bill (exposed culmen), 6.6–7.6 (7.4); tarsus, 15.0–17.0 (16.0); middle toe without claw, 8.1–8.6 (8.4). *Adult female*: Wing, 46.5–51.1 (49.0); tail, 50.0–56.9 (53.8); bill, 6.6–7.6 (7.1); tarsus, 15.0–16.5 (15.7); middle toe, 7.6–8.6 (8.4).

RANGE: S.e. Arizona and s. New Mexico, south to n.e. Sonora and Trans-Pecos and Edwards Plateau Texas.

TEXAS: *Resident*: Collected in Jeff Davis and Brewster cos. Two summer specimens, but no evidence of nesting: Kerr Co., Kerrville (June 6, 1937, D. W. Lay); Kinney Co. (July 13, 1956, R. R. Graber).

NESTING: *Nest*: In canyons and on slopes and mesas of mountains and hills; forests and their margins; suspended from limb of tree or bush, such as oak or juniper; long pensile bag with entrance at side; composed of various vegetable fibers, such as grasses, ferns, lichens, and moss; lined with wool or feathers. *Eggs*: 5–7; ovate; pure white, without markings; average size, 14.7 × 10.7 mm.

Nuthatches: Sittidae

WHITE-BREASTED NUTHATCH, *Sitta carolinensis*
Latham

SPECIES ACCOUNT

A small, chunky, "topsy-turvy" tree climber; strong, spikelike bill; large head, feet (hind claw especially strong); stubby tail. Largely bluish gray above with black cap, nape; large dark eyes on white face; white-edged tail; white below with tawny flanks, crissum. Length, 5¾ in.; wingspan, 10¾; weight, ¾ oz.

RANGE: Extreme s. Canada, south through most of United States and highland Mexico to s. Baja California, Guerrero, Oaxaca, c. Veracruz, U.S. Gulf states, and c. Florida; limited seasonal movement noted. Largely absent from Great Plains.

TEXAS: (See map.) *Breeding*: Early Mar. to late June, perhaps later (eggs, Mar. 26 to Apr. 2) from about 50 (rarely) to 8,500 ft. Fairly common locally to uncommon in forested mountains of Trans-Pecos; scarce to rare in northeastern counties of state (most numerous along middle Trinity River in Anderson and Henderson cos., fide C. D. Fisher); rare and irregular in southeastern section, south to Lee and northern Harris cos. Eastern races formerly west to Edwards Plateau, where recorded during all seasons, but actual nesting evidence never obtained. *Winter*: Early Oct.— occasionally late Aug.—to mid-Apr. (extremes: July 26, May 13). Common to fairly common throughout regular breeding range; uncommon and irregular in El Paso region and northern Panhandle; scare to rare in central and southeastern portions; casual at Midland, Del Rio, and on central coast.

HAUNTS AND HABITS: The Sittidae contains a controversial number of species—seventeen to twenty-nine. Among the four U.S. nuthatches, the White-breasted is the largest and least fidgety member of its family; therefore human observers often term it a sedate, earnest, rather stoic little bird. In Texas it ranges coniferous and deciduous woodlands and groves of the Trans-Pecos and Edwards Plateau—although formerly much more plentiful—and in the northeast corner of the state. In yards and parks of towns and cities, especially during winter, it is attracted to shade trees as well as feeding stations well supplied with suet. Ordinarily not gregarious, the Whitebreast moves singly or with its mate. Even in winter, members of a pair keep in touch with conversational *yank* notes as they roam. Loose groups form during cooler months, often with small woodpeckers, chickadees, and Brown Creepers, an association that is due largely to a similarity in diet.

Flight is strong, swift, and undulating much like a woodpecker's. Quite agile on the wing, the bird has been observed catching falling nuts in mid-air. The Whitebreast's long toes and claws give it a remarkable purchase on bark, allowing it to run about tree trunks —typically head downward—or out on limbs as well as on the undersides of branches or terminal twigs; it seldom if ever uses its tail for a prop as do woodpeckers. In trees and occasionally on the ground around the roots, it gleans beetles, caterpillars, bugs, ants, spiders; also nuts, acorns, wild berries, and seeds.

One call of the White-breasted Nuthatch is a nasal *yank* or *quank*, a number of times repeated; it is stronger, louder, and lower pitched than that of its smaller relative, the Red-breasted. Another note, likewise nasal, is *tootoo*. Its song is a rapid, resonant se-

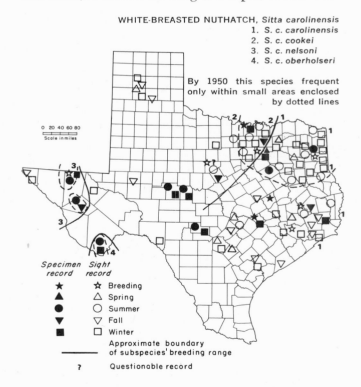

WHITE-BREASTED NUTHATCH, *Sitta carolinensis*
1. *S. c. carolinensis*
2. *S. c. cookei*
3. *S. c. nelsoni*
4. *S. c. oberholseri*

By 1950 this species frequent only within small areas enclosed by dotted lines

0 20 40 60 80
Scale in miles

Specimen record	Sight record	
★	☆	Breeding
▲	△	Spring
●	○	Summer
▼	▽	Fall
■	□	Winter

——— Approximate boundary of subspecies' breeding range

? Questionable record

quence of notes on the same pitch: *hah, hah, hah, hah, hah, hah; whi, whi, whi, whi, whi, whi;* or *who, who, who,* etc.

CHANGES: The White-breasted Nuthatch is another of the numerous birds of northern origin which retreated northward with climatic warming and drying during the first half of the twentieth century. Within this time span the species largely faded from central and southeastern Texas; it also declined somewhat in the Chisos Mountains, southernmost of the Trans-Pecos ranges.

Since about 1950, the word has gone out from some climatologists and other pontificators that the Northern Hemisphere is again growing cooler. Regardless of any tenuous cause-and-effect relationship that may exist, it is of interest that a White-breasted Nuthatch returned to the Austin region of central Texas after having been apparently completely absent since at least 1940. At frequent intervals through 1970 a lone but lively individual was viewed by many bird watchers in and near Austin's Eastwoods Park. This bird usually progressed in proper nuthatch manner by jerking along head downward on main trunks of big pecans (*Carya illinoensis*), live oaks (*Quercus virginiana*), and cedar elms (*Ulmus crassifolia*).

DETAILED ACCOUNT: FOUR SUBSPECIES

FLORIDA WHITE-BREASTED NUTHATCH, *Sitta carolinensis carolinensis* Latham

DESCRIPTION: *Adult male, nuptial plumage:* Acquired by wear from winter plumage. Pileum and hindneck glossy black; remainder of upper surface between slate gray and neutral gray; middle pair of tail feathers neutral gray; remainder of tail black, except for large white subterminal spots on three outer pairs of rectrices which are largest on outermost pair and occupy approximately half outer web and nearly one-third inner web; secondaries dark chaetura drab, changing to dark fuscous on primaries; several of middle primaries have white or grayish white spot on median portion of inner webs, outer primaries have white at extreme base; wing-coverts edged with color of back and greater series tipped narrowly with grayish white; wing-quills edged externally with neutral gray, the tertials neutral gray or light neutral gray, with a broad dull black stripe on inner webs (which on two inner feathers occupies entire web, on third only a portion of tip), also the outer web of third tertial mostly dull black, this with a broadly rounded posterior margin; sides of head, together with lower parts, dull white or grayish white, sometimes slightly tinged with buff; lower flanks and crissum much mixed with russet or tawny; lining of wing black. Bill slate, blackish plumbeous, slate black, or black, basal two-thirds of mandible cinereous, french gray, or plumbeous, cutting edges dull white; iris chocolate; legs and feet brownish black, broccoli brown, seal brown, clove brown, slate color, or mouse gray; feet olive, dark brown, olive drab, or like legs; claws dull black or slate black. *Adult male, winter:* Acquired by complete postnatal molt. Practically same as nuptial adult male. *Adult female, nuptial:* Acquired by wear from winter plumage. Similar to nuptial adult male, but pileum usually duller, more brownish, often more or less mixed with slate color; legs drab to clove brown; feet hair brown to olive. *Adult female, winter:* Acquired by complete postnuptial molt. Like nuptial adult female. *Male and female, first nuptial:* Acquired by wear from first winter. Like corresponding sex of nuptial adults, except for wing-quills retained from juvenal, also pileum which in male is duller. *Male and female, first winter:* Acquired by partial postjuvenal molt. Like corresponding sex

in first nuptial. *Juvenal:* Acquired by complete postnatal molt. Similar to nuptial adults, but bill smaller; pileum duller and more brownish; remainder of upper parts darker and more tinged with brown; edges of wing-coverts and of secondaries brown or buff. *Natal:* Pale smoke gray or drab gray. Bill and feet pinkish buff tinged with brown.

MEASUREMENTS: *Adult male:* Wing, 85.1–91.9 (average, 87.4) mm.; tail, 40.9–47.0 (44.7); bill (exposed culmen), 18.0–19.6 (18.5); tarsus, 18.0–19.6 (18.3); middle toe without claw, 14.0–16.5 (15.7). *Adult female:* Wing, 82.6–89.9 (86.4); tail, 39.9–47.5 (43.9); bill, 17.0–19.0 (18.0); tarsus, 17.0–18.5 (18.0); middle toe, 15.0–16.5 (15.7).

RANGE: N.e. Texas to s. Virginia, south to s.e. Texas and e. Florida.

TEXAS: *Breeding:* Altitudinal range, about 50 (rarely) to 2,300 ft. Collected north to Dallas, south to Navarro cos.; formerly (19th century) farther south to Lee, and in summer (breeding suspected) in Kerr cos. Uncommon. *Winter:* Taken north to Dallas, southeast to Hardin, west to Kerr cos. Fairly common.

NESTING: *Nest:* On uplands and lowlands, in swamps, on slopes, level land, sometimes cultivated areas, usually deep woodlands, even in vicinity of human dwellings; 2–60 ft. above ground, in hole in tree, either natural or excavated by the birds, or in deserted woodpecker burrow; material, placed nearly level to nest entrance, comprised of fine grass, leaves, strips of bark, fur, hair, and feathers; lining of bark strips, leaves, rabbit fur, other hair, and feathers. *Eggs:* 4–10, usually 5–6; ovate or rounded ovate, sometimes elliptical ovate; white, creamy white, or pinkish white; much speckled with reddish brown and lilac, markings sometimes most numerous about larger end; average size, 17.8 × 14.5 mm.

CANADA WHITE-BREASTED NUTHATCH, *Sitta carolinensis cookei* Oberholser

DESCRIPTION: *Adult male and female, nuptial plumage:* Similar to *S. c. carolinensis* but larger; upper parts lighter; lower surface more purely white. Bill relatively less slender.

MEASUREMENTS: *Adult male:* Wing, 86.1–97.1 (average, 90.4) mm.; tail, 43.9–50.5 (46.8); bill (exposed culmen), 16.5–21.1 (19.0); tarsus, 18.0–20.1 (18.8); middle toe without claw, 14.5–16.5 (15.7). *Adult female:* Wing, 85.1–92.5 (88.1); tail, 41.9–49.5 (46.8); bill, 16.5–19.6 (18.3); tarsus, 17.0–19.0 (18.3); middle toe, 15.0–17.0 (15.7).

RANGE: S. Manitoba to n. Nova Scotia, south to c. Texas, s. Ohio, and e. Virginia.

TEXAS: *Breeding:* Altitudinal range, 400 to 1,900 ft. Collected in Cooke (eggs) and Collin cos.; collected in summer (breeding suspected) in Concho and Tom Green cos. Scarce and local. *Winter:* Taken in Cooke (1 specimen), Kerr (1), Concho (1), and Tom Green (1) cos. Scarce.

NESTING: Similar to that of *S. c. carolinensis*, but average egg size, 19.3 × 14.5 mm.

ROCKY MOUNTAIN WHITE-BREASTED NUTHATCH, *Sitta carolinensis nelsoni* Mearns

DESCRIPTION: *Adult male and female, nuptial plumage:* Similar to *S. c. cookei,* but bill longer; middle toe shorter; gray of upper parts darker; flanks more strongly washed with gray; second tertial (from inner side) with more black on base of outer web, black on outer web of third tertial more or less pointed at tip instead of rounded.

MEASUREMENTS: *Adult male:* Wing, 88.4–95.5 (average, 91.2) mm.; tail, 42.9–52.1 (48.3); bill (exposed culmen), 18.0–23.1 (19.8); tarsus, 17.0–19.0 (18.0); middle toe without claw, 13.0–15.0 (14.5). *Adult female:* Wing, 87.1–94.0 (90.7); tail, 42.9–51.1 (45.2); bill, 17.0–20.1 (18.8); tarsus, 17.0–18.5 (17.8); middle toe, 14.0–15.5 (14.2).

RANGE: Montana, south to n. Sonora and n. Trans-Pecos Texas.

TEXAS: *Breeding:* Altitudinal range, 5,200 to 8,500 ft. Collected in Guadalupe Mts., Culberson Co.; and Davis Mts., Jeff Davis Co. Fairly common. *Winter*: One specimen: Culberson Co., Guadalupe Mts., The Bowl (Jan. 1, 1939, G. H. Lowery, Jr.).

NESTING: *Nest*: Chiefly on mountains, hills, and slopes, and in canyons; preferably in deep forests but also more open areas; in trunk, branch, or stub of oak, pine, aspen, Douglasfir, cottonwood, or other tree; at almost any height from ground, in natural cavity or those excavated by the bird itself or by woodpeckers; nest materials mostly fur, grass, bark, and feathers; lined with bark strips, hair, fur of various animals, and feathers. *Eggs*: 4–9, usually 5; rounded ovate to elliptical ovate; white, much speckled with reddish brown and lilac, chiefly at larger end; average size, 20.3 × 15.2 mm.

CHISOS WHITE-BREASTED NUTHATCH, *Sitta carolinensis oberholseri* Brandt

Race not in A.O.U. check-list, 1957 (see Appendix A).

DESCRIPTION: *Adult male and female, nuptial plumage*: Similar to *S. c. nelsoni*, but bill, wing, and middle toe shorter; upper surface darker; under parts somewhat more deeply colored, somewhat darker, more grayish (less whitish).

MEASUREMENTS: *Adult male*: Wing, 85.6–90.9 (average, 88.1) mm.; tail, 44.4–48.5 (47.3); bill (exposed culmen), 16.5–19.0 (17.8); tarsus, 17.0–19.0 (18.3); middle toe without claw, 13.0–14.0 (13.7). *Adult female*: Wing, 84.1–88.4 (86.9); tail, 45.0–47.0 (46.3); bill, 17.3–19.0 (17.8); tarsus, 17.3–18.5 (17.8); middle toe, 13.0–14.0 (13.5).

RANGE: S. Trans-Pecos Texas, south to s. Coahuila.

TEXAS: *Breeding*: Altitudinal range, 5,200 to 7,800 ft. Collected in Chisos Mts., Brewster Co. Uncommon. *Winter*: Taken in Brewster Co. (5 specimens). Uncommon.

NESTING: Similar to that of *S. c. nelsoni*.

RED-BREASTED NUTHATCH, *Sitta canadensis* Linnaeus

SPECIES ACCOUNT

Bluish gray above with black cap; side of head white

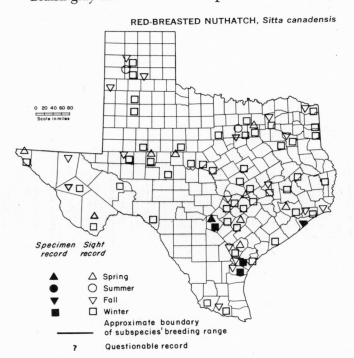

RED-BREASTED NUTHATCH, *Sitta canadensis*

0 20 40 60 80
Scale in miles

Specimen Sight
record   record

▲   △ Spring
●   ○ Summer
▼   ▽ Fall
■   □ Winter

──── Approximate boundary of subspecies' breeding range

?   Questionable record

with black stripe through eye; tawny below (becoming paler anteriorly, fading to whitish on throat). Length, 4½ in.; wingspan, 8¼; weight, ½ oz.

RANGE: S.e. Alaska and s. Yukon to Newfoundland, south to mountains of s. California and s.e. Arizona, Colorado, s.w. South Dakota, Great Lakes region, and s. New England, and in Appalachians to e. Tennessee and w. North Carolina; also Guadalupe Island off Baja California. Winters chiefly from s. Canada irregularly to s. United States.

TEXAS: (See map.) *Winter*: Mid-Oct. to mid-Apr. (extremes: Aug. 30, May 4). Irregularly fairly common (usually eastern parts) to scarce in most sections north of 29th parallel; increasingly rare south to Corpus Christi; casual in Rio Grande delta.

HAUNTS AND HABITS: The Red-breasted Nuthatch, ranging farther north into Canada than the Whitebreasted, confines its breeding chiefly to coniferous forests. For a nest it selects a cavity in a decaying tree limb or stump, sometimes excavating it further, or in a discarded woodpecker hole; the bird lines the hole with bark strips, grasses, weed fibers, and feathers and also smears pitch on the entrance. The few Redbreasted Nuthatches that migrate in winter to Texas seek woods (often deciduous), thickets, cliffs, even bare rocky places, gardens and orchards about country dwellings, or shade trees and feeders in yards and parks of towns.

Flight is usually swift and strong, rarely sustained, and undulating, these undulations more apparent as the bird travels a longer distance. More animated than the larger, calmer Whitebreast, the Redbreast runs nimbly on tree trunks and branches, where it forages for insects, their eggs and larvae, and spiders, as well as seeds of conifers; it also does a good bit of fly-catching. Unlike jays and chickadees, a nuthatch does not use its feet to brace a nut or seed on a limb to crack it; instead the bird wedges it in a crack or crevice of bark to hammer it open.

The common note of the Red-breasted Nuthatch is a series of *ank*'s, sometimes sounding more like *enk*. The bird varies the quality of this call either by uttering the notes in a rapid-fire sequence, by slowing the series so it sounds more measured and deliberate, or by drawing out a single *ank* into a whine. Higher pitched and more nasal than that of the Whitebreast, this call is said by some listeners to resemble a blast from a tiny tin horn. Song is a greatly prolonged *yaaaaa, yaaaaa, yaaaaa*. The bird sings infrequently on its northern breeding ground. In Texas, its note is often heard; the song, almost never.

DETAILED ACCOUNT: ONE SUBSPECIES

EASTERN RED-BREASTED NUTHATCH, *Sitta canadensis canadensis* Linnaeus

No races recognized by A.O.U. check-list, 1957 (see Appendix A).

DESCRIPTION: *Adult male, nuptial plumage*: Acquired by wear from winter plumage. Pileum glossy black; remainder of upper surface slate gray; middle pair of tail feathers similar but lighter

Red-breasted Nuthatch, *Sitta canadensis*

and duller; remainder of tail brownish black, outer two pairs of feathers with large subterminal white spots; wings dark hair brown or chaetura drab, upper wing-coverts having edges of quills between neutral gray and dark gull gray, narrow outer edges of primaries paler, rather more buffy; loral stripe, post-ocular region, and sides of neck black; broad white superciliary stripe extending back to nape; chin, cheeks, and upper throat buffy white; remainder of lower surface between ochraceous buff and ochraceous tawny, darker posteriorly; lining of wing brownish white or buffy white. Bill black, blackish slate, or slate black, but basal half of mandible cinereous or pale gull gray; iris vandyke brown or black; legs and feet dull greenish yellow, dull grayish yellow, raw umber, or hair brown; claws hair brown. *Adult male, winter*: Acquired by complete postnuptial molt. Similar to nuptial adult male, but lower parts, particularly flanks, darker and more richly colored. *Adult female, nuptial*: Acquired by wear from winter. Similar to nuptial adult male but paler above; top of head and sides of neck duller—slate or blackish slate, instead of black; pileum sometimes almost concolor with back. *Adult female, winter*: Acquired by complete postnuptial molt. Similar to nuptial adult female but somewhat darker below. *Male and female, first nuptial*: Acquired by wear from first winter. Similar to corresponding sex of nuptial adults, but pileum somewhat duller and less sharply defined from sides of head; lower parts paler. *Male and female, first winter*: Acquired by partial postjuvenal molt. Similar to corresponding sex of adults in winter. *Male, juvenal*: Acquired by complete postnatal molt. Similar to nuptial adult male, but head duller, less glossy black; remainder of upper surface darker and duller, more brownish— to deep neutral gray; lower parts paler and more or less mixed with gray. Maxilla black or slate black; basal half of mandible pale green or dull blue, terminal half slate gray with tip black; iris black; feet greenish slate. *Female, juvenal*: Acquired by complete postnatal molt. Similar to nuptial adult female, but pileum and sides of neck more brownish—deep mouse gray; lower parts duller and paler.

MEASUREMENTS: *Adult male*: Wing, 66.5–70.1 (average, 68.3) mm.; tail, 35.6–39.1 (37.3); bill (exposed culmen), 13.5–17.5 (14.7); tarsus, 15.0–17.0 (16.3); middle toe without claw, 10.9–13.0 (11.9). *Adult female*: Wing, 63.0–68.1 (65.3); tail, 33.0–37.6 (34.8); bill, 12.4–14.5 (13.7); tarsus, 14.2–16.5 (15.7); middle toe, 10.9–11.9 (11.4).

RANGE: Identical with that of species with exception of range of *S. c. clariterga* Burleigh described from Clearwater Co., Idaho.

TEXAS: *Winter*: Taken in Bexar, Galveston (Oct. 25), San Patricio, and Nueces cos.

BROWN-HEADED NUTHATCH, *Sitta pusilla*
Latham

SPECIES ACCOUNT

A very small nuthatch. Neutral gray above with brown cap bordered by narrow, dark brown streak through eye; whitish nape-spot; dull white below. Length, 4½ in.; wingspan, 7¾.

RANGE: Extreme s.e. Oklahoma to s. Delaware, south to s.e. Texas, U.S. Gulf coast, s. Florida, and Grand Bahama.

TEXAS: (See map.) *Resident*: Breeds, mid-Feb. to late May (eggs, Mar. 21 to Apr. 19; young in nest as early as Mar. 11) from near sea level to about 300 ft. Common locally to uncommon in pine forests of eastern quarter; rare and erratic winter visitor south to Freeport. One report from Lee Co. (observed in Mar., Apr., May, 1882, H. Nehrling).

HAUNTS AND HABITS: The Brown-headed Nuthatch is

the second phylogenetically of four bird species endemic (or nearly so) to the pinelands of the southeastern United States. It is not as rigid in its habitat requirements as is the absurdly overspecialized Redcockaded Woodpecker; neither is it as adaptable as the Pine Warbler. The migratory warbler has settled down to proliferate in the isolated pines in Bastrop County, Texas; the sedentary nuthatch has apparently never found Bastrop's "lost pines." An advantage of the migratory habit seems demonstrated here. *Sitta pusilla* lives almost exclusively in pine forests, generally the more open parts but sometimes in fairly dense pine-oak as well. It also appears on woodland borders, along fence rows, in scattered trees of old fields, and even on telephone poles along highways.

Flight is rather undulating and at times swift, although ordinarily the bird does not fly any great distance. Not particularly shy, it frequents tops of tall trees, saplings, or fence posts. Often in winter it moves in small flocks of up to twenty individuals. Quick, active, and restless, the Brown-headed Nuthatch flies from tree to tree gleaning bark insects and their larvae and eggs; rarely it adds a few spiders and pine seeds to its diet. On a tree it runs up and down the trunk, branches, and twigs, turning about as do other nuthatches, examining bark and bases of pine needles. Occasionally it descends to the ground and hops about, flipping over dead leaves in search of food.

Rather noisy, the Brown-headed Nuthatch has several chattery notes uttered either on the wing or as the bird runs about on a tree. Most frequent is a rapid *kit, kit, kit*. A squeaky *ki-day* or *ki-dee-dee* is heard in spring and is probably the song; individuals keep in touch with one another by means of their *kit* notes all year long.

BROWN-HEADED NUTHATCH, *Sitta pusilla*
S. p. pusilla

0 20 40 60 80
Scale in miles

Specimen record	Sight record	
★	☆	Breeding
▲	△	Spring
●	○	Summer
▼	▽	Fall
■	□	Winter

——— Approximate boundary of subspecies' breeding range

? Questionable record

DETAILED ACCOUNT: ONE SUBSPECIES

COMMON BROWN-HEADED NUTHATCH, *Sitta pusilla pusilla* Latham

DESCRIPTION: *Adults, nuptial plumage*: Acquired by wear from winter plumage. Pileum buffy brown to rufescent drab, tips of feathers often paler, thus imparting spotted or mottled appearance; middle of nape with more or less conspicuous spot of dull white; remainder of upper surface deep neutral gray to near neutral gray; middle pair of tail feathers similar but rather lighter or duller; most of remainder of tail brownish black, terminal portion of three outer tail feathers dull hair brown subterminally, on two outermost pairs grayish white or brownish white; wings fuscous, edgings of wing-coverts and of wing-quills similar to color of back but on primaries more brownish; lores and postocular streak dark olive brown or clove brown; cheeks and chin grayish white or buffy white; remainder of lower surface dull cream buff, but sides and flanks neutral gray; lining of wing dark neutral gray; axillars dull buffy white or gray, edge of wing creamy white. Bill dark brown, base of mandible plumbeous; iris dark brown; legs and feet dull brown. *Adults, winter*: Acquired by complete postnuptial molt. Similar to nuptial adults, but pileum much darker and more uniform; lower parts much more deeply buff. *First nuptial*: Acquired by wear from first winter. Similar to nuptial adults. *First winter*: Acquired by partial postjuvenal molt. Similar to adults in winter, but colors somewhat darker. *Juvenal*: Acquired by complete postnatal molt. Similar to nuptial adults, but pileum hair brown to mouse gray; back deep mouse gray, thus darker and duller; lower surface darker, duller, and much mixed with gray; flanks overlaid with dull buff; white spot on nape less conspicuous. *Natal*: Drab to light drab. Bill and feet light sepia.

MEASUREMENTS: *Adult male*: Wing, 62.5–68.8 (average, 66.0) mm.; tail, 29.9–34.5 (32.3); bill (exposed culmen), 13.5–16.0 (14.7); tarsus, 14.5–16.0 (15.2); middle toe without claw, 10.9–11.9 (11.4). *Adult female*: Wing, 62.5–67.6 (65.0); tail, 29.4–33.0 (31.8); bill, 13.5–16.0 (14.7); tarsus, 13.0–15.5 (14.7); middle toe, 10.4–11.9 (11.4).

RANGE: Extreme s.e. Oklahoma to c. Alabama and s. Delaware, south to s.e. Texas and s.e. Georgia.

TEXAS: *Resident*: Collected in Walker, Trinity, Polk, Tyler, Jasper, Hardin, Harris (eggs), and Montgomery cos.

NESTING: *Nest*: On uplands or bottomlands, mostly in open pine or mixed pine-oak forests; in cavity in tree, 2–50 ft. above ground, either excavated by the birds in dead stub or limb of tree, or in natural cavity; nest composed of grass, parts of pine seeds, bits of cotton, wool, and feathers; lining of similar materials, but sometimes eggs laid on bare floor of cavity. *Eggs*: 4–7; short ovate; white, cream white, or dull white; profusely marked with reddish brown, purplish brown, or lavender gray; average size, 15.5 × 12.4 mm.

PYGMY NUTHATCH, *Sitta pygmaea* Vigors

SPECIES ACCOUNT

Closely resembles its southeastern U.S. counterpart, the Brown-headed Nuthatch (the two are allopatric), but has grayer cap; broader, blacker stripe through eye. Length, 4¼ in.; wingspan, 8; weight, ¼ oz.

RANGE: S. interior British Columbia to s.w. South Dakota, south through w. United States to n. Baja California and extreme s. Rockies, and through highland Mexico (chiefly Sierra Madre Occidental, c. highlands; local elsewhere) to Michoacán and Puebla.

TEXAS: (See map.) *Breeding*: Probably late Apr. to late July (no egg dates available, but nest located in Guadalupe Mts. by F. R. Gehlbach) from about 7,500 to 8,500 ft. Uncommon in Guadalupe Mts.; rare in Davis Mts. *Winter*: Early Sept. to late Apr. Fairly common in Guadalupe Mts.; uncommon and irregular at El Paso; scarce and highly erratic in northern Panhandle, Davis Mts., and Chisos Mts.; accidental at Dallas.

HAUNTS AND HABITS: Western mountain relative to the Brown-headed Nuthatch is the Pygmy. It lives on mountain tops, their slopes, canyons, and gulches, chiefly in open or dense coniferous or mixed pine-oak forest. Only very rarely does an individual descend to purely deciduous woods. It seems to be most attracted to large conifers, especially western yellow pine (*Pinus ponderosa*) and Douglasfir (*Pseudotsuga mucronata*). The only extensive stand in Texas of these two trees grows along the 8,000-foot contour line in the Guadalupe Mountains; among these evergreens live the only regularly breeding Pygmy Nuthatches in the state. To a Texas bird watcher it is an astounding sight to see within this state the crown of a Douglasfir hopping with these little birds—like animated Christmas tree ornaments. The Pygmy gathers at most times of the year in loose companies, small or large, which troop through the forest, moving from tree to tree in a restless procession. These companies sometimes associate with other small forest-inhabiting birds, such as the Mountain Chickadee, Plain Titmouse, and Audubon's Warbler.

Ordinarily the bird does not fly far, its normal regimen being from one tree to another, but it is capable of longer flights and at times is rather swift. Ever active and alert, the Pygmy remains usually on trees; here it searches both trunk and terminal foliage for insects and an occasional spider. Infrequently it is seen on the ground. It readily climbs about trunks and branches,

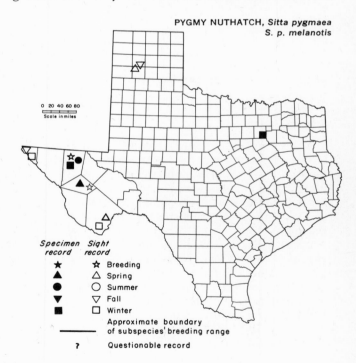

PYGMY NUTHATCH, *Sitta pygmaea*
S. p. melanotis

0 20 40 60 80
Scale in miles

Specimen record   *Sight record*
★   ☆ Breeding
▲   △ Spring
●   ○ Summer
▼   ▽ Fall
■   □ Winter
——— Approximate boundary of subspecies' breeding range
?   Questionable record

head downward like other nuthatches. More than some of its larger relatives, it is inclined to hunt on leaves, small twigs, and terminal foliage. Not a shy bird, it pays little attention to human observers even near its nest.

The usual note of the Pygmy is a rapid *kit, kit, kit,* practically identical with that of its extremely close relative, the Brown-headed Nuthatch. The high-pitched song, *ki-dee,* differs a wee bit, however. Note is heard all year; song issues in spring and early summer.

DETAILED ACCOUNT: ONE SUBSPECIES

BLACK-EARED PYGMY NUTHATCH, *Sitta pygmaea melanotis* van Rossem

DESCRIPTION: *Adults, nuptial plumage:* Acquired by wear from winter plumage. Pileum and hindneck deep grayish olive to dark olive gray, sometimes with more brownish tinge, hindneck with large more or less concealed buffy white or pale buff spot; remainder of upper surface deep slate gray or between slate gray and neutral gray; middle tail feathers neutral gray, medially white at base; remainder of tail feathers brownish black, all tipped, chiefly on outer webs, with deep neutral gray or deep mouse gray, two outer pairs with broad diagonal subterminal white band; wings fuscous to chaetura drab, tertials, lesser and median wing-coverts, and broad edgings of secondaries and of greater and primary coverts like back, primaries edged externally with paler gray, their inner margins basally whitish; sides of neck like crown; lores and postocular region forming broad stripe through eye chaetura black; cheeks and lower surface pale cream color; sides and flanks dull light neutral gray; lining of wing grayish white or buffy white, some of coverts hair brown. Bill slate color, black, or slate black, but basal half of mandible dull white, pale russian blue, or light king blue; iris dark vandyke brown, argus brown, or fuscous black; legs and feet dark plumbeous, plumbeous black, dark olive gray, or hair brown; claws fuscous black. *Adults, winter:* Acquired by complete postnuptial molt. Similar to nuptial adults, but lower parts cinnamon buff or pinkish buff, light nuchal spot more concealed and often more deeply buff. *First nuptial:* Acquired by wear from first winter. Practically identical with nuptial adults. *First winter:* Acquired by partial postjuvenal molt. Practically same as adults in winter. *Juvenal:* Acquired by complete postnatal molt. Similar to nuptial adults, but upper parts duller, more brownish and somewhat paler; pileum paler, more grayish or dull drab; lower parts duller, more grayish; sides and flanks strongly tinged with dull buff. *Natal:* Drab gray.

MEASUREMENTS: *Adult male:* Wing, 62.0–68.1 (average, 65.0) mm.; tail, 31.5–35.6 (34.0); bill (exposed culmen), 13.5–15.5 (14.5); tarsus, 14.0–15.5 (14.7); middle toe without claw, 10.9–11.9 (11.4). *Adult female:* Wing, 63.0–65.5 (63.8); tail, 33.0–35.1 (33.8); bill, 14.0–15.0 (14.5); tarsus, 14.0–15.5 (14.7); middle toe, 10.9–11.4 (11.2).

RANGE: S. British Columbia, south to s.e. California and Trans-Pecos Texas.

TEXAS: *Breeding:* Collected in Guadalupe Mts., Culberson Co. *Winter:* Three specimens: Culberson Co., The Bowl (Jan. 1, 1939, G. H. Lowery, Jr.); Jeff Davis Co., Davis Mts., north side of Mount Livermore (Apr. 9, 1937, J. Van Tyne); Dallas Co., Irving (Dec. 31, 1966, W. M. Pulich).

NESTING: *Nest:* On mountain slopes, mesas, or in canyons; forests, their margins, or even more open country; in hole in tree or crevice in bark, 20 or more ft. above ground; cavity stuffed with vegetable down, fibers, and feathers; lined with down, wool, feathers, and hair. *Eggs:* 6–9; ovate, without gloss; white, thickly spotted with dull red, pale reddish brown, and lilac, most numerously about large end; average size, 14.5 × 11.4 mm.

Creepers: Certhiidae

BROWN CREEPER, *Certhia familiaris* Linnaeus

SPECIES ACCOUNT

A small bird that creeps spirally up tree trunks; has long, slender, sharp, slightly decurved bill; stiff pointed tail feathers; short legs, large feet. Brown above streaked with whitish or grayish; whitish eye-stripe; dull white below. Length, 5¼ in.; wingspan, 7¾; weight, ¼ oz.

RANGE: In Eurasia, largely resident from Arctic Circle, south (somewhat locally) to s. Europe, Asia Minor, Himalayas, and Japan. In Western Hemisphere, from s.e. Alaska to Newfoundland, south to c. California coast, s. Great Lakes region, and s. New England, and through western mountain system to s. California, s. Nevada, Trans-Pecos Texas, Guerrero, Chiapas, Guatemala, and Nicaragua, and through Appalachians to North Carolina; migratory races (Pacific races mainly resident) winter chiefly south of Canada to n. Mexico and extreme s. United States.

TEXAS: (See map.) *Breeding*: Probably early May to late July (no egg dates available, but nest located in Guadalupe Mts. by F. R. Gehlbach) from 8,000 to about 8,500 ft. Uncommon in Guadalupe Mts. *Winter*: Late Oct. to late Mar.—occasionally late Apr. (extremes: Aug. 1, June 27). Common to fairly common in most of eastern three-quarters north of 29th parallel; uncommon in western quarter; uncommon (some years) to scarce in south Texas.

HAUNTS AND HABITS: *Certhia familiaris* is the only North American representative of the six-species Certhiidae—a family of small birds whose predominantly brown, black, and white plumages resemble the bark of trees on which they creep. Forests, groves, swamps, and timber along streams attract the retiring Brown Creeper. At times, it frequents even trees near dwellings and in city parks. Particularly when migrating, it appears in more open country. Small and protectively colored, it is hard to spot and often passes unnoticed as it forages on trees for bark-dwelling insects, their pupae, larvae, and eggs. It is sometimes found in the company of tits, chickadees, small woodpeckers, and warblers, but also is seen singly or in pairs.

Flight is usually not prolonged, generally from tree to tree, swift, and diving, usually from a higher to a lower position. In typical creeper fashion it flies to the base of a tree and then by successive hops or hitches climbs up the trunk spirally, using its stiff tail as a prop. All the time it investigates the bark for food.

The Brown Creeper's ordinary call is a single, long, very high-pitched *seeee*. This note resembles the trebled *see-see-see* of the Golden-crowned Kinglet. Song of this creeper, likewise high-pitched, is a clear *see-see-see ti-ti see* or variant thereof. Song period in the Guadalupe Mountains is probably from about mid-March to early July. Migrating and wintering Brown Creepers are seldom heard singing in Texas.

DETAILED ACCOUNT: THREE SUBSPECIES

AMERICAN BROWN CREEPER, *Certhia familiaris americana* Bonaparte

DESCRIPTION: *Adults, nuptial plumage*: Acquired by wear from winter plumage. Lores brownish black; anterior upper parts, including sides of head, sepia, streaked on each feather with dull buff or grayish white; conspicuous superciliary stripe of same; back cinnamon brown, mixed with ochraceous tawny, feathers with shaft streaks of dull light ochraceous gray; rump and upper tail-coverts tawny, ochraceous orange, or bright cin-

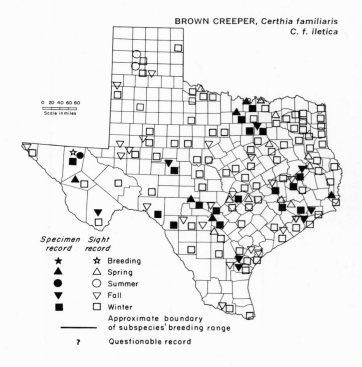

BROWN CREEPER, *Certhia familiaris*
C. f. iletica

0 20 40 60 80
Scale in miles

Specimen record — Sight record
★ / ☆ Breeding
▲ / △ Spring
● / ○ Summer
▼ / ▽ Fall
■ / □ Winter

Approximate boundary of subspecies' breeding range

? Questionable record

namon rufous; stiff and pointed tail feathers buffy brown, centrally hair brown, shafts dull cinnamon; wings rather dark hair brown or light fuscous, secondaries and inner primaries crossed about middle by broad oblique bar of dull buff or buffy white, wing-quills tipped with very pale buff or dull white and margined on outer webs for considerable distance near tips with very pale buff or dull white, inner webs of tertials and tips and outer margins ochraceous, russet, or drab, leaving only narrow streak on outer web near shaft dark hair brown or fuscous; greater coverts tipped with dull white, buffy white, or pale buff; median coverts with broad terminal shaft streaks of very pale buff or buffy white; lesser coverts similar to back but with narrower streaks; lower parts dull grayish white or buffy white, often much soiled, crissum pale dull buff; lining of wing white. Bill black, slate black, brownish black, or clove brown, basal half of mandible dull pale yellow, dull white, flesh color, pale lilac, or pinkish vinaceous; iris hazel or vandyke brown; legs and feet hair brown, brownish slate color, olive, light drab, drab, dark drab, light yellowish drab, or seal brown; claws slightly darker. *Adults, winter*: Acquired by complete postnuptial molt. Similar to nuptial adults but somewhat more rufescent above; posterior lower parts somewhat more strongly buff. *First nuptial*: Acquired by wear from first winter. Similar to nuptial adults, but upper parts rather paler; lower parts rather duller. *First winter*: Acquired by partial postjuvenal molt. Like adults in winter but somewhat lighter. Maxilla and tip of mandible brownish black; rest of mandible vinaceous; iris vandyke brown; legs and feet broccoli brown. *Juvenal*: Acquired by complete postnatal molt. Similar to adults, but upper surface presenting more spotted appearance, lighter areas more extensive and whole tone of plumage paler, more buffy or ochraceous; upper tail-coverts decidedly paler and duller—cinnamon buff to clay color; lower parts duller, more grayish and buffy. Maxilla brownish black; mandible pinkish white, dull light hair brown, or clove brown. *Natal* (this plumage of this race not seen in Texas): Hair brown. Bill and feet pinkish buff.

MEASUREMENTS: *Adult male*: Wing, 62.0–68.1 (average, 65.5) mm.; tail, 61.0–66.0 (63.8); bill (exposed culmen), 11.9–15.0 (13.7); tarsus, 14.5–16.0 (15.2); middle toe without claw, 10.4–11.4 (10.9). *Adult female*: Wing, 59.9–67.1 (62.7); tail, 55.1–65.0 (61.2); bill, 11.9–15.0 (12.7); tarsus, 14.5–16.0 (15.0); middle toe, 10.4–11.4 (11.2).

RANGE: W. Manitoba to n. Nova Scotia, south to s.e. Nebraska and n. New Jersey. Winters from s. Manitoba and c. Nova Scotia to s. Texas and s. Florida.

TEXAS: *Winter*: Taken north to Cooke, east to Orange (Mar. 2), south to Nueces (Nov. 18), west to Kinney and Brewster (Nov. 9) cos. Fairly common.

NESTING: (This race does not nest in Texas.) *Nest*: On uplands or lowlands, in forests or swamps; usually not high above ground, on old stub or trunk of coniferous or deciduous tree, such as pine, oak, or elm, behind loose hanging bark or in knot hole or deserted woodpecker nest; nest composed of pine or other kinds of bark, twigs, moss, bits of wood, lichens, plant down, and grass; lined sometimes with a few spider cocoons, feathers, and hair, all bound together with spider webs. *Eggs*: 4–9; nearly ovate to short rounded ovate; slightly glossy; pure white, grayish, or cream white, spotted and dotted with reddish brown, sometimes with purplish brown, largely about greater end; average size, 15.2 × 12.2 mm.

ROCKY MOUNTAIN BROWN CREEPER, *Certhia familiaris montana* Ridgway

DESCRIPTION: *Adults, nuptial plumage*: Similar to *C. f. americana*, but tail, and particularly bill, longer; upper parts rather darker and more grayish (less rufescent or ochraceous), light streaks more whitish or grayish (less buffy); lower parts more purely white, less buffy laterally.

MEASUREMENTS: *Adult male*: Wing, 63.0–67.6 (average, 66.0) mm.; tail, 64.0–70.1 (65.3); bill (exposed culmen), 14.2–16.5 (15.5); tarsus, 14.5–15.5 (15.2); middle toe without claw, 10.9–11.4 (11.2). *Adult female*: Wing, 61.5–66.5 (63.8); tail, 61.5–66.0 (63.8); bill, 13.0–14.5 (13.7); tarsus, 14.5–15.5 (15.2); middle toe, 10.4–11.4 (10.9).

RANGE: C. British Columbia to c. Alberta, south to c. Arizona and s. New Mexico. Winters from breeding range to s.e. California and w. Texas (casually).

TEXAS: *Winter*: Two specimens from western portion: Jeff Davis Co., 1 mi. north of Fort Davis (Mar. 17, 1937, J. Van Tyne); Tom Green Co., Concho River near San Angelo (Jan. 18, 1887, W. Lloyd). One specimen from Trinity Co., 1 mi. east of Trinity (Jan. 5, 1937, P. D. Goodrum).

PECOS BROWN CREEPER, *Certhia familiaris iletica* Oberholser, new subspecies (see Appendix A)

DESCRIPTION: *Adults, nuptial plumage*: Similar to *C. f. montana*, but tail, bill, and middle toe shorter; upper parts less ochraceous, especially on light areas. *Natal*: Probably similar to *C. f. americana*.

MEASUREMENTS: *Adult male*: Wing, 64.0–65.0 (average, 64.5) mm.; tail, 56.4–60.5 (57.7); bill (exposed culmen), 14.5–15.7 (15.0); tarsus, 15.0–16.0 (15.2); middle toe without claw, 10.4–10.9 (10.7). *Adult female*: Wing, 59.4–65.0 (62.7); tail, 56.9–65.0 (62.1); bill, 12.4–13.5 (13.2); tarsus, 14.0–16.0 (15.2); middle toe, 9.9–10.9 (10.4).

TYPE: Adult female, no. 341640, U.S. National Museum, Biological Surveys collection; The Bowl, Guadalupe Mts., Culberson Co., Texas; May 19, 1938, T. D. Burleigh, original no., 5068.

RANGE: N. Trans-Pecos Texas. Winters from breeding range to Val Verde Co., Texas.

TEXAS: *Breeding*: Collected in Guadalupe Mts., Culberson Co. *Winter*: Taken in Culberson, Jeff Davis (Mar. 16), and Val Verde cos. Fairly common.

NESTING: Similar to that of *C. f. americana*, but restricted to mountain forests.

Dippers: Cinclidae

DIPPER, *Cinclus mexicanus* Swainson

SPECIES ACCOUNT

Also called American Dipper and Water Ouzel. Suggests a big plump wren. A robust, dark gray bird of fast-running mountain streams; has broad rounded wings and stubby tail; frequently teeters and bobs. Length, 7¼ in.; wingspan, 11½.

RANGE: Aleutian Islands, c. Alaska, c. Alberta, and s.w. South Dakota, south to s. California and c. New Mexico, thence through highlands of Mexico and Central America to w. Panama. Casual wanderer to c. Texas.

TEXAS: *Casual*: Seven records, all of single birds, one substantiated by color photographs: Kerr Co., on Johnson Creek, tributary of Guadalupe River (July or early Aug., 1919, Aug. 19, 1921, Bessie Reid); Kimble Co., Seven Hundred Springs near headwaters of Llano River (May 6, 1925, Aug. 30, 1937, Reid); Crosby Co., Silver Falls on White River (May 2, 1969, S. D. Casto, H. W. Garner; photographed in color on May 3, 1969, Mr. and Mrs. R. W. Wiley; one of these photos subsequently reproduced in black and white, see Casto and Garner, 1969, *Bull. Texas Ornithological Society* 3: 29; nos. 37 a & b in Texas Photo-Record File, Texas A&M University). Wilbarger Co., at an earthen tank 8 mi. south of Vernon (May 14, 1939, R. L. More, G. E. Maxon); Baylor Co., western end of Lake Kemp (May 14, 1939, More and Maxon; probably not same individual as in Wilbarger Co.).

HAUNTS AND HABITS: Dippers are the only passerines which habitually swim and dive; they are built to withstand the rigors of swift cold mountain streams. Like the four other members of Cinclidae, the American Dipper has firm and dense plumage with a thick undercoat of down. Additional adaptations are an enlarged oil gland for waterproofing feathers, and nostril flaps which close when the bird is submerged. Its bulky domed nest is placed on a rock ledge, behind a waterfall, on a rock or fallen log in a watercourse, or it is wedged in a hollow in a wall, between tree roots or bridge girders. This well-camouflaged, ovenlike structure of moss and grass holds usually four or five unmarked, satiny white eggs. The Dipper often raises two broods a year.

Cinclus mexicanus is solitary. It is also distinctly restive. Like many small birds that dwell by water, it is an exuberant teeterer—sometimes bobbing forty to sixty times in a minute. Flight is buzzy, brief, swift, and close to the water. From a midstream or bankside perch on a rock or snag, the Dipper dives or walks into rushing current or cascading rapids. As it swims underwater in pursuit of its prey it "flies" with its short broad wings which are well concaved on the under surface; its brief tail cuts down on drag. It frequently appears to walk on the bottom. While the bird is submerged or in the midst of heavy spray, the flashing white of its nictitating membrane can be seen as it blinks away excess water. The Dipper forages mainly in shallows along stream margins by dipping in the water and upturning pebbles and leaves with its bill. It eats chiefly insects (especially larvae of black flies, caddis flies, and mosquitoes), also small crustaceans and mollusks, fish eggs, and tiny fish. The only bird observed feeding in Texas, the Silver Falls individual, was taking black fly (Simuliidae) larvae anchored to stream rocks.

The Dipper's note is a sharp *zeet*, sounded singly or repeatedly. Its variable song is a rapid, wrenlike collection of trills and flutelike notes; the bird sings year-round except when molting in late summer. All vocalizations, especially the call note, are loud, so as to be heard above roaring water. The bird sings from the air or from a rock or similar vantage.

DETAILED ACCOUNT: ONE SUBSPECIES

NOTE: Although none of the birds sighted in Texas can safely be identified to subspecies, H. C. Oberholser believed that Dippers occurring in the state probably belonged to the Rocky Mountain race, which description follows.

ROCKY MOUNTAIN DIPPER, *Cinclus mexicanus unicolor* Bonaparte

C. m. unicolor of A.O.U. check-list, 1957, is considered as two races in the present work.

DESCRIPTION: *Adults, nuptial plumage*: Acquired by wear from winter plumage. Pileum and anterior part of hindneck olive brown to fuscous or light fuscous, passing on posterior hindneck into mouse gray, thence to rather deep mouse gray of remaining upper parts; tail fuscous or verging toward deep mouse gray, shafts of feathers rather darker and middle rectrices edged with mouse gray; wing-quills fuscous, inner margins hair brown, outer vanes margined with color of back, this on tertials occupying nearly all outer vane; sides of head like pileum but slightly lighter, small elongated white or buffy white spot just above eye; sides of neck similar but shading posteriorly into gray of upper surface; chin and throat rather dull buffy brown to rather light olive brown; remainder of lower surface rather light mouse gray, under tail-coverts tipped with dull white or buffy white; lining of wing like lower surface, outer edge somewhat paler, feathers tipped with white or buffy white. Bill plumbeous black or drab, but extreme base of mandible brownish white or dull pale yellow or yellowish white; iris burnt umber or bright hazel; legs and feet light flesh color, toes rather darker; claws tinged with brown. *Adults, winter*: Acquired by complete postnuptial molt. Similar to nuptial adults, but upper parts darker and duller with slight brownish appearance imparted by brownish tips of feathers; obscurely scalelike appearance of feathers more evident than in nuptial; wing-quills tipped rather conspicuously with dull white; many feathers of lower parts tipped with dull pale buff, buffy white, or dull white, whitish tips of lower tail-coverts broader and more conspicuous. Base of bill more yellowish. *First nuptial*: Acquired by wear from first winter. Similar to nuptial adults, but pileum, chin, and throat more grayish, often almost purely so (less distinctly brown); plumage both above and below averaging more purely gray (less brownish). *First winter*: Acquired by partial postjuvenal molt, which does not involve wing-quills or tail. Similar to adults in winter, but upper surface averaging rather lighter and still more purely grayish (less brownish), pileum still appreciably more brownish than back; below distinctly lighter and somewhat more purely gray; white and buffy edgings on lower parts broader and more numerous. *Juvenal*: Acquired by complete postnatal molt. Similar to first winter male and female, but upper surface averaging somewhat lighter, pileum scarcely or not at all brownish, and feathers with appreciably more scalelike dark margins; lower parts decidedly paler; chin white or very pale buff, sometimes mottled with drab gray or smoke gray; remainder of lower parts between smoke gray and drab gray or between drab gray and mouse gray, much mottled with dull white, buffy white, or very pale buff; sides, flanks, and crissum mouse gray, wood brown, avellaneous, or dull cinnamon buff, these colors often much mixed. Maxilla and tip of mandible dull plumbeous or bone brown; remainder of mandible orange salmon color or wood brown, but base of maxilla and cutting edges of bill similar although duller or maize yellow; iris raw umber; legs and feet light flesh color or tilleul buff, but posterior part of tarsus, soles of toes, and tips of claws avellaneous.

MEASUREMENTS: *Adult male*: Wing, 90.9–100.1 (average, 95.8) mm.; tail, 47.0–57.7 (52.6); bill (exposed culmen), 15.5–19.0 (17.0); tarsus, 28.9–31.8 (30.5); middle toe without claw, 20.1–23.6 (21.6). *Adult female*: Wing, 83.1–91.9 (87.1); tail, 43.9–52.1 (47.5); bill, 16.0–18.0 (17.0); tarsus, 25.9–29.9 (28.2); middle toe, 18.5–22.1 (20.9).

RANGE: N.w. Alaska and c. Yukon to s.w. South Dakota, south (exclusive of Pacific Coast Ranges, which are occupied by *C. m. mortoni*) to s.e. California, s.e. Arizona, and c. New Mexico. Casual to c. Texas.

TEXAS: *Casual*: See species account.

Wrens: Troglodytidae

HOUSE WREN, *Troglodytes domesticus* (Wilson)

SPECIES ACCOUNT

Troglodytes aedon of A.O.U. check-list, 1957 (see Appendix A). Northern House Wren of many authors. Small, plump body; thin, longish bill; short, rounded wings; narrow, rounded tail often cocked over back. A plain wren; brown above; lacks any distinct eye-stripe; wings and tail finely barred with dark brown; brownish or grayish below (palest on throat, belly). Length, 4¾ in.; wingspan, 6½; weight, ½ oz.

RANGE: S. Canada, south to n. Baja California, s.e. Arizona, New Mexico, n. Texas (irregularly), Tennessee, n. Georgia, and North Carolina. Winters from s. United States through Mexico to Isthmus of Tehuantepec.

TEXAS: (See map.) *Breeding*: Probably late Apr. to late July (no egg dates available, but nests located in Guadalupe Mts. by F. R. Gehlbach; 2 nests at Weatherford, Parker Co., May, 1922, S. J. Rucker) from about 400 to 8,000 ft. Uncommon in The Bowl, Guadalupe Mts.; rare and highly irregular in northern Panhandle (bird carrying food into hole in cottonwood, Palo Duro State Park, July 15, 1935, Paul Russell) and Dallas–Fort Worth area (last suspected nesting: Dallas, summer 1958, Mrs. E. E. Winford). *Migration*: Late Mar. to early May; mid-Sept. to mid-Nov. (extremes: Mar. 4, June 12; Sept. 2, Nov. 25). Very common to fairly common through eastern two-thirds; fairly common through western third. *Winter*: Mid-Oct. to late Apr. Common to fairly common in much of eastern half, but normally uncommon north of Austin and Bryan–College Station; uncommon in western half south of Lubbock; probably absent most years from northern Panhandle.

HAUNTS AND HABITS: The sixty-three members of the Troglodytidae are active, inquisitive little songbirds, supposedly close kin to the thrashers and thrushes. All but one—the Winter Wren—dwell exclusively in the New World. The House Wren, one of nine wrens found in Texas, lives chiefly in woodland undergrowth. This bird dodges continually about bushes, old logs, and thickets near the ground; it frequents also cultivated areas, fence rows, and the vicinity of houses, and particularly in summer, farm or ranch buildings. This wren prefers to move singly or in pairs but occasionally associates with several individuals of its own kind in the brush.

Flight is usually not prolonged, but the bird is strong on the wing, flying rather directly and at times swiftly with rapid wing-beats. It is quick of movement, very active, and often seen with its tail elevated. Amid low bushes and tangled brush, this wren devours grasshoppers, locusts, crickets, beetles, gnats, ants, wasps; also spiders, millipedes, and snails. Sometimes it ascends to roofs, chimney tops, poles, and posts about farm and garden. It does not, however, much frequent the ground. In the northern United States where House Wrens are common breeders, some individuals have been observed puncturing eggs of other bird species found within their nesting territories.

The call notes of the House Wren include a rapidly repeated *chur* and a harsh "scold." The song, of poor musical quality, is a fizzing bubbling chatter that wells up then fizzles at the end. The few House Wrens which have nested in Texas probably sang chiefly from mid-March to early August; wintering or migrating individ-

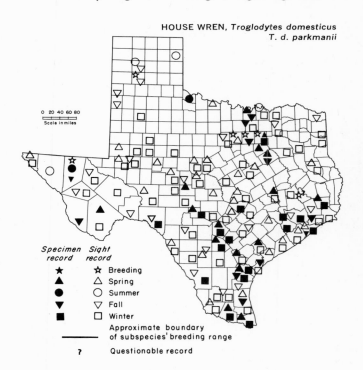

HOUSE WREN, *Troglodytes domesticus*
T. d. parkmanii

0 20 40 60 80
Scale in miles

Specimen record	Sight record	
★	☆	Breeding
▲	△	Spring
●	○	Summer
▼	▽	Fall
■	☐	Winter

——— Approximate boundary of subspecies' breeding range

?   Questionable record

uals occasionally burst into song, especially in March and April.

Detailed Account: Three Subspecies

EASTERN HOUSE WREN, *Troglodytes domesticus domesticus* (Wilson)

Troglodytes aedon aedon of A.O.U. check-list, 1957 (see Appendix A).

DESCRIPTION: *Adults, nuptial plumage*: Acquired by wear from winter plumage. Upper parts cinnamon brown, anteriorly somewhat more grayish, back crossed by numerous narrow more or less obsolete bars; rump and upper tail-coverts russet with many more or less concealed white subterminal shaft spots and blackish brown bars; tail dull russet, sometimes more grayish terminally and even whitish on outermost pair of feathers, with a number of fuscous black bars; wing-quills between buffy brown and hair brown, tertials and outer webs of primaries and secondaries with broad bars of cinnamon brown, upper wing-coverts like back, lesser coverts rather more grayish, and all narrowly barred with rufescent hair brown; lores and rather indistinct superciliary stripe buffy gray, sides of head dull grayish buff, obscurely and finely streaked with buffy brown or dull buffy brown, narrowly streaked with buff or brownish white; lower parts dull white, washed with dull pale buff or dull vinaceous buff, chin and throat usually paler, middle of abdomen more purely white, sides dull avellaneous, sometimes with obscure darker spots or inconspicuous narrow bars; flanks and crissum cinnamon brown or snuff brown with narrow, sometimes obscure, buffy brown or fuscous bars, crissum with broader fuscous black bars and sometimes dull white interspaces particularly on longer lower tail-coverts; lining of wing dull brownish white. Bill black, slate black, or blackish brown, basal half of mandible mouse gray, cinereous, vinaceous, fawn, flesh color, dull yellow, or dull white; inside of mouth deep naples yellow; corner of mouth pale yellow; iris dark brown or raw umber; legs and feet drab gray, drab, ecru drab, or hair brown. *Adults, winter*: Acquired by complete postnuptial molt. Similar to nuptial adults, but upper parts darker, somewhat more sooty; lower parts more deeply colored and more suffused with drab and vinaceous; fine spots on breast drab. *First nuptial*: Acquired by wear from first winter. Very similar to nuptial adults. *First winter*: Acquired by partial postjuvenal molt. Like adults in winter but paler above, somewhat more brownish (less grayish); lower parts sometimes somewhat marked with brown. *Juvenal*: Acquired by complete postnatal molt. Similar to adults in winter but somewhat more uniform, less distinctly barred above; lower parts darker; sides and flanks sayal brown to dull cinnamon rufous and nearly uniform, bars almost obsolete; anterior lower surface much more heavily spotted and finely barred with drab and dark brown than in adults. Maxilla black or dull brown; mandible bluish gray or yellow; legs and feet brown. *Natal* (this plumage of this race not seen in Texas): Sepia. Bill and feet buffy sepia.

MEASUREMENTS: *Adult male*: Wing, 49.5–53.6 (average, 51.3) mm.; tail, 41.9–45.5 (44.2); bill (exposed culmen), 11.4–13.5 (12.2); tarsus, 16.5–17.5 (17.0); middle toe without claw, 10.9–13.0 (12.2). *Adult female*: Wing, 46.5–51.6 (48.8); tail, 37.6–43.9 (40.9); bill, 10.9–12.7 (11.7); tarsus, 16.0–18.0 (16.8); middle toe, 10.9–13.0 (12.2).

RANGE: N. New Brunswick, south to Virginia. Winters from c. Texas and s.e. South Carolina to s. Tamaulipas and s. Florida.

TEXAS: *Migration*: Collected in Cooke (1 specimen), Arkansas (1), Jim Wells (1), and Kenedy (1) cos. Uncommon. *Winter*: Three specimens: Travis Co., Austin (Jan. 20, 1905, E. Perry, Jr.); Cameron Co., Brownsville (Jan. 14, 1911, Feb. 12, 1907, A. P. Smith).

OHIO HOUSE WREN, *Troglodytes domesticus baldwini* Oberholser

DESCRIPTION: *Adults, nuptial plumage (brown phase)*: Simi-

lar to *T. d. domesticus*, but upper surface darker, duller, much less rufescent (more sooty); sides and flanks less rufescent (more grayish); remainder of lower surface more grayish (less buffy). *Adults, nuptial (gray phase)*: Similar to brown phase, but upper parts much more grayish (less rufescent). In this plumage more like *T. d. parkmanii* (see below), but darker.

MEASUREMENTS: *Adult male*: Wing, 46.0–52.1 (average, 49.8) mm.; tail, 38.1–44.4 (41.7); bill (exposed culmen), 10.7–13.2 (11.7); tarsus, 16.0–18.0 (17.0); middle toe without claw, 11.4–13.0 (11.9). *Adult female*: Wing, 46.5–50.0 (48.8); tail, 38.1–41.9 (40.6); bill, 10.4–11.9 (11.4); tarsus, 16.5–18.0 (17.0); middle toe, 11.4–12.4 (11.9).

RANGE: W. Michigan to s. Quebec, south to e. Tennessee and e. North Carolina. Winters from Trans-Pecos Texas and s. South Carolina to s. Texas and s. Florida.

TEXAS: *Migration*: Collected in Dallas (1 specimen), Hardin (1), Chambers (1), Galveston (1), and Culberson (1) cos. Uncommon. *Winter*: Taken in Bexar (1 specimen), Hardin (1), Harris (1), Fort Bend (1), and Hidalgo (1) cos. Uncommon.

WESTERN HOUSE WREN, *Troglodytes domesticus parkmanii* Audubon

DESCRIPTION: *Adults, nuptial plumage*: Similar to *T. d. baldwini* but much paler and sometimes more grayish above; sides and flanks paler, rather more rufescent; rest of lower parts paler, more buffy. Similar to *T. d. domesticus*, but very much paler, both above and below, and much more grayish. *Natal*: Probably similar to *T. d. domesticus*.

MEASUREMENTS: *Adult male*: Wing, 49.5–53.6 (average, 51.3) mm.; tail, 41.9–45.5 (44.2); bill (exposed culmen), 11.4–13.5 (12.2); tarsus, 16.5–17.5 (17.0); middle toe without claw, 10.9–13.0 (12.2). *Adult female*: Wing, 49.0–52.3 (51.1); tail, 41.9–47.0 (44.7); bill, 10.9–12.7 (11.7); tarsus, 16.0–18.0 (16.8); middle toe, 10.9–13.0 (12.2).

RANGE: S.w. British Columbia to c. Ontario, south to n.w. Baja California, w. Tamaulipas, and s.w. Kentucky. Winters from c. California, s. Mississippi, and s.e. South Carolina to s. Baja California and s.w. Mexico.

TEXAS: *Breeding*: Collected in Guadalupe Mts., Culberson Co. Sight records of nesting activity in Randall, Parker, Tarrant, and Dallas cos. apparently of this subspecies (see species account). *Migration*: Collected north to Cooke, east to Navarro and Brazos, south to Cameron, west to Brewster cos. Common. *Winter*: Taken north to Dallas, east to Waller, south to Cameron, west to Val Verde cos. Common.

NESTING: *Nest*: In more or less open country, on edges of woods, in pastures, orchards, especially in vicinity of human habitations, and on buildings themselves, usually no more than 8–10 ft. above ground; in various nooks about house, in martin, wren, or other bird box, hollow tree, woodpecker hole, other cavity in tree, log, or stump, in fact, anywhere a suitable cavity is discovered; loosely constructed of interlaced sticks, often these being surprisingly large for size of the bird; weeds and grass fill cavity in which nest is built, leaving small hole for entrance; lined with various soft substances (e.g., fur, feathers, hair, and wool), fine weed stems, rootlets, and bits of bark. *Eggs*: 4–9; ovate; pinkish white, thickly spotted with reddish brown or purplish brown; average size, 16.3 × 12.7 mm.

WINTER WREN, *Nannus troglodytes* (Linnaeus)

Species Account

Troglodytes troglodytes of A.O.U. check-list, 1957 (see Appendix A). Tiny, rotund, dark body; very slender bill; cocked, stub tail; bobs on limbs, logs. Rusty brown above; pale buff eye-stripe; dull buff below (paler on throat); flanks heavily barred with dark brown. Length, 4 in.; wingspan, 6; weight, ¼ oz.

RANGE: Breeds throughout cooler parts of Eurasia, on many boreal islands, and in North America from s. Alaska across forested Canada to Newfoundland, south to c. California, c. Idaho, Great Lakes region, and s. New England, and in Appalachians to Georgia. In North America winters south to extreme s. United States.

TEXAS: (See map.) *Winter*: Mid-Nov.—often as early as Oct.—to late Mar. (extremes: Sept. 1, May 2). Fairly common to uncommon in eastern half north of 29th parallel; uncommon to scarce in remainder of state, but rare in northern Panhandle and Rio Grande delta.

HAUNTS AND HABITS: The Winter Wren is the northernmost ranging of the true wrens; it is also the only American bird species which has successfully colonized large portions of Eurasia. This wren is appropriately named as far as Texas is concerned; here it is very much a bird of winter. On its breeding grounds it inhabits dense coniferous forests, swamps, and deep thickets removed from cultivated areas. It constructs a bulky but compact nest of twigs, moss, fur, and feathers in a cavity of a tree or log, in a brush heap, or on the ground among tangled roots. When wintering in Texas it remains primarily in thickets, brush piles, cane or cattail patches, woodland undergrowth, and streamside bushes particularly in bottomlands. Sometimes it may be found about farms or even in parks or yards of towns if shrubbery is especially dense. Only very occasionally is it seen in more open country, on bare rocks, or in grass.

The Winter is active and quick but seldom flies far. Exceedingly shy and elusive, it hides about hollow

logs, upturned roots, and crevices of brushy undergrowth. In these places it also searches for insects, their larvae, and spiders. As it forages, it nervously flits about, often with stubby tail vertical and head raised. It is rarely seen except singly; at most, in twos or threes.

Ordinary calls of the Winter Wren are a low *chirr*, *chuck*, and *kip* (the last sometimes doubled). Its song, one of the most beautiful heard in North America, is a succession of liquid notes, tinkling warbles, and high trills, the whole extending sometimes for nine seconds —much longer than most bird songs. Unfortunately this splendid performance is seldom heard in Texas, both because this species rarely sings in winter, and because few noise-damaged, mid-twentieth-century human ears can hear its exceptionally high notes.

DETAILED ACCOUNT: FOUR SUBSPECIES

EASTERN WINTER WREN, *Nannus troglodytes hiemalis* (Vieillot)

DESCRIPTION: *Adults, nuptial plumage*: Acquired by wear from winter plumage. Upper surface cinnamon brown or prout brown, but upper tail-coverts more rufescent, and all except pileum and hindneck, barred obscurely with fuscous or fuscous black, as well as to some extent, particularly on scapulars, with dull brownish white, feathers of rump with rather large concealed silvery or grayish white subterminal spots; tail reddish brown like upper tail-coverts, narrowly and numerously barred with fuscous; wings fuscous, broadly barred on tertials and outer webs of secondaries and of inner primaries with cinnamon brown or prout brown, on outer webs of primaries narrowly barred with dull brown, dull buff, or even dull white; wing-coverts like back, barred very narrowly with fuscous, median coverts with small buffy white spots terminally; sides of head dull cinnamon buff mixed with cinnamon brown, lores and conspicuous superciliary stripe pale dull buff; postocular stripe dull cinnamon brown; lower surface in general dull cinnamon buff or dull light pinkish buff, more or less mottled or barred with darker and conspicuously spotted on sides with fuscous, but flanks and crissum fuscous or chaetura drab, barred narrowly with dull grayish white, cinnamon brown, or dull buff; lining of wing buff or grayish white, narrowly barred with fuscous or hair brown. Maxilla brownish black or dull brown; mandible vinaceous, dull light yellow, or drab; inside of mouth orange; iris dark burnt umber; legs and feet brownish flesh color, wood brown, light drab, drab, or pale yellow. *Adults, winter*: Acquired by complete postnuptial molt. Like nuptial adults. *First nuptial*: Acquired by wear from first winter. Often identical with nuptial adults but often less conspicuously barred. *First winter*: Acquired by partial postjuvenal molt, which does not involve wing-quills. Similar to adults in winter but somewhat more rufescent; barring of plumage not so heavy. Maxilla black; mandible seal brown; iris vandyke brown; legs, feet, and claws mummy brown. *Juvenal*: Acquired by complete postnatal molt. Similar to adults in winter, but upper surface darker, more sooty (less rufescent), and less evidently barred, sometimes practically plain; superciliary stripe and postocular stripe indistinct or wanting; lower surface darker, duller, more grayish; throat barred and feathers tipped conspicuously with fuscous. Maxilla slate color or clove brown; mandible slate gray, with basal two-thirds yellowish white or flesh color; iris dark brown; legs and feet prout brown or broccoli brown.

MEASUREMENTS: *Adult male*: Wing, 45.0–50.0 (average, 47.8) mm.; tail, 27.9–32.0 (30.2); bill (exposed culmen), 10.9–11.9 (11.2); tarsus, 18.0–19.6 (18.5); middle toe without claw, 11.9–13.0 (12.7). *Adult female*: Wing, 39.9–47.0 (43.7); tail, 24.9–29.9 (27.7); bill, 10.4–11.9 (11.2); tarsus, 17.0–18.0 (17.8); middle toe, 10.9–13.0 (11.9).

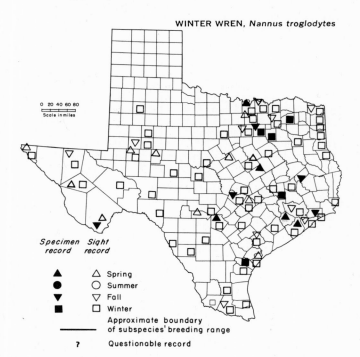

WINTER WREN, *Nannus troglodytes*

0 20 40 60 80
Scale in miles

Specimen   Sight
record   record

▲   △ Spring
●   ○ Summer
▼   ▽ Fall
■   □ Winter

——— Approximate boundary
      of subspecies' breeding range

? Questionable record

RANGE: C. Alberta to c. Nova Scotia, south to c. Minnesota and e. West Virginia. Winters from n.e. Nebraska and s. Maine to s. Texas and s. Florida.

TEXAS: *Winter*: Taken north to Dallas and Hopkins, east to Chambers (Oct. 21), south to Brazoria (Mar. 2) and San Patricio, west to Brewster (Oct. 22) cos. Fairly common.

ALLEGHENY WINTER WREN, *Nannus troglodytes pullus* Burleigh

DESCRIPTION: *Adults, nuptial plumage*: Similar to *N. t. hiemalis*, but bill slenderer; upper parts darker, more sooty (less rufescent); lower surface lighter, but barring on flanks and abdomen heavier.

MEASUREMENTS: *Adult male*: Wing, 47.3–50.5 (average, 48.8) mm.; tail, 28.9–32.0 (30.7); bill (exposed culmen), 10.7–11.4 (11.2); tarsus, 18.0–19.6 (18.8); middle toe without claw, 10.7–11.9 (11.7). *Adult female*: Wing, 42.9–50.0 (45.7); tail, 27.4–29.9 (28.7); bill, 10.7–11.4 (11.2); tarsus, 17.8–19.0 (18.3); middle toe, 10.9–11.9 (11.4).

RANGE: In mountains of West Virginia and n.w. Maryland, south to n. Georgia. Winters at lower altitudes in breeding range to c. Louisiana and s. South Carolina; casual in Texas.

TEXAS: *Winter*: One specimen: Kaufman Co., 20 mi. east of Dallas (Jan. 8, 1939, W. A. Mayer).

NEWFOUNDLAND WINTER WREN, *Nannus troglodytes aquilonaris* (Burleigh and Peters)

Race not in A.O.U. check-list, 1957 (see Appendix A).

DESCRIPTION: *Adults, nuptial plumage*: Similar to *N. t. hiemalis* but darker, more sooty (less rufescent) above; under surface somewhat paler, though bars on flanks and abdomen heavier and more extensive. Resembling *N. t. pullus*, but upper parts paler and more grayish or sooty (less rufescent).

MEASUREMENTS: Practically identical with those of *N. t. hiemalis*. (Only averages given.) *Adult male*: Wing, 48.0 mm.; tail, 30.5; bill (exposed culmen), 10.7. *Adult female*: Wing, 45.5; tail, 28.2; bill, 10.4.

RANGE: Newfoundland. Winters from s. New England (probably) to c. Louisiana and s. South Carolina; casual in Texas.

TEXAS: *Winter*: One specimen: Cooke Co., Red River north of Gainesville (Mar. 18, 1879, G. H. Ragsdale).

IDAHO WINTER WREN, *Nannus troglodytes salebrosus* (Burleigh)

Race not in A.O.U. check-list, 1957 (see Appendix A).

DESCRIPTION: Similar to *N. t. hiemalis*, but upper parts much darker, more sooty (less rufescent), feathers of back and rump with very obscure or no dark bars; anterior lower surface decidedly more deeply colored.

MEASUREMENTS: *Adult male*: Wing, 44.5–50.0 (average, 47.3) mm.; tail, 28.0–33.0 (30.5); bill (exposed culmen), 10.0–12.0 (11.0). *Adult female*: Wing, 42.0–48.0 (45.0); tail, 27.0–30.5 (28.2); bill, 10.0–12.0 (11.0).

RANGE: S. British Columbia and s.w. Alberta, south to n.e. Oregon and w. Montana. Winters from w. Washington and w. Idaho to w. Nevada; casual in Trans-Pecos Texas.

TEXAS: *Winter*: One specimen: Brewster Co., Hot Springs (Oct. 22, 1937, A. E. Borell).

BEWICK'S WREN, *Thryomanes bewickii* (Audubon)

SPECIES ACCOUNT

Jerks, swings, and cocks long, mobile tail. Brown or grayish brown above; prominent white eye-stripe; white-edged blackish tail; clear whitish below. Length, 5¼ in.; wingspan, 7; weight, ¼ oz.

RANGE: Largely resident from s.w. British Columbia,

s. Nevada, s.w. Wyoming, Colorado, w. Nebraska, s. Kansas, s.e. Nebraska, extreme s. Great Lakes region, and Virginia, south to Texas and n. parts of Gulf states, thence to s. Baja California and mainland Mexico (chiefly highlands) to Oaxaca and Tamaulipas. Northern races winter south to n. Gulf coast and s. Florida.

TEXAS: (See map.) *Breeding*: Early Feb. to mid-Aug. (eggs, Feb. 26 to July 22) from near sea level to 8,500 ft. Common to fairly common through most of western two-thirds, east to Hunt, Navarro, Brazos, and Matagorda cos., where uncommon; scarce in San Jacinto Co.; very rare on upper coast (last recorded breeding: near Beaumont, July 4, 1916, Bessie Reid). *Winter*: Mid-Oct. to late Apr. (extremes: Sept. 18, May 11). Common to fairly common throughout breeding range; fairly common to uncommon in much of eastern third, but scarce on upper coast.

HAUNTS AND HABITS: The Bewick's Wren is a thicket and brush bird. It seems to thrive best in hilly, semiarid localities; the bushes it lives within may or may not grow near water. This habitat contrasts with that of the Carolina Wren—a bird which is rather closely restricted to streamside woody vegetation, at least in the dry western two-thirds of Texas. Although the Bewick's Wren comes freely about ranch woodpiles and houses (where it is frequently called "house wren" by Texas ranchmen), it disappears from excessively cleared, over-urbanized areas. The bird is not ordinarily gregarious, although sometimes a few are seen together, this probably being a family group.

Flight is commonly not prolonged—most often from one bush or small tree to another; it is not particularly swift but is performed with rapid wing-beats. The Bewick's hops about with an erect tail which the bird frequently jerks to one side. Although not shy, it is

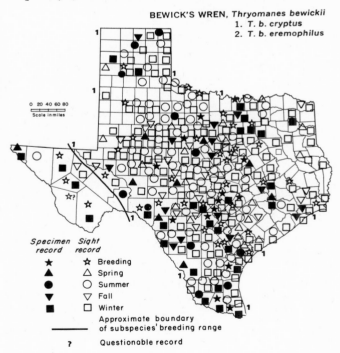

BEWICK'S WREN, *Thryomanes bewickii*
1. *T. b. cryptus*
2. *T. b. eremophilus*

0 20 40 60 80
Scale in miles

Specimen / Sight record
★ / ☆ Breeding
▲ / △ Spring
● / ○ Summer
▽ / ▽ Fall
■ / □ Winter
—— Approximate boundary of subspecies' breeding range
? Questionable record

exceeedingly active and quickly disappears if frightened, slipping through vines, bushes, and lower parts of trees with much agility. Amid thickety vegetation the bird gleans chiefly insects and spiders; also a few seeds.

The common call note of the Bewick's Wren has been variously represented as *chee, chick,* or *plit;* this note, usually given in a series, is commonly described as having a "rasping" or "scolding" quality. Its fine song is a long, sweet, varied warble, much resembling that of the Song Sparrow; however, some of the notes are higher pitched, especially a frequently given closing trill. There is much more variation in this bird's song than is apparent in that of the Canyon Wren or even that of the Carolina Wren. In singing it perches on a twig or branch of a low tree or bush, fence post, wire, or roof, generally with its head well up and tail hanging down; sometimes the bird sings as it looks for food. Song period is mostly from mid-February to early August.

DETAILED ACCOUNT: FIVE SUBSPECIES

COMMON BEWICK'S WREN, *Thryomanes bewickii bewickii* (Audubon)

DESCRIPTION: *Adults, nuptial plumage*: Acquired by wear from winter plumage. Upper surface prout brown to light cinnamon brown; rump with large concealed subterminal white spots; tail brownish black, middle pair of feathers broadly and numerously barred with hair brown, remaining rectrices broadly tipped with neutral gray and barred on terminal portion of external web of two outer feathers with grayish white; wings between buffy brown and hair brown, tertials and outer webs of primaries and secondaries rather broadly barred with color of back, becoming lighter and more buffy on terminal portions of feathers and on outer primaries; wing-coverts like back but rather lighter, and all but lesser series narrowly barred with fuscous; lores and superciliary stripe dull white; lores mixed with fuscous; postocular stripe brown like pileum but rather darker; cheeks and auriculars mixed fuscous and grayish white; lower surface dull white, somewhat washed with gray or brown, sides of breast shaded with brownish gray, flanks washed with buffy brown, but crissum buffy white or pale buff, more or less distinctly and narrowly barred with fuscous or fuscous black; lining of wing grayish white. Bill black, chaetura drab, or brownish black, but base of mandible light neutral gray, pale brown, or cinereous; iris mars brown or auburn; legs, feet, and claws dull pale brown or light quaker drab. *Adults, winter*: Acquired by complete postnuptial molt. Similar to nuptial adults but darker and somewhat more brightly colored above—brussels brown to dull auburn; middle tail feathers more brownish; sides and flanks more strongly washed with brown; lower tail-coverts usually more brownish. *First nuptial*: Acquired by wear from first winter and differing little. *First winter*: Acquired by partial postjuvenal molt, which does not involve wing-quills. Similar to adults in winter, but feathers of jugulum somewhat edged with dull gray or brownish gray; lower tail-coverts more brownish and less distinctly barred. *Juvenal*: Acquired by complete postnatal molt. Similar to nuptial adults but averaging somewhat darker and duller above; middle tail feathers similar in color to back; lower surface duller and darker anteriorly, feathers margined narrowly with mouse gray or drab, producing mottled or somewhat barred appearance; crissum more strongly tinged with dull brown and slightly or very obscurely barred, though sometimes plain.

MEASUREMENTS: *Adult male*: Wing, 51.6–56.4 (average, 54.3) mm.; tail, 48.0–55.9 (52.6); bill (exposed culmen), 12.4–14.5 (13.2); tarsus, 17.0–18.5 (17.8); middle toe without claw, 11.4–13.0 (12.2). *Adult female*: Wing, 51.6–53.1 (52.3); tail, 49.0–53.1 (50.8); bill, 13.0–14.0 (13.5); tarsus, 17.0–18.0 (17.3); middle toe, 11.4–13.0 (12.2).

RANGE: C. Nebraska to s.e. Ontario, south to w. Arkansas and w. Tennessee. Winters from s. Illinois and s. Indiana to c. Texas and c. Florida.

TEXAS: *Winter*: Taken north to Cooke, east to Chambers (Oct. 19), southwest to Karnes (Sept. 19) cos. Uncommon.

APPALACHIAN BEWICK'S WREN, *Thryomanes bewickii altus* Aldrich

DESCRIPTION: *Adults, nuptial plumage*: Similar to *T. b. bewickii*, but upper surface darker and more sooty (less rufescent).

MEASUREMENTS: *Adult male*: Wing, 51.6–55.9 (average, 54.3) mm.; tail, 48.0–55.1 (51.8); bill (exposed culmen), 13.0–14.5 (13.5); tarsus, 17.0–18.5 (17.8); middle toe without claw, 11.4–13.5 (12.4). *Adult female*: Wing, 49.0–55.1 (51.8); tail, 46.0–52.6 (50.0); bill, 11.9–14.0 (13.5); tarsus, 17.0–18.5 (17.5); middle toe, 11.9–13.5 (12.4).

RANGE: N. Ohio and n.e. Pennsylvania, south to n.w. Alabama and c. South Carolina. Winters from West Virginia to c. Louisiana and n. Florida; casual in Texas.

TEXAS: *Winter*: One specimen: Camp Co., Pittsburg (Dec. 8, 1943, T. D. Burleigh).

TEXAS BEWICK'S WREN, *Thryomanes bewickii cryptus* Oberholser

DESCRIPTION: *Adults, nuptial plumage*: Similar to *T. b. bewickii* but larger; upper parts paler and more grayish. *Natal*: Drab.

MEASUREMENTS: *Adult male*: Wing, 54.6–61.0 (average, 57.2) mm.; tail, 52.1–61.0 (56.1); bill (exposed culmen), 13.5–15.5 (14.2); tarsus, 17.5–19.0 (18.3); middle toe without claw, 11.9–12.4 (12.2). *Adult female*: Wing, 53.1–54.1 (53.8); tail, 54.6–55.9 (55.3); bill, 13.5–14.5 (14.0); tarsus, 18.0–18.5 (18.3); middle toe, 11.9–13.0 (12.4).

RANGE: S. Kansas, south to n. Nuevo León and c. Tamaulipas. Winters from n. Oklahoma to Nuevo León and Tamaulipas.

TEXAS: *Breeding*: Altitudinal range, near sea level to 3,800 ft. Collected north to Randall, east to Cooke, south to Refugio and Cameron, west to Val Verde cos. Common. *Winter*: Taken north to Oldham, east to Kaufman, south to Cameron, west to Jeff Davis cos. Common.

NESTING: *Nest*: On hills and flatlands, in brushy, somewhat open country or on edges of woods, often on ranches, even in immediate vicinity of human dwellings; in stump, hole in tree, deserted woodpecker excavation, hollow log, nook about building or in fence, in bird box, mail box, tin can, or even in pocket of scarecrow, also in bush or cactus; open cup, not roofed over, rather loosely constructed, and decidedly bulky; composed of grass, sticks, thorny twigs, plant stems, rootlets, bark, string, weed stems, wool, cotton, feathers, and spider webs; lined with almost any soft substance, such as hair, fur, rootlets, and feathers. *Eggs*: 4–11; ovate, rather broad; without gloss; white or pinkish white; speckled with light and dark reddish brown, chestnut, lilac, and lavender, usually forming wreath about large end; average size, 16.0 × 11.4 mm.

DESERT BEWICK'S WREN, *Thryomanes bewickii eremophilus* Oberholser

DESCRIPTION: *Adults, nuptial plumage*: Similar to *T. b. cryptus*, but upper surface still more grayish. Two distinct color phases—a gray and a brown—found in this race, involving, however, only upper parts. In gray phase upper parts are hair brown, verging somewhat toward buffy brown; in brown, upper parts between sayal brown and buffy brown.

MEASUREMENTS: *Adult male*: Wing, 55.1–59.9 (average, 57.4) mm.; tail, 50.5–63.5 (57.7); bill (exposed culmen), 13.0–15.0 (14.0); tarsus, 17.5–18.5 (18.3); middle toe without claw, 10.9–11.9 (11.4). *Adult female*: Wing, 51.1–54.1 (52.6); tail,

50.5–55.9 (54.3); bill, 13.0–14.5 (13.7); tarsus, 15.0–18.5 (17.5); middle toe, 9.9–11.9 (11.2).

RANGE: S.e. California, s.w. Utah, and Trans-Pecos Texas, south to c. Zacatecas. Winters from breeding range to c. Texas and n.e. Tamaulipas.

TEXAS: *Breeding*: Altitudinal range, 1,800 to 8,500 ft. Collected in El Paso, Culberson, Jeff Davis, and Brewster cos. Fairly common. *Winter*: Taken northeast to Eastland (Nov. 3), south to Maverick, west to Brewster and El Paso cos. Fairly common.

NESTING: Similar to that of *T. b. cryptus*, but average egg size, 16.5 × 12.2 mm.

COLORADO BEWICK'S WREN, *Thryomanes bewickii niceae* Sutton

Race not in A.O.U. check-list, 1957 (see Appendix A).

DESCRIPTION: *Adults, nuptial plumage*: Similar to *T. b. eremophilus*, but tail usually having only outer two rectrices on each side with broad gray tips.

MEASUREMENTS: *Adult male*: Wing, 54.1–58.9 (average, 57.2) mm.; tail, 54.6–62.0 (59.2); bill (exposed culmen), 13.0–14.5 (14.2); tarsus, 18.5–20.6 (19.3); middle toe without claw, 9.9–11.9 (10.7). *Adult female*: Wing, 54.1–56.4 (54.8); tail, 53.1–62.0 (56.6); bill, 12.2–13.7 (13.2); tarsus, 17.5–19.0 (18.3); middle toe, 10.4–10.9 (10.7).

RANGE: S.w. Wyoming to w. Kansas, south to n.e. New Mexico and n.w. Oklahoma. Winters from New Mexico to c. Texas.

TEXAS: *Breeding* (probably): Altitude, 2,430 ft. One specimen: Lipscomb Co., Lipscomb (July 4, 1903, A. H. Howell). *Winter*: Two specimens: Kendall Co. (Feb. 3, 1880, N. C. Brown); Val Verde Co., Del Rio (Jan. 31, 1890, V. Bailey).

NESTING: Similar to that of *T. b. cryptus*.

CAROLINA WREN, *Thryothorus ludovicianus* Latham

SPECIES ACCOUNT

A rather large, especially rusty wren. Reddish brown above; prominent white eye-stripe; rich buff below (paler on throat). Length, 5¾ in.; wingspan, 7¾; weight, ¾ oz.

RANGE: S.e. Nebraska, extreme s. Great Lakes region, and s. New England, south to n.e. Mexico, U.S. Gulf coast, and s. Florida. Largely resident, but limited movement noted.

TEXAS: (See map.) *Resident*: Breeds, mid-Feb. to late Aug. (eggs, Feb. 26 to Aug. 13) from near sea level to 3,500 ft. Common to fairly common through most of eastern half, but uncommon to scarce and irregular as far west as northern Panhandle, San Angelo (last nest record, 1885, W. Lloyd), and northern Val Verde Co. (nested, 1970), and as far south as Uvalde, McMullen Co., and Corpus Christi; rare southward along coast to Rio Grande delta, where formerly common. Scarce to rare visitor (nonbreeder) during all seasons in Panhandle, Trans-Pecos, and most of south Texas brush country (including delta).

HAUNTS AND HABITS: The Carolina Wren is a woodland and underbrush bird. In west Texas it is restricted to trees and bushes along streams, but in the more humid eastern portion of the state it is widespread over the landscape. Here it inhabits bottoms and uplands, particularly about forest margins, in clearings, under-

growth, and cutover pine woods containing a mixed growth of timber. It frequents swamps and swampy woods along streams and about lake shores. Trees, roots, vines, and tangled thickets furnish good hiding along creek banks and streams, as well as in gulches and canyons. It is also at home in cultivated areas, where it visits fields near woods, fence rows, log piles, brush heaps, old mills and similar buildings, farm houses and their outbuildings, and yards and buildings of towns. It is less partial to rocky places than some of the other wrens and very seldom occurs on open prairies or plains.

Flight of this wren, usually not prolonged, is quick, nervous, and performed with very rapid wing-beats. Generally shy, it is at times difficult to observe in its tangled habitat. The Carolina is active and sometimes inquisitive, often holding its tail upward and turning its head this way and that. Often when pursued, it runs, hops, or flits about on the ground dodging through the interstices of thicket or underbrush. It hunts in dark corners and secluded places—on bark of old trunks, stumps, and prostrate logs, under fallen leaves, in brush heaps, etc.—for caterpillars, moths, crickets, beetles, boll weevils, spiders, millipedes, snails, and occasionally some wild fruit. The Carolina Wren is one of two Texas birds which very commonly suns its rump—the other is the Roadrunner. A sunning bird relaxes in a patch of light, partially spreads its wings and tail, and parts its back and rump feathers so that sunlight reaches the bare skin. Often it remains in this highly relaxed position for several minutes.

A frequent call note of the Carolina Wren is a long trilled *chirrrr*. Sometimes portions of songs are used as calls. Songs of this wren are loud, musical whistles that would seem to belong to a bird about twice its size. A

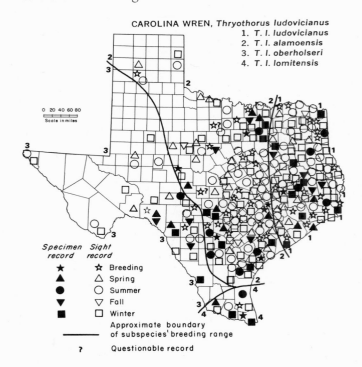

CAROLINA WREN, *Thryothorus ludovicianus*
1. *T. l. ludovicianus*
2. *T. l. alamoensis*
3. *T. l. oberholseri*
4. *T. l. lomitensis*

0 20 40 60 80
Scale in miles

Specimen record / Sight record
★ ☆ Breeding
▲ △ Spring
● ○ Summer
▼ ▽ Fall
■ □ Winter

— Approximate boundary of subspecies' breeding range

? Questionable record

few variations particularly resemble phrases of the Cardinal. However, the Carolina's whistles are more rapidly uttered, usually in triplets, and have been represented by the words *tea kettle, tea kettle, tea kettle, tea.* Another common song goes something like *chirpity, chirpity, chirpity, chip.* The bird delivers its song usually while feeding; seldom does it use a fixed, exposed song perch. The season is a very long one. In fact, the Carolina Wren is probably the only Texas bird which literally sings all year long.

CHANGES: Carolina Wren populations in Texas have remained fairly stable into the early 1970's except in the extreme south. The Lomita Carolina Wren, *T. l. lomitensis,* of the Rio Grande delta in Texas and Tamaulipas appears to be largely exterminated. Although J. C. Arvin, in a 1972 nesting report, recorded a remarkable fourteen pairs on the Santa Maria tract (Cameron Co.), he tempered his find with the comment that the species "seems to be on its way out" as a breeder in the delta.

Decimating factors since the great freeze of 1951 include excessive brush and some citrus tree removal, very high Bronzed Cowbird populations, and regular and heavy use of hard pesticides. Birds are still occasionally heard, especially in fall and winter, in far south Texas, but these individuals probably largely represent upstate races that have wandered south. The Carolina's habit of singing all year complicates identification of breeding ranges.

DETAILED ACCOUNT: FOUR SUBSPECIES

SOUTHERN CAROLINA WREN, *Thryothorus ludovicianus ludovicianus* (Latham)

DESCRIPTION: *Adults, nuptial plumage:* Acquired by wear from winter plumage. Upper surface rufescent prout brown to auburn or russet, somewhat less rufescent (sepia) on forehead and crown, but more so on rump and upper tail-coverts; feathers of rump with more or less concealed large, rather roundish white spots; tail snuff brown, becoming sayal brown or buffy brown terminally, narrowly barred with fuscous or fuscous black and spotted on outer webs of two outer pairs of tail feathers with white or buffy white; wings between olive brown and hair brown, tertials and outer webs of primaries and secondaries broadly barred with snuff brown or deep ochraceous tawny, becoming more buffy on outer webs of primaries; wing-coverts dull sepia, greater series barred with fuscous, these and median coverts mostly with small buffy white terminal spots, forming two poorly defined wing-bars; broad superciliary stripe white or buffy white, bordered above by narrow blackish line; lores sepia; postocular stripe and sides of neck russet or auburn; cheeks cream buff or grayish white, speckled with fuscous; chin grayish white; flanks cinnamon buff, rarely barred with fuscous; remainder of lower surface cream buff, paler medially, crissum narrowly barred with fuscous or fuscous black; lining of wing grayish or buffy white, outer under wing-coverts hair brown or fuscous. Bill blackish slate, slate gray, or brownish slate, mandible dull white with slaty or cinereous tip and flesh-colored base and edges, or white tinged with vinaceous; iris hazel or chocolate; legs and feet flesh color, ecru drab, drab gray, dull fawn color, or brown. *Adults, winter:* Acquired by complete postnuptial molt. Similar to nuptial adults but much more richly colored; upper parts auburn to bay; superciliary stripe more buffy (less whitish); lower surface darker—ochraceous buff to ochraceous tawny; crissum light hazel. *First nuptial:* Acquired by wear from first winter. Very similar to nuptial

adults, but wing-quills somewhat more worn, since they are retained from juvenal. *First winter:* Acquired by partial postjuvenal molt, which does not involve wing-quills. Similar to adults in winter, but jugulum with some dark brown edgings on feathers. *Juvenal:* Acquired by complete postnatal molt. Similar to nuptial adults, but upper parts of much paler cinnamon brown to light russet, pileum spotted with paler brown, back obsoletely barred with darker brown; breast and sometimes flanks speckled or obsoletely barred with fuscous. Bill shorter. *Natal:* Drab. Bill and feet pinkish buff.

MEASUREMENT: *Adult male:* Wing, 56.9–63.8 (average, 60.7) mm.; tail, 47.5–57.4 (51.8); bill (exposed culmen), 15.5–18.0 (16.5); tarsus, 21.1–23.1 (21.4); middle toe without claw, 14.0–15.0 (14.7). *Adult female:* Wing, 54.1–62.0 (57.2); tail, 47.0–52.1 (49.8); bill, 14.2–17.0 (15.7); tarsus, 20.1–22.6 (21.4); middle toe, 14.0–15.0 (14.7).

RANGE: S. Michigan to s. Virginia, south to s.e. Texas and e. Georgia. Winters from breeding range to n. Florida.

TEXAS: *Resident:* Altitudinal breeding range, near sea level to 500 ft. Collected north to Bowie, south to Orange, southwest to Matagorda cos. Common.

NESTING: *Nest:* On uplands or lowlands; swamps or dry country, often in cultivated areas, woodlands, thickets, or more open areas, wherever suitable sites are found, usually less than 10 ft. above ground; placed in hollow tree or stump, fence post, rock or wood pile, brush heap, woodpecker hole, nook about building, such as corner of barn; bulky, dome-shaped nest, sometimes arched over, opening at side only large enough to allow the bird to enter; composed of all kinds of rubbish, sticks, grass, weed stems, interlaced with moss, leaves, cornstalks, corn silk, straw, hair, and feathers; lined with moss, leaves, fine dry grasses, thin black roots, poultry or other feathers, horsehair and various other kinds of hair. *Eggs:* 3–6; of variable shape, but usually short ovate; dull or rather glossy; white, cream white, pinkish white, or salmon buff; extensively dotted with light reddish brown, pale chestnut, dark reddish brown, dull pink, and lilac, most numerously about large end, where sometimes forming wreath; average size, 18.8 × 15.2 mm.

BEXAR CAROLINA WREN, *Thryothorus ludovicianus alamoensis* Godfrey

Race not in A.O.U. check-list, 1957 (see Appendix A).

DESCRIPTION: *Adults, nuptial plumage:* Most closely resembles Northern Carolina Wren, *T. l. carolinianus,* but upper parts paler and duller; light bars on tail more grayish (less rufescent).

MEASUREMENTS: *Adult male:* Wing, 59.9–61.5 (average, 60.5) mm.; tail, 48.5–52.6 (50.5); bill (exposed culmen), 15.7–17.5 (16.8); tarsus, 21.4–23.6 (22.4); middle toe without claw, 15.0–15.2 (15.1). *Adult female:* Wing, 55.1–59.4 (56.6); tail, 46.0–51.8 (48.8); bill, 14.7–17.0 (16.0); tarsus, 19.3–21.9 (21.1); middle toe, 15.0–15.2 (15.0)

RANGE: E. Minnesota and s. Indiana, south to c. Texas.

TEXAS: *Resident:* Altitudinal breeding range, near sea level to 3,500 ft. in Panhandle. Collected north to Cooke, east to Trinity, south to Washington (eggs) and Nueces, west to Tom Green cos.; taken outside regular breeding range, west to Kinney and Webb cos. Common.

NESTING: Similar to that of *T. l. ludovicianus.*

SOUTHWESTERN CAROLINA WREN, *Thryothorus ludovicianus oberholseri* Lowery

Race not in A.O.U. check-list, 1957 (see Appendix A).

DESCRIPTION: *Adults, nuptial plumage:* Similar to *T. l. ludovicianus,* but above decidedly darker, more sooty (less rufescent); below also averaging more deeply rufescent.

MEASUREMENTS: *Adult male:* Wing, 58.9–62.5 (average, 60.7) mm.; tail, 49.5–53.6 (51.8); bill (exposed culmen), 15.2–17.0 (16.8); tarsus, 20.1–22.6 (21.6); middle toe without claw, 13.5–15.0 (13.7). *Adult female:* Wing, 55.6–59.4 (57.9); tail, 47.0–49.5 (48.3); bill, 16.0–16.5 (16.3); tarsus, 20.6–22.6 (21.9); middle toe, 14.0–15.0 (14.2).

RANGE: Edwards Plateau of Texas.

TEXAS: *Resident*: Altitudinal breeding range, 900 to 2,200 ft. Collected in Kimble, Kerr, and Val Verde cos. Fairly common.

NESTING: Similar to that of *T. l. ludovicianus*.

LOMITA CAROLINA WREN, *Thryothorus ludovicianus lomitensis* Sennett

DESCRIPTION: *Adults, nuptial plumage*: Similar to *T. l. ludovicianus* but smaller, except bill, which is actually as well as relatively larger; upper parts duller, less rufescent; lower parts paler, less rufescent; flanks usually barred with fuscous. *Juvenal*: Similar to nuptial adults but with little or no barring on flanks.

MEASUREMENTS: *Adult male*: Wing, 55.9–59.9 (average, 58.2) mm.; tail, 46.5–52.1 (49.5); bill (exposed culmen), 16.5–18.5 (17.3); tarsus, 20.6–23.1 (21.6); middle toe without claw, 13.5–16.5 (15.2). *Adult female*: Wing, 52.1–57.4 (54.3); tail, 42.9–48.0 (45.7); bill, 16.0–17.5 (16.5); tarsus, 20.1–21.6 (20.3); middle toe, 14.5–15.0 (14.7).

RANGE: Extreme s. Texas and extreme n.e. Tamaulipas.

TEXAS: *Resident*: Altitudinal breeding range, near sea level to about 250 ft. Collected in Kenedy, Cameron, Hidalgo, and Starr cos. Rare (formerly common).

NESTING: *Nest*: Similar to that of *T. l. ludovicianus*. *Eggs*: Usually 5; short ovate; white; much speckled with light reddish brown and purplish brown; average size, 18.3 × 14.2 mm.

CACTUS WREN, *Campylorhynchus brunneicapillus* (Lafresnaye)

SPECIES ACCOUNT

A very large wren. Brown above (often becoming rusty anteriorly) with whitish streaks on back, and whitish barring on wings and outer tail feathers; broad white eye-stripe; whitish below (buffy on sides, flanks, belly) with black spots, these largest and densest on breast. Length, 8½ in.; wingspan, 11; weight, 1½ oz.

RANGE: S. California, s. Nevada, s.w. Utah, w. and s. Arizona, s. New Mexico, and s.w. Texas, south to s. Baja California, Sinaloa, and Tamaulipas, and in highland Mexico to Michoacán, State of México, and Hidalgo.

TEXAS: (See map.) *Resident*: Breeds, late Feb. to late Aug.—occasionally later (eggs, Mar. 12 to Aug. 6; young just out of nest, Sept. 11) from near sea level to 6,000 ft. Common to fairly common over most of southwestern half north to Lubbock, east to San Angelo, San Antonio, and Rockport, but uncommon and local on Edwards Plateau; northeast irregularly from San Antonio to extreme southern Travis Co., where scarce. Casual visitor (nonbreeder) in Potter, Young, Washington, San Jacinto, and Galveston cos.

HAUNTS AND HABITS: The Cactus Wren, a giant among wrens, inhabits plains, broad valleys, scrubby flats, brushy mesas, cactus and mesquite tracts, gulches, canyons, and hills, either near or at a considerable distance from water. Sometimes it approaches ranch houses, particularly in brush country; at times it comes into gardens and yards on outskirts of towns or even into more populated portions. On occasion the species is found in small flocks, although for the most part it appears singly or in pairs.

Flight, commonly not protracted, is short and jerky. The Cactus Wren is generally shy and remains well hidden but at times appears inquisitive. If pursued, however, it briskly dives into a thicket, bush, or cactus patch, usually spreading its tail as it quickly slips out of sight. If perching, it often jerks its tail at intervals much in the manner of some flycatchers. On the ground it hops about, actively searching among rocks, cactus, and aridland brush for weevils, beetles, bees, wasps, grasshoppers, caterpillars, and spiders; also, less frequently, fruits of hackberry, pricklypear, and other wild plants.

In addition to the usual nests for raising young, Cactus Wrens build nests for roosting; the only other southwestern songbird which commonly constructs dormitories is the Verdin. Both species tend to be late sleepers on cold or rainy days; in fact, if the weather is very nasty these birds may stay in their nests all day long!

The Cactus Wren's ordinary scolding or alarm note is a harsh *chut* several times repeated. Its so-called song, which is monotonous and not melodious, may be represented by the words *choo, choo, choo, choo*. Sometimes the series sounds more like *chug, chug, chug, chug*. Unlike woodland wrens, the Cactus often sings from an exposed perch. When the bird is singing, its tail droops almost vertically below the branch and its head is raised until the bill extends at a sharp angle upward, sometimes almost vertically. When young are leaving the nest this wren, like other members of *Campylorhynchus*, is frequently extraordinarily responsive to the bird watcher's back-of-the-hand kissing or "squeak." The Cactus Wren is reported to sing all year long, but this bird spends so much time sleeping, building nests, feeding young, and flying toward squeakers, that its singing hours must be considerably curtailed!

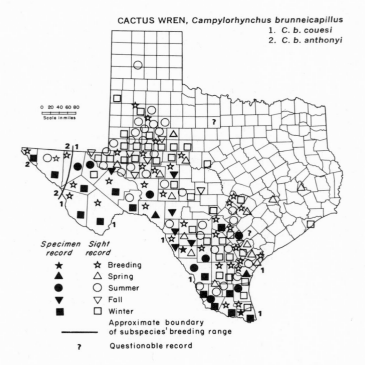

CACTUS WREN, *Campylorhynchus brunneicapillus*
1. *C. b. couesi*
2. *C. b. anthonyi*

0 20 40 60 80
Scale in miles

Specimen record / Sight record
★ / ☆ Breeding
▲ / △ Spring
● / ○ Summer
▼ / ▽ Fall
■ / □ Winter

——— Approximate boundary of subspecies' breeding range
? Questionable record

DETAILED ACCOUNT: TWO SUBSPECIES

NORTHERN CACTUS WREN, *Campylorhynchus brunneicapillus couesi* Sharpe

DESCRIPTION: *Adults, nuptial plumage*: Acquired by wear from winter plumage. Forehead and crown mummy brown to dull cinnamon; occiput prout brown to cinnamon brown, without light markings; back between drab and buffy brown with broad stripes and irregular streaks of white and irregular spots of chaetura drab and chaetura black; upper tail-coverts light hair brown, broadly barred with chaetura black; feathers of rump with large concealed subterminal white spots; middle tail feathers light hair brown, numerously and rather irregularly barred with chaetura black or brownish black; remainder of tail brownish black tipped with hair brown and with broad subterminal bar of white, which on next to middle pair of rectrices sometimes becomes light hair brown, this pair of feathers more or less mottled or spotted on outer webs with hair brown, next two feathers slightly spotted on outer webs with white or grayish white, next to outer pair with additional broad white bar on terminal portion of inner webs, and narrow whitish or grayish white bars on outer webs, external pair barred or spotted on both webs with white; wings rather rufescent hair brown, tertials irregularly barred, inner secondaries barred on outer webs with dull pale buff, and on inner webs, except terminal portion, imperfectly barred with white; primaries spotted on outer webs and barred on inner webs with dull or buffy white, except on terminal portions; lesser wing-coverts hair brown, more or less barred with chaetura drab and spotted or streaked with dull white; median and greater coverts chaetura drab, irregularly barred, spotted, and edged with hair brown, rufescent hair brown, and dull gray or buffy white; broad superciliary stripe white; lores grayish white, mixed with dull black, postocular stripe bister or sepia; cheeks grayish white, streaked or speckled with dull black or sepia; chin, throat, and upper breast white, throat and jugulum heavily spotted with roundish spots of black, which are sometimes coalescent; sides and flanks ochraceous buff to ochraceous tawny; middle of abdomen and crissum similar but paler, middle of abdomen with numerous elongated spots, and sides, flanks, and crissum with roundish spots of black; longest lower tail-coverts broadly barred with black; lining of wing grayish or buffy white, spotted with black or chaetura black. Bill deep plumbeous, lighter below; iris orange or dark red; legs and feet light gray. *Adults, winter*: Acquired by complete postnuptial molt. Like nuptial adults. *First nuptial*: Acquired by wear from first winter. Practically identical with nuptial adults, but anterior lower parts somewhat less heavily spotted. *First winter*: Acquired by partial postjuvenal molt. Essentially like first nuptial. *Juvenal*: Acquired by complete postnatal molt. Resembling nuptial adults, but pileum clove brown or between hair brown and fuscous; back drab or washed with wood brown to cinnamon brown, light markings of upper surface more inconspicuous and blended, ranging from dull white to dull buff or snuff brown; bars and spots on wing-quills more buffy or pinkish; cinnamomeous of posterior lower parts, including flanks, much paler, dull light ochraceous buff; spots on lower surface very much smaller, chaetura drab or chaetura black, sometimes nearly absent, particularly on posterior portion. *Natal*: Pale tilleul buff or dull pale pinkish buff.

MEASUREMENTS: *Adult male*: Wing, 80.0–88.9 (average, 85.6) mm.; tail, 75.9–82.6 (78.7); bill (exposed culmen), 22.1–25.9 (23.4); tarsus, 26.4–28.4 (27.9); middle toe without claw, 18.5–20.1 (19.3). *Adult female*: Wing, 79.0–87.9 (83.3); tail, 70.0–82.0 (74.7); bill, 20.6–23.1 (22.4); tarsus, 25.9–28.9 (27.4); middle toe, 17.5–20.1 (18.8).

RANGE: E. Trans-Pecos and c. Texas, south to n. Coahuila, Nuevo León, and Tamaulipas.

TEXAS: *Resident*: Altitudinal breeding range, near sea level to 6,000 ft. Collected north to Tom Green, east to Bexar and Karnes, southeast to Cameron, west to Presidio and Culberson cos. Common locally.

NESTING: *Nest*: On mesas, slopes, in canyons, and washes; brush and margins of low woodlands; usually not high above ground, in bush, thicket, cactus (especially pricklypear and cholla), yucca, catclaw, mesquite, and various other thorny shrubs; large retort-shaped structure with opening at one end; composed of various kinds of plant stems, grasses, thorny twigs, and feathers; lined with feathers. *Eggs*: 3–7; short ovate to ovate; slightly glossy; cream white, buff, or pale pinkish cinnamon; very thickly speckled with pale reddish brown, almost so thick as to obscure ground color, these markings sometimes confluent in wreath at large end; average size, 24.4 × 16.5 mm.

ARIZONA CACTUS WREN, *Campylorhynchus brunneicapillus anthonyi* (Mearns)

Race not in A.O.U. check-list, 1957 (see Appendix A).

DESCRIPTION: *Adults, nuptial plumage*: Similar to *C. b. couesi*, but wing and tail longer; upper parts lighter, more rufescent (less grayish), spots on jugulum and throat larger and more confluent; barring on upper surface of middle tail feathers broader and more conspicuous.

MEASUREMENTS: *Adult male*: Wing, 83.6–91.9 (average, 87.6) mm.; tail, 79.0–86.1 (83.3); bill (exposed culmen), 20.6–25.1 (22.9); tarsus, 27.4–29.9 (28.7); middle toe without claw, 18.0–20.1 (19.3). *Adult female*: Wing, 80.0–86.1 (83.3); tail, 71.9–84.1 (80.2); bill, 19.6–23.9 (21.9); tarsus, 25.4–28.9 (27.7); middle toe, 17.5–19.0 (18.8).

RANGE: S. California to s.w. Utah, south to n.e. Baja California and Trans-Pecos Texas.

TEXAS: *Resident*: Altitudinal breeding range, 3,300 to 5,000 ft. Collected in El Paso, Hudspeth, Culberson, and Reeves (no evidence of nesting) cos. Fairly common.

NESTING: Similar to that of *C. b. couesi*.

LONG-BILLED MARSH WREN, *Telmatodytes palustris* (Wilson)

SPECIES ACCOUNT

Slender bill; cocked, stubby tail; skulks in cattails, rushes. Reddish brown above with broad black and white stripes on back; prominent whitish eye-stripe; dull white below. Length, 5 in.; wingspan, 6½; weight, ½ oz.

RANGE: S. Canada, south to extreme n. Baja California, c. New Mexico, U.S. Gulf coast, and s. Florida; also c. Mexico. Winters over much of breeding range (very sparingly, when present, in far northern parts), south to s. Mexico.

TEXAS: (See map.) *Breeding*: Mid-Apr. to early Sept. (eggs, July 7 to Aug. 21) from near sea level to 3,750 ft. Locally fairly common to uncommon along coast, south to Corpus Christi; scarce and extremely local in Trans-Pecos (along Rio Grande) and along Red River boundary of state. *Winter*: Late Sept. to late Apr. (extremes: Sept. 3, May 12). Locally common to fairly common along coast and Rio Grande; uncommon and local in remainder of southern two-thirds; scarce in northern third.

HAUNTS AND HABITS: Well named, the Long-billed Marsh Wren is distinctively a bird of the marsh. It lives in various kinds of wetlands, but especially at the edges of lakes and ponds where cattails, tall grass, reeds, or rushes grow. Occasionally, migrants linger briefly in patches of weeds on absolutely dry ground. Sometimes so many individuals are present in a certain marsh that they form a loose colony and at times dur-

Cactus Wren, *Campylorhynchus brunneicapillus,*
on cholla (*Opuntia*)

ing the nonbreeding season they gather into small companies.

Flight of the Longbill is weak and usually very short. When flushed it flies with rapidly beating wings, rather laboriously, barely clearing tops of the vegetation; soon it drops down out of sight. It is well adapted to life in the marsh, for it can creep or sidle up stems of cattails, reeds, and rushes with agility, twisting its body into strange positions and switching its tail down, over its back, or from side to side. In fact, it appears highly nervous as it flits among the reeds searching for grass-hoppers, locusts, mosquitoes, flies, ants, wasps, water bugs, beetles, and other marsh insects. It is also shy and remains well concealed in the dense growth of its habitat.

The ordinary alarm note of the Long-billed Marsh Wren, difficult to represent in syllables, is something like *tsuk*. The song is a rapid, weak, bubbling sound, that somewhat resembles the song of the House Wren, but concludes with a guttural rattle. The bird sings while perched on a reed stem or marsh grass or as it flies up—then floats down into the vegetation. A per-sistent singer, it may be heard at almost all times of the day, often for considerable periods. It frequently sings at night. The note, of course, is heard all year; song is chiefly from March to early August.

DETAILED ACCOUNT: SEVEN SUBSPECIES

COMMON LONG-BILLED MARSH WREN, *Telmatodytes palustris palustris* (Wilson)

DESCRIPTION: *Adults, nuptial plumage:* Acquired by practically complete prenuptial molt. Similar to *T. p. dissaëptus* (see be-low), but tail averaging about 3 percent shorter, wing slightly so; upper parts and flanks less rufescent and averaging slightly paler.

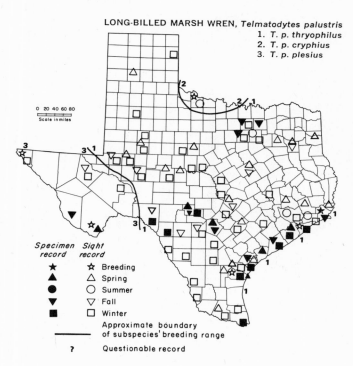

LONG-BILLED MARSH WREN, *Telmatodytes palustris*
1. *T. p. thryophilus*
2. *T. p. cryphius*
3. *T. p. plesius*

0 20 40 60 80
Scale in miles

Specimen   Sight
record   record
★   ☆ Breeding
▲   △ Spring
●   ○ Summer
▼   ▽ Fall
■   □ Winter
─── Approximate boundary
     of subspecies' breeding range
?   Questionable record

MEASUREMENTS: *Adult male:* Wing, 47.0–53.1 (average, 49.8) mm.; tail, 38.1–44.4 (41.1); bill (exposed culmen), 12.4–15.0 (13.7); tarsus, 18.5–21.6 (20.1); middle toe without claw, 10.9–15.0 (13.0). *Adult female:* Wing, 43.9–51.1 (46.5); tail, 36.1–41.7 (38.6); bill, 11.9–14.0 (13.0); tarsus, 18.0–20.6 (18.8); middle toe, 9.9–13.0 (11.9).

RANGE: S. Connecticut, south to n. and s.e. Virginia. Winters from s. New Jersey to w. Florida; casual in Texas.

TEXAS: *Winter:* Two specimens: Refugio Co., Tivoli (Oct. 8, 1915, A. P. Smith); Calhoun Co., Seadrift (May 3, 1916, A. P. Smith).

NORTHEASTERN LONG-BILLED MARSH WREN, *Telmatodytes palustris dissaëptus* (Bangs)

DESCRIPTION: *Adults, nuptial plumage:* Similar to *T. p. thryo-philus* (see below), but larger, particularly wing and tail; upper parts lighter, less sooty (more rufescent); brown of sides and flanks lighter, less spread over rest of lower parts.

MEASUREMENTS: *Adult male:* Wing, 49.0–52.3 (average, 51.1) mm.; tail, 41.1–43.9 (42.7); bill (exposed culmen), 12.4–14.5 (13.7); tarsus, 20.1–21.6 (20.9); middle toe without claw, 10.9–12.7 (11.9). *Adult female:* Wing, 47.3–49.5 (48.3); tail, 39.9–42.4 (40.6); bill, 12.4–13.5 (13.0); tarsus, 18.5–22.1 (20.1); middle toe, 10.9–12.7 (11.7).

RANGE: S.w. Quebec to s. Maine, south to Connecticut and Rhode Island. Winters from s. Texas to s.e. Georgia.

TEXAS: *Winter:* Collected in Nueces, Refugio (Oct. 8), Gal-veston (Oct. 29), and Jefferson (Oct.) cos. Uncommon.

OHIO LONG-BILLED MARSH WREN, Telmatodytes palustris canniphonus Oberholser, new subspecies (see Appendix A)

DESCRIPTION: *Adults, nuptial plumage:* Similar to *T. p. dis-saëptus*, but wing averaging 3 percent longer; upper surface and flanks darker, much less rufescent (more sooty).

MEASUREMENTS: *Adult male:* Wing, 50.5–54.3 (average, 52.3) mm.; tail, 40.4–46.0 (43.4); bill (exposed culmen), 13.0–14.7 (14.0); tarsus, 20.6–22.1 (21.4); middle toe without claw, 11.4–13.0 (12.2). *Adult female:* Wing, 47.0–51.6 (49.0); tail, 37.1–41.4 (40.1); bill, 11.9–13.7 (13.0); tarsus, 20.1–20.6 (20.1); middle toe, 10.9–11.9 (11.4).

TYPE: Adult male, no. 29985, Cleveland Museum of Natural History; Bay Point, 4 mi. north of Sandusky, Ottawa Co., Ohio; May 26, 1931, J. W. Aldrich, original no., 1125.

RANGE: Ohio and n.w. Pennsylvania. Winters from n.w. Ohio to s. Mississippi and w. Florida; casual in Texas.

TEXAS: *Winter:* One specimen: Matagorda Co., Matagorda (Apr. 22, 1935, H. H. Kimball).

LOUISIANA LONG-BILLED MARSH WREN, *Telmatodytes palustris thryophilus* Oberholser

DESCRIPTION: *Adults, nuptial plumage:* Acquired by prac-tically complete prenuptial molt. Similar to *T. p. palustris* but smaller, except tarsus which is longer; brown of upper parts duller, usually more or less tinging entire breast; pileum sepia with more or less mixture of blackish, usually confined to sides of crown, giving top of head a broadly striped appearance; re-mainder of upper surface light sepia to cinnamon brown, tri-angular area in middle of back dull fuscous black with conspic-uous broad white streaks; middle tail feathers broadly but some-what irregularly barred with brown of upper parts, remaining tail feathers barred except on middle portions with same color; wings fuscous, wing-coverts and broad bars on outer webs of wing-quills cinnamon brown, becoming somewhat lighter and more buffy on primaries; broad superciliary stripe grayish or buffy white; lores buffy white, somewhat mixed with dull brown; postocular stripe fuscous; sides of head and neck buffy avel-laneous, somewhat mixed with grayish white; lower parts, in-cluding lining of wing, white, sides and flanks cinnamon brown to saccardo umber, breast washed with dull buff or brownish buff, sometimes with small obscure umber spots, sides and flanks sometimes obscurely barred with dark brown; crissum tawny olive, narrowly barred with fuscous or cinnamon brown. Bill black, slate black, or olive brown, cutting edges and basal two-thirds of mandible pale vinaceous, dull white, olive gray, ecru drab, brownish or flesh color; inside of mouth yellow or buff yellow; tongue white; iris raw umber, prout brown, or hazel; legs and feet broccoli brown, sepia, brownish white tinged with lilaceous, yellowish drab gray, or drab; toes darker; claws hair brown or drab. *Adults, winter:* Acquired by complete post-nuptial molt. Similar to nuptial adults, but upper parts, sides, and flanks darker and duller. *First nuptial:* Acquired by nearly complete prenuptial molt. Very similar to nuptial adults; becomes very much worn and more grayish by summer. *First winter:* Acquired by partial postjuvenal molt, which does not involve wing-quills. Similar to first nuptial, but tertials and wing-coverts less heavily barred; wings and tail feathers somewhat less grayish. *Juvenal:* Acquired by complete postnatal molt. Similar to adults, but pileum and hindneck dull brownish black, nearly uniform; back without distinct white streaks and only a few blackish markings; white superciliary stripe indistinct or practically absent; posterior lower parts paler. Bill ecru drab, but tip darker; inside of mouth lemon yellow; iris dark brown; legs and feet buff yellow; claws broccoli brown. *Natal:* White, slightly buffy or tilleul buff. Bill and feet dull pinkish buff.

MEASUREMENTS: *Adult male:* Wing, 45.5–49.0 (average, 47.8) mm.; tail, 36.1–41.4 (40.4); bill (exposed culmen), 13.0–14.5 (14.0); tarsus, 20.1–23.1 (21.1); middle toe without claw, 11.9–13.0 (12.2). *Adult female:* Wing, 45.0–48.5 (46.8); tail, 37.1–40.4 (39.1); bill, 12.7–13.7 (13.2); tarsus, 18.0–21.1 (20.1); middle toe, 10.9–12.2 (11.7).

RANGE: S.e. Texas and s. Louisiana (except extreme eastern corner). Winters from s. Texas to w. Florida.

TEXAS: *Breeding:* Altitude, near sea level. Collected in Jefferson Co. (nest and eggs). Nesting activity observed in Chambers and Nueces cos. Locally fairly common. *Winter:* Taken northeast to Jefferson (Sept. 2), southwest to Matagorda and Nueces (Mar. 26) cos. Fairly common.

NESTING: *Nest:* In marshes along rivers, lakes, or bays, or on other wet ground, often in scattered colonies; rarely in high weeds or on dry ground, firmly attached to rushes, wildrice, sedges, flags, or bushes, a few to 6 ft. above water or ground; globular nest with long axis vertical and entrance at side, in appearance very much like a coconut, well constructed and well protected from rain; composed of sedges, rushes, reeds, flags, and various kinds of other marsh vegetation, sometimes cemented together with mud or clay; lined with fine grass, soft warm vegetable substances, such as down of cattail and milkweed, and feathers, and down of ducks and other birds. Male often builds several incomplete nests while female is constructing the one for the eggs. *Eggs:* 5–10, usually 5–6; ovate to nearly oval; pale brown to dark chocolate, but so thickly marked with dots and blotches of dark chocolate or dark mahogany as to be almost of uniform color; average size, 16.5 × 11.7 mm.

PRAIRIE LONG-BILLED MARSH WREN, Telmatodytes palustris cryphius Oberholser, new subspecies (see Appendix A)

DESCRIPTION: *Adults, nuptial plumage:* Similar to *T. p. dissaëptus,* but wing and middle toe longer; bill somewhat shorter; upper parts paler, more ochraceous; lower parts lighter.

MEASUREMENTS: *Adult male:* Wing, 50.5–54.1 (average, 52.3) mm.; tail, 37.1–46.0 (42.9); bill (exposed culmen), 11.9–14.7 (13.2); tarsus, 17.5–22.1 (20.6); middle toe without claw, 11.7–15.0 (13.0). *Adult female:* Wing, 48.0–52.6 (49.8); tail, 37.1–41.9 (39.6); bill, 11.9–14.0 (13.0); tarsus, 18.0–22.1 (19.6); middle toe, 11.2–14.0 (12.7).

TYPE: Adult male, no. 259563, U.S. National Museum, Biological Surveys collection; Blackmer, North Dakota; June 10, 1915, H. H. Sheldon, original no., 95.

RANGE: N. North Dakota to n. Indiana, south to Kansas and s. Indiana; rarely to Texas. Winters from c. Colorado and e. North Carolina to s. Texas and s. Florida.

TEXAS: *Breeding:* Altitude, about 1,200 ft. No specimen, but observations in Wilbarger Co., Watt Lake (nest discovered, May 5, 1926; bird sighted, early May, 1930, R. L. More) thought to be of this subspecies. *Winter:* Taken north to Collin (Sept. 30), east to Galveston, south to Nueces and Cameron, west to Kerr cos. Fairly common.

NESTING: Similar to that of *T. p. thryophilus.*

ALBERTA LONG-BILLED MARSH WREN, Telmatodytes palustris iliacus Ridgway

DESCRIPTION: *Adults, nuptial plumage:* Similar to *T. p. thryophilus* but larger; very much paler, particularly on upper parts, sides, and flanks; general coloration more ochraceous.

MEASUREMENTS: *Adult male:* Wing, 52.1–55.9 (average, 53.3) mm.; tail, 41.9–48.0 (45.2); bill (exposed culmen), 11.9–15.0 (13.0); tarsus, 19.0–21.6 (20.3); middle toe without claw, 11.9–14.0 (13.0). *Adult female:* Wing, 47.0–53.6 (50.8); tail, 39.9–47.5 (44.7); bill, 11.9–13.5 (13.0); tarsus, 19.0–21.1 (20.1); middle toe, 11.4–13.0 (11.9).

RANGE: Alberta to Manitoba. Winters from s. Texas to Jalisco.

TEXAS: *Winter:* Collected north to Denton (Oct. 21), east to Matagorda (Oct. 30), south to Cameron, west to Kerr (Oct. 19), and Presidio (Sept. 14) cos. Uncommon.

WESTERN LONG-BILLED MARSH WREN, Telmatodytes palustris plesius (Oberholser)

DESCRIPTION: *Adults, nuptial plumage:* Similar to *T. p. cryphius,* but wing and tail decidedly longer; upper parts somewhat paler and more grayish; upper tail-coverts distinctly barred with darker brown; lower tail-coverts usually more distinctly barred; sides and flanks duller and paler, pale wood brown, pale isabella color, or pale broccoli brown.

MEASUREMENTS: *Adult male:* Wing, 52.1–56.9 (average, 55.1) mm.; tail, 44.2–50.5 (47.5); bill (exposed culmen), 12.7–14.0 (13.5); tarsus, 19.6–21.6 (20.3); middle toe without claw, 11.9–13.5 (12.4). *Adult female:* Wing, 49.5–54.1 (51.6); tail, 40.4–47.0 (43.4); bill, 11.9–13.7 (12.4); tarsus, 17.5–20.6 (19.0); middle toe, 10.9–11.9 (11.4).

RANGE: S. British Columbia to n. Montana, south to e. California and Trans-Pecos Texas. Winters from s. British Columbia and n. Colorado to s. Baja California, Jalisco, and c. Veracruz.

TEXAS: *Breeding:* Altitudinal range, 1,700 to 3,750 ft. Collected in Brewster Co. Nest discovered in El Paso Co., El Paso (Apr. 10, 1938, Lena McBee). *Winter:* Taken northwest to Presidio (Sept. 27) and Val Verde, east to Bexar (Nov. 14) and Matagorda (Oct. 30), south to Cameron cos. Uncommon.

NESTING: *Nest:* Similar to that of *T. p. thryophilus. Eggs:* 5–10; ovate to nearly oval; pale chocolate color, marked with fine spots of darker shades of chocolate; average size, 16.3 × 12.2 mm.

SHORT-BILLED MARSH WREN, Cistothorus platensis (Latham)

SPECIES ACCOUNT

Also known as Sedge Wren. Tiny; short, slender bill; short tail, often cocked; lurks in grassy or sedgy marshes, meadows. Brownish and blackish above with fine whitish streaks on crown and back; buffy below (richest on crissum). Length, 4¼ in.; wingspan, 5¾; weight, ¼ oz.

RANGE: S.e. Saskatchewan to New Brunswick, south to n.w. Oklahoma (irregularly), Arkansas, and Virginia; also locally from Michoacán and Veracruz through

Central America and South America to Tierra del Fuego and Falkland Islands. Northernmost race winters chiefly from Gulf states and Maryland to n.e. Mexico and s. Florida.

TEXAS: (See map.) *Migration*: Late Mar. to early May; late Sept. to early Nov. (extremes: Mar. 5, May 18; July 31, Nov. 5). Common (some years; usually upper coast) to fairly common along coast; uncommon to scarce in rest of eastern half; rare in northern Panhandle. *Winter*: Early Nov.—often late Oct. along coast—to late Mar. Common to uncommon along coast; scarce to rare in remainder of eastern two-thirds; rare from southern Panhandle to Big Bend and Del Rio regions.

HAUNTS AND HABITS: Marsh grass, fresh and salt, is prime habitat for the Short-billed Marsh Wren. It frequents marshy or swampy borders of rivers, streams, and lakes, low grassy meadows, wet or dry, sedgy areas, old weedy fields, prairies covered with dense grass or weeds. Its small, coconut-shaped nest is well concealed in dense vegetation, preferably in sedges or grasses. In Texas this species ordinarily leaves cattail and tall-reed wetlands to its relative, the Long-billed Marsh Wren. Although not gregarious, it occurs at times with the Longbill; in the northern United States it has even occasionally nested in a colony of this species. Also, sometimes in spring or during the breeding season it gathers into small colonies in marshes.

Flight, awkward, weak, and fluttering, is performed with rapid wing-beats. If flushed, the Shortbill flies out weakly but soon drops out of sight. Shy and retiring, even more so than the Longbill, it is much more frequently heard than seen. Like its relative, it can cling with its feet to stems and sidle up and down these with alacrity, tipping its tail and twisting its body. As it slips through grass, it gleans moths, caterpillars,

crickets, locusts, grasshoppers, weevils, beetles, ants, and a few spiders.

The Short-billed Marsh Wren calls its *chap* or delivers its song from a grass stem, sometimes a weed or even a bush, occasionally for a considerable period. The song is rather sharp, metallic, and not particularly musical, sounding something like *tsip, tsip, tse-tse-tse-tse*, the first two or three notes rather slowly, the rest rapidly, uttered. Sometimes, the rendition resembles a series of accelerating *chap*'s. The bird sings in early morning and late evening and sometimes at night; in Texas, individuals sing mostly in March and almost entirely in the daytime.

DETAILED ACCOUNT: ONE SUBSPECIES

NORTHERN SHORT-BILLED MARSH WREN, *Cistothorus platensis stellaris* (Naumann)

DESCRIPTION: *Adults, nuptial plumage (light cinnamon phase)*: Acquired by practically complete prenuptial molt. Pileum deep fuscous black or fuscous, numerously streaked with buffy brown, dull cinnamon, sayal brown, or even buffy white; forehead of these colors but nearly uniform; hindneck buffy brown or dull cinnamon but usually darker and duller, forming a definite broad collar, this sometimes narrowly streaked with fuscous black or even dull white; triangular area on middle of back fuscous black, streaked with dull white or buffy white, sometimes with buff or light cinnamon posteriorly; remainder of upper surface sayal brown to light cinnamon brown; rump and upper tail-coverts light cinnamon brown, rump more or less streaked or spotted with fuscous black and grayish white; upper tail-coverts narrowly barred with fuscous black; tail dull tawny to hair brown; wings hair brown, but wing-coverts mostly sayal brown, dull buff, or dull pale buff, as are also numerous bars on outer webs of wing-quills, except on terminal portions of primaries and secondaries, becoming buffier on outer primaries; outer webs of tertials black with spots or bars of dull buff or buffy white; sides of head dull cinnamon buff, mixed with darker and lighter; narrow postocular streak fuscous; chin and middle of abdomen dull white or buffy white; breast dull ocher or cinnamon buff; sides, flanks, and crissum cinnamon buff to deep ochraceous tawny, unbarred; lining of wing buffy white or very light buff. Bill black or dull dark brown, but cutting edges and basal two-thirds or more of mandible pale dull flesh color or brownish white; iris prout brown or hazel; legs and feet light brown, ecru drab, or brownish flesh color, but soles of toes dull yellow. *Adults, nuptial (dark cinnamon phase)*: Similar to light cinnamon phase, but light areas of upper surface much darker, more rufescent; sides of head and of body, with flanks and crissum, also darker. *Adults, nuptial (light gray phase)*: Similar to light cinnamon phase but much more grayish, light markings buffy white to dull clay color, tawny olive, and between buffy brown and drab; sides and flanks very dull cinnamon buff to dull cinnamon. *Adults, nuptial (dark gray phase)*: Similar to light gray phase, but upper parts decidedly, sides and flanks somewhat, darker. *Adults, nuptial (blackish phase)*: Similar to dark cinnamon phase, but ground color of upper surface largely dull black, even forehead, this practically eliminating light brown nuchal collar; remainder of upper parts with minimum of cinnamon or rufescent brown markings, although with numerous but narrow white or pale buff streaks. *Adults, winter*: Acquired by complete postnuptial molt. Similar to nuptial adults but more deeply colored, particularly light areas of upper surface and lower parts—cinnamon buff areas, such as breast, sides, flanks, and crissum, sometimes show obscure terminal pale grayish spots or a few dull brown subterminal spots or bars. *First nuptial*: Acquired by practically complete prenuptial molt. Practically identical with nuptial adults. *First winter*: Acquired by partial postjuvenal molt. Like adults in winter. *Juvenal*: Acquired by complete postnatal molt. Similar to adults in winter, but pileum and hindneck almost uniform clove brown to between

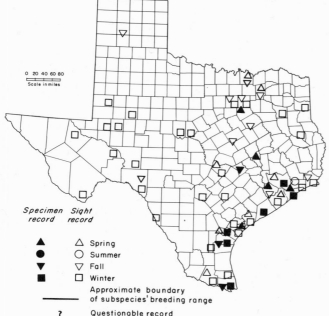

SHORT-BILLED MARSH WREN, *Cistothorus platensis*

0 20 40 60 80
Scale in miles

Specimen   Sight
record   record

▲   △   Spring
●   ○   Summer
▼   ▽   Fall
■   ☐   Winter

          Approximate boundary
———   of subspecies' breeding range

  ?   Questionable record

buffy brown and fuscous or olive brown; remainder of upper surface ochraceous tawny or dull tawny to between cinnamon brown and saccardo umber, streaked with clove brown or dull brownish black; median dorsal blackish area very much reduced in extent, sometimes represented chiefly by a few blackish streaks; rump and upper tail-coverts cinnamon brown to russet, unbarred; wings and tail hair brown, wings edged with ochraceous tawny and dark ochraceous tawny or sayal brown; sides of head pinkish buff, lores tinged with brown of pileum; postocular streak fuscous; rictal streak extending to below auriculars fuscous black; malar region, chin, throat, and median lower parts deep colonial buff; sides of breast ochraceous tawny to tawny olive, crissum cinnamon or sayal brown to tawny olive; sides of neck and of body dull cinnamon buff; remainder of lower surface buffy white to colonial buff.

MEASUREMENTS: *Adult male*: Wing, 42.9–47.0 (average, 45.0) mm.; tail, 36.1–41.4 (38.9); bill (exposed culmen), 9.9–10.9 (10.4); tarsus, 15.0–17.5 (16.8); middle toe without claw, 9.9–11.9 (11.2). *Adult female*: Wing, 40.9–45.5 (42.9); tail, 35.1–38.1 (36.8); bill, 9.4–10.4 (10.2); tarsus, 15.5–17.0 (16.3); middle toe, 9.9–11.9 (10.9).

RANGE: C. Saskatchewan to s.e. Maine and New Brunswick, south to n.w. Oklahoma (casually), n.e. Kansas, Arkansas, and e. Virginia. Winters from s.e. Michigan (casually) and New Jersey to s.e. San Luis Potosí and s. Florida.

TEXAS: *Winter*: Taken north to Ellis (Apr. 27), east to Harris and Galveston, southwest to Cameron cos.

CANYON WREN, *Catherpes mexicanus* (Swainson)

SPECIES ACCOUNT

Also spelled Cañon Wren. Creeps over ledges and cliffs; has long slender bill. Brownish above (finely dotted with whitish), becoming reddish brown posteriorly; clear white throat and breast contrasting with dull rusty belly and crissum (narrowly barred with whitish). Length, 5¾ in.; wingspan, 7½.

RANGE: S. interior British Columbia to s.w. South Dakota, south through w. United States and Mexico to Chiapas.

TEXAS: (See map.) *Resident*: Breeds, late Feb. to late July (eggs, Mar. 4 to July 7; young in nest to July 27) from 400 to 7,800 ft., probably higher. Common to fairly common in northern Panhandle (local), Trans-Pecos, and Edwards Plateau, east locally to Clay, Palo Pinto, McLennan, Caldwell, and Atascosa cos. Rare visitor during nonbreeding season east to Denton, south to Dimmit cos.

HAUNTS AND HABITS: Among all the avian inhabitants of Texas canyons, none is more delightful than the Canyon Wren. The spectacular Santa Elena and other canyons of the Rio Grande as well as less imposing rock cliffs of the Trans-Pecos and Edwards Plateau are its favored habitat. In contrast to the Rock Wren, which frequently perches on sunlit desert rocks and soil, the Canyon seeks shaded crevices, shallow caves, and shelters in rocky cliffs. While the Canyon Wren is most at home in wild deep canyons and gulches, it lives also about other rocky places of hills and mountains, bluffs along streams, and even among stone and brick— sometimes even wood—buildings of cities, where walls provide a substitute for its native cliffs.

In the 1940's and 1950's, one or more pairs of Canyon Wrens nested in the dome of the state capitol at Austin. Nesting was not their only indoor activity. Ralph Bickler and other bird watchers who worked in and near the capitol frequently witnessed these wrens flitting and creeping like mice along walls and ceiling pipes as they searched for spiders, flies, and crickets. At the end of the 1950's, the entrance hole (a broken window) was repaired; thus was the nation's largest wren house put out of business.

Active and restless, the Canyon Wren flits in and out of crevices, stopping now and then to sing or to utter its peculiar "jeering" note. Then with a flirt of its expanded tail, it disappears behind a boulder, pipe, or rafter only to pop out at some unexpected point. It seems not to be very shy. When creeping about walls it clings to them very much in the fashion of a nuthatch, that is without the use of its tail.

Navigation within man-made structures is far superior to that shown by most songbirds. In Burnet County at a country residence formerly owned by the Texas writer, J. Frank Dobie, William M. and Pauline Edwards made many indoor observations on a pair of Canyon Wrens. For several years during the 1960's, these birds nested inside a light fixture which hung from the ceiling in the parlor of the Edwards' home. When the young birds were being fed in the nest their parents were obliged to fly in and out of the house all day long. Entrance was down the chimney, across the fireplace room, and into the light in the parlor. The Edwards had to keep electricity switched off during the season to avoid burning the nest. Exit route was sometimes the same as the entrance route; at other times one or both parents flew from the parlor through the dining room, thence through the kitchen, and finally to their exit out a hole in the floor of the back porch. Probably the Canyon Wren's thousands of years of practice inside caves accounts for its extraordinary direction-

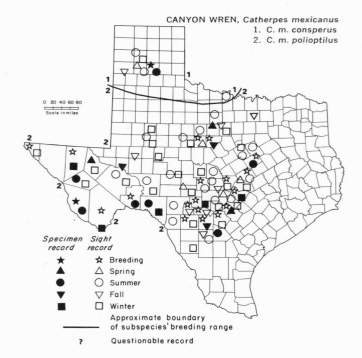

CANYON WREN, *Catherpes mexicanus*
1. *C. m. conspersus*
2. *C. m. polioptilus*

0 20 40 60 80
Scale in miles

Specimen record | Sight record
★ | ☆ Breeding
▲ | △ Spring
● | ○ Summer
▼ | ▽ Fall
■ | □ Winter

——— Approximate boundary of subspecies' breeding range

? Questionable record

finding ability within houses. When Cardinals, Blue Grosbeaks, and other finches—supposedly the most highly developed of birds—enter a simple one-room chicken house they are usually unable to find their way out again, as witnessed by many observers in Texas and elsewhere.

The Canyon Wren's note is a rather low *peupp*, often repeated several times. The loud song is one of the enchanting features of west Texas canyons. Vernon Bailey, U.S. Biological Survey field naturalist, recounted the following incident to H. C. Oberholser. In early August, 1902, in a canyon in the foothills of the Davis Mountains, Bailey was chasing a fox at sunrise with fifteen hounds in full bay. All around, Canyon Wrens were excitedly answering back with their ringing songs that echoed even above the voices of the dogs! The song is a series of seven to twelve clear, gushing, ringing notes (*tee*'s followed by *tew*'s) beginning high and descending an octave or more, sometimes ending with a harsh call. The Canyon Wren sings from jutting rocks, chimneys, roofs, or even inside caves or buildings, usually from late February to early November.

DETAILED ACCOUNT: TWO SUBSPECIES

COLORADO CANYON WREN, *Catherpes mexicanus conspersus* Ridgway

DESCRIPTION: *Adults, nuptial plumage*: Similar to *C. m. polioptilus* (see below), but smaller, particularly bill; lighter and more rufescent (less grayish) on upper parts, particularly head. MEASUREMENTS: *Adult male*: Wing, 56.4–61.5 (average, 59.7) mm.; tail, 51.1–54.1 (52.3); bill (exposed culmen), 19.0–22.6 (20.6); tarsus, 17.5–18.5 (18.3); middle toe without claw, 11.9–13.5 (12.7). *Adult female*: Wing, 55.1–60.5 (57.2); tail, 46.0–50.0 (48.3); bill, 17.0–20.1 (18.3); tarsus, 17.0–17.5 (17.3); middle toe, 11.9–12.4 (12.2).
RANGE: N. Nevada to c. Colorado, south to s.e. California and s. Oklahoma.
TEXAS: *Resident*: Altitudinal breeding range, 900 to 3,700 ft. One specimen: Armstrong Co., Rush Creek (June, 1910, J. K. Strecker, Jr.). Bird heard singing in Clay Co., Henrietta (early July, 1900, H. C. Oberholser) thought to be of this subspecies. Fairly common in Panhandle canyons.
NESTING: Similar to that of *C. m. polioptilus* (see below), but average egg size, 17.8 × 13.2 mm.

TEXAS CANYON WREN, *Catherpes mexicanus polioptilus* Oberholser

Race not in A.O.U. check-list, 1957 (see Appendix A).
DESCRIPTION: *Adults, nuptial plumage*: Acquired by wear from winter plumage. Pileum hair brown to drab, shading on back through wood brown, buffy brown, or dull cinnamon to tawny on rump and upper tail-coverts, feathers everywhere with subterminal spots of hair brown or fuscous and with small terminal spots of white or buffy white or of dull cinnamon to hazel; tail cinnamon to hazel with numerous more or less irregular bars of fuscous or fuscous black; wings dark buffy brown, coverts like back, those of greater series more brightly rufescent, lesser coverts with small spots of hair brown and dull white, median and lesser coverts each with subterminal spot of hair brown and terminal spot of dull white, also with tertials and outer webs of primaries and secondaries numerously barred with cinnamon, and tertials with subterminal shaft spot of buffy white; sides of head and of neck like pileum; short obscure superciliary stripe beginning above middle of eye buffy or grayish white; lores dull grayish white mixed with dark drab; anterior lower parts white; posterior lower surface anteriorly pale cinnamon rufous shading behind to russet; sides, flanks, and abdomen with numerous spots, some more or less transverse, clove brown or fuscous; lower tail-coverts spotted or narrowly barred more or less with dull white; lining of wing dull white or brownish white, somewhat washed with pale cinnamon and somewhat spotted with hair brown. Bill slate color, but base of mandible paler and tinged with olivaceous; iris umber brown; legs and feet dark brown or dull slate black. *Adults, winter*: Acquired by complete postnuptial molt. Practically identical with nuptial adults. *First nuptial*: Acquired by wear from first winter. Scarcely distinguishable from nuptial adults. *First winter*: Acquired by partial postjuvenal molt, which does not involve wing-quills or tail. Practically identical with first nuptial. *Juvenal*: Acquired by complete postnatal molt. Similar to nuptial adults, but dark markings of upper parts larger and more inclining to bars, white or whitish dots few or absent entirely; posterior lower parts duller, mostly unspotted or unbarred, between russet and cinnamon brown, bars if present usually indistinct. *Natal*: Dull tilleul buff, pale vinaceous buff, or drab.
MEASUREMENTS: *Adult male*: Wing, 61.5–65.0 (average, 63.8) mm.; tail, 53.1–55.6 (54.3); bill (exposed culmen), 20.1–23.1 (21.9); tarsus, 19.0–21.6 (20.1); middle toe without claw, 13.0–14.5 (13.7). *Adult female*: Wing, 58.4–64.0 (60.7); tail, 51.6–55.1 (53.1); bill, 19.0–21.6 (19.8); tarsus, 17.5–20.6 (19.0); middle toe, 11.9–14.0 (12.7).
RANGE: S.e. Arizona to Trans-Pecos and c. Texas.
TEXAS: *Resident*: Altitudinal breeding range, 400 to 7,800 ft., probably higher. Collected north to Stephens, east to McLennan and Travis, south to Atascosa, west to Val Verde, Presidio, and Culberson cos. Locally common.
NESTING: *Nest*: On rocky slopes, in canyons or ravines; in crevice among rocks or in shallow cave; loose cup of leaves, grasses, twigs, and weed stalks; thickly lined with down and feathers. *Eggs*: 3–7; rounded ovate; glossy; white; blotched and speckled with reddish brown, rufous, lilac, lavender gray, and vinaceous, mostly at large end, where markings often form wreath; average size, 18.3 × 13.5 mm.

ROCK WREN, *Salpinctes obsoletus* (Say)

SPECIES ACCOUNT

A large pale wren; bobs on rocks. Gray-brown above, finely spotted with whitish; whitish eye-stripe; buffy or cinnamon rump, flanks, corners of tail; broad black subterminal tail-band; dull white below with faint dusky breast-streaks. Length, 6 in.; wingspan, 9; weight, ½ oz.
RANGE: S. British Columbia to w. North Dakota, south through w. United States and deserts and highlands of Mexico to n.w. Costa Rica. Northern race winters from n. California, c. Colorado, and w. Nebraska southward.
TEXAS: (See map.) *Breeding*: Mid-Mar. to late Aug. (eggs, Apr. 2 to July 3; young in nest as late as Aug. 15) from 400 to 8,500 ft. Common to uncommon in northern Panhandle, Trans-Pecos, and on western Edwards Plateau; local, but apparently regular, in remainder of western half east to Wichita, Travis, and Starr cos. Last recorded nesting in Rio Grande delta: Cameron Co., 6 mi. southeast of Loma Alta (2 nests, 1 in construction, Mar. 14, 1919, R. W. Quillin). *Winter*: Late Sept. to mid-Apr. Common to fairly common through most of western third; uncommon in remainder of western half, becoming scarce east to Denton, Waco, Beeville, and Rio Grande delta.
HAUNTS AND HABITS: As its name asserts, the Rock Wren is attracted to rough rocky places: bare talus

slides, gulches, canyons, dry washes, valleys, dams, cliffs, and ledges along streams and elsewhere. It lives also in thin brush and scrub and, indeed, almost everywhere throughout arid and semiarid regions. Sometimes it frequents clearings in brush or woods, but it avoids forests. Some individuals even come to towns. In settlements it is likely to appear on stone fences and garden walls where it creeps, jumps, and bobs about so much that Mexicans long ago named it—as well as the Canyon Wren, whose town habits are similar—*saltapared* (leaps on wall). Although Rock and Canyon Wren habitats overlap a bit, the Rock is especially attracted to boulders and bare ground; the Canyon seeks shadowy canyons, bold rock cliffs, and shallow caves. The Rock Wren is frequently conspicuous as it hops about on rocks or sings from a point of vantage atop a stone.

Flight is usually quick, jerky, and short; the bird spreads its ample tail conspicuously just before it alights. When startled, the Rock Wren may fly to a rock and excitedly bob its body up and down or even from side to side. It is always active and ordinarily not very shy, but sometimes suspicious. Darting in and out of crevices and between rocks, it raises its head and tail as it hops about, often in search of grasshoppers, beetles, bugs, ants, caterpillars, spiders, and snails.

The Rock Wren's call note has been variously represented as *tik-ear*, *ti-keer*, or *tu-ree*. Its rather rambling song begins with two or three notes somewhat like *ti-ou*, *ti-ou*, *ti-ou*, or a variation of this, with a more varied ending. Volume is not great, but the metallic and ringing character makes it a well-carrying sound, although as a complete performance it is rather monotonous. To some ears the song seems Mockingbird-like, but without imitations. Singing is chiefly from March into July.

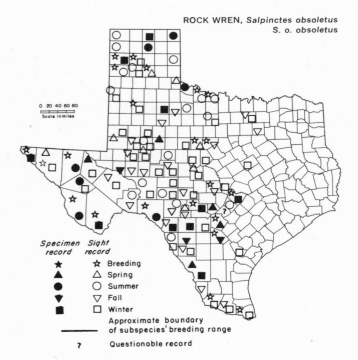

ROCK WREN, *Salpinctes obsoletus*
S. o. obsoletus

0 20 40 60 80
Scale in miles

Specimen record / Sight record

★ / ☆ Breeding
▲ / △ Spring
● / ○ Summer
▼ / ▽ Fall
■ / □ Winter

——— Approximate boundary of subspecies' breeding range

? Questionable record

DETAILED ACCOUNT: ONE SUBSPECIES

COMMON ROCK WREN, *Salpinctes obsoletus obsoletus* (Say)

DESCRIPTION: *Adults, nuptial plumage:* Acquired by wear from winter plumage. Upper parts drab to between drab and wood brown, but rump pinkish cinnamon or between cinnamon and orange cinnamon; everywhere above, though less so on rump, finely and obscurely spotted with hair brown and dull buff or grayish white; tail hair brown, middle rectrices and outer webs of all but outermost pair narrowly barred with chaetura drab or dark hair brown, with broad subterminal irregular bar of light pinkish buff or cinnamon buff tipped with light hair brown or drab, above this a broad bar of brownish black, outermost pair of tail feathers with additional cinnamon buff bar on inner webs, and several broad bars or spots on outer web; wings light hair brown, superior coverts like back, greater series barred or spotted on outer webs with dark hair brown or chaetura drab, each with small whitish shaft dot; tertials and outer webs of primaries and secondaries, except at tips, barred or spotted with color of back; sides of head mostly like crown, with distinct superciliary stripe dull buff or brownish white; cheeks and lores dull white somewhat mixed with dull drab; anterior lower surface dull or brownish white, throat, jugulum, and upper breast rather narrowly streaked with hair brown or drab; posterior lower parts dull white or white washed with pinkish cinnamon; sides, flanks, and sometimes crissum light pinkish cinnamon, crissum barred with fuscous or fuscous black; under wing-coverts white spotted with hair brown, axillars light pinkish cinnamon or avellaneous. Bill slate color or brownish white, basal part of mandible vinaceous or dull pale yellow; iris olive, olivaceous drab, or grayish umber; legs, feet, and claws black or slate black. *Adults, winter:* Acquired by postnuptial molt. Very similar to nuptial adults, but upper parts darker and more grayish, of less rufescent brown—rather light hair brown; terminal white or whitish spots larger and more conspicuous; rump more pinkish—fawn color; sides, flanks, and crissum of duller avellaneous; remainder of lower surface darker and with more wash of fawn color or avellaneous. *First nuptial:* Acquired by wear from first winter. Practically identical with nuptial adults. *First winter:* Acquired by partial postjuvenal molt. Very similar to adults in winter. *Juvenal:* Acquired by complete postnatal molt. Similar to nuptial adults, but above paler, more buffy posteriorly, pileum almost unmarked, and back wood brown, obscurely and narrowly barred with drab or hair brown; rump and upper tail-coverts much more buffy, between avellaneous and pinkish cinnamon, little or not at all spotted or barred; posterior lower parts lighter—pale pinkish buff. Maxilla brownish plumbeous; mandible, except dull brown tip, flesh color; legs and feet brownish plumbeous. *Natal:* Tilleul buff.

MEASUREMENTS: *Adult male:* Wing, 68.1–74.9 (average, 71.4) mm.; tail, 50.5–58.9 (53.8); bill (exposed culmen), 15.5–19.6 (17.8); tarsus, 18.5–23.1 (21.4); middle toe without claw, 12.4–14.5 (13.7). *Adult female:* Wing, 67.1–71.9 (69.3); tail, 48.5–57.4 (52.3); bill, 16.0–19.0 (17.5); tarsus, 19.0–21.6 (20.9); middle toe, 12.4–14.5 (13.2).

RANGE: S. British Columbia to s.w. North Dakota, south to s. Baja California and Tamaulipas. Winters from n. California and c. Colorado to southern limits of breeding range in Mexico.

TEXAS: *Resident:* Collected north to Oldham and Hardeman, east to Travis, south to Webb, west to Val Verde, Brewster, and El Paso cos. One specimen outside known breeding range: Lipscomb Co., Lipscomb (June 30, 1903, A. H. Howell).

NESTING: *Nest:* On rocky slopes, mesas, and about cliffs or uninhabited rocky open lands, along streams or not; in crevices of various kinds, under overhanging rocks, on ground under rocks, in hollow tree stump, crevice of building, such as log cabin, or hole of adobe structure; entrance to nesting cavity paved with small stones and bits of rock; loose cup of grass, bits of wood, bark, roots, moss, and hair; lined with rootlets, fine strips of bark, goat hair, or wool. *Eggs:* 4–10, usually 5; ovate; pure white, finely dotted with reddish brown, chiefly about large end; average size, 18.5 × 14.0 mm.

Mockingbirds and Thrashers: Mimidae

MOCKINGBIRD, *Mimus polyglottos* (Linnaeus)

Species Account

Also known as Northern Mockingbird. Trim body; thin, almost straight bill; longish wings; long, mobile tail. *Adult*: gray above; whitish below; large white patches on blackish wings and tail; pale yellow eyes. *Immature*: similar but spotted with grayish brown on breast. Length, 10 in.; wingspan, 14; weight, 1¾ oz.

RANGE: N. interior California to South Dakota and New Jersey (casually to s. Canada), south over s. United States and Mexico to Isthmus of Tehuantepec; also Bahamas, Greater Antilles, Virgin Islands. Naturalized in Hawaii. In winter, some individuals withdraw from northern limits.

TEXAS: (See map.) *Resident*: Breeds, mid-Feb. to late Aug.—occasionally later (eggs, Mar. 6 to Aug. 25; young just out of nest as late as Oct. 19) from near sea level to 6,000 ft. Very common to common in most areas, but uncommon and local, especially in winter, in parts of northern Panhandle where bushes and trees are scarce.

HAUNTS AND HABITS: The Mockingbird is one of thirty members of the strictly New World Mimidae. Probably no other native perching bird, unless it be the Scissor-tailed Flycatcher, is more widely known in Texas than the Mockingbird, official state bird, whose remarkable song and wide distribution make it so conspicuous. Though rare or absent on treeless plains and in deep forests, it is found almost everywhere else, particularly in bushy places and thickety edges of dry or wet woodlands. It also frequents roadsides, vicinity of country houses, and cemeteries, gardens, yards, and streets of towns and cities. It is not a gregarious bird and is usually seen singly or in pairs, although in the non-breeding season, particularly in autumn, a few birds, perhaps comprising family parties, sometimes congregate.

Flight is usually not long continued, although the bird is capable of flying rapidly for a considerable distance. Its ordinary flights from bush to bush or tree to tree are jerky and performed with more or less fanning and/or lowering of the tail. It remains mostly in lower branches of trees and in bushes but also perches on houses (particularly on the ridge of a roof or on a chimney), on posts, and in treetops for purposes of

singing or resting. Along roads it is one of the birds frequently seen on poles or wires. But it is just as much at home on the ground, where it walks or hops about hunting its food of caterpillars, grasshoppers, locusts, crickets, ants, bees, termites, beetles, flies, chinch bugs, millipedes, sowbugs, and snails. In bushes and trees it plucks many berries, including mulberry, elderberry, pokeberry, blackberry, Virginia creeper, and hackberry. When foraging on the ground, the Mockingbird frequently lifts its wings in a "wing-flashing" gesture the significance of which is controversial, but which perhaps has the effect of flushing grasshoppers out of the turf.

In character perhaps the Mockingbird is not quarrelsome, but at the same time it tends to be master of its neighborhood. At a feeding tray it often drives other birds away until it has satisfied its own appetite. It confronts birds not only similar to it in size, but also larger ones—a hawk, jay, or crow—or even a cat or dog. At the time young are leaving the nest, parents are especially fierce and repeatedly swoop at the heads of

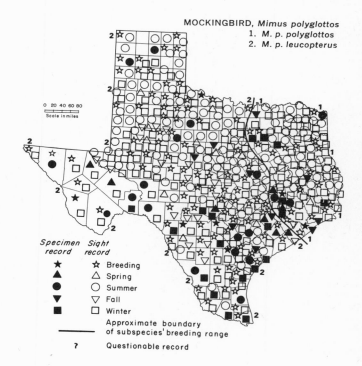

MOCKINGBIRD, *Mimus polyglottos*
1. *M. p. polyglottos*
2. *M. p. leucopterus*

0 20 40 60 80
Scale in miles

Specimen record	Sight record	
★	☆	Breeding
▲	△	Spring
●	○	Summer
▼	▽	Fall
■	□	Winter

—— Approximate boundary of subspecies' breeding range

? Questionable record

human beings and other intruders. Usually a Mocker's onslaught is so persistent that it comes out the victor.

The Mockingbird has many call notes, two of the most common being a harsh *shack* and *tchair*. Its song ranks among the top ten U.S. bird songs in quality, and is number one in both variety and quantity. Delivery is loudest and most frequent by the male, but the female also sings well. In the breeding season, the male Mocker is an indefatigable songster at all times of day and even at night, particularly if the moon is shining. It often performs for an hour or more without cessation. A typical song is a medley of its own notes and phrases, interspersed with imitations of those of other birds; sometimes an individual mocks a mammal or even creaky machinery. A favorite imitation is the food-begging squeal of the spotted-breasted young. Usually, a singer rapidly repeats each note or phrase about six times then rushes on to an entirely different set of notes. Many imitations are so accurate that only a sudden change of song tells a listener that the singer is the Mocker and not the mocked.

Mimus polyglottos usually mimics only birds it hears locally, but there are exceptions. For example, on the western edge of Austin, April 16, 1972, a Mockingbird repeatedly sang vocalizations of neotropical species— Chachalaca, Groove-billed Ani, Couch's Tropical Kingbird, Kiskadee Flycatcher, and Green Jay; imitations of the ani's *tee-ho* call were good, but other sounds were poorly reproduced (E. B. Kincaid, Jr., Suzanne Winckler). None of these mocked species normally occurs closer than 275 miles south of Austin. This unusual happening apparently can be explained in several ways: (1) the Mocker wasn't really mocking, but some of his highly varied phrases by coincidence sounded like those of other birds; (2) this Mockingbird was more migratory than most individuals of his species and had spent the winter in deep south Texas or in Mexico amid birds he was imitating; (3) the Mocker was mimicking a series of Mockingbirds stationed between Austin and the Rio Grande delta, thus picking up his neotropical notes from other individuals of *Mimus polyglottos* instead of from direct sources. Of central Texas naturalists, Roy Bedichek favored explanation (1); Charles Hartshorne favors (2) or (3).

While singing, the bird spreads its tail, drops or raises its wings, or even tosses itself several feet into the air and parachutes down to its perch. Less frequently it engages in its remarkable flight song, which is delivered as the bird is either hovering in air, flying, or dropping toward the ground. With its springtime day and night singing and long song season (i.e., most of the year, except less vigorously in winter and rarely in August), the Mockingbird gets in many more hours of singing than any other U.S. bird. So much singing would be monotonous and largely ignored by would-be invaders of the Mocker's breeding and feeding territories, if it were not for the frequent imitations; hence the great amount of song makes the imitations biologically necessary—or so holds a modern ornithological theory.

DETAILED ACCOUNT: TWO SUBSPECIES

EASTERN MOCKINGBIRD, *Mimus polyglottos polyglottos* (Linnaeus)

DESCRIPTION: *Adult male, nuptial plumage*: Acquired by wear from winter plumage. Upper surface plain hair brown to grayish hair brown; tail dark fuscous, two outer pairs of rectrices white or mostly so, third pair with outer web mostly fuscous, inner web often largely so, except at tip and base, fourth pair similar or fuscous except at tip; wings fuscous or dark fuscous, large area on base of primaries white, as are primary coverts with exception of tips; tertials and secondaries broadly edged exteriorly with color of back, with white or whitish tips; wing-coverts like back, but median coverts with broad grayish white tips, greater series broadly margined with color of back and tipped with white or grayish white; sides of head similar to crown but paler; cheeks whitish; sometimes obscure grayish white superciliary stripe; lores chaetura drab, sometimes mixed with pale gray; lower surface dull white, breast washed with pale gray or pale buff; flanks and crissum dull cartridge buff, crissum often whitish; lining of wing white, marked with hair brown. Bill black, base of mandible pale dull yellow or light brown; iris sulphine yellow, light brown, or dark brown; legs and feet black or dark brown, but hind portion of tarsus usually yellowish and soles of toes dull pale yellow. *Adult female, nuptial*: Acquired by wear from winter. Similar to nuptial adult male but smaller; outer tail feathers with dark portions more extensive. *Adult male and female, winter*: Acquired by complete postnuptial molt. Similar to nuptial adults, but more grayish (less brownish) above and somewhat darker—light grayish hair brown to dark grayish hair brown. *Male and female, first nuptial*: Acquired by wear from first winter. Practically identical with nuptial adults, though wing-quills and tail feathers are, at least in part, retained from juvenal. *Male and female, first winter*: Acquired by partial postjuvenal molt. Similar to adults in winter, except for wings and tail. *Juvenal*: Acquired by complete postnatal molt. Similar to adults in winter, but upper surface usually paler—dark rufescent hair brown; pileum dull light drab, back dark drab, rump dull avellaneous; in some individuals these colors much darker and somewhat more grayish; lower surface more purely white, with throat, breast, jugulum, sides, and flanks thickly marked with large and small spots of hair brown. Bill, legs, and feet dull brown. *Natal*: Pale sepia. Bill, legs, and feet pinkish buff shaded with brown.

MEASUREMENTS: *Adult male*: Wing, 105.9–119.9 (average, 111.3) mm.; tail, 110.0–134.1 (119.6); bill (exposed culmen), 17.0–18.5 (17.8); tarsus, 29.4–34.0 (32.5); middle toe without claw, 19.0–20.6 (20.3). *Adult female*: Wing, 100.1–111.5 (104.6); tail, 100.6–114.6 (108.5); bill, 16.0–18.0 (17.0); tarsus, 30.5–34.0 (31.8); middle toe, 18.5–21.6 (19.8).

RANGE: C. South Dakota to New Jersey, south to s.e. Texas and s. Florida; also n. Bahamas.

TEXAS: *Resident*: Altitudinal breeding range, near sea level to 1,000 ft. Collected north to Bowie, south to Chambers, west to Waller and Dallas cos. Common.

NESTING: *Nest*: On uplands and bottomlands, in all kinds of more open country, in wild and cultivated areas, even close to human dwellings, in pastures, and along highways; in tree or bush, usually not very high above ground—but ranging 1–50 ft., in dense thicket, fence corner, brush heap, and even in hollow top of stump or post; rather bulky, somewhat loosely built bowl of twigs, grasses, leaves, weed stalks, bark strips, moss, cotton, rags, string, rootlets, hair, tree blooms, various vegetable fibers, and feathers; lined with rootlets, horsehair, fine grass, gray moss, or cotton. *Eggs*: 3–6, usually 4; short ovate to elliptical ovate; dull greenish blue, bluish green, dark green, bright blue to buffy gray; spotted with reddish or yellowish brown, sometimes chocolate and dull purple or lilac; average size, 24.4 × 18.8 mm.

WESTERN MOCKINGBIRD, *Mimus polyglottos leucopterus* (Vigors)

DESCRIPTION: *Adult male and female, nuptial plumage*: Similar to *M. p. polyglottos* but larger with relatively shorter tail; upper parts lighter, more brownish; lower surface more strongly tinged with buff.

MEASUREMENTS: *Adult male*: Wing, 103.1–122.5 (average, 115.3) mm.; tail, 109.5–132.6 (119.6); bill (exposed culmen), 17.5–20.1 (18.3); tarsus, 29.9–34.5 (32.8); middle toe without claw, 19.0–23.1 (21.1). *Adult female*: Wing, 104.1–118.6 (110.7); tail, 105.1–127.5 (115.3); bill, 17.0–18.5 (17.5); tarsus, 30.5–33.5 (32.3); middle toe, 19.0–22.6 (20.9).

RANGE: E. California to s.w. South Dakota, south through w. United States to s. Baja California and in mainland Mexico to Isthmus of Tehuantepec.

TEXAS: *Resident*: Altitudinal breeding range, near sea level to 6,000 ft. Collected north to Oldham, east to Falls and Wharton, south to Cameron, west to Brewster and El Paso cos. Common.

NESTING: Similar to that of *M. p. polyglottos*, but average egg size, 25.1 × 18.3 mm.

BLACK CATBIRD, *Melanoptila glabrirostris* Sclater

SPECIES ACCOUNT

Dumetella glabrirostris of some authors. Resembles Catbird (see below), but entire plumage glossy violet black (slightly duller underneath). Length, 8 in.; weight, ca. 1¼ oz.

RANGE: Yucatán Peninsula (including Isla Cozumel), n. Guatemala, and n. Honduras.

TEXAS: *Accidental*: One specimen, first for United States: at or near Brownsville (male, June 21, 1892, Frank B. Armstrong). Bird was included in large collection gathered by Armstrong around Brownsville and sent to Josiah Hoopes of Philadelphia without comment and apparently without identification by Armstrong. Later identified by Robert Ridgway, but record never published. Skin now in Academy of Natural Sciences of Philadelphia collection.

There has long been a bit of cloud over the locality records of Armstrong, a professional bird collector. It was said that he was not above dipping into Mexico to obtain rare specimens for his clients, even though all of them wanted their birds collected at least one inch inside the U.S.A. Ludlow Griscom claimed that Armstrong placed "Brownsville, Texas" tags on everything he or his Mexican helpers shot anywhere between Corpus Christi, central Texas coast, and Tampico, on the Tamaulipas-Veracruz border. However, the Black Catbird could just as well have been taken at Brownsville as at Tampico, since this Yucatán species is equally unlikely at either town. Furthermore, according to investigations by H. C. Oberholser, neither Armstrong nor his associates did any collecting on the Mexican side of the Rio Grande until 1895 or later. It is noteworthy that the Brownsville *Melanoptila glabrirostris* was taken in 1892 on a date near the beginning of hurricane season.

HAUNTS AND HABITS: Very little is known about the Black Catbird, but in appearance and behavior it seems to be similar to our U.S. Catbird. The chief distinction of *M. glabrirostris* is that the bird's metropolis is on Isla Cozumel—where it is one of the most abundant species—while on its mainland range it is rare and local.

The Black Catbird is a lowlander of semiarid tropical woods and underbrush. It stays usually well hidden and low in thickets, at woodland edges, and in abandoned *milpas* (cornfields). Occasionally it gets into cutover areas of rain forests. Seldom is it seen above mid-level of vegetation or flying in the open. During the breeding season, however, a bird often moves to a conspicuous perch to sing its song: a persistent, high-pitched series of rising, then descending, phrases, usually repeated in rapid sequence.

DETAILED ACCOUNT: NO SUBSPECIES

R. A. Paynter, Jr., described the subspecies *cozumelana* from Isla Cozumel in 1954.

DESCRIPTION: *Adult male, nuptial plumage*: Acquired by partial prenuptial molt. Upper parts uniform glossy dusky slate violet; lower parts similar but rather duller, the abdomen with little or no gloss; tail metallic dull greenish black, inner webs of more outer feathers chaetura black; wings chaetura black, exposed surfaces of closed wing metallic dull greenish black, except anterior lesser coverts which are like back. Bill black; iris dark brown; legs and feet black or blackish brown, soles of toes dull pale yellow. *Adult female, nuptial*: Acquired by partial prenuptial molt. Similar to nuptial adult male but averaging somewhat smaller; plumage duller, particularly lower surface, where throat and chin are often decidedly brownish with little or no metallic sheen. *Adult male and female, winter*: Acquired by complete postnuptial molt. Similar to corresponding sex of nuptial. *Juvenal*: Unknown.

MEASUREMENTS: *Adult male*: Wing, 87.9–98.1 (average, 90.7) mm.; tail, 88.9–97.1 (93.0); bill (exposed culmen), 16.5–21.6 (19.3); tarsus, 26.4–29.9 (27.9); middle toe without claw, 18.0–20.1 (18.8). *Adult female*: Wing, 86.1–88.9 (87.4); tail, 81.0–90.9 (86.9); bill, 16.0–20.1 (17.8); tarsus, 25.9–28.4 (27.2); middle toe, 17.0–19.0 (18.3).

TEXAS: *Accidental*: One specimen (see species account).

CATBIRD, *Lucar carolinense* (Linnaeus)

SPECIES ACCOUNT

Dumetella carolinensis of A.O.U. check-list, 1957 (see Appendix A); Gray Catbird of recent authors. Trim; jerks and flips long tail. Uniform blackish gray (somewhat paler below) with black cap, rusty crissum. Length, 8½ in.; wingspan, 11½; weight, 1¼ oz.

RANGE: S. British Columbia to Nova Scotia, south to e. Oregon, c. Arizona, e. Texas, c. and s. (locally) Gulf states, s. Georgia, and n. Florida (rarely); also Bermuda. Winters from s.e. United States (a few north along Atlantic seaboard to Long Island) through e. and s. Mexico to Panama; also Bermuda, West Indies.

TEXAS: (See map.) *Breeding*: Mid-Apr. to mid-Aug. (eggs, May 5 to July 28) from 300—formerly 50—to 3,700 ft. Fairly common to uncommon in northeastern Panhandle east along Red River boundary to northeastern counties, south to Dallas, Brazos, Polk, and Nacogdoches cos.; scarce to rare southwest to Waco and Bastrop. Apparently summers very occasionally on upper coast, but last nesting evidence was in 19th century: northern Harris Co. (nest with 1 egg, May 5, 1881, H. Nehrling). *Migration*: Mid-Apr. to mid-May; late Sept. to late Oct. (extremes: Mar. 20, May 31;

PLATE 23: Cliff Swallow, *Petrochelidon pyrrhonota* (left), Barn Swallow, *Hirundo rustica* (right)

PLATE 24: Western Bluebird, *Sialia mexicana*, perched on *Juniperus*
immature male (top), adult male (bottom)

Aug. 7, Dec. 3). Very common (usually along coast) to uncommon through most of eastern two-thirds; uncommon to scarce in Panhandle; rare to casual in Trans-Pecos (one specimen, not identified to race: Brewster Co., Big Bend Nat. Park, May 7, 1971, R. H. Wauer). *Winter*: Late Nov. to Mar. Uncommon to scarce along coast; rare in remainder of eastern two-thirds and in northern Panhandle; casual in Trans-Pecos.

HAUNTS AND HABITS: The Catbird inhabits chiefly thickets and undergrowth, but is not so partial to heavy forests. Rather, it is found about woodland edges, in swamps, vine and briar tangles, and even on prairies with scattered bushes. During migration it is more apt to frequent cultivated areas, brushy fence rows, borders of fields, and orchards, gardens, yards, parks, and hedges in towns. Less shy than the Brown Thrasher, it oftentimes lives close to human habitations, either in country or town. Not much given to gathering into companies of any size, it may be seen in parties comprised of a few individuals, chiefly during migration.

Flight is ordinarily not long but quick and rather jerky, sometimes smooth and sailing when more prolonged, and generally with spread tail which is flirted either up or down. Wherever common, the Catbird is usually not suspicious and is much in evidence. In fact, it is rather inquisitive and can easily be attracted by imitating the sound of a wounded or alarmed bird. It is very active and certainly aggressive. The Catbird works not only in trees and bushes, but also frequently hops about on the ground; it flits through brush with ease, apparently just as much at home in the interior of a bush as in outer foliage. In Texas, favorite shrubbery foods are mulberries and pokeberries; on the ground the bird seeks especially ants and grasshoppers. When

excited, it at times pauses, then raises and spreads its tail.

Its common note is a curious catlike mewing. This thrasher's song is pleasing, but not so musical as that of either the Brown Thrasher or Mockingbird; a rather squeaky or complaining quality makes it thinner, less voluble, and less melodious. The Catbird does, however, have much tenacity and sings sometimes for long periods with practically no interruption save the occasional introduction of its peculiar *mee-ew*. It ordinarily does not repeat a song phrase; this contrasts with the Brown Thrasher which sings paired phrases and the Mockingbird which repeats itself rapidly about six times before passing to the next song. Not only is the Catbird a songster in its own right, but it can also mimic songs and calls of other birds, though not as proficiently as the Mockingbird. Occasionally it attempts to imitate even nonavian sounds. Song delivery is typically from the interior of a bush. *Lucar carolinense* sings mostly from March to July, chiefly by day, but also at night, though not then so avidly as the Mocker. In September, October, and early November, males which have nested in or near Texas may occasionally render a "whisper" song. This is rarely heard, however, since most individuals are south of the state by mid-October.

DETAILED ACCOUNT: THREE SUBSPECIES

COMMON CATBIRD, *Lucar carolinense carolinense* (Linnaeus)

No races recognized by A.O.U. check-list, 1957 (see Appendix A).

DESCRIPTION: *Adult male, nuptial plumage*: Acquired by wear from winter plumage. Pileum blackish brown, distinctly defined from back which ranges from deep mouse gray to deep neutral gray; tail blackish mouse gray, tips of outer feathers paler; wing-quills fuscous black, exposed portions similar to back in color; wing-coverts like upper surface; sides of head and of neck, including superciliary stripe, together with lower parts, neutral gray to rather dark neutral gray, lightest on middle of abdomen and on chin; lower tail-coverts bay to chestnut; lining of wing light neutral gray. Bill black, mandible slate black, blackish slate, or brownish slate; inside of mouth slate color; iris dark brown; legs and feet black, slate black, blackish slate, slate, brownish slate, clove brown, or vandyke brown, but feet and claws sometimes olive. *Adult female, nuptial*: Acquired by wear from winter. Similar to nuptial adult male, but upper parts averaging somewhat more brownish; chestnut of lower tail-coverts usually more mixed with gray. *Adult male and female, winter*: Acquired by complete postnuptial molt. Similar to corresponding sex of nuptial adult. *Male and female, first nuptial*: Acquired by wear from first winter. Like corresponding sex of nuptial adult. *Male and female, first winter*: Acquired by partial postjuvenal molt, which does not involve wing-quills or tail. Similar to adults in winter, but wings and tail somewhat more brownish. *Juvenal*: Acquired by complete postnatal molt. Similar to nuptial adults, but throat decidedly more brownish; posterior upper parts chaetura drab; lower surface hair brown washed with fuscous, most so anteriorly; crissum russet, paler than in adult. *Natal* (this plumage of this race not seen in Texas): Neutral gray. Bill and feet pinkish buff tinged with brown; inside of mouth orange, instead of slate color.

MEASUREMENTS: *Adult male*: Wing, 86.1–96.0 (average, 91.2) mm.; tail, 88.9–103.1 (95.8); bill (exposed culmen), 15.0–18.0 (16.3); tarsus, 26.9–29.0 (27.7); middle toe without claw, 18.0–20.1 (19.3). *Adult female*: Wing, 84.1–90.9 (87.9); tail, 82.0–

CATBIRD, *Lucar carolinense*
L. c. meridianum

0 20 40 60 80
Scale in miles

Specimen Sight
record record

★ ☆ Breeding
▲ △ Spring
● ○ Summer
▼ ▽ Fall
■ □ Winter

——— Approximate boundary
of subspecies' breeding range

? Questionable record

97.0 (91.6); bill, 15.0–17.0 (16.3); tarsus, 27.0–28.5 (27.7); middle toe, 18.0–20.1 (19.3).

RANGE: S.e. Manitoba to c. Nova Scotia, south to Kansas and e. Tennessee. Winters from Texas (casually) and e. North Carolina through e. Mexico and Central America to Colombia (probably); also Bahamas, Cuba.

TEXAS: *Migration*: Collected in Denton, Tarrant, Dallas, and Ellis cos. Uncommon.

NESTING: (This race does not nest in Texas.) *Nest*: On uplands or bottomlands, in swamps or dry areas, in wild or cultivated regions, on edges of forests, or in more or less open land; along fence rows, borders of fields, in gardens, parks, cemeteries, ornamental grounds; in bush or vines in immediate vicinity of house, in thicket, bush, or low tree, 3–10 ft. above ground, often along stream; rough, bulky, and rather loosely built bowl; composed of twigs, rootlets, grasses, weed stalks, leaves, strips of bark, various vegetable fibers, trash, pieces of paper, and similar materials; lined with strips of grapevine and other bark, tendrils of vines, rootlets, leaves, and fine grass. *Eggs*: 3–6, usually 4; generally ovate or elliptical ovate; glossy, bright bluish green, unmarked; average size, 24.1 × 17.8 mm.

WESTERN CATBIRD, *Lucar carolinense ruficrissum* (Aldrich)

No races recognized by A.O.U. check-list, 1957 (see Appendix A).

DESCRIPTION: *Adult male and female, nuptial plumage*: Resembling *L. c. carolinense*, but under parts lighter, particularly abdomen and crissum.

MEASUREMENTS: *Adult male*: Wing, 86.6–97.0 (average, 91.0) mm.; tail, 91.0–104.1 (96.3); bill (exposed culmen), 15.0–17.0 (16.0); tarsus, 26.4–30.0 (28.5); middle toe without claw, 17.0–20.1 (18.5). *Adult female*: Wing, 83.6–93.5 (88.4); tail, 88.4–97.5 (93.5); bill, 15.4–17.0 (16.0); tarsus, 27.0–29.0 (28.0); middle toe, 17.5–19.0 (18.3).

RANGE: S.w. British Columbia to s.w. Manitoba, south to c. Arizona and n. New Mexico. Winters chiefly in e. Mexico.

TEXAS: *Migration*: Collected north to Tarrant, Dallas, and Wood, south to Galveston cos. Uncommon.

SOUTHEASTERN CATBIRD, *Lucar carolinense meridianum* (Burleigh)

No races recognized by A.O.U. check-list, 1957 (see Appendix A).

DESCRIPTION: *Adult male and female, nuptial plumage*: Similar to *L. c. carolinense*, but upper and lower parts much paler. Like *L. c. ruficrissum*, but black of pileum definitely more brownish; gray of upper and lower surfaces decidedly brownish, not as clear; and in female, more whitish, thus less uniform gray. *Natal*: Probably similar to *L. c. carolinense*.

MEASUREMENTS: *Adult male*: Wing, 85.0–92.5 (average, 90.5) mm.; tail, 86.0–97.0 (93.0); bill (exposed culmen), 14.0–17.5 (16.1). *Adult female*: Wing, 82.5–92.0 (87.5); tail, 82.0–95.0 (90.3); bill, 14.0–16.0 (15.8).

RANGE: N. Texas to s.w. Maryland, south to s.e. Texas and Florida. Winters from breeding range through e. Mexico to Nicaragua; also Bahamas, Cuba.

TEXAS: *Breeding*: Collected north to Cooke, south to Robertson (eggs) and Brazos cos. *Migration*: Collected north to Tarrant, east to Galveston, south to Nueces and Cameron, west to Kerr and Menard cos. Common. *Winter*: Taken northeast to Fannin, southwest to Victoria, Aransas, and Cameron cos. Uncommon to scarce.

NESTING: Similar to that of *L. c. carolinense*.

BROWN THRASHER, *Toxostoma rufa* (Linnaeus)

SPECIES ACCOUNT

Toxostoma rufum of A.O.U. check-list, 1957 (see

Appendix A). Sleek, with long tail; fairly long, very slightly decurved blackish bill, dull whitish at base; yellow eyes. Reddish brown above; buffy or grayish cheeks; two whitish wing-bars; heavily brown-streaked whitish below. Length, 11¼ in.; wingspan, 13⅓; weight, 2¼ oz.

RANGE: U.S.-Canada border from s.e. Alberta to n. and s.w. Maine, south to s.e. Texas, Gulf coast, and s. Florida. Winters from Texas and e. Oklahoma to s. Maryland, south to U.S. Gulf coast and s. Florida.

TEXAS: (See map.) *Breeding*: Mid-Mar. to late June (eggs, Apr. 19 to June 3; young in nest, Apr. 16 to June 13) from about 50—rarely lower—to 2,500 ft. Fairly common to uncommon from northern Panhandle along Red River, south to Fort Worth, Dallas, and Tyler; uncommon and local south to Austin and Houston; scarce in Lavaca and Chambers cos.; casual at Corpus Christi (pair carrying nesting material, Apr. 2, 1967, Kay McCracken; birds occupied nest site to May 29). *Winter*: Late Sept. to early May (extremes: Sept. 5, May 23). Very common to uncommon through eastern half with exception of extreme southern part (south of Corpus Christi), where rare; uncommon to rare in most of western half.

HAUNTS AND HABITS: The Brown Thrasher lives in thickets and bushes on the edges, or in open portions, of woodlands and forests. In Texas this bird seeks wintertime shelter and food especially in yaupon (*Ilex vomitoria*) thickets. In search of insects, seeds, grain, and berries, it frequents also cultivated areas, fence and brush rows, gardens, yards, and shrubbery about farms and other houses. Vines on porches of houses are sometimes visited, and even yards, gardens, and parks of towns. It is not a gregarious bird and only at times

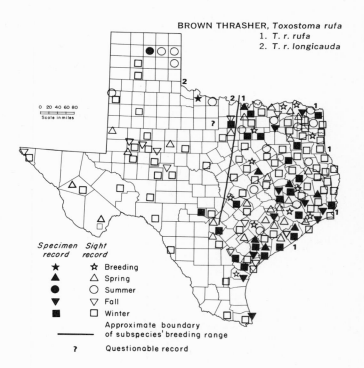

BROWN THRASHER, *Toxostoma rufa*
1. *T. r. rufa*
2. *T. r. longicauda*

0 20 40 60 80
Scale in miles

Specimen record	Sight record	
★	☆	Breeding
▲	△	Spring
●	○	Summer
▼	▽	Fall
■	□	Winter

—— Approximate boundary of subspecies' breeding range

? Questionable record

during nonbreeding seasons is it found occasionally in small companies.

On the wing, it is quick and more or less jerky, with often a downward flirt of the tail; except during migration, its flights are usually brief, from bush to bush or from thicket to copse. Occasionally, however, an individual may be seen higher in the air passing from one grove to another. Rather shy, this bird retreats at the approach of an intruder, slips into shrubs, and either flies away or dashes through vegetation to escape observation. When the bird takes up in cultivated areas, however, it loses something of its shyness; some individuals can even be enticed out of bushes by proffered shelled peanuts. It is at home in treetops, bushes, or on the ground and frequently seeks beetles and earthworms, scratching with its bill among leaves and other debris.

The distinctive call note of the Brown Thrasher is a resounding, guttural *tsack*. Another note, much sounded from yaupon thickets in winter, can only be described as a low, gentle rasp. Its song, one of the best of those of eastern birds, is rich, voluble, and melodious. This song sounds Mockingbird-like, but each phrase is usually sung as a pair (instead of the Mocker's rapid repetition of a phrase up to six or even more times) with few or no obvious imitations. Brown Thrasher songs are a bit lower in pitch and a little more "fruity," hence more pleasant to some human ears. When singing the bird ordinarily perches well up in a bush or tree, with long tail hanging down and head upraised. It sings much from early spring into July, but infrequently at other times of the year.

DETAILED ACCOUNT: TWO SUBSPECIES

EASTERN BROWN THRASHER, *Toxostoma rufa rufa* (Linnaeus)

DESCRIPTION: *Adults, nuptial plumage*: Acquired by wear from winter plumage. Upper surface dull cinnamon rufous or between tawny and cinnamon brown, but paler in worn nuptial; forehead dull buffy brown, centers of feathers narrowly olive brown, upper tail-coverts and rump brighter, more rufescent than rest of upper surface; tail similar to back, outer edges of feathers rather duller; wing-quills hair brown, wing-coverts and exterior margins of quills like back, margins of outer primaries somewhat paler and more grayish, median and greater coverts with broad buffy white tips forming two wing-bars and with darker fuscous or hair brown subterminal spots; sides of head and neck buffy brown mixed with dull buff; lower surface dull buffy white, strongly tinged with pale buff on throat and upper breast; sides, flanks, and crissum warm buff; jugulum, breast, sides, and flanks with numerous conspicuous longitudinal spots of fuscous or fuscous black; lining of wing light buff or pale cinnamon buff. Bill black or slate black; base of mandible dull white or dull pale yellow; iris light yellow or chrome yellow; legs and feet mouse gray, drab, or flesh color; claws light brown. *Adults, winter*: Acquired by complete postnuptial molt. Like nuptial adults, but somewhat darker above, more buffy below. *First nuptial*: Acquired by wear from first winter. Like nuptial adults. *First winter*: Acquired by partial postjuvenal molt, which does not involve wing-quills or tail. Practically same as adults in winter, but iris sometimes gray. *Juvenal*: Acquired by complete postnatal molt. Similar to adults in winter, but bill shorter; pileum usually duller; back and scapulars, occasionally pileum, streaked with dull fuscous black; wing-bars dull cinnamon buff

or light buff; rump and upper tail-coverts paler and more or less spotted with fuscous, feathers sometimes with pale buff tips, crissum paler, streaks on lower parts narrower and more numerous. Bill seal brown, black, or slate black, but basal half of mandible dull pale yellow, dull white, or tinged with pink; iris pale yellow, gray, or hair brown; legs and feet mouse brown, drab, or dark drab; soles of toes dull white. *Natal*: Deep brownish drab. Bill, legs, and feet dull pinkish buff.

MEASUREMENTS: *Adult male*: Wing, 99.1–105.9 (average, 103.6) mm.; tail, 116.1–128.0 (122.5); bill (exposed culmen), 23.6–27.4 (24.9); tarsus, 33.5–35.6 (34.5); middle toe without claw, 22.1–24.4 (23.1). *Adult female*: Wing, 95.5–104.1 (100.3); tail, 109.0–125.5 (118.9); bill, 22.1–25.9 (24.4); tarsus, 32.5–34.5 (33.8); middle toe, 21.6–23.9 (23.4).

RANGE: Minnesota to n. Maine, south to s.e. Texas and c. Florida. Winters from n.e. Oklahoma and e. North Carolina to s. Texas and s. Florida.

TEXAS: *Breeding*: Altitudinal range, 50 to 600 ft. Collected north to Red River (Oct. 20), south to Orange (Feb. 24) and Chambers (Sept. 29), west to Austin (Oct. 29) and Dallas (Feb. 20) cos. Uncommon. *Winter*: Taken outside regular breeding range south to Brazoria (Mar. 1), Matagorda, and Nueces (Mar. 30) cos. Common. One specimen collected in Rio Grande delta, probably of this race: Cameron Co., s. Padre Island, 8 mi. north of Port Isabel (1 found dead, Oct. 27, 1972, G. W. Blacklock; skin in Welder Wildlife Refuge collection).

NESTING: *Nest*: On uplands and bottomlands, slopes and level areas; usually 3–8 ft. above ground, in bush or low tree or even on ground, in fence corner, cluster of vines, briars, brush heap, sometimes in orchard tree; rough bulky bowl, somewhat flat but strongly built; made of twigs, sticks, strips of bark, grasses, weed stalks, roots, and leaves, all firmly interwoven; lined with grapevine and other bark, fine roots, grass, weed stalks, dead leaves, horsehair, and a few feathers. *Eggs*: 3–6, usually 4; ovate to elliptical ovate; ground color greenish white, pale buff, bluish white, or very pale gray; finely speckled with reddish brown and yellowish brown, these markings ordinarily confluent about large end; average size, 27.2 × 20.3 mm.

WESTERN BROWN THRASHER, *Toxostoma rufa longicauda* (Baird)

DESCRIPTION: *Adults, nuptial plumage*: Similar to *T. r. rufa*, but wing, and especially tail, much longer; upper parts somewhat paler.

MEASUREMENTS: *Adult male*: Wing, 106.9–115.1 (average, 110.2) mm.; tail, 123.0–136.9 (130.3); bill (exposed culmen), 23.1–28.9 (26.4); tarsus, 33.5–35.6 (34.8); middle toe without claw, 22.6–24.9 (23.6). *Adult female*: Wing, 104.1–114.0 (108.2); tail, 119.1–141.0 (128.3); bill, 23.9–28.9 (26.7); tarsus, 33.0–35.1 (34.0); middle toe, 22.1–24.4 (23.6).

RANGE: E. Alberta to n.e. North Dakota, south to n.w. Texas and c. Oklahoma. Winters from n. and s.e. Texas to s. Mississippi.

TEXAS: *Breeding*: Altitudinal range, 1,205 to perhaps 2,500 ft. in Panhandle. No skin, but eggs collected: Wilbarger Co., Vernon, 1,205 ft. (June 1, 1931, R. L. More). Uncommon. *Winter*: Taken north to Cooke, east to Bowie and Jefferson (late Oct.), south to Brazoria and Nueces (Oct. 1), west to Kerr cos. Common.

NESTING: Similar to that of *T. r. rufa*, but average egg size, 27.4 × 20.3 mm.

LONG-BILLED THRASHER, *Toxostoma longirostris* (Lafresnaye)

SPECIES ACCOUNT

Toxostoma longirostre of A.O.U. check-list, 1957 (see Appendix A). Texas race known as Sennett's Thrasher in older works. Resembles Brown Thrasher, but grayish (not rufous) brown above; grayer cheeks; black streaks below; longer, more decurved, entirely blackish bill. Length, 11½ in.; wingspan, 13¼.

RANGE: S. Texas, south at low and moderate altitudes through e. Mexico to c. Veracruz. Accidental in Colorado (Barr, one specimen).

TEXAS: (See map.) *Resident*: Breeds, mid-Mar. to late July (eggs, Mar. 26 to June 25; nest building as late as July 1) from near sea level to 1,000 ft. Locally fairly common from Del Rio, Sabinal, San Antonio, Beeville, and Rockport south to mouth of Rio Grande; somewhat irregular along northern limits; nonbreeding individuals sighted in Jeff Davis Co., southern Brewster Co., Gonzales Co., and Victoria.

HAUNTS AND HABITS: The Long-billed Thrasher (excluding the Colorado specimen) is a found-in-the-U.S.-only-in-Texas specialty. Among these specialties, the Pauraque, Long-billed Thrasher, Black-headed Oriole (some years), and Olive Sparrow are the only brushland species whose resident range extends up from Mexico over most of—but not farther north than—the area called South Texas Plains by botanists, Tamaulipan Biotic Province (Texas section) by zoogeographers, and south Texas brush country by ordinary Texas mortals.

The Long-billed and the Curve-billed (both have long bills that decurve about equally) are the only resident thrashers in brushy south Texas. Longbills concentrate in bottomland willow (*Salix*), huisache (*Acacia farnesiana*), mesquite (*Prosopis*), *Condalia*, and various other bushes; Curvebills seek well-drained elevations where mesquite is low and pricklypear cactus (*Opuntia*) is high. In Mexico, *Toxostoma longirostris* ranges locally as high as five thousand feet in the humid Sierra Madre Oriental, but in semiarid south Texas this bird is strictly a lowlander, since here only low, nearly level ground retains enough moisture to grow thickets tall and dense enough to suit the species.

This thrasher is not gregarious and is seen singly or in pairs, even where common. It is shy and wary, particularly in the neighborhood of human habitations, and under ordinary circumstances is not easy to study. Owing to its dense and tangled habitat, it is much more likely to be heard than seen; usually it does not come out into the open. The Longbill's brief and jerky flights and quick movements remind one very much of the Brown Thrasher for which it is often mistaken. The present species gathers its food of antlions, ants, beetles, bugs, and termites largely on the ground in thickets. Here, like other thrashers, it swings its bill from side to side to flick away dead leaves, twigs, and loose soil that cover its prey. Upon occasion it ascends to treetops, chiefly for the purpose of eating hackberries and singing in springtime.

Some of its call notes seem to be identical with those of the Brown Thrasher; others are higher pitched and sharper. Song is highly similar to that of its kinsbird, but perhaps repetition of phrases is not quite so frequent. Longbills sing at least snatches of their song much of the year except when weather is extremely cold or overly hot. However, the main singing season—and about the only time these birds perch atop mesquites to sing—is from March to July.

DETAILED ACCOUNT: ONE SUBSPECIES

SENNETT'S LONG-BILLED THRASHER, *Toxostoma longirostris sennetti* (Ridgway)

DESCRIPTION: *Adults, nuptial plumage*: Acquired by wear from winter plumage. Similar to Eastern Brown Thrasher, *T. rufa rufa*, but upper parts darker and duller, more brownish or grayish (less rufescent); sides of head and neck more grayish, dark spots on lower surface more conspicuous because more blackish. Pileum between hair brown and buffy brown to between cinnamon brown and russet, but forehead more grayish brown and darker centers of feathers giving pileum rather mottled appearance; back rufescent buffy brown washed with gray to between cinnamon brown and russet; tail cinnamon brown to russet or between saccardo umber and light cinnamon brown, tips of outermost rectrices paler, even buffy white; wingquills light olive brown, outer edges dull cinnamon, inner margins, except at tips, dull pinkish cinnamon; lesser wing-coverts fuscous, margined with grayish cinnamon; median and greater coverts broadly tipped with white forming two wing-bars and with subterminal fuscous shaft spots; sides of head and anterior part of neck between hair brown and drab, somewhat mixed with paler brown; cheeks buffy white, finely streaked or spotted with chaetura drab; lower parts white or often washed with pale buff; crissum light buff; throat, jugulum, breast, sides, and flanks with numerous large longitudinal spots of chaetura black; under wing-coverts white or buffy white, more or less spotted with hair brown; axillars pinkish buff or pale pinkish buff. Bill dark brown, mandible paler at base; iris bright yellow; legs and feet dull brown. *Adults, winter*: Acquired by complete postnuptial molt. Similar to nuptial adults but more richly colored. *First nuptial*: Acquired by wear from first winter. Like nuptial adults. *First winter*: Acquired by partial postjuvenal molt. Very much like adults in winter. *Juvenal*: Acquired by complete postnatal molt. Similar to adults in winter, but bill shorter; upper parts

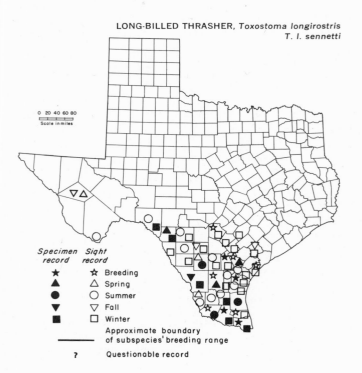

LONG-BILLED THRASHER, *Toxostoma longirostris T. l. sennetti*

0 20 40 60 80
Scale in miles

Specimen record / Sight record

★ / ☆ Breeding
▲ / △ Spring
● / ○ Summer
▼ / ▽ Fall
■ / □ Winter

—— Approximate boundary of subspecies' breeding range

? Questionable record

duller, feathers with appreciably darker centers, those of hind-neck and rump with paler tips; wing-bars deep buff or dull cinnamon, instead of white; spots on lower surface less sharply defined. *Natal*: Unknown.

MEASUREMENTS: *Adult male*: Wing, 95.0–103.1 (average, 99.6) mm.; tail, 116.1–132.1 (125.7); bill (exposed culmen), 24.9–29.9 (27.2); tarsus, 35.1–37.1 (35.6); middle toe without claw, 23.1–24.9 (23.6). *Adult female*: Wing, 93.0–103.1 (98.8); tail, 121.9–128.0 (124.7); bill, 24.9–26.7 (26.2); tarsus, 33.0–37.1 (35.3); middle toe, 22.6–24.9 (23.6).

RANGE: C. Coahuila and s. Texas, south to s. San Luis Potosí and s.e. Tamaulipas.

TEXAS: *Resident*: Collected northwest to Val Verde, east to La Salle, Live Oak, and Nueces, south to Cameron and Hidalgo cos.

NESTING: *Nest*: On level or slightly rolling areas; in timber along streams, or in brush, thicket, hedge, bush, or low tree; 4–8 ft. above ground, often in dense undergrowth of heavy timber or in cactus or yucca; rather rude, bulky bowl; composed of twigs, pieces of vines, rootlets, straw, and coarse weed stems; lined with fine roots, grasses, bark, and Spanishmoss. *Eggs*: 2–5, usually 3–4; between ovate and elliptical ovate; dull white or pale greenish white or yellowish white; much speckled with reddish brown, sometimes over entire surface, often more thickly at large end; average size, 27.4 × 20.9 mm.

[BENDIRE'S THRASHER, *Toxostoma bendirei* (Coues)

Resembles Curve-billed Thrasher (see below), but has shorter, less decurved bill (note virtually straight lower mandible) with whitish or buff (not blackish) ramus; clear yellow eyes; whitish tail-corners, but no wing-bars. Breast-spots of Bendire's are shaped like tiny arrowheads pointing upward; Curvebill's chest-spots are large, round, and blurry. Beware of young Curvebill which has fairly short, rather straight bill. Length, ca. 9½ in.

RANGE: S.e. California, s. Nevada, s. Utah, Arizona, and s.w. New Mexico, south to s. Sonora. Winters from s. Arizona to s. Sinaloa.

TEXAS: *Hypothetical*: Three careful sightings, all in Randall Co.: Palo Duro Canyon (1 seen, Apr. 14, 1955, Mr. and Mrs. J. C. Creager, Bess Smith); Palo Duro Club near Canyon (1 seen, Apr. 16, 1955, Peggy Acord); and Canyon (1 watched for entire day at close range, Nov. 9, 1956, J. H. Bailey). Other sightings (Maverick Co., etc.) apparently based on misidentifications.]

CURVE-BILLED THRASHER, *Toxostoma curvirostris* (Swainson)

SPECIES ACCOUNT

Toxostoma curvirostre of A.O.U. check-list, 1957 (see Appendix A). Long decurved bill; red or orange eyes. Grayish brown above; buffy white wing-bars and tail-corners, these sometimes absent; whitish throat, bordered on each side by grayish brown stripe; remaining under parts grayish with large, pale brown breast-spots. Length, 10¾ in.; wingspan, 13½; weight, 3¼ oz.

RANGE: S. Arizona to extreme n.w. Oklahoma and w.

and s. Texas, south over deserts and Central Plateau of Mexico to Oaxaca.

TEXAS: (See map.) *Resident*: Breeds, early Mar. to late Aug. (eggs, Mar. 17 to Aug. 12; young in nest to Aug. 20) from near sea level to 6,200 ft. Very common (some winters) to fairly common in Trans-Pecos, southern Panhandle, and south Texas brush country; uncommon in middle Panhandle, on western Edwards Plateau, and along northeastern limits of south Texas from San Antonio to Beeville and Rockport; north locally and irregularly to northern Panhandle (nonbreeders) and Austin, where scarce. Accidental in Walker Co., Huntsville area (1 observed and photographed, Sept. 16, 1968–Feb. 1, 1969, K. B. Bryan).

HAUNTS AND HABITS: The Curve-billed is the most numerous and widely distributed of thrashers in arid-land Texas. It lives preferably in thorn scrub and thickets on the edge of woods, among *Opuntia* and other cacti, yuccas, mesquites, and other semidesert shrubs in valleys, canyons, and washes, and on plains, mesas, and slopes. It is found frequently, however, in open brushy woodlands, brush heaps, occasionally trees on borders of fields, or rarely in close vicinity of human habitations. It lives, for the most part, singly or in pairs, and rarely do more than a few gather together in any one place.

Flight is usually quick, more or less jerky, and accompanied often by a downward movement of the spread tail characteristic of thrashers. The Curvebill flies mostly from bush to bush, but at times it wings swiftly for a longer distance, generally near the ground. Ordinarily shy and rather wild, it keeps out of sight as much as possible and retreats rapidly at appearance of any intruder. Sometimes it mounts to the top of a mesquite or other bush to obtain a singing perch or view

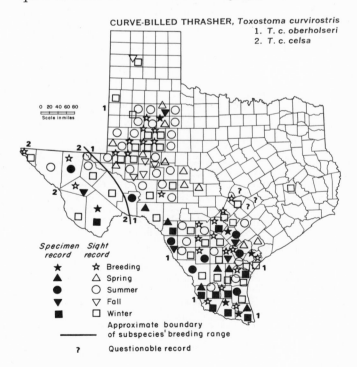

CURVE-BILLED THRASHER, *Toxostoma curvirostris*
1. *T. c. oberholseri*
2. *T. c. celsa*

0 20 40 60 80
Scale in miles

Specimen record / Sight record
★ / ☆ Breeding
▲ / △ Spring
● / ○ Summer
▼ / ▽ Fall
■ / □ Winter

——— Approximate boundary of subspecies' breeding range

? Questionable record

of the surroundings. Walking about much on the ground, it inspects nooks and crannies for beetles, other insects, and wild fruits.

The alarm note of the Curve-billed Thrasher is a rather sharp *whit, whit* or *whit-wheet*. Its song is a few-syllabled, melodious warble, rich and full, that bears a general resemblance to the songs of other mimids, particularly the Mockingbird. The Curvebill is a bit harsher than the Mocker, does not repeat itself so much, gives fewer obvious imitations of other birds, and intersperses more *whit-wheet*'s. This thrasher's song season is also shorter, chiefly from March into July, and it seldom sings at night, neither does it have a vigorous revival of song in autumn.

DETAILED ACCOUNT: TWO SUBSPECIES

BROWNSVILLE CURVE-BILLED THRASHER, *Toxostoma curvirostris oberholseri* Law

DESCRIPTION: *Adults, nuptial plumage*: Acquired by wear from winter plumage. Upper surface light grayish hair brown; tail light clove brown, but middle pair of rectrices olive brown or buffy brown, all, except middle pair, with broad white or buffy white tips; wing between buffy brown and hair brown, lesser coverts and very narrow edgings of other coverts and quills like back, median coverts and greater series tipped with white forming two rather inconspicuous wing-bars; sides of head and neck like crown, cheeks more or less mixed with white or buffy white, very inconspicuous paler superciliary stripe; chin and middle of throat white or buffy white, bordered by more or less indistinct grayish brown submalar stripe; rest of lower surface dull buffy white; flanks and crissum cinnamon buff; jugulum, breast, sides of throat, and less conspicuously sides and flanks, with large, roundish, sometimes confluent spots of light hair brown; sides of body rather rufescent hair brown; under wing-coverts buffy white spotted with hair brown; axillars dull wood brown. Bill dull black or dark brown, but basal portion of mandible paler; iris bright red or yellow next to pupil with outer orange ring; legs and feet dark brown. *Adults, winter*: Acquired by complete postnuptial molt. Like nuptial adults but darker and less brownish (more grayish) above; spots on anterior lower parts larger and darker. *First nuptial*: Acquired by wear from first winter. Practically identical with nuptial adults. *First winter*: Acquired by partial postjuvenal molt. Like adults in winter. *Juvenal*: Acquired by complete postnatal molt. Similar to adults in winter, but bill shorter; upper parts decidedly more brownish—dark grayish buffy brown; upper tail-coverts much more rufescent—dark snuff brown—and much more contrasted with back; edges of wings more rufescent, light tips of wing-coverts deep buff instead of white, posterior parts lighter; jugulum strongly tinged with buff; crissum cinnamon buff; spots on lower surface more brownish, smaller, and more in form of streaks. *Natal*: Above chaetura drab or sayal brown; below lighter or somewhat whitish. Inside of mouth ocher yellow.
MEASUREMENTS: *Adult male*: Wing, 101.1–109.0 (average, 105.1) mm.; tail, 101.6–117.1 (107.4); bill (exposed culmen), 25.9–31.8 (27.7); tarsus, 32.0–35.1 (33.0); middle toe without claw, 22.6–25.4 (24.1). *Adult female*: Wing, 98.1–104.9 (101.3); tail, 98.8–107.4 (102.9); bill, 23.1–27.9 (26.7); tarsus, 29.9–34.0 (31.8); middle toe, 22.1–25.4 (23.6).
RANGE: E. Trans-Pecos and c. Texas, south to c. Coahuila and e. Tamaulipas.
TEXAS: *Resident*: Altitudinal breeding range, near sea level to 2,500 ft. Collected north to Dickens, southeast to Bexar, Refugio (eggs), Nueces, and Cameron, west to Terrell cos. Common.
NESTING: *Nest*: On mesas and lowlands, in mesquite or similar thickets, often on edges of woodlands, or in cultivated areas, such as garden or courtyard of house, also along roadsides;

placed 2–10 ft. above ground in thickets, dense, often thorny bushes, or cacti; bulky bowl, rough outside, edges guarded by thorny twigs, sometimes, however, nearly flat with little depression for eggs; composed of sticks, roots, and grasses; lined with finer grasses, straw, and rootlets. *Eggs*: 3–5, usually 3 or 4; ovate to between ovate and elliptical ovate; light bluish green or light niagara green to deep greenish blue or pale yellowish blue; profusely dotted over entire surface with reddish brown; average size, 28.4 × 20.1 mm.

PLATEAU CURVE-BILLED THRASHER, *Toxostoma curvirostris celsa* Moore

DESCRIPTION: *Adults, nuptial plumage*: Similar to Mexican Curve-billed Thrasher, *T. c. curvirostris*, from c. and s. Mexico, but wing shorter; bill longer; upper parts averaging somewhat paler and more grayish (less brownish). Similar to *T. c. oberholseri* but larger; somewhat darker and more grayish (less brownish) above; spots on anterior lower parts averaging larger.
MEASUREMENTS: *Adult male*: Wing, 106.9–115.6 (average, 110.0) mm.; tail, 107.4–117.1 (112.5); bill (exposed culmen), 27.4–31.5 (29.7); tarsus, 32.0–35.6 (33.8); middle toe without claw, 23.1–25.9 (24.1). *Adult female*: Wing, 104.6–111.0 (108.7); tail, 101.6–116.6 (109.5); bill, 27.4–31.0 (29.2); tarsus, 31.0–34.5 (32.5); middle toe, 23.1–24.4 (23.6).
RANGE: S.e. Arizona to extreme n.w. Oklahoma, south to Durango and Guanajuato.
TEXAS: *Resident*: Altitudinal breeding range, 1,800 to 6,200 ft. Collected in Culberson, Jeff Davis, and Brewster cos. Common.
NESTING: Similar to that of *T. c. oberholseri*, but average egg size, 27.4 × 19.8 mm.

CRISSAL THRASHER, *Toxostoma dorsalis* Henry

SPECIES ACCOUNT

Toxostoma dorsale of A.O.U. check-list, 1957 (see Appendix A). A large thrasher with a long, well-decurved bill; yellowish or brownish eyes; rusty crissum. Grayish brown above; white throat bordered on each side by distinct black stripe; plain pale gray below. Length, 12 in.; wingspan, 12¾.
RANGE: S.e. California, s. Nevada, s.w. Utah, c. Arizona, New Mexico, and Trans-Pecos Texas, south to n. interior Baja California, c. Sonora, and locally to Zacatecas and Hidalgo.
TEXAS: (See map.) *Resident*: Breeds, early Mar. to late Aug. (eggs, Mar. 25 to Aug. 17; young in nest as early as Mar. 25) from about 1,900 to 5,600 ft. Fairly common to uncommon in much of Trans-Pecos, but scarce in Pecos River Valley (species reported during all seasons, but nesting unconfirmed).
HAUNTS AND HABITS: The Crissal Thrasher has a more decurved bill than does the Curve-billed Thrasher; it is, in fact, number one among Texas songbirds in the sickle-bill department. The present species also inhabits, for the most part, more arid and elevated regions. Texas Crissal Thrashers live, ordinarily well concealed, in two habitats—mesquite or willow thickets beside desert rivers, such as the Rio Grande in Big Bend, and juniper-pinyon-oak hill slopes, as in the Chisos Mountains. Of the two habitats, the bird prefers the riverside thickets. While it generally does not haunt the vicinity of human habitations, it infrequently will live about

Curve-billed Thrasher, *Toxostoma curvirostris*,
on mesquite (*Prosopis*)

ranch houses, where it becomes less shy than in its wild desert surroundings.

Ordinarily retiring, the Crissal flies relatively little. When it does, its movements are usually quick, jerky, short, and chiefly from bush to bush, where it can dart rapidly out of sight. On occasion, in order to cross a broad valley, it takes to the air and travels far, often gliding on steady wings for a considerable distance. A terrestrial bird, it runs swiftly, then stands and quickly raises its tail. On the ground it digs with its bill for caterpillars, beetles, grasshoppers, bugs, and scorpions. When in bushes it eats wild grapes and other berries. To mount to the crown of a bush it skips from branch to branch in the interior portion until reaching the top. The Crissal is seen singly and in pairs, but toward the end of breeding and in autumn, small groups, apparently family parties, congregate.

The Crissal Thrasher has a harsh call note, which may be represented by *cha*. Another note resembles *chideary*. Its song is sweet and of considerable variety, rich and full, but apparently not imitative as is sometimes the song of the Brown Thrasher. In singing it perches often atop a bush or small tree with its tail hanging down, head uplifted, and sickle bill opening wide. Rather frequently, however, it sings while standing on the ground. The song period extends over the greater part of the year, although it is usually quiet during July and August.

DETAILED ACCOUNT: ONE SUBSPECIES

COMMON CRISSAL THRASHER, *Toxostoma dorsalis dorsalis* Henry

DESCRIPTION: *Adults, nuptial plumage (gray phase)*: Acquired by wear from winter plumage. Upper parts plain hair brown; tail somewhat darker and slightly more rufescent; wing-quills

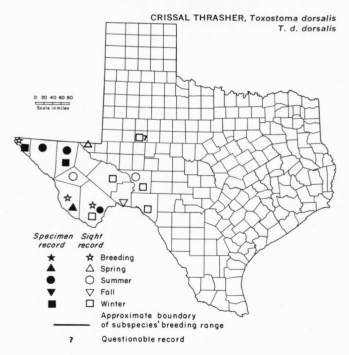

CRISSAL THRASHER, *Toxostoma dorsalis*
T. d. dorsalis

0 20 40 60 80
Scale in miles

Specimen Sight
record record

★ ☆ Breeding
▲ △ Spring
● ○ Summer
▼ ▽ Fall
■ □ Winter

———— Approximate boundary of subspecies' breeding range

? Questionable record

hair brown, wing-coverts and edgings of secondaries drab; outer edges of primaries similar but paler; sides of head drab, posterior ear-coverts somewhat more buffy; cheeks and auriculars finely streaked with dull white, rictal streak and submalar streak of chaetura black, enclosing malar streak of pale buff or buffy white; chin and middle of upper throat white; crissum bright russet; remainder of lower surface grayish light drab; lining of wing vinaceous buff. Bill dark brown or dull black; iris golden yellow, brownish straw color, light brown, or dull white; legs and feet slightly reddish brown, blackish brown, or dull olive brown; claws plumbeous black. *Adults, nuptial (brown phase)*: Similar to gray phase, but upper parts more or less tinged with ochraceous; lower parts strongly tinged with same. This phase well marked from gray phase and discernible in juvenal as well as in nuptial and winter adults. *Adults, winter*: Acquired by complete postnuptial molt. Similar to nuptial adults in corresponding phase but usually somewhat darker above and below. *First nuptial*: Acquired by wear from first winter. Like corresponding phase of nuptial adults. *First winter*: Acquired by partial post-juvenal molt. Similar to corresponding phase of adults in winter. *Juvenal*: Acquired by complete postnatal molt. Similar to nuptial adults, but upper parts more rufescent, rump and upper tail-coverts decidedly so—dull mikado brown; lower parts more strongly tinged with buff or ochraceous; crissum pale russet. Iris very pale brown. *Natal*: Drab.

MEASUREMENTS: *Adult male*: Wing, 96.0–104.9 (average, 100.3) mm.; tail, 133.1–150.6 (140.2); bill (exposed culmen), 34.0–38.6 (35.8); tarsus, 31.5–34.5 (32.8); middle toe without claw, 21.6–22.6 (21.9). *Adult female*: Wing, 93.5–102.6 (98.8); tail, 123.0–144.0 (135.4); bill, 34.5–37.6 (35.3); tarsus, 30.5–34.5 (31.8); middle toe, 19.0–23.1 (21.1).

RANGE: S.e. California to n.e. New Mexico, south to c. Sonora and Trans-Pecos Texas.

TEXAS: *Resident*: Collected in El Paso, Hudspeth, Culberson, Presidio, and Brewster cos.

NESTING: *Nest*: On arid mountains, mesas, and in valleys; in pinyon-oak scrub on semiarid mountains or in *Condalia*-mes-quite-tornillo-*Acacia* thickets along desert streams; usually not high above ground in densely branched shrub; large bulky bowl, often very poorly constructed, with but slight depression for eggs; composed of coarse, often thorny, twigs, sticks, and rootlets; lined with finer vegetable material, such as dead grass, small twigs, rootlets, feathers, grass, bark, and horse and other hair. *Eggs*: 2–4, usually 3; ovate; pale greenish blue to light niagara green or bluish green, unmarked; average size, 27.7 × 19.0 mm.

SAGE THRASHER, *Oreoscoptes montanus*
(Townsend)

SPECIES ACCOUNT

A relatively short-billed, short-tailed thrasher; has yellow eyes. Gray-brown above; whitish eye-stripe, wing-bars; white tail-corners; blackish-streaked whitish below. Length, 8¾ in.; wingspan, 12½; weight, 1¾ oz.

RANGE: Great Basin and Rocky Mts. regions from interior s.w. Canada (locally), south to s. California, s. Nevada, n. New Mexico, and extreme w. Oklahoma (casually). Winters from c. California, n. Arizona, s. New Mexico, w. Oklahoma, and w. Texas to deserts of n. Mexico, south sparingly on Central Plateau of Mexico to Guanajuato.

TEXAS: (See map.) *Summer*: Specimen: Culberson Co., Bell Creek (Aug. 18, 1940, B. E. Ludeman). Sightings: El Paso (Aug. 17, 1921, A. H. McLellan); Big

Sage Thrasher, *Oreoscoptes montanus*

Bend Nat. Park (July 24, 1964, Dick Rasp, fide R. H. Wauer). Regarded as permanent resident by Panhandle birders; widely reported in literature to breed in northwestern Texas, but closest actual nesting record seems to be in southern Cimarron Co., Oklahoma. *Winter*: Early Oct. to mid-Apr. (extremes: Aug. 28, May 26). Common to uncommon, though virtually absent some years, west of 100th meridian and along Rio Grande from Eagle Pass to delta; irregularly uncommon to rare in remainder of western two-thirds, east to Dallas, Waco, Austin, and Rockport areas; casual on upper coast.

HAUNTS AND HABITS: In Texas the Sage Thrasher winters in brush and scrubby thickets in drier, more open parts of the countryside, rather than bottomland thickets or timber along streams; but also at times it ventures into cultivated fields. On its breeding grounds in the Rocky Mountains and northern Great Basin it lives largely in sagebrush of valley slopes, mesas, and foothills. It also sometimes occurs in cemeteries or other places near or on the outskirts of towns. It stays mostly in bushes or on the ground, but frequents also bare rocks.

During the breeding season it is seen mostly singly or in pairs, but in autumn sometimes congregates in small companies. It is rather shy, particularly in summer, and when disturbed runs away rapidly on the ground or dives into the brush; sometimes it flies a considerable distance low over the ground in a rather circuitous flight to another bush. While on the ground it runs and stands not unlike an American Robin and, at times, scurries along with tail raised. Here it feeds on weevils, crickets, grasshoppers, and berries, the latter particularly in cooler months. Flight is swift, but usually not elevated or prolonged, being confined mostly to travels from one bush or thicket to another.

The Sage's usual note is a guttural *chuck*, sometimes more than once repeated; there is also a high-pitched rally note. Its song, while not as strong as that of the Brown Thrasher or Catbird, is still pleasing and varied; its warbles and trills at first recall the song of the Ruby-crowned Kinglet. Sometimes the singer progresses to a rich, Black-headed Grosbeak–like outpouring. The rapid, clear phrases are typically given in a continuous warble; these phrases, unlike those of the Brown and other thrashers, are only occasionally repeated and do not seem to be imitative of other birds. The bird, though it sometimes sings on the wing, usually delivers its melody from atop a bush; occasionally the singer turns his head from side to side while singing. The song period usually begins in March, but at first the songs are not as elaborate or fine as they become a little later. While nesting, the bird apparently sings little, but late in autumn its urge revives. The Sage Thrasher is not very often heard in Texas.

DETAILED ACCOUNT: NO SUBSPECIES

DESCRIPTION: *Adults, nuptial plumage (gray phase)*: Acquired by wear from winter plumage. Upper parts mouse gray, feathers of head with darker centers, giving pileum slightly streaked appearance; back almost uniform, but with slightly darker feather centers; tail fuscous to dark fuscous, palest on middle feathers, three outer pairs of feathers with broad white tips, outermost pair narrowly margined externally with white, and all but outermost pair edged with paler; wings dull hair brown, lesser coverts like back, remaining coverts and wing-quills edged with color of back or with paler gray, greater and median series of wing-coverts narrowly tipped with brownish white forming two wingbars; auriculars dark drab, more or less mixed with dull white; superciliary stripe dull brownish white; lores chaetura drab, mixed with whitish; cheeks dark drab, rather more grayish and more or less mixed with dull white; malar streak pale buff or whitish; submalar streak chaetura black; lower parts white washed with pinkish buff, chiefly on lower throat, breast, and sides; flanks and crissum cinnamon buff; jugulum, breast, sides, and flanks with numerous triangular spots of fuscous to fuscous black, becoming more like streaks on posterior lower parts; lining of wing pale buff or buffy white, under wing-coverts spotted with hair brown. Bill dull black or brownish black, but basal half of mandible pale brown, yellowish slate, or faintly yellow; inside of mouth deep yellow; iris chrome yellow or gamboge yellow; legs brownish olive green, olive gray, greenish slate, or olive brown; toes dark sepia, soles straw color. *Adults, nuptial (brown phase)*: Similar to gray phase, but more brownish or deeply buff; upper parts rather dark grayish buffy brown, verging toward hair brown; tail warm fuscous; lower parts more strongly tinged with cinnamon buff, this color more spread over lower parts. *Adults, winter*: Acquired by complete postnuptial molt. Similar to nuptial adults, but light or whitish margins of tertials broader; upper parts more purely grayish (less brownish); lower parts more deeply tinged with buff. *First nuptial*: Acquired by wear from first winter. Practically identical with corresponding phase of nuptial adults. *First winter*: Acquired by partial postjuvenal molt. Like corresponding phases of nuptial adults. *Juvenal (gray phase)*: Acquired by complete postnatal molt. Similar to nuptial adults, but upper parts light buffy gray, everywhere streaked conspicuously with fuscous, these streaks smallest on rump; lower parts pale pinkish buff on breast and crissum, elsewhere white or buffy white, streaks rather less well defined and those on sides and flanks smaller than in adult. *Juvenal (brown phase)*: Acquired by complete postnatal molt. Upper parts buffy brown, streaks olive brown; breast and crissum cinnamon buff; else-

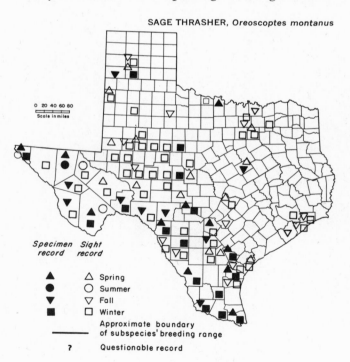

SAGE THRASHER, *Oreoscoptes montanus*

0 20 40 60 80
Scale in miles

Specimen record / Sight record

▲ △ Spring
● ○ Summer
▼ ▽ Fall
■ □ Winter

—— Approximate boundary of subspecies' breeding range

? Questionable record

where mostly pale pinkish buff or buffy white. Bill black or dull black, but mandible bluish black, its basal half more or less yellow or lilaceous; interior of mouth dull yellow or greenish yellow; iris lemon or greenish yellow; legs dull greenish yellow, dark yellowish green, or yellowish brown; toes dull black, but soles yellow. *Natal*: Dull black.

MEASUREMENTS: *Adult male*: Wing, 95.0–103.1 (average, 98.9) mm.; tail, 87.1–95.0 (90.7); bill (exposed culmen), 14.5–17.5 (16.3); tarsus, 28.4–31.5 (30.2); middle toe without claw, 18.0–21.1 (19.3). *Adult female*: Wing, 94.0–100.1 (96.3); tail, 85.1–91.9 (88.4); bill, 15.0–17.0 (16.3); tarsus, 28.9–32.0 (30.7); middle toe, 17.0–20.1 (18.5).

TEXAS: *Summer*: See species account. *Winter*: Taken north to Oldham (Oct. 8) and Randall, east to Clay (Apr. 11) and Mc-Lennan (Oct. 12), south to Nueces and Cameron, west to Presidio (Oct. 5) and El Paso cos.

NESTING: *Nest*: On mesas or slopes; in sage or other brush; in bush, cactus, or low tree, usually about 10 in.–3 ft. above ground; a loose, bulky bowl, substantial but inartistic, sometimes a little domed with a deep inner cavity; composed of thorny twigs, twigs of sage, greasewood, and other shrubs, strips of bark from sage and other bushes, coarse grasses, heavy plant stems; lined with rootlets, fine plant stems, grasses, hair, and fur. *Eggs*: 3–5, usually 4; ovate or short ovate to nearly elliptical oval; highly glossy; greenish blue; spotted with bright reddish brown, clove brown, chocolate, or umber brown, with shell markings of plumbeous gray and lilac gray; average size, 24.4 × 17.8 mm.

Thrushes: Turdidae

ROBIN, *Turdus migratorius* Linnaeus

SPECIES ACCOUNT

American Robin of many authors. A large thrush. *Nuptial male*: blackish gray above (darkest on head); incomplete white "spectacles"; black-streaked white throat; brick red breast; white lower belly, crissum; blackish tipped yellow bill. *Female, winter male*: somewhat duller, paler. *Immature*: large blackish spots on breast. Length, 9 in.; wingspan, 16; weight, 2¾ oz.

RANGE: Tree-limit of North America, south to s. California, Gulf states, and s. Georgia; also south through highland Mexico to Guerrero and Oaxaca. Winters from U.S.-Canada border to Guatemala, Gulf coast, and s. Florida; also Bahamas, w. Cuba.

TEXAS: (See map.) *Breeding*: Early Mar. to Aug. (no egg dates available, but young in nest from Mar. 28 to Aug.) from near sea level to 8,000 ft. Common to fairly common in eastern quarter; uncommon and local in remainder of state north of 29th parallel, but Trans-Pecos nesting evidence confined to El Paso and Guadalupe Mts.; scarce on central coast south to Corpus Christi. *Winter*: Early Nov.—occasionally mid-Oct.—to late Mar.—a few to mid-Apr. (extremes: Aug. 23, May 21). Irregularly abundant to fairly common throughout.

HAUNTS AND HABITS: The 304-species Turdidae is an almost world-wide family of predominantly woodland songbirds. The American Robin, a familiar winter bird of Texas, occurs over practically the entire state. *Turdus migratorius* is numerous almost everywhere: forests and their undergrowth, thickets on prairies and in pastures and orchards, about cultivated fields and their woodland fringes, as well as timber along streams. It is also frequent about farmhouses and in streets, yards, lawns, gardens, and parks of towns and cities. Robins oftentimes gather into considerable loose flocks and at night—particularly in autumn and winter—assemble into large roosts, either in trees, high weeds, or tall grass of prairies or reeds of marshes. At times these roosts contain an almost unbelievable number of individuals. Ordinarily Robin roosts are not shared by other birds, but sometimes other species in greater or lesser numbers associate with this thrush.

Flight of the American Robin is strong and capable of being long sustained. Whenever traveling any distance, it flies direct, steadily, with fairly rapid but intermittent wing-beats, and sometimes high in the air.

However, moving from tree to tree or bush to bush, it is quick and jerky, often spreading its tail to permit a quick stop. Frequently the bird is seen perched high atop a tree or bush that offers a good view of the surroundings. The American Robin is not shy. In fact, it is an unusually familiar bird, apparently not disturbed by the presence of human beings.

Although more or less arboreal, the bird is perfectly at home on the ground, where it hops, walks, or runs about, rapidly on occasion, often seeking its favored earthworms. In searching, it frequently pauses, turns its head as though listening or looking for prey, then suddenly pokes its bill into the ground to pull out a long, juicy earthworm. Occasionally an earthworm is hard to extract and the bird braces itself for a hard pull. If, under these circumstances, the worm suddenly gives way the bird may fall backward with such force that it virtually turns a complete somersault. Juniper berries are much sought after in fall and winter.

The nearly omnivorous American Robin has another food habit which has been much remarked upon by Texans. During some winters in San Antonio and other Texas cities and towns, flocks of these birds gorge on the fruit of Chinaberry (*Melia azedarach*), a seminat-

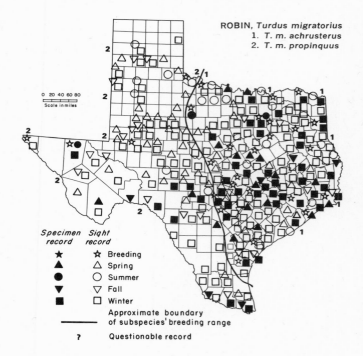

ROBIN, *Turdus migratorius*
1. *T. m. achrusterus*
2. *T. m. propinquus*

0 20 40 60 80
Scale in miles

Specimen record	Sight record	
★	☆	Breeding
▲	△	Spring
●	○	Summer
▼	▽	Fall
■	□	Winter

——— Approximate boundary of subspecies' breeding range

? Questionable record

uralized ornamental tree of Oriental origin. During some years more than others, a few Chinaberries will make a Robin tipsy, more will make it drunk, and a big overindulgence will kill the individual. The sight of numerous birds lying about a lawn like Bowery bums seems to amuse some people.

This bird has many calls, sometimes uttered with an accompanying jerk of the tail. A common note is a quick *tut, tut.* Its rather musical song is usually represented by *cheerily, cheer up, cheerily, cheer up.* The American Robin is one of the earliest morning songsters, and in spring it sings as soon as it arrives on breeding territory. Its song period continues from February more or less intermittently until late October. Singing is infrequent in Texas during August and September, however.

CHANGES: During the historic period, the Robin has been only a local breeder in Texas, except in the forested eastern quarter. Most of the state is too hot, dry, and deficient in woodlands to induce enthusiastic nesting. Between 1925 and 1940 there was an increase in tree planting and lawn sprinkling in Texas communities. As a result of these well-spaced trees, increased humidity, and mud for nest-wall construction, breeders increased in north Texas and spread south to Waco, Austin, San Antonio, and by 1967 had reached Corpus Christi. Robins were rearing a spotted-breasted youngster in Austin as late as the spring of 1970 according to the observations of Bertha McKee Dobie and others, but future breeding prospects seem poor. Increasing pollution of earthworms, mud, and water coupled with a recent upsurge in Starling nesting are ominous.

DETAILED ACCOUNT: FOUR SUBSPECIES

EASTERN ROBIN, *Turdus migratorius migratorius* Linnaeus

DESCRIPTION: *Adult male, nuptial plumage:* Acquired by wear from winter plumage. Top and sides of head brownish black, but broad spot above posterior portion of lores, also spots on upper and lower eyelids, white; upper surface dull mouse gray, feathers with darker centers, but not conspicuous; rump and upper tail-coverts clear mouse gray; tail deep fuscous black, outer feathers terminally hair brown, outermost pair with broad white tips, broadest on inner webs, second and third feathers more narrowly tipped with white, and all feathers narrowly edged on outer webs with mouse gray; wing-quills fuscous, narrowly edged externally with light mouse gray, basal portion of inner webs of secondaries dull cinnamon buff or pinkish buff; lesser wing-coverts like back but slightly more ochraceous; remainder of wing-coverts edged with similar colors; chin white; throat white, finely streaked with brownish black; middle of lower abdomen and crissum white, crissum more or less spotted or streaked with mouse gray, particularly on middle feathers; thighs and posterior portion of flanks mouse gray; remainder of lower surface, including lining of wing, between hazel and russet. Bill orange, deep chrome, cadmium yellow, ocher yellow, buff yellow, or wax yellow, but tip of maxilla, sometimes of mandible, chaetura drab, brownish black, blackish slate, or fuscous; inside of mouth chrome yellow; tongue dull white; iris fuscous black or vandyke brown; legs, feet, and claws seal brown, prout brown, fuscous, or chaetura drab, but soles of toes somewhat yellow. *Adult female, nuptial:* Acquired by wear from winter. Similar to nuptial adult male but lighter and duller in color throughout, head particularly so, and more brownish or slaty; upper surface less purely gray; rufescent portions of lower sur-

face dull cinnamon rufous. Bill dark brown, black, or blackish slate, basal one-half or two-thirds of mandible chrome yellow or deep chrome, or else bill cadmium yellow, maize yellow, or ochraceous, except brown or brownish black tip; tongue and inside of mouth ochraceous; iris vandyke brown; legs and feet dark fawn, broccoli brown, dark drab gray, or seal brown; claws black. *Adult male and female, winter:* Acquired by complete postnuptial molt. Resembling corresponding sex of nuptial adults, but upper surface suffused with light olive, feathers of head edged with same; feathers of lower parts broadly tipped with dull white. *Male and female, first nuptial:* Acquired by wear from first winter. Similar to corresponding sex of nuptial adults but somewhat more brownish on upper surface; pileum lighter; white terminal tail-spots rather smaller. *Male and female, first winter:* Acquired by partial postjuvenal molt, which does not involve wing-quills. Similar to adults in winter, but head lighter; remainder of upper parts more brownish; white tail-spots smaller. *Male, juvenal:* Acquired by complete postnatal molt. Similar to nuptial adult male, but back, scapulars, and rump deep grayish olive to mouse gray, each feather with broad terminal bar of dull black or chaetura drab, many feathers with white or buffy white spots of shaft streaks; greater and median coverts more or less tipped with buffy white; lesser coverts spotted and streaked with pale buff or russet; middle of throat buffy white or light cinnamon buff, unstreaked; rest of lower parts white or suffused with dull cinnamon; jugulum, breast, abdomen, and sides conspicuously spotted or narrowly barred with fuscous or brownish black. Bill brownish or blackish slate, mandible more or less tinged with yellow; iris dark brown; legs and feet clove brown, blackish slate, or drab gray. *Female, juvenal:* Acquired by complete postnatal molt. Similar to juvenal male, but upper parts lighter; lower surface paler, more extensively whitish; sides and flanks clay color. Bill brownish slate, blackish slate, brownish black, or slate gray, tinged with yellow or ochraceous on sides of cutting edges and on mandible, sometimes base of mandible ochraceous or deep chrome; inside of mouth ochraceous; iris brown; legs and feet olive drab gray, dark drab gray, mars brown, or mouse gray. *Natal* (this plumage of this race not seen in Texas): Mouse gray. Bill, legs, and feet dull pinkish buff.

MEASUREMENTS: *Adult male:* Wing, 130.0–138.4 (average, 134.4) mm.; tail, 100.1–105.4 (102.4); bill (exposed culmen), 19.6–20.6 (20.3); tarsus, 32.0–34.5 (33.3); middle toe without claw, 20.1–23.6 (21.9). *Adult female:* Wing, 120.9–130.6 (125.7); tail, 91.4–103.1 (97.3); bill, 17.5–20.6 (18.8); tarsus, 30.5–35.1 (31.8); middle toe, 20.1–23.1 (21.1).

RANGE: N.w. Alaska to s. Quebec, south to s.e. Kansas and w. North Carolina. Winters from s.e. South Dakota and Massachusetts to s. Texas and s. Florida; also Bahamas, w. Cuba.

TEXAS: *Winter:* Taken north to Cooke, east to Bowie and Orange, south to Cameron, west to Kinney and Sutton cos. Common.

NESTING: (This race does not nest in Texas.) *Nest:* In almost all kinds of country except deep forests and treeless plains—in open woodlands, city parks, pastures, orchards, other cultivated lands, along highways; placed on ground or up to 70 ft. in a tree, also found in bush, thicket, corner of fence, stump, telephone pole, stone wall, or even shutters on house, inside of building, nook about bridge, on wagon, car, boat, railroad car, or equally strange place; large compact cup; composed of grasses, twigs, weed stalks, straw, rags, roots, twine, leaves, lichens, hair, wool, and similar materials, cupped on inside with mud; lined with fine grasses, rootlets, seaweed, bits of cloth, string, yarn, cotton, and paper. *Eggs:* 3–6, usually 4; ovate to elongate ovate; glossy; greenish blue ("robin's-egg blue"), ordinarily unmarked, though very rarely with inconspicuous spots of reddish brown; average size, 29.2 × 20.1 mm.

SOUTHERN ROBIN, *Turdus migratorius achrusterus* (Batchelder)

DESCRIPTION: *Adult male and female, nuptial plumage:* Similar to *T. m. migratorius* but smaller, duller, and paler; black of pileum usually more mixed with gray on tips of feathers; back more brownish (less purely gray). *Natal*: Probably similar to *T. m. migratorius*.

MEASUREMENTS: *Adult male*: Wing, 121.9–132.1 (average, 126.2) mm.; tail, 88.9–103.1 (96.8); bill (exposed culmen), 17.0–20.1 (18.0); tarsus, 30.7–34.5 (32.8); middle toe without claw, 19.6–23.1 (21.1). *Adult female*: Wing, 120.9–128.0 (124.7); tail, 90.9–98.6 (94.7); bill, 17.0–20.6 (18.3); tarsus, 29.9–34.0 (32.8); middle toe, 20.1–22.6 (21.4).

RANGE: E. Oklahoma to c. Maryland, south to s.e. Texas and s. Georgia. Winters throughout breeding range to s. Florida.

TEXAS: *Breeding*: Altitudinal range, near sea level to 2,000 ft. Collected northwest to Haskell, east to Dallas, southeast to Hardin cos. Fairly common locally. *Winter*: Taken north to Cooke, east to Chambers, south to Nueces, west to Kerr and Val Verde cos. Common.

NESTING: Similar to that of *T. m. migratorius*.

WESTERN ROBIN, *Turdus migratorius propinquus* Ridgway

DESCRIPTION: *Adult male and female, nuptial plumage*: Similar to *T. m. migratorius* but larger, especially tail, wing, and tarsus; upper parts paler and more olivaceous; lower parts averaging also slightly paler; pileum more abruptly defined posteriorly against color of back; outer tail feathers with very narrow or no white tips. *Natal*: Probably similar to *T. m. migratorius*.

MEASUREMENTS: *Adult male*: Wing, 132.1–145.0 (average, 139.7) mm.; tail, 102.6–111.5 (105.1); bill (exposed culmen), 18.5–21.6 (20.3); tarsus, 32.5–37.1 (34.5); middle toe without claw, 20.1–23.1 (21.6). *Adult female*: Wing, 130.0–142.0 (135.4); tail, 95.0–105.9 (100.8); bill, 18.0–21.6 (20.1); tarsus, 32.0–35.1 (33.3); middle toe, 19.6–22.6 (21.1).

RANGE: S. British Columbia to c. North Dakota, south to Durango and Trans-Pecos Texas. Winters from n. Washington and c. Nebraska through Mexico to Guatemala (probably).

TEXAS: *Breeding*: Altitudinal range, 3,500 to 8,000 ft. Collected in Guadalupe Mts., Culberson Co. Uncommon. *Winter*: Taken north to Cooke, east to Navarro (ca. 1880), south to Aransas, west to Kinney and Culberson cos. Uncommon.

NESTING: *Nest*: On mountains, hills, slopes, and mesas, at edges of timber or in open woodlands, also more open parts of country, and in cultivated areas; usually at moderate height in tree, such as ponderosa pine, Douglasfir, oak, willow, or similar tree, or in bush; compact, well-constructed, though bulky cup; composed of twigs, weed stems, leaves, grasses, various kinds of trash, string, pine needles, plastered on inside with mud; lined with fine plant stems and rootlets. *Eggs*: 3–6, usually 4; ovate to elongate ovate; glossy; greenish blue, unspotted; average size, 29.7 × 20.7 mm.

CALIFORNIA ROBIN, *Turdus migratorius aleucus* Oberholser, new subspecies (see Appendix A)

DESCRIPTION: *Adult male and female, nuptial plumage*: Similar to *T. m. propinquus* but decidedly smaller. Similar to *T. m. achrusterus*, but wing and tail longer; upper and lower surface paler, with no white tip on tail or at least with very slight indication of this.

MEASUREMENTS: *Adult male*: Wing, 123.5–137.4 (average, 131.8) mm.; tail, 96.0–108.5 (102.4); bill (exposed culmen), 17.5–19.0 (18.3); tarsus, 32.0–35.1 (33.8); middle toe without claw, 21.6–23.6 (22.4). *Adult female*: Wing, 124.5–131.5 (127.8); tail, 94.0–101.1 (98.3); bill, 17.0–18.5 (17.8); tarsus, 31.0–34.0 (32.8); middle toe, 20.1–22.1 (21.4).

TYPE: Adult male, no. 196766, U.S. National Museum, Biological Surveys collection; South Yollo Bolly Mt., California; July 31, 1905; J. F. Ferry, original no., 26.

RANGE: N. Oregon through California. Winters throughout breeding range to w. Nevada and Baja California (probably); accidental in Texas.

TEXAS: *Winter*: One specimen: Nueces Co., Corpus Christi (Jan. 22, 1887, C. W. Beckham).

[RUFOUS-BACKED ROBIN, *Turdus rufo-palliatus* Lafresnaye

A pale robin. *Male*: gray head and hindneck, reddish brown back, scapulars, wing-coverts; remaining upper parts grayish brown; white throat, streaked with dark brown; tawny brown breast, sides; white belly, crissum; mainly yellow bill. *Female*: similar but paler and duller. *Immature*: buffy-streaked above; spotted with black below; clear white throat; dusky bill. Length, 9–9½ in.

RANGE: W. Mexico, from s. Sonora to Oaxaca; also Tres Marías Islands. Casual in s. Arizona.

TEXAS: *Hypothetical*: Two careful sightings, neither substantiated by photograph: Brewster Co., Big Bend Nat. Park, Rio Grande Village (lone bird observed amid dense mesquite and baccharis, Oct. 23–31, 1966, R. H. Wauer, Sharon Wauer); Hidalgo Co., Santa Ana Nat. Wildlife Refuge, shore of North Lake (1 observed drinking at edge of lake, Sept. 15, 1972, W.A. Shifflett, Cruz Martinez).]

CLAY-COLORED ROBIN, *Turdus grayi* Bonaparte

SPECIES ACCOUNT

Gray's Robin, Gray's Thrush, and Tamaulipas Thrush (northeastern race) of various authors. *Adult*: similar to a faded Robin, but grayish brown above (darker on wings and tail); pale buffy throat, streaked vaguely with olive; tawny olive on breast becoming paler—buffy olive—posteriorly; bill yellowish brown or greenish. *Immature*: brown-spotted on breast. Length, 9 in.

RANGE: S. Nuevo León, s.e. San Luis Potosí, and s. Tamaulipas, south through s. Mexico and Central America to n. Colombia (Santa Marta region). Casual in extreme s. Texas.

TEXAS: *Casual*: Six careful sightings, one substantiated by photographs: Cameron Co., along resaca just northwest of Brownsville (1 carefully studied by observer long familiar with the species in Mexico, Mar. 10, 17, 1940, L. I. Davis); Hidalgo Co., Bentsen–Rio Grande Valley State Park (1 seen, May 14–June 8, 1959, initially by Mrs. L. H. McConnell, later by L. C. Goldman, Alexander Sprunt IV, et al.; photographed in color by P. B. Myers, slide on file at Louisiana State University Museum; see P. James, 1960, *Auk* 77: 475–476); Hidalgo Co., Santa Ana Nat. Wildlife Refuge (1 seen, Mar. 2–5, 1962, J. E. Lieftinck, R. J. Fleetwood; 1 observed, Feb. 24, 1963, John Morony, Jr., fide Fleetwood); Hidalgo Co., Anzalduas tract (1 singing persistently, June 14, 28, 1972, J. C. Arvin, W. A. Shifflett, C. E. Hudson); Cameron Co., Laguna Atascosa Nat. Wildlife Refuge (1 observed, Dec. 10, 1972, C. E. Hudson, P. T. Moore).

HAUNTS AND HABITS: *Turdus grayi* is the most common tropical counterpart of the American Robin. An adaptable species, it is found from near sea level to at least 5,000 feet (8,000 in Costa Rica) in a variety of situations: semiarid regions, where it frequents riverside thickets and woods; coffee fincas, other plantations, and orchards; and wet broad-leaved rain and cloud forests. Throughout its range, it is more numerous in cultivated areas and second growth than in virgin forests. Nest sites are equally variable, but a densely foliaged tree or tall bush is most frequently used for its bulky, open cup. The 1959 visitor to the Rio Grande delta lingered in thick riparian brush—Texas ebony (*Pithecellobium flexicaule*), mesquite (*Prosopis*), and other trees, mixed with shrubs and large weeds.

Its flight and behavior, for the most part, are similar to those of *Turdus migratorius*, although the Claycolor is more retiring. It forages in secluded thickets, where it quietly gathers earthworms, slugs, caterpillars, an occasional lizard, and other animal food; also wild figs (*Ficus*), bananas, and other fruit. It seldom exposes itself on an open lawn or pasture. During the nesting season, its liquid song pervades its haunts; however, in the nonbreeding period, it is very quiet and withdrawn.

Calls of the Clay-colored Robin include a clearly whistled *meeoo, meert,* or *mee-roit* and a low-pitched *pup-up-up.* The song, similar to the Robin's but slower (delivery takes 7½ seconds), is a series of smooth, melodious, measured phrases; one rendition is *farmer-farmer feed-that-cow feed-it feed-it feed-it now* (L. I. Davis).

DETAILED ACCOUNT: ONE SUBSPECIES

TAMAULIPAS CLAY-COLORED ROBIN, *Turdus grayi tamaulipensis* (Nelson)

NOTE: Although no specimen has been taken in Texas, the Cameron Co. individual was identified by L. I. Davis as *T. g. tamaulipensis*; Mr. Davis studied the bird closely and compared his notes with individuals in Tamaulipas and San Luis Potosí. The other birds identified in Texas, judging from the range of *tamaulipensis*, were also likely of this race.

DESCRIPTION: *Adults, nuptial plumage*: Acquired by wear from winter plumage. Upper surface rather light, slightly grayish, saccardo umber to between citrine drab and buffy brown, centers of feathers slightly darker; tail light olive brown, feathers edged on outer webs with color of back; wing-quills between olive brown and fuscous, outer edgings like back, but tips and outer edges of greater coverts, and sometimes tips of median wing-coverts, somewhat lighter; inner margins of primaries and secondaries, except at tips, cinnamon buff to dull pinkish buff; sides of head grayish wood brown to saccardo umber; chin pinkish buff to pale pinkish buff, rather broadly streaked with light saccardo umber or buffy brown; lower parts light dull tawny olive to dull, rather light ochraceous buff on crissum; middle of abdomen between dull pinkish buff or light buff and dull warm buff; lining of wing light ochraceous tawny, between ochraceous tawny and ochraceous orange. Bill dull dark brown, terminal portion and cutting edges more or less extensively dull light yellow; iris dark brown; legs and feet rather light brown. *Adults, winter*: Acquired by complete postnuptial molt. Similar to nuptial adults but much darker, more deeply tinged with ochraceous on upper parts; much more deeply ochraceous (less grayish) on lower surface. *First nuptial*: Acquired by wear from first winter. Similar to nuptial adults, but wing and tail shorter. *First winter*: Acquired by partial postjuvenal molt, which does not involve primaries and secondaries. Similar to first nuptial male and female but much more tinged with ochraceous and otherwise more richly colored. *Juvenal*: Acquired by complete postnatal molt. Upper parts saccardo umber, centers of feathers on head and hindneck lighter, those of back, scapulars, and rump with conspicuous long guttate shaft markings of tawny olive to clay color; wings and tail like those of adult, except greater and median wing-coverts are tipped with tawny olive or clay color, and lesser wing-coverts have broad conspicuous guttate shaft markings of same color; sides of head like hindneck—saccardo umber with streaks of clay color; lower parts ochraceous buff, darker on jugulum and paling to light buff on middle of abdomen; also duller and lighter on throat; throat indistinctly spotted with light saccardo umber; jugulum, breast, and sides heavily spotted or barred with same color; lining of wing cinnamon buff. Bill pale reddish brown; iris dark brown; legs and feet dull light brown.

MEASUREMENTS: *Adult male*: Wing, 116.1–128.0 (average, 122.2) mm.; tail, 91.9–107.4 (100.1); bill (exposed culmen), 20.1–23.1 (21.4); tarsus, 30.5–34.0 (32.3); middle toe without claw, 20.1–23.1 (20.9). *Adult female*: Wing, 116.6–128.0 (123.0); tail, 91.9–103.1 (98.8); bill, 19.6–22.1 (21.4); tarsus, 31.8–34.0 (32.5); middle toe, 20.1–22.1 (21.1).

RANGE: S. Nuevo León, s.e. San Luis Potosí, and s. Veracruz, south to n. Tabasco, Campeche, Yucatán, and Quintana Roo (including Isla Cozumel and Islas Mujeres).

TEXAS: *Casual*: See species account.

VARIED THRUSH, *Ixoreus naevius* (Gmelin)

SPECIES ACCOUNT

Resembles Robin but has orange eye-stripe and wing-bars; black band across bright rusty breast. *Female*: gray breast-band. *Immature*: breast-band broken; spotted with dusky on under parts. Length, 9½ in.; wingspan, 15–16.

RANGE: N. central Alaska to n.w. Mackenzie, south to n.w. California, n.e. Oregon, n. Idaho, and n.w. Montana. Winters mainly on Pacific slope from s. British Columbia to n. Baja California. Casual east to Saskatchewan, Quebec, Colorado, and Texas.

TEXAS: *Casual*: Four, possibly five, sight records of single birds, one or two substantiated by photographs: El Paso (1 present in yard of Mary Belle Keefer, Feb. 12–16, 1956, and this, or another individual, Mar. 7–21; photographed in color, Feb. 12, by George Burrows, and on Mar. 8, by Mrs. D. T. Johnson); Nacogdoches Co. (1 seen, Nov. 28, 1969, Mr. and Mrs. C. E. Booger); Chambers Co., Cove (1 seen, Nov. 4, 6, 1935, A. K. McKay); Galveston Co. Park (1 observed, Feb. 13, 1965, E. N. McHenry; bird present through Mar. 15, T. B. Feltner, Bill Pettit, J. B. Strickling, et al.).

HAUNTS AND HABITS: The Varied Thrush is one of the northern American birds which inhabits dense, dark, coniferous forests—the kind that used to be called gloomy in the years before smog palls demonstrated what true gloom really is. It spends most of its time on or near the ground and generally sings from a low perch. The nest is placed against the trunk of a small conifer or in an upright crotch of a deciduous tree or bush. The female lays three brown-dotted pale blue eggs in a substantial cup of twigs, dead leaves, rotten wood, and grass. In the colder months, many of these birds winter in the fog-swept redwood forests of north-western California; some fly south to oak-sycamore woods in the smog-shrouded southern part of the former Golden State. In short, the bird prefers dense forests at all times of the year but in winter it sometimes accepts light woods, even shade trees about houses.

Flight of the Varied Thrush is Robin-like but is not as long sustained; ordinarily the present species makes only brief, quiet, shadowy flittings within the woodland understory. *Ixoreus naevius* forages mostly amid fallen leaves on damp soil. Here it gathers millipedes, earthworms, snails, spiders, beetles, ants, bugs, and caterpillars. Its vegetable food includes fruit of manzanita, dogwood, honeysuckle, sumac, and mistletoe, with some acorns.

All-year calls of the Varied Thrush are a twangy *zeeeee* and a low *took*. The breeding-territory song begins with a long quavering whistle, then after several seconds of silence comes another whistle, either on a higher or lower pitch. The song is described as very slow and eerie by most listeners.

DETAILED ACCOUNT: ONE SUBSPECIES

NORTHERN VARIED THRUSH, *Ixoreus naevius meruloides* (Swainson)

NOTE: Dr. Oberholser wrote: "Mrs. D. T. Johnson took a color photograph on March 8 [1956] which was so good that the bird could easily be subspecifically identified therefrom." However, Ridgway, to whom Oberholser refers the reader for a detailed description and measurements of the Varied Thrush, was unable to recognize any subspecies in *Ixoreus naevius*.

DESCRIPTION: *Adult male and female, nuptial plumage*: Acquired by wear from winter plumage. See Ridgway, 1907, *Bull. U.S. Nat. Mus.*, no. 50, pt. 4, pp. 131–132. *Adult male, winter*: Acquired by complete postnuptial molt. Similar to nuptial male but darker, including ochraceous wing-bars; feathers of upper parts obscurely edged and tipped with olive. *Adult female, winter*: Acquired by complete postnuptial molt. Like nuptial female but somewhat darker and more ochraceous above (less grayish). *Male, first nuptial*: Acquired by wear from first winter. Similar to nuptial adult male but upper surface duller, somewhat more brownish, particularly on head. *Male, first winter*: Acquired by partial postjuvenal molt. Resembling first nuptial male but still duller and more brownish above; feathers of jugular band much tipped with tawny or ochraceous. *Female, first nuptial*: Acquired by wear from first winter. Resembling nuptial adult female, but upper parts somewhat more rufescent. *Female, first winter*: Acquired by partial postjuvenal molt. Similar to first nuptial female but still more rufescent above. *Juvenal*: Acquired by complete postnatal molt. Pileum and hindneck sepia to olive brown, centers of feathers lighter, sayal brown to tawny olive; back light brownish olive to olive brown, the tips darker; rump and upper tail-coverts dull hair brown to buffy brown; tail bister, three outer feathers with small white tips; wings dark olive brown, but a few lesser coverts, broad tips of median and greater coverts, middle part of outer webs of primaries, secondaries, and outer webs and tips of tertials dull cinnamon to bright ochraceous tawny, these forming three conspicuous wing-bars; chin and throat dull ochraceous buff, sides of throat and all of jugulum of same color but darker, the sides of throat with small spots of buffy brown, jugulum heavily spotted with saccardo umber to fuscous; breast dark ochraceous buff, somewhat spotted with buffy brown; abdomen white, laterally tinged with ochraceous buff; crissum mixed with white and ochraceous buff.

MEASUREMENTS: Ibid., p. 132.

RANGE: Identical with that of species with exception of Yakutat Bay (s.e. Alaska) south on w. slope of Coast and Cascade

ranges in British Columbia, Washington, and Oregon to n.w. California, which encompasses the range of *I. n. naevius*. Winters from s. British Columbia to Baja California.

TEXAS: *Casual*: See species account.

WOOD THRUSH, *Hylocichla mustelina* (Gmelin)

SPECIES ACCOUNT

Plump. Reddish brown above (brightest on head); whitish eye-ring; white below with numerous large, rounded, blackish spots on breast and sides. Length, 7¾ in.; wingspan, 12¾; weight, 1¾ oz.

RANGE: S.e. South Dakota, s. Great Lakes region, and s. Quebec, south to s.e. Texas and n. Florida. Winters from e. and s. Mexico (chiefly Caribbean slope) to Panama.

TEXAS: (See map.) *Breeding*: Mid-Apr. to probably late July (eggs, Apr. 29 to May 2) from near sea level to about 600 ft. Common locally to uncommon in forested regions of eastern third. *Migration*: Mid-Apr.—often early Apr.—to early May; mid-Sept. to mid-Nov. (extremes: Mar. 1, June 6; Aug. 29, Dec. 5). Common (chiefly along upper coast) to uncommon in spring through eastern half, though often scarce between 98th and 99th meridians; scarce to very rare in western half. Uncommon to scarce in fall through eastern half; very rare in northern Panhandle and in Midland Co. *Winter*: Dec. 12 to Jan. 26. No specimen, but a scattering of sightings along coast and in Rio Grande delta. Inland sightings: Fort Worth (Dec. 24, 1925, F. B. Isely); Austin (1 observed, Jan. 16–Apr. 8, 1970, Fred and Marie Webster); San Antonio (Dec. 27, 1964, Juanita Edmison, Wayne Jessup).

HAUNTS AND HABITS: The Wood Thrush is distinctly

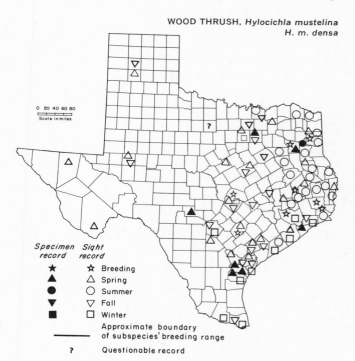

WOOD THRUSH, *Hylocichla mustelina*
H. m. densa

0 20 40 60 80
Scale in miles

Specimen record	Sight record	
★	☆	Breeding
▲	△	Spring
●	○	Summer
▼	▽	Fall
■	□	Winter

——— Approximate boundary of subspecies' breeding range

? Questionable record

a bird of moist woodlands, even densely wooded swamps. In Texas it is almost entirely an inhabitant of heavy deciduous and mixed woods and thickets, particularly along streams, both on uplands and bottomlands, but preferably valleys. The bird seems to avoid pine woods unless there is a considerable mixture of deciduous trees. This bird is not gregarious, but in migration several may be found together.

On the wing, it is quick, though graceful, and can fly for long distances, at which time it flies rather high and direct. Ordinarily its flights are from one part of its tree or thicket habitat to another, where its movements are generally swift and darting. This thrush is not excessively shy, simply retiring, and with care may be approached without difficulty. It may perch in either the upper or lower parts of a tall tree or even in a small sapling or bush. Much on the ground, it hops about with ease, scratching or probing with its bill in search of food—beetles, caterpillars, ants, wasps, bees, earthworms, snails, sowbugs; also, especially in fall, elderberries and other small, wild fruit.

The Wood Thrush has several calls. One is a guttural *quoit* or *quirt*; another sounds like *tuck, tuck*. A sharp *pit* several times repeated seems to be the alarm note. Naturalists often rate the Wood Thrush's song as second only to that of the Hermit Thrush in U.S. bird music. A sizeable minority would place the Wood equal or even superior to the Hermit. Musical construction of the latter's song is probably somewhat better, but the lower pitch of the Wood's notes renders them more pleasant to many human ears. The liquid, flutelike song contains *ee-o-lay*'s, pauses, and occasional gutturals. This serene, effortless singing sounds most exquisite on quiet or misty days. As is generally true of thrushes, the Wood sings most frequently early in the morning and late in the afternoon; however, in April and May the bird often sings all day from dark thickets. Song season in Texas lasts from mid-April to near the end of July.

DETAILED ACCOUNT: ONE SUBSPECIES

SOUTHERN WOOD THRUSH, *Hylocichla mustelina densa* (Bonaparte)

No races recognized by A.O.U. check-list, 1957 (see Appendix A).

DESCRIPTION: *Adults, nuptial plumage (ochraceous phase)*: Acquired by wear from winter plumage. Pileum sanford brown to russet; back sudan brown to amber brown; rump light brownish olive; tail and wing-quills light olive brown, wing-coverts and outer surface of wing-quills, except at tips, brown like back, but rather lighter and more ochraceous; inner webs of secondaries and inner primaries with spot of pale buff at base; cheeks and sides of head fuscous, narrowly streaked with dull white or pale buff; lores whitish or mixed with dull gray; submalar streak black, and malar streak white, sometimes slightly spotted with dull black; sides of neck mostly like crown, posteriorly like back; eye-ring dull white; lower parts white strongly tinged with light buff on breast and jugulum, often slightly so elsewhere, all lower parts—excepting middle of abdomen, chin, throat, and crissum—marked with triangular or roundish spots of fuscous; lining of wing buffy white or hair brown, spotted with fuscous. Bill blackish slate, slate black, brownish slate, blackish brown, or hair brown, basal half or two-thirds of mandible flesh color, vina-

ceous buff, lavender white, cream white, or dull pale yellow; iris prout brown; legs and feet flesh color, pale vinaceous, or lavender white; claws light brown. *Adults, nuptial (gray phase)*: Similar to ochraceous phase, but upper surface lighter and less rufescent (more olivaceous or grayish); pileum russet to sudan brown; back dresden brown to saccardo umber. *Adults, winter*: Acquired by complete postnuptial molt. Similar to nuptial adults in corresponding phase but rather brighter; lower parts more deeply tinged with buff. *First nuptial*: Acquired by wear from first winter. Like nuptial adults in corresponding phase. *First winter*: Acquired by partial postjuvenal molt, which does not include wing-quills or tail. Like winter adults in corresponding phase. *Juvenal*: Acquired by complete postnatal molt. Similar to adults in winter, but bill shorter; pileum, neck, and back with conspicuous streaks of ochraceous tawny, these on hindneck shortest and more like spots; spots on lower surface smaller and less clearly defined. *Natal*: Mouse gray to light olive brown. Bill, legs, and feet pale pinkish buff.

MEASUREMENTS: *Adult male*: Wing, 100.1–105.4 (average, 103.1) mm.; tail, 67.3–71.7 (69.3); bill (exposed culmen), 16.0–17.3 (16.5); tarsus, 31.0–32.5 (31.8); middle toe without claw, 17.0–18.5 (17.5). *Adult female*: Wing, 98.1–105.4 (101.3); tail, 64.0–68.6 (65.8); bill, 16.0–17.5 (16.5); tarsus, 29.4–31.5 (30.2); middle toe, 16.3–17.8 (17.3).

RANGE: C. Oklahoma and s. Indiana to South Carolina, south to s.e. Texas and n. Florida. Winters in Florida, and from Tabasco probably into Central America.

TEXAS: *Breeding*: One specimen: Smith Co., Tyler (Apr. 20, 1880, G. H. Ragsdale). *Migration*: Collected northwest to Young (ca. 1890), east to Dallas and Galveston, south to Nueces cos.

NESTING: *Nest*: In woodlands and swamps, on both uplands and bottoms, preferably damp situations, such as thickets along streams or fringes of timber about edges of marshes, also in cultivated areas, such as ornamental grounds, even near human dwellings, or in city parks or on streets; usually 4–20 ft. above ground in tree or bush, either in crotch or on horizontal limb; bulky, rather compact cup, more or less ornamented by pieces of paper or leaves hanging on outside; composed of leaves, grass, straw, grapevine and other bark, pieces of paper, weed stalks, strings, rags, sealed with leaf mold or mud; lined with fine rootlets and fine grass. *Eggs*: 2–5, usually 4; ovate to rather broad elliptical ovate; glossy; greenish blue, unspotted; average size, 26.4 × 18.5 mm.

HERMIT THRUSH, *Hylocichla guttata* (Pallas)

SPECIES ACCOUNT

Jerks upward, then slowly lowers, rusty tail. Olive brown above, becoming rusty on rump; whitish below with blackish spots on breast and sides of throat. Length, 7 in.; wingspan, 11¼; weight, 1 oz.

RANGE: C. Alaska across c. Canada to Newfoundland, south to high mountains of s.w. United States, n. Great Lakes region, and s. New York, and in Appalachians to w. Maryland. Winters from s. British Columbia and coastal (except n. New England) and s. United States through Mexico to Guatemala.

TEXAS: (See map.) *Breeding*: Probably late Apr. to late July (no egg dates available, but nest located at 8,000 ft. by F. R. Gehlbach). Uncommon in The Bowl, Guadalupe Mts. *Migration*: Mar. to mid-Apr.—mid-May in western third; late Oct.—occasionally early Oct.—to late Nov. (extremes: mid-Feb., June 10; Sept. 10, mid-Dec.). Common to uncommon throughout. *Winter*: Nov. to early Apr. Common to uncommon in most parts; fairly common (some years) to uncommon on Edwards Plateau; irregular and uncommon in Panhandle.

HAUNTS AND HABITS: In both summer and winter the Hermit Thrush bears out the tradition of its name. On its sole Texas breeding ground in the Guadalupe Mountains, it frequents the most remote pine, Douglasfir, and oak groves above 7,800 feet. In the non-nesting season it lives in cedar, pine, and deciduous thickets of all kinds, especially those along streams, but also shrubbery at almost any altitude in mountains, hills, and flatlands. The Hermit generally prefers seclusion of the country but sometimes migrating individuals will linger in extensive plantings of shrubs in city parks. During the breeding season it is found only singly and in pairs, but in migration and winter it may accumulate in small companies, which are sometimes associated with other thrushes and even with sparrows and other small birds.

Its flight is at times swift and more or less direct, even elevated, but ordinarily the bird flits from bush to bush or branch to branch, disappearing quietly and quickly at approach of an intruder. It is frequently on the ground looking for insects, spiders, snails, and earthworms under leaves and other debris. This thrush is able to winter farther north than do its close relatives because it includes a higher proportion of small fruits in its diet; berries of cedar, hackberry, dogwood, and many others are avidly eaten. As it hops about, when it pauses, or even as it lands in a tree or bush, it has the distinctive habit of lifting its tail. In summer the Hermit is especially shy, retiring, and difficult to observe; during the cold season it is less wary.

The ordinary call note of this bird is a soft *chuck* or

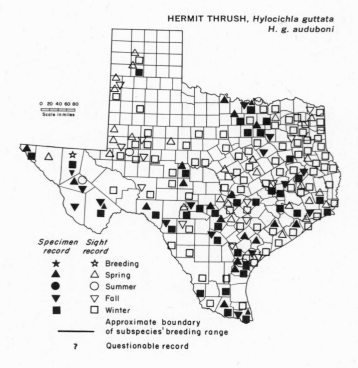

HERMIT THRUSH, *Hylocichla guttata*
H. g. *auduboni*

0 20 40 60 80
Scale in miles

Specimen record

★
▲
●
▼
■

Sight record

☆ Breeding
△ Spring
○ Summer
▽ Fall
□ Winter

——— Approximate boundary of subspecies' breeding range

? Questionable record

tuck. Other calls are a rough *tuck-tuck-tuck* and a harsh *pay*. The clear, flutelike song is regarded by most naturalists as the finest vocalization that comes from any U.S. bird. Its three or four phrases are on different pitch levels; each phrase is prefaced by a long introductory note. The song sounds deliberate, serene, relaxed. Singing is most frequent from tall conifers in late afternoon and evening. In the Guadalupe Mountains the main song season is from April to mid-July. Unlike the Swainson's, the Hermit Thrush seldom sings away from its nesting territory.

DETAILED ACCOUNT: TEN SUBSPECIES

ALASKAN HERMIT THRUSH, *Hylocichla guttata guttata* (Pallas)

DESCRIPTION: *Adults, nuptial plumage (gray—normal—phase):* Acquired by wear from winter plumage. Upper surface grayish deep olive, passing into ochraceous tawny or russet on longer upper tail-coverts and on base of tail; end of tail light sepia; wings light olive brown, lesser coverts like back, median and greater coverts as well as tertials and outer webs of secondaries and primaries margined with same, but lighter and more brownish—between color of back and color of wing-quills, outer margins of outer primaries still paler, and large spot on base of secondaries and inner primaries cinnamon buff or pinkish buff; sides of head and of neck like upper parts, lores more or less mixed with dull buff or dull gray, cheeks and auriculars somewhat spotted or streaked with same; lower parts dull white, but breast pale pinkish buff, sides and flanks mouse gray, throat, jugulum, and breast conspicuously marked with more or less triangular spots of chaetura drab; lining of wing dull drab, washed with light buff; axillars basally dull white. Bill brownish black, dark brown, brownish slate, slate color, slate black, or black, base of mandible flesh color, cream yellow, lilaceous white, or dull yellow; interior of mouth and rictus dull or rich yellow; iris deep bister; legs and feet dull flesh color, vinaceous gray, lilac gray, drab, or ecru drab, but soles of toes dull yellow or cream color; claws light brown. *Adults, nuptial (brown phase):* Similar to gray phase, but pileum and remainder of upper parts much more rufescent; back between brownish olive and saccardo umber. *Adults, winter:* Acquired by complete postnuptial molt. Similar to corresponding phase of nuptial adults, but colors brighter, above more olive brownish; upper tail-coverts and tail somewhat more rufescent; anterior lower parts more deeply buff. *Second winter:* Acquired by complete postnuptial molt. Similar to corresponding phase of adults in winter. *First nuptial:* Acquired by wear from first winter. Similar to corresponding phase of nuptial adults, but differs in retention of wing-quills, tail feathers, and particularly some upper wing-coverts from juvenal. *First winter:* Acquired by partial postjuvenal molt, which does not involve wing-quills, tail feathers, or all upper wing-coverts. Similar to first nuptial, but somewhat more richly colored. *Juvenal:* Acquired by complete postnatal molt. In both gray and brown phases similar to adults in winter, but upper surface somewhat more rufescent, even in gray phase; everywhere more or less streaked or spotted with pale buckthorn brown or light buff; spots on breast more numerous and often more like bars; middle of abdomen, sides, and flanks more or less spotted or barred with chaetura drab or fuscous. Bill black, but base of mandible yellow; iris black; feet brown. *Natal* (this plumage of this race not seen in Texas): Rather dark hair brown.

MEASUREMENTS: *Adult male:* Wing, 82.8–89.4 (average, 87.4) mm.; tail, 63.5–68.6 (67.1); bill (exposed culmen), 10.4–11.9 (11.7); tarsus, 28.4–29.9 (29.2); middle toe without claw, 16.0–17.0 (16.3). *Adult female:* Wing, 81.0–84.1 (82.8); tail, 58.4–66.0 (63.5); bill, 10.4–12.2 (11.7); tarsus, 26.9–29.4 (28.4); middle toe, 16.0–16.5 (16.3).

RANGE: C. Alaska to n. British Columbia. Winters from Washington, Texas, and w. North Carolina to s. Baja California and Jalisco.

TEXAS: *Winter*: Taken north to Randall, southeast to Bexar and Cameron, west to Brewster and El Paso (May 8) cos. Uncommon.

VANCOUVER HERMIT THRUSH, *Hylocichla guttata vaccinia* Cumming

Race not in A.O.U. check-list, 1957 (see Appendix A).

DESCRIPTION: *Adults, nuptial plumage*: Similar to *H. g. guttata*, but wing and bill longer, upper surface darker, more sooty (less rufescent).

MEASUREMENTS: *Adult male*: Wing, 84.1–93.5 (average, 90.7) mm.; tail, 64.5–73.9 (68.3); bill (exposed culmen), 11.2–13.0 (12.4); tarsus, 27.9–29.9 (29.2); middle toe without claw, 15.0–17.0 (15.7). *Adult female*: Wing, 85.1–91.4 (88.1); tail, 64.0–68.6 (65.8); bill, 10.9–12.7 (12.2); tarsus, 27.4–29.4 (28.7); middle toe, 16.0–17.0 (16.3).

RANGE: S.w. British Columbia and n.w. Washington. Winters from s.e. California to Trans-Pecos and s. Texas.

TEXAS: *Winter*: Taken in Culberson (3 specimens) and Jeff Davis (1, Oct. 3) cos.; one specimen collected on Nueces River (county unknown). Scarce.

MONTEREY HERMIT THRUSH, *Hylocichla guttata slevini* Grinnell

DESCRIPTION: *Adults, nuptial plumage*: Similar to *H. g. oromela* (see below), but much smaller; in fact, smallest of all races of Hermit Thrush. In brown phase more rufescent than same phase of *oromela*, but in gray phase somewhat more grayish.

MEASUREMENTS: *Adult male*: Wing, 81.5–87.1 (average, 85.3) mm.; tail, 63.0–70.1 (66.3); bill (exposed culmen), 11.7–14.5 (13.2); tarsus, 27.4–29.9 (28.2); middle toe without claw, 13.5–15.5 (14.7). *Adult female*: Wing, 78.0–86.1 (82.6); tail, 57.9–68.1 (64.3); bill, 11.4–14.2 (13.0); tarsus, 25.9–29.4 (27.2); middle toe, 13.5–16.0 (14.7).

RANGE: S.w. Oregon to c. California. Winters from s. Baja California and s. Sonora to Trans-Pecos and s. Texas.

TEXAS: *Winter*: Two specimens: Brewster Co., Chisos Mts., Boot Spring (May 5, 1932, M. M. Peet); Bexar Co., San Antonio (Mar. 19, 1890, H. P. Attwater).

CASCADE HERMIT THRUSH, *Hylocichla guttata oromela* Oberholser

Race not in A.O.U. check-list, 1957 (see Appendix A).

DESCRIPTION: *Adults, nuptial plumage*: Similar to *H. g. guttata*, in both gray and brown phases, and to *H. g. vaccinia*, but upper parts paler, more grayish; dark brown (chaetura drab) spots on jugulum averaging smaller. Bill larger than that of *H. g. guttata*. Resembling *H. g. euboria* (see below), but bill averaging somewhat larger; wing and tail shorter; upper parts paler and more grayish.

MEASUREMENTS: *Adult male*: Wing, 87.1–92.5 (average, 88.9) mm.; tail, 64.5–71.1 (67.3); bill (exposed culmen), 11.9–13.5 (12.7); tarsus, 27.9–29.9 (28.7); middle toe without claw, 15.0–17.0 (15.7). *Adult female*: Wing, 82.3–87.9 (85.3); tail, 62.0–67.1 (64.8); bill, 11.4–13.5 (12.7); tarsus, 25.9–29.4 (28.2); middle toe, 14.5–17.0 (15.7).

RANGE: S. British Columbia to w. Alberta, south to n. California. Winters from n.w. Alberta, s. Arizona, and n.w. Arkansas to s. Baja California and Nuevo León.

TEXAS: *Winter*: Taken north to Clay (Apr. 21) and Cooke, south to San Patricio, Cameron (Nov. 18), and Hidalgo, west to Brewster and Culberson cos. Fairly common.

YUKON HERMIT THRUSH, *Hylocichla guttata euboria* Oberholser

Race not in A.O.U. check-list, 1957 (see Appendix A).

DESCRIPTION: *Adults, nuptial plumage*: Similar to *H. g. guttata*, in both gray and brown phases, but larger, except its relatively smaller bill.

MEASUREMENTS: *Adult male*: Wing, 89.9–96.0 (average, 92.7) mm.; tail, 67.6–75.9 (72.2); bill (exposed culmen), 10.9–13.5 (12.2); tarsus, 26.4–29.9 (28.9); middle toe without claw, 15.0–17.3 (15.7). *Adult female*: Wing, 89.9–93.5 (91.9); tail, 67.8–71.9 (69.3); bill, 11.4–12.7 (12.2); tarsus, 27.9–30.5 (29.2); middle toe, 15.5–16.0.

RANGE: S. Yukon to c. British Columbia. Winters from c. California and n. Oklahoma to Nuevo León.

TEXAS: *Winter*: Taken north to Kerr, east to Bexar and Nueces (Nov. 21), south to Cameron, west to Brewster (Apr. 27) and Presidio (Sept. 26) cos. Uncommon.

SIERRA HERMIT THRUSH, *Hylocichla guttata sequoiensis* (Belding)

DESCRIPTION: *Adults, nuptial plumage*: Resembling *H. g. oromela* but larger; coloration of upper parts darker, more rufescent. Similar to *H. g. euboria*, but wing and particularly bill larger; upper parts somewhat lighter. In this race, gray and brown phases seem to be more noticeably marked than in most other races.

MEASUREMENTS: *Adult male*: Wing, 90.9–99.1 (average, 94.7) mm.; tail, 68.1–80.0 (72.3); bill (exposed culmen), 12.4–15.2 (14.0); tarsus, 27.4–30.5 (28.9); middle toe without claw, 16.0–17.0 (16.3). *Adult female*: Wing, 87.9–94.5 (91.2); tail, 65.5–76.5 (70.4); bill, 12.4–14.5 (13.7); tarsus, 26.9–29.9 (28.9); middle toe, 14.5–16.5 (15.7).

RANGE: E. California to s. Baja California. Winters from s.e. California and Texas through Mexico to Guatemala.

TEXAS: *Winter*: Taken north to Cooke, south to Nueces (Mar. 21) and Cameron (Mar. 29), west to Brewster (May 4) and Jeff Davis (Oct. 1) cos. Uncommon.

MONO HERMIT THRUSH, *Hylocichla guttata polionota* Grinnell

DESCRIPTION: *Adults, nuptial plumage*: Much like *H. g. sequoiensis* but more grayish (less brownish) on upper surface. Similar to *H. g. euboria* but larger, particularly bill; upper parts more grayish. In this race, brown phase is apparently not well defined.

MEASUREMENTS: *Adult male*: Wing, 93.5–101.9 (average, 98.3) mm.; tail, 70.1–78.2 (74.2); bill (exposed culmen), 12.2–16.0 (13.5); tarsus, 28.7–31.2 (29.7); middle toe without claw, 15.0–17.5 (16.3). *Adult female*: Wing, 91.9–96.5 (94.2); tail, 67.6–72.9 (70.6); bill, 11.7–15.0 (13.2); tarsus, 26.9–30.5 (29.2); middle toe, 15.5–17.0 (16.3).

RANGE: S.e. Washington to n.w. Utah, south to e. California and s.w. New Mexico. Winters from s. Texas through Mexico to Guatemala.

TEXAS: *Winter*: Taken northwest to Culberson (Oct. 8), east to Menard (May 11) and Kerr (Mar. 15), south to Kinney, west to Brewster (Apr. 25) cos. Fairly common.

AUDUBON'S HERMIT THRUSH, *Hylocichla guttata auduboni* (Baird)

DESCRIPTION: *Adults, nuptial plumage*: Similar to *H. g. polionota* but decidedly larger; paler above; in brown phase, decidedly more brownish or ochraceous than that form in corresponding phase. In this race the two color phases are well marked. *Natal*: Probably similar to *H. g. guttata*.

MEASUREMENTS: *Adult male*: Wing, 97.1–107.4 (average, 103.4) mm.; tail, 71.7–79.5 (76.2); bill (exposed culmen), 13.0–16.0 (14.7); tarsus, 28.9–31.0 (29.9); middle toe without claw, 16.0–19.0 (17.8). *Adult female*: Wing, 89.9–102.1 (97.3); tail, 70.1–73.9 (72.2); bill, 13.5–15.5 (14.5); tarsus, 28.4–30.5 (29.7); middle toe, 15.0–18.0 (16.8).

RANGE: N. Montana, south to s. New Mexico and extreme n. Trans-Pecos Texas. Winters from Texas through Mexico to Guerrero.

TEXAS: *Breeding*: Five specimens: Culberson Co., Guadalupe Mts., The Bowl (July 11, 1938, G. H. Lowery, Jr.; May 2, June 14, 15, 1939, T. D. Burleigh; Aug. 20, 1940, B. E. Ludeman). *Winter*: Taken northeast to Cooke (Mar. 23), south to Kinney, west to Brewster (Apr. 25) and Jeff Davis (Sept. 29) cos. Uncommon.

NESTING: *Nest*: On mountains, mesas, or slopes or in valleys; in forests, open woods, or swampy areas; usually 3–10 ft. above ground, in pine, oak, or other tree or bush; rather bulky, though compact, cup with thick walls; composed of grasses, leaves, roots, strips of bark, twigs, straw, and moss; lined with fine rootlets or moss. *Eggs*: 3–5, usually 4; between oval and ovate; bluish green, ordinarily unspotted; average size, 22.9 × 17.0 mm.

EASTERN HERMIT THRUSH, *Hylocichla guttata faxoni* Bangs and Penard

DESCRIPTION: *Adults, nuptial plumage*: Similar to *H. g. guttata* but larger, especially bill; much more rufescent on upper parts, flanks, and sides. Resembling *H. g. auduboni* but smaller, darker, and more strongly rufescent above. Similar to *H. g. euboria*, but bill much larger; wing, tarsus, and middle toe also larger; upper parts, sides, and flanks much more rufescent. The two color phases are well marked in this race. Bill black, but base of mandible fawn color; tongue and inside of mouth ocher yellow; legs and feet fawn color; claws seal brown.

MEASUREMENTS: *Adult male*: Wing, 88.9–99.1 (average, 94.2) mm.; tail, 66.0–74.9 (69.8); bill (exposed culmen), 13.5–15.5 (14.2); tarsus, 28.9–32.0 (30.5); middle toe without claw, 16.5–19.0 (17.8). *Adult female*: Wing, 86.1–96.5 (90.7); tail, 64.5–73.9 (66.3); bill, 13.0–15.0 (13.7); tarsus, 27.9–31.5 (29.7); middle toe, 16.0–19.0 (17.5).

RANGE: S.w. Mackenzie to s.e. Labrador, south to c. Alberta and Maryland. Winters from Oklahoma and Massachusetts through e. Mexico to c. Veracruz, and along U.S. Gulf coast to s. Florida.

TEXAS: *Winter*: Taken north to Cooke, east to Jefferson, south to Cameron, west to Kinney cos. Common.

NEWFOUNDLAND HERMIT THRUSH, *Hylocichla guttata crymophila* Burleigh and Peters

DESCRIPTION: *Adults, nuptial plumage*: Resembling *H. g. faxoni*, but upper surface darker, less rufescent; flanks more grayish (less brownish).

MEASUREMENTS: (Only averages given.) *Adult male*: Wing, 93.5 mm.; tail, 68.8; bill (exposed culmen), 12.7. *Adult female*: Wing, 90.2; tail, 66.5; bill, 11.9.

RANGE: Newfoundland. Winters probably in s. New England, and from s. Texas to w. North Carolina.

TEXAS: *Winter*: Collected in Kinney (1 specimen), Real (1), Bexar (1), and Cameron (1, Nov. 24) cos. Scarce.

SWAINSON'S THRUSH, *Hylocichla ustulata* (Nuttall)

SPECIES ACCOUNT

Olive-backed Thrush and Russet-backed Thrush of many authors. Olive brown or gray-brown above; buffy eye-ring (conspicuous), cheeks, breast; whitish below with blackish spots on sides of throat and breast. Length, 7 in.; wingspan, 11¾; weight, 1¼ oz.

RANGE: C. Alaska across Canada to Newfoundland, south to California, c. Colorado, n. Great Lakes region, and in mountains to West Virginia. Winters from Nayarit and s. Tamaulipas through Central America to n. Argentina.

TEXAS: (See map.) *Migration*: Mid-Apr. to mid-May

—occasionally late May; mid-Sept. to early Nov. (extremes: Mar. 2, June 7; Aug. 26, Dec. 6). Common to fairly common in spring through eastern half; uncommon through most of western half. *Winter*: Nov. 18 to Feb. 12. No specimen, but a number of sightings along coast; a few sightings from Waco and San Antonio areas. One sighting in northern Panhandle: Canyon (Jan. 21, 27, 1935, Miss A. I. Hibbets). Insufficient evidence on winter sighting from Big Bend.

HAUNTS AND HABITS: The Swainson's Thrush frequents woodlands, cottonwood groves, willows, and other trees and thickets along streams, rivers, and creeks. In northern forests and swamps, often near water, the bird conceals its nest of pine needles and moss. In more arid regions it is especially attracted to pools in canyons, preferably with nearby trees. During migration it associates at times in small, scattered flocks with related thrushes, such as the Gray-cheeked and Veery. In its travels through Texas it also visits shrubbery, trees, ornamental bushes about houses, orchards, gardens, and parks in towns and cities, here sometimes keeping company with sparrows (chiefly White-crowned or White-throated) and juncos.

Flight of the Swainson's is rather swift and capable of being long sustained, as its extensive migratory journeys to South America necessitate. When traveling for any distance it flies high and direct, but in short flights is rather swift, sometimes irregular and flitting, but generally easy and graceful. A shy bird, it slips through undergrowth and thickets quietly—almost like a shadow—although sometimes it appears rather tame. On the ground it hops about searching carefully among leaves for insects in a manner somewhat similar to that of the Robin. Spring migrants in Texas relish mulberries.

Night-flying migrants emit a *heep* note; on the

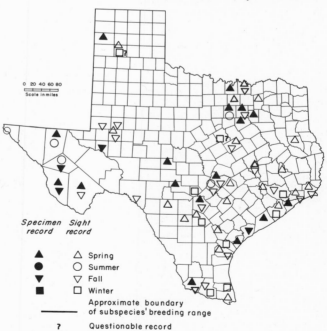

SWAINSON'S THRUSH, *Hylocichla ustulata*

0 20 40 60 80
Scale in miles

Specimen record / Sight record

▲ △ Spring
● ○ Summer
▼ ▽ Fall
■ □ Winter

—— Approximate boundary of subspecies' breeding range

? Questionable record

ground the call sounds more like *whit*. The breezy, rather high-pitched song is somewhat flutelike; most phrases climb upward. Unlike many migrants, the Swainson's Thrush sings a great deal in Texas. Its song is heard especially from the vicinity of mulberry trees in late afternoon and early morning during April and May.

DETAILED ACCOUNT: THREE SUBSPECIES

RUSSET-BACKED SWAINSON'S THRUSH, *Hylocichla ustulata ustulata* (Nuttall)

DESCRIPTION: *Adults, nuptial plumage*: Acquired by wear from winter plumage. Upper parts rufescent brownish olive to dark saccardo umber; tail rather light sepia; wing-quills rather grayish olive brown, exposed surface of closed wing very much like back, but on outer webs of primaries and secondaries somewhat more rufescent, large pinkish buff spot on inner webs of secondaries and inner primaries; sides of head like crown; superciliary stripe, lores, and eye-ring warm buff; cheeks and auriculars finely streaked with dull buff; sides of neck like back; posterior lower surface mostly white; jugulum and upper breast warm buff; chin and upper throat paler; sides and flanks light brownish olive; submalar streak, streaks on sides of throat, subtriangular spots on jugulum and breast brownish olive to chaetura drab; lining of wing dull cinnamon buff. Bill slate black, brownish black, or brownish slate, but basal half of mandible flesh color, dull straw yellow, pale drab, or yellowish drab; interior of mouth yellow; iris sepia, very dark brown, or black; legs drab, ecru drab, lilac gray, or very pale brown; toes darker. In adults, though not in young, two color phases are so slight as to be of little importance. *Adults, winter*: Acquired by complete postnuptial molt. Similar to nuptial adults but somewhat more deeply and brightly colored, crissum more strongly buff. *Second winter*: Acquired by complete postnuptial molt. Similar to nuptial adults. *First nuptial*: Acquired by wear from first winter. Similar to nuptial adults, but differs chiefly by reason of buff-marked pale upper wing-coverts retained from juvenal. *First winter*: Acquired by partial postjuvenal molt, which does not involve wing-quills, tail feathers, nor all upper wing-coverts. Similar to adults in winter, but differs by reason of retained juvenal wing-coverts. *Juvenal (gray phase)*: Acquired by complete postnatal molt. Similar to corresponding phase of adults in winter but darker and duller above—rather rufescent brownish olive; crown, back, scapulars, and lesser wing-coverts streaked with pale buff; buff of anterior lower surface paler; spots usually smaller and more inclined to become bars; sides and flanks also narrowly and indistinctly barred with brownish olive. *Juvenal (brown phase)*: This phase differs from adults more than gray phase, being darker, much more rufescent on upper parts, including wings—between snuff brown and saccardo umber—and streaked on most of upper parts, including lesser coverts, with cinnamon buff anteriorly and ochraceous tawny on rump and upper tail-coverts.

MEASUREMENTS: *Adult male*: Wing, 93.0–103.6 (average, 97.8) mm.; tail, 67.1–79.5 (72.9); bill (exposed culmen), 13.0–15.0 (13.7); tarsus, 26.9–31.0 (28.2); middle toe without claw, 16.0–18.5 (17.3). *Adult female*: Wing, 88.4–98.1 (94.5); tail, 64.5–72.4 (68.8); bill, 13.0–14.5 (13.7); tarsus, 25.9–29.4 (28.2); middle toe, 15.5–17.5 (16.5).

RANGE: S.e. Alaska to n.w. California. In migration, east to Texas (casually). Winters from Mexico through Central America to Ecuador.

TEXAS: *Migration*: Two specimens: Presidio Co. (May 12, 1890, W. Lloyd); Bexar Co., San Antonio (Apr. 25, 1890, H. P. Attwater).

OLIVE-BACKED SWAINSON'S THRUSH, *Hylocichla ustulata swainsoni* (Tschudi)

DESCRIPTION: *Adults, nuptial plumage*: Similar to *H. u. ustu-* *lata* but much paler, more grayish or olivaceous (less rufescent) above; also more grayish (less deeply buff) below, particularly on sides and flanks; breast more yellowish buff or cream buff; spots on breast averaging broader and darker. Bill black or brownish black, but base of mandible dull white, dull yellow, flesh color, or cream color; tongue and inside of mouth yellow or chrome yellow; iris fuscous black or vandyke brown; legs and feet light drab, drab, light brown, flesh color, or light gray, soles of toes yellow or flesh color.

MEASUREMENTS: *Adult male*: Wing, 96.5–104.9 (average, 101.9) mm.; tail, 66.0–77.5 (71.1); bill (exposed culmen), 11.4–14.5 (13.0); tarsus, 25.9–30.5 (28.2); middle toe without claw, 15.0–18.0 (16.5). *Adult female*: Wing, 90.4–102.6 (97.3); tail, 62.0–73.9 (67.3); bill, 11.4–13.5 (12.7); tarsus, 25.4–27.9 (26.7); middle toe, 15.0–18.0 (16.3).

RANGE: C. Alaska to s. Labrador, south to e. California and s. Colorado. Winters from s.e. Mexico through Central America and w. South America to Argentina.

TEXAS: *Migration*: Collected north to Dallas and Kaufman, south to Calhoun, west to Menard and Brewster cos. Uncommon.

EASTERN SWAINSON'S THRUSH, *Hylocichla ustulata clarescens* Burleigh and Peters

DESCRIPTION: *Adults, nuptial plumage*: Similar to *H. u. swainsoni*, but upper parts, sides, and flanks darker and more brownish (less grayish). Intermediate in color between *H. u. ustulata* and *H. u. swainsoni*, though not intermediate in distribution. Bill black, but basal part of mandible pinkish white; inside of mouth and tongue ocher yellow; iris vandyke brown; legs and feet ecru drab; claws drab.

MEASUREMENTS: *Adult male*: Wing, 96.5–104.1 (average, 99.8) mm.; tail, 64.5–73.9 (69.3); bill (exposed culmen), 11.9–14.0 (13.2); tarsus, 26.4–29.4 (27.7); middle toe without claw, 15.5–18.0 (16.8). *Adult female*: Wing, 92.5–102.1 (97.1); tail, 63.0–71.7 (66.5); bill, 11.9–14.0 (13.0); tarsus, 25.9–28.9 (27.4); middle toe, 15.5–18.0 (16.8).

RANGE: E. Minnesota to s. Nova Scotia, south to c. West Virginia. Winters from Costa Rica to Peru.

TEXAS: *Migration*: Collected north to Oldham, east to Dallas and Galveston, south to Starr, west to Jeff Davis cos. Common.

GRAY-CHEEKED THRUSH, *Hylocichla minima* (Lafresnaye)

SPECIES ACCOUNT

A drab thrush, olive gray or olive brown above; gray cheeks; dull, inconspicuous eye-ring; grayish white below with blackish spots on sides of throat and breast. Length, 7½ in.; wingspan, 12¼; weight, 1¼ oz.

RANGE: N.e. Siberia and Alaska across far n. Canada to Newfoundland, south to n.e. British Columbia and n.w. Massachusetts. Winters from Nicaragua to n. South America; also Hispaniola (a few).

TEXAS: (See map.) *Migration*: Late Apr. to mid-May; late Sept. to mid-Nov. (extremes: Mar. 6, May 25; Sept. 17, Nov. 28). Fairly common to uncommon in spring along coast; uncommon to scarce in remainder of eastern half; rare to casual in western portion. Rare in fall through eastern half; extremely rare in Trans-Pecos. *Winter*: Dec. 23 to Feb. 5. No specimen, but a scattering of sightings in northern Panhandle and eastern half.

HAUNTS AND HABITS: In its migrations through Texas and elsewhere, the Gray-cheeked Thrush frequents thickets, brush, and tangles of vines along streams and in open woodlands on uplands, lowlands, and swampy areas. Occasionally it is found along roads and paths through woodlands and occurs, at times, in shrubbery about human dwellings and in yards and parks of towns. Ordinarily it does not gather in flocks, even in migration, but rather is scattered through woods, sometimes more or less associated with its relatives, the Swainson's Thrush and Veery. The Graycheek is shy and retiring as it flits through the dim aisles of forests, shady thickets, or swamps. On its breeding ground, where it is even more shy than during migrations, it builds an intricately woven nest on or near the ground in stream valleys, on mountain slopes, or forest fringes.

Its flight is quick, strong, and capable of being long sustained, but the bird is usually seen winging gracefully from ground to bush or vice versa. It often descends to the ground to hunt and pick among leaves for insects, worms, or berries.

The Graycheek's note is a somewhat harsh, rather drawn out *queep*. The song is a musical, but thin and sibilant performance of several syllables which often rises steeply at the end: *whee-wheeoo-titi-wheee*. This bird apparently sings much less in Texas than does the Swainson's Thrush.

DETAILED ACCOUNT: ONE SUBSPECIES

NORTHERN GRAY-CHEEKED THRUSH, *Hylocichla minima minima* (Lafresnaye)

DESCRIPTION: *Adults, nuptial plumage (gray phase)*: Acquired by wear from winter plumage. Upper parts plain grayish olive; tail between sepia and brownish olive, feathers edged with color of back; wings rather grayish olive brown, upper wing-coverts and outer edgings of wing-quills similar to back; lighter, however, on outer webs of primaries, large spot on in-

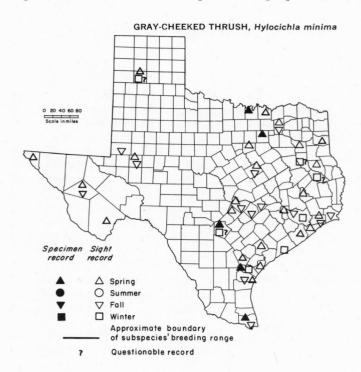

GRAY-CHEEKED THRUSH, *Hylocichla minima*

0 20 40 60 80
Scale in miles

*Specimen   Sight
record   record*

▲   △ Spring
●   ○ Summer
▼   ▽ Fall
■   □ Winter

─── Approximate boundary
     of subspecies' breeding range

?   Questionable record

ner webs of secondaries and inner primaries light buff; sides of head like crown but rather lighter and more or less obscurely streaked and spotted with grayish white or buffy white, particularly on lores and cheeks; lower parts white, but sides of throat, with jugulum and breast, light buff, chin and middle of throat of same color or grayish white; sides and flanks between light grayish olive and mouse gray, this tinging outer lower tail-coverts which otherwise are plain white; submalar streak, streaks on sides of throat, and small more or less triangular spots on jugulum and 'breast chaetura black, posteriorly becoming grayish olive; under wing-coverts hair brown; axillars light grayish olive tinged with buff. Bill slate black or brownish black, but basal half of mandible flesh color, fawn color, buff yellow, or dull yellow; tongue and inside of mouth chrome yellow; iris vandyke brown; legs dark drab, drab gray, fawn, or flesh color; feet somewhat darker and soles of toes paler; claws dark drab or fawn color. *Adults, nuptial (brown phase)*: Acquired by wear from winter. Similar to corresponding sex in gray phase, but upper surface brownish olive instead of grayish olive. *Adults, winter*: Acquired by complete postnuptial molt. Similar to corresponding phase of nuptial adults but somewhat more brightly colored, buff on jugulum even deeper. Maxilla and terminal half of mandible black; base of mandible drab gray; inside of mouth, tongue, and cutting edges of bill ocher yellow; front of legs and toes drab gray, hind part white; claws drab gray. *Second winter*: Acquired by complete postnuptial molt. Like adults in winter. *First nuptial*: Acquired by wear from first winter. Similar to nuptial adults, but upper wing-coverts usually with some buffy spots or edgings, since these feathers are retained from juvenal. *First winter*: Acquired by partial postjuvenal molt, which does not involve wing-quills, tail feathers, or greater and medial wing-coverts. Similar to adults in winter, except for buff edgings or spots on some of upper wing-coverts. *Juvenal*: Acquired by complete postnatal molt. Similar to adults in winter but darker and rather more rufescent—brownish olive—above; streaked and spotted on pileum, sides of head, hindneck, back, and scapulars with cartridge buff, on upper tail-coverts, also on lesser wing-coverts, with cinnamon buff; tips of greater wing-coverts pale buff; a spot on tips of tertials pale buff; lower parts decidedly more whitish, flanks and breast paler, less buffy or olive grayish; spots on lower parts larger, more inclined to bars, and more extended posteriorly, sometimes over entire lower surface, and even obscurely on crissum.

MEASUREMENTS: *Adult male*: Wing, 99.1–109.0 (average, 104.1) mm.; tail, 65.0–78.5 (72.9); bill (exposed culmen), 13.0–15.0 (14.2); tarsus, 27.9–32.5 (30.2); middle toe without claw, 15.5–18.5 (17.3). *Adult female*: Wing, 97.1–107.4 (100.1); tail, 63.0–77.0 (67.8); bill, 12.4–14.5 (13.7); tarsus, 26.9–31.5 (29.7); middle toe, 15.0–18.5 (17.3).

RANGE: N.e. Siberia and n.w. Mackenzie to e. Labrador, south to n.w. British Columbia and w. Newfoundland. Winters in n.w. South America.

TEXAS: *Migration*: Collected in Cooke (1 specimen), Dallas (1), Bexar (2), San Patricio (1), and Cameron (1) cos.

VEERY, *Hylocichla fuscescens* (Stephens)

SPECIES ACCOUNT

A thrush uniformly reddish brown above; whitish below with a few indistinct brownish breast-spots; lack of eye-ring makes eye appear dark and beady. Length, 7¼ in.; wingspan, 12; weight, 1 oz.

RANGE: S. Canada and n. United States, south in mountains to n.e. Arizona and n. Georgia. Winters from Central America to n. South America; casually north to coastal Texas.

TEXAS: (See map.) *Migration*: Late Apr. to mid-

May; mid-Sept. to early Oct. (extremes: Feb. 27, June 15; Sept. 12, Oct. 19). Fairly common (some years) to uncommon in spring along coast; scarce through remainder of eastern half; rare in northern Panhandle and Midland Co. Extremely rare in fall through eastern half; casual in northern Panhandle and Midland Co. *Winter*: Late Dec. to mid-Feb. (extremes: Dec. 22, Feb. 20). Casual along coast and in Rio Grande delta.

HAUNTS AND HABITS: In northern wooded regions the shy Veery secludes itself in streamside thickets, open woods, and wooded swamps, here placing its nest on or very near the ground in a clump of shoots or beside a bush, stump, or boulder. During its migration through the southern United States it sometimes leaves strict woodlands long enough to be seen in towns, gardens, and parks. This bird is not gregarious, but at times a number may appear together in a loose company.

In flight this bird is sometimes swift but ordinarily it does not fly far. It is capable, however, of long-sustained flights when it migrates to and from South America, during which time it usually flies at a moderate altitude, but sometimes rather high. The Veery easily escapes observation by slipping quietly and swiftly through underbrush. When seen, it is frequently on the ground where it moves about quickly hunting its food of insects, earthworms, snails, and berries.

The ordinary call note of this thrush has been well described as a low *phew*. Its song is breezy and wheels downward: *vee-ur, vee-ur, veer, ver*. To some ears this sounds like *veery, veery, ver, rrr*; hence the common name Veery. This bird is apparently not very often heard in Texas.

DETAILED ACCOUNT: TWO SUBSPECIES

COMMON VEERY, *Hylocichla fuscescens fuscescens* (Stephens)

DESCRIPTION: *Adults, nuptial plumage*: Acquired by wear from winter plumage. Upper parts sudan brown to antique brown, pileum rather darker, rump and upper tail-coverts somewhat lighter, more rufescent; tail rufescent saccardo umber, basally edged with color of upper tail-coverts; wings light olive brown, wing-coverts and outer edges of quill feathers like back, but on outer webs of primaries rather lighter, large cinnamon buff spot on base of inner webs of secondaries and inner primaries; sides of head similar to back, but more grayish and more or less mixed with dull pale buff, lores mostly pale gray; lower parts white, throat and jugulum dull cinnamon buff or dull clay color, submalar stripe, narrow stripes on throat, and small subtriangular spots on jugulum saccardo umber; sides and flanks mouse gray; lining of wing dull brownish white or buffy white, under wing-coverts more or less spotted or mottled with saccardo umber; axillars white, more or less tinged with dull buff or pale brown. Bill slate gray, blackish slate, or brownish slate, mandible, at least basal half, flesh color or dull white with drab tip; iris dark brown; legs and feet ecru drab or drab, toes darker; claws brown. *Adults, winter*: Acquired by complete postnuptial molt. Similar to nuptial adults but usually somewhat brighter on upper surface; somewhat more deeply buff on anterior lower parts. *Second winter*: Acquired by complete postnuptial molt. Like adults in winter. *First nuptial*: Acquired by wear from first winter. Similar to nuptial adults but with spots of buff retained from juvenal on terminal portion of many upper wing-coverts. *First winter*: Acquired by partial post-juvenal molt, which does not involve wing-quills, tail feathers,

or part of upper wing-coverts. Similar to adults in winter, but upper parts rather paler and greater wing-coverts with terminal spots of buff. *Juvenal*: Acquired by complete postnatal molt. Similar to nuptial adults, but all upper parts numerously spotted or marked with short streaks of ochraceous tawny to buckthorn brown; lesser and middle wing-coverts also thus marked and greater series tipped with small spots of same colors, feathers of upper parts more or less spotted or with obscure narrow bars of darker brown; jugulum and breast cinnamon buff, sometimes suffusing remainder of lower parts, anterior lower parts heavily spotted or barred; sides and flanks narrowly or less conspicuously barred or spotted with olive brown.

MEASUREMENTS: *Adult male*: Wing, 98.6–104.9 (average, 102.4) mm.; tail, 69.6–78.5 (74.2); bill (exposed culmen), 13.5–15.5 (14.2); tarsus, 28.4–32.0 (30.2); middle toe without claw, 16.5–17.5 (17.3). *Adult female*: Wing, 94.5–101.1 (96.3); tail, 65.5–72.4 (68.5); bill, 13.0–14.0 (13.7); tarsus, 27.4–29.4 (28.7); middle toe, 15.5–17.5 (16.3).

RANGE: S.e. Ontario to n. Nova Scotia, south to n.e. Georgia. In migration, west rarely to Texas. Winters in n. South America; accidental in Texas.

TEXAS: *Migration*: One specimen: Bexar Co., San Antonio (May 18, 1891, H. P. Attwater). *Winter*: One specimen: Cameron Co., Brownsville (Jan. 1, 1877, J. C. Merrill).

WESTERN VEERY, *Hylocichla fuscescens salicicola* Ridgway

DESCRIPTION: *Adults, nuptial plumage*: Similar to *H. f. fuscescens* but duller in color, upper surface darker, duller, more sooty (less rufescent)—cinnamon brown to between cinnamon brown and mummy brown; spots or streaks on jugulum larger and darker—olive brown to clove brown. Bill black or brownish black, but basal portion of mandible yellow, salmon yellow, or flesh color; iris dark brown; legs and feet fawn color, drab, light drab, or flesh color, toes sometimes light brown.

MEASUREMENTS: *Adult male*: Wing, 96.0–103.6 (average, 100.6) mm.; tail, 70.1–79.0 (74.2); bill (exposed culmen), 13.0–15.0 (14.2); tarsus, 28.9–31.0 (29.7); middle toe without claw, 16.0–17.5 (17.0). *Adult female*: Wing, 88.9–100.1 (97.6); tail, 69.6–74.4 (71.7); bill, 13.5–14.5 (13.7); tarsus, 27.9–30.5 (29.2); middle toe, 16.5–18.5 (17.0).

RANGE: C. British Columbia to c. Ontario, south to n. New Mexico, s. North Dakota, and n. Indiana. Winters from n. Venezuela to w. Brazil; accidental in Texas.

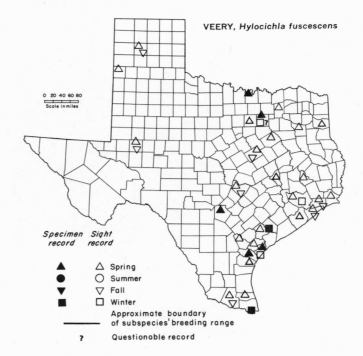

VEERY, *Hylocichla fuscescens*

TEXAS: *Migration*: Collected in Cooke (1 specimen), Dallas (1), San Patricio (1), and Aransas (1) cos. Fairly common to scarce. *Winter*: One specimen: Jackson Co., Lavaca Forks (Feb. 20, 1885, D. H. Talbot).

EASTERN BLUEBIRD, *Sialia sialis* (Linnaeus)

SPECIES ACCOUNT

Hunched, round-shouldered posture. *Male*: blue above; rusty throat, breast, flanks; white belly, crissum. *Female*: much duller above; paler below. Length, 6¾ in.; wingspan, 12¼; weight, 1 oz.

RANGE: S. Saskatchewan to Nova Scotia, south to extreme n.e. Mexico (formerly), U.S. Gulf coast, and s. Florida; also s.e. Arizona, south locally over Mexican highlands to n. Nicaragua. Northernmost race winters from s.e. South Dakota, s. Great Lakes region, and s. New England to n.e. Mexico and Gulf states; also w. Cuba (rarely).

TEXAS: (See map.) *Breeding*: Mid-Feb. to late July —occasionally Sept. (eggs, Mar. 2 to July 15; young in nest as early as Mar. 6) from near sea level to 4,000 ft. Common to fairly common in most of eastern two-thirds; uncommon and local in northern Panhandle, south Texas brush country. Last recorded breeding from Rio Grande delta: Brownsville, prior to 1923 (nest with broken eggs taken, R. D. Camp). One record from Trans-Pecos: Big Bend Nat. Park, Rio Grande Village (adult male observed feeding 4 young, Apr. 15–May 2, 1972, R. H. Wauer). *Winter*: Early Nov. to late Mar. (extremes: Oct. 2, Apr. 16). Common to fairly common over most of eastern two-thirds; irregularly uncommon to rare in western third with exception of western Trans-Pecos, where casual.

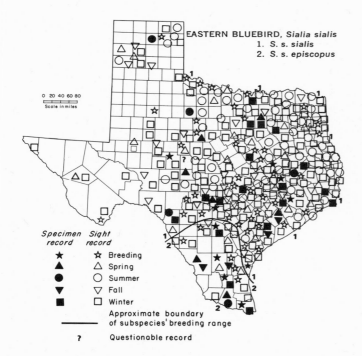

EASTERN BLUEBIRD, *Sialia sialis*
1. *S. s. sialis*
2. *S. s. episcopus*

0 20 40 60 80
Scale in miles

Specimen / Sight record

★ / ☆ Breeding
▲ / △ Spring
● / ○ Summer
▼ / ▽ Fall
■ / □ Winter

Approximate boundary of subspecies' breeding range

? Questionable record

HAUNTS AND HABITS: Both uplands and bottomlands —almost everywhere except treeless prairies and deepest forests—suit the Eastern Bluebird. It inhabits particularly pine-oak and other open woodlands and their margins, groves, forest clearings, deadenings, and meadows; also fence rows, highways, railroads, orchards, fields, the vicinity of farmhouses, and yards and streets of towns. During autumn and winter it often assembles into sizeable flocks. Individuals sometimes pass the night in old nests of other birds.

The ordinary flight of the Eastern Bluebird is not strong and is more or less irregular unless the bird is traveling a long distance. Its short flights are usually not at a great height. It often perches on terminal branches of trees, on telephone wires, fence posts, and even houses, as well as low trees and bushes. It often descends to the ground long enough to pick up insects and berries. Notwithstanding its apparent mild disposition, the Eastern Bluebird can be pugnacious, especially when seeking a nest hole coveted by a pair of House Wrens, Starlings, or House Sparrows. This bluebird holds its own with House Wrens, but where Starling and House Sparrow populations are heavy, as in the Midwest and East, these two aliens appropriate most nest sites.

The ordinary note of this bird is a two-syllabled call that has been represented by *turr-wee* or *tru-ly*. It also has a rather harsh alarm note. Its musical song is a repetition of a two-syllabled call somewhat like the ordinary call note, but mellower. This, like its call, is heard either when the bird is on the wing or when perching. Territory-courtship performance consists of a fluttering song flight by the male. He ascends fifty or one hundred feet into the air and then floats down to a bush or tree, fluttering about the female and even offering her food. In Texas, he has been heard singing from mid-February to July.

CHANGES: Since 1950 the Eastern Bluebird has declined moderately in Texas, instead of drastically as in the North and East (up to 90 percent reduction in some areas, fide Lawrence Zeleny). Milder climate, a comparatively thin (but increasing) population of breeding Starlings, and less urbanization in the Lone Star State have favored the species. Other anti-bluebird factors—a dense population of House Sparrows and rather high pesticide pollution levels—seem to be as detrimental here as in other states.

The south Texas race, *S. s. episcopus*, has not been found nesting in the Rio Grande delta since 1923, but Eastern Bluebirds, possibly of this race, are still present (1950 into 1970's) locally in the live oak (*Quercus virginiana*) areas from just north of the delta (nesting, Kenedy Co., June 9, 1968, B. A. Fall) to the vicinity of San Antonio.

DETAILED ACCOUNT: TWO SUBSPECIES

COMMON EASTERN BLUEBIRD, *Sialia sialis sialis* (Linnaeus)

DESCRIPTION: *Adult male, nuptial plumage*: Acquired by wear from winter plumage. Above prussian blue to rood blue; rump and upper tail-coverts spectrum blue; tail similar but rather duller, feathers brownish on inner margins and externally edged with color of upper tail-coverts; wing-quills chaetura black, but outer edges of primaries and secondaries, except tips, and exposed surfaces of wing-coverts, blue like back; sides of head below eyes chaetura drab, more or less washed with blue of upper parts; lores dull mouse gray; chin light mouse gray washed with blue; center of throat, with jugulum and upper breast, dull russet or dull hazel; sides and flanks dull cinnamon rufous; rest of lower parts dull white, sometimes washed with gray or brown; lining of wing slate gray mixed with pale gray or dull white. Bill black; tongue and inside of mouth ocher yellow; iris dark brown or black; legs and feet black or slate black. *Adult male, winter*: Acquired by complete postnuptial molt. Similar to nuptial adult male but duller above, feathers of hindneck, back, and scapulars much tipped with dull cinnamon rufous, russet portions of anterior lower parts duller. *Adult female, nuptial (blue phase)*: Acquired by wear from winter. Somewhat resembling adult male but much duller in color. Upper surface deep mouse gray with wash of prussian blue, rump and upper tail-coverts light methyl blue to salvia blue; wings and tail fuscous black, tail more or less washed with blue of upper tail-coverts, lesser wing-coverts and outer webs of primaries and of outer secondaries edged with blue, lighter than blue of back; sides of head and of neck hair brown or chaetura drab, washed with blue or with cinnamon rufous; throat, sometimes also chin, with jugulum, upper breast, sides, and flanks, dull cinnamon or dull cinnamon rufous; middle of abdomen and crissum dull white; lining of wing white, under wing-coverts spotted with dull hair brown. Bill and feet black; iris prout brown. *Adult female, nuptial (brown phase)*: Similar to blue phase, but upper parts hair brown or dull buffy brown; very slightly washed with blue, upper tail-coverts clear windsor blue, blue edgings of wings and tail more greenish. *Adult female, winter*: Acquired by complete postnuptial molt. Similar to nuptial adult female, but colors both above and below duller and more blended, tertials margined with dull buff or dull tawny. *Male, first nuptial*: Acquired by wear from first winter. Similar to nuptial adults, but colors not quite so rich and chin with somewhat less blue. *Male and female, first winter*: Acquired by partial postjuvenal molt, which does not involve wing-quills. Similar to corresponding sex and phase of adults in winter, but colors rather lighter and chin with less blue. *Male, juvenal*: Acquired by complete postnatal molt. Upper parts dark hair brown to fuscous; hindneck, back, and scapulars more or less conspicuously streaked with white or dull buff, rump and upper tail-coverts sometimes obscurely streaked with paler brown; wings and tail as in nuptial adult male but usually somewhat more greenish, most of wing-coverts with small terminal spots or short streaks of dull white or buffy white; greater coverts and tertials edged with pale buff or tawny; sides of head and lower parts dull white, on sides of head and on breast washed with buff; sides of head and of neck, anterior lower parts, and sides of body with numerous broad feather edgings of olive brown to snuff brown, imparting scaled appearance; middle of abdomen and crissum dull white; lining of wing dull white with a few hair brown markings. Bill black; iris dark brown; feet seal brown, blackish slate, clove brown, or black. *Female, juvenal*: Acquired by complete postnatal molt. Similar to juvenal male, but blue of wings and tail lighter, duller, and more greenish, outermost primary and outermost tail feather with white outer webs, tertials and wing-coverts brown, edgings duller, and primaries and secondaries with darker tips; dark markings of lower parts usually heavier and more extended posteriorly. *Natal*: Dark drab. Bill, legs, and feet pinkish buff tinged with brown.

MEASUREMENTS: *Adult male*: Wing, 96.5–104.6 (average, 100.3) mm.; tail, 59.4–68.6 (63.8); bill (exposed culmen), 10.9–14.0 (12.2); tarsus, 19.0–21.6 (20.3); middle toe without claw, 15.0–17.5 (16.3). *Adult female*: Wing, 93.0–101.6 (98.3); tail, 56.4–66.5 (60.7); bill, 10.9–13.5 (12.2); tarsus, 18.0–21.1 (20.1); middle toe, 15.0–17.5 (16.3).

RANGE: S.w. Saskatchewan to c. Nova Scotia, south to s.e. Texas and n. Florida. Winters from s.e. South Dakota and Rhode Island to s. Texas and c. Florida; also Bermuda.

TEXAS: *Breeding*: Altitudinal range, near sea level to 4,000 ft. Collected north to Haskell, east to Walker, south to Bee and Nueces (eggs), west to Tom Green (eggs) cos. Fairly common. *Winter*: Taken north to Cooke, east to Jefferson, south to Cameron (Nov. 27), west to Kinney cos. Common.

NESTING: *Nest*: In rather open country, on slopes and level land, wild or cultivated; in open woodlands, along fence rows or highways, in yards in country or towns; 3–30 ft. above ground, in tree cavity (natural or deserted by woodpeckers), in fence, post, suitable nook about building, or crevice about rocks, or in Purple Martin or other bird box; exceptionally saddled on limb of a tree; sometimes no material in cavity, but usually a rather smoothly constructed cup of grasses, leaves, rootlets, feathers, fine twigs, hair, bark strips, sedges, straw, and other similar vegetable materials; lined with fine grasses and feathers. *Eggs*: 3–7, usually 5; ovate to nearly oval; glossy; pale greenish or bluish white, rarely pure white, unspotted; average size, 20.9 × 15.7 mm.

RIO GRANDE EASTERN BLUEBIRD, *Sialia sialis episcopus* Oberholser

DESCRIPTION: *Adult male and female, nuptial plumage*: Similar to *S. s. sialis*, but blue of upper parts lighter and more greenish. Similar to Azure Eastern Bluebird, *S. s. fulva*, of Arizona, but russet of lower parts much darker.

MEASUREMENTS: *Adult male*: Wing, 98.6–101.1 (average, 99.6) mm.; tail, 65.5–67.1 (66.3); bill (exposed culmen), 10.9–11.9 (11.2); tarsus, 19.0–21.6 (20.3); middle toe without claw, 14.0–16.8 (15.2). *Adult female*: Wing, 93.5–95.0 (94.2); tail, 59.9–63.0 (61.5); bill, 10.9–11.9 (11.4); tarsus, 19.3–20.6 (19.8); middle toe, 15.0–16.0 (15.5).

RANGE: S. Texas and Tamaulipas (at least formerly).

TEXAS: *Breeding*: Altitudinal range, near sea level to 700 ft. Collected in Atascosa (eggs), Duval (eggs), Brooks (eggs), Hidalgo, and Cameron (eggs) cos. Uncommon and local. One summer specimen from Kinney Co., Fort Clark (June 12, 1893, E. A. Mearns). *Winter*: Taken in Atascosa, Brooks, Cameron, and Webb (Nov. 21) cos. Uncommon.

NESTING: Similar to that of *S. s. sialis*.

WESTERN BLUEBIRD, *Sialia mexicana* Swainson

SPECIES ACCOUNT *See colorplate 24*

Male: resembles Eastern Bluebird, but throat and upper breast blue; back, shoulders rusty (usually). *Female*: resembles Eastern, but darker (throat grayer, upper parts browner). Length, 6¾ in.; wingspan, 12¾; weight, 1 oz.

RANGE: S. British Columbia and c. Montana, south through mountains to n. Baja California and Trans-Pecos Texas, and through Mexican highlands to Morelos and Veracruz; descends in winter to lower elevations.

TEXAS: (See map.) *Breeding*: Early May to mid-Aug. (no egg dates available, but nest located in Guadalupe Mts. by F. R. Gehlbach) from 6,000 to 8,500 ft. Fairly common in Guadalupe Mts.; uncommon and irregular in Davis Mts. *Winter*: Late Oct. to mid-Apr. (extremes: Sept. 16, May 31). Common (some years) to fairly common in Trans-Pecos; irregularly uncommon to scarce in remainder of western third; rare to casual east of 100th meridian to Hunt, Brazos, and Bastrop cos., central coast, and Rio Grande delta.

HAUNTS AND HABITS: The Western Bluebird is a bird of open juniper-pine-oak forest and woodland edge of the West. Summer in Texas finds this species confined almost entirely to timbered canyons and slopes of Trans-Pecos mountains. At other times it may appear on hilly or even flat farm and ranch lands. During cool months it moves in small companies, sometimes in large, loose flocks, which often include other birds such as Mountain Bluebirds, Robins, and Audubon's and other warblers.

Flight of the Western is very similar to that of the Eastern Bluebird. It is ordinarily rather hesitating and not at great heights unless prolonged. Sometimes, particularly when the bird is going a long distance, it flies more strongly and will ascend to considerable height. The Western is not an active bird, but rather quiet and deliberate in its actions. It spends much time perching calmly in a round-shouldered position; however, it frequently flies out with considerable dash to snap up an insect or berry.

This bluebird has a chattering note, *cut-cut-cut*. More frequently heard is a soft *kew*. In the early breeding season individuals fly around above trees in predawn darkness to give a chorus of *kew*'s; this song is only occasionally heard in daylight.

DETAILED ACCOUNT: ONE SUBSPECIES

CHESTNUT-BACKED WESTERN BLUEBIRD, *Sialia mexicana bairdi* Ridgway

DESCRIPTION: *Adult male, nuptial plumage*: Acquired by wear from winter plumage. Upper parts smalt blue, but back and most of scapulars chestnut brown to auburn; tail similar to upper parts but sometimes lighter (gentian blue), inner margins, and sometimes tips, of feathers mouse gray or rather deep neutral gray; wing-quills chaetura black, all exposed surfaces,

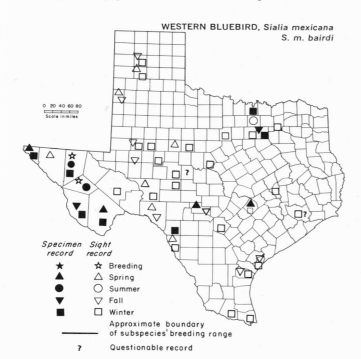

WESTERN BLUEBIRD, *Sialia mexicana S. m. bairdi*

0 20 40 60 80
Scale in miles

Specimen Sight
record   record

★   ☆ Breeding
▲   △ Spring
●   ○ Summer
▼   ▽ Fall
■   □ Winter

——— Approximate boundary of subspecies' breeding range

?   Questionable record

except tips of quills, blue like upper parts; sides of head mouse gray or chaetura drab and, excepting lores, much washed with blue of upper parts; chin, throat, and jugulum gentian blue; lower breast and upper abdomen also frequently tinged with this color; breast, sides, and sometimes flanks russet or chestnut; abdomen bluish white or buffy white; crissum bluish white or pale grayish blue—light gentian blue; lining of wing tyrian blue or windsor blue, more or less mixed with gray or grayish white. Bill black; iris bister or very dark brown; interior of mouth chrome yellow; legs and feet black. *Adult male, winter*: Acquired by complete postnuptial molt. Similar to nuptial adult male, but blue of upper and lower parts duller; chestnut brown areas both above and below more or less obscured by light dull buff or grayish brown edgings; wings and tail with very narrow whitish tips. *Adult female, nuptial*: Acquired by wear from winter. Very much duller than nuptial adult male; pileum hair brown or mouse gray, mantle light olive brown to rufescent sepia; rump and upper tail-coverts grayish violaceous blue to vanderpoel blue; tail chaetura black to hair brown, edged with color of upper tail-coverts, with narrow white line along most of basal portion of outer web and rather broad white margins on outer web of outermost tail feathers; wings fuscous, but lesser wing-coverts blue like rump; remaining wing-coverts and inner secondaries margined with dull buff, tertials with dull ochraceous, the inner primaries and outer secondaries with inner webs, except at tips, greenish blue, rather more greenish than on rump; sides of head and of throat between hair brown and drab, but with dull white supraloral line and cheeks mixed with pale gray; chin dull white; throat dull brownish gray; jugulum and breast dull cinnamon rufous or dull hazel; abdomen dull grayish white or buffy white, lower tail-coverts mouse gray margined with dull white; lining of wing hair brown or light mouse or neutral gray mixed with white. Bill black; iris medium brown; legs and feet black. *Adult female, winter*: Acquired by complete postnuptial molt. Similar to nuptial adult female, but cinnamon of upper and lower parts rather brighter, pileum more bluish, and chestnut below darker. *Male, first nuptial*: Acquired by wear from first winter. Similar to nuptial adult male, but colors somewhat lighter, greater coverts hair brown or chaetura drab, instead of blue. *Male, first winter*: Acquired by partial postjuvenal molt, which does not involve wing-quills. Similar to adult male in winter, but blue of head and throat somewhat lighter, light edgings of both upper and lower surfaces paler; greater coverts hair brown or chaetura drab, light edgings of wing-quills broader, tertials light snuff brown on margins; lining of wing less bluish. *Female, first nuptial*: Acquired by wear from first winter. Similar to nuptial adult female, but colors somewhat duller. *Female, first winter*: Acquired by partial postjuvenal molt. Similar to adult female in winter, but colors somewhat duller, lighter, and more brownish. *Male, juvenal*: Acquired by complete postnatal molt. Pileum dark rufescent hair brown; back sooty hays brown with narrow streaks of mikado brown; upper tail-coverts rather dark brownish neutral gray, on rump passing into color of back; wings and tail similar to those of first winter male, but median coverts with brownish white apical spots, blue areas dull violet blue or grayish violaceous blue; sides of head similar to pileum but paler and slightly more brownish; chin whitish with dull bars of brownish gray; breast, jugulum, and sides sepia with numerous short streaks and spots of snuff brown; abdomen and crissum buffy brown or cream white; flanks and crissum spotted or mottled with dull hair brown or mouse gray. *Female, juvenal*: Acquired by complete postnatal molt. Similar to juvenal male, but upper parts paler, more grayish (less rufescent); streaks white or pale buff; lower parts paler anteriorly, light streaks broader; lower tail-coverts less mottled; blue of wings and tail lighter and more greenish. *Natal*: Drab to dark drab.

MEASUREMENTS: *Adult male*: Wing, 104.9–117.1 (average, 110.7) mm.; tail, 63.5–71.1 (67.8); bill (exposed culmen), 10.9–13.0 (11.9); tarsus, 19.0–21.6 (20.3); middle toe without claw, 14.0–16.0 (14.7). *Adult female*: Wing, 101.6–109.5 (105.1); tail, 57.9–68.1 (63.5); bill, 10.9–13.0 (12.2); tarsus, 18.5–20.6 (19.6); middle toe, 13.5–15.0 (14.2).

RANGE: N. Utah and s. Wyoming, south to s.w. Durango. Winters from s.w. Nevada and w. Texas to Zacatecas.

TEXAS: *Breeding*: Collected in Culberson and Jeff Davis cos. *Winter*: Taken north to Cooke, south to Dallas and Bastrop (Mar. 24), west to Kinney, Brewster, Presidio, and El Paso cos.

NESTING: *Nest*: On slopes and in canyons of mountains, in more or less open forests, and in still more open country, and cultivated areas; in woodpecker hole or other cavity in tree, stump, or post, or even under loose bark of dead tree, such as pine, or in bird box; cup, usually rather loosely put together, composed mostly of dry grasses; lined with finer grass. *Eggs*: 4–6, usually 4; ovate to nearly oval; uniform pale blue, unmarked; average size, 27.7 × 16.5 mm.

MOUNTAIN BLUEBIRD, *Sialia currucoides* (Bechstein)

SPECIES ACCOUNT

Also known as Arctic Bluebird. Erect (not hunched) posture; hovers frequently. *Male*: turquoise blue (somewhat lighter below); whitish belly, crissum. *Female*: dull gray-brown (paler, buffier below); bluish rump, tail, wings. Length, 7 in.; wingspan, 13¼; weight, 1 oz.

RANGE: C. Alaska to s.w. Manitoba, south chiefly in mountains to s. California, s. New Mexico, and w. Oklahoma. Winters from s. British Columbia, w. Montana, and Kansas to n. Baja California, Sinaloa, Michoacán, and Guanajuato.

TEXAS: (See map.) *Summer*: Sighted in northern Panhandle: Palo Duro Canyon (between June 15 and Sept. 15, 1933, K. D. Carlander); Amarillo (June 23, 1933, K. D. Carlander). Recorded in Trans-Pecos: Davis Mts. (July, fide R. T. Peterson). No good evidence of breeding. *Winter*: Nov.—often Oct. in north-

MOUNTAIN BLUEBIRD, *Sialia currucoides*

0 20 40 60 80
Scale in miles

Specimen record / Sight record

▲ △ Spring
● ○ Summer
▼ ▽ Fall
■ □ Winter

—— Approximate boundary of subspecies' breeding range

? Questionable record

western third—to late Mar. (extremes: Sept. 3, May 29). Common to fairly common in northern Panhandle and northern Trans-Pecos; irregularly fairly common to scarce in remainder of northwestern two-thirds, southeast to Dallas, Bastrop, San Antonio, and Laredo areas; rare on central coast, south to Rio Grande delta; casual on upper coast.

HAUNTS AND HABITS: The Mountain Bluebird is attracted to cool, open country more than to mountains as such. Meadows, plains, and clearings made nearly (but not entirely) treeless by cold, aridity, axe, fire, or even the plow, constitute its habitat in both summer and winter. In northern open country it places its nest in woodpecker holes in the few trees available, in crevices of cliffs and rocks, or in birdhouses. In Texas, it winters mostly in the drier parts of the state since here there is more bare ground. In nonbreeding seasons it often moves in flocks, possibly some of the smaller companies being family groups.

Flight is not very swift, often rather fluttering, like that of other bluebirds, but sometimes sustained for long periods. When traveling it usually flies high, but ordinarily its flight is not at a great distance from the ground. This bird often feeds by hovering in the air a few feet above a meadow. After a few seconds or minutes, it drops to the ground to pick up what it spied—usually an insect or berry.

The Mountain Bluebird—the male of soul-satisfying blue—seems to be a species on the way to an almost complete loss of voice. The note is a weak *chur* or *phew*. Almost the only singing the species does is a low, short warble; normally even this is given only just before dawn and in the height of breeding season!

DETAILED ACCOUNT: NO SUBSPECIES

DESCRIPTION: *Adult male, nuptial plumage (blue phase)*: Acquired by wear from winter plumage. Upper parts between cerulean blue and mathews blue, but slightly paler, more greenish on forehead; rump rather lighter and brighter; tail similar to back but rather duller, though edged with brighter color of upper tail-coverts, inner margins of feathers neutral gray; wings fuscous black, coverts and outer webs of primaries, secondaries, and tertials, margined with color of back, but of slightly more purplish (less greenish) blue; lores chaetura drab or chaetura black; jugulum, breast, sides, and lining of wing light cerulean blue or light methyl blue; chin, cheeks, and throat similarly colored, but lighter and somewhat more greenish; abdomen and crissum white or creamy white, crissum sometimes washed with blue. Bill black; interior of mouth light naples yellow; iris hazel, black, or dark brown; legs and feet black. *Adult male, nuptial (green phase)*: Acquired by wear from winter. Similar to blue phase, but blue much less purplish (more greenish) above, between italian blue and cerulean blue or dark cendre blue; below rather dark calamine blue. *Adult male, winter*: Acquired by complete postnuptial molt. Similar to nuptial adult male, but blue of upper surface duller; pileum, hindneck, back, and scapulars edged with drab or dark drab; wing-coverts secondaries, and tertials margined with grayish white or brownish white; anterior lower parts duller, feathers with broad tips of avellaneous or vinaceous buff. *Adult female, nuptial (blue-gray phase)*: Acquired by wear from winter. Upper parts between neutral gray and mouse gray, strongly washed with dull greenish blue; rump, upper tail-coverts, and tail from china blue to mathews blue; tail feathers margined on outer webs with light fuscous, outermost rectrix edged externally with dull white; wing-quills fuscous, margined on outer webs and on wing-coverts with porcelain blue; anterior lower parts, including sides of head, light dull buffy drab; sides between drab and mouse gray; remainder of lower surface white, washed with drab or dull buff; lining of wing mouse gray or hair brown and white, more or less washed with pale greenish blue. *Adult female, nuptial (brown phase)*: Acquired by wear from winter. Similar to blue-gray phase, but anterior upper surface between drab and mouse gray; sides of head and anterior lower parts brighter, more cinnamomeous, avellaneous, or light wood brown. *Adult female, winter*: Acquired by complete postnuptial molt. Similar to nuptial adult female, but upper parts more uniform and rather darker, light edgings on wing-quills and wing-coverts broader; anterior lower parts darker and colors more blended. *Male and female, first nuptial*: Acquired by wear from first winter. Similar to corresponding sex and phase of nuptial adults but somewhat duller. *Male and female, first winter*: Acquired by partial postjuvenal molt, which does not include wing-quills. Similar to corresponding sex and phase of adults in winter but duller. *Male, juvenal*: Acquired by complete postnatal molt. Anterior upper parts, including back and scapulars, buffy brown or brownish drab, but pileum duller, often streaked or spotted with dull white or buff, sometimes pileum obscurely barred with fuscous; rump and upper tail-coverts mouse gray, sometimes narrowly and indistinctly barred with fuscous, but without trace of blue; tail china or mathews blue, tips deep mouse gray, inner margins of feathers paler gray; wing-quills fuscous black, margined on outer webs with china blue or mathews blue; lesser wing-coverts margined with color of back; greater wing-coverts, tertials, and secondaries margined with dull brownish white or pale buffy brown, latter chiefly on tertials; lower parts dull white, anteriorly much spotted and streaked with dull buffy brown and mouse gray, these spots becoming smaller and less conspicuous on sides, flanks, and middle of abdomen; breast like back; crissum almost immaculate. *Female, juvenal*: Acquired by complete postnatal molt. Similar to juvenal male, but blue of wings and tail decidedly more greenish—light terre verte or porcelain blue; upper parts darker and anteriorly more brownish. *Natal*: Rather dark drab.

MEASUREMENTS: *Adult male*: Wing, 112.5–121.4 (average, 117.9) mm.; tail, 68.6–75.9 (71.9); bill (exposed culmen), 12.4–14.0 (13.2); tarsus, 21.6–23.9 (22.9); middle toe without claw, 14.5–17.0 (15.5). *Adult female*: Wing, 106.9–116.1 (111.8); tail, 64.5–73.9 (68.3); bill, 11.9–14.5 (13.2); tarsus, 21.6–23.6 (22.4); middle toe, 14.5–16.0 (15.0).

TEXAS: *Winter*: Taken north to Oldham and Hutchinson (Mar. 6), east to Dallas, south to Hidalgo, west to Presidio and El Paso (Mar. 9) cos.

NESTING: *Nest*: About cliffs, canyons, and slopes in mountains, on level land, in cultivated areas, about human dwellings, even in towns; in hole in tree or other suitable cavity, abandoned woodpecker hole, crevice in old building or in cliff, or even deserted mine shaft; bulky cup, composed mostly of dry grass, with cedar and other bark and feathers; lined with fine grasses or similar material, sometimes wool or a few feathers. *Eggs*: 3–7, usually 5; oval to ovate; pale greenish blue, rarely pure white, unmarked; average size, 21.6 × 16.0 mm.

TOWNSEND'S SOLITAIRE, *Myadestes townsendi* (Audubon)

SPECIES ACCOUNT

Slim body; short bill; long, notched tail; erect posture. Gray body (paler below); white eye-ring and sides of tail; buffy wing-patches. Length, 8½ in.; wingspan, 13½; weight, 1 oz.

RANGE: S.e. Alaska to s.w. South Dakota, south in mountains to s. California, Durango, and w. Zacatecas.

Winters at lower elevations from s. British Columbia and w. Nebraska to Baja California, n.w. Jalisco, and Coahuila.

TEXAS: (See map.) *Winter*: Late Oct.—occasionally Sept.—to mid-Apr.—often May (extremes: Aug. 28, June 10). Fairly common in western third; increasingly uncommon east to Hunt Co., Bastrop Co., and Rockport, where rare; casual in Rio Grande delta.

HAUNTS AND HABITS: The somewhat reclusive Townsend's Solitaire is a Rocky Mountain inhabitant, chiefly of evergreen forests, sometimes even the densest portions. It favors canyons and mountain slopes and occurs in summer in brush and thickets or on brush- or tree-covered ridges, where it nests under overhanging banks or in crevices about tree roots, stumps, or hollow logs. In winter it often descends to valleys and canyons, rocky places, and juniper-covered ridges. When wintering in Texas it frequents thickets and timber along streams, canyons, cedar brakes, and other similar secluded retreats. The Townsend's is usually seen singly, in pairs, or in family parties; however, during migration and in winter, a considerable number may be attracted to a food or water source. It is a retiring and shy bird, especially during summer.

Its flight, ordinarily not rapid or prolonged, resembles somewhat that of the Cedar Waxwing and is performed commonly with rather slow, irregular wingbeats. The Townsend's favorite perch, from where it occasionally flycatches, is a projecting branch, high or low, or the top of a dead tree, but it is often seen on the ground, on rocks, or in bushes. It moves about readily, picking up insects and berries (often those of cedar and mistletoe) or bathing in rocky or other streams. Sometimes on the ground it is seen moving its wings up and down slowly as if to stretch.

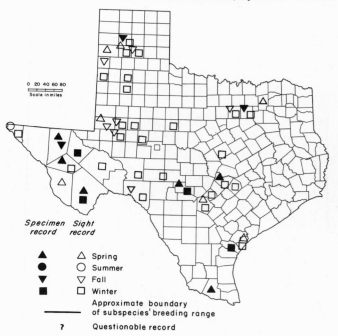

TOWNSEND'S SOLITAIRE, *Myadestes townsendi*

0 20 40 60 80
Scale in miles

Specimen record | Sight record
▲ | △ Spring
● | ○ Summer
▼ | ▽ Fall
■ | □ Winter
——— Approximate boundary of subspecies' breeding range
? Questionable record

The Townsend's *eek* note gives little hint that it, together with all the other members of its genus *Myadestes*, is a good singer. (*M. unicolor*, the Slate-colored Solitaire of Mexican and Guatemalan cloud forests, may be the world's best songster.) Townsend's long-warbled song—delivered from a high branch or from the air—sounds somewhat like a fast Black-headed Grosbeak's. This solitaire is said to sing nearly all year. However, on the Edwards Plateau, a favorite Texas wintering ground, the species is seldom heard.

Detailed Account: No Subspecies

DESCRIPTION: *Adults, nuptial plumage (gray phase)*: Acquired by wear from winter plumage. Upper parts mouse gray, slightly rufescent on longest upper tail-coverts; tail clove brown to dark clove brown, but middle pair of rectrices dull olive brown, outermost feather on each side with outer web, except extreme base and terminal third of inner web, brownish white, second pair of feathers broadly tipped with brownish white, and sometimes a narrow tip on third pair; wing-quills fuscous; basal portion of secondaries and broad band on all but two or three outer primaries ochraceous buff to cinnamon buff, outer webs of secondaries and inner primaries with broad band of dull cinnamon to cinnamon buff; lesser wing-coverts and edges of outer coverts similar to back but rather more brownish, greater series narrowly tipped with brownish white; tertials broadly tipped with same and their outer margins edged with pale gray; sides of head and neck like upper parts, auriculars rather more rufescent; cheeks somewhat mottled or obscurely barred with pale gray; eye-ring dull white; lower surface between mouse gray and light drab, but middle of abdomen and chin paler, throat also obscurely barred with same pale gray, lower tail-coverts tipped with pale gray like middle of abdomen; lining of wing grayish white or pale gray, coverts mottled with mouse gray. Bill black; iris dark brown; legs, feet, and claws black or dark brown. *Adults, nuptial (brown phase)*: Similar to gray phase, but upper parts dull rufescent hair brown; lower surface dull drab. *Adults, winter*: Acquired by complete postnuptial molt. Similar to corresponding phase of nuptial adults. *Second winter*: Acquired by complete postnuptial molt. Like adults in winter. *First nuptial*: Acquired by wear from first winter. Similar to nuptial adults, except for buff-tipped upper wing-coverts and wing-quills retained from juvenal. *First winter*: Acquired by partial postjuvenal molt, which does not involve wing-quills or all upper wing-coverts. Similar to first nuptial but slightly darker. *Juvenal (gray phase)*: Acquired by complete postnatal molt. Upper surface hair brown, with numerous more or less triangular spots of white, buffy white, or light buff, feathers more or less broadly tipped with chaetura black; wings and tail as in adult, but all secondary coverts with broad white, buffy white, or pale buff tips; lower parts dull pale gray as in adult, but everywhere with broad, more or less scalelike tips of chaetura black. *Juvenal (brown phase)*: Acquired by complete postnatal molt. Similar to juvenal gray phase, but upper surface deep buffy brown, feather tips fuscous black, subterminal spots deep buff or ochraceous; lower parts more buffy, breast dull pinkish buff, scalelike tips of feathers fuscous black.

MEASUREMENTS: *Adult male*: Wing, 112.5–123.0 (average, 117.3) mm.; tail, 95.0–109.5 (103.4); bill (exposed culmen), 11.9–13.0 (12.2); tarsus, 20.1–22.1 (20.9); middle toe without claw, 15.0–16.5 (15.5). *Adult female*: Wing, 110.5–115.6 (113.8); tail, 95.0–104.9 (97.6); bill, 10.9–12.4 (11.7); tarsus, 19.6–21.1 (20.3); middle toe, 14.5–16.0 (15.2).

TEXAS: *Winter*: Taken north to Potter (Sept. 27), east to Dallas (Nov. 24), south to Nueces and Hidalgo (Mar. 5), west to Brewster and Culberson (Oct. 3) cos.

Gnatcatchers and Kinglets: Sylviidae

BLUE-GRAY GNATCATCHER, *Polioptila caerula*
(Linnaeus)

SPECIES ACCOUNT

Tiny, slender body; thin bill; cocks and flips long, rounded tail. Bluish above; whitish below; white eye-ring; white-edged black tail (underside largely white). Male has narrow black band on forehead. Length, 4¾ in.; wingspan, 6½; weight, ¼ oz.

RANGE: California to extreme s. Ontario and New Jersey, south to s. Baja California, Guatemala, Isla Cozumel, U.S. Gulf coast, and Bahamas. Northern races winter from s. United States through Mexico to Guatemala; also Cuba.

TEXAS: (See map.) *Breeding*: Late Mar. to late July (eggs, Apr. 4 to July 3; young in nest to July 11) from near sea level to 7,500 ft. Common to uncommon through much of state; scarce and local in south Texas brush country. *Migration*: Mid-Mar. to mid-Apr.; mid-Aug. to mid-Oct. (extremes: Feb. 28, May; July, Nov. 24). Very common to fairly common through most parts; uncommon in middle and southern Panhandle. *Winter*: Late Nov. to late Feb. Very common to uncommon south of 30th parallel; scarce and irregular north to Amarillo, Denton, and Texarkana.

HAUNTS AND HABITS: Gnatcatchers and kinglets are often placed with the Old World Warblers, Sylviidae, a nearly cosmopolitan family of some 313 species. The trim Blue-gray Gnatcatcher lives on hills, in their valleys and gulches, or in rolling or flat country. It frequents oak, juniper, and other woodlands, heavy or open. During the breeding season in Texas it favors oaks; at other times of the year it seeks tiny insects and their eggs in almost any species of woody vegetation.

Flight, normally for short distances from tree to tree or thicket to thicket, is strong and at times swift but not direct; sometimes a bird may fly higher in the air over trees or brush. The Blue-gray is exceedingly active and sprightly. It often darts through its haunts as if someone were chasing it, spreading and twitching its tail and raising its wings. As it searches for gnats, flies, caddis flies, and other small insects, it gives the impression of a most indefatigable worker. Occasionally it descends from thickets to forage on the ground. Not particularly shy, it usually comes readily to investigate a bird watcher's squeaks.

The ordinary call of the Blue-gray is a thin *tsee*, sometimes drawn out and very much shriller. Its song,

infrequently heard, is short, thin, and insectlike. It has been represented as *zee-u, zee-u, ksee, ksee, ksee, ksu*. Singing lasts from March well into July.

DETAILED ACCOUNT: TWO SUBSPECIES

EASTERN BLUE-GRAY GNATCATCHER, *Polioptila caerulea caerulea* (Linnaeus)

DESCRIPTION: *Adult male, nuptial plumage*: Acquired by partial prenuptial molt. Forehead and narrow line bordering crown on each side black; rest of upper surface grayish delft blue; tail black, all but two middle pairs of tail feathers more or less tipped with white, this on outermost feather occupying about two-thirds of both webs, somewhat less on next pair; on third pair merely a broad tip, and on fourth pair a narrow tip; wing-quills dark mouse gray, inner edges of secondaries paler, almost whitish at base; lesser wing-coverts like back; remaining wing-coverts, with primaries and secondaries, edged on outer webs with brownish gray; tertials dark mouse gray, broadly edged with dull white; sides of head pale neutral gray; eye-ring white; sides of neck like back; lower parts white, but sides of breast, sides of body, and flanks pale neutral gray; lining of wing white or grayish white, outer under wing-coverts slightly spotted with mouse gray. Bill black, mandible sometimes burn blue on middle part, pale dull yellow, or plumbeous at base; iris mars brown; legs and feet black. *Adult female, nuptial*: Acquired by partial prenuptial molt. Similar to nuptial adult male but smaller; gray of upper surface not so bluish, near slate gray;

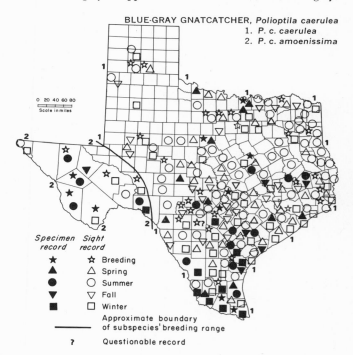

BLUE-GRAY GNATCATCHER, *Polioptila caerulea*
1. *P. c. caerulea*
2. *P. c. amoenissima*

0 20 40 60 80
Scale in miles

Specimen Sight
record   record
★   ☆   Breeding
▲   △   Spring
●   ○   Summer
▼   ▽   Fall
■   □   Winter
────── Approximate boundary
        of subspecies' breeding range
  ?   Questionable record

no black on forehead; no black line on sides of crown. *Adult male and female, winter*: Acquired by complete postnuptial molt. Similar to corresponding sex of nuptial adults. *Male, first nuptial*: Acquired by partial prenuptial molt. Like nuptial adult male. *Male, first winter*: Acquired by partial postjuvenal molt, not involving wing-quills or tail. Similar to adult female in winter but larger; gray of upper surface more bluish. Similar to adult male in winter, but without black markings on head, and upper surface lighter and more grayish. *Female, first nuptial*: Acquired by partial prenuptial molt. Like nuptial adult female. *Female, first winter*: Acquired by partial postjuvenal molt. Similar to adult female in winter, but gray of upper surface duller, rather bluish—neutral gray or mouse gray. *Juvenal*: Acquired by complete postnatal molt. Similar to first winter female, but gray of upper parts rather paler and more brownish, head mouse gray, back rather brownish neutral gray. Bill, legs, and feet dull black. *Natal*: Light bluish gray. Bill, legs, and feet pinkish buff.

MEASUREMENTS: *Adult male*: Wing, 49.0–54.6 (average, 52.3) mm.; tail, 48.0–54.1 (50.3); bill (exposed culmen), 8.9–10.9 (9.7); tarsus, 16.5–18.0 (17.3); middle toe without claw, 8.4–8.9 (8.6). *Adult female*: Wing, 50.0–52.1 (50.8); tail, 47.5–54.1 (50.0); bill, 8.9–10.4 (9.7); tarsus, 16.0–18.0 (17.3); middle toe, 8.4–8.9 (8.6).

RANGE: C. Nebraska and n.w. Wisconsin to New Jersey, south to s. Texas and w. Florida. Winters from c. Texas and s. South Carolina through e. Mexico (including Cozumel) to islands off coast of Honduras; also Cayman Islands, Cuba, and Bahamas.

TEXAS: *Breeding*: Altitudinal range, near sea level to at least 3,800 ft. in the Panhandle. Collected north to Cooke, east to Galveston, south to Cameron, west to Kerr cos. Common. *Winter*: Taken north to Bexar, east to Bee and Nueces, south to Brooks and Cameron cos. Common.

NESTING: *Nest*: On slopes of uplands and in valleys; along stream beds and thickets or at edge of open forests; saddled on horizontal branch or crotch of tree or bush, 10–60 ft. above ground; beautiful, compact cup with high, well-constructed walls; resembles very much a large nest of Ruby-throated Hummingbird, though walls are much higher and thicker; main portion consists of fine grasses, plant down, moss, shreds of bark, leaves, plant stems, feathers, milkweed, thistle or other down, felted and closely woven together with spider webs, covered on outside with lichens to match branch on which it rests; lined with plant down, hair, various cottony substances, withered blossoms, silky down of milkweed, thistle down, fine wiry grasses, stems of old leaves, and sometimes feathers from the bird itself. *Eggs*: 4–6, usually 5; ovate to rounded ovate; bluish white, greenish white, or plain white; dotted or speckled with chestnut, rufous, umber, dull purple, slate color, and lilac, most heavily at large end; average size, 14.5 × 11.2 mm.

WESTERN BLUE-GRAY GNATCATCHER, *Polioptila caerulea amoenissima* Grinnell

DESCRIPTION: *Adult male and female, nuptial plumage*: Similar to *P. c. caerulea*, but wing shorter; upper surface slightly duller; black on base of inner web of outermost tail feather more extensive, white terminal portion therefore shorter.

MEASUREMENTS: *Adult male*: Wing, 48.0–51.6 (average, 49.8) mm.; tail, 49.5–55.6 (51.8); bill (exposed culmen), 9.4–10.9 (10.2); tarsus, 16.0–18.0 (17.3); middle toe without claw, 8.4–8.9 (8.6). *Adult female*: Wing, 47.0–51.6 (48.5); tail, 47.0–54.1 (50.3); bill, 8.9–10.4 (9.7); tarsus, 16.5–18.5 (17.5); middle toe, 8.1–8.9 (8.6).

RANGE: N. California to n.w. Oklahoma, south to n. Baja California and Trans-Pecos Texas. Winters from s. California and s. Texas to s. Baja California and Colima.

TEXAS: *Breeding*: Altitudinal range, 1,700 to 7,500 ft. Collected in Culberson, Jeff Davis, Brewster, and Presidio cos. Fairly common. *Winter*: Two specimens: Val Verde Co., Del Rio (Jan. 31, 1890, V. Bailey); Webb Co., Laredo (1886, H. B. Butcher).

NESTING: Similar to that of *P. c. caerulea*.

BLACK-TAILED GNATCATCHER, *Polioptila melanura* Lawrence

SPECIES ACCOUNT

Plumbeous Gnatcatcher of many authors. Resembles Blue-gray Gnatcatcher, but underside of tail largely black. Nuptial male has black cap. Length, 4½ in.; wingspan, 5½; weight, ¼ oz.

RANGE: S. California and s. Nevada to s.w. Texas, south to n. Mexico.

TEXAS: (See map.) *Resident* (largely): Breeds, mid-Apr. to late Aug. (eggs, Apr. 13 to Aug. 13) from near sea level (formerly) to about 5,500 ft.—occasionally 6,500 ft. Common to fairly common in deserts of Trans-Pecos, especially along Rio Grande and its drainage; uncommon downriver from Del Rio to Rio Grande City (formerly south to Brownsville: eggs discovered, Apr. 13, 1892, F. B. Armstrong). Some seasonal movement evident; i.e., nonbreeding birds irregularly occur east to San Antonio, Rockport, and Rio Grande delta, where casual.

HAUNTS AND HABITS: The Black-tailed Gnatcatcher has the distinction of being the smallest Texas songbird. Its average weight is .18 of an ounce; the Blue-gray Gnatcatcher weighs in at .22 of an ounce. In Texas, as elsewhere, *Polioptila melanura* is the desert version of *P. caerulea*. Where the two live side-by-side, as in the Trans-Pecos, the Blue-gray resides in pinyon-oak mountain woodlands while the present bird inhabits desert thornbrush. Mesquite-acacia-lined arroyos and brush-choked gullies near the Rio Grande constitute prime habitat for the Blacktail, although some individuals range out into creosotebush (*Larrea*) flats—one of the very few bird species to do so. Here, in

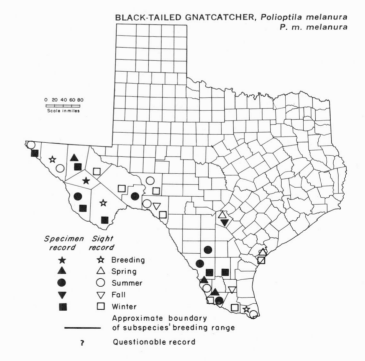

BLACK-TAILED GNATCATCHER, *Polioptila melanura*
P. m. melanura

0 20 40 60 80
Scale in miles

Specimen record / Sight record
★ ☆ Breeding
▲ △ Spring
● ○ Summer
▼ ▽ Fall
■ ☐ Winter
——— Approximate boundary of subspecies' breeding range
? Questionable record

summer, temperatures may reach the vicinity of 110° F. for many days at a time. At this season the male even wears a heat-absorbing black cap over his thin skull. In spite of the terrific heat, this gnatcatcher is fully as active as is its relative of cool mountain woodlands. It dashes about within thorn bushes, often flirting its tail from side to side and darting into the air after tiny insects.

The call note of this bird is a harsh, mewing sound, something like *chee, chee, chee*. This contrasts with the single clear *chee* or *tsee* of the Blue-gray. Its song is a weak, thin, and rather harsh insectlike ditty, resembling *tsee-dee-dee-dee-dee*. It suggests in quality and form some chickadee songs. Singing is from March into July.

DETAILED ACCOUNT: ONE SUBSPECIES

PLUMBEOUS BLACK-TAILED GNATCATCHER,
Polioptila melanura melanura Lawrence

DESCRIPTION: *Adult male, nuptial plumage*: Acquired by partial prenuptial molt. Pileum and its sides down to and including eyes, upper edge of auriculars, and lores glossy, slightly bluish or greenish black; however, lores sometimes wholly or partly grayish white, and eye-ring sometimes partly white; remainder of upper surface deep neutral gray, sometimes verging toward slate gray; tail black, outer web of outermost feather, except extreme base, and about half or more of inner web of same feather white, next pair similar, but white terminal portion less extensive, on third pair reduced to a broad white tip, and on fourth feather sometimes a very narrow white tip; wings fuscous, lesser and median coverts edged with color of back, greater coverts slightly more brownish gray, as are also narrow outer edges of wing-quills; remainder of sides of head and neck and entire lower surface white, washed with pale neutral gray on breast; lining of wing grayish white. Bill black, but mandible gray basally; iris mars brown; legs and feet black. *Adult male, winter*: Acquired by complete postnuptial molt. Similar to nuptial male, but black feathers of pileum, particularly posteriorly, more or less extensively tipped and margined with gray of upper surface. *Adult female, nuptial*: Acquired by wear from winter. Resembles nuptial adult male but duller, more brownish, and without black on head; pileum deep mouse gray or deep neutral gray; back more or less tinged with dark dull buffy brown to drab. *Adult female, winter*: Acquired by complete postnuptial molt. Similar to nuptial adult female, but upper parts, as well as wings, rather lighter and more brownish. *Male, first nuptial*: Acquired by partial prenuptial molt, not involving wing-quills. Similar to adult male in winter, but without black on pileum which is dark neutral gray or dark mouse gray; back duller, more brownish; lower surface duller and somewhat washed with light brown or dull buff. *Female, first nuptial*: Acquired by partial prenuptial molt. Like nuptial adult female. *Female, first winter*: Acquired by partial postjuvenal molt. Similar to adult female in winter, but upper parts darker, decidedly more brownish; back rather bright buffy brown; rump snuff brown; lower surface more buffy, particularly on posterior portion; crissum light cinnamon buff. *Juvenal*: Acquired by complete postnatal molt. Pileum drab to brownish neutral gray; rest of upper surface dull drab to dark drab; wing-coverts hair brown margined with drab or dark drab, greater coverts and tertials edged with dull vinaceous buff; lower parts washed with dull brown, particularly on breast, sides, flanks, and crissum. *Natal*: Unknown.
MEASUREMENTS: *Adult male*: Wing, 45.5–49.0 (average, 47.3) mm.; tail, 49.5–54.6 (51.8); bill (exposed culmen), 8.6–9.9 (9.1); tarsus, 16.5–18.0 (17.5); middle toe without claw, 7.6–8.9 (9.4). *Adult female*: Wing, 46.0–49.5 (48.0); tail,

51.1–55.9 (52.6); bill, 8.9–9.9 (9.1); tarsus, 16.5–18.5 (17.8); middle toe, 7.6–8.1 (7.9).
RANGE: S.w. Texas, south to Nuevo León and Tamaulipas.
TEXAS: *Resident* (largely): Collected northwest to El Paso and Culberson, southeast to Terrell, Duval, and Starr cos. One specimen outside breeding range: Bexar Co., San Antonio River (Sept. 30, 1863, H. E. Dresser).
NESTING: *Nest*: On slopes and mesas or along stream valleys; usually in brush or near it; in mesquite or other bush, low tree, vine, or bunch of mistletoe; tiny deep cup with rather thick, firm, and well-built walls, though of soft materials; composed of fine hemplike vegetable fibers, shreds of bark, cotton, downy substances, and fragments of cocoons, closely felted together but with no lichens as adornment on outside; lined with silky down of various plants, feathers, and animal hair. *Eggs*: 2–5, usually 4; rounded ovate; pale greenish white or pale greenish blue, finely speckled with reddish brown, black, and dull purple; average size, 13.5 × 10.7 mm.

GOLDEN-CROWNED KINGLET, *Orchilus satrapa* (Lichtenstein)

SPECIES ACCOUNT

Regulus satrapa of A.O.U. check-list, 1957 (see Appendix A). Tiny, plump body; stubby tail; flicks wings. Olive gray above; dingy white below; white eye-stripe; orange crown-patch bordered narrowly by yellow, then by black (in female, crown-patch all yellow, bordered by black); whitish wing-bars. Length, 4 in.; wingspan, 6½; weight, ¼ oz.
RANGE: S. Alaska to Newfoundland, south to c. California, s.e. Arizona, U.S.-Canada border, and w. North Carolina; also highlands from c. Mexico to Guatemala. Northern races winter south to extreme n. Mexico, U.S. Gulf coast, and n. Florida.
TEXAS: (See map.) *Winter*: Late Oct. to late Mar.

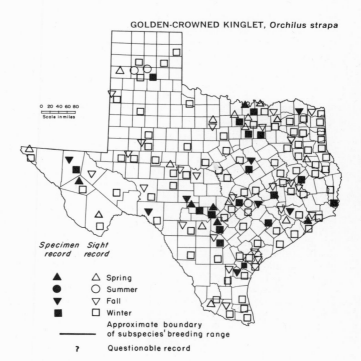

GOLDEN-CROWNED KINGLET, *Orchilus strapa*

0 20 40 60 80
Scale in miles

Specimen record	Sight record	
▲	△	Spring
●	○	Summer
▼	▽	Fall
■	□	Winter

—— Approximate boundary of subspecies' breeding range

? Questionable record

PLATE 25: Golden-cheeked Warbler, *Dendroica chrysoparia*, perched on cedar (*Juniperus ashei*)
adult female (lower left), adult male (center)

PLATE 26: Bullock's Oriole, *Icterus bullockii*, perched on cottonwood (*Populus*) immature male (top), adult male (bottom)

(extremes: Sept. 14, June 4). Irregularly common to uncommon in most parts, but often scarce south of 28th parallel.

HAUNTS AND HABITS: The Golden-crowned Kinglet lives in boreal conifer forests, where it suspends its globular nest of bark strips, moss, and lichens from twigs of a pine or spruce. During migration and winter in Texas it seems to prefer trees to brush and undergrowth, but it also forages for insects and their larvae in thickets and scrub. It moves often in scattered flocks of its own kind or associated with small birds of other species. These mixed troops drift through woodlands and groves, gleaning as they go, and are at all times lively companies.

In flight it is much like the Ruby-crowned Kinglet, often quick, sometimes rather fluttering, erratic, and jerky, as it works through vegetation; but at times it flies much longer distances, sometimes high in the air, but seldom directly. The Goldencrown is an active, restless mite, one of the smallest Texas bird inhabitants; it often forages at or near the ends of tree branches or even hovers in the air in front of these. Its diet is largely insects—wasps, bugs, flies, beetles, plant lice; some plant food is taken in autumn and winter.

The commonly heard note is a very high, wiry *tee-tee-tee*. Song is a long series of *tee*'s which rise in pitch, then drop into a wee chatter. The Golden-crowned Kinglet is said to sing very seldom in Texas. However, its song is so high pitched that doubtless few men over thirty can hear it!

DETAILED ACCOUNT: THREE SUBSPECIES

EASTERN GOLDEN-CROWNED KINGLET, *Orchilus satrapa satrapa* (Lichtenstein)

DESCRIPTION: *Adult male, nuptial plumage*: Acquired by wear from winter plumage. Center of crown orange chrome or cadmium orange, bordered on each side by lemon yellow or lemon chrome, this in turn bordered on each side by black which extends across forehead and back to occiput; extreme forehead and broad superciliary stripe grayish white, dull pale gray, or grayish olive; nape deep grayish olive, sometimes more or less brownish; back yellowish olive; rump shading toward light yellowish olive; tail chaetura drab or dark hair brown, edged externally with color of rump, narrow inner margin of feathers whitish; wings chaetura drab, lesser coverts deep grayish olive, greater and primary coverts edged with yellowish olive, greater series broadly tipped with yellowish white, broad bar on outer webs of secondaries posterior to white wing-bar on coverts chaetura black or fuscous black; secondaries and all but outer primaries margined for remainder of terminal portion with light yellowish olive, this becoming still paler on exposed basal portions of outer webs of primaries; tertials and inner secondaries broadly tipped with brownish white; streak through eye chaetura black; lores whitish or pale grayish olive; rest of sides of head and of neck like nape but lighter; lower parts dull brownish white but strongly washed on sides, flanks, and crissum, sometimes also on breast, with grayish olive; lining of wing white. Bill black, slate black, blackish brown, or dark olive brown, but base of mandible sometimes somewhat paler; iris black or vandyke brown; legs drab, prout brown, hair brown, light olive, clove brown, or seal brown; feet broccoli brown, light olive, prout brown, burnt umber, seal brown, clove brown, or tawny olive; soles of toes dull yellow; claws black or tawny olive. *Adult male, winter*: Acquired by complete postnuptial molt. Similar to nuptial adult male, but colors usually brighter,

posterior upper surface more yellowish or greenish (less grayish); lower parts more strongly tinged with light buffy olive. *Adult female, nuptial*: Acquired by wear from winter. Similar to nuptial adult male, but middle of crown entirely lemon chrome, replacing orange of middle of crown in male. *Adult female, winter*: Acquired by complete postnuptial molt. Like nuptial adult female but somewhat more richly colored. *Male, first nuptial*: Acquired by wear from first winter. Like nuptial adult male. *Male, first winter*: Acquired by partial postjuvenal molt, which does not involve wing-quills or tail. Little, if any, different from adult male in winter. *Female, first winter*: Acquired by partial postjuvenal molt. Practically identical with adult female in winter. *Juvenal*: Acquired by complete postnatal molt. Similar to nuptial adult female, but crown entirely without yellow, being wholly dull grayish hair brown; remainder of upper surface dull light brownish olive. Bill black or slate black; iris very dark brown; legs clove brown, seal brown, or broccoli brown; feet prout brown, clove brown, broccoli brown, or tawny olive.

MEASUREMENTS: *Adult male*: Wing, 56.4–59.9 (average, 58.2) mm.; tail, 41.9–46.5 (44.2); bill (exposed culmen), 6.1–8.6 (7.6); tarsus, 16.5–17.5 (17.3); middle toe without claw, 8.1–9.4 (8.6). *Adult female*: Wing, 55.1–57.9 (56.1); tail, 41.4–45.0 (42.7); bill, 7.1–8.6 (7.9); tarsus, 16.0–17.0; middle toe, 8.1–8.9 (8.6).

RANGE: N.e. Alberta to c. Labrador, south to c. Montana, n.w. Michigan, and s.w. North Carolina. Winters from e. Nebraska and c. Nova Scotia to n.e. Tamaulipas and c. Florida.

TEXAS: *Winter*: Taken north to Armstrong, east to Red River (Nov. 10) and Orange, south to Nueces (Nov. 23), west to Jeff Davis (Apr. 8) cos. Fairly common.

ARIZONA GOLDEN-CROWNED KINGLET, *Orchilus satrapa apache* (Jenks)

DESCRIPTION: *Adult male and female, nuptial plumage*: Similar to *O. s. satrapa*, but male's bill longer and more slender; nasal plumes averaging smaller; upper surface rather lighter, much more brightly yellowish olive; crown more deeply reddish orange; black of plumage rather duller; lower surface somewhat lighter. Female shows similar differences, also darker yellow crown.

MEASUREMENTS: *Adult male*: Wing, 55.1–57.9 (average, 56.6) mm.; tail, 40.4–43.4 (41.7); bill (exposed culmen), 7.6–8.6 (8.4); tarsus, 17.8–19.0 (18.3); middle toe without claw, 8.1–9.4 (8.6). *Adult female*: Wing, 54.1–55.9 (55.3); tail, 39.9–45.0 (42.2); bill, 7.9–8.9 (8.4); tarsus, 17.8–18.3 (18.0); middle toe, 8.1–8.9 (8.6).

RANGE: E. Arizona and c. New Mexico. Winters from s.e. Arizona (probably) to Trans-Pecos Texas.

TEXAS: *Winter*: Three specimens, all from Guadalupe Mts., Culberson Co.: McKittrick Canyon (2 on Jan. 3, 1939, T. D. Burleigh); The Bowl (Jan. 5, 1939, Burleigh).

WESTERN GOLDEN-CROWNED KINGLET, *Orchilus satrapa olivaceus* (Baird)

DESCRIPTION: *Adult male and female, nuptial plumage*: Similar to *O. s. satrapa*, but wing and tail much shorter; bill more slender; upper parts brighter, of more greenish or brownish (less grayish) olive; sides and flanks more brownish.

MEASUREMENTS: *Adult male*: Wing, 53.1–56.9 (average, 54.8) mm.; tail, 38.6–42.4 (40.6); bill (exposed culmen), 6.6–8.1 (7.1); tarsus, 15.5–18.0 (17.3); middle toe without claw, 8.1–8.9 (8.6). *Adult female*: Wing, 52.6–55.1 (53.6); tail, 38.1–41.9 (39.6); bill, 7.1–8.9 (7.9); tarsus, 16.0–18.0 (16.8); middle toe, 8.1–8.9 (8.6).

RANGE: S.w. Alaska to n. Alberta, south to s. California. Winters from s. British Columbia to s. California and New Mexico; casual in Texas.

TEXAS: *Winter*: One specimen: Lee Co., Giddings (Nov. 15, 1887, J. A. Singley).

RUBY-CROWNED KINGLET, *Regulus calendula* (Linnaeus)

SPECIES ACCOUNT

Tiny, plump body; stubby tail; flicks wings. Olive gray above; dingy buff below; conspicuous whitish eye-ring (incomplete on top), wing-bars. Male has red crown-patch (often concealed). Length, 4¼ in.; wingspan, 7; weight, ¼ oz.

RANGE: Alaska across Canada to Newfoundland, south in mountains to s. California, c. New Mexico, n. Michigan, and Nova Scotia; also Guadalupe Island off Baja California. Winters from s. British Columbia, c. United States, and Maryland to Guatemala, Gulf coast, and Florida.

TEXAS: (See map.) *Winter*: Late Sept. to early May (extremes: Aug. 23, May 30). Very common to fairly common in most parts; uncommon to scarce in northern Panhandle, though often common during migrations.

HAUNTS AND HABITS: The Ruby-crowned Kinglet breeds in evergreen forests of the far north and of western mountains. Here, the twigs of a conifer are often chosen from which to hang the mossy nest typically bound with spider webs. Less specialized on its Texas wintering grounds, this sprightly kinglet frequents all types of woodlands and brush. It visits fence rows, old fields, gardens, and yards and parks of towns and cities. The Rubycrown is not a closely gregarious bird but is often seen in scattered groups, these associated with Golden-crowned Kinglets, nuthatches, woodpeckers, chickadees, and other small birds.

Flight is usually jerky and irregular and ordinarily only from tree to tree; a bird sometimes flies longer distances, somewhat erratically but swiftly. The Ruby-

crown darts about nervously—almost constantly flicking its wings—in trees or bushes, either in interior or outer foliage. Here it gleans small insects and their eggs, also an occasional gall or wild berry. It rarely descends to the ground.

Note is a distinctive, hurried *ji-dit*. The male's song is a reedy warble, rapidly uttered and remarkably loud for so small a bird. The song usually starts with some squeaky *tee*'s, drops in pitch for a series of *tew*'s, then concludes with three or more emphatic *ti-dadee*'s. While the Rubycrown sojourns in Texas, it sings its melody occasionally in the fall but most commonly in February, March, and April.

DETAILED ACCOUNT: TWO SUBSPECIES

EASTERN RUBY-CROWNED KINGLET, *Regulus calendula calendula* (Linnaeus)

DESCRIPTION: *Adult male, nuptial plumage*: Acquired by wear from winter plumage. Upper surface grayish olive, back sometimes more greenish, passing into light yellowish olive on rump and upper tail-coverts; center of crown with large patch of grenadine red or vermilion, usually concealed by olive gray feathers; wings and tail hair brown, tail feathers edged on outer webs with light yellowish olive, inner margins of feathers paler, almost whitish; lesser wing-coverts and margins of greater coverts grayish olive, broad tips of greater coverts and narrow tips of median coverts ivory yellow or dull white, forming two light wing-bars; posterior to tips of greater coverts is a broad fuscous black band across outer webs of secondaries and innermost primaries; posterior to this band the outer webs of primaries and secondaries are margined narrowly on outer webs with light yellowish olive, tertials broadly margined on outer webs with yellowish white; sides of head and neck like crown but rather paler; conspicuous yellowish or greenish white eye-ring, which is incomplete on upper eyelid; lower surface olive buff or deep olive buff; lining of wing paler, sometimes whitish. Bill black, olivaceous black, or slate black, basal portion of mandible sometimes brownish slate color or even dull yellow; iris vandyke brown or fuscous black; legs black, brownish black, seal brown, clove brown, or olive drab; feet seal brown, clove brown, chocolate, or prout brown; soles of toes dull yellow; claws seal brown. *Adult male, winter*: Acquired by complete postnuptial molt. Similar to nuptial adult male, but upper surface lighter and brighter, more olivaceous (less grayish); lower surface more deeply olive buff. *Adult female, nuptial*: Acquired by wear from winter. Similar to nuptial adult male, but lacking red patch on crown. *Adult female, winter*: Acquired by complete postnuptial molt. Similar to nuptial adult female but brighter, more olivaceous (less grayish) above; darker, less grayish, olive buff below. *Male and female, first nuptial*: Acquired by limited prenuptial molt and wear from first winter. Similar to corresponding sex of nuptial adults. *Male and female, first winter*: Acquired by partial postjuvenal molt, which does not involve wing-quills or tail. Like corresponding sex of adults in winter. *Juvenal*: Acquired by complete postnatal molt. Upper surface buffy olive to light brownish olive; wings and tail similar to those of adult, broad light wing-bar on tips of greater coverts ivory yellow to cartridge buff; sides of head like pileum; anterior lower parts dull light grayish olive; posterior lower surface dull olive buff, but middle of abdomen dull white. Bill becoming dull brown, paler at base; legs and feet dark brown; toes somewhat yellowish.

MEASUREMENTS: *Adult male*: Wing, 56.4–61.5 (average, 58.7) mm.; tail, 40.4–45.0 (42.7); bill (exposed culmen), 7.1–9.4 (8.6); tarsus, 18.0–20.1 (19.0); middle toe without claw, 8.9–10.4 (9.7). *Adult female*: Wing, 54.1–57.9 (56.1); tail, 40.4–43.9 (42.2); bill, 7.6–9.4 (8.6); tarsus, 17.5–19.6 (18.8); middle toe, 8.9–9.9 (9.1).

RANGE: S. Mackenzie to e. Labrador, south to c. Saskatche-

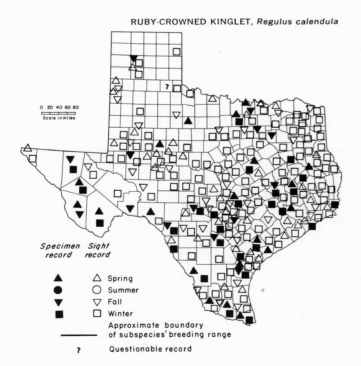

RUBY-CROWNED KINGLET, *Regulus calendula*

0 20 40 60 80
Scale in miles

Specimen Sight
record   record

▲ △ Spring
● ○ Summer
▼ ▽ Fall
■ □ Winter

⎯⎯⎯ Approximate boundary of subspecies' breeding range

? Questionable record

wan, n. Michigan, and c. Nova Scotia. Winters from n.e. Nebraska to s. Tamaulipas, and along U.S. Gulf coast to s. Florida.

TEXAS: *Winter*: Taken north to Potter (Sept. 27), east to Wise and Orange, south to Cameron, west to Brewster and Culberson (Oct. 10) cos. Common.

WESTERN RUBY-CROWNED KINGLET, *Regulus calendula cineraceus* Grinnell

DESCRIPTION: *Adult male and female, nuptial plumage*: Similar to *R. c. calendula* but larger, particularly tail; upper parts paler and more grayish.

MEASUREMENTS: *Adult male*: Wing, 57.9–63.0 (average, 60.5) mm.; tail, 42.9–47.5 (45.7); bill (exposed culmen), 7.6–8.9 (8.1); tarsus, 18.0–20.1 (19.3); middle toe without claw, 8.6–9.9 (9.1). *Adult female*: Wing, 53.1–59.9 (57.2); tail, 39.9–46.0 (42.9); bill, 7.6–8.9 (8.4); tarsus, 18.0–19.0 (18.5); middle toe, 8.1–9.4 (8.6).

RANGE: C. Alaska to w. Yukon, south to s.w. California and c. New Mexico. Winters from s. British Columbia, Utah, and w. Texas to s. Baja California, and through s.w. Mexico to Guatemala.

TEXAS: *Winter*: Taken north to Haskell (May 15), east to Travis and Victoria (May 5), south to Hidalgo, west to Brewster and Culberson cos. Uncommon.

Water Pipit, *Anthus spinoletta*

Pipits: Motacillidae

WATER PIPIT, *Anthus spinoletta* (Linnaeus)

SPECIES ACCOUNT

A small, streaked ground bird with white outer tail feathers; slender, warblerlike bill; walks, rather than hops; wags tail. Plain gray-brown above; brown-streaked buffy below; blackish legs. Length, 6½ in.; wingspan, 10¾; weight, ½ oz.

RANGE: Circumpolar in arctic and arctic-alpine zones; winters in milder climes over much of Northern Hemisphere. In Western Hemisphere breeds from Alaska, far n. Canada, and w. Greenland, south in high western mountains to n. New Mexico; winters chiefly from coastal (except New England) and s. United States to Guatemala.

TEXAS: (See map.) *Winter*: Mid-Oct. to late Apr. (extremes: Aug. 6, June 30). Very common to fairly common in most parts; uncommon in Panhandle, though often common during migrations.

HAUNTS AND HABITS: The world's forty-eight Motacillidae are represented in Texas by only two species. During the breeding season, the Water Pipit inhabits cold barren tundra and high western mountains. Here it shelters its bulky nest of grasses and forbs beside a rock or grass tuft. In migration and winter it occurs in Texas most numerously on plains, prairies, meadows, golf courses, unused football fields, road shoulders, and muddy or grassy margins of rivers, water holes, lakes, and bays. At this season the bird seeks open country at any altitude. As the name indicates, this species is more likely to forage beside water than is the Sprague's Pipit. *Anthus spinoletta* often associates with Horned Larks and longspurs.

Flight is strong, erratic, and ordinarily undulating. When a flock is disturbed, the birds may rise high into the air, hover, and then return to earth. The Water Pipit feeds on the ground, singly or sometimes in large but scattered flocks. It walks gracefully or runs easily, bobbing its head and tipping its tail. When foraging, it scours old fields or newly turned furrows for insects (beetles, caterpillars, grasshoppers, others) and seeds (especially of spurge). It also patrols shores of pond or stream, even at times wading into shallows to catch an invertebrate. Occasionally the Water Pipit alights in a low tree, on a fence, high wire, or even a building.

Its ordinary note is rather plaintive and lispy, some-thing like *tsee-tseep* or *pi-pit*. The *chee-whee, che-whee, che-whee* flight song is almost never heard in Texas.

DETAILED ACCOUNT: FOUR SUBSPECIES

HUDSON BAY WATER PIPIT, *Anthus spinoletta ludovicianus* (Gmelin)

Race not in A.O.U. check-list, 1957 (see Appendix A).

DESCRIPTION: *Adults, nuptial plumage*: Acquired by partial prenuptial molt. Upper surface between hair brown and dark grayish olive, sometimes with olive buff tinge or verging toward drab, but centers of feathers dark hair brown, fuscous, or chaetura drab, imparting somewhat mottled appearance to upper surface; upper tail-coverts somewhat more rufescent, these and rump practically uniform, without markings; tail fuscous black, with very narrow edgings of grayish olive, outermost tail feather white for terminal two-thirds of length on outer web, and nearly as much next to shaft on inner web, although edge of inner web, except at tip, is brown like rest of tail, also there is a narrow subtriangular white tip on next to outermost tail feathers; sometimes similar tip on third pair; wings fuscous, margins of wing-coverts and tertials dull drab, wing-coverts and shorter tertials dull drab, longest tertials margined on outer webs with brownish or olivaceous white, outer webs of secondaries and primaries narrowly edged, except at tips, with dark grayish olive;

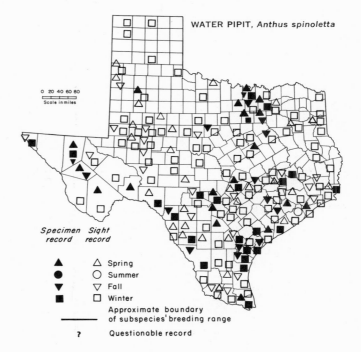

WATER PIPIT, *Anthus spinoletta*

0 20 40 60 80
Scale in miles

Specimen   Sight
record   record

▲ △ Spring
● ○ Summer
▼ ▽ Fall
■ □ Winter

——— Approximate boundary of subspecies' breeding range

?   Questionable record

superciliary stripe pale pinkish buff or pale olive buff; auriculars buffy drab; remainder of sides of head and neck similar, but rather lighter and more or less mixed and blended with dark brown; lower surface pale pinkish buff or almost white to cinnamon buff; jugulum, sides of throat, of breast, and of body streaked and spotted with fuscous, these streaks more numerous on sides of throat and on jugulum; lining of wing olivaceous or buffy white, outer under wing-coverts more or less spotted with hair brown or mouse gray. Bill black, brownish black, or dark olive brown, but basal part of mandible clove brown, light brown, or even dull yellow; iris vandyke brown, hazel, or black; legs and feet dark brown, blackish brown, or dark drab, but soles of toes greenish yellow; claws black. *Adults, winter*: Acquired by complete postnuptial molt. Similar to nuptial adults, but upper parts darker, more brownish or buffy—brownish olive to buffy brown or light olive brown; lower parts darker, more deeply buff—dull light cinnamon buff to clay color. *First nuptial*: Acquired by partial prenuptial molt. Like nuptial adults. *First winter*: Acquired by partial postjuvenal molt, which does not involve wing-quills or tail. Similar to adults in winter but still more brownish above and more deeply buffy below. *Juvenal*: Acquired by complete postnatal molt. Similar to adults in winter, but less uniform above, conspicuous dark centers of feathers chaetura drab or chaetura black, and colors more blended; lower surface lighter. Iris and tarsus dark brown.

MEASUREMENTS: *Adult male*: Wing, 82.0–87.6 (average, 84.1) mm.; tail, 61.0–69.1 (64.5); bill (exposed culmen), 10.4–13.0 (12.4); tarsus, 21.1–24.4 (22.6); middle toe without claw, 13.0–14.7 (13.5); white on inner web of outermost tail feather, 28.9–39.9 (35.8). *Adult female*: Wing, 77.0–83.1 (80.5); tail, 59.9–63.0 (61.5); bill, 10.9–13.5 (11.9); tarsus, 21.1–23.1 (22.1); middle toe, 13.0–14.5 (13.5); white on inner web, 26.9–38.1 (33.5).

RANGE: N.e. Siberia to Somerset Island and n. Keewatin, south to s. Mackenzie and w. Quebec. Winters from s.w. British Columbia, c. Kansas, and New Jersey to s. Baja California, mainland Mexico, and c. Florida; also probably Guatemala.

TEXAS: *Winter*: Taken north to Cooke, east to Orange, south to Cameron, west to El Paso cos. Common.

ROCKY MOUNTAIN WATER PIPIT, *Anthus spinoletta alticola* Todd

DESCRIPTION: *Adults, nuptial plumage*: Similar to *A. s. ludovicianus*, but upper parts paler, more grayish; lower parts more deeply and uniformly cinnamon (not so buffy); breast and jugulum usually almost unmarked.

MEASUREMENTS: *Adult male*: Wing, 83.6–90.4 (average, 86.9) mm.; tail, 63.5–70.1 (66.3); bill (exposed culmen), 11.4–13.7 (12.4); tarsus, 21.1–23.6 (22.6); middle toe without claw, 11.9–14.5 (13.5); white on inner web of outermost tail feather, 31.5–39.9 (36.1). *Adult female*: Wing, 78.0–83.1 (81.5); tail, 59.9–62.5 (61.0); bill, 10.9–12.7 (12.2); tarsus, 21.1–23.1 (22.1); middle toe, 11.9–14.0 (13.2); white on inner web, 33.0–35.6 (33.8).

RANGE: C. Idaho and n. Montana, south to n. New Mexico. Winters from c. California and Texas to State of México.

TEXAS: *Winter*: Taken north to Lubbock (Apr. 1), east to Collin (Mar. 22) and Dallas (Apr. 10), southwest to Brewster (Apr. 11) and Culberson (Apr. 26) cos. Uncommon.

PACIFIC WATER PIPIT, *Anthus spinoletta pacificus* Todd

DESCRIPTION: *Adults, nuptial plumage*: Similar to *A. s. geophilus* (see below), but lower parts much lighter and more whitish; upper surface slightly paler. Similar to *A. s. ludovicianus*, but not so dark above; lower parts much lighter and more whitish.

MEASUREMENTS: *Adult male*: Wing, 81.0–86.8 (average, 84.1) mm.; tail, 62.5–67.6 (65.3); bill (exposed culmen), 11.2–13.2 (12.4); tarsus, 21.1–23.6 (22.4); middle toe without claw, 13.0–14.5 (13.5); white on inner web of outermost tail feather, 32.5–39.9 (36.1). *Adult female*: Wing, 74.4–81.0 (78.5); tail,

56.4–64.5 (59.7); bill, 11.2–12.7 (11.9); tarsus, 22.1–23.6 (22.4); middle toe, 12.4–14.0 (13.2); white on inner web, 29.9–39.9 (35.3).

RANGE: S.e. Alaska and s. Yukon, south to n.e. Oregon. Winters from s.w. British Columbia, n. Texas, and s.w. Louisiana to s. Baja California and c. Mexico.

TEXAS: *Winter*: Taken northeast to Collin, south to Aransas and Cameron, west to Val Verde and Culberson cos. Fairly common.

ALASKAN WATER PIPIT, *Anthus spinoletta geophilus* Oberholser

Race not in A.O.U. check-list, 1957 (see Appendix A).

DESCRIPTION: *Adults, nuptial plumage*: Similar to *A. s. ludovicianus*, but upper surface paler. Similar to *A. s. alticola*, but upper parts somewhat darker, less grayish (more brownish); lower surface paler or more whitish and more buffy (less cinnamomeous); jugulum usually heavily streaked with dark brown.

MEASUREMENTS: *Adult male*: Wing, 78.0–87.1 (average, 83.8) mm.; tail, 62.5–69.1 (65.0); bill (exposed culmen), 10.9–11.9 (11.7); tarsus, 21.6–23.1 (22.4); middle toe without claw, 13.0–14.2 (13.7); white on inner web of outermost tail feather, 33.5–39.9 (37.8). *Adult female*: Wing, 75.4–83.6 (78.7); tail, 57.9–64.0 (61.2); bill, 11.4–11.9 (11.7); tarsus, 20.1–22.1 (21.4); middle toe, 12.2–14.0 (13.0); white on inner web, 29.4–38.6 (33.8).

RANGE: C. and s. Alaska. Winters from Washington to s. California and s. Texas through w. Mexico to Oaxaca.

TEXAS: *Winter*: Taken north to Cooke (Nov. 21) and Dallas (Apr. 10), south to Cameron (Nov. 29), west to Culberson (Oct. 6) cos. Uncommon.

SPRAGUE'S PIPIT, *Anthus spragueii* (Audubon)

SPECIES ACCOUNT

Resembles Water Pipit, but has blackish streaks on buffy back; pinkish or yellowish legs. Length, 6½ in.; wingspan, 10¾.

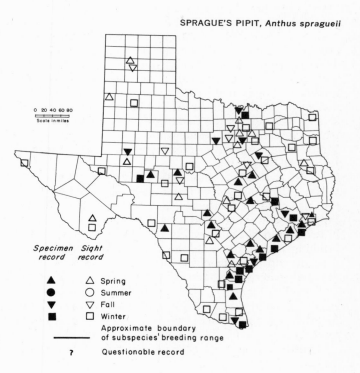

SPRAGUE'S PIPIT, *Anthus spragueii*

0 20 40 60 80
Scale in miles

Specimen | Sight
record | record

▲ | △ Spring
● | ○ Summer
▼ | ▽ Fall
■ | □ Winter

——— Approximate boundary of subspecies' breeding range

?   Questionable record

RANGE: N. Alberta to c. Manitoba, south to Montana and n.w. Minnesota. Winters from Sonora, Texas, Oklahoma, and n.w. Mississippi to s. Mexico (Guerrero to Veracruz).

TEXAS: (See map.) *Migration*: Mid-Mar. to early May; late Sept. to mid-Nov. (extremes: Mar. 7, June 4; July 21, Nov. 22). Fairly common to scarce through most parts; rare in Trans-Pecos. *Winter*: Late Nov. to late Mar. Uncommon to scarce in most areas; extremely rare in northern Panhandle and Trans-Pecos.

HAUNTS AND HABITS: Dubbed "Missouri Skylark" by Audubon, the Sprague's Pipit is an elusive songster of open country. At home on the northern Great Plains, this pipit frequents short-grass prairies, where it constructs a bulky, often loosely arched nest in a grassy clump or depression in the ground. During migration and winter in Texas, as elsewhere, Sprague's may be found hunting insects and seeds in weedy fields and the vicinity of airports as well as in a wide variety of grasslands. Very low turf on dry ground seems to be the favorite feeding ground in both summer and winter. At times it associates, especially during winter and migration, with Baird's Sparrows, Chestnut-collared Longspurs, Horned Larks, and sometimes Savannah Sparrows.

The Sprague's is a timid bird and sometimes will remain motionless, even on bare ground, at the approach of an intruder, attempting thereby to escape observation. However, it usually hides in the grass, where its coloration makes detection even more difficult. When the bird flushes, it sometimes "skyrockets," often uttering its lisping note, then drops like a rock. A flock may fly away for a considerable distance or may return and alight near where it was before. Flight is strong, quick, and undulating, usually erratic and jerky, but capable of being well sustained. On the ground, the Sprague's walks gracefully or runs rapidly, frequently tipping its tail as does the Water Pipit.

This pipit's typical call note is a single *tsip*, uttered in series and mostly while the bird is on the wing; it is rather harsher, sharper, and squeakier than the note of the Water Pipit. The Sprague's remarkable flight song draws the attention of almost all observers who have seen it on the bird's breeding ground. In fact, it was this activity that first called Audubon's attention to the species. The male rises from the ground, sometimes to a height of three hundred feet, where it flies in circles. Spreading its tail and holding its wings V-shaped, it thus sails and sings. It remains in the air, sometimes for twenty minutes or more, circling and singing, after which it fixes its wings, dives at great speed back to earth, and alights on the ground, later to repeat the performance. The song, seldom heard in Texas, is a soft tinkling melody of eight or more notes on a descending scale; it resembles somewhat the song of a thrush.

DETAILED ACCOUNT: NO SUBSPECIES

DESCRIPTION: *Adults, nuptial plumage*: Acquired by partial prenuptial molt. Above dull cinnamon buff, pinkish buff, or clay color, heavily streaked on pileum, slightly so on hindneck, with fuscous to dull olive brown, heavily spotted or streaked with same colors on back, less conspicuously so on rump and upper tail-coverts; tail fuscous black, middle pair of tail feathers fuscous, broadly edged with wood brown, drab, or light drab, which becomes whitish when worn; two outer tail feathers white, except edge of inner webs which for basal two-thirds of feathers is more or less narrowly brown; third feather with outer web and tip of inner web partly or wholly white; wings between buffy brown and hair brown or dark drab, inner webs of secondaries palest; wing-coverts edged with dull light cinnamon buff, outer edgings of wing-quills similar, but rather darker on tertials; tips of primaries, secondaries, and tertials dull white; sides of head dull cinnamon buff to clay color, very narrowly and obscurely streaked, except on lores, with dull brown, rather poorly defined superciliary stripe dull buffy white; lower parts white or buffy white; jugulum and upper breast dull warm buff, narrowly and rather sparsely streaked with fuscous or fuscous black; sides and flanks tawny olive or isabella color; lining of wing white or buffy white, outer under wing-coverts with small spots of hair brown or fuscous. Maxilla brownish black, slate black, or dull brown; tip of mandible drab; basal portion of mandible and edges of maxilla flesh color, dull white, ecru drab, or straw color; iris vandyke brown; legs and feet light ecru drab, flesh color, or pale flesh color; claws isabella color. *Adult male, winter*: Acquired by complete postnuptial molt. Similar to nuptial adults, but upper and lower parts darker and more richly colored; ground color of upper surface darker—dull cinnamon buff or clay color; breast, sides, and flanks cinnamon buff to light clay color; streaks on jugulum broader and more blended. *First nuptial*: Acquired by partial prenuptial molt. Similar to nuptial adults. *First winter*: Acquired by partial postjuvenal molt, which does not involve wing-quills or tail. Similar to adults in winter, but more extensively blackish above; breast and sides more pinkish buff. *Juvenal*: Acquired by complete postnatal molt. Upper parts light buff or cinnamon buff, boldly spotted with dull black or brownish black, feathers with lighter, sometimes whitish, tips, imparting squamate appearance, particularly on back; jugulum and breast warm buff or pale cinnamon buff, usually lighter than nuptial adults; streaks on jugulum and breast usually more numerous than in adults and extending to sides of body. Bill with no yellow; otherwise similar to nuptial adults.

MEASUREMENTS: *Adult male*: Wing, 77.0–84.6 (average, 81.3) mm.; tail, 54.1–61.0 (57.9); bill (exposed culmen), 10.9–12.4 (11.7); tarsus, 22.1–24.4 (23.1); middle toe without claw, 15.0–17.0 (16.0). *Adult female*: Wing, 75.4–85.1 (79.2); tail, 50.5–62.0 (57.7); bill, 11.4–13.0 (11.9); tarsus, 22.6–24.4 (23.4); middle toe, 15.5–17.5 (16.5).

TEXAS: *Winter*: Taken north to Cooke, east to Chambers (Apr. 15), south to Cameron, west to Martin (Sept. 29) cos.

Waxwings: Bombycillidae

BOHEMIAN WAXWING, *Bombycilla garrulus*
(Linnaeus)

SPECIES ACCOUNT

Bombycilla garrula of A.O.U. check-list, 1957 (see Appendix A). Resembles Cedar Waxwing (see below), but larger and grayer (especially on under parts, where gray replaces yellow of Cedar); has rusty crissum; conspicuous white and yellow wing-markings. Length, 8¼ in.; wingspan, 13¾; weight, 2 oz.

RANGE: Coniferous forests of n. Scandinavia, n. Russia, and n. Siberia, and of n.w. North America from c. Alaska to n. Manitoba, south to c. Washington and n.w. Montana. Winters south erratically to s. Eurasia, and in North America to California, Texas, Arkansas, and Nova Scotia.

TEXAS: (See map.) *Winter*: Late Nov. to Apr. (extremes: Nov. 9, May 4). Extremely rare visitor to northern Panhandle; casual in remainder of northern portion, south to Midland, Fort Worth, Dallas, and Tyler. Reported from College Station (3 birds, Apr., ca. 1929, Mrs. E. L. Scoates), San Antonio (Jan. 27–28, 1970, C. R. Bender, G. B. Harding), and Corpus Christi (May 3, 1946, F. M. Packard); other sightings from southern half lack substantiation.

HAUNTS AND HABITS: The Bohemian Waxwing is one of three members of the Bombycillidae—a family of sleek, crested birds given to sporadic wandering, especially in winter, in search of food, mainly fleshy fruits. In North America, *Bombycilla garrulus* dwells, as long as food is available, in northern coniferous forests. Here it places its nest well up in an isolated pine, spruce, or tamarack growing in open muskeg; nesting often takes place in loose colonies, which may or may not be reused in subsequent years.

The Bohemian is found at times in enormous flocks; some winters the species irrupts in almost unbelievable numbers south of the breeding range, though during other winters, flocks are virtually absent. Thus far, these throngs have stopped far short of Texas. Berries are the chief food; a bit of flycatching is done in summer. During winter months, troops of *B. garrulus* scour residential areas for trees and shrubs bearing small fruit—mountain ash, hawthorn, crab apple, juniper, others. When the Bohemian finds plants in good fruit it settles down for however long it takes to exhaust the supply. The bird is a voracious eater and, like the Cedar Waxwing, will often gorge itself to repletion, then sit about the trees waiting for its meal to digest before wandering on in search of other fruitful grounds.

Its ordinary vocalization can scarcely be termed a song. Though rather weak, it is rougher, louder, and more far carrying than that of the Cedar Waxwing, and has been represented by the syllables *te-e-e-e-e* or *zir-r-r-r*.

DETAILED ACCOUNT: ONE SUBSPECIES

AMERICAN BOHEMIAN WAXWING, *Bombycilla garrulus carolinensis* (Miller)

Race not in A.O.U. check-list, 1957 (see Appendix A).

DESCRIPTION: *Adult male, nuptial plumage (cinnamon phase)*: Acquired by wear from winter plumage. Narrow line across forehead, with nasal tufts, black; remainder of forehead and sides of anterior crown russet; middle of crown and short, pointed crest between wood brown and drab; hindneck wood brown; back drab; upper tail-coverts rather light mouse gray; base of tail like upper tail-coverts; tail feathers broadly tipped with yellow—between lemon chrome and light cadmium; remainder of tail shading from dark mouse gray to blackish mouse gray subter-

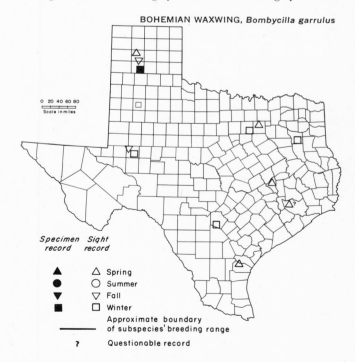

BOHEMIAN WAXWING, *Bombycilla garrulus*

0 20 40 60 80
Scale in miles

Specimen Sight
record   record

▲   △   Spring
●   ○   Summer
▼   ▽   Fall
■   □   Winter
——— Approximate boundary of subspecies' breeding range
?   Questionable record

minally; outer webs of primaries blackish mouse gray to dark mouse gray, inner webs deep mouse gray to dark mouse gray, inner edges mouse gray to rather light mouse gray, with broad lemon chrome terminal stripe on outer webs, turning more or less to white and becoming narrower and shorter on outer primaries and practically disappearing on outermost feather; all primaries, except usually outermost two, also tipped with white on inner webs, becoming narrower toward inner margin which joins yellow on outer webs, producing very conspicuous Z-shaped light markings; secondaries rather deep mouse gray, lighter on inner edges, with short, broad, terminal stripe of white on outer webs, and each feather with narrow scarlet red waxlike appendage; tertials rather dark drab; primary coverts blackish mouse gray, broadly tipped with white; remainder of upper wing-coverts between drab and hair brown; black loral stripe continuous with black stripe on anterior forehead and extending as superciliary stripe, also under eye to its middle; white or whitish streak on posterior portion of lower eyelid; malar stripe white to cream color, this posteriorly and sometimes entirely light tawny, broadening out posteriorly to below eye; sides of neck like upper surface, but rather lighter, ear-coverts dull fawn color; chin black, sometimes distinctly defined posteriorly, however, usually merging more or less broadly into dull wood brown of jugulum; breast, abdomen, and sides rather light drab with a concealed silky white tuft on each side opposite lower breast or upper abdomen; anal region light colonial buff; flanks between light grayish olive and light drab; lower tail-coverts light russet to light hazel; lining of wing rather light mouse gray, outwardly more or less irregularly spotted with mouse gray. *Adult male, nuptial (gray phase)*: Similar to cinnamon phase, but entire plumage more grayish, crest drab, back between hair brown and drab, jugulum drab, abdomen and breast rather light mouse gray; in worn summer plumage decidedly paler above in both phases. Bill black or blackish plumbeous, but plumbeous, pale slate blue, or purple at base of mandible; iris black, claret brown, or dark red; legs and feet black or grayish black. *Adult male, winter*: Acquired by complete postnuptial molt. Similar to corresponding phase of nuptial adult male, but somewhat darker, particularly on pileum and back. *Adult female, nuptial*: Acquired by wear from winter. Similar in both phases to nuptial adult male, but yellow tip of tail narrower; red waxlike tips of secondaries smaller, particularly narrower and fewer; yellow terminal stripes on outer webs of primaries averaging slightly paler and smaller (shorter or narrower); white tips on inner webs of primaries narrower; black chin-patch smaller and less clearly black (more brownish or grayish), particularly on hind portion. In worn summer plumage, like male, decidedly paler than in spring. *Adult female, winter*: Acquired by complete postnuptial molt. Similar to nuptial adult female but somewhat darker, particularly on upper surface. *Male, first nuptial*: Similar to nuptial adult male, but wing-quills duller, more brownish, and rather lighter; red waxlike tips on secondaries much smaller and usually fewer; terminal streaklike spots at tips of outer webs of primaries narrower or shorter and mostly white to wax yellow or citrine yellow, thus much paler than in fully adult bird; inner webs of primaries entirely without white tips. *Male, first winter*: Similar to first nuptial male but somewhat darker, particularly on upper surface. *Female, first nuptial*: Similar to nuptial adult female, but wing-quills lighter, more brownish, red waxlike tips of secondaries smaller and fewer, streaklike tips of outer webs of primaries smaller and white or very pale yellow, inner webs without white tips. *Female, first winter*: Acquired by partial postjuvenal molt, not involving wing-quills or tail. Like first nuptial female but somewhat darker, particularly above. *Male, juvenal*: Acquired by postnatal growth. Upper surface between hair brown and drab, but forehead paler; wings and tail much as in first winter, but wing-coverts darker and duller; crest shorter; loral stripe and superciliary stripe chaetura drab to chaetura black; postocular stripe grayish white or buffy white; auriculars dull drab; chin and upper part of throat light cartridge buff to dull light pinkish buff; remainder of lower surface hair brown to between hair brown and deep grayish olive, rather obscurely streaked with buffy white or pale dull buff, middle of breast and abdomen buffy

white or pale dull buff, and lower tail-coverts dull cinnamon to dull cinnamon rufous. Bill black; iris dark brown or red; legs and feet black. *Female, juvenal*: Acquired by postnatal growth. Similar to juvenal male, but yellow tail-tip narrower; long streaklike tips on outer webs of primaries more whitish or of paler yellow and smaller (shorter); red waxlike tips of secondaries smaller and usually fewer.

MEASUREMENTS: *Adult male*: Wing, 110.0–119.1 (average, 114.0) mm.; tail, 58.9–70.1 (63.8); bill (exposed culmen), 10.4–11.9 (11.7); tarsus, 20.1–21.6 (20.6); middle toe without claw, 16.0–19.0 (17.0). *Adult female*: Wing, 110.0–120.9 (114.3); tail, 58.9–70.1 (63.2); bill, 9.9–11.9 (10.9); tarsus, 19.0–21.6 (20.9); middle toe, 15.0–19.0 (17.0).

RANGE: C. Alaska to c. Mackenzie, south to c. Washington and n.w. Montana. Winters from s. Alaska and Newfoundland to California, Texas, and New Jersey.

TEXAS: *Winter*: One specimen: Randall Co., Palo Duro Canyon State Park (Dec. 26, 1936, T. F. Smith).

CEDAR WAXWING, *Bombycilla cedrorum* Vieillot

SPECIES ACCOUNT

Gregarious. Sleek; crested; silky brown plumage; black mask; short, yellow-tipped tail; often with red waxlike spot on wing (secondaries); yellowish flanks, belly; white crissum. Length, 7 in.; wingspan, 11½; weight, 1¼ oz.

RANGE: S.e. Alaska across c. Canada to Newfoundland, south to c. United States, and in Appalachians to Georgia. Winters erratically in extreme s. Canada and throughout most of United States, Mexico, and Central America; also Greater Antilles (rarely).

TEXAS: (See map.) *Winter*: Nov.—mid-Oct. some years—to late May (extremes: Aug. 2, July 19). Irregularly abundant to fairly common throughout.

HAUNTS AND HABITS: On its gypsy wanderings, the

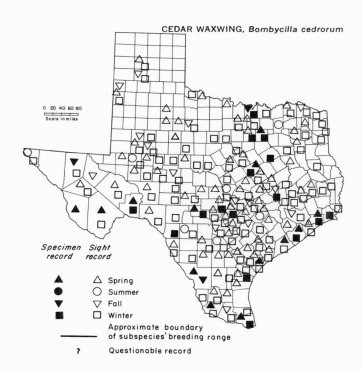

CEDAR WAXWING, *Bombycilla cedrorum*

0 20 40 60 80
Scale in miles

Specimen record   Sight record

▲   △ Spring
●   ○ Summer
▼   ▽ Fall
■   □ Winter

——— Approximate boundary of subspecies' breeding range

?   Questionable record

Cedar Waxwing ranges swamps, valleys, hills, mesas, open and even dense woodlands, as well as second growth. It is frequently found in cultivated areas—along borders of fields, in orchards, and in ornamental trees about houses, streets, dooryards, and parks of cities and towns. It seems to prefer the vicinity of trees; therefore, in drier portions of its range, it frequents mostly streams and canyons with their timber and brush. For nest support in its northern home this species usually selects a horizontal branch of a deciduous or coniferous tree or bush. Nesting, of necessity, begins very late since the waxwing—unlike many other song birds, especially finches—feeds mostly adult food (berries) to its nestlings. It must wait until small fruit in the northern United States and Canada has had time to develop. However, the bird also does a wee bit of flycatching and caterpillar gleaning.

Often, Cedar Waxwings enter Texas with the first cold norther, which may occur as early as late October or early November. They soon spread over the entire state. While numbers are greatest throughout the coldest period of winter, a few birds may linger into late May—even in southern Texas. However, this species is very erratic in its migrations, apparently being more or less influenced by the location of ample food supplies. It moves much in flocks, often of large size, until the very beginning of the breeding period. A wandering flock, having settled momentarily into a large fruit-bearing pyracantha, native cedar (*Juniperus*), or hackberry (*Celtis*) will avidly devour berries, sometimes denuding the plant in a matter of minutes. Individuals that remain as late as May feed largely on mulberries (*Morus*).

Flight of this bird, whether in flocks or singly, is rather easy, at times swift, often somewhat undulating; it can be long sustained. The Cedar moves with rapid and numerous wing-beats, except for short distances it may glide on set wings. When a flock alights in a tree, the birds often sit close together, usually upright, and almost always facing into the wind. While it descends to the ground for bathing, drinking, and feeding, it prefers trees, especially, and bushes. It is a very sociable bird. The following well-known observation illustrates the attraction Cedar Waxwings have for one another: An individual at the end of a row of birds perching on a limb will pick a cherry and pass it to the next bird, which in turn passes it to the one beyond. Sometimes the fruit will be passed all the way to the end of the line and even back again. Vernon Bailey noted at Navasota (Grimes Co.), December 16, 1904, an interesting behavior of the species. A flock of nine came down to the Navasota River to drink, and found on the steep bank a tree bent down and trailing one of its limbs in the water. The birds alighted on the upper part, slowly made their way down the branch to the water and, thus clinging, drank until satisfied.

This bird has a very weak voice. Virtually its only vocalization is a lisping call that is audible for only a short distance; it is fairly well indicated by the syllable *see* several times repeated.

DETAILED ACCOUNT: TWO SUBSPECIES

SOUTHERN CEDAR WAXWING, Bombycilla cedrorum cedrorum Vieillot

No races recognized by A.O.U. check-list, 1957 (see Appendix A).

DESCRIPTION: *Adults, nuptial plumage (gray phase)*: Acquired by wear from winter plumage. Forehead, lores, and broad stripe through eye black; behind this black a very narrow dull white line; pileum, including short crest, warm buffy brown; hindneck and back between hair brown and buffy brown; rump rather brownish neutral gray; tail dark mouse gray, broadly tipped with wax yellow; wing-quills between deep mouse gray and hair brown, most of secondaries tipped with narrow waxlike scarlet tips, inner margins of basal portion of secondaries brownish white; wing-coverts like back; sides of head sayal brown; sides of throat and breast similar to back but paler; chin dull black; middle of lower breast paler; flanks and abdomen olive ocher to dull olive yellow; lining of wing dull drab gray or light dull drab; lower tail-coverts dull grayish white or yellowish white. Bill black, basal half of mandible sometimes dull brown; iris dark brown or dark red; legs, feet, and claws black. *Adults, nuptial (brown phase)*: Acquired by wear from winter. Similar to gray phase, but both upper and lower parts much more reddish or cinnamon brown; pileum cinnamon brown; back sepia, slightly grayish, and breast between sayal brown and snuff brown. *Adults, winter*: Acquired by complete postnuptial molt. Similar to nuptial adults but upper parts averaging somewhat darker. *First nuptial*: Acquired by wear from first winter. Similar to nuptial adults but lacks red waxlike tips of secondaries or, if present, very small and few. *First winter*: Acquired by partial postjuvenal molt, which does not involve wing-quills or tail. Like first nuptial male and female but averaging somewhat darker above. *Juvenal*: Acquired by postnatal growth. Lores and narrow line across forehead dull black; another narrow line across forehead, together with superciliary stripe, grayish white; upper parts between hair brown and drab, slightly streaked or mottled with paler color; sides of head dull light buffy brown; cheeks streaked with whitish; chin light buff or warm buff; jugulum, lateral part of breast, with sides and flanks, between hair brown and grayish olive, anterior lower parts streaked narrowly and obscurely with dull white or buffy white, and on sides and flanks broadly with dull white; abdomen, crissum, and middle of breast dull white or greenish white; wings and tail as in adult. Bill brownish black, paler at base; feet plumbeous.

MEASUREMENTS: *Adult male*: Wing, 90.9–98.1 (average, 93.7) mm.; tail, 52.6–61.0 (56.1); bill (exposed culmen), 8.9–10.9 (9.9); tarsus, 16.0–17.5 (16.8); middle toe without claw, 13.0–15.5 (14.2). *Adult female*: Wing, 90.9–99.1 (92.7); tail, 51.1–59.9 (53.8); bill, 8.9–10.4 (9.4); tarsus, 16.0–18.0 (16.8); middle toe, 13.0–15.0 (14.2).

RANGE: Colorado and n. Arkansas to Massachusetts, south to Oklahoma and n. Georgia. Winters irregularly from n.e. United States through Mexico to Panama; also Greater Antilles (rarely).

TEXAS: *Winter*: Taken north to Cooke, east to Jefferson, south to Cameron, west to Culberson (Oct. 11) cos. Irregularly abundant.

IDAHO CEDAR WAXWING, Bombycilla cedrorum larifuga Burleigh

No races recognized by A.O.U. check-list, 1957 (see Appendix A).

DESCRIPTION: *Adults, nuptial plumage*: Similar to *B. c. cedrorum* and of same size, but paler above and below.

RANGE: S.e. British Columbia to s. Manitoba, south to Oregon and s. Montana. Winters irregularly from breeding range through Mexico and Central America to Colombia.

TEXAS: *Winter*: Two specimens: lower Rio Grande Valley (no date, G. B. Sennett); Brazoria Co., 12 mi. northwest of Columbia (Mar. 2, 1892, W. Lloyd).

Silky Flycatchers: Ptilogonatidae

PHAINOPEPLA, *Phainopepla nitens* (Swainson)

Species Account

Silky Flycatcher of older authors. Slim-bodied; pointed crest; long tail; red eyes. *Male*: glossy blue-black; large white wing-patch (apparent only in flight). *Female*: dark gray (paler below); small whitish wing-patch. Length, 7½ in.; wingspan, 11½; weight, 1 oz.

RANGE: C. California to Trans-Pecos Texas, south through deserts to n.w. Mexico and over Mexican Plateau to Puebla and Veracruz. Largely withdraws from northern limits in winter; occasionally wanders into contiguous areas along eastern border of U.S. range.

TEXAS: (See map.) *Breeding*: Apr. to June (eggs, May 10 to May 19; active nest, June 3) from about 1,800 to 5,500 ft. Scarce and local west of Pecos River. *Winter*: Aug. to Apr. (extremes: July 24, May 27). Uncommon west of Pecos River, where chiefly resident (as a species); rare visitor to Midland vicinity and extreme western Edwards Plateau; casual in south Texas brush country north to Kerr, Bexar, and Victoria cos.

HAUNTS AND HABITS: The Phainopepla is the only U.S. representative of the four-species, waxwinglike Ptilogonatidae, the silky flycatchers of Middle American highlands. This sleek, wing-flashing bird lives chiefly in tall brush and scattered trees about springs, along streams, and in irrigated plots. It also frequents dense scrub and various kinds of woods—juniper, oak, mesquite, others—on hillsides, mountain slopes and canyons, desert washes and flats. Trees parasitized by mistletoe are especially favored since mistletoe berries are a prime food. *P. nitens* also occurs in the vicinity of cultivated areas, particularly ornamental trees about dwellings. In the Trans-Pecos—only part of Texas where the Phainopepla occurs with any regularity—this bird is to be looked for in tall cottonwoods or pecans about isolated ranch houses. Like the White-winged Dove, Hooded Oriole, and various other arid-land species, it seems to seek out the tallest vegetation available in the landscape. This species, as does its relative the Gray Silky Flycatcher, *Ptilogonys cinereus*, of Mexico, usually perches on or near tops of trees, bushes, or cacti. Where the bird is numerous it is gregarious and flocks of fifty and upward are frequent.

(But not in Texas; here even one Phainopepla is an event!)

Phainopepla's ordinary flight is rather short and nervous, but buoyant; when prolonged it is even and direct, though not especially swift. Starting out for a longer flight, a bird rises, often at an upward angle from a treetop, then moves on a straight and level course with a light and graceful movement, displaying its white wing-patches. This silky flycatcher is restless, shy, and suspicious, and if alarmed usually dashes into the brush. When disturbed, it jerks its tail and raises its crest—actions which give it a very "authoritative" appearance.

In spring, the male Phainopepla gives a delightful performance which apparently serves the dual function of asserting territorial rights and attracting the female. Singing all the while, he launches into the air and executes somersaults and other evolutions, frequently with crest raised and wings held in a V. Call notes are varied. An alarm note, somewhat harsh and querulous, resembles the syllables *ka-rak*. A more frequently heard "conversational" note is a low, soft *wurp*. Phain-

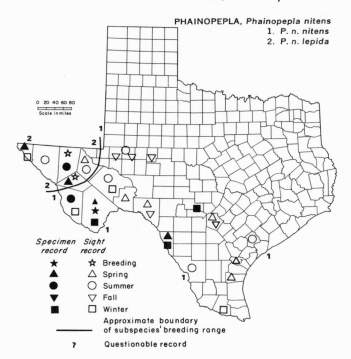

PHAINOPEPLA, *Phainopepla nitens*
1. *P. n. nitens*
2. *P. n. lepida*

0 20 40 60 80
Scale in miles

Specimen record	Sight record	
★	☆	Breeding
▲	△	Spring
●	○	Summer
▼	▽	Fall
■	□	Winter

——— Approximate boundary of subspecies' breeding range

? Questionable record

opepla song is a weak, wheezy disconnected warble. Males sing infrequently from April into June.

DETAILED ACCOUNT: TWO SUBSPECIES

MEXICAN PHAINOPEPLA, *Phainopepla nitens nitens* (Swainson)

DESCRIPTION: *Adult male, nuptial plumage*: Acquired by wear from winter plumage. Above and below, including crest, glossy greenish blue-black; tail black, inner webs of rectrices fuscous black, outer edges greenish or bluish black, like upper parts, or somewhat less glossy; wings chaetura black or fuscous black, upper wing-coverts, outer edges of primaries and secondaries, and tertials similar to back, but rather duller; large white area in middle of wing formed by white portions of inner webs of middle part of primaries, occupying almost half length of feathers. Bill black; iris carmine; legs and feet black. *Adult male, winter*: Acquired by complete postnuptial molt. Similar to nuptial adult male but duller; abdomen and crissum narrowly edged with dull white or pale gray. *Adult female, nuptial*: Acquired by wear from winter. Upper surface olivaceous mouse gray, but middle portion of crest feathers dark mouse gray, though margins like rest of upper surface; tail fuscous black, outermost feathers fuscous, outer web of outermost tail feather very narrowly margined with brownish white, remainder of feathers narrowly edged externally with color of upper surface; wing fuscous, margins of wing-coverts like back, outermost lesser coverts with paler edges, median and greater series tipped conspicuously with brownish white, which on greater series extends as narrow edgings on distal half of feathers; wing-quills edged with color of back; tertials narrowly margined with brownish white; sides of head and neck like upper parts; lower parts similar but slightly paler, sometimes posterior lower surface strongly tinged with dull brown, and crissum paler, feathers tipped with brownish white; lining of wing rather light mouse gray with some darker spots on outer lower wing-coverts. *Adult female, winter*: Acquired by complete postnuptial molt. Similar to nuptial adult female, but light edgings of wing-coverts and tertials broader; lesser wing-coverts tipped with gray or grayish white, brownish white tips of feathers of crissum and lower abdomen broader. *Male, first nuptial*: Acquired by wear from first winter. Similar to nuptial adult male but duller, posterior lower parts often decidedly brownish, wing-quills more brownish black with less metallic sheen. *Male, first winter*: Acquired by complete postjuvenal molt. Similar to adult male in winter, but lesser wing-coverts narrowly, greater coverts and tertials very broadly, tipped with grayish white or buffy white, feathers of posterior lower parts broadly, those of remainder of plumage narrowly, tipped with drab. *Female, first nuptial*: Acquired by wear from first winter. Similar to nuptial adult female, but lower parts paler, particularly abdomen. *Female, first winter*: Acquired by complete postjuvenal molt. Practically identical with first nup-

tial, except somewhat darker. *Juvenal*: Similar to nuptial adult female, but much more brownish above, feathers of crest fuscous or fuscous black without conspicuously paler margins; paler and more brownish below, abdomen decidedly paler than anterior lower parts; whitish margins of wing-quills and coverts rather more brownish or buffy and somewhat more extensive; tips of lower tail-coverts much less distinct. *Natal*: Cream white.

MEASUREMENTS: *Adult male*: Wing, 96.0–103.1 (average, 98.8) mm.; tail, 93.5–104.9 (100.3); bill (exposed culmen), 9.9–10.9 (10.7); tarsus, 17.5–19.0 (18.3); middle toe without claw, 13.5–14.5 (14.2). *Adult female*: Wing, 89.9–97.1 (94.7); tail, 90.9–98.1 (94.2); bill, 9.9–10.9 (10.4); tarsus, 17.0–19.0 (18.0); middle toe, 13.0–15.0 (14.0).

RANGE: Trans-Pecos Texas to s.w. Tamaulipan highlands, south to n.w. Durango and s.e. Oaxaca.

TEXAS: *Breeding*: Altitudinal range, 1,800 to 5,500 ft. Collected in Brewster and Presidio cos. Scarce. *Winter*: Two specimens: Kerr Co., 10 mi. west of Kerrville (Feb. 9, 1895, H. Lacey); Maverick Co., Eagle Pass (Feb., 1864, H. E. Dresser).

NESTING: Similar to that of *P. n. lepida* (see below).

NORTHERN PHAINOPEPLA, *Phainopepla nitens lepida* Van Tyne

DESCRIPTION: *Adult male and female, nuptial plumage*: Similar to *P. n. nitens* but decidedly smaller, particularly wing and tail.

MEASUREMENTS: *Adult male*: Wing, 89.9–98.1 (average, 93.7) mm.; tail, 90.9–101.1 (94.7); bill (exposed culmen), 9.9–11.9 (10.9); tarsus, 16.0–18.0 (17.0); middle toe without claw, 11.9–15.0 (13.7). *Adult female*: Wing, 86.1–91.9 (88.6); tail, 83.1–93.0 (88.1); bill, 10.9–11.9 (11.2); tarsus, 17.0–19.0 (18.3); middle toe, 11.9–14.0 (13.2).

RANGE: C. California to s.w. Utah, south to s. Baja California and Trans-Pecos Texas.

TEXAS: *Breeding*: Altitudinal range, 3,000 to 5,000 ft. Two specimens: Culberson Co., 7 mi. north of Pine Spring (Aug. 18, 1940, D. Quimby); Jeff Davis Co., 21 mi. west of Fort Davis (May 23, 1938, G. H. Lowery, Jr.). *Migration*: Collected in El Paso (1 specimen) and Brewster (3) cos. Scarce. *Winter*: One specimen: Brewster Co., 22 mi. south of Alpine (Feb. 28, 1935, J. Van Tyne).

NESTING: *Nest*: In more or less open country, in brushy thickets or open woods, often near water, in cultivated areas or in towns; placed in cottonwood, willow, mesquite, elderberry, sycamore, live oak, or other tree or bush, usually 8–25 ft. above ground; rather flat saucer, shallow, loosely constructed of twigs, plant stems, weeds, grasses, soft down, cotton, and other vegetable fibers; lined with finer materials of same character. *Eggs*: 2–4, usually 3; ovate; light gray, yellowish gray, or greenish white; spotted with black or olive brown, with violet gray and faint lilac shell markings, confluent in wreath at large end; average size, 22.4 × 16.5 mm.

Shrikes: Laniidae

NORTHERN SHRIKE, *Lanius excubitor* Linnaeus

SPECIES ACCOUNT

Great Grey Shrike of Old World authors. *Male*: resembles Loggerhead (see below), but black mask does not extend across forehead; faintly barred breast, flanks; less white in wings, tail; pale base to lower mandible (more apparent in winter). *Female*: somewhat darker above than male; duller, buffier below. Length, 10 in.; wingspan, 14¼; weight, 2¼ oz.

RANGE: Eurasia, n. Africa, Alaska, and n. Canada. Largely resident in Old World. In North America, winters south irregularly to n. California, n. New Mexico, and Maryland; highly erratic farther south.

TEXAS: (See map.) *Winter*: Nov. to Jan. (extremes: Oct. 13, Jan. 31). Rare and very irregular in northern third; casual south to upper and central coasts.

HAUNTS AND HABITS: Members of Laniidae are songbirds with bold, hawklike habits. Two of the sixty-seven species in the family are found in North America and both occur in Texas. In arctic and subarctic areas of the Western Hemisphere, the Northern Shrike is an inhabitant of scattered growths, open woods, thickets, and brushy swamps and bogs. Its bulky nest is usually well concealed in the branches of a dense tree, typically a small conifer. During the nonbreeding season, it moves south into the northern United States, where this sentinel retains its preference for open and semi-open country. Fence posts, treetops, or high wires provide advantageous lookouts.

The flight and other behavior of the Northern Shrike is very much like that of the Loggerhead (see below), although its wing-beats are apparently not quite as rapid. It can move very swiftly and turn quickly in the air if necessary. It often catches birds on the wing after the manner of a hawk, but with beak, not talons. When perched, it sits upright and sometimes moves its tail up and down. If a mouse or other small rodent is observed, the bird dashes downward and picks up the victim. Occasionally it hovers over an object in the grass, much as does a Sparrow Hawk. Large insects—grasshoppers, beetles, caterpillars, others—are important in its diet. The Northern is ordinarily wary, but sometimes becomes so intent on pursuit of prey that it seems unaware of human observers. It hunts as long as it can find anything to kill, often as if just for pleas-

ure, and after satisfying its hunger hangs what is left on thorns or fence barbs—seemingly for future use, though certainly much that it thus disposes of is never again visited.

The ordinary call of *Lanius excubitor* is somewhat harsh and not frequently heard. This shrike has also a fairly musical song, which is a rather soft whistle composed of several trills but interspersed with harsher notes. The song is almost never heard in Texas.

DETAILED ACCOUNT: ONE SUBSPECIES

GREAT NORTHERN SHRIKE, *Lanius excubitor invictus* Grinnell

DESCRIPTION: *Adult male, nuptial plumage*: Acquired by partial prenuptial molt. Upper surface pale, rather brownish, neutral gray to brownish light neutral gray, anterior part of forehead, superciliary stripe, ends of scapulars and upper tail-coverts white, grayish white, or very pale gray; tail fuscous black or brownish black, two middle pairs of feathers narrowly tipped with dull white or brownish white, four outer pairs of feathers with broad white tips, broadest on outermost and on outer web of outermost rectrix extending to base; primaries fuscous, with conspicuous white spot near base occupying both webs, visible

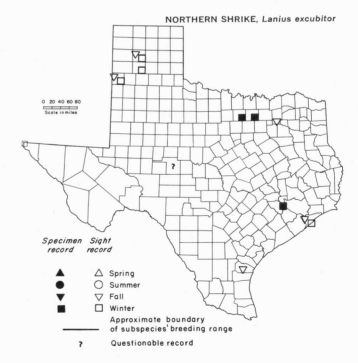

NORTHERN SHRIKE, *Lanius excubitor*

0 20 40 60 80
Scale in miles

Specimen record	Sight record	
▲	△	Spring
●	○	Summer
▼	▽	Fall
■	□	Winter

——— Approximate boundary of subspecies' breeding range

? Questionable record

as relatively small spot in closed wing; secondaries and tertials fuscous black or brownish black, broad tips of secondaries, narrow tips of tertials, and inner primaries white or grayish white; lesser coverts similar to color of back, but rather more brownish; greater and median coverts brownish black; primary coverts fuscous or fuscous black; broad postocular stripe extending below eyes black, this color not reaching across forehead; lores black, more or less mixed with dark gray; lower surface, cheeks, and sides of throat and of breast white or dull white, much vermiculated on all but chin, throat, and middle of abdomen with narrow bars of gray like back, abdomen and crissum sometimes slightly washed with buff; lining of wing white, under wing-coverts sometimes slightly mottled with mouse gray. Bill black, but base of mandible paler; iris burnt umber; legs and feet black or grayish black. *Adult male, winter*: Acquired by complete postnuptial molt. Similar to nuptial adult male, but bill black, dull slate color, or dull brown, base and cutting edges of maxilla purplish white, dull white, flesh color, dull yellowish, grayish white, or slate color; iris dark brown; legs and feet black. *Adult female, nuptial*: Acquired by partial prenuptial molt. Similar to nuptial adult male, but upper parts somewhat darker; light gray on anterior part of forehead more conspicuous; lower surface usually a little more buffy. *Adult female, winter*: Acquired by complete postnuptial molt. Similar to nuptial adult female, but sometimes feathers of back with slight mouse gray tips; breast and jugulum sometimes washed with vinaceous buff. Bill brown, base light flesh color. *Male and female, second winter*: Acquired by complete postnuptial molt. Like corresponding sex of adults in winter. *Male, first nuptial*: Acquired by partial prenuptial molt. Similar to nuptial adult male but duller, gray of upper surface more overlaid with buffy brown or light brownish olive; white of upper tail-coverts more or less washed with gray, bars and vermiculations of lower surface usually more conspicuous and extensive; black of sides of head more or less obscured by brown or gray. *Male, first winter*: Acquired by partial post-juvenal molt. Similar to first nuptial male and female, but upper parts very much more brownish, back buffy brown, upper tail-coverts light pinkish cinnamon, barred with buffy brown or fuscous, tips of scapulars pinkish cinnamon or cinnamon; tail fuscous black, tipped with white as in adults; wing-quills fuscous, tipped with light buff or buffy white, white spot at base of primaries very much reduced or practically absent, lesser wing-coverts dull cinnamon, as are tips of greater and median coverts; sides of head similar to upper parts except space around eye dull cinnamon buff, and auriculars and postocular region fuscous, replacing black stripe of adult; lower parts much washed with cinnamon, dark gray or brownish vermiculations very conspicuous. Bill dull slaty brown, base of mandible flesh color. *Female, first nuptial*: Acquired by partial prenuptial molt. Like first nuptial male, but plumage somewhat darker both above and below, lower surface more often suffused with vinaceous buff. *Female, first winter*: Acquired by partial postjuvenal molt. Similar to first winter male, but upper and lower parts darker. *Juvenal*: Acquired by complete postnatal molt. Similar to first winter male and female, but pileum, sides of head and of neck, hindneck, scapulars, upper tail-coverts, and rump finely vermiculated with hair brown or mouse gray. Bill black, slate color, or blackish slate, but base flesh color, yellow, cream color, light gull gray, or deep gull gray; iris dark brown; legs and feet dark slate color.

MEASUREMENTS: *Adult male*: Wing, 114.8–119.6 (average, 118.1) mm.; tail, 115.1–124.2 (117.9); bill (exposed culmen), 17.0–18.5 (17.8); tarsus, 26.2–29.7 (27.2); middle toe without claw, 11.9–13.2 (12.4). *Adult female*: Wing, 109.2–116.8 (113.0); tail, 108.7–117.1 (113.0); bill, 16.5–18.5 (17.8); tarsus, 26.7–27.9 (27.2); middle toe, 12.2–12.7 (12.4).

TEXAS: *Winter*: Six specimens: Wise Co., Decatur (Jan. 22, 1889, J. A. Donald; Jan. 5, 1890, W. Lloyd); Denton Co., Lake Dallas (male, Oct. 23, 1945, H. P. Kirby and W. A. Mayer; Dallas Museum of Natural History collection, no. 2469); Denton Co., 30 mi. north of Dallas (male, Nov. 29, 1945, Kirby and Mayer; Dallas Museum collection, no. 2488); Waller Co., near Hempstead (2 on Dec. 13, 1876, A. L. Kumlien and R. E. Earll).

LOGGERHEAD SHRIKE, *Lanius ludovicianus* Linnaeus

SPECIES ACCOUNT

Heavy, hook-tipped blackish bill; large rounded head; stooped posture; rapid, undulating flight; hawk-like behavior. Black mask meets on forehead; gray above; whitish below; white patches in black wings and tail. Length, 9 in.; wingspan, 12¾; weight, 1¾ oz.

RANGE: S. Canada, south to s. Baja California, mainland Mexico (in mountains to Guerrero and Oaxaca), Texas (except extreme south), U.S. Gulf coast, and s. Florida. Migrant races winter mainly in middle and southern breeding range to c. Mexico.

TEXAS: (See map.) *Breeding*: Mar. to late Aug. (eggs, Mar. 6 to June 15; feeding young, Aug. 23) from near sea level to 7,000 ft. Locally common to uncommon in northern half, Trans-Pecos, and eastern third; irregular on central prairie; uncommon to scarce and very local on southern Edwards Plateau and in south Texas brush country, south to Duval Co. and Corpus Christi. *Winter*: Late Aug. to early Apr. Very common to fairly common throughout.

HAUNTS AND HABITS: This shrike, like the other species in its family, seems a paradox. It is both a sweet singer and a hook-billed killer of animals approaching itself in size. The peculiar habit of impaling its prey—usually large insects or small birds and mammals (mice, shrews)—on thorns and barbed wire has earned for it the name "butcher bird." It dwells in open or semiopen country, where scattered trees, thorn brush, hedgerows, and wood margins provide acceptable nesting sites. It is found regularly and commonly along highways and railroads where it is given to perching,

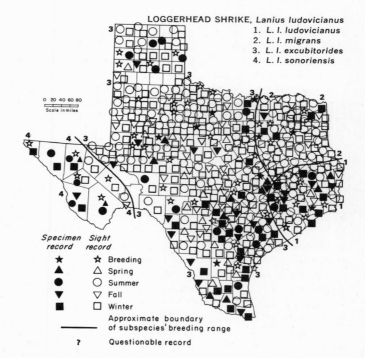

LOGGERHEAD SHRIKE, *Lanius ludovicianus*

1. *L. l. ludovicianus*
2. *L. l. migrans*
3. *L. l. excubitorides*
4. *L. l. sonoriensis*

0 20 40 60 80
Scale in miles

Specimen record / Sight record

★ / ☆ Breeding
▲ / △ Spring
● / ○ Summer
▼ / ▽ Fall
■ / □ Winter

——— Approximate boundary of subspecies' breeding range

? Questionable record

conspicuously and invariably alone, on wires, fences, weed stalks, and tops of bushes and trees.

The flight of the Loggerhead is usually low, swift, and direct and performed by very rapid, continuous wing-beats. Its habit of dropping suddenly from a high perch, flying just above the ground for a considerable distance, then sweeping steeply up to its second perch enables this bird to move inconspicuously from one lookout to another. This shrike seems to be awkward on the ground and is seldom found there except in pursuit of prey.

A typical call of the Loggerhead is a rather harsh note that E. H. Forbush has represented as *jo-ree*. The bird often sounds off with a drawn out *shack, shack* or *shank, shank*. The infrequent song consists of a slow, pleasing series of light trills rather like those of the Catbird or Brown Thrasher but not as smooth and musical. Males normally sing from March into July.

DETAILED ACCOUNT: SIX SUBSPECIES

SOUTHERN LOGGERHEAD SHRIKE, *Lanius ludovicianus ludovicianus* Linnaeus

DESCRIPTION: *Adult male, nuptial plumage*: Acquired by partial prenuptial molt. Upper surface almost uniform deep neutral gray to rather brownish neutral gray, upper tail-coverts sometimes slightly paler, ends of scapulars pale gray or even dull white; tail dull black, four outer pairs of feathers broadly tipped with white, broadest on outermost pair of feathers, which are white on outer webs almost to base; wing-quills chaetura black to black, outer webs of inner secondaries and of tertials dull black, with conspicuous white spot near base of most of primaries, showing as small white spot in closed wing; secondaries and tertials rather broadly tipped with dull white or grayish white; lesser wing-coverts like back; remaining coverts dull black or chaetura black; lores, narrow band across forehead, and broad stripe across side of head, including eyes, black; cheeks, sides of throat, and entire under parts white and, excepting chin and throat, more or less washed with neutral gray and sometimes crossed by slight shadowy narrow grayish bars, these perhaps indication of immaturity. Bill black, but base drab gray; interior of mouth whitish flesh color; lower eyelid bluish cinereous; iris bister or vandyke brown; legs, feet, and claws black. *Adult male, winter*: Acquired by complete postnuptial molt. Similar to nuptial adult male, but bill brown instead of black. *Adult female, nuptial*: Acquired by partial prenuptial molt. Similar to nuptial adult male, but pileum and back somewhat darker; black at base of culmen more restricted; lower parts often washed with pale gray and slightly vermiculated. *Adult female, winter*: Acquired by complete postnuptial molt. Like nuptial adult female, but bill brown. *Male and female, second winter*: Acquired by complete postnuptial molt. Like corresponding sex of adult in winter. *Male, first nuptial*: Acquired by partial prenuptial molt. Similar to nuptial adult male, but somewhat darker above, lower parts more washed and lightly vermiculated with gray, and parts of primaries and secondaries, as well as primary coverts retained from juvenal. *Male, first winter*: Acquired by partial postjuvenal molt. Similar to first nuptial male, but bill more brownish. *Female, first nuptial*: Acquired by partial prenuptial molt. Like first nuptial male, but coloration somewhat darker. *Female, first winter*: Acquired by partial postjuvenal molt, which does not involve parts of primaries, secondaries, and primary coverts. Similar to first winter male but slightly darker; jugulum and breast more often vermiculated. *Juvenal*: Acquired by complete postnatal molt. Upper surface between drab and mouse gray, crown and upper tail-coverts washed with dull light buff, scapulars paler than back; pileum, hindneck, scapulars,

rump, and upper tail-coverts with narrow bars or vermiculations of dark gray or fuscous; tail brownish black, but middle tail feathers tipped with dull buff; wing-quills fuscous black or chaetura black; tips of greater and median wing-coverts dull light pinkish cinnamon and narrowly barred with dark brown, lesser wing-coverts similar to pileum; tips of secondaries and tertials pale buff or buffy white; lores like crown or mixed with dull black, spot in front of eye blackish, and stripe beginning under eye and extending to sides of neck fuscous black or chaetura black; lower parts creamy white, breast and sometimes crissum pinkish buff; jugulum, breast, sides, and occasionally crissum, vermiculated or narrowly barred with dull brownish gray; lining of wing dull white or buffy white. Bill brownish black, base of mandible dull flesh color; iris dark brown; legs and feet dull brown. *Natal*: White, scanty, almost absent. Skin of newly hatched bird orange. Bill and feet apricot yellow.

MEASUREMENTS: *Adult male*: Wing, 90.9–99.1 (average, 95.0) mm.; tail, 91.4–104.1 (99.1); bill (exposed culmen), 14.5–17.5 (16.0); tarsus, 25.7–28.2 (26.7); middle toe without claw, 12.2–13.2 (12.7). *Adult female*: Wing, 87.9–98.1 (93.0); tail, 88.9–101.1 (96.3); bill, 15.5–16.5 (16.0); tarsus, 24.9–27.7 (26.4); middle toe, 11.7–13.2 (12.7).

RANGE: N.e. Louisiana to c. Virginia, south to s.e. Texas and s. Florida.

TEXAS: *Breeding*: Altitudinal range, near sea level to 400 ft. One collection: Chambers Co., Mont Belvieu (young birds captured, May 30, July 22, 1930. A. R. Shearer). *Winter*: Taken in Washington (1 specimen), Waller (1), and Chambers (2) cos. Fairly common.

NESTING: *Nest*: On slopes, uplands, and bottoms, usually in more open areas; in edges of woodlands, hedges, brushy tangles, and scattered bushes, often thorny, also in cultivated areas, along roadsides, in fields, along streams, or even railroad rights-of-way; in tree or bush, either in upright fork or on outer more or less horizontal limb, 5–30 ft. above ground; large, bulky, open-topped nest, rather loosely constructed, sometimes relatively flat and shallow; composed of weeds, grasses, cornstalks, roots, strips of inner bark, twigs, straw, paper, wool, cotton, and feathers; thickly lined with fine grasses, stems of herbaceous plants, cotton, and poultry and other feathers. *Eggs*: 4–6, usually 5; ovate; somewhat glossy; grayish white, yellowish white, or light greenish white, spotted and blotched with light brown, umber, yellowish brown, dull purple, and purplish gray; average size, 24.6 × 18.5 mm.

MIGRANT LOGGERHEAD SHRIKE, *Lanius ludovicianus migrans* Palmer

DESCRIPTION: *Adult male and female, nuptial plumage*: Similar to *L. l. ludovicianus*, but bill smaller (shorter and slenderer); wing longer; tail shorter and decidedly shorter than wing; upper parts lighter, upper tail-coverts often so.

MEASUREMENTS: *Adult male*: Wing, 95.0–102.1 (average, 98.3) mm.; tail, 86.1–98.1 (94.5); bill (exposed culmen), 13.5–16.0 (14.7); tarsus, 25.1–27.7 (26.4); middle toe without claw, 12.2–13.2 (12.7). *Adult female*: Wing, 91.9–101.1 (96.5); tail, 87.9–97.1 (93.0); bill, 14.0–16.0 (14.7); tarsus, 25.7–27.2 (26.7); middle toe, 12.2–13.5 (13.0).

RANGE: S.e. Manitoba to s.e. Quebec, south to n.e. Texas and Maryland. Winters from s. Wisconsin and Massachusetts to s. Texas and s.e. South Carolina.

TEXAS: *Breeding*: Altitudinal range, 250 to 500 ft. Two specimens: Ellis Co., 20 mi. south of Dallas (May 14, 1941, W. A. Mayer); Smith Co., Troup (May, 1932, S. A. Krom). *Winter*: Taken north to Cooke, east to Bowie and Galveston, south to Cameron, west to El Paso cos. Fairly common.

NESTING: Similar to that of *L. l. ludovicianus*, but average egg size, 24.1 × 17.8 mm.

WHITE-RUMPED LOGGERHEAD SHRIKE, *Lanius ludovicianus excubitorides* Swainson

DESCRIPTION: *Adult male and female, nuptial plumage*: Similar to *L. l. migrans*, but tail longer, upper parts lighter, upper tail-coverts not concolor with back but much paler, nearly or quite white; breast and sides more whitish, flanks lighter.

MEASUREMENTS: *Adult male*: Wing, 95.5–102.9 (average, 99.1) mm.; tail, 90.0–104.6 (97.3); bill (exposed culmen), 13.7–15.5 (14.7): tarsus, 26.2–27.9 (27.2); middle toe without claw, 12.7–13.7 (13.2). *Adult female*: Wing, 92.5–101.9 (96.8); tail, 89.4–97.6 (92.5); bill, 13.5–15.5 (14.2); tarsus, 25.9–27.7 (26.7); middle toe, 12.7–13.7 (13.2).

RANGE: C. Alberta to s. Manitoba, south to c. Chihuahua and n. Tamaulipas. Winters from s.e. Wyoming and n.w. Nebraska through Mexico to Oaxaca.

TEXAS: *Breeding*: Altitudinal range, 300 to 4,200 ft. Collected north to Oldham and Roberts, east to Cooke and Milam, south to Duval (eggs collected, May 28, year unknown but probably in 19th century, specimens in British Museum), west to Edwards and Mitchell cos. Locally fairly common. *Winter*: Taken north to Cooke, east to Kaufman, south to Victoria and Cameron, west to Kinney cos. Common.

NESTING: Similar to that of *L. l. ludovicianus*, but average egg size, 24.6 × 18.3 mm.

SONORA LOGGERHEAD SHRIKE, *Lanius ludovicianus sonoriensis* Miller

DESCRIPTION: *Adult male and female, nuptial plumage*: Similar to *L. l. excubitorides*, but tail much longer; bill larger; wing slightly longer; upper surface paler and rather more brownish gray; below more purely white, white tip on inner web of outer rectrix much (about 8 percent) smaller, white spot on primaries also smaller.

MEASUREMENTS: *Adult male*: Wing, 99.3–105.6 (average, 102.4) mm.; tail, 101.9–112.0 (106.7); bill (exposed culmen), 15.0–16.5 (15.7); tarsus, 26.7–28.7 (27.7); middle toe without claw, 12.7–14.2 (13.2). *Adult female*: Wing, 98.6–104.6 (101.3); tail, 101.3–109.5 (105.1); bill, 14.7–16.0 (15.2); tarsus, 25.7–28.7 (27.2); middle toe, 11.9–14.2 (13.7).

RANGE: S.e. California to Trans-Pecos Texas, south to s. Sinaloa and Durango.

TEXAS: *Breeding*: Altitudinal range, 1,700 to 7,000 ft. Collected in El Paso, Hudspeth, Culberson, Jeff Davis, Presidio, Brewster, and Pecos cos. Locally fairly common. One summer specimen: Kerr Co., 1 mi. north of Kent (July 28, 1940, W. B.

Davis). *Winter*: Taken in El Paso, Hudspeth, Culberson, and Presidio cos. Fairly common.

NESTING: Similar to that of *L. l. ludovicianus*.

NEVADA LOGGERHEAD SHRIKE, *Lanius ludovicianus nevadensis* Miller

Race not in A.O.U. check-list, 1957 (see Appendix A).

DESCRIPTION: *Adult male and female, nuptial plumage*: Similar to *L. l. excubitorides*, but tail and bill longer; hook of bill longer and more sharply curved; white tip on inner web of outermost tail feather 20 to 30 percent shorter; upper parts darker, duller, less bluish gray.

MEASUREMENTS: *Adult male*: Wing, 98.6–102.9 (average, 100.3) mm.; tail, 97.3–106.7 (102.4); bill (exposed culmen), 14.0–16.0 (15.2); tarsus, 25.4–28.2 (27.2); middle toe without claw, 13.0–13.7 (13.2). *Adult female*: Wing, 94.7–101.1 (98.3); tail, 96.3–104.4 (100.3); bill, 14.5–16.0 (15.2); tarsus, 25.9–28.2 (27.2); middle toe, 12.2–13.7 (13.2).

RANGE: S.e. Oregon to n.w. Colorado, south to c. California and n.w. New Mexico. Winters from breeding range to Sonora and Trans-Pecos Texas.

TEXAS: *Winter*: Taken in Randall (Sept. 26), Culberson (Mar. 6), and Brewster (Mar. 26) cos. Rare.

CALIFORNIA LOGGERHEAD SHRIKE, *Lanius ludovicianus gambeli* Ridgway

DESCRIPTION: *Adult male and female, nuptial plumage*: Similar to *L. l. nevadensis*, but white spot on primaries somewhat smaller; pale anterior edge of forehead narrower; remainder of upper parts darker and duller, upper tail-coverts darker, less whitish; breast and flanks darker, less whitish.

MEASUREMENTS: *Adult male*: Wing, 96.5–102.9 (average, 99.8) mm.; tail, 97.1–105.1 (102.4); bill (exposed culmen), 14.0–16.0 (15.2); tarsus, 26.2–28.7 (27.7); middle toe without claw, 12.7–14.0 (13.2). *Adult female*: Wing, 94.2–99.8 (97.3); tail, 96.5–101.9 (100.1); bill, 14.7–16.0 (15.5); tarsus, 25.1–28.7 (27.2); middle toe, 12.2–14.2 (13.2).

RANGE: S. British Columbia to w. Montana, south to n.w. Baja California. Winters from breeding range to s. Baja California and Morelos.

TEXAS: *Winter*: Taken in Armstrong (1 specimen, Aug. 23), Kerr (1), and Atascosa (3) cos. Rare.

Starlings: Sturnidae

STARLING, *Sturnus vulgaris* Linnaeus

SPECIES ACCOUNT

Also called Common Starling and European Starling. A chunky, short-tailed "blackbird" with spikelike bill; resembles meadowlark in shape; pointed wing suggests that of Purple Martin, but is shorter and broader at base. *Nuptial adult*: glossy black (appears purplish above; greenish on face, under parts, wings) with brownish spots on back; yellow bill. *Winter adult*: duller, browner above, body heavily speckled with buff and white "stars"; bill blackish, usually into January. *Immature*: brownish or dusky gray. Length, 8½ in.; wingspan, 15¼; weight, 2¾ oz.

RANGE: Native to palearctic region from Iceland and Azores to c. Asia. Winters from southern breeding range to n. Africa and plains of India. Naturalized in North America, Jamaica, South Africa, Australia, and New Zealand. Winters in America from s. Canada to n. Mexico; locally to s. Mexico. Apparently resident in other parts of introduced range.

TEXAS: (See map.) *Breeding*: Early Mar. to mid-July (no egg dates available, but nest building as early as Mar. 12; tending young as late as July 9) from near sea level to about 3,600 ft. Common to uncommon in northeastern two-thirds, southwest to Midland, San Antonio, and Corpus Christi; scarce and local south to Rio Grande delta. No nesting evidence as yet (1970) west of Pecos River or on western Edwards Plateau. *Winter*: Mid-Oct. to late Mar. (extremes: Sept. 17, May 5). Abundant to common east of Pecos River, though irregular and usually increasingly less numerous southward from 29th parallel; locally fairly common to scarce west of Pecos River.

HAUNTS AND HABITS: Members of Sturnidae constitute an Old World family of often silky-plumaged, usually gregarious, generally garrulous birds. Three of its 103 species are naturalized in the United States: two in the contiguous states—Starling and Crested Myna, *Acridotheres cristatellus*; and one in Hawaii—Indian Myna, *A. tristis. Sturnus vulgaris* is by far the most widespread of this trio of introduced aliens.

The species' current multimillion American population apparently got its start from a mere sixty birds which were released in New York City in 1890, and forty more in the same city in 1891. Success of this

hardy species in North America stems in large part from the huge and ever-increasing supply of suitable Starling habitat found here—open fields, livestock feedlots, suburbs, cities, garbage dumps, parks, cutover woodlands, and bulldozed scrub. The bird is absent from heavy forests and high mountains.

The Starling is more or less resident in North America, although there is a southwestward movement in fall and a northeasterly return in spring. This pattern differs somewhat from the more north-south routes of many native migrants but is interestingly comparable to a southwest-northeast movement of the Starling in Europe. After numerous Starling generations in the New World, the species still seems to be following the shape of Europe, rather than of North America. Occasionally, autumn migrants thrust far southwest. On November 13, 1961, the senior editor watched a Starling alight on the *S. S. Hawaiian Farmer*. This freighter, having embarked from Hawaii, was sailing in the Pacific 1,160 nautical miles from Honolulu and 920 nautical miles from the San Francisco light vessel. Three Starlings accompanied the *Farmer* until she was 887

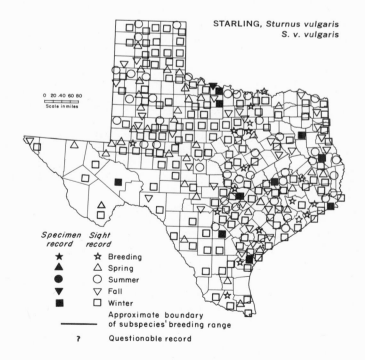

STARLING, *Sturnus vulgaris*
S. v. vulgaris

0 20 .40 60 80
Scale in miles

Specimen record	Sight record	
★	☆	Breeding
▲	△	Spring
●	○	Summer
▼	▽	Fall
■	□	Winter

——— Approximate boundary of subspecies' breeding range

? Questionable record

nautical miles from San Francisco. These birds were almost certainly migrants, since *Sturnus vulgaris*—published statements to the contrary—has never been naturalized in Hawaii.

Flight of the Starling is moderate to fast (it has been clocked by automobile up to 55 m.p.h.) and direct—not steeply undulating like that of most American black-plumaged birds. Periods of quick flapping alternate with sailing on fixed wings; frequently, however, flapping is steady, without glides. From late summer to spring, Starlings share communal night roosts, often with grackles, cowbirds, Red-winged Blackbirds, and other songbirds. Toward late afternoon, birds gravitate to a marsh or grove of trees. *Sturnus vulgaris*, much more addicted to sleeping on buildings than are its common associates, often roosts on houses. Prior to settling, birds perform vesper flights of amazing synchrony. Starlings sometimes breed in colonies, though more often a pair nests in isolation.

The Starling perches almost anywhere and is frequently on the ground. It stands quite upright and walks with short brisk steps, swinging its body from side to side and bobbing its head with each step, not unlike a pigeon. City and suburb birds are generally not shy and can be approached with relative ease; Starlings in rural areas tend to be more wary. Usually rather randomly, birds forage on the ground for an assortment of insects (beetles, weevils, grasshoppers, crickets, caterpillars), spiders, and millipedes; also many kinds of fruit (especially mulberry and cherry) and grains, both wild and cultivated.

Heard all year, Starling vocalizations include a number of creaks, chatters, chuckles, squeaks, and clear whistles. Commonly uttered in Texas is a sound like that of an unoiled metal sign swinging in the wind; the Bronzed (Red-eyed) Cowbird emits similar squeaks. Other calls are a harsh *tseeer* and a *whoo-ee* whistle. Apparently, Starlings can mimic sounds within the range of 1,200 and 8,250 vibrations per second; thus, they attempt to imitate songs of other birds and even whistles of people. Starling imitations, at least those heard in Texas, tend to be low-volumed and jumbled—not loud and clear as are various imitations by the Mockingbird. Starlings are usually silent when flying.

CHANGES: The European Starling and the English House Sparrow are the only two wild bird species which man his imported with tremendous success into the North American continent. Rather oddly, early Starling transplants did not take hold. Locations and years of unsuccessful introductions were: Cincinnati, Ohio (1872–73); Quebec, Canada (1875); Worcester, Massachusetts (1884); Tenafly, New Jersey (1884); New York City (1877, 1887); Portland, Oregon (1889, 1892); Allegheny, Pennsylvania, and Springfield, Massachusetts (1897); Bay Ridge, New York (ca. 1900). In Central Park, New York, Eugene Scheifflin and associates liberated sixty Starlings in 1890, and forty more in 1891. This brood stock of one hundred is officially credited as the one which produced the millions of

birds which, by 1960, were overrunning all forty-eight contiguous United States and southern Alaska.

First Texas record of *Sturnus vulgaris* was established when one was found dead at Cove (Chambers Co.) in late December, 1925, by A. R. Shearer. It was next taken at Beaumont (Jefferson Co.) January 8, 1926, by H. D. Anastasas. Both of these localities are on the upper coast.

Just a decade later, the Starling, sweeping down from the northeast, conquered Texas as a winter bird. By February 23, 1936, it had penetrated Port Isabel (Cameron Co.) in the extreme south (L. I. Davis). El Paso in the far west was reached by a scout on November 15, 1939 (T. M. Kirksey). First great upsurge in numbers was in the winter of 1933–34. Another tremendous Starling winter was in 1952–53; during this season, huge coalesced flocks of *S. vulgaris* hung over the city of San Antonio like a thick pall of black oil smoke. Some of the overflow from south Texas flew down to points south of the Tropic of Cancer. A Christmas Count at Tampico on the Tamaulipas-Veracruz boundary, January 1–2, 1953, turned up twenty-seven European Starlings (L. I. Davis, Pauline James, Marshall Johnston, E. B. Kincaid, Jr., John Morony, Jr.). These Starlings apparently were a first record for the New World's continental Torrid Zone.

The Starling was slow to nest in Texas, probably because it is programmed to reproduce most successfully in a chilly humid climate, such as obtains in its native western Europe. Nevertheless, by 1970 it was nesting fairly freely in the state's northeastern two-thirds (see TEXAS section above). Through 1939 the extensive investigations of H. C. Oberholser revealed no record of Starling breeding within Texas. Probably *Sturnus vulgaris* started laying its bluish white eggs in the Lone Star State during World War II, but unfortunately written records are scanty. Kent and Roddy Rylander reported that nesting Starlings showed an increase at Denton in 1956, thus implying that the species had been doing some nesting in the region previously. Next reported breeding activity was on the McAllen Ranch (Hidalgo Co.), some 530 miles south of Denton. On this ranch in extreme south Texas one of two Starlings was carrying insects into brush—apparently to hidden young—on April 20, 1958 (J. C. Arvin, Pauline James). On the upper coast, where the first Texas individuals were taken, two pairs were found nesting in the summer of 1959 (A. K. McKay). During the 1960's, nesting activity was witnessed at widely scattered places within each major subregion of Texas, except west of the Pecos River and the western Edwards Plateau. In less dry years of the near future, Starlings will probably carry nesting material even into these two desert fortresses.

DETAILED ACCOUNT: ONE SUBSPECIES

EUROPEAN STARLING, *Sturnus vulgaris vulgaris* Linnaeus

DESCRIPTION: *Adult male, nuptial plumage:* Acquired by wear from winter plumage. Pileum, sides of head, chin, and throat metallic dull bluish green; nape and upper back metallic vinaceous purple or metallic dark vinaceous purple; lower back, rump, and upper tail-coverts metallic deep dull yellowish green, upper surface, except pileum, with numerous small, rather triangular terminal spots of tawny olive to sayal brown, these smallest on occiput and nape, and all spots on upper parts sometimes practically absent through wear of feathers during summer; upper tail-coverts sometimes margined with same color; tail deep mouse gray, shafts of feathers and narrow stripes along outer edges blackish mouse gray, feathers narrowly edged and tipped with tawny olive; wing-quills and tertials fuscous, but outer webs of primaries, outer margins of secondaries, and tips of tertials fuscous black, this, in turn, very narrowly edged externally with tawny olive, except on tips of primaries; wing-coverts fuscous, and with tertials, edged on outer webs with metallic dusky greenish blue, lesser and median coverts with terminal tawny olive spots like back; lesser wing-coverts with very narrow margins of same color; sides of neck anteriorly metallic green, like throat, succeeded by metallic vinaceous purple like nape, and posteriorly metallic green like back; chin dull black with metallic green or purple gloss; jugulum metallic vinaceous purple or metallic dark vinaceous purple; breast and upper abdomen metallic dark green; sides and flanks metallic indigo blue to madder blue; lower abdomen and crissum dull black, more or less washed with metallic dark green, feathers of crissum with broad buffy tips; lining of wing fuscous or chaetura drab, margined with dull cinnamon buff. Bill lemon yellow; iris seal brown or vandyke brown; legs and feet burnt umber, chestnut, or buffy brown; claws drab or slate black. *Adult male, winter*: Similar to nuptial adult male, but practically entire plumage, including wing-coverts, with numerous conspicuous light spots—dull ochraceous tawny on upper surface and white or buffy white below—which are much larger than those of summer plumage; chin sometimes almost entirely white due to spots on that portion. Bill dark brown, but base of mandible dull yellow. *Adult female, nuptial*: Acquired by wear from winter. Similar to nuptial adult male, but coloration duller, both above and below, with metallic colors on wings of less extent, feathers of body shorter, somewhat broader, and usually not so acutely pointed, and light tips of feathers usually rather larger. Iris brown, but with narrow yellowish white outer or inner ring; iris sometimes all brown. *Adult female, winter*: Acquired by complete postnuptial molt. Differs from nuptial adult female as adult male in winter differs from nuptial adult male. *Male and female, first nuptial*: Acquired by wear from first winter. Similar to corresponding sex in nuptial adults, but duller; secondaries and greater wing-coverts with less metallic sheen; entire body more spotted with buff or tawny. *Male and female, first winter*: Acquired by complete postjuvenal molt. Similar to corresponding sex of winter adult, but feathers of breast broader, tips less acuminate, and broader; spots both above and below somewhat larger; metallic colors rather duller. *Juvenal*: Acquired by complete postnatal molt. Upper surface plain dark hair brown to dull buffy brown; wings and tail similar but rather lighter, wing-quills edged externally with light buff or dull cinnamon buff, greater coverts also edged narrowly with same, as are tail feathers; chin and middle of throat creamy white or brownish white; sides of head and neck and rest of lower parts like upper surface, but paler (grayish drab or light grayish drab), middle of breast and abdomen more or less streaked with grayish white or buffy white; lining of wing like lower surface but still paler, feathers edged with dull vinaceous buff. Bill dull brown; iris grayish brown; legs and feet light dull reddish brown or dull buffy brown. *Natal*: Drab gray or grayish white. Bill, legs, and feet pinkish buff.

MEASUREMENTS: *Adult male*: Wing, 125.2–131.8 (average, 129.0) mm.; tail, 62.2–64.8 (63.8); bill (exposed culmen), 23.9–27.9 (25.9); tarsus, 28.4–32.5 (30.5); middle toe without claw, 22.4–24.1 (22.9). *Adult female*: Wing, 124.7–127.5 (125.7); tail, 56.6–62.5 (59.2); bill, 23.4–26.9 (25.4); tarsus, 29.4–32.0 (30.7); middle toe, 21.4–22.9 (22.4).

RANGE: Native to Europe (except Faeroe Islands, Shetland Islands, c. Russia, Rumania, and Greece which are occupied by other races). Winters from breeding range south to n. Africa and Asia Minor. Introduced in North America, Jamaica, South Africa, Australia, and New Zealand. Winters in America from s. Canada to Baja California, Arizona, n. Tamaulipas (occasionally to Veracruz and Yucatán), and s. Florida.

TEXAS: *Breeding*: No specimen (see species account). *Winter*: Taken north to Wichita, east to Nacogdoches and Jefferson, south to San Patricio, west to Pecos cos.

NESTING: *Nest*: In all sorts of country except dense forests and treeless deserts, on uplands, bottoms, and slopes, but particularly in cultivated land, about human habitations, and in cities; in crevice in cliff or high rocks, stone heap, any convenient hole, abandoned woodpecker excavation, or similar tree cavity; eaves of house or other nook of building (e.g., old tower, church steeple, outbuilding, cornice), crevice in billboard; rather loosely constructed cup of twigs, straw, grasses, and various kinds of trash; lined with feathers, and sometimes wool, leaves, or moss. *Eggs*: 4–8; short ovate; somewhat glossy; pale bluish green or bluish white, sometimes almost pure white; unmarked; average size, 30.2 × 21.3 mm.

Vireos: Vireonidae

BLACK-CAPPED VIREO, *Vireo atricapillus*
Woodhouse

SPECIES ACCOUNT

Vireo atricapilla of A.O.U. check-list, 1957 (see Appendix A). *Male*: jet black head; conspicuous white "spectacles" (suggested by eye-ring and loral stripe); red eyes; bright olive above; white below with greenish yellow flanks; yellowish wing-bars. *Female*: slightly duller; dark slaty head; whitish under parts, wingbars. Length, 4½ in.; wingspan, 6¾.

RANGE: C. Oklahoma (formerly bred north to c. Kansas, occurred to s.e. Nebraska), south locally through c. Texas (southwest to Big Bend, where breeds sporadically) and c. Coahuila. Winters chiefly in w. Mexico from s. Sonora to Guerrero.

TEXAS: (See map.) *Breeding*: Early Apr. to mid-July (eggs, Apr. 20 to June 24; young being fed, Apr. 22 to July 1) from about 500 to 4,000 ft. Locally fairly common on eastern and southern Edwards Plateau, though formerly nested northwest across most of Plateau to Reagan Co. and San Angelo and north along outlying ridges to Oklahoma border; uncommon to rare and irregular in southern Trans-Pecos (Chisos Mts. and near mouth of Pecos River) and in southwestern Dallas Co. *Migration*: Late Mar. to early May; early Aug. to mid-Sept. (extremes: Mar. 13, mid-May; July 2, Sept. 25). Fairly common to uncommon through most of breeding range; rare through former nesting grounds and slightly east of Edwards Plateau; casual in Rio Grande delta.

HAUNTS AND HABITS: Forty-one species are usually placed in the Vireonidae, a strictly New World, mostly neotropical family. Vireos—small, slightly hook-billed birds all—dwell in forest or brushland. They are plain of plumage, lethargic of movement, and the females lay speckled eggs. The very special Blackcap violates these rules: It is bold in pattern, quick in action, and lays pure white eggs.

Summer haunts of the furtive Black-capped Vireo consist of dense, low (chiefly 4 to 10 ft.), ragged-topped thickets growing in brilliant sunlight on hilly, stony ground in—as George Finlay Simmons wrote—the hottest imaginable places. The usually dry limestone hilltops, ridges, slopes, and gulches of the Edwards Plateau support most of the bushes used by this vireo. Here the Blackcap inhabits clumps of oaks (*Quercus*

breviloba, Q. virginiana, Q. texana, Q. laceyi, others), Texas mountainlaurel (*Sophora secundiflora*), or sumacs (*Rhus copallina lanceolata, R. trilobata, R. virens*). Often there is some cedar (*Juniperus ashei*) associated with these shrubs. In Oklahoma and Coahuila, bushes used for feeding and nesting differ in species, but conform to the low-in-height, densely foliaged standard. In late summer, birds migrate—some via the Barranca del Cobre, Mexico's rival of the Grand Canyon—to semiarid tropical brush, sometimes mixed with palms, in Pacific foothills and flatlands. In late March, *Vireo atricapillus* flies back along similar routes to Texas.

The Blackcap is an extremely active but reclusive vireo. It keeps mostly to the interior of shrubs, where it remains low and is usually heard rather than seen. If it emerges from cover it is ordinarily but for a brief flitting to another thicket. Flight is quick, nervous, and rarely sustained. *V. atricapillus* eats mainly insects (small beetles, caterpillars of moths and butterflies) and occasionally a few spiders and tiny fleshy fruits.

This vireo's "scolding" note is a rasping screechy

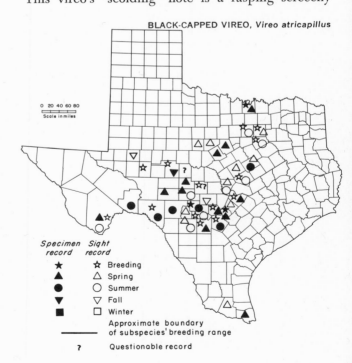

BLACK-CAPPED VIREO, *Vireo atricapillus*

0 20 40 60 80
Scale in miles

Specimen   Sight
record   record

★   ☆ Breeding
▲   △ Spring
●   ○ Summer
▼   ▽ Fall
■   □ Winter

———— Approximate boundary
     of subspecies' breeding range

?   Questionable record

squeak, harsher than similar notes of its relatives. The song of the Blackcap is decidedly vireonine; it somewhat suggests that of a White-eyed Vireo, but is faster, more burry, and quite varied. The bird seems to make repeated efforts to pronounce its English name: *black-cap V, b-cap vee-reeo, bee-cap-vee veereeor, vee-vee-ree-poo, wick-kuh-poo, wick-kuh-poo-chee-ee-e, black-cap* (G. F. Simmons). To many human listeners, the phrases sound hurried, restless, even waspish. A persistent vocalizer, the male sings from arrival in late March until departure in the last half of August. Midday heat, so depressive of most bird song, seems to have a stimulating effect on *V. atricapillus*. Usual song perch is an interior twig of a bush, but occasionally individuals sing briefly from atop a shrub or dead limb. Outbursts of singing occur frequently while the vireo is feeding, or even when it is sitting on the nest, but rarely while flying. The female sings also, but neither as much nor as well.

CHANGES: The limited breeding range of the Blackcapped Vireo is gradually becoming smaller. The species has apparently lost the state of Kansas (last known nesting, Comanche Co., May 11, 1885, N. S. Goss), and it has become much reduced in Oklahoma, Texas, and Coahuila. Long-term warming and drying of the climate, culminating in the intense drought of 1950–57, killed many of the bushes upon which it depends. Since 1933, federal subsidies to ranchers for brush clearance have stimulated bush elimination by axe, fire, herbicide, and bulldozer. In most of the vireo's range—especially the Edwards Plateau, "Angora goat capital of the world"—goats eat shrubs in places too steep for bulldozers. Near the extreme eastern and southern edges of this plateau, the goat population has actually declined somewhat since 1950, but urban sprawl from Fort Worth, Dallas, Waco, Austin, and San Antonio is doing away with the large clumps of dense scrub that furnish food, shelter, and nest sites for the Blackcap. Each pair must have a breeding habitat of between 2½ and 4½ acres; surface water in or near this territory is not necessary. To maintain a viable population there must be available at least 10 to 12 acres of suitable shrubs arranged in rectangular or oval—not linear—form.

Housing developments and ranching activities extirpate Blackcaps by outright habitat destruction and by thinning of scrub; these actions, in turn, increase populations of the Brown-headed Cowbird, a bird of open country. In addition, numbers of cowbirds are further inflated by man's practice of feeding grain to livestock in the country and to wild birds in suburban areas; the latter activity is rapidly increasing in popularity.

In the 1950's before the situation became as critical as it is now (1972), Jean Graber found, in her studies in Oklahoma, Texas, and Coahuila, that out of 243 Black-capped Vireo eggs only 43 (17.6 percent) hatched and developed to the stage of leaving the nest. The major cause of reproductive failure was cowbird parasitism. Ninety-seven eggs (72.3 percent of those lost) and 25 chicks (29.7 percent of the viable chicks) died because of cowbirds.

The Blackcap does have one important trait that helps it survive. It accepts either thickets of dwarf woody plants (such as *Quercus breviloba*) or young of taller growing trees (*Q. texana*, large sumacs, and others). The bird is quick to move in when second growth springs up after a bulldozer or fire. On the Edwards Plateau, Black-capped Vireos are often heard in patches of lance-leaved sumac (*Rhus copallina lanceolata*) that commonly cover a burned area three to ten years after a fire. In short, *V. atricapillus* has the unusual ability to use both virgin and second growth. For further details, the reader is referred to Jean W. Graber, 1961, Distribution, Habitat Requirements, and Life History of the Black-capped Vireo (*Vireo atricapilla*), *Ecological Monographs* 31(4): 313–336.

DETAILED ACCOUNT: NO SUBSPECIES

DESCRIPTION: *Adults, nuptial plumage*: Acquired by wear from winter plumage. Top and sides of head and cervix rather glossy black; sides of forehead, lores, and eye-ring white; remainder of upper surface rather grayish or yellowish olive green; wings and tail light chaetura drab, tail and wing-quills edged with serpentine green, but not tertials; lesser wing-coverts like back, tips of median and greater coverts, with outer webs of tertials, broadly barium yellow, forming two wing-bars; sides of neck like back; lower parts white or creamy white; sides and flanks serpentine green, mixed with citrine yellow; lower tail-coverts washed with citrine yellow; lining of wing citrine yellow. Bill above black; mandible plumbeous; cutting edges and tip of bill dull white; iris light brick red; legs and feet plumbeous. *Adults, winter*: Acquired by complete postnuptial molt. Similar to nuptial adults, but upper parts brighter, of rather more yellowish (less grayish) olive green, feathers of occiput and cervix edged with deep neutral gray. *Second nuptial*: Acquired by wear from second winter. Similar to nuptial adults, but posterior half or third of pileum, along with hindneck, dark olive gray, or between mouse gray and neutral gray, and washed with olive gray, instead of wholly black; lores black, anterior portion somewhat more brownish; loral stripe and lower parts not so purely white, but somewhat more washed with buff. *Second winter*: Acquired by complete postnuptial molt. Similar to second nuptial male and female. *First nuptial*: Acquired by partial prenuptial molt. Similar to second nuptial male and female, but entire pileum and hindneck dark olive gray, centers of feathers somewhat darker; lower parts still duller, washed with olive buff or yellowish olive; upper parts duller and somewhat more brownish olive green. *First winter*: Acquired by partial postjuvenal molt. Similar to first nuptial male and female, but upper parts duller, decidedly more brownish olive; pileum dark hair brown to rather light brownish olive, brownish citrine drab, or deep olive; back and rump citrine or olive citrine; upper tail-coverts similar but somewhat more yellowish; wings and tail similar to those of nuptial adults, but olive green edgings of wing-quills and coverts somewhat more brownish or yellowish (less grayish); extreme forehead, lores, and eye-ring pinkish buff to cinnamon buff; remainder of sides of head dark hair brown to light hair brown; sides of neck olive citrine; throat, jugulum, breast, sides, and flanks pinkish buff to light cinnamon buff, olive buff, warm buff, or on flanks buffy citrine; remainder of lower parts buffy white; lining of wing cream color to white; axillars and edge of wing naphthalene yellow to barium yellow. *Juvenal*: Acquired by complete postnatal molt. Upper surface dull drab; wings and tail similar to those of first winter male and female, but wing-coverts more brownish drab; loral stripe and eye-ring light buff; remainder of sides of head dull buff; all lower parts buffy white. *Natal*: None; chick hatches naked (G. M. Sutton).

MEASUREMENTS: *Adult male*: Wing, 53.1–57.4 (average, 55.3) mm.; tail, 40.9–47.0 (42.9); bill (exposed culmen), 8.9–10.9

(9.7); tarsus, 18.0–20.1 (19.0); middle toe without claw, 8.6–10.4 (9.1). *Adult female*: Wing, 51.6–55.1 (53.6); tail, 41.4–43.4 (42.4); bill, 8.9–9.9 (9.1); tarsus, 18.5–19.0 (18.8); middle toe, 8.6–9.9 (9.1).

TEXAS: *Breeding*: Collected northeast to Cooke, south to Erath, McLennan, Travis, Comal, Bexar, and Medina, west to Kerr, Edwards, Val Verde, Terrell (nesting unconfirmed), and Tom Green cos. *Migration*: One specimen outside breeding range: Cameron Co., Brownsville (Mar. 29, 1894, F. B. Armstrong).

NESTING: *Nest*: On rocky hill tops, slopes, and mesas, in valleys, canyons, and gulches; in thickets of scrub oak, elm, sumac, etc., 3–8 ft., occasionally 15 ft., above the ground; very small, pensile basket, strongly woven with moderately thick walls, and hung usually between fork of branch; composed of pieces of bleached leaves, shreds of bark, grasses, catkins, dry leaves, fine weed stems, sheep wool, mohair, spider or caterpillar silk, spider cocoons, and silklike down from plants; lined with fine shreds of bark, fine grasses, rootlets, and sometimes with slender leaves from coniferous (chiefly juniper) trees. *Eggs*: 3–5, usually 4; ovate; without gloss; pure white or grayish white, unmarked; average size, 18.0 × 13.2 mm.

WHITE-EYED VIREO, *Vireo griseus* (Boddaert)

SPECIES ACCOUNT

White eyes; yellow "spectacles"; olive above; two whitish wing-bars; whitish below with pale yellow flanks. Young are duller; have brown or gray eyes. Length, 5 in.; wingspan, 7¾; weight, ½ oz.

RANGE: E. Nebraska to New York, south to c. Mexico, U.S. Gulf coast, and s. Florida; also Bermuda. Winters chiefly from s. Texas, Gulf coast (a few), and s. Georgia to Guatemala and Honduras; also Bahamas, Cuba, Isle of Pines, and Swan Island.

TEXAS: (See map.) *Breeding*: Mar. to mid-July (eggs, Apr. 1 to July 4) from near sea level to 1,900 ft.

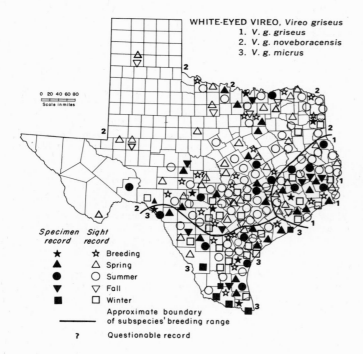

WHITE-EYED VIREO, *Vireo griseus*
1. *V. g. griseus*
2. *V. g. noveboracensis*
3. *V. g. micrus*

0 20 40 60 80
Scale in miles

Specimen record / Sight record
★ / ☆ Breeding
▲ / △ Spring
● / ○ Summer
▼ / ▽ Fall
■ / □ Winter
——— Approximate boundary of subspecies' breeding range
? Questionable record

Common to fairly common east of 100th meridian; irregularly fairly common in Del Rio region. *Migration*: Mid-Mar. to mid-May; late Aug. to late Oct. (extremes: Feb. 23, May 20; July 14, Nov. 26). Common to fairly common through eastern two-thirds; rare in northern Panhandle and vicinity of Midland; casual west of Pecos River. *Winter*: Early Dec. to Mar. Fairly common to uncommon south of 29th parallel; uncommon to scarce north through breeding range to 31st parallel; rare in Tyler vicinity.

HAUNTS AND HABITS: Tangled thickets—preferably near water, thick undergrowth, and damp bushy canyons are favored summer haunts of the White-eyed Vireo. Because of this vireo's ability to supplement its insect diet with various berries, individuals sometimes remain throughout the winter in southern U.S. locales, where they seek shelter within evergreen shrubs. Evergreen sumac (*Rhus virens*), yaupon (*Ilex vomitoria*), and live oak (*Quercus virginiana*) thickets are favored in central, east, and south Texas, respectively. In the Rio Grande delta, where in mild years mesquite (*Prosopis glandulosa*) tends to keep its leaves through the winter, White-eyed Vireos live in the few patches which the bulldozer has somehow overlooked.

The White-eye's flight is usually short, quick, and flitting. The bird remains most of the time in thickets and bushes near ground; infrequently it ascends to upper branches of trees. It is a lively vireo, sometimes very active, though at other times more or less deliberate in its search for food—mostly caterpillars, moths, bugs, beetles, ants, and spiders—in the undergrowth.

Usual note of this species is harsh, somewhat drawn out, and scolding. The song, startlingly loud and emphatic for so small a bird, attracts attention to its author; however, the White-eye, though not particularly shy, is adept at keeping mostly out of sight. Robert Ridgway has rendered the song as *chick-ty-beaver, limber-stick*, although the last three syllables are often omitted. Sometimes the White-eye seems to imitate the notes or songs of other birds, including the Catbird, Carolina Wren, and even the Whip-poor-will. Its song is one of the most continuously heard in thickets, even during midday. In Texas, *V. griseus* sings from March well into September, though with diminishing vigor after July; individuals occasionally sing in winter.

DETAILED ACCOUNT: THREE SUBSPECIES

SOUTHERN WHITE-EYED VIREO, *Vireo griseus griseus* (Boddaert)

DESCRIPTION: *Adults, nuptial plumage*: Acquired by wear from winter plumage. Upper parts yellowish olive green, sometimes tinged with mouse gray on occiput and hindneck; nape mouse gray; lores and sides of forehead strontian yellow or empire yellow; tail dark hair brown, edged externally with citrine, inner webs of feathers margined with yellowish or buffy white; wings dark hair brown, primaries and secondaries with narrow external edges of yellowish citrine, lesser wing-coverts and edges of others like back; median and greater coverts broadly tipped with barium yellow, forming two conspicuous wing-bars, tertials margined on outer webs with same; eye-ring yellow like lores; sides of neck down to eyes like upper parts, below and on cheeks becoming paler and rather grayish light drab or light grayish olive; anterior lower parts grayish white or very pale olive gray; posterior lower parts creamy or yellowish white; sides and flanks citrine yellow mixed with serpentine green; lining of wing citrine yellow, coverts more or less spotted with mouse gray. Bill blackish slate, black, slate black, or slate color, but mandible plumbeous, cinereous, or slaty white; cutting edges of bill and tip of mandible white; tongue white; iris white, dull white, or dark gray; legs and feet plumbeous or cinereous. *Adults, winter*: Acquired by complete postnuptial molt. Similar to nuptial adults, but coloration somewhat richer. *First nuptial*: Acquired by wear from first winter. Similar to nuptial adults, but iris gray or broccoli brown instead of white. *First winter*: Acquired by partial postjuvenal molt. Essentially same as adults in winter, except iris gray instead of white. *Juvenal*: Acquired by complete postnatal molt. Similar to nuptial adults, but bill smaller and coloration duller; upper parts, particularly forehead, decidedly more brownish—buffy olive or light brownish olive; wing-bars buff; sides of head duller, more brownish; lores mouse gray, dark olive buff, or deep colonial buff; supraloral and orbital region very pale dull yellow or yellowish white; chin and throat more buffy (less purely gray); breast pale buff, washed with yellow; sides and flanks paler and duller olive yellow; crissum more deeply yellow. Iris dull white. *Natal*: Unknown.

MEASUREMENTS: *Adult male*: Wing, 58.4–63.0 (average, 60.7) mm.; tail, 48.0–51.1 (49.0); bill (exposed culmen), 9.9–11.4 (10.7); tarsus, 18.5–20.6 (19.8); middle toe without claw, 9.9–10.9 (10.2). *Adult female*: Wing, 55.6–62.5 (59.4); tail, 44.4–51.6 (49.0); bill, 9.7–11.4 (10.7); tarsus, 18.8–20.6 (19.8); middle toe, 9.1–10.4 (9.7).

RANGE: S.e. Texas to n.e. North Carolina, south to s. Florida. Winters from s. Texas and s.e. South Carolina through e. Mexico to Yucatán.

TEXAS: *Breeding*: Altitudinal range, near sea level to 400 ft. Collected north to Shelby, south to Jefferson and Brazoria, west to Waller and Walker cos. Fairly common. *Migration*: Collected north to Dallas, east to Tyler, south to Atascosa, west to Kinney cos. Fairly common. *Winter*: Two specimens: Hidalgo Co., Lomita Ranch (Feb. 26, 1880, M. A. Frazar); Cameron Co., Brownsville (Feb. 15, 1911, A. K. Fisher).

NESTING: *Nest*: On bottomlands, uplands, in swamps and stream valleys; in open woodlands, also about their edges, and timber along streams, tangled thickets of vines and weeds; in bush, vine, or low tree, 2–8 ft. above ground, usually not over 4 ft.; deeply cupped nest, rather large for size of bird, suspended from forked branch; composed of grass, leaves, bark, bits of wood, weeds, grasses, mosses, lichens, hemplike plant fibers, fragments of palmetto fronds or pine needles, various other vegetable substances, and pieces of paper; lined usually with fine grasses. *Eggs*: 3–5, usually 4; short ovate to elliptical ovate; clear white, sparingly and minutely dotted with black, dark purplish brown, and light lilac; average size, 19.3 × 14.2 mm.

NORTHERN WHITE-EYED VIREO, *Vireo griseus noveboracensis* (Gmelin)

DESCRIPTION: *Adults, nuptial plumage*: Similar to *V. g. griseus*, but yellowish color of sides and flanks more golden yellow (less greenish) and more extensive.

MEASUREMENTS: *Adult male*: Wing, 61.0–65.0 (average, 62.2) mm.; tail, 46.0–52.1 (49.5); bill (exposed culmen), 9.4–10.4 (9.9); tarsus, 18.0–20.1 (19.3); middle toe without claw, 8.9–10.9 (9.9). *Adult female*: Wing, 58.9–63.0 (61.0); tail, 43.9–51.1 (47.8); bill, 9.4–10.9 (10.2); tarsus, 19.0–21.1 (20.1); middle toe, 9.9–10.9 (10.4).

RANGE: E. Nebraska to New Hampshire, south to c. Texas and North Carolina. Winters from c. Texas and c. Georgia through e. Mexico to Honduras; also Bahamas, Cuba, and Isle of Pines.

TEXAS: *Breeding*: Altitudinal range, 400 to 1,800 ft. Collected north to Cooke, east to Fannin and Brazos, south to Bexar, west to Kerr and Menard cos. Fairly common. *Migration*: Collected

north to Clay, east to Hardin, south to Cameron, west to Val Verde cos. Fairly common. *Winter*: Two specimens: Cameron Co., Brownsville (Dec. 5, 1909, A. P. Smith); Webb Co., Laredo (Dec. 4, 1885, F. B. Armstrong).

NESTING: Similar to that of *V. g. griseus*.

RIO GRANDE WHITE-EYED VIREO, *Vireo griseus micrus* Nelson

DESCRIPTION: *Adults, nuptial plumage*: Similar to *V. g. griseus* but smaller, except tarsus and middle toe; upper parts of duller, more grayish olive; flanks duller, lighter, and more grayish (less yellowish) olive green.

MEASUREMENTS: *Adult male*: Wing, 55.1–58.9 (average, 57.2) mm.; tail, 43.9–49.0 (47.3); bill (exposed culmen), 8.1–8.9 (8.6); tarsus, 19.0–20.1 (19.8); middle toe without claw, 8.9–10.9 (10.2). *Adult female*: Wing, 54.1–57.9 (56.1); tail, 43.9–49.0 (46.3); bill, 8.9–9.9 (9.7); tarsus, 19.6–20.1 (19.8); middle toe, 9.9–10.9 (10.2).

RANGE: C. Coahuila and s. Texas, south to San Luis Potosí and s.e. Tamaulipas.

TEXAS: *Breeding*: Altitudinal range, near sea level to 1,900 ft. Collected northwest to Val Verde, east to Matagorda, south to Cameron cos. Fairly common locally; now scarce in Rio Grande delta. *Winter*: Taken in Matagorda, Bee, Brooks, Cameron, and Hidalgo cos. Fairly common to uncommon.

NESTING: Similar to that of *V. g. griseus*.

HUTTON'S VIREO, *Vireo huttoni* Cassin

SPECIES ACCOUNT

Resembles Ruby-crowned Kinglet, but moves deliberately; has heavier, slightly hooked bill; prominent whitish loral spot; and distinct voice. Grayish olive above; whitish "spectacles" (incomplete above eyes), wing-bars; dingy buff below with yellow wash on flanks. Length, 5 in.; wingspan, 8¼.

RANGE: S.w. British Columbia, south along Pacific coast to Baja California; also c. Arizona, s.w. New

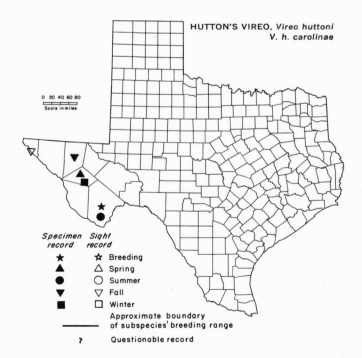

HUTTON'S VIREO, *Vireo huttoni*
V. h. carolinae

0 20 40 60 80
Scale in miles

Specimen record   Sight record
★   ☆ Breeding
▲   △ Spring
●   ○ Summer
▼   ▽ Fall
■   □ Winter

———— Approximate boundary of subspecies' breeding range

?   Questionable record

Mexico, and s. Trans-Pecos Texas, south through Mexican highlands to Guatemala. Withdraws in winter from c. to s.e. Arizona.

TEXAS: (See map.) *Breeding*: Late Apr. to June, probably later (eggs collected: Glass Mts., May 22, 1913, E. F. Pope; nest building: Chisos Mts., Basin, Apr. 29, 1935, G. M. Sutton, and Laguna Meadow, May 17, 1969, fide R. H. Wauer) from 5,800 to 7,500 ft. Fairly common in Chisos Mts., Big Bend Nat. Park, where observed during every month but Nov.; uncommon and irregular on nearby mountains in Brewster Co. *Migration*: Mid-Apr. to mid-May; mid-Sept. to late Oct. (extremes: Apr. 9, late May; Sept. 7, Nov. 9). Fairly common in Chisos Mts.; uncommon to scarce in remainder of Trans-Pecos mountains; rare at El Paso. *Winter*: Dec. to Mar. Fairly common to uncommon in Chisos Mts.; scarce in Davis Mts.

HAUNTS AND HABITS: The Hutton's Vireo lives chiefly in mountains, canyons, gulches, and on rocky slopes. It is found primarily in junipers, pinyons, and oaks, and appears to be more attracted to scrub and low trees than to thickets and underbrush. The Hutton's, rather tame, assiduously peers about in its deliberate search for insects and other food. In marked contrast to its "double," the Ruby-crowned Kinglet, this vireo very seldom twitches its wings when it perches or moves through branches.

It has a hoarse, monotonous vocalization, which is not nearly so emphatic as that of the White-eyed Vireo, nor as musical as that of the Solitary Vireo. A common variation has been well interpreted as *zu-weep*, uttered with rising inflection. *Day dee dee* is another vocalization. Males sing often from late March to August.

DETAILED ACCOUNT: TWO SUBSPECIES

SOUTHWESTERN HUTTON'S VIREO, *Vireo huttoni stephensi* Brewster

DESCRIPTION: *Adults, nuptial plumage*: Acquired by wear from winter plumage. Upper surface grayish olive, passing into light yellowish olive on rump and upper tail-coverts; tail rather dark hair brown, edged on outer webs of feathers with light yellowish olive, outer web of outermost tail feather very narrowly margined with yellowish white; wings dark hair brown, but primaries and secondaries narrowly edged externally with light yellowish olive, tertials broadly margined on outer webs with very light yellowish olive or yellowish white, secondaries and basal portions of primaries edged on inner webs with yellowish white or very pale gray, lesser wing-coverts edged with color of back, median and greater coverts broadly tipped with yellowish white, forming two well-marked wing-bars; lores dull cartridge buff, somewhat mixed with light grayish olive; sides of head similar to back but somewhat more buffy; eye-ring dull buffy white or greenish white; lower surface dull dark olive buff, posteriorly dull primrose yellow, sides washed with olivaceous or yellow; lining with marguerite yellow, outer under wing-coverts somewhat mottled with mouse gray. Bill dull brown, mandible paler; iris dark brown; legs and feet dull brownish slate or dull black. *Adults, winter*: Acquired by complete postnuptial molt. Similar to nuptial adults, but colors somewhat darker and richer. *First nuptial*: Acquired by wear from first winter. Similar to nuptial adults. *First winter*: Acquired by partial postjuvenal molt. Similar to adults in winter. *Juvenal*: Acquired by complete postnatal molt. Similar to nuptial adults, but upper parts rather paler and decidedly more brownish (less greenish); sides

of head and neck duller, more uniform, and decidedly more buffy; below paler, more whitish (less yellowish), particularly on abdomen; wing-bars decidedly buffy. *Natal* (this plumage of this race not seen in Texas): Pale tilleul buff to very pale drab gray.

MEASUREMENTS: *Adult male*: Wing, 66.0–71.9 (average, 68.8) mm.; tail, 49.5–54.1 (51.3); bill (exposed culmen), 8.9–9.9 (9.7); tarsus, 18.0–19.0 (18.3); middle toe without claw, 8.9–10.4 (9.9). *Adult female*: Wing, 67.1–68.6 (67.8); tail, 52.1–52.6 (52.3); bill, 9.4–10.9 (10.2); tarsus, (18.5); middle toe, 9.4–9.9 (9.7).

RANGE: S. Arizona and s.w. New Mexico, south to Sinaloa and n.w. Durango; in winter south to Nayarit and Zacatecas.

TEXAS: *Migration*: One specimen: Culberson Co., Pine Spring Canyon (Oct. 8, 1938, T. D. Burleigh).

NESTING: (This race does not nest in Texas.) *Nest*: On slopes and valleys, chiefly in mountains; usually in forest or scrub, or thickets along streams; in oak, or other low tree or bush; cup-shaped pensile nest, hung between forks of twig, 12 ft. or more above ground; composed of grass tops, moss, buff plant down, fine grass, and moss, bound together by cobwebs, materials very compactly put together, rather scantily lined with grass tops and similar materials. *Eggs*: 3–4; ovate; with little gloss; pure white; very sparsely dotted with umber brown and brownish red at large end; average size, about 17.8 × 12.7 mm.

CHISOS HUTTON'S VIREO, *Vireo huttoni carolinae* Brandt

DESCRIPTION: *Adults, nuptial plumage*: Similar to *V. h. stephensi*, but upper surface much darker; lower parts rather darker. *Natal*: Probably similar to *V. h. stephensi*.

MEASUREMENTS: *Adult male*: Wing, 63.0–69.1 (average, 66.8) mm.; tail, 48.5–55.1 (52.3); bill (exposed culmen), 9.1–11.9 (9.7); tarsus, 18.5–20.6 (19.3); middle toe without claw, 9.1–10.4 (9.7). *Adult female*: Wing, 64.0–68.6 (65.3); tail, 50.0–55.1 (52.6); bill, 8.9–10.7 (9.7); tarsus, 18.0–20.6 (19.3); middle toe, 9.1–9.9 (9.7).

RANGE: S. Trans-Pecos Texas, south to s. Coahuila and s.w. Tamaulipas.

TEXAS: *Breeding*: Collected in Chisos Mts., Brewster Co. *Migration*: Collected in Jeff Davis and Brewster cos. Uncommon. *Winter*: One specimen: Jeff Davis Co., Limpia Canyon (Dec., 1885, W. Lloyd).

NESTING: Similar to that of *V. h. stephensi*.

BELL'S VIREO, *Vireo bellii* Audubon

SPECIES ACCOUNT

Nondescript. Olive gray above; faint whitish "spectacles," wing-bars; whitish below with pale yellowish wash on flanks. Length, 5 in.; wingspan, 7; weight, ¼ oz.

RANGE: Central Valley of California, extreme s. Nevada, c. Arizona, s.w. New Mexico, e. Colorado, s.e. South Dakota, and n. Illinois, south to n. Baja California, n. mainland Mexico, Texas, and n.w. Louisiana. Winters from Mexico to Nicaragua.

TEXAS: (See map.) *Breeding*: Late Mar. to late Aug. (eggs, Mar. 30 to Aug. 6) from near sea level to 5,000 ft. Common to uncommon in most parts, though irregular in vicinity of Midland; rare in western Panhandle (except along streams), southeastern portion, and southern tip. *Migration*: Late Mar. to early May; late Aug. to late Sept. (extremes: Mar. 3, May 11; Aug. 20, Nov. 9). Very common locally to fairly common through regular breeding range; uncommon to scarce in remainder of state. *Winter:* Late Dec. to late Feb. Casual in south Texas brush country.

HAUNTS AND HABITS: Summer home of the Bell's Vireo is usually a mesquite (*Prosopis*) flat, streamside thicket (especially near willows and cottonwoods), or open stand of scrub oaks. During migration the Bell's frequents brush and open woods almost anywhere along its route.

This vireo normally flits rather nervously from twig to twig or bush to bush. However, it is capable of long-sustained flight, and when it travels any distance, flight is swift, although somewhat irregular. *Vireo bellii* feeds at times in the very tops of trees, but ordinarily it prefers the lower and interior foliage; thus, it is more frequently heard than seen.

A frequent call of the Bell's, rather harsh, particularly when used as an alarm, sounds something like *too-weea-skee*. Its decidedly vireolike song, not loud or strong, is rather distinctive, but does suggest that of the White-eyed Vireo and, to a lesser extent, that of the Warbling Vireo. Roger Tory Peterson's frequently quoted rendition is *cheedle cheedle chee?—cheedle cheedle chew!* In spring and early summer, the Bell's Vireo is a persistent songster, continuing even throughout the hot portions of the day; sometimes it even sings on the nest. Commonly, males sing from their arrival in spring well into August.

DETAILED ACCOUNT: THREE SUBSPECIES

NORTHERN BELL'S VIREO, *Vireo bellii bellii* Audubon

DESCRIPTION: *Adults, nuptial plumage:* Acquired by wear from winter plumage. Pileum and hindneck between citrine drab and hair brown; back and scapulars grayish light yellowish olive or between light yellowish olive and buffy olive; rump light yellowish olive; longer upper tail-coverts similar but

BELL'S VIREO, *Vireo bellii*
1. *V. b. bellii*
2. *V. b. medius*
3. *V. b. arizonae*

0 20 40 60 80
Scale in miles

Specimen record / Sight record
★ / ☆ Breeding
▲ / △ Spring
● / ○ Summer
▼ / ▽ Fall
■ / □ Winter
——— Approximate boundary of subspecies' breeding range
? Questionable record

somewhat more brownish; tail rather dark hair brown, margined on outer webs of feathers with light yellowish olive, inner margins narrowly dull yellowish or greenish white; wings rather dark hair brown, lesser coverts and margins of greater coverts and of external webs of wing-quills like back, tips of quills very narrowly pale grayish or brownish white, inner margins of quills, except terminal portion of primaries, brownish or yellowish white; most of median and greater coverts broadly tipped with buffy or yellowish white, forming two indistinct wing-bars; indistinct supraloral stripe and narrow eye-ring dull white or buffy white; small dull dark brownish spot in front of eye; remainder of sides of head similar to pileum but somewhat paler; sides of neck like back; lower parts buffy or yellowish white, anteriorly pale buff or dull pale yellow, but sides, flanks, and crissum straw yellow, all but crissum washed with citrine; lining of wing straw yellow. Bill dull dark brown or blackish brown, mandible of paler brown or brownish white, base and cutting edges of bill pale dull lilaceous; iris dark brown, light brown, rufous, or dark hazel; legs, feet, and claws plumbeous. *Adults, winter:* Acquired by complete postnuptial molt. Similar to nuptial adults, but colors somewhat darker and brighter. *First nuptial:* Acquired by wear from first winter. Similar to nuptial adults. *First winter:* Acquired by partial postjuvenal molt. Similar to adults in winter, but upper surface decidedly more brownish and rather darker; breast more buffy; sides and flanks more brownish. *Juvenal:* Acquired by complete postnatal molt. Pileum and hindneck between wood brown and drab; remainder of upper surface dull buffy brown, upper tail-coverts somewhat olivaceous; wings and tail similar to those of first winter male and female, but wing-coverts still more brownish, lesser wing-coverts wood brown like crown; lower parts dull buffy white or yellowish white, sides and crissum very pale dull yellow; sides of breast washed with drab. *Natal:* Hatches naked (G. M. Sutton).

MEASUREMENTS: *Adult male:* Wing, 52.1–58.4 (average, 55.6) mm.; tail, 41.4–46.5 (44.7); bill (exposed culmen), 8.9–9.9 (9.7); tarsus, 18.0–19.0 (18.8); middle toe without claw, 9.4–10.4 (9.7). *Adult female:* Wing, 53.1–56.4 (55.3); tail, 43.9–47.0 (45.2); bill, 8.9–9.9 (9.7); tarsus, 18.0–19.6 (18.8); middle toe, 9.4–10.9 (9.9).

RANGE: N. Nebraska to s. Wisconsin, south to Texas and s.w. Tamaulipas. Winters from s. Texas (casually) through w. Mexico to Guatemala.

TEXAS: *Breeding:* Altitudinal range, near sea level to 2,500 ft. Collected north to Lipscomb, east to Bowie and Harris (nest and eggs), south to Starr, west to Mitchell cos. Fairly common. *Migration:* Collected north to Clay, east to Collin, south to Hidalgo, west to Pecos cos. Fairly common. *Winter:* One specimen: Bexar Co., San Antonio (Feb. 19, 1890, H. P. Attwater).

NESTING: *Nest:* On uplands and bottomlands, in wild or cultivated areas; in thicket along stream, bush, or tree, usually not at great elevation; cup-shaped nest, hung between forks of branch or twig, compactly and beautifully woven; composed of strips of bark, flaxlike vegetable fibers of various plants, bits of leaves; lined with fine grasses, vegetable down, rootlets, feathers, hair, and thin weed stems. *Eggs:* 3–4, usually 4; ovate; white; dotted with reddish brown or umber, mostly about large end; average size, 17.8 × 12.7 mm.

TEXAS BELL'S VIREO, *Vireo bellii medius* Oberholser

DESCRIPTION: *Adults, nuptial plumage:* Similar to *V. b. bellii*, but tail averaging somewhat longer; upper parts more grayish (less greenish); lower surface more whitish, sides, flanks, lower tail-coverts, and axillars paler.

MEASUREMENTS: *Adult male:* Wing, 53.1–55.6 (average, 54.3) mm.; tail, 45.0–47.0 (46.3); bill (exposed culmen), 8.9–9.9 (9.7); tarsus, 18.0–19.0 (18.8); middle toe without claw, 9.4–9.9 (9.7). *Adult female:* Wing, 53.6–55.9 (54.6); tail, 45.0–48.0 (46.5); bill, 9.4–9.9 (9.7); tarsus, 18.5–19.0 (18.8); middle toe, 9.4–9.9 (9.7).

RANGE: Trans-Pecos Texas to s.e. Coahuila. Winters from Coahuila and n.w. Durango to Guanajuato.

TEXAS: *Breeding:* Altitudinal range, 1,800 to 5,000 ft. Collected in Reeves, Jeff Davis, Brewster, and Presidio cos. Locally common. *Migration*: One specimen outside breeding range: Kinney Co., Fort Clark (May 7, 1898, E. A. Mearns). Fairly common.

NESTING: Similar to that of *V. b. bellii*.

ARIZONA BELL'S VIREO, *Vireo bellii arizonae* Ridgway

DESCRIPTION: *Adults, nuptial plumage*: Similar to *V. b. medius*, but tail much longer; tarsus somewhat longer; upper parts paler, more grayish, and more uniform; olive yellow of sides and flanks lighter and less evident.

MEASUREMENTS: *Adult male*: Wing, 53.6–56.9 (average, 54.3) mm.; tail, 48.0–54.1 (50.3); bill (exposed culmen), 8.9–9.9 (9.7); tarsus, 18.5–20.1 (19.3); middle toe without claw, 9.4–10.4 (10.2). *Adult female*: Wing, 53.1–56.9 (54.8); tail, 49.0–51.6 (49.8); bill, 8.9–9.9 (9.7); tarsus, 18.5–20.1 (19.3); middle toe, 9.4–10.4 (9.7).

RANGE: S.e. California and s.w. Utah to extreme w. Texas, south to s.w. Sinaloa and w. Chihuahua. Winters from c. Sonora to s. Sinaloa.

TEXAS: *Breeding*: Altitudinal range, 3,500 to 3,800 ft. Two specimens: Hudspeth Co., Fort Hancock (June 8, 14, 1893, E. A. Mearns).

NESTING: Similar to that of *V. b. bellii*, but average egg size, 17.5 × 12.2 mm.

GRAY VIREO, *Vireo vicinior* Coues

SPECIES ACCOUNT

Drab; jerks longish tail. Uniform gray above; narrow whitish eye-ring; single faint grayish wing-bar; whitish below. Length, 5½ in.; wingspan, 8¼.

RANGE: S. California and n. Baja California, east across s.w. United States to extreme n.w. Oklahoma and Trans-Pecos Texas. Winters chiefly in s. Baja California and Sonora.

TEXAS: (See map.) *Breeding*: Probably late Apr. to

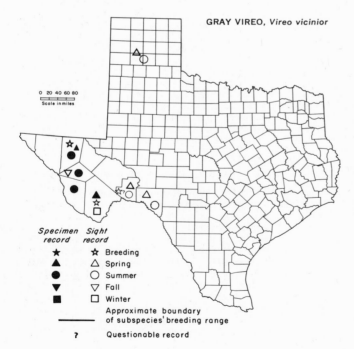

GRAY VIREO, *Vireo vicinior*

0 20 40 60 80
Scale in miles

Specimen record | Sight record
★ | ☆ Breeding
▲ | △ Spring
● | ○ Summer
▼ | ▽ Fall
■ | □ Winter

—— Approximate boundary of subspecies' breeding range

? Questionable record

mid-July (no egg dates available, but nest located, Guadalupe Mts., F. R. Gehlbach) from about 2,400 to 6,000 ft. Locally fairly common to uncommon in foothills and mountain slopes of Trans-Pecos; rare in northern Panhandle canyons (nesting unconfirmed). *Migration*: Early Apr. to early May; late Aug. to late Sept. (extremes: Mar. 17, May 9; early Aug., Sept. 25). Fairly common to uncommon through Trans-Pecos breeding range; scarce to rare in northern Panhandle. *Winter*: No specimen, but three sightings, all in Big Bend Nat. Park (Dec. 24, 1950, K. W. Haller; Dec. 30, 1970, and Jan. 3, 1971, J. Barlow, R. H. Wauer).

HAUNTS AND HABITS: The Gray Vireo is a bird of moderate altitudes in arid foothills and mountains. Ordinarily it summers where desert thorn scrub is intermixed with junipers and small oaks. In Texas it normally lives higher than the Bell's Vireo of riverside willows and mesquites, but a little lower than the Hutton's, and much lower than the Plumbeous Solitary Vireo, a mountain forest bird.

Shy and difficult to observe, the Gray is usually seen alone, rarely ever showing signs of gregariousness. It is probably the second most active vireo; the Black-capped Vireo ranks first in the quick movement department. As the Gray inspects leaves and twigs for its insect prey, it flops its tail about more in the manner of a gnatcatcher than a vireo. It forages mostly in upper portions of bushes and small trees, usually from six to twelve, rarely fifteen feet, above the ground. Its flight is quick, not usually prolonged, and principally from bush to bush. Even on the wing the bird has a tendency to keep hidden, so that much of the time its presence is detected chiefly by its notes and song.

The song consists of three or four phrases of liquid whistling notes rather slowly given, although sometimes more rapidly, and is one of the finest of western vireo songs. In general character it resembles that of the Solitary Vireo, but is usually more rapid. Mrs. Lena McBee thus describes its phrases: *chee-wee, chick-bur, chee-bur*; *chee-be, chee-bur, ve-ree, ve-che-bur*; and *vee-re, vee-che-bur, ve-che*. While the male is chief songster, the female also has a song, but it is not as impressive. The male is heard in Texas from April into August.

DETAILED ACCOUNT: NO SUBSPECIES

DESCRIPTION: *Adults, nuptial plumage*: Acquired by wear from winter plumage. Upper surface plain gray—between neutral gray and mouse gray; rump and upper tail-coverts deep grayish olive; tail rather dark hair brown, outermost pair of feathers margined externally with brownish white, others narrowly margined on outer webs with color of rump, inner margins very narrowly brownish white; wings rather dark hair brown, quills margined on outer webs narrowly with dull pale gray that is lighter and more brownish than back, and edged on basal portion of inner webs with brownish white, median coverts very obscurely tipped with paler gray, greater series more broadly with brownish white or dull yellowish white; sides of head and neck like pileum but rather paler, lores and conspicuous eye-ring dull white or grayish white; lower parts white with tinge of smoke gray anteriorly, sides and flanks washed with grayish olive; lining of wing white, mottled with hair brown. Bill plumbeous, but somewhat paler on cutting edges and on mandible; inside of mouth bluish white; iris dark brown; legs and feet plumbeous or light plumbeous. *Adults, winter*: Acquired by complete postnuptial molt. Similar to nuptial adults but somewhat darker above and less purely grayish (more olivaceous or brownish), light edgings of wing-quills and greater wing-coverts broader; lower parts less purely white; breast washed with drab or gray. *First nuptial*: Acquired by wear from first winter. Like nuptial adults. *First winter*: Acquired by partial postjuvenal molt. Similar to adults in winter. *Juvenal*: Acquired by complete postnatal molt. Similar to nuptial adults, but upper parts decidedly paler and more brownish; pileum dark drab, back light hair brown; wings also decidedly more brownish, lesser wing-coverts drab, edgings of remaining coverts and of wing-quills more yellowish or greenish; lower surface duller, distinctly washed with pale buff. *Natal*: Dull white.

MEASUREMENTS: *Adult male*: Wing, 62.0–67.1 (average, 64.8) mm.; tail, 57.9–61.0 (58.4); bill (exposed culmen), 8.9–11.7 (10.4); tarsus, 18.0–20.6 (19.6); middle toe without claw, 8.9–10.4 (9.7). *Adult female*: Wing, 61.0–64.0 (62.5); tail, 55.1–58.9 (57.2); bill, 8.9–10.9 (9.7); tarsus, 18.0–20.6 (19.3); middle toe, 9.4–10.9 (9.9).

TEXAS: *Breeding*: Collected in Culberson, Jeff Davis, Presidio, and Brewster cos. *Migration*: Collected in Culberson, Brewster, and Terrell cos.

NESTING: *Nest*: On slopes and mesas and in valleys; in juniper-oak scrub or thickets along streams; in bush or low tree, usually 4–6 ft. above ground; nest cup usually semipensile (less so when in a crotch), ordinarily attached by rim to fork of branch or twig, somewhat loosely constructed; composed of strips of bark, grasses, and dead leaves; lined with fine grasses. *Eggs*: 3–4; rounded ovate; white, with dots of reddish brown, umber brown, or dull black, mostly about large end; average size, 18.5 × 14.2 mm.

YELLOW-THROATED VIREO, *Lanivireo flavifrons* (Vieillot)

SPECIES ACCOUNT

Vireo flavifrons of A.O.U. check-list, 1957 (see Appendix A). Yellow "spectacles," throat, breast; olive green above; gray rump; white belly, wing-bars. Length, 5¾ in.; wingspan, 9¾; weight, ¾ oz.

RANGE: S. Manitoba, Great Lakes region, and c. New England, south to c. and e. Texas, Gulf states, and c. Florida. Winters chiefly from s. Mexico to Panama; also Bahamas and w. Greater Antilles.

TEXAS: (See map.) *Breeding*: Early Apr. to mid-July (eggs, Apr. 15 to June; feeding fledged Brown-headed Cowbird, July 13) from near sea level to about 1,900 ft. Fairly common to uncommon in eastern third; locally uncommon to scarce in remainder of eastern two-thirds north of 29th parallel. *Migration*: Late Mar. to mid-May; early Aug. to late Oct. (extremes: Mar. 6, May 22; July 17, Nov. 23). Common (some springs; usually upper coast) to uncommon through eastern two-thirds; scarce to casual in western third. *Winter*: Late Dec. to late Feb. No specimen, but scattered sightings along coast and in Rio Grande delta; recorded inland at Huntsville, Bryan, and San Antonio.

HAUNTS AND HABITS: This slow-moving, slow-singing bird is an inhabitant of tall shade trees in deciduous or mixed woodlands. In Texas it seems especially attracted to woods growing on flood plains of rivers and creeks, canyons and gulches, and about lakes and other bodies of water. However, it occasionally lives in more open country where there are trees or groves, and it is at home—at least during migration—in streets, parks, and yards of towns.

The Yellow-throated is more of a tree-loving species than some vireos, such as the White-eye, and it usually feeds deliberately in treetops. Only in migration is it seen commonly in bushes. Its flight is quick and rather swift and is accomplished by strong, moderately frequent wing-beats, though not as many as those of the Red-eyed Vireo.

The common scolding note of the Yellow-throated Vireo is notably harsh and loud. Its song, rich and mellow, is very deliberate with long pauses; it is louder and more burry than that of the Redeye. It consists usually of five notes in two phrases and has been well represented by the words: *de-ar-ié, come-herè*. A concluding phrase often sounds like *three-eight*. *L. flavifrons* normally sings from April into September.

DETAILED ACCOUNT: ONE SUBSPECIES

TEXAS YELLOW-THROATED VIREO, *Lanivireo flavifrons flavifrons* (Vieillot)

DESCRIPTION: *Adult male, nuptial plumage*: Acquired by wear from winter plumage. Similar to Northeastern Yellow-throated Vireo, *L. f. sylvicola*, but decidedly smaller; yellow of anterior lower parts more golden (less greenish). Pileum, hindneck, and back warbler green or dark warbler green; scapulars, rump, and upper tail-coverts neutral gray; tail deep mouse gray, three or four middle pairs of rectrices edged basally with color of rump; rest of feathers narrowly margined on inner and outer webs with grayish white, more broadly on outer feathers; wings chaetura drab, but primaries and secondaries narrowly margined on outer webs with pale olivaceous gray, inner margins at base white or brownish white, and also very narrowly tipped with

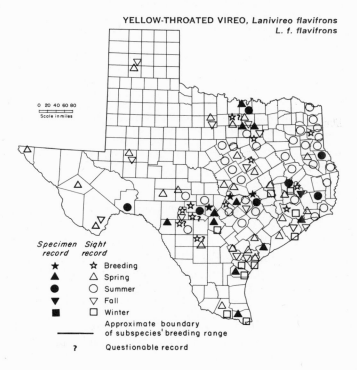

YELLOW-THROATED VIREO, *Lanivireo flavifrons*
L. f. flavifrons

0 20 40 60 80
Scale in miles

Specimen record / Sight record

★ / ☆ Breeding
▲ / △ Spring
● / ○ Summer
▼ / ▽ Fall
■ / □ Winter

——— Approximate boundary of subspecies' breeding range

? Questionable record

dull white; tertials deep mouse gray broadly edged with dull white or yellowish white; lesser wing-coverts like scapulars, slightly washed with warbler green; all but innermost median and greater coverts broadly tipped on outer webs with white, forming two conspicuous wing-bars; sides of head and of neck yellowish warbler green, but supraloral stripe and broken eye-ring (interrupted in front and behind) lemon chrome, and loral stripe dull black or fuscous; chin, throat, and breast lemon chrome instead of wax yellow, as in *sylvicola*; abdomen and crissum white; sides and flanks light neutral gray to neutral gray; lining of wings mostly white, washed with yellow and mottled with neutral gray or deep mouse gray. Bill plumbeous, olivaceous black, or plumbeous black, but mandible lighter; iris dark reddish brown; legs and feet plumbeous or plumbeous black. *Adult female, nuptial*: Acquired by wear from winter. Almost identical with nuptial adult male, but yellow of head and under surface averaging somewhat lighter and duller. *Adult male and female, winter*: Acquired by complete postnuptial molt. Similar to corresponding sex of nuptial adults. *Male and female, first nuptial*: Acquired by wear from first winter. Essentially same as corresponding nuptial adult. *Male and female, first winter*: Acquired by partial postjuvenal molt. Similar to corresponding sex of adults in winter, but warbler green of upper surface rather more yellowish; rump less purely gray (more washed with olivaceous). *Juvenal*: Acquired by complete postnatal molt. Very different from nuptial adults; pileum dull light drab, changing to brownish drab on back and rump; wings and tail similar to those of adults, but lesser coverts brownish drab, tertials and inner secondaries broadly margined on outer webs with olive yellow; sides of head dull mustard yellow; supraloral stripe and eye-ring, with chin, throat, and jugulum, pale straw yellow; remainder of lower surface white; sides and flanks scarcely washed with grayish. Bill and feet dull brown. *Natal*: Drab. Bill and feet pinkish buff; iris dark hazel.

MEASUREMENTS: *Adult male*: Wing, 70.6–74.4 (average, 72.9) mm.; tail, 47.0–51.1 (48.3); bill (exposed culmen), 10.4–12.4 (11.4); tarsus, 18.0–20.1 (19.0); middle toe without claw, 9.9–11.4 (10.4). *Adult female*: Wing, 70.6–73.9 (72.9); tail, 47.5–51.1 (48.8); bill, 11.4–12.4 (11.9); tarsus, 18.5–20.1 (19.3); middle toe, 9.9–11.9 (11.2).

RANGE: C. Texas to n. South Carolina, south to s.e. Texas and n.e. Florida. Winters from Oaxaca through Central America to Venezuela; also Bahamas.

TEXAS: *Breeding*: Collected north to Cooke, east to Shelby, southwest to Kendall, Kerr, and Kinney cos. *Migration*: Collected north to Cooke, east to Galveston, south to Cameron, west to Terrell (summer) cos.

NESTING: *Nest*: On uplands and bottoms; in forests, open country, and cultivated lands; in tree or bush, usually deciduous, 3–50 ft. above ground; beautiful basketlike cup, suspended from forked twig; composed of fine strips of bark, grasses, lichens, pine or juniper needles, various plant fibers, soft plant down, paper from hornets' nests, ornamented on outside with lichens and plant down, and bound together with caterpillar and spider silks, and insect cocoons; lined with hair, fine grass, and other plants. *Eggs*: 3–5, usually 4; short ovate; pinkish white or cream white; dotted chiefly at large end with purplish, brown, reddish brown, and black; average size, 20.6 × 15.2 mm.

SOLITARY VIREO, *Solivireo solitarius* (Wilson)

SPECIES ACCOUNT

Vireo solitarius of A.O.U. check-list, 1957 (see Appendix A). Blue-gray or gray head; white "spectacles," under parts, wing-bars; olive or gray back; yellowish or grayish flanks. Length, 5½ in.; wingspan, 9½; weight, ½ oz.

RANGE: N.e. British Columbia and s.w. Mackenzie to Nova Scotia, south in mountains through w. United States to s. Baja California and El Salvador, also in e. United States to n.e. Ohio and Georgia. Winters from s. United States to n. Nicaragua; also Cuba.

TEXAS: (See map.) *Breeding*: Probably mid-May to early Aug. (no egg dates available, but nests located: Guadalupe Mts., F. R. Gehlbach; Davis Mts., Anne LeSassier, Pansy Espy; Paradise Canyon, 4 mi. southwest of Alpine, G. M. Sutton, J. Van Tyne) from 5,000 to 8,000 ft. Fairly common to scarce in mountains of Trans-Pecos. *Migration*: Early Apr. to mid-May; early Sept. to early Nov. (extremes: Mar. 2, June 21; July 14, Nov. 30). Common to uncommon through most parts. *Winter*: Mid-Dec. to early Apr. Fairly common to uncommon in southern half east of Pecos River; scarce to rare west of Pecos River and in northern half.

HAUNTS AND HABITS: The Solitary Vireo inhabits coniferous-hardwood forests. In montane Trans-Pecos, sole breeding outpost in Texas for this recluse, preferred mixed woodlands are generally scrubby and above 5,000 ft. Here the Solitary lives on juniper-pine-oak slopes and along creeks and draws lined with oaks, maples, and occasional cottonwoods. During migration and winter, however, it may be found in a wide variety of woods, as well as coastal scrub, tall brush, and isolated mottes.

On the wing, the Solitary Vireo is strong and swift. Tree-to-tree or bush-to-bush flights are quick and sometimes diving. While the Solitary seeks seclusion of dense vegetation, it is not especially shy, particularly in the nonbreeding season. It frequents tall trees, bushes, thickets, and undergrowth but is not commonly seen on the ground. Most movements are deliberate, after the fashion of many vireos, although the bird is capable of moving quickly when occasion demands.

Its ordinary scolding note is similar to that of the

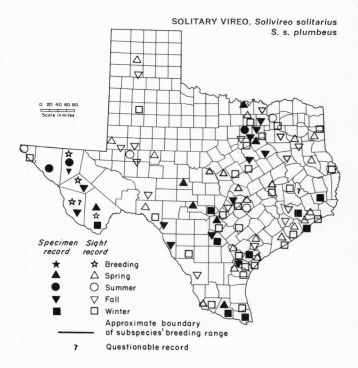

SOLITARY VIREO, *Solivireo solitarius*
S. s. *plumbeus*

0 20 40 60 80
Scale in miles

Specimen record | Sight record
★ | ☆ Breeding
▲ | △ Spring
● | ○ Summer
▼ | ▽ Fall
■ | □ Winter
——— Approximate boundary of subspecies' breeding range
? Questionable record

Red-eyed Vireo but not quite as emphatic. Its song, among the best of the vireos, resembles that of a somewhat slow Redeye, but with much of the rich quality of the Yellow-throated Vireo. Throughout Texas, males sing much in April and May; on breeding territory they may sing well into August.

DETAILED ACCOUNT: FIVE SUBSPECIES

BLUE-HEADED SOLITARY VIREO, *Solivireo solitarius solitarius* (Wilson)

DESCRIPTION: *Adult male, nuptial plumage:* Acquired by wear from winter plumage. Pileum and hindneck deep neutral gray; remainder of upper surface kronberg green, somewhat mixed with neutral gray on back and rather more yellowish on rump and upper tail-coverts; tail rather dark mouse gray, outer web of outermost feather dull white, remaining rectrices narrowly margined on outer webs with yellowish olive green, on inner margins with dull white or yellowish white, most broadly on outer feathers where these edgings become broad oblique tips terminally; wings deep mouse gray, primaries and secondaries narrowly margined externally with color of back, inner webs, except at tips, dull white or brownish white, tertials broadly margined on outer webs with dull olive yellow; wing-coverts margined with color of back, greater and median coverts broadly tipped with yellowish or greenish white, forming two conspicuous wing-bars; sides of head and anterior part of neck like crown, but sides of forehead, anterior and upper parts of lores, and broad eye-ring white or grayish white, and posterior part of lores dull black or dark neutral gray; sides of neck like back; lower surface white, but sides and flanks citrine yellow washed with neutral gray and serpentine gray; under wing-coverts deep mouse gray, broadly edged with white or yellowish white; axillars citrine yellow. Bill black, slate black, or slate color, with basal half or more of mandible plumbeous; iris burnt umber or deep bister; legs and feet plumbeous or slate color. *Adult female, nuptial:* Acquired by wear from winter. Similar to nuptial adult male, but upper parts duller and more uniform, crown more olivaceous or brownish, olive green of rest of upper surface rather lighter and more yellowish; lower parts usually more or less washed with buff. *Adult male and female, winter:* Acquired by complete postnuptial molt. Similar to corresponding sex in nuptial adult, but wing-bars white or whitish and edges of tertials broader. *Male and female, first nuptial:* Acquired by wear from first winter. Similar to respective sex in nuptial adult, but pileum duller, more washed with olive or dull brown (not so clearly gray); wing-quills somewhat more brownish. *Male and female, first winter:* Acquired by partial postjuvenal molt, which does not involve wing-quills or tail. Similar to corresponding sex of adult in winter but duller; pileum more brownish or olivaceous; olive green of remaining upper parts somewhat more brownish; lower surface more tinged with buff. *Juvenal:* Acquired by complete postnatal molt. Upper surface dull buffy olive; wings and tail similar to those of adults in winter but more brownish; sides of head paler and much more brownish than in adults—drab or rather light drab; lower parts dull white or buffy white; sides and flanks white, somewhat washed with light yellow. *Natal* (this plumage of this race not seen in Texas): Buffy white. Bill, legs, and feet pinkish buff.

MEASUREMENTS: *Adult male:* Wing, 71.9–75.9 (average, 74.7) mm.; tail, 48.0–55.1 (52.8); bill (exposed culmen), 9.4–9.9 (9.7); tarsus, 17.5–19.0 (18.3); middle toe without claw, 10.9–11.4 (11.2). *Adult female:* Wing, 71.1–74.9 (73.4); tail, 47.0–54.1 (50.8); bill, 9.4–10.9 (10.2); tarsus, 18.0–19.0 (18.8); middle toe, 9.9–11.9 (10.9).

RANGE: S.w. Mackenzie to Nova Scotia, south to n.e. North Dakota and s.w. Pennsylvania. Winters from Texas and North Carolina through Mexico to n. Nicaragua; also e. Cuba.

TEXAS: *Migration:* Collected north to Cooke, south to Navarro and Cameron, west to Val Verde cos. Fairly common. *Winter:*

Taken northwest to Kendall, east to Galveston, south to Cameron and Hidalgo cos. Uncommon.

NESTING: (This race does not nest in Texas.) *Nest:* In mountains and valleys; in forests or on their margins, sometimes in more open country; in evergreen or other tree or bush, 5–12 ft. above ground; well-made, basketlike, hemispherical pensile nest, usually hanging from forks of horizontal twig or branch; composed of strips of grapevine or other bark, leaves, lichens, catkins, fine dry grass, mosses, and plant down, covered or ornamented on outside with paper from hornets' nests, and bound together with caterpillar or spider silk; lined with fine grasses, pine needles, and hair. *Eggs:* 3–5; ovate to elliptical ovate; white with faint creamy tinge; speckled, chiefly at large end, with chestnut, umber brown, or black; average size, 20.6 × 15.0 mm.

MOUNTAIN SOLITARY VIREO, *Solivireo solitarius alticola* (Brewster)

DESCRIPTION: *Adult male and female, nuptial plumage:* Similar to S. s. *solitarius* but larger, especially bill and wing; upper parts more grayish (less olive green).

MEASUREMENTS: *Adult male:* Wing, 78.0–83.6 (average, 80.2) mm.; tail, 52.1–56.9 (55.1); bill (exposed culmen), 10.9–11.9 (11.7); tarsus, 18.0–20.1 (19.3); middle toe without claw, 11.9–13.0 (12.2). *Adult female:* Wing, 75.9–82.0 (78.7); tail, 51.1–57.9 (55.6); bill, 10.9–11.9 (11.7); tarsus, 18.5–20.1 (19.3); middle toe, 10.9–13.0 (12.2).

RANGE: S.e. Kentucky and w. Virginia, south to n. Georgia and w. North Carolina. Winters from Texas (casually) and South Carolina to c. Florida.

TEXAS: *Winter:* One specimen: Hardin Co., Silsbee (Jan. 16, 1917, A. P. Smith).

PLUMBEOUS SOLITARY VIREO, *Solivireo solitarius plumbeus* (Coues)

DESCRIPTION: *Adult male and female, nuptial plumage:* Similar to S. s. *alticola*, but tail longer; middle toe shorter; upper parts paler, very much less olive greenish—from dull neutral gray on crown to rather dark olive gray on remainder of upper surface; rump and upper tail-coverts deep grayish olive; sides and flanks much less strongly washed with greenish yellow; edgings of wings and tail pale gray or white instead of olive green. *Natal:* Probably similar to S. s. *solitarius.*

MEASUREMENTS: *Adult male:* Wing, 77.0–81.0 (average, 79.5) mm.; tail, 55.9–59.9 (58.2); bill (exposed culmen), 9.7–10.9 (10.4); tarsus, 18.5–20.6 (19.8); middle toe without claw, 10.4–11.7 (11.2). *Adult female:* Wing, 76.5–80.0 (78.2); tail, 55.1–58.9 (56.6); bill, 9.7–11.4 (10.7); tarsus, 18.0–20.1 (19.3); middle toe, 9.4–11.9 (10.9).

RANGE: N. New Mexico to Trans-Pecos Texas. Winters in s.w. New Mexico.

TEXAS: *Breeding:* Collected in Culberson, Jeff Davis, and Brewster cos.

NESTING: Similar to that of S. s. *solitarius,* but average egg size, 20.1 × 15.0 mm.

JACKSON'S SOLITARY VIREO, *Solivireo solitarius jacksoni* Oberholser, new subspecies (see Appendix A)

DESCRIPTION: *Adult male and female, nuptial plumage:* Similar to S. s. *plumbeus,* but bill larger; upper surface more olivaceous (less grayish), also a little lighter; flanks less washed with olive green (more grayish).

MEASUREMENTS: *Adult male:* Wing, 77.5–83.1 (average, 80.7) mm.; tail, 55.9–59.9 (57.9); bill (exposed culmen), 10.9–12.4 (11.7); tarsus, 19.0–21.1 (20.1); middle toe without claw, 10.4–11.9 (11.2). *Adult female:* Wing, 77.0–82.6 (79.2); tail, 55.9–60.5 (57.7); bill, 10.7–13.0 (11.7); tarsus, 19.6–21.6 (20.3); middle toe, 10.7–11.9 (11.2).

TYPE: Adult female, no. 268418, U.S. National Museum, Biological Surveys collection; 16 mi. south of Roundup, Montana, Aug. 6, 1918; M. A. Hanna.

RANGE: N.e. Nevada, c. Montana, and s.w. South Dakota, south to n.e. Sonora; perhaps extreme w. Texas (breeding unconfirmed). Winters from s. Sonora to e. Guerrero.

TEXAS: *Summer*: Five specimens: Hudspeth Co., Fort Hancock, 3,517 ft. (June 9, 10, 11, 12, 21, 1893, E. A. Mearns).

CASSIN'S SOLITARY VIREO, *Solivireo solitarius cassinii* (Xantus)

DESCRIPTION: *Adult male and female, nuptial plumage*: Similar to *S. s. solitarius*, but upper parts duller and more uniform with less contrast between pileum and back; wing-bars narrower and more whitish; head lighter and duller; back duller, of less greenish (more brownish) olive; sides and flanks paler, less yellowish.

MEASUREMENTS: *Adult male*: Wing, 70.1–77.0 (average, 72.2) mm.; tail, 49.0–55.9 (52.3); bill (exposed culmen), 9.9–10.9 (10.2); tarsus, 18.0–20.1 (18.8); middle toe without claw, 10.9–11.9 (11.2). *Adult female*: Wing, 70.1–74.9 (72.2); tail, 49.5–54.1 (52.1); bill, 8.9–10.9 (9.7); tarsus, 18.0–20.1 (19.3); middle toe, 10.9–11.9 (11.2).

RANGE: S.w. British Columbia to s.w. Alberta, south to n. Baja California. Winters mainly through Mexico to Guatemala.

TEXAS: *Migration*: Collected in Culberson, Jeff Davis, Presidio, and Brewster cos. Rare. *Winter*: One specimen: Brewster Co., Chisos Mts. (Feb. 24, 1935, J. Van Tyne).

BLACK-WHISKERED VIREO, *Vireosylva calidris* (Linnaeus)

SPECIES ACCOUNT

Vireo altiloquus of A.O.U. check-list, 1957 (see Appendix A). Northern (Florida) race is *Vireosylva calidris barbatula* fide Robert Ridgway, 1904. Resembles Red-eyed Vireo (see below), but has narrow blackish streak on each side of throat ("whisker"); upper parts a little duller; bill larger. Length, 6½ in.

RANGE: Mangroves of s. coastal Florida (especially Florida keys) and West Indies. Floridian, Bahaman, and most Greater Antillean birds winter chiefly in n. South America; many Hispaniolan and Lesser Antillean individuals are resident.

TEXAS: *Accidental*: One specimen: Galveston Co., Galveston Island (bird first seen on Apr. 28, 1965, by a number of birders; taken, Apr. 29, by J. O. Ellis. Bird confiscated by law enforcement agents for use as evidence in court trial; in 1973, skin was turned over by Texas Parks and Wildlife Department to U.S. National Museum; catalog no. 566527; skin identified as *Vireo altiloquus barbatulus* by Roxie C. Laybourne and J. S. Weske). One sighted: Aransas Co., Rockport (Apr. 24, 1966, Mr. and Mrs. H. A. J. Evans; Apr. 28, W. V. Mealy; Apr. 30, Sumner Dana, J. A. Middleton).

It is noteworthy that over the last decade the species has occurred repeatedly during spring and summer in s. Louisiana, and that nesting is suspected (see *American Birds* 25 [1971]: 868).

HAUNTS AND HABITS: The Black-whiskered Vireo, eyes just as red, is the West Indian representative of the Red-eyed Vireo. Like the Mangrove Cuckoo, *Coccyzus minor*, the Blackwhisker inhabits coastal mangrove woods almost exclusively in Florida, but farther south it also occurs in various other genera and species of scrubby tropical trees. Nest of the Blackwhisker is a deep cup—sometimes composed largely of seaweed—suspended from a horizontally forked mangrove twig. The three white or pinkish eggs are sparingly dotted with brown.

Flits of the present vireo are usually short, between interior branches of mangroves. However, A. H. Howell once collected an individual from the top of a large oak growing a mile inland from Old Tampa Bay. The Blackwhisker eats spiders, caterpillars, beetles, wasps, bees, true bugs, earwigs; also barberries and ragweed seed.

Song of *V. calidris* resembles that of the Red-eyed Vireo but is somewhat more hesitating and emphatic (F. M. Chapman).

DETAILED ACCOUNT: ONE SUBSPECIES

NORTHERN BLACK-WHISKERED VIREO, *Vireosylva calidris barbatula* (Cabanis)

Vireo altiloquus barbatulus of A.O.U. check-list, 1957.
DESCRIPTION: See Robert Ridgway, 1904, *Bull. U.S. Nat. Mus.*, no. 50, pt. 3, pp. 141–143.
MEASUREMENTS: Ibid., pp. 141–142.
RANGE: S. Florida (north on Gulf coast to Anclote Keys, on Atlantic to Miami area), Bahamas, Cuba, Isle of Pines, and Little Cayman.
TEXAS: *Accidental*: One specimen (see species account).

YELLOW-GREEN VIREO, *Vireosylva flavoviridis* (Cassin)

SPECIES ACCOUNT

Vireo flavoviridis of A.O.U. check-list, 1957 (see Appendix A); often regarded as conspecific with Red-eyed Vireo. Resembles Red-eyed Vireo (see below), but sides and crissum washed with yellow; head-stripes less defined. Length, 6½ in.

RANGE: C. Sonora, c. Nuevo León, and Rio Grande delta of Texas (rarely), south to Panama. Winters chiefly from s. Panama to upper Amazon Basin.

TEXAS: (See map.) *Breeding*: Probably mid-May to mid-July (no egg dates available, but nests located: Cameron Co., 13 mi. southwest of Harlingen, June 20, Sept. 5, 1943, L. I. Davis; probably nested: Hidalgo Co., Santa Ana Nat. Wildlife Refuge, present all summer and 1 adult and 3 "birds of the year" noted, July 29, 1960, R. J. Fleetwood) from near sea level to perhaps 150 ft. Rare in Rio Grande delta. *Migration*: May 6 to May 14; July 3 to Oct. 13. Rare in Rio Grande delta; casual at Austin and along coast northeast to Chambers Co.; accidental in Big Bend (see detailed account). *Winter*: No specimen, but three records from Rio Grande delta: Cameron Co., Harlingen (Dec. 27, 1947, Ruby Sandmeyer); Hidalgo Co., Santa Ana Refuge (Dec. 20, 1961, Audubon Christmas Bird Count, R. J. Fleetwood, compiler); Hidalgo Co., Bentsen–Rio Grande Valley State Park (Dec. 23, 1965, Pauline James).

HAUNTS AND HABITS: The Yellow-green Vireo, continental tropical counterpart of the Red-eyed Vireo, breeds in lowlands and at moderate altitudes in Mexico and Central America. Unlike many tropical species, the Yellow-green is highly migratory; most individuals spend the nonbreeding season in South America. During spring and summer, it is a bird primarily of woodlands, shady plantations and roadsides, forest margins and clearings, thin second-growth woods, and even brushy pastures. In the Rio Grande delta of Texas it is irregularly found in scattered timber along the Rio Grande, in residential shade trees, especially tepeguaje (*Leucaena pulverulenta*), and in tall thickets and brushy tangles bordering resacas and levees. Except at the extremes of its range, the Yellow-green, like the Redeye in unpoisoned U.S. woodlands, is usually numerous. Behavior is likewise similar to that of its close relative.

Song of the two is fairly close, but the Yellow-green's has a chirpy, noticeably House Sparrow–like quality. Singing lasts from late March into August.

DETAILED ACCOUNT: ONE SUBSPECIES

NORTHEASTERN YELLOW-GREEN VIREO, *Vireosylva flavoviridis flavoviridis* Cassin

DESCRIPTION: *Adults, nuptial plumage*: Acquired by wear from winter plumage. Pileum and hindneck mouse gray to light hair brown; remainder of upper surface citrine; tail between citrine drab and deep olive, feathers margined on outer webs with citrine and on inner webs with dull straw yellow; wings dark hair brown, inner margins, except at tips of primaries, dull straw yellow, primaries (except at tips), secondaries, and tertials margined on outer webs with pyrite yellow, remainder of tertials like tail; lesser and median wing-coverts like back; greater series edged on outer webs with same color, outermost with pyrite yellow; superciliary stripe light drab or drab gray, above this a narrow rather ill-defined streak somewhat, or not at all, darker than crown; lores dull drab, becoming rather darker just in front of eye; region below eye yellowish drab washed with citrine; sides of neck like back, becoming paler and more yellowish on auriculars; chin, throat, and middle of breast and of abdomen grayish or buffy white; sides of throat, of breast, and of body, also flanks, olive yellow; crissum between pale lemon yellow and empire yellow; lining of wing similar, outer under wing-coverts somewhat spotted with darker. Bill dull brown, but mandible and cutting edges pale bluish gray; iris dark red or brownish red; legs and feet bright bluish plumbeous. *Adults, winter*: Acquired by complete postnuptial molt. Almost identical to nuptial adults. *First nuptial*: Acquired by wear from first winter. Similar to nuptial adults, except for retained juvenal wing-quills and tail feathers. *First winter*: Acquired by partial postjuvenal molt, which does not include wing-quills or tail. Similar to adults in winter. *Juvenal*: Acquired by complete postnatal molt. Pileum, hindneck, back, scapulars, rump, and lesser wing-coverts dull wood brown; superciliary stripe brownish or buffy white; wing-quills and tail similar to those of nuptial adults; lower parts white; sides and flanks primrose yellow; crissum between citrine yellow and amber yellow. Bill dull brown, but basal portion of mandible tinged with blue; iris dark brown. *Natal*: Drab gray.

MEASUREMENTS: *Adult male*: Wing, 74.9–82.0 (average, 78.2) mm.; tail, 50.0–59.9 (55.3); bill (exposed culmen), 14.0–15.0 (14.2); tarsus, 18.0–19.0 (18.8); middle toe without claw, 9.9–10.9 (10.7). *Adult female*: Wing, 73.9–80.0 (76.2); tail, 49.0–55.1 (51.8); bill, 13.0–15.0 (14.0); tarsus, 17.0–19.0 (18.3); middle toe, 9.9–10.9 (10.7).

RANGE: Nuevo León, Rio Grande delta of Texas, and Tamaulipas, south through e. Mexico to Nicaragua. Winters from Colombia to e. Ecuador.

TEXAS: *Breeding*: One specimen: Cameron Co., Brownsville (June 7, 1892, F. B. Armstrong). *Migration*: Two specimens outside breeding range: Matagorda Co., Matagorda (May 9, 1938, H. H. Kimball); San Patricio Co., Ingleside (female, May 10, 1966, J. I. Richardson). One specimen (perhaps of this race) from Brewster Co.: Big Bend Nat. Park, Cottonwood Campground (1 singing male, July 13, 1972, Dave Easterla, fide R. H. Wauer).

NESTING: *Nest*: Along streams or on uplands, in forests or their margins or more open country; in tree or bush, sometimes resting on ground, and usually not more than 10 ft. above, sometimes over water, and at times well concealed; pensile nest, like that of other vireos, strongly woven and compact, suspended between forks of twig; composed of strips of bark, weeds, and various other vegetable fibers, soft dry leaves, with pieces of string or paper woven into sides, all bound together on outside with spider webs and egg cases; lined with fine vegetable fibers and fine dry grass. *Eggs*: 3–4; ovate to elliptical ovate; white, rather sparsely dotted with burnt umber, orange rufous, and black; average size, 20.6 × 14.5 mm.

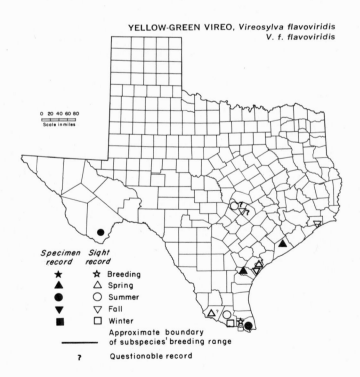

YELLOW-GREEN VIREO, *Vireosylva flavoviridis*
V. f. flavoviridis

0 20 40 60 80
Scale in miles

Specimen record | Sight record
★ | ☆ Breeding
▲ | △ Spring
● | ○ Summer
▼ | ▽ Fall
■ | □ Winter
——— Approximate boundary of subspecies' breeding range
? Questionable record

RED-EYED VIREO, *Vireosylva virescens* (Vieillot)

SPECIES ACCOUNT

Vireo olivaceus of A.O.U. check-list, 1957 (see Appendix A). Gray crown; black-bordered white eyestripe; red eyes; olive above; white below. Length, 6 in.; wingspan, 10; weight, ½ oz.

RANGE: S.w. British Columbia and s.w. Mackenzie to Nova Scotia, south to n. Oregon, c. Colorado, c. Texas, Gulf states, and c. Florida. Winters in Amazon Basin.

TEXAS: (See map.) *Breeding*: Late Apr. to early Aug. (eggs, May 6 to June 18; young in nest, July 28) from near sea level to about 2,000 ft. Locally common to uncommon in eastern half south irregularly to 29th parallel; locally fairly common to scarce in canyons of

Edwards Plateau. *Migration*: Early Apr. to mid-May; mid-Aug. to mid-Oct. (extremes: Mar. 2, June 10; July 6, Nov. 16). Very common to uncommon through eastern two-thirds; increasingly scarce west of 100th meridian to El Paso region, where casual.

HAUNTS AND HABITS: Within Texas the Red-eyed Vireo makes its home in open woodlands, preferably broad-leaved though often mixed. It also frequents shade trees about houses, along town streets, and in parks. In the breeding season this vireo requires tall timber; therefore, through the western part of its range in this state it occurs mostly along rivers. Even in eastern Texas it is seldom found away from tall streamside baldcypress (*Taxodium distichum*), cottonwood (*Populus deltoides*), black willow (*Salix nigra*), and American sycamore (*Platanus occidentalis*).

Flight, whether from one branch to another or from tree to tree, is oftentimes rapid, on other occasions deliberate, and performed with powerful, quick, though not numerous, wing-beats. The Redeye is capable, however, of making long journeys, as its annual migration to South America well indicates. On a protracted flight across open spaces it often flies high, fast, and more or less unevenly. It hunts insects with great diligence, slipping through the canopy and lower foliage like a warbler or hanging to terminal twigs almost like a titmouse; on this account *V. virescens* is often mistaken for other avian species. This vireo supplements its animal diet with fruits of Virginia creeper, dogwood, elderberry, blackberry, magnolia, others.

The alarm note of the Red-eyed Vireo is a rather drawn out, querulous cry, something like *creee* or *chway*. Its song is a mellow succession of short phrases, very much like that of a Robin though, of course, not as loud. Throughout the day in spring and early summer this bird is such a persistent and emphatic repeater of his phrases that long ago country folk named him "preacher." *You see it—you know it—do you hear me?—do you believe it?* was one interpretation. It occasionally sings while sitting on the nest. The song period lasts well into late summer, sometimes into September —beyond that of most Texas summer birds.

DETAILED ACCOUNT: TWO SUBSPECIES

EASTERN RED-EYED VIREO, *Vireosylva virescens virescens* (Vieillot)

No races recognized by A.O.U. check-list, 1957 (see Appendix A).

DESCRIPTION: *Adults, nuptial plumage*: Acquired by wear from winter plumage. Pileum mouse gray to deep mouse gray; remainder of upper surface roman green to dull citrine; tail hair brown, but inner margins of feathers slightly paler, particularly on outer rectrices, and outer webs of feathers margined with color of rump; wings dark hair brown, inner edges of primaries and secondaries, except at tips of primaries, yellowish or brownish white, outer margins olive green like upper surface; tertials similar but somewhat duller; lesser wing-coverts and outer margins of other coverts similar to back, but on outer webs of greater coverts light yellowish olive; broad superciliary stripe dull white to drab gray, above this a well-defined line of blackish mouse gray; lores and short postocular stripe dull hair brown; cheeks and auriculars light citrine drab; sides of neck like back; lower parts dull white, washed with gray or dull light green; sides of body and flanks light yellowish olive; crissum whitish yellow; lining of wing primrose yellow or colonial buff, with some darker markings on outer coverts. Maxilla plumbeous, blackish slate, slate black, or brownish plumbeous; mandible cinereous, slate gray, plumbeous, or french gray, base slightly pink, whitish, or with tinge of flesh color, and tip sometimes dull white; iris dark red, red brown, maroon, or bright indian red; legs, feet, and claws plumbeous, slate gray, or slate color. *Adults, winter*: Acquired by complete postnuptial molt. Very much like nuptial adults, but slightly brighter and more richly colored. *First nuptial*: Acquired by wear from first winter. Practically identical with nuptial adults, except perhaps for rather more brownish wings and tail retained from juvenal. *First winter*: Acquired by partial postjuvenal molt, which does not involve wing-quills or tail. Practically identical with adults in winter. *Juvenal*: Acquired by complete postnatal molt. Upper surface, including lesser wing-coverts, wood brown to avellaneous or buffy brown; rest of wings and tail like those of nuptial adults; broad superciliary stripe dull white or buffy white; narrow loral streak and postocular streak dark brownish gray; lower parts white, but crissum straw yellow and flanks sometimes slightly washed with same. Maxilla black or blackish slate, mandible french gray, plumbeous, or dull white, base flesh color or tinged with pink; iris dull reddish brown, reddish brown, or burnt umber; feet plumbeous. *Natal*: Pale drab gray. Bill, legs, and feet pinkish buff; iris walnut brown.

MEASUREMENTS: *Adult male*: Wing, 77.0–85.1 (average, 81.0) mm.; tail, 51.1–59.9 (55.1); bill (exposed culmen), 10.9–14.0 (12.7); tarsus, 17.0–19.0 (18.0); middle toe without claw, 10.9–12.4 (11.4). *Adult female*: Wing, 73.9–83.1 (78.2); tail, 47.0–55.9 (52.6); bill, 11.9–13.0 (12.2); tarsus, 17.0–19.0 (18.0); middle toe, 10.2–11.9 (10.7).

RANGE: S.w. British Columbia and s.w. Mackenzie to Nova Scotia, south to c. Texas and c. Florida. Winters in Amazon Basin.

TEXAS: *Breeding*: Collected north to Cooke, east to Marion, south to Bexar, west to Kinney cos. *Migration*: Collected north to Clay, east to San Jacinto, south to Cameron, west to Val Verde and Tom Green cos. Common.

NESTING: *Nest*: On uplands and bottomlands; in forests, also more open country, as well as parks and yards in towns; in various trees, such as elm and maple, 4–50 ft. above ground,

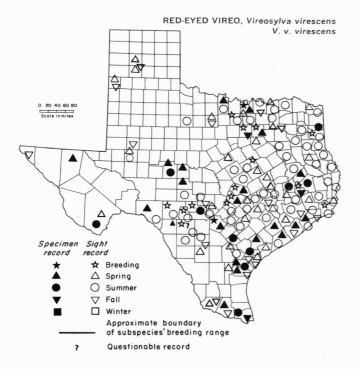

RED-EYED VIREO, *Vireosylva virescens*
V. v. virescens

0 20 40 60 80
Scale in miles

Specimen record	Sight record	
★	☆	Breeding
▲	△	Spring
●	○	Summer
▼	▽	Fall
■	□	Winter

——— Approximate boundary of subspecies' breeding range

? Questionable record

PLATE 27: Brewer's Blackbird, *Euphagus cyanocephalus*

usually not over 10 ft., sometimes even bottom of nest resting on ground; very well made, strongly woven, cup-shaped, pensile nest, so durable it often resists effects of winter storms, attached to horizontal fork of twig or branch; composed of strips of bark, fine grasses, leaves, weeds, or vines, and other vegetable fibers, bits of string, paper from hornets' or wasps' nests, and bound together with spider webs, cocoons, and bits of caterpillar silk; lined with finer similar materials, sometimes also with bark fibers, hairlike stems and rootlets, hair, or pine needles. *Eggs:* 3–5, usually 4; ovate to elliptical ovate; white; sparingly speckled with reddish brown, light brown, deep umber, and black, chiefly at large end; average size, 21.6 × 14.2 mm.

NORTHWESTERN RED-EYED VIREO, *Vireosylva virescens caniviridis* (Burleigh)

No races recognized by A.O.U. check-list, 1957 (see Appendix A).

DESCRIPTION: *Adults, nuptial plumage:* Resembling *V. v. virescens,* but pileum lighter; remainder of upper surface paler, more grayish (less olive greenish); blackish line on each side of pileum less well marked; lower parts more clearly white, with little or no yellowish olive on sides and flanks.

MEASUREMENTS: *Adult male:* Wing, 81.0–83.0 (average, 81.9) mm., tail, 53.0–58.0 (56.5); bill (exposed culmen), 11.0–12.5 (11.7). *Adult female:* Wing, 78.0–80.0 (78.8); tail, 54.0–58.5 (56.8); bill, 11.0–12.0 (11.6).

RANGE: Washington, n. Oregon, and Idaho. In migration, east to Texas. Winters probably in South America.

TEXAS: *Migration:* Collected in Brewster (1 specimen, June 10), Galveston (1), and San Patricio (1, July 6) cos. Rare.

PHILADELPHIA VIREO, *Vireosylva philadelphica* (Cassin)

SPECIES ACCOUNT

Vireo philadelphicus of A.O.U. check-list, 1957 (see Appendix A). Gray head; whitish eye-stripe; blackish line through eye; grayish olive above; yellowish below

PHILADELPHIA VIREO, *Vireo philadelphica*

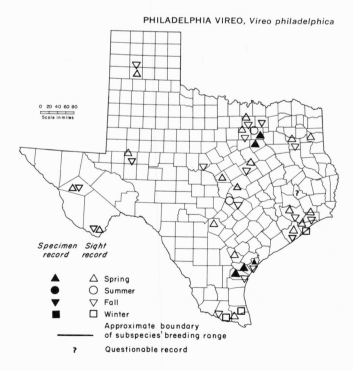

0 20 40 60 80
Scale in miles

Specimen   Sight
record   record

▲ △ Spring
● ○ Summer
▼ ▽ Fall
■ □ Winter

——— Approximate boundary of subspecies' breeding range

?   Questionable record

(paler on throat, crissum). Length, 5¼ in.; wingspan, 8¼; weight, ½ oz.

RANGE: N.e. British Columbia and c. Alberta to Newfoundland, south to n. North Dakota and c. Maine. Winters from Guatemala to n.w. Colombia.

TEXAS: (See map.) *Migration:* Late Apr. to mid-May; late Aug. to late Oct. (extremes: Mar. 21, May 21; Aug. 2, Nov. 14). Uncommon (some springs) to rare (most falls) through eastern half; extremely rare in northern Panhandle and Trans-Pecos. *Winter:* Dec. 22 to Jan. 2. No specimen, but several sightings on upper coast and in Rio Grande delta.

HAUNTS AND HABITS: In its summer home, actually well north of the City of Brotherly Love, the Philadelphia Vireo inhabits scrubby second growth, woodland edges, moist thickets along streams or about lakes, and, to some extent, open mixed woods with heavy understory. Here it may hang its tight, cuplike nest—often ragged with usnea lichen—on horizontal twigs of a tall deciduous tree or in the crown of a deciduous sapling. During migration through Texas, as elsewhere, it frequents woodlands and visits shade trees in parks and yards and along streets of cities.

The Philadelphia's flight is similar to that of the Red-eyed Vireo, but swifter with powerful, though not rapid, wing-beats. It lives mostly in higher parts of trees, sometimes in their very tops, but it also descends to lower branches and to bushes. This species is rather retiring and keeps much within foliage, although occasionally it flies out into the air to catch an insect. Feeding and singing alternately, it hops more or less deliberately from branch to branch with a slow lifting motion of the wings. It is, however, quicker in movements than the Redeye. The Philadelphia feeds also about the terminal twigs and leaves, even clinging upside down like a chickadee. Particularly in the interior foliage, it peers deliberately about, turning its head from side to side in search of insects.

The rather harsh call note is quite like the Warbling Vireo's. The Philadelphia's ordinary song, resembling that of the Red-eyed Vireo, is usually more slowly delivered (about half the speed of the Redeye's) and rather sweeter, clearer, and higher in pitch. It has been represented by the following: *chur-r-ee, chur-wee, pst-i-ree, psr-r-ree.* Within Texas, males are occasionally found in song in May.

DETAILED ACCOUNT: NO SUBSPECIES

DESCRIPTION: *Adults, nuptial plumage:* Acquired by wear from winter plumage. Pileum between mouse gray and dark olive gray; remainder of upper surface greenish deep grayish olive; tail dark hair brown, margined externally with color of rump, feathers margined on inner edges with yellowish white, broadest toward tips; wings rather dark hair brown, inner edges of quills yellowish or brownish white, quills margined on outer webs with color of back, lesser and median wing-coverts edged with same, greater coverts with dull rather light grayish olive; superciliary stripe and sides of forehead dull buffy white or dull cartridge buff; lores and postocular streak dull hair brown; cheeks and auriculars between light drab and deep olive buff, spot below eye paler; sides of neck dark olive buff; throat and breast straw yellow to amber yellow; chin dull white; abdomen buffy white; sides and flanks similar to breast but somewhat washed with olive gray; crissum straw yellow; lining of wing barium yellow, more or less mottled with hair brown or mouse gray. Bill black, blackish brown, or grayish brown, but mandible plumbeous; iris hazel or black; legs and feet plumbeous. *Adults, winter*: Acquired by complete postnuptial molt. Essentially identical with nuptial adults, but colors rather brighter and deeper. *First nuptial*: Acquired by wear from first winter. Practically identical with nuptial adults, except perhaps for slightly more worn wing-quills retained from juvenal. *First winter*: Acquired by partial postjuvenal molt, which does not involve wing-quills or tail. Similar to adults in winter, but pileum more olivaceous; lower parts more deeply and extensively yellow—auburn yellow to penard yellow. *Juvenal*: Acquired by complete postnatal molt. Above olive brown, head, nape, and rump paler; wings and tail similar to those of nuptial adults, but wing-coverts much more brownish; sides of head buffy yellow; eye-ring pale dull yellow; loral and postocular streak dull brown; lower surface pale primrose yellow, but sides and flanks darker. Maxilla dark brown; mandible french gray, base dull white or tinged with flesh color; iris black or dark brown; legs and feet cinereous; claws tipped with white.

MEASUREMENTS: *Adult male*: Wing, 65.0–69.1 (average, 66.8) mm.; tail, 43.9–48.0 (45.7); bill (exposed culmen), 8.9–9.9 (9.1); tarsus, 16.0–18.0 (17.3); middle toe without claw, 8.9–9.9 (9.7). *Adult female*: Wing, 62.0–66.0 (64.8); tail, 42.9–46.0 (44.7); bill, 8.6–9.4 (8.9); tarsus, 17.0–18.0 (17.5); middle toe, 8.9–9.9 (9.4).

TEXAS: *Migration*: Collected in Dallas (1 specimen), Ellis (1), Aransas (1), San Patricio (1), and Nueces (1) cos.

WARBLING VIREO, *Melodivireo gilvus* (Vieillot)

SPECIES ACCOUNT

Vireo gilvus of A.O.U. check-list, 1957 (see Appendix A). Pale and drab. Grayish olive head, upper parts; whitish eye-stripe, under parts; buffy wash on sides. Length, 5½ in.; wingspan, 8¾; weight, ½ oz.

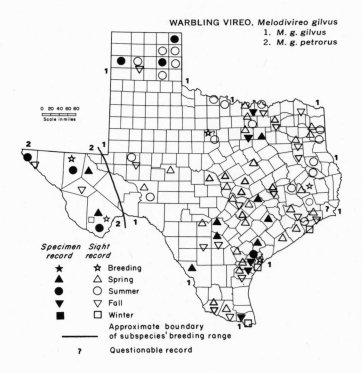

WARBLING VIREO, *Melodivireo gilvus*
1. *M. g. gilvus*
2. *M. g. petrorus*

0 20 40 60 80
Scale in miles

Specimen / Sight record

★ / ☆ Breeding
▲ / △ Spring
● / ○ Summer
▼ / ▽ Fall
■ / □ Winter

——— Approximate boundary of subspecies' breeding range

? Questionable record

RANGE: N. British Columbia and s. Mackenzie to Nova Scotia, south to Baja California, s. Mexico (locally), Texas, Louisiana, and e. Virginia. Winters from s. Sonora and Veracruz to El Salvador.

TEXAS: (See map.) *Breeding*: Early May to late July (no egg dates available, but nest being incubated, Guadalupe Mts., June 29, 1960, F. R. Gehlbach; nest located, Chisos Mts., June 8, 1968, R. H. Wauer; pair observed nest building, Rockport, May 10, 1939, Connie Hagar) from near sea level to 8,000 ft. Fairly common in Guadalupe Mts.; uncommon and local in other Trans-Pecos mountains and in northern Panhandle (nesting suspected); scarce and very local in north central portion, casually south to central coast. Recent nesting observed in east Texas: Polk Co., along Trinity River (1972, C. D. Fisher). *Migration*: Mid-Apr. to mid-May; mid-Aug. to late Oct. (extremes: Mar. 13, May 28; July 27, Nov. 26). Common (some springs) to uncommon (most falls) through eastern half; uncommon to scarce through western half. *Winter*: Dec. 23 to Feb. 21. No specimen, but several sightings along coast and in Rio Grande delta; isolated sight record: Big Bend Nat. Park, mouth of Tornillo Creek (Dec. 25, 1934, Lovie Whitaker).

HAUNTS AND HABITS: The Warbling Vireo makes its home in tall, broad-leaved trees, preferring those that grow along streams and in open woodlands to those of dense forests. It lives also in orchards, about country houses, in streets, parks, and dooryards of towns, where its pleasing song is more often heard than the bird is seen. During migration it is likely to be found in a wide variety of woodlands and shade trees.

In flight this bird is like the Red-eyed Vireo, and ordinarily its movements on the wing are short. It usually remains high in the trees though at times, particularly during migration, it descends to bushes and even to weed patches along streams. The Warbling glides in and out of the canopy unobtrusively, at times rather deliberately—as is the habit of vireos—singing the while and gleaning insects carefully from leaves and branches. Whether in trees or bushes, it stays mostly in interior growth. It rarely descends to the ground.

The Warbling Vireo's call note sounds like *tshay* or *twee*. Song is a continuous, languid warble, not broken into phrases as are the songs of other vireos. Its song period lasts well into summer, though not as long as that of the Red-eyed Vireo.

DETAILED ACCOUNT: TWO SUBSPECIES

EASTERN WARBLING VIREO, *Melodivireo gilvus gilvus* (Vieillot)

DESCRIPTION: *Adults, nuptial plumage*: Acquired by partial prenuptial molt. Pileum deep grayish olive, remainder of upper surface grayish olive, but somewhat more greenish on rump and upper tail-coverts; tail rather dark hair brown, feathers margined on outer webs with color of rump, narrowly on inner webs with brownish or yellowish white; wings rather dark hair brown, wing-quills margined on inner webs, except at tips of primaries, with pale brownish or brownish white, on outer webs with color of back; edgings of wing-coverts like back but rather more grayish; narrow superciliary stripe grayish or buffy white; lores posteriorly like crown, this extending through eye as dull brown postocular streak; cheeks between vinaceous buff and deep olive buff, passing into dark olive buff on sides of breast and posterior part of sides of neck; lower parts dull white, washed with grayish buff or yellow on anterior portion and slightly so posteriorly, but sides, flanks, crissum, and lining of wing yellowish olive buff, last often dull white, and more or less mottled with hair brown or mouse gray. Maxilla slate, slate black, seal brown, or brownish slate; mandible cinereous, mouse gray, or drab gray, but paler, even white, at base; iris vandyke brown, claret brown, or burnt umber; legs and feet plumbeous—light plumbeous to black. *Adults, winter*: Acquired by complete postnuptial molt. Practically identical with nuptial adults. *First nuptial*: Acquired by partial prenuptial molt. Practically identical with nuptial adults, except for perhaps somewhat more brownish wings and tail retained from juvenal. *First winter*: Acquired by partial postjuvenal molt, which does not involve wing-quills or tail. Similar to adults in winter, but upper parts somewhat more brownish or buffy, greater wing-coverts tipped with buff or pale buffy olive; sides and flanks usually somewhat more yellowish. *Juvenal*: Acquired by complete postnatal molt. Pileum and hindneck light vinaceous buff; back dark drab; wings and tail similar to those of nuptial adults, but lesser wing-coverts drab, other wing-coverts and edges more brownish; lower parts white, crissum colonial buff. Bill blackish slate, but base of mandible dull white or yellow; iris dark brown; legs and feet dark plumbeous. *Natal*: Pale wood brown. Bill, legs, and feet pinkish buff; iris dark hazel.

MEASUREMENTS: *Adult male*: Wing, 67.1–73.9 (average, 70.6) mm.; tail, 49.0–55.1 (52.1); bill (exposed culmen), 9.9–10.9 (10.7); tarsus, 17.0–19.0 (18.0); middle toe without claw, 9.9–10.9 (10.2). *Adult female*: Wing, 66.0–71.1 (69.1); tail, 47.0–53.1 (50.3); bill, 9.9–10.9 (10.4); tarsus, 17.0–19.0 (18.0); middle toe, 9.9–10.9 (10.2).

RANGE: C. Saskatchewan and Great Lakes region to Prince Edward Island, south to Texas and North Carolina. Winters in s. Florida and from Durango to Guatemala.

TEXAS: *Breeding*: Altitudinal range, near sea level to perhaps 3,200 ft., though nesting unconfirmed at latter height. Pair building nest at Rockport (Aransas Co.) probably of this subspecies (see species account). Summer specimens collected in Lips-comb (1 specimen), Oldham (1), and Gray (1) cos. Rare. *Migration*: Collected north to Dallas, south to Colorado and San Patricio, southwest to Webb cos. Fairly common.

NESTING: *Nest*: On uplands and lowlands, in rather open country, about edges of forests, timber along streams, and in cultivated areas, such as orchards and ornamental grounds; in tree or bush, usually 6–70 ft. above ground, suspended from fork of twig; cup-shaped, well-woven nest; composed of strips of bark and various vegetable fibers and held together by spider webs; lined with hair or fine grasses and thin stems of plants. *Eggs*: 3–5; ovate to short ovate; pure white, with fine spots of umber, reddish brown, black, and lilac, mostly about large end; average size, 19.0 × 14.0 mm.

WYOMING WARBLING VIREO, Melodivireo gilvus petrorus Oberholser, new subspecies (see Appendix A)

DESCRIPTION: *Adults, nuptial plumage*: Similar to M. g. *gilvus*, but upper surface darker, back and flanks more olivaceous (less grayish). Similar to Western Warbling Vireo, M. g. *swainsonii*, of Pacific coast region of North America, but larger and somewhat more grayish (less olivaceous) on upper parts.

MEASUREMENTS: *Adult male*: Wing, 67.6–73.4 (average, 70.6) mm.; tail, 50.0–55.1 (52.6); bill (exposed culmen), 8.9–9.9 (9.7); tarsus, 16.5–18.3 (17.5); middle toe without claw, 8.9–10.2 (9.9). *Adult female*: Wing, 64.5–70.6 (68.6); tail, 46.5–53.1 (50.3); bill, 8.9–10.9 (9.7); tarsus, 17.0–18.5 (17.8); middle toe, 9.4–10.9 (10.2).

TYPE: Adult male, no. 228538, U.S. National Museum; Fort Steele, Wyoming; May 30, 1911, H. E. Anthony, original no., 380.

RANGE: S. British Columbia and s. Alberta, south to n. Sonora and Trans-Pecos Texas. Winters from s. Sonora to Guatemala.

TEXAS: *Breeding*: Altitudinal range, 5,500 to 8,000 ft. Collected in Culberson Co. One summer specimen from El Paso Co., Ysleta (July 30, 1901, L. A. Fuertes). Fairly common to uncommon. *Migration*: Collected northeast to Cooke, south to Cameron, west to Brewster and Reeves cos. Fairly common.

NESTING: Similar to that of M. g. *gilvus*; average egg size the same.

American Wood Warblers: Parulidae

BLACK-AND-WHITE WARBLER, *Mniotilta varia*
(Linnaeus)

Species Account

A creeping wood warbler. Striped black and white; white crown stripe. *Male*: black cheek, throat. *Female*: largely white below. Length, 5¼ in.; wingspan, 8½; weight, ½ oz.

RANGE: N.e. British Columbia and s.w. Mackenzie to Newfoundland, south through e. United States (chiefly east of Great Plains) to c. Texas, s. Louisiana, and c. South Carolina. Winters from n. Mexico, Gulf coast (a few), and c. Florida through Central America and West Indies to n. South America.

TEXAS: (See map.) *Breeding*: Early Apr. to early July (eggs, Apr. 11 to May 25) from near sea level to 2,000 ft. Fairly common but local on Edwards Plateau and in wooded eastern third. *Migration*: Mid-Mar.—early Mar. some years—to mid-May; mid-July to late Oct. (extremes: Feb. 22, June 13; July 2, Dec. 29). Very common (some springs) to fairly common through most parts east of 100th meridian; uncommon to scarce in western portions. Dec. sightings in Trans-Pecos probably represent late migrants. *Winter*: Late Dec. to late Feb. Uncommon to scarce along coast and in Rio Grande delta; rare in central portions from Fort Worth to Bryan, Beeville, and San Antonio.

HAUNTS AND HABITS: Most of the 110 American wood warblers glean insects from leaves and twigs of trees; the Black-and-white Warbler gathers its bugs and spiders largely from more wooden parts of trees—trunks and large limbs. During its breeding season in Texas, the Black-and-white haunts canyons overgrown with mountain cedar (*Juniperus ashei*), Spanish oak (*Quercus texana*) and various shrubs on the edges of the Edwards Plateau. In east Texas woodlands, where it is also a local nester, it inhabits pines (*Pinus echinata, P. palustris, P. taeda*) mixed with American beech (*Fagus grandifolia*), oaks (*Q. alba, Q. falcata,* others) and sweetgum (*Liquidambar styraciflua*). As is true of other migrants, this warbler frequents a great variety of trees when it is migrating and wintering. It is usually seen singly or in pairs, but winter birds often associate with bands of other small insectivorous passerines.

In flight the Black-and-white is swift and somewhat erratic, and it sometimes flies a considerable distance from one group of trees to another. It seems to be equally at home in tops of tall trees and low in shrubs or undergrowth. It is rather nuthatchlike as it creeps around trunks and branches, but works much less often with its head down. Though deliberate and methodical in its foraging movements, it intermittently flits and hops and occasionally extends its wings.

The Black-and-white is largely insectivorous, but will take spiders and harvestmen, small snails, and some seeds. H. C. Oberholser even found remains of a small lizard in the stomach contents of one specimen. The normal diet includes mostly wood-boring beetles and weevils, leaf beetles, moths, cankerworms, tent caterpillars, plant lice, scale insects, leaf- and tree-hoppers, stink bugs, ants, flies and their larvae, earwigs, walkingsticks, crickets, grasshoppers, and katydids.

The Black-and-white has two call notes, a weak *tsip* and a louder sharp *pit* suggesting the *chip* of the Blackpoll Warbler. Its song is a thin, insectlike *squeaky* or *weesee* repeated six or more times at the same high pitch and at moderate speed. It is similar to one vocalization of the American Redstart, but ends without the

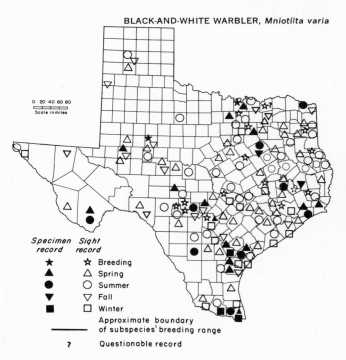

BLACK-AND-WHITE WARBLER, *Mniotilta varia*

0 20 40 60 80
Scale in miles

	Specimen record	Sight record	
	★	☆	Breeding
	▲	△	Spring
	●	○	Summer
	▼	▽	Fall
	■	□	Winter

—— Approximate boundary of subspecies' breeding range

? Questionable record

particular emphasis of the latter's song. It is heard in Texas from early March through June.

CHANGES: The Black-and-white Warbler, first of the American wood warblers, is a bit atypical because of its wood-creeping feeding habit, but it is like nearly all the other species in that it requires woodland and tree insects at all times of the year.

Deforestation in Mexico, the West Indies, Central America, and northern South America—chief wintering grounds of U.S. warblers—has been extremely spectacular since World War II (1939–1945). During and since this war, control of malaria (largely with DDT applied to mosquitoes) and yellow fever (by means of vaccine and slaughter of wild monkeys) has become general over the Tropics, thereby removing effective controls on human population increase. As a result more and more people reach adulthood to breed more and more. Also, newly constructed roads allow these hordes—nearly all agrarians—to invade wilderness areas.

Tropical rural people live by the slash-burn (*milpa*) system of agriculture, whereby they chop down all the trees on a plot of ground, burn the wood, and plant corn, rice, sugarcane, beans, bananas, grass (for cattle), and other crops in the ashes. In most localities the soil wears out in only two years. Another patch of forest is then cut and burned, and so on and on. The *milpa* system has been going on for many hundreds of years. In former times the original plot was often left alone for a century or more to regain its fertility and trees. No significant harm was done so long as human populations remained thin and large sections of forest remained inaccessible. Now, people are so numerous and land so scarce that each plot is repeatedly burned and there is no chance for forest regeneration. To all those who know present-day conditions in the Tropics, it was no surprise that the astronauts of 1968, 1969, and the early 1970's were unable to see any spots of green on planet Earth.

Tree removal on the warblers' temperate nesting territories has been perhaps somewhat less rapid since World War II. However, tonnage of herbicides and insecticides dumped on "developed" countries has been terrific. The year 1970 say the first slackening (feeble) of pesticide application in northern climes; in tropical lands, poison broadcasts are still accelerating.

In short, the Black-and-white Warbler, together with its insect-eating relatives, is finding its habitat decimated and its food poisoned. All warblers are declining. (Under the following species accounts changes will be mentioned only when they are unusual.)

DETAILED ACCOUNT: NO SUBSPECIES

DESCRIPTION: *Adult male, nuptial plumage*: Acquired by partial prenuptial molt. Pileum and hindneck black, with broad central stripe of white; remainder of upper surface black, conspicuously streaked with white or grayish white; tail deep mouse gray, feathers narrowly margined on outer webs with neutral gray, two outer feathers with broad terminal white spots on inner webs, others with very narrow white edgings on terminal portion of inner webs, and middle feathers with shaft stripe blackish mouse gray; primaries and secondaries deep mouse gray, edged on outer webs very narrowly with neutral gray; tertials and upper wing-coverts black, tertials margined broadly on outer webs with white, all wing-quills and tertials with inner margins, except at tips of primaries, white, and median and greater coverts broadly tipped with white, as are also inner webs of terminal portion of alula; sides of head black; broad white superciliary stripe extending to sides of forehead; lores, and sometimes remaining part of head, narrowly streaked with white, but auriculars usually solid black; broad submalar streak white; chin, throat, and jugulum black, narrowly streaked white, or often chin and middle of throat solid black; remaining lower parts white, but sides of breast and of body, flanks, and crissum broadly streaked with black; lining of wing white. Bill black, slate black, blackish slate, or slate color, but basal half of mandible dull white or french gray; iris dark brown or black; legs plumbeous, greenish slate, slate gray, slate black, or slate color; feet greenish slate, slate gray, slate color, or olive gray; claws olivaceous hair brown, broccoli brown, or olivaceous yellow. *Adult male, winter*: Acquired by complete postnuptial molt. Similar to nuptial adult male, but throat much more extensively white, sometimes with only narrow streaks or spots of black. Bill more brownish. *Adult female, nuptial*: Acquired by partial prenuptial molt. Similar to nuptial adult male but duller and somewhat more brownish, upper parts, particularly posteriorly, somewhat washed with cream buff; sides of head dull pale buff, auriculars and cheeks with no well-marked dark streaks; lower parts dull white with slight dull buffy tinge, blackish streaks much duller, more grayish, and much narrower, and median portion without any sharply defined streaks or spots, flanks and crissum strongly tinged with vinaceous buff or dull chamois; lining of wing dull white, outer portion with small spots of hair brown or mouse gray. *Adult female, winter*: Acquired by complete postnuptial molt. Similar to nuptial adult female but still more brownish, both above and below, particularly on posterior lower parts. *Male, first nuptial*: Acquired by partial prenuptial molt. Similar to nuptial adult male, but primary coverts brown instead of black, and chin often not solidly black. *Male, first winter*: Acquired by partial postjuvenal molt, which does not involve wing-quills or tail. Similar to adult male in winter, but upper surface duller, black more brownish and decidedly tinged with buff; sides of head wholly or largely white except for blackish postocular stripe; middle portion of entire lower parts mostly white except for occasional blackish streaks on breast; streaks on sides narrower, more obscured by whitish; and posterior lower parts much washed with deep buff. *Female, first nuptial*: Acquired by partial prenuptial molt. Practically identical with nuptial adult female. *Female, first winter*: Acquired by partial postjuvenal molt. Similar to adult female in winter but still more brownish both above and below, brown areas on upper surface much washed or overlaid on posterior portion with hair brown, white areas strongly tinged with cream buff; cheeks and sides of head chamois or deep cartridge buff; anterior lower parts cartridge buff; sides, flanks, and crissum cinnamon buff, chamois, or clay color. *Juvenal*: Acquired by complete postnatal molt. Similar to first winter female but even more strongly buffy or brownish on upper surface and anterior lower parts; above brownish black or fuscous black with numerous spots of dull buff, dull tawny, or brownish ochraceous, edgings of greater and median wing-coverts buffy white; chin dull buffy white; throat and jugulum buffy drab; remainder of lower parts grayish or dull buffy white, entire lower surface, except chin, more or less spotted or finely streaked with fuscous or chaetura black. Bill slate color or blackish slate, but mandible french gray or dull white, sometimes its tip slate gray; iris dark brown or black. *Natal*: Mouse gray to deep mouse gray. Bill and feet pinkish buff.

MEASUREMENTS: *Adult male*: Wing, 66.5–71.7 (average, 68.8) mm.; tail, 42.7–51.1 (48.5); bill (exposed culmen), 10.2–12.7 (11.2); tarsus, 16.5–18.5 (17.3); middle toe without claw, 11.9–13.5 (12.7). *Adult female*: Wing, 65.0–69.1 (67.3); tail, 45.5–48.5 (46.5); bill, 10.2–12.2 (11.2); tarsus, 16.3–17.5 (16.8); middle toe, 11.9–13.0 (12.4).

TEXAS: *Breeding*: Collected north to Cooke, east to Bowie and

Jefferson, south to Bexar, west to Kerr cos.; at least formerly (19th century) to Mitchell Co. *Migration*: Collected north to Cooke, east to Jefferson, south to Cameron, west to Brewster cos. *Winter*: Taken in Bee, Hidalgo, and Cameron cos.

NESTING: *Nest*: On uplands and bottoms, preferably on hillsides and other slopes, also on more level land; usually in woodlands, deciduous or partly evergreen; on ground, commonly in depression under shelter of stump, fallen log, stone, or plants; bulky cup, but rather compact, sometimes more or less roofed over and very well concealed; composed of grasses, strips of grapevine, cedar or other bark, rootlets, moss, and various other plant fibers, sometimes bits of decayed wood; lined with hairs and hairlike roots, fine grasses, down from ferns and other plants. *Eggs*: 4–6, usually 5; white or cream white; spotted and dotted with chestnut, umber, hazel, slate color, lilac, and lavender, ordinarily in form of wreath about large end; average size, 16.8 × 13.5 mm.

PROTHONOTARY WARBLER, *Protonotaria citrea* (Boddaert)

SPECIES ACCOUNT

Bill and eyes large, blackish, conspicuous. *Male*: orange-yellow head, under parts (lighter on belly); greenish yellow back; blue-gray wings, rump, tail; white crissum, underside of tail. *Female*: somewhat paler. Length, 5½ in.; wingspan, 8¾; weight, ½ oz.

RANGE: S. Great Lakes region and New Jersey, south to e. Texas, Gulf coast, and c. Florida. Winters chiefly from Yucatán Peninsula through Central America to n. Colombia and n. Venezuela.

TEXAS: (See map.) *Breeding*: Mid-Apr. to July (eggs, Apr. 25 to June 4; young just out of nest, June 22) from near sea level to 700 ft. Very locally common (some years) to uncommon in eastern third, west to Gainesville, Fort Worth, Palmetto State Park, and Vic-

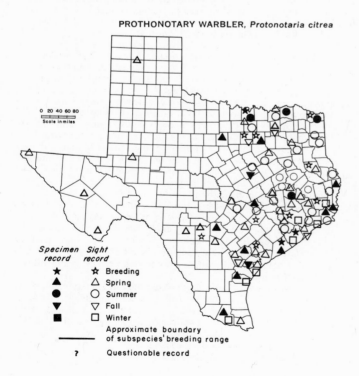

PROTHONOTARY WARBLER, *Protonotaria citrea*

Specimen record / Sight record

★ / ☆ Breeding
▲ / △ Spring
● / ○ Summer
▼ / ▽ Fall
■ / □ Winter

Approximate boundary of subspecies' breeding range

? Questionable record

toria; increasingly rare west to Medina Co., where casual. *Migration*: Late Mar. to mid-May; early Aug. to late Sept. (extremes: Feb. 21, June 3; July 21, Oct. 15). Common (some springs) to uncommon (most falls) along coast and in eastern third; uncommon to rare through remainder of state east of 100th meridian; casual in western parts. First documented record from Trans-Pecos: Brewster Co., Big Bend Nat. Park (bird photographed, Apr. 28, 1971, Aline and Forrest Romero; no. 29 in Texas Photo-Record File, Texas A&M University). *Winter*: Late Dec. to mid-Feb. No specimen, but a scattering of sightings along coast.

HAUNTS AND HABITS: In the Old South, the Prothonotary Warbler is a bird of bottomland and bayou country. This beautiful species is attracted to trees and shrubs growing in or beside still or sluggish water. In most localities low limbs of baldcypress (*Taxodium distichum*) and black willow (*Salix nigra*) furnish singing perches, from which the male advertises his presence by loud sweet song. He further proclaims his breeding territory by exposing his bright feathers to view as he flits about in his somber domain of dark brown water, green-gray gloom of baldcypress foliage, and long streamers of Spanishmoss (*Tillandsia usneoides*). At this time, especially if he flies through a shaft of sunlight, he resembles a tiny detached bit of golden swamp-fire. No doubt about it: He and even his paler mate are the most brilliant summer birds in the swamp.

The reclusive Prothonotary's flight is swift and strong, more direct and less erratic than that of most warblers. It forages primarily in understory and often on the ground. In gleaning prey, most Prothonotaries are not as given to creeping along trunks as are Black-and-white Warblers, but they often spend considerable time inspecting large limbs and even driftwood, where they occasionally take small snails and crustaceans. The normal diet, however, consists primarily of insects (caterpillars, leaf and leaf-eating beetles, bees, ants, flies, and many aquatic insects); also spiders and occasional seeds.

The usual call note is a mild *tsip*, but an alarmed bird utters a sharper, more guttural note, resembling that of the Louisiana Waterthrush. The Prothonotary's territorial song—the essence of baldcypress country in spring and early summer—is a penetrating *peet tweet tweet tweet tweet tweet tweet*, all on the same pitch. An aerial nuptial song, delivered while the bird hovers butterflylike, sometimes at considerable height, is longer, softer, and more complexly melodious.

CHANGES: Astoundingly enough, in a world where wildlife habitat depletion is practically universal, Prothonotary Warbler habitat may be increasing. Since World War II, there has been a constant orgy of dam building in Texas. Currently (1970), the two largest lakes in the history of the state—Sam Rayburn and Toledo Bend reservoirs—are filling, and in the process, drowning thousands of deciduous trees and some pine in and near Angelina and Sabine national forests. If dead timber is left standing in shallow water, decay, wind, and woodpeckers should provide many nest cavities for Prothonotary pairs. It is, however, too early to tell whether man's flooding activities will result in an actual increase in *Protonotaria citrea*.

DETAILED ACCOUNT: NO SUBSPECIES

DESCRIPTION: *Adult male, nuptial plumage*: Acquired by wear from winter plumage. Entire head and neck between light cadmium and lemon chrome or between light cadmium and cadmium yellow; forehead sometimes cadmium yellow; back and scapulars yellowish orange citrine to yellowish citrine; rump and upper tail-coverts neutral gray; middle pair of tail feathers deep neutral gray, their broad tips and narrow shaft stripes blackish neutral gray; remainder of tail mostly white, outer webs and tips of feathers deep neutral gray to blackish neutral gray; wings deep mouse gray, but inner margins of secondaries and primaries, except at tips of primaries, white, outer margins of wing-quills, except at tips of primaries, neutral gray; lesser and median wing-coverts like back, greater series neutral gray on outer webs, washed with orange citrine of back; lower parts between light cadmium and cadmium yellow, sometimes verging toward lemon chrome, but flanks washed with citrine or yellowish citrine; under wing-coverts white or grayish white, mottled with hair brown, axillars yellow like under parts, but mixed with white or grayish white; edge of wing yellow like under parts; crissum and middle of lower abdomen white or cream white. Bill black; iris dark brown or hazel; legs and feet dark plumbeous. *Adult male, winter*: Acquired by complete postnuptial molt. Similar to nuptial adult male, but back of head more or less washed with olive or citrine. Bill brown. *Adult female, nuptial*: Acquired by wear from winter. Similar to nuptial adult male, but upper parts duller and more uniform, pileum practically like back; white areas of tail less extensive; yellow of lower surface paler and duller, abdomen more extensively white. *Adult female, winter*: Acquired by complete postnuptial molt. Similar to nuptial adult female. Bill light brown. *Male and female, first nuptial*: Acquired by wear from first winter. Similar to corresponding sex of nuptial adults. *Male and female, first winter*: Acquired by partial postjuvenal molt, which does not involve wing-quills or tail. Similar to adult female in winter but duller and more brownish or olivaceous; upper surface washed with citrine or olive green; sides of head and of neck more washed with olivaceous; yellow of anterior lower parts very much washed with olive. *Juvenal*: Acquired by complete postnatal molt. Pileum dull grayish citrine or buffy citrine; back dark citrine; rump dull deep grayish olive; tail with very little or no white, this sometimes reduced to narrow edgings on inner webs of outer feathers; sides of head and anterior lower parts pale yellowish olive, but chin and throat rather lighter; posterior lower parts dull yellowish white, but sides and flanks dull light gray washed with yellowish olive, middle of abdomen very pale yellow or yellowish white, lower tail-coverts mouse gray, all feathers broadly tipped with white; lining of wing dull mouse gray washed with dull yellow. *Natal*: Brownish mouse gray. Bill, legs, and feet pinkish buff.

MEASUREMENTS: *Adult male*: Wing, 69.1–74.9 (average, 71.7) mm.; tail, 43.9–51.6 (47.3); bill (exposed culmen), 13.0–15.5 (14.2); tarsus, 18.0–20.6 (19.3); middle toe without claw, 10.4–12.4 (11.7). *Adult female*: Wing, 65.3–69.3 (67.3); tail, 39.9–48.5 (45.5); bill, 11.9–14.5 (13.7); tarsus, 18.0–20.1 (18.8); middle toe, 11.4–13.0 (11.9).

TEXAS: *Breeding*: Collected north to Cooke, east to Bowie, south to Matagorda, west to Lee cos. *Migration*: Collected north to Cooke, east to Orange, south to Hidalgo, west to Bexar and Palo Pinto cos.

NESTING: *Nest*: Usually on bottomlands, in swamps, or along streams, sometimes in vicinity of human habitations; in cavity or abandoned woodpecker hole in stump or tree trunk, or in bird box or gourd; often over water, 2–15 ft. above water or ground, though usually not over 4 or 5 ft.; the cavity, however large, is usually filled to within about 4 or 5 in. of entrance with leaves, moss, twigs, grapevine and other bark, fine grasses, straw, roots,

lichens, decayed wood and other vegetable substances; depression for eggs lined with shreds of bark, fine grasses, moss, leaves of baldcypress and other trees, fine rootlets, grass culms, hair, or feathers. *Eggs*: 3–8, usually 5 or 6; rounded ovate to short ovate; glossy; yellowish white, cream white, or buff; blotched, spotted, and speckled, chiefly at large end, with chestnut, cinnamon brown, and purplish brown, with shell markings of lilac and purplish gray (such bold markings are unusual for a cavity-nesting species); average size, 17.8 × 14.5 mm.

SWAINSON'S WARBLER, *Limnothlypis swainsonii* (Audubon)

SPECIES ACCOUNT

Long billed for a warbler. Solid brown crown; whitish eye-stripe; uniform olive brown above; plain dingy buff below. Length, 5½ in.; wingspan, 8¾.

RANGE: Locally from n.e. Oklahoma to s. Ohio and s.e. Maryland, south to s.e. Texas and n. Florida. Winters mainly on Yucatán Peninsula, in British Honduras, Cuba, and Jamaica.

TEXAS: (See map.) *Breeding*: Probably mid-Apr. to late July (nest with 1 egg located, Bowie Co., July 6, 1888, B. T. Gault) from about 100 to 450 ft. Scarce and extremely local in eastern quarter, west to Bryan (nesting suspected). Recent observations: Little Thicket Nature Sanctuary, San Jacinto Co. (adults and 2 begging young, July 4, 1964, V. L. Emanuel, J. L. Rowlett; adults feeding 1 tiny fledgling, July 14, 1971, J. L. Rowlett, Rose Ann Rowlett). *Migration*: Early Apr. to mid-May; mid-Aug. to late Sept. (extremes: Mar. 2, June 14; Aug. 16, Oct. 21). Uncommon (some springs) to rare (most falls) through eastern third and along coast south to Corpus Christi; rare in remainder of eastern half.

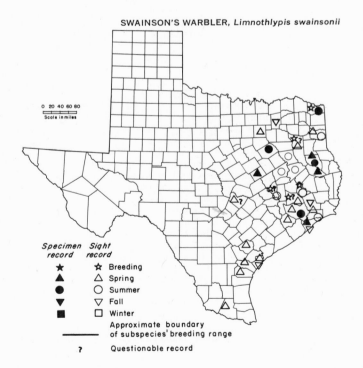

SWAINSON'S WARBLER, *Limnothlypis swainsonii*

0 20 40 60 80
Scale in miles

Specimen record	Sight record	
★	☆	Breeding
▲	△	Spring
●	○	Summer
▽	▽	Fall
■	□	Winter

———— Approximate boundary of subspecies' breeding range

? Questionable record

HAUNTS AND HABITS: Surprisingly, the Swainson's Warbler breeds in both highlands and almost sea-level lowlands. One population nests in alder and rhododendron thickets beside rocky Appalachian streams. Texas birds all use "classical" habitat, similar to that in which the Rev. John Bachman, Audubon's best friend, discovered this species in the South Carolina low country in 1832. The Swainson's skulks in dense undergrowth growing in muddy (but usually not watery), acidic soil in bottomland woods. Dense patches of cane, bushes, and briars along rivers or creeks are sometimes frequented. This warbler is a solitary bird, almost always seen singly or in pairs.

Flight is swift and strong though usually short. Swainson's spends considerable time foraging on the ground, where it walks about with deliberate, thrush-like movements, sometimes drooping its wings but not pumping its tail. Food consists chiefly of insects (caterpillars, ground beetles, ants, bees, flies), but includes some spiders, centipedes, and millipedes. The Swainson's is a rather secretive bird and, when disturbed, may remain motionless in one place for some time.

The territory defended by the male is used primarily for mating and feeding, the nest being located usually along its margin and sometimes entirely outside. The dull-colored, normally invisible Swainson's, unlike the Prothonotary (plumage showy, song monotonous), must depend almost entirely upon his complex song to proclaim territorial rights. This vocalization, sometimes written as *whee, whee, whee, whip-poor-will*, is subject to at least five common variations. It is surprisingly ventriloquial in quality and resembles the song of the Louisiana Waterthrush. Indeed, it is among the best American warbler songs. Delivery is- normally from a low perch or even the ground; rarely does the male move much during singing. Swainson's Warblers usually sing in Texas from mid-April to early August. The usual call note is a soft *tchip*.

DETAILED ACCOUNT: NO SUBSPECIES

DESCRIPTION: *Adults, nuptial plumage*: Acquired by wear from winter plumage. Pileum dresden brown; remainder of upper surface light brownish olive; tail plain olive brown, outer margins of feathers light brownish olive; wings rather light olive brown, wing-quills basally paler on inner webs (pale brown or dull buff), outer webs of primaries and secondaries margined with rather lighter olive brown, edgings of coverts like back; broad superciliary stripe and cheeks dull primrose yellow or light primrose yellow; lores and postocular streak brown like back; remainder of sides of head and of neck grayish olive; lower surface dull primrose yellow or light primrose yellow, breast with obscure markings or blotches of very light grayish olive; sides and flanks grayish olive; lining of wing grayish olive washed with primrose yellow. Bill light brown above, paler on mandible; iris dark brown or hazel; legs and feet flesh color. *Adults, winter*: Acquired by complete postnuptial molt. Very similar to nuptial adults. *First nuptial*: Acquired by wear from first winter. Like nuptial adults. *First winter*: Acquired by partial postjuvenal molt, which does not involve wing-quills or tail. Practically identical with adults in winter. *Juvenal*: Acquired by complete postnatal molt. Pileum and hindneck buffy brown, dull cinnamon brown, or between sayal brown and saccardo umber; remainder of upper surface between olive brown and natal brown or between snuff brown and sepia; wings hair brown or dull olive brown, outer margins of wing-quills between brownish olive and saccardo umber; lesser and greater wing-coverts margined on outer webs with dull buffy brown, and median and greater coverts tipped with sayal brown; sides of head like pileum but somewhat darker, particularly on auriculars, and with very obscure postocular streak of darker brown; jugulum, breast, and sides of body dull snuff brown or between sayal brown and cinnamon; chin and upper throat paler; lower breast and abdomen cream color or yellowish white with large spots of dull snuff brown, saccardo umber, or between sayal brown and cinnamon; crissum pale dull clay color. *Natal*: Dark, rather brownish drab. Bill, legs, and feet pale pinkish buff.

MEASUREMENTS: *Adult male*: Wing, 67.6–72.4 (average, 70.4) mm.; tail, 46.5–52.1 (49.3); bill (exposed culmen), 15.0–16.5 (15.2); tarsus, 17.0–19.0 (17.8); middle toe without claw, 12.4–14.0 (13.2). *Adult female*: Wing, 66.0–71.9 (69.1); tail, 46.5–52.1 (49.3); bill, 14.7–16.0 (15.2); tarsus, 17.0–19.0 (18.3); middle toe, 12.4–14.0 (13.2).

TEXAS: *Breeding*: Three specimens: Bowie Co., Geans Plantation (1 on July 4, 1888; 2 on July 6, 1888, B. T. Gault). *Migration*: Collected in Dallas, Navarro (Aug. 24), Falls, Harris (summer), and Galveston cos.

NESTING: *Nest*: Chiefly on bottomlands, in wooded swamps, and canebrakes, although sometimes on high dry land at a distance from water; in palmetto, cane, bush, or low tree, or in vine, 2–10 ft. above ground, sometimes in small colonies; large, open-topped nest, somewhat bulky for size of bird, composed of leaves of sweetgum, holly, water oak, cane, and other trees and bushes, together with moss; lined with pine needles, fine roots, and dry moss. *Eggs*: 2–4, usually 3; rounded ovate; with little or no gloss; cream white or plain white with faint bluish tinge; nearly always unmarked, but rarely with a few dots of dark brown; average size, 19.0 × 15.0 mm.

WORM-EATING WARBLER, *Vermivora americ* Linnaeus

SPECIES ACCOUNT

Helmitheros vermivorus of A.O.U. check-list, 1957 (see Appendix A). Prominent black stripes on buffy head; brownish olive above; plain buff below (paler on throat, belly). Length, 5½ in.; wingspan, 8¾.

RANGE: S. Iowa, n. Illinois, Ohio River Valley, s.e. New York, and s. New England, south to n.e. Texas, Louisiana (locally), c. Alabama, and n.w. South Carolina. Winters chiefly from s. Mexico to Panama, and in West Indies; regularly a few north to s. Tamaulipas and c. Florida.

TEXAS: (See map.) *Breeding*: Four records: Bowie Co., Geans Plantation (young bird found just able to care for itself, July 3, 1888, B. T. Gault; species reported fairly common in this locality June 19–July 12, 1888); Houston Co., Radcliff Lake (pair carrying nest material, May, ca. 1966, F. R. Gehlbach); San Jacinto Co., Little Thicket Nature Sanctuary (adults feeding 2 fledglings, June 26, 1971, V. L. Emanuel, J. L. Rowlett); Cass Co., 10 mi. south of Atlanta (adult feeding 1 juvenal, the latter collected, June 14, 1973, C. D. Fisher; skin in Stephen F. Austin State University collection). *Migration*: Late Mar. to early May; late Aug. to early Oct. (extremes: early Mar., June 11; Aug. 8; Oct. 21). Common (some springs) to scarce (most falls) on upper coast; fairly common to scarce along central coast and in Rio Grande delta; scarce to rare inland east of 98th meridian; scarce to casual in western half. *Winter*: Early Dec. to mid-Feb. No specimen, but scattered sightings along coast and in Rio Grande delta; inland sightings from Haskell (Dec. 3) and Henderson (Feb. 18) cos.

HAUNTS AND HABITS: In spring and summer, the Worm-eating Warbler is a bird of undergrowth in deciduous forest. Within woods, it is attracted to damp, dark situations on hillsides, ravines, along streams, and in bushy bogs. It is a rather solitary bird, normally seen singly in Texas.

Flight is usually flitting and ordinarily low and for short distances. The Worm-eating usually forages by walking on the ground or creeping about in bushes; only occasionally does it ascend into trees. As it walks about probing and scratching, it frequently bobs its head and carries its tail elevated. In common with most warblers, it ingests many caterpillars, but seldom takes true worms. Other constituents of its diet are moths, weevils and other beetles, dragonflies, walking-sticks, scale insects, cicadas, ants, bumblebees, and small grasshoppers as well as spiders.

The Worm-eating's usual call note is a rather sharp *chip* or *dzt*. Its simple, monotonous song is a thin buzzy trill, *che-e-e-e-e-e-e*, somewhat Chipping Sparrow-like. A more varied song may be uttered while the bird is on the wing. Song period is April to July, sometimes until late August. The insipid vocalizations and dull plumage of this warbler render it little noticed in Texas and practically unobserved in its Latin American winter quarters.

DETAILED ACCOUNT: NO SUBSPECIES

DESCRIPTION: *Adults, nuptial plumage*: Acquired by wear from winter plumage. Pileum broadly striped on each side with brownish black or dull black, center of crown with broad stripe of chamois, honey yellow, or cream buff; remainder of upper surface yellowish olive or dull citrine; tail hair brown, margined externally with yellowish olive or dull citrine; wings hair brown, inner edges of wing-quills, except tips of primaries, dull pale buff or brownish white, wing-quills and all wing-coverts edged with color of back; sides of head, including superciliary stripe, like median crown stripe; broad postocular stripe, extending to nape, dull black or fuscous black; under parts cream buff to honey yellow, but throat lighter and brighter, crissum light mouse gray, its feathers broadly tipped with colonial buff, sides and flanks light isabella color; lining of wing deep colonial buff. Maxilla drab, brownish black, or blackish brown; mandible on terminal half ecru drab, basally ecru drab or pale vinaceous buff; tongue white; iris dark brown; legs and feet brownish flesh color, flesh color, or pale vinaceous buff. *Adults, winter*: Acquired by complete postnuptial molt. Similar to nuptial adults but more deeply colored; upper parts more greenish (less grayish) olive; sides of head and anterior lower parts more deeply ochraceous; abdomen more buffy. *First nuptial*: Acquired by wear from first winter. Like nuptial adults. *First winter*: Acquired by partial postjuvenal molt, which does not involve wing-quills or tail. Practically identical with adults in winter. *Juvenal*: Acquired by complete postnatal molt. Two lateral stripes on pileum light hair brown to saccardo umber; broad median stripe clay color to pinkish buff; remainder of upper surface buffy brown to dull russet, but tips of greater and median wing-coverts tawny olive to cinnamon buff; wings and tail similar to those of adult; sides of head and lower parts ochraceous tawny to cinnamon buff, postocular stripe brown like crown stripes, posterior lower surface paler than breast. Bill drab; gape maize yellow; legs and feet whitish. *Natal*: Brownish mouse gray. Bill, legs, and feet pinkish buff.

MEASUREMENTS: *Adult male*: Wing, 66.3–72.7 (average, 69.3) mm.; tail, 47.8–51.1 (49.3); bill (exposed culmen), 12.7–14.5 (13.7); tarsus, 17.3–18.3 (18.0); middle toe without claw, 11.4–13.0 (12.2). *Adult female*: Wing, 64.5–67.3 (65.8); tail, 44.7–47.8 (46.5); bill, 12.7–13.7 (13.2); tarsus, 17.8–19.3 (18.3); middle toe, 11.4–12.4 (11.9).

TEXAS: *Breeding*: Two specimens: Bowie Co., Geans Plantation (bird taken, perhaps fledgling, but age or sex not recorded, July 3, 1888, B. T. Gault); Cass Co. (see species account). *Migration*: Collected north to Cooke (June 11), east to Jefferson, south to Cameron, west to Brewster and Jeff Davis cos.

NESTING: *Nest*: On hillsides and bottomlands; in swamps, along streams, and in ravines; in forests or more open country, but usually in depression in ground, commonly at foot of tree or bush, beside fallen log, underneath bush or even on level ground in an open place, ordinarily, however, near a stream in damp woods, sometimes not particularly concealed, but at other times well hidden; open-topped nest, large for size of bird; composed mostly of leaves and moss, with lining of hairlike moss, fine grass, stems of maple seeds, fine roots, and horsehair. *Eggs*: 3–6, usually 4 or 5; short ovate to ovate; white; blotched and spotted, chiefly about large end, with light and dark chestnut and lilac brown, with shell markings of lavender; average size, 17.5 × 13.5 mm.

GOLDEN-WINGED WARBLER, *Helminthophila chrysoptera* (Linnaeus)

SPECIES ACCOUNT

Vermivora chrysoptera of A.O.U. check-list, 1957 (see Appendix A). *Male*: yellow forehead, crown, wing-patch; black throat, broad band through eye; white facial stripes, under parts; gray upper parts. *Female*: duller; gray replaces black. Length, 5 in.; wingspan, 7½.

RANGE: S. Great Lakes region and s. New England,

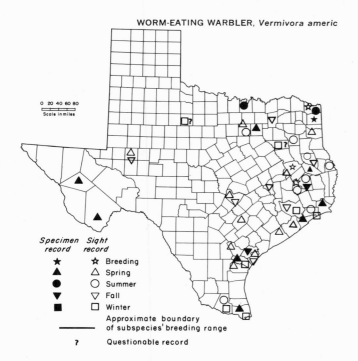

WORM-EATING WARBLER, *Vermivora americ*

0 20 40 60 80
Scale in miles

Specimen record / Sight record

★ / ☆ Breeding
▲ / △ Spring
● / ○ Summer
▼ / ▽ Fall
■ / □ Winter

———— Approximate boundary of subspecies' breeding range

? Questionable record

south to s.e. Iowa, s. Ohio, and n. New Jersey, and in Appalachians to Georgia and South Carolina. Winters from Guatemala to c. Colombia and n.e. Venezuela.

TEXAS: (See map.) *Migration*: Mid-Apr. to early May; mid-Sept. to early Oct. (extremes: Apr. 7, May 19; Aug. 28, Oct. 23). Fairly common to uncommon in spring along coast; scarce to rare through remainder of state east of 99th meridian; casual in northern Panhandle and Midland vicinity; accidental in Big Bend Nat. Park (May 9, 1970, C. F. Crabtree, Jr., and R. H. Wauer). Uncommon (some years) to scarce in fall along coast; rare inland to Austin and San Antonio.

HAUNTS AND HABITS: The trim Golden-winged Warbler nests on the ground in open woodlands or their edges in states northeast of Texas. During migration, it frequents planted saltcedar (*Tamarix gallica*) and native live oak (*Quercus virginiana*) along the Gulf coast; inland it flits through a variety of deciduous and evergreen trees, saplings in overgrown fields, and bushy undergrowth. It seldom occurs in numbers but often associates with other warblers.

Flight is quick and erratic and usually not prolonged. As it searches the canopy of both trees and shrubs for insects, this species frequently hunts head downward as does its close relative, the Bluewing. It is most often found in the lower tree levels and frequently utilizes the ground. Preferred food is caterpillars, many of which are injurious—cankerworm, tent caterpillar, and those of the leaf-roller moth. Beetles and their larvae, other insects, and certain spiders are taken as well.

The Goldenwing's sharp *chip* note is the vocalization most often heard in Texas. But occasionally this species pauses to deliver its insectlike, buzzy song: *bee-bz-bz-bz*, the first note higher in pitch.

GOLDEN-WINGED WARBLER, *Helminthophila chrysoptera*

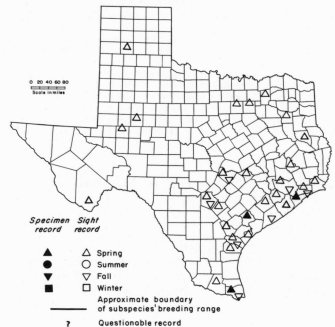

Specimen Sight
record record

▲ △ Spring
● ○ Summer
▼ ▽ Fall
■ □ Winter

——— Approximate boundary
of subspecies' breeding range

? Questionable record

DETAILED ACCOUNT: NO SUBSPECIES

DESCRIPTION: *Adult male, nuptial plumage*: Acquired by wear from winter plumage. Forehead and crown yellow (between lemon chrome and light cadmium yellow); remainder of upper surface between slate gray and neutral gray, rump slightly paler; tail dark mouse gray, but middle tail feathers rather lighter (deep neutral gray), outer tail feathers of still lighter neutral gray, outer four pairs of tail feathers with large white subterminal or terminal spots on inner webs, these spots largest on outermost feathers and reduced to small oblong spot on fourth feather; wings dark hair brown, inner margins of primaries and secondaries, except at tips of secondaries, dull white or brownish white, quills narrowly edged externally with color of back, tertials exteriorly with dull yellowish olive green; lesser wing-coverts like back; remaining coverts lemon yellow to lemon chrome, forming large spot on wing; broad superciliary stripe white; lores and broad stripe through eye to nape black; broad malar strip extending to sides of neck white or grayish neutral gray; sides of neck like back; chin, throat, and jugulum black; middle of remaining lower surface white, including crissum; sides and flanks light neutral gray to pale neutral gray; lining of wing white with a few hair brown or chaetura drab spots on outer portion. Bill black or brownish black; iris black or dark brown; legs clove brown; feet and claws sepia. *Adult male, winter*: Acquired by complete postnuptial molt. Similar to nuptial adult male, but upper surface, including crown, washed more or less with warbler green, as are also black throat patch and posterior lower parts. *Adult female, nuptial*: Acquired by wear from winter. Much duller in color than nuptial adult male; forehead and crown gamboge yellow, much overlaid with warbler green or entirely warbler green; back neutral gray washed with warbler green; wings and tail similar to those of male, but wings much more extensively margined on secondaries and tertials with yellowish warbler green, yellow on wing-coverts of less extent and wax yellow or lemon chrome; superciliary stripe dull white; broad stripe on sides of head chaetura drab instead of black; chin and throat between light neutral gray or neutral gray and light mouse gray or mouse gray; remaining lower parts dull grayish white, tinged with buff, and on breast sometimes with pale yellow; sides and flanks smoke gray to light drab. *Adult female, winter*: Acquired by complete postnuptial molt. Like nuptial adult female. *Male, first nuptial*: Acquired by wear from first winter. Similar to nuptial adult male, but upper parts often with more olive green edgings, and black of throat somewhat obscured by light gray or dull white tips of feathers. *Male, first winter*: Acquired by partial postjuvenal molt, which does not involve wing-quills or tail. Similar to adult male in winter but still more washed with yellowish olive, particularly on upper parts, and crown more overlaid with olive green; chin dull white like malar stripes; black area of throat often smaller and somewhat obscured by dull gray or olivaceous tips of feathers. *Female, first nuptial*: Acquired by wear from first winter. Similar to nuptial adult female. *Female, first winter*: Acquired by partial postjuvenal molt. Similar to adult female in winter but still more washed with yellowish olive green, both on upper and lower parts. *Juvenal*: Acquired by complete postnatal molt. Upper parts deep olive; pileum and rump yellowish olive; tail as in first winter female; wings rather deep mouse gray; two rather narrow wing-bars, formed by tips of greater and median coverts, dull primrose yellow to dull colonial buff; rest of coverts and wing-quills margined with yellowish olive green to dull citrine; lower parts grayish olive anteriorly, light grayish olive posteriorly. Bill, legs, and feet brownish buff or light brown.

MEASUREMENTS: *Adult male*: Wing, 59.7–65.0 (average, 62.2) mm.; tail, 43.2–48.5 (46.3); bill (exposed culmen), 10.9–12.4 (11.7); tarsus, 17.0–18.5 (17.8); middle toe without claw, 8.9–10.9 (10.2). *Adult female*: Wing, 57.7–63.5 (59.7); tail, 44.2–48.0 (45.5); bill, 10.4–11.9 (11.2); tarsus, 17.0–18.5 (17.8); middle toe, 8.9–10.4 (9.7).

TEXAS: *Migration*: Collected in Galveston, Victoria, and Cameron cos.

BLUE-WINGED WARBLER, *Helminthophila pinus* (Linnaeus)

SPECIES ACCOUNT

Vermivora pinus of A.O.U. check-list, 1957 (see Appendix A). *Male:* yellow crown, face, under parts; black line through eye; greenish upper parts; bluish gray wings with two white bars. *Female:* slightly duller. Length, 4¾ in.; wingspan, 7½; weight, ¼ oz.

RANGE: E. Nebraska to s.e. Minnesota and s. New England, south to e. Oklahoma (locally), Kentucky, and Delaware, and in Appalachians to Alabama and Georgia. Winters chiefly from c. Mexico and Yucatán Peninsula to Nicaragua; rarely to Panama.

TEXAS: (See map.) *Summer:* Sighted at Fort Worth on four occasions between June 1 and July 2, 1951; nesting suspected, but unconfirmed (L. McCart, W. Wilson). *Migration:* Early Apr. to early May; mid-Aug. to early Oct. (extremes: Mar. 10, May 30; July 29, Nov. 8). Common (some years) to uncommon in spring along coast; scarce to rare through remainder of eastern half; casual in Trans-Pecos. Uncommon to scarce in fall along coast; rare inland east of 98th meridian. *Winter:* One sight record: Brazos Co., College Station (Dec. 29, 1972, Betty and Larry Dillon).

HAUNTS AND HABITS: The Blue-winged Warbler and the very closely related Golden-winged Warbler breed in, and migrate through, virtually the same habitat, and their geographic distributions coincide closely (although the Bluewing nests a bit farther south in a few localities). The stage is thus set for hybridization; in actual practice, interbreeding between the two species has produced what is probably the most famous set of

hybrids known among wild birds. These hybrids are of two main forms: Brewster's Warbler (white throat, belly) and Lawrence's Warbler (black or gray throat, yellow under parts).

Within Texas the "dominant" Brewster's has been sighted (up to 1972) along the coast in Galveston, Aransas, San Patricio, and Hidalgo counties; inland, in Travis County. The "recessive" Lawrence's has been seen in Travis, Chambers, Galveston, Aransas, and Nueces counties.

Nesting, flight, and foraging behavior of the Bluewing and of both hybrid forms is very similar to that of the Goldenwing. Analysis of stomach contents reveals a similar diet of beetles, bugs, flies, ants, and caterpillars, together with many other insects, their eggs and larvae, as well as some spiders.

The call note of this warbler is a light *chip*. Its song, occasionally heard in Texas, is a sibilant *bee-e-e-e bz-z-z-z*, the first part of rising inflection and the second descending, suggesting inhalation and exhalation.

DETAILED ACCOUNT: NO SUBSPECIES

DESCRIPTION: *Adult male, nuptial plumage:* Acquired by wear from winter plumage. Forehead and crown lemon chrome to light cadmium; remainder of upper surface warbler green to yellowish warbler green, but rump and upper tail-coverts verging toward pyrite yellow; tail dark mouse gray or deep mouse gray, middle feathers and outermost rather lighter, darker feathers edged on outer webs with lighter gray, outer four tail feathers with large terminal or subterminal white spots on inner webs, which on outermost pair of feathers occupy nearly two-thirds of web, though on fourth feather from outside this white is reduced to oblong subterminal spot; wing-quills hair brown to deep mouse gray, inner margins of primaries and secondaries, except at tips of secondaries, brownish white, wing-quills edged narrowly on outer webs with mouse gray; wing-coverts neutral gray, greater series washed slightly with yellowish olive green, median and greater coverts broadly tipped with dull white or yellowish white, forming two conspicuous wing-bars; lores and short postocular streak black; sides of neck like back; remainder of sides of head and entire lower parts gamboge yellow, crissum white or dull yellowish white; sides and flanks pyrite yellow, washed with warbler green; lining of wing dull white, outer coverts slightly mottled with mouse gray. Bill black, but terminal portion of cutting edges paler, somewhat brownish; tongue white; iris dark brown; feet blackish slate, olive, or olive brown; claws and soles of toes light greenish yellow or yellowish tawny olive, claws sometimes seal brown. *Adult male, winter:* Acquired by complete postnuptial molt. Similar to nuptial adult male, but yellow feathers of crown more or less extensively tipped with warbler green. *Adult female, nuptial:* Acquired by wear from winter. Similar to nuptial adult male, but upper surface duller and more uniform, crown usually only slightly more yellowish than back, yellow much overlaid by olive green; white spots of tail smaller; wing-bars dull light grayish olive, narrow and inconspicuous; loral streak duller chaetura drab; yellow of under surface duller, between wax yellow and primuline yellow. *Adult female, winter:* Acquired by complete postnuptial molt. Similar to nuptial adult female, but upper parts brighter, more yellowish (less grayish); lower surface somewhat brighter, whitish wing-bars more conspicuous. *Male, first nuptial:* Acquired by wear from first winter. Similar to nuptial adult male. *Male, first winter:* Acquired by partial postjuvenal molt, which does not involve wing-quills or tail. Similar to adult male in winter, but yellow of crown still more obscured by warbler green; wing-bars much washed with olive green. *Female, first*

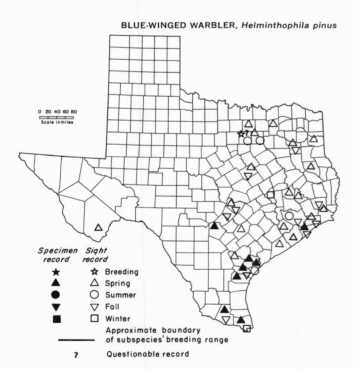

BLUE-WINGED WARBLER, *Helminthophila pinus*

nuptial: Acquired by wear from first winter. Like nuptial adult female. *Female, first winter*: Acquired by partial postjuvenal molt, which does not involve wing-quills or tail. Similar to adult female in winter, but upper parts rather duller, crown still less yellowish; throat and breast more or less obscured by olivaceous tips of feathers. *Juvenal*: Acquired by complete postnatal molt. Upper parts olive yellow, but back somewhat darker; wings and tail mouse gray with lighter margins, wing-coverts and tertials edged with olive yellow, greater and median coverts tipped with pale yellow or yellowish white; lores dull brown. Bill and feet dull brown. *Natal*: Mouse gray. Bill, legs, and feet pinkish buff.

MEASUREMENTS: *Adult male*: Wing, 57.4–63.5 (average, 59.9) mm.; tail, 42.4–48.5 (46.3); bill (exposed culmen), 10.4–12.4 (11.2); tarsus, 16.3–19.0 (17.8); middle toe without claw, 8.9–10.4 (9.7). *Adult female*: Wing, 54.1–60.5 (57.2); tail, 40.9–47.8 (43.7); bill, 10.2–12.2 (11.2); tarsus, 16.5–18.8 (17.3); middle toe, 8.6–10.4 (9.7).

TEXAS: *Migration*: Collected north to Bexar, east to Galveston, south to Cameron and Hidalgo cos.

NESTING: *Nest*: In open country overgrown with thickets, bushes, or low trees, sometimes in heavy forests; on ground, in a thicket or clump of bushes, or amid grass, small sprouts, or vines; deeply cupped, bulky, of varying shape; composed of leaves, strips of grapevine or other bark, blades of grass, shreds of corn leaves, and various other vegetable fibers; lined with shreds of grapevine bark, fine grass, shreds of grass stems, and horsehair. *Eggs*: 3–5; short ovate to ovate; white, slightly creamy; sometimes unmarked, but usually more or less speckled with burnt umber, seal brown, chestnut, and purplish brown, with shell markings of lilac and lavender; average size, 16.3 × 13.0 mm.

[BACHMAN'S WARBLER, *Helminthophila bachmanni* (Audubon)

SPECIES ACCOUNT

Vermivora bachmanii of A.O.U. check-list, 1957. *Male*: olive green above; yellow face and under parts; black crown, throat-patch. *Female*: resembles male, but lacks black patches; instead has bluish gray crown and cheeks, entirely yellow throat, and yellow eye-ring. Song is wiry buzzing trill on one pitch. Length, 4¼ in.

RANGE: *Nearly extinct*. Formerly lowland swamps and adjacent pinelands of s.e. United States. Wintered in Cuba.

TEXAS: *Hypothetical*: No specimen, photograph, or plausible sight record. Sightings apparently based on Hooded, Wilson's, Nashville, and other warblers, or even on young Orchard Oriole. Reported at Fort Worth (Oct. 3, 1945) and Texarkana, Texas (3 birds, May 30–June 21, 1971). In addition, said to occur in Big Thicket region of eastern quarter (1946, Edna Miner); currently listed as one of the representative birds of the Big Thicket (1971, A. Y. Gunter, *The Big Thicket*, p. 153).]

TENNESSEE WARBLER, *Helminthophila peregrina* (Wilson)

SPECIES ACCOUNT

Vermivora peregrina of A.O.U. check-list, 1957 (see Appendix A). *Male*: bluish gray forehead, crown, nape; olive green upper parts; white eye-stripe, under parts. *Female*: more extensively olive green above; slightly yellowish below. *Fall adults*: greenish above with trace of wing-bar; yellowish eye-stripe; dingy yellow wash below but usually retains white crissum. Length, 4¾ in.; wingspan, 7¾; weight, ¼ oz.

RANGE: S. Yukon to Newfoundland, south to interior British Columbia, U.S.-Canadian border, and extreme n.e. United States. Winters from s. Mexico through Central America to n.w. Colombia and n. Venezuela.

TEXAS: (See map.) *Migration*: Early Apr. to mid-May; mid-Sept. to late Oct. (extremes: Mar. 1, May 27; Aug. 24, Nov. 27). Very common (some springs) to fairly common (most falls) in coastal vicinities; common to uncommon inland east of 99th meridian; scarce west to San Angelo and Uvalde; casual in Trans-Pecos. *Winter*: Late Dec. to mid-Feb. Rare and irregular in Rio Grande delta; casual north along Rio Grande to Laredo and along coast to Freeport.

HAUNTS AND HABITS: The Tennessee Warbler nests on damp mossy or ferny ground in a variety of coniferous forest habitats chiefly in Canada. In spring it rushes through Texas and in fall slips silently past, some years going almost unnoticed. During these migrations, it rests and feeds in any available tree or bush. It shows some preference, however, for pecans (*Carya illinoensis*) and oaks in spring. It often occurs in small numbers associated with other migrant warblers.

Flight is quick and jerky, as are the bird's foraging movements. The Tennessee feeds amid catkins or foliage often near the tops of tall trees. Food consists largely of insects, their larvae and eggs (flies, weevils, fireflies, ants, cankerworms and other caterpillars,

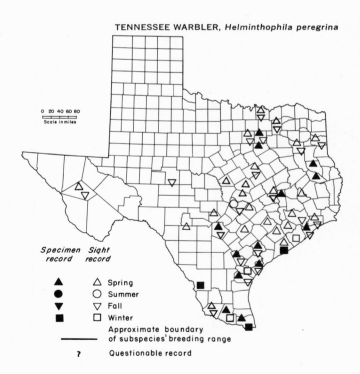

TENNESSEE WARBLER, *Helminthophila peregrina*

0 20 40 60 80
Scale in miles

Specimen record	Sight record	
▲	△	Spring
●	○	Summer
▼	▽	Fall
■	□	Winter

——— Approximate boundary of subspecies' breeding range

? Questionable record

locusts, grasshoppers, caddis flies, plant lice, leaf- and tree-hoppers, and waterbugs), but includes some spiders and snails and occasionally seeds and berries (poison-ivy, grapes).

The usual call note is an indistinctive *chip*. In April and May in Texas, Tennessees frequently sing their loud, staccato, usually two-part song: *k'see-k'see-xee-xee-see-see, see-e-e-e*, the second part of which is like an emphatic Chipping Sparrow's but louder at the end.

DETAILED ACCOUNT: NO SUBSPECIES

DESCRIPTION: *Adult male, nuptial plumage*: Acquired by partial prenuptial molt. Pileum and hindneck deep mouse gray to deep olive drab; back, rump, and scapulars warbler green to grayish warbler green; upper tail-coverts yellowish warbler green; tail hair brown, feathers edged basally with yellowish warbler green, two or three outer feathers with dull white spots on terminal portion of inner webs, these spots sometimes reduced to mere whitish edgings; wings hair brown, inner margins of primaries and secondaries, except at tips of primaries, dull white or brownish white, outer margins of primaries and secondaries yellowish citrine, except on tips of primaries; lesser coverts like back; outer edgings of remaining coverts yellowish citrine; grayish white or yellowish white superciliary stripe; throat and sides of head olive buff or pale olive buff, more or less obscurely streaked or mottled with mouse gray, but streak through lores and back of eye mouse gray to dark mouse gray; posterior sides of neck warbler green like back; lower parts white, faintly washed with pale buff or pale yellow; sides and flanks light yellowish olive; lining of wing white, outer portion slightly mottled with mouse gray; axillars white, washed with pale yellow. Bill slate, blackish slate, blackish brown, or brownish black, but cutting edges and base of mandible mouse gray; iris prout brown; legs and feet drab or drab gray, but feet sometimes greenish yellow or olive. *Adult male, winter*: Acquired by complete postnuptial molt. Similar to nuptial adult male, but crown much washed with olive green; lower parts more or less washed with olive green or olive yellow; sides, flanks, and breast more or less washed with olive yellow. *Adult female, nuptial*: Acquired by partial prenuptial molt. Similar to nuptial adult male, but crown more brownish and much washed with olive; olive green of upper parts usually duller and more yellowish (less grayish); superciliary stripe, sides of head, and anterior part of neck pale olive yellow; lower surface much more tinged with pale yellow. *Adult female, winter*: Acquired by complete postnuptial molt. Similar to nuptial adult female, but crown much more overlaid with olive green; lower parts more washed with yellow or yellowish warbler green. *Male and female, first nuptial*: Acquired by partial prenuptial molt. Similar to corresponding sex of nuptial adult. *Male and female, first winter*: Acquired by partial postjuvenal molt, which does not involve wing-quills or tail. Similar to adult female in winter, but upper parts more yellowish warbler green, making these almost uniform; sides of head and of neck, including superciliary stripe, more strongly yellowish, inclining to olive ocher; lower surface much more strongly washed with yellow, olive yellow, or light yellowish olive, except for median portion of breast and abdomen which is more whitish; tips of greater and median wing-coverts conspicuously paler yellow, forming two indistinct wing-bars. *Juvenal*: Acquired by complete postnatal molt. Upper parts dull deep olive; lower parts anteriorly citrine drab, posteriorly dull colonial buff; wings and tail like those in first winter. Bill and feet blackish slate, but base of mandible dull white or yellowish-white; feet clove brown.

MEASUREMENTS: *Adult male*: Wing, 62.5–67.8 (average, 64.5) mm.; tail, 40.9–46.0 (42.2); bill (exposed culmen), 9.1–11.4 (10.2); tarsus, 15.5–17.8 (16.8); middle toe without claw, 9.4–10.9 (10.2). *Adult female*: Wing, 58.2–63.5 (60.7); tail, 37.6–43.4 (40.4); bill, 8.9–11.4 (10.2); tarsus, 15.7–17.3 (16.3); middle toe, 9.4–10.9 (10.2).

TEXAS: *Migration*: Collected north to Dallas, east to Galveston, south to Cameron, west to Bexar cos. *Winter*: Taken in Matagorda, Cameron, and Webb cos.

ORANGE-CROWNED WARBLER, *Helminthophila celata* (Say)

SPECIES ACCOUNT

Vermivora celata of A.O.U. check-list, 1957 (see Appendix A). Plain, dingy. *Nuptial*: orange crown-patch (seldom visible); drab olive green above; greenish yellow below with faint breast-streaks. *Winter*: more grayish (less greenish); smudgy breast, faint breast-streaks usually present; retains yellow crissum. Length, 4¾ in.; wingspan, 7½; weight, ¼ oz.

RANGE: Alaska to n.w. Quebec, south to n.w. Baja California, s.e. Arizona, n. Trans-Pecos Texas, s. Manitoba, and c. Ontario. Winters from n. California, c. Arizona, Gulf states, and South Carolina to Guatemala and s. Florida.

TEXAS: (See map.) *Breeding*: Probably early May to mid-Aug. (no egg dates available, but nest located at 8,000 ft. by F. R. Gehlbach). Fairly common in The Bowl, Guadalupe Mts. *Migration*: Mid-Mar. to early May; mid-Sept. to early Nov. (extremes: Mar. 11, May 24; Aug. 16, Nov. 11). Very common to fairly common through eastern half; fairly common to uncommon through western half. *Winter*: Mid-Oct. to late Apr. Common to fairly common in southern half; uncommon to scarce in northern half with exception of northern and middle Panhandle, where rare.

HAUNTS AND HABITS: In Texas the Orange-crowned

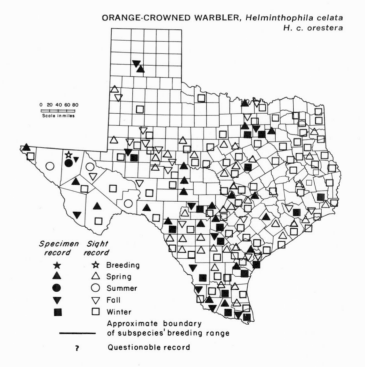

ORANGE-CROWNED WARBLER, *Helminthophila celata*
H. c. orestera

0 20 40 60 80
Scale in miles

Specimen record	Sight record	
★	☆	Breeding
▲	△	Spring
●	○	Summer
▼	▽	Fall
■	□	Winter

—————— Approximate boundary of subspecies' breeding range

? Questionable record

Warbler nests on the ground amidst grasses and forbs, bushes, oaks, pines, and Douglasfir (*Pseudotsuga*) high in the Guadalupe Mountains. In migration and winter it is able to live in almost all parts of the state. Unlike most other warblers, it does not require woods. Mesquites and other shrubs, with or without thorns, apparently suit it nearly as well as do trees. Although it seldom occurs in numbers, individuals or small groups commonly associate with mixed flocks of warblers or other insectivorous species.

Flight is quick and jerky. The bird forages restlessly through foliage of bushes and trees, apparently preferring the lower levels, and often descends to the ground. The Orangecrown's warm-season diet consists of about one-tenth vegetable matter (fruit, leaf galls, seeds) and nine-tenths animal matter, primarily insects (leaf bugs, leaf-hoppers, plant lice, scale insects, weevils, ladybirds, caterpillars, wasps, ants, flies), together with a few spiders. In winter, a somewhat higher proportion of plant products is taken.

Its call note is a sharp *chip*; its song, a low-pitched, musical trill that drops in energy and may change in pitch at the end. Song is infrequently heard away from nesting territory.

DETAILED ACCOUNT: TWO SUBSPECIES

EASTERN ORANGE-CROWNED WARBLER, *Helminthophila celata celata* (Say)

DESCRIPTION: *Adult male, nuptial plumage*: Acquired by partial prenuptial molt. Upper parts dull citrine, but rump yellowish citrine; crown rich ochraceous tawny, more or less obscured by dull citrine of upper parts; tail hair brown, narrowly margined on outer webs, chiefly at base, with yellowish citrine; wings hair brown, basal portion of primaries and secondaries with inner margins brownish white, lesser coverts and outer edges of remaining coverts and of wing-quills like back; usually narrowly edged on bend of wing with yellowish or whitish; superciliary stripe wax yellow; rest of sides of head light yellowish olive, but cheeks slightly streaked with dull yellow; anterior lower parts wax yellow; more or less obscurely streaked with light yellowish or grayish olive; posterior lower parts amber yellow to citrine yellow, but sides and flanks light yellowish olive; lining of wing amber yellow, slightly mottled with light yellowish olive. Bill blackish brown, dull black, or brownish slate, but cutting edges and mandible plumbeous, darker at tip and yellow at base; iris vandyke brown, burnt sienna, or black; legs dull plumbeous or dull brown; feet olive, dark greenish slate, dull brown, or greenish yellow; soles of toes greenish yellow; claws dark brown. *Adult male, winter*: Acquired by complete postnuptial molt. Similar to nuptial adult male but rather more yellowish (less grayish) olive green, though feathers are slightly tipped with pale brown or grayish brown, making upper surface somewhat more brownish; sides of head and neck somewhat more brownish, as are also sides and flanks. *Adult female, nuptial*: Acquired by partial prenuptial molt. Similar to nuptial adult male but duller, somewhat more grayish above; paler, somewhat more grayish below; tawny crown-patch duller, less extensive, or even absent. Bill black or slate black, but tip dull white and mandible dull brown or yellow at base; iris prout brown; legs and feet hair brown, brownish yellow, or hair brown; claws dark drab or hair brown with lower surface yellow. *Adult female, winter*: Acquired by complete postnuptial molt. Similar to nuptial adult female, but upper parts more brownish and more yellowish olive (less grayish); colors more blended and, therefore, entire upper surface more uniform; sides of head likewise more brownish; coloration of lower parts more blended, sides and flanks more brownish; remainder of lower surface usually more yellowish. *Male, first nuptial*: Acquired by partial prenuptial molt. Like nuptial adult. *Male, first winter*: Acquired by partial postjuvenal molt, which does not involve wing-quills or tail. Similar to adult male in winter but duller, still more brownish above and below; tawny crown-patch very small or obsolete. *Female, first nuptial*: Acquired by partial prenuptial molt. Like nuptial adult female. *Female, first winter*: Acquired by partial postjuvenal molt. Similar to first winter male but smaller; tawny crown-patch always absent. *Juvenal*: Acquired by complete postnatal molt. Pileum and hindneck between dull mouse gray and dull hair brown; back dull buffy olive; rump buffy citrine; wings and tail as in first winter female, except greater and lesser coverts conspicuously tipped with tawny olive to isabella color, forming two conspicuous wing-bars; chin, throat, and breast buffy light drab, somewhat washed with light gray, chin dull white; superciliary stripe buffy white; lores mouse gray, more or less mixed with dull white; auriculars like crown but lighter; sides and flanks gray, washed with dull light citrine or dull buff; abdomen dull cream white; crissum citrine yellow to amber yellow; under wing-coverts buff or pale dull yellow, slightly mottled with mouse gray; axillars citrine yellow. Maxilla chaetura black, dark olive brown; mandible hair brown or slate blue, but lighter or dull pale yellow at base; rictus pale yellow; iris vandyke brown; legs and feet olivaceous hair brown or dark slate color. *Natal* (this plumage of this race not seen in Texas): Dark gray. Bill, legs, and feet pinkish buff.

MEASUREMENTS: *Adult male*: Wing, 59.4–64.0 (average, 61.2) mm.; tail, 47.0–53.1 (49.3); bill (exposed culmen), 8.9–10.9 (9.7); tarsus, 16.5–18.5 (17.8); middle toe without claw, 9.4–11.4 (10.7). *Adult female*: Wing, 57.2–59.2 (58.2); tail, 45.2–49.3 (47.3); bill, 9.1–10.7 (9.9); tarsus, 17.5–18.5 (18.0); middle toe, 9.4–10.7 (10.2).

RANGE: Alaska to Manitoba. Winters from c. California, Texas, and South Carolina to s. Baja California, n. Mexico, and U.S. Gulf coast.

TEXAS: *Migration*: Collected north to Potter, east to Cooke and Kaufman, south to Cameron, west to Culberson cos. Fairly common. *Winter*: Taken north to Dallas, east to Hardin, south to Cameron, west to Kinney cos. Fairly common.

NESTING: (This race does not nest in Texas.) *Nest*: In mountains or stream valleys, or on more level land; in undergrowth of open woodlands, in thickets or similar places, sometimes on side of bank; on ground and often well concealed; large for size of bird and deeply cupped; composed of long strips of bark interwoven with dry grass, plant stems, leaves, and weeds; lined with fine grass, hair, or fur. *Eggs*: 4–6; ovate to rounded ovate; white or cream white; speckled, chiefly at large end, with reddish brown, pale brown, chestnut, and purplish slate, with shell markings of lilac and lavender; average size, 16.0 × 12.4 mm.

ROCKY MOUNTAIN ORANGE-CROWNED WARBLER, *Helminthophila celata orestera* Oberholser

DESCRIPTION: *Adult male and female, nuptial plumage*: Similar to *H. c. celata*, but wing longer; upper parts more yellowish olive; lower surface more deeply and extensively yellow. Similar to Lutescent Orange-crowned Warbler, *H. c. lutescens*, but much larger; less yellowish above and below; also somewhat more grayish on upper surface. *Natal*: Probably similar to *H. c. celata*.

MEASUREMENTS: *Adult male*: Wing, 61.5–66.0 (average, 63.2) mm.; tail, 48.5–53.1 (50.3); bill (exposed culmen), 9.9–10.9 (10.2); tarsus, 17.5–19.6 (18.3); middle toe without claw, 9.9–10.9 (10.2). *Adult female*: Wing, 57.4–61.0 (59.2); tail, 46.0–49.0 (47.5); bill, 9.4–10.9 (9.9); tarsus, 17.0–19.0 (18.3); middle toe, 9.9–10.4 (10.2).

RANGE: S.w. Yukon to s. Saskatchewan, south to e. California and Trans-Pecos Texas. Winters from c. Washington, c. Arizona, and c. Texas to s. Baja California, Sinaloa, Guerrero, and Veracruz.

TEXAS: *Breeding*: Collected in Culberson Co. *Migration*: Collected north to Tarrant, east to Travis, south to Webb, west to

El Paso cos. Fairly common. *Winter*: Taken north to Bexar, east to Nueces, south to Cameron, west to Kinney cos. Fairly common.

NESTING: Similar to that of *H. c. celata*, but in Texas restricted to mountains.

NASHVILLE WARBLER, *Helminthophila ruficapilla* (Wilson)

SPECIES ACCOUNT

Vermivora ruficapilla of A.O.U. check-list, 1957 (see Appendix A). Gray head; white eye-ring; chestnut crown-patch (often concealed); olive green above; yellow throat, breast, crissum; whitish lower abdomen. Length, 4¾ in.; wingspan, 7¼; weight, ¼ oz.

RANGE: S. British Columbia to Nova Scotia, south (largely excluding Rockies) to c. California, n. Utah, s. Great Lakes region, and Pennsylvania. Winters from n. Mexico and s. Texas to Guatemala; also s. Florida.

TEXAS: (See map.) *Migration*: Late Mar. to mid-May; early Sept. to late Oct. (extremes: Mar. 17, May 27; July 4, Nov. 15). Very common to fairly common east of 100th meridian (numbers greater in spring inland, in fall on upper coast); uncommon through remainder of state with exception of western Trans-Pecos, where rare in fall. *Winter*: Late Nov. to mid-Mar. Fairly common (some years) to uncommon in Rio Grande delta; increasingly scarce north to Houston where rare, and to Austin and Del Rio where rare to casual; sightings from San Angelo (Dec. 23), Fort Worth (Jan. 1–3), and Hunt Co. may represent extremely late fall stragglers.

HAUNTS AND HABITS: On their breeding grounds in the north, Nashville Warblers show preference for two different habitat types: (1) forest-bordered bogs with a sprinkling of conifers and a moist ground cover of moss; and (2) open stands of dry, young second-growth forest where deciduous trees, such as birch and aspen, mingle with evergreens. In both habitats, the nest is built on the ground.

In springtime central Texas, the Nashville is usually the most numerous of purely migrant warblers. In common with related species, it favors deciduous trees and shrubs along rivers and creeks. In good years, however, numbers can be found even in hilltop cedars. In fall, this bird appears to migrate by a somewhat different route; at this season its numbers are down in central Texas but up on the northern Gulf coast. Where common, Nashvilles often occur in loose flocks and frequently associate with other migrant warblers.

Flight is quick and erratic, and the Nashville darts about nervously gleaning insects from vegetation high and low. Food consists chiefly of caterpillars (tent, cankerworms), beetles (including wood-boring), flies, grasshoppers, locusts, leaf-hoppers, plant lice, and their larvae and eggs, together with a few spiders.

The call note of this species is a weak *chip*. Nashville Warbler song is a variable *seebit seebit seebit seebit, ti-ti-ti-ti* of rather sibilant quality and descending at the end. Spring migrants sing often in Texas.

DETAILED ACCOUNT: TWO SUBSPECIES

EASTERN NASHVILLE WARBLER, *Helminthophila ruficapilla ruficapilla* (Wilson)

DESCRIPTION: *Adult male, nuptial plumage*: Acquired by partial prenuptial molt. Pileum neutral gray, slightly washed with olivaceous, center of crown auburn, more or less obscured by gray feather tips; back and scapulars warbler green; rump and upper tail-coverts between warbler green and pyrite yellow; tail hair brown, inner webs of outer feathers edged with whitish, all feathers edged narrowly on outer webs with color of rump; wings hair brown, coverts and quills edged with color of back, quills rather more brownish, basal edge of primaries and secondaries brownish white; lores dull white, mixed with gray of forehead; sides of head neutral gray, conspicuous eye-ring white or yellowish white; lower parts, including lining of wing, gamboge yellow, becoming more or less whitish on lower abdomen, sides and flanks slightly washed with olive. Bill plumbeous, chaetura black, clove brown, slate black, or brownish black, but cutting edges of maxilla somewhat paler or even whitish; mandible, except slate or dull brown tip, plumbeous white, drab, tawny olive, or dull lilaceous, but its base dull yellow; tongue white; iris burnt umber or fuscous black; legs plumbeous or raw umber; feet olivaceous, olive brown, olive gray, olivaceous slate, or raw umber; claws raw umber. *Adult male, winter*: Acquired by complete postnuptial molt. Similar to nuptial adult male, but upper parts more grayish or brownish and more uniform, all but rump and upper tail-coverts much obscured by dull brownish gray including brown crown-patch; sides of head more brownish; lower parts duller, yellow much obscured by olive gray or brownish tips of feathers. *Adult female, nuptial*: Acquired by partial prenuptial molt. Similar to nuptial adult male, but duller, pileum somewhat more brownish, auburn crown-patch very much smaller or absent; lower surface somewhat paler. *Adult female, winter*: Acquired by complete postnuptial molt. Similar to nuptial adult female, but pileum more brownish, auburn crown-patch, if present, obscured by brownish feather tips, back more grayish or brownish, yellow of lower parts duller, more or less obscured by pale brown or gray tips of feathers. *Male, first nuptial*: Acquired by partial prenuptial molt. Similar to nup-

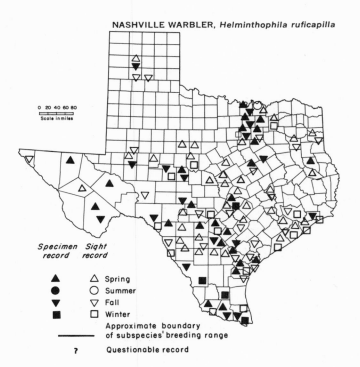

NASHVILLE WARBLER, *Helminthophila ruficapilla*

0 20 40 60 80
Scale in miles

Specimen Sight
record record

▲ △ Spring
● ○ Summer
▼ ▽ Fall
■ □ Winter

—— Approximate boundary
of subspecies' breeding range

? Questionable record

tial adult male. *Male, first winter*: Acquired by partial post-juvenal molt not involving wing-quills or tail. Similar to adult male in winter, but upper parts duller and more brownish, anteriorly pale brownish citrine drab, auburn crown-patch much smaller or absent, yellow of lower parts duller, chin inclining to white. *Female, first nuptial*: Acquired by partial prenuptial molt. Like nuptial adult female. *Female, first winter*: Acquired by partial postjuvenal molt. Similar to first winter male, but auburn crown-patch nearly always absent. *Juvenal*: Acquired by complete postnatal molt. Upper surface dull citrine drab, passing on upper tail-coverts into citrine; greater and lesser wing-coverts tipped with pale buff or yellowish white, forming two rather obvious light wing-bars; chin inclining to white; throat and breast light citrine drab; abdomen dull reed yellow; crissum light olive yellow. Bill slate black, but base of mandible olive gray, becoming yellowish white at base; legs blackish slate; toes and claws olive above, dull wax yellow below.

MEASUREMENTS: *Adult male*: Wing, 57.9–62.0 (average, 60.2) mm.; tail, 42.4–46.5 (43.9); bill (exposed culmen), 8.9–9.9 (9.7); tarsus, 16.5–17.5 (17.0); middle toe without claw, 9.4–10.4 (9.9). *Adult female*: Wing, 54.8–61.0 (56.9); tail, 39.1–46.0 (42.2); bill, 9.1–9.9 (9.7); tarsus, 16.5–17.8 (17.3); middle toe, 9.4–10.9 (10.2).

RANGE: S.w. Saskatchewan to s.e. Quebec, south to c. Minnesota, e. West Virginia, and s. Maine. Winters from s. Texas through Mexico to s.e. Guatemala.

TEXAS: *Migration*: Collected north to Potter, east to Chambers, south to Cameron, west to Culberson cos. Common. *Winter*: Taken in Webb, Brooks, and Cameron cos. Uncommon to scarce.

CALAVERAS NASHVILLE WARBLER, *Helminthophila ruficapilla gutturalis* (Ridgway)

Vermivora ruficapilla ridgwayi of A.O.U. check-list, 1957 (see Appendix A).

DESCRIPTION: *Adult male and female, nuptial plumage*: Similar to *H. r. ruficapilla*, but tail slightly longer; back more golden (less greenish) olive; rump brighter, more yellowish (less greenish); yellow of lower parts more golden (less greenish); wing-coverts lighter, more yellowish; lower abdomen averaging more extensively dull white.

MEASUREMENTS: *Adult male*: Wing, 58.4–62.0 (average, 60.5) mm.; tail, 42.7–48.0 (44.7); bill (exposed culmen), 9.4–10.7 (9.9); tarsus, 16.5–18.0 (17.3); middle toe without claw, 9.4–10.4 (9.9). *Adult female*: Wing, 55.1–59.9 (57.2); tail, 40.4–46.5 (43.2); bill, 8.9–10.4 (9.7); tarsus, 15.5–18.0 (16.8); middle toe, 9.1–9.9 (9.7).

RANGE: S.w. British Columbia to n.w. Idaho, south to c. California and s.e. Wyoming. Winters from s. Texas (a few) through w. Mexico to s.w. Guatemala.

TEXAS: *Migration*: Collected north to Concho, southeast to Bexar and Cameron, west to Brewster cos. Uncommon. *Winter*: Two specimens: Travis Co., Austin (Feb. 14, 1913, E. Perry, Jr.); Cameron Co., Brownsville (Feb. 22, 1910, A. P. Smith).

COLIMA WARBLER, *Helminthophila crissalis*
Salvin and Godman

SPECIES ACCOUNT

Vermivora crissalis of A.O.U. check-list, 1957 (see Appendix A). *Nuptial male*: gray head; brownish back; grayish below; chestnut crown-patch; yellow rump, crissum. *Female, fall male*: somewhat duller; more brownish. Length, 5¼ in.

RANGE: Chisos Mts. of Trans-Pecos Texas, south in Sierra Madre Oriental through Coahuila to s.w. Tamaulipas. Winters in w. Mexico from s. Sinaloa to Guerrero.

TEXAS: (See map.) *Breeding*: Late Apr. to mid-July (eggs, May 12 to May 28; nestlings, May 25 to July 6) from 5,900 to 7,500 ft. Locally common in the Chisos Mts., Big Bend Nat. Park, where recorded from Mar. 15 to Sept. 19. Yearly censuses taken in the second week of May yielded a total of 92 birds in 1967; 130 in 1968; 166 in 1969; and 118 in 1970 (R. H. Wauer, et. al.).

HAUNTS AND HABITS: The Chisos Mountains of Big Bend have the distinction of supporting the only colony of Colima Warblers in the United States. Even within this small mountain group, the species is restricted chiefly to forested canyons and slopes at altitudes between 6,000 and 7,000 feet; most birds are seen in Boot Canyon or along Laguna Meadow on the South Rim trail. Here it places its nest—not found until 1932—among fallen oak leaves on rocky slopes.

In the immediate vicinity of Boot Spring the bird spends much time catching caterpillars and other insects in Arizona cypress (*Cupressus arizonica*) and in neighboring vegetation. Farther from the spring the Colima lives mostly in thickets of oak (*Quercus emoryi, Q. gravesii, Q. grisea*, others) and maple (*Acer grandidentatum*). The Colima is deliberate and somewhat vireolike in its movements, but may sally forth for an airborne insect or drop to the ground for a caterpillar. Females pull off (with their beaks) strips of drooping juniper (*Juniperus flaccida*) bark for their nests.

Males usually sing from low trees—oaks, maple, madrone (*Arbutus texana*); occasionally they use as a singing perch a high branch of a ponderosa pine (*Pinus ponderosa*). They persistently sing while foraging, even when the sky is overcast. The song is a musical trill much like that of a Chipping Sparrow, but ending

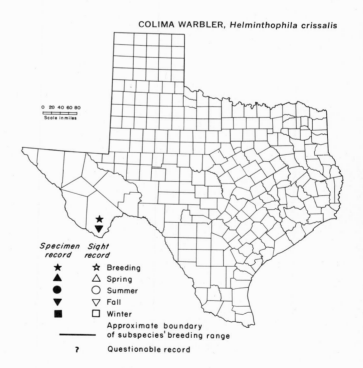

COLIMA WARBLER, *Helminthophila crissalis*

0 20 40 60 80
Scale in miles

Specimen record   Sight record

★ ☆ Breeding
▲ △ Spring
● ○ Summer
▼ ▽ Fall
■ □ Winter

——— Approximate boundary of subspecies' breeding range

? Questionable record

with two lower notes. May and June are the chief singing months. The call note is an abrupt, sharp *psit*.

DETAILED ACCOUNT: NO SUBSPECIES

DESCRIPTION: *Adult male, nuptial plumage*: Acquired probably by partial prenuptial molt. Pileum dull neutral gray; crown centrally cinnamon rufous to sanford brown; back and scapulars between buffy brown and deep olive; rump pyrite yellow; upper tail-coverts orange citrine; tail dark hair brown, feathers narrowly edged basally on outer webs with color of back; wings dark hair brown, wing-coverts and quills edged with color of back; sides of head and of neck mouse gray, neck rather darker; lores mixed with paler gray; narrow white eye-ring; throat between light grayish olive and light mouse gray; jugulum, breast, and abdomen similar, but jugulum somewhat washed with brown; sides and flanks light brownish olive, middle of abdomen dull white; crissum analine yellow or between analine yellow and cadmium yellow; lining of wing grayish white. Bill plumbeous, but base of mandible paler; inside of mouth pale straw yellow; iris very dark brown; legs and feet plumbeous. *Adult male, winter*: Acquired by complete postnuptial molt. Similar to nuptial adult male, but colors duller and richer, particularly upper parts which are more deeply brown; rufous crown-patch more obscured by brown tips of feathers; gray of anterior lower parts more washed with brown; sides and flanks more deeply brown. *Adult female, nuptial*: Acquired probably by partial prenuptial molt. Similar to nuptial adult male but averaging somewhat darker; under surface more brownish. *Male and female, first nuptial*: Acquired probably by partial prenuptial molt. Not seen, but probably similar to corresponding sex of nuptial adults. *Male and female, first winter*: Acquired probably by partial postjuvenal molt. Similar to nuptial adults, but upper parts, particularly head and hindneck, more brownish (less grayish); lower parts, particularly anteriorly, but also breast and abdomen, more buffy or brownish (less grayish). *Juvenal*: Acquired by complete postnatal molt. Similar to adult male in winter but duller; crown with no cinnamon rufous patch; upper surface slightly more greenish olive; pileum and hindneck dull, rather grayish, light brownish olive; back brownish olive; rump rather lighter and more greenish; upper tail-coverts yellow ocher, but longest feathers darker; tail dark hair brown, edged with deep olive; wing-quills between dark mouse gray and chaetura drab, inner edges of primaries and secondaries, except at tips, brownish white, edges of outermost few primaries mouse gray, those of rest of primaries and of secondaries brownish olive; wing-coverts margined on outer webs with brownish to light brownish olive, median and greater wing-coverts also tipped with dull cream buff or colonial buff, forming two obvious wing-bars; lores mixed with mouse gray and grayish white; eye-ring yellowish white; remainder of sides of head and sides of neck mouse gray, overlaid or washed with light brownish olive; chin buffy white; throat and jugulum dull light grayish olive; abdomen dull grayish white or buffy white; crissum greenish yellow ocher; lining of wing massicot yellow. *Natal*: Unknown.

MEASUREMENTS: *Adult male*: Wing, 62.5–67.6 (average, 64.5) mm.; tail, 52.6–57.9 (55.3); bill (exposed culmen), 10.9–11.9 (11.4); tarsus, 18.0–21.1 (19.0); middle toe without claw, 9.9–10.9 (10.4). *Adult female*: Wing, 58.4–63.0 (60.2); tail, 51.1–56.4 (52.8); bill, 10.7–11.9 (11.2); tarsus, 17.5–19.0 (18.5); middle toe, 9.4–10.9 (10.2).

TEXAS: *Breeding*: Collected in Chisos Mts., Brewster Co.

NESTING: *Nest*: In mountains; in open low woods of stream canyons or slopes; on ground, not particularly well concealed, embedded in oak leaves and arched over, with entrance on side, rather loosely or neatly woven; composed of grasses, green moss, juniper or other bark, and leaves; lined with fine grass, hair, and fur. *Eggs*: 4; ovate; cream white, spotted and blotched with light vinaceous fawn, light brownish drab, and cinnamon drab, forming wreath at large end; average size, 18.3 × 13.5 mm.

LUCY'S WARBLER, *Helminthophila luciae* (Cooper)

SPECIES ACCOUNT

Vermivora luciae of A.O.U. check-list, 1957 (see Appendix A). A tiny desert warbler. *Nuptial male*: gray above; chestnut crown-patch (often concealed) and upper tail-coverts; whitish below tinged with buff. *Female, winter male*: buffier. Length, 4¼ in.; wingspan, 6¾.

RANGE: S. Nevada, s. Utah, and s.w. Colorado, south to n.e. Baja California, n. Sonora, s.w. New Mexico, and occasionally Trans-Pecos Texas. Winters from Jalisco to Guerrero.

TEXAS: *Breeding*: One record: Hudspeth Co., Sierra Blanca (1 adult seen feeding young Brown-headed Cowbird, June 8, 1958, Mr. and Mrs. D. T. Johnson). Rare to casual in spring and summer in El Paso region and Big Bend. Records from Big Bend Nat. Park: Rio Grande Village (Apr. 8, 1970, Noberto Ortega and R. H. Wauer; 2 seen, May 3, 1970, Wauer; lone birds singing, Apr. 4, and 23, 1972, Wauer); Boquillas (singing male collected, Apr. 17, 1970, Wauer). *Casual*: Two sightings outside Trans-Pecos: Navarro Co., Corsicana (May 21, 22, 1929, Connie Hagar); Brazoria Co., Freeport (Dec. 27, 1964, Mr. and Mrs. J. B. Strickling). *Winter*: Reports from El Paso region need substantiation.

HAUNTS AND HABITS: The Lucy's Warbler is the smallest of the American wood warblers and sole member of its family that nests mainly on the Lower Sonoran desert of the southwestern United States and northwestern Mexico. It is a bird of extensive mesquite groves and of willows and cottonwoods along streams that course through hot deserts.

Preferred foraging is in mesquites where it actively flits, gleaning insects. Little is known of its diet.

Lucy's call note is a rather loud *tseep* which resembles that of a White-crowned Sparrow. The song is a lively, double-pitched *weeta weeta weeta che che che che che*, similar in quality to that of a Yellow Warbler.

DETAILED ACCOUNT: NO SUBSPECIES

DESCRIPTION: *Adult male, nuptial plumage*: Acquired by wear from winter plumage. Crown auburn to bay, usually somewhat streaked or spotted with gray of upper parts; upper tail-coverts chestnut to light auburn with a narrow, almost obscure dull whitish, white, or buffy white bar across lower rump; remainder of upper surface between light neutral gray and mouse gray; wings and tail hair brown to dark hair brown, outermost pair of tail feathers with dull white subterminal area on inner margin of terminal portion of inner webs, but rectrices, except middle pair, margined more or less on their inner webs with dull white or buffy white, and on outer webs with gray of upper surface; lesser coverts, outer margins of other coverts, and all wing-quills gray like back, but outer edges of tertials dull light drab; eye-ring buffy white; sides of head, throat, and breast between cartridge buff and cream color, this tinged with gray on sides of head, and becoming nearly pure gray on sides of neck, but paler than upper surface; chin and remainder of lower surface buffy white or very pale buff; sides and flanks shaded with light gray; lining of wing buffy white, slightly mottled, particularly on outer edge, with drab gray. Culmen dull brown; sides of maxilla and all of mandible lighter, more inclining to plumbeous; iris dark brown; legs and feet dark brown or black. *Adult male, winter*: Acquired by complete postnuptial molt. Similar to nuptial adult male, but crown-patch with very broad grayish feather tips, back more tinged with pale brown or buff; upper tail-coverts tipped with pale buff or dull white; pale tips and margins of wing-coverts broader; lower parts more deeply and richly colored; throat and breast ochraceous buff; sides and flanks between cream buff and deep olive buff. *Adult female, nuptial*: Acquired by wear from winter. Similar to nuptial adult male but smaller; crown-patch of less extent; upper tail-coverts paler; gray of upper surface less pure (more buffy or brownish); lower surface averaging more deeply buff. Bill black, but mandible plumbeous; iris dark brown; legs and feet dull black. *Adult female, winter*: Acquired by complete postnuptial molt. Similar to nuptial adult female, but crown-patch more obscured by gray tips and margins of feathers; lower parts more deeply buff. *Male, first nuptial*: Acquired by wear from first winter. Similar to nuptial adult male, but upper surface averaging less purely gray (more brownish or buffy); upper parts averaging somewhat more deeply buff. *Male, first winter*: Acquired by partial postjuvenal molt, which does not involve wing-quills or tail. Similar to adult male in winter, but upper surface much more washed with light brown or buff; lower surface still more deeply buff; differs also from first nuptial male in much the same way, only more decidedly, also in the less conspicuous auburn crown-patch, which is almost entirely obscured by brownish gray tips of feathers. *Female, first nuptial*: Acquired by wear from first winter. Similar to nuptial adult female, but lower surface more deeply buff. *Female, first winter*: Acquired by partial postjuvenal molt, which does not involve wing-quills or tail. Similar to adult female in winter but still more buffy below. *Male, juvenal*: Acquired by complete postnatal molt. Similar to first winter male but lacking reddish brown crown-patch; all body plumage of looser character common to juvenal birds; upper surface lighter, less brownish; rump and upper tail-coverts lighter—clay to ochraceous tawny; middle and greater wing-coverts tipped with dull buff, forming two wing-bars; outer edgings of tertials tinged with dull buff; lower parts more whitish (much less buffy). *Female, juvenal*: Acquired by complete postnatal molt. Similar to juvenal male but smaller; lower surface averaging more buffy. *Natal*: Pale tilleul buff.

MEASUREMENTS: *Adult male*: Wing, 55.3–58.2 (average, 56.6) mm.; tail, 41.1–43.7 (42.7); bill (exposed culmen), 8.4–9.4 (8.9); tarsus, 16.0–16.5 (16.3); middle toe without claw, 8.6–9.9 (9.1). *Adult female*: Wing, 51.8–52.8 (52.3); tail, 37.3–39.6 (38.9); bill, 7.9–8.9 (8.4); tarsus, 15.5–16.0 (15.7); middle toe, 8.6–9.9 (9.1).

TEXAS: *Breeding*: See species account.

NESTING: *Nest*: On mesas and slopes but chiefly in valleys; in desert brush, thickets along streams, and fringes of timber along rivers; in bush, tree, or giant cactus, 2–20 ft. above ground, in fork or almost any nook of tree, in loose bark on tree trunk, in woodpecker or other deserted hole in giant cactus or tree, or among tree roots on river bank; rather small cup of grass, straw, leaves, twigs, weed stalks, horsehair, and feathers; lined with horsehair, sometimes cow hair and feathers. *Eggs*: 3–6, usually 4; short ovate; white or cream white, rather sparsely dotted, chiefly at larger end, with umber, reddish brown, and black, and with shell markings of violet gray; average size, 15.0 × 11.9 mm.

VIRGINIA'S WARBLER, *Oreothlypis virginiae* (Baird)

SPECIES ACCOUNT

Vermivora virginiae of A.O.U. check-list, 1957 (see Appendix A). Resembles Colima Warbler, but smaller, slightly paler; yellow on breast. Length, 4¾ in.; wingspan, 7½; weight, ¼ oz.

RANGE: Mountains of c. Nevada to s.e. Idaho and n. Colorado, south to s.e. California, c. and s.e. Arizona, and e. New Mexico. Winters in w. Mexico from Jalisco and Guanajuato to Oaxaca.

TEXAS: (See map.) *Breeding*: Two specimens: Culberson Co., Guadalupe Mts., Upper Dog Canyon (1 female, June 20, 1972, at 6,500 ft., and 1 fledgling, June 22, 1972, 6,350 ft., G. A. Newman; original nos., 314, 319, Texas A&M University collection). *Migration*: Late Apr. to mid-May; late Aug. to late Sept. (extremes: Apr. 8, June 16; Aug. 21, Sept. 24). Fairly common to uncommon in majority of Trans-Pecos counties, but scarce in Pecos River Valley; rare, though very irregularly uncommon, east to Amarillo and Midland; casual at Corpus Christi. *Winter*: No specimen, but individual sighted at Laguna Atascosa Nat. Wildlife Refuge, Cameron Co. (Dec. 29, 1960, C. R. Bender).

HAUNTS AND HABITS: The Virginia's Warbler is the Rocky Mountain version of the Chisos–Sierra Madre Oriental's Colima Warbler. Both species frequent similar habitat, although the Virginia's is rather more closely confined to scrubby oak thickets. Nesting and foraging habits are similar to those of the Colima, but the Virginia's is more shy and retiring and stays closer to the ground. Known food consists of spiders and such insects as caterpillars, carpenter ants, stink bugs, and weevils.

Virginia's call note is a sharp *chip*. Its song is much like the Colima's although louder, more variable, and usually rising in pitch at the end.

DETAILED ACCOUNT: NO SUBSPECIES

DESCRIPTION: *Adult male, nuptial plumage*: Acquired by partial prenuptial molt. Pileum and hindneck dull neutral gray, but center of crown auburn; back brownish mouse gray; rump and upper tail-coverts yellowish sulphine yellow; tail hair brown,

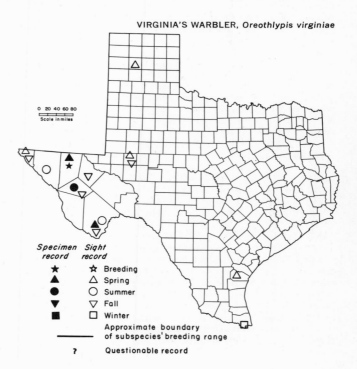

VIRGINIA'S WARBLER, *Oreothlypis virginiae*

0 20 40 60 80
Scale in miles

Specimen record / Sight record

★ / ☆ Breeding
▲ / △ Spring
● / ○ Summer
▼ / ▽ Fall
■ / □ Winter

———— Approximate boundary of subspecies' breeding range

? Questionable record

but inner margins of feathers narrowly whitish, narrow outer margins basally mouse gray; wings hair brown, narrow inner edge of primaries and secondaries, except at tips of primaries, brownish white, coverts and outer webs of wing-quills edged with color of back, which, except on lesser coverts, is somewhat more brownish; sides of head and of neck similar to crown but rather paler, lores mixed with pale gray or dull white with conspicuous white orbital ring; chin grayish white, washed more or less strongly with yellow; center of jugulum, and sometimes most of upper breast, gamboge yellow; sides of breast smoke gray; lower breast and abdomen creamy white; sides and flanks drab gray; crissum gamboge yellow; lining of wing grayish white, washed with yellow. Bill plumbeous black, but mandible and cutting edges paler with lilaceous tinge; iris dark brown; legs and feet olivaceous; soles of toes dull pale yellow. *Adult male, winter*: Acquired by complete postnuptial molt. Similar to nuptial adult male, but upper parts much more brownish, auburn crown-patch more obscured, sometimes entirely, with brownish gray tips of feathers; sides of head somewhat more brownish; yellow of jugulum duller, much obscured by buffy tips of feathers; posterior lower parts more strongly buffy. *Adult female, nuptial*: Acquired by partial prenuptial molt. Similar to nuptial adult male, but upper parts duller, back and head more brownish, auburn chestnut patch smaller, sometimes nearly absent; lower parts more buffy; yellow of lower tail-coverts paler; yellow of jugulum paler and much less extensive, sometimes nearly absent. *Adult female, winter*: Acquired by complete postnuptial molt. Similar to nuptial adult female, but upper parts duller and more brownish; auburn crown-patch more obscured by brownish tips of feathers; lower parts much more strongly buffy; sides and flanks more brownish; yellow of jugulum obscured by buffy tips of feathers. *Male, first nuptial*: Acquired by partial prenuptial molt. Similar to nuptial adult male, but upper parts more brownish. *Male, first winter*: Acquired by partial postjuvenal molt. Similar to adult female in winter, but auburn crown-patch still more obscured; yellow of rump and upper tail-coverts duller, yellow of jugulum much reduced in extent and more obscured by buffy tips of feathers. *Female, first nuptial*: Acquired by partial prenuptial molt. Similar to nuptial adult female, but upper parts more brownish. *Female, first winter*: Acquired by partial postjuvenal molt. Similar to first winter male but smaller; upper parts more brownish; upper tail-coverts somewhat duller; lower parts duller; yellow of breast less in extent or absent. *Juvenal*: Acquired by complete postnatal molt. Upper parts between hair brown and buffy brown, but rump and upper tail-coverts dull primrose yellow; wings and tail as in first winter female, but greater and lesser wing-coverts conspicuously tipped with dull vinaceous buff; sides of head like crown but somewhat paler; anterior lower parts between mouse gray and light drab, jugulum with little or no yellow; sides and flanks washed with same color; abdomen dull white. Iris brown. *Natal*: Unknown.

MEASUREMENTS: *Adult male*: Wing, 58.9–62.5 (average, 61.2) mm.; tail, 46.7–51.0 (48.5); bill (exposed culmen), 8.9–10.9 (9.9); tarsus, 16.5–18.5 (17.3); middle toe without claw, 9.4–10.4 (10.2). *Adult female*: Wing, 53.6–59.4 (57.4); tail, 45.0–47.0 (46.2); bill, 8.9–10.2 (9.6); tarsus, 16.0–18.0 (17.3); middle toe, 8.9–10.4 (9.4).

TEXAS: *Breeding*: Two specimens (see species account). *Migration*: Collected in Culberson, Jeff Davis (Aug. 21), and Brewster cos.

NESTING: *Nest*: On mountain slopes, mesas, and along streams; in low oak or other scrub, or more open brush; sunk in a depression on the ground, well concealed in grass or under branches of bush; rather slight and loosely built cup of fine strips of inner bark of mountainmahogany (*Cercocarpus*) and other trees, fine grasses, roots, moss, and straw; lined with finer materials of same and with fur and hair of mammals. *Eggs*: 3–5, usually 4; rounded ovate to short ovate; cream white or white with slight roseate tinge; much blotched and dotted with purplish brown, reddish brown, and vinaceous brown, these markings confluent about large end, and with shell markings of lilac and purplish gray; average size, 16.8 × 12.4 mm.

PARULA WARBLER, *Parula americana* (Linnaeus)

SPECIES ACCOUNT

Nuptial male: bluish above with yellow-green back-patch; yellow throat and breast with blackish-and-rusty band; broken white eye-ring; white wing-bars, belly. *Female, fall male*: somewhat duller; lack breast-bands. Length, 4½ in.; wingspan, 7½; weight, ¼ oz.

RANGE: S.e. Manitoba to Nova Scotia, south to c. and e. Texas and c. Florida. Winters chiefly in e. and s. Mexico, n. Central America, s. Florida, and West Indies.

TEXAS: (See map.) *Breeding*: Early Apr. to mid-July (eggs, Apr. 20 to May 30) from near sea level to 1,800 ft. Locally common to uncommon in eastern portion north of 28th parallel, west irregularly to Fort Worth, Austin, Kerrville, and Live Oak Co.; nested beside Anzalduas levee, Hidalgo Co. (1966, J. C. Arvin). *Migration*: Mid-Mar. to mid-May; mid-Aug. to late Oct. (extremes: Feb. 21, May 28; June 30, Nov. 23). Common locally (most springs) to uncommon (most falls) east of 100th—98th north of Austin—meridian; increasingly scarce west to Amarillo, Midland, and Big Bend Nat. Park (bird collected at Rio Grande Village, Nov. 27, 1968, not identified to race, R. H. Wauer); casual in remainder of Trans-Pecos. *Winter*: Mid-Dec. to mid-Feb. One specimen (not identified to race): Kenedy Co., King Ranch, 10 mi. east of Rudolf (male, Feb. 4, 1969, B. A. Fall). Scattering of sightings along coast and locally along Rio Grande to Big Bend; single sight records from Fort Worth, Harrison Co., and Austin lack substantiation.

HAUNTS AND HABITS: The ascending trill of the Parula Warbler enlivens woodlands of east Texas in spring

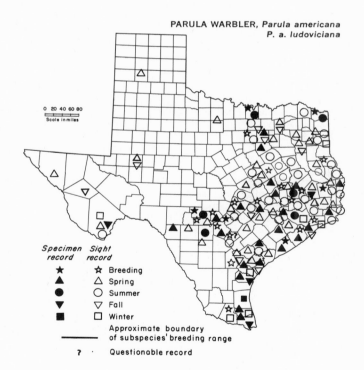

PARULA WARBLER, *Parula americana*
P. a. *ludoviciana*

0 20 40 60 80
Scale in miles

	Specimen record	Sight record
Breeding	★	☆
Spring	▲	△
Summer	●	○
Fall	▼	▽
Winter	■	□

―――― Approximate boundary of subspecies' breeding range

? Questionable record

and early summer. This species inhabits both upland and bottomland forests—coniferous as well as deciduous—particularly along creeks and in swamps. Its summer distribution in Texas appears to be largely determined by the presence of Spanishmoss (*Tillandsia usneoides*) and the long, gray-green lichen *Usnea*, in either of which it almost invariably places its nest. During migration, however, the Parula is not so particular; along with other warblers, it visits a variety of habitats, pausing in both woodlands and brush.

Its flight is quick and erratic, performed by rapid though not numerous wing-beats. When flying a long distance it often ascends to considerable height, but normal flight is from tree to tree. It is exceedingly active, continually creeping about branches—especially in tree canopy—and readily hanging upside down in a manner reminiscent of chickadee or titmouse. It also forages in the understory, but only occasionally descends to the ground. Although bud scales (rarely) and a few spiders enter the diet, food consists mostly of insects, their eggs and larvae: ants, wasps, bees; weevils and other beetles; caterpillars (cankerworm, tent), moths; two-winged flies, locusts, scale insects, plant lice, lace-winged flies, and mayflies. The Parula is not shy and thus may be approached and studied with relative ease.

The usual call is a rather sharp *chip*. The male's song is a distinctive performance, very insectlike and what might be termed buzzy or wheezy in quality; it is given on a rising scale until the last note which descends abruptly. A common variation may be represented as follows: *zip-er zip-er zip-er zeeeeeeee-up*. Singing is heard from March throughout July.

DETAILED ACCOUNT: THREE SUBSPECIES

SOUTHERN PARULA WARBLER, *Parula americana americana* (Linnaeus)

No races recognized by A.O.U. check-list, 1957 (see Appendix A).

DESCRIPTION: *Adult male and female, nuptial plumage*: Similar to *P. a. ludoviciana* (see below), but bill somewhat larger; anterior lower parts duller; blackish slate band of male narrower or absent, cinnamon rufous or chestnut paler and less extended.

MEASUREMENTS: *Adult male*: Wing, 55.6–61.0 (average, 58.4) mm.; tail, 40.4–45.0 (42.4); bill (exposed culmen), 9.9–11.4 (10.7); tarsus, 15.5–17.5 (16.8). *Adult female*: Wing, 52.1–58.4 (54.8); tail, 37.6–41.9 (39.6); bill, 9.9–10.9 (10.2); tarsus, 15.5–17.0 (16.3).

RANGE: N. Virginia and s. Maryland, south to s. Alabama and c. Florida. In migration, west to Texas. Winters from s.e. Georgia and c. Florida to Campeche and Yucatán; also West Indies.

TEXAS: *Migration*: Collected in Brazos (1 specimen), Jefferson (1), and Cameron (1) cos. Rare.

WESTERN PARULA WARBLER, *Parula americana ludoviciana* (Gmelin)

No races recognized by A.O.U. check-list, 1957 (see Appendix A).

DESCRIPTION: *Adult male, nuptial plumage*: Acquired by partial prenuptial molt. Upper parts rather bluish dark or deep green-blue gray, but rump somewhat greenish light slate gray; large triangular area on back citrine to yellowish warbler green;

tail dark mouse gray, middle feathers broadly, and other feathers narrowly, edged on outer webs with color of upper tail-coverts, two outer tail feathers with broad squarish subterminal spots of white on inner webs, remainder of feathers with narrow white terminal edgings on inner webs; wings deep mouse gray, tertials chaetura drab, primaries and secondaries margined on inner webs with dull white, except at tips of primaries, and edged on outer webs with grayish olive or with color of upper parts; lesser wing-coverts and outer margins of others like color of upper parts; greater and median coverts broadly tipped with white, forming two wing-bars (on greater coverts this white occupies only outer webs of the outermost coverts); lores black or dull black, as is often malar region; narrow white eye-ring broken before and behind; remainder of sides of head and of neck like hindneck; chin and throat wax yellow or primuline yellow, often washed with ochraceous tawny; jugulum with broad band of blackish slate washed or more or less overlaid with yellow, and below this a somewhat narrower band of cinnamon rufous to chestnut, also more or less washed or overlaid with yellow; lower breast wax yellow; remainder of lower surface dull white, but sides more or less streaked with chestnut; lining of wing white, outer portion often mottled with mouse gray or neutral gray. Bill black, but cutting edges and mandible yellow or yellow ocher; iris vandyke brown or hazel; legs yellowish brown or tawny olive; toes more yellowish. *Adult male, winter*: Acquired by complete postnuptial molt. Similar to nuptial adult male, but jugulum and breast more overlaid with yellow; conspicuous white spot above, and another below, eye; upper parts more or less washed with olive green. *Adult female, nuptial*: Acquired by partial prenuptial molt. Much like adult male in winter, but colors duller, upper parts often still more strongly washed with olive green; lores chaetura drab; yellow of anterior lower parts lighter, jugulum and breast without well-defined band of slate or dull black, often with little or none of this color and with much less of cinnamon or rufous tinge; sides and flanks duller and more brownish or olivaceous gray. *Adult female, winter*: Acquired by complete postnuptial molt. Similar to nuptial adult female, but bluish areas of upper surface still more tinged with olive green; more or less conspicuous dull white spot above and below eye; sometimes narrow white supraloral line; breast still less tinged with chestnut. *Male, first nuptial*: Acquired by partial prenuptial molt. Like nuptial adult male, but with tail, wing-quills, and particularly primary coverts, decidedly more brownish, primary coverts less conspicuously edged with bluish gray, and gray edgings of outer webs of secondaries more greenish (less bluish); blackish slate band on jugulum narrower or replaced by bay. *Male, first winter*: Acquired by partial postjuvenal molt, which does not involve wing-quills or tail. Similar to adult male in winter, but bluish areas of upper surface more heavily overlaid with olive green; sides of head and neck more tinged with olive green; slate or bay of jugulum, as well as cinnamon rufous of breast, much more overlaid with dull yellow on tips and margins of feathers; narrow whitish or yellowish supraloral streak. *Female, first winter*: Acquired by partial postjuvenal molt. Very similar to adult female in winter but still more strongly olive green on upper surface; white wing-bars duller, more washed with olivaceous; lower parts duller, yellow less tinged with chestnut; sides and flanks more strongly olivaceous. *Juvenal*: Acquired by complete postnatal molt. Upper parts deep grayish olive, more or less washed with olive green; wings and tail similar to those of nuptial adult female, but white wing-bars much narrower and duller; chin and upper throat pale straw yellow; jugulum dull neutral gray or light smoke gray; remainder of lower surface dull white. Maxilla black; mandible yellow ocher; iris vandyke brown; legs clove brown; toes and claws isabella color. *Natal*: Smoke gray. Bill pinkish buff or dark prout brown; inside of mouth and gape gamboge yellow; legs vinaceous buff or pinkish buff; feet white or pinkish buff; claws vinaceous buff.

MEASUREMENTS: *Adult male*: Wing, 54.6–61.5 (average, 57.4) mm.; tail, 39.1–45.0 (40.6); bill (exposed culmen), 8.1–10.9 (9.7); tarsus, 16.0–17.0 (16.5); middle toe without claw, 8.9–10.9 (9.7). *Adult female*: Wing, 51.1–55.1 (53.3); tail, 37.6–

40.4 (38.9); bill, 8.9–10.4 (9.4); tarsus, 14.5–16.8 (16.0); middle toe, 8.6–9.4 (9.1).

RANGE: S. Manitoba to n. Michigan, south to s.e. Texas and s.w. Alabama. Winters from s. Tamaulipas, Tabasco, and Yucatán through Central America to Nicaragua; also Haiti and Puerto Rico.

TEXAS: *Breeding*: Collected north to Cooke, east to Bowie and Tyler, south to Matagorda, west to Kerr cos. *Migration*: Collected north to Cooke, east to Galveston, south to Cameron, west to Kinney cos. Common.

NESTING: *Nest*: In forests and their margins, in swamps, and sometimes in parks or other ornamental grounds, 5–40 ft. above ground, in tree or bush, coniferous or deciduous; pensile in shape with entrance at side, or semipensile, or not at all so with opening at top; when pensile it hangs below limb, either supported by twigs or by strands of Spanishmoss; composed of Spanishmoss, twigs, leaves, rootlets, rubbish, and sometimes a few hairs; lined with fine grass, hair, and sometimes lichens or Spanishmoss. *Eggs*: 3–7, usually 4 or 5; ovate to short ovate; white to cream white, dotted and spotted, sometimes in wreath about large end, with chestnut and other shades of dark brown, and with shell markings of lilac and lavender gray; average size, 16.3 × 11.7 mm.

NORTHERN PARULA WARBLER, *Parula americana pusilla* (Wilson)

No races recognized by A.O.U. check-list, 1957 (see Appendix A).

DESCRIPTION: *Adult male and female, nuptial plumage*: In color similar to *P. a. ludoviciana*, but larger; male with somewhat broader blackish and cinnamon rufous or chestnut bands on jugulum. Similar to *P. a. americana*, but wing longer, though bill shorter; colors darker and richer; male with blackish and chestnut on throat, jugulum, and breast more conspicuous and extensive.

MEASUREMENTS: *Adult male*: Wing, 56.9–63.0 (average, 60.7) mm.; tail, 39.6–45.0 (42.4); bill (exposed culmen) 8.9–10.9 (9.7); tarsus, 15.5–18.0 (16.8). *Adult female*: Wing, 54.1–59.4 (56.6); tail, 38.6–41.9 (40.1); bill, 8.9–10.4 (9.7); tarsus, 16.0–17.0 (16.5).

RANGE: C. Ontario to n.e. Nova Scotia, south to e. Tennessee and e. New Jersey. In migration, west to Texas. Winters from Veracruz, Oaxaca, and Tabasco through Central America to Nicaragua; also West Indies.

TEXAS: *Migration*: Collected in Cameron Co. (4 specimens). Uncommon.

OLIVE-BACKED WARBLER, *Parula pitiayumi* (Vieillot)

SPECIES ACCOUNT

Also called Pitiayumi Warbler and Tropical Parula; Texas race formerly known as Sennett's Warbler. Resembles Parula, of which it is a tropical representative, but lacks eye-ring, breast-band; white wing-bars smaller. Male has black mask; orange wash on breast. Length, 4½ in.; wingspan, 6½.

RANGE: E. Sonora and s.w. Chihuahua, and n.e. Coahuila to extreme s. Texas, south locally through Mexico, Central America, and South America to n. Argentina, Uruguay, and s. Brazil. Largely withdraws in winter from northern limits of range.

TEXAS: (See map.) *Breeding*: Mid-Apr. to mid-July (eggs, May 2 to May 23; young in nest to July 5) from near sea level to 200 ft. Scarce, though common prior

to 1951, in Rio Grande delta from early Mar. to early Oct. *Winter*: Mid-Dec. to mid-Feb. Formerly scarce, and since 1951 extremely rare, in Hidalgo and Cameron cos. Population recently discovered in Kenedy Co.; nesting as yet undetermined (see CHANGES section).

HAUNTS AND HABITS: The Olive-backed is one of three (formerly four) warblers whose U.S. nesting range is confined to Texas. Here, it is a bird of woods, dense or open, and undergrowth, brush, and trees along edges of rivers and resacas. It remains much in upper branches of trees and in places is sometimes very common. Although scarcely to be called gregarious, it may be seen at times in small companies of three or more. In habitat and behavior it is very similar to the Parula. Its song, virtually identical with that of its close relative, is an ascending buzzy trill with a drop at the end. Males sing from March into July.

CHANGES: Habitat in the Rio Grande delta remained adequate for *P. pitiayumi* from the J. C. Merrill–G. B. Sennett days of bird study in the late 1870's until the great freeze of January 29–February 1, 1951. This disaster resulted in a switch in dominant agri-business from citrus to cotton, grain sorghum, and cows. By 1956, Olive-backed Warblers had become noticeably less numerous. Between 1961 and 1965, there were apparently no nestings on U.S. soil. However, during the spring of 1966, at least five breeding pairs returned to the Anzalduas tract (Hidalgo Co.), the best remaining delta habitat; in 1967, about an equal number of birds was present—one pair per ten acres (J. C. Arvin). As of 1972, there apparently has not been much recolonization of other parts of deep south Texas. In the live oaks of the King Ranch (Kenedy Co.) there were seven sightings in July and August, 1968; in January, 1969, there were three records, including a male specimen

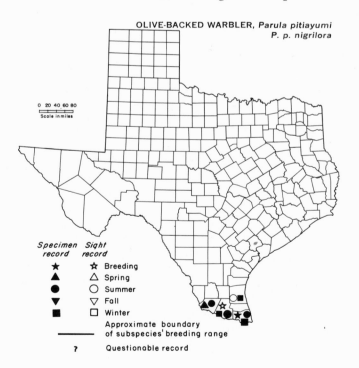

OLIVE-BACKED WARBLER, *Parula pitiayumi*
P. p. nigrilora

0 20 40 60 80
Scale in miles

Specimen record	Sight record	
★	☆	Breeding
▲	△	Spring
●	○	Summer
▼	▽	Fall
■	□	Winter

——— Approximate boundary of subspecies' breeding range

? Questionable record

(B. A. Fall). It is unknown whether these birds represent a recent range extension or a reoccupation.

Three factors have probably caused the decimation of this warbler in the delta: reduced Spanishmossy woodlands, heavy pesticide pollution, and a mushrooming population of Red-eyed Bronzed Cowbirds.

It is noteworthy that as late as the early 1970's in southwestern Tamaulipas, Mexico, especially between Gómez Farías and Rancho del Cielo, the Sennett's Olive-backed Warbler continued to be numerous (F. S. Webster, Jr., et al.). This area contained large groves of trees bearing Spanishmoss and other epiphytes of the genus *Tillandsia*. Here, presence of heavy forest and remoteness from modern farms have kept pesticide pollution, cows, and Bronzed Cowbirds within tolerable limits.

DETAILED ACCOUNT: ONE SUBSPECIES

SENNETT'S OLIVE-BACKED WARBLER, *Parula pitiayumi nigrilora* Coues

DESCRIPTION: *Adult male, nuptial plumage*: Acquired by partial prenuptial molt. Upper parts rather bluish dark or deep green-blue gray, but rump rather greenish light slate gray; large triangular area on back citrine to yellowish warbler green; tail dark mouse gray, middle feathers broadly, and other feathers narrowly, edged on outer webs with color of upper tail-coverts, outer two tail feathers on each side with broad squarish subterminal spots of white on inner webs, other feathers with narrow white terminal edgings on inner webs; wings deep mouse gray, but tertials chaetura drab, primaries and secondaries margined on inner webs with dull white, except at tips of primaries; wing-quills edged on outer webs with grayish olive or with color of upper parts; lesser wing-coverts and margins of others like color of upper parts, greater and median coverts broadly tipped with white, this on greater coverts occupying only outer web, and only outermost coverts; lores and region below eye black, latter sometimes more or less washed with gray; no white eyering; sides of neck like hindneck; chin and throat rich gamboge yellow; jugulum raw sienna or mars yellow; breast and upper abdomen gamboge yellow; remainder of abdomen and lower tail-coverts white; sides and flanks dark gull gray to slate gray, neutral gray, or pale neutral gray; lining of wing white, outer edge sometimes more or less mottled with dark neutral gray. Bill black or brownish black above, but mandible yellow; iris dark brown; legs and feet light fleshy brown. *Adult male, winter*: Acquired by complete postnuptial molt. Similar to nuptial adult male, but upper parts, particularly pileum and hindneck, overlaid with olive green. *Adult female, nuptial*: Acquired by partial prenuptial molt. Similar to nuptial adult male but smaller; coloration in general paler and duller; upper parts lighter and duller, also more greenish gray, without black on sides of head, these parts being in color similar to pileum; wings and tail more brownish; lower surface lighter; jugulum dull light cadmium, apricot yellow, or gamboge yellow, only slightly tinged with raw sienna; chin sometimes lemon chrome. *Adult female, winter*: Acquired by complete postnuptial molt. Similar to nuptial adult male, but upper parts, including wings, together with sides of neck, overlaid with olive green. *Male, first nuptial*: Acquired by partial prenuptial molt. Similar to nuptial adult male, but upper parts—particularly pileum, hindneck, and rump —not so clearly bluish gray, but duller, more washed with olive green or brown; wings and tail lighter, duller, and more brownish, edgings more olivaceous. *Male, first winter*: Acquired by partial postjuvenal molt, which does not involve wing-quills or tail. Similar to adult male in winter but duller; wing-quills and tail feathers, together with edgings, as well as upper parts and sides of head, even more washed with olive green, and wings and tail also more brownish (less slaty or grayish). *Female, first*

nuptial: Acquired by partial prenuptial molt. Similar to nuptial adult female, but upper parts somewhat duller, more washed with olivaceous (less clearly bluish); sides of head less bluish (more greenish or olivaceous); wing-quills and tail feathers lighter, duller, and more brownish, edgings somewhat more olivaceous; jugulum little or not at all tinged with raw sienna. *Female, first winter*: Acquired by partial postjuvenal molt, which does not involve wing-quills or tail. Similar to nuptial adult female, but upper parts strongly washed with olive green; wings and tail duller, more brownish, and more washed with olivaceous; yellow of anterior lower parts duller and lighter—lemon chrome; jugulum less tinged with raw sienna; abdomen washed with olive yellow. *Juvenal*: Acquired by complete postnatal molt. Above between drab and deep grayish olive; wings and tail like first winter, but wing-coverts light hair brown, greater and median series tipped with dull white, edgings of wing-quills somewhat more brownish; lower parts dull white, but chin and jugulum washed with olive yellow. *Natal*: Unknown.

MEASUREMENTS: *Adult male*: Wing, 50.0–53.1 (average, 51.3) mm.; tail, 37.6–40.4 (38.9); bill (exposed culmen), 8.9–10.7 (9.7); tarsus, 15.5–16.5 (16.0); middle toe without claw, 8.4–8.9 (8.6). *Adult female*: Wing, 46.0–49.0 (47.8); tail, 32.5–37.6 (35.3); bill, 8.9–9.9 (9.7); tarsus, 15.5–16.8 (15.7); middle toe, 8.6–9.4 (8.9).

RANGE: Coahuila to s. Texas, south to s.e. San Luis Potosí and s. Tamaulipas.

TEXAS: *Breeding*: Collected in Starr, Hidalgo, and Cameron cos. *Winter*: Taken in Hidalgo and Cameron cos. One specimen from Kenedy Co., 8 mi. east of Rudolf (male, Jan. 16, 1969, B. A. Fall; Texas A&M University collection, no. 7808).

NESTING: *Nest*: On more or less level land along rivers, in tall brush or timber along streams; in bush or tree, ordinarily 8–40 ft. above ground, in hanging streamers of Spanishmoss or in other air plants, sometimes at extremity of branch of tree or bush; a pocket composed of Spanishmoss, and lined with a few horsehairs and cottony woody fibers. *Eggs*: 3; ovate to short ovate; dull white, spotted with dark brown, with shell markings of lilac, scattered over entire surface, or also in wreath about large end; average size, 17.0 × 11.7 mm.

[OLIVE WARBLER, *Peucedramus taeniatus* (Du Bus)

Male: rich tawny hood; bold black stroke through eye; gray back; blackish wings with two white bars; blackish tail with white outer feathers; whitish belly. *Female*: greenish gray above; yellowish head, neck, throat, breast; dim dusky cheek-patch; white areas on dark wings and tail essentially as in male. Length, 5 in.

RANGE: S.e. Arizona and s.w. New Mexico, south to n. Nicaragua. In winter, largely withdraws from United States.

TEXAS: *Hypothetical*: Two careful sightings in Chisos Mts., Big Bend Nat. Park: near South Rim (1 on Aug. 19, 1966, C. R. Bender and W. V. Mealy); Boot Canyon (1 on Sept. 19, 1970, R. H. Wauer).]

YELLOW WARBLER, *Dendroica petechia* (Linnaeus)

SPECIES ACCOUNT

Nuptial male: yellow head, under parts, tail-spots; greenish yellow above; reddish breast-streaks. *Female, fall male*: duller; breast-streaks faint or absent. Length, 5 in.; wingspan, 7½; weight, ¼ oz.

RANGE: Alaska to Newfoundland, south to n. Baja California, c. New Mexico, n. Texas, c. Oklahoma, c. Alabama (irregularly), and c. Georgia; also on Mexican Central Plateau from s. Guanajuato to c. Michoacán and Distrito Federal. Winters from Mexico to Peru and n. Brazil. Tropical races breed chiefly in mangroves from s. Baja California, s. Tamaulipas, and West Indies, south locally to n. South America.

TEXAS: (See map.) *Breeding*: Early May to late July (eggs, May 17 to July 13; young in nest, June 4 to July 24) from about 50 to 5,000 ft., possibly slightly higher. Formerly fairly common, but local, north of 29th parallel. Last well-documented records of nesting: Kerr Co., Kerrville (known definitely to nest, May 18, 1938, F. F. Nyc, Jr.); Travis Co., Indian Cove on Lake Austin (2 birds feeding young cowbird, June, 1967, David Simon). May still breed irregularly and locally. *Migration*: Mid-Apr.—often early Apr.—to late May; early Aug. to early Oct. (extremes: Mar. 14, June 20; July 11, Nov. 30). Common (some years) to fairly common through most parts. *Winter*: Mid-Dec. to late Feb. Extremely rare along upper coast and in Rio Grande delta; single sightings from Eagle Pass (Dec. 27) and College Station (Dec. 24) lack substantiation.

HAUNTS AND HABITS: Most widely distributed of the warblers, the Yellow occurs in a great variety of habitats. During the breeding season, it may be found in open woodlands and on brushy slopes, riparian associations (especially with willows and cottonwoods), and various ecotonal situations. It is usually absent from deep forests, swamps, and open plains, except where thickets occur. In some places where the only woody vegetation is confined along watercourses crossing the plains, the Yellow is at times common locally. While migrating through Texas it occasionally appears in

large numbers and at such seasons frequents an even greater diversity of vegetation types, including those of urban, suburban, and many agricultural areas.

The Yellow is noted for its repeated attempts to curb the success of the cowbird, by which it is frequently victimized. Some individuals isolate the parasite's egg by covering it with a new nest floor, thus often producing a multi-storied nest.

Flight—whether long or short—is quick and rather erratic. In Texas the Yellow seems to prefer undergrowth, thickets, and the lower portions of trees, where it actively forages in subcanopy and interior zones. Because its colors blend so readily with the greens and golds of leaves, it is frequently more easily heard than seen.

Food consists almost entirely of insects. Ants, bees, wasps, and sawflies constitute about one-third of the bird's diet; it also takes caterpillars (including tent, cankerworm, and measuringworm), moths, beetles (cotton-boll weevil, leaf, ladybird, soldier, scavenger, ground, bark, and boring), craneflies, gnats, plant lice, leaf hoppers, scale insects, grasshoppers, crickets, mayflies, and dragonflies. The remainder of the diet consists of a few spiders and myriopods and 2 to 3 percent vegetable matter (fruit, as of mulberry and dogwood).

The Yellow utters a rather emphatic *chip* or *chilp* when alarmed and a distinctive *zup* during flight. Its song is a variable warble of moderate loudness which may be confused with that of the Chestnut-sided Warbler, but it lacks the emphatic ending of the regular song of the latter. One of its common songs sounds much like *wee-chee, wee-chee, wee*. Another is well represented by the syllables *we-che, che, che, che, cheery, wee*. A very persistent singer, it vocalizes from April into August, though less enthusiastically after July.

CHANGES: The Yellow Warbler seems to be almost out of the breeding business in the state. Climatic warming and drying in the first half of the twentieth century plus, in later years, rapidly increasing pollution and destruction of streamside vegetation are probably major factors in reduction of *D. petechia*. Brown-headed Cowbirds have also increased greatly since 1950. Apparently the Yellow Warbler's famous sometime habit of flooring over cowbirds' eggs in its nest has not been sufficient to save this warbler as a viable nester in Texas.

DETAILED ACCOUNT: SIX SUBSPECIES

NEWFOUNDLAND YELLOW WARBLER, *Dendroica petechia aestiva* (Gmelin)

DESCRIPTION: *Adult male and female, nuptial plumage*: Similar to *D. p. flava* (see below), but male darker, less yellowish on upper parts, yellow of forehead duller, less extensive, edges of wing-quills narrower and duller yellowish color; lower parts averaging duller, less golden (more greenish yellow); female duller, less yellowish (more grayish) above. Similar to *D. p. rubiginosa* (see below), but forehead and crown yellowish, and upper parts somewhat lighter, more yellowish (less greenish).

MEASUREMENTS: *Adult male*: Wing, 57.7–63.5 (average, 61.2) mm.; tail, 42.4–46.5 (45.5); bill (exposed culmen), 8.9–9.9

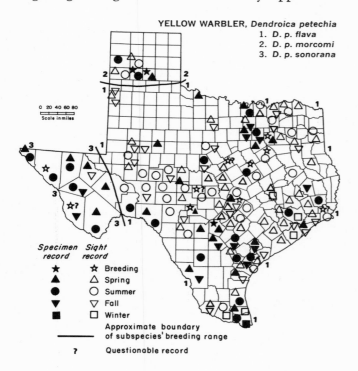

YELLOW WARBLER, *Dendroica petechia*
1. *D. p. flava*
2. *D. p. morcomi*
3. *D. p. sonorana*

0 20 40 60 80
Scale in miles

Specimen record / Sight record
★ / ☆ Breeding
▲ / △ Spring
● / ○ Summer
▼ / ▽ Fall
■ / □ Winter

——— Approximate boundary of subspecies' breeding range
? Questionable record

(9.4); tarsus, 17.8–20.1 (19.3); middle toe without claw, 9.4–10.4 (10.2). *Adult female*: Wing, 55.9–59.2 (57.7); tail, 39.9–45.0 (42.7); bill, 9.1–10.2 (9.7); tarsus, 18.0–20.1 (18.8); middle toe, 9.4–10.4 (9.7).

RANGE: N. Alaska to s.e. Labrador, south to c. British Columbia and s.e. Newfoundland. Winters from s. Mexico to Costa Rica; also Grenada Island and Surinam.

TEXAS: *Migration*: Collected north to Denton and Kaufman, south to Cameron, west to Brewster cos. Uncommon.

ALASKAN YELLOW WARBLER, *Dendroica petechia rubiginosa* (Pallas)

DESCRIPTION: *Adult male and female, nuptial plumage*: Similar to *D. p. aestiva*, but crown uniform olive green like back or with slight yellowish tinge on forehead; remainder of upper parts darker, somewhat less yellowish. From *D. p. flava* (see below), it differs as does *D. p. aestiva*, also in having crown and forehead much less or scarcely at all yellowish.

MEASUREMENTS: *Adult male*: Wing, 59.9–63.0 (average, 61.7) mm.; tail, 40.9–46.0 (43.2); bill (exposed culmen), 9.9–10.4 (10.2); tarsus, 18.0–20.1 (19.0); middle toe without claw, 9.4–10.9 (10.7). *Adult female*: Wing, 56.9–60.5 (58.7); tail, 40.9–45.5 (42.9); bill, 9.4–9.9 (9.7); tarsus, 18.0–19.6 (18.5); middle toe, 9.4–10.9 (10.2).

RANGE: Alaska. Winters from s. Texas through Mexico to Panama; probably into South America.

TEXAS: *Migration*: Collected north to Denton, south to Cameron, west to Jeff Davis (Aug. 21) cos. Uncommon. *Winter*: Taken in Cameron Co. (3 specimens). Rare to casual.

EASTERN YELLOW WARBLER, *Dendroica petechia flava* (Vieillot)

Race not in A.O.U. check-list, 1957 (see Appendix A).

DESCRIPTION: *Adult male, nuptial plumage*: Acquired by partial prenuptial molt. Forehead and crown between cadmium yellow or light cadmium and primuline yellow, occasionally with obscure streaks of chestnut or burnt sienna; hindneck and back light pyrite yellow to yellowish warbler green, back obscurely and slightly streaked with dull olive green or with dull reddish brown; upper tail-coverts between lemon chrome and sulphine yellow; tail light brownish olive, outer webs of feathers narrowly margined with greenish wax yellow or yellowish warbler green, inner webs of all feathers, except middle pair, more or less extensively lemon chrome or lemon yellow, this occupying most of feathers except tips; wings brownish olive, inner edges of primaries and secondaries, except tips of primaries, broadly lemon yellow, outer webs of tertials greenish wax yellow, lesser wing-coverts like back, greater and median series margined on outer webs with greenish wax yellow or dull lemon chrome; lower surface rich yellow, between lemon chrome and light cadmium, broadly and numerously streaked on jugulum, breast, and sides with chestnut; sides of head and of anterior part of neck yellow like under parts, but slightly tinged with olive green posteriorly; lining of wing yellow like lower surface. Maxilla black, slate black, or yellowish gray; mandible and cutting edges of maxilla olive gray, smoke gray, or plumbeous; iris dark brown; legs and feet isabella color, wood brown, brownish yellow, wax yellow, or light olive brown. *Adult male, winter*: Acquired by complete postnuptial molt. Similar to nuptial adult male, but crown much more nearly uniform with back, and lacking any chestnut tinge; yellow of lower surface duller, chestnut streaks smaller and much less numerous and less conspicuous, sometimes very lightly streaked. *Adult female, nuptial*: Acquired by partial prenuptial molt. Upper parts similar to those of adult male in winter but duller, less yellowish—yellowish warbler green; pileum but little more yellowish than back; back more uniform; tail as in adult male in winter; wings brownish olive to chaetura drab, edgings more greenish (less brightly yellow); lower surface duller—wax yellow to primuline yellow, very narrowly or scarcely streaked on sides of breast and of body with orange rufous; lining of wing lemon chrome. Bill dull plumbeous or dark olive, but base of mandible lighter, bluish white, or dull

yellow; legs and feet yellowish brown. *Adult female, winter*: Acquired by complete postnuptial molt. Similar to nuptial adult female but rather paler and slightly duller and more greenish both above and below. *Male, first nuptial*: Acquired by partial prenuptial molt. Like nuptial adult male but less heavily streaked with chestnut below. *Male, first winter*: Acquired by partial postjuvenal molt, which does not involve wing-quills or tail. Similar to adult male in winter, but primary coverts more brownish, less conspicuously edged with yellow or olive green, yellow of plumage paler and duller, somewhat more greenish below; chestnut streaks absent or very small and inconspicuous. Similar to adult female in winter, but colors above and below more golden, chestnut streaks of lower surface more often present and more conspicuous. *Female, first nuptial*: Acquired by partial prenuptial molt. Very similar to nuptial adult female. *Female, first winter*: Acquired by partial postjuvenal molt. Similar to adult female in winter, but upper parts duller, more grayish or brownish (less yellowish); yellow of tail paler; wing-coverts and wing edgings more brownish; lower surface duller, paler, and more buffy (less greenish) yellow, sometimes almost white, tinged with olive yellow. *Juvenal*: Acquired by complete postnatal molt. Upper parts hair brown to drab, more or less obscurely streaked or spotted, particularly on back and rump; tail and most of wings as in first winter female, but wing-coverts more brownish, lesser wing-coverts drab or hair brown; chin, throat, and jugulum between light drab and light grayish olive; posterior lower parts dull grayish white or buffy white. Maxilla drab, or olive brown edged with paler brown; mandible pale yellow or flesh color; iris dark brown; legs and feet dull light yellow, dull brown, olive drab, or olive brown; or maxilla dull greenish white; iris bister; legs and feet dull yellowish brown. *Natal*: Mouse gray. Bill, legs, and feet pinkish buff.

MEASUREMENTS: *Adult male*: Wing, 59.9–66.0 (average, 62.7) mm.; tail, 41.9–51.1 (44.2); bill (exposed culmen), 9.9–10.9 (10.2); tarsus, 17.0–20.1 (18.8); middle toe without claw, 9.9–11.9 (10.9). *Adult female*: Wing, 56.9–59.9 (58.7); tail, 39.1–45.0 (42.2); bill, 8.9–10.4 (9.9); tarsus, 17.0–20.1 (18.8); middle toe, 9.9–11.9 (10.7).

RANGE: E. Montana to Maine, south to s.e. Texas (at least formerly) and e. Georgia. Winters from s. Mexico through Central America to n. South America; also St. Vincent and Trinidad islands.

TEXAS: *Breeding*: Altitudinal range, from ca. 50 to 1,900 ft. Collected north to Cooke and Kaufman, east to Hardin (formerly), south to Bexar, west to Kerr cos. Rare; recent breeding doubtful. *Migration*: Collected north to Wilbarger, east to Polk and Galveston, south to Cameron, west to Mitchell cos. Common.

NESTING: *Nest*: On uplands and bottoms; along stream valleys, about lakes, in cultivated areas, fence rows, and along roadsides; in many kinds of trees, shrubbery, hedges, bushes, or briars, 3–40 ft. above ground, but usually under 10 ft.; securely fastened to nearly or quite upright twigs; compact, beautiful, more or less symmetrical, thick-walled cup with deep cavity for eggs; composed of fine stems of plants, leaves, grayish hemp and other fibers, strips of bark, silky pappus from plants, down from catkins of willow and other trees or shrubs, bits of paper, cotton, and down from ferns; lined with soft plant down, wool, hair, fine grasses, cotton, and feathers. *Eggs*: 2–6, usually 4; ovate to short ovate; bluish white, greenish white, or grayish white to light green, sometimes almost pure white; spotted and blotched, usually in a wreath about large end or in the middle, sometimes heavily marked all over, with umber, dull black, purplish brown, and slate gray, and with shell markings of lilac gray; average size, 16.8 × 12.7 mm.

WESTERN YELLOW WARBLER, *Dendroica petechia morcomi* Coale

DESCRIPTION: *Adult male and female, nuptial plumage*: Similar to *D. p. flava*, but adult male duller above, less heavily streaked with chestnut below; female duller, more grayish (less greenish) on upper surface.

MEASUREMENTS: *Adult male*: Wing, 58.9–64.0 (average, 61.7)

mm.; tail, 43.9–48.0 (46.3); bill (exposed culmen), 8.6–10.4 (9.7); tarsus, 17.8–19.0 (18.3); middle toe without claw, 9.4–10.9 (10.4). *Adult female*: Wing, 54.1–64.0 (60.2); tail, 39.1–46.5 (43.9); bill, 9.1–9.9 (9.7); tarsus, 18.0–19.6 (18.8); middle toe, 9.9–11.4 (10.7).

RANGE: S. British Columbia to n.w. Montana, south to e. California and n.w. Texas. Winters from s. Texas (casual) and s.w. Mexico to Panama; probably into South America.

TEXAS: *Breeding*: Altitudinal range, 2,500 to 3,600 ft. Collected in Oldham (1 specimen), Randall (1), and Armstrong (1) cos. Eggs collected: Randall Co., Cañoncito Blanco (June 6, 1876, C. A. H. McCauley); Armstrong Co., Prairie Dog Fork of Red River (May 30, 1876, McCauley). Formerly fairly common. *Migration*: Collected north to Denton, east to Polk, south to Cameron, west to Jeff Davis and Culberson cos. Fairly common. *Winter*: Taken in Cameron Co. (2 specimens). Rare to casual.

NESTING: Similar to that of *D. p. flava*, but average egg size, 17.3 × 12.7 mm.

ARIZONA YELLOW WARBLER, Dendroica petechia
hypochlora Oberholser, new subspecies (see Appendix A)

DESCRIPTION: *Adult male and female, nuptial plumage*: Similar to *D. p. morcomi* but slightly smaller, except bill; male above much more yellowish, below considerably less heavily streaked with chestnut; female with upper surface paler and more grayish, lower surface much paler, less yellowish (more grayish or whitish). Differs from *D. p. sonorana* (see below) in smaller size, excepting bill; and darker upper parts.

MEASUREMENTS: *Adult male*: Wing, 57.9–62.5 (average, 60.2) mm.; tail, 42.9–47.5 (45.2); bill (exposed culmen), 9.4–10.9 (10.2); tarsus, 18.5–19.6 (18.8); middle toe without claw, 9.4–10.9 (10.2). *Adult female*: Wing, 57.4–62.0 (58.7); tail, 41.9–47.0 (44.2); bill, 9.4–10.4 (9.7); tarsus, 17.5–20.1 (19.3); middle toe, 9.4–10.4 (10.2).

TYPE: Adult male, no. 258487, U.S. National Museum, Biological Surveys collection; 3 mi. north of Fort Whipple, near Prescott, Arizona, 3,000 ft.; July 5, 1916; W. P. Taylor, original no., 97.

RANGE: S.e. Nevada to s. Utah, south to c. Arizona. In migration, east to Trans-Pecos Texas. Winters from Oaxaca through Central America to Ecuador.

TEXAS: *Migration*: Collected in Culberson (Aug. 16), Pecos, and Brewster cos. Uncommon.

SONORA YELLOW WARBLER, Dendroica petechia sonorana
Brewster

DESCRIPTION: *Adult male and female, nuptial plumage*: Similar to *D. p. morcomi* but a little larger, decidedly paler, both above and below. Adult male much lighter and more yellowish olive green above, back usually more or less conspicuously streaked with chestnut, yellow pileum with little or no pronounced greenish tinge; upper tail-coverts and lower part of rump yellow with slight olive green streaks, all wing edgings yellow; lower surface paler and with very narrow, sometimes indistinct, streaks of chestnut. Adult female very much paler than female of *D. p. morcomi*; upper parts sometimes very pale gray; yellow of lower parts ordinarily decidedly very pale and buffy tinged.

MEASUREMENTS: *Adult male*: Wing, 58.9–66.0 (average, 63.2) mm.; tail, 45.0–49.0 (47.3); bill (exposed culmen), 9.9–10.9 (10.2); tarsus, 18.0–20.1 (19.0); middle toe without claw, 9.9–11.9 (10.7). *Adult female*: Wing, 56.9–61.0 (58.7); tail, 41.9–45.0 (43.2); bill, 9.9–10.4 (10.2); tarsus, 18.5–19.6 (19.0); middle toe, 9.4–10.4 (9.9).

RANGE: S.e. California to c. New Mexico, south to n.e. Baja California and Trans-Pecos Texas. Winters from Baja California through w. Mexico to Guatemala.

TEXAS: *Breeding*: Altitudinal range, 3,500 to 5,000 ft., possibly higher. Collected in Hudspeth and Jeff Davis cos. Formerly fairly common. *Migration*: Collected in El Paso, Culberson, Reeves, Jeff Davis, Presidio, and Brewster cos. Fairly common.

NESTING: *Nest*: On mesas and in river canyons; often in thickets and low timber along streams; 10–25 ft. above ground, in cottonwood, willow, or mesquite tree, usually in upright fork; well-built cup of various kinds of grasses, vegetable fibers, stems of vines, wild hemp, and similar materials; lined with cotton from cottonwood tree or other vegetable down. *Eggs*: Usually 4, shapes similar to those of other races; colors paler than those of *D. p. flava*; average size, 17.5 × 13.0 mm.

MAGNOLIA WARBLER, Dendroica lutea
(Linnaeus)

SPECIES ACCOUNT

Dendroica magnolia of A.O.U. check-list, 1957 (see Appendix A). *Nuptial male*: largely blackish above; black-streaked yellow below; white wing-patch, tail-band. *Female, fall male*: duller; grayish olive above; black streaks narrower, sparser (usually restricted to flanks in fall). Length, 5 in.; wingspan, 7½; weight, ¼ oz.

RANGE: S.w. Mackenzie to Newfoundland, south to c. British Columbia, s. Manitoba, n. Great Lakes region, extreme n.e. Ohio, and n. Massachusetts; locally south in Appalachians to w. Virginia. Winters chiefly from Gulf lowlands of Mexico through Central America to Panama; also Bahamas, Greater Antilles.

TEXAS: (See map.) *Migration*: Late Apr.—often mid-Apr.—to mid-May; early Sept. to late Oct. (extremes: Mar. 5, June 2; Aug. 21, Nov. 25). Very common (some springs) to fairly common (most falls) east of 99th meridian (although abundant some springs on upper coast); increasingly scarce westward to Amarillo and Big Spring; casual in Trans-Pecos. *Winter*: Early Dec. to mid-Feb. Extremely rare along coast and in Rio Grande delta; casual inland in eastern half.

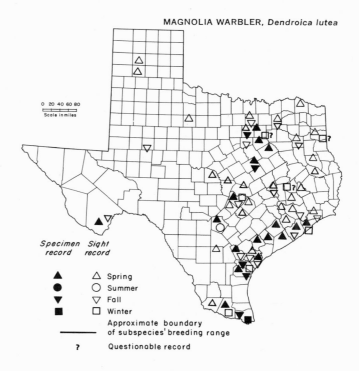

MAGNOLIA WARBLER, *Dendroica lutea*

0 20 40 60 80
Scale in miles

Specimen   Sight
record   record

▲ △ Spring
● ○ Summer
▼ ▽ Fall
■ □ Winter

——— Approximate boundary of subspecies' breeding range

? Questionable record

HAUNTS AND HABITS: In its northern summer home, the Magnolia lives mostly in coniferous forests and about their edges; here it places its nest in a small pine, fir, or spruce. During migration and in winter this species is often found in largely deciduous woods and in broad-leaved evergreens (including *Magnolia grandiflora*). It seems especially attracted to thickets along watercourses, but it also pauses on mesquite (*Prosopis*) and other brush flats. This warbler also visits ornamental trees about dwellings and orchards. *D. lutea* is seen usually singly or in pairs, although at times it appears in small companies, which may be associated with the troops of warblers that constitute such an attractive feature of Texas migrations.

In flight the Magnolia is similar to the Black-throated Blue Warbler (see below), and is at times rather erratic. It is an active bird, sometimes engaging in considerable fluttering and spreading of tail as it moves quickly about in the branches. Individuals frequent both upper and lower parts of trees, as well as undergrowth and thickets, and utilize the interior of trees more than terminal foliage. Food consists of insects, their eggs and larvae, particularly the smaller winged species, and includes click and leaf beetles, weevils, craneflies, moths, cankerworms, plant lice, leaf-hoppers, scale insects, ants, sawfly larvae, parasitic wasps and bees. A few spiders and harvestmen are also taken.

Magnolia's usual call note is a soft *tlep*. The male has a number of advertising songs, the common one being represented by the syllables *weely, weely, wichy*. Migrants in Texas sing a good bit in April and May.

DETAILED ACCOUNT: NO SUBSPECIES

DESCRIPTION: *Adult male, nuptial plumage*: Acquired by partial prenuptial molt. Forehead black; pileum and hindneck between neutral gray and slate gray; remainder of upper parts black, but rump lemon chrome, feathers of lower back more or less edged with citrine, warbler green, or pyrite yellow; scapulars edged with grayish olive or dull olive green; tail black, outer webs of feathers very narrowly edged, particularly at base, with neutral gray, tail feathers, except middle pair, with large square white spot on terminal half, beginning near middle of tail; wing-quills between deep mouse gray and chaetura drab, inner margins of primaries and secondaries, except at tips of primaries, dull white or grayish white, tertials chaetura black or brownish black; lesser wing-coverts black edged with neutral gray, tips of lesser coverts and broad terminal portion of greater coverts white, forming conspicuous white patch on wing with a few black streaks in center, outer greater coverts edged with neutral gray and with slight tips of white on outer webs; wing-quills edged on outer webs with neutral gray; broad white stripe beginning above eye and extending back to nape, and below this, a broad black stripe through eye and lores connecting with forehead; long white spot on lower eyelid; sides of neck mostly neutral gray, washed with yellow and spotted with black; abdomen and crissum white, abdomen sometimes tinged with buff or yellow; remainder of lower surface lemon chrome or between lemon chrome and light cadmium, but lower tail-coverts white, jugulum, breast, sides, and flanks broadly streaked with black, this sometimes almost confluent on jugulum; lining of wing and axillars white. Bill black; iris dark brown; legs, feet, and claws bister or olive brown; soles of toes dull greenish yellow. *Adult male, winter*: Acquired by complete postnuptial molt. Very different in appearance from nuptial adult male; colors duller and more blended; pileum deep neutral gray, sometimes verging to-

ward deep grayish olive, back and scapulars warbler green, centers of feathers dull black; rump, upper tail-coverts, and tail as in nuptial adult male; wing-quills as in nuptial adult male, but white patch replaced by two narrow white wing-bars formed by tips of median and greater wing-coverts; yellow of lower parts as in nuptial adult male, but jugulum without conspicuous streaks or spots and somewhat shaded with dull gray; on remaining lower surface black streaks very much reduced in number and extent, general appearance of lower parts thus more or less uniform, slightly broken on sides and flanks with black streaking, many streaks on lower parts partly concealed by yellow tips of feathers. *Adult female, nuptial*: Acquired by partial prenuptial molt. Similar to adult male in winter but paler and duller, pileum and hindneck light mouse gray to deep mouse gray, back warbler green, sometimes much mixed with deep grayish olive, feathers usually with conspicuous dull black or chaetura black centers; rump with band of olive yellow; wings and tail chaetura drab to hair brown, greater and lesser coverts more broadly tipped with white, forming two conspicuous wing-bands but not a white patch; lower parts gamboge yellow, except white abdomen and crissum; jugulum and breast with more conspicuous, but narrower, dull black streaks, these becoming chaetura black or chaetura drab on sides and flanks, and very much narrower than in adult male in winter. Bill slate black; feet brownish drab. *Adult female, winter*: Acquired by complete postnuptial molt. Similar to nuptial adult female, but pileum and hindneck more brownish; warbler green of back more brownish and practically without blackish spots; white wing-bars duller and somewhat narrower; sides of head more brownish, similar to crown but somewhat paler, white streak above and behind eye obsolete; practically no dark streaks on lower parts except on sides and flanks; jugulum pale dull gray, washed with yellow, forming distinct grayish band. *Male, first nuptial*: Acquired by partial prenuptial molt. Similar to nuptial adult male, but wings and tail, particularly primary coverts, more brownish and usually more worn. *Male, first winter*: Acquired by partial postjuvenal molt, which does not involve wing-quills or tail. Similar to adult male in winter, but primary coverts, wing-quills, and tail somewhat more brownish (less blackish); back somewhat duller with few and inconspicuous blackish spots or streaks, entire upper surface thus more uniform, lower surface scarcely or not at all streaked, such streaks as are present confined to sides and flanks; grayish jugular band more pronounced. *Female, first nuptial*: Acquired by partial prenuptial molt. Similar to nuptial adult female, but primary coverts, wing-quills, and tail feathers more brownish. *Female, first winter*: Acquired by partial postjuvenal molt. Similar to adult female in winter, but primary coverts, wing-quills, and tail feathers somewhat more brownish; upper surface more brownish and more uniform, yellow of rump somewhat duller; streaks on sides and flanks narrower and less blackish. Similar to first winter male, but upper parts duller, lighter, more brownish, and with almost no blackish streaks or spots on upper surface; jugulum more buffy or yellowish; streaks on sides and flanks duller and narrower. *Juvenal*: Acquired by complete postnatal molt. Upper surface olive brown, head somewhat lighter, verging toward natal brown, back with more or less faintly indicated darker brown markings; wing-quills and tail as in first winter female, lesser coverts brown like upper surface, greater and median series tipped with pale buffy yellow; breast and jugulum grayish olive to hair brown; sides of head very much like crown but slightly paler; lower breast, abdomen, crissum, chin, and throat dull primrose yellow to marguerite yellow. Bill slate gray or brownish drab, but mandible slightly paler—to drab gray; iris dark brown; legs olive drab, olive buff, or greenish slate; feet greenish gray, olive drab, or olive buff.

MEASUREMENTS: *Adult male*: Wing, 57.9–63.5 (average, 60.7) mm.; tail, 47.5–50.5 (48.8); bill (exposed culmen), 8.9–9.9 (9.7); tarsus, 16.5–18.5 (17.8); middle toe without claw, 8.9–10.4 (9.7). *Adult female*: Wing, 55.9–59.4 (57.9); tail, 46.5–49.5 (47.8); bill, 8.6–9.9 (9.1); tarsus, 17.0–18.5 (17.8); middle toe, 8.6–10.4 (9.7).

TEXAS: *Migration*: Collected north to Dallas, east to Galveston, south to Cameron, west to Brewster cos. *Winter*: Two specimens: Cameron Co., Brownsville (Dec. 16, 1896, Jan. 19, 1897, F. B. Armstrong).

CAPE MAY WARBLER, *Dendroica tigrina* (Gmelin)

SPECIES ACCOUNT

Nuptial male: largely olive green above, streaked with black; black-streaked yellow below; chestnut cheek; yellow neck-spot, rump; white wing-patch. *Female, winter male*: much duller; grayish cheek-patch; smaller, duller yellow neck-spot; whitish wing-bars. Length, 5 in.; wingspan, 8¼; weight, ½ oz.

RANGE: S.w. Mackenzie and n.e. British Columbia to s. Quebec, south to n.e. North Dakota, U.S.-Canada border, Maine, and c. Nova Scotia. Winters chiefly in Bahamas, Greater Antilles; rarely in Lesser Antilles, on Tobago, and on Yucatán Peninsula.

TEXAS: (See map.) *Migration*: Apr. 14 (once as early as Mar. 31) to May 13; only one fall record. No specimen, but numerous spring sightings, one substantiated with photographs: Moore Co. (Apr., 1972, photographed by Catherine Stallwitz; no. 19 in Texas Photo-Record File, Texas A&M University); also male banded: Galveston Co., High Island (Apr. 16, 1969, F. O. Novy). Scarce (some years) to rare along coast—sightings predominantly from Chambers and Galveston cos.; rare to casual in eastern half and northern Panhandle; casual in southern Trans-Pecos. Fall sight record: Randall Co., Canyon (Oct. 16, 1936, Miss I. A. Hibbets, Mrs. L. Saunders). Three winter sightings: Galveston Co., High Island (Dec. 19, 1972, David Wolf); Chambers Co., Cove (Dec. 25, 1945, A. K. Mc-Kay); Cameron Co., Brownsville (Dec. 22, 1925, C. W. Townsend).

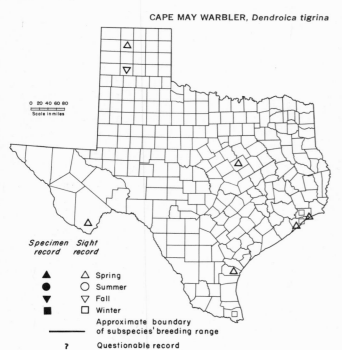

CAPE MAY WARBLER, *Dendroica tigrina*

0 20 40 60 80
Scale in miles

Specimen record / Sight record

▲	△	Spring
●	○	Summer
▼	▽	Fall
■	□	Winter

——— Approximate boundary of subspecies' breeding range

? Questionable record

HAUNTS AND HABITS: The Cape May Warbler nests far to the north of Texas and winters far southeast; nearly all individuals migrate east of the state. In its northern summer home, this warbler nests high in coniferous trees, usually tall ones. However, it also frequents dense deciduous woods, particularly during migration, when it additionally occurs in second-growth pine, oak, and other timber, on both uplands and lowlands. It seems to prefer the drier, scrubbier situations. While not strictly gregarious, it often migrates in small companies, with Blackpoll, Bay-breasted, and other wood warblers.

Flight of the Cape May is quick and jerky, even when sustained. The bird usually does not fly much above the tops of the tallest trees, except in migration. In its search for food, it examines branches and foliage usually in the interior, sometimes within the canopy. The Cape May is rather more deliberate in its movements than most other arboreal warblers, but at times it moves quickly. This warbler occasionally eats vegetable matter, such as grapes and mulberries, but insects and their larvae (weevils, flea and click beetles; bees, wasps, ants; moths, caterpillars; flies, leaf-hoppers, termites, and dragonflies) comprise the main part of the diet. A small number of spiders and harvestmen are taken also.

The Cape May's note is usually a weak *chip*. Its rather monotonous song suggests those of both the Black-and-white Warbler and the Blackpoll. It has been represented by the syllables *zee, zee, zee, zee*.

DETAILED ACCOUNT: NO SUBSPECIES

DESCRIPTION: *Adult male, nuptial plumage*: Acquired by partial prenuptial molt. Pileum brownish black or chaetura black, feathers narrowly edged with yellowish olive or dull citrine, sometimes more or less with chestnut, these edgings more numerous posteriorly; rump wax yellow or primuline yellow; upper tail-coverts fuscous black or chaetura black, edged with yellowish olive or dull citrine; remainder of upper surface yellowish olive or dull citrine, centers of feathers fuscous or fuscous black; tail dull clove brown, feathers narrowly edged on outer webs with dull citrine or yellowish olive, two outer tail feathers with large white subterminal oblique spots on inner webs, third pair of feathers with small white subterminal spot on inner webs; wing-quills dull clove brown, edged externally with dull citrine, and inner margins of primaries and secondaries, except tips of primaries, brownish white or very pale dull brown; wing-coverts chaetura black, edged with yellowish olive or dull citrine, lesser coverts with broad white or yellowish white tips; outer greater coverts margined on outer webs with rather light grayish olive; superciliary stripe (as far as middle of the eye), sides of neck (which almost meet as a collar across hindneck), chin, throat, and breast lemon chrome to orange; posterior part of superciliary stripe, subocular region, and auriculars chestnut to burnt sienna; lores narrowly chaetura black or fuscous black; throat, jugulum, breast, sides, and flanks broadly streaked with black; posterior lower parts dull white or yellowish white, or somewhat washed with yellow; lining of wing mostly white, sometimes washed with yellow, outer portion mottled or spotted with chaetura black or hair brown. Bill black or slate black, but base of mandible dull white; iris vandyke brown; legs black, toes and claws seal brown. *Adult male, winter*: Acquired by complete postnuptial molt. Similar to nuptial adult male, but upper parts much more uniform; black of pileum more or less obscured by broad feather margins of mouse gray or olive gray, giving pileum a spotted effect; remainder of upper surface lighter, black spots of back and scapulars mostly concealed by olive green tips of feathers, chestnut of sides of head much reduced in extent and replaced by yellow; black streaks of lower surface more or less obscured by yellow or gray tips of feathers, the yellow somewhat duller. Bill decidedly brown. *Adult female, nuptial*: Acquired by partial prenuptial molt. Upper surface dull yellowish olive, pileum and hindneck often more grayish, pileum and back more or less obscurely and finely streaked or spotted by chaetura drab centers of feathers; rump pyrite yellow, more or less obscurely streaked with chaetura drab; wings and tail similar to those of nuptial adult male, but third rectrix from outermost without white subterminal spot, wing-coverts duller, more grayish, less olivaceous, and white edgings of median coverts much narrower; sides of head grayish olive, more or less streaked or spotted with a darker color; superciliary stripe and sides of neck dull primuline yellow or dull grayish wax yellow; throat and breast wax yellow to primrose yellow to dull reed yellow; remainder of lower surface dull yellowish or buffy white; middle of throat, jugulum, breast, sides, and flanks rather narrowly but numerously streaked with chaetura drab to deep grayish olive, these streaks palest and least conspicuous on sides and flanks; lining of wing dull white, edge of wing mottled with hair brown. *Adult female, winter*: Acquired by complete postnuptial molt. Similar to nuptial adult female, but upper surface duller, more brownish, colors more blended; olive green of upper parts more yellowish and much overlaid by mouse gray feather tips; edgings of wings broader and more brownish; yellow of rump more golden and somewhat obscured by grayish tips of feathers; sides of head and of neck duller; lower parts duller and more uniform, blackish streaks much obscured by dull gray or dull yellow tips of feathers. *Male, first nuptial*: Acquired by partial prenuptial molt. Similar to nuptial adult male, but wing-quills and tail feathers somewhat more brownish (less blackish). *Male, first winter*: Acquired by partial postjuvenal molt, which does not involve wing-quills or tail. Similar to adult male in winter, but upper parts duller and more uniform, blackish spots still more overlaid by gray or olive green edgings of feathers, so that dark markings are still less conspicuous; yellow of rump duller and more greenish; sides of head much duller, chestnut areas replaced by olive gray or dull yellow; yellow of sides of neck almost completely obscured by olive gray tips of feathers; white wing-coverts somewhat duller; yellow of lower parts lighter and duller, less golden, black streaks much obscured by grayish edgings of feathers. Maxilla black; mandible yellowish wood brown; iris vandyke brown; legs and feet black. *Female, first nuptial*: Acquired by partial prenuptial molt. Similar to nuptial adult female, but wing-quills and tail somewhat more brownish. *Female, first winter*: Acquired by partial postjuvenal molt. Similar to adult female in winter, but upper parts more grayish (less yellowish or brownish); sides of head and of neck duller, less yellowish; lower surface more grayish (less yellowish), and somewhat paler, dark streaks less sharply defined. *Juvenal*: Acquired by complete postnatal molt. Upper parts dull olive brown; lower parts dull brownish gray; breast and sides somewhat tinged with buff. Bill slate black, but base of mandible yellowish white; iris dark brown; feet clove brown.

MEASUREMENTS: *Adult male*: Wing, 64.0–70.4 (average, 66.3) mm.; tail, 44.7–49.5 (47.3); bill (exposed culmen), 9.1–10.2 (9.7); tarsus, 16.3–18.8 (17.8); middle toe without claw, 11.7–12.7 (12.2). *Adult female*: Wing, 61.0–65.8 (63.8); tail, 43.2–47.5 (45.7); bill, 9.1–10.2 (9.7); tarsus, 17.5–18.3 (17.8); middle toe, 11.2–12.2 (11.7).

TEXAS: *Migration*: See species account.

BLACK-THROATED BLUE WARBLER, *Dendroica caerulescens* (Gmelin)

SPECIES ACCOUNT

Male: blue above; black face, throat, sides; white breast, belly, wing-spot. *Female*: plain; olive above;

buffy below; whitish eye-stripe, wing-spot (usually visible). Length, 5 in.; wingspan, 7¾; weight, ¼ oz.

RANGE: W. Ontario to Nova Scotia, south to U.S.-Canada border and Connecticut, and in Appalachians to Georgia. Winters chiefly in Bahamas and Greater Antilles.

TEXAS: (See map.) *Migration*: Late Apr. to mid-May; late Sept. to late Oct. (extremes: Mar. 2, June 22; Sept. 2, Dec. 9). Rare in eastern half, south to San Antonio and Corpus Christi; increasingly rare west of 99th meridian—where recorded in fall only—to Randall Co., Midland, and Kerrville; casual west of Pecos River (spring and fall records) and Rio Grande delta. One summer record from Big Bend Nat. Park, Panther Junction (female found dead, June 22, 1971, Patty Easterla).

HAUNTS AND HABITS: The Black-throated Blue is a "far eastern" warbler—so eastern that, for the most part, only off-course migrants get as far west as Texas. This bird's color, blue, is unusual in the wood warbler family, but its habitat is standard. It is a bird of forests, both deciduous and partly or wholly evergreen. On its breeding grounds it inhabits thickets and second-growth, cutover, and open woodlands. The nest, bulky for a warbler, is placed low in a small tree or shrub.

During migration the species occurs also in more open country: in pastures wherever there are bushes, thickets, or low trees, in cultivated areas, along fence rows, in borders of fields near woodlands, and in parks and yards of cities and towns. It does not often congregate in flocks as do the Myrtle and other related species; it is usually seen singly or in pairs.

Flight, quick and jerky, is most often from bush to bush or tree to tree. The Black-throated Blue forages in woodland undergrowth, and in trees as well, usually

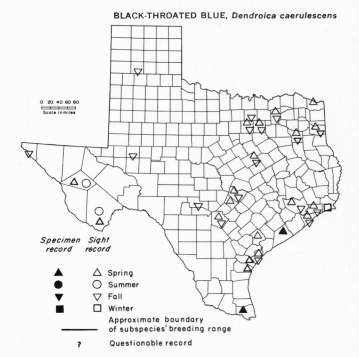

BLACK-THROATED BLUE, *Dendroica caerulescens*

0 20 40 60 80
Scale in miles

Specimen   Sight
record   record

▲   △ Spring
●   ○ Summer
▼   ▽ Fall
■   □ Winter
——— Approximate boundary of subspecies' breeding range
?   Questionable record

in interior foliage—high or low. Sometimes it descends
to the ground. It is fairly deliberate in its movements
but at times more active, though not as much so as the
American Redstart. Like the latter, it may hold its
wings partly open when perched or even when moving
along a branch. Food consists chiefly of insects, which
are often taken on the wing. Included are plant lice,
lanternflies, scale insects, tent and other caterpillars,
moths, ants, curculios, engraver beetles, other weevils,
flea and longhorn beetles, and two-winged flies; it also
captures a few spiders. In autumn and winter, small
seeds may constitute a substantial element of the diet.

The Black-throated Blue's call note is a short *chuk*.
Its usual song, a very wheezy insectlike performance,
has numerous variations, but generally resembles the
syllable *zwee*, repeated three or four times, the last
note with rising inflection.

Detailed Account: One Subspecies

NORTHERN BLACK-THROATED BLUE WARBLER,
Dendroica caerulescens caerulescens (Gmelin)

DESCRIPTION: *Adult male, nuptial plumage*: Acquired by partial prenuptial molt. Upper parts between deep slate blue and
delft blue, pileum somewhat paler, and everywhere more or less
obscurely and finely mottled by somewhat darker edgings or
centers of feathers; tail deep mouse gray, outer webs of feathers
narrowly margined with color of back, outermost three pairs of
rectrices with large subterminal more or less oblique white spots
on inner webs, remaining pairs, except middle pair, with narrow
white edgings near tips; wing-quills chaetura drab, inner margins broadly dull white except on tips of primaries, conspicuous
even in closed wing; wing-quills edged externally with color of
back; tertials mouse gray; lesser wing-coverts like crown; remaining wing-coverts chaetura black, and, with exception of primary coverts, edged externally with color of back; sides of head
—including forehead, superciliary stripe, and anterior portion of
sides of neck—dull black, as are chin, throat, and sides of body;
sides of neck posteriorly like back; remainder of lower parts
white; lining of wing white; edge of wing slate blue like upper
surface but mixed with dull black. Bill black; iris dark brown;
legs and feet clove brown, hair brown, or olive brown. *Adult
male, winter*: Acquired by complete postnuptial molt. Like nuptial adult male, but upper surface, particularly back and rump,
with very narrow olive green feather edgings; black of throat,
breast, sides, and flanks of less extent and very narrowly tipped
with grayish white or pale gray. Mandible dull dark brown instead of black. *Adult female, nuptial*: Acquired by partial prenuptial molt. Upper surface dull yellowish olive, but forehead
sometimes bluish; tail between deep mouse gray and chaetura
drab, outer feathers rather paler; exterior edges of feathers margined with color of upper parts, outermost feather with subterminal whitish or drab spot on inner web, this sometimes obscure
or almost absent; wings dark hair brown, basal portion of inner
webs of primaries and secondaries margined with brownish white
or pale dull brown; dull white or greenish white spot at base of
middle primary, showing as small whitish spot in closed wing;
all wing-coverts and outer margins of wing-quills like upper
surface but slightly more bluish; lores fuscous; narrow superciliary stripe dull yellowish or greenish white; remainder of sides
of head and of neck similar to upper parts, but ear-coverts rather
more brownish; greenish white or dull yellowish white spot on
lower and upper eyelid, latter extending backward for short distance over auriculars; lower surface olive buff to dark dull colonial buff; sides and flanks buffy olive; lining of wing dull olive
buff, somewhat mottled with chaetura drab or hair brown. Bill
slate black, but mandible clove brown; iris dark brown; legs and
feet olive brown to broccoli brown. *Adult female, winter*: Ac-

quired by complete postnuptial molt. Similar to nuptial adult
female, but upper surface averaging more greenish or brownish
(less grayish); lower surface usually more distinctly yellow; sides
and flanks more strongly tinged with olive. *Male, second winter*: Acquired by complete postnuptial molt. Like adult male in
winter. *Male, first nuptial*: Acquired by partial prenuptial molt.
Similar to nuptial adult male, but upper parts showing slight
olive green feather edgings; wing-quills, tail feathers, and particularly primary coverts more brownish and margined with
olive as in first winter male, instead of with slaty blue; chin and
throat usually with more or less distinct whitish feather edgings.
Male, first winter: Acquired by partial postjuvenal molt, which
does not involve wing-quills, tail, or primary wing-coverts. Similar to adult male in winter, but upper parts much washed with
olive green; wing-quills lighter, more brownish—between hair
brown and chaetura drab, their outer edgings, together with
those of primary coverts, dull olive green; black of chin, throat,
sides of head, and sides of body much more broadly edged with
white, pale gray, or buffy white; chin and throat sometimes
nearly all white; abdomen, sides, and flanks strongly tinged with
buff. *Female, first nuptial*: Acquired by prenuptial molt. Similar
to nuptial adult female, but wings, tail, and primary coverts
somewhat more brownish. *Female, first winter*: Acquired by partial postjuvenal molt. Similar to adult female in winter, but upper parts more greenish and without bluish tinge; lower parts
somewhat more yellowish or buffy; superciliary stripe dull yellow. *Male, juvenal*: Acquired by complete postnatal molt. Upper
parts brownish olive, pileum sometimes light brownish olive; tail
as in adult male in winter; wing-quills as in first winter male;
upper wing-coverts brownish olive; superciliary stripe dull colonial buff; lores chaetura black; ear-coverts olivaceous black or
dark brownish olive; chin and throat light brownish olive; remainder of lower surface pale dull colonial buff or ivory yellow.
Bill brownish slate, but mandible slate gray; iris dark brown;
legs and feet drab or olive buff. *Female, juvenal*: Acquired by
complete postnatal molt. Similar to juvenal male but paler, lores
and ear-coverts less distinctly blackish; wings and tail as in first
winter female.

MEASUREMENTS: *Adult male*: Wing, 62.0–67.1 (average, 65.3)
mm.; tail, 49.0–54.1 (51.3); bill (exposed culmen), 8.9–10.4
(9.7); tarsus, 17.5–19.6 (18.8); middle toe without claw, 10.4–
11.9 (11.2). *Adult female*: Wing, 59.9–63.0 (61.2); tail, 47.5–
51.1 (48.5); bill, 8.9–10.4 (9.7); tarsus, 18.0–19.0 (18.8); middle toe, 9.9–10.9 (10.7).

RANGE: W. Ontario to n.e. Nova Scotia, south to c. Wisconsin
and s. Connecticut. In migration, west to Wyoming and Texas.
Winters in s.w. Florida (a few), Bahamas, and Greater Antilles;
rarely from Guatemala to n. Peru.

TEXAS: *Migration*: Two specimens: Matagorda Co., Mata-
gorda (Apr. 23, 1936, H. H. Kimball); Cameron Co., Green
Island (May 11, 1924, R. D. Camp). Bird found dead in Big
Bend Nat. Park not identified as to race (see species account).

MYRTLE WARBLER, *Dendroica coronata*
(Linnaeus)

Species Account

Nuptial (female duller): bluish gray above with
yellow on crown, rump, and sides of breast; black
cheeks, breast, sides; white throat, belly, wing-bars.
Winter: brownish above; brown-streaked whitish below; yellow rump. Length, 5½ in.; wingspan, 8¾;
weight, ½ oz.

RANGE: Alaska to Newfoundland, south to n. British
Columbia, n. Great Lakes region, and Massachusetts.
Winters from Kansas, s. Great Lakes region, and s. New
England through s.e. United States and e. and s. Mexi-

co to c. Panama, and in the West Indies; also along Pacific coast from n.w. Oregon to n. Baja California.

TEXAS: (See map.) *Migration*: Mid-Mar. to late Apr.; mid-Oct. to mid-Dec. (extremes: Mar. 10, June 12; Sept. 13, Dec. 20). Abundant (some decline since 1960) to common through most parts, though less numerous in northern Panhandle and Trans-Pecos where local and often uncommon; rare in El Paso region. *Winter*: Early Nov. to mid-Apr. Very common to fairly common east of 100th meridian; fairly common to uncommon west to Balmorhea, Fort Davis, and Big Bend; rare in northern Panhandle.

HAUNTS AND HABITS: The Myrtle Warbler adds myrtle berries and many other small fruits to the usual warbler insect diet. Since its dependence on crawling and flying insects is much reduced, it, more than most of its relatives, is able to winter in colder regions. Even though it does not breed in Texas, the Myrtle is without doubt the state's most numerous warbler from mid-November to mid-April. During late spring and early summer this warbler, good *Dendroica* that it is, usually builds its nest in a pine, spruce, or fir. At other seasons, however, it is not at all restricted to coniferous forests and, in fact, seems rather partial to deciduous woodlands. Migrants occur in many places: slopes and uplands with scattered cedar (*Juniperus*) and other trees and shrubs, canyons, various streamside and swamp vegetation, thickets and bushes skirting bayous, ditches, fields, fence rows, and highways, and yards and parks of towns and cities, also marshes and even sandy beaches along the Gulf coast. At times it appears in large flights or in companies of considerable size (though more or less scattered) and often associated with other warbler species.

The Myrtle's flight is ordinarily easy and fluttering

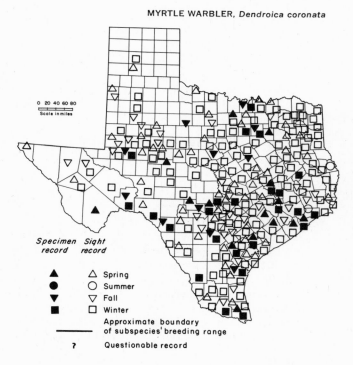

MYRTLE WARBLER, *Dendroica coronata*

0 20 40 60 80
Scale in miles

Specimen   Sight
record   record

▲   △ Spring
●   ○ Summer
▼   ▽ Fall
■   □ Winter

——— Approximate boundary
    of subspecies' breeding range

?   Questionable record

and performed with a minimum of wing-beats; when prolonged, it is usually much swifter and somewhat erratic. Found from highest treetops to the ground, this bird is at home in almost any situation. In trees and shrubs it gleans insects from foliage and terminal twigs. It can also hover briefly while it picks an insect off a leaf. At times it sallies into the air, flycatcher-style, to snap up a passing moth or fly. Upon returning to its perch it commonly flicks its tail and utters its call note. It is not at all shy and is easily approached.

Its food preferences have been studied more thoroughly than those of most other warblers. In addition to spiders and harvestmen, the Myrtle consumes large quantities of injurious insects, their larvae and eggs: leaf-rollers, measuringworms, cankerworms, cotton-boll weevil, leaf chafers, longhorn and lamellicorn beetles and their larvae, scale insects, jumping plant lice, woolly apple tree aphis, plant lice and their eggs, mosquito eggs, gnats, house flies, caddis flies, ichneumon flies, and ants. In winter the Myrtle is a frequent visitor to fruit-bearing plants, such as junipers, dogwoods (*Cornus*), sumacs (*Rhus*), and yaupon (*Ilex vomitoria*); even a well-stocked feeding tray, especially if it contains suet, may entice it.

Its usual call note, heard all year, is a low guttural *tschut* or *check*, louder than that of most arboreal warblers. Its song is spritely, and may be represented by the syllables *wee-see-see-see*, sometimes repeated at a somewhat higher pitch. Before departing Texas for its northern summer home, it sings much in March and April.

DETAILED ACCOUNT: TWO SUBSPECIES

EASTERN MYRTLE WARBLER, *Dendroica coronata coronata* (Linnaeus)

DESCRIPTION: *Adult male, nuptial plumage*: Acquired by partial prenuptial molt. Narrow line across forehead black; pileum and hindneck deep slate gray, but broad central portion of crown lemon chrome, and forehead and hindneck narrowly, sides of crown broadly, streaked with black; back and scapulars neutral gray, broadly streaked with black, lower back sometimes strongly tinged with buffy brown; rump lemon yellow to lemon chrome; upper tail-coverts black, edged with neutral gray; tail chaetura black, margined on outer webs of feathers with neutral gray, outer feathers partly with whitish, and outer three rectrices with large slightly oblique subterminal spots of white; wing-quills chaetura drab, inner margins of all but tertials and tips of primaries brownish white or pale brown; wing-quills and tertials edged externally with dull hair brown, margins of tertials paler, sometimes warmer brown; upper wing-coverts dull black, margined with neutral gray, greater and median series broadly tipped with white, forming two conspicuous wing-bars; superciliary stripe and short streak on lower eyelid white; lores and sides of head below eyes mostly black; sides of neck like hindneck; lower surface white, but jugulum and sides of breast mostly black, streaked with white, with large patch of lemon chrome on each side of breast; sides and flanks broadly streaked with black; lining of wing white, outer portion mottled with chaetura drab. Bill black or slate black, but basal portion of mandible slate gray or seal brown; iris dark brown; legs and feet black to broccoli brown. *Adult male, winter*: Acquired by complete postnuptial molt. Duller and very much less brightly colored than nuptial adult male; upper parts between hair brown and buffy brown or snuff brown, back with a few spots and streaks of black; yellow of crown partially or entirely obscured by brown tips of feathers; rump and upper tail-coverts as in nuptial adult male; wing edgings much more brownish; wing-bars avellaneous to wood brown, sometimes partly brownish white; lower parts dull buffy white; sides of head more or less brown like upper parts, black areas obscured or obliterated; throat brownish white; breast strongly washed with brown of upper surface; rest of lower parts dull white or buffy white, but jugulum, breast, sides, and flanks obscurely streaked with dull black or chaetura drab; yellow patches on sides of breast duller and more or less obscured by grayish or brownish tips of feathers. *Adult female, nuptial*: Acquired by partial prenuptial molt. Similar to nuptial adult male but smaller and coloration duller; yellow patches on crown, rump, and sides of breast paler (lemon yellow) and usually smaller; pileum and hindneck between neutral gray and mouse gray to between mouse gray and drab, very narrowly streaked with dull black or chaetura black; back dark drab to dull buffy brown, rather broadly streaked with dull black; tail dark chaetura drab, edged on outer webs of feathers with neutral gray, outer two or three pairs of tail feathers with large subterminal white spots on inner webs; wings fuscous, edgings of wing-coverts dull brown, similar to color of back; white wing-bars narrower; sides of head similar to nape; whitish spot on lower eyelid and white superciliary stripe; lower parts like nuptial adult male, but only breast streaked with black; sides and flanks much less distinctly and heavily streaked with chaetura drab or dull black, these streaks much narrower and more sharply defined than in nuptial adult male. Bill, legs, and feet black; iris dark brown. *Adult female, winter*: Acquired by complete postnuptial molt. Similar to adult male in winter but smaller; upper parts more uniform dull buffy brown, blackish streaks less conspicuous; wings more brownish, yellow patch on crown practically concealed; yellow rump paler; lower parts duller, more brownish, breast deep drab to drab, less distinctly streaked, streaks less blackish (more grayish or brownish); yellow patch on each side of breast smaller and much overlaid with brown. *Male, first nuptial*: Acquired by partial prenuptial molt. Similar to nuptial adult male, but wing-quills, tail feathers, and particularly primary wing-coverts usually more brownish, and edgings of primary coverts usually more clearly gray (less brownish). *Male, first winter*: Acquired by partial postjuvenal molt, which does not involve wing-quills, primary coverts, or tail. Similar to adult male in winter, but wing-quills, primary coverts, and tail feathers more brownish, and margins less clearly gray, particularly those of primary coverts; upper surface more distinctly brownish, yellow crown-patch still more nearly concealed; lower parts decidedly more brownish, yellow patches on sides of breast duller, smaller, and more tinged with brown. Similar to adult female in winter but larger; upper parts more brownish and more plainly streaked with black; streaks of lower parts more blackish. *Female, first nuptial*: Acquired by complete prenuptial molt. Similar to nuptial adult female, but wing-quills, tail feathers, and primary coverts lighter and more brownish. *Female, first winter*: Acquired by partial postjuvenal molt. Similar to adult female in winter, but wing-quills and tail somewhat more brownish, edgings of these feathers somewhat more brownish (less purely gray); upper parts more brownish (less grayish) and rather darker—between olive brown and snuff brown to between snuff brown and buffy brown; yellow of crown and sides of breast less in extent, duller, latter more tinged with brown and sometimes practically absent; lower surface more tinged with brown. Bill black; iris vandyke brown; legs and feet black or greenish black. *Juvenal*: Acquired by complete postnatal molt. Upper parts light hair brown to dull rufescent buffy brown; numerously streaked with fuscous and dull black, rump slightly paler; wings and tail as in first winter female; sides of head brownish like upper parts; superciliary stripe almost obsolete, slight whitish mark on lower eyelid; lower parts dull white, yellowish white, or buffy white, jugulum and upper breast sometimes dull pale gray and everywhere, except on middle of abdomen, conspicuously streaked with fuscous to dull black. Bill slate black, slate gray, or brownish slate, basal portion of mandible dull white or yellowish white; iris dark brown; legs and feet flesh color, cream buff, broccoli brown, or even dull black.

MEASUREMENTS: *Adult male*: Wing, 71.1–74.9 (average, 72.9) mm.; tail, 52.8–57.4 (54.8); bill (exposed culmen), 8.1–9.4 (8.9); tarsus, 18.5–19.8 (19.3); middle toe without claw, 10.4–11.7 (11.2). *Adult female*: Wing, 67.6–72.4 (69.8); tail, 51.3–54.8 (52.8); bill, 7.9–9.7 (8.9); tarsus, 18.0–19.8 (18.8); middle toe, 10.4–11.4 (10.9).

RANGE: N.e. Saskatchewan to s. Labrador, south to c. Minnesota and Massachusetts. Winters from c. Kansas and s.w. Maine through s.e. United States and e. and s. Mexico to Panama; also West Indies.

TEXAS: *Winter*: Taken north to Dallas, east to Trinity and Galveston, south to Cameron, west to Kinney cos. Common.

HOOVER'S MYRTLE WARBLER, *Dendroica coronata hooveri* McGregor

DESCRIPTION: *Adult male and female, nuptial plumage*: Similar to *D. c. coronata* but larger; adult male with less black on lower surface, that on jugulum and on sides of neck more streaked or mottled with white; yellow of rump averaging paler; adult female more grayish (less rufescent) brown above, and with yellow of rump usually somewhat lighter. *First winter and juvenal*: Usually darker, duller, of less rufescent brown than individuals of *D. c. coronata* of same age.

MEASUREMENTS: *Adult male*: Wing, 75.7–78.0 (average, 76.7) mm.; tail, 56.4–60.5 (58.4); bill (exposed culmen), 8.6–9.9 (9.1); tarsus, 18.8–20.6 (19.6); middle toe without claw, 10.9–11.9 (11.2). *Adult female*: Wing, 70.4–75.2 (72.9); tail, 54.1–57.9 (56.4); bill, 8.4–9.9 (9.1); tarsus, 19.0–19.8 (19.3); middle toe, 10.4–11.9 (10.9).

RANGE: N.w. Alaska to c. Mackenzie, south to British Columbia and e. Alberta. Winters from s.w. Oregon, c. Oklahoma, and South Carolina to s. Baja California and Veracruz.

TEXAS: *Winter*: Taken north to Cooke, east to Chambers, south to Cameron, west to Brewster (Mar. 15) cos. Common.

AUDUBON'S WARBLER, *Dendroica auduboni* (Townsend)

SPECIES ACCOUNT

Resembles Myrtle, but has yellow throat. Male has white shoulder-patch. Length, 5½ in.; wingspan, 9; weight, ½ oz.

RANGE: C. British Columbia to w. South Dakota, south in mountains to n. Baja California and s. Durango, possibly to Guanajuato. Winters from s.w. British Columbia, s.w. Utah, c. New Mexico, and Texas through Mexico to Costa Rica.

TEXAS: (See map.) *Breeding*: Probably early May to mid-Aug. (no egg dates available, but nest located at 8,000 ft. by F. R. Gehlbach). Fairly common summer resident above 7,000 ft. in Guadalupe Mts.; breeding confirmed, however, only in The Bowl. Occasionally summers at high altitude in Davis Mts., but no good evidence of nesting. *Migration*: Late Mar. to late Apr.—mid-May in Trans-Pecos; late Sept. to late Nov. (extremes: Mar. 20, June 5; Aug. 25, Dec. 1). Common to fairly common west of 100th meridian; uncommon (most springs) to scarce (most falls) east to Dallas, Bastrop, Rockport, and Brownsville; rare on upper coast. *Winter*: Mid-Dec. to late Mar. Common in Trans-Pecos; irregularly fairly common in remainder of state west of 100th meridian with exception of northern Panhandle where scarce; scarce eastward to 97th meridian; very rare on upper coast.

HAUNTS AND HABITS: The Audubon's Warbler is the western version of the Myrtle. During the breeding season it replaces its very close relative in most of the western United States, but during migration and on wintering grounds in Texas and elsewhere the two often associate. Audubon's lives during summer in evergreen and deciduous forests of mountains; during migration and winter it frequents woodlands and groves as well as brushy canyons and hillsides, open plains, and orchards. Occasionally it migrates or winters in considerable flocks, which may be associated with other warblers or even with bluebirds.

Flight of an Audubon's Warbler when hovering about a tree is fluttering, but at other times it is swift (however somewhat erratic), performed with moderate though powerful wing-beats, and capable of being long sustained. It haunts tops of tall trees and is exceedingly active in its feeding operations, flitting about terminal branches rather than interior foliage, often catching insects on the wing. Although it prefers upper branches of trees, the Audubon's also forages low in thickets, undergrowth, and even in grass or on the ground.

Food, even in winter, consists of at least 85 percent animal matter, primarily insects, but including a few spiders as well. Wasps and ants comprise about one-fourth of the diet; flies, gnats, and craneflies, about one-sixth; bugs, including olive scales, plant lice, stink bugs, leaf- and tree-hoppers, about one-fifth. Caterpillars, moths and their cocoons, weevils, carrion and ladybird beetles are also taken. The vegetable portion consists chiefly of wild fruit, weed seed, and seeds of poison-oak.

The standard call note is a loud, low-pitched *tchip*, very similar to, but softer than, that of the Myrtle.

Though not loud or elaborate, its regular song is pleasing. It has been represented by the syllables *si-wi, si-wi, si-wi, sissle, sissle, see-see,* but its other songs vary considerably from this one. The Audubon's sings from late April well into July.

DETAILED ACCOUNT: TWO SUBSPECIES

PACIFIC AUDUBON'S WARBLER, *Dendroica auduboni auduboni* (Townsend)

DESCRIPTION: *Adult male, nuptial plumage*: Acquired by partial prenuptial molt. Upper surface between neutral gray and slate gray, but upper rump sometimes mouse gray, lower rump lemon chrome; large patch in center of crown between lemon chrome and light cadmium; pileum finely streaked with black, hindneck with a few inconspicuous streaks of same, back, scapulars, and upper tail-coverts broadly streaked with black on central parts of feathers; tail dull black or fuscous black, outer webs of feathers at base narrowly edged with neutral gray, outermost two feathers edged with white on outer webs, middle pair of tail feathers edged with white on inner webs subterminally, and four or five of other feathers on each side with large more or less transverse white subterminal spots on their inner webs; primaries and secondaries, except at tips of primaries, edged on inner webs with brownish white; narrow outer margins of primaries and secondaries neutral gray; tertials chaetura drab to chaetura black, broad outer edges grayish white or brownish white; wing-coverts dull black, lesser coverts broadly edged with neutral gray, outer greater coverts edged with pale neutral gray, inner ones sometimes narrowly tipped with white, greater coverts broadly margined with white on outer webs and tipped with same; median coverts broadly tipped with white, these white areas forming conspicuous patch on wing; lores, malar region, and region below eye black or grayish black; long white spot on upper and lower eyelids; rest of sides of head and sides of neck like upper parts; chin, throat, and conspicuous patch on each side of breast between lemon chrome and light cadmium; jugulum and breast black, usually more or less streaked or mottled with white or very pale gray, though jugulum is sometimes solidly black; middle of breast, abdomen, sides, flanks, and crissum white or buffy white, but sides and flanks broadly streaked with black; lining of wing white, outer edge of wing somewhat mottled with chaetura drab. Bill dull black; iris burnt umber or hazel; legs and feet black, brownish black, or dark brown. *Adult male, winter*: Acquired by complete postnuptial molt. Decidedly different in appearance from nuptial adult male, upper parts much washed with buffy brown, which much obscures yellow crown-patch and black streaks on back; edges of wing feathers and coverts much more brownish, white edgings of wing-coverts less extensive and washed with brown; white tips of greater and median coverts showing chiefly as two more or less obscured wing-bars; sides of head paler and more brownish than in nuptial; yellow of throat and of sides of breast duller and rather paler; sides of breast sometimes tinged with brown; black areas of lower surface very much obscured by light gray, dull white, or drab edgings of feathers, black markings sometimes barely showing. *Adult female, nuptial*: Acquired by partial prenuptial molt. Similar to nuptial adult male, but upper parts duller, more brownish mouse gray or toward neutral gray; yellow crown-patch smaller, more or less obscured by brown or gray tips of feathers; black streaks of upper parts much smaller and less conspicuous; yellow of rump slightly paler; white spots on tail smaller; wing more brownish, white edgings and tips of wing-coverts less extensive and often somewhat washed with brown or buff; sides of head and of neck like upper parts, lores without black; white spots on eyelids duller and less conspicuous; yellow of throat less extensive, usually becoming white or whitish on chin; yellow patch on each side of breast much smaller and duller; remainder of lower surface buffy white, but sides and flanks streaked with chaetura drab, sometimes washed with buffy brown; jugulum and breast smoke gray to drab gray with narrow streaks or roundish spots of dull black

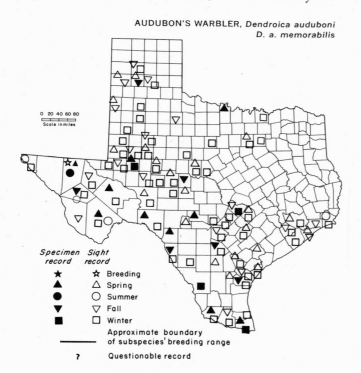

AUDUBON'S WARBLER, *Dendroica auduboni*
D. a. memorabilis

0 20 40 60 80
Scale in miles

Specimen record	Sight record	
★	☆	Breeding
▲	△	Spring
●	○	Summer
▼	▽	Fall
■	□	Winter

———— Approximate boundary of subspecies' breeding range

? Questionable record

PLATE 28: Bronzed Cowbird, *Tangavius aeneus*
males showing expanded neck-ruffs

and chaetura drab. Similar to adult male in winter, but upper parts less brownish (more grayish), yellow crown-patch smaller; wings more brownish; sides of head paler; yellow of throat usually less extensive and somewhat brighter, that on sides of breast much less extensive; dark markings on breast, jugulum, sides, and flanks smaller. Bill and feet black. *Adult female, winter*: Acquired by complete postnuptial molt. Similar to nuptial adult female, but upper parts very much more uniform and more brownish—dull buffy brown to between snuff brown and saccardo umber, yellow crown-patch almost entirely obscured, black streaks on upper surface very much less conspicuous or obsolete; yellow rump-patch usually paler; wings very much more brownish, edgings of feathers, including tips of greater and lesser coverts, dull buff; sides of head and of neck similar to upper parts but paler; lower surface much duller and more uniform—dull warm buff, dull avellaneous, dull vinaceous buff, or smoke gray, but middle of breast, abdomen, and crissum sometimes white or dull white, black markings of breast and jugulum absent or only faintly indicated by dark brown or chaetura drab streaks or mottlings; yellow of throat of less extent and duller, almost entirely obscured and much washed with buff; sides and flanks streaked obscurely with dull brown or chaetura drab; yellow patches on sides of breast duller and much obscured by brown. Similar to adult male in winter but much smaller and differing in coloration as from nuptial adult female. *Male, first nuptial*: Acquired by partial prenuptial molt. Similar to nuptial adult male, but wing-quills, tail feathers, and primary coverts, particularly outer margins, more brownish, less purely blue-gray. *Male, first winter*: Acquired by partial postjuvenal molt, which does not involve wing-quills or tail. Similar to adult male in winter, but upper parts more brownish, more or less washed or suffused with saccardo umber, dull buffy brown, or snuff brown; yellow crown-patch more obscured by tips of feathers; wings and light edgings more brownish; lower parts duller, more uniform, and more brownish; yellow throat-patch very much less in extent, duller, more buffy, or even absent; jugulum, sides, and flanks dull vinaceous buff, dull drab gray, and smoke gray to dull mouse gray, dark streaks and spots on lower surface very much less conspicuous, sometimes nearly absent and reduced to narrow streaks of dull black, chaetura drab, or olive gray on jugulum, breast, sides, and flanks; yellow patches on sides of breast smaller, duller, and much tinged with brown, sometimes almost absent. Similar to adult female in winter but decidedly larger, upper surface more grayish (less brownish), yellow crown-patch not usually so much obscured; lower surface lighter, less brownish (more grayish or whitish), and more noticeably streaked or spotted, though obscurely, with dull black or dark gray; yellow of throat and sides of breast usually more extensive and brighter, but some specimens difficult to distinguish except by size. *Female, first nuptial*: Acquired by partial prenuptial molt. Similar to nuptial adult female, but wing-quills, primary coverts, and tail feathers more brownish. *Female, first winter*: Acquired by partial postjuvenal molt, exclusive of wing-quills, primary coverts, and tail feathers. Similar to adult female in winter but still darker, duller, and more brownish on upper surface; yellow crown-patch smaller and almost completely covered by brown; dark streaks on back much narrower and more inconspicuous, leaving upper surface more uniform than in adult female, though often feathers of hindneck and back have very narrow, obscure, paler brown tips, imparting faintly barred appearance; less white in tail but usually some on fourth feather; lower surface duller, more brownish, particularly jugulum, but even less evidently streaked with dark brown or brownish gray, yellow of throat duller, not infrequently absent, and replaced by dull buff; occasionally some specimens difficult to distinguish from adult female in winter. *Juvenal*: Acquired by complete postnatal molt. Upper surface dull buffy brown or between drab and hair brown, narrowly streaked and spotted on pileum, broadly marked on mantle, with chaetura drab or chaetura black, fuscous black, and fuscous; rump buffy or grayish white, narrowly streaked with fuscous; wings and tail as in young in first autumn, but greater coverts tipped, not margined, with dull white; sides of head similar to pileum, lores rather darker, auriculars dull drab, inconspicuous dull buffy white spot on each eyelid; lower surface pale dull

olive buff or dull white, streaked everywhere except on chin and center of lower abdomen, but most conspicuously on jugulum, breast, and sides, with chaetura drab to chaetura black. *Natal* (this plumage of this race not seen in Texas): Light drab.

MEASUREMENTS: *Adult male*: Wing, 71.7–77.0 (average, 74.7) mm.; tail, 55.1–59.9 (58.2); bill (exposed culmen), 9.4–10.7 (10.2); tarsus, 18.5–20.1 (18.8); middle toe without claw, 10.9–12.4 (11.7). *Adult female*: Wing, 69.8–73.7 (71.7); tail, 55.6–57.9 (56.6); bill, 9.9–10.9 (10.2); tarsus, 19.0–19.8 (19.3); middle toe, 10.4–11.4 (10.9).

RANGE: C. British Columbia to s. California. In migration, east to Trans-Pecos Texas and Coahuila. Winters from s.w. British Columbia to s. Baja California and through w. Mexico to Guatemala.

TEXAS: *Migration*: Collected in Culberson (2 specimens) and Brewster (3) cos. Uncommon.

NESTING: (This race does not nest in Texas.) *Nest*: On mountains, their slopes and canyons; farther north, on lower land in spruce, pine, fir, or other evergreen or deciduous forests, sometimes in more open country; in bush or tree, usually on outer branch, 3–30 ft. above ground, well-made, bulky structure with rather deep inner cup; composed of strips of bark, grass, leaves, small twigs, pine needles, lichens, mosses, roots, weed stalks, catkins, and even pieces of cotton cloth; lined with rootlets, hair, grass, and feathers. *Eggs*: 3–5, usually 4; rounded ovate to short ovate; dull white, greenish white, or bluish white to pale green or even pale blue; blotched and spotted with blackish brown, olive brown, purplish brown, with shell markings of lilac and lavender, sometimes covering entire egg, but in others with wreath about large end; average size, 17.0 × 13.2 mm.

ROCKY MOUNTAIN AUDUBON'S WARBLER, *Dendroica auduboni memorabilis* Oberholser

DESCRIPTION: *Adult male and female, nuptial plumage*: Similar to *D. a. auduboni* but larger; male with breast and jugulum nearly always more solidly and more extensively black, sides of head also with more black. *Natal*: Probably similar to *D. a. auduboni*.

MEASUREMENTS: *Adult male*: Wing, 77.2–83.6 (average, 80.5) mm.; tail, 59.9–66.8 (63.0); bill (exposed culmen), 9.4–10.9 (10.2); tarsus, 18.0–21.1 (19.8); middle toe without claw, 11.4–12.4 (11.9). *Adult female*: Wing, 71.9–78.0 (74.4); tail, 55.1–61.0 (58.2); bill, 9.4–10.9 (10.2); tarsus, 18.0–20.1 (19.3); middle toe, 10.9–11.9 (11.4).

RANGE: W. Alberta and s.w. Saskatchewan through Rocky Mts. to Trans-Pecos Texas. Winters from s. California and s.w. Texas through Mexico to Costa Rica.

TEXAS: *Breeding*: Collected in Guadalupe Mts., Culberson Co. *Migration*: Collected north to Randall, east to Clay, south to Nueces and Cameron, west to Culberson cos. Fairly common. *Winter*: Taken northwest to Jeff Davis (Nov. 3), east to Travis, south to Cameron cos. Fairly common.

NESTING: Similar to that of *D. a. auduboni*, but average egg size, 18.0 × 14.2 mm.

BLACK-THROATED GRAY WARBLER, *Dendroica nigrescens* (Townsend)

SPECIES ACCOUNT

Male: black crown, cheeks, throat, and streaks on sides; white facial stripes, under parts, wing-bars; gray upper parts; yellow loral spot. *Female*: duller; whitish throat. Length, 5 in.; wingspan, 7½.

RANGE: S.w. British Columbia to c. Colorado, south in mountains to n. Baja California, n.e. Sonora, and Trans-Pecos Texas (probably). Winters from coastal and s. California, s. Arizona, and s. Texas to s. Baja California, Oaxaca, and Veracruz.

TEXAS: (See map.) *Breeding* (probably): Perhaps early May to mid-July (no egg dates available, but bird in apparent juvenal plumage located, Aug. 2, 1960, by F. R. Gehlbach). Uncommon in Guadalupe Mts. *Migration*: Late Mar. to late Apr.; early Sept. to late Nov. (extremes: –May 8; Aug. 13–). Uncommon (most falls) to scarce (most springs) in Trans-Pecos; scarce in western Panhandle; rare (most falls) to extremely rare (most springs) in eastern half south of 32nd parallel. *Winter*: Late Nov. to mid-Apr. Numerous sightings; one specimen (not identified to race): Kenedy Co., King Ranch, 8 mi. east of Rudolf (Jan. 16, 1969, B. A. Fall; Texas A&M University collection, no. 7809). Uncommon to scarce in and near Rio Grande delta; rare in southern Trans-Pecos, central portions, and along coast.

HAUNTS AND HABITS: The Black-throated Gray Warbler is a summer inhabitant of juniper-pinyon-oak scrub growing at moderate altitudes on slopes, foothills, and in canyons. However, it also frequents denser, wetter woodlands, where it occurs in undergrowth among scattered timber and in thickets, often at the edge of clearings. It may even nest high in a conifer. While it apparently prefers dry situations, it occasionally occurs in swampy places. As with most birds, its habitat requirements during the nonbreeding season are considerably more flexible. Though often seen singly or in pairs, the Black-throated Gray at times gathers into small companies, especially while migrating, and it may or may not be associated with Audubon's and other warblers.

Its flight is rather quick, somewhat flitting and erratic, and ordinarily not much prolonged. It forages not only in tops of tall trees, but also in their lower

parts, and even in bushes and thickets. The bird is retiring and where foliage is thick may remain inconspicuous. Its movements are not as rapid or nervous as those of some warblers. *D. nigrescens* apparently spends little time on the ground, being eminently a bird of trees and shrubs. It feeds largely on insects (moths, butterflies, caterpillars, dragonflies, leaf-eating and June beetles, weevils, grasshoppers, true bugs, and ants), along with a few spiders and leaf galls.

Usual call note is a sharp *chit*. It has several territorial songs, one of which has been represented by *ze, ze, ze*, another by *tsewey, tsewey, tsewey, tsewey-tsew*. There are other variations, the quality of all recalling that of the more deliberate song of the Black-throated Green Warbler. In the Guadalupe Mountains, male Black-throated Grays sing from late April through July.

DETAILED ACCOUNT: TWO SUBSPECIES

PACIFIC BLACK-THROATED GRAY WARBLER, *Dendroica nigrescens nigrescens* (Townsend)

No races recognized by A.O.U. check-list, 1957 (see Appendix A).

DESCRIPTION: *Adult male and female, nuptial plumage*: Similar to *D. n. halseii* (see below), but smaller; white area on second and third rectrices from outside of tail much less extensive, dark area on basal part of these feathers, therefore, much greater; gray of upper parts averaging slightly darker; black streaks on sides and flanks not so heavy.

MEASUREMENTS: *Adult male*: Wing, 58.9–63.0 (average, 61.0) mm.; tail, 48.0–51.1 (49.3); bill (exposed culmen), 8.9–9.9 (9.7); tarsus, 16.5–18.0 (17.3); middle toe without claw, 8.9–9.9 (9.7); white on inner web of second outer tail feather, 26.9–35.6 (31.2). *Adult female*: Wing, 56.9–62.7 (58.7); tail, 44.4–51.1 (47.8); bill, 8.6–9.9 (9.7); tarsus, 17.0–18.5 (17.8); middle toe, 8.9–9.9 (9.1); white on inner web, 24.9–33.0 (29.4).

RANGE: S.w. British Columbia to n.w. California. In migration, east to s. Texas. Winters from n.w. California into Mexico.

TEXAS: *Migration*: One specimen: Cameron Co., Brownsville (Apr. 2, 1910, A. P. Smith).

ARIZONA BLACK-THROATED GRAY WARBLER, *Dendroica nigrescens halseii* (Giraud)

No races recognized by A.O.U. check-list, 1957 (see Appendix A).

DESCRIPTION: *Adult male, nuptial plumage*: Acquired by wear from winter plumage. Pileum black; remainder of upper surface neutral gray or somewhat bluish neutral gray; back, scapulars, and upper tail-coverts conspicuously streaked with black; tail black, middle tail feathers and basal portions of most of other rectrices edged narrowly on basal portions of external webs with neutral gray, outer two tail feathers nearly all white except for narrow terminal shaft streak broader toward end of feathers, remaining pairs with decreasingly large white terminal areas on inner webs, middle feathers without white markings except occasionally for narrow whitish terminal edgings on inner webs; primaries and secondaries chaetura drab, inner webs broadly edged with dull white or grayish white, except at tips of primaries, these edgings occupying on innermost secondaries a large part of webs; outer edges of primaries and secondaries neutral gray; tertials chaetura black, broadly margined on outer webs with pallid neutral gray or grayish white; wing-coverts dull black, lesser coverts mostly like back, greater coverts narrowly edged with neutral gray on outer webs, and broadly tipped, as are median coverts, with white, forming two broad wing-bars;

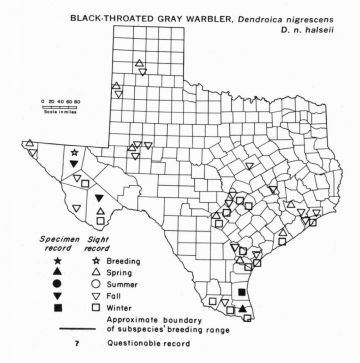

BLACK-THROATED GRAY WARBLER, *Dendroica nigrescens*
D. n. halseii

0 20 40 60 80
Scale in miles

Specimen   Sight
record   record

★   ☆ Breeding
▲   △ Spring
●   ○ Summer
▼   ▽ Fall
■   □ Winter

—— Approximate boundary of subspecies' breeding range

?   Questionable record

sides of head black, but small spot on black lores lemon chrome to orange, broad postocular stripe and broad malar stripe extending to sides of neck white; chin, throat, and jugulum black; remainder of lower surface, including lining of wing, white, sides and flanks broadly streaked with black. Bill black; iris dark sepia; legs and feet black or brownish black, but soles of toes yellow. *Adult male, winter*: Acquired by complete postnuptial molt. Similar to nuptial adult male, but black of crown, and particularly on occiput, somewhat obscured by dull brown or dull gray tips of feathers; remainder of upper surface more or less washed with brown, black streaks of nuptial plumage much or entirely obscured; black of sides of head somewhat obscured by small dark gray tips of feathers; margins of feathers on throat narrowly dull gray or dull white, black streaks on sides and flanks less sharply defined and more or less obscured by whitish tips of feathers. Bill dark brown. *Adult female, nuptial*: Acquired by wear from winter. More or less similar to nuptial adult male, but upper parts duller and more brownish, between mouse gray and neutral gray, back and upper tail-coverts very narrowly or not at all streaked with dull black, black of pileum much streaked with gray; wings and tail more brownish, white wing-bars narrower, inner margins of primaries and secondaries light drab gray or pale dull vinaceous fawn instead of white, these edgings much narrower; yellow spot on lores usually paler—lemon yellow or lemon chrome; chin white; throat largely white, streaked or spotted with dull black; large dull black spot on each side of jugulum; occasionally entire middle of throat and jugulum solid black with some dull white or pale grayish tips of feathers; remainder of lower surface grayish or buffy white; sides and flanks streaked with black or chaetura drab; lining of wing dull white, outer portion mottled with hair brown. Bill black, but base of mandible slightly tinged with lilaceous. *Adult female, winter*: Acquired by complete postnuptial molt. Similar to nuptial adult female, but upper parts darker and more uniform—hair brown to rufescent hair brown, black of pileum almost completely obscured by gray tips of feathers, blackish streaks on back practically covered by brownish tips of feathers; sides of head duller, more grayish, due to edgings of feathers; black of anterior lower parts much obscured by whitish or buffy tips of feathers, as are streaks on sides and flanks; posterior lower surface more strongly washed with buff, particularly on sides and flanks. *Male, first nuptial*: Acquired by wear from first winter. Similar to nuptial adult male, but wings and tail somewhat more brownish. *Male, first winter*: Acquired by partial postjuvenal molt. Similar to adult male in winter, but upper surface much more washed with brown, black of pileum more obscured by this color, center of pileum mostly like back, blackish streaks on back and upper tail-coverts nearly or entirely concealed; wings somewhat more brownish, inner margins of primaries and secondaries light drab gray or pale dull vinaceous fawn instead of white, these edgings much narrower; chin white; black of throat very much obscured by dull white tips and edgings of feathers; sides and flanks more tinged with buff. *Female, first nuptial*: Acquired by wear from first winter. Similar to nuptial adult male, but wings and tail somewhat more brownish. *Female, first winter*: Acquired by partial postjuvenal molt. Similar to adult female in winter, but upper surface more distinctly brownish—between hair brown and buffy brown; wings and tail somewhat more brownish. *Juvenal*: Acquired by complete postnatal molt. Upper parts between hair brown and buffy brown; pileum somewhat darker; rump a little paler; wings and tail as in first winter female; broad postocular stripe dull white; lower parts dull gray; abdomen dull white; breast lightly streaked with dull brown. *Natal*: Drab gray to pale drab gray.

MEASUREMENTS: *Adult male*: Wing, 63.0–69.1 (average, 65.3) mm.; tail, 50.8–55.1 (53.6); bill (exposed culmen), 9.1–10.2 (9.7); tarsus, 16.8–18.5 (17.8); middle toe without claw, 9.1–9.9 (9.7); white on inner web of second outer tail feather, 33.0–52.1 (38.9). *Adult female*: Wing, 59.9–63.8 (61.5); tail, 49.0–52.1 (50.3); bill, 8.4–9.9 (9.1); tarsus, 17.0–19.0 (17.8); middle toe, 8.6–9.4 (9.1); white on inner web, 32.0–36.1 (34.3).

RANGE: N. Oregon to c. Colorado, south to n. Baja California and n. Trans-Pecos Texas. Winters from s. Arizona and s. Texas to s. Baja California and Oaxaca.

TEXAS: *Breeding*: No specimen, but apparent juvenal observed in Culberson Co. was probably of this subspecies (see species account). *Migration*: Three specimens: Culberson Co., Pine Springs Canyon (Oct. 8, 1938, T. D. Burleigh); Brewster Co., Pine Canyon (Sept. 2, 7, 1936, T. F. Smith).

NESTING: *Nest*: On slopes or mesas; in open woodlands or denser tree growths, thickets of alders and willows along streams, manzanita chaparral, in pines of forests, sometimes in thickets of oaks, ordinarily on dry land, 4–50 ft. above ground; very well built, well-cupped nest; composed of fine grasses, weed stalks, soft moss, sometimes trash, feathers, and spiders' egg cases; lined with hair of horse, rabbit, cow, or other mammals, fur, or stems of moss flowers. *Eggs*: 3–5, usually 4; ovate to short ovate; white, cream white, or greenish white; spotted with cinnamon rufous, reddish brown, umber, and black, chiefly about large end, where markings are confluent, also with shell markings of pale lavender and lilac gray; average size, 17.5 × 13.2 mm.

TOWNSEND'S WARBLER, *Dendroica townsendi* (Townsend)

SPECIES ACCOUNT

Nuptial male: black crown, cheeks, throat, side-streaks; yellow facial stripes, breast; olive green upper parts; white wing-bars. *Female, fall male*: duller; dark olive green crown, cheeks; yellow throat. Length, 5 in.; wingspan, 8.

RANGE: S. Alaska and s. Yukon, south to c. Oregon and n.w. Wyoming. Winters chiefly in coastal and s. California, and from Sinaloa and Nuevo León to Nicaragua.

TEXAS: (See map.) *Migration*: Late Apr. to mid-May; late Aug. to early Oct. (extremes: Mar., May 31;

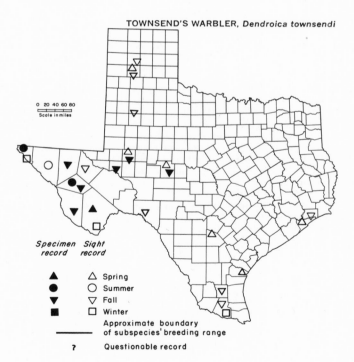

TOWNSEND'S WARBLER, *Dendroica townsendi*

0 20 40 60 80
Scale in miles

Specimen record
Sight record

▲ △ Spring
● ○ Summer
▼ ▽ Fall
■ □ Winter

—— Approximate boundary of subspecies' breeding range

? Questionable record

July 31, Nov. 25). Common (some years) to fairly common in Trans-Pecos; uncommon to scarce in remainder of state west of 100th meridian; extremely rare east of 100th meridian (all sightings south of 30th parallel). *Winter*: Dec. to Feb. No specimen, but apparently regular (a few) in Chisos Mts., Big Bend Nat. Park; sightings from El Paso and Rio Grande delta.

HAUNTS AND HABITS: In summer the Townsend's Warbler is a bird of cool evergreen forests where it nests chiefly in firs growing on mountains, in valleys, and along canyons. During migration through Texas, it occurs not only in the conifers of Trans-Pecos mountains, but in canyons sprinkled with madrones (*Arbutus texana*), on oak-covered slopes and ridges, in streamside vegetation, and even on open brushy deserts and scrubby coastal plains. Though it sometimes travels in small companies, occasionally associated with other warblers, it most often occurs singly or in pairs.

The Townsend's has a quick, if more or less irregular, flight. It frequents tops of tall conifers, where it moves about nervously, seeking insects along branches; at times it descends to the lower parts and even into smaller trees, undergrowth, and thickets. It feeds almost entirely on animal matter, principally insects. Stink-bugs, scales and leaf-hoppers, wasps, ants, and weevils (including engraver beetles) comprise the major portion of the diet; the remainder consists of caterpillars and a small number of spiders, and scarcely 5 percent vegetable matter consisting of seeds and leaf galls.

Usual call note of the Townsend's is a rather high *tseep*. Its song is a brief *zee, zee, zee, slee-slick* or *zee, zee, ziddy, zee*. It is somewhat similar to the song of the Black-throated Gray Warbler.

DETAILED ACCOUNT: NO SUBSPECIES

DESCRIPTION: *Adult male, nuptial plumage*: Acquired by partial prenuptial molt. Pileum and hindneck black, but feathers of hindneck more or less edged with yellowish warbler green; longest upper tail-coverts mouse gray with broad shaft markings of dull black; remainder of upper surface yellowish warbler green, verging on rump and anterior upper tail-coverts toward pyrite yellow, all broadly streaked or spotted with dull black or chaetura black; tail chaetura black, middle feathers edged externally with mouse gray, outer three rectrices on each side with terminal portions largely white—on outermost feather this white occupying all but basal portion of inner web and terminal shaft portion of both webs, on second pair occupying nearly as much, but on third feather confined to long terminal spot on inner web; primaries and secondaries chaetura drab, but margined narrowly on outer webs with grayish olive, on inner webs with dull brownish white or pale brown, except on tips of primaries; tertials chaetura black, edged with grayish olive; wing-coverts dull black, lesser coverts edged with warbler green, outer greater coverts with grayish olive, tips of outer greater coverts and tips of median coverts broadly white, forming two conspicuous wing-bars; broad superciliary stripe, long spot underneath eye, and broad submalar stripe which extends on sides of head and meets superciliary stripe behind black auricular lemon chrome or toward light cadmium; remainder of sides of head black; sides of posterior portion of neck like back; chin, throat, and jugulum black; breast lemon chrome or between lemon chrome and light cadmium; rest of lower surface white or buffy white, but sides of breast and of abdomen, as well as flanks, broadly streaked with black; lining of wing white. Bill black or brownish black; iris dark brown or black; legs and feet dull brown, black, or olivaceous black, but soles of toes yellow. *Adult male, winter*: Acquired by complete postnuptial molt. Similar to nuptial adult male, but black of pileum much obscured by warbler green edges of feathers, black markings of rest of upper surface more or less concealed by olive green tips of feathers; black on sides of head slightly obscured by olive green tips of feathers; black throat much tipped with lemon yellow or yellowish white; black streaks of sides and flanks somewhat obscured by light tips of feathers. *Adult female, nuptial*: Acquired by partial prenuptial molt. Similar to nuptial adult male but smaller; pileum everywhere broadly streaked with warbler green; remainder of upper parts duller with inconspicuous, sometimes obsolete, blackish markings; wings and tail more brownish, white wing-bars somewhat narrower; sides of head deep olive instead of black; yellow of anterior lower parts duller; throat and jugulum yellow with small irregular black blotch on each side of jugulum, center of jugulum frequently with more or less concealed black markings; streaks on sides and flanks much narrower and obscure; flanks washed with buff. *Adult female, winter*: Acquired by complete postnuptial molt. Similar to nuptial adult female, but upper parts more uniform, crown and back with few or no visible blackish streaks; general color of upper parts more brownish or yellowish (less greenish)—between citrine and orange citrine; ear-coverts paler, more brownish—brownish olive; yellow of lower parts duller—gamboge yellow, blackish markings of anterior portion much duller and obscured by tips of feathers; sides and flanks washed with dull brownish buff, and streaks less well defined. *Male, first nuptial*: Acquired by partial prenuptial molt. Similar to nuptial adult male, but posterior part of pileum more mixed with olive green; throat duller, somewhat mixed with yellow; chin more extensively yellow; black of throat also duller. *Male, first winter*: Acquired by partial postjuvenal molt. Similar to adult male in winter, but black of pileum almost entirely obscured by olive green of upper surface, thus reduced to narrow streaks or spots; black markings of back and rump almost entirely concealed by tips of feathers; olive green of upper surface somewhat more brownish; yellow of sides of head and under parts paler and duller; lores and cheeks, including auriculars, deep olive or brownish olive; anterior lower parts yellow with few black markings on throat; streaks on sides and flanks narrower and duller. Similar to adult female in winter but larger, pileum noticeably streaked with black, and remainder of upper parts usually with a few black streaks or spots; white wing-bars broader; sides of head darker; more blackish markings on anterior lower surface; streaks on sides of body darker and broader. *Female, first nuptial*: Acquired by partial prenuptial molt. Very similar to nuptial adult female. *Female, first winter*: Acquired by partial postjuvenal molt. Similar to adult female in winter, but upper parts somewhat darker; yellow of anterior lower parts and of sides of head paler, with fewer and much more obscure dark markings; sides and flanks more strongly tinged with light brown or buff. *Juvenal*: Acquired by complete postnatal molt. Pileum between hair brown and light brownish olive; wings and tail light chaetura drab, light markings similar to first winter female; broad superciliary stripe dull cartridge buff; cheeks between hair brown and deep grayish olive; submalar stripe dull colonial buff; chin, throat, sides, and flanks dull light drab; remainder of lower surface yellowish white or buffy white; posterior lower parts, except middle of abdomen, obscurely streaked with mouse gray or deep mouse gray.

MEASUREMENTS: *Adult male*: Wing, 65.0–69.1 (average, 67.3) mm.; tail, 48.0–52.1 (50.0); bill (exposed culmen), 8.1–9.9 (9.1); tarsus, 18.0–19.0 (18.8); middle toe without claw, 9.9–11.9 (10.9). *Adult female*: Wing, 63.0–66.0 (64.5); tail, 47.0–52.6 (49.3); bill, 8.1–9.9 (9.1); tarsus, 18.0–19.0 (18.8); middle toe, 8.9–10.9 (9.9).

TEXAS: *Migration*: Collected northwest to El Paso (Aug. 24), east to Midland and Tom Green, south to Brewster and Presidio cos.

BLACK-THROATED GREEN WARBLER,
Dendroica virens (Gmelin)

SPECIES ACCOUNT

Nuptial male: olive green upper parts; yellow cheeks; deep olive streak through eye; black throat, upper breast, side-streaks; whitish under parts, often washed with yellow; white wing-bars, outer tail feathers. *Female, fall male*: duller; black much reduced and mixed with yellowish. Length, 5 in.; wingspan, 7¾; weight, ¼ oz.

RANGE: S. Mackenzie to Newfoundland, south to Great Lakes region and n. New Jersey, and in Appalachians to Alabama and Georgia; also on Atlantic coastal plain south to South Carolina. Winters chiefly from extreme s. Texas (irregularly) through e. and s. Mexico to Panama; also s. Florida, West Indies.

TEXAS: (See map.) *Migration*: Late Mar. to mid-May; early Sept. to early Nov. (extremes: Mar. 11, June 8; July 8, Dec. 18). Common (most springs) to uncommon in eastern two-thirds; scarce in northern Panhandle, Midland Co., and Del Rio region; extremely rare west of Pecos River. *Winter*: Late Dec. to late Mar. Fairly common (some years) to scarce in Rio Grande delta; rare on eastern edge of Edwards Plateau and along coast.

HAUNTS AND HABITS: In its summer home the Black-throated Green Warbler frequents a diversity of habitats, including cool coniferous forests, northern hardwoods, other deciduous as well as mixed woodlands, and baldcypress swamps. Favorite nest tree is a conifer. During migration through Texas, it occurs in various types of woods in both uplands and bottoms, their

thickets and undergrowth, riparian associations, thorn and other brush, coastal scrub, and parks, cemeteries, and yards of towns and cities. It often associates with other migrating warblers.

When flying from one tree to another, even when the distance is considerable, the Black-throated Green is jerky, swift, and erratic. It remains much of the time in upper parts of trees, particularly in summer, where it gleans insects not only from the interior branches but also from terminal foliage, as it forages industriously. It descends often, however, to lower parts of trees and to smaller trees and bushes—especially in the non-breeding season, but it rarely goes to the ground, except for bathing, drinking, or gathering nest material. Although usually active and somewhat restless, it does not seem to be particularly shy. Food consists largely of insects (moths, clouded sulphur and other butterflies, leaf-rollers, cankerworms, measuringworms, Hymenopterans, curculios and other beetles, gall flies, gnats, other two-winged flies, locusts, and plant lice), but includes some spiders and mites. It also eats berries of juniper and poison-ivy.

The call note of the Black-throated Green is a rather loud *tsip*. Its usual song sounds much like *zee, zee, zu, zee*, sometimes expanded into seven notes, the next to the last usually on a lower pitch. This deliberate, somewhat prolonged performance has many variations, but is usually identifiable by these characteristics. The bird is a persistent singer and often utters an incredible number of songs within a short period: up to 466 repetitions have been counted in a single hour! Normally males sing from their arrival in March throughout May, after which time most have completed their northern passage through Texas.

DETAILED ACCOUNT: TWO SUBSPECIES

NORTHERN BLACK-THROATED GREEN WARBLER,
Dendroica virens virens (Gmelin)

DESCRIPTION: *Adult male, nuptial plumage*: Acquired mostly by wear and by limited prenuptial molt. Upper surface olive green, dark warbler green to yellowish warbler green—forehead lemon chrome mixed with olive green, back and rump usually with a few small blackish spots or streaks; upper tail-coverts mouse gray with shaft streaks of fuscous or chaetura black; tail chaetura black, middle feathers basally edged on outer webs with mouse gray, outer two tail feathers white, except for shaft and terminal portion of outer web and small oblong terminal part of inner web; third feather similar except dark base of inner web; fourth feather with only terminal oblique white spot on inner web; primaries and secondaries chaetura drab, outer margins of primaries and secondaries narrowly mouse gray, inner margins of primaries and secondaries, except at tips, brownish white or pale brown; tertials chaetura black, edged on outer webs with mouse gray; wing-coverts chaetura black, margins of lesser coverts grayish olive or dull grayish olive green, as are outer margins of greater coverts; median and greater coverts broadly tipped with white, forming two conspicuous wing-bars; sides of head and anterior part of sides of neck, lemon chrome to gamboge yellow, lores and postocular streak deep olive, region below eye somewhat washed with olive; posterior sides of neck like back; chin, throat, and jugulum black; remainder of lower surface dull white, yellowish white, or buffy white, but

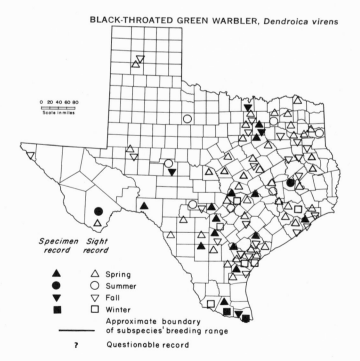

BLACK-THROATED GREEN WARBLER, *Dendroica virens*

0 20 40 60 80
Scale in miles

Specimen record / Sight record

▲ △ Spring
● ○ Summer
▼ ▽ Fall
■ □ Winter

—— Approximate boundary of subspecies' breeding range

? Questionable record

breast often much washed with lemon yellow, sides and flanks broadly streaked with black; lining of wing white, sometimes a few hair brown or mouse gray spots on outer portion. Bill black; iris very dark brown; legs and feet black, greenish black, olive brown, or clove brown; soles of toes greenish yellow or olive. *Adult male, winter*: Acquired by complete postnuptial molt. Similar to nuptial adult male, but forehead somewhat more uniformly olive green; back more uniform, mostly obscuring black markings; black of lower surface—tips of feathers anteriorly and tips and margins of feathers on sides and flanks—veiled with yellowish or grayish white, warbler green, or pale yellow. *Adult female, nuptial*: Acquired mostly by wear and limited prenuptial molt from winter. Similar to adult male in winter, but forehead more yellow; upper surface duller, thus somewhat less yellowish (more grayish); wings and tail lighter, more brownish, white wing-bars narrower; white areas of tail less extensive; chin and throat wax yellow or primuline yellow; jugulum dull black, feathers tipped with white, pale gray, or pale yellow, sometimes much obscuring black; streaks on sides and flanks narrower, chaetura drab or dull black. *Adult female, winter*: Acquired by complete postnuptial molt. Similar to nuptial adult female, but upper parts more uniform; yellow of forehead overlaid with warbler green; lower parts brighter, more yellowish or brownish; less black on jugulum and upper breast, this much more overlaid with pale dull yellowish or grayish tips of feathers; black streaks on sides and flanks more obscured, as is yellow of chin and of throat; sides of head duller, more brownish. *Male, first nuptial*: Acquired by partial prenuptial molt. Similar to nuptial adult male, but wing-quills and tail somewhat more brownish, edgings duller. *Male, first winter*: Acquired by partial postjuvenal molt, which does not involve wing-quills or tail. Similar to adult female in winter but larger, upper parts lighter, brighter, more yellowish; anterior lower parts usually with more black, partly overlaid by light tips of feathers; throat usually with more yellow. *Female, first nuptial*: Acquired by partial prenuptial molt. Similar to nuptial adult female, but wing-quills and tail somewhat more brownish. *Female, first winter*: Acquired by partial postjuvenal molt. Similar to adult female in winter, but upper parts averaging rather duller; sides of head somewhat duller, yellow rather less extensive; anterior lower parts with little or no black and with little or no pronounced yellow, but mostly dull colonial buff to dull yellowish white or dull dark olive buff; blackish streaks on sides and flanks duller and less conspicuous. *Juvenal*: Acquired by postnatal molt. Upper surface dull grayish brown, feathers of back edged with olive green; sides of head dull slate color; superciliary stripe brownish white; lower surface dull white spotted or streaked with slate or dull black. Bill, legs, and feet dull light brown; iris dark brown.

MEASUREMENTS: *Adult male*: Wing, 61.5–66.0 (average, 63.8) mm.; tail, 46.5–50.5 (48.8); bill (exposed culmen), 9.0–10.5 (9.5); tarsus, 16.5–18.8 (17.8); middle toe without claw, 9.4–10.4 (10.2). *Adult female*: Wing, 56.9–62.0 (59.2); tail, 44.4–49.5 (47.0); bill, 8.9–9.7 (9.1); tarsus, 16.8–18.5 (17.8); middle toe, 9.4–10.9 (9.7).

RANGE: S. Mackenzie to Newfoundland, south to s. Minnesota, w. Virginia, and Connecticut. Winters from s. Texas through Mexico and Central America to n. Colombia (casually); also West Indies.

TEXAS: *Migration*: Collected north to Cooke, east to Galveston, south to Cameron, west to Brewster (probably this race, Aug. 8, 1969, R. H. Wauer) cos. Common. One summer specimen: Walker Co., Loma (June 25, 1936, W. P. Taylor). *Winter*: Taken in Hidalgo (1 specimen) and Cameron (3) cos. Uncommon.

WAYNE'S BLACK-THROATED GREEN WARBLER,
Dendroica virens waynei Bangs

DESCRIPTION: *Adult male and female, nuptial plumage*: Like *D. v. virens*, but bill decidedly smaller, tail shorter, and otherwise slightly smaller.

MEASUREMENTS: *Adult male*: Wing, 61.0–65.0 (average, 62.5) mm.; tail, 45.0–47.0 (46.0); bill (exposed culmen), 8.1–8.9

(8.6); tarsus, 17.0–18.0 (17.5). *Adult female*: Wing, 57.9–61.0 (59.9); tail, 45.0–47.0 (46.0); bill, 8.1–8.6 (8.4); tarsus, 16.0–19.0 (17.8); middle toe, 8.9–10.9 (9.9).

RANGE: S.e. Kentucky to s.e. Virginia, south to c. Alabama and s.e. South Carolina. In migration, west to Texas. Winters from South Carolina and n.w. Florida to western Cuba.

TEXAS: *Migration*: One specimen: Galveston Co., Point Bolivar Lighthouse (Apr. 17, 1904, H. C. Claiborne).

GOLDEN-CHEEKED WARBLER, *Dendroica chrysoparia* Sclater and Salvin

SPECIES ACCOUNT   *See colorplate 25*

Male: yellow cheeks, strikingly outlined in black; resembles Black-throated Green, but upper parts black; prominent black line through eye; lower breast and belly pure white (not tinged with yellow). *Female*: duller; black-streaked olive green above; yellowish throat, usually speckled with black; blackish upper breast. Length, 5¼ in.; wingspan, 7¾.

RANGE: C. Texas, along more broken parts of Edwards Plateau and outlying hills from Palo Pinto and Dallas (rare), south to Bosque, McLennan (formerly), Coryell, Lampasas, Burnet, Williamson, Travis, Hays, Comal, and Bexar, west to Medina, Uvalde, Kinney, Edwards, and Kimble cos. Migrates chiefly via Edwards Plateau and Sierra Madre Oriental. Winters in highlands from c. Mexico (possibly) through Guatemala to Honduras and Nicaragua.

TEXAS: (See map.) *Breeding*: Mid-Mar. to mid-July (eggs, Mar. 10 to June 27) from 600 to about 1,700 ft. Locally common to fairly common on southeastern Edwards Plateau; uncommon and increasingly disjunct north of Austin along hilly outcroppings to Palo Pinto

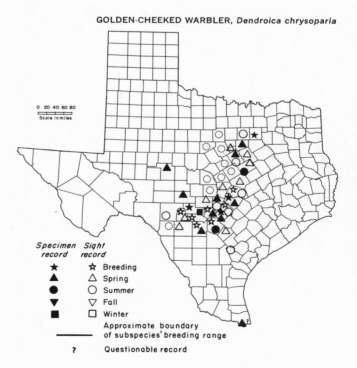

GOLDEN-CHEEKED WARBLER, *Dendroica chrysoparia*

0 20 40 60 80
Scale in miles

Specimen   Sight
record   record

★   ☆ Breeding
▲   △ Spring
●   ○ Summer
▼   ▽ Fall
■   □ Winter

——— Approximate boundary
of subspecies' breeding range

?   Questionable record

and Somervell cos.; rare and extremely local in southwestern Dallas Co. *Migration*: Mid-Mar.—early Mar. some years—to mid-Apr.; early July to early Aug. (extremes: Feb. 15, May 13; July 1, Aug. 28). Locally common to uncommon through breeding range, though rare on northeastern extremity; scarce beyond breeding range to Tom Green, Tarrant, Bastrop, Wilson, and Atascosa cos.; very casual at Beeville and Brownsville. Unconfirmed sightings at Big Bend Nat. Park, Welder Wildlife Refuge (San Patricio Co.), and Rockport (Aransas Co.). *Winter*: Two specimens: Kerr Co., Camp Verde (both taken on Jan. 20, 1902, M. Cary).

HAUNTS AND HABITS: The beautiful Golden-cheeked Warbler has the distinction of being the only generally recognized full species of bird whose nesting range is entirely confined within Texas. During the first three weeks in March, adult males—followed one day to a week later by the females—arrive from Central American wintering mountains to stake out their song-proclaimed breeding territories in the canyons and slopes of the Edwards Plateau region. Nesting habitat consists of mature mountain (post) cedar (*Juniperus ashei*) and Spanish oak (*Quercus texana*) growing on broken terrain. While the Goldencheek forages much among the leaves and twigs of these two small (10–40 ft.) trees, it also hunts insects in other woody vegetation. In stream canyons, the bird flits about cedar elm (*Ulmus crassifolia*), escarpment blackcherry (*Prunus serotina eximia*), live oak (*Quercus virginiana*), walnuts (*Juglans*), pecan (*Carya illinoensis*), Carolina basswood (*Tilia caroliniana*), and other species. Such a wooded canyon with rocky sides covered with cedar, small oaks, Texas ash (*Fraxinus texensis*), sumacs (*Rhus*), Texas mountainlaurel (*Sophora secundiflora*), and rock redbud (*Cercis canadensis texensis*) is prime Goldencheek country. In the upper Sabinal River canyon (Bandera Co.), this warbler also gleans caterpillars from the area's special maple (*Acer grandidentatum sinuosum*).

Roy W. Quillin observed nesting of *Dendroica chrysoparia* at the J. P. Classen Ranch, eighteen miles north of San Antonio: "I have examined about twenty-five or thirty nests, occupied and old, and only three of them have been in cedars, and those cedars were in creek beds. With the exception of one nest, all were in trees either in the dry creek beds or the narrow flats bordering them. The other nest was about a quarter of a mile from a creek on an open flat. I have never seen a nest, either here or in the Frio Canyon [Real Co.] on the dry hot hill tops. I hunted the hill tops for years but never found a nest there. The males sing there but their mates are below them.

"On April 18, 1937, I found a nest with four eggs, twelve feet up in a slender bushy elm. On May 1, 1938, I saw a male feeding two grown young with caterpillars from one to two inches long; the larger ones he crammed down as far as he could reach into the mouths of the young birds, then he gathered up the loose ends and tucked them inside.

"The nests are well hidden, as the birds are very clever in selecting sites which are screened by tufts of leaves and masses of twigs. I use a mirror but even with this it is difficult to see into any nest on account of the protecting leaves and twigs. Nests are partly made of the naturally curved gray strips of bark from old cedars. These form the outer part and the rim; under this there are fine strips of any kind of cedar bark intermixed with fine grass or bits of weeds. The rim is constricted, being about a quarter of an inch smaller than the bottom of the cup. All nests are heavily lined with feathers (Gray-tailed Cardinal feathers usually) and some horsehair. Most of the nests are well made, heavy-walled, and compact. The females are very tame when flushed and while the nests are being examined usually come within two or three feet of one. They frequently spread the wings and tail, much like an American Redstart, and utter a drawn-out zissing sound which can evidently be heard at a distance as the male responds very quickly and joins in the protest. He is an extremely shy bird which dives for cover the instant he realizes that he is being-watched."

The female Golden-cheeked Warbler builds the nest and performs the duty of incubation and brooding; the male probably feeds her on the nest. Eggs hatch in twelve days; young leave the nest in eight or nine (W. M. Pulich). Nesting sometimes occurs in the same tree for two or more years in succession. The female is extremely quick and agile. In returning to her duty of incubation, she dashes through the foliage with scarcely a reduction in her great speed until she is actually on the nest; in leaving, she often flies with the same quick, almost unfollowable, dash. When the young are hatched, both male and female assist in their feeding. A pair raises only one brood—either its own or cowbirds—per year.

Should the nest contain fresh eggs, the parents do not betray its location by their actions, and even when the male is singing in the vicinity, the female does not appear at all. If a nest containing young is endangered, both parents utter their alarm notes close at hand, sometimes becoming very demonstrative. The female will even pretend to be injured and flutter down a limb to the ground. On his ranch in Kerr County, Howard Lacey watched a Goldencheek drive a Brownheaded Cowbird away from its nest on May 27, 1918. Other pairs are not so fortunate in protecting their broods from cowbird parasitism.

Grown young, which more or less keep together, wander about hillsides and canyons, still, to a certain extent, being fed by the adults. This continues until the birds are thoroughly able to take care of themselves. Then, perhaps early in July, these groups break up and the birds become independent. Fall migration begins in July, and most birds are gone by the last week of this month; only a few linger into August. Thus, the canyon-haunting Golden-cheeked Warbler comes to the Edwards Plateau earlier and leaves earlier than the Black-capped Vireo of hilltop scrub.

Flight of *Dendroica chrysoparia*—the "golden-cheeked tree dweller"—is quick and jerky, usually not prolonged except, of course, during migration, which occurs mostly at night. It is an active bird, flying much from branch to branch in its search for insects. In spring it gleans many caterpillars which infest new leaves of oaks (*Quercus texana, Q. virginiana*, others). The bird pinches a caterpillar with its bill and then beats it against a branch until it is limp enough to swallow. Adults also feed their young on caterpillars. In addition, H. P. Attwater found small black plant lice (*Aphis*) in the stomachs of young birds. Ants and thread-legged bugs are also consumed, chiefly by adults. The Goldencheek sometimes dashes into the air in the manner of a Myrtle Warbler to snap up flies, small moths, and other winged insects. A captive kept by Warren M. Pulich ate up to twenty bagworms per day; it also drank water.

As it forages in its territory, an adult Goldencheek frequently utters its *chip* or *tick* notes. While gleaning, and also from a treetop song perch, the male gives out its buzzy song. Some interpretations are *wee-che-wee, che-wee-che* (H. P. Attwater); *tsrr weasy-weasy tweah* (W. H. Werner); a buzzy *tweah-tweah-twee-sy* (W. M. Pulich); and *buzzz, layzee, dayzee* (various listeners). Often a *chip* introduces a song, and *tick*'s between songs are frequent. Sometimes, a male will follow its regular song with a short series of rattles (suggestive of those of a Field Sparrow, or even an Olive Sparrow). At a distance, the song of *D. chrysoparia* can sound like that of a Bewick's Wren. In fact, many Texas Hill Country birders, straining to hear the first Goldencheek of spring, have been fooled, at least momentarily, by the resident wren. The Golden-cheeked Warbler has a short season. The bird is in song when it arrives in March, but singing starts dwindling in mid-May and has virtually ceased by the end of June; young males of the year sometimes contribute to the sparse June singing.

CHANGES: Within the historic period, nesting range of the Golden-cheeked Warbler has always been very small for a continental species—approximately 200 miles north-south by 200 miles west-east, as late as the early 1930's. In contrast, the Black-throated Green Warbler, apparently the Goldencheek's closest relative, enjoys a breeding range of roughly 1,000 miles by 1,000 miles.

So many *Juniperus ashei* trees have died (as a result of the drought of 1950–1957) or been eradicated on the western and central parts of the Edwards Plateau that *Dendroica chrysoparia* breeding range has shrunk to something like a wedge shape, with the southern base about 150 miles wide and the northern apex perhaps 50 miles across. Even within this tiny range the bird is extremely localized.

Chief force pushing the Goldencheek to extinction is the U.S. Soil Conservation Service—termed "U.S. soil erosion service" by friends of the warbler. Since 1933, branches of this "service," each with the official name of Agricultural Stabilization and Conservation– County Committee, have operated in every one of Texas' 254 counties. The ASCCC subsidizes ranchers to clear cedar, oak, and other woody vegetation by means of axe, bulldozer, rootplow, and herbicide. In addition, fire—subsidized or not—often breaks out in cedar brakes. Theoretically, this clearance allows livestock-nourishing grasses to grow, but in actual practice it mostly turns the 24,000,000-acre Edwards Plateau into piles of bare rock. In 1948, after fifteen years of brush eradication, there were still about 19,000,000 acres in cedar. By 1962 this juniper acreage was down to less than 10,000,000. At that time, Warren M. Pulich, chief Goldencheek researcher of recent years, estimated that there were approximately 15,000 of these birds left in the world. From 1962 through 1972, destruction of habitat has continued at the rate of 5,000 to 10,000 acres per county per year.

In addition, numerous dams built on the Colorado and other Edwards Plateau rivers since 1930 have resulted in the drowning of many square miles of habitat and the attraction of hordes of recreation-seeking people.

Nowadays (1972), there are no large tracts of Goldencheek nesting habitat left—only bits and pieces. These scraps are mostly near cities—Dallas, Waco, Austin, and San Antonio—where the land is being held at astronomical prices for housing developments. When houses are built, not only is habitat destroyed, but also many home owners proceed to install dooryard bird feeders. This practice attracts and maintains a huge population of Brown-headed Cowbirds, which, in turn, lay their eggs in the nests of various songbirds. This heavy parasitism has had considerable effect on the breeding success of the Goldencheek, although, as yet, the warbler has not suffered as much as the Black-capped Vireo.

There are many noble plans, and even negotiations, for saving some cedar-oak, but so far (1972) only one sanctuary specifically for Goldencheeks has been set aside. This is the Travis Audubon Society's 94-acre plot in western Travis County; as of March 31, 1973, Travis Audubon was in the midst of a vigorous effort to increase its Goldencheek sanctuary to 620 acres. A few state parks, maintained by Texas Parks and Wildlife Department, contain some Goldencheek habitat. These are Dinosaur Valley (Somervell Co.), 1,221 acres; Meridian (Bosque Co.), 461 acres; Mother Neff (Coryell Co.), 259 acres; Pedernales Falls (Blanco Co.), 4,860 acres; and Garner (n. Uvalde Co.), 630 acres. In April, 1973, Texas Parks and Wildlife had completed purchase of about 1,200 acres of juniper-maple habitat for a state park in Sabinal Canyon (Bandera Co.). In addition, Texas Parks and Wildlife owns the Kerr Wildlife Management Area (Kerr Co.), 6,493 acres. However, *Juniperus-Quercus* acreage in the reserves just named is probably not enough to save Texas' special *Dendroica* from extinction.

One practice prevalent in Texas does tend to prolong the life of the species. This is the hunting-lease system, whereby owners of large ranches derive substantial income from leasing their land to hunters. Most of these land owners have never heard of the Golden-cheeked

Warbler, but some of them are beginning to realize that oaks and cedar brakes shelter and provide food for valuable big game animals—chiefly White-tailed Deer and Wild Turkey. Both mammal and bird habitually eat acorns and cedar "berries." Landowners who eradicate all cedar-oak from their pastures generally get less income from hunters. Money talks. Another lesser economic reason, at least formerly, for conserving some cedar was that it was valued for posts in fence building.

In the final analysis, many more people are working to exterminate *Juniperus ashei* than to conserve it. Besides those people trying to grow grass for cattle or sheep, there are a surprising number of persons who are allergic to *J. ashei* pollen, which blows about the central Texas landscape in winter and early spring. *Dendroica chrysoparia* and its cedar brakes are unlikely to reach the twenty-first century alive, but then, who is?

DETAILED ACCOUNT: NO SUBSPECIES

DESCRIPTION: *Adult male, nuptial plumage*: Acquired probably by wear from winter plumage. Upper surface black, but rump more or less mixed with mouse gray; center of forehead and anterior part of crown with short median stripe of lemon chrome; tail chaetura black, basal portion of middle feathers edged externally with mouse gray, the outermost feathers nearly all white except for the dark shaft and long guttate spot along shaft involving all outer web and part of inner, the second feather from outer side similar but with less black terminally, the base of third feather black with base of inner web and entire outer web black and same guttate spot along terminal portion of shaft, the fourth feather with oblique terminal spot on inner web not reaching shaft, and the next pair of feathers only slightly edged with white subterminally on inner webs; wing-quills chaetura drab to chaetura black, outer webs edged with mouse gray, inner webs of secondaries broadly white on inner margins, basal portions of primaries edged with brownish white on inner webs; wing-coverts black, median and greater series broadly tipped with white, forming two conspicuous wing-bars, that on median coverts broader; superciliary stripe cadmium yellow, paling posteriorly to gamboge yellow or warm lemon chrome; anterior part of lores yellow mixed with dull white; posterior part of lores next to eye, together with postocular streak, dull black; remainder of cheeks and anterior sides of neck gamboge yellow or warm lemon chrome; remainder of sides of neck, with chin, throat, jugulum, and sides of breast, black, the latter sometimes more or less mixed with dull white; remainder of lower surface, including lining of wing, white, but sides and flanks broadly streaked with black, as are lower tail-coverts usually. Bill, legs, and feet brownish black; iris dark brown. *Adult male, winter*: Acquired by complete postnuptial molt. Similar to nuptial adult male, but black feathers of throat and jugulum narrowly margined with dull white or pale yellow. *Adult female, nuptial*: Acquired by wear from winter. Upper parts yellowish olive green or warbler green, but scapulars deep mouse gray, pileum, hindneck, back, and upper tail-coverts numerously streaked with black, dull black, fuscous black, or olive, these broadest on back and upper tail-coverts; tail chaetura black, middle feathers basally margined exteriorly with mouse gray; white markings on outer three tail feathers similar to those in male, but rather less extensive; wings dark hair brown or light fuscous, lesser and median wing-coverts deep mouse gray, greater wing-coverts chaetura black, both median and greater series broadly tipped with white; sides of head, including superciliary stripe, lemon chrome; posterior part of lores and narrow postocular stripe chaetura drab or chaetura black; remainder of sides of head lemon chrome; center of throat anteriorly dull lemon

chrome or lemon yellow, mixed with buffy white and dull black; rest of throat dull pale buff or dull pale yellow, more or less mixed with black; jugulum black, overlaid by grayish white or buffy white tips of feathers; sides of breast and of body, with flanks, broadly streaked with black, which becomes chaetura drab on flanks; remainder of lower surface white; lining of wing dull white, outer portion more or less finely mottled with hair brown or chaetura drab. *Adult female, winter*: Acquired by complete postnuptial molt. Similar to nuptial adult female but upper surface brighter, almost uniform warbler green, black of sides of breast more veiled with dull white or gray edgings of feathers. *Male and female, third winter*: Like corresponding sex in adult winter. *Male and female, second nuptial*: Acquired by wear from second winter. Like corresponding sex in nuptial adult, but male not so solidly black on back. *Male and female, second winter*: Acquired by complete postnuptial molt. Like corresponding sex in adult winter. *Male, first nuptial*: Acquired probably by partial prenuptial molt. Similar to first winter male, but feathers of upper parts with fewer olive green edgings; sides of head rather brighter; chin, throat, and jugulum almost solidly black with few, if any, white, pale gray, or yellowish feather tips; black streaks on sides and flanks more sharply defined. *Male, first winter*: Acquired by partial postjuvenal molt. Similar to nuptial adult male, but upper parts mostly yellowish olive green or warbler green, broadly streaked or spotted with black; wings and tail much as in adult, but white wing-bars somewhat narrower; sides of head rather duller, postocular stripe and posterior part of lores not so deeply blackish; chin mostly buffy white or dull yellowish laterally, black of chin, throat, and jugulum much overlaid with dull white or pale dull yellow on tips of feathers; black streaks on sides and flanks much obscured by dull white or very pale gray edgings of feathers. Similar to nuptial adult female but smaller, with much broader black streaks above; throat much more extensively and solidly black. *Female, first nuptial*: Acquired by partial prenuptial molt. Similar to nuptial adult female but somewhat duller. *Female, first winter*: Acquired by partial postjuvenal molt. Similar to adult female in winter, but upper surface darker, duller, more brownish, or grayish (less yellowish)—yellowish olive or dark yellowish olive; yellow of sides of head duller, somewhat more brownish; center of throat mostly dull buff with faint wash of yellow on posterior part of chin; very little blackish on anterior lower parts, this overlaid by dull pale buff or grayish white; jugulum dull white or pale colonial buff; blackish streaks on sides and flanks narrower, duller, more brownish and more obscured. *Juvenal*: Acquired by complete postnatal molt. Upper surface light brownish olive, slightly mottled with darker olive; wings and tail chaetura drab to dark chaetura drab; lesser wing-coverts hair brown; white wing-bars washed with brown; sides of head dull light vinaceous buff; throat and breast between dull light drab and smoke gray; posterior lower parts dull buff or grayish white, obscurely streaked with dull drab or light hair brown. *Natal*: Rather light hair brown.

MEASUREMENTS: *Adult male*: Wing, 62.2–65.8 (average, 64.0) mm.; tail, 51.6–54.8 (53.3); bill (exposed culmen), 9.1–10.9 (9.9); tarsus, 17.0–18.8 (18.0); middle toe without claw, 10.2–11.2 (10.7). *Adult female*: Wing, 57.9–61.7 (60.2); tail, 47.8–52.3 (50.8); bill, 9.7–10.7 (9.9); tarsus, 17.8–18.8 (18.3); middle toe, 10.2–10.9 (10.4).

TEXAS: *Breeding*: Collected northeast to Dallas, south to Bosque, McLennan (formerly), Travis, Bexar, and Medina, west to Kerr and Kimble cos. *Migration*: Collected northwest to Tom Green, east to Travis, south to Bexar cos. One specimen considerably outside breeding range: Cameron Co., Brownsville (Mar. 26, 1894, F. B. Armstrong). *Winter*: Two specimens (see species account).

NESTING: *Nest*: On slopes and in canyons in broken country; in cedar (juniper) or other small tree; in forks or on horizontal branches, 5–30 ft. above ground; neat compact cup, composed chiefly of strips of inner bark of mountain cedar (*Juniperus ashei*), woven with spider webs; very well concealed because it so closely resembles the bark of the tree; lined with hair and feathers. *Eggs*: 3–5, usually 4; ovate; with slight gloss; white or cream white; spotted and dotted with shades of cinnamon rufous to burnt umber and chestnut, with shell spots of lilac gray and lavender; average size, 19.3 × 14.2 mm.

HERMIT WARBLER, *Dendroica occidentalis* (Townsend)

SPECIES ACCOUNT

Male: yellow head; blackish nape; streaked gray back; black throat; white under parts, wing-bars. *Female*: duller; blackish smudge on throat. Length, 5¼ in.; wingspan, 8.

RANGE: S.w. Washington, south through Coast Ranges and Sierra Nevada to c. California. Winters chiefly from c. Mexico to Nicaragua; rarely in coastal California.

TEXAS: (See map.) *Migration*: Late Apr. to mid-May; early Sept. to mid-Oct. (extremes: Apr. 26, May 14; Aug. 5, Dec. 31). Scarce in mountains of Trans-Pecos; casual at Midland. Accidental: Willacy Co., 8 mi. east of Raymondville (1 male, Apr. 18, 1965, Harold Werner); Galveston Co., High Island (1 female, Mar. 29–30, 1972, Jenny Huey, Guy McCaskie, et al.).

HAUNTS AND HABITS: The Hermit Warbler is an inhabitant of moderately dense coniferous forests of "far western" mountains, where it breeds on northerly slopes, lower ridges, and in canyons—usually not at great altitudes. The bird saddles its nest on a high horizontal branch of a conifer. During migration, it frequents pines and other species in mountains and their gulches. Despite its preference for conifers throughout the year, it may be found in willows, oaks, and, very exceptionally, mesquites, particularly along streams and on slopes.

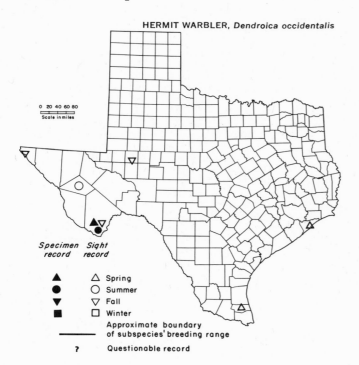

HERMIT WARBLER, *Dendroica occidentalis*

0 20 40 60 80
Scale in miles

Specimen Sight
record record

▲ △ Spring
● ○ Summer
▼ ▽ Fall
■ □ Winter

——— Approximate boundary of subspecies' breeding range

? Questionable record

It frequently perches in the very tops of even the tallest trees, but also descends to the lower parts, and even to undergrowth and thickets along streams. Insect food is sought chiefly in the canopy. The Hermit characteristically ascends to the treetops by successive hops from branch to branch, not unlike a jay. It occasionally descends to the ground as well. Food consists mainly of insects, such as caterpillars, bark beetles, true bugs, plant lice, Hymenopterans, and two-winged flies; also included are small spiders and a few conifer seeds.

The Hermit's call note is a weak *tseet*. Of its several songs, one has been transliterated as *zeegle, zeegle, zeegle, zeek*; another as *tsit, tsit, tsit, tsit, chee, chee, chee*, the latter part of which is uttered more rapidly than the first. Its voice, though not loud, is rather far carrying and somewhat resembles that of the Audubon's Warbler.

DETAILED ACCOUNT: NO SUBSPECIES

DESCRIPTION: *Adult male, nuptial plumage*: Acquired by partial prenuptial molt. Pileum lemon chrome to light cadmium, crown and occiput more or less spotted with black; hindneck mixed with olive green, grayish olive green, and black; remainder of upper surface deep olive gray, broadly streaked, rump least so, with dull black; tail chaetura black, outer webs of feathers except outer pairs edged with deep olive gray, outer three feathers with large terminal oblique spots of white on inner webs, these largest on outermost feathers, but leaving long guttate terminal dark shaft spot; outer webs of outermost three tail feathers white on middle portions; wing-quills and tertials chaetura drab, margined on exterior vanes with mouse gray, these becoming broader on outer webs of tertials; inner webs of primaries and secondaries margined with brownish white, except on tips of primaries; lesser wing-coverts chaetura black, edged with deep olive gray; greater wing-coverts narrowly edged externally with same; both median and greater series broadly tipped with white, forming two conspicuous wing-bars of which the anterior is wider; sides of head and of neck yellow like pileum; chin, throat, and middle of jugulum black; remainder of lower surface, including lining of wing, dull white; but sides and flanks faintly washed with pale gray, obscurely and narrowly streaked with chaetura drab or dull gray. Bill black or dull black; iris dark brown; legs and feet dark brown. *Adult male, winter*: Acquired by complete postnuptial molt. Similar to nuptial adult male, but pileum more overlaid, yellow thus obscured by olive, yellowish olive, or dull black; upper surface more greenish and more uniform, dark markings somewhat hidden by olivaceous tips of feathers; sides of head duller, more or less obscured by olive tips of feathers; black of throat and jugulum much veiled by dull white, pale yellow, or pale gray tips of feathers; posterior lower surface more or less washed with buff; sides of body somewhat more brownish. *Adult female, nuptial*: Acquired by partial prenuptial molt. Similar to nuptial adult male but smaller; yellow of head paler and duller; upper parts lighter, duller, less purely grayish—deep grayish olive, only slightly streaked or spotted with darker olive, except on posterior part of pileum and hindneck; tail chaetura drab, white markings less extensive than in male; wings dark hair brown, but inner edges of wing-quills pale brown, outer edges hair brown to drab, wing-coverts like back but somewhat more brownish; white wing-bars narrower, less conspicuous, and washed with brown; chin dull gamboge yellow or dull pale yellowish buff; throat and jugulum with more or less black, this sometimes nearly absent and always more or less veiled by pale gray, dull white, or yellowish edgings or tips of feathers, and less in extent than in male; sides and flanks more brownish. *Adult female, winter*: Acquired by complete postnuptial molt. Similar to nuptial adult female, but crown much more overlaid with olive green or olive; upper parts grayish deep olive with a few darker streaks on back, but often numerous blackish streaks on pileum; yellow of sides of head more overlaid with olive; black markings of throat and jugulum much more veiled by buffy edgings of feathers; remainder of lower surface much more buffy—dull cream buff to dull chamois; flanks between vinaceous buff and deep olive buff. *Male, first nuptial:* Acquired by partial prenuptial molt. Similar to nuptial adult male, but throat much mixed or overlaid with light yellow or light gray. *Male, first winter:* Acquired by partial postjuvenal molt. Similar to adult female in winter but larger; upper surface more greenish (less brownish); pileum more yellowish; throat and jugulum more extensively black, although much obscured by pale yellow, pale gray, or dull white tips of feathers. *Female, first nuptial:* Acquired by partial prenuptial molt. Similar to nuptial adult female. *Female, first winter:* Acquired by partial postjuvenal molt. Similar to adult female in winter, but upper surface duller, more brownish, yellow of pileum almost entirely hidden by darker tips of feathers; yellow of sides of head duller and more obscured by olive or dull gray tips of feathers; throat and jugulum with very little or no black, entire lower surface usually much more deeply buff. *Juvenal:* Acquired by complete postnatal molt. Upper parts between hair brown and dark grayish olive, back slightly streaked with dull fuscous; wings and tail as in first winter female; postocular streak dull white; throat and breast dull light gray; posterior lower parts dull brownish white, somewhat mottled by feather tips of blackish brown.

MEASUREMENTS: *Adult male:* Wing, 63.0–69.1 (average, 66.0) mm.; tail, 49.0–52.1 (50.5); bill (exposed culmen), 9.4–10.9 (10.2); tarsus, 18.0–21.1 (19.3); middle toe without claw, 10.9–11.9 (11.2). *Adult female:* Wing, 61.0–68.1 (63.8); tail, 46.5–51.1 (48.3); bill, 8.9–9.9 (9.7); tarsus, 16.5–20.1 (18.3); middle toe, 9.9–12.4 (11.2).

TEXAS: *Migration:* Two specimens, both from Big Bend Nat. Park, Brewster Co.: Basin, 5,300 ft. (May 3, 1935, G. M. Sutton); Boot Canyon, 6,000 ft. (Aug. 8, 1969, R. H. Wauer).

CERULEAN WARBLER, *Dendroica cerulea*
(Wilson)

SPECIES ACCOUNT

Male: blue above; white below; narrow black line across upper breast; black streaks on upper parts and sides; white wing-bars. *Female:* much duller; streaks fainter; has whitish eye-stripe; buffy white under parts. Length, 4¾ in.; wingspan, 7¾; weight, ¼ oz.

RANGE: S.e. Nebraska, s. Great Lakes region, and s.e. New York, south to n.e. Texas (irregularly), Louisiana, and c. North Carolina. Winters in w. South America from Venezuela to Bolivia.

TEXAS: (See map.) *Breeding:* Probably mid-Apr. to early July (nest and one egg taken: Cooke Co., Gainesville, Apr. 26, 1887, G. H. Ragsdale; nest with eggs located: Dallas Co., Bachman Lake, Apr. 17, 1932, C. Kelley) from 250 to 750 ft. Rare in summer in Red River Valley from Gainesville to Texarkana, where recorded from Apr. 7 to July 12; extremely rare south to Dallas. *Migration:* Early Apr. to early May; late July to mid-Sept. (extremes: Mar. 16, May 25; July 4, Sept. 27). Fairly common (some years) to uncommon in spring along coast; scarce through remainder of eastern half. Extremely rare in fall.

HAUNTS AND HABITS: The Cerulean Warbler, tiny and blue, is a summer inhabitant of riverbank woodlands, rich swamps, and bottomlands. In spring, this trans-Gulf migrant rarely stops along the coast unless grounded by a rainy cool front. Then it may be found, with other warblers, in a variety of situations. Early to depart from its breeding grounds, it probably starts its southward flight across the Gulf from well inland, being virtually unknown along the coastal plain in fall. Rarely are more than two individuals seen at one time in Texas.

Flight is quick, flitting, and usually restricted, especially in its woodland summer home. Generally, the Cerulean is a bird of treetops and it seems to prefer the tallest trees, making it difficult to observe and study. It feeds chiefly on insects and their larvae (weevils, ladybird beetles, fireflies, wasps, caterpillars, and ants), together with a few spiders; at times it will eat small berries and weed seeds.

The call note of the Cerulean is a weak *tsip*. The male's song is high pitched, loud, and incessantly uttered during the short breeding season. It resembles the song of the Parula but is easily distinguished. Two variations have been represented as follows: *zwee-zwee, zwee, zwee*; and *tse, tse, tse, tsee, te-e-e-e-e-e-e-e*, the last part on an ascending scale. Males sing from late April to early July and again sometimes in August.

DETAILED ACCOUNT: NO SUBSPECIES

DESCRIPTION: *Adult male, nuptial plumage:* Acquired by partial prenuptial molt. Above grayish blue—deep orient blue to porcelain blue—but back somewhat mixed with neutral gray, rump paler, and crown brighter and more bluish (less grayish); pileum, back, and scapulars more or less broadly streaked with dull black, upper tail-coverts dull black tipped with grayish blue of rump; tail dull blackish mouse gray, middle feathers edged

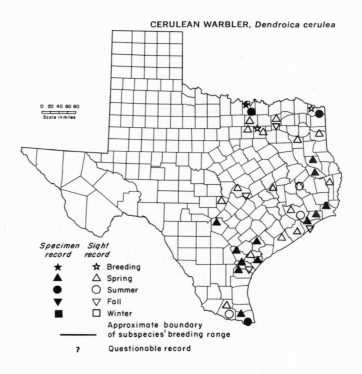

CERULEAN WARBLER, *Dendroica cerulea*

0 20 40 60 80
Scale in miles

Specimen record / Sight record
★ / ☆ Breeding
▲ / △ Spring
● / ○ Summer
▼ / ▽ Fall
■ / □ Winter
—— Approximate boundary of subspecies' breeding range
? Questionable record

externally with color of rump, rectrices, except middle pair, with more or less squarish subterminal white spots on inner webs, middle feathers sometimes narrowly edged with white on subterminal portion of inner web; wings rather deep mouse gray, but tertials blackish mouse gray, primaries and secondaries edged externally with deep green blue-gray, inner edges of primaries and secondaries, except at tips, broadly white, though becoming somewhat grayish on primaries; tertials edged externally with dull gull gray; wing-coverts blackish mouse gray, lesser and greater coverts edged on outer webs with grayish blue of back, median and greater coverts broadly tipped with white, the latter chiefly on outer webs, and forming two conspicuous wing-bars; sides of head and of neck like back, but rather duller and more grayish; lores chaetura drab; lower parts dull white, broad band across jugulum and broad streaks on sides and flanks blackish slate, somewhat overlaid by lighter bluish gray; lining of wing white, outer portion more or less mottled with chaetura drab or chaetura black. Bill black, but mandible slate color or plumbeous at base; iris dark brown or brownish black; legs and feet plumbeous. *Adult male, winter*: Acquired by complete postnuptial molt. Similar to nuptial adult male, but upper parts duller and more overlaid by pale brown or gray tips of feathers; general tone of upper parts duller and slightly more greenish, band across jugulum much more obscured by whitish tips of feathers and, for this reason, sometimes incomplete. *Adult female, nuptial*: Acquired by partial prenuptial molt. Pileum dull stone green to rather dark american green; back and scapulars andover green to dull sage green, rump rather paler and more yellowish; tail dark mouse gray, outer feathers deep neutral gray, feathers edged externally, outer ones chiefly basally, with color of upper tail-coverts; nearly all feathers except middle pair with more or less conspicuous subterminal, somewhat squarish, white spots, largest on outermost feathers; primaries and secondaries dark hair brown, primaries and secondaries edged on outer webs with color of back and primaries except tips edged on inner webs with brownish white, secondaries thus edged with yellowish or greenish white; tertials deep mouse gray edged externally with pale yellowish glaucous; lesser wing-coverts like back; greater coverts margined very narrowly with same on outer webs, greater and median coverts broadly tipped with yellowish white, forming two conspicuous wing-bars; superciliary stripe dull white or dull pale yellow; lores mixed with fuscous and dull yellowish white, posterior portion usually chaetura drab, sometimes like rest; short postocular streak of olive gray, short streak below eye dull yellowish white or pale greenish yellow, and below this a rictal streak of dull bluish green like back; lower surface between primrose yellow and deep colonial buff, more whitish on throat, deepest on jugulum and breast, and paler, even whitish, on middle of abdomen and sometimes on crissum; lining of wing dull yellowish white, outermost portion mottled with hair brown, sometimes washed with glaucous blue; sides and flanks obscurely streaked with grayish olive. *Adult female, winter*: Acquired by complete postnuptial molt. Similar to nuptial adult female, but upper surface duller, more uniform, and more greenish; sides of head more greenish or yellowish (less bluish or grayish); lower surface much more deeply and more extensively yellow. *Male, first nuptial*: Acquired by partial prenuptial molt. Similar to nuptial adult male, but wing-quills and tail more brownish, duller, and often more worn. *Male, first winter*: Acquired by partial postjuvenal molt, which does not involve wing-quills or tail. Similar to adult male in winter but duller and less clearly blue, wing-quills and tail more brownish, edgings duller and less clearly bluish gray. Similar to nuptial adult female but larger; upper parts more bluish; lower surface rather more bluish (less yellowish); streaks on sides and flanks much darker, more numerous, and more distinct. *Female, first nuptial*: Acquired by partial prenuptial molt. Similar to nuptial adult female, but wings and tail somewhat more brownish. *Female, first winter*: Acquired by partial postjuvenal molt. Similar to adult female in winter, but upper parts duller, rather paler, and more grayish or brownish (less greenish); lower parts paler, less deeply yellowish, streaking on sides and flanks obsolete. *Juvenal*: Acquired by complete postnatal molt. Upper surface hair brown, very slightly washed with olive, broad median stripe on pileum dull brownish; sides of head buffy white, long postocular streak hair brown, wings and tail as in first winter young; lower surface dull buffy white. Bill, legs, and feet dull brown; iris dark brown. *Natal*: Light mouse gray to light drab. Bill, legs, and feet pinkish buff; iris blackish.

MEASUREMENTS: *Adult male*: Wing, 62.0–67.8 (average, 65.5) mm.; tail, 43.2–47.8 (45.0); bill (exposed culmen), 9.1–10.4 (9.7); tarsus, 15.7–17.0 (16.5); middle toe without claw, 8.6–9.9 (9.7). *Adult female*: Wing, 58.4–62.7 (61.2); tail, 39.9–43.4 (41.2); bill, 9.1–10.4 (9.7); tarsus, 15.5–17.0 (16.3); middle toe, 8.9–9.9 (9.4).

TEXAS: *Breeding*: Collected in Cooke and Bowie cos. *Migration*: Collected north to Cooke, east to Jefferson, south to Cameron, west to Bexar cos.

NESTING: *Nest*: Usually in bottomlands, in heavy forests; on horizontal branch of tree, usually some distance from trunk, or in small tree, either coniferous or deciduous, 15–90 ft. above ground, usually 20–60 ft.; very compactly built cup, saddled on limb, often in fork; composed of fine dry grass, weeds, fibers of bark, moss, and bits of wasps' nests and snake skin, bound together with spider webs; lined with strips of grapevine and other bark, fine grasses, stems of blossoms, hair, soft moss, cotton, horse and other hair, and feathers, together with caterpillar or spider webs. *Eggs*: 3–5; usually 4; ovate to rounded ovate; white, dull greenish, bluish, or cream white; dotted with reddish brown, with lavender shell markings, chiefly at large end, sometimes in form of wreath, usually scattered over entire egg; average size, 17.3 × 13.2 mm.

BLACKBURNIAN WARBLER, *Dendroica fusca* (Müller)

SPECIES ACCOUNT

Nuptial male: black and white with orange headstripes, throat, and upper breast; two white stripes on back. *Female, fall male*: much duller, paler; retain stripes on back. Length, 5 in.; wingspan, 8¼; weight, ¼ oz.

RANGE: S. Saskatchewan to Nova Scotia, south to Great Lakes region and Massachusetts, and in Appalachians to Georgia. Winters from Guatemala to c. Peru and Venezuela.

TEXAS: (See map.) *Migration*: Mid-Apr. to mid-May; early Sept. to early Nov.—occasionally mid-Dec. in Rio Grande delta (extremes: Mar. 13, June 6; Aug. 15, Dec. 30). Common (some springs) to scarce (most falls) east of 100th meridian; rare in northern Panhandle; extremely rare in Trans-Pecos. One mid-summer sighting: Travis Co., Austin (singing male, July 5, 1965, F. S. Webster, Jr.).

HAUNTS AND HABITS: The fiery orange and black Blackburnian Warbler is primarily an inhabitant of dense woodlands, especially hemlock, spruce, and pine forests of the north and pine-oak-hickory ridges of the Appalachians. It generally positions its nest well out on a limb of a large conifer. During migrations through Texas and elsewhere, it may pause in scrubby growth on rocky hillsides, woodland understory, thickets and timber along creeks, both on uplands and bottomlands, even in bushes and trees along fence rows, roadsides, railroad rights-of-way, and in cities and towns.

Its flight is quick and jerky and usually from tree to

tree. The bird frequents tops of tall trees, but also utilizes lower branches and undergrowth at times, and occasionally descends to the ground. It forages briskly along interior limbs and in the canopy and sometimes darts, flycatcherlike, after a flying insect. Food consists mainly of various insects and their larvae: leaf beetles, moths, caterpillars, ants, ichneumon flies, craneflies, and bugs. At times, particularly when insects are scarce, some berries are taken.

The Blackburnian's usual call note is a weak *chip*, similar to that of many other warblers. Its song is extremely varied, insectlike, high pitched, and lisping. A common variation is represented by the syllables *zip zip zip zip titi tseeeeee*, the last note high and slurred.

DETAILED ACCOUNT: NO SUBSPECIES

DESCRIPTION: *Adult male, nuptial plumage*: Acquired by partial prenuptial molt. Upper parts black, but broad stripe on middle of crown, sometimes extending to middle of forehead, cadmium yellow to light cadmium; sides of back, with scapulars and rump, more or less broadly streaked with yellowish or buffy white, lateral upper tail-coverts edged on outer webs with same; tail dull black, outer two or three rectrices mostly white, except for brownish black shafts and terminal shaft spot, remaining feathers, except middle pair, with large more or less oblique white spots on inner webs, middle pair edged narrowly on inner webs near tips with dull white; primaries and secondaries chaetura drab, margined on outer webs with light grayish olive or deep grayish olive; on inner webs secondaries edged with white or brownish white, primaries with pale brownish white except at tips; tertials chaetura black, edged on outer webs with dull white; upper wing-coverts black, median coverts and middle greater coverts with narrow tips of outer feathers white, forming conspicuous white wing-patch; superciliary stripe cadmium yellow, verging toward orange anteriorly; lores, cheeks, and auriculars black, relieved by long cadmium yellow patch below eye, the black extending in curved stripe to side of throat; anterior portion of neck behind auriculars cadmium yellow; chin, throat, and jugulum cadmium yellow to cadmium orange; breast

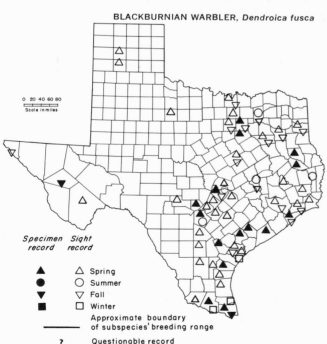

BLACKBURNIAN WARBLER, *Dendroica fusca*

0 20 40 60 80
Scale in miles

Specimen Sight
record   record

▲ △ Spring
● ○ Summer
▼ ▽ Fall
■ ☐ Winter

Approximate boundary
——— of subspecies' breeding range

? Questionable record

dull colonial buff to primuline yellow, passing on abdomen into dull pale buff, buff, or yellowish white; crissum white or yellowish white; sides of breast and of body, together with flanks, broadly streaked with black; lining of wing white, outer portion slightly washed with yellow, and occasionally with a few mottlings of hair brown or mouse gray. Bill black, slate black, or blackish slate, but basal portion dull white or slate gray; iris very dark brown; legs and feet olive brown, hair brown, or brownish drab; claws dark brown. *Adult male, winter*: Acquired by complete postnuptial molt. Similar to nuptial adult male, but black areas of head and upper surface more obscured by olive gray or brownish tips and edgings of feathers; white area of wing very much reduced, forming two wing-bars instead of white patch; orange of sides and anterior lower parts somewhat paler and more or less obscured by buffy tips of feathers; black streaks on sides and flanks narrower and much obscured by pale yellow or light gray edgings of feathers. *Adult female, nuptial*: Acquired by partial prenuptial molt. Similar to nuptial adult male but very much duller, paler, and more brownish, both above and below; center of crown primuline yellow or wax yellow, upper parts dull buffy citrine or saccardo olive, but rump grayish olive; everywhere above streaked with dull black, streaks broadest on back and upper tail-coverts; wings and tail more brownish, tail with much less white and wings with two white wing-bars, instead of white patch; dark areas of sides of head dull buffy citrine instead of black; orange throat much paler, and streaks on sides and flanks narrower, duller, and more brownish; abdomen primuline yellow to dull buff. *Adult female, winter*: Acquired by complete postnuptial molt. Similar to nuptial adult female, but yellow crown-patch almost hidden by darker brown edgings of feathers; entire upper surface duller, more brownish, and more uniform, blackish streaks on back largely overlaid by brownish edgings and tips of feathers, thus they appear narrower; anterior lower parts paler, duller, and less orange (more yellowish), and lower parts more uniform; color of jugulum passing more gradually into buff or pale yellow of posterior lower surface. *Male, first nuptial*: Acquired by partial prenuptial molt. Similar to nuptial adult male, but wing-quills, tail, and particularly primary coverts more brownish. *Male, first winter*: Acquired by partial postjuvenal molt, which does not involve wing-quills or tail. Similar to adult male in winter, but wing-quills and tail somewhat more brownish. Similar to nuptial adult female but larger; dark areas on sides of head darker, more blackish; throat and breast paler, duller, and more yellowish (less orange), usually between wax yellow and primuline yellow, ranging sometimes toward light cadmium or cadmium yellow; blackish streaks on sides and flanks broader and more conspicuous; wings and tail darker, more blackish, and with more white on tail as in adult male. *Female, first nuptial*: Acquired by partial prenuptial molt. Similar to nuptial adult female, but crown with fewer dark spots and lower surface duller; wings and tail somewhat more brownish. *Female, first winter*: Acquired by partial postjuvenal molt. Similar to adult female in winter, but upper parts still more brownish and less conspicuously streaked—between olive brown and deep olive or between hair brown and deep olive, crown-patch entirely hidden by dull brownish tips of feathers; white wing-bars narrower; anterior lower surface much duller yellow, sometimes mostly dull white or very pale buff; usually somewhat less white on outer tail feather; streaks on posterior lower surface duller, more buffy or grayish, streaks on sides and flanks paler—light brownish olive or grayish olive. *Juvenal*: Acquired by complete postnatal molt. Upper surface dull bister; back more or less streaked or spotted with dull buff; wings and tail much as in first winter female; superciliary stripe, broad postocular streak, and streak down side of neck dull pinkish buff; auricular region brown like upper surface; throat pale grayish drab; breast and jugulum drab, more or less obscurely spotted with hair brown; remainder of lower surface dull white or buffy white, but sides and flanks lightly streaked or spotted with hair brown. Bill brownish slate or blackish slate; iris dark brown; legs and feet hair brown or drab.

MEASUREMENTS: *Adult male*: Wing, 66.5–71.7 (average, 68.3) mm.; tail, 45.5–50.5 (48.0); bill (exposed culmen), 8.9–10.9

(9.9); tarsus, 17.5–18.5 (17.8); middle toe without claw, 9.9–10.9 (10.2). *Adult female*: Wing, 63.0–70.6 (65.0); tail, 42.4–49.0 (45.7); bill, 9.4–10.4 (9.9); tarsus, 17.3–19.0 (18.0); middle toe, 9.1–10.9 (9.7).

TEXAS: *Migration*: Collected north to Dallas, east to Nacogdoches and Galveston, south to Cameron, west to Jeff Davis cos.

YELLOW-THROATED WARBLER, *Dendroica dominica* (Linnaeus)

SPECIES ACCOUNT

Gray above; yellow throat, upper breast; black face, side-streaks; white eye-stripe, neck-spot, belly, wingbars. Length, 5¼ in.; wingspan, 8¼.

RANGE: S.e. Nebraska, extreme s. Great Lakes region, and c. New Jersey, south to c. and e. Texas, Gulf coast, c. Florida; also n. Bahamas. Winters from s. Texas through e. and s. Mexico to Costa Rica, and from s. South Carolina to s. Florida; also Bahamas and Greater Antilles.

TEXAS: (See map.) *Breeding*: Late Apr. to mid-July, exceptionally to early Sept. (eggs, May 15 to July 1) from near sea level to 1,700 ft. Fairly common locally to uncommon in eastern quarter, west to Gainesville and Brazoria Co.; scarce on southeastern Edwards Plateau. *Migration*: Mid-Mar. to late Apr.; late July to late Nov. (extremes: Mar. 7, May 13; July 18, Dec. 12). Common (some springs) to uncommon (most falls) through eastern third; uncommon to rare in remainder of state east of 100th meridian; extremely rare in northern Panhandle and Trans-Pecos. *Winter*: Mid-Dec. to late Mar. Uncommon in Rio Grande delta; scarce to very rare in remainder of eastern two-thirds.

HAUNTS AND HABITS: The Yellow-throated Warbler

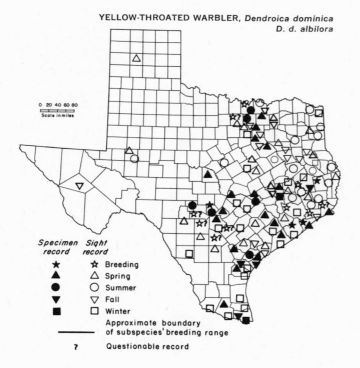

YELLOW-THROATED WARBLER, *Dendroica dominica*
D. d. albilora

0 20 40 60 80
Scale in miles

Specimen Sight
record   record
★   ☆ Breeding
▲   △ Spring
●   ○ Summer
▼   ▽ Fall
■   □ Winter
————   Approximate boundary
              of subspecies' breeding range
  ?   Questionable record

typically breeds in open pine forests and in baldcypress–American sycamore woodlands along rivers and bayous; sometimes the bird will accept deciduous forest growing on well-drained soil. The female often builds her nest in a clump of Spanishmoss. During migration and in winter the Yellow-throated is likely to occur in any stand of woods, coastal scrub, or tall brush.

In flight this warbler is on occasion quick and nervous, and it seldom flies far. In the South, Alexander Sprunt, Jr., twice found dead birds which had flown into and become entangled in the golden web of the huge Carolina silk spider. When foraging, *Dendroica dominica* is more deliberate than most of its relatives, creeping along limbs and branches in a manner similar to that of the Pine Warbler. It also spends considerable time high in trees searching the foliage of canopy and subcanopy. And, at times, it descends to undergrowth, particularly during migration. Food consists of moths, caterpillars and other larvae, flies, scale insects, grasshoppers, locusts, crickets, beetles, ants; also spiders.

The Yellow-throated Warbler's song is spirited and melodious, its quality reminiscent of the song of the Indigo Bunting. It is a series of clear notes of high carrying quality: *twsee-twsee-twsee, twsee-see*, the last two syllables with rising inflection and terminated with strong emphasis. Males sing, often from a preferred perch, from April into July.

DETAILED ACCOUNT: THREE SUBSPECIES

EASTERN YELLOW-THROATED WARBLER, *Dendroica dominica dominica* (Linnaeus)

DESCRIPTION: *Adult male and female, nuptial plumage*: Similar to *D. d. albilora* (see below), but eyebrow wholly or partly yellow; yellow of throat less rich, that is, less orange; wing averaging slightly longer.

MEASUREMENTS: *Adult male*: Wing, 63.8–68.1 (average, 66.3) mm.; tail, 47.0–53.6 (50.5); bill (exposed culmen), 11.9–13.7 (12.7); tarsus, 16.8–18.0 (17.5); middle toe without claw, 9.9–11.9 (11.2); white on inner web of outermost tail feather, 20.1–26.9 (22.6). *Adult female*: Wing, 60.5–69.1 (64.5); tail, 47.0–52.1 (49.8); bill, 10.9–13.2 (12.7); tarsus, 16.5–18.0 (17.3); middle toe, 10.7–12.7 (11.7); white on inner web, 19.6–26.4 (22.4).

RANGE: E. Mississippi to c. Virginia, south to s. Alabama and c. Florida. Winters from Mexico to Honduras, and from South Carolina to s. Florida; also West Indies.

TEXAS: *Migration*: One specimen: Aransas Co., Rockport (Mar. 23, 1892, H. P. Attwater).

INDIANA YELLOW-THROATED WARBLER, *Dendroica dominica axantha* Oberholser, new subspecies (see Appendix A)

DESCRIPTION: *Adult male and female, nuptial plumage*: Similar to *D. d. albilora* (see below), but smaller, particularly bill and wing; throat less deeply orange; white on outer tail feather somewhat less in extent.

MEASUREMENTS: *Adult male*: Wing, 62.5–67.6 (average, 65.0) mm.; tail, 48.5–54.1 (50.5); bill (exposed culmen), 10.7–11.9 (11.4); tarsus, 16.0–18.0 (17.0); middle toe without claw, 10.4–11.4 (10.9); white on inner web of outermost tail feather, 23.1–25.9 (23.9). *Adult female*: Wing, 59.9–64.0 (62.2); tail, 45.0–55.9 (49.3); bill, 10.2–11.9 (11.2); tarsus, 16.0–17.5 (16.8); middle toe, 9.9–10.9 (10.7); white on inner web, 21.1–23.9 (22.9).

TYPE: Adult male, no. 25339, Cleveland Museum of Natural History; Lucasville, Scioto Co., Ohio; May 6, 1925; A. B. Fuller.

RANGE: S.e. Nebraska to West Virginia, south to s. Missouri and c. Tennessee. Winters from Yucatán to Nicaragua; also Isla Cozumel and Cayman Islands.

TEXAS: *Migration*: Collected north to Denton (Aug. 23), east to Galveston, southwest to Cameron cos. Uncommon.

SYCAMORE YELLOW-THROATED WARBLER, *Dendroica dominica albilora* Ridgway

DESCRIPTION: *Adult male, nuptial plumage*: Acquired by wear from winter plumage. Forehead and crown black with short, narrow, white line in center of forehead; remainder of upper surface neutral gray to dark gull gray or between slate gray and deep neutral gray; tail chaetura black, most feathers edged externally with color of upper parts, three outer tail feathers with large white squarish terminal spot on inner webs, remainder of feathers more or less broadly margined with white on terminal portion, this very narrow on central pair of feathers; primaries and secondaries chaetura drab, margined on inner webs with dull white or brownish white, primaries edged narrowly on outer webs with gray of back; tertials chaetura black, broadly edged on outer webs and at tips with mouse gray, inner tertials also narrowly tipped with white; lesser wing-coverts like back; greater and median wing-coverts dull black to chaetura black, broadly tipped with white, forming two conspicuous wing-bars, median coverts also narrowly edged on outer webs with gray of back; broad superciliary stripe white; elongated vertical patch on middle of side of neck also white, as well as large somewhat elongated spot on lower eyelid; remainder of sides of head, including lores and sides of throat, black; remainder of sides of neck like upper surface; chin and middle of throat and of jugulum light cadmium to near lemon chrome; rest of lower surface, including lining of wing, white, but sides and flanks broadly streaked with black. Bill black; iris dark brown; legs, feet, and claws olive brown; soles of toes greenish yellow. *Adult male, winter*: Acquired by complete postnuptial molt. Similar to nuptial adult male, but gray of upper surface distinctly washed with brown or olivaceous; posterior lower parts pale buff or washed with buff. *Adult female, nuptial*: Acquired by wear from winter. Similar to nuptial adult male but smaller; upper parts lighter, duller, and more brownish; crown with less black; black of sides of head and of neck less extensive; streaks on sides and flanks narrower. *Adult female, winter*: Acquired by complete postnuptial molt. Similar to nuptial adult female, but upper surface distinctly washed with brown; posterior lower parts tinged with buff, particularly on sides and flanks. *Male, first nuptial*: Acquired by wear from first winter. Similar to nuptial adult male, but wing-quills, and particularly primary coverts, also sometimes tail, more brownish. *Male, first winter*: Acquired by partial postjuvenal molt, which does not involve wing-quills or tail. Similar to adult male in winter, but wing-quills, tail, and particularly primary coverts, somewhat more brownish; entire upper surface duller and much more strongly brownish; black of fore part of crown almost entirely obscured by brownish or gray tips of feathers; posterior lower parts still more strongly tinged with buff; sides and flanks dull avellaneous. Similar to adult female in winter but much larger. *Female, first nuptial*: Acquired by wear from first winter. Similar to nuptial adult female, but wing-quills and tail somewhat more brownish. *Female, first winter*: Acquired by partial postjuvenal molt. Similar to adult female in winter, but upper parts duller, paler, much more brownish, and without black on pileum; black areas on sides of head and neck duller, more veiled with brown; superciliary stripe washed with dull buff; lower parts duller, abdomen and flanks still more strongly buff, flanks duller, more deeply avellaneous, the streaks on sides and flanks narrower, duller, paler, and more brownish, often much obscured by lighter tips of feathers. Similar to first winter male but smaller, upper surface somewhat paler with little or no visible black on forehead, posterior lower parts rather more brownish or buffy. *Juvenal*: Acquired by complete postnatal molt. Pileum drab to dark drab; remainder of upper surface hair brown to benzo brown, but scapulars drab to light

drab; wings and tail as in first winter, but drab edges of tertials rather broader; wing-bars washed with brown or buff; sides of head light drab, though auriculars, lores, and region below eye hair brown, chin and throat drab gray or dull white; remainder of lower parts dull white or vinaceous white, but jugulum, breast, sides, and flanks more or less obscurely streaked or spotted with hair brown. Bill dull brown, but base of mandible lighter; iris dark brown; legs and feet dull brown. *Natal*: Drab. Bill, legs, and feet brownish black.

MEASUREMENTS: *Adult male*: Wing, 64.0–71.7 (average, 67.8) mm.; tail, 46.0–54.1 (50.8); bill (exposed culmen), 11.2–13.2 (12.4); tarsus, 17.0–18.3 (17.5); middle toe without claw, 10.9–11.9 (11.4); white on inner web of outermost tail feather, 22.6–29.9 (25.9). *Adult female*: Wing, 62.0–69.1 (64.3); tail, 46.0–52.3 (48.8); bill, 11.9–13.0 (12.2); tarsus, 16.5–18.0 (17.3); middle toe, 10.4–11.4 (10.9); white on inner web, 20.1–26.4 (23.6).

RANGE: C. Texas to Mississippi. Winters from s. Texas through e. and s. Mexico to Costa Rica.

TEXAS: *Breeding*: Collected north to Cooke, east to Tyler (eggs) and Galveston (eggs), south to Matagorda, west to Kerr cos. *Migration*: Collected north to Cooke, east to Jefferson, south to Cameron, west to San Saba cos. Fairly common. *Winter*: Taken in Grimes (1 specimen) and Cameron (3) cos. Scarce.

NESTING: *Nest*: On bottomlands and hill slopes, damp or dry; in mixed or deciduous woodlands, in pine or other tree; on horizontal limb or in fork, 10–120 ft. above ground, ordinarily concealed in Spanishmoss or foliage, usually cup-shaped, but when made of Spanishmoss more or less pensile; composed of short twigs, strips of bark, Spanishmoss, weed stems, fine grass, silky vegetable down, and caterpillar silk; lined with soft hairlike vegetable down, moss, cotton, horsehair, blossoms of moss, and feathers. *Eggs*: 3–5, usually 4; short ovate; dull greenish or grayish white; spotted with sepia, umber, and dull black, with pale lavender and purplish gray shell markings, almost all near large end and sometimes forming wreath; average size, 17.5 × 13.5 mm.

GRACE'S WARBLER, *Dendroica graciae* Baird

SPECIES ACCOUNT

Gray above; yellow stripe over eye, becoming white posteriorly; yellow throat and breast; black streaks on crown, back, sides; white belly, wing-bars. Length, 5 in.; wingspan, 7¾.

RANGE: S. Utah and s.w. Colorado, south in mountains through w. and s. Mexico to n. Nicaragua, and through s.e. Rockies to n. Trans-Pecos Texas. Winters from Sinaloa southward.

TEXAS: (See map.) *Breeding*: Probably mid-May to mid-Aug. (no egg dates available, but nest located in Guadalupe Mts. by F. R. Gehlbach), usually above 7,000 ft. Uncommon but regular in Guadalupe Mts. Occasionally summers in Davis Mts., but no good evidence of nesting. *Migration*: Late Apr. to late May; mid-Aug. to late Sept. (extremes: Apr. 21, June 1; Aug. 8, Sept. 24). Fairly common in Guadalupe Mts.; uncommon in Davis and Chisos mts.; scarce in El Paso region; very rare at Midland.

HAUNTS AND HABITS: The Grace's Warbler is one of the less known North American wood warblers, possibly because of its limited distribution and rather retiring habits. It breeds in pine-oak forests of the Transition Zone, where it inhabits mountain canyons, slopes, and summits. Even in the nonbreeding season, it is principally a bird of mountains. It is generally not gregarious but may be found in small groups during migration.

Grace's flight is quick, erratic, and somewhat undulating. This warbler seems to prefer tall pines, although it sometimes descends to feed in oaks and undergrowth. It is an active bird and does considerable flycatching in mid-air. Its diet is poorly known, but is probably mainly insects.

Its call note resembles *tsip*, rather quickly uttered. One common variation of its song is a weak repetition of notes very similar to those of the Chipping Sparrow. A finer version is composed of two or three whistling notes followed by a trill: *cheedle cheedle che che che che*. Males, usually from the treetops, may sing from late April into August.

DETAILED ACCOUNT: ONE SUBSPECIES

NORTHERN GRACE'S WARBLER, *Dendroica graciae graciae* Baird

DESCRIPTION: *Adult male, nuptial plumage*: Acquired by wear from winter plumage. Upper parts rather dark neutral gray to mouse gray, but forehead black with short narrow yellow median line, sides of crown broadly streaked with black, center of pileum, back, and upper tail-coverts also streaked with black, streaks narrowest on pileum; tail blackish mouse gray, outermost two feathers on each side with large oblique white terminal spots on inner webs, outer webs also white except at tips, third feather from outermost with elongated subterminal white spot on inner web, remainder of tail feathers narrowly edged on outer webs with neutral gray; primaries and secondaries chaetura drab, margined narrowly on outer webs with rather light neutral gray, base of inner webs, except at tips of primaries, brownish white or pale dull brown; lesser wing-coverts like back; greater and median coverts dull black, latter narrowly edged on outer webs with mouse gray or neutral gray, both me-

dian and greater coverts broadly tipped with white (on greater coverts, however, chiefly on outer feathers), forming two conspicuous wing-bars; broad superciliary stripe lemon chrome, changing to dull white behind eye; lores chaetura black, duller and more brownish anteriorly; streak on lower eyelid light yellow; remainder of sides of head, with sides of neck, gray like upper surface, but auriculars somewhat darker; chin, throat, and jugulum light to dark lemon chrome; remainder of lower parts, including lining of wing, white, sides of breast, of body, and flanks broadly streaked with black. Bill dull black; iris dark brown or dull black; legs and feet dark brown or brackish brown; soles of toes dull yellow. *Adult male, winter*: Acquired by complete postnuptial molt. Similar to nuptial adult male, but upper parts duller, more or less decidedly washed with brown, black of crown more or less obscured by gray or brownish gray tips of feathers, and streaks on back likewise obscured, sometimes none visible; black streaks of lower parts more or less hidden by lighter tips of feathers; posterior lower parts more tinged with buff, colors thus more blended. *Adult female, nuptial*: Acquired by wear from winter. Similar to nuptial adult male but smaller; upper surface decidedly duller and somewhat more brownish, with fewer and smaller black streaks on pileum and back; white wing-bars narrower, rather duller, and somewhat washed with brown or buff; sides of head rather paler and duller; yellow of anterior lower surface lighter, blackish streaks on sides and flanks narrower and less blackish. *Adult female, winter*: Acquired by complete postnuptial molt. Similar to nuptial adult female, but upper parts decidedly more brownish, black markings partly or entirely concealed by brownish tips of feathers; sides of head duller and more brownish; yellow of anterior lower parts duller, somewhat tinged with buff; posterior lower parts strongly washed with buff; streaks on sides and flanks narrower, paler, and more brownish. Similar to adult male in winter but smaller, more brownish, dark markings on forehead, crown, and back still more obscured; dark streaks on sides and flanks narrower, much duller, and more brownish; yellow of anterior lower surface duller. *Male, first nuptial*: Acquired by wear from first winter. Similar to nuptial adult male, but upper parts duller and more brownish. *Male, first winter*: Acquired by partial postjuvenal molt. Similar to adult male in winter, but upper parts much more uniform and more brownish—between hair brown and light olive brown; black streaks on pileum and back almost or quite covered by brown tips of feathers; sides of head and of neck paler and more brownish; yellow of throat rather lighter; posterior lower parts still more strongly washed with brown or buff, blackish streaks on sides and flanks narrower and much more obscured. Similar to adult female in winter but larger, upper parts rather darker; anterior part of superciliary stripe more deeply yellow; yellow of throat and jugulum rather paler; streaks on sides and flanks more blackish and somewhat broader. *Female, first nuptial*: Acquired by wear from first winter. Similar to nuptial adult female, but upper parts duller, more brownish; yellow of throat also duller. *Female, first winter*: Acquired by partial postjuvenal molt. Similar to adult female in winter but duller and still more brownish on upper surface—between hair brown and fuscous; posterior lower surface more deeply buff and laterally more brownish; streaks on sides and flanks still more obscure. *Male, juvenal*: Acquired by complete postnatal molt. Upper surface between hair brown and fuscous; wings and tail as in first winter; supraloral line faint pale buff or dull white; sides of head like upper parts; lower parts dull buffy white, breast and jugulum sometimes dull drab, under surface more or less spotted and streaked with hair brown, fuscous, or chaetura drab. *Female, juvenal*: Acquired by complete postnatal molt. Similar to juvenal male but lighter and more brownish above, including wings and tail. *Natal*: Unknown.

MEASUREMENTS: *Adult male*: Wing, 62.5–68.1 (average, 65.8) mm.; tail, 50.0–55.1 (51.6); bill (exposed culmen), 9.1–10.4 (9.7); tarsus, 16.0–17.5 (17.0); middle toe without claw, 9.9–10.9 (10.4). *Adult female*: Wing, 59.9–65.5 (62.2); tail, 47.5–53.1 (49.8); bill, 9.4–10.4 (9.9); tarsus, 16.5–17.8 (17.0); middle toe, 9.7–11.4 (10.2).

RANGE: S. Utah and s.w. Colorado (casual), south to s.e. So-

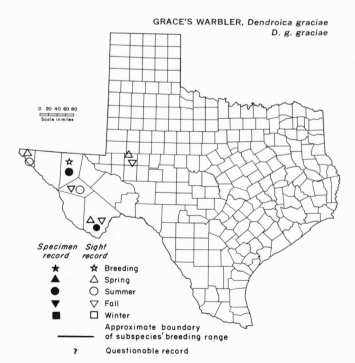

GRACE'S WARBLER, *Dendroica graciae*
D. g. graciae

0 20 40 60 80
Scale in miles

Specimen   Sight
record   record

★   ☆ Breeding
▲   △ Spring
●   ○ Summer
▼   ▽ Fall
■   □ Winter

              Approximate boundary
———   of subspecies' breeding range

?   Questionable record

nora and n. Trans-Pecos Texas. Winters from Nayarit to Michoacán.

TEXAS: *Breeding*: Collected in Guadalupe Mts., Culberson Co. *Migration*: One specimen: Brewster Co., Big Bend Nat. Park, Boot Canyon (Aug. 8, 1969, R. H. Wauer).

NESTING: *Nest*: On mountains and mesas; in coniferous forests; in pine, Douglasfir, or other tree, juniper or other bush; on limb, up to 60 ft. above ground; very compact cup of vegetable fibers, such as catkins, bud scales of oak, wool, and vegetable down, also string and straw; lined with dry grass, feathers, and horse and cow hair. *Eggs*: 3–4, usually 3; ovate; cream white; spotted over entire surface, but more so at large end, with light umber and chestnut, with lilac shell markings; average size, 17.5 × 12.7 mm.

CHESTNUT-SIDED WARBLER, *Dendroica pensylvanica* (Linnaeus)

SPECIES ACCOUNT

Nuptial male: yellow crown; chestnut side-stripe; black and white face; black-streaked yellowish above; white below; whitish wing-bars. *Nuptial female*: duller; side-stripe narrow or broken. *Fall birds*: greenish above; whitish below (side-stripe absent or reduced to chestnut streaks); white eye-ring; yellowish wing-bars. Length, 5 in.; wingspan, 7¾; weight, ½ oz.

RANGE: C. Saskatchewan to Nova Scotia, south to e. Nebraska, s. Great Lakes region, and c. New Jersey, and in Appalachians to Georgia. Winters from s. Nicaragua to Panama.

TEXAS: (See map.) *Migration*: Mid-Apr. to mid-May; mid-Sept. to late Oct. (extremes: Mar. 4, June 10; Aug. 27, Dec. 31). Common (abundant some years on upper coast) to uncommon in spring east of 100th me-

ridian; scarce to very rare in Panhandle; rare to casual in Trans-Pecos. Uncommon to rare in fall through eastern half; extremely rare in northern Panhandle; casual in Trans-Pecos.

HAUNTS AND HABITS: The Chestnut-sided Warbler—so rare in the first half of the nineteenth century that Audubon saw it but once—has actually increased its population and breeding range with the regrowth of cutover land. It inhabits scrubby, open, second-growth woodland (usually where broad-leaved species predominate) during an early stage of regeneration. It places its nest low in a shrub or small tree. When the young trees grow to form a closed-canopy woodland, the Chestnut-sided vanishes from the area. During its migrations through Texas, however, it occurs in all types of thickets and woods—even deep forests, deciduous or evergreen.

Flight is light, quick, and rarely prolonged. The Chestnut-sided is usually quite active and has the habit of simultaneously puffing its breast, elevating its tail, and drooping its wings. It generally forages in terminal foliage and at times darts out after insects flycatcher-like. Its insect diet includes larvae of wood-boring species, cankerworms, tent caterpillars, measuringworms, grasshoppers, leaf-hoppers, plant lice, plant bugs, craneflies, bees, ants, parasitic Hymenoptera, and bark and wood-boring beetles. It also takes a few spiders and, rarely, wild fruit and a few grass or weed seeds.

Its call note is a mild *tsip*. Song, similar to that of the Yellow Warbler, is a more emphatic *te, te, te, te, wé, chu* or *please please pleased to meétcha*, the last note dropping abruptly. Males often pause to sing as they migrate through Texas in April and May.

DETAILED ACCOUNT: NO SUBSPECIES

DESCRIPTION: *Adult male, nuptial plumage*: Acquired by partial prenuptial molt. Pileum gamboge yellow to wax yellow; center of occiput usually with spot of white or pale yellow; nape pale mouse gray, streaked with black; remainder of upper surface pyrite yellow to warbler green, broadly streaked with black, streaks on rump more or less obscured by tips of feathers; tail chaetura black, feathers edged on outer webs with neutral gray, outer pair basally with white, outer three pairs of feathers with more or less oblique terminal white spots on inner webs, smallest on third pair of feathers, largest on outermost, remainder of feathers narrowly edged with dull white on terminal portion of inner webs; primaries and secondaries chaetura drab to fuscous, edged on outer webs with warbler green, inner edges of primaries and secondaries dull white on secondaries to dull buff on primaries except at tips; tertials chaetura drab to fuscous, sometimes chaetura black; edges warbler green, but often paler, yellowish olive buff; lesser wing-coverts neutral gray, more or less washed with olive green, feathers with centers of chaetura black; median and greater wing-coverts chaetura black, inner and outer greater coverts edged on outer webs with warbler green, middle ones broadly edged, median and greater coverts tipped with strontian yellow to citrine yellow, and subterminally on median coverts with white, forming two conspicuous wing-bars which sometimes coalesce into yellow wing-patch; narrow superciliary stripe and very narrow orbital ring white; lores, postocular stripe, and malar stripe black; rest of sides of head and of anterior part of neck white; posterior sides of neck white streaked with black and more or less washed with warbler green; sides of breast and flanks chestnut or streaked with chestnut; re-

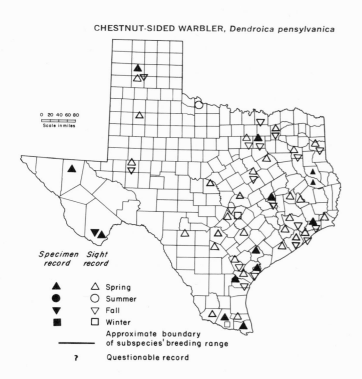

CHESTNUT-SIDED WARBLER, *Dendroica pensylvanica*

0 20 40 60 80
Scale in miles

Specimen   Sight
record   record

▲ △ Spring
● ○ Summer
▼ ▽ Fall
■ □ Winter

————— Approximate boundary
of subspecies' breeding range

? Questionable record

mainder of lower parts, including lining of wing, white, outer under wing-coverts sometimes more or less finely spotted with hair brown. Bill black, slate black, or blackish slate, but basal portion of mandible slate gray, blackish slate, dull white, or slightly yellow; iris dark brown; legs and feet slate color, plumbeous, hair brown, or seal brown. *Adult male, winter*: Acquired by complete postnuptial molt. Entire upper surface warbler green or yellowish warbler green, some edgings of upper tail-coverts neutral gray, showing through to some extent on nape; posterior part of rump and upper tail-coverts broadly streaked with black, remainder of rump, with back and scapulars, showing small more or less obscured spots or streaks of black, these sometimes almost obsolete; wings and tail as in nuptial adult; sides of head and of neck light mouse gray or neutral gray with whitish eye-ring; lower parts dull white, sides and flanks broadly streaked with chestnut. *Adult female, nuptial*: Acquired by partial prenuptial molt. Similar to nuptial adult male but smaller; upper parts duller, pileum between pyrite yellow and warbler green; remainder of upper surface warbler green; hindneck and upper tail-coverts more or less gray; blackish streaks on upper parts much narrower and less numerous; white spots of tail somewhat smaller; yellow wing-bars narrower and outer webs of greater coverts edged with warbler green; black areas of sides of head duller, more brownish, less extensive, often mottled with dull white or pale gray, sometimes almost entirely replaced by dull gray; chestnut of sides and flanks usually much less extensive. *Adult female, winter*: Similar to adult male in winter but smaller; upper parts rather lighter, more uniform, black streaks on back much less evident, entirely obscured by tips of feathers or only slightly indicated; yellow wing-bars somewhat narrower; sides and flanks with little or no chestnut. Bill black or blackish plumbeous; iris dark brown; legs and feet slate black or blackish plumbeous. *Male, first nuptial*: Acquired by partial prenuptial molt. Similar to nuptial adult male, but wing-quills and tail more brownish. *Male, first winter*: Acquired by partial postjuvenal molt, which does not involve wing-quills or tail. Similar to adult male in winter, but upper surface paler, more uniform, with few or no black streaks on back; wing-quills and tail somewhat more brownish; chestnut on sides and flanks reduced to a few streaks. Similar to adult female in winter but larger; upper parts averaging lighter, with somewhat less black streaking; yellow wing-bars somewhat broader; sides and flanks usually with more chestnut. *Female, first nuptial*: Acquired by partial prenuptial molt. Similar to nuptial adult female, but wing-quills and tail somewhat more brownish. *Female, first winter*: Acquired by partial postjuvenal molt. Similar to adult female in winter, but upper parts lighter, more yellowish, and more uniform, with usually little or no indication of streaks on back; jugulum, breast, sides, and flanks with more or less wash of warbler green; sides and flanks without chestnut. Similar to first winter male but smaller, yellow wing-bars averaging somewhat narrower; jugulum, breast, sides, and flanks more washed with warbler green; sides and flanks entirely without chestnut. *Juvenal*: Acquired by complete postnatal molt. Upper parts saccardo olive, dull orange citrine, or dull buffy citrine, upper tail-coverts more brownish, obscurely streaked or spotted with olive brown or clove brown, particularly on back; wings and tail as in first winter female, but edgings of wings and their coverts more brownish; yellow wing-bars paler—dull primrose yellow; sides of head and of neck pale brownish olive; chin and throat dull pale buff; jugulum light buffy olive, more or less mottled with dull white; remainder of lower surface dull white. Bill brownish slate or blackish slate, but base of mandible dull white, tip of mandible slate gray; iris dark brown; legs and feet slate color.

MEASUREMENTS: *Adult male*: Wing, 60.5–67.3 (average, 63.2) mm.; tail, 48.5–52.8 (50.3); bill (exposed culmen), 9.1–10.4 (9.9); tarsus, 17.0–19.6 (18.3); middle toe without claw, 9.4–11.2 (9.9). *Adult female*: Wing, 57.7–63.0 (60.2); tail, 45.0–48.5 (46.8); bill, 8.9–9.9 (9.4); tarsus, 17.0–18.5 (17.8); middle toe, 9.4–10.4 (9.9).

TEXAS: *Migration*: Collected north to Potter, east to Dallas and Chambers, south to Cameron, west to Brewster and Culberson cos.

BAY-BREASTED WARBLER, *Dendroica castanea* (Wilson)

SPECIES ACCOUNT

Nuptial male: chestnut crown, throat, breast, sides; black mask; buffy neck-patch, belly; black-streaked gray above; white wing-bars. *Nuptial female*: much duller, paler. *Fall birds*: olive green above; buffy below (including crissum); breast-streaks (if any) indistinct; trace of chestnut on flanks (most adults); blackish legs. Length, 5½ in.; wingspan, 8¾; weight, ½ oz.

RANGE: C. Manitoba to Nova Scotia, south to n. Great Lakes region and n. New England. Winters from c. Panama to n. Colombia and w. Venezuela.

TEXAS: (See map.) *Migration*: Late Apr. to mid-May; late Sept. to late Oct. (extremes: Apr. 20, May 26; Sept. 9, Dec. 29). Common (abundant some years on upper coast) to uncommon in spring through eastern half; very rare in northern Panhandle and in Midland Co. Scarce to rare in fall east of 99th meridian; casual in northern Panhandle and Midland Co.

HAUNTS AND HABITS: The Bay-breasted Warbler is an inhabitant of cool northern forests—primarily evergreen though occasionally deciduous—and their edges. Whether in bogs, on slopes, or in small clearings on level terrain, this warbler usually places its nest in a small conifer. During its brief passage through Texas it appears to prefer trees but occasionally flits through bushes and scrub, especially along the coast.

Flight from one feeding site to another is flitting and somewhat jerky; longer flights are steadier though still slightly erratic. The Baybreast works at all heights in trees and bushes and is a rather deliberate forager. Its diet consists largely of insects, a few spiders, and, par-

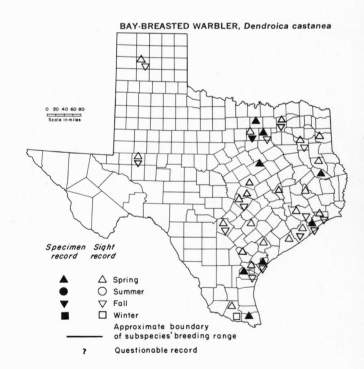

BAY-BREASTED WARBLER, *Dendroica castanea*

0 20 40 60 80
Scale in miles

Specimen record / Sight record

▲ △ Spring
● ○ Summer
▼ ▽ Fall
■ □ Winter

———— Approximate boundary of subspecies' breeding range

? Questionable record

ticularly in autumn, a small amount of vegetable matter, such as berries of Virginia creeper (though mulberries may be taken in spring). The insects include beetles (striped squash, ladybird, click, leaf-eating, June) and their larvae, two-winged flies (house, gall), mayflies, ants, lace-winged flies, ichneumon flies, moths and their cocoons, caterpillars (cankerworms, measuringworms), locusts, grasshoppers, leaf-hoppers, and dragonflies, together with eggs and larvae.

The Baybreast's usual call is a sharp *tsip*. The song it sings in spring migration is similar to that of the Black-and-white Warbler. Normally it is a series of thin, high-pitched, sibilant *wiss* notes, louder in the middle and diminishing at the end.

DETAILED ACCOUNT: NO SUBSPECIES

DESCRIPTION: *Adult male, nuptial plumage*: Acquired by partial prenuptial molt. Forehead dull black; crown and occiput dark chestnut; hindneck, back, scapulars, and rump between deep grayish olive and mouse gray, but upper tail-coverts mouse gray, hindneck and upper back sometimes strongly tinged with warm buff, back, scapulars, and upper tail-coverts broadly streaked with black, rump with a few streaks or spots of black; tail chaetura black, margined on outer webs of feathers with mouse gray, outer two tail feathers with squarish subterminal spots of white on inner webs, third feather sometimes with small white subterminal spot on inner web, remainder of tail feathers narrowly edged with white on terminal portion of inner webs; primaries and secondaries chaetura drab to hair brown, edged narrowly on outer webs with deep grayish olive, edges of inner webs, except at tips of primaries, buffy white on secondaries to dull buff on primaries; tertials hair brown, broadly edged on outer webs with light grayish olive; wing-coverts chaetura black, lesser coverts tipped and edged with light grayish olive to mouse gray, greater series edged on outer webs with mouse gray or grayish olive, median and greater coverts broadly tipped with white or buffy white, forming two conspicuous wing-bars; sides of head, including superciliary stripe, dark brownish black, sometimes slightly and narrowly streaked with dull buff or dull pale gray, and feathers sometimes obscurely tipped with chestnut; broad vertical stripe on sides of neck warm buff, posterior portion of sides of neck like hindneck; chin, throat, jugulum, sides, and flanks russet; remainder of lower surface warm buff, but middle of abdomen sometimes paler; lining of wing dull white, outer portion spotted with hair brown. Bill brownish black, but base of mandible sometimes plumbeous; iris dark brown; legs and feet dull plumbeous. *Adult male, winter*: Acquired by complete postnuptial molt. Upper surface yellowish warbler green to dull citrine, changing to mouse gray on upper tail-coverts; everywhere more or less streaked with dull black, crown usually with some chestnut, this more or less concealed; wings and tail as in nuptial adult male, but wing-coverts more or less washed with warbler green, wing-bars yellowish rather than buffy white; superciliary stripe dull pale greenish yellow; lores mouse gray, more or less washed with yellow; cheeks mixed with dull grayish olive green and dull white; sides of neck olive ocher to light greenish citrine; lower surface dull light buff, sometimes much washed with olive on sides and breast; jugulum sometimes olive ocher; sides and flanks more or less extensively russet; crissum dull warm buff. *Adult female, nuptial*: Acquired by partial prenuptial molt. Similar to nuptial adult male but smaller, duller, and with much less chestnut, pileum olive green or olive gray, numerously streaked or spotted with dull black or dull olive, with greater or lesser admixture of chestnut, sometimes forming considerable patch on posterior part of crown; remainder of upper surface much less heavily streaked than in adult male and somewhat more clearly gray; sides of head much paler, mostly dull buff or dull gray, mixed with chaetura drab; lower surface paler, chestnut everywhere

lighter and of much less extent, mixed particularly on throat and jugulum with dull buff; buff of remainder of lower parts paler. *Adult female, winter*: Acquired by complete postnuptial molt. Similar to adult male in winter but smaller, upper parts lighter, more uniform, with slightly evident blackish streaks, these reduced to slight blackish or dull brown spots or streaks and almost entirely obscured or practically absent, crown without chestnut; lower surface lighter, less deeply buff, and chestnut on sides and flanks much reduced, sometimes almost absent. *Male, first nuptial*: Acquired by partial prenuptial molt. Similar to nuptial adult male, but wing-quills, primary coverts, and tail lighter and more brownish. *Male, first winter*: Acquired by partial postjuvenal molt, which does not involve wing-quills or tail. Similar to adult male in winter, but upper surface averaging lighter, brighter, more yellowish, and much less, sometimes almost not at all, streaked with black, also with very little or no chestnut on crown; wing-quills and tail somewhat more brownish; chestnut of sides and flanks duller and of less extent. Similar to adult female in winter but larger; upper parts usually with blackish streaks less evident, and chestnut on sides and flanks somewhat more extensive. *Female, first nuptial*: Acquired by partial prenuptial molt. Similar to nuptial adult female, but colors somewhat duller, with wing-quills and tail somewhat more brownish. *Female, first winter*: Acquired by partial postjuvenal molt. Similar to adult female in winter, but upper parts averaging somewhat lighter, with rather less evident blackish streaks on back; lower surface duller and more yellowish, less buffy, crissum paler, sometimes even whitish; sides and flanks dark olive buff without chestnut, except occasionally slight wash on flanks. Similar to first winter male but smaller, upper parts averaging duller, lower surface duller, more yellowish, and with less strongly buffy suffusion, crissum of paler buff or even whitish; sides and flanks more greenish with little or no indication of chestnut; very similar to young of Blackpoll Warbler, *Dendroica breviunguis*, but upper surface usually lighter and brighter; lower surface decidedly duller, less brightly yellowish, more inclined to buff, particularly on flanks and lower tail-coverts. Legs and feet plumbeous instead of brown. *Juvenal*: Acquired by complete postnatal molt. Pileum dull tilleul buff; remainder of upper surface between light grayish olive and drab, becoming more brownish on upper tail-coverts, everywhere streaked or spotted, or on pileum irregularly barred, with fuscous or fuscous black; these markings broadest on hindneck, back, and scapulars; wings and tail as in first winter female; sides of head dull olive yellow, somewhat spotted with fuscous; chin pale buff; throat pale drab; breast and upper abdomen dull white or buffy white; remainder of abdomen and crissum dull cream buff, lower parts everywhere spotted, except on crissum, with chaetura drab and chaetura black. Bill, legs, and feet dull brown; iris dark brown.

MEASUREMENTS: *Adult male*: Wing, 71.7–76.2 (average, 73.2) mm.; tail, 51.8–56.1 (53.3); bill (exposed culmen), 9.9–11.2 (10.2); tarsus, 17.5–20.3 (18.3); middle toe without claw, 10.2–11.7 (11.2). *Adult female*: Wing, 67.8–73.7 (69.8); tail, 48.0–52.8 (50.0); bill, 9.1–10.9 (9.9); tarsus, 17.8–19.3 (18.3); middle toe, 10.2–11.7 (10.7).

TEXAS: *Migration*: Collected north to Denton, east to Angelina and Galveston, south to Cameron cos.

BLACKPOLL WARBLER, *Dendroica breviunguis* (Spix)

SPECIES ACCOUNT

Dendroica striata of A.O.U. check-list, 1957 (see Appendix A). Adult and immature of both sexes show white crissum, wing-bars; yellowish (usually) legs. *Nuptial male*: black cap; white cheeks; black-streaked gray above; white below; black malar stripe, side-streaks. *Female, fall male*: black-streaked greenish or gray above; yellowish white below with black streaks on sides. In autumn, white crissum and yellowish legs help distinguish Blackpoll from Baybreast. Length, 5½ in.; wingspan, 8¾; weight, ½ oz.

RANGE: Alaska to Newfoundland, south to c. British Columbia, c. Prairie provinces, s.e. Canada, and n.e. United States. Winters in South America from Colombia (chiefly east of Andes) and Venezuela to c. Chile.

TEXAS: (See map.) *Migration*: Late Apr. to mid-May; late Aug. to late Sept. (extremes: Apr. 6, May 18 —once to June 11; Aug. 27, Dec. 28). Irregularly common (very occasionally) to scarce (most years) in spring along upper and central coasts; rare along lower coast; extremely rare inland east of Pecos River; casual west of Pecos River. Very rare in fall, reported only along upper coast and in Rio Grande delta.

HAUNTS AND HABITS: The Blackpoll Warbler, so named because of its conspicuous black cap, is one of the most numerous warblers and one of the latest to reappear on its far northern breeding grounds. A transcontinental inhabitant of stunted coniferous forests, the Blackpoll is likely to place its nest low in a small spruce, though in some arctic areas perhaps in a dense alder thicket or even on the ground. In Texas, this far eastern migrant varies in numbers from one spring to the next, but when present is most often found in trees and bushes along the coast.

From breeding to wintering grounds, the Blackpoll migrates at least 3,500 miles; some birds probably travel 10,000 miles annually. Flight on these long journeys is slower and steadier than are short flights from tree to tree. While foraging, this warbler is sometimes very active, feeding occasionally in the outermost canopy, but more often in interior foliage. Food consists mostly of insects, some of which are caught on the wing: scale insects, cankerworms, fall webworms,

measuringworms, larvae of boring beetles, weevils, locusts, grasshoppers, ants, sawflies, parasitic wasps, bees, gnats, mosquitoes, mayflies, and termites. Additional items are mites, spiders, and sometimes, particularly in autumn, seeds and berries.

The call of the Blackpoll is a guttural *chuck*, lighter than that of the Myrtle Warbler, and with a muffled quality that is different from the ordinary sharp *chip* of many warblers. Its song, though subject to variation in form, is a thin, insectlike repetition of the syllable *tsee* or *tsit*, all on the same pitch, the notes usually rather evenly spaced and deliberately uttered.

DETAILED ACCOUNT: ONE SUBSPECIES

WESTERN BLACKPOLL WARBLER, *Dendroica breviunguis lurida* Burleigh and Peters

No races recognized by A.O.U. check-list, 1957 (see Appendix A).

DESCRIPTION: *Adult male, nuptial plumage (olive phase)*: Acquired by partial prenuptial molt. Pileum glossy black down to eyes; remainder of upper surface grayish olive, slightly more grayish posteriorly, narrow whitish collar around hindneck, this and remaining upper parts streaked with black, back most broadly; tail chaetura drab to fuscous or fuscous black, edged exteriorly with color of upper tail-coverts, two outer feathers with large terminal, somewhat squarish, spots of white on inner webs, third feather sometimes with smaller spot, remaining rectrices narrowly edged with white on terminal portion of inner webs; primaries and secondaries fuscous to chaetura drab, tertials chaetura black to fuscous black, all edged on outer webs narrowly with citrine drab, terminal edges of tertials dull pale olive yellow or pale grayish olive, inner edges of secondaries brownish white, of primaries pale brown; wing-coverts chaetura black, edged with color of back, median series tipped with dull white, greater series tipped with pale yellow or yellowish white, forming two conspicuous wing-bars; sides of head below eyes white; sides of neck grayish white, streaked with dull black; lower surface, including lining of wing, white; broad black stripe or series of broad black streaks on side of throat meeting across chin and extending as chain along sides of breast and of body onto flanks; outer under wing-coverts more or less spotted with chaetura drab or chaetura black and sometimes washed with yellow. Bill black, slate color, or blackish slate, but base of mandible dull brown, dull white, yellow, yellowish white, or dull flesh color; iris vandyke brown; legs and feet hair brown, broccoli brown, yellowish green, deep chrome, or pale orange; claws seal brown. *Adult male, nuptial (gray phase)*: Acquired by partial prenuptial molt. Similar to olive phase, but back and posterior upper surface much more clearly grayish—rather brownish neutral gray—without olive tinge; wing-bars very faintly if at all washed with yellow. *Adult male, winter*: Acquired by complete postnuptial molt. Upper surface dull warbler green or serpentine green, rump and upper tail-coverts between mouse gray and neutral gray, washed with green of back; back, rump, and upper tail-coverts broadly, anterior parts narrowly, streaked with chaetura black; wings and tail as in nuptial adult male but somewhat washed with warbler green, and wing-bars primrose yellow or yellowish white; superciliary stripe dull citrine yellow; sides of head light yellowish olive; anterior lower parts dull white or yellowish white, tinged with pale olive yellow or amber yellow, deepest on breast and jugulum, remaining lower surface washed with same color, but sides and flanks light grayish olive or light brownish olive, sides of breast and of body and flanks obscurely streaked with dark olive gray; crissum white or yellowish white. *Adult female, nuptial (olive phase)*: Acquired by partial prenuptial molt. Similar to adult male in winter but smaller; upper surface usually somewhat more heavily streaked; wings and tail more brownish; sides of throat, of breast, and of

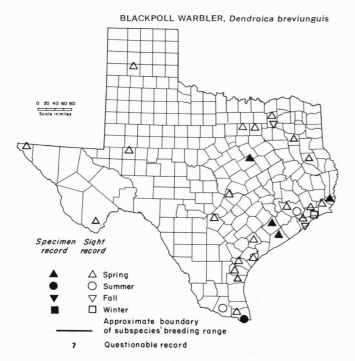

BLACKPOLL WARBLER, *Dendroica breviunguis*

0 20 40 60 80
Scale in miles

Specimen   Sight
record   record

▲   △ Spring
●   ○ Summer
▼   ▽ Fall
■   □ Winter

Approximate boundary
of subspecies' breeding range

?   Questionable record

body, with flanks, more conspicuously dark-streaked; lower surface often more strongly tinged with yellow. *Adult female, nuptial (gray phase)*: Acquired by partial prenuptial molt. Similar to nuptial adult male in gray phase, but deep olive gray to mouse gray above, crown not so black but streaked with chaetura black as are hindneck, back, and longest upper tail-coverts; wing-bars rather more yellowish; superciliary stripe yellowish white; sides of neck brownish gray like upper surface, narrowly streaked with chaetura black; lower surface dull white; sides of throat, of breast, and of body with narrow chaetura drab streaks. *Adult female, winter*: Acquired by complete postnuptial molt. Similar to nuptial adult female in olive phase, but upper parts rather more brightly olive green, black streaks much obscured by olive green edges and tips of feathers, streaks on pileum narrower and more inconspicuous or usually entirely absent; lower surface much more strongly tinged with yellow; blackish streaks on sides of breast and of body practically absent or very slightly indicated, lower parts thus more uniform. Similar to adult male in winter but smaller, upper parts duller, somewhat more uniform, streaks narrower and less conspicuous, even entirely absent, from pileum; rump and upper tail-coverts more uniformly olive green (less grayish); lower surface more brightly and more uniformly yellow. *Male, first nuptial*: Acquired by partial prenuptial molt. Similar to nuptial adult male, but wing-quills and tail more brownish. *Male, first winter*: Acquired by partial postjuvenal molt, which does not involve wing-quills or tail. Similar to adult male in winter, but upper parts usually more yellowish and more obscurely streaked; rump and upper tail-coverts less grayish but more uniformly olive green; wing-quills and tail more brownish (less blackish); lower surface, except crissum, much more brightly and more extensively yellow—deep amber yellow or mustard yellow; streaks on sides and flanks often obsolete. Similar to adult female in winter but larger; upper surface averaging somewhat brighter, more yellowish; yellow wing-bars usually broader; lower surface more brightly yellow. Very easily confused with same plumage of Bay-breasted Warbler, *Dendroica castanea*, but differs in having pure white or yellowish white, instead of buffy, under tail-coverts; more brightly yellowish lower parts with little or no buffy tinge; and legs and feet brownish instead of plumbeous. Bill brownish slate, blackish slate, or slate color, but basal half of mandible dull white, yellowish white, or even deep chrome, iris dark brown, prout brown, broccoli brown, or olive; feet similar, or even raw umber or very dark brown. *Female, first nuptial*: Acquired by partial prenuptial molt. Similar to nuptial adult female, but wing-quills and tail somewhat more brownish. *Female, first winter*: Acquired by partial postjuvenal molt, which does not involve wing-quills or tail. Similar to adult female in winter, but upper parts somewhat more uniform and more brightly yellowish, with less evident streaks on back; lower parts more brightly yellowish. Similar to first winter male but smaller, averaging rather lighter, more uniform, and less streaked with blackish above. Maxilla and tip of mandible black; remainder of mandible yellowish white; iris vandyke brown; legs seal brown; toes and claws tawny olive. *Juvenal*: Acquired by complete postnatal molt. Pileum drab; remainder of upper surface drab or between drab and light grayish olive, everywhere spotted or barred, most broadly on back, with dull black or chaetura black; sides of head dark olive buff, somewhat mixed with dull black; lower surface buffy white or grayish white, numerously barred and spotted everywhere, least so on crissum and middle of abdomen, with chaetura black; wings and tail as in first winter female, wing-bars very narrow and yellowish or buffy white, outer edgings of primaries and secondaries citrine drab.

MEASUREMENTS: *Adult male*: Wing, 71.4–77.7 (average, 74.2) mm.; tail, 48.8–54.1 (51.3); bill (exposed culmen), 9.1–10.7 (10.2); tarsus, 18.3–20.3 (19.3); middle toe without claw, 10.7–13.0 (11.9). *Adult female*: Wing, 69.1–74.9 (71.7); tail, 45.0–51.1 (48.3); bill, 8.9–10.9 (9.9); tarsus, 18.0–20.1 (19.3); middle toe, 10.4–11.9 (11.4).

RANGE: N.w. Alaska and Alberta to n. Quebec, south to c. British Columbia and s. Manitoba. Winters from c. Venezuela to w. Chile.

TEXAS: *Migration*: Collected north to McLennan, east to Orange, south to Cameron (Aug.) cos.

PINE WARBLER, *Dendroica pinus* (Wilson)

SPECIES ACCOUNT

Nuptial (female somewhat duller): olive green above; yellow throat, breast (faintly streaked with olive); white belly, wing-bars. *Winter adults and immature*: paler; more brownish or grayish; some birds without yellow. Length, 5½ in.; wingspan, 8¾; weight, ½ oz.

RANGE: S. Manitoba to s. Quebec and c. Maine, south to e. Texas, Gulf coast, Florida; also Bahamas and Hispaniola. Winters in southern half of breeding range and slightly southwest into s. Texas and extreme n.e. Mexico (rarely).

TEXAS: (See map.) *Breeding*: Probably late Mar. to late July (no egg dates available, but adults seen feeding young, Bastrop State Park, Rose Ann Rowlett) from near sea level to 400 ft. Common to fairly common in pine woods of eastern quarter and in and near Bastrop and Buescher state parks, Bastrop Co. *Migration*: Mid-Mar. to late Apr.; late Sept. to late Nov. (extremes: Mar. 9, May 19; Aug. 27, Dec. 3). Common within breeding range; uncommon to scarce in remainder of eastern half. *Winter*: Mid-Dec. to mid-Mar. Common (most years) to fairly common within breeding range; fairly common locally to scarce in remainder of state east of 100th meridian, but rare in Rio Grande delta; extremely rare at Del Rio. Sighted once at El Paso.

HAUNTS AND HABITS: Within Texas, the Pine Warbler breeds in lowland pine forests. During winter this bird preserves its affinity for lowlands but it no longer re-

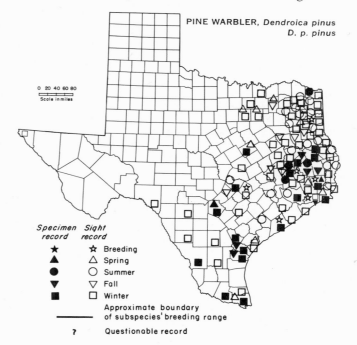

PINE WARBLER, *Dendroica pinus*
D. p. pinus

0 20 40 60 80
Scale in miles

Specimen record / Sight record

★ / ☆ Breeding
▲ / △ Spring
● / ○ Summer
▼ / ▽ Fall
■ / □ Winter

——— Approximate boundary of subspecies' breeding range

? Questionable record

quires pines. In fact, it often occurs in mixed ever-green and deciduous woodlands far from piney woods. Its migratory habit and its ability to live without pines has enabled it to colonize (apparently sometime prior to 1925) Bastrop's "lost pines," an isolated *Pinus* island surrounded by deciduous trees and prairies.

Its usual flight is quick and erratic and seldom much prolonged. On longer journeys, however, it is steadier. In search of food the Pine Warbler ranges high amongst terminal pine needle tufts or searches bark crevices of larger branches and trunks, where it creeps much like a Black-and-white Warbler though not so actively. At times it catches insects on the wing; in winter it often goes to the ground to feed. Its diet includes insects and their larvae (moths, caterpillars, beetles, ants, gall flies, plant lice, locusts, grasshoppers, and crickets), some spiders, and even suet. In winter it consumes considerable vegetable matter: pine seeds, and berries of sumac, dogwood, poison-ivy, Virginia creeper, bayberry, yaupon, and wild grape.

A weak *chip* or *tip* is the call note of the Pine Warbler. Its song is a rapid, monotonous repetition of a single note much like that of the Chipping Sparrow, but slower, softer, and more liquid and musical. It sings while sitting still—lifting its head to utter its song —or during its search for food. The period of persistent singing begins in February and continues into July, but males may be heard sporadically throughout the winter.

DETAILED ACCOUNT: ONE SUBSPECIES

NORTHERN PINE WARBLER, *Dendroica pinus pinus* (Wilson)

DESCRIPTION: *Adult male, nuptial plumage*: Acquired by wear from winter plumage. Upper parts between citrine and warbler green, slightly and obscurely mottled by darker centers of feathers; tail dark hair brown to chaetura drab, basal portion of feathers margined on outer webs with mouse gray, two outer tail feathers with large terminal oblique spots on inner webs, middle portion of outer web of outermost feather dull white; primaries and secondaries chaetura drab to fuscous; tertials similar, but somewhat darker; outer webs of these feathers narrowly margined with dull drab, inner edges of secondaries brownish white, those of primaries pale brown or brownish white except at tips; lesser wing-coverts warbler green like back, and remaining coverts dark hair brown, but greater coverts edged on outer webs with dull drab and median and greater coverts, except innermost, broadly tipped with brownish white or very pale drab, forming two rather broad wing-bars; superciliary stripe gamboge yellow; lores warbler green or chaetura drab, sometimes mixed with buff; remainder of sides of head similar to crown; lower surface, except abdomen and crissum, gamboge yellow, but breast, jugulum, sides of body, and flanks more or less streaked, often obscurely, with olive; abdomen and crissum dull white or grayish white or dull pale buff, flanks often washed with gamboge yellow, particularly on edge of wing, outer under wing-coverts somewhat spotted with hair brown. Bill slate black, blackish slate, or brownish black, but mandible often plumbeous at base with dull yellowish tinge, dull white, pale yellow, or flesh color; cutting edges of bill lighter; iris dark reddish brown; legs prout brown, russet, yellowish brown, or hair brown; feet broccoli brown, hair brown, yellowish brown, or russet. *Adult male, winter*: Acquired by complete postnuptial molt. Similar to nuptial adult male, but upper surface usually somewhat lighter,

more brownish or grayish, and usually more uniform, feathers, particularly on back and scapulars, tipped with dull brown or dull gray; yellow of lower parts brighter but usually more or less veiled with white or pale buff edges and tips of feathers; dark streaks on lower parts less distinct and much obscured by yellow or buffy tips of feathers. Bill more brownish, basal part of mandible noticeably paler. *Adult female, nuptial (gray phase)*: Acquired by wear from winter. Much smaller and much less brightly colored than nuptial adult male, yellow duller, paler, less extensive, and entire plumage more grayish. Forehead and crown citrine, nape, and sometimes occiput, deep grayish olive to mouse gray; back saccardo olive to light brownish olive; upper tail-coverts dull citrine; wing and tail as in nuptial adult male, but white spots on tail smaller and light wing-bars narrower and somewhat more brownish or buffy; superciliary stripe dull strontian yellow; lores and auriculars dull mouse gray, latter sometimes washed with yellow; dull whitish spot below eye; cheeks and sides of neck similar to auriculars, but rather paler; chin and throat dull white, slightly washed with yellow; jugulum and breast between dull wax yellow and dull primuline yellow; remainder of lower surface dull buffy white, but sides and flanks buffy grayish olive; lining of wing dull grayish drab. *Adult female, nuptial (yellow phase)*: Acquired by wear from winter. Similar to gray phase, but upper surface with very much more yellow, back orange citrine; anterior lower parts decidedly more deeply and extensively yellowish from chin to lower breast; sides and flanks more strongly brownish; crissum pale buff. Much smaller and less brightly colored than nuptial adult male. *Adult female, winter (gray and yellow phases)*: Acquired by complete postnuptial molt. Similar to nuptial adult female, but upper surface more brownish, more uniform and blended, due to more brownish tips and edgings of feathers; light wing-bars more brownish or buffy; yellow of anterior lower parts obscured by pale gray, pale brown, or buff tips of feathers; sides and flanks more brownish. *Male, first nuptial*: Acquired by wear from first winter. Similar to nuptial adult male, but wing-quills and tail somewhat more brownish. *Male, first winter*: Acquired by partial postjuvenal molt, which does not involve wing-quills or tail. Similar to adult male in winter, but upper parts much duller, more brownish, a light olive brown or buffy brown color overlying dull citrine of basal part of plumage; wing-quills and tail somewhat more brownish; lower surface duller; yellow of anterior lower parts paler and much veiled by light buffy gray or dull white edgings of feathers, darker streaks still fainter and more obscured. Similar to adult female in winter, yellow phase, but much larger; white spots on tail feathers larger; upper parts lighter and much more yellowish; yellow of lower surface much brighter and more extensive. *Female, first nuptial*: Acquired by wear from first winter. Similar to nuptial adult female, but wing-quills and tail somewhat more brownish. *Female, first winter*: Acquired by partial postjuvenal molt. Similar to adult female in winter but smaller; in gray phase somewhat lighter above and paler and duller below, particularly yellow of anterior portion which is much overlaid by pale buffy edgings of feathers, rest of lower parts more buffy, sides and flanks more brownish; in yellow phase upper surface lighter than in adult female, more uniformly brownish with very little greenish or yellowish tint, usually light brownish olive, lower parts paler and duller with little or no yellow on anterior portion, sides of head dull drab, flanks light buffy brown to drab. *Male, juvenal*: Acquired by complete postnatal molt. Upper surface between cinnamon brown and dresden brown; wings and tail as in first winter; sides of head similar to crown, but paler; superciliary stripe and area below eye still paler; sides of throat pale buffy brown or cream color; lower surface dull straw yellow, pale dull brown, or buffy white; breast and jugulum thickly spotted, sometimes almost solidly, with buffy olive to light brownish olive, middle of chin and throat not spotted, posterior lower parts usually lightly spotted or obscurely streaked, except on flanks and sides which are darker and more heavily marked—sometimes almost uniformly brown. Bill blackish slate, but cutting edges lighter, mandible, except for dark tip, flesh color or dull whitish; iris dark brown; legs broccoli brown; feet hair brown or russet. *Female, juvenal*: Acquired by complete postnatal molt. Similar to juvenal male, but white tail spots smaller. *Natal*: Sepia. Bill, legs, and feet pinkish buff tinged with brown.

MEASUREMENTS: *Adult male*: Wing, 67.6–75.9 (average, 73.2) mm.; tail, 51.6–57.9 (54.6); bill (exposed culmen), 9.9–11.4 (10.7); tarsus, 17.5–19.6 (18.8); middle toe without claw, 11.9–13.5 (12.7). *Adult female*: Wing, 66.5–70.6 (68.3); tail, 50.5–53.6 (51.8); bill, 9.7–10.9 (10.2); tarsus, 17.0–19.0 (18.3); middle toe, 11.9–13.5 (12.2).

RANGE: S. Manitoba to Nova Scotia, south to e. Texas and n.e. Florida. Winters from Massachusetts (rarely) through s.e. United States to n.e. Tamaulipas.

TEXAS: *Breeding*: Collected north to Bowie, south to Hardin, west to Montgomery and Walker cos. *Migration*: Collected north to Trinity, east to Tyler and Chambers, south to Nueces, west to Bexar cos. *Winter*: Taken north to McLennan, east to Angelina and Jefferson, south to Cameron, west to Webb cos.

NESTING: *Nest*: In forests, chiefly in pine or mixed woods; ordinarily on pine tree, usually on horizontal bough, often toward end of limb, usually 18–50 ft.—sometimes 130 ft.—above ground, and well concealed; well built and deeply cupped, though sometimes much thinner and less solid; composed of pine needles, oak and other leaves, sedges, strips of grapevine and other bark, bits of weeds, stems of leaves, small twigs, grasses, fine webs of cocoons, and caterpillar silk; lined with dead tops of sedges, fine rootlets, fibers of bark, grasses, string, pine needles, down from ferns, hair, bristles, chicken and other feathers, as well as fur of mammals, with silky down of plants. *Eggs*: 3–5; usually 4; short ovate to ovate; dull white, grayish white, bluish white, purplish white, or cream white; spotted and dotted with burnt umber, madder brown, purplish brown, and dull black, with shell markings of lavender and lilac gray, usually more numerous near large end and forming wreath; average size, 18.3 × 13.7 mm.

PRAIRIE WARBLER, *Dendroica discolor* (Vieillot)

SPECIES ACCOUNT

Wags tail; in most plumages shows blackish spot on side of neck. *Nuptial male*: olive green above; yellow below; black stripes on face, sides; chestnut streaks on back; whitish wing-bars. *Female, fall male*: slightly duller; back-streaks (if any) more obscure. Length, 4¾ in.; wingspan, 7; weight, ¼ oz.

RANGE: S.e. South Dakota, s. Great Lakes region, and s. New Hampshire, south to e. Oklahoma, Louisiana, c. Gulf states, and s. Florida. Winters chiefly from c. Florida through West Indies, and on islands off Mexico and Central America from Quintana Roo to Costa Rica.

TEXAS: (See map.) *Breeding*: Probably late May to late July (no egg dates available, but adults nest building, May 30–June 5, and feeding young, July 4–10, 1955, O. C. Sheffield). Scarce and irregular in eastern quarter, definite nesting records from Smith, Sabine, Jasper, and Newton cos.; nesting highly likely in Hardin Co. (4 singing males presumed to be on territory, May 5, 1972, T. B. Feltner, J. A. Lane). *Migration*: Late Apr. to early May; early Aug. to late Sept. (extremes: Apr. 11, May 21; July 26, Nov. 14). Fairly common to uncommon in northeastern portion (north of 31st parallel, east of 96th meridian); uncommon (some falls; usually upper coast) to rare (most springs) in remainder of eastern half; extremely rare in northern

Panhandle; casual in Midland Co. *Winter*: Late Dec. to late Feb. A scattering of sightings along upper coast; one from Rio Grande delta, Starr Co. (Dec. 28, 1971, G. F. Oatman, Jr.); one reported inland at Austin (Feb. 13, 1953, W. D. Anderson). Dead individual found in car grill near Beaumont (Jan. 29, 1956, J. C. Arvin).

HAUNTS AND HABITS: Inaptly named, the Prairie Warbler does not inhabit prairies. Rather, when seeking a nesting site, it inspects heavily cut or burned areas partially overgrown with deciduous saplings and bushes, low, open second-growth pine stands with scrubby understory, margins of woodlands, and mangroves (in Florida). Probably because of the temporary character of the plant communities it inhabits, its distribution is spotty and inconstant. During migration and winter in Texas it most often frequents open woodlands and thickets.

The Prairie's flight is quick and somewhat nervous and ordinarily not long sustained; longer flights are swift but still erratic. A low-ranging forager, it slips rather easily and quickly through the branches, constantly tilting its tail and often fluttering its wings. Food of the Northern Prairie Warbler consists almost entirely of animal matter, very largely insects, their eggs and larvae. Moths, butterflies, caterpillars, deerflies, lanternflies, stink bugs, grasshoppers, locusts, beetles (flea, ladybird, leaf, long-horn, and click), weevils, and ants comprise the main diet, together with a few spiders.

The usual call note of this warbler is a weak *chip*. The Prairie's song, often delivered from the top of a bush or low tree, is one of the most distinctive of warbler songs. It is a thin, but somewhat mellow, series of

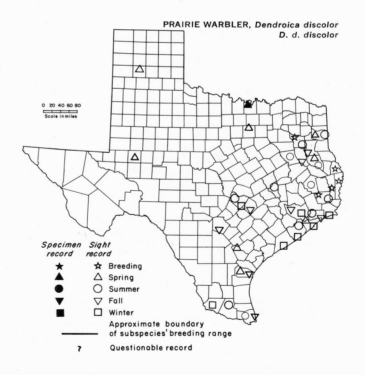

PRAIRIE WARBLER, *Dendroica discolor*
D. d. discolor

0 20 40 60 80
Scale in miles

Specimen record / Sight record

★ / ☆ Breeding
▲ / △ Spring
● / ○ Summer
▼ / ▽ Fall
■ / □ Winter

——— Approximate boundary of subspecies' breeding range

? Questionable record

lisping *tze*-like notes on a rising scale. Males may sing from their appearance in spring until July.

CHANGES: During the 1950's, sightings of the Prairie Warbler in Texas were more numerous than they had been in previous years. This decade probably represented the time when much sprout-land had reached the proper stage to interest the Prairie, and pesticides had not yet built up dangerously in most parts of this bird's environment.

DETAILED ACCOUNT: ONE SUBSPECIES

NORTHERN PRAIRIE WARBLER, *Dendroica discolor discolor* (Vieillot)

DESCRIPTION: *Adult male, nuptial plumage*: Acquired by partial prenuptial molt. Upper parts yellowish warbler green, back with numerous spots or short broad streaks of bay, chestnut, or auburn; tail chaetura black, outer webs of feathers narrowly margined basally with olive gray or dull citrine, two outer pairs with long, white, more or less oblique, terminal spots on inner webs, third feather with more squarish subterminal spot of white on inner web, outer web of outermost feather white on middle portion; primaries and secondaries dark hair brown, secondaries margined on inner webs basally with dull white or brownish white, inner edges of primaries except at tips pale brown, outer edges of primaries and secondaries like upper surface but somewhat duller; tertials light chaetura drab, outer edges similar to back but paler and more brownish; lesser wing-coverts like back, greater and median series chaetura black, lesser wing-coverts broadly tipped with dull lemon yellow or yellowish white, forming broad wing-bar, greater series margined on outer web like primaries, outer webs broadly tipped with pale dull yellow, dull buff, or brownish white, forming another, though rather poorly defined, wing-bar; superciliary stripe gamboge yellow to light cadmium; lores black, small spot behind eye dull black; black rictal streak extending in curve to auriculars; black spot on each side of throat; remainder of sides of head dull gamboge yellow; sides of neck like upper surface; crissum baryta yellow; remainder of lower surface gamboge yellow, but sides of throat, of breast, and of body broadly streaked with black; lining of wing lemon yellow or brownish white washed with yellow; outer under wing-coverts somewhat spotted with mouse gray. Bill olive brown, olivaceous black, or blackish slate, but basal half of mandible pale yellow; iris dark brown; legs, feet, and claws clove brown; soles of toes greenish yellow. *Adult male, winter*: Acquired by complete postnuptial molt. Similar to nuptial adult male, but chestnut spots of back more or less obscured by olive green margins of feathers, sometimes entirely hidden; black streaks of lower parts less distinct, more obscured by yellow tips of feathers. *Adult female, nuptial*: Acquired by partial prenuptial molt. Similar to nuptial adult male but smaller, olive green of upper parts somewhat paler, noticeably duller, less yellowish (more grayish); chestnut spots on back smaller and less numerous, sometimes wanting; wing-bars duller and less conspicuous, dull drab, dull buff, or pale buffy olive; sides of head duller; black markings usually replaced by olive or mouse gray; yellow of sides of head mixed or washed with olive, except superciliary stripe; yellow of lower parts rather lighter and duller, and black streaks on lower parts narrower, more grayish, often on flanks absent or obsolete. *Adult female, winter*: Acquired by complete postnuptial molt. Similar to nuptial adult female, but upper parts with colors more blended and more uniform, sometimes with wash of gray due to very narrow edgings of feathers; sides of head usually more grayish and duller, superciliary stripe often less distinct; chestnut spots of back overlaid and hidden by margins of feathers; yellow of lower surface rather duller, dark streaks on sides still more obscured by yellow tips of feathers; sometimes almost entirely covered. *Male, first nuptial*: Acquired by partial prenuptial molt in which wing-quills and tail of juvenal are retained. Similar to nuptial adult male. *Male, first winter*: Acquired by partial postjuvenal molt, which does not involve wing-quills or tail. Similar to adult male in winter, but upper surface darker, duller, more brownish or grayish; wing-bars duller, more brownish or olive, bar on median coverts much less yellowish; sides of head much duller, more grayish, black markings obscured or replaced by olive or gray; superciliary stripe less distinct, paler, sometimes yellowish white; yellow of lower surface duller and paler, black streaks narrower, and more obscured by lighter edgings of feathers; chin and throat usually decidedly paler than breast, chin often buffy, even whitish. Bill paler brown. Similar to adult female in winter but larger, upper surface averaging darker, chestnut spots on back, although covered by olive green tips of feathers, are larger and more evident. *Female, first nuptial*: Acquired by partial prenuptial molt. Similar to first winter female, except somewhat paler. *Female, first winter*: Acquired by partial postjuvenal molt, which does not involve wing-quills or tail. Similar to adult female in winter, but upper parts darker, more brownish; back between light brownish olive and snuff brown; crown and rump light yellowish olive to buffy olive; chestnut spots on back often absent; sides of head more grayish (less yellowish) olive, usually mostly drab, auriculars sometimes darker; yellow of lower surface paler, streaks still fainter, and more obscured; sides and flanks usually more brownish, chin and throat decidedly paler than breast, chin pale buff or almost white. Similar to first winter male but smaller; chestnut spots on back smaller or absent; lower surface paler, streaks on sides and flanks duller, less blackish, and much more obscured. *Juvenal*: Acquired by complete postnatal molt. Pileum between drab and buffy brown; remainder of upper surface dull buffy brown; tail light chaetura drab, three outer feathers with large white spots on inner webs, as in adult; wing-quills light hair brown, lesser coverts like back, tips of greater and median coverts dull cream buff or dull light chamois; sides of head like crown but rather paler, and with narrow, faint superciliary line of dull white, lores hair brown, and light spot below eye; throat and jugulum deep olive buff or wood brown; chin similar, but paler; remainder of lower surface pale yellow—dull marguerite yellow, streaked, except on middle of abdomen, with buffy olive. Bill olive brown, but mandible pale brown or dull white at base; iris dark brown or hazel; legs and feet olive brown. *Natal*: Drab to dark drab. Bill, legs, and feet pinkish buff.

MEASUREMENTS: *Adult male*: Wing, 52.1–58.9 (average, 56.6) mm.; tail, 41.9–50.0 (46.8); bill (exposed culmen), 8.6–9.9 (9.4); tarsus, 17.0–19.6 (18.3); middle toe without claw, 9.9–10.9 (10.2). *Adult female*: Wing, 51.1–55.1 (53.3); tail, 40.9–46.5 (44.2); bill, 8.9–9.9 (9.1); tarsus, 17.0–19.0 (17.8); middle toe, 8.9–9.9 (9.6).

RANGE: S.e. South Dakota to s. New Hampshire, south to e. Oklahoma and n. Florida. Winters from s.e. South Carolina through West Indies, and on islands off Mexico and Central America from Quintana Roo to Honduras.

TEXAS: *Migration*: Two specimens: Cooke Co., Gainesville (May 21, 1885, G. H. Ragsdale); Harris–Fort Bend county line, Buffalo Bayou (ca. 1880, H. Nehrling).

NESTING: *Nest*: On slopes and level land, usually dry situations, rather open country with scattered bushes and trees, often near streams or lakes, in dry, rocky, bushy pastures, and scrubby open woodlands; in bush or low tree, usually in fork, 1–12 ft. above ground; beautiful, deep cup, ordinarily compactly built and well concealed; composed of fine grass, pieces of various wild plants, straw, feathers, dry leaves, inner bark of red cedar and other trees, down of dandelion, milkweed, ferns, and other plants, cottony fibers of various kinds; lined with hair and very fine straw, rootlets, moss stems, plant down, and feathers. *Eggs*: 3–6, usually 4; ovate to rounded ovate; white or pale greenish white; blotched, spotted, and dotted, often gathered in wreath at large end, with purplish brown, chestnut brown, burnt umber, vandyke brown, and shell markings of lilac, lavender, and lavender gray; average size, 16.5 × 12.2 mm.

PALM WARBLER, *Dendroica palmarum* (Gmelin)

SPECIES ACCOUNT

Wags tail. *Nuptial* (sexes similar): brownish above; chestnut-streaked yellow below (western race has whitish belly); chestnut crown; yellow eye-stripe, crissum. *Winter*: duller, paler. Length, 5¼ in.; wingspan, 6¾; weight, ½ oz.

RANGE: S.w. Mackenzie to Newfoundland, south to n. Great Lakes region, Maine, and Nova Scotia. Winters from coastal Texas and North Carolina (occasionally farther north) through West Indies to Yucatán Peninsula and Honduras.

TEXAS: (See map.) *Migration*: Mid-Apr.—early Mar. along coast—to early May; late Sept. to early Nov. (extremes: late Feb., May 22; Aug. 31, Nov. 16). Fairly common (some falls) to uncommon (most springs) along upper coast; scarce to rare in remainder of eastern half; extremely rare in northern Panhandle and in Midland Co. A specimen of yellow race, *hypochrysea*, collected in Big Bend (see detailed account). *Winter*: Early Dec. to late Mar. Fairly common (some years) to uncommon along upper coast; scarce along central coast; rare on lower coast, in Rio Grande delta, and inland in eastern half—where recorded at Tyler, Austin, and San Antonio.

HAUNTS AND HABITS: On its northern, chiefly Canadian, breeding ground, the Palm Warbler exhibits preference for open spruce-tamarack muskegs and bogs. Typically, the nest is set in sphagnum moss growing on damp ground under a water- or cold-stunted tree. At other seasons, however, it occurs in almost any kind of coniferous or broad-leaved woodland or thicket; also

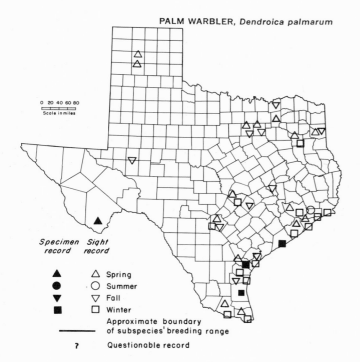

PALM WARBLER, *Dendroica palmarum*

0 20 40 60 80
Scale in miles

Specimen Sight
record record

▲   △ Spring
●   ○ Summer
▼   ▽ Fall
■   □ Winter
         Approximate boundary
——————— of subspecies' breeding range

?   Questionable record

in open, weedy fields and edges; and even about towns and gardens. During winter it often assembles in considerable numbers—but rather loose flocks—frequently associating with Myrtle and other warblers.

Its usual flight is rather flitting and performed with moderately rapid wing-beats. Longer flight is more direct but still erratic. This warbler probably spends more time feeding in low bushes and on the ground than does any other *Dendroica*. It eats chiefly insects and their larvae, a few spiders, and in winter some berries and seeds. Insects taken include weevils and other beetles, grubs; house flies, mosquitoes, gnats; moths, butterflies, cottonworms; ants; plant lice; grasshoppers, and mayflies. While foraging, it almost constantly pumps its tail up and down. In fact, the bird bobs its tail when it is resting; some bright graduate student should investigate whether this motion continues even when the Palm is asleep!

Its usual call note is a weak *tsip* or *chip*. Its common song has been described as a weak, Chipping Sparrow–like trill: *tsee-tsee-tsee-tsee*, with a distinct swell.

DETAILED ACCOUNT: TWO SUBSPECIES

WESTERN PALM WARBLER, *Dendroica palmarum palmarum* (Gmelin)

DESCRIPTION: *Adult male, nuptial plumage*: Acquired by partial prenuptial molt. Forehead dull black with narrow median line of lemon yellow or strontian yellow; pileum dark chestnut to burnt sienna; hindneck, back, and rump light brownish olive, but becoming somewhat more yellowish on rump, centers of feathers dull olive brown, giving slight streaked or mottled appearance; upper tail-coverts dull olive yellow, central portions or shaft stripes buffy olive; tail fuscous to fuscous black, outermost feather edged terminally with light brown, basally, with other feathers, edged exteriorly with light yellowish olive, outermost two tail feathers with large terminal white spots on inner webs; wings fuscous, inner margins of wing-quills light fuscous, primaries edged on outer webs very narrowly with citrine drab, tertials rather more broadly with light fuscous; all upper wing-coverts tipped and edged exteriorly with dull wood brown or avellaneous to tilleul buff, those on greater and median coverts forming rather poorly defined wing-bars; sides of head grayish buffy brown, mixed with fuscous, fuscous black, grayish white, and yellowish white, last chiefly on region below eye, and lores mostly fuscous or fuscous black continuous with postocular streak of fuscous and bounded below by another dark streak on side of throat; superciliary stripe, chin, throat, jugulum, and breast strontian yellow to lemon yellow, jugulum and breast often much mixed with dull buff; sides of throat, of jugulum, and of breast with narrow streaks or spots of fuscous, fuscous black, tawny, and russet to cinnamon brown; abdomen barium yellow, often more or less mixed with buff or yellowish white; crissum strontian yellow; sides of body and flanks dull buffy brown, washed with yellow; edge of wing amber yellow; lining of wing smoke gray, spotted, particularly outwardly, with hair brown and washed with pale yellow. Bill black or blackish brown, but base of mandible drab; tongue white, but tip blackish; iris dark brown; legs, feet, and claws seal brown or olive brown; soles of toes greenish yellow. *Adult male, winter*: Acquired by complete postnuptial molt. Similar to nuptial adult male, but chestnut of crown much or almost entirely hidden by brown tips of feathers; colors of upper parts more blended because of much broader tips of feathers and broader, more conspicuous lighter edgings of wing and tail; superciliary stripe much paler—yellowish white, buffy white, or dull buff instead of bright yellow; lower surface much duller, more grayish, less brightly yellow; throat dull brownish white, grayish white, or pale dull buff, dark streaks on sides of throat and on jugulum much less conspicuous, more blended, due to broad light tips of feathers, yellow of breast and posterior lower parts much obscured by overlying gray tips of feathers. *Adult female, nuptial*: Acquired by partial prenuptial molt. Similar to nuptial adult male but smaller; chestnut of pileum of less extent; lower surface somewhat duller and less extensively yellow; upper tail-coverts usually somewhat duller. *Adult female, winter*: Acquired by complete postnuptial molt. Differs from nuptial adult female, as does adult male in winter from nuptial adult male; differs from adult male in winter as does nuptial adult female from nuptial adult male. *Male, first nuptial*: Acquired by partial prenuptial molt. Similar to nuptial adult male, but chestnut of pileum of lesser extent; lower parts duller, less strongly and less extensively yellow; streaks on jugulum and sides of throat and of body narrower, less numerous, and of lighter color (less dark brownish or blackish). *Male, first winter*: Acquired by partial postjuvenal molt, not including wing-quills or tail. Similar to adult male in winter, but pileum with little or no chestnut; lower parts more buffy and often less heavily streaked. Bill black, but base of mandible dull white; iris prout brown; legs and feet black, but soles of toes dull yellowish white. *Female, first nuptial*: Acquired by partial prenuptial molt. Similar to nuptial adult female, but chestnut crown-patch smaller, lower surface duller, less yellowish, and less heavily streaked. *Female, first winter*: Acquired by partial postjuvenal molt. Similar to adult female in winter, but without chestnut crown-patch or, at most, with only a few chestnut feathers; lower surface duller, less yellowish, and less conspicuously streaked, in fresh plumage more buffy. *Juvenal*: Acquired by complete postnatal molt. Pileum isabella color; remainder of upper surface saccardo umber to light brownish olive, everywhere irregularly spotted and streaked, on back irregularly barred, with fuscous, olive brown, or fuscous black; upper tail-coverts yellowish olive, mixed with tawny; wings and tail as in first winter, but lesser wing-coverts dull buffy citrine, median and greater coverts tipped with dull buff, and margins of tertials cinnamon brown; lower surface yellowish white, much streaked and spotted with fuscous.

MEASUREMENTS: *Adult male*: Wing, 62.0–67.3 (average, 64.5) mm.; tail, 50.5–53.8 (52.8); bill (exposed culmen), 9.1–10.2 (9.7); tarsus, 19.8–20.9 (20.3); middle toe without claw, 11.7–12.7 (12.2). *Adult female*: Wing, 59.7–62.7 (60.7); tail, 47.8–51.8 (49.0); bill, 9.7–10.2 (9.9); tarsus, 19.0–19.8 (19.6); middle toe, 11.2–12.7 (11.7).

RANGE: S.w. Mackenzie to w. Ontario, south to c. Alberta and c. Michigan. Winters from s.e. Texas, South Carolina, and Florida through West Indies to Yucatán Peninsula and Honduras.

TEXAS: *Winter*: Three specimens: Matagorda Co., Colorado River (Jan. 17, 1936, Feb. 16, 1937, H. H. Kimball). San Patricio Co., Welder Wildlife Refuge (Dec. 29, 1964, C. Cottam; skin in Welder collection).

YELLOW PALM WARBLER, *Dendroica palmarum hypochrysea* Ridgway

DESCRIPTION: *Adult male and female, nuptial plumage*: Similar to *D. p. palmarum* but larger; all lower parts conspicuously yellow in all plumages; upper surface, except head, more olivaceous (less brownish).

MEASUREMENTS: *Adult male*: Wing, 64.3–70.6 (average, 67.1) mm.; tail, 51.8–56.9 (54.6); bill (exposed culmen), 9.6–10.2 (9.9); tarsus, 19.3–20.6 (20.1); middle toe without claw, 11.9–12.9 (12.4). *Adult female*: Wing, 62.0–65.8 (64.1); tail, 51.3–53.1 (52.3); bill, 9.6–10.2 (9.9); tarsus, 19.3–20.3 (19.6); middle toe, 11.9–12.4 (12.2).

RANGE: Ontario to Newfoundland, south to Maine and Nova Scotia. Winters from Tennessee and Connecticut to Texas (rarely) and Florida.

TEXAS: *Migration*: One specimen: Brewster Co., Big Bend Nat. Park, Boquillas Crossing (Apr. 1, 1970, R. H. Wauer). *Winter*: Two specimens: Kenedy Co., 8 mi. northeast of Rudolf (Feb. 5, 1969, B. A. Fall; Texas A&M University collection, nos. 7836, 7837).

OVENBIRD, *Seiurus aurocapillus* (Linnaeus)

SPECIES ACCOUNT

Suggests small Wood Thrush. Olive brown above; blackish-streaked white below; black-bordered orange crown-stripe; whitish eye-ring; pinkish legs. Length, 6 in.; wingspan, 9½; weight, ¾ oz.

RANGE: N.e. British Columbia and s. Mackenzie to Newfoundland, south to e. Colorado, s.e. Oklahoma, and n. Georgia. Winters from Sinaloa, Nuevo León, U.S. Gulf coast (a few rarely), and n. Florida (casually South Carolina) to n. Colombia, n. Venezuela, and West Indies (locally).

TEXAS: (See map.) *Migration*: Mid-Apr. to mid-May; early Sept. to late Oct. (extremes: Mar. 2, June 7; Aug. 13, Dec. 6). Common (some years) to uncommon in eastern half; increasingly scarce west of 99th meridian to Amarillo, Midland, Davis Mts., and Big Bend; casual at El Paso. *Winter*: Late Dec. to early Feb. Rare along coast and in Rio Grande delta; extremely rare inland in eastern half, where sighted at Texarkana and San Antonio.

HAUNTS AND HABITS: The Ovenbird appears like a wee thrush as it walks about on the floor of its northern deciduous woodland home. Here, on the ground among fallen leaves, it conceals its domed nest, shaped somewhat like an old-fashioned bread-baking oven. In Texas and elsewhere along its migration route, this bird seeks habitat similar to that in which it breeds. Not a gregarious species, it is normally found singly or in pairs, though sometimes within a relatively limited area a number of pairs will breed. During migration, it occasionally associates with other species and rarely appears in flocks of its own kind.

Normally, this warbler, like most other songbirds, migrates by flying considerable distances during nights

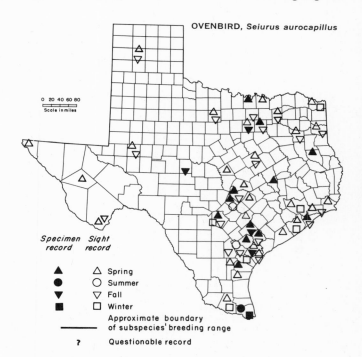

OVENBIRD, *Seiurus aurocapillus*

0 20 40 60 80
Scale in miles

Specimen record — Sight record

▲ △ Spring
● ○ Summer
▼ ▽ Fall
■ □ Winter
— Approximate boundary of subspecies' breeding range
? Questionable record

and spending days resting and feeding. Flight is rapid, strong, and fairly direct even when only a short distance is involved. It moves with relatively few wing-beats, but these are powerful and give the bird strong impetus in the air.

The Ovenbird is adapted for foraging primarily on the ground and amid forest undergrowth; it does, however, sometimes ascend to treetops. On the ground it walks deliberately, often with wings slightly drooped and tail somewhat upraised, but without the pronounced wagging motion of the waterthrushes. It gathers mainly invertebrate food amid fallen leaves on the forest floor. Food items are not taken selectively, but eaten in the approximate proportions in which they are available. Food consists chiefly of insects, including leaf and click beetles, weevils, caterpillars (cankerworm, gypsy moth), moths, butterflies, crickets, grasshoppers, walkingsticks, flies, ants, bugs, and plant lice; also included are spiders and their egg cases, snails, slugs, earthworms, myriapods, and an occasional tree toad, as well as small grass seeds and wild fruit. The Ovenbird swallows a quantity of grit also, evidently to assist in digesting its food.

Its standard call note is a weak *chip* or *cheep* and its alarm note a loud *chuck*. The ordinary territorial song is commonly represented by the word *teacher*, seven to ten times repeated, with the accent on the last syllable, and with a gradual increase in volume from the beginning to about the sixth *teacher*. It is loud, ringing, and not particularly musical, but exceedingly characteristic; it serves readily to identify this warbler in the woods. In addition, the Ovenbird sounds a clear, melodious flight song, sometimes during the middle of the day or in the morning, but chiefly in the evenings, at times into the night, especially if the moon is up. The bird flies into the air, singing as it rises, sometimes one hundred to two hundred feet above ground; when the song is completed the bird partly closes its wings and dives downward back into the depths of the forest. Occasionally this song is delivered as the bird flies through the trees or as it is fluttering up through the branches, and sometimes it is given even from a perch. There is considerable individual variation in these territory-advertising songs, and the birds themselves can distinguish between songs of different individuals, reacting more aggressively toward songs of nonadjacent birds than toward songs of their neighbors. Though the nuptial flight song is not heard in Texas, a spring male may reveal his presence with a spontaneous *teacher* song.

Detailed Account: Four Subspecies

MASSACHUSETTS OVENBIRD, *Seiurus aurocapillus aurocapillus* (Linnaeus)

DESCRIPTION: *Adult male, nuptial plumage (gray phase)*: Acquired by wear from winter plumage. Center of pileum light raw sienna or mars yellow, feathers tipped with grayish olive; on each side a broad stripe of dull black; remainder of upper surface rather greenish buffy olive or buffy olive; tail hair brown to dark hair brown, outer margins of feathers like upper surface; wing-quills between buffy brown and hair brown, edged with color of upper surface, inner webs of secondaries dull pinkish buff, of primaries, except at tips, dull light brown; tertials and wing-coverts like wing-quills, but edgings of tertials and greater and median wing-coverts somewhat more brownish; sides of head between drab and grayish olive or between wood brown and grayish olive, including broad superciliary stripe, but lores more or less mixed with grayish white; broad malar stripe white; narrow submalar streak black; eye-ring dull white; sides of neck like back; remainder of lower surface mostly white, but flanks light brownish olive or isabella color, jugulum, upper breast, sides, and flanks broadly streaked with black; lining of wing dull primrose yellow mottled with mouse gray. Bill black, purplish slate color, or slate gray, base of mandible pale pinkish vinaceous or flesh color; iris dark brown; legs and feet pale pinkish vinaceous, ecru drab, or flesh color. *Adult male, nuptial (olive brown phase)*: Similar to gray phase, but upper surface much more yellowish brown—between orange citrine and medal bronze; pileum darker, more brownish—dull xanthine orange. *Adult male, winter*: Acquired by complete postnuptial molt. Similar to nuptial adult male, but upper surface darker and more richly colored, center of pileum more obscured by olive green feather edgings; breast sometimes washed with buff; flanks somewhat more brownish. *Adult female, nuptial*: Acquired by wear from winter. Similar to nuptial adult female, but center of crown averaging paler and more obscured by olive green tips of feathers. *Adult female, winter*: Acquired by complete postnuptial molt. Similar to nuptial adult female, but colors somewhat darker and richer, crown sometimes often more obscured by olive tips of feathers. Similar to adult male in winter, but middle of pileum somewhat lighter. *Male and female, first nuptial*: Acquired by wear from first winter. Practically identical with corresponding sex of nuptial adult. *Male and female, first winter*: Acquired by partial postjuvenal molt, though wing-quills and tail feathers not involved. Very much like corresponding sex of adult in winter, but streaks on lower parts somewhat lighter, as is middle of crown. *Juvenal*: Acquired by complete postnatal molt. Crown tawny olive, spotted with fuscous; remainder of upper surface buckthorn brown to sayal brown, streaked or spotted, most numerously on rump, with olive brown or fuscous; wings and tail as in nuptial adult female, but lesser wing-coverts and broad tips of median and greater series clay color; sides of head similar to crown but rather paler; chin and throat cinnamon buff, slightly streaked or spotted on sides with fuscous; jugulum, sides of body, and flanks dull pale buff and streaked with fuscous; remainder of lower surface dull white or buffy white, breast also streaked with fuscous. Bill drab or brownish slate, but mandible dull white with darker tip; gape lemon yellow or gamboge yellow; iris dark brown; legs, feet, and claws pale flesh color, vinaceous buff, or brownish white.

MEASUREMENTS: *Adult male*: Wing, 70.9–79.0 (average, 75.2) mm.; tail, 49.8–58.4 (54.3); bill (exposed culmen), 11.2–12.4 (11.7); tarsus, 20.3–22.9 (21.9); middle toe without claw, 11.9–14.7 (13.5). *Adult female*: Wing, 69.8–73.2 (71.9); tail, 49.8–52.8 (51.1); bill, 11.4–11.9 (11.7); tarsus, 20.3–22.4 (21.4); middle toe, 12.7–14.2 (13.2).

RANGE: E. Saskatchewan to Quebec, south to n.w. Louisiana, s.w. Tennessee, and e. New Jersey. Winters from Nuevo León and extreme s. Texas (rarely) through Mexico and Central America to n. Colombia, and from s.e. South Carolina (casually) to s. Florida and West Indies (locally).

TEXAS: *Migration*: Collected north to Cooke and Dallas, east to Nacogdoches (probably this race), south to Victoria and Cameron, west to Concho cos. Fairly common. *Winter*: One specimen: Cameron Co., Brownsville (Feb. 4, 1892, F. B. Armstrong).

SOUTHEASTERN OVENBIRD, *Seiurus aurocapillus canivirens* Burleigh and Duvall

Race not in A.O.U. check-list, 1957 (see Appendix A).

DESCRIPTION: *Adult male and female, nuptial plumage*: Resembling *S. a. aurocapillus*, but upper surface lighter and more grayish (less greenish).

MEASUREMENTS: (Only averages given.) *Adult male*: Wing, 74.5 mm.; tail, 53.3; bill (exposed culmen), 13.5; tarsus, 23.8;

middle toe without claw, 13.5. *Adult female*: Wing, 72.5; tail, 52.0; bill, 12.0; tarsus, 21.3; middle toe, 13.5.

RANGE: Kentucky to Maryland, south to Alabama and South Carolina. In migration, west rarely to Texas. Winters from Florida through West Indies; also Isla Cozumel.

TEXAS: *Migration*: Three specimens: Nueces Co., Corpus Christi (2 on May 7, 1951, I. N. Gabrielson; May, 1961, C. Cottam).

NEWFOUNDLAND OVENBIRD, *Seiurus aurocapillus furvior* Batchelder

DESCRIPTION: *Adults, nuptial plumage*: Similar to *S. a. aurocapillus* and *S. a. canivirens*, but upper parts darker and decidedly more brownish, including broad middle crown stripe which is amber brown; markings on lower surface darker.

MEASUREMENTS: (Only averages given.) *Adult male*: Wing, 72.5 mm.; tail, 51.9; bill (exposed culmen), 12.3; tarsus, 20.7; *Adult female*: Wing, 74.7; tail, 54.1; bill, 13.2; tarsus, 22.6.

RANGE: C. and s. Newfoundland. Winters chiefly from Guatemala to Costa Rica and Panama; also Bahamas and Cuba.

TEXAS: *Migration*: One specimen: Galveston Co., High Island (May 3, 1929, Bessie Reid).

GRAY OVENBIRD, *Seiurus aurocapillus cinereus* A. H. Miller

DESCRIPTION: *Adult male and female, nuptial plumage*: Similar to *S. a. aurocapillus*, but upper parts, including outer webs of tail feathers, more grayish or sooty (less greenish) and somewhat paler; auriculars and sides of neck less tawny. More like *S. a. canivirens* but darker and more grayish above, with scarcely any or very little tinge of olive green.

MEASUREMENTS: (Only averages given.) *Adult male*: Wing, 72.5 mm.; tail, 51.9; bill (exposed culmen), 12.3; tarsus, 20.7; middle toe without claw, 13.0. *Adult female*: Wing, 75.5; tail, 51.5; bill, 11.8; tarsus, 22.3; middle toe, 12.5.

RANGE: S. Mackenzie to Saskatchewan, south to Colorado and Nebraska. Winters from Chihuahua and Sinaloa to Costa Rica.

TEXAS: *Migration*: Two specimens: Brazos Co., College Station (May 11, 1940, T. F. Smith); Nueces Co., Corpus Christi (May 7, 1951, I. N. Gabrielson).

NORTHERN WATERTHRUSH, *Seiurus noveboracensis* (Gmelin)

SPECIES ACCOUNT

Also called Small-billed Waterthrush. Teeters as it walks; feeds at water's edge. Brown upper parts; buffy or whitish eye-stripe; pale yellow or whitish under parts, streaked with blackish (*including throat*). Compare carefully with Louisiana Waterthrush. Length, 6 in.; wingspan, 9½; weight, ½ oz.

RANGE: Alaska to Newfoundland, south to c. British Columbia, n. Idaho, n. Great Lakes region, and Massachusetts, and in Appalachians to c. West Virginia. Winters mainly from s. Baja California, Sinaloa, San Luis Potosí, and Yucatán Peninsula to Ecuador, n.e. Peru, s. Venezuela, and Guianas; also s. Florida and West Indies.

TEXAS: (See map.) *Migration*: Mid-Apr. to mid-May; late Aug. to early Oct. (extremes: Mar. 14, June 1; July 14, Oct. 21). Common (some years) to uncommon in eastern two-thirds; uncommon (some years) to rare in western third. *Winter*: Mid-Dec. to late Feb. Rare in southern half, though more likely to occur along coast or in Rio Grande delta.

HAUNTS AND HABITS: The Northern Waterthrush inhabits cool, shaded forest undergrowth about shores of lakes, pools, and streams of all kinds, though it occurs also in damp woodlands, either evergreen or deciduous, and in northern wooded swamps and shrub-grown bogs; here it shelters its mossy nest in a bank cavity, under a tree root, or at the base of a stump. During migration through Texas, however, it is found near both running and stagnant water in open woodlands and thickets almost anywhere; it is also seen bobbing daintily under garden shrubbery, in city parks, residential yards, ditches, brushy fence rows, and next to rain puddles in woods. While not gregarious in the ordinary sense, it often occurs in considerable numbers within a small area.

Flight, quick and strong, is performed with relatively few, but vigorous, wing-beats. Though capable of direct, sustained flight, its efforts are usually for short distances, in which case it is erratic. The Northern Waterthrush spends considerable time walking over mossy rocks, leaves, and bare ground, wagging its tail up and down with such vigor that it moves the posterior part of the body as well. For this habit it has been dubbed "wagtail warbler." When not in motion the tail is held at an upward angle. A low-ranging forager, the Northern turns over leaves with it bill in search of food amid litter of the forest floor. Although the bird sometimes takes small seeds, it eats mainly animal matter, largely insects and their larvae: beetles (water scavenger, ground flea, curculio and other weevils), moths, measuringworms, mosquitoes, flower flies, ants, water boatmen, other aquatic bugs, lanternflies, grasshoppers, crickets, dragonflies, and damselflies. The non-insect portion is composed of snails, slugs, small crabs

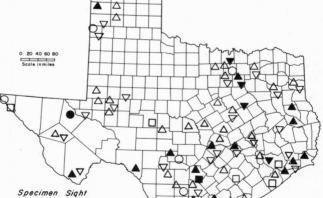

NORTHERN WATERTHRUSH, *Seiurus noveboracensis*

0 20 40 60 80
Scale in miles

Specimen   Sight
record   record

▲ △ Spring
● ○ Summer
▼ ▽ Fall
■ □ Winter

——— Approximate boundary of subspecies' breeding range

?   Questionable record

and other crustaceans, worms, and rarely even small minnows.

The call of this waterthrush is a sharp *chink*, which often advertises the bird's presence before it is viewed. Its song is a loud, clear, musical performance, very different from that of its close relative, the Louisiana Waterthrush. It has been represented by *sweet sweet sweet chu-chu-wee-chu*, the first three notes rather staccato. It also has a remarkable flight song delivered as the male flies either through or above the trees on his breeding territory. This is similar to the regular song but faster and with more frills. The male seldom sings even his ordinary song in Texas.

DETAILED ACCOUNT: THREE SUBSPECIES

COMMON NORTHERN WATERTHRUSH, *Seiurus noveboracensis noveboracensis* (Gmelin)

DESCRIPTION: *Adults, nuptial plumage*: Acquired by wear from winter plumage. Upper parts olive brown; tail and wings, including upper wing-coverts, similar but rather lighter; margins of inner webs of primaries and secondaries, except at tips of primaries, somewhat paler; broad superciliary stripe primrose yellow to olive buff or cinnamon buff; lores and broad postocular streak same color as upper parts; auriculars similar but paler, sometimes streaked with dull buff; broad malar stripe below eyes primrose yellow to straw yellow, speckled or slightly streaked with chaetura drab; sides of neck like back; submalar streak olive brown; lower surface primrose yellow to straw yellow, but sides and flanks washed with buffy brown, and crissum naphthalene yellow, throat, jugulum, breast, sides, and flanks broadly streaked with dull black or chaetura drab; lining of wing drab, outer part spotted with hair brown. Bill slate black or brownish black, but base of mandible seal brown, drab gray, or dull gray; iris reddish brown or dark vandyke brown; legs and feet brownish yellow, drab, broccoli brown, clay color, or fawn color. *Adults, winter*: Acquired by complete postnuptial molt. Similar to nuptial adults, but superciliary stripe averaging more deeply buff. *First nuptial*: Acquired by wear from first winter. Similar to nuptial adults, but wing-quills and tail somewhat lighter. *First winter*: Acquired by partial postjuvenal molt, which does not involve wing-quills or tail. Similar to adults in winter, but wing-quills and tail somewhat lighter and streaks of lower parts rather narrower. *Juvenal*: Acquired by complete postnatal molt. Upper parts olive brown, most feathers with subterminal clove brown bars and tips of buffy brown to dull buff, giving pileum finely spotted appearance and rest of upper surface distinctly barred effect; wings as in adults in winter, but wing-coverts more brownish and edged with pale buff or dull buffy brown; sides of head and of neck olive brown, lores and sides of neck much streaked with pale dull buffy yellow; postocular stripe above eye dull cream buff; anterior lower parts dull cartridge buff, posterior surface straw yellow; flanks washed with color of back; chin, throat, breast, and sides of body heavily streaked with dark olive brown or clove brown. Bill, legs, and feet dull brown; iris dark brown.

MEASUREMENTS: *Adult male*: Wing, 75.4–80.0 (average, 76.7) mm.; tail, 45.0–53.6 (51.3); bill (exposed culmen), 11.9–14.7 (13.0); tarsus, 19.8–22.4 (21.4); middle toe without claw, 13.0–14.0 (13.5). *Adult female*: Wing, 68.3–75.7 (73.2); tail, 45.0–52.1 (49.5); bill, 10.7–13.2 (12.4); tarsus, 20.3–21.6 (21.1); middle toe, 12.4–13.7 (13.2).

RANGE: E. Ontario to e. Labrador, south to West Virginia and Maryland. In migration, west to Texas. Winters from South Carolina and w. Florida through Mexico and Central America to Venezuela; also Bahamas and Cuba.

TEXAS: *Migration*: Collected northeast to Navarro, south to Nueces and Cameron, west to Bexar cos. Uncommon.

GRINNELL'S NORTHERN WATERTHRUSH, *Seiurus noveboracensis notabilis* Ridgway

DESCRIPTION: *Adults, nuptial plumage*: Similar to *S. n. noveboracensis*, but tail, and especially bill, longer; upper surface darker, more sooty (less brownish) olive; superciliary stripe and lower surface less deeply yellowish (more whitish).

MEASUREMENTS: *Adult male*: Wing, 73.7–81.3 (average, 77.2) mm.; tail, 50.8–57.2 (53.3); bill (exposed culmen), 12.2–16.0 (13.7); tarsus, 20.1–22.4 (21.9); middle toe without claw, 12.7–14.2 (13.7). *Adult female*: Wing, 73.2–78.7 (75.7); tail, 48.8–57.9 (53.3); bill, 12.2–14.2 (13.2); tarsus, 21.4–22.4 (21.9); middle toe, 12.2–13.7 (13.2).

RANGE: W. Alaska to c. Quebec, south to s.w. Montana and n.w. Pennsylvania. Winters from s. Texas to s. Baja California through w. Mexico and Central America to Venezuela; also West Indies.

TEXAS: *Migration*: Collected north to Oldham, east to Cooke and Jefferson, south to Cameron, west to Brewster and Reeves (Aug. 29) cos. Fairly common. *Winter*: Two specimens: Bexar Co., San Antonio (Dec., 1863, H. E. Dresser); Webb Co., Laredo (Jan. 30, 1886, F. B. Armstrong).

BRITISH COLUMBIA NORTHERN WATERTHRUSH, *Seiurus noveboracensis limnaeus* McCabe and Miller

DESCRIPTION: *Adults, nuptial plumage*: Similar to *S. n. notabilis*, but wing and tail shorter; color of upper surface darker; lower parts with usually more yellow.

MEASUREMENTS: *Adult male*: Wing, 69.8–76.2 (average, 73.7) mm.; tail, (51.7); tarsus, (21.5); middle toe without claw, (13.5). *Adult female*: Wing, 73.0–74.0 (73.5); tail, 49.0–52.0 (50.5); bill, (12.0); tarsus, (21.0); middle toe, 13.0–14.0 (13.5).

RANGE: British Columbia. In migration, east to Texas. Winters from s. Baja California to Panama and Colombia.

TEXAS: *Migration*: Two specimens: Dallas Co., Cedar Hill (Oct. 15, 1960, W. M. Pulich; identified by J. W. Aldrich); Nueces Co., Corpus Christi (May 6, 1951, Pauline James; identified by I. N. Gabrielson).

LOUISIANA WATERTHRUSH, *Seiurus motacilla* (Vieillot)

SPECIES ACCOUNT

Also called Large-billed Waterthrush. Similar to Northern Waterthrush, but has larger bill, *unstreaked* white upper throat, and white eye-stripe; whitish below. Length, 6 in.; wingspan, 10; weight, ¾ oz.

RANGE: S. Great Lakes region and s. New England, south to e. Texas, Gulf states, and s. Georgia. Winters from n. Mexico through Central America to n. South America; also West Indies.

TEXAS: (See map.) *Breeding*: Mid-Apr. to mid-July (eggs, Apr. 22 to June 13; young in nest, May 8 to June 13) from 75 to 1,000 ft. Uncommon and local in wooded eastern portion west to 98th meridian and south to 30th parallel. *Migration*: Late Mar. to late Apr.; early Aug. to mid-Sept. (extremes: Mar. 6, May 31; July 6, Oct. 6). Common (some years; usually along coast) to uncommon in eastern half; increasingly scarce west to Randall Co., Midland, Del Rio region, and Laredo; casual in Chisos and Davis mts. *Winter*: Late Dec. to mid-Feb. No specimen, but single adults banded at Waco (Feb. 12, 1929, Mrs. W. W. Woodson) and Palmetto State Park, Gonzales Co. (Jan. 28, 1965, F. O.

Novy); the individual banded at Palmetto was recaptured there the following year (Jan. 31, 1966, Novy). Extremely rare east of 98th meridian, though casual north of 32nd parallel.

HAUNTS AND HABITS: Deep within moist, thicketed woodlands, along a dark, secluded stream the Louisiana Waterthrush is at home. Here it hides its bulky nest in a bank, an upturned tree root, or a stump. Occasionally it abandons running water to build in a swamp or about the margin of a lake. In Texas, as elsewhere, this unusual warbler, even during migration, is generally found teetering along a creek bank or deliberately walking about over a protruding rock or log in search of aquatic insects. It is almost always a solitary bird, found at most in pairs.

The Louisiana can fly swiftly with powerful wing-beats but more often it flies rather jerkily near the water surface or along the water margin. It walks deliberately over rocks and pebbly shores or on the ground; or it perches on some low bush or limb. Wherever foraging, it continually pumps its tail, for which habit—along with the Northern Waterthrush—it has acquired the name "water wagtail." Food of this warbler consists largely of animal matter, chiefly insects: beetles (ground, leaf, water, long-horned), grasshoppers, cockroaches, scale insects, tree-hoppers, dragonflies, crane-fly larvae, borborid flies, moths, ants, parasitic wasps, and ant lions. Other animal items are small worms, mollusks (bivalves and snails), scorpions, spiders, crustaceans, tree toads, and killifishes. A few small seeds and fruits are also consumed. The Louisiana is a very shy warbler and, for this reason, is ordinarily difficult to approach closely or to study.

Its usual call note is a loud *chink*, almost identical to that of the Northern Waterthrush. Its song, however, is decidedly different. It is a clear, somewhat shrill, stressed melody, the introductory phrases of which are slurred, followed by a rapid, descending jumble of notes; it has been transliterated by William Brewster as *pseur pseur per-see-ser*. In delivery, the male perches either on a rock, a bush, or a low branch and seems to put all his strength into his song, throwing back his head and singing with vigorous movements of his body. His flight song, which is even more elaborate, is performed as he flies up above the treetops and then descends. He sings from the time of his spring arrival well into July.

DETAILED ACCOUNT: NO SUBSPECIES

DESCRIPTION: *Adults, nuptial plumage*: Acquired by wear from winter plumage. Pileum between clove brown and dark olive; remainder of upper surface between brownish olive and olive; wings and tail rather dark olive brown, inner edges of secondaries a little paler; tips of primaries and margins of tertials somewhat lighter; sides of head and of neck like upper surface, cheeks and anterior sides of neck rather paler and streaked or spotted with pale buff; broad superciliary stripe, malar stripe, and lower parts light colonial buff; sides, flanks, and crissum chamois to cinnamon buff or light clay color; long submalar streak, fine spots on sides of throat, and broad streaks on jugulum, upper breast, sides, and flanks olive brown to clove brown or chaetura drab; lining of wing dull drab to hair brown, coverts edged with dull buff. Bill brownish black or dull brown, but base of mandible paler; iris dark brown; legs and feet flesh color. *Adults, winter*: Acquired by complete postnuptial molt. Similar to nuptial adults, but buff of posterior lower parts usually darker. *First nuptial*: Acquired by wear from first winter. Similar to nuptial adults. *First winter*: Acquired by partial postjuvenal molt, which does not involve wing-quills or tail. Like adults in winter. *Juvenal*: Acquired by complete postnatal molt. Pileum olive brown, back between cinnamon brown and russet, upper tail-coverts brighter, rather dull russet; wings and tail like nuptial adults, but wing-coverts more rufescent, greater series with narrow tips of sayal brown, forming wing-bar; sides of head olive brown but largely mixed with dull pale buff, with white superciliary stripe obsolete anteriorly but broad behind eye, and conspicuous olive brown postocular stripe; lower surface dull pale pinkish buff or buffy white; abdomen dull cream buff; flanks cinnamon buff; throat, jugulum, breast, and sides heavily streaked with olive brown. Bill, legs, and feet dull brown; iris dark brown. *Natal*: Dark olive brown to mouse gray. Bill, legs, and feet pinkish buff.

MEASUREMENTS: *Adult male*: Wing, 75.7–84.3 (average, 80.7) mm.; tail, 49.5–55.3 (51.8); bill (exposed culmen), 12.2–13.5 (13.2); tarsus, 21.9–22.9 (22.4); middle toe without claw, 14.0–15.2 (14.5). *Adult female*: Wing, 75.9–81.0 (78.7); tail, 49.5–52.8 (50.8); bill, 12.7–14.2 (13.5); tarsus, 21.9–23.4 (22.9); middle toe, 14.0–15.0 (14.5).

TEXAS: *Breeding*: Collected northwest to Cooke, east to Harrison (eggs), Nacogdoches, and Orange cos. *Migration*: Collected north to Wise, east to Galveston, south to Cameron, west to Val Verde (July 18) cos.

NESTING: *Nest*: Usually in wooded stream valleys or in wooded swamps; on ground, in bank of stream, or upturned roots of fallen tree, about old logs, stumps, or similar places, but nearly always in moist situations; bulky cup of partially decayed leaves with mud attached, grasses, roots, bits of moss, dead grass, sometimes a few twigs; lined with rootlets, pine needles, dead grass, and occasionally hair. *Eggs*: 3–7, usually 5; pure white to deep cream white; profusely blotched, spotted, and dotted, most heavily near large end, with cinnamon rufous and chestnut, with shell markings of lilac and lavender; average size, 19.6 × 15.5 mm.

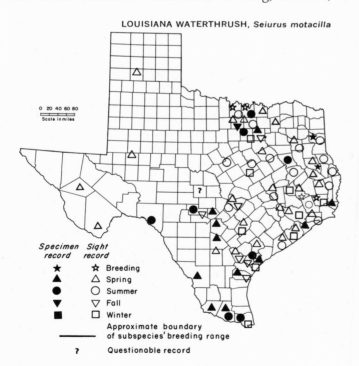

LOUISIANA WATERTHRUSH, *Seiurus motacilla*

0 20 40 60 80
Scale in miles

Specimen record / Sight record

★ / ☆ Breeding
▲ / △ Spring
● / ○ Summer
▼ / ▽ Fall
■ / □ Winter

——— Approximate boundary of subspecies' breeding range

? Questionable record

KENTUCKY WARBLER, *Oporornis formosus* (Wilson)

Species Account

Black forehead and "sideburns"; yellow eye-stripe, incomplete eye-ring; olive green upper parts; yellow under parts. Length, 5¼ in.; wingspan, 8¼; weight, ½ oz.

RANGE: S.e. Nebraska to s.e. New York, south to c. Texas, Gulf states, and n.w. Florida. Winters mainly from s. Mexico to extreme n. South America.

TEXAS: (See map.) *Breeding*: Late Apr. to mid-July (eggs, May 6 to June 19) from near sea level to 1,700 ft. Fairly common to uncommon in eastern third north of 30th parallel; irregularly uncommon to scarce and increasingly local west to Wise Co., Waco, Austin, Kerrville, and extreme southeastern edge of Edwards Plateau. *Migration*. Mid-Apr. to early May; mid-Aug. to mid-Sept. (extremes: Mar. 18, June 5; July 17, Dec. 10). Common (most springs) to uncommon through eastern third; uncommon to scarce in remainder of state east of 100th meridian; rare in northern Panhandle; extremely rare in Midland vicinity; accidental in Davis Mts. (recorded in Apr., Pansy Espy). *Winter*: Late Dec. to early Feb. No specimen, but occasional sightings along coast and in Rio Grande delta; one inland sight record: Decatur, Wise Co. (Jan. 29, 1890, J. A. Donald).

HAUNTS AND HABITS: The Kentucky Warbler constructs its bulky nest at the base of a bush or amid rank grasses and forbs growing in damp bottomland woods —usually deciduous, though sometimes mixed—with extensive undergrowth and tangles; in central Texas it favors shady pecan (*Carya illinoensis*) groves and

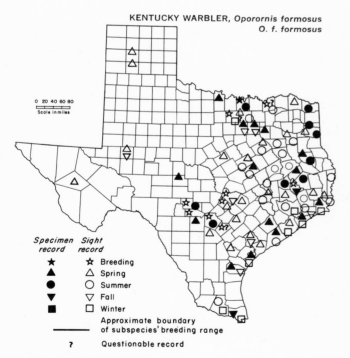

KENTUCKY WARBLER, *Oporornis formosus*
O. f. formosus

0 20 40 60 80
Scale in miles

Specimen Sight
record   record
★   ☆ Breeding
▲   △ Spring
●   ○ Summer
▼   ▽ Fall
■   □ Winter
          Approximate boundary
          of subspecies' breeding range
?   Questionable record

moist, wooded canyons with dense, low-growing vegetation. During migration, it ventures into more open localities, such as parks, dooryards, cemeteries, and coastal scrub. It is usually found singly or in pairs, not often associated with other species. Though tending to remain in the seclusion of its sometimes impenetrable haunts, it is not so shy as many of its relatives.

The Kentucky's flight is rather strong, swift, and capable of being long sustained. During its summer sojourn, however, it has little occasion for protracted flights. In foraging it prefers bushes, undergrowth, and low tree limbs, often overhanging water; it seldom goes high in the trees. *O. formosus* is more deliberate in movement than are many other warblers, showing little nervousness in its behavior. It is also frequently observed on the ground, where it quietly walks about in its search for food, reminding one a little of an Ovenbird. Its diet is composed of insects and their larvae (caterpillars, grasshoppers, locusts, ants, beetles, bugs, plant lice, and moths), some spiders, and at times small berries, such as poke (*Phytolacca americana*) and hackberry (*Celtis*).

Its ordinary call is a low-pitched, guttural *chip*, *check*, or *chuck*. The delightful song is a ringing, whistled melody surprisingly like that of the Carolina Wren, though it is slower and not as loud. It is fairly well represented by the syllables *ter-wheeter*, the last several times repeated. The male sings from a low, often exposed branch, a bush, or even from the ground. He also delivers a nuptial flight song in spring. The song period continues from mid-April well into July.

Detailed Account: One Subspecies

SOUTHERN KENTUCKY WARBLER, *Oporornis formosus formosus* (Wilson)

No races recognized by A.O.U. check-list, 1957 (see Appendix A).

DESCRIPTION: *Adult male, nuptial plumage*: Acquired by partial prenuptial molt. Forehead and crown black, but many crown feathers, particularly behind, tipped with mouse gray; remainder of upper surface light olive green, somewhat paler on upper tail-coverts; tail light brownish olive, edged on outer webs of rectrices with dull warbler green; wings between drab and hair brown, inner margins of primaries and secondaries, except tips of primaries, dull light drab, quills and coverts edged exteriorly with dull warbler green; superciliary stripe and eye-ring rich lemon chrome, eye-ring broken anteriorly by black of lores which color also covers cheeks and auriculars and extends in broad stripe along sides of throat; remainder of sides of neck light dull warbler green; lower surface rich lemon chrome, but sides and flanks dull warbler green or citrine; lining of wing lemon chrome, outer portion spotted with mouse gray. Bill dark brown or brownish black, but mandible paler and light flesh color at base; iris dark brown; legs, feet, and claws pinkish flesh color or pinkish cream color. *Adult male, winter*: Acquired by complete postnuptial molt. Similar to nuptial adult male, but black feathers of crown more broadly and numerously tipped with mouse gray, and black at sides of throat more or less veiled by dull yellow tips of feathers. *Adult female, nuptial*: Acquired by partial prenuptial molt. Similar to nuptial adult male but somewhat duller, particularly on upper surface; black on head and sides of throat duller, the latter less extensive and somewhat obscured by olive green tips of feathers, black of crown more obscured by mouse gray tips of feathers. *Adult female, winter*: Acquired by

Kentucky Warbler, *Oporornis formosus*,
on sassafras (*Sassafras albidum*)

PLATE 29: Western Tanager, *Piranga ludoviciana*, perched on cottonwood (*Populus*)
male (top), female (bottom)

complete postnuptial molt. Similar to nuptial adult female, but black of pileum almost hidden by more numerous and larger mouse gray or dull brownish tips of feathers; black on sides of head still more obscured by lighter feather tips; yellow of lower parts rather deeper and richer. *Male, first nuptial*: Acquired by partial prenuptial molt. Similar to nuptial adult male. *Male, first winter*: Acquired by partial postjuvenal molt, which does not involve wing-quills or tail. Similar to adult male in winter, but black of crown more obscured by hair brown or mouse gray tips of feathers; black on sides of head duller and more obscured by lighter tips of feathers; sides of breast more or less obscurely spotted with olive. Similar to nuptial adult female but larger, crown more obscured by gray or brown tips of feathers, and black on sides of head and of neck more extensive. Similar to adult female in winter but larger; crown not so much obscured by light brown or gray tips of feathers; black on sides of head and of neck less obscured and more extensive. *Female, first nuptial*: Acquired by partial prenuptial molt. Similar to nuptial adult female. *Female, first winter*: Acquired by partial postjuvenal molt. Similar to adult female in winter, but black of head often entirely obscured by dull or rufescent hair brown tips of feathers; upper surface rather duller; sides of head duller, blackish areas still more obscured by olive; sides of breast and of jugulum usually with obscure olive spots. *Juvenal*: Acquired by complete postnatal molt. Pileum dull buffy brown to rather light brownish olive; back saccardo umber to cinnamon brown or prout brown, somewhat mottled by darker tips of feathers; wings and tail as in adult female in winter, but lesser coverts and tips of greater and median coverts buckthorn brown, forming two conspicuous wing-bars, edgings of coverts also more brownish than in adult; sides of head and of neck like upper parts but somewhat lighter; jugulum and upper breast between citrine and orange citrine; chin and throat somewhat paler; abdomen wax yellow to light olive ocher; sides and flanks yellowish buckthorn brown. *Natal*: Olive brown. Bill, legs, and feet flesh color.

MEASUREMENTS: *Adult male*: Wing, 64.5–69.1 (average, 67.1) mm.; tail, 47.8–54.1 (49.5); bill (exposed culmen), 9.9–13.0 (11.4); tarsus, 21.6–23.6 (22.4); middle toe without claw, 11.4–14.0 (12.7). *Adult female*: Wing, 61.0–66.0 (63.8); tail, 46.5–49.0 (47.8); bill, 10.9–12.4 (11.7); tarsus, 21.6–23.6 (22.9); middle toe, 11.4–13.0 (12.2).

RANGE: E. Nebraska to e. North Carolina, south to s.e. Texas and s.e. South Carolina. Winters mainly from s. Mexico through Central America to n.w. Venezuela.

TEXAS: *Breeding*: Collected north to Cooke, east to Polk, southwest to Bexar and Kerr cos. *Migration*: Collected north to Clay, east to Jefferson, south to Cameron, west to Menard cos.

NESTING: *Nest*: In lowlands, swamps, stream valleys of uplands, brushy hillsides (if moist), and wooded bottomlands; on ground, usually at foot of bush or in weeds, in low bush, on low limb of tree or bush, only a short distance above ground; bulky cup, loosely built and usually well concealed by bushes and other vegetation, sometimes nearly arched over and with entrance on side; composed of grasses, leaves, weed stalks, rootlets, strips of grapevine and other bark, sometimes green leaves of dogwood, blossoms of oak, pith of wood; lined with rootlets, pine needles, or horsehair. *Eggs*: 4–6, usually 4–5; rounded ovate to short ovate; sometimes glossy; white or cream white, spotted and speckled, more heavily at large end, where markings sometimes form wreath or confluent mass, with burnt umber, cinnamon rufous, reddish brown, and lilac gray; average size, 18.5 × 14.5 mm.

CONNECTICUT WARBLER, *Oporornis agilis*
(Wilson)

SPECIES ACCOUNT

Adult: gray hood (paler in female); complete white eye-ring; olive green above; yellow below; under tail-coverts extend almost entire length of tail. *Immature*:

similar but duller; eye-ring buffy. Compare carefully in all plumages with Mourning Warbler (see below); the length of under tail-coverts considered to be most important field mark, especially in fall. Length, 5½ in.; wingspan, 8¾; weight, ½ oz.

RANGE: E. British Columbia to n.w. Quebec, south to n.w. Great Lakes region. Winters from n. Venezuela to n.w. and c. Brazil.

TEXAS: (See map.) *Migration*: Mid-Apr. to mid-May; late Aug. to early Oct. Apparently rare along upper and central coasts; rare to casual through remainder of eastern half. The Connecticut Warbler's close resemblance to the Mourning Warbler, especially in fall, makes evaluation of its status quite difficult. Oberholser recorded only one specimen for *O. agilis*, collected in the 19th century (see detailed account); the whereabouts of the skin is seemingly unknown. Apparently the species has not been collected within Texas in the 20th century.

HAUNTS AND HABITS: In its cool summer home, far to the north of Texas, the Connecticut Warbler lives in brushy spruce and tamarack bogs or dense undergrowth in upland poplar-aspen country. Here its compact nest, composed largely of leaves and grass, is usually cupped on or near the ground in a mound of moss, a vine tangle, or a grassy clump. During migration through Texas and other places, it frequents undergrowth, thickets, weed patches, hedgerows, swamps, and brushy ditches, even low trees about houses, dooryard shrubbery, and parks in towns.

On the wing, the Connecticut is strong and swift and usually quite direct. It is capable of long-sustained flight as evidenced by its extensive migrations, but normally flight is short and performed by a few powerful strokes. This warbler stays much on the ground, where

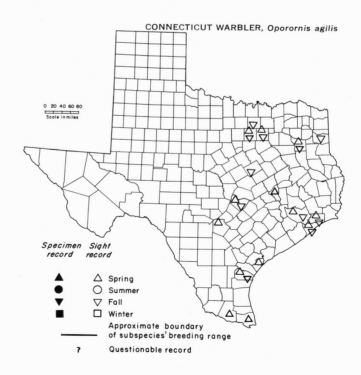

CONNECTICUT WARBLER, *Oporornis agilis*

0 20 40 60 80
Scale in miles

Specimen record / Sight record

▲ △ Spring
● ○ Summer
▼ ▽ Fall
■ □ Winter

——— Approximate boundary of subspecies' breeding range

? Questionable record

it is usually shy and elusive and not easily located. Throughout its range it seems to wander at times in what might be termed flights, these lasting for several days. The bird is everywhere local and very irregular in occurrence, particularly in Texas. On the ground it is deliberate and slow; frequently it sits for a time almost motionless on a perch, unless disturbed. Food consists largely of beetles and small caterpillars, but spiders and snails are also taken, together with some seeds and berries.

Connecticut's call note is a sharp, somewhat metallic *plink* or *peek*. Its song has been described as a loud, jerky *fru-chapple, fru-chapple, fru-chapple, whoit,* or a monotonous *beecher, beecher, beecher, beecher, beech.* In singing, the male seems to take the performance seriously, entering so heartily into the execution that he vibrates all over, fluttering his wings simultaneously.

DETAILED ACCOUNT: NO SUBSPECIES

DESCRIPTION: *Adult male, nuptial plumage*: Acquired by partial prenuptial molt. Pileum deep mouse gray; remainder of upper surface light olive citrine to dark roman green, hindneck washed or tinged with gray of pileum; tail dull hair brown, feathers edged exteriorly with dull citrine; wings hair brown, without spots or bars, outer edges saccardo olive to olive citrine; sides of head deep mouse gray like pileum or somewhat lighter, with conspicuous dull white or yellowish white eye-ring; sides of neck light olive citrine, more or less washed or tinged with gray of jugulum; sides of head and anterior lower parts gray, chin between pale smoke gray and pallid neutral gray, shading over throat to neutral gray or between neutral gray and deep neutral gray on jugulum, posterior line of gray jugulum more or less sharply defined against yellow of posterior lower parts; breast strontian yellow or wax yellow, passing into amber yellow or citrine yellow on lower tail-coverts; sides and flanks ecru olive to light yellowish olive; lining of wing drab, feathers edged and tipped with amber yellow to citrine yellow, which is also color of axillars. Maxilla and tip of mandible dull brown, cutting edges lighter, mandible flesh color, except at tip; iris dark brown; legs and feet flesh color. *Adult male, winter*: Acquired by complete postnuptial molt. Similar to nuptial adult male but darker and more richly colored throughout, gray of pileum obscured by brownish olive tips, and that of throat by dull buff or light brown edges of feathers. *Adult female, nuptial*: Acquired by partial prenuptial molt. Similar to nuptial adult male but smaller; upper surface somewhat lighter, crown almost uniform in color with back or only slightly grayish, shading on sides of head and on jugulum to grayish olive or light grayish olive; chin and throat dull buff. Bill brownish slate, mandible dull white, but tip and cutting edges brownish; iris dark brown; legs and feet drab gray. *Adult female, winter*: Acquired by complete postnuptial molt. Similar to nuptial adult female, but upper surface darker and more brownish, especially on pileum; sides and flanks darker; throat and jugulum more brownish. *Male, first nuptial*: Acquired by partial prenuptial molt. Similar to nuptial adult male, but pileum nearly or quite uniform in color with back; chin, throat, jugulum, and sides of head and of neck more brownish or buffy (less purely gray); yellow of lower parts rather duller. *Male, first winter*: Acquired by partial postjuvenal molt, which does not involve wing-quills or tail. Similar to adult male in winter, but upper surface still more brownish; sides of head and of neck, chin, throat, and jugulum much more brownish (less grayish), jugulum citrine drab; yellow of posterior lower parts duller. Similar to adult female in winter but larger; throat and jugulum somewhat more grayish (less brownish). Maxilla brown, blackish brown, or black; mandible pale dull yellow or light drab; iris hazel or prout brown; legs and feet dull

white, light drab, pinkish gray, brownish gray, or pale yellow slightly tinged with flesh color. *Female, first nuptial*: Acquired by partial prenuptial molt. Similar to nuptial adult female, but upper surface somewhat more brownish, pileum less grayish; throat and jugulum decidedly more brownish or buffy. *Female, first winter*: Acquired by partial postjuvenal molt. Similar to adult female in winter, but averages above rather darker, and also somewhat more brownish or yellowish olive; sides of head and of neck, chin, throat, and jugulum more brownish or buffy. *Juvenal*: Acquired by complete postnatal molt. Pileum olive brown, back rather light clove brown; wings chaetura drab; throat and jugulum buffy brown; sides saccardo umber; flanks rather dark buckthorn brown; breast and abdomen mustard yellow.

MEASUREMENTS: *Adult male*: Wing, 70.9–75.2 (average, 73.2) mm.; tail, 46.8–52.8 (49.8); bill (exposed culmen), 11.2–12.2 (11.7); tarsus, 20.6–23.1 (21.4); middle toe without claw, 13.2–14.7 (14.2). *Adult female*: Wing, 67.3–71.7 (69.3); tail, 46.8–49.3 (48.0); bill, 11.4–11.9 (11.7); tarsus, 19.0–21.9 (20.9); middle toe, 13.5–14.0 (13.7).

TEXAS: *Migration*: One specimen: Cooke Co., Gainesville (adult female, 1878, G. H. Ragsdale).

MOURNING WARBLER, *Oporornis philadelphia* (Wilson)

SPECIES ACCOUNT

Adult: gray hood (on nuptial male, becoming black on chin, throat, and upper breast); *no eye-ring*; dull olive green above; yellow below; under tail-coverts extend only about one-half length of tail. *Fall female and immature*: incomplete white eye-ring (broken in front). Compare in all plumages with Connecticut Warbler. Length, 5½ in.; wingspan, 7¾; weight, ½ oz.

RANGE: C. Alberta to Newfoundland, south to n.e. North Dakota, s. Great Lakes region, and s.e. New York, and in higher Appalachians to e. West Virginia.

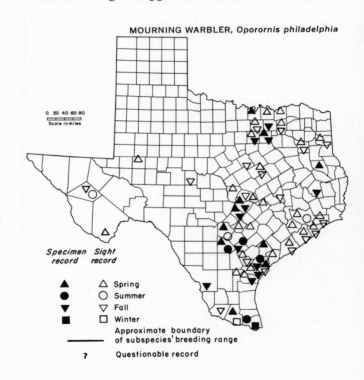

MOURNING WARBLER, *Oporornis philadelphia*

0 20 40 60 80
Scale in miles

Specimen | Sight
record | record

▲ | △ Spring
● | ○ Summer
▼ | ▽ Fall
■ | □ Winter

——— Approximate boundary of subspecies' breeding range

?   Questionable record

Winters from Nicaragua to Ecuador and w. Venezuela.

TEXAS: (See map.) *Migration*: Late Apr. to late May; late Aug. to mid-Oct. (extremes: Mar. 29, June 5; July 9, Nov. 9). Common (some years; usually between 96th and 98th meridians) to scarce in eastern half; increasingly rare west to Midland; casual in Davis and Chisos mts. *Winter*: Casual in Rio Grande delta.

HAUNTS AND HABITS: Dense thickets bordering cool northern bogs and extensive briar patches in overgrown clearings provide optimum summer habitat for the Mourning Warbler. Well concealed within these often impenetrable tangles, its bulky, grassy nest is generally cradled in a fern clump, berry vine, or rank growth of forbs. During the nonbreeding season, in Texas as elsewhere, the Mourning retains its preference for low-growing vegetation, frequenting woodland and streamside undergrowth, shrubbery in yards and parks, tall weeds, and brushy fence rows.

This warbler's flight is largely confined to short, flitting dashes from one bush to another. It is, however, capable of longer flights, on which it travels less erratically. The Mourning rarely ascends far from the ground and is furtive and difficult to observe. It forages low through the bushes, taking mainly spiders and insects (flies, leaf-eating beetles, weevils, cottonworms, and leaf-hoppers).

The Mourning's call is a sharp *peenk*. Its song, a pleasing performance, is a clear, rather rapidly uttered *tee, te-o, te-o, te-o, we-se*, the last phrase emphasized and on a higher pitch. During their northward passage through Texas, males sing on occasion, usually in May.

DETAILED ACCOUNT: NO SUBSPECIES

DESCRIPTION: *Adult male, nuptial plumage*: Acquired by partial prenuptial molt. Pileum and hindneck neutral gray to deep neutral gray; back and scapulars dull olive green to yellowish olive, passing into light olive green on rump and upper tail-coverts; tail dull citrine, inner edges of most of feathers, except middle pair, verging to dull buffy brown; wings between hair brown and buffy brown, inner edges of primaries and secondaries dull vinaceous buff, becoming darker and duller on primaries, except at tips; lesser wing-coverts warbler green, outer edges of remaining coverts and of wing-quills citrine; sides of head and neck like pileum but of somewhat paler neutral gray; lores chaetura black or chaetura drab, sometimes mixed with neutral gray; chin, throat, and jugulum dull black, this usually much veiled by neutral gray edgings of feathers, black sometimes nearly absent or entirely obscured on chin and throat, thus confined to central patch on jugulum; sides and flanks warbler green; remainder of lower surface, including lining of wing, lemon yellow to lemon chrome. Maxilla black or brownish slate color; mandible brownish white or pinkish white; iris very dark brown; legs ecru drab or flesh color; feet and claws drab or flesh color. *Adult male, winter*: Acquired by complete postnuptial molt. Similar to nuptial adult male, but upper surface duller and more brownish (less grayish), also more uniform, gray pileum sometimes almost entirely concealed by olive green or dull brown edgings of feathers; sides of head and neck more brownish or washed with olive; black feathers on throat and jugulum more obscured by broader gray tips of feathers; yellow of lower surface duller, more washed with buff. *Adult female, nuptial*: Acquired by partial prenuptial molt. Similar to adult male, but duller, more uniform above, with less difference between pileum and remainder of upper surface; pileum and hindneck mouse gray to deep grayish olive, washed with brown; back dull olive,

passing into yellowish olive on rump and upper tail-coverts; wings and tail as in nuptial adult male; sides of head much lighter, duller, and more brownish, lores dull gray, mixed with paler gray or pale buffy brown; supraloral stripe grayish white or pale buff; chin, throat, and jugulum without black, instead light vinaceous buff to tilleul buff washed with pale drab or smoke gray and varying posteriorly to mouse gray washed with dull buff—chin and center of throat usually palest; remainder of lower surface as in nuptial adult male, but flanks duller and yellow usually paler, somewhat more golden (less greenish). *Adult female, winter*: Acquired by complete postnuptial molt. Similar to nuptial adult female, but upper surface duller, more uniform, and somewhat more brownish, gray of head practically concealed by brownish tips of feathers; throat more tinged with buff or even washed with pale dull yellow; acquires narrow elongated dull buffy white spot on each eyelid, interrupted anteriorly. *Male, first nuptial*: Acquired by partial prenuptial molt. Similar to nuptial adult male, but upper parts duller, rather lighter, pileum duller, less clearly plumbeous (more brownish or washed with olivaceous); throat and jugulum usually with less black and more veiled with gray. *Male, first winter*: Acquired by partial postjuvenal molt, not including wing-quills and tail. Similar to adult male in winter, but upper parts duller, usually more brownish; throat and jugulum paler, much more brownish or olivaceous, jugulum with very much less black and this usually in small spots which are obscured by pale olive gray or dull yellowish tips of feathers, throat sometimes entirely without black, this then dull gray washed with yellow and buff; posterior lower parts duller, often more golden; sides and flanks usually darker. Similar to adult female in winter but larger; throat and jugulum usually darker and with some black on jugulum, although nearly always obscured by yellow or pale gray tips of feathers; specimens without black on jugulum very similar to adult female in winter, but still usually darker on jugulum. *Female, first nuptial*: Acquired by partial prenuptial molt. Similar to nuptial adult female, but chin, throat, and jugulum lighter, almost uniform with less gray tinge posteriorly and laterally. *Female, first winter*: Acquired by partial postjuvenal molt. Similar to adult female in winter, but upper surface usually more uniform and more brownish, particularly pileum; chin, throat, and jugulum much paler, much washed with yellow, sometimes nearly as yellow as posterior lower parts, though paler. *Juvenal*: Acquired by complete postnatal molt. Upper surface dark olive brown; wings and tail similar to first winter female, but middle and greater wing-coverts with cinnamon brown tips; anterior lower surface and sides of body similar but paler and with more yellowish buff. Bill, legs, and feet dull brown; iris dark brown.

MEASUREMENTS: *Adult male*: Wing, 58.2–65.0 (average, 61.5) mm.; tail, 46.3–52.3 (49.0); bill (exposed culmen), 10.7–12.2 (11.4); tarsus, 20.3–21.9 (20.9); middle toe without claw, 12.7–14.0 (13.7). *Adult female*: Wing, 54.8–61.7 (58.7); tail, 42.7–49.8 (46.8); bill, 10.2–11.7 (11.2); tarsus, 20.9–21.4 (21.1); middle toe, 12.2–13.2 (12.7).

TEXAS: *Migration*: Collected north to Cooke, east to Polk and Angelina, south to Cameron, west to Webb and Bexar cos. *Winter*: One specimen: Cameron Co., Brownsville (Feb. 21, 1894, F. B. Armstrong).

MacGILLIVRAY'S WARBLER, *Oporornis tolmiei* (Townsend)

SPECIES ACCOUNT

Also known as Tolmie's Warbler. *Nuptial male*: incomplete white eye-ring (broken fore and aft); gray hood with blackish smudge on throat and upper breast; olive green above; yellow lower breast and belly. *Nuptial female*: similar, but hood duller; lacks blackish on throat and upper breast. *Fall adults*: somewhat duller, more brownish. *Immature*: still duller, more brownish. Length, 5¼ in.; wingspan, 7½.

RANGE: S. Alaska to s.w. Saskatchewan, south in mountains to c. California, c. Arizona, and c. New Mexico; also locally in Nuevo León. Winters from s. Baja California, s. Sonora, and Nuevo León to Panama.

TEXAS: (See map.) *Migration*: Late Apr. to late May; late Aug. to late Sept. (extremes: Mar. 15, June 6; Aug. 16, Nov. 25). Common (some years) to fairly common in Trans-Pecos; fairly common to uncommon in remainder of state east to 100th meridian; increasingly scarce eastward to Gainesville, Dallas, Waco, Austin, Beeville, Rio Grande delta; casual on upper coast.

HAUNTS AND HABITS: In behavior as well as appearance the MacGillivray's Warbler so closely resembles its eastern counterpart, the Mourning Warbler, that without careful observation it is difficult to distinguish. In its western summer home the MacGillivray's lives and feeds near the ground within dense thickets—usually along streams or near other water—in valleys and canyons and within second-growth tangles in burned or heavily logged forests; it may also inhabit dry, brushy slopes. Here it generally places its small, ragged nest on or near the ground in rank forbs or occasionally several feet up in a bush. As it migrates through Texas it frequents whatever heavy underbrush or tall weeds are available. It is a rather solitary bird, usually seen singly or in pairs.

This warbler's flight is quick and flitting, and the bird rarely makes long journeys, except during migrations; these sustained flights are more direct. It is a low-ranging forager, ordinarily shy and elusive. Sometimes, however, particularly in spring and summer, it does ascend to branches well above ground. Ground insects—beetles (flea, dung, click, weevils) and cater-

pillars—comprise most of its food. Though a rather active feeder, MacGillivray's frequently pauses to utter its song.

One variation of its pleasing song resembles that of the Mourning Warbler; another variation has been interpreted as *sizik-sizik-sizik, lipik-lipik*. It is usually May before males even occasionally sing in Texas. The often heard call note is a loud *chip* or *click*.

DETAILED ACCOUNT: FOUR SUBSPECIES

PACIFIC MacGILLIVRAY'S WARBLER, *Oporornis tolmiei tolmiei* (Townsend)

DESCRIPTION: *Adult male, nuptial plumage*: Acquired by partial prenuptial molt. Pileum and hindneck neutral gray to rather deep neutral gray; remainder of upper surface rather dark warbler green to serpentine green, becoming lighter and more yellowish on rump and upper tail-coverts; tail citrine, inner edges of feathers light brownish olive; wings dark hair brown, inner edges of primaries and secondaries, except tips of primaries, paler, inner edges of basal portion of secondaries dull vinaceous buff; wing-coverts and wing-quills edged on external margins with citrine, lesser wing-coverts verging toward warbler green; sides of head and of neck similar to pileum but rather paler; dull black lores; elongated white spot on upper and lower eyelids; throat mouse gray to deep mouse gray, feathers margined with pallid neutral gray to brownish neutral gray; middle of jugulum dull black to deep mouse gray, feathers margined with mouse gray to pallid neutral gray, black never so extensive as is usually the case in the Mourning Warbler, *Oporornis philadelphia*; sides and flanks light olive green to yellowish citrine; remainder of posterior lower surface lemon chrome; lining of wing yellowish citrine, edge of wing lemon chrome. Bill brownish black, dark brown, chaetura black, or brownish plumbeous, but cutting edges and mandible flesh color, ecru drab, light drab, yellow, or dull white, tip darker; iris grayish sepia or hazel; legs and feet light brown, light drab, flesh color, brownish flesh color, or brownish white. *Adult male, winter*: Acquired by complete postnuptial molt. Similar to nuptial adult male, but gray of pileum more or less obscured by edgings of buffy brown; feathers of throat and jugulum more broadly tipped with pale gray or dull white. *Adult female, nuptial*: Acquired by partial prenuptial molt. Similar to nuptial adult male but decidedly smaller, duller; upper surface, particularly pileum, more brownish or olivaceous; sides of head paler, more brownish; throat and jugulum much lighter—pallid mouse gray or rather light neutral gray to rather light mouse gray, nearly uniform, and entirely without black or blackish on jugulum; also chin and middle of throat usually somewhat paler than jugulum. *Adult female, winter*: Acquired by complete postnuptial molt. Similar to nuptial adult female, but upper surface duller and decidedly more brownish and more uniform, gray feathers of crown almost completely concealed by brownish tips of feathers; chin, throat, and jugulum much less clearly gray, more strongly washed with dull vinaceous buff, sometimes almost entirely of this color. *Male and female, second winter*: Acquired by complete postnuptial molt. Like corresponding sex in adult winter. *Male, first nuptial*: Acquired by partial prenuptial molt. Similar to nuptial adult male, but upper parts duller, somewhat paler, pileum less clearly plumbeous, more washed with olivaceous or tinged with brown; throat and jugulum commonly with less black and more obscured by gray. *Male, first winter*: Acquired by partial postjuvenal molt, which does not involve wing-quills or tail. Similar to adult male in winter, but upper surface duller, more brownish, particularly pileum, which is almost uniformly warm olive brown to dull buffy brown; sides of head paler and more brownish or olivaceous, throat and jugulum lighter—dark neutral gray or deep mouse gray washed with light drab and with little or no blackish on jugulum. Similar to adult male in winter but larger; throat and jugulum paler, less grayish, and much more uniformly buffy or more deeply tinged with buff; jugulum never

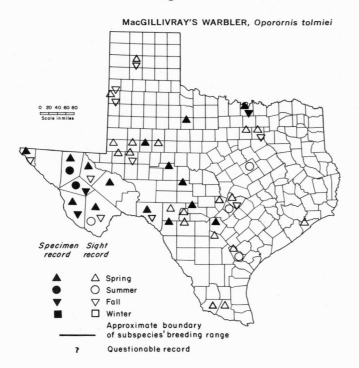

MacGILLIVRAY'S WARBLER, *Oporornis tolmiei*

0 20 40 60 80
Scale in miles

Specimen   Sight
record   record

▲   △   Spring
●   ○   Summer
▼   ▽   Fall
■   □   Winter

Approximate boundary
of subspecies' breeding range

?   Questionable record

with blackish or dark grayish feather centers. Maxilla chaetura drab or chaetura black; mandible flesh color; iris fuscous black or dark brown; legs and feet buff or flesh color. *Female, first nuptial*: Acquired by partial prenuptial molt. Similar to nuptial adult female, but pileum dull brown instead of clear gray; anterior lower parts paler, somewhat less tinged with gray. *Female, first winter*: Acquired by partial postjuvenal molt, which does not involve wing-quills or tail. Similar to adult female in winter but still more brownish (less greenish) on upper surface; throat and jugulum still more strongly buffy (less grayish); yellow of lower surface duller, more tinged with buff from more buffy tips of feathers. *Juvenal*: Acquired by complete postnatal molt. Similar to first winter female, but upper parts still more brownish; sides of head somewhat more brownish. Maxilla dull brown, mandible yellow, but tip brown; feet light yellow.

MEASUREMENTS: *Adult male*: Wing, 54.6–61.5 (average, 57.7) mm.; tail, 47.0–54.6 (51.6); bill (exposed culmen), 9.9–11.2 (10.4); tarsus, 19.0–22.6 (20.6); middle toe without claw, 11.9–13.0 (12.4). *Adult female*: Wing, 55.1–56.4 (55.6); tail, 49.0–54.1 (51.3); bill, 9.9–10.9 (10.2); tarsus, 19.6–20.6 (20.3); middle toe, 11.9–13.0 (12.4).

RANGE: S.e. Alaska and s.w. British Columbia, south through Cascade Mts. to w. California. Winters from s. Baja California through w. Mexico to Costa Rica.

TEXAS: *Migration*: One specimen: Culberson Co., Pine Springs Canyon, 5,800 ft. (May 1, 1939, T. D. Burleigh).

INTERMEDIATE MacGILLIVRAY'S WARBLER, *Oporornis tolmiei intermedius* Phillips

Race not in A.O.U. check-list, 1957 (see Appendix A).

DESCRIPTION: *Adult male and female, nuptial plumage*: Similar to *O. t. tolmiei*, but upper and lower parts somewhat duller; wings somewhat, tail moderately, longer.

MEASUREMENTS: *Adult male*: Wing, 53.8–63.8 (average, 59.9) mm.; tail, 50.0–56.4 (54.1); bill (exposed culmen), 10.2–11.2 (10.7); tarsus, 19.8–21.4 (20.9); middle toe without claw, 12.2–13.2 (12.7). *Adult female*: Wing, 55.3–60.5 (57.4); tail, 51.3–55.1 (52.6); bill, 9.4–11.2 (10.4); tarsus, 20.3–20.9 (20.6); middle toe, 11.4–13.5 (12.7).

RANGE: N.w. British Columbia and c. Oregon to w. Nevada. Winters from s. Baja California through w. Mexico to w. Panama.

TEXAS: *Migration*: Collected northwest to Jeff Davis (Aug. 22) and Pecos, southeast to Kinney and Kerr cos. Uncommon.

NORTHEASTERN MacGILLIVRAY'S WARBLER, *Oporornis tolmiei austinsmithi* Phillips

Race not in A.O.U. check-list, 1957 (see Appendix A).

DESCRIPTION: *Adult male and female, nuptial plumage*: Resembling *O. t. intermedius*, but upper parts duller, more grayish (less yellowish); posterior lower parts slightly duller, more greenish (gamboge yellow to strontian yellow).

MEASUREMENTS: *Adult male*: Wing, 55.6–65.0 (average, 59.9) mm.; tail, 51.6–56.4 (54.1); bill (exposed culmen), 10.2–10.7 (10.4); tarsus, 19.8–21.4 (20.9); middle toe without claw, 12.7–13.5 (13.0). *Adult female*: Wing, 55.1–61.0 (57.7); tail, 49.8–54.3 (51.3); bill, 9.7–11.2 (10.2); tarsus, 19.0–20.9 (20.1); middle toe, 11.4–13.0 (12.7).

RANGE: S.e. British Columbia to s.w. Saskatchewan, south to w. Wyoming and w. South Dakota. Winters from s. Sinaloa to w. Panama.

TEXAS: *Migration*: Collected north to Haskell and Cooke, south to Bexar, west to El Paso cos. Fairly common.

MOUNTAIN MacGILLIVRAY'S WARBLER, *Oporornis tolmiei monticola* Phillips

DESCRIPTION: *Adult male and female, nuptial plumage*: Similar to *O. t. austinsmithi*, but tail relatively (95 percent of wing, instead of 90) as well as actually much longer; wing also longer.

MEASUREMENTS: *Adult male*: Wing, 57.9–67.8 (average, 61.7)

mm.; tail, 55.1–62.2 (58.4); bill (exposed culmen), 10.2–11.4 (10.4); tarsus, 21.6–22.4; middle toe without claw, 11.9–13.5 (13.0). *Adult female*: Wing, 56.1–67.6 (61.2); tail, 55.1–62.2 (58.4); bill, 9.9–10.4 (10.2); tarsus, 20.1–21.1 (20.6); middle toe, 11.9–13.5 (12.7).

RANGE: E. Oregon to s.e. Wyoming, south to c. Arizona and e. New Mexico. Winters from Colima and Morelos to Guatemala.

TEXAS: *Migration*: Collected north to Culberson and Reeves, east to Menard, south to Val Verde, west to Presidio cos. Fairly common.

YELLOWTHROAT, *Geothlypis trichas* (Linnaeus)

SPECIES ACCOUNT

Also known as Maryland Yellowthroat, U.S. Yellowthroat, and Common Yellowthroat. *Male*: black mask with whitish upper border; olive green above; yellow throat, breast; whitish belly. *Female*: lacks mask; olive brown above; yellow throat; buffy yellow breast; whitish belly. Length, 5 in.; wingspan, 7; weight, ½ oz.

RANGE: S.e. Alaska to Newfoundland, south to n. Baja California, Oaxaca, U.S. Gulf states, and s. Florida. Winters from n. California, s. Arizona, Gulf states, and South Carolina to Panama; also Greater Antilles.

TEXAS: (See map.) *Breeding*: Early Apr. to mid-July, occasionally to late Sept. (eggs, Apr. 9 to June 22; nestling, Sept. 20) from near sea level to 4,000 ft. Formerly fairly common to scarce in northern Panhandle, eastern third (south to Austin, Eagle Lake, Houston), Rio Grande delta, Big Bend, and El Paso region (along Rio Grande), but increasingly rare and local. *Migration*: Mid-Apr. to mid-May; mid-Sept. to late Oct. (extremes: Mar. 13, June 4; July 4, Nov. 10). Very common to fairly common in eastern two-thirds and Panhandle; locally fairly common to uncommon on western

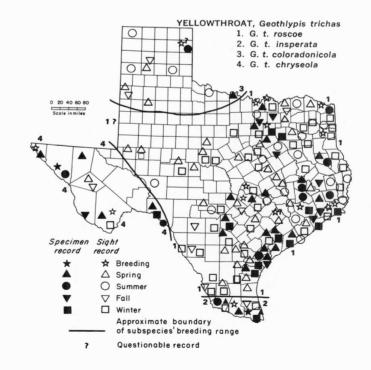

YELLOWTHROAT, *Geothlypis trichas*
1. *G. t. roscoe*
2. *G. t. insperata*
3. *G. t. coloradonicola*
4. *G. t. chryseola*

0 20 40 60 80
Scale in miles

Specimen record / Sight record
★ / ☆ Breeding
▲ / △ Spring
● / ○ Summer
▼ / ▽ Fall
■ / □ Winter

——— Approximate boundary of subspecies' breeding range
? Questionable record

Edwards Plateau and in Trans-Pecos. *Winter*: Mid-Nov. to late Mar. Very common to common along coast; common to fairly common in south Texas brush country and up Rio Grande to Big Bend (irregular); uncommon to scarce in remainder of eastern two-thirds north of 30th parallel; casual at Midland.

HAUNTS AND HABITS: The few Yellowthroats that still breed in Texas usually seek optimum habitat—cattail (*Typha*) ponds, marshes, and swamps. During winter these birds normally continue to live beside water, but they inhabit a variety of tall grasses, sedges, forbs (often *Aster spinosus*) and bushes. Only during large migrations, nowadays diminished, are Yellowthroats widespread over the countryside. They then may occur almost anywhere.

Yellowthroat flight is labored and short—usually from bush to bush or within the interior of a bush—and is performed by rapid wing-beats. At times, however, the bird seems capable of moving rapidly for a short distance. Much like the Long-billed Marsh Wren, it flits from branch to branch or moves up and down within cattails or reeds. It is also at home on the ground, where it hops about searching for food or nesting material. Its food consists almost entirely of insects, many of which—grasshoppers, crickets, cankerworms, fall webworms, mourning-cloak butterflies, leafworms, and plant lice—are at times destructive. The Yellowthroat also takes other butterflies, moths, ants, parasitic wasps, bees, beetles (scavenger, ground, squash, ladybird, flea, cotton-boll weevil, curculio), scales, tree- and leaf-hoppers, leaf bugs, craneflies, mayflies, dragonflies, and gnats. Spiders, harvestmen, small mollusks, and occasionally a few seeds make up the remainder of its diet.

Its ordinary call note is a distinctive *tchep*. Its usual song, heard from early spring sometimes into October, has many variations; it is commonly rendered as *wichity, wichity, wichity,* or *whittitee, whittitee, whittitee.* A flight song, delivered on rare occasions, is a prolonged repetition of its ordinary musical notes. The bird ascends six to fifteen, even twenty feet, begins singing at the height of its flight, then glides downward—as if it were sliding down the scale of its own music. Once in a while, it seems to imitate another bird's song, though not particularly well.

CHANGES: The Yellowthroat is by a wide margin the most plastic bird that nests within Texas: Dr. Oberholser has identified a full twenty races within the state. This extreme plasticity, however, appears to have little survival value. Of the four breeding subspecies, the Brownsville Yellowthroat, *G. t. insperata*, has been rare or extinct since 1951, if not earlier; the Sonora Yellowthroat, *G. t. chryseola*, has apparently not nested in this state since 1934, when A. H. McLellan reported a nest with eggs on May 23 at Valverde (El Paso Co.). However, two youngsters, perhaps of this race, were observed at the silt pond, Rio Grande Village, Big Bend National Park on July 9, 1968 (R. H. Wauer). Actual nesting of the Colorado Yellowthroat, *G. t. coloradonicola*, seemingly has never been verified; very

little hard evidence of breeding by the Arkansas Yellowthroat, *G. t. roscoe*, has been forthcoming since 1945. Gradual warming and drying of the Texas climate during the first half of the twentieth century plus accelerating disturbance and destruction of habitat and increasing pollution, especially since the mid-1940's, are probably major factors in Yellowthroat decline. Cowbird increase has very likely hurt the species also.

DETAILED ACCOUNT: TWENTY SUBSPECIES

ATHENS YELLOWTHROAT, *Geothlypis trichas trichas* (Linnaeus)

DESCRIPTION: *Adult male and female, nuptial plumage*: Somewhat like *G. t. marilandica* (see below), but larger; coloration darker, richer, and more brownish, both above and below. Similar to *G. t. restricta* (see below), but smaller, particularly tail, bill, and wing; male with upper and lower parts rather lighter, somewhat less brownish, yellow of throat and jugulum rather less orange, and flanks a little lighter brown; in female bill decidedly smaller and upper parts average somewhat more greenish (less brownish).

MEASUREMENTS: *Adult male*: Wing, 50.5–56.4 (average, 53.8) mm.; tail, 47.0–55.1 (51.3); bill (exposed culmen), 9.4–11.7 (10.7); tarsus, 20.1–22.9 (21.4); middle toe without claw, 10.9–13.0 (12.2). *Adult female*: Wing, 49.0–53.6 (51.8); tail, 47.5–53.1 (50.0); bill, 9.9–11.2 (10.4); tarsus, 20.1–22.1 (21.1); middle toe, 11.4–12.4 (11.9).

RANGE: C. Alabama to s.e. Virginia. Winters from n. Nuevo León, s. Texas, and South Carolina to Nicaragua; also Greater Antilles.

TEXAS: *Winter*: Taken northeast to Harris and Jefferson, southwest to Cameron cos. Uncommon.

FLORIDA YELLOWTHROAT, *Geothlypis trichas restricta* Maynard

Race not in A.O.U. check-list, 1957 (see Appendix A).

DESCRIPTION: *Adult male and female, nuptial plumage*: Similar to *G. t. trichas*, but wing, tail, and bill longer. Upper parts of male somewhat darker, more brownish (less greenish); yellow of throat and jugulum somewhat more orange. Female with bill decidedly larger than female of *G. t. trichas*; upper surface averaging somewhat more brownish (less greenish).

MEASUREMENTS: *Adult male*: Wing, 53.6–59.2 (average, 55.6) mm.; tail, 51.6–62.0 (54.8); bill (exposed culmen), 10.9–12.4 (11.7); tarsus, 20.1–24.9 (21.9); middle toe without claw, 10.9–14.0 (12.7). *Adult female*: Wing, 50.0–55.1 (51.8); tail, 43.9–55.1 (49.8); bill, 9.9–12.4 (11.4); tarsus, 20.1–22.1 (21.4); middle toe, 10.9–13.0 (12.2).

RANGE: S.e. Louisiana to s.e. South Carolina, south to s. Florida. Winters from breeding range through s. Texas to Costa Rica; also Greater Antilles.

TEXAS: *Migration*: Two specimens: Chambers Co., Anahuac (Oct. 23, 1916, A. P. Smith); Galveston Co., Bolivar Point (May 7, 1907, H. C. Claiborne). *Winter*: Taken in Galveston (1 specimen), Jackson (1), and Cameron (2) cos. Rare.

ARKANSAS YELLOWTHROAT, *Geothlypis trichas roscoe* (Audubon)

Race not in A.O.U. check-list, 1957 (see Appendix A).

DESCRIPTION: *Adult male and female, nuptial plumage*: Similar to *G. t. restricta* but much smaller; above much less brownish; yellow of throat lighter, less orange tinted; flanks much paler, more grayish (less brownish). Similar to *G. t. marilandica* (see below), but tail about 3 percent shorter. Upper surface of male paler, often more grayish; forehead averaging paler, more creamy (less grayish); yellow of anterior lower surface more orange (less greenish). Female lighter above, averaging more yellowish than *marilandica*; also yellow of throat more orange;

lower surface more buffy, flanks more brownish (less grayish). *Natal*: Probably similar to *G. t. marilandica* (see below).

MEASUREMENTS: *Adult male*: Wing, 49.5–54.6 (average, 51.8) mm.; tail, 44.4–49.8 (47.0); bill (exposed culmen), 9.7–11.4 (10.7); tarsus, 18.5–21.6 (20.1); middle toe without claw, 11.4–13.0 (11.9). *Adult female*: Wing, 47.5–50.5 (49.0); tail, 41.4–46.5 (45.5); bill, 9.7–10.7 (10.4); tarsus, 19.0–20.6 (19.8); middle toe, 10.4–11.9 (11.4).

RANGE: N.w. Iowa to s.w. Ohio, south to s.e. Texas and c. Tennessee. Winters from s. Texas and s. Mississippi through Mexico to British Honduras.

TEXAS: *Breeding*: Altitudinal range, near sea level to 750 ft. Collected north to Cooke, east to Bowie, south to Jefferson and Galveston, west to Travis cos. Formerly fairly common; increasingly rare. *Migration*: Collected north to Cooke, east to Galveston, south to Cameron, west to Presidio cos. Fairly common.

NESTING: *Nest*: On uplands or bottomlands, usually in moist situations; in open woodlands, thickets on edges of woods, tangles of briars, marshes, swamps, bushy meadows, swampy thickets, and about streams, ponds, lakes, bushy pastures, and tangles of vegetation often near water; on ground or in vegetation as high as 5 ft. above ground, hidden at base of bush or bunch of weeds, in tuft of grass, cattails, or similar location, usually well concealed; bulky and rather loosely made, usually an open cup but sometimes globular and domed with entrance on side; composed of grasses, leaves, grapevine or other bark, pieces of weeds, ferns, sedges, small twigs, and various fibers of vegetable material; lined with fine grasses, tendrils, rootlets, sedges, and sometimes horsehair and feathers. *Eggs*: 3–6, usually 4; ovate to rounded ovate and to nearly elliptical oval; somewhat glossy; pure white or cream white; spotted, blotched, dotted, and sometimes lined, mostly about large end, and sometimes in form of wreath, with dark umber, reddish brown, purplish black, chestnut, and purplish brown, with shell markings of lavender and lilac. No egg measurements available for *roscoe*; average egg size of Florida Yellowthroat, 17.7 × 13.4 mm. (A. C. Bent).

BROWNSVILLE YELLOWTHROAT, *Geothlypis trichas insperata* Van Tyne

DESCRIPTION: *Adult male and female, nuptial plumage*: Similar to *G. t. roscoe* but larger, bill decidedly so. General coloration of female above somewhat paler; yellow of throat rather more greenish (less orange); flanks and abdomen lighter. *Juvenal*: Similar to juvenal of *G. t. marilandica* (see below), but with larger bill. *Natal*: Probably similar to *G. t. marilandica* (see below).

MEASUREMENTS: *Adult male*: Wing, 53.1–56.9 (average, 55.1) mm.; tail, 48.0–55.9 (52.3); bill (exposed culmen), 10.9–12.2 (11.4); tarsus, 21.1–23.1 (21.9); middle toe without claw, 11.4–14.0 (12.4). *Adult female*: Wing, 49.0–52.1 (50.8); tail, 46.0–50.5 (48.8); bill, 10.9–11.9 (11.2); tarsus, 21.1–22.1 (21.6); middle toe, 11.9–13.0 (12.4).

RANGE: S. Texas. Winters from s. Texas to n. Veracruz.

TEXAS: *Breeding*: Altitudinal range, near sea level to 250 ft. Collected in Cameron, Hidalgo, and Starr cos. Formerly fairly common; increasingly rare. *Vagrant*: Two specimens outside breeding range: Refugio Co., Tivoli (Aug. 7, 1915, A. P. Smith); Aransas Co., Rockport (Oct. 6, 1891, H. P. Attwater).

NESTING: Similar to that of *G. t. roscoe*.

MARYLAND YELLOWTHROAT, *Geothlypis trichas marilandica* (Wilson)

Race not in A.O.U. check-list, 1957 (see Appendix A).

DESCRIPTION: *Adult male, nuptial plumage*: Acquired by partial prenuptial molt. Forehead, fore part of crown, and broad band extending diagonally downward across sides of head, including eyes, and extending to sides of neck black; behind this a narrower pale dull smoke gray band extending from center of crown around posterior end of black band to sides of throat; occiput dull grayish olive to light olive brown; back and scapulars dull yellowish olive to between saccardo olive and olive citrine, upper tail-coverts somewhat lighter and more yellowish; tail plain citrine, edged on exterior webs with light citrine; wings hair brown, inner margins of wing-quills paler, becoming dull pinkish buff on basal portions of outer webs of all wing-quills, wing-coverts light citrine, but lesser coverts rather more grayish; posterior sides of neck behind pale gray band like back; chin, throat, and breast lemon chrome to gamboge yellow; crissum similar but paler; abdomen pale buff or buffy white, sometimes washed with yellow; sides and flanks isabella color to light isabella color; lining of wing buffy white or yellowish white, outer portion mottled with mouse gray and washed with yellow or almost entirely lemon chrome. Bill black, slate black, or clove brown, but basal half of mandible often flesh color, drab, yellow, or brownish white; tongue white; iris bister, reddish brown, hazel, or black; legs and feet sepia, cinnamon, clay color, flesh color, light fawn color, or cream color. *Adult male, winter*: Acquired by complete postnuptial molt. Similar to nuptial adult male, but upper parts duller, more brownish (less greenish), and usually darker—olive brown to light vandyke brown, posterior portion of gray on pileum overlaid by brown edgings of feathers, and anterior part of gray with small brown feather tips; black of sides of head more or less tipped with gray, particularly along sides of throat; lower surface more buffy, sides and flanks darker. *Adult female, nuptial*: Acquired by partial prenuptial molt. Upper parts saccardo olive to dull deep olive, but pileum more brownish, sometimes cinnamon brown or verging toward dull russet; wings and tail similar to those of adult male but rather more brownish; sides of head and of neck dull grayish olive or dull saccardo umber; dull, pale, buffy streak on lower eyelid and rather obscure pale grayish or buff superciliary stripe; chin and throat wax yellow to primuline yellow, chin sometimes whitish; jugulum similar but darker and duller, usually more or less tinged with buff; sides and flanks light isabella color; crissum dull primuline yellow or wax yellow; remainder of lower surface pale colonial buff; axillars pale isabella color; under wing-coverts rather light mouse gray edged with dull wax yellow. Bill clove brown, but basal half of mandible dull pale yellow or brownish white; iris light brown or dark brown; legs and feet clay color. *Adult female, winter*: Acquired by complete postnuptial molt. Similar to nuptial adult female, but upper parts darker, more brownish, and rather more uniform; also somewhat brighter on sides of head and of neck; lower surface darker, much more brownish, particularly on jugulum; sides, flanks, and yellow of chin and throat more washed with buff. *Male, first nuptial*: Acquired by partial prenuptial molt, which does not involve wing-quills or tail feathers. Similar to nuptial adult male. *Male, first winter*: Acquired by partial postjuvenal molt, which does not involve wing-quills or tail. Similar to adult male in winter, but upper surface darker and more brownish; black forehead and gray of anterior part of crown entirely concealed by brown tips of feathers or else practically absent; sides of head much duller, with much less or no black on mask, and whenever present largely or entirely concealed by brownish or dull pale gray tips of feathers; dull, light brownish, yellowish, or grayish superciliary stripe; remainder of sides of head and of neck brownish or dull brownish gray similar to upper surface but lighter; light grayish or pale dull yellowish streak on lower eyelid; yellow of chin, throat, and jugulum duller, more brownish or buffy; sides and flanks darker and more brownish; remainder of lower surface more tinged with buff. Similar to adult female in winter but larger; sides of head with more or less concealed black; yellow of anterior lower parts less buffy (more clearly yellow). Maxilla dull brown; mandible yellow; iris sepia; legs and feet flesh color or light brown. *Female, first nuptial*: Acquired by partial prenuptial molt. Similar to nuptial adult female. *Female, first winter*: Acquired by partial postjuvenal molt, which does not involve wing-quills or tail. Similar to adult female in winter, but general appearance of lower surface lighter; yellow of throat and of jugulum paler, duller, and more buffy, often replaced almost entirely by buff and scarcely tinged with yellow; posterior lower parts more buffy; sides and flanks darker. Bill brown, but base of mandible flesh color; iris sepia; feet brown. *Juvenal*: Acquired by complete postnatal molt. Upper surface citrine to dull orange citrine; rump and upper tail-coverts usually somewhat paler and more yellowish; wings and tail as in first winter female, but lesser wing-coverts more brownish like upper surface, greater and median wing-coverts more or less distinctly tipped with dull clay color, forming one or two rather indistinct wing-bars; sides of head and of neck dull isabella color or light brownish olive; chin chamois; throat and jugulum isabella color or between honey yellow and isabella color; sides and flanks similar to lower breast; abdomen and crissum dull chamois to honey yellow. Maxilla brownish slate; mandible dull white or pale flesh color, with dull brownish tip; iris sepia; legs and feet clay color, pale drab, or olive tinged with flesh color. *Natal* (this plumage of this race not seen in Texas): Sepia. Bill, legs, and feet pinkish buff.

MEASUREMENTS: *Adult male*: Wing, 50.0–52.6 (average, 51.6) mm.; tail, 47.0–50.5 (48.5); bill (exposed culmen), 9.9–10.9 (10.4); tarsus, 19.0–21.6 (19.6); middle toe without claw, 11.4–13.0 (11.9). *Adult female*: Wing, 46.0–52.1 (49.5); tail, 41.9–49.5 (46.5); bill, 9.9–11.4 (10.4); tarsus, 18.5–21.1 (19.6); middle toe, 10.9–11.9 (11.4).

RANGE: N. Pennsylvania and New Jersey, south to c. Virginia and Delaware. Winters from s. Mississippi and North Carolina (probably casually from Texas) to e. Nicaragua; also Greater Antilles.

TEXAS: *Migration*: One specimen: Bexar Co., San Antonio (Apr. 4, 1890, H. P. Attwater).

NORTHERN YELLOWTHROAT, *Geothlypis trichas brachidactyla* (Swainson)

G. t. brachidactylus of A.O.U. check-list, 1957 (see Appendix A).

DESCRIPTION: *Adult male and female, nuptial plumage*: Similar to *G. t. marilandica*, but wing and tail longer. Male with olive green of upper surface more yellowish or brownish (less grayish), lighter and brighter; light band on forehead lighter and brighter, more whitish or creamy (less grayish); yellow of anterior lower parts more orange (less greenish) and usually more extended posteriorly; flanks more brownish (less grayish). Female lighter above, more yellowish (less grayish or brownish); yellow of throat more orange; flanks more rufescent (less grayish).

MEASUREMENTS: *Adult male*: Wing, 52.6–58.4 (average, 55.9) mm.; tail, 46.5–53.3 (50.0); bill (exposed culmen), 9.9–11.4 (10.7); tarsus, 19.6–22.1 (20.9); middle toe without claw, 11.4–13.0 (12.2). *Adult female*: Wing, 49.0–54.1 (52.1); tail, 43.9–48.5 (46.3); bill, 9.9–10.9 (10.4); tarsus, 19.0–20.6 (20.1); middle toe, 10.9–11.9 (11.7).

RANGE: E. New York and s. New Hampshire, south to n. New Jersey and e. Massachusetts. Winters from s. Texas and Mississippi to Guatemala; also Greater Antilles.

TEXAS: *Migration*: Collected in Travis, Nueces, and Cameron cos. Uncommon. *Winter*: Taken in Cameron Co. (4 specimens). Rare.

NOVA SCOTIA YELLOWTHROAT, *Geothlypis trichas novascoticola* Oberholser

Race not in A.O.U. check-list, 1957 (see Appendix A).

DESCRIPTION: *Adult male and female, nuptial plumage*: Similar to *G. t. marilandica*, but wing and tail longer. Male with upper parts decidedly darker, somewhat more brownish (less grayish). Female darker above and more greenish (less grayish or brownish); yellow of throat deeper; flanks darker.

MEASUREMENTS: *Adult male*: Wing, 52.0–57.0 (average, 55.1) mm.; tail, 47.0–53.0 (50.3); bill (exposed culmen), 10.0–12.0 (10.8); tarsus, 19.0–21.5 (20.3); middle toe without claw, 11.0–12.5 (11.7). *Adult female*: Wing, 47.5–53.0 (51.1); tail, 44.5–50.0 (47.8); bill, 9.9–11.3 (10.8); tarsus, 19.0–21.0 (20.1); middle toe, 11.0–12.0 (11.5).

RANGE: Nova Scotia. In migration, west to s. Texas (casually). Winters from n. Florida and Bahamas to Honduras and Jamaica.

TEXAS: *Migration*: One specimen: Nueces Co. (?), 17 mi. east of Padre Island (Apr. 18, 1952, H. R. Bullis, Jr.).

QUEBEC YELLOWTHROAT, *Geothlypis trichas quebecicola* Oberholser

Race not in A.O.U. check-list, 1957 (see Appendix A).

DESCRIPTION: *Adult male, nuptial plumage*: Similar to *G. t. brachidactyla*, but tail averaging somewhat longer (about 2 percent); upper surface darker, duller, and more brownish (less yellowish) olive, gray frontal band narrower; yellow of throat and jugulum less orange and more confined to anterior lower surface, its posterior border well defined.

MEASUREMENTS: *Adult male*: Wing, 51.6–58.9 (average, 55.3) mm.; tail, 48.0–55.1 (51.1); bill (exposed culmen), 9.9–10.9 (10.4); tarsus, 20.1–22.4 (21.1); middle toe without claw, 11.4–12.4 (12.2). *Adult female*: Wing, 52.1–56.1 (54.1); tail, 49.0–52.1 (50.5); bill, 10.2–10.9 (10.7); tarsus, 20.1–21.6 (20.9); middle toe, 11.4–12.4 (11.9).

RANGE: Extreme s.e. Ontario and s. Quebec to Newfoundland. Winters from s. Texas and South Carolina to Guatemala; also West Indies.

TEXAS: *Winter*: Taken in Bexar (1 specimen) and Cameron (3 cos.) cos. Rare.

OHIO YELLOWTHROAT, *Geothlypis trichas ohionicola* Oberholser

Race not in A.O.U. check-list, 1957 (see Appendix A).

DESCRIPTION: *Adult male, nuptial plumage*: Resembling *G. t. novascoticola*, but upper surface lighter, more yellowish; yellow of throat more orange hued and more extended posteriorly, suffusing most of abdomen.

MEASUREMENTS: *Adult male*: Wing, 52.0–59.5 (average, 55.7) mm.; tail, 45.5–53.5 (50.0); bill (exposed culmen), 10.0–11.3 (10.9); tarsus, 19.5–21.3 (20.3); middle toe without claw, 11.3–13.0 (11.9). *Adult female*: Wing, 50.0–53.5 (52.4); tail, 45.5–50.5 (48.1); bill, 10.0–11.3 (10.4); tarsus, 19.5–20.5 (20.1); middle toe, 11.0–12.3 (11.7).

RANGE: S.w. Michigan to c. Pennsylvania, south to n. Georgia and w. North Carolina. Winters from s. Mississippi, s. Florida, and Bahamas to Jamaica and Guatemala.

TEXAS: *Migration*: One specimen: Nueces Co. (?), 17 mi. east of Padre Island (Apr. 18, 1952, H. R. Bullis, Jr.).

MINNESOTA YELLOWTHROAT, *Geothlypis trichas minnesoticola* Oberholser

Race not in A.O.U. check-list, 1957 (see Appendix A).

DESCRIPTION: *Adult male, nuptial plumage*: Similar to *G. t. brachidactyla*, but upper parts lighter; light band on forehead behind black mask decidedly more whitish (less grayish); yellow of throat more golden and more extensive; sides and flanks more brownish.

MEASUREMENTS: *Adult male*: Wing, 53.6–57.9 (average, 55.3) mm.; tail, 46.0–54.1 (50.0); bill (exposed culmen), 10.2–11.7 (11.2); tarsus, 19.6–21.9 (20.6); middle toe without claw, 11.9–13.0 (12.2). *Adult female*: Wing, 50.5–54.6 (52.3); tail, 45.5–53.6 (48.5); bill, 10.2–11.4 (10.7); tarsus, 19.6–21.6 (21.1); middle toe, 11.9–13.0 (12.4).

RANGE: S.w. Manitoba and w. Ontario, south to c. Nebraska, s. Minnesota, and n. Illinois. Winters from Texas and probably s. Mississippi through Mexico to Nicaragua.

TEXAS: *Migration*: Collected north to Clay and Collin, south to Atascosa and Cameron cos. Fairly common. *Winter*: Taken north to Dallas, south to Bexar and Cameron, west to Val Verde cos. Fairly common.

ALBERTA YELLOWTHROAT, *Geothlypis trichas alberticola* Oberholser

Race not in A.O.U. check-list, 1957 (see Appendix A).

DESCRIPTION: *Adult male and female, nuptial plumage*: Similar to *G. t. minnesoticola*, but bill decidedly shorter. In male, tail averaging about 2 percent shorter; upper parts rather darker, much more grayish (less greenish, yellowish, or brownish); frontal band more whitish (less grayish or creamy); yellow of anterior lower parts less extensive; flanks less brownish (more grayish). In female, upper surface more grayish (less greenish or yellowish); yellow of throat less orange (more greenish); remainder of lower surface paler, more grayish or whitish (less buffy).

MEASUREMENTS: *Adult male*: Wing, 54.1–57.7 (average, 56.1) mm.; tail, 47.5–51.6 (49.0); bill (exposed culmen), 9.9–10.9 (10.4); tarsus, 19.0–21.6 (20.9); middle toe without claw, 11.9–12.4 (12.2). *Adult female*: Wing, 49.5–54.1 (52.3); tail, 46.8–52.1 (49.5); bill, 9.7–9.9 (9.8); tarsus, 20.6–21.6 (21.1); middle toe, 11.4–12.2 (11.9).

RANGE: Alberta and s. Saskatchewan. Winters in Texas and probably into Mexico.

TEXAS: *Migration*: Two specimens: Brewster Co., 4 mi. south of Marathon (Apr. 23, 1935, J. B. Semple); Cameron Co., 2 mi. west of Boca Chica (Mar. 9, 1938, G. M. Sutton). *Winter*: Taken in Kaufman (1 specimen) and Cameron (4) cos. Uncommon.

YUKON YELLOWTHROAT, *Geothlypis trichas yukonicola* Godfrey

Race not in A.O.U. check-list, 1957 (see Appendix A).

DESCRIPTION: *Adult male, nuptial plumage*: Similar to *G. t. alberticola*, but tail slightly longer; upper surface decidedly more grayish (less greenish or brownish); posterior lower breast and abdomen much more whitish, with only slight tinge of yellow; sides and flanks paler, more grayish (less yellowish or brownish).

MEASUREMENTS: *Adult male*: Wing, 55.0–57.5 (average, 55.4) mm.; tail, 46.1–53.2 (50.5); bill (exposed culmen), 10.1–11.5 (10.5); tarsus, 19.8–20.9 (20.3). *Adult female* (averages): Wing, 52.6; tail, 50.2; bill, 10.5; tarsus, 20.8.

RANGE: S. Yukon and probably n. British Columbia. Winters in s. Texas.

TEXAS: *Winter*: One specimen: San Patricio Co., Welder Wildlife Refuge (Feb. 16, 1956, C. Cottam).

MONTANA YELLOWTHROAT, *Geothlypis trichas campicola* Behle and Aldrich

DESCRIPTION: *Adult male and female, nuptial plumage*: Similar to *G. t. minnesoticola*, but upper parts of male paler, more grayish or brownish (less yellowish or greenish), light frontal band nearly pure white and broader; yellow of anterior lower parts much more golden. In female, upper parts lighter, more grayish (less greenish or yellowish); lower surface paler, yellow of throat somewhat more orange tinted but lighter and less extensive.

MEASUREMENTS: *Adult male*: Wing, 53.1–56.9 (average, 54.6) mm.; tail, 47.0–53.1 (50.0); bill (exposed culmen), 10.4–11.9 (10.9); tarsus, 19.6–22.1 (20.9); middle toe without claw, 11.2–13.0 (12.4). *Adult female*: Wing, 50.0–55.1 (52.3); tail, 45.0–52.1 (47.8); bill, 10.4–11.4 (10.7); tarsus, 19.6–21.6 (20.3); middle toe, 11.4–12.4 (11.9).

RANGE: Montana, s.w. Saskatchewan, and n.w. North Dakota, south to n.e. Wyoming. Winters from s. Texas to Nuevo León and s.e. Tamaulipas.

TEXAS: *Migration*: Collected north to Dallas, south to Cameron, west to Brewster and Presidio cos. Fairly common. *Winter*: Taken in Nueces (2 specimens) and Cameron (3) cos. Fairly common.

COLORADO YELLOWTHROAT, *Geothlypis trichas coloradonicola* Oberholser

Race not in A.O.U. check-list, 1957 (see Appendix A).

DESCRIPTION: *Adult male and female, nuptial plumage*: Similar to *G. t. campicola*, but male with upper parts more yellowish (less brownish or grayish); yellow of throat deeper, more orange, and more extended posteriorly. Female lighter above, more greenish or yellowish (less brownish or grayish); yellow of throat averaging darker and more extended posteriorly.

MEASUREMENTS: *Adult male*: Wing, 52.8–56.4 (average, 54.8)

mm.; tail, 49.5–52.1 (50.5); bill (exposed culmen), 10.9–11.9 (11.2); tarsus, 20.1–21.6 (21.1); middle toe without claw, 11.9–13.0 (12.4). *Adult female*: Wing, 51.8–55.9 (53.8); tail, 46.5–52.6 (50.0); bill, 9.9–11.2 (10.7); tarsus, 20.1–22.1 (21.1); middle toe, 10.9–12.4 (11.9).

RANGE: S.w. North Dakota, south to c. New Mexico and n.w. Texas. Winters from n. Baja California and Texas to Chiapas.

TEXAS: *Breeding* (no actual nests found): Altitudinal range, probably 1,200 to 3,800 ft. One summer specimen: Hemphill Co., Canadian (July 14, 1903, A. H. Howell). *Migration*: Collected north to Cooke, south to Jackson and Cameron, west to Presidio and Culberson cos. Fairly common. *Winter*: Taken northeast to Harris and Galveston, southwest to Cameron cos. Fairly common.

NESTING: Similar to that of *G. t. roscoe*.

UTAH YELLOWTHROAT, *Geothlypis trichas utahicola* Oberholser

Race not in A.O.U. check-list, 1957 (see Appendix A).

DESCRIPTION: *Adult male and female, nuptial plumage*: Similar to *G. t. campicola*, but tail of male averaging about 10 percent longer; upper parts of male more rufescent, brownish, or yellowish (less grayish or greenish); yellow of anterior lower parts more golden and somewhat more extended posteriorly. Female more brownish above (less greenish or yellowish).

MEASUREMENTS: *Adult male*: Wing, 53.1–59.9 (average, 56.6) mm.; tail, 51.1–59.4 (55.1); bill (exposed culmen), 10.4–11.9 (10.9); tarsus, 20.1–21.6 (20.9); middle toe without claw, 11.9–13.5 (12.7). *Adult female*: Wing, 50.5–54.1 (52.8); tail, 47.0–54.6 (49.5); bill, 9.4–10.9 (10.2); tarsus, 19.0–22.6 (20.6); middle toe, 11.4–13.0 (11.9).

RANGE: Utah and w. Wyoming. Winters from w. Sonora (probably casually from Texas) to n. Veracruz.

TEXAS: *Migration*: One specimen: Bexar Co., San Antonio (May 9, 1900, H. P. Attwater).

IDAHO YELLOWTHROAT, *Geothlypis trichas idahonicola* Oberholser

Race not in A.O.U. check-list, 1957 (see Appendix A).

DESCRIPTION: *Adult male and female, nuptial plumage*: Similar to *G. t. campicola*, but larger, wing and tail decidedly longer. Upper parts of male averaging more yellowish or greenish (less grayish or brownish), and rather darker; light forehead band averaging broader and rather more creamy white; yellow of throat darker, of more orange tint; flanks darker. Female with upper parts averaging somewhat more greenish or grayish (less brownish).

MEASUREMENTS: *Adult male*: Wing, 55.6–61.0 (average, 58.4) mm.; tail, 51.1–58.9 (55.3); bill (exposed culmen), 10.2–12.2 (10.9); tarsus, 19.6–22.6 (21.1); middle toe without claw, 11.4–13.0 (12.4). *Adult female*: Wing, 52.1–55.9 (53.8); tail, 48.5–55.1 (51.8); bill, 10.2–11.2 (10.7); tarsus, 20.1–21.6 (21.1); middle toe, 11.4–12.4 (11.9).

RANGE: E. Oregon and c. Idaho, south to n. Utah. Winters from Texas and Tamaulipas to Guanajuato.

TEXAS: *Migration*: Two specimens: Atascosa Co., 7 mi. southwest of Somerset (May 4, 1935, A. J. Kirn); Starr Co., Rio Grande City (Apr. 7, 1880, M. A. Frazar). *Winter*: Two specimens: Cameron Co., Brownsville (Dec. 21, 1888, Jan. 4, 1892, F. B. Armstrong).

OREGON YELLOWTHROAT, *Geothlypis trichas oregonicola* Oberholser

Race not in A.O.U. check-list, 1957 (see Appendix A).

DESCRIPTION: *Adult male and female, nuptial plumage*: Similar to *G. t. idahonicola* but tail shorter. Upper parts of male lighter, more grayish (less brownish, greenish, or yellowish). Female with upper surface lighter, more grayish (less greenish), particularly in autumn; yellow of throat averaging less orange (more greenish).

MEASUREMENTS: *Adult male*: Wing, 55.6–61.5 (average, 57.9)

mm.; tail, 47.5–55.6 (52.8); bill (exposed culmen), 10.4–11.4 (11.2); tarsus, 20.6–22.4 (21.6); middle toe without claw, 11.9–13.2 (12.7). _Adult female_: Wing, 52.8–56.6 (54.3); tail, 48.3–53.1 (51.3); bill, 9.7–10.9 (10.4); tarsus, 20.1–22.1 (21.1); middle toe, 11.4–13.0 (12.2).

RANGE: C. Oregon and probably n.w. California and n.w. Nevada. In migration, east to Trans-Pecos Texas. Winters in Mexico at least to Nayarit.

TEXAS: _Migration_: Two specimens, both from Brewster Co.: 3 mi. west of San Vicente (May 10, 1933, G. M. Sutton); Lajitas (May 8, 1935, J. B. Semple).

WESTERN YELLOWTHROAT, _Geothlypis trichas occidentalis_ Brewster

DESCRIPTION: _Adult male and female, nuptial plumage_: Similar to _G. t. oregonicola_, but tail decidedly longer. Upper parts of male darker, more brownish or yellowish (less grayish); white frontal band broader. Female with upper surface more brownish or yellowish (less grayish); ventral surface more buffy or yellowish; flanks darker.

MEASUREMENTS: _Adult male_: Wing, 55.9–60.5 (average, 58.2) mm.; tail, 52.6–56.4 (55.3); bill (exposed culmen), 9.9–11.9 (11.2); tarsus, 20.6–22.9 (21.9); middle toe without claw, 12.4–13.7 (13.0). _Adult female_: Wing, 55.1–55.9 (55.6); tail, 51.1–54.1 (52.3); bill, 10.4–10.9 (10.7); tarsus, 20.6–21.6 (21.1); middle toe, 12.4–13.0 (12.7).

RANGE: W. Nevada. Winters from n.e. Baja California (probably casually from Texas), apparently into Mexico.

TEXAS: _Migration_: Two specimens: Hidalgo Co., Lomita Ranch (May 11, 1878, G. B. Sennett); Starr Co., Rio Grande City (Mar. 13, 1890, F. B. Armstrong).

ARIZONA YELLOWTHROAT, _Geothlypis trichas arizonicola_ Oberholser

Race not in A.O.U. check-list, 1957 (see Appendix A).

DESCRIPTION: _Adult male and female, nuptial plumage_: Similar to _G. t. chryseola_ (see below), but upper parts of male decidedly paler, less yellowish (more grayish or brownish); yellow of anterior lower parts less extended posteriorly, posterior lower parts thus less uniformly yellow. Female with upper surface much more grayish (less yellowish); lower parts paler, more whitish or grayish (less buffy).

MEASUREMENTS: _Adult male_: Wing, 56.4–59.4 (average, 57.7) mm.; tail, 53.1–57.4 (55.3); bill (exposed culmen), 10.2–11.9 (11.2); tarsus, 20.1–22.6 (21.6); middle toe without claw, 11.4–13.5 (12.4). _Adult female_: Wing, 52.1–56.4 (54.1); tail, 51.6–55.9 (53.1); bill, 9.9–11.9 (10.7); tarsus, 21.1–21.9 (21.4); middle toe, 11.9–13.0 (12.7).

RANGE: S.w. Utah, south to n.e. Baja California and c. Arizona. In migration, east to Trans-Pecos Texas. Winters from s.e. Arizona (probably) to Jalisco.

TEXAS: _Migration_: Collected in Brewster Co. (4 specimens). Rare.

SONORA YELLOWTHROAT, _Geothlypis trichas chryseola_ van Rossem

DESCRIPTION: _Adult male and female, nuptial plumage_: Similar to _G. t. occidentalis_, but male above decidedly more yellowish (less brownish); below more extensively yellow. Female with upper parts lighter, more yellowish; below also lighter.

MEASUREMENTS: _Adult male_: Wing, 54.6–59.4 (average, 57.2) mm.; tail, 53.6–56.4 (55.3); bill (exposed culmen), 10.9–11.9 (11.4); tarsus, 20.6–22.1 (21.4); middle toe without claw, 11.9–13.5 (12.4). _Adult female_: Wing, 51.6–54.1 (52.6); tail, 49.0–51.1 (50.0); bill, 9.9–11.2 (10.7); tarsus, 20.1–20.6 (20.3); middle toe, 11.4–13.0 (11.9).

RANGE: S. Arizona to Trans-Pecos Texas, south to n. Sonora and c. Coahuila. Winters from s.e. California and s. Texas (probably) to c. Sonora and Coahuila.

TEXAS: _Breeding_: Altitudinal range, 3,200 to 4,000 ft. Collected in El Paso, Hudspeth, and Brewster cos. One summer specimen from Val Verde Co., Del Rio (June 16, 1939, T. D. Burleigh). Formerly fairly common; increasingly rare. _Migration_: Collected northwest to Presidio and Val Verde, southeast to Victoria and Cameron cos. Uncommon.

NESTING: Similar to that of _G. t. roscoe_.

GROUND-CHAT, _Chamaethlypis poliocephala_ (Baird)

SPECIES ACCOUNT

Sometimes put in genus _Geothlypis_. Thick-billed Yellowthroat, Gray-crowned Yellowthroat, Gray-headed Groundchat, Mexican Ground-chat, Rio Grande Ground-chat, and Meadow Warbler are frequently used common names; Rio Grande Yellowthroat formerly was applied to race which occurred in Texas. A thick-billed, long-tailed warbler. _Male_: gray head; narrow black forehead band and lores (lacks Yellowthroat's extensive black face mask); broken white eye-ring; olive above; yellow below. _Female_: similar to male, but paler; lacks gray of head, black on forehead, and distinctly black lores. Best told from female Yellowthroat, which it resembles, by larger body and bill, and entirely yellow under parts. Length, 5½ in.

RANGE: Sinaloa and s. Tamaulipas (formerly extreme s. Texas), south through lowlands of Mexico and Central America to w. Panama.

TEXAS: _Breeding_ (formerly): Late Apr. to late June (eggs, May 1 to June 17; eggs collected, Hidalgo Co., Lomita Ranch, 1880, J. B. Bourbois; Paisano, Cameron or Hidalgo Co., 1902, G. Thomas, fide A. C. Bent) from near sea level to about 125 ft. Casual visitor, formerly apparently fairly common, in Rio Grande delta. All skins are from Cameron Co.; almost all of them were taken in 1890's. Last observed at Brownsville (1 male, June 14, 1959, J. A. Grom, K. Holtz) and Bentsen–Rio Grande Valley State Park (Apr. 25, 1965, L. T. Adams, Elizabeth Henze). _Winter_: Mid-Sept. to late Feb. Formerly uncommon to rare in Cameron Co. Recent sightings: Hidalgo Co., near McAllen (1 seen, Sept. 16, 20, 1956, and 2 seen, Sept. 24, 1956, J. C. Arvin).

HAUNTS AND HABITS: In its Latin American home, preferred habitat of the Ground-chat is open meadows of tall coarse grass with scattered low trees and bushes or clumps of coarse bracken fern. The species apparently does not occur in saltgrass. North of the border the Meadow Warbler formerly inhabited similar grassy openings in the subtropical thorny brushland of the Rio Grande delta. Even when common, it was probably not seen in flocks.

Similar in behavior to the Yellowthroat, this species forages low in grass or bushes and usually remains concealed save for short flights from clump to clump. Food is little known, but is probably mainly insects.

Call notes include a musical, rhythmic _peet-a-loo_, descending in pitch (E. P. Edwards). Song is a long mellow warble, extremely complex and varied. According to Alexander Skutch, it is one of the finest of wood warbler songs; others have called the vocalization bright and buntinglike. It is delivered from a high perch amid the herbage where the songster usually lurks.

CHANGES: Judging by the twenty-four skins collected in the breeding season and the six taken in winter, the Ground-chat was at least fairly common in Cameron County during the 1890's. In or about 1900 it seems to have been virtually extirpated from the southern tip of Texas, its only toehold in the United States. Twentieth-century sight records are clouded by the fact that until the 1950's there was a breeding race of the Yellow-breasted Chat, *Icteria virens*, and of the Yellowthroat, *Geothlypis trichas*, in the extreme southern portion of the state. These species are often confused with the Ground-chat. To compound the confusion, the resident *G. trichas* was often called Rio Grande Yellowthroat—the same English name that was generally applied to *Chamaethlypis (Geothlypis) poliocephala*.

In the vicinity of Brownsville during the nineteenth century, *milpa* agriculture—the slash-and-burn technique of farming—was practiced, just as it still is in the true Tropics all over the world. This practice in the Rio Grande delta suppressed trees and, to some extent, bushes, but encouraged growth of rank green grass—prime Ground-chat habitat. In the twentieth century, fire departments put out fires soon after they start; also the cattle, citrus, and cotton industries, along with housing developments and highway construction, have eliminated all extensive tall-grass meadows with scattered brush. Also there were large freshwater marshes, with associated tall grasses, around Brownsville in the nineteenth century. These marshes disappeared shortly after 1900. Nowadays, one must travel south of the Tropic of Cancer to encounter good Meadow Warbler habitat.

DETAILED ACCOUNT: ONE SUBSPECIES

RALPH'S GROUND-CHAT, *Chamaethlypis poliocephala ralphi* (Ridgway)

Also known as Rio Grande Yellowthroat.

DESCRIPTION: *Adult male, nuptial*: Acquired by partial prenuptial molt. Narrow black band across forehead, including nasal tufts and lores, and extending below eye; pileum light neutral gray to neutral gray, washed and more or less narrowly streaked with buffy citrine; remainder of upper surface saccardo olive to buffy citrine, rather lighter on rump and upper tail-coverts; tail rather greenish citrine, inner edges of feathers dull light brownish olive, without markings; wings between hair brown and buffy brown, inner edges of primaries and secondaries, except at tips of former, pale brown or very pale brown; outer edgings of wing-quills and coverts like back, edgings of primaries rather more greenish; short streak or spot on upper eyelid, also most of lower eyelid, dull white; sides of neck and of head behind eyes like crown but paler, and auriculars more or less washed with yellow; chin, throat, jugulum, and upper breast amber yellow to between wax yellow and primuline yellow, this more or less mixed with, or even in places replaced by, pale buff; crissum wax yellow washed with buff; flanks cream buff to dull clay color; abdomen pale buff or buffy white, often washed with yellow of breast; axillars and edge of wing yellow like anterior lower parts; remainder of under wing-coverts grayish white or buffy

white, often washed with yellow, and more or less mottled with mouse gray. Bill dark brown, but cutting edges and mandible, except at tip, decidedly paler; legs and feet light brown or flesh color. *Adult male, winter*: Acquired by complete postnuptial molt. Similar to nuptial adult male, but gray of pileum, particularly of occiput, more or less tipped with buffy brown or light olive brown; remainder of upper surface more rufescent; yellow of anterior lower parts much overlaid with buff, due to buffy tips of feathers; posterior lower surface more extensive and more pronounced buff (less grayish). *Adult female, nuptial*: Acquired by partial prenuptial molt. Similar to nuptial adult male but smaller; upper surface somewhat duller, also nearly uniform buffy olive, pileum nearly concolor with back (not conspicuously gray)—dark dull light brownish olive, faintly washed with gray; forehead brownish like crown, instead of black; lores lighter, duller—chaetura drab or chaetura black; yellow of lower parts paler, less extensive, bright area often confined chiefly to chin and throat; crissum chamois or cream buff, slightly tinged with yellow; remainder of lower surface dull pale buff, more or less washed with yellow. *Adult female, winter*: Acquired by complete postnuptial molt. Similar to nuptial adult female, but upper surface more brownish (less grayish); lores duller and lighter—fuscous or fuscous mixed with light dull brownish gray; short, brownish white or dull buff superciliary stripe; lower surface darker and much more buffy; yellow of throat darker, duller, and much washed with buff. *Male, first nuptial*: Acquired by partial prenuptial molt. Similar to adult male in winter, but upper surface duller and more uniform; gray of crown practically hidden by olive brown tips of feathers, as is black of forehead; yellow of jugulum more overlaid with buff; sides and flanks rather darker. Similar to adult female in winter but larger; upper surface darker, crown showing more grayish; lores black; no lighter superciliary stripe; yellow of anterior lower parts darker. *Female, first nuptial*: Acquired by partial prenuptial molt. Similar to nuptial adult female. *Female, first winter*: Acquired by partial postjuvenal molt. Similar to adult female in winter, but upper parts still darker and duller, somewhat more brownish; lower parts darker, more brownish. *Juvenal*: Acquired by complete postnatal molt. Similar to first winter female but still duller; upper parts still more uniform. *Natal*: Unknown.

MEASUREMENTS: *Adult male*: Wing, 55.9–58.9 (average, 57.7) mm.; tail, 59.9–65.5 (62.7); bill (exposed culmen), 10.9–11.9 (11.4); tarsus, 22.1–23.6 (22.9); middle toe without claw, 14.0–16.0 (14.7). *Adult female*: Wing, 51.1–55.9 (53.8); tail, 56.4–61.0 (58.7); bill, 11.4–11.9 (11.7); tarsus, 20.1–23.6 (22.1); middle toe, 14.0–14.5 (14.2).

RANGE: Rio Grande delta of Texas and probably adjacent Tamaulipas.

TEXAS: *Breeding* (formerly): Two sets of eggs collected (see species account). At least 24 specimens collected in Cameron Co. First specimen: Brownsville (June 8, 1890, F. B. Armstrong). Last: Brownsville (May 25, 1894, Armstrong). *Winter*: Six specimens taken in Cameron Co. First: Brownsville (Feb. 26, 1892, Armstrong). Last: 20 mi. east of Brownsville (Jan. 11, 1927, G. S. Wing).

NESTING: *Nest*: One collected in Rio Grande delta at Paisano, Texas, was a small cup in clump of coarse grass near a road; outside was of dry grass, interior of fine grass with inner lining of horsehair. *Eggs*: 3–5; rounded ovate; cream white with small spots and dots of dull brown and black, and shell markings of drab, mostly at large end, and sometimes in form of wreath; average size, 17.5 × 14.0 mm.

YELLOW-BREASTED CHAT, *Icteria virens* (Linnaeus)

SPECIES ACCOUNT

The largest U.S. warbler. Thick, blunt bill; white eye-stripe and broken white eye-ring give "spectacled" look; olive green upper parts; yellow throat, breast; white belly. Length, 7¼ in.; wingspan, 9¾; weight, 1 oz.

RANGE: S. British Columbia to s. Great Lakes region and c. New England, south to c. Baja California, Morelos, s. Tamaulipas (formerly), Gulf coast (rarely), and n. Florida. Winters from s. Baja California, s. Sinaloa, and Nuevo León to w. Panama.

TEXAS: (See map.) *Breeding*: Early Apr. to mid-Aug.—occasionally to late Sept. (eggs, Apr. 6 to Sept. 15) from near sea level to 5,000 ft. Locally common to uncommon in most parts north of 29th parallel, though rare in middle and southern Panhandle and on upper coast; very rare in lowland south Texas brush country (last reported breeding: nest with 2 young, 1 egg, Santa Maria, Cameron Co., July 4, 1935, Mrs. C. H. Miller). *Migration*: Early Apr. to early May; mid-Aug. to mid-Oct. (extremes: Mar. 17, May 26; July 4, Dec. 6). Very common to fairly common through most parts; scarce in middle and southern Panhandle. *Winter*: Early Dec. to late Feb. Rare along coast and in Rio Grande delta; casual inland to Bryan, Austin, San Antonio, and Laredo.

HAUNTS AND HABITS: The Yellow-breasted Chat inhabits thickets, briar tangles, and woodland undergrowth near rivers and swamps and juniper or oak scrub on drier uplands and slopes. Sometimes it even frequents hedges, fence rows, and overgrown fields. A solitary bird, it is generally found singly or in pairs.

Flight is quick, jerky, and seldom prolonged, except during migration. This warbler usually feeds low, where it lurks in dense foliage. The animal part of its diet consists of insects (weevils, grasshoppers, tent caterpillars, currantworms, butterflies, moths, ants, wasps, bees, bugs, and mayflies), and occasionally spiders and

crustaceans. At times it feeds rather extensively on wild fruits, such as strawberries, raspberries, blackberries, elderberries, huckleberries, and wild grapes.

Although *Icteria virens* normally remains secluded, its song betrays its presence at all times of day and even during the night. The regular vocalization consists of one or two harsh notes followed by clear whistling calls, cackles, chuckles, rattles, squawks, and pops; these are on the same or different pitches and intermingled in almost endless variety. The ventriloquial quality of these phrases often makes it difficult to determine the singer's exact location. The chat's varied repertoire sometimes sounds Mockingbird-like and, thus, seemingly imitative of other birds.

In the early part of the breeding season, the male frequently engages in a curious aerial performance. While uttering his usual oddball squeaks and squawks, he flutters up into the air and then slowly pitches and jerks—typically with head and tail upraised, feet dangling—anywhere from five to thirty feet above his patch of bushes. He then appears like a suspended puppet being moved slowly across a stage by an invisible elastic rubber band. In Texas, his flight song is given mostly in April and May; singing from a perch continues frequently into July.

CHANGES: The Yellow-breasted Chat has virtually ceased nesting in the south Texas brush country since 1900; from 1933 it has declined somewhat on the Edwards Plateau. Climatic warming plus excessive bulldozing and overgoating of thickets seem to be the chief chat inhibitors.

DETAILED ACCOUNT: FOUR SUBSPECIES

EASTERN YELLOW-BREASTED CHAT, *Icteria virens virens* (Linnaeus)

DESCRIPTION: *Adult male, nuptial plumage*: Acquired by wear from winter plumage. Upper surface olive citrine to rather deep olive, pileum somewhat more grayish and usually with more or less indication of spotting, due to dark chaetura drab or chaetura black centers of feathers; tail fuscous, feathers edged on outer webs with olive or citrine, most of feathers, except two middle pairs, edged terminally very narrowly on inner webs with dull white or grayish white; wings dark hair brown, primaries and secondaries edged on inner webs, except at tips of primaries, with dull white or brownish white, forming very sharply defined line on all feathers; lesser wing-coverts and outer edges of wing-quills citrine; superciliary stripe white; lores and short stripe below eye black or slate black; lower eyelid white; auriculars deep mouse gray; sides of neck like hindneck; short malar stripe white; chin, throat, and breast between lemon chrome and light cadmium; sides and flanks grayish olive to drab; remainder of lower surface white; lining of wing lemon chrome. Bill black, but base of mandible sometimes somewhat lighter; inside of mouth black; iris dark brown or hazel; legs and feet slate color, dark olive brown, or plumbeous. *Adult male, winter*: Acquired by complete postnuptial molt. Similar to nuptial adult male, but upper surface and sides of head more brownish or olivaceous (less grayish); breast and jugulum more or less washed, spotted, or streaked obscurely with olive; sides and flanks more buffy or drab. Bill dark brown or blackish brown, but cutting edges and mandible, except tip, dull grayish white. *Adult female, nuptial*: Acquired by wear from winter. Similar to nuptial adult male but smaller; upper parts usually duller; lores lighter, duller, dark mouse gray; yellow of anterior lower parts paler and less orange. Bill dark brown or blackish brown, cutting edges and basal por-

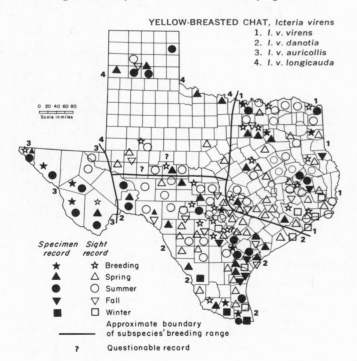

YELLOW-BREASTED CHAT, *Icteria virens*

1. *I. v. virens*
2. *I. v. danotia*
3. *I. v. auricollis*
4. *I. v. longicauda*

0 20 40 60 80
Scale in miles

Specimen record / Sight record

★ / ☆ Breeding
▲ / △ Spring
● / ○ Summer
▼ / ▽ Fall
■ / □ Winter

——— Approximate boundary of subspecies' breeding range

? Questionable record

tion of mandible plumbeous or grayish white; legs and feet plumbeous. *Adult female, winter*: Acquired by complete postnuptial molt. Similar to nuptial adult female, but upper surface rather lighter, more greenish or brownish (less grayish); yellow of anterior lower parts more or less mottled or veiled with olive; sides and flanks more brownish (less grayish). *Male, first nuptial*: Acquired by wear from first winter. Similar to nuptial adult male but somewhat duller, particularly on upper surface. *Male, first winter*: Acquired by complete postjuvenal molt. Similar to adult female in winter, but upper surface decidedly darker and more brownish; lores somewhat lighter, more grayish; yellow of anterior lower parts much more overlaid with olive; sides and flanks still darker and more brownish. *Female, first nuptial*: Acquired by wear from first winter. Similar to nuptial adult female but plumage rather duller. *Female, first winter*: Acquired by complete postnatal molt. Practically identical with adult female in winter. *Juvenal*: Acquired by complete postnatal molt. Upper surface dull deep grayish olive to between olive brown and deep olive; wings and tail as in first winter female; sides of head like crown but slightly paler and without indication of superciliary stripe or eyelid spots; lower surface cream white, but throat, jugulum, upper breast, and sides of body heavily spotted or mottled with dull light grayish olive or between drab and grayish olive; flanks pinkish buff. Bill dark brown above, pale below; iris dark brown; legs and feet light brown. *Natal*: None; bird hatched unfeathered.

MEASUREMENTS: *Adult male*: Wing, 73.4–81.0 (average, 76.7) mm.; tail, 71.1–83.6 (74.4); bill (exposed culmen), 13.0–14.5 (13.7); tarsus, 24.9–26.9 (26.2); middle toe without claw, 15.5–17.0 (16.3). *Adult female*: Wing, 71.9–77.0 (74.2); tail, 69.1–74.9 (71.7); bill, 13.0–14.0 (13.5); tarsus, 24.9–26.9 (25.7); middle toe, 15.0–16.5 (15.7).

RANGE: S.w. Minnesota to c. New York, south to s.e. Texas and n. Florida. Winters from Texas (a few) and s.w. Louisiana through Mexico to n.w. Panama.

TEXAS: *Breeding*: Altitudinal range, near sea level to 750 ft. Collected north to Cooke, east to Bowie, south to Fort Bend, west to Travis cos. Locally common. *Migration*: Collected north to Clay, east to Polk, south to Cameron (Aug. 26), west to Tom Green cos. Common. *Winter*: One specimen: Cameron Co., Brownsville (Feb. 23, 1911, A. K. Fisher).

NESTING: *Nest*: On uplands and bottomlands, sometimes in scattered colonies; in bushy or brushy areas, edges of woodlands, and thickets along fence rows and roadsides; in tangle of briars, thicket, small tree, or bush, 1–5 ft. above ground, or even in old box near house; bulky, somewhat rudely built cup, but ordinarily well concealed; composed of grasses, leaves, strips of grapevine and other bark, stems of weeds and of other plants, and roots; lined with finer grasses, tendrils, wiry plant stems, pine needles, sometimes roots and hair. *Eggs*: 3–5, ordinarily 4; nearly oval to short ovate; glossy white or slightly greenish white; spotted and speckled, either over entire surface or in wreath about large end, with cinnamon rufous, chestnut, and light red, with shell markings of lavender or lilac; average size, 22.9 × 17.8 mm.

BROWNSVILLE YELLOW-BREASTED CHAT, Icteria virens danotia Oberholser, new subspecies (see Appendix A)

DESCRIPTION: *Adult male and female, nuptial plumage*: Similar to *I. v. longicauda* (see below), but smaller; averaging slightly more grayish on upper surface; flanks and crissum averaging more whitish or grayish (much less buffy). Similar to *I. v. virens*, but tail slightly longer than wing (instead of shorter); upper surface much more grayish; sides and flanks more whitish or grayish (less buffy).

MEASUREMENTS: *Adult male*: Wing, 72.9–78.5 (average, 76.2) mm.; tail, 70.6–82.6 (77.5); bill (exposed culmen), 13.0–15.0 (14.0); tarsus, 25.9–28.4 (26.7); middle toe without claw, 13.5–16.0 (14.7). *Adult female*: Wing, 71.9–77.5 (74.7); tail, 73.9–77.5 (75.7); bill, 14.0–15.0 (14.7); tarsus, 25.9–27.4 (26.7); middle toe, 14.5–16.5 (15.2).

TYPE: Adult male, no. 363609, U.S. National Museum, Bio-

logical Surveys collection; 20 mi. west of Mountain Home, Kerr Co., Texas; June 18, 1937, B. E. Ludeman, original no., 80.

RANGE: N.e. Coahuila to c. and s. Texas. Winters from s. Texas into Mexico.

TEXAS: *Breeding*: Altitudinal range, near sea level (formerly) to 1,800 ft. Collected north to Gillespie, east to Bee, south to Cameron cos. Locally fairly common on s. Edwards Plateau; apparently no recent (since 1935) nesting record in lowlands (below 500 ft.). *Migration*: Collected north to Menard, east to Victoria and Aransas, south to Cameron, west to Val Verde cos. Fairly common. *Winter*: Two specimens: Webb Co., Laredo (Jan. 23, 27, 1886, F. B. Armstrong).

NESTING: Similar to that of *I. v. virens*, also to that of *longicauda* (see below).

MEXICAN YELLOW-BREASTED CHAT, Icteria virens auricollis (Lichtenstein)

DESCRIPTION: *Adult male and female, nuptial plumage*: Similar in size to *I. v. longicauda* (see below), but upper parts averaging darker, more grayish (less greenish) olive; sides and flanks lighter, decidedly more grayish (less buffy). Similar to *I. v. danotia* but larger; upper parts averaging somewhat darker, more grayish (less greenish) olive; sides and flanks darker and somewhat more buffy.

MEASUREMENTS: *Adult male*: Wing, 74.9–83.1 (average, 78.7) mm.; tail, 75.9–86.1 (81.8); bill (exposed culmen), 14.0–15.7 (14.7); tarsus, 24.9–28.4 (26.7); middle toe without claw, 14.0–16.5 (14.7). *Adult female*: Wing, 73.9–75.9 (74.7); tail, 78.0–79.0 (78.5); bill, 14.5–15.5 (15.0); tarsus, 25.9–26.9 (26.4); middle toe, 14.0–15.5 (14.5).

RANGE: W. Sonora to Trans-Pecos Texas, south to Jalisco and Puebla. Winters from n. Mexico (probably) to Morelos.

TEXAS: *Breeding*: Altitudinal range, 1,800 to 5,000 ft. Collected in El Paso, Hudspeth, Jeff Davis, Presidio, and Brewster cos. Locally common. *Migration*: Collected in El Paso and Brewster cos. Common.

NESTING: Similar to that of *I. v. longicauda* (see below).

LONG-TAILED YELLOW-BREASTED CHAT, Icteria virens longicauda (Lawrence)

DESCRIPTION: *Adult male and female, nuptial plumage*: Similar to *I. v. virens*, but wing, tail, and bill longer; tail longer than wing (instead of shorter); upper surface more grayish; white on malar region more extensive; sides and flanks even more buffy, crissum somewhat so; yellow of anterior lower surface deeper, more inclining to orange.

MEASUREMENTS: *Adult male*: Wing, 74.9–84.1 (average, 79.2) mm.; tail, 76.5–86.1 (81.3); bill (exposed culmen), 13.5–15.0 (14.5); tarsus, 25.9–27.9 (26.4); middle toe without claw, 15.0–17.5 (16.3). *Adult female*: Wing, 72.9–80.0 (77.7); tail, 71.9–82.0 (78.0); bill, 13.5–15.0 (14.5); tarsus, 25.9–26.9 (26.2); middle toe, 14.5–16.5 (15.2).

RANGE: S.w. British Columbia to n.w. North Dakota, south to c. Baja California, n. Arizona, and n.w. Texas. Winters from s. Sinaloa to Oaxaca.

TEXAS: *Breeding*: Altitudinal range, 900 to 2,500 ft. Collected in Hemphill, Armstrong, and Randall cos. Uncommon and local. *Migration*: Collected in Deaf Smith (1 specimen), Armstrong (1), Wilbarger (1), and Kaufman (1) cos. Uncommon.

NESTING: Similar to that of *I. v. virens*, but average egg size, 21.4 × 16.3 mm.

[RED-FACED WARBLER, Cardellina rubrifrons (Giraud)

Adult: bright red mask covering forehead, lores, throat, upper breast, and sides of neck; black crown, auriculars; white nape, rump; gray back, wings, tail;

whitish below. *Immature*: duller; red of face replaced with flesh pink; white areas tinged with buff. Length, 5 in.

RANGE: Mountains of c. Arizona and s.w. New Mexico, south to Durango. Winters from Sinaloa and Durango to Chiapas, Veracruz, and Guatemala.

TEXAS: *Hypothetical*: Five sightings: El Paso (flock of 4–8, Aug. 1, 1956, Lena G. McBee, Mary Belle Keefer, Mr. and Mrs. D. T. Johnson, Caroline McClintock, et al.); Brewster Co., Boot Spring in Chisos Mts. (1 seen, June 5, 1964, B. A. Mack); Midland (1 seen, May 5, 1956, Anne LeSassier); San Antonio (1 studied for an hour in backyard, May 30, 1966, Col. and Mrs. E. R. Diggs, fide Hazel Kush); San Saba Co. (3 observed for ca. 4½ hours, May 5, 1973, Lillian Brown, Gerald Raun, Lou Barnette).]

HOODED WARBLER, *Wilsonia citrina* (Boddaert)

SPECIES ACCOUNT

Male: black hood; yellow forehead, face, under parts; olive green upper parts; white tail-spots. *Female*: similar, but lacks black hood; usually shows tinge of black about head. Length, 5½ in.; wingspan, 8; weight, ½ oz.

RANGE: S.e. Nebraska to s. Great Lakes region and s. New England, south to s.e. Texas, U.S. Gulf coast, and n. Florida. Winters in humid lowlands from Mexico to Panama.

TEXAS: (See map.) *Breeding*: Probably mid-Apr. to July (nest with eggs located, Matagorda Co., May 2, 1938, F. F. Nyc; young following parents, Bowie Co., July 5, 1888, B. T. Gault; adult feeding young, San Ja-

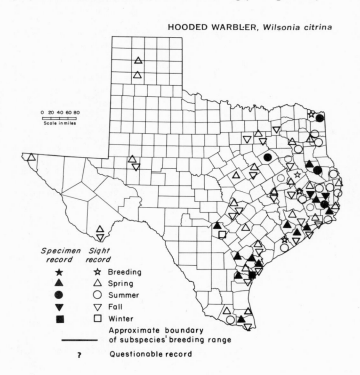

HOODED WARBLER, *Wilsonia citrina*

0 20 40 60 80
Scale in miles

Specimen record	Sight record	
★	☆	Breeding
▲	△	Spring
●	○	Summer
▼	▽	Fall
■	□	Winter

—— Approximate boundary of subspecies' breeding range

? Questionable record

cinto Co., July 19, 1972, Suzanne Winckler) from near sea level to approximately 250 ft., rarely higher. Locally common to fairly common along eastern border and in southeastern portion; rare west to about 95th meridian; last nesting record south of 30th parallel: Matagorda Co. (nest with eggs, May 2, 1938, F. F. Nyc). *Migration*: Late Mar. to early May; late Aug. to mid-Oct. (extremes: Mar. 1, June 13; Aug. 12, Nov. 21). Very common (some springs; usually upper coast) to fairly common in eastern quarter and along coast; uncommon to scarce in remainder of eastern half; scarce to very rare in western half. *Winter*: One specimen: San Patricio Co., Welder Wildlife Refuge (male, Feb. 19, 1956, Clarence Cottam; Welder collection, no. 213). One sighting: Bexar Co., San Antonio (male, Dec. 27, 1964, Mr. and Mrs. G. B. Harding).

HAUNTS AND HABITS: The Hooded Warbler's Texas summer home is amid thickets of forested river and stream valleys. Well hidden in the bushes, the Hooded can be heard singing but is often difficult to find. During migration it retains a preference for dense, shady undergrowth, but occurs in a wide variety of habitats along its route. It is almost always seen singly or in pairs but does occur sometimes in migrating companies with other warblers.

Its flight is quick and strong but usually short; occasionally it flies backwards for a short distance. *W. citrina* has a habit of spreading its tail, somewhat redstartlike, which it sometimes does even in flight. Although commonly found in the lower strata of the forest, it occasionally ascends to treetops and at times sings from a high perch. Assiduously it gleans insects from branches and foliage, also descending to the ground to feed. When foraging, it flits about actively, occasionally turning somersaults in the air or catching insects on the wing. Sometimes without pausing in flight, it seizes insects from leaves as it passes. Although food consists mostly of insects (beetles, bugs, mosquitoes, flies, ants, wasps, grasshoppers, locusts, plant lice, caddis flies, caterpillars, moths, and butterflies), some spiders are taken as well, and probably certain wild berries.

Call notes of the Hooded have been described as a somewhat sharp *chirp* or *churp* and a metallic *chink*. Its song is loud and clear with a decided whistling quality. One variation may be represented by *che-whee-whee-whee-a-wheer*, accented strongly on the last syllable. Renditions often include a slurred *tee-o* near the end. The song season in Texas lasts from April into early July.

DETAILED ACCOUNT: NO SUBSPECIES

DESCRIPTION: *Adult male, nuptial plumage*: Acquired by wear from winter plumage. Forehead, anterior part of crown, sides of head, including superciliary stripe, yellow—between lemon chrome and light cadmium; remainder of pileum, sides of neck, chin, throat, and jugulum black; remainder of upper surface warbler green to dark warbler green; tail light chaetura drab to hair brown, edged on outer webs of feathers with warbler green, outer three tail feathers with large oblique terminal white areas on inner webs, these largest on outermost feathers; wings light chaetura drab, lesser coverts and edgings of others, with edgings of wing-quills, like back, inner edges of secondaries brownish white, of primaries, except at tips, light brown; breast, abdomen, and crissum lemon chrome to between lemon chrome and light cadmium; sides and flanks washed with olivaceous; lining of wing lemon chrome, outer portions somewhat mottled with smoke gray. Bill black or brownish black, but mandible somewhat lighter; iris dark brown; legs light flesh color; feet and claws similar but darker. *Adult male, winter*: Acquired by complete postnuptial molt. Similar to nuptial adult male, but bill lighter, more brownish; black of head and throat often slightly veiled by dull buff or pale yellowish tips of the feathers. *Adult female, nuptial (yellow-throated phase)*: Acquired by wear from winter. Similar to nuptial adult male, but upper parts duller, posterior part of pileum and sides of neck dull black or dark olive, much mixed with warbler green; yellow of sides of head duller, that of lower parts duller, paler, and usually more greenish; no black on under surface but occasionally a few olivaceous spots on side or middle of jugulum. *Adult female, nuptial (black-throated phase)*: Acquired by wear from winter. Similar to above phase, but throat and jugulum as extensively black as in male, though duller and often washed with yellow or olive green, and black on upper part of throat often mixed with these same colors. Most specimens are variously intermediate between these two phases, black on throat varying from mere indication to fully black throat and jugulum like adult male. *Adult female, winter*: Acquired by complete postnuptial molt. Like nuptial adult female. *Male and female, second winter*: Acquired by complete postnuptial molt. Like corresponding sex of adult in winter. *Male, first nuptial*: Acquired by wear from first winter. Very closely resembling nuptial adult male. *Male, first winter*: Acquired by partial postjuvenal molt, not involving wing-quills or tail. Similar to adult male in winter, but upper parts rather lighter, black of pileum more edged with warbler green to pale dull yellow, as are black areas on anterior lower surface and on sides of head; yellow of lower parts paler and more greenish. *Female, first nuptial*: Acquired by wear from first winter. Like nuptial adult female, but without black on either head or throat. *Female, first winter*: Acquired by partial postjuvenal molt, which does not involve wing-quills or tail. Similar to adult female in winter, but with no black on either head or throat. *Juvenal*: Acquired by complete postnatal molt. Pileum light brownish olive, remainder of upper surface rather darker; wings and tail similar to those of first winter female, but lesser wing-coverts light brownish olive, greater and median coverts edged with same; auriculars light brownish olive, washed with dull yellow; chin, throat, and jugulum buffy citrine; breast and abdomen dull colonial buff, breast much spotted with buffy citrine. *Natal*: Light sepia. Bill, legs, and feet pinkish buff.

MEASUREMENTS: *Adult male*: Wing, 64.0–71.9 (average, 66.5) mm.; tail, 54.1–64.0 (57.9); bill (exposed culmen), 9.9–11.4 (10.7); tarsus, 19.0–21.6 (20.3); middle toe without claw, 10.4–11.9 (10.9). *Adult female*: Wing, 58.4–65.0 (62.7); tail, 50.0–57.9 (54.3); bill, 8.9–10.9 (10.2); tarsus, 19.0–20.9 (20.3); middle toe, 10.4–11.4 (10.7).

TEXAS: *Breeding*: Collected north to Bowie, south to Hardin cos. (see species account). *Migration*: Collected north to Navarro (late Aug.), east to Tyler and Jefferson, south to Cameron, west to Bexar cos. *Winter*: See species account.

NESTING: *Nest*: Ordinarily in lowlands, occasionally on slopes, in forested areas, swamps with dense undergrowth, often along streams, in undergrowth, thickets, or canebrakes, in bush, low tree, or herbaceous vegetation, often in fork of branch, 1–5 ft. above ground; compactly woven cup of leaves, small strips of bark, leaves of cane and other plants, parts of weeds and sedges, scales of beech buds, cottonlike vegetable substances, catkins, fuzz from hickory and oak trees, fibrous roots and grasses, bound together with spider webs; lined with horse or cattle hair, shreds of grapevine or other bark, fine grasses, dry weeds, rootlets, blackish moss, and pine needles. *Eggs*: 3–5, usually 4; ovate to short ovate, to nearly oval; white, cream white, or pale yellowish white, with spots and dots, sometimes blotches, principally near large end where often forming wreath, of chestnut, burnt

umber, chestnut red, purplish red, with shell markings of pale lavender; average size, 18.3 × 13.5 mm.

WILSON'S WARBLER, *Wilsonia pusilla* (Wilson)

SPECIES ACCOUNT

Black-capped Warbler and Pileolated Warbler are frequently used common names. *Male*: olive green above with rounded black cap; yellow forehead, face, under parts. *Female*: similar, but cap faint or lacking. Length, 5 in.; wingspan, 6¾.

RANGE: Alaska and Canada, south to s. California, c. Nevada, and n. New Mexico, and into n. New England. Winters chiefly from Mexico (excluding Yucatán Peninsula) to w. Panama.

TEXAS: (See map.) *Migration*: Mid-Apr. to mid-May; late Aug. to early Oct. (extremes: Mar. 8, June 21; Aug. 6, Nov. 25). Very common to fairly common through most parts. *Winter*: Late Dec. to mid-Mar. Uncommon locally to scarce along coast and in Rio Grande delta; rare in remainder of state south of 30th parallel; casual at El Paso and Austin.

HAUNTS AND HABITS: In its northern home, the Wilson's Warbler nests on or near the ground in sedgy, mossy, bushy portions of deciduous and evergreen woods on both uplands and lowlands. During its twice-annual trip through Texas this warbler occurs in thickets, borders of woods, mesquite, bushy hillsides, trees and bushes along fence rows and roadsides, orchards, and ornamental trees in country, town, and city. Generally it is found singly or in pairs, but during a big migration a hefty number may be found together in a loose flock.

While it prefers shrubs and forest undergrowth, it

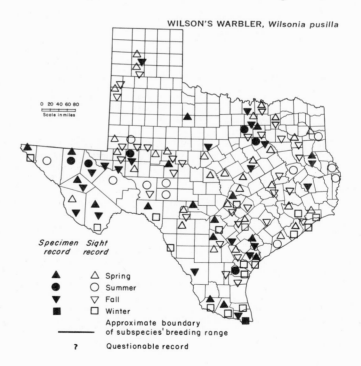

WILSON'S WARBLER, *Wilsonia pusilla*

0 20 40 60 80
Scale in miles

Specimen record | Sight record

▲ △ Spring
● ○ Summer
▼ ▽ Fall
■ □ Winter

——— Approximate boundary of subspecies' breeding range

? Questionable record

is seen also in higher parts of trees. The Wilson's is an active species and busily works all parts of the vegetation. At times it flits its tail and also its wings. Its flight is rather quick and darting, and the bird often engages in flycatching. Food consists chiefly of small insects (flies, gnats, plant lice, grasshoppers, caterpillars), together with some spiders.

The ordinary note of the Wilson's is a slightly harsh *cheet* or *chep*. Its usual song is a rapid chatter which drops in pitch at the end: *chi-chi-chi-chi-chi chet chet*. One of its simpler songs might be represented by *chee-chee-chee*, sometimes followed by a trill.

DETAILED ACCOUNT: TWO SUBSPECIES

EASTERN WILSON'S WARBLER, *Wilsonia pusilla pusilla* (Wilson)

DESCRIPTION: *Adult male, nuptial plumage*: Acquired by partial prenuptial molt. Forehead gamboge yellow to wax yellow; crown metallic blue-black; remainder of upper surface warbler green; tail hair brown, feathers narrowly edged on outer webs with warbler green, with no white markings; wings dark hair brown, lesser wing-coverts yellowish warbler green, as are outer edgings of greater and median coverts; outer margins of wing-quills dull warbler green to olive green; inner margins of primaries and secondaries, except at tips of primaries, dull white or brownish white; lores, superciliary stripe, and entire lower surface gamboge yellow to wax yellow; sides of head and of body and flanks pyrite yellow; lining of wing wax yellow. Bill black, brownish black, blackish olive, or brownish slate, but mandible and cutting edges pale wood brown, ecru drab, plumbeous white, yellow, or yellowish white; tip sometimes drab; iris dark brown (sepia or hazel); legs, feet, and claws light yellowish brown, pale olivaceous yellow, wood brown, or light brown; soles of toes greenish yellow. *Adult male, winter*: Acquired by complete postnuptial molt. Similar to nuptial adult male, but feathers of black crown more or less conspicuously tipped with citrine or warbler green. *Adult female, nuptial*: Acquired by partial prenuptial molt. Similar to nuptial adult male but smaller; usually duller above and below, black of crown less extensive and more or less mixed or overlaid with warbler green, or crown entirely warbler green, though occasionally intense black as in male. Similar to adult male in winter but smaller; coloration duller, black of crown more restricted or absent and more overlaid with warbler green, lower surface averaging paler and duller. Bill black or dull brown, but mandible yellow, except dull brown tip; iris brown; legs and feet brownish black. *Adult female, winter*: Acquired by complete postnuptial molt. Similar to nuptial adult female, but colors both above and below usually richer. *Male and female, second winter*: Acquired by complete postnuptial molt. Like corresponding sex of adult in winter. *Male, first nuptial*: Acquired by partial prenuptial molt, which does not include wing-quills or tail. Like nuptial adult male. *Male, first winter*: Acquired by partial postjuvenal molt, which does not involve wing-quills or tail. Similar to adult male in winter, but superciliary stripe and forehead duller, more greenish— deep wax yellow; black feathers of crown more broadly tipped with warbler green or citrine. *Female, first nuptial*: Acquired by partial prenuptial molt. Like nuptial adult female. *Female, first winter*: Acquired by partial postjuvenal molt, which does not involve wing-quills or tail. Similar to adult female in winter but much duller, both above and below, and black of crown either absent or almost entirely concealed by warbler green edgings of feathers; lower parts paler and duller. Similar to first winter male but smaller; in color differs as from adult female in winter. *Juvenal*: Acquired by complete postnatal molt. Upper surface hair brown; wings and tail similar to those of first winter female, but wing-coverts tipped with brownish white to form two wing-

bars; anterior lower parts dull, rather light brown, as are sides; abdomen yellowish white. Bill, legs, and feet pale brown; iris dark brown.

MEASUREMENTS: *Adult male*: Wing, 53.1–57.4 (average, 55.6) mm.; tail, 46.5–50.3 (48.3); bill (exposed culmen), 7.1–8.9 (8.1); tarsus, 17.0–19.0 (18.3); middle toe without claw, 8.9–10.7 (9.9). *Adult female*: Wing, 52.1–55.1 (53.8); tail, 46.0–49.5 (47.5); bill, 8.1–8.9 (8.6); tarsus, 17.0–18.5 (17.8); middle toe, 8.9–10.7 (9.9).

RANGE: W. Mackenzie to Labrador, south to c. Alberta, e. Vermont, and s.e. Newfoundland. Winters from s. Texas through Mexico to Costa Rica.

TEXAS: *Migration*: Collected north to Cooke, east to Polk and Nacogdoches (probably this race), south to Cameron, west to Culberson cos. Common. *Winter*: Taken in Cameron Co. Scarce.

NORTHERN WILSON'S WARBLER, *Wilsonia pusilla pileolata* (Pallas)

DESCRIPTION: *Adult male and female, nuptial plumage*: Similar to *W. p. pusilla*, but wing, tail, and tarsus averaging longer; forehead brighter, more golden (less greenish) yellow; remainder of upper surface brighter, more golden yellowish (less greenish) olive green, particularly on rump; lower parts of deeper, more golden (less greenish) yellow.

MEASUREMENTS: *Adult male*: Wing, 55.1–59.9 (average, 57.4) mm.; tail, 47.0–52.1 (50.3); bill (exposed culmen), 7.1–8.9 (8.4); tarsus, 18.0–20.1 (18.8); middle toe without claw, 9.4–10.4 (9.9). *Adult female*: Wing, 54.6–56.9 (55.3); tail, 47.5–50.0 (48.3); bill, 7.6–8.9 (8.6); tarsus, 18.0–19.6 (18.8); middle toe, 8.9–10.9 (9.9).

RANGE: W. Alaska to n.w. Mackenzie, south to c. California and n. New Mexico. Winters from s. Texas through Mexico to Panama.

TEXAS: *Migration*: Collected north to Potter, east to Eastland and Victoria, south to Hidalgo, west to El Paso cos. Common. *Winter*: Taken in Cameron Co. (3 specimens). Rare.

CANADA WARBLER, *Wilsonia canadensis* (Linnaeus)

SPECIES ACCOUNT

Male: gray upper parts; yellow under parts, "spectacles"; necklace of black streaks across breast. *Female*: duller; necklace fainter. Length, 5¼ in.; wingspan, 7¾; weight, ¼ oz.

RANGE: N. Alberta to s. Quebec and New Brunswick, south to Great Lakes region, s.e. New York, and Connecticut, and in Appalachians to Georgia. Winters from Colombia and n.w. Venezuela to c. Peru.

TEXAS: (See map.) *Migration*: Late Apr. to mid-May; late Aug. to early Oct. (extremes: Mar. 24, June 4; Aug. 8, Dec. 16). Common to uncommon through eastern half; scarce west to Panhandle and western Edwards Plateau; extremely rare in Trans-Pecos. *Winter*: Late Dec. to late Feb. Casual along coast and in Rio Grande delta.

HAUNTS AND HABITS: In the cool, moist North Woods, the Canada Warbler nests on or near the ground in ferny clumps amid stumps and roots. In Texas, where it is known as a late spring migrant—chiefly in May— this warbler is to be looked for in forests, undergrowth, and thickets near water. During the big migration waves of yesteryear it was widespread throughout all kinds of bushes and trees in country, town, and city. It generally occurs singly or in pairs, but during migration associates at times with various other warblers.

Flight is rather strong and more direct than that of the American Redstart. It is an active bird and frequents usually bushes or lower branches of trees— sometimes, however, their very tops—gleaning food from branches and foliage; it occasionally descends to the ground. Like the Wilson's Warbler, it catches insects on the wing. Food consists chiefly of insects, their eggs and larvae, including flies, mosquitoes; small beetles, Hymenoptera, moths, and hairless caterpillars, such as the cankerworm, together with a few spiders.

The Canada's call note is a harsh *tchip* or *tchack*. Its rather clear, liquid song is varied and rapidly given; it may be represented by *rup-it-che, rup-i-chip-it* or by *tle-we* several times repeated and ending *tl-it-wit*. Notes in this irregularly arranged song may be slurred together to suggest the Yellowthroat's *witchity*.

DETAILED ACCOUNT: NO SUBSPECIES

DESCRIPTION: *Adult male, nuptial plumage*: Acquired by wear from winter plumage. Forehead black with short, narrow median stripe of dull lemon yellow; crown also black, feathers so broadly edged with neutral gray as to impart black-spotted appearance; remainder of upper surface neutral gray or mouse gray, sometimes, particularly on back and scapulars, washed with deep olive gray; tail chaetura drab, feathers without white markings, and narrowly edged on outer webs with gray of upper surface; wings rather dark hair brown, outer edgings of feathers like back; primaries margined on inner webs, except at tips, with light brown; secondaries with inner edges dull vinaceous buff; supraloral stripe dull lemon yellow to gamboge yellow; posterior part of lores and broad submalar stripe dull black; eye-ring pale dull yellow or dull white; sides of neck like back; lower parts

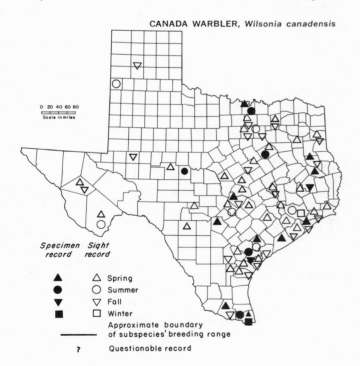

CANADA WARBLER, *Wilsonia canadensis*

0 20 40 60 80
Scale in miles

Specimen Sight
record   record

▲ △ Spring
● ○ Summer
▼ ▽ Fall
■ □ Winter

——— Approximate boundary of subspecies' breeding range

? Questionable record

dull lemon yellow to gamboge yellow with numerous dull black to chaetura black spots on jugulum, upper breast, and sides of throat, forming conspicuous necklace; sides and flanks slightly washed with warbler green; lower tail-coverts white, sometimes washed with pale yellow; lining of wing dull white or brownish white, wing-coverts mottled with hair brown, sometimes washed with yellow. Bill brownish black, olivaceous black, or brownish slate, but mandible, excepting prout brown tip, bluish olive or dull white; tongue and inside of mouth white; iris dark brown; legs and feet clay color, yellowish clay color, pale yellow, flesh color, or pale tawny olive. *Adult male, winter*: Acquired by complete postnuptial molt. Similar to nuptial adult male, but upper surface washed with dull olive green, feathers of forehead, as well as of crown, edged and tipped with gray; black spots on jugulum more or less veiled by pale yellow edgings of feathers. *Adult female, nuptial*: Acquired by wear from winter. Similar to nuptial adult male but smaller; upper surface duller, somewhat more olivaceous (less purely gray); forehead with little if any black, and more or less washed with dull yellow; black malar stripe absent, this as well as black on posterior part of lores replaced by olive gray; yellow of lower surface duller, dark spots on jugulum duller, lighter, less clearly defined, and deep olive or citrine drab, instead of black. *Adult female, winter*: Acquired by complete postnuptial molt. Similar to nuptial adult female, but upper surface duller and more olivaceous (less grayish); forehead and anterior part of crown more yellowish; dark spots on breast less distinct. *Male and female, second winter*: Acquired by complete postnuptial molt. Like corresponding sex in winter adult. *Male, first nuptial*: Acquired by partial prenuptial molt, not including wing-quills or tail. Similar to nuptial adult male. *Male, first winter*: Acquired by partial postjuvenal molt, which does not involve wing-quills or tail. Similar to adult male in winter, but upper surface more washed with olive green, forehead and anterior part of crown more washed with yellow or tinged with buffy brown, black on forehead and crown less extensive and concealed by brown or gray tips of feathers; yellow of lower surface duller and more greenish; spots on jugulum duller, less sharply defined, and dark grayish olive instead of black. Similar to adult female in winter but larger; upper surface averaging rather more grayish, often with concealed black spots on forehead or anterior part of crown; dark spots on jugulum rather more distinct and darker. Similar to nuptial adult female but more olivaceous above, head more brownish; sides of head usually duller and more brownish, spots on jugulum darker and more sharply defined. *Female, first nuptial*: Acquired by partial prenuptial molt. Essentially identical with nuptial adult female. *Female, first winter*: Acquired by partial postjuvenal molt, which does not involve wing-quills or tail. Similar to adult female in winter but averaging somewhat more brownish or olivaceous above, particularly on pileum and back; spots on jugulum averaging rather smaller and less numerous. Similar to first winter male but smaller; upper surface duller, more olivaceous, crown more brownish and always without hidden blackish spots; dark spots on jugulum duller, smaller, less numerous, and less sharply defined. *Juvenal*: Acquired by complete postnatal molt. Upper parts saccardo umber or broccoli brown; wings and tail as in first winter female, but wing-coverts much more brownish, median and greater series broadly tipped with dull vinaceous buff, forming two conspicuous wing-bars; throat and jugulum between isabella color and saccardo umber; remainder of lower surface dull wax yellow to barium yellow. Bill, legs, and feet dull pale brown; iris dark brown.

MEASUREMENTS: *Adult male*: Wing, 64.5–67.3 (average, 66.3) mm.; tail, 54.8–57.2 (56.1); bill (exposed culmen), 10.2–11.2 (10.7); tarsus, 18.0–19.8 (19.0); middle toe without claw, 10.7–11.7 (11.2). *Adult female*: Wing, 60.2–64.5 (62.5); tail, 51.1–53.3 (52.8); bill, 9.7–11.2 (10.7); tarsus, 17.8–19.0 (18.3); middle toe, 9.1–11.7 (10.7).

TEXAS: *Migration*: Collected north to Cooke, east to Nacogdoches, Polk, and Galveston, south to Cameron, west to Concho (Aug. 28) cos. *Winter*: One specimen: Cameron Co., Brownsville (Feb. 3, 1891, F. B. Armstrong).

GOLDEN-CROWNED WARBLER, *Basileuterus culicivorus* (W. Deppe)

SPECIES ACCOUNT

Brasher's Warbler of older authors. Grayish olive above; yellow below; yellow crown-stripe bordered broadly by black. Length, 5 in.

RANGE: Moderate altitudes in mountains of w. (very locally) and e. Mexico, south through Central America (except e. Panama) to e. Bolivia, n. Argentina, and Uruguay.

TEXAS: *Accidental*: Two specimens and one sight record, all from Cameron Co.: Brownsville (2 males collected, Jan. 6, 20, 1892, F. B. Armstrong; skins in Josiah Hoopes Collection, Academy of Natural Sciences, Philadelphia); sighting along Resaca de los Fresnos about 4 mi. south of Harlingen (Sept. 5, 1945, L. I. Davis, Bayard Auchinclose).

HAUNTS AND HABITS: The Brasher's Warbler is the sole representative of its large, primarily South American genus that has been collected in the United States. It inhabits tropical and subtropical forest undergrowth where it frequents coffee *fincas*, woodland thickets, and second-growth timber on slopes and in canyons as well as on more level terrain. The domed nest of moss and leaves is situated on the ground.

In places, especially in southern portions of Mexico's Sierra Madre Oriental, the Goldencrown is a common bird, occurring singly, in pairs, or during the nonbreeding season often in small bands and frequently in company with other species. Restlessly, it hunts for insects in low trees and bushes, searching trunks as well as twigs and leaves. If approached, this warbler seems quite suspicious and usually is quick to investigate an intruder, especially a squeaking or *pssh*-ing bird watcher. In flitting from branch to branch, it often droops its wings and partly expands its tail.

The call of this warbler is a rapid series of weak *tick*'s. It has a slight, somewhat musical song, which consists usually of five rapidly ascending notes; the last two notes are diagnostic (F. S. Webster, Jr.).

DETAILED ACCOUNT: ONE SUBSPECIES

BRASHER'S GOLDEN-CROWNED WARBLER, *Basileuterus culicivorus brasierii* (Giraud)

B. c. brasherii of Robert Ridgway, 1902. The subspecies was named for Philip Brasher of Brooklyn, New York.

DESCRIPTION: *Adults, nuptial plumage (yellow-crowned phase)*: Acquired by partial prenuptial molt. Middle of crown lemon yellow to lemon chrome, more or less obscured by yellowish olive tips of feathers; broad dull black or olivaceous black stripe on each side of crown, extending back over hindneck and narrowing on forehead where it sometimes disappears; forehead and superciliary stripe light yellowish olive, forehead sometimes more grayish; remainder of upper surface grayish olive to deep grayish olive; tail plain hair brown, feathers basally edged with color of back; wings hair brown, edgings of quills and coverts like back, inner margins of primaries and secondaries, except at tips of primaries, white or brownish white, becoming pale brown on outer primaries; lores like forehead; small spot in front of eye dull olive to mouse gray; sides of head and of neck light yellowish olive to citrine drab, portion below eye rather darker and duller; auriculars sometimes obscurely streaked with paler yellowish olive; streak on upper and lower eyelids pale dull yellow; lower surface gamboge yellow, but sides and flanks slightly washed with olive; lining of wing lemon yellow, outer part slightly mottled with mouse gray. Bill dark brown, but mandible paler; iris dark brown; legs and feet light flesh color or brownish flesh color. *Adults, nuptial (rufous-crowned phase)*: Similar to yellow-crowned phase, but middle of crown orange rufous or sanford brown. *Adults, winter*: Acquired by complete postnuptial molt. Similar to nuptial adults, but middle of crown lemon yellow to orange chrome. *First winter*: Acquired by partial postjuvenal molt. Similar to first nuptial male and female but somewhat brighter. *Juvenal*: Acquired by complete postnatal molt. Pileum between saccardo umber and olive brown; back cinnamon brown to between prout brown and mummy brown; lores clove brown; remainder of sides of head dull light isabella color, somewhat mottled with saccardo umber; wing-quills as in nuptial adults, but upper wing-coverts edged on outer webs with brown—between saccardo umber and snuff brown—and tipped with tawny olive; chin and throat dull warm buff to dull naples yellow; remainder of lower surface amber yellow to citrine yellow, but blotched, mottled, or spotted with light brownish olive to dresden brown, most so on jugulum, breast, sides, and flanks.

MEASUREMENTS: *Adult male*: Wing, 58.4–64.0 (average, 61.7) mm.; tail, 51.6–56.9 (54.8); bill (exposed culmen), 9.4–10.4 (9.9); tarsus, 19.6–20.1 (19.8); middle toe without claw, 9.9–11.9 (11.2). *Adult female*: Wing, 56.9–57.9 (57.7); tail, 51.0–55.1 (52.6); bill, 9.9–10.9 (10.4); tarsus, 19.6–21.1 (20.1); middle toe, 11.4–12.4 (11.9).

RANGE: Nuevo León, Tamaulipas, and San Luis Potosí.

TEXAS: *Accidental*: Two specimens (see species account).

[RUFOUS-CAPPED WARBLER, *Basileuterus rufifrons* (Swainson)

SPECIES ACCOUNT

A small plump warbler with long tail, frequently uptilted. *Adult*: brownish olive back, wings, and tail; rufous pileum and side of head; line over eye and malar stripe white; posterior border of auriculars also finely edged with white; most races yellow on throat and breast with white abdomen and crissum (*B. r. salvini*, of s. Mexico, entirely yellow below); no wing-bars or tail-patches. *Immature*: dull brownish olive above (including head and auriculars); buffy white eye-line; two buffy wing-bars; buffy below with olive tinge on sides. Length, 4½–5 in.

RANGE: Sonora and Nuevo León, south in foothills and mountains (generally 1,000–7,000 ft.) to Guatemala and Honduras.

TEXAS: *Hypothetical*: One sighting: Starr Co., along Rio Grande ca. ¼ mi. below Falcon Dam, 341 ft. (bird in adult plumage, Feb. 10, 1973, J. L. Rowlett, V. L. Emanuel). These two skilled observers were previously familiar with the species in Mexico. After giving the bird watchers a close view, the bird disappeared and could not be located the next day when additional observers and a photographer were present.

The winter of 1972–73 was unusually cold, even in northern Mexico. Cold weather tends to push tropical species to lowlands in search of food. It is of interest that Starr Co. is the closest point in Texas to the Sierra Madre Oriental west of Monterrey, Nuevo León, Mexico, where *Basileuterus rufifrons* occurs regularly; the low Mexican mountains visible from Falcon Dam probably harbor this warbler at least occasionally.

Emanuel and Rowlett took branches of the shrubs on which the Rufous-capped Warbler perched. These were identified by Marshall C. Johnston as *Celtis pallida, Clematis drummondii,* and *Baccharis glutinosa.*]

AMERICAN REDSTART, *Setophaga ruticilla* (Linnaeus)

SPECIES ACCOUNT

A fly-catching, butterflylike warbler. *Male*: black with orange patch on each wing, sides of breast, and each side of tail; white belly. *Female*: grayish olive above; white below; orange areas of male replaced with yellow. Length, 5¼ in.; wingspan, 7½; weight, ¼ oz.

RANGE: S.e. Alaska, n. British Columbia, and s. Mackenzie to Newfoundland, south to e. Oregon, n. Colorado, e. Oklahoma, e. Texas, s. Louisiana, and c. Georgia. Winters chiefly in humid lowlands from Mexico to n. South America; also West Indies.

TEXAS: (See map.) *Breeding*: Formerly perhaps fairly common in northeastern corner (species reported "common," in Bowie Co.: June 19–July 12, 1888, G. T. Gault; June 23–30, 1902, H. C. Oberholser). Nests located, Lavaca Co., Hallettsville (1861–1864, J. D. Mitchell); nest found, Victoria Co. (1900, Mitchell). Recent indications of breeding: Liberty Co., along Trinity River (2 males with enlarged testes collected, and 30 singing males observed, summer 1972, C. D.

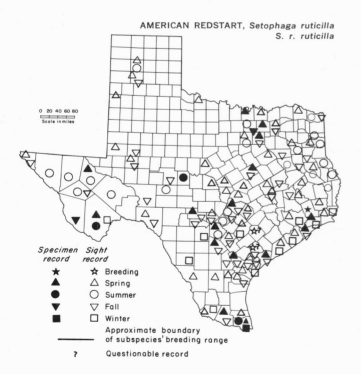

AMERICAN REDSTART, *Setophaga ruticilla*
S. r. ruticilla

0 20 40 60 80
Scale in miles

Specimen record / Sight record
★ / ☆ Breeding
▲ / △ Spring
● / ○ Summer
▼ / ▽ Fall
■ / □ Winter
— Approximate boundary of subspecies' breeding range
? Questionable record

Fisher); Bowie-Cass county line, Sulphur River (at least 100-125 singing birds counted along ca. 15 mi. of river, June 15, 1973, C. D. Fisher, Suzanne Winckler). One recent mid-summer record from Hays Co., Pedernales River (1 observed periodically, June 16–Aug. 1, 1968, L. T. Adams, et al.). *Migration*: Mid-Apr. to mid-May; late Aug. to mid-Oct. (extremes: Mar. 2, June 27; late July, Dec. 5). Very common (abundant some years on upper coast) to fairly common through eastern half; fairly common to uncommon through western half. *Winter*: Late Dec. to late Feb. Rare along coast and in Rio Grande delta; extremely rare in remainder of state south of 30th parallel.

HAUNTS AND HABITS: One of the most dainty and winsome of all small American woodland birds is the American Redstart. In Texas, it migrates through all kinds of forests and undergrowth, preferably deciduous, in bottomlands and uplands; in canyons, along streams, about ponds and lakes, and on slopes. It also occurs in cultivated areas and in gardens and parks of cities and towns. It is not gregarious nor does it much associate with flocks of other migrating warblers.

Flight, appearing rather weak and flitting, is normally not long sustained and performed with few wing-beats. The American Redstart occurs not only in thickets and undergrowth, but also in tops of tall trees, ranging interior as well as terminal foliage. Ever on the move, it flutters about with wings drooped and tail spread, and it has the habit of flitting from side to side. At times it moves along branches very much like some of the other creeping warblers. Often it flies into the air to seize insects, which constitute the major portion of its diet. Caterpillars, moths, butterflies; plant lice, lanternflies, scale insects, tree- and leaf-hoppers, spittle insects; mayflies; gnats, craneflies; long-horned beetles, flea, ladybird, and leaf beetles, weevils; grasshoppers, ants, bees, wasps, ichneumon flies, termites, and various larvae and eggs all fall prey to its untiring industry. In addition to insects, some spiders and harvestmen and occasional seeds (e.g., magnolia) are consumed.

Its ordinary call note is a *tseet*. Other vocalizations are highly varied, but a frequently heard song with its high-pitched, sibilant quality resembles that of the Black-and-white Warbler, although stronger and usually with a decidedly lower note at the end. Other songs end on a high note; some are double noted. Songs are often alternated. Migrating American Redstarts sing a good bit in Texas, especially in April and May.

CHANGES: It is presently unknown whether recent observations of probable nesting American Redstarts in east Texas (Bowie-Cass cos., Liberty Co.) represent a retaking of old territory or an expansion of range. It is also conceivable that the species has always been present, but gone undetected, in this relatively under-birded region of the state. However, C. D. Fisher suspects that the species currently (early 1970's) breeds in bottomland forests along many major streams in east Texas.

DETAILED ACCOUNT: TWO SUBSPECIES

SOUTHERN AMERICAN REDSTART, *Setophaga ruticilla ruticilla* (Linnaeus)

DESCRIPTION: *Adult male, nuptial plumage*: Acquired by wear from winter plumage. Upper surface dull metallic black with faint bluish gloss; tail dark clove brown, basal half of outer three or four pairs of rectrices and part of outer web of next pair cadmium orange to capucine buff, these spots occupying about two-thirds length of tail; primaries and secondaries fuscous, tertials fuscous black or dark clove brown, basal portion of primaries and secondaries cadmium orange to capucine buff, showing as conspicuous wing-spot; remaining portions of basal part of inner webs of feathers pale yellow, dull pale buff, or pinkish buff, outer webs of primaries and secondaries beyond orange wing area narrowly margined with cinnamon brown; sides of head and of neck, with chin, throat, and jugulum, glossy metallic black like upper surface, which color often extends in streaks or blotches along sides of body; sides of breast and of body between orange cadmium and flame scarlet; remainder of lower surface white, sometimes washed with orange, particularly on breast, which is often mottled with black; lining of wing orange cadmium, outer edge mottled with dull black. Bill black or very dark brown, but somewhat paler below; iris dark brown; legs and feet clove brown, brownish black, or black. *Adult male, winter*: Acquired by complete postnuptial molt. Similar to nuptial adult male and often indistinguishable, but feathers of upper surface often narrowly and obscurely tipped with pale dull brown. *Adult female, nuptial*: Acquired by wear from winter. Pileum mouse gray to hair brown; remainder of upper surface dull citrine drab; tail fuscous to fuscous black, almost two-thirds of basal area on outer three or four feathers amber yellow to straw yellow, middle feathers narrowly edged on outer webs with color of back; wings dark hair brown to fuscous, basal portion of secondaries, extending also narrowly to inner primaries, straw yellow or amber yellow, forming wing-spot similar to that in male; outer webs of primaries and secondaries outside this area narrowly edged externally with citrine, inner edges of primaries outside yellow area pale brown or brownish white; edges of wing-coverts like back; superciliary stripe dull pale buff or brownish white; rest of sides of head between drab and mouse gray; lower parts dull cream buff or grayish white, sides of breast and of body broadly amber yellow to primuline yellow, also tinging flanks; longest lower tail-coverts dull buff or pale brown, sides and flanks sometimes washed with buffy brown or olive gray; lining of wing straw yellow, outermost under wing-coverts somewhat mottled with mouse gray. Bill clove brown or slate black, but base of mandible drab; iris dark brown; legs and feet hair brown or clove brown. *Adult female, winter*: Acquired by complete postnuptial molt. Similar to nuptial adult female, but upper surface more brownish and somewhat more uniform, with less difference between pileum and back; throat and breast suffused with dull buff. *Male and female, second winter*: Acquired by complete postnuptial molt. Similar to corresponding sex of adults in winter. *Male, first nuptial*: Acquired by partial prenuptial molt. Similar to nuptial adult female but larger; upper surface darker, usually more strongly brownish or olivaceous, with occasional, often with many, scattered black feathers; yellow area in tail and yellow wing-patch averaging darker; lower surface with at least a few scattered black feathers; yellow patch on each side of breast often strongly tinged with orange and ranging from gamboge yellow to orange. *Male, first winter*: Acquired by partial postjuvenal molt, which does not involve wing-quills or tail. Similar to first nuptial male, but upper surface darker, more olivaceous, and both upper and lower parts without any black feathers. Similar to adult female in winter, but upper parts darker, more brownish or olivaceous; sides of breast more tinged with orange. *Female, first nuptial*: Acquired by partial prenuptial molt. Similar to nuptial adult female, but yellow wing-patch much smaller. *Female, first winter*: Acquired by partial postjuvenal molt, which does not involve wing-quills or tail. Similar to adult female in winter, but wing-patch much smaller, often entirely concealed. Similar to first nuptial female, but upper parts darker, more strongly olive green, throat more strongly tinged with buff (less whitish). *Juvenal*: Acquired by complete postnatal molt. Pileum dark buffy brown or dull drab; remainder of upper surface cinnamon brown to between saccardo umber and snuff brown; wings and tail similar to first winter female, but wing-coverts more brownish, greater and median series broadly tipped with light buff or naples yellow, forming two conspicuous wing-bars; sides of head and of neck dull wood brown or light drab; throat and breast dull light drab or between light drab and grayish olive; lower breast, abdomen, and crissum dull white or sometimes washed with pale yellow. Bill, legs, and feet dull brown; iris dark brown. *Natal*: Hair brown to drab. Bill, legs, and feet pinkish buff tinged with brown.

MEASUREMENTS: *Adult male*: Wing, 62.2–68.3 (average, 65.8) mm.; tail, 55.1–59.9 (57.2); bill (exposed culmen), 8.6–9.9 (9.1); tarsus, 16.5–18.0 (17.3); middle toe without claw, 8.9–10.4 (10.2). *Adult female*: Wing, 58.9–64.5 (62.2); tail, 54.1–58.9 (56.6); bill, 8.6–9.4 (9.1); tarsus, 16.5–17.8 (17.3); middle toe, 9.4–10.9 (10.2).

RANGE: S. Minnesota to Nova Scotia, south to e. Texas and c. Georgia. Winters from s. Texas (rarely) through Mexico to n.w. South America; also West Indies.

TEXAS: *Breeding*: Two specimens collected in Liberty Co. probably of this race (see species account). *Migration*: Collected northwest to Concho (Aug. 31), east to Chambers, south to Cameron cos. Fairly common. *Winter*: One specimen: Cameron Co., Brownsville (Jan. 24, 1893, F. B. Armstrong).

NESTING: *Nest*: On uplands and bottomlands; in woodlands and their margins, sometimes in more open country, pastures, orchards, and even ornamental grounds near dwellings; placed in upright crotch or on horizontal branch, 2–40 ft., ordinarily not more than 15 ft., above ground, usually in maple, beech, elm, or other tree or bush; compact, beautifully made, cuplike structure; composed of stalks of plants, cottony hemplike fibers, shreds of bark, grasses, rootlets, weeds, pine needles, soft vegetable wool, thistle down, bits of newspaper, sometimes ornamented on outside with white egg cases of insects and fine green moss stems, all bound together with spider webs and spider cocoons, and lined with fine grasses, rootlets or rootlike fibers, fine shreds of bark, chiefly inner bark, small pine needles, horse and other hair, and feathers. *Eggs*: 3–5, usually 4; ovate to rounded ovate; white, grayish white, greenish white, bluish white, or cream white, with spots and dots, chiefly about large end, of cinnamon brown, reddish, yellowish, purplish, or dull light brown, and shell markings of lilac gray, lilac, and grayish lavender; average size, 16.3 × 12.4 mm.

NORTHERN AMERICAN REDSTART, *Setophaga ruticilla tricolora* (Müller)

DESCRIPTION: *Adult male and female, nuptial plumage*: Similar to *S. r. ruticilla* but smaller, except tail which is longer; male with smaller orange or yellow wing speculum; female with upper surface paler and more grayish (less conspicuously olivaceous).

MEASUREMENTS: *Adult male*: Wing, 61.0–65.5 (average, 63.8) mm.; tail, 55.6–61.0 (58.4); bill (exposed culmen), 8.1–9.4 (8.6); tarsus, 16.0–17.8 (17.0); middle toe without claw, 8.9–10.9 (9.7). *Adult female*: Wing, 55.9–63.0 (57.7); tail, 51.1–58.4 (54.3); bill, 8.1–9.1 (8.6); tarsus, 16.0–17.5 (16.8); middle toe, 8.9–10.4 (9.7).

RANGE: S.e. Alaska to Newfoundland, south to e. Oregon, n. Colorado, and n. Michigan. Winters from s.e. Mexico to n. South America.

TEXAS: *Migration*: Collected north to Cooke, east to Galveston, south to Cameron, west to Presidio and Reeves cos. Fairly common.

PAINTED REDSTART, *Setophaga picta* Swainson

SPECIES ACCOUNT

Moves about with half-spread wings and tail like

American Redstart. Mainly black with large white patch on wing and each side of tail; red breast; white lower belly and wing-linings. Length, 5¾ in.; wing-span, 8½.

RANGE: N.w. Arizona to s.w. New Mexico, s. Trans-Pecos Texas (irregularly), and c. Nuevo León, south through highlands of Mexico and Central America to n. Nicaragua. Winters chiefly from Sonora and Chihuahua southward.

TEXAS: (See map.) *Breeding*: Probably late Apr. to mid-July (nest with 3 eggs located, Boot Spring, 6,000 ft. in Chisos Mts., May 13, 1937, H. W. Brandt). Very irregular in Chisos Mts., Big Bend Nat. Park, where recorded from Mar. 19 to Aug. 27. *Migration*: Late Mar. to mid-May (extremes: Mar. 10, May 21). Uncommon during spring in Chisos Mts.; casual at Midland (specimen) and Del Rio. Accidental in spring on upper coast: Galveston Co., High Island (1 bird observed, May 5–6, 1973, Kathleen Brannan, et al.). One fall sighting at El Paso (Oct. 7–15, 1953, J. Wooldridge, et al.).

HAUNTS AND HABITS: The strikingly butterflylike Painted Redstart dwells chiefly in timbered desert mountains, canyons, gulches, and rugged slopes, sometimes in more open valleys. It is a bird of evergreen and deciduous woodlands, particularly pines and oaks, and is especially attracted to thickets and oaks in secluded canyons near streams. For the most part, the Painted is found singly and in pairs; rarely (except for family parties) in companies or in association with other warblers.

Its flight is flitting and usually not prolonged. The bird is often seen moving jerkily, but more or less deliberately, from bush to bush or tree to tree with wings and tail spread, showing off its beautiful plumage. Frequently it clings to a tree trunk much like a creeper; from a perch it often flies out into the air to seize an insect. Its food is probably similar to that of the American Redstart.

An unwarblerlike *peep* or *clee-ip* is its call note. A common song is sometimes written *weeta, weeta, weeta, wee*. The Painted Redstart seldom nests in Texas, but when it does it sings from late March into July.

DETAILED ACCOUNT: ONE SUBSPECIES

NORTHERN PAINTED REDSTART, *Setophaga picta picta* Swainson

DESCRIPTION: *Adults, nuptial plumage*: Acquired by wear from winter plumage. Entire upper surface glossy bluish black; tail brownish black to fuscous black, outer two tail feathers white, except for bases, and third pair with broad oblique white tip occupying on outer web at least half the feather; wing-quills and tertials fuscous, chaetura drab, fuscous black, or chaetura black, inner margins of secondaries dull white or brownish white, of primaries, except at base, brownish white to pale brown, outer webs of tertials and innermost secondaries conspicuously edged with white; large white patch on wing-coverts involves greater and median series, excepting innermost and primary coverts; lesser wing-coverts glossy black, inner greater wing-coverts brownish black on inner webs; primary coverts fuscous or fuscous black; sides of head and of neck, chin, throat, jugulum, sides of breast and of body, and flanks black like upper surface, flanks and sometimes sides of body more or less mixed with dull white or mouse gray; breast and upper abdomen scarlet red to between scarlet red and spectrum red; lower abdomen white; crissum mouse gray or dull black, feathers more or less tipped with white or grayish white; lining of wing white, outer edge of wing slightly mottled with hair brown or dull black. Bill, legs, and feet black; iris dark brown. *Adults, winter*: Acquired by complete postnuptial molt. Like nuptial adults. *First nuptial*: Acquired by wear from first winter. Like nuptial adults, but upper parts duller with less metallic sheen; wings and tail more brownish. *First winter*: Acquired by partial postjuvenal molt, which does not involve wing-quills or tail. Similar to adults in winter but duller, less glossy. *Juvenal*: Acquired by complete postnatal molt. Upper parts dark fuscous or fuscous black, including wings and tail; white areas of wing and tail as in nuptial adults; lower surface hair brown to dull drab, anterior lower parts very obscurely spotted with fuscous; breast and abdomen more evidently so and with larger markings; feathers of crissum broadly tipped with buffy white or grayish white, middle of abdomen sometimes more or less streaked with buffy white. *Natal*: Pale smoke gray to pallid smoke gray.

MEASUREMENTS: *Adult male*: Wing, 68.1–74.9 (average, 71.7) mm.; tail, 61.0–68.1 (63.2); bill (exposed culmen), 8.1–8.9 (8.6); tarsus, 16.0–17.0 (16.8); middle toe without claw, 9.9–11.4 (10.7). *Adult female*: Wing, 67.1–70.1 (68.8); tail, 59.9–64.5 (62.2); bill, 8.4–8.9 (8.6); tarsus, 16.0–17.0 (16.3); middle toe, 10.4–11.4 (10.9).

RANGE: N.w. Arizona to s. Trans-Pecos Texas, south through Mexico to Oaxaca. Winters mainly from Chihuahua to Oaxaca.

TEXAS: *Breeding*: Collected in Chisos Mts., Brewster Co. *Migration*: One specimen: Midland Co., Midland (May 22, 1967, J. C. Henderson; Welder Wildlife Refuge collection, no. 1551).

NESTING: *Nest*: On hillsides, mountainsides, in valleys or canyons; on ground, in cavity, ordinarily near stream, in bank, under stones, projecting rock, bunch of grass, or at base of bush, sunk in ground; rather large, flat, shallow bowl, however, often arched over; composed of dry grass, strips of bark, parts of weed stems, leaves, horsehair, and other hair; lined with fine grass, horsehair and other hair. *Eggs*: 3–4, usually 4; ovate to short ovate; white or pearl white; spotted and dotted over surface and in wreath about larger end, with brownish red, light and dark reddish brown, with shell markings of lilac and lavender gray; average size, 16.5 × 12.7 mm.

PAINTED REDSTART, *Setophaga picta*
S. p. picta

0 20 40 60 80
Scale in miles

Specimen record / Sight record

★ ☆ Breeding
▲ △ Spring
● ○ Summer
▼ ▽ Fall
■ □ Winter

——— Approximate boundary of subspecies' breeding range

? Questionable record

House Sparrow, *Passer domesticus*
male (top) female (bottom)

Weaver Finches: Ploceidae

HOUSE SPARROW, *Passer domesticus* (Linnaeus)

SPECIES ACCOUNT

English Sparrow of many authors. Bill thick; legs short. *Male*: gray crown; chestnut nape; whitish cheek; brown and black streaks on back; black bib; pale gray belly. *Female*: brownish above with dull black streaks on back; plain dingy whitish below; buffy eye-stripe. Length, 6¼ in.; wingspan, 9½; weight, 1 oz.

RANGE: Mainly resident. Native to Eurasia and n. Africa. Naturalized in North America (general in temperate and subtropical regions), West Indies (local), South America (southern half), Africa (far south), s.e. Australia (including Tasmania), and New Zealand; also on many continental islands and some oceanic ones (Hawaii, Bermuda, Mascarene Islands).

TEXAS: (See map.) *Resident*: Breeds throughout year but mainly early Feb. to late July (eggs, Mar. 14 to June 23) from near sea level to 5,200 ft. Abundant to common in all settled areas.

HAUNTS AND HABITS: *Passer domesticus* is by far the most widespread of the Ploceidae, an Old World family of some 263 species. In Texas, the House Sparrow and Mourning Dove share the distinction of being the only wild birds which have written occurrence records in all 254 counties. Both species thrive in grain-growing, gardening, livestock- and poultry-raising districts. The sparrow has the edge, however, because it also likes places with lots of houses.

A very gregarious species, it often gathers into large foraging flocks and noisy communal roosts. Flight is fairly rapid and direct though somewhat laborious; it is performed with rapid and numerous wing-beats and is usually at low or moderate heights.

The food habits of the House Sparrow are, ironically, largely detrimental. It was originally imported for the purpose of destroying injurious caterpillars, but less than 5 percent of its diet is composed of insects. It feeds largely on cultivated fruits and grains, showing some preference for grapes and wheat, but also consuming large quantities of peas, beans, corn, lettuce, oats, rye, barley, sorghum, buckwheat, rice, and cultivated grass. It also eats weed seeds to some extent, including those of dandelion and smartweed. At times it has been an effective destroyer of alfalfa weevils, and may take a considerable variety of insects, especially

when nestlings are being fed—but even the nestlings' diet consists of at least one-third vegetable matter, chiefly grain. The House Sparrow exemplifies an ill-advised introduction of a foreign species into a new country where the effective population controls of its natural home are absent.

The most common vocalizations are garrulous *cheep*'s, *chissick*'s, and an occasional twittering song which is essentially a series of chirps. Varied harsh utterances are sounded during encounters between territorial competitors.

CHANGES: The House Sparrow's conquest of Texas from bases in New York and Galveston is of interest. Nicolas Pike, then a director of the Brooklyn Institute, brought the first English House Sparrows to North America in 1850 for the purpose of controlling cankerworms. These and subsequent shipments he caused to be liberated around New York City in 1851, 1852, and 1853. The sparrows quickly bred up a heavy population in the Atlantic states. Probably some of these birds rode to Texas in railway boxcars.

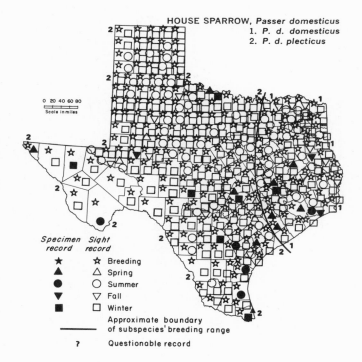

HOUSE SPARROW, *Passer domesticus*
1. *P. d. domesticus*
2. *P. d. plecticus*

0 20 40 60 80
Scale in miles

Specimen record	Sight record	
★	☆	Breeding
▲	△	Spring
●	○	Summer
▼	▽	Fall
■	□	Winter
—		Approximate boundary of subspecies' breeding range
?		Questionable record

Texas' chief House Sparrow base was established at Galveston in 1867 when one J. M. Brown imported a small colony. Dates of first recorded appearance in other cities and towns of the state follow: Houston, 1882; Jefferson, about 1882; San Saba, 1886; Gainesville, Nov. 25, 1892; Petty, Feb. 13, 1894; San Angelo, about 1895; San Antonio, Apr. 21, 1896; Kerrville, Dec. 12, 1897; Nuevo Laredo on Texas-Tamaulipas border, specimen, Dec. 30, 1901 (E.W. Nelson and E. A. Goldman); Corpus Christi and Brownsville, about 1905.

The much discussed mid-twentieth-century decrease in House Sparrow numbers, said to be pronounced in the northern and eastern United States, was up to 1972 not noticeable in Texas. Sparrow populations appear to have remained fairly stable since the 1920's, except of course in places where DDT saturation approaches 100 percent.

After less than a century in the western United States, House Sparrows in this region had become pale enough for H. C. Oberholser to describe this population as a new subspecies, *P. d. plecticus*. Apparently evolution proceeds at a somewhat more rapid pace than is generally recognized.

DETAILED ACCOUNT: TWO SUBSPECIES

ENGLISH HOUSE SPARROW, *Passer domesticus domesticus* (Linnaeus)

DESCRIPTION: *Adult male, nuptial plumage*: Acquired by wear from winter plumage. Pileum and anterior of hindneck brownish mouse gray to deep mouse gray; hindneck liver brown to bay, feathers of median portion tipped with brownish mouse gray or dull brown; back and scapulars russet to ochraceous tawny, broadly streaked with black; rump and upper tail-coverts mouse gray to between mouse gray and drab; tail hair brown, becoming darker, usually chaetura drab, at tips of feathers, middle rectrices margined basally with color of rump; primaries and secondaries hair brown, becoming darker terminally and drab or light drab on inner edges, except at tips of primaries; tertials fuscous, broadly margined on outer webs with dull ochraceous tawny or sayal brown, which color also forms a spot on several outer webs of outer primaries at tips of primary coverts, secondaries, and outer primaries basally, narrowly margined with same; lesser wing-coverts chestnut; median wing-coverts with dull black subterminal bar and broadly tipped with white, forming conspicuous wing-bar; greater wing-coverts fuscous, broadly edged on outer margin with dull russet to ochraceous tawny, which becomes paler at tips, sometimes even pale buffy white; dull white supraloral streak; lores, malar region, and stripe extending backward below eye to behind eye black; auriculars, posterior parts of cheeks and lower part of sides of neck extending to sides of throat in large patch, smoke gray or dark smoke gray; sides of head dark bay behind eye above black stripe, this extending forward to above middle of eye, backward to sides of neck, and downward in point along sides of neck and invading smoke gray patch; chin, middle of throat, and broad jugular crescent black or brownish black; sides dull buffy smoke gray or between light grayish olive and light drab; remainder of lower surface dull grayish or buffy white; lining of wing and edge of wing grayish white, outer under wing-coverts mottled with hair brown or mouse gray. Bill black, brownish black, or bluish black; iris hazel or dark brown; legs and feet prout brown, burnt umber, or light brown. *Adult male, winter*: Acquired by complete postnuptial molt. Similar to nuptial adult male, but upper parts lighter, more brownish, and more uniform, pileum and rump, as well as blackish streaks of interscapulum, more or less overlaid with buffy brown; edgings of wings

and tail broader, lower surface much washed with dull buff, black of anterior lower parts more or less veiled with light gray, dull white, or dull buff tips and edgings of feathers. Bill dull brown, base of mandible yellowish. *Adult female, nuptial*: Acquired by wear from winter. Pileum dark drab to dark dull buffy brown; rump and upper tail-coverts similar, but paler; back and scapulars sayal brown, cinnamon brown, or dark snuff brown, with dull black streaks; tail between buffy brown and hair brown, rectrices edged on outer webs with color of rump; wing-quills like tail but rather darker, tertials and wing-coverts clove brown, outer edgings of lesser and greater coverts, tertials, primaries, and secondaries brown like interscapulum, those on tertials and inner secondaries broad, those on primaries narrow, and median wing-coverts broadly tipped with dull pinkish buff, forming conspicuous wing-bar; sides of head, including lores, between drab and light drab, or between drab and light buffy brown; darker postocular streak of light dull olive brown, and above this a broad postocular streak of rather buffy avellaneous; sides and flanks between drab and wood brown; remainder of lower surface dull smoke gray, usually with wash of light dull buff; chin, middle of throat, and abdomen whitish; lining of wing pale drab or buffy drab; outer under wing-coverts mottled with hair brown, smoke gray, or drab. Bill bluish black or dull brown, but base of mandible flesh color, light brown, or pale yellow; iris dark brown; legs and feet dark fawn color, flesh color, or grayish flesh color. *Adult female, winter*: Acquired by complete postnuptial molt. Similar to nuptial adult female, but upper surface duller, colors more blended by edgings of feathers; lower surface more strongly washed with buff. *Male and female, second winter*: Acquired by complete postnuptial molt. Similar to corresponding sex of adults in winter. *Male, first nuptial*: Acquired by wear from first winter. Like nuptial adult male, but chin with more white on tips of feathers. *Male, first winter*: Acquired by complete postjuvenal molt. Similar to adult male in winter, but chin usually with more extensive dull white or pale buff edgings on feathers. Iris hazel; legs and feet brown. *Female, first nuptial*: Acquired by wear from first winter. Similar to nuptial adult female. *Female, first winter*: Acquired by complete postjuvenal molt. Like adult female in winter. *Male, juvenal*: Acquired by postnatal growth. Similar to adult female in winter, but bill smaller; plumage looser and more fluffy; pileum with paler feather edges, imparting slightly mottled appearance; remainder of upper surface averaging paler, black streaks on interscapulum lighter, duller, smaller, narrower, and less blackish olive brown; wings and tail somewhat more brownish and lighter, tail more or less indistinctly barred or spotted with fuscous; lower parts duller; throat at first slightly vermiculated or even slightly barred with olive gray or fuscous, and both jugulum and throat darker; center of throat brownish deep mouse gray; sides and flanks light buffy brown. *Female, juvenal*: Acquired by postnatal growth. Similar to juvenal male, but middle of throat all dull white or dull pale buff. Bill slate gray, but mandible dull white with yellowish tinge at base; iris dark brown; legs and feet hair brown. *Natal*: None. Bird hatched unfeathered. Bill, legs, and feet pinkish buff.

MEASUREMENTS: *Adult male*: Wing, 71.7–79.0 (average, 75.9) mm.; tail, 52.8–58.2 (54.8); bill (exposed culmen), 12.2–13.5 (12.7); tarsus, 18.3–20.3 (19.3); middle toe without claw, 13.2–16.0 (15.0). *Adult female*: Wing, 74.2–76.5 (75.2); tail, 52.3–55.6 (54.3); bill, 11.7–13.0 (12.4); tarsus, 18.0–20.3 (19.3); middle toe, 13.7–15.7 (15.0).

RANGE: Mainly resident. Native to Europe (except Italy) and n.w. Africa. Naturalized in e. North America (including e. Mexico), Bermuda, and West Indies (local); also in temperate and subtropical parts of South America, South Africa, Australia, New Zealand, and Hawaii.

TEXAS: *Resident*: Altitudinal breeding range, near sea level to 600 ft. Collected north to Nacogdoches, southeast to Chambers, southwest to Wharton, northwest to Brazos cos. Abundant to common. One specimen from Cameron Co. (July 11, 1924, R. D. Camp).

NESTING: *Nest*: In more open country, preferably near human dwellings, also in cities and towns; in all sorts of locations:

branch of tree or bush, up to 50–60 ft. above ground, in vines, all kinds of crevices about buildings, hole in tree, woodpecker hole, burrow of Bank Swallow, box put up for other birds (especially bluebird and Purple Martin houses), etc.; if in tree branches, usually globular, with opening on side, although sometimes open; if in cavity, much less material is used, ordinarily rather untidy; composed of grass, hay, straw, rubbish of various kinds, paper, string, rags, and even bits of wire, or steel shavings from a lathe, and feathers of all kinds; lined with feathers, fine grass, and similar materials. *Eggs*: 4–9, usually 5–6; ovate to nearly elliptical oval; dull white, grayish white, to purplish gray, and even olive brown; very thickly dotted or blotched and otherwise marked over entire surface with reddish brown, dark brown, black, various shades of gray, slate color, and olive, with shell markings of purplish gray; average size, 22.1 × 15.5 mm.

PALE HOUSE SPARROW, Passer domesticus plecticus
Oberholser, new subspecies (see Appendix A)

DESCRIPTION: *Adult male and female, nuptial plumage*: Simi-lar to *P. d. domesticus*, but male with pileum and rump somewhat more clearly grayish (less buffy); lower surface more whitish and grayish (less buffy); female decidedly more grayish (less buffy or ochraceous) above, and averaging somewhat darker; and lower parts lighter, more grayish (less buffy).

MEASUREMENTS: *Adult male*: Wing, 74.9–80.5 (average, 77.7) mm.; tail, 55.1–59.4 (57.2); bill (exposed culmen), 11.4–12.7 (11.9); tarsus, 19.0–20.6 (19.8); middle toe without claw, 14.5–16.0 (15.2). *Adult female*: Wing, 72.9–78.0 (75.4); tail, 53.6–57.9 (55.9); bill, 11.4–13.0 (12.2); tarsus, 18.5–20.6 (19.6); middle toe, 14.0–15.5 (14.7).

TYPE: Adult male, no. 419466, U.S. National Museum; Gray, Bonneville Co., Idaho; May 29, 1951, T. D. Burleigh, original no., 13855.

RANGE: S.w. British Columbia to North Dakota, south to Baja California, Coahuila, and Texas.

TEXAS: *Resident*: Altitudinal breeding range, near sea level to 5,200 ft. Collected northwest to El Paso, east to Brazos and Colorado, south to Victoria and Cameron cos. Abundant to common.

NESTING: Similar to that of *P. d. domesticus*.

Meadowlarks, Blackbirds, and Orioles: Icteridae

BOBOLINK, *Dolichonyx oryzivorus* (Linnaeus)

SPECIES ACCOUNT

Finchlike bill; pointed tail feathers. *Nuptial male*: buff nape; bold areas of white on black upper parts; black head and under parts. *Female, fall male*: streaked dark brown and buffy on upper parts, striped with same on crown; rich buffy on breast. Length, 7¼ in.; wingspan, 11¾; weight, 1¼ oz.

RANGE: S.e. British Columbia across s. Canada to Nova Scotia, south (east of Cascades) to n.e. California, thence across n. United States to New Jersey. Migrates chiefly through eastern United States, West Indies, e. Central America, and n. South America. Winters in South America from w. Brazil to n. Argentina and Paraguay.

TEXAS: (See map.) *Migration*: Late Apr. to mid-May; late Aug. to mid-Oct. (extremes: Mar. 16, June 8; Aug. 15, Nov. 28). Fairly common (some years) to scarce in spring along upper coast; rare in remainder of state east of 99th meridian; casual in northern Panhandle. Very rare in fall through eastern portion west to San Angelo. *Winter*: Sight record: Galveston Co. (Dec. 31, 1966, E. N. McHenry).

HAUNTS AND HABITS: The Bobolink is the number one long distance migrant among the Icteridae, a strictly New World family of eighty-eight species. On its nesting grounds, the Bobolink requires extensive fields of tall grass or grain where it conceals its nest on the ground. During its long migrations from grassy daisy meadows of North America to marsh grass of the Gran Chaco in central South America, this famous species passes mostly east of Texas. Outside the breeding season, the Bobolink is highly gregarious and in days gone by assembled into great flocks which often moved in dense formations while migrating and foraging. Upper and central coast marshes, prairies, and rice fields still furnish landing places for a few individuals, but large flocks of handsome spring males singing their bubbling and tinkling *bob-o-link*'s are of the past.

Flight is ordinarily somewhat hovering but is swift and strong during migration. The bird often perches on fence posts, in bushes and reeds, and on the ground, as well as in tall grass where it mainly feeds. Despite its famed autumnal depredations on cultivated rice in the Carolinas, the Bobolink is too scarce in Texas to cause concern. Food in fall is cultivated or wild rice, but oats, wheat, barley, buckwheat, and seeds of smartweed, ragweed, sorrel, barn grass, and panicum are also eaten. During spring and summer, however, insects comprise well over 50 percent of the diet and include curculios, other weevils, leaf-chafers, predacious ground beetles, May, click, and lamellicorn beetles; ants, ichneumon flies, parasitic wasps; moths, caterpillars (cottonworm, cankerworm, cutworm); mayflies, grasshoppers, crickets, dragonflies, bugs; and house flies. A few spiders and millipedes are also taken.

The Bobolink's chief note is a clear, metallic *pink* or *clink*; nocturnal migrants use this call to keep in touch. The male's spring song, often delivered on the wing, is an ecstatic, bubbling jumble of notes; sometimes it is given in chorus. H. C. Oberholser described the vocalizations of a flock of six hundred males as one of the most remarkable exhibitions of concert singing to be heard in the wild.

CHANGES: The Bobolink played a much larger part

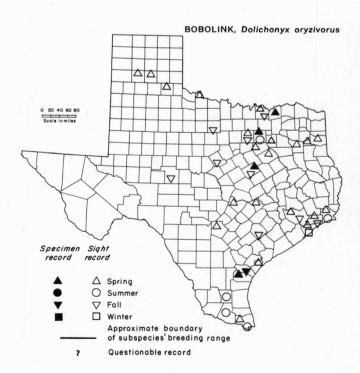

BOBOLINK, *Dolichonyx oryzivorus*

0 20 40 60 80
Scale in miles

Specimen Sight
record   record

▲ △ Spring
● ○ Summer
▼ ▽ Fall
■ □ Winter

——— Approximate boundary of subspecies' breeding range

? Questionable record

in American life in the nineteenth century than it has in the twentieth. It was popular with poets and cage bird fanciers because of its sprightly song; gourmets considered Bobolinks fattened in South Carolina rice fields the epitome of "first-rate eating."

The twentieth century has seen a great decline in Bobolink numbers. The hayfields where it nests are now mostly machine-mowed so early in the season that many nestlings are killed. In addition, nesting sites are rapidly being transformed into subdivisions and automobile parking lots. Other fields have even been allowed to grow up into scrubby second-growth woods. Carolina rice, which in fall used to fuel huge flocks of these birds for their long flight to South America, is not grown much any more. Finally, the winter range in southwestern Brazil, northern Argentina, and Paraguay is largely converted to agricultural uses. Many of the birds which still arrive to winter are quite likely to be cooked Italian style by the hordes of immigrants who now heavily ranch and farm the region. No wonder that nowadays (early 1970's) the sight of even one Bobolink in Texas is an event. Proof that miracles are still possible was demonstrated in 1973. In the upper coast marshes between High Island and Sabine Pass, thirty "skunk blackbirds" appeared on May 2; on May 6, fourteen Bobolinks, including one female and one partially albino male, were viewed in the same marshes (V. L. Emanuel, et al.).

DETAILED ACCOUNT: NO SUBSPECIES

DESCRIPTION: *Adult male, nuptial plumage*: Acquired by complete prenuptial molt and subsequent wear. Pileum black or brownish black, feathers more or less tipped with pale dull buff; hindneck warm buff to clay color, somewhat clouded by dull gray edgings of feathers; center of back like hindneck but somewhat streaked with dull black; sides of back black with edgings of dull buff, clay color, or buffy white; scapulars dull white, much overlaid with dull buff, clay color, or mouse gray; rump mouse gray, more or less washed with dull light grayish olive; upper tail-coverts white, more or less overlaid with light grayish olive; tail fuscous black, all feathers tipped irregularly and more or less margined terminally with hair brown, these edgings broadest on inner webs of middle pair; wing-quills fuscous black or brownish black, terminal portion of primaries and secondaries fuscous, inner webs of wing-quills without paler margins; outer primaries margined narrowly on outer webs and tertials broadly on both webs with pale dull buffy drab, saccardo umber, or dull wood brown; lesser wing-coverts black, slightly tipped with dull white, remainder of wing-coverts dull black, inner greater coverts broadly margined with paler buff or pale brown of tertials, outer greater coverts narrowly tipped with buffy white or pale buff; entire lower surface, including lining of wing, dull black, feathers more or less tipped everywhere, usually most broadly on flanks and crissum, with light buff or cream color. Bill black, slate black, or bluish black, but base of mandible plumbeous; iris vandyke brown; legs and feet black or dull dark brown. *Adult male, worn nuptial*: Acquired wholly by wear from fresh nuptial. Similar to fresh nuptial, but entire head and lower parts slightly brownish black without lighter feather edgings; hindneck lighter, light cream color to deep naples yellow, with almost no dull margins on feathers; middle of back dull white or pale buff with a few narrow black streaks; scapulars almost pure grayish white or dull buffy white with much less clouding than in fresh nuptial; black of back with little or no admixture of buff or dull white on edges of feathers; upper tail-coverts white or very pale buff with little or no grayish wash; rump mouse gray

or between mouse gray and neutral gray; wings dull black with but few buffy or whitish edgings, these chiefly on edges of outer primaries and on tertials. *Adult male, winter*: Acquired by complete postnuptial molt. Similar to nuptial adult female, but larger; upper surface much darker, more brownish; lower surface much more deeply yellowish, brownish, or buffy, jugulum and breast ranging from pale dull chamois to buckthorn brown. Bill dull brown or reddish brown, mandible and often base of maxilla decidedly paler; iris dark brown. *Adult female, nuptial*: Acquired by complete prenuptial molt and subsequent wear. Upper surface between light brownish olive or isabella color and tawny olive, rump somewhat more grayish or grayish olive, nape more buffy, pileum mostly fuscous black or brownish black with cinnamon buff tips of feathers and central stripe of cream buff or dull cinnamon buff, remainder of upper surface broadly streaked, most broadly on back and scapulars, with fuscous black or brownish black; tail dark hair brown to fuscous, feathers edged terminally with dull pale buff, as are outer webs narrowly throughout most of length; primaries and secondaries dark hair brown to fuscous, narrowly edged on both outer webs and at tips with pale buffy white or pale buff, inner margins of secondaries rather paler; tertials and wing-coverts fuscous black; lesser wing-coverts grayish olive; median and greater wing-coverts edged on outer webs and tipped with pale dull buff; broad superciliary stripe chamois or dull cartridge buff; narrow postocular streak fuscous black; remainder of sides of head and of neck honey yellow to chamois, lores somewhat more grayish, and auriculars sometimes duller and darker; lower surface white, buffy white, or dull pale yellowish buff, lightest on chin, upper throat, and abdomen, but jugulum and upper breast strongly washed with chamois, dull cartridge buff, or pale dull gray and darker than rest of lower surface; remainder of lower surface often much washed with dull pale buff and sides and flanks more or less broadly streaked with fuscous black; lining of wing dull white or buffy white, outer portion mottled with drab or mouse gray. Maxilla seal brown or reddish brown, but cutting edges and base cinnamon, mandible white or flesh color; iris light brown or vandyke brown; legs and feet drab or light brown. *Adult female, worn nuptial*: Similar to fresh nuptial, but upper surface lighter, somewhat more grayish (less buffy or brownish), blackish streaks broader, more numerous, and more sharply defined; lower surface usually paler and somewhat more yellowish (less buffy). *Adult female, winter*: Acquired by complete postnuptial molt. Similar to nuptial adult female, but upper surface much more brownish and darker; lower surface darker and more deeply yellow or buffy; jugulum and breast honey yellow to tawny olive or dull chamois. Similar to adult male in winter but smaller; upper surface averaging somewhat lighter, less brownish; lower surface usually averaging somewhat less brownish with less broadly streaked sides and flanks. *Male, first nuptial*: Acquired by complete prenuptial molt. Similar to nuptial adult male, but yellowish edgings of feathers broader. *Male, first winter*: Acquired by partial postjuvenal molt, which does not involve wing-quills or tail feathers. Similar to adults in winter, but upper surface lighter, more ochraceous, and with usually lighter and brighter buffy edgings; lower surface usually much more deeply and uniformly buff or yellow; streaks on sides and flanks more veiled by lighter edgings of feathers. *Female, first nuptial*: Acquired by complete prenuptial molt. Similar to nuptial adult female. *Female, first winter*: Acquired by partial postjuvenal molt. Similar to adult female in winter. Maxilla walnut brown, but its tip black; mandible ecru drab; tip of tongue and inside of mouth white; iris prout brown; legs, feet, and claws fawn color. *Juvenal*: Acquired by complete postnatal molt. Similar to first winter birds, but more buffy, particularly below; breast and jugulum with some dark spots; sides and flanks with almost no blackish streaks. Bill clay color, but tip dull brown; feet vandyke brown.

MEASUREMENTS: *Adult male*: Wing, 93.7–101.9 (average, 97.6) mm.; tail, 62.7–68.8 (65.3); bill (exposed culmen), 14.0–16.0 (14.7); height of bill at base, 8.9–9.9 (9.7); tarsus, 26.2–28.4 (27.2); middle toe without claw, 20.3–22.4 (21.4). *Adult female*: Wing, 85.3–89.7 (87.4); tail, 58.7–64.5 (61.0); bill,

13.0–15.0 (13.7); height of bill, 8.4–9.4 (9.1); tarsus, 24.6–27.2 (25.7); middle toe, 18.5–21.4 (20.3).

TEXAS: *Migration*: Collected in Fannin Co. (300 shot, spring 1884, H. F. Peters); Dallas Co. (3 on May 8, 1898, W. A. Mayer); McLennan Co. (1 on May 14, 1931, T. F. Smith); San Patricio Co. (female, Oct. 21, 1955, C. Cottam; Welder Wildlife Refuge collection, no. 67); Nueces Co. (male, Apr. 30, 1965, K. Baker; Welder collection, no. 1229).

EASTERN MEADOWLARK, *Sturnella magna* (Linnaeus)

SPECIES ACCOUNT

Also known as Common Meadowlark. *Song*: high-pitched; two clear, slurred whistles. Chunky body; sturdy, spikelike bill; flattish crown; short, wide tail; bird alternately flaps and sails. Streaked brown (appears dark) above; whitish malar area; yellow throat and breast with black V; white outer tail feathers. Heavy blackish cross-bars on central tail feathers and on secondaries and tertials usually coalesce along shafts of feathers (compare with Western Meadowlark). Length, 9½ in.; wingspan, 15; weight, 3¾ oz.

RANGE: N.w. Arizona, s. New Mexico, s.w. South Dakota, Great Lakes region, and Nova Scotia, south through c. and e. United States, Mexico, Cuba, and Central America to Colombia, Venezuela, British Guiana, and n. Brazil. Migratory races winter chiefly in United States and n. Mexico.

TEXAS: (See map.) *Breeding*: Early Mar. to late Aug. (eggs, mid-Mar. to Aug. 8) from near sea level to 6,100 ft. Common to fairly common in many parts east of Pecos River, but south of 29th parallel largely restricted to coast; locally fairly common in Trans-Pecos. *Winter*: Mid-Sept. to mid-Apr. (extremes: Sept.

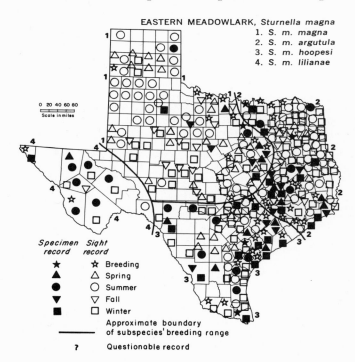

EASTERN MEADOWLARK, *Sturnella magna*
1. *S. m. magna*
2. *S. m. argutula*
3. *S. m. hoopesi*
4. *S. m. lilianae*

0 20 40 60 80
Scale in miles

Specimen | Sight
record | record

★ | ☆ Breeding
▲ | △ Spring
● | ○ Summer
▼ | ▽ Fall
■ | □ Winter

—— Approximate boundary of subspecies' breeding range

? Questionable record

2, Apr. 27). Very common to common in eastern third and along coast to southern tip; uncommon to rare west to El Paso region; rare to casual in northern Panhandle.

HAUNTS AND HABITS: The Eastern Meadowlark nests in tall grass meadows and fields; it also breeds in wooded country, provided there is grass growing between trees. On lush prairies in spring and summer almost every other fence post is topped by a male tirelessly proclaiming territory. In the nonbreeding season it is fairly gregarious, often appearing in scattered flocks of rather large size.

The meadowlark is generally low flying. Periods of vigorous flapping alternate with periods of gliding on stiff-set, downward-bowed wings. Birds walk briskly over both grassy and bare ground, where they dig food from the earth with their beaks. Almost three-quarters of their food consists of insects—a remarkably large percentage of them grasshoppers, locusts, and crickets. In fact, contents of a single stomach examined by F. E. L. Beal included thirty common grasshoppers, four green grasshoppers, and ten crickets! Beetles (May, flea, leaf, potato, curculio, cotton-boll weevil), bugs, caterpillars, moths, ants, wasps, flies, dragonflies; a few spiders; ticks; millipedes; snails and crustaceans; and occasionally even a small frog or toad form a lesser component of the animal diet. The vegetable portion consists of seeds of forbs and grasses, and in autumn, waste grain.

The ordinary call is a metallic, somewhat nasal *peent* with some guttural chatter. The loud, clear whistled song is a high-pitched *tee-yah* (or *tee-yee*) *tee-yair*, sometimes more loosely translated as *spring is here*. It is usually uttered from an elevated perch where the male sits upright with tail pointing down and bill uplifted in song. It may be heard throughout the year, but is more frequent in warmer months.

CHANGES: The remarkable thing about the Eastern Meadowlark is that it has maintained its numbers so well in spite of drastic and far-reaching alterations of its habitat. Other grassland birds are sinking toward extinction (prairie chickens) or they are much reduced (Bobolink, longspurs), but the Eastern Meadowlark seemingly holds its own against all the destruction of the terrible twentieth century.

DETAILED ACCOUNT: FOUR SUBSPECIES

NORTHERN EASTERN MEADOWLARK, *Sturnella magna magna* (Linnaeus)

DESCRIPTION: *Adult male, nuptial plumage*: Acquired by wear from winter plumage. Crown dull black or brownish black, streaked narrowly with cartridge buff, dull russet, or cinnamon brown, and with broad central stripe of cartridge buff to chamois, streaks on crown narrowest and sometimes almost absent on forehead; feathers of remainder of upper surface centrally dull black or brownish black, these centers smallest on hindneck and broadest on back, all feathers margined and tipped with dull russet, cinnamon brown, tawny olive, or sayal brown, palest on rump and upper tail-coverts, where centers of feathers are also more or less longitudinal and subterminally mottled with same color as are lighter edgings, this also occurring on some scapulars; tail fuscous, outer three feathers white, except for extreme bases and for narrow streak on outer webs, and also broad dark area on inner edge of inner web of third feather, this occupying also a third of entire basal portion of feather, fourth feather with long white shaft streak running almost entire length of feather, basally on outer and terminally on inner web, remainder of tail with broken bars of hair brown to drab, fuscous bars thus confluent along shafts of feathers; primaries and secondaries between fuscous and hair brown, outer webs of primaries except at tips and excepting two outer feathers, broadly barred with dull drab; secondaries still more broadly barred with fawn to wood brown; tertials wood brown to sayal brown, with partly separated and partly confluent bars of dull black or brownish black; upper wing-coverts fuscous to brownish black, lesser series edged with mouse gray, median coverts broadly tipped and margined on both webs with dull light buff; greater coverts barred on outer webs with pale dull buff and fawn color or wood brown; superciliary stripe above lores gamboge yellow, and posteriorly dull cream buff; anterior part of lores dull black, as is also broad postocular streak below superciliary stripe; remainder of sides of head pale cartridge buff or buffy grayish white, sides of neck similar, but often gradually verging into color of upper surface, and narrowly and numerously streaked with dull black; anterior part of chin dull white; remainder of chin and middle of throat, together with breast and middle of abdomen, gamboge yellow or between lemon chrome and light cadmium, with broad black crescent on jugulum; sides of breast with large black spots on whitish or buffy white ground, sometimes slightly tinged with yellow; sides, flanks, under tail-coverts, and thighs cartridge buff, cinnamon buff, or chamois, broadly streaked with black or fuscous, thighs with narrower streaks; lining of wing dull white, grayish white, or buffy white, more or less mottled or streaked with dull light olive brown or dull black; edge of wing lemon yellow or lemon chrome. Tip of bill white; terminal third of maxilla and terminal half of mandible dull, blackish slate, mouse gray, or chestnut; basal two-thirds of maxilla fawn color; iris hazel or prout brown; basal half of mandible cinereous, lavender gray, bluish white, or dull pale flesh color; tongue and inside of mouth white; legs and feet ecru drab, olive gray, drab gray, vinaceous white, or vinaceous buff; claws brown or drab. *Adult male, winter*: Acquired by complete postnuptial molt. Similar to nuptial adult male, but light areas of upper surface darker, more brownish, buffy areas of head and neck more deeply colored; black centers of feathers on back, scapulars, and rump largely concealed by brown or buffy edgings of feathers (in fresh plumage these light buffy edgings extend entirely around tips of feathers); wings and tail also darker; yellow of lower parts as well as black jugular crescent much overlaid with dull buff, pale gray, and pale buffy brown edgings of feathers; sides, flanks, and crissum more deeply buff, streaks more or less veiled by light edgings of feathers. *Adult female, nuptial*: Acquired by wear from winter. Similar to nuptial adult male, but decidedly smaller; black stripes on pileum more broadly streaked with brown; black postocular stripe much mixed with streaks of brown, often mostly dull brown streaked with black; sides of head and neck less whitish (more buffy); black jugular crescent usually smaller and tipped, often broadly, with grayish white or buffy white; yellow of lower parts somewhat duller. *Adult female, winter*: Acquired by complete postnuptial molt. Similar to nuptial adult female, but upper surface more brownish, brown tips of feathers more extensive and often nearly covering black centers; light areas of upper surface more deeply buff, as are sides of head and neck; yellow of lower parts duller, veiled by buffy white or pale buff edgings and tips of feathers; black jugular crescent more extensively broken by pale gray or dull buffy edgings of feathers; sides and flanks more deeply buff. Maxilla brown; mandible plumbeous; iris hazel; legs and feet brown, tinged with flesh color. *Male, first nuptial*: Acquired by wear from first winter. Very similar to nuptial adult male. *Male, first winter*: Acquired by complete postjuvenal molt. Similar to adult male in winter, but central crown stripe, hindneck, and edgings of rump and upper tail-coverts, more deeply buff; sides of head and of neck more deeply buff, particularly superciliary stripe, yellow anterior portion of this much overlaid by buff; yellow of lower parts as well as black of jugular crescent more veiled with buff; sides and flanks more deeply buff. *Female, first nuptial*: Acquired by wear from first winter. Like nuptial adult female. *Female, first winter*: Acquired by complete postjuvenal molt. Similar to adult female in winter, but edgings of rump and upper tail-coverts more deeply buff, as well as sides of head and neck; yellow superciliary stripe and yellow of throat almost entirely obscured by buffy edgings of feathers; yellow of remainder of lower surface much more overlaid by buff; black jugular crescent almost entirely hidden by buffy edges and tips of feathers; sides and flanks more deeply buff. *Juvenal*: Acquired by complete postnatal molt. Similar to adults in winter, but bill shorter; upper surface brownish black to fuscous black, feathers of pileum narrowly margined with cartridge buff to rood brown, broad central stripe on pileum cartridge buff to honey yellow; feathers of hindneck more broadly margined with buff; feathers of back, scapulars, tertials, and wing-quills more or less mottled with rood brown, and margined and tipped with cartridge buff or buffy white, producing squamate effect; feathers of rump and upper tail-coverts margined and more or less spotted or barred with cartridge buff to chamois; wings and tail similar to first winter female, but lesser wing-coverts fuscous, margined with pale buff, very pale yellow, or yellowish white, greater series and primary coverts tipped with pale buff or buffy white; superciliary stripe cartridge buff, more or less spotted with fuscous; postocular stripe fuscous or fuscous black; auriculars dull buff; lower surface deep colonial buff to cream buff or dull wax yellow, chin sometimes whitish, throat often paler than remainder of lower surface; breast, sides, and flanks more deeply buff; jugulum broadly and heavily spotted with dull black; sides of breast with smaller spots of fuscous black to hair brown; sides, flanks, and crissum spotted or streaked with same. Bill slaty; feet dull clay color. *Natal*: Light drab to drab gray. Bill, legs, and feet pinkish buff.

MEASUREMENTS: *Adult male*: Wing, 114.3–129.0 (average, 122.2) mm.; tail, 67.6–86.6 (78.7); bill (from base), 30.7–36.8 (34.3); tarsus, 38.9–46.3 (41.7); middle toe without claw, 27.2–32.3 (30.2). *Adult female*: Wing, 103.6–113.8 (107.2); tail, 65.8–73.7 (67.8); bill (from base), 26.7–31.5 (29.9); height of bill at base, 36.3–40.6 (37.3); middle toe, 25.1–29.9 (27.2).

RANGE: N. Great Lakes area and s.e. Canada, south through c. United States to n.w. and c. Texas, w. North Carolina, and Virginia. Winters from s. Great Lakes area and n.e. United States to c. and s.e. Texas and w. Florida.

TEXAS: *Breeding*: Altitudinal range, 250 to 4,200 ft. Collected northwest to Hemphill, southeast to Navarro and Falls cos. Common. *Winter*: Taken northwest to Dickens, east to Hardin (Mar. 26), south to Calhoun (Apr. 6) cos. Common.

NESTING: *Nest*: In open country, prairies, and cultivated areas, pastures, meadows, and fields; usually in depression on ground, often in a bunch of thick weeds, tuft of grass, clover, or similar vegetation; rather well made, usually more or less domed, with covered entrance, even with two such entrances, thus very difficult to discover; composed of coarse grasses, weeds, and other vegetation, and lined with similar finer materials. *Eggs*: 3–8, usually 5; usually ovate, but varying to short ovate, elongate ovate, elliptical oval, or practically oval; white or pale greenish white; thickly spotted or speckled, sometimes blotched, with umber, chocolate brown, purplish brown, and ferruginous, with shell markings of lilac, pale heliotrope purple, and lavender; occasionally unspotted; average size, 27.9 × 20.3 mm.

SOUTHERN EASTERN MEADOWLARK, *Sturnella magna argutula* Bangs

DESCRIPTION: *Adult male and female, nuptial plumage*: Similar to S. *m. magna* but much smaller and darker; upper surface rather more blackish, light areas darker, as well as sides of head; yellow of lower parts deeper, more orange; white on two outer tail feathers of less extent.

MEASUREMENTS: *Adult male*: Wing, 104.9–118.9 (average, 111.8) mm.; tail, 67.8–78.5 (72.7); bill (from base), 30.5–35.3

(32.8); tarsus, 39.4–43.7 (41.1); middle toe without claw, 27.2–31.8 (29.2). *Adult female*: Wing, 94.2–101.9 (99.3); tail, 60.2–67.3 (63.0); bill (from base), 27.7–30.2 (28.7); tarsus, 36.3–40.6 (38.4); middle toe, 25.7–30.2 (27.2).

RANGE: E. Oklahoma to North Carolina, south to e. Texas, s.e. United States, and s. Florida. Winters from n.e. Oklahoma and c. Georgia to southern portion of breeding range.

TEXAS: *Breeding*: Altitudinal range, near sea level to 750 ft. Collected north to Cooke, east to Bowie, south to Galveston, west to Brazos cos. Common locally. *Winter*: Taken north to Cooke, east to Jefferson (Sept. 7), southwest to Cameron (Apr. 15) cos. Common.

NESTING: Similar to that of *S. m. magna*.

RIO GRANDE EASTERN MEADOWLARK, *Sturnella magna hoopesi* Stone

DESCRIPTION: *Adult male and female, nuptial plumage*: Similar to *S. m. magna* but smaller; upper parts much paler, more grayish (less brownish), black centers of feathers smaller or more broken by brown bars, these centers on upper tail-coverts more in form of bars rather than streaks; bars on tertials and middle feathers of tail narrower and more widely separated, often not confluent, somewhat as in the Interior Western Meadowlark, *S. ludoviciana ludoviciana*, sides and flanks paler; yellow of lower surface much more tinged with orange. Similar to *S. m. argutula* but larger.

MEASUREMENTS: *Adult male*: Wing, 115.6–121.4 (average, 117.1) mm.; tail, 68.1–79.0 (75.2); bill (exposed culmen), 32.5–35.6 (34.3); tarsus, 40.4–44.4 (42.4); middle toe without claw, 26.9–29.9 (28.4). *Adult female*: Wing, 100.1–108.5 (105.6); tail, 63.0–71.1 (67.8); bill, 28.9–34.0 (31.2); tarsus, 38.6–41.4 (39.6); middle toe, 24.9–27.4 (25.9).

RANGE: C. and s. Texas, south to n. and s.e. Coahuila and e. Tamaulipas.

TEXAS: *Breeding*: Altitudinal range, near sea level to 2,450 ft. Collected north to Kerr, east to Goliad (eggs), south to Cameron, west to Edwards cos. Common locally. *Winter*: Taken north to Travis and Lee, east to Waller and Matagorda, south to Cameron, west to Webb cos. Common.

NESTING: Similar to that of *S. m. magna*, but average egg size, 29.4 × 20.3 mm.

LILIAN'S EASTERN MEADOWLARK, *Sturnella magna lilianae* Oberholser

DESCRIPTION: *Adult male and female, nuptial plumage*: Similar to *S. m. hoopesi* but larger; upper surface much paler, more grayish, dark bars on tertials and middle tail feathers still narrower and more widely separated; dark streaks on pileum less solidly black, more mixed with buff or brown; yellow of lower surface averaging more deeply golden or orange.

MEASUREMENTS: *Adult male*: Wing, 114.6–124.0 (average, 118.9) mm.; tail, 65.5–82.0 (71.9); bill (exposed culmen), 29.9–34.0 (32.5); tarsus, 39.1–43.4 (41.1); middle toe without claw, 23.9–26.9 (24.9). *Adult female*: Wing, 104.1–108.0 (104.9); tail, 58.4–62.0 (60.2); bill, 28.7–31.5 (30.2); tarsus, 37.1–39.9 (38.9); middle toe, 22.6–25.9 (24.6).

RANGE: C. Arizona to Trans-Pecos Texas, south to s.e. Sonora and n.w. and c. Chihuahua.

TEXAS: *Breeding*: Altitudinal range, 1,000 to 6,100 ft. Collected in Culberson, Reeves, Pecos, Brewster, Presidio, and Jeff Davis cos. Uncommon. *Winter*: Taken in El Paso (1 specimen) and Kinney (3) cos. Uncommon.

NESTING: Similar to that of *S. m. magna*.

WESTERN MEADOWLARK, *Sturnella ludoviciana* (Linnaeus)

SPECIES ACCOUNT

Sturnella neglecta of A.O.U. check-list, 1957 (see Appendix A). *Song*: low-pitched; seven to ten gurgling notes. Streaked brown (appears somewhat pale) above; yellow malar area; yellow throat and breast with black V; white outer tail feathers. Fine blackish cross-bars on central tail feathers and on secondaries and tertials usually don't coalesce along shafts of feathers. Length, 9½ in.; wingspan, 15½; weight, 3½ oz.

RANGE: C. British Columbia to w. Great Lakes region, south through w. and c. United States to n.w. Baja California, n. Sonora, Zacatecas, c. Nuevo León, n.w. Texas, and n. Louisiana. Winters south to s. Baja California, c. Mexico, Texas, and Mississippi; largely withdraws from n. and n.e. parts of breeding range.

TEXAS: (See map.) *Breeding*: Mid-Mar. to mid-Aug. (eggs, Mar. 27 to July 24) from 300 to 5,000 ft. Fairly common in northern Panhandle; uncommon to scarce in rest of northwestern third; increasingly scarce southeast to Fort Worth and Waco. *Winter*: Mid-Oct. to early Apr. (extremes: July 21, June 25). Very common to fairly common in western two-thirds; uncommon to rare in eastern third.

HAUNTS AND HABITS: The Western Meadowlark inhabits prairies, meadows, and fields; so does the Eastern Meadowlark. Habitat details frequently differ, however. In Texas this difference is best illustrated in the northern Panhandle. During spring and summer the Western nests on uplands where grass is comparatively dry and short; the Eastern occupies stream floodplains or moist fields where grasses and weeds are taller. In winter, habitat preferences are less marked; both meadowlarks occur together in almost all parts of the state. Even in the nonbreeding season, though, the Western is a little more likely to forage on bare, desert-like ground.

Habits of the Western are similar to those of the

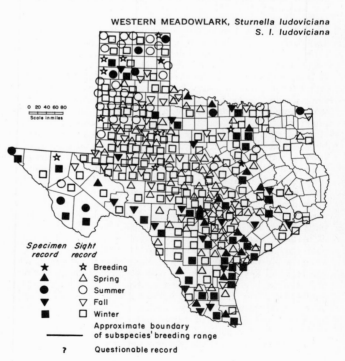

WESTERN MEADOWLARK, *Sturnella ludoviciana*
S. l. *ludoviciana*

0 20 40 60 80
Scale in miles

Specimen record	Sight record	
★	☆	Breeding
▲	△	Spring
●	○	Summer
▼	▽	Fall
■	□	Winter

—— Approximate boundary of subspecies' breeding range

? Questionable record

Eastern. Its food consists of about 70 percent animal matter, chiefly insects, and 30 percent vegetable, principally seeds. The insects are similar to those taken by the Eastern, and like the Eastern, this species is one of the best destroyers of boll weevils. The Western also takes some spiders, sowbugs, and snails. The vegetable portion of its diet consists of grain (corn, oats, wheat, barley), a little fruit pulp, and weed seeds.

The Western's call, distinctive from that of the Eastern, is a penetrating *chuck*, followed by rolling notes. Its song, also entirely different, is a loud, rich melody of seven to ten flutelike notes with a bubbling or gurgling quality.

CHANGES: As a species, the Eastern Meadowlark nests in far more climes than does the Western. In spite of this fact, the Western Meadowlark seems to be maintaining its numbers just as well as the Eastern. Apparently, man's landscape-altering activities compensate for the Western's comparative lack of adaptability. Ranching, farming, and road building have converted much tall-grass prairie and open grassy woodland—Eastern Meadowlark habitat—into land more suited to the Western species—short grass (both wild and cultivated) and bare, desertlike ground.

DETAILED ACCOUNT: TWO SUBSPECIES

INTERIOR WESTERN MEADOWLARK, *Sturnella ludoviciana ludoviciana* (Linnaeus)

DESCRIPTION: Similar to Lilian's Eastern Meadowlark, *S. magna lilianae*, but wing and tail longer; tarsus shorter; sides of head more whitish or grayish (less buffy); yellow of throat extending over much of malar region; yellow of lower surface lighter, less orange; sides and flanks less deeply buff. Similar to Rio Grande Eastern Meadowlark, *S. m. hoopesi*, but wing longer; tail, bill, tarsus, and particularly middle toe, shorter; dark crown stripes much more streaked or mottled with buff or brown, thus less deeply blackish; remainder of upper surface usually lighter, less rufescent (more grayish), middle tail feathers and tertials with dark bars narrower and somewhat more widely separated, seldom confluent; sides of head and of neck somewhat more grayish (less buffy); yellow of lower surface rather lighter, less golden, yellow of throat also extending over much of malar region; sides and flanks less deeply buff, blackish streaks on sides and flanks more frequently and extensively mottled with dull buffy brown; black jugular crescent averaging narrower. Maxilla seal brown, but cutting edges lilac gray; mandible basally cinereous, changing to lavender gray on middle portion to dull black at tip; iris prout brown; legs and feet pale dull gray; claws light seal brown. *Adult male, nuptial (gray—normal—phase)*: Acquired by wear from winter plumage. Similar to *S. m. hoopesi*, but upper parts very much paler, more grayish, black bars on tertials and middle tail feathers narrower and more widely separated; yellow of lower surface lighter and less golden, and extending over much of malar region; sides and flanks paler, less buffy (more whitish). *Adult male, nuptial (brown phase)*: Similar to *S. m. hoopesi*, but upper surface slightly less rufescent and black bars on tertials and middle tail-coverts somewhat narrower, less confluent; sides of head somewhat more grayish, lower surface differing as in gray phase. Bill black or dark olive brown, but cutting edges and basal two-thirds of mandible delft blue or plumbeous; iris burnt umber or hazel; legs and feet flesh color, tinged with dull blue, purple, or cinereous; claws dull brown. *Adult male, winter*: Acquired by complete postnuptial molt. Similar to nuptial adult male, but more buffy on upper surface, and colors paler and more blended, broad brown tips of feathers nearly covering

black centers, and feathers with narrower margins and tips of white or very pale buff, imparting squamate appearance to upper surface; sides of head more buffy, yellow of lower parts as well as black jugular crescent more or less overlaid with buff or pale buff; sides, flanks, and crissum more deeply buff. *Adult female, nuptial*: Acquired by wear from winter. Similar to nuptial adult male, but much smaller; sides of head and of neck more buffy; yellow of anterior portion of superciliary stripe less extensive; yellow of throat usually duller and extending over less of malar region; yellow of remaining lower parts duller; jugular crescent smaller. *Adult female, winter*: Acquired by complete postnuptial molt. Differs from nuptial adult female as does male in winter from nuptial male. *Male and female, first nuptial*: Acquired by wear from first winter. Similar to corresponding sex of nuptial adults. *Male and female, first winter*: Acquired by complete postjuvenal molt. Similar to corresponding sex of winter adults, but colors somewhat richer. *Juvenal*: Acquired by complete postnatal molt. Similar to juvenal of *S. m. hoopesi*, but upper and lower parts paler and upper surface more mottled, jugulum with usually smaller fuscous or fuscous black spots. Bill brownish plumbeous or light sepia, but cutting edges of mandible, except at tip, vinaceous white or dull vinaceous; iris burnt umber; legs and feet brownish white, dull vinaceous white, or pale vinaceous gray; toes somewhat darker. *Natal*: Pale cartridge buff.

MEASUREMENTS: *Adult male*: Wing, 118.4–129.0 (average, 125.0) mm.; tail, 68.3–82.8 (75.7); bill (from base), 29.7–36.8 (33.3); tarsus, 36.8–41.7 (38.9); middle toe without claw, 25.1–28.4 (26.7). *Adult female*: Wing, 104.6–116.8 (110.7); tail, 61.0–72.2 (65.8); bill (from base), 27.7–32.5 (30.5); tarsus, 33.5–37.8 (36.3); middle toe, 22.9–26.7 (25.1).

RANGE: S.w. British Columbia, Saskatchewan, and e. Michigan, south to c. Baja California and n.w. Texas; casual in s.w. Alaska, n.e. Alberta, and n.e. Manitoba. Winters from western breeding range, east to Montana, s.e. South Dakota, and s. Wisconsin, and south to s. Baja California, Michoacán, e. Tamaulipas, s. Texas, and Mississippi.

TEXAS: *Breeding*: Collected north to Deaf Smith and Lipscomb, southeast to McLennan (eggs), west to El Paso cos. *Winter*: Taken north to Oldham, east to Galveston (Nov. 1), south to Cameron, west to El Paso cos. Common.

NESTING: *Nest*: In open country, such as fields and pastures, often in cultivated land or natural grassy meadows; on ground, in slight depression, either natural or dug out by the birds; nest rather loosely woven, but usually arched over, sometimes with a covered passage for entrance; composed of grass and weeds; lined with fine material of same. *Eggs*: 3–7, usually 5; elliptical ovate to oval; white or sometimes with very pale greenish tinge; dotted or more heavily spotted with chocolate, vinaceous russet, purplish brown, and very dark purple, with shell markings of shades of lilac and vinaceous gray, most markings at larger end; average size, 28.4 × 20.6 mm.

PACIFIC WESTERN MEADOWLARK, *Sturnella ludoviciana confluenta* Rathbun

DESCRIPTION: *Adult male and female, nuptial plumage*: Resembling *S. l. ludoviciana* but upper parts more deeply colored, with black markings broader; bars on tertials and tail wider and decidedly more confluent; blackish markings on flanks, sides of body and of breast larger; yellow of lower parts a little darker.

MEASUREMENTS: *Adult male*: Wing, 118.0–132.0 (average, 124.8) mm.; tail, 75.0–82.0 (78.2); bill (exposed culmen), 31.0–34.0 (32.8); tarsus, 35.5–39.0 (36.8); middle toe without claw, 24.0–28.0 (26.6). *Adult female*: Wing, 108.0–115.0 (110.7); tail, 62.0–70.0 (65.9); bill, 28.0–30.0 (29.1); tarsus, 34.0–36.0 (35.1); middle toe, 23.0–26.5 (25.0).

RANGE: S.w. and c. British Columbia, south to w. Washington, Oregon, and w. Idaho. Winters from breeding range to Baja California and s. Texas.

TEXAS: *Winter*: Three specimens: San Patricio Co., Welder Wildlife Refuge (Nov. 14, and Dec. 15, 1955, Feb. 6, 1956, C. Cottam; identified by J. W. Aldrich).

YELLOW-HEADED BLACKBIRD, *Xanthocephalus xanthocephalus* (Bonaparte)

SPECIES ACCOUNT

Male: yellow head and chest; black body; white wing-patch. *Female*: brown with buffy throat; dull yellow chest; white streaks on lower breast. Length, 9½ in.; wingspan, 15¾; weight, 2½ oz.

RANGE: C. British Columbia, n.e. Alberta, and c. Saskatchewan to s.w. Great Lakes region, south through w. United States to n.e. Baja California, s.w. and c. Arizona, n. New Mexico, Kansas, and n.e. Missouri; very locally south in highlands to c. Mexico. Winters chiefly from c. California, c. Arizona, s. New Mexico, Texas, and s.w. Louisiana (rarely) to Guerrero, Puebla, and Veracruz.

TEXAS: (See map.) *Breeding*: One definite record: Armstrong Co. (nest located between May 18 and 30, 1876, C. A. H. McCauley). Thought to have bred in Oldham (1899), Mason (1884, 1886), and Culberson (1939) cos. *Migration*: Mid-Apr. to mid-May; mid-July to early Nov. (extremes: Mar. 7, June 24; July 4, Nov. 26). Very common to fairly common in western two-thirds; uncommon to scarce in eastern third, but rare in fall along upper coast. *Winter*: Mid-Dec. to late Mar. Common (some years) to virtually absent in southwestern Trans-Pecos; uncommon to scarce in remainder of southwestern third; increasingly scarce north and east to Lubbock, Hunt Co., and Beaumont.

HAUNTS AND HABITS: The handsome Yellow-headed Blackbird nests in cattail or tule marshes in the arid West. The head of a singing male—as he perches atop a cattail in the nesting colony—resembles a yellow flower, but his voice sounds somewhat like a buzz saw biting into a hard log. During its visits in Texas, this species frequents open farmlands, cow pastures, and livestock pens, where it feeds in flocks, often associated with other blackbirds.

On the wing, Yellowheads may be direct and steady, or they may whirl erratically above a marsh in very close formation. Evening flights to established roosts, which sometimes contain hundreds of birds, add a lively touch to west Texas sunsets.

A considerable portion of the food is gathered from the ground as the bird walks deliberately, often with head held downward. The Yellowhead consumes about two-thirds vegetable and one-third animal matter. It seems to prefer grain (oats, corn, wheat), but also eats many weed seeds (barngrass, ragweed, smartweed, sorrel), especially in winter. Beetles, caterpillars, and grasshoppers (especially in midsummer) comprise the bulk of its animal diet.

Usual call is a hoarse, guttural croak or *chack*. The so-called song is a jumble of harsh, squealing notes that seem to be uttered with great effort and are accompanied by swelling of the bird's body plumage and spreading of its tail.

CHANGES: The Yellow-headed Blackbird offers a noteworthy example of a bird whose nesting habitat has undergone drastic diminution without notably changing the status of the species. This bird's scarce desert and prairie marsh habitat has long been growing scarcer, but so far (to 1972) the Yellowhead has maintained its numbers well.

DETAILED ACCOUNT: NO SUBSPECIES

DESCRIPTION: *Adult male, nuptial plumage*: Acquired by wear from winter plumage. Pileum and hindneck cadmium yellow to orange; remainder of upper surface brownish black, slightly glossy; wings and tail fuscous black, primaries somewhat lighter, primary wing-coverts white, tipped with fuscous or fuscous black, outer greater wing-coverts and inner webs of few adjoining greater coverts white; remainder of wing-coverts like back; lores and narrow area around eye black or chaetura black; remaining sides of head and anterior parts of sides of neck yellow like crown; rest of sides of neck brownish black; chin, throat, jugulum, and upper breast gamboge yellow to cadmium yellow, often ending posteriorly in point on breast, posterior edge of yellow often spotted with black, as are sides and sometimes all of chin; remainder of lower surface, including lining of wing, dull black or chaetura black; anal region more or less extensively dull light yellow to orange. Bill black or bluish black; iris prout brown or hazel; legs and feet black. *Adult male, winter*: Acquired by complete postnuptial molt. Similar to nuptial adult male, but pileum and hindneck flame scarlet to grenadine red, this very much obscured by black tips of feathers; black of upper surface duller, due to dull dark brown edgings of feathers; sides of head and anterior part of neck, together with chin, throat, and jugulum, much more reddish—orange chrome to flame scarlet, paling to orange on posterior edge of this color on breast, the feathers there barred or spotted with dull black; sides of head and neck more or less obscured by black or dull brown tips of feathers; remainder of lower surface with narrow inconspicuous and often obsolete tips of dull brown. *Adult female, nuptial*: Acquired by wear from winter. Entire upper surface, including wings and tail, light clove brown or dark olive brown, wings without white, narrow line across forehead dull buff or ochraceous buff; superciliary stripe yellow ocher to dull ochraceous orange; lores and auriculars olive brown, lores sometimes slightly mixed with grayish white or buffy white, auriculars sometimes narrowly streaked with same; cheeks naples yellow to dull light cadmium, rather irregular

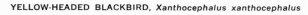

YELLOW-HEADED BLACKBIRD, *Xanthocephalus xanthocephalus*

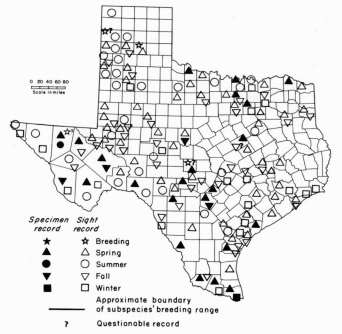

Specimen record	Sight record	
★	☆	Breeding
▲	△	Spring
●	○	Summer
▼	▽	Fall
■	□	Winter

────── Approximate boundary of subspecies' breeding range

? Questionable record

PLATE 30: top: male Summer Tanager, *Piranga rubra*
bottom: male Scarlet Tanager, *Piranga olivacea*, perched on white oak (*Quercus alba*)

broken submalar streak of olive brown sometimes extending backward to join brown of sides of neck; sides of neck olive brown, more or less narrowly streaked with buffy white; chin and center of throat dull pale buff to naples yellow; jugulum naples yellow to dull light cadmium, more or less spotted or streaked with olive brown; remainder of lower surface, including lining of wing, olive brown or light clove brown, rather lighter than upper surface, breast more or less streaked with dull white. Bill dark brown or blackish brown, but mandible paler, particularly at base; iris dark brown; legs and feet dull black. *Adult female, winter*: Acquired by complete postnuptial molt. Similar to nuptial adult female, but duller and darker, feathers of pileum and hindneck tipped with paler brown, feathers of remaining upper surface obscurely margined or tipped with slightly lighter brown, general color of upper surface between dark fuscous and olive brown; sides of head and of neck more extensively yellow, superciliary stripe, auriculars, and cheeks more deeply ochraceous orange; throat and jugulum more deeply yellow or orange, ranging from bright yellow ocher to dark ochraceous orange; breast more broadly streaked with white, feathers of breast, middle of abdomen, and crissum tipped obscurely with dull white or very pale buff; rest of lower parts light olive brown to dark fuscous. *Male, second winter*: Acquired by complete postnuptial molt. Like adult male in winter. *Male, first nuptial*: Acquired by partial prenuptial molt. Similar to nuptial adult female, but upper parts rather darker clove brown; lores and orbital region dull black or chaetura black; sides of head more extensively yellow; forehead and superciliary stripe more broadly yellow; black spot on each side of chin sometimes prolonged into very short malar stripe; chin, throat, and jugulum darker and solid yellow—lemon chrome to cadmium yellow, with occasional patches of orange, but without conspicuous brown streaks or spots, except occasionally at posterior margin. *Male, first winter*: Acquired by partial postjuvenal molt, which does not affect wing-quills or tail. Similar to first nuptial male, but upper surface darker; superciliary stripe, extreme forehead, cheeks, chin, throat, and jugulum much darker and duller, between mars orange and dull flame scarlet; yellow of superciliary stripe and sides of head much less extensive. *Female, first nuptial*: Acquired by partial prenuptial molt. Like nuptial adult female. *Female, first winter*: Acquired by partial postjuvenal molt, which does not involve wing-quills or tail. Similar to adult female in winter, but tips of primaries, secondaries, and tertials paler, more whitish, or light buff, and somewhat broader, more conspicuous; whitish or pale buffy edgings of thighs broader; chin and middle of throat less deeply yellow, usually pale buff or buffy white. *Juvenal*: Acquired by complete postnatal molt. Pileum cinnamon to ochraceous tawny, or dark ochraceous tawny, forehead sometimes paler, pinkish cinnamon to cinnamon; upper surface fuscous, middle of back and tips of feathers more or less broadly pinkish cinnamon to dark ochraceous tawny, dull cinnamon, or cinnamon buff; wings, tail, and back fuscous, tertials tipped with dull cinnamon; longer lesser coverts, median coverts, and broad tips of greater coverts dull white to cinnamon, forming conspicuous wing-bar; sides of head and neck like crown, but sides of head somewhat paler; lores and orbital region chaetura drab, mixed with dull white or pale buff; middle of chin and throat light pinkish buff; jugulum cinnamon to dark ochraceous tawny; much of remainder of lower surface light dull pinkish buff, darker and more or less obscurely spotted with fuscous on sides and flanks, but sides of breast and of abdomen buffy white, and posterior lower parts often more or less obscurely spotted with fuscous. Bill drab gray, whitish at tip; commissure primrose yellow; iris slate black; front of tarsus and toes ecru drab; posterior part of tarsus buff yellow; soles of toes cream color; claws drab, their tips white. *Natal*: Light pinkish buff.

MEASUREMENTS: *Adult male*: Wing, 135.4–145.5 (average, 141.2) mm.; tail, 93.0–108.5 (102.9); bill (from base), 21.4–25.1 (22.9); height of bill at base, 10.7–13.2 (12.2); tarsus, 33.3–37.3 (35.8); middle toe without claw, 23.4–26.2 (24.6). *Adult female*: Wing, 110.0–117.9 (113.8); tail, 78.7–87.6 (82.0); bill (from base), 19.8–21.4 (20.3); height of bill, 9.7–10.7 (10.2); tarsus, 29.7–31.5 (30.5); middle toe, 20.3–22.4 (21.4).

TEXAS: *Breeding*: See species account. *Migration*: Collected north to Wilbarger, east to Red River, south to Cameron, west to El Paso cos. *Winter*: One specimen: Cameron Co., Brownsville (Dec. 22, 1925, C. W. Townsend).

NESTING: *Nest*: In open country, about lakes, along watercourses, in marshes, edges of swamps and sloughs; in cattails, bulrushes, or other tall marsh vegetation, usually in colonies; placed on stalks of grass or reeds, usually over water, ½–3 ft. above surface; rather light structure, much like a basket, bulky, but well made and well cupped with thick walls; composed of grasses, sedges, rushes, weeds, cattails, and reeds; lined with fine grass, fine tules, reeds, rushes, and similar vegetation. *Eggs*: 2–6, usually 4; ovate to short ovate to elliptical ovate; dull grayish white, pale grayish green, bluish gray, or greenish white, with small spots, blotches, dots, and lines of umber, snuff brown, mikado brown, warm sepia, rufous, black, and gray, and with shell markings of drab and pearl gray, rather thickly and evenly distributed over surface; average size, 28.9 × 19.8 mm.

RED-WINGED BLACKBIRD, *Agelaius phoeniceus* (Linnaeus)

SPECIES ACCOUNT

Male: black; red shoulder-patch ("epaulet") tipped with buff or yellow. *Female*: brownish above; heavily blackish- and whitish-streaked below. Length, 8¼ in.; wingspan, 14; weight, 2 oz.

RANGE: Canada and United States, south through Mexico and Central America to Costa Rica; also West Indies. Canadian and U.S. races winter to s. United States and n. Mexico.

TEXAS: (See map.) *Breeding*: Mid-Apr. to late July (eggs, Apr. 17 to July 19) from near sea level to 4,000 ft. Locally common to fairly common in most parts, though uncommon in Trans-Pecos. *Winter*: Late July to late Apr. Locally abundant to common in all parts.

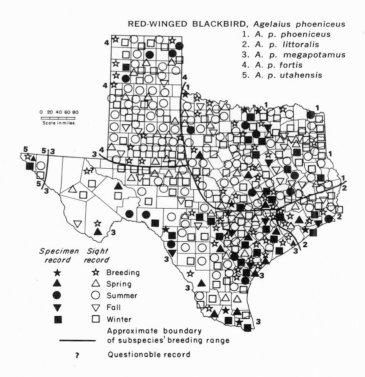

RED-WINGED BLACKBIRD, *Agelaius phoeniceus*
1. *A. p. phoeniceus*
2. *A. p. littoralis*
3. *A. p. megapotamus*
4. *A. p. fortis*
5. *A. p. utahensis*

0 20 40 60 80
Scale in miles

Specimen record / Sight record

★ △ Breeding
▲ △ Spring
● ○ Summer
▼ ▽ Fall
■ □ Winter

——— Approximate boundary of subspecies' breeding range

? Questionable record

HAUNTS AND HABITS: In Texas the Red-winged Blackbird nests in loose colonies in freshwater marshes and floodplains—often in cattails and *Baccharis* bushes. Males are polygynous and avidly defend their territories against intruders of either sex, once bonds are established. During cooler months, however, flocks—sometimes immense—feed in croplands, wet prairies, and pastures, often in association with other blackbirds, cowbirds, and grackles.

The Redwing may travel considerable distance to a favorite roost site; these long flights are steady and direct. Sometimes, members of an enormous flock, as they settle for the night, whirl and turn with fantastic coordination, shifting together with a whirring of wings. During courtship flights, males ascend to considerable height, hover with fluttering wings—their red epaulets ablaze—then dive again into the marsh and disappear.

Foraging parties often advance over a field by the "roller coaster" method. Birds at the rear of the column, presumably having exhausted the food supply there, rise and fly forward to settle in front of the flock; repetition by those in the rear often results in a continuous stream of birds in the air, the flock advancing in this way sometimes for hours. Because of its flocking behavior, this species is potentially destructive to croplands. But F. E. L. Beal has shown that grain constitutes only a small percentage of the total food, and that much of this is waste gleaned after harvest. Though three-quarters of the diet is vegetable, only in July—when the birds are widely dispersed—is the proportion of grain significant. In fall and winter, grass and weed seeds (barngrass, ragweed, pigweed, smartweed, amaranth, sorrel, panicum, joint grass, sunflower, gromwell, plantain, wildrice, and chickweed) furnish a large portion of the diet. During spring and summer, insects—many of them injurious—comprise most of the animal food. Grasshoppers, caterpillars (including armyworm and tent), and beetles (weevils, click, leaf, May, and predaceous) are important prey.

The Redwing's usual call note is a guttural chucking *cack*; the alarm whistle is a long, high-pitched, nasal *peeeah*. Its song is a liquid *o-ka-leee* or *konk-la-ree*, rising in pitch and ending with a trill.

CHANGES: Since rice growing became important on the upper Texas coast beginning in the early years of the twentieth century, winter flocks of Redwings, Brewer's Blackbirds, grackles, and cowbirds have been frequently enormous. Particularly in the 1930's and 1940's, flocks of blackbirds flying over rice fields resembled dark billows of drifting oil smoke. In the 1950's, 1960's, and early 1970's, these flocks appeared smaller, but the Red-winged Blackbird is still an abundant wintertime bird in Texas.

DETAILED ACCOUNT: NINE SUBSPECIES

EASTERN RED-WINGED BLACKBIRD, *Agelaius phoeniceus phoeniceus* (Linnaeus)

DESCRIPTION: *Adult male, nuptial*: Acquired by wear from winter plumage. Upper surface deep black with faint greenish blue gloss and practically immaculate; tail black with slight greenish sheen, inner edges of feathers very slightly brownish, particularly at base; wing-quills brownish black with faint greenish sheen, inner edges of primaries and secondaries fuscous black; lesser wing-coverts scarlet red to scarlet without black streaks or spots; median wing-coverts ochraceous tawny to ochraceous buff; greater wing-coverts glossy black like upper surface; lower surface, including lining of wing, black with same sheen as upper surface, but somewhat duller posteriorly. Bill black or slate black, but mandible black or slate gray; iris hazel, prout brown, vandyke brown, or red; legs and feet black, bluish black, or clove brown. *Adult male, winter*: Acquired by complete postnuptial molt. Similar to nuptial adult male, but feathers of upper surface, particularly hindneck, back, and scapulars, narrowly tipped, also wing-quills, upper tail-coverts, and other parts narrowly tipped or edged with russet, tawny, or dull buff; feathers of posterior lower parts very slightly tipped with dull pale buff or grayish white; red of lesser wing-coverts duller; buff of median wing-coverts darker and duller. Bill dull black, slate black, or brownish black, with mandible somewhat lighter. *Adult female, nuptial*: Acquired by wear from winter. Upper surface fuscous to fuscous black, more or less streaked everywhere with russet to dull buff, buffy brown, and even dull white, this streaking broadest on back and scapulars, on rump taking appearance rather of scalelike markings which are usually mouse gray; tail fuscous black to fuscous, outer edges of feathers very narrowly margined with pale dull buff or buffy white, inner webs narrowly tipped with same; wing-quills and tertials fuscous, very slightly paler on inner margins, primaries and secondaries edged on outer webs with pale buff, tertials with dull cinnamon to buffy white; anterior lesser wing-coverts dull blood red to scarlet, more or less mixed with fuscous black and buffy brown; median wing-coverts dull black, rather broadly tipped with buffy white or very light buff; greater wing-coverts fuscous, very narrowly edged on outer webs and more broadly tipped with buffy white; lores fuscous to dull buff; superciliary stripe light buff, cinnamon pink, to onion-skin pink, anteriorly becoming dull light buff, or even whitish posteriorly; postocular stripe fuscous; short rictal stripe and narrow submalar stripe fuscous or fuscous black; auriculars between drab and buffy brown; stripe below eye and malar stripe, together with chin and upper throat, cinnamon pink to onion-skin pink, occasionally pale colonial buff; sides of neck like hindneck; remainder of lower surface dull white or buffy white, broadly streaked with fuscous or fuscous black, but lower tail-coverts solidly of this color, tipped broadly with buffy white or pale buff; lining of wing fuscous, sometimes with pinkish or reddish wash on outer edge. Bill black, dull black, bluish black, or brownish black, but mandible lighter and more brownish; iris hazel or vandyke brown; legs and feet black, bluish black, or dull black. *Adult female, winter*: Acquired by complete postnuptial molt. Similar to nuptial adult female, but upper surface much more buffy or rufescent brown on account of very broad edgings of feathers, these edgings ranging from buffy white to tawny and chestnut; red on lesser wing-coverts darker and duller; light edgings of wings and tail broader; posterior lower surface much more buffy or ochraceous, this tinge extending over breast; dark streaks of lower surface much less sharply defined owing to paler edgings of feathers, thus, colors below much more blended; sides of head more rufescent. *Male, fourth winter*: Acquired by complete postnuptial molt. Like adult male in winter. *Male, third nuptial*: Acquired by wear from third winter. Similar to nuptial adult male but appreciably smaller, black of upper and lower surfaces duller, more brownish, sometimes with remains of pale edges of previous plumage; red and buff of wing-coverts paler, a little mixed with brownish black, the red more orange. *Male, third winter*: Acquired by complete postnuptial molt. Similar to adult male in winter but differs as third nuptial differs from nuptial adult, and additionally in that edgings of upper parts (including wings) and particularly of lower parts are much broader and more numerous. *Male, second nuptial*: Acquired by wear from second winter. Similar to third nuptial male, but median wing-coverts largely black, and red lesser wing-coverts usually with much black. *Male, second winter*: Acquired by complete postnuptial molt. Similar to third winter male, but median wing-coverts largely black, and red lesser wing-coverts usually much mixed with black; edgings of buff and tawny on upper and lower surfaces somewhat broader. *Male, first nuptial*: Acquired by wear from first winter. Similar to second nuptial male, but median wing-coverts nearly all black, except buff or gray tips, lesser coverts largely, sometimes almost wholly, black with little orange or red. Some individuals are very much like those in third nuptial. *Male, first winter*: Acquired by partial or complete postjuvenal molt. Similar to second winter male, except for wing-coverts, in which it differs as does first nuptial from second nuptial male. Similar to adult male in winter but smaller; entire plumage, except wings and tail, more brownish with less gloss; entire upper surface, together with wings, edged with russet, tawny, dull buff, buffy white, and grayish white; feathers of lower surface edged more or less with grayish white, buffy white, or dull pale buff; median wing-coverts more or less extensively dull black, median and greater coverts tipped with dull buff or buffy white; red of lesser coverts duller—grenadine red to orange chrome—sometimes much mixed with buff and more or less with dull black. *Female, fourth winter*: Acquired by complete postnuptial molt. Like adult female in winter. *Female, third nuptial*: Acquired by wear from third winter. Similar to nuptial adult female, but red on lesser wing-coverts less extensive, more mixed with black or brown and usually duller; chin and throat averaging somewhat less brightly and less deeply salmon or pinkish (more yellowish or buffy). *Female, third winter*: Acquired by complete postnuptial molt. Similar to adult female in winter, but differs on lesser wing-coverts as does third nuptial female from nuptial adult female; throat and chin somewhat less pinkish or salmon colored. *Female, second nuptial*: Acquired by wear from second winter. Similar to third nuptial female, but only with small amount of red on lesser wing-coverts; chin and throat averaging less pinkish or salmon colored (more buffy or yellowish). *Female, second winter*: Acquired by complete postnuptial molt. Similar to third winter female, but differs as second nuptial female does from third nuptial female. *Female, first nuptial*: Acquired by partial prenuptial molt and wear from first winter. Similar to second nuptial female, but without reddish in plumage; chin and throat with very little or no trace of salmon or pink, but dull white, yellow, or pale buff. *Female, first winter*: Acquired by partial or complete postjuvenal molt. Very much like second winter female, but lesser wing-coverts without red; chin and throat with very little or no trace of salmon or pink. Maxilla olive brown or slate color, mandible olive gray; iris dark brown; legs and feet olive brown. *Male, juvenal*: Acquired by complete postnatal molt. Similar to adult female in winter, but upper parts somewhat more blackish with paler, more buffy or whitish edgings, these less russet and more buffy, cream buff, cream color, or ochraceous buff, and also narrower, thus showing much more ground color; bend of wing (lesser wing-coverts) without red; lower surface lighter, usually not so heavily or distinctly streaked, streaks fuscous black or brownish black, and often showing spotted rather than streaked appearance, ground color pinkish buff, ochraceous buff, or mustard yellow. Bill dark olive brown, blackish slate, slate black, or black, but mandible slate black, dull yellowish buff, or blackish slate, paler at base; iris dark brown or light brown; legs and feet slate black, blackish slate, or clove brown. *Female, juvenal*: Acquired by complete postnatal molt. Similar to juvenal male, but upper surface decidedly lighter and more brownish (less blackish); lower surface lighter, usually less heavily streaked, these streaks also not so blackish (more brownish). Bill slate color or slate black, but mandible slate gray; iris blackish brown; legs and feet clove brown. *Natal*: Pale mouse gray, buffy white, drab, or light drab. Bill olive brown or slate color; iris blackish brown; legs and feet olive brown or drab; claws drab.

MEASUREMENTS: *Adult male*: Wing, 114.0–121.9 (average, 118.9) mm.; tail, 84.1–94.0 (90.7); bill (exposed culmen), 21.1–23.1 (21.9); height of bill at base, 10.9–12.4 (11.9); tarsus, 27.9–30.5 (29.2); middle toe without claw, 20.9–22.9 (21.9). *Adult female*: Wing, 97.6–102.1 (99.8); tail, 71.9–

78.0 (75.4); bill, 17.5–19.6 (18.8); height of bill, 9.4–10.9 (10.2); tarsus, 23.9–26.4 (25.4); middle toe, 17.3–19.3 (18.3).

RANGE: C. Ontario to Nova Scotia, south to c. Texas and n. Florida. Winters from e. Nebraska and n. Indiana to s. Texas and c. Florida; casual in n.e. United States and s.e. Canada.

TEXAS: *Breeding*: Altitudinal range, 200 to 1,800 ft. Collected north to Cooke, east to Bowie, south to Travis, west to Haskell cos. Locally common. *Winter*: Taken north to Cooke, east to Angelina, south to Cameron, west to Travis cos. Common.

NESTING: *Nest*: In rather open country, in marshes and meadows, usually along streams or in vicinity of water, also in swamps, and sometimes in grassy upland fields, often in colonies; on or near ground in tuft of grass, reeds, or other vegetation, in bush, or even in tree as high as 40 ft. above ground; bulky, though substantial, basket; composed of strips of grass, rushes, sedges, reeds, weeds, leaves of other plants, or even pieces of string; lined with finer grasses, fine strips of other plants, and occasionally horsehair. *Eggs*: 2–6, usually 4; ordinarily ovate; bluish white, pale bluish green, or even light blue or pale olive buff; spotted, blotched, marbled, lined, and clouded, often almost entirely about larger end, with black, light brown, umber, other shades of dark brown, purplish red, and dark purple; average size, 24.6 × 17.5 mm.

GULF COAST RED-WINGED BLACKBIRD, *Agelaius phoeniceus littoralis* Howell and van Rossem

DESCRIPTION: *Adult male and female, nuptial plumage*: Similar to *A. p. phoeniceus*, but wing and tail shorter; female averaging darker above, streaks on lower parts averaging broader and more deeply blackish. Bill longer and somewhat more slender.

MEASUREMENTS: *Adult male*: Wing, 110.0–118.1 (average, 114.6) mm.; tail, 85.1–93.0 (88.6); bill (exposed culmen), 23.4–26.9 (25.1); height of bill at base, 11.2–13.2 (11.9); tarsus, 27.4–30.2 (28.9); middle toe without claw, 19.3–22.4 (21.1). *Adult female*: Wing, 89.9–98.1 (93.2); tail, 68.1–72.9 (70.4); bill, 19.3–23.1 (21.1); height of bill, 9.9–11.4 (10.7); tarsus, 24.4–26.9 (25.4); middle toe, 16.5–19.0 (18.0).

RANGE: S.e. Texas, east through Gulf states to n.w. Florida. Winters within breeding range and slightly south along Texas coast.

TEXAS: *Breeding*: Altitudinal range, near sea level to 400 ft. Collected north to Walker, east to Jefferson, south to Galveston, west to Waller cos. Common. *Winter*: Taken north to Liberty, east to Jefferson (Mar. 13), southwest to Refugio (Aug. 11) cos. Common.

NESTING: Similar to that of *A. p. phoeniceus*.

RIO GRANDE RED-WINGED BLACKBIRD, *Agelaius phoeniceus megapotamus* Oberholser

DESCRIPTION: *Adult male and female, nuptial plumage*: Resembling *A. p. phoeniceus*, but smaller, except for tarsus and middle toe; bill more slender; female lighter above on both ground color and edgings; lower surface also paler, streaks narrower and lighter, chin more pinkish, less salmon or buff. Similar to *A. p. littoralis*, but bill shorter; female differs in color as from *A. p. phoeniceus*, but even more decidedly.

MEASUREMENTS: *Adult male*: Wing, 112.5–120.1 (average, 115.1) mm.; tail, 82.8–91.9 (86.9); bill (exposed culmen), 20.9–26.7 (23.1); height of bill at base, 9.9–10.9 (10.4); tarsus, 25.9–31.2 (28.9); middle toe without claw, 20.3–22.1 (21.4). *Adult female*: Wing, 88.9–97.6 (94.0); tail, 63.0–72.7 (68.8); bill, 18.5–21.4 (19.6); height of bill, 8.6–10.4 (9.7); tarsus, 24.6–26.2 (25.7); middle toe, 17.0–19.0 (18.0).

RANGE: S. Texas, south to n.e. Coahuila, Nuevo León, and n. Veracruz.

TEXAS: *Breeding*: Altitudinal range, near sea level to 1,600 ft. Collected north to Lee, east to Brazoria, south to Cameron, west to Val Verde cos. Common. *Winter*: Taken north to Lee (Nov. 14), east to Matagorda, south to Cameron, west to Kinney cos.

Common. One specimen from Callahan Co. (Apr. 29, 1926, A. J. Kirn).

NESTING: Similar to that of *A. p. phoeniceus.*

THICK-BILLED RED-WINGED BLACKBIRD, *Agelaius phoeniceus fortis* Ridgway

DESCRIPTION: *Adult male and female, nuptial plumage:* Similar to *A. p. megapotamus,* but wing and tail larger; female pale below as in that race. Bill shorter and stouter.

MEASUREMENTS: *Adult male:* Wing, 121.4–132.1 (average, 127.3) mm.; tail, 88.9–104.9 (95.8); bill (exposed culmen), 22.1–24.9 (23.4); height of bill at base, 11.9–13.0 (12.2); tarsus, 28.4–32.5 (30.7); middle toe without claw, 19.6–22.6 (20.3). *Adult female:* Wing, 98.1–104.9 (102.4); tail, 72.4–79.0 (75.7); bill, 17.5–19.8 (18.4); height of bill, 9.4–10.9 (10.2); tarsus, 23.9–28.4 (26.2); middle toe, 16.5–20.1 (18.3).

RANGE: S.w. South Dakota, south to n.w. Texas and c. Oklahoma. Winters from n. Colorado and n.e. Kansas to s.w. New Mexico and n.w. Louisiana.

TEXAS: *Breeding:* Altitudinal range, 2,300 to 4,000 ft. Collected northeast to Lipscomb and Hemphill, southwest to Deaf Smith cos. Fairly common. *Winter:* Taken north to Oldham, east to Harris (Mar. 15), south to Bee, west to Brewster and El Paso cos. Common.

NESTING: Similar to that of *A. p. phoeniceus.*

GIANT RED-WINGED BLACKBIRD, *Agelaius phoeniceus arctolegus* Oberholser

DESCRIPTION: *Adult male and female, nuptial plumage:* Similar to *A. p. phoeniceus* but larger, particularly wing and bill, latter longer and stouter; male with buff of median wing-coverts somewhat paler; female in autumn on upper surface with more extensive ochraceous edgings, throat usually more pinkish or salmon colored.

MEASUREMENTS: *Adult male:* Wing, 121.4–127.5 (average, 125.2) mm.; tail, 87.9–100.1 (92.5); bill (exposed culmen), 22.9–26.4 (23.9); height of bill at base, 11.4–14.0 (12.7); tarsus, 28.4–32.5 (29.9); middle toe without claw, 19.0–21.6 (20.3). *Adult female:* Wing, 97.1–106.9 (102.6); tail, 71.9–79.0 (75.4); bill, 17.0–20.1 (18.8); height of bill, 8.6–10.9 (10.2); tarsus, 23.9–28.9 (26.2); middle toe, 17.0–18.5 (17.8).

RANGE: British Columbia and s.e. Mackenzie to Manitoba, south to Iowa, Wisconsin, and n.w. Michigan. Winters from s.w. Idaho and n. Michigan to U.S. Gulf coast.

TEXAS: *Winter:* Taken north to Dallas, east to Smith, south to Bee, west to Val Verde cos. Fairly common.

COLORADO RED-WINGED BLACKBIRD, *Agelaius phoeniceus stereus* Oberholser, new subspecies (see Appendix A)

DESCRIPTION: *Adult male and female, nuptial plumage:* Like *A. p. arctolegus,* but wing and tail longer; bill shorter and less stout; male with buffy median wing-coverts darker; female somewhat more brownish (less blackish), in winter with more light edgings on upper surface, these edgings also rather paler; throat paler, usually more buffy, yellowish, or whitish (instead of salmon). Like *A. p. phoeniceus,* but wing and tail very much longer, bill relatively shorter (actually of about same length) and tarsus longer; female lighter (less blackish); in winter, edgings of upper surface more numerous, broader, and lighter; below paler, white streaks broader and dark streaks not so deeply black.

MEASUREMENTS: *Adult male:* Wing, 121.9–132.1 (average, 128.3) mm.; tail, 87.9–104.9 (97.8); bill (exposed culmen), 20.1–23.9 (22.4); height of bill at base, 11.2–12.4 (12.2); tarsus, 28.9–32.0 (30.7); middle toe without claw, 19.0–21.6 (20.1). *Adult female:* Wing, 100.6–107.4 (104.4); tail, 72.9–86.1 (77.5); bill, 17.0–20.1 (18.3); height of bill, 9.9–11.9 (10.7); tarsus, 25.4–28.4 (27.2); middle toe, 16.5–18.5 (17.3).

TYPE: Adult female, no. 206000, U.S. National Museum, Bio-

logical Surveys collection; Barr, Adams Co., Colorado; June 28, 1908; R. B. Rockwell.

RANGE: Montana and North Dakota, south to Wyoming and Colorado. Winters from s. Montana to c. Arizona, n. Chihuahua, and w. and c. Texas.

TEXAS: *Winter:* Taken northwest to El Paso, east to Colorado, south to Atascosa (Mar. 8) cos. Uncommon.

IDAHO RED-WINGED BLACKBIRD, **Agelaius phoeniceus zastereus** Oberholser, new subspecies (see Appendix A)

DESCRIPTION: *Adult male and female, nuptial plumage:* Similar to *A. p. fortis,* but bill decidedly more slender; female in autumn rather darker and duller above; and throat usually more pinkish (not buffy or whitish). Resembling *A. p. nevadensis* (a California race described by A. J. van Rossem in 1926), but wing, tail, and tarsus longer; bill and middle toe shorter; female lighter below, black of posterior portion not so extensive.

MEASUREMENTS: *Adult male:* Wing, 122.5–136.4 (average, 127.8) mm.; tail, 87.9–102.1 (95.0); bill (exposed culmen), 21.1–25.4 (23.4); height of bill at base, 10.4–12.2 (11.4); tarsus, 29.9–33.5 (31.2); middle toe without claw, 19.6–22.6 (20.6). *Adult female:* Wing, 101.1–111.0 (105.1); tail, 71.9–85.6 (76.7); bill, 17.0–20.1 (19.3); height of bill, 9.4–10.9 (9.9); tarsus, 26.4–28.4 (27.7); middle toe, 17.0–18.5 (17.8).

TYPE: Adult female, no. 32316, Cleveland Museum of Natural History; Boise, 2,700 ft., Ada Co., Idaho; Mar. 31, 1932; Pierce Brodkorb, original no., 9655.

RANGE: Idaho and w. Montana. Winters from c. Idaho and s.w. Montana to Utah and Trans-Pecos Texas.

TEXAS: *Winter:* Two specimens: Brewster Co., 4 mi. south of Marathon (Apr. 18, 1935, J. B. Semple).

UTAH RED-WINGED BLACKBIRD, *Agelaius phoeniceus utahensis* Bishop

Race not in A.O.U. check-list, 1957 (see Appendix A).

DESCRIPTION: *Adult male and female, nuptial plumage:* Similar to *A. p. stereus,* but tail decidedly shorter; bill longer and relatively more slender; male in autumn with light edgings of upper surface lighter; female much paler above, including ground color as well as edgings, and edgings more numerous; below paler with white areas increased, dark streaks paler and narrower.

MEASUREMENTS: *Adult male:* Wing, 119.6–131.5 (average, 126.5) mm.; tail, 88.9–99.1 (93.2); bill (exposed culmen), 20.6–24.9 (22.9); height of bill at base, 10.9–12.4 (11.7); tarsus, 27.9–32.5 (29.7); middle toe without claw, 18.0–21.6 (20.3). *Adult female:* Wing, 101.1–106.9 (104.4); tail, 70.1–80.0 (75.4); bill, 17.0–19.6 (18.3); height of bill, 9.7–10.4 (10.2); tarsus, 25.4–27.9 (26.2); middle toe, 17.0–19.6 (18.0).

RANGE: S.e. Idaho, south to Arizona and extreme w. Texas. Winters from c. Utah to c. Sinaloa and Trans-Pecos Texas.

TEXAS: *Breeding:* Altitudinal range, 3,650 to 3,760 ft. Collected in El Paso Co. Uncommon. *Winter:* Taken northwest to El Paso, southeast to Val Verde cos. Uncommon.

NESTING: Similar to that of *A. p. phoeniceus.*

NEW MEXICAN RED-WINGED BLACKBIRD, **Agelaius phoeniceus heterus** Oberholser, new subspecies (see Appendix A)

DESCRIPTION: *Adult male and female, nuptial plumage:* Like *A. p. fortis,* but wing somewhat shorter; bill decidedly shorter and relatively not so slender; male with buffy wing-coverts more deeply colored; female with upper and lower surfaces lighter, more brownish (less blackish); pileum more uniform, lower parts usually rather more narrowly streaked; throat usually pinkish.

MEASUREMENTS: *Adult male:* Wing, 120.9–127.0 (average, 123.7) mm.; tail, 88.9–97.6 (92.7); bill (exposed culmen), 20.6–22.4 (21.6); height of bill at base, 10.9–11.9 (11.7); tarsus, 28.9–31.5 (30.2); middle toe without claw, 19.6–21.1

(20.3). *Adult female*: Wing, 100.6–103.9 (102.4); tail, 71.1–80.0 (74.2); bill, 16.5–19.0 (17.8); height of bill, 8.9–10.4 (9.7); tarsus, 25.9–27.9 (26.9); middle toe, 17.0–18.5 (17.5).

TYPE: Adult female, no. 196857, U.S. National Museum, Biological Surveys collection; Fort Wingate, n.w. New Mexico; June 23, 1905; Ned Hollister, original no., 864.

RANGE: N. Arizona and New Mexico. Winters from breeding range to Trans-Pecos Texas and n. Chihuahua.

TEXAS: *Winter*: Taken northwest to El Paso, southeast to Brewster (Apr. 18) and Val Verde (Apr. 26) cos. Uncommon.

ORCHARD ORIOLE, *Icterus spurius* (Linnaeus)

SPECIES ACCOUNT

Male: black head, back, wings, tail (shows some whitish edgings on wing and tail feathers); deep chestnut rump, under parts. *Female*: olive above; greenish yellow below; whitish wing-bars. *Immature male*: resembles female but has black throat-patch. Length, 6¾ in.; wingspan, 9¾; weight, ¾ oz.

RANGE: S. Manitoba to Massachusetts, south through c. and e. United States to n.e. Mexico, Gulf states, and n. Florida; also south in Mexican highlands to Oaxaca. Winters chiefly from c. Mexico to Colombia and n.w. Venezuela.

TEXAS: (See map.) *Breeding*: Late Apr. to late July (eggs, Apr. 30 to July 21) from near sea level to 5,000 ft. Common to fairly common in most parts; uncommon in middle and southern Panhandle, northern Trans-Pecos, and Rio Grande delta. *Migration*: Early Apr. to early May; early July to mid-Sept. (extremes: Mar. 5, May 21; June 22, Nov. 6). Very common (some years) to fairly common in all parts with exception of western Panhandle, where scarce. *Winter*: Mid-Nov. to Mar. Casual along coast and in Rio Grande Valley

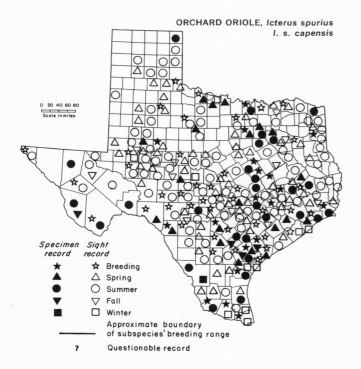

ORCHARD ORIOLE, *Icterus spurius*
I. s. capensis

Specimen record	Sight record	
★	☆	Breeding
▲	△	Spring
●	○	Summer
▼	▽	Fall
■	□	Winter

——— Approximate boundary of subspecies' breeding range

? Questionable record

south of Laredo; inland sight records from Midland and McCulloch Co.

HAUNTS AND HABITS: The Orchard Oriole inhabits rural and suburban country with an abundance of scattered trees. Of native Texas species, it prefers mesquite (*Prosopis glandulosa*), in which it often nests; here it might well be called the "little mesquite oriole." It is not a gregarious species, but small companies may occur during migration.

In the United States the Orchard feeds almost entirely on insects, including cabbageworm and cankerworm and other destructive larvae; moths, mayflies, grasshoppers, beetles, plant lice, flies, ants, and parasitic flies; also a few spiders. In cotton-growing districts it is one of the most useful of all birds in destroying the cotton-boll weevil. On its wintering grounds in Mexico and Central America it is one of the nectar-sipping orioles.

Call notes include a blackbirdlike *cluck* and a chattering, "fussing" call. The male often rises above the treetops, then pours forth a burst of song as he drops again treeward. The song is a variable, somewhat Robin-like series of loud, clear, musical notes, fairly high in pitch and usually ending in a downward-slurred call.

CHANGES: Prior to the 1940's, Orchard Orioles inhabited cultivated orchards, but nowadays these places are heavily dosed with pesticides and herbicides. Even this oriole's favorite native tree is disappearing; by 1968, six million acres of mesquite brushland had been cleared in south Texas alone. Fortunately the Orchard Oriole will use a rather large variety of small, widely spaced trees and the intervening grassy, weedy patches for its singing, nesting, and insect-hunting activities. Population decline has so far been moderate. This sprightly songster still occupies all its Texas range, though nesting has been very infrequent in the Rio Grande delta since the 1950's.

DETAILED ACCOUNT: TWO SUBSPECIES

EASTERN ORCHARD ORIOLE, *Icterus spurius spurius* (Linnaeus)

No races recognized by A.O.U. check-list, 1957 (see Appendix A).

DESCRIPTION: *Adult male, nuptial plumage*: Acquired by wear from winter plumage. Pileum, hindneck, upper back, and scapulars black with slight bluish sheen; remainder of upper surface chestnut; tail pale dull black or brownish black, feathers more brownish on inner edges and outer two or three pairs narrowly tipped with buffy white or pale brown; primaries and secondaries fuscous to dark hair brown, narrowly margined on outer webs with pale pinkish buff, broadly edged on inner webs, except tips of primaries, with dull pinkish buff or light brown; tertials brownish black or fuscous black, edged on outer webs, as are innermost secondaries, with dull pale pinkish buff, innermost tertials tawny or light chestnut; lesser and median wing-coverts chestnut, greater wing-coverts dull black, margined terminally on outer webs with buffy white mixed a little with light chestnut; sides of head and of neck, chin, throat, and upper jugulum black with slight bluish gloss; remainder of lower surface, including lining of wing, chestnut, burnt sienna, or sanford brown, often paler on middle of abdomen. Bill black, bluish black, or slate color, but base of mandible paler, more plumbeous; inside of mouth blackish; tongue white; iris dark brown; legs and feet bluish black or dark plumbeous; claws slate black. *Adult male, winter*: Acquired by complete postnuptial molt. Similar to nuptial adult male, but black of anterior upper surface, chiefly that of back and scapulars, with feathers more or less tipped with pale grayish olive, dull chestnut, or dull buffy gray; feathers of chestnut area of rump and posterior lower surface tipped with olive yellow or yellowish olive. *Adult female, nuptial*: Acquired by wear from winter. Pileum and hindneck yellowish citrine to olive lake; back and scapulars light yellowish olive or somewhat darker, edges of feathers citrine drab or dull citrine, giving feathers of back an obscurely mottled appearance; rump and upper tail-coverts pyrite yellow or sulphine yellow; tail citrine, shaft portion of middle feathers and terminal portions of rest rather light dull brownish olive; wings hair brown, outer margins of quills narrowly light yellowish olive, outer edges of inner secondaries and tertials pale dull yellowish or buffy white, inner margins of primaries and secondaries, except tips of primaries, dull olive buff or light brown, palest on inner secondaries; lesser wing-coverts edged with color of back; median wing-coverts broadly tipped with olive buff, greater coverts tipped on outer webs with same color, but rather lighter, and edged on outer margins with color of back, light tips of median and greater coverts forming two conspicuous wing-bars; lores dull mouse gray, sometimes washed with dull olive green; narrow superciliary stripe and remainder of sides of head and of neck, together with lower parts, olive ocher to wax yellow or between wax yellow and primuline yellow, but flanks yellowish citrine or grayish olive; middle of abdomen and often middle of throat, somewhat paler than rest of lower parts; lining of wing light buff; axillars and edge of wing often yellow. Bill dull plumbeous or brownish slate, mandible lighter; iris dark brown; legs and feet dull brown or slate color. *Adult female, winter*: Acquired by complete postnuptial molt. Similar to nuptial adult female, but upper surface more uniform, somewhat more brownish or greenish (less yellowish or grayish); lower surface duller, more brownish, particularly on jugulum, sides, and flanks. Maxilla and tip of mandible dark brown; base of mandible plumbeous; iris brown; legs and feet plumbeous. *Male, second nuptial*: Acquired by wear from second winter. Similar to nuptial adult male, but primary coverts and outer edges of basal part of secondaries brown instead of black; posterior lower parts usually with more olive yellow mixture, and wing-quills lighter brown. *Male, second winter*: Acquired by complete postnuptial molt. Similar to second nuptial male, but with black of upper parts more or less tipped with pale grayish olive, chestnut, or gray; feathers of chestnut area of rump and posterior lower surface tipped with olive yellow or yellowish olive. *Male, first nuptial*: Acquired by wear from first winter. Similar to nuptial adult female but usually larger; upper surface often with admixture of black feathers; rump and upper tail-coverts sometimes with admixture of chestnut; chin and middle of throat always black, usually solidly; lower surface frequently with greater or lesser admixture of chestnut feathers. *Male, first winter*: Acquired by partial postjuvenal molt, not involving wing-quills or tail. Similar to adult female in winter but larger; upper surface more greenish, yellowish, or brownish; lower parts brighter, more yellowish (less buffy). *Female, first nuptial*: Acquired by wear from first winter. Like nuptial adult female. *Female, first winter*: Acquired by partial postjuvenal molt. Similar to adult female in winter, but averaging somewhat more brownish above and somewhat more brightly yellow below. Similar to first winter male but smaller; upper surface averaging duller; lower surface usually paler, duller, rather less brightly yellowish. *Juvenal*: Acquired by complete postnatal molt. Pileum light orange citrine; back and scapulars dull orange citrine; rump and upper tail-coverts similar to pileum but somewhat lighter; wings and tail in general like first winter female, but lesser wing-coverts dull citrine, greater and median series broadly tipped with dull cinnamon buff or dull chamois, forming two conspicuous wing-bars; tertials broadly tipped and margined on outer webs with light isabella color; sides of head similar to crown, but auriculars and cheeks more or less mixed or washed with primuline yellow;

lores dull gray, washed with yellow; lower surface primuline yellow, duller and lighter posteriorly; sides and flanks olive ocher. Bill dull brown, maxilla slaty; iris dark brown; legs and feet dark wood brown or dull black. *Natal* (this plumage of this race not seen in Texas): Between pale drab gray and tilleul buff. Bill pinkish; legs and feet olive gray.

MEASUREMENTS: *Adult male*: Wing, 75.9–82.6 (average, 79.7) mm.; tail, 69.6–74.9 (71.4); bill (exposed culmen), 15.5–17.3 (16.3); height of bill at base, 6.9–7.9 (7.4); tarsus, 21.6–23.1 (22.4); middle toe without claw, 13.0–14.5 (13.7). *Adult female*: Wing, 73.4–78.0 (75.7); tail, 67.1–71.9 (68.8); bill, 15.0–17.0 (16.3); height of bill, 6.6–7.1 (6.9); tarsus, 21.1–23.6 (22.4); middle toe, 12.7–15.0 (13.7).

RANGE: W. Wisconsin to e. Massachusetts, south to Louisiana and n. Florida. Winters from Chiapas and Yucatán through Central America to n.w. Venezuela.

TEXAS: *Migration*: Collected north to Menard, east to Calhoun, south to Cameron, west to Kinney cos. Rare.

NESTING: (This race does not nest in Texas.) *Nest*: In semi-open country, rarely in dense forests; in trees or bushes, seldom coniferous, 5–40 ft., though usually 10–20 ft., above ground; small, partially pensile basket, in upright crotch often resting against twigs, or attached at rim and also usually at sides; composed of green grass, which becomes yellowish in drying, or of other grasses or Spanishmoss; lined with fine grasses, vegetable down, catkins, cotton, animal wool, bits of yarn, and feathers, sometimes not lined. *Eggs*: 3–7, usually 5; mostly ovate, sometimes elliptical oval; pale bluish white or grayish white, with spots, dots, irregular lines, and sometimes blotches of dark purplish brown and various other shades of brown, black, and gray, and with shell markings of pale purple, lilac, and lavender, most near large end; average size, 20.6 × 14.5 mm.

TEXAS ORCHARD ORIOLE, *Icterus spurius capensis* (Gmelin)

No races recognized by A.O.U. check-list, 1957 (see Appendix A).

DESCRIPTION: *Adult male and female, nuptial plumage*: Similar to *I. s. spurius* but smaller; female paler above, back more grayish brown (less olive green); and lower surface averaging somewhat lighter. *Natal*: Probably similar to that of *I. s. spurius*.

MEASUREMENTS: *Adult male*: Wing, 74.9–79.0 (average, 76.2) mm.; tail, 64.0–70.6 (68.3); bill (exposed culmen), 14.0–16.0 (15.2); height of bill at base, 6.4–7.4 (6.9); tarsus, 20.1–23.1 (21.9); middle toe without claw, 13.0–14.5 (13.7). *Adult female*: Wing, 69.6–72.9 (70.9); tail, 63.5–67.1 (65.3); bill, 14.0–15.5 (14.7); height of bill, 6.4–7.1 (6.9); tarsus, 20.1–22.6 (21.4); middle toe, 11.9–14.5 (13.2).

RANGE: S. Manitoba, south through c. United States to n.e. Mexico; also south through highland Mexico to Oaxaca. Winters from Colima and Puebla through s. Mexico and Central America to n.w. Colombia and n.w. Venezuela; casually in s. Texas.

TEXAS: *Breeding*: Collected north to Lipscomb, east to Bowie and Jefferson, south to Cameron, west to Presidio and Culberson cos. *Winter*: Two specimens: Webb Co., Laredo (Feb. 24, 1932, C. C. Sperry).

NESTING: Similar to that of *I. s. spurius*, but average egg size, 19.6 × 14.2 mm.

FUERTES' ORIOLE, *Icterus fuertesi* Chapman

SPECIES ACCOUNT

Also known as Ochre Oriole; considered a race of Orchard Oriole by some authors. *Male*: black on head, back, wings, and tail (shows some whitish edgings on wing and tail feathers); buff or ochraceous rump, patch at bend of wing, lower breast, belly, and under tail-coverts. *Female and immature*: dull olive gray above; blackish gray wings with two white wing-bars; mostly dull buffy yellow below. *First year male:* similar to female but with black throat-patch. Length, 6¼ in.

RANGE: Lowlands of s. Tamaulipas, e. San Luis Potosí, and Veracruz. In winter recorded from Guerrero (Feb. and Sept.).

TEXAS: *Accidental:* One specimen, first record for United States: Cameron Co., Brownsville (adult male collected, Apr. 3, 1894, F. B. Armstrong; Museum of Comparative Zoology collection, no. 258513). The skin, mislabeled *Icterus spurius,* was correctly identified by R. W. Dickerman (1964, *Auk* 81: 433).

Frank B. Armstrong's localities have been doubted by numerous ornithologists, but according to investigations of H. C. Oberholser, Armstrong collected only on the Texas side of the Rio Grande until 1895 or later. His Brownsville *Icterus fuertesi* is dated Apr. 3, 1894. Furthermore, the Fuertes' Oriole is strongly migratory, and it would be relatively easy, at least in theory, for an individual in spring to overshoot its southern Tamaulipas breeding grounds.

HAUNTS AND HABITS: The Fuertes' Oriole was named by ornithologist Frank M. Chapman for the bird artist Louis Agassiz Fuertes, who, at dawning of the twentieth century, painted the bird pictures reproduced in this book. Together, the two friends discovered the species in second-growth shrubbery on the south bank of the Río Tamesí, thirty-five miles northwest of Tampico, Tamaulipas, east coast of Mexico. Since that April 6, 1910, this tiny oriole has been a subject of controversy, even mystery. Is it a species apart from the Orchard Oriole, *Icterus spurius?* Has it really occurred in the United States? How is it able to survive in the deadly modern world? What are its migration routes?

Icterus fuertesi is one of several birds that are endemic as nesters within the Tamaulipan Biotic Province. Prior to widespread deforestation, the species was probably restricted to the narrow belt of coastal vegetation growing on and near dunes that fringe the Gulf of Mexico. Here, birds usually nest in dense clumps of majagua (*Hibiscus tiliaceus*) and mango negro (*Conocarpus erecta*). However, in striking contrast to most endemics—many of which are dying all over the world along with the indigenous plants on which they depend —the Fuertes' Oriole promptly moves into second-growth shrubs and imported ornamental trees. Thus, from July 11 to 13, 1970, at Ciudad Mante, Tamaulipas (elevation, 280 ft.), in midday tropical sunshine, male Fuertes' Orioles were seen vigorously singing from perches on wires and in trees. Males frequently sang from high in largely bare flamboyants (*Delonix regia*), an import from Madagascar, that lined canals between Mante and its water source, the *nacimiento*. The almost warbler-sized orioles appeared minute amid the giant (2 ft. long) seed pods of the flamboyant trees. Landscape here has, since the 1950's, been sprayed with potent agricultural pesticides; egg-eating Great-tailed Grackles and parasitic Red-eyed Bronzed Cowbirds abound. It is a mystery how *Icterus fuertesi* is able to maintain a viable population in the face of the same adverse factors that seem, since 1960, to have virtually wiped out *I. spurius* as a breeder in the Rio Grande delta. The smallest New World oriole appears to be one of the toughest.

Fuertes' Orioles are fast fliers—they must be to escape Great-tailed Grackles which seem to regard them as possible food morsels. They also have to be strong on the wing for their considerable migrations. The species has been found in the cool season at Chilpancingo, Guerrero (4,600 ft.). Since 280 feet appears to be its maximum summer elevation, *I. fuertesi* winters, at least occasionally, higher than it breeds. It is unusual for a tropical bird to be strongly migratory and most extraordinary for it to winter in a temperate climate. Migration routes are unknown, but the shortest distance between the summer range and Guerrero is via Mexico City (7,370 ft.), where the altitude and smog are hard on most lowlanders. Apparently little is known of the specific diet of the Fuertes' Oriole. However, Jean and Richard Graber (1954, *Condor* 56: 274–282) in their studies of the species in the coastal dunes of Tamaulipas noted that adults feeding young "almost always flew to the low vegetation of the dunes to catch insects." They also saw at least one pair "flutter before the large, yellow, bell-shaped flowers of *Hibiscus* only a few feet from their nest and probe repeatedly." These birds were probably gleaning both insects and nectar.

Most who hear vocalizations of the Fuertes' Oriole compare them to those of the Orchard Oriole. F. M. Chapman in the article accompanying his original description of *I. fuertesi* wrote that the song ". . . while unmistakably of the Orchard Oriole type, differs materially from the song of that species. It is less rich and loud, and lacks a certain distinctiveness of articulation and finish which characterize the song of *Icterus spurius.*"

CHANGES: In 1910, breeding ranges of *I. fuertesi* and *I. spurius* were separated by a gap in Tamaulipas of approximately 250 miles. By the 1960's the separation was closer to 300 miles and growing wider. The Orchard Oriole is retreating northward as a nester. Those who lust to find interbreeding between the two birds had better hurry.

DETAILED ACCOUNT: NO SUBSPECIES

NOTE: Following description and measurements are taken from the original description of *Icterus fuertesi* by Frank M. Chapman (1911, *Auk* 28: 1–4).

CHARACTERISTICS OF SPECIES: Most nearly related to *I. spurius,* but smaller with chestnut areas of that species replaced by a color which varies from buff to ochraceous. *Type:* American Museum Nat. History collection, no. 95909; Paso del Haba, south shore of Río Tamesí, 35 mi. northwest of Tampico, Mexico, Apr. 6, 1910; collected and presented by L. A. Fuertes.

DESCRIPTION: *Adult male:* Head, throat, center of chest, foreback, and scapulars black, the two latter slightly edged with grayish brown; rest of body, including upper and under tail-coverts, rich buff with a slight yellowish cast, particularly medially on under parts (color here is much like buffy tips to fall plumage of adult males of *I. spurius*), and with a cinnamon shade on rump; wings black, edged externally with whitish, lesser, median, and under wing-coverts cinnamon buff, greater wing-coverts black, bordered terminally with white; tail black, the outer feathers graduated and narrowly tipped with whitish. *Adult female*: Similar in color to corresponding plumage of *I. spurius*, but size smaller. *Immature male*: Similar in color to corresponding plumage of *I. spurius* but smaller.

MEASUREMENTS: *Adult male*: Wing, 71 mm.; tail, 64; bill (exposed culmen), 15. *Adult female*: Wing, 68; tail, 63.5; bill, 14.5 (no. 95908, Río Tamesí, Mexico, Apr. 7, 1910, F. M. C.). *Immature male*: Wing, 72; tail, 65.5; bill, 15 (no. 95907, Río Tamesí, Mexico, Apr. 7, 1910, F. M. C.).

TEXAS: *Accidental*: One specimen (see species account).

BLACK-HEADED ORIOLE, *Icterus graduacaudus* Lesson

SPECIES ACCOUNT

Icterus graduacauda of A.O.U. check-list, 1957. Audubon's Oriole of older authors. *Male*: yellow body, tinged with greenish on back; black head, wings, tail (shows some whitish edgings on wing feathers). *Female*: slightly duller. Length, 9½ in.; wingspan, 12½.

RANGE: Jalisco and s. Texas, south at low and moderate elevations to n.w. Guatemala.

TEXAS: (See map.) *Resident* (individuals or pairs may wander): Breeds, late Mar. to mid-July, occasionally to mid-Sept. (eggs, Apr. 6 to June 28) from near sea level to 450 ft. Locally fairly common (some years) to scarce from Laredo, Live Oak Co., and Beeville, south to the Rio Grande. Breeding recorded in Val Verde Co., Del Rio (2 nests with eggs, 1 with young, June 28, 1941, T. C. Meitzen). Sometimes drifts north after breeding, infrequently as far as Eagle Pass, San Antonio, and Bastrop.

HAUNTS AND HABITS: In Texas the curious slow "boy-

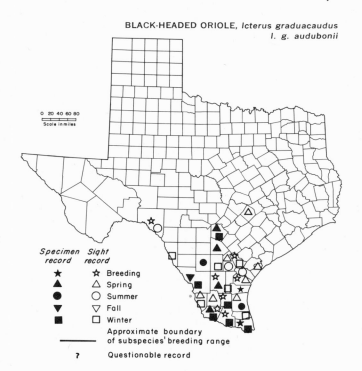

BLACK-HEADED ORIOLE, *Icterus graduacaudus I. g. audubonii*

0 20 40 60 80
Scale in miles

Specimen Sight
record record

★ ☆ Breeding
▲ △ Spring
● ○ Summer
▼ ▽ Fall
■ □ Winter

——— Approximate boundary of subspecies' breeding range

? Questionable record

like" whistled song of the Black-headed Oriole issues usually from mesquite woods in warm months and from evergreen trees—live oak (*Quercus virginiana*), huisache (*Acacia farnesiana*), and Texas ebony (*Pithecellobium flexicaule*)—in winter. From fall through December it often forages in willows (*Salix*) and hackberries (*Celtis*), provided these still retain leaves. In short, this oriole, like the Green Jay, spends much of its time hiding behind thick cover of leaves; both species tend to choose the tallest and densest trees in the landscape. The Black-headed Oriole is able to inhabit somewhat lower brush than does the Green Jay; apparently this is why it is rather more likely to be found north of the Rio Grande delta. It seems to be a rather sedentary bird and is frequently found in pairs throughout the year.

Flight is strong but seldom much prolonged. Birds forage quietly in trees and bushes, taking mostly insects (beetles, moths, others), but also some small fruits, such as hackberries and mesquite beans.

The Black-headed Oriole's song is a series of low, mellow whistled notes of a human quality, slow and disjointed, and with half-tones. Singing occurs in all seasons but is very much reduced in cold weather. The species sounds an *ike, ike, ike* note that resembles the Altamira Oriole's but is much higher pitched.

CHANGES: Beginning in the 1920's, the mesquite and ebony woodlands of the Rio Grande delta have been increasingly cleared to make room for citrus, cotton, grain, vegetables, and livestock. This clearing greatly reduced the habitat of all woodland birds. Furthermore, the opening up of the country and introduction of cattle increased the cowbird population. Black-headed Orioles are frequent victims of cowbirds, especially of the Red-eyed Bronzed form. *Icterus graduacaudus* still occupies most of its old range in the United States (meaning south Texas), but its density since the 1920's has been low. By the 1960's, its population was so thin that an Audubon Christmas Bird Count of four individuals in any locality was usually sufficient to ensure a high count for the nation.

DETAILED ACCOUNT: ONE SUBSPECIES

AUDUBON'S BLACK-HEADED ORIOLE, *Icterus graduacaudus audubonii* Giraud

DESCRIPTION: *Adult male, nuptial plumage*: Acquired by wear from winter plumage. Pileum and anterior hindneck somewhat glossy black; posterior part of hindneck gamboge yellow, shading gradually into greenish analine yellow of back and scapulars, and becoming dull gamboge yellow on rump and upper tail-coverts, there often washed with olive green; tail dull black to brownish black, very slightly glossy, outer two pairs of feathers more or less tipped, usually narrowly, and mostly on outer web, with mouse gray; primaries and secondaries dark chaetura gray, margined on outer webs, except tips, with black, and middle portion of primaries and terminal portion of secondaries narrowly margined with dull white; tertials black or brownish black, broadly margined on outer webs with white or yellowish white; lesser and median wing-coverts naples yellow to straw yellow; remainder of wing-coverts black, greater series tipped on outer webs with straw yellow, yellowish white, or white; sides of head, chin, throat, and jugulum glossy black, posterior rounded edge of this color on jugulum streaked with yellow of under surface; remainder of lower surface lemon chrome to light cadmium; lining of wing lemon chrome. Bill black or plumbeous black, but base of mandible plumbeous; iris brown; legs and feet plumbeous or dull black. *Adult male, winter*: Acquired by complete postnuptial molt. Similar to nuptial adult male but somewhat duller above, black feathers of hindneck and occiput tipped with dull orange or yellowish citrine. *Adult female, nuptial*: Acquired by wear from winter. Similar to nuptial adult male but smaller; upper parts duller, more uniform, back, scapulars, rump, and upper tail-coverts bright yellowish warbler green; tail duller, more brownish (fuscous black to fuscous), most feathers narrowly tipped with mouse gray, outermost pair and sometimes next two, margined on middle portions of outer webs with yellowish olive green, mouse gray, or grayish white, outermost feather with terminal oblong spot of dull citrine on inner web and of dull mouse gray on outer web, this showing sometimes to some extent on next pair of feathers; lower surface averaging rather paler—gamboge yellow—and more greenish (less golden yellow); edge of wing olive buff to pale colonial buff. *Adult female, winter*: Acquired by complete postnuptial molt. Similar to nuptial adult female, but upper parts rather duller, black feathers of occiput more or less tipped with dark brown, giving pileum more brownish cast. *Male, first nuptial*: Acquired by partial prenuptial molt. Similar to nuptial adult female but larger; long spot on inner web of outermost tail feather usually lighter and more yellowish; lesser wing-coverts duller, more greenish yellow; edgings at tips of outer webs of greater coverts longer, giving appearance of broader wing-bar; primary coverts fuscous or olive brown, instead of black; primaries and secondaries lighter, more brownish (hair brown or dark hair brown). Similar to nuptial adult male, but in color differing as from adult female, and additionally in more brownish tail, and duller, more greenish (less clearly yellow) back and posterior upper parts. *Male, first winter*: Acquired by partial postjuvenal molt, which does not involve wing-quills or tail. Similar to first nuptial male, but primaries and secondaries somewhat lighter, more brownish; tail light clove brown or olive brown, outermost pair of feathers and outer webs of next three pairs, together with terminal portions, dull yellowish old gold, terminal portion of two middle feathers somewhat washed with this color, and narrowly margined on external webs basally with yellowish white; yellow of lower surface lighter and more greenish (less golden). *Female, first nuptial*: Acquired by partial prenuptial molt. Similar to nuptial adult female,· but wing-quills and tail feathers usually duller, somewhat more brownish. *Female, first winter*: Acquired by partial postjuvenal molt, which does not involve wing-quills or tail. Similar to adult female in winter, but upper surface much duller, more grayish, and much tinged with neutral gray or mouse gray, because of broad edgings of feathers; tail more grayish or brownish, middle pairs of feathers margined on outer webs with mouse gray; lesser wing-coverts duller yellow; light margins of outer webs of greater coverts duller, less yellowish (more grayish); wing-quills lighter, more brownish; primary coverts olive brown or light fuscous instead of black; yellow of lower surface duller and lighter, more greenish (less golden). Similar to first winter male, but smaller; upper surface still duller, more grayish or greenish (less yellowish); outer feathers of tail duller olive lake or buffy citrine, thus more brownish or greenish. *Juvenal*: Acquired by complete postnatal molt. Upper surface yellowish warbler green or dull orange citrine, without black on head, hindneck and upper tail-coverts somewhat lighter, more yellowish; wings and tail similar to first winter female, fuscous to light fuscous, outer tail feathers citrine to buffy citrine; lower surface uniform dull lemon yellow, without black on anterior parts; sides and flanks washed with olive gray. *Natal*: Unknown.

MEASUREMENTS: *Adult male*: Wing, 96.3–102.4 (average, 100.8) mm.; tail, 102.9–106.1 (104.6); bill (from base), 25.7–28.2 (26.2); height of bill at base, 10.7–11.2 (10.9); tarsus, 26.7–27.7 (27.2); middle toe without claw, 17.5–19.8 (18.5). *Adult female*: Wing, 94.0–98.1 (96.0); tail, 99.8–105.6 (102.9); bill (from base), 21.9–26.2 (24.6); height of bill, 9.7–10.7

(10.2); tarsus, 24.6–27.2 (26.7); middle toe, 17.5–19.3 (18.5).

RANGE: S. Texas, south to Nuevo León, s.e. San Luis Potosí, and s.e. Tamaulipas.

TEXAS: *Resident* (largely): Collected north to Bexar (nonbreeder), east to Nueces (eggs), south to Cameron, west to Webb and La Salle cos.

NESTING: *Nest*: In lowlands; in woods along streams, or in open woods or thickets; in tree or bush, 6–14 ft. above ground; small, partly pensile basket; similar to that of Orchard Oriole, and attached to upright terminal branches; composed of dry grass, sometimes of Spanishmoss, in which it is placed; lined with finer grass and grass tops. *Eggs*: 3–5; ovate to elliptical ovate; without gloss; pale bluish or grayish white, with spots, splashes, and irregular lines of chestnut brown, dull purple, or black, and lilac or lavender shell markings, principally at larger end; average size, 24.9 × 18.0 mm.

HOODED ORIOLE, *Icterus cucullatus* Swainson

SPECIES ACCOUNT

Male: orange (or yellow) head, nape, rump, under parts; black throat, back, wings, tail; two white wingbars. *Female*: brownish olive above; dull yellow below; whitish wing-bars. Length, 8 in.; wingspan, 10½.

RANGE: C. California to s.w. Texas, south to s. Mexico and n. British Honduras. Winters mainly in Mexico.

TEXAS: (See map.) *Breeding*: Late Mar. to mid-Aug. (eggs, Apr. 3 to Aug. 9) from near sea level to 1,900 ft., probably higher. Locally common (some years) to fairly common along Rio Grande (usually within 80 mi. of river) from Big Bend to western Starr Co.; scarce (formerly very common) in Rio Grande delta; uncommon to scarce on lower coast, though fairly common on King Ranch (fide B. A. Fall); occasional north to Corpus Christi; probably breeds irregularly

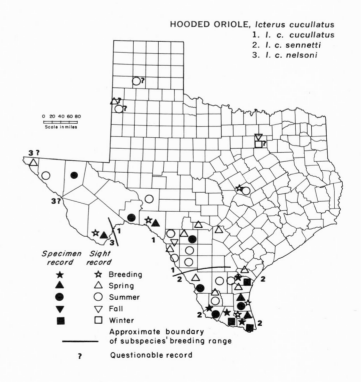

HOODED ORIOLE, *Icterus cucullatus*
1. *I. c. cucullatus*
2. *I. c. sennetti*
3. *I. c. nelsoni*

Specimen record / Sight record

★ / ☆ Breeding
▲ / △ Spring
● / ○ Summer
▼ / ▽ Fall
■ / □ Winter

——— Approximate boundary of subspecies' breeding range

? Questionable record

along Rio Grande in El Paso and Hudspeth cos. One specimen from Culberson Co. presumably represents northward extension of range: Frijole, 5,500 ft. (singing male of a pair of adults, testis 10 mm., June 14, 1972, G. A. Newman; original no., 289). Accidental in Bell Co. (pair feeding nestlings, June 8–9, 1961, Velma Geiselbrecht). *Winter*: Early Oct. to mid-Mar. Scarce to casual in Rio Grande delta. One specimen from Nueces Co. (see detailed account); one sighting in Dallas Co. (Oct. 3, 1956, Hazel Nichols, et al.).

HAUNTS AND HABITS: Before 1951 the then numerous Hooded Oriole sang and displayed in both town and country in the Rio Grande delta. Within built-up areas, ornamental palms of the genera *Washingtonia* and *Sabal* were favorite nest trees; countryside patches of Texas ebony and mesquite brush likewise supported a high population of this oriole. North of the delta, *Icterus cucullatus* was, and is, closely restricted to towns. Here it nests in palm and pecan (*Carya illinoensis*) trees. Mesquites on the surrounding ranches it leaves to Orchard and Bullock's orioles.

The Hooded ordinarily occurs singly, in pairs, or in small family parties. Flight is quick and direct, performed with powerful though not rapid wing-beats. This oriole gleans food from trees and shrubs with deliberate motions and is active throughout the day. It feeds mostly on caterpillars and grasshoppers and various other insects and larvae, together with spiders. It also consumes some nectar and wild fruit.

CHANGES: The disastrous freeze of January 29–February 1, 1951, appears to be the event which indirectly caused the collapse of the Hooded Oriole from very common (up to 100 per half-day in prefreeze days) to scarce in the Rio Grande delta. This cold wave killed so many orange and grapefruit trees that it brought about a switch from citrus to cotton and cattle as the dominant agricultural pursuits. The rise of King Cotton and his many pests greatly increased the tonnage of DDT, herbicides, and defoliants dumped onto the lands along the lower Rio Grande. C. E. Hudson, Jr., a resident (near San Benito) farmer and bird watcher, repeatedly observed Hooded Orioles feeding at the edge of highly poisoned cotton fields in the 1950's.

A substantial number of citrus groves were replaced by cattle feed lots, sorghum fields, and improved pastures. The increase of cattle, cow food, and treeless areas favors the Red-eyed Bronzed Cowbird, which species very frequently imposes its eggs upon the delicate Hooded Oriole. In short, *Icterus cucullatus* found its insect food poisoned, and the few relatively unpolluted patches of habitat heavily infested with Bronzed Cowbirds. It is of note that upriver from the delta, especially in the town of Del Rio where there is little spraying and a scarcity of Bronzed Cowbirds, the Hooded Oriole was still nesting in 1967. Of further interest is the Hooded Oriole population on the relatively unpoisoned but cowbird-infested King Ranch; during May and June of 1969, B. A. Fall recorded daily totals of up to fifteen birds.

DETAILED ACCOUNT: THREE SUBSPECIES

MEXICAN HOODED ORIOLE, *Icterus cucullatus cucullatus* Swainson

DESCRIPTION: *Adult male, nuptial plumage*: Acquired by wear from winter plumage. Forehead, lores, and eye-ring black; rest of pileum and hindneck cadmium orange to orange chrome; back and scapulars slightly glossy black; rump and upper tail-coverts orange to cadmium orange; base of tail under upper tail-coverts lemon chrome to yellowish white; tail brownish black, outer two pairs of tail feathers narrowly tipped with light drab to brownish white; primaries and secondaries chaetura drab to light chaetura drab, darkest on outer webs, inner edges of secondaries and basal part of primaries dull drab gray, outer margins of outer webs darker, more blackish, outer primaries, except outermost, narrowly edged on middle portion with yellowish or buffy white; tertials black, these and innermost secondaries conspicuously margined on outer webs with yellowish or buffy white; lesser and greater wing-coverts black; median wing-coverts and bases of greater coverts white, forming conspicuous white or yellowish white bar on wing; greater coverts margined at tips on outer webs with dull white or yellowish white; cheeks, chin, middle of throat and of jugulum somewhat glossy black; sides of head behind eyes, sides of neck, together with remainder of lower surface, deep orange chrome to cadmium yellow, somewhat paler and less orange posteriorly; lining of wing gamboge yellow. Bill black or bluish black, but base of mandible pale bluish gray or bluish white; legs and feet dark plumbeous. *Adult male, winter*: Acquired by complete postnuptial molt. Similar to nuptial adult male, but upper surface duller, pileum, hindneck, and rump somewhat washed with olivaceous; black feathers of back broadly tipped with citrine, dull light citrine drab, or light grayish olive; tertials more broadly edged with dull white or very pale yellow; yellow of lower parts duller. *Adult female, nuptial*: Acquired by wear from winter. Upper surface between light brownish olive and citrine drab, but rump lighter, centers of feathers darker; forehead and upper tail-coverts rich analine yellow to dull cadmium yellow; remainder of pileum and hindneck more or less tinged with this color; tail orange citrine to medal bronze, middle feathers darkest, and most of feathers edged on outer webs narrowly with analine yellow; wing-quills rather dark hair brown, inner margins of primaries and secondaries, except tips of primaries, pale brown or avellaneous to tilleul buff; outer margins of primaries, secondaries, and tertials brownish white or dull light drab, broadest on tertials; lesser wing-coverts edged with dull brown—between hair brown and deep grayish olive; median wing-coverts broadly tipped with brownish white; greater wing-coverts narrowly edged with drab and narrowly tipped with brownish white; lores dull mouse gray; superciliary stripe dull cadmium yellow; sides of head and of anterior part of neck, and most of lower parts dull light cadmium or dull cadmium yellow, sides of head and neck more or less washed with grayish olive, and much duller than lower surface; jugulum darkest; abdomen dull pale buff, more or less washed with yellow, its middle palest; crissum like jugulum; sides and flanks washed with grayish olive; lining of wing dull light drab, edge of wing primuline yellow. Base of mandible bluish gray. *Adult female, winter*: Acquired by complete postnuptial molt. Similar to nuptial adult female, but upper surface duller and darker, colors more blended and more washed with dull gray, light edgings of tertials broader; lower surface more clouded with gray on tips of feathers; sides and flanks duller, more extensively gray. *Male, first nuptial*: Acquired by partial prenuptial molt. Similar to nuptial adult female but larger; yellow of upper surface brighter; tail fuscous black, outer two or three pairs of feathers more or less mottled or broadly tipped, chiefly on inner webs, with citrine or yellowish citrine; lesser, median, and greater coverts darker, but with same brown primary coverts as compared to black primary coverts of adult male; yellow of lower parts darker, often brighter; lores, anterior part of cheeks, chin, middle of throat and of jugulum black, sometimes mixed with yellow on posterior margin of jugulum. *Male, first winter*: Acquired by partial postjuvenal molt, which does not involve wing-quills or tail. Similar to first nuptial male, but sides and flanks darker. *Female, first nuptial*: Acquired by partial prenuptial molt. Similar to nuptial adult male but paler above, yellow of pileum, hindneck, and rump paler, less orange hue; yellow of sides of head and of neck, together with lower parts, paler, more greenish (less orange)—light gamboge yellow. *Female, first winter*: Acquired by partial postjuvenal molt, which does not concern wing-quills or tail. Similar to first nuptial female, but upper surface darker and duller, colors more blended because of broad olive gray edgings of feathers; light margins of tertials broader; lower surface darker and duller, feathers much tipped with dull light gray, particularly on jugulum; sides and flanks darker. *Juvenal*: Acquired by complete postnatal molt. Similar to first winter female, but bill shorter; upper surface paler and more brownish; edgings of wing-quills and coverts light dull buff; yellow of lower surface lighter and duller. *Natal*: Tilleul buff.

MEASUREMENTS: *Adult male*: Wing, 83.3–86.4 (average, 84.8) mm.; tail, 89.7–98.1 (94.0); bill (from base), 19.8–20.9 (20.3); height of bill at base, 7.9–9.1 (8.6); tarsus, 21.9–23.6 (22.9); middle toe without claw, 15.5–16.8 (16.0). *Adult female*: Wing, 80.2–81.5 (81.0); tail, 85.9–90.2 (87.4); bill (from base), (19.8); height of bill, 7.4–7.9 (7.6); tarsus, 22.4–23.4 (22.9); middle toe, 15.2–15.7 (15.5).

RANGE: Texas-Mexico border (chiefly Del Rio region), south through aridlands to c. Coahuila, s. Tamaulipas, s. San Luis Potosí, and c. Veracruz. Winters from Jalisco to Guerrero, State of México, and c. Veracruz.

TEXAS: *Breeding*: Altitudinal range, ca. 700 to ca. 1,300 ft. Specimens: Terrell Co., Hicks Ranch (adult male, testes enlarged, 8.2 mm., July 7, 1949, W. A. Thornton, no. 335; identified by G. M. Sutton, no. 420 in Texas Natural History collection, University of Texas at Austin); Val Verde Co., mouth of Pecos River (Apr. 25, 1939, T. D. Burleigh). Sight record: Val Verde Co., Del Rio (4 individuals, adults carrying food and feeding young, July 30, 1967, J. L. Rowlett). Locally fairly common. One specimen apparently outside breeding range: Brewster Co., 13 mi. south of Marathon (Apr. 17, 1935, G. M. Sutton).

NESTING: *Nest*: Similar to *I. c. nelsoni* (see below), but bird more often places its nest among pecan leaves or suspends it from underside of a palm frond. *Eggs*: 3–5, usually 4; ovate to elliptical ovate; without gloss; bluish white, buffy white, or grayish white, with irregular lines, scratches, and spots of seal brown, claret brown, dark gray, dark purple, and black, and shell markings of pearl gray and lavender; average size, similar to that of *I. c. nelsoni*.

SENNETT'S HOODED ORIOLE, *Icterus cucullatus sennetti* Ridgway

DESCRIPTION: *Adult male and female, nuptial plumage*: Similar to *I. c. cucullatus*, but wing and tail averaging shorter; yellow areas on upper and lower surface of male paler, more greenish (less orange); female lighter both above and below; yellow of pileum and upper tail-coverts paler and more greenish; remainder of upper surface lighter, more clearly grayish (less brownish).

MEASUREMENTS: *Adult male*: Wing, 80.5–85.3 (average, 83.3) mm.; tail, 87.6–99.3 (91.7); bill (from base), 19.8–20.9 (20.3); height of bill at base, 7.9–8.4 (8.1); tarsus, 21.9–23.4 (22.9); middle toe without claw, 15.2–15.7 (15.5). *Adult female*: Wing, 78.0–81.3 (79.5); tail, 83.8–88.1 (86.4); bill (from base), 18.3–19.8 (19.3); height of bill, 7.9–8.4 (8.1); tarsus, 20.9–22.9 (22.4); middle toe, 15.2–15.7 (15.5).

RANGE: S. Texas, south to n. Tamaulipas. Winters from s. Texas (rarely) to n. Guerrero and Morelos.

TEXAS: *Breeding*: Altitudinal range, near sea level to 450 ft., possibly slightly higher. Collected northwest to Webb, east to Kenedy, south to Cameron cos. Uncommon to scarce. One speci-

men outside breeding range: Val Verde Co., Langtry (Apr. 27, 1901, L. A. Fuertes). *Winter*: Taken in Hidalgo and Cameron cos. Rare. One specimen from Nueces Co. (Feb., 1898, collection of J. A. Weber).

NESTING: *Nest*: Similar to that of *I. c. nelsoni* (see below), but bird more often builds nest in and of Spanishmoss. *Eggs*: Similar in color to those of *I. c. cucullatus*; average egg size, 21.6 × 15.2 mm.

ARIZONA HOODED ORIOLE, *Icterus cucullatus nelsoni* Ridgway

DESCRIPTION: Similar to *I. c. sennetti*, but wing decidedly longer; bill also longer; tail shorter. *Adult male, nuptial*: Yellow of upper and lower surface much paler—cadmium yellow to near light cadmium; lining of wing lemon chrome; no black on forehead. *Adult female, nuptial*: Similar to adult female, *I. c. sennetti*, but pileum rather dull pyrite yellow; rump olive lake; upper tail-coverts analine yellow; back between grayish olive and drab; yellow of lower surface decidedly paler and more greenish (less golden)—between primuline yellow and light cadmium. *Juvenal*: Similar to adult female of this race but duller, more brownish above, wing-bars and edgings of wing feathers more buffy; lower surface paler, duller, more buffy yellow—amber yellow to between wax yellow and primuline yellow.

MEASUREMENTS: *Adult male*: Wing, 86.4–90.2 (average, 88.1) mm.; tail, 81.8–96.0 (89.9); bill (from base), 20.9–22.4 (21.9); height of bill at base, 6.9–7.4 (7.1); tarsus, 21.9–23.4 (22.4); middle toe without claw, 15.5–16.8 (16.0). *Adult female*: Wing, 80.7–82.8 (81.8); tail, 80.5–83.3 (82.0); bill (from base), 19.8–20.9 (20.3); height of bill, 6.9–7.4 (7.1); tarsus, 21.9–22.4 (22.1); middle toe, 14.5–16.0 (15.2).

RANGE: S.e. California to Trans-Pecos Texas, south to c. Sonora and n. Chihuahua. Winters from c. Sonora to Guerrero.

TEXAS: *Breeding*: One specimen from Brewster Co.: 1 mi. west of Boquillas, ca. 1,900 ft. (May 18, 1935, G. M. Sutton); one recent specimen from Culberson Co. (see species account).

NESTING: *Nest*: Mostly on flatlands; chiefly in palm, yucca, pecan, cottonwood, willow, elm, or ash tree, sometimes in bunch of mistletoe; cup-shaped and semipensile structure, securely fastened to twigs or stiff leaves; composed of green grass, which dries to bright straw color, coarse dry grasses, palm and yucca fibers; lined with finer green or dry grasses, plant fibers, cotton waste, horsehair, cottonwood, willow, and other vegetable down, wool, and rarely feathers. *Eggs*: 3–7, usually 4–5; white or bluish white; dotted, blotched, marbled, and irregularly lined with various shades of brown, purple, and black, chiefly at larger end, with shell markings of purplish gray; average size, 21.6 × 15.5 mm.

SCOTT'S ORIOLE, *Icterus parisorum* Bonaparte

SPECIES ACCOUNT

Male: black head, breast, back, wings; yellow belly, crissum, rump; black and yellow tail; white wing-bar and white edgings on tertials. *Female*: greenish yellow body with blackish mottled back; yellow rump; dusky cheek; two white wing-bars. Length, 8½ in.; wingspan, 12½.

RANGE: S.e. California, s. Nevada, Utah, c. New Mexico, and w. Texas, south to s. Baja California and Oaxaca. Winters mainly in Mexico.

TEXAS: (See map.) *Breeding*: Late Apr. to mid-July (eggs, May 13 to June 21) from approximately 1,200 to 8,000 ft. Fairly common west of Pecos River; fairly common (some years) to scarce on southwestern Edwards Plateau; rare and local on southeastern Plateau: Kendall Co. (fide C. R. Bender) and Comal Co. (nest with 4 eggs located, 2 young seen being fed, nest subsequently collected and deposited in Witte Museum in San Antonio, June 21–July 15, 1966, Col. and Mrs. W. Jessup, J. A. Middleton). *Migration*: Early Apr. to mid-May; mid-July to mid-Oct. (extremes: Mar. 25, June 10; mid-July, mid-Dec.). Common to fairly common west of Pecos River; fairly common to uncommon on southwestern Edwards Plateau; rare to casual north of breeding range to Midland and Camp Barkeley, near Abilene. *Winter*: No specimen, but 3 individuals sighted in Chisos Mts., Brewster Co. (Dec. 23, 1968, R. H. Wauer); inexplicable sight record, Hardin Co. (Jan. 15–16, 1957, Corrie Hooks, Mrs. H. B. Lindsay, Bessie Reid).

HAUNTS AND HABITS: The Scott's Oriole is a bird of elevated arid country. In the Southwest it occupies both juniper-oak woods in mountains and yucca-strewn desert flats. Probably the best habitat of Scott's Oriole in Texas is found in Brewster County, site of Big Bend National Park. Here this oriole occurs at all altitudes from Rio Grande level (1,700 ft. in the extreme southeastern part of the county) to near the top of Mt. Emory (7,835 ft.). By the time the Rio Grande has flowed down to Del Rio (948 ft.), its valley is apparently too low for nesting Scott's Orioles, although the species summers on ocotillo-clad hills to the north and northwest of this town. Downstream, from Laredo (438 ft.) on south to sea level, another yellow-and-black oriole, the Black-headed, takes over.

In summer the Scott's is usually observed singly, in pairs, or in trios—generally an adult male, female, and immature bird. In spring and fall, however, it is sometimes seen in flocks of up to twelve or so individuals;

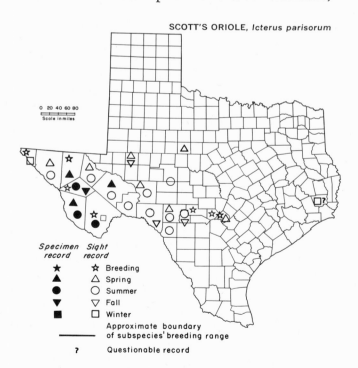

SCOTT'S ORIOLE, *Icterus parisorum*

0 20 40 60 80
Scale in miles

Specimen   Sight
record   record
★   ☆ Breeding
▲   △ Spring
●   ○ Summer
▼   ▽ Fall
■   □ Winter

—————— Approximate boundary
        of subspecies' breeding range

?   Questionable record

and small groups sometimes gather at water holes to drink.

Flight is commonly low and somewhat undulating; when alarmed this oriole often flies swiftly for a long distance. It roosts at night in yuccas or other desert shrubs. It forages deliberately, climbing about trees and shrubs rather than using its wings. Food consists of various insects (beetles, grasshoppers, ants, bugs, butterflies, and caterpillars), spiders, lizards, and at times wild berries and fruits. When yucca and agave are in bloom, it feeds on nectar and insects in the flowers.

The song of the Scott's, one of the finest of oriole songs, consists of a few rich, whistled notes strikingly similar to those of the Western Meadowlark. Immature males sing as well as adults, and even the female occasionally sings—usually from atop a yucca or similar perch. One of the most persistent singers of desert birds, it may be heard any time of day from early April to August, or occasionally mid-September.

DETAILED ACCOUNT: NO SUBSPECIES

DESCRIPTION: *Adult male, nuptial*: Acquired by wear from winter plumage. Pileum, hindneck, back, and scapulars black, slightly glossy; rump and upper tail-coverts gamboge yellow to lemon chrome; basal portion of tail yellow like rump, this occupying on outer feathers about two-thirds of tail, but on two middle pairs only basal portion; remainder of tail brownish black to fuscous black, most feathers tipped with dull yellowish white, most broadly on outermost pair; primaries and secondaries fuscous, inner margins paler—even pale brown—except at tips of primaries; tertials and outer webs of primaries and secondaries fuscous black or brownish black, tertials narrowly tipped and margined on outer webs, and outer primaries (except outermost) narrowly edged on subterminal portion with dull white or yellowish white; lesser and median coverts lemon chrome, latter tipped with white; greater coverts dull black, tipped on outer margins with white, and inner greater coverts with inner veins mostly white, forming conspicuous white wing-bar; sides of head and of neck, and anterior lower parts, including breast, black, slightly glossy, posterior margin of this color rounded, but at edge the black of feathers somewhat mixed with yellow; remainder of lower surface, including lining of wing, gamboge yellow to lemon chrome. Bill black or bluish black, but base of mandible plumbeous; iris dark brown or black; legs and feet slate color or brownish slate. *Adult male, winter*: Acquired by complete postnuptial molt. Similar to nuptial adult male, but upper surface duller, feathers of pileum tipped with dull gray or brown, feathers of back with broad pale olive gray or whitish tips, yellow of rump and upper tail-coverts much washed with gray; white edgings of wing-quills and coverts, particularly greater coverts and tertials, much broader; black of sides of neck more or less obscured by dull yellow or olive gray tips of feathers; yellow of lower surface duller, more or less obscured by dull yellow or olive gray tips of feathers; yellow of lower surface duller, more or less obscured by olivaceous or deep buff feather tips; flanks washed with gray or olive. *Adult female, nuptial*: Acquired by wear from winter. Much duller than nuptial adult male; upper surface light yellowish olive or dull light yellowish olive; pileum, back, and scapulars heavily streaked or spotted with blackish brown, fuscous black, fuscous, or chaetura black, hindneck less conspicuously so; rump sulphine yellow to bright analine yellow, upper tail-coverts duller and darker; tail olive brown to near dark olive, extreme base of two middle pairs of tail feathers, together with basal two-thirds or three-quarters of remaining feathers, like rump, the middle tail feathers shading off to next pair and to tips of all rectrices, olive brown to dark

male Scott's Oriole, *Icterus parisorum*,
on ocotillo (*Fouquieria splendens*)

olive brown, outer feathers narrowly tipped with brownish white; wing-quills fuscous, inner edge of all but tips of primaries and inner tertials between light drab and avellaneous, outer webs of quills margined narrowly with dull light drab, brownish white, or pale tilleul buff; lesser and median wing-coverts fuscous black, lesser coverts broadly margined with dark wax yellow, but centers of feathers presenting mottled or spotted appearance on covert area; median wing-coverts broadly tipped with buff or yellowish white, greater series very narrowly margined on outer webs with dull drab, and broadly tipped with brownish white or yellowish white; sides of head and of neck like upper surface, more or less extensively mottled or spotted with fuscous black or chaetura black, although sides of head sometimes almost solidly black; chin and throat more or less extensively fuscous black or chaetura black, sometimes almost solidly, usually with admixture of olive or dull yellow; remainder of lower surface between wax yellow and primuline yellow to dull gamboge yellow; sides and flanks light citrine; lining of wing gamboge yellow. *Adult female, winter*: Acquired by complete postnuptial molt. Similar to nuptial adult female, but dark brown or blackish areas of upper surface much obscured by olive green or olive gray edges of feathers; wing-quills more broadly tipped with dull white; black of throat and jugulum much obscured by yellow or olive green edgings and tips of feathers; breast, sides, and flanks more washed or tinged with olivaceous or mouse gray. *Male, first nuptial*: Acquired by partial prenuptial molt. Similar to nuptial adult female, but head all around, together with breast and jugulum, more extensively and more solidly black, that on jugulum extending farther behind; dark streaks and spots of back and scapulars more blackish (less brownish); middle tail feathers entirely or partly brownish black or fuscous black, sometimes also terminal portion of most other feathers of same color; wing-coverts and tertials black or fuscous black. *Male, first winter*: Acquired by partial postjuvenal molt. Similar to first nuptial male, but feathers of black areas of pileum and back broadly edged with olive, olive green, or grayish olive, much obscuring dark centers of feathers; black feathers of sides of head, jugulum, and breast broadly tipped with yellowish olive green, dull yellow, or yellowish olive. *Female, first nuptial*: Acquired by partial prenuptial molt. Similar to nuptial adult female, but upper surface paler, duller, and more uniform, head without black, centers of feathers on pileum and back much less blackish, more olive brown, giving upper surface much more uniform appearance; sides of head and neck much paler, duller, with little or no blackish; lower surface much lighter, duller, and more uniform, chin, throat, and jugulum without black, though occasionally with small broken olive brown patch in middle of throat. *Female, first winter*: Acquired by partial postjuvenal molt. Similar to first nuptial female, but upper surface duller, more brownish, and more uniform, dark feather centers of pileum and back more obscured by lighter edgings of feathers; tertials more broadly tipped with dull white or yellowish white; lower parts darker, breast, jugulum, sides, and flanks more strongly tinged with ochraceous. Similar to adult female in winter, but upper surface more brownish, and dark feather centers still more obscured by lighter edgings; sides of head more brownish, anterior lower surface without black, breast, sides, and flanks more strongly tinged with ochraceous (less grayish or olive). *Juvenal (dark phase)*: Acquired by complete postnatal molt. Similar to first winter female, but bill usually shorter; upper surface paler and commonly more uniform, there being fewer dark markings on back and almost none on pileum, and these olive brown or buffy brown; rump and upper tail-coverts pale old gold or light isabella color, two outer pairs of tail feathers broadly tipped with amber yellow, remaining tail feathers more narrowly tipped with pale yellow or yellowish white; wing-bars pale buff or pale yellow, instead of dull white; lower surface usually paler, breast, abdomen, and crissum amber yellow, wax yellow, or dull gamboge yellow, jugulum, sides, and flanks much less strongly ochraceous (more greenish or olivaceous), jugulum light citrine. *Juvenal (light phase)*: Similar to dark phase, but upper surface averaging lighter, sometimes practically uniform and without darker markings; lower surface very much

paler, breast and abdomen straw yellow or pale straw yellow. Bill black, but base of mandible bluish; iris dark brown; legs and feet dark plumbeous. *Natal*: Pale drab gray to tilleul buff.

MEASUREMENTS: *Adult male*: Wing, 98.8–106.7 (average, 104.4) mm.; tail, 79.2–91.7 (88.1); bill (exposed culmen), 20.9–24.6 (22.9); height of bill at base, 8.6–9.7 (9.1); tarsus, 22.9–25.1 (23.6); middle toe without claw, 17.0–19.3 (18.0). *Adult female*: Wing, 94.5–102.4 (97.8); tail, 81.3–88.1 (84.3); bill, 20.3–22.9 (21.4); height of bill, 8.4–9.7 (8.9); tarsus, 23.4–24.6 (24.1); middle toe, 16.3–19.8 (17.5).

TEXAS: *Breeding*: Collected in Culberson, Pecos, Brewster, Presidio, and Jeff Davis cos. *Migration*: No specimen collected outside of Trans-Pecos.

NESTING: *Nest*: Usually on mesas or slopes, but even in broad valleys; in brush or among scattered timber; in tree, such as juniper, pinyon, or cottonwood, or in yucca, usually 15–20 ft. above ground, occasionally in mesquite or cactus, or in vine hanging from rocks; semipensile structure, attached to under side of leaves of yucca or to twigs of tree; similar to nests of other orioles, but usually very firmly attached to surroundings, and, though basketlike, not free swinging like that of Bullock's Oriole; composed of yucca fibers, fine grass of various kinds, pine needles, cotton waste, twine, and cotton batting; lined with fine grasses, seed pappus of plants, hemplike plant fibers, cotton waste, and horsehair. *Eggs*: 2–5, usually 3; ovate to elliptical ovate; dull white with bluish tint, with small blotches, dots, and sometimes zigzag markings of black, purplish brown, claret brown, russet, and ferruginous, and shell markings of mouse gray, pearl gray, and lavender, principally about larger end; average size, 23.9 × 17.0 mm.

WAGLER'S ORIOLE, *Icterus wagleri* Sclater

SPECIES ACCOUNT

Black-vented Oriole of some authors. *Adult*: black head, back, chest, wings (entirely without white), tail, and crissum; bright orange shoulder-patch, rump, lower breast, and belly (race in Sonora and Chihuahua and some individuals elsewhere show chestnut band bordering black of upper breast). *Immature*: may require three years to reach adulthood, hence plumage variable. Mainly olive above; yellow-orange on forequarters and under parts; sometimes streaked with blackish on back; face and throat irregularly spotted with black, or entirely black; wings blackish olive; orangish shoulder-patch spotted with black; tail black with outer feathers greenish yellow. Length, 8 in.

RANGE: Sonora, Chihuahua, Coahuila, and Nuevo León, south to Guatemala, El Salvador (apparently only in winter), Honduras, and n. Nicaragua.

TEXAS: *Accidental*: One sighting, first documented record for United States: Brewster Co., Big Bend Nat. Park, Rio Grande Village (1 adult, first seen Sept. 27, 1968; rediscovered Apr. 28, 1969, and present until Sept. 27; captured, banded, and photographed, July 4, 1969, R. H. Wauer, et al.). For more details, including close-up photo of bird's vent region, see Wauer, 1970, *Auk* 87: 811–812; a photo by T. Hotchkiss is no. 31 in Texas Photo-Record File, Texas A&M University.

HAUNTS AND HABITS: Surprisingly, the neotropical Wagler's Oriole shares, in northern and central Mexico, a wide range of habitats with the nearctic Scott's Oriole. In Chihuahua, both birds forage from Sierra Madre pines, junipers, and oaks through canyon sycamores to lowland yucca, scrub, and cactus deserts. At Zimapán, Hidalgo, both eat the small tunas (fruit) of the local big candelabra cactus. The Wagler's does, however, range into hotter terrain; it is much more likely to eat tropical figs and is somewhat more apt to weave its nest of palm, rather than of yucca, fiber— interestingly, both plants are called *palma* by Mexicans.

Icterus wagleri is usually seen singly or in pairs. It is conspicuous when it flies from one distant aridland tree to another but it can seclude itself among dense foliage. The Texas individual—which showed no sign of having been caged—ranged within a one-quarter-square-mile area which included essentially two habitats: (1) dense Rio Grande floodplain mesquite brush, and (2) planted willow, cottonwood, sycamore, and honeylocust trees scattered over a bermuda grass lawn.

Stomachs of two birds collected in extreme northern Mexico contained insects and caterpillars (Joe T. Marshall).

Call is a short weak nasal *dur* or *nur* (L. I. Davis). Song consists of about six notes, some musical, with the last note often a metallic buzz (E. P. Edwards). Call is heard more frequently than the song.

NOTE: Wauer sent close-up photographs of the Texas *Icterus wagleri* to Mexican bird expert A. R. Phillips, who pronounced the race to be *I. w. wagleri*. However, it is the policy of the present book not to give subspecies write-ups to species whose occurrence in Texas is documented solely by photos.

BALTIMORE ORIOLE, *Icterus galbula* (Linnaeus)

SPECIES ACCOUNT

Male: black head, back, wings, tail; orange under parts, shoulder-patch, rump, and tail-corners (the latter sometimes yellow); white wing-bar and white edgings on tertials. *Female*: orange olive above; orange-yellow below; two whitish wing-bars. Length, 7½ in.; wingspan, 11¾; weight, 1¼ oz.

RANGE: C. Alberta to Nova Scotia, south to e. Oklahoma, n. and e. Texas, and n. Georgia. Winters chiefly from s. Mexico through Central America to n. Colombia and n.w. Venezuela.

TEXAS: (See map.) *Breeding*: Mid-May to late July (eggs collected, June 1, 1922, Wilbarger Co., G. E. Allman) from 25 to 2,500 ft. Scarce to casual, formerly fairly common to uncommon, from northeastern Panhandle east along Oklahoma border to Harrison Co., also in San Jacinto Co. (nested, 1961, J. M. Heiser, and May, 1965, T. B. Feltner) and Jefferson Co. (nest, 1914, Bessie Reid); summer records from Nacogdoches, Liberty, and Hardin cos. (C. D. Fisher); nesting in Waco and Houston unconfirmed. Accidental: Observed nesting near Fabens, El Paso Co., at approximately 3,600 ft. (May 22, 30, 1959, Roy Fisk, Mary Belle Keefer). *Migration*: Mid-Apr. to early May; late Aug. to early Oct. (extremes: Mar. 9, June 29; July 4,

Nov. 30). Very common (some years) to fairly common in spring east of 100th meridian; scarce to rare in Panhandle; casual in Trans-Pecos. Irregularly common to uncommon in fall east of 100th meridian; increasingly rare westward to Trans-Pecos, where casual. *Winter*: Mid-Dec. to late Feb. No specimen, but a scattering of sightings along coast. Casual inland in Gonzales Co. (immature male, Dec. 5, 1970; adult male, Dec. 4, 1971, F. S. Webster, Jr., et al.).

HAUNTS AND HABITS: The Baltimore Oriole is a bird of open, deciduous woodlands. Its rich, piping whistles are frequently heard from timber along streams, and it often hunts bagworms and berries within shade trees in residential areas. Like other northeastern U.S. nesters, it seems to require fairly cool and humid surroundings for successful hatching and raising of its young. Though not gregarious, Baltimores frequently appear in small groups during migration.

Flight is swift but somewhat jerky and uneven. Amidst foliage this oriole is graceful and quick in its search for food. More than 95 percent of its diet consists of insects, some of which are destructive and eaten by relatively few other avian species. It displays a preference for caterpillars (cankerworms, fall webworm, tent, forest tent, spiny elm, and tussock moth caterpillars), sometimes taking as many as one hundred at a meal! Beetles are another important element; included are metallic, long-horned wood-borers, click, wireworms, June, May, and leaf beetles, and weevils (nut, oak, and cotton-boll). In addition to many other species of insects, a few spiders and snails are taken, as well as some wild fruit and vegetable galls.

The Baltimore's usual call is a whistled *hew-li*; a loud, harsh rattle serves as an alarm note. The song is

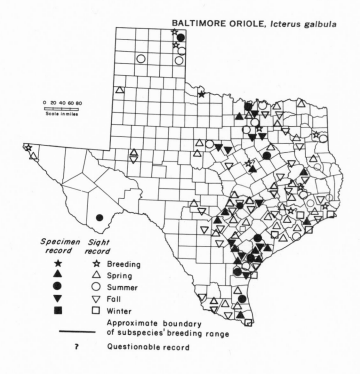

BALTIMORE ORIOLE, *Icterus galbula*

Specimen record	Sight record	
★	☆	Breeding
▲	△	Spring
●	○	Summer
▼	▽	Fall
■	□	Winter

——— Approximate boundary of subspecies' breeding range

? Questionable record

a variable elaboration of the call note, consisting of a series of clear, mellow whistled notes, low in pitch.

CHANGES: The Baltimore Oriole, along with other avian insect-eaters, is facing environmental deterioration in the twentieth century. The Baltimore's crisis may be a bit more severe than average. It favors big, living American elms (*Ulmus americana*) for nesting and feeding. Since about 1950, this elm either has died, or is in the process of doing so, throughout most of the Baltimore's breeding range. Tons of DDT and other potent insecticides were sprayed on these trees to slow the progress of Dutch elm disease and other accidentally imported killers of the favorite Yankee shade tree. Thus, the oriole has found many nesting sites destroyed and its food often poisoned or nonexistent.

In Texas as of 1972, *Icterus galbula* was still apparently numerous as a migrant, but it was practically out of the nesting business. The decline of the Baltimore as a breeder in Texas started in the 1920's, long before the first application of DDT in the 1940's. A trend toward a hotter and drier climate was perhaps responsible.

DETAILED ACCOUNT: NO SUBSPECIES

DESCRIPTION: *Adult male, nuptial plumage (orange phase)*: Acquired by wear from winter plumage. Pileum, hindneck, upper back, and scapulars glossy black, but feathers of hindneck light cadmium subterminally and dull white basally, this light portion entirely covered by black tips; lower back, rump, and upper tail-coverts between orange chrome and flame scarlet; corners of tail yellow ocher to dull cadmium yellow, remainder of tail (i.e., a broad irregular median band, usually entire length of middle pair of feathers, and sometimes terminal portion of next pair) brownish black or dull black; primaries and secondaries chaetura drab to dull black, inner edges, except on tips of primaries, dull white, brownish white, or very pale brown, outer webs margined narrowly, outer webs of secondaries more broadly, with white; tertials dull black, broadly edged on outer webs with white; lesser and median wing-coverts orange like rump; greater coverts black, broadly tipped with white on outer webs, forming conspicuous wing-bar; sides of head and of upper part of neck, with chin, throat, and narrow triangular area in center of jugulum, rather glossy black; remainder of lower surface between orange chrome and flame scarlet; lining of wing cadmium yellow to orange. Bill slate, bluish slate, or bluish black, but mandible cinereous or plumbeous; iris dark brown; legs and feet plumbeous. *Adult male, nuptial (yellow phase)*: Similar to orange phase, but yellow of rump, lower surface, and lesser wing-coverts cadmium yellow to orange, light portion of tail cadmium, hidden yellow on nape lemon chrome. *Adult male, winter*: Acquired by complete postnuptial molt. Similar to nuptial adult male, but hindneck, back, and scapulars broadly tipped with sudan brown, sanford brown, or mouse gray; white edgings of tertials and secondaries broader; rump much washed with olive; orange of lower surface somewhat duller. *Adult female, nuptial*: Acquired by wear from winter. Upper surface rather dull light orange citrine, passing on extreme forehead and upper tail-coverts into dull saffron yellow; pileum, hindneck, back, and scapulars conspicuously spotted with chaetura black to chaetura drab, these spots being centers of feathers; tail between yellow ocher and raw sienna, middle rectrices saccardo umber, this often tinging tips of feathers; primaries and secondaries dark hair brown, tertials approaching fuscous, but inner margins of primaries and secondaries, except tips of primaries, very pale brown or brownish white, outer webs of primaries, secondaries, and tertials edged with white, those of inner secondaries and tertials most broadly; lesser wing-coverts cadmium yellow, more or less spotted with

chaetura black, particularly on outermost feathers; median wing-coverts chaetura black, very broadly tipped with white, this showing as wing-bar; greater wing-coverts dark hair brown, broadly tipped on outer margins with dull white, forming second wing-bar, and narrowly margined on remaining portion of outer webs with dull pale gray; sides of head and of neck like crown, and similarly spotted, auriculars sometimes almost without spots, lores and region below eye dull buff, buffy gray, or dull grayish white; lower surface dull orange to light cadmium, jugulum and crissum usually brightest and deepest in color, abdomen palest, more or less washed with light gray; chin grayish white, yellowish white, or pale yellow, with middle of throat spotted dull black or chaetura drab, sometimes forming more or less well-defined patch; sides and flanks somewhat washed with orange citrine; lining of wing yellow like lower surface. Maxilla black; mandible, legs, and feet cinereous; claws drab gray. Individuals vary much in colors. *Adult female, winter*: Acquired by complete postnuptial molt. Similar to nuptial adult female, but colors of upper surface more blended, dark markings much obscured by orange citrine or grayish tips of feathers; outer edgings of secondaries and tertials, as well as greater wing-coverts, broader. *Male and female, second winter*: Acquired by complete postnuptial molt. Like that of corresponding sex in adult winter. *Male, first nuptial*: Acquired by partial prenuptial molt. Similar to nuptial adult male, but black feathers of back usually with orange edgings; orange parts somewhat paler; and wing-quills, as well as sometimes other feathers in wing, more brownish, being retained from juvenal. *Male, first winter*: Acquired by partial postjuvenal molt, not involving wing-quills or tail. Similar to adult female in winter, but larger; upper surface duller, dark centers of feathers of pileum entirely overlaid by lighter edgings; rump and upper tail-coverts decidedly duller, much overlaid by olive gray on tips of feathers; lower surface duller, particularly on breast and abdomen, where less yellow, more mixed with dull light gray or olive gray; throat and jugulum without black. *Female, first nuptial*: Acquired by partial prenuptial molt. Similar to nuptial adult female, but wing-quills, and sometimes other feathers on wings, more brownish. *Female, first winter*: Acquired by partial postjuvenal molt not involving wing-quills or tail. Similar to first winter male, but smaller; upper parts still duller and more grayish; rump light grayish isabella; sides of head more grayish, with little if any orange tinge; lower parts dull cream buff, with little orange except as wash on jugulum and crissum, on jugulum becoming dull saffron. *Male, juvenal*: Acquired by complete postnatal molt. Similar to first winter male, but upper surface more uniform and more brownish— between buffy brown and saccardo umber to dull light olive brown; rump and upper tail-coverts duller and decidedly lighter —light raw sienna or dark buckthorn brown; back and scapulars with little or no indication of spots or streaks; wing-bars pale buff or dull pale buffy yellow; sides of head duller, more grayish or olivaceous, less washed with orange; lower surface duller and paler. Bill slate color, slate gray, or brownish slate, but mandible pale flesh color; iris dark brown; legs and feet olive gray or plumbeous. *Female, juvenal*: Acquired by complete postnatal molt. Similar to juvenal male, but upper surface lighter, more grayish (less brownish); lower surface decidedly paler, particularly behind, less orange or saffron tinged, but more yellowish; sides of head duller, less brownish (more yellowish or olivaceous). Maxilla olive gray; mandible light olive gray; legs and feet cinereous; claws drab gray. *Natal*: Pale tilleul buff or buffy white. Bill, legs, and feet pinkish buff.

MEASUREMENTS: *Adult male*: Wing, 91.2–102.4 (average, 97.1) mm.; tail, 70.9–80.0 (75.7); bill (exposed culmen), 17.5–19.8 (18.3); height of bill at base, 9.1–10.7 (9.7); tarsus, 22.9–25.1 (23.6); middle toe without claw, 15.2–16.8 (15.7). *Adult female*: Wing, 85.3–91.7 (88.6); tail, 66.0–71.7 (68.8); bill, 16.0–18.0 (17.5); height of bill, 8.4–10.2 (9.1); tarsus, 22.4–23.6 (23.4); middle toe, 14.7–16.5 (15.5).

TEXAS: *Breeding*: Collected north to Lipscomb, south to Wilbarger (eggs) and Trinity cos. *Migration*: Collected north to Cooke, east to Galveston, south to Cameron, west to Brewster (summer) cos.

NESTING: *Nest*: On uplands and bottomlands; in woods or more open country, sometimes along streams, frequently in cultivated lands (e.g., vicinity of country house, park, ornamental ground), even streets of towns and cities; in bush or tree, 4–90 ft. above ground; remarkably close-woven pensile basket, much longer than wide, occasionally roofed over with entrance at one side, but usually open at top, suspended usually at or near extremity of horizontal or nearly horizontal branch, often by rim to forked twig; composed of long tough grasses, strips of bark, various other plant fibers, moss, yarn, wrapping twine, rags, paper, horse and cow hair, strips of cloth, and even human hair, all woven into clothlike pouch, so strong that it often withstands storms of two winters; lined with plant down, tree moss, other similar soft warm material, such as cotton, string, yarn, rags, tow, fine grass, plant down, and hair. *Eggs*: 3–7, usually 4–5; elliptical ovate to ovate; white with bluish tint, or pale grayish white, with spots, blotches, lines, and scrawls—thickest about larger end and often forming wreath—of black, gray, umber, and other shades of dark brown, and shell markings of lavender and pearl gray; rarely unmarked; average size, 23.1 × 15.5 mm.

BULLOCK'S ORIOLE, *Icterus bullockii* (Swainson)

SPECIES ACCOUNT   *See colorplate 26*

Often considered conspecific with *Icterus galbula*; Northern Oriole is then its English name. *Male*: black crown, back, line through eye, throat; bright orange cheeks, under parts; large white wing-patch near shoulder; golden outer feathers on black tail. *Female*: olive gray above; yellow cheeks, breast; white belly; two whitish wing-bars. *Immature male*: resembles female but has black throat-patch. Length, 7¾ in.; wing-span, 12¼.

RANGE: S. British Columbia to s.w. Saskatchewan and c. South Dakota, south through w. United States to n. Baja California, Durango, and n. Tamaulipas. Winters chiefly from Mexico to n.w. Costa Rica.

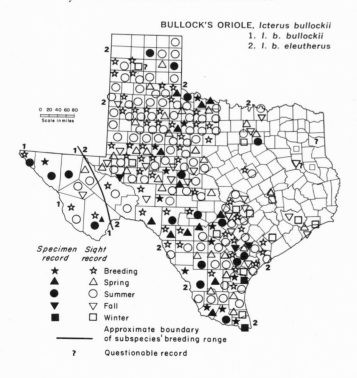

BULLOCK'S ORIOLE, *Icterus bullockii*
1. *I. b. bullockii*
2. *I. b. eleutherus*

0 20 40 60 80
Scale in miles

Specimen Sight
record   record
★   ☆   Breeding
▲   △   Spring
●   ○   Summer
▼   ▽   Fall
■   □   Winter

——— Approximate boundary of subspecies' breeding range

?   Questionable record

TEXAS: (See map.) *Breeding*: Early Apr. to mid-July (eggs, Apr. 7 to July 5) from near sea level to 5,700 ft. Locally common in Panhandle and in north central Texas east to 98th meridian; locally fairly common in Trans-Pecos and south Texas brush country; locally uncommon on Edwards Plateau; rare east to 97th meridian. *Migration*: Late Mar. to mid-May; late July to late Sept. (extremes: Mar. 20, May 22; July 27, Nov. 22). Very common (some years) to fairly common through regular breeding range; scarce in Fort Worth–Dallas–Waco area and along upper coast. *Winter*: Late Nov. to late Mar. Scarce along coast and in Rio Grande delta; rare to casual in remainder of western two-thirds; casual in wooded eastern portion.

HAUNTS AND HABITS: Throughout much of the western United States the Bullock's is the only breeding oriole. In Texas, it is characteristic of areas where mature mesquite (*Prosopis*) predominates. Since this rather big oriole often chatters and sings in, and swings its nest from, big mesquite trees, it has double claim to the colloquial title "big mesquite oriole." Other favored trees are streamside willows (*Salix*) and cottonwoods (*Populus*). Near the Sabinal River in Uvalde County in the 1920's and 1930's, this bird inhabited chiefly leafy crowns of cultivated pecan trees (Lucile McKee Kincaid, E. B. Kincaid, Jr.). The Bullock's, like other western orioles, lives in areas where woody vegetation is well spaced, often with grass and wild flower patches between; in western Texas and wide stretches of the arid West, it often accepts countryside where trees are extremely far apart. It prefers flatlands. The species sometimes interbreeds with the Baltimore Oriole on the Great Plains, but the resulting hybrids are seldom seen in Texas.

Flight is rather jerky, performed with relatively few, but powerful, wing-beats. Feeding birds, searching trees, shrubs, and edges of fields, may make foraging trips far from the nest. More than 75 percent of the diet consists of animal matter—largely insects, but also a few spiders, lizards, and mollusks. Beetles—including tiger, ladybird, and cotton-boll weevil—comprise nearly half the insect element. Others are ants, wasps, scale insects, stink bugs, leaf-hoppers, tree-hoppers, plant lice, grasshoppers, and moths, their pupae and caterpillars. Vegetable matter eaten is nearly all fruit; occasionally it eats buds of certain desert shrubs.

The call note of the Bullock's is a sharp *skip*; a persistent chatter is uttered in alarm. The male's song is a series of loud, clear double notes similar to that of its close relative, the Baltimore Oriole, but not so piping or musical. During the breeding season the female occasionally sings also.

DETAILED ACCOUNT: THREE SUBSPECIES

ARIZONA BULLOCK'S ORIOLE, *Icterus bullockii bullockii* (Swainson)

DESCRIPTION: *Adult male, nuptial plumage (orange phase)*: Acquired by wear from winter plumage. Forehead and superciliary stripe between orange chrome and flame scarlet; rest of pileum, hindneck, back, and scapulars black, a little glossy, also tinged slightly with brownish, concealed subterminal portions of feathers of hindneck and occiput light cadmium to cadmium yellow; rump dull orange to mars yellow; upper tail-coverts similar, but often brighter; tail cadmium yellow to yellow ocher, terminal half or two-thirds of middle pair of tail feathers, with most of terminal half of next pair, and more or less broad tips chiefly on outer webs of remaining pairs, fuscous black or brownish black, amount and distribution of this exceedingly variable, outer two or three pairs of tail feathers often terminally partly or entirely dresden brown or fuscous; primaries and secondaries dark hair brown, margins of inner webs, except tips of primaries, broadly white, becoming brownish white on outer primaries; tertials fuscous black, broadly edged on outer webs, as are secondaries, with white, primaries also narrowly edged on outer margins with white; lesser wing-coverts cadmium yellow to orange, but outer row black; lesser wing-coverts and outer webs of greater series white, forming large wing-patch; inner webs of greater wing-coverts fuscous black; primary coverts fuscous black; lores, narrow postocular streak, small malar spot, chin, and center of throat (the latter ending posteriorly in more or less a point) black, as is also posterior part of sides of neck, this reaching down to sides of throat somewhat in a point; remainder of sides of head and of anterior part of neck, extending upward, reaching halfway across hindneck, with remainder of lower parts, between orange chrome and flame scarlet, passing on abdomen into orange or cadmium yellow, where sometimes slightly washed with gray; lining of wing orange or cadmium yellow. Bill black, but cutting edges and mandible bluish gray, cinereous, or light plumbeous, tip dull white; iris dark brown or hazel; legs, feet, and claws plumbeous, cinereous, or dull bluish gray; claws dark mouse gray. *Adult male, nuptial (yellow phase)*: Similar to orange phase but rather more yellow than orange; rump dull light cadmium, as are also yellow parts of tail; lower surface gamboge yellow to orange. *Adult male, winter*: Acquired by complete postnuptial molt. Similar to nuptial adult male, but feathers of pileum narrowly and often inconspicuously, those on hindneck, back, and scapulars broadly, tipped with mouse gray or raw sienna, feathers of rump and upper tail-coverts tipped with mouse gray or grayish olive, thus much obscuring yellow or orange of these parts; orange of auriculars and sides of neck sometimes washed with olivaceous or gray; lower surface duller, feathers more or less margined and tipped with very pale gray or dull white; tail narrowly tipped with mouse gray. *Adult female, nuptial*: Acquired by wear from winter. Pileum and hindneck analine yellow to bright old gold, sometimes slightly grayish or brownish on occiput; back and scapulars between grayish olive and drab, centers of feathers rather darker, often imparting somewhat spotted or obscurely barred appearance; rump light grayish olive or verging toward drab; upper tail-coverts and tail old gold to analine yellow, inner feathers on inner webs and terminal portions of all, sometimes with middle pair of feathers, light brownish olive to between light brownish olive and hair brown; wings dark hair brown, inner margins of primaries and secondaries, except tips of primaries, more or less narrowly light brown, or at base of inner secondaries brownish white, outer webs of primaries, except at tips, narrowly margined with brownish white; tertials and inner secondaries more broadly edged on outer webs with dull light drab; lesser wing-coverts margined narrowly on outer webs with light drab, and broadly tipped on outer webs with brownish white, forming somewhat obscure wing-bar; superciliary stripe dull cadmium yellow or analine yellow; lores light drab or grayish light drab, remainder of sides of head and anterior part of sides of neck, with throat, jugulum, and sometimes breast, dull cadmium yellow to dull light cadmium; middle of chin and throat more or less black or chaetura black, sometimes forming long narrow solid patch, chin sometimes whitish; remainder of lower surface pale buff or grayish white, but breast and crissum somewhat washed with pale yellow, sides and flanks smoke gray to dull drab gray; lining of wing dull drab gray washed with yellow, edge of wing cadmium yellow. Bill dark brown or blackish brown, but cutting edges and mandible dull pale gray; iris dark brown; legs and feet dull bluish gray. *Adult*

female, winter: Acquired by complete postnuptial molt. Similar to nuptial adult female, but upper surface rather darker and duller, pileum more brownish; light edgings of tertials broader; lower parts duller, colors more blended; black or dark brown of throat more or less obscured by yellow tips of feathers; yellow of anterior lower parts duller and more orange, veiled by pale buff or buffy white tips of feathers, as are also sides of head and neck. *Male and female, second winter*: Acquired by complete postnuptial molt. Like that of corresponding sex of nuptial adult. *Male, first nuptial*: Acquired by partial prenuptial molt. Similar to nuptial adult female but usually larger; upper parts darker, with scattered black feathers; crown and occiput sometimes almost solidly brown; black spots on upper surface sometimes reduced to a feather or two; wings and tail as in nuptial adult female; lores black; sides of head and of neck more orange; chin black; throat usually with broad black center almost as large as in adult male, but sometimes this black much mixed with yellow; yellow of lower surface deeper, more orange, and more extended posteriorly, sometimes tinging entire lower surface. *Male, first winter*: Acquired by partial postjuvenal molt, not involving wing-quills or tail. Similar to first nuptial male, but upper surface more blended, tertials with broader whitish edgings; dark brown centers of feathers of back mostly concealed by lighter margins of feathers; upper surface without black feathers, or these feathers practically concealed by lighter edgings; pileum usually more brownish; sides of head and of neck usually somewhat darker, more orange; chin and throat sometimes without black. Similar to adult female in winter, but larger; upper surface darker—light brownish olive; sides of head usually more deeply orange, as are also throat and jugulum, black on throat usually more conspicuous. *Female, first nuptial*: Acquired by partial prenuptial molt. Similar to nuptial adult female but somewhat lighter above, yellow of head and foreneck usually paler and without black on throat. *Female, first winter*: Acquired by partial postjuvenal molt. Similar to first nuptial female, but head and sides of neck darker, of more brownish orange (less clearly yellow), as are also upper tail-coverts; upper surface more uniform, colors more blended, light wing edgings broader; throat more brownish orange (less clearly yellowish). *Male, juvenal*: Acquired by complete postnatal molt. Similar to first winter female, but wing and tail longer; upper surface lighter; coloration variable, back buffy brown, between hair brown and drab, or between vinaceous buff and drab; rump dull vinaceous buff; wing-bars more buffy—tilleul buff; tertials and secondaries with broader dull buffy or whitish edgings; cheeks primuline yellow to orange; lower surface usually paler, more clearly yellow, but crissum brighter—gamboge yellow to light cadmium. *Female, juvenal*: Similar to juvenal male, but wing and tail shorter; pileum less strongly tinged with yellow (more brownish or grayish); yellow of sides of head, of neck, and of anterior lower parts, as well as crissum, paler; remainder of lower surface averaging somewhat lighter. *Natal*: White.

MEASUREMENTS: *Adult male*: Wing, 99.1–104.9 (average, 102.4) mm.; tail, 75.4–83.6 (79.5); bill (exposed culmen), 16.5–19.6 (18.3); tarsus, 23.1–25.9 (24.4); middle toe without claw, 15.0–18.8 (16.8). *Adult female*: Wing, 91.4–98.1 (95.2); tail, 71.1–78.5 (74.4); bill, 17.0–19.0 (17.8); tarsus, 23.9–25.9 (25.1); middle toe, 15.5–17.5 (16.8).

RANGE: S. British Columbia to s.w. Manitoba (casually), south to s.e. California, n.w. Durango, Trans-Pecos Texas, and e. Coahuila. Winters from Chihuahua to Jalisco, n. Michoacán, Guerrero, and Morelos.

TEXAS: *Breeding*: Altitudinal range, 1,800 to 5,700 ft. Collected in El Paso, Hudspeth, Culberson, and Brewster cos. Locally fairly common. *Migration*: Collected north to Wichita, southeast to Duval and Cameron, west to Brewster (Aug. 11) cos. Fairly common.

NESTING: *Nest*: On mesas and in lowlands, very rarely in high mountains; in woodlands, usually not dense, or in more open country, including cultivated lands (irrigated areas, vicinity of ranches, etc.), and streets and parks of towns and cities; in tree, commonly cottonwood or willow, sometimes in mistletoe; on twigs, often on terminal portion of branch; a handsome, well-woven pouch (about twice as deep as Orchard Oriole's), usually pensile, but occasionally attached at side; composed of soft plant fibers, such as grasses, long narrow leaves, shreds of wild flax, inner bark of willow and similar trees, string, cotton, twine, horsehair, and other hair, woven into a fabric as tough as that of the Baltimore Oriole; lined with down of plants, grasses, wool, fine straw, horsehair, and feathers. *Eggs*: 2–6, usually 4–5; often elliptical ovate, but also ovate to short ovate; grayish or bluish white to pale buffy white, with streaks, lines, and spots, sometimes blotches, chiefly about larger end, of deep reddish brown, umber, black, and deep purple, and shell markings of lilac; average size, 23.9 × 16.0 mm.

TEXAS BULLOCK'S ORIOLE, Icterus bullockii eleutherus
Oberholser, new subspecies (see Appendix A)

DESCRIPTION: *Adult male and female, nuptial plumage*: Similar to *I. b. bullockii*, but orange of male much deeper on both under parts and rump; four middle tail feathers usually solidly black; female darker above.

MEASUREMENTS: *Adult male*: Wing, 98.6–104.9 (average, 102.1) mm.; tail, 73.9–85.6 (80.5); bill (exposed culmen), 17.5–20.1 (18.3); tarsus, 23.9–25.4 (24.6); middle toe without claw, 16.0–17.8 (17.0). *Adult female*: Wing, 96.0–101.1 (98.6); tail, 81.3–82.0 (81.8); bill, 18.3–18.8 (18.5); tarsus, 24.4–24.9 (24.6); middle toe, 16.0–17.0 (16.5).

TYPE: Adult male, no. 186125, U.S. National Museum, Biological Surveys collection; Del Rio, Texas; May 23, 1903; J. H. Gaut, original no., 166.

RANGE: W. Oklahoma and n. Texas, south through w. and s. Texas to n. Tamaulipas. Winters in Mexico and Guatemala; a few in Arizona, Texas, Arkansas, and Louisiana.

TEXAS: *Breeding*: Altitudinal range, near sea level to 4,200 ft. Collected north to Hutchinson, east to Wilbarger, south to Refugio and Cameron, west to Val Verde and Crane (Sept. 12) cos. Common locally. *Migration*: One specimen outside breeding range: Dallas Co., Dallas (July 27, 1897, W. A. Mayer). Common within breeding range. *Winter*: Taken in Nueces (1 specimen) and Cameron (3) cos. Rare.

NESTING: Similar to that of *I. b. bullockii*, but birds more often place nests in mesquite and pecan trees.

CALIFORNIA BULLOCK'S ORIOLE, Icterus bullockii parvus
van Rossem

DESCRIPTION: *Adult male and female, nuptial plumage*: Similar to *I. b. bullockii* but much smaller, male somewhat more yellowish (less orange); female paler above, with yellow of anterior lower parts less orange (more clearly yellow).

MEASUREMENTS: *Adult male*: Wing, 94.0–101.6 (average, 97.8) mm.; tail, 71.1–78.5 (73.4); bill (exposed culmen), 17.0–19.3 (17.8); tarsus, 22.6–24.9 (23.6); middle toe without claw, 15.0–17.0 (16.0). *Adult female*: Wing, 86.1–93.0 (89.7); tail, 70.1–77.5 (72.2); bill, 16.0–18.0 (17.3); tarsus, 22.6–24.9 (23.6); middle toe, 15.0–17.0 (16.3).

RANGE: California and n. Baja California. In migration, from w. Sonora and Trans-Pecos Texas to e. Coahuila. Winters from Durango to Colima.

TEXAS: *Migration*: One specimen: Brewster Co., 15 mi. south of Marathon (May 18, 1901, H. C. Oberholser).

LICHTENSTEIN'S ORIOLE, *Andriopsar gularis* (Wagler)

SPECIES ACCOUNT

Icterus gularis of A.O.U. check-list, 1957 (see Appendix A). Altamira Oriole, Black-throated Oriole, and "oropendola" are frequently used common names. Large; heavy bill. *Adult*: bright orange with black

throat, back, wings, tail; upper wing-bar orange or yellow, lower wing-bar white. *Immature*: yellow head, rump, under parts; otherwise mostly brownish. Length, 10 in.; wingspan, 14¼.

RANGE: Rio Grande delta of Texas, south through e. and s. Mexico (chiefly lowlands and foothills) to Nicaragua.

TEXAS: (See map.) *Resident*: Breeds, late Mar. to mid-July (no egg dates available, but young in nest, July 4, 1951) from near sea level to 200 ft. Fairly common (formerly casual) in Rio Grande delta upriver to Falcon Dam. Accidental: El Paso, Dec. 7–17, 1956 (see detailed account); Bexar Co., Fort Sam Houston (summer, 1957, Maurine McFarland).

HAUNTS AND HABITS: Even though no part of Texas is frost-free, a few truly tropical birds and plants manage to survive the one, two, or three freezing northers that sweep down into the Rio Grande delta each winter. Two of these tropicals are the showy Altamira Lichtenstein's Oriole and the tepeguaje (*Leucaena pulverulenta*), a leguminous tree with delicate, fernlike leaves, the leaflets of which fold or "sleep" at night. Typically, an Altamira's nest—which can be up to twenty-five inches deep—droops and sways gracefully from the tip of a high tepeguaje branch. This big oriole also suspends its pouch from a mesquite, willow, or other tree with slender, strong, and flexible terminal twigs. Usually this bird avoids hanging its "stocking" from a Texas ebony, since the branches of this tree are so strong and stiff that rats and other mammalian predators can easily climb to the outermost tips. The avoidance of ebony is by no means total, however: On April 25, 1970, a golden female was busily constructing her nest of Spanishmoss in the Big Ebony—said to be the largest in the United States—in Santa Ana National

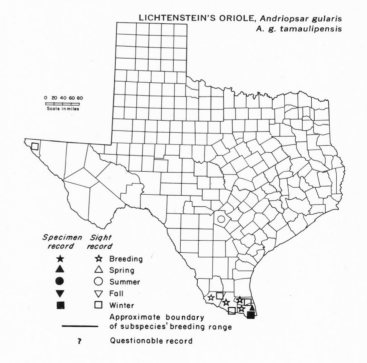

LICHTENSTEIN'S ORIOLE, *Andriopsar gularis*
A. g. tamaulipensis

0 20 40 60 80
Scale in miles

Specimen record	Sight record	
★	☆	Breeding
▲	△	Spring
●	○	Summer
▼	▽	Fall
■	▢	Winter

——— Approximate boundary of subspecies' breeding range

? Questionable record

Wildlife Refuge, Hidalgo County (Bertha McKee Dobie and E. B. Kincaid, Jr.).

Flight, rather quick and jerky, is ordinarily only from branch to branch or from one tree to another. Apparently the Altamira does not engage in majestic trans-horizon flights, as sometimes does the crow-sized *Gymnostinops montezuma*, a true oropendola which swings its fifty-inch-deep nest in great trees from southeastern Mexico to Panama. In its lightly wooded haunts, *Andriopsar gularis* forages for insects and wild fruits—hackberries (*Celtis*) and tropical figs (*Ficus*) are favorites—from tree tops to ground (occasionally). Sometimes, as at Santa Ana and Bentsen–Rio Grande Valley State Park, the bird inspects automobile radiators for grasshoppers, as well as high wires for nest support.

Lichtenstein's Oriole chatters a low-pitched, rasping *ike, ike, ike* and sings disjointed whistles, some loud and flutelike. Vocalizations are sounded chiefly from a tree perch, but sometimes notes are given in flight. Song season is all year, but singing is very infrequent on cool winter days. The male seems to depend more on his fiery orange-and-black coloration than upon song to proclaim his breeding territory. The female, almost equally brilliant, makes no attempt to hide either herself or her highly conspicuous nest.

CHANGES: Almost alone among the world's gorgeous tropical woodland birds, the Altamira Lichtenstein's Oriole is increasing, at least in Tamaulipas and Texas. The gradual rise of this species is indicated by Audubon Christmas Bird Counts taken in the Rio Grande delta of south Texas during the past quarter century:

Christmas Season	Delta Counts	Altamira Orioles
1947	1	1
1948	1	0
1949	4	0
1950	3	2
1951	1	0
1952	2	0
1953	2	0
1954	2	1
1955	2	0
1956	2	4
1957	2	3
1958	2	6
1959	4	0
1960	4	13
1961	2	25
1962	4	25
1963	4	15
1964	3	50
1965	4	10
1966	4	39
1967	4	13
1968	5	27
1969	5	30
1970	6	28
1971	6	48

When the first active Altamira nest discovered in Texas was photographed on July 4, 1951, *A. gularis* was the rarest Rio Grande delta oriole. Other nesting orioles in order of high to low abundance were Hooded,

Bullock's, Orchard, and Black-headed. From 1960 into the 1970's, the most successful breeder has been the Altamira. Why the rather rapid switch from low to high oriole on the totem pole?

Delta land in the 1950's and 1960's was about equally cleared—over 90 percent. The chief ecological change, other than mounting pesticide pollution, has been the increase in Red-eyed Bronzed Cowbirds, which has continued from the early 1950's through the present (1972). The phenomenal rise in Bronzed Cowbird numbers can be explained, at least in part, by the increase in cattle raising and grain growing in the delta following the freeze of January 29–February 1, 1951, that killed most of the citrus, previously the dominant crop in the Rio Grande Valley.

All south Texas species smaller than the cowbird nowadays seem to have trouble combating this parasite. A theory holds that only the Altamira among orioles is big and aggressive enough to defend itself successfully from nest parasitism. Perhaps also the large oriole's deep nest stocking appears like a trap to cowbirds. *A. gularis* does raise some cowbirds but, for whatever reason, it appears better able to survive heavy cowbird pressure.

DETAILED ACCOUNT: ONE SUBSPECIES

ALTAMIRA LICHTENSTEIN'S ORIOLE, *Andriopsar gularis tamaulipensis* (Ridgway)

DESCRIPTION: *Adult male, nuptial plumage*: Acquired by wear from winter. Top and sides of head and of neck between flame scarlet and orange chrome; upper back and scapulars black; lower back, rump, and upper tail-coverts similar to head, but usually somewhat lighter and duller; tail fuscous black to brownish black, its concealed base pale yellow, feathers with white shafts in this area; wings dark fuscous, inner edges somewhat lighter, outer webs and tertials brownish black, base of outer webs of primaries, margins of outer webs of terminal half of secondaries, and entire length of outer webs of tertials, together with broad tips of outer webs of greater wing-coverts, white; lesser and median wing-coverts cadmium yellow to orange; lores, narrow eye-ring, chin, middle of throat, and middle of jugulum broadly black; breast like sides of head; posterior lower parts cadmium orange to cadmium yellow, middle of abdomen lightest; lining and edge of wing cadmium yellow to orange, passing into yellowish white posteriorly. Bill black, basal portion of mandible light grayish or plumbeous blue; iris dark brown; legs and feet bluish gray or plumbeous blue. *Adult male, winter*: Acquired by complete postnuptial molt. Similar to nuptial adult male, but white edges of tertials broader, black of back edged with ochraceous orange to yellow ocher. *Adult female, nuptial*: Acquired by wear from winter. Similar to nuptial adult male, but black and yellow areas somewhat duller; black of throat of less extent; upper part of rump with olive green suffusion. *Adult female, winter*: Acquired by complete postnuptial molt. Differs from nuptial adult female as does adult male in winter from nuptial adult male. *Third winter*: Acquired by complete postnuptial molt. Like corresponding sex of adult in winter. *Second nuptial*: Acquired by wear from second winter. Similar to corresponding sex of nuptial adult, but averaging less intensely orange, some of median wing-coverts with blackish shaft streaks or spots. *Second winter*: Acquired by complete postnuptial molt. Similar to corresponding sex in second nuptial, but white edgings of tertials broader, black area of back edged with ochraceous orange to dull light cadmium. *First nuptial*: Acquired by partial prenuptial molt. Similar to corresponding sex in second nuptial, but orange and yellow areas duller (less purely orange);

back and scapulars not black, but between orange citrine and analine yellow to between analine yellow and raw sienna; upper tail-coverts between raw sienna and cadmium yellow; tail medal bronze, edged on outer webs of feathers with orange citrine; wings dull hair brown to chaetura drab, primaries and secondaries edged on outer webs with pale brown or brownish white, tertials margined exteriorly with brownish white, median and lesser coverts chaetura drab to chaetura black, median coverts broadly tipped with analine yellow to yellowish white, lesser coverts edged with orange citrine, greater coverts broadly tipped on outer webs with dull white. *First winter:* Acquired by partial postjuvenal molt. Similar to first nuptial, but upper surface duller, somewhat overlaid by gray or olivaceous, white edgings of tertials broader. Bill black, but base of mandible light bluish gray; iris dark brown; legs and feet dull plumbeous. *Juvenal:* Acquired by complete postnatal molt. Pileum and hindneck between primuline yellow and analine yellow; upper back and scapulars between buffy citrine and light brownish olive, shading on rump to between sulphine yellow and analine yellow, and on upper tail-coverts to between yellow ocher and light cadmium; tail as in first winter, but somewhat more grayish brown, tips of feathers dull lemon yellow; wing-quills hair brown to dark hair brown, outer webs of bases of primaries broadly white, outer webs of remaining portions of primaries and of secondaries also dull white, inner secondaries and tertials broadly margined on outer webs with dull white, greater coverts on outer webs and median coverts on both webs broadly tipped with naphthalene yellow to amber yellow, lesser coverts more or less broadly tipped and edged with analine yellow; sides of head and of neck like pileum, but slightly more tinged with orange, lores dull dark brown, somewhat mixed with olivaceous; lower surface, including lining of wings, dull lemon yellow to light cadmium, throat sometimes with a few spots of light brownish olive or chaetura drab. *Natal:* Unknown.

MEASUREMENTS: *Adult male:* Wing, 108.2–118.1 (average, 114.3) mm.; tail, 97.3–111.0 (104.4); bill (from base), 24.6–26.7 (25.7); height of bill at base, 13.0–14.7 (13.7); tarsus, 29.4–31.0 (29.9); middle toe without claw, 19.3–21.9 (20.3). *Adult female:* Wing, 105.4–110.7 (108.2); tail, 95.0–103.4 (99.8); bill, 23.6–25.7 (24.6); height of bill, 12.7–14.0 (13.2); tarsus, 28.7–29.9 (29.4); middle toe, 19.6–22.4 (20.3).

RANGE: Rio Grande delta of Texas, south along Gulf of Mexico slope to Puebla, Tabasco, and extreme w. Campeche.

TEXAS: *Resident:* Three specimens: Cameron Co. (Apr. 11, May 9, 1890, F. B. Armstrong; Jan. 7, 1938, T. D. Burleigh). First active nest discovered: Cameron Co., Santa Maria (bird and nest photographed in color, July 4, 1951, C. T. Gill). No specimen from Hidalgo Co., but birds and nests photographed scores of times at Santa Ana Nat. Wildlife Refuge and Bentsen–Rio Grande Valley State Park (e.g., see Robert Murphy, 1968, *Wild Sanctuaries,* p. 103, for color photo of *A. gularis* at nest in Santa Ana). Accidental in El Paso Co. (immature bird, Dec. 7–17, 1956, photographed in color on 8 mm. film, Dec. 17, by Mrs. D. T. Johnson; bird identified by Mary Belle Keefer).

NESTING: *Nest:* In lowlands and on hill slopes; in woodlands or cultivated areas; in tree, 12–35 ft. above ground, or utility line; a long (1–2 ft.), pensile pouch, fastened to ends of mostly horizontal branches, composed of Spanishmoss, palm, and other vegetable fibers; lined with grass, plant down, and similar materials. Starting at the top and working down, the female with her bill weaves nest in 18 to 26 days. *Eggs:* 3–4; ovate to near elliptical oval; slightly glossy; pale grayish white; streaked, lined, spotted, and dotted with dark chocolate brown and lavender, these confined chiefly to larger end; average size, 26.4 × 18.8 mm.

RUSTY BLACKBIRD, *Euphagus carolinus* (Müller)

SPECIES ACCOUNT

Slender bill; moderate tail (not elongated); pale yel-

low eyes (both sexes). *Male:* black (lacks iridescence). *Female:* slaty. *Winter birds:* rusty bars on body; buffy eye-stripe. Length, 9¼ in.; wingspan, 14¼; weight, 2¼ oz.

RANGE: Alaska, Canada, and extreme n.e. United States. Winters mainly in e. United States (east of Rocky Mts.) from Canadian border to Gulf coast.

TEXAS: (See map.) *Winter:* Early Nov. to late Mar. (extremes: July 14, May 4). Common locally (some years) to uncommon in eastern half, but increasingly scarce west of 98th meridian to western Panhandle and Trans-Pecos, where casual. Not recorded south of 28th parallel.

HAUNTS AND HABITS: The Rusty Blackbird ordinarily, in both winter and summer, lives in very different habitat from that used by its "look-alike," the Brewer's Blackbird. This is indeed fortunate; otherwise, bird watchers would confuse the two species most of the time, instead of much of the time. Basically the Rusty likes woods and wetness; the Brewer's seeks plains and dryness. From chilly northern woody and bushy bogs—where it nests in shrubs or conifers near water—the Rusty migrates to the Gulf and Atlantic states to winter in damp woods surrounding pools.

In Texas, availability of prime habitat is very erratic, due largely to inconsistent amounts of rainfall. In wet years, woodland pools may be plentiful, and in dry years nearly all of them may be dusty. As a consequence of this and probably other factors, the species varies tremendously in numbers from winter to winter. These yearly fluctuations tend to mask any long-term changes in status that may be taking place.

In winter the Rusty is gregarious and sometimes gathers in flocks of considerable size, often associated with Red-winged Blackbirds, cowbirds, or grackles. In

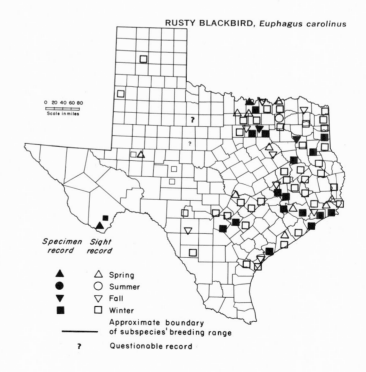

RUSTY BLACKBIRD, *Euphagus carolinus*

0 20 40 60 80
Scale in miles

Specimen record	Sight record	
▲	△	Spring
●	○	Summer
▼	▽	Fall
■	□	Winter

——— Approximate boundary of subspecies' breeding range

? Questionable record

flight, flocks are somewhat swifter and more compact than those of the Redwing. At pool margins, Rusties actively walk and wade with deliberation, constantly babbling a variety of clucks and whistles. When flushed, the flock retreats temporarily to branches of a nearby tree.

The Rusty eats more insects than other North American blackbirds. It feeds largely on beetles and their larvae (predaceous forms, May, leaf, and aquatic beetles, and weevils), caterpillars, and grasshoppers. Moths, ants, bugs, flies, dragonflies, caddis flies, and mayflies also fall prey to the Rusty. Spiders, millipedes, a few snails, small fishes, and salamanders, together with many crustaceans, compose the rest of its animal food. The vegetable portion of its diet consists largely of grain, preferably rice, great quantities of waste being ingested in the old rice stubble. Various weed seeds and wild fruit also form part of its food.

The most common call of the Rusty is a harsh, grating *tschak*, once or twice repeated; but it also emits a variety of gracklelike clucks and whistles. Its "song" is a penetrating *koo-a-lee*, much like the creak of a rusty hinge.

DETAILED ACCOUNT: ONE SUBSPECIES

CONTINENTAL RUSTY BLACKBIRD, *Euphagus carolinus carolinus* (Müller)

DESCRIPTION: *Adult male, nuptial plumage*: Acquired by wear from winter plumage. Upper surface metallic dull greenish black or metallic greenish slate black, very slightly more bluish on pileum; tail same color, inner margins of feathers chaetura black to fuscous black; wings fuscous black, coverts and outer edgings of quills like upper surface; lower surface like upper surface, but somewhat duller, under tail-coverts narrowly tipped with pale gray. Bill black; iris primrose yellow, straw yellow, or white; legs and feet black or brownish black. *Adult male, winter*: Acquired by complete postnuptial molt. Similar to nuptial adult male, but feathers of entire upper surface, particularly pileum, hindneck, back, and scapulars, broadly tipped with auburn or light auburn, these tips often almost entirely covering black of pileum, involving, usually to a less degree, rump and upper tail-coverts, tips of tertials, and tips of some wing-coverts, where these markings are narrower; conspicuous superciliary stripe, ochraceous tawny to dull cream buff; tips of feathers on sides of head and of neck, particularly cheeks, mostly pinkish buff, dull cinnamon buff, or grayish white, but cheeks dull cinnamon buff, as are edgings of lower parts, with exception of middle of abdomen which is sometimes immaculate. Bill brownish black, but base of mandible paler. *Adult female, nuptial*: Acquired by wear from winter. Upper surface deep mouse gray or dark mouse gray, sometimes slightly overlaid with olive brown, and slightly glossed with dull green; tail fuscous black with gloss of metallic dull greenish black; wings fuscous to fuscous black, outer margins of quills and coverts similar to upper surface, but secondaries, tertials, and greater coverts sometimes distinctly edged with dull dark brown; sides of head and of neck, together with entire lower parts, similar to upper surface, but somewhat paler, between deep mouse gray and mouse gray. Iris light yellow. *Adult female, winter*: Acquired by complete postnuptial molt. Similar to nuptial adult female, but pileum, hindneck, back, and scapulars much obscured by broad auburn or light auburn tips of feathers; this of less extent on upper tail-coverts, tertials, inner secondaries, and greater wing-coverts; tail feathers sometimes with narrow brownish or buffy tip; conspicuous superciliary stripe light auburn to dull ochraceous, sometimes almost obsolete; sides of head and of neck much overlaid with ochraceous tawny to dull cream buff; lower surface paler than nuptial

—mouse gray, most of feathers, except sometimes those on middle of abdomen, broadly tipped with pinkish buff to dull cinnamon or grayish white. *Male and female, second winter*: Acquired by complete postnuptial molt. Like that of corresponding sex in nuptial adult. *Male, first nuptial*: Acquired by wear from first winter. Similar to nuptial adult male, but upper and lower surface duller and less glossy; superciliary area and chin with usually some dull pale buff or whitish feathers; upper surface of body and sometimes anterior lower parts with narrow brown edgings, these appearing also on scapulars, greater wing-coverts, and tertials. *Male, first winter*: Acquired by complete postjuvenal molt. Similar to adult male in winter, but feathers of upper surface usually more broadly edged with lighter brown—light auburn to ochraceous tawny, pileum and back sometimes almost solidly brown, and edgings on tertials and wing-coverts broader and lighter; sides of head and of neck more broadly, sometimes almost solidly, edged with same browns and buffs; edgings on lower surface more numerous, broader, and paler, jugulum often solidly clay color to cinnamon buff, giving lower surface lighter appearance than in adult. Bill black; iris light sage green or naples yellow; legs, feet, and claws black. *Female, first nuptial*: Acquired by wear from first winter. Similar to nuptial adult female, but upper surface lighter and more brownish, this appearance imparted by more numerous and broader auburn and light auburn edgings of feathers; secondaries, tertials, and greater wing-coverts also with broader dark brown edgings; lower surface usually paler, feathers with more numerous and broader edgings and tips of brown or dull buff, and often with distinct demarcation between throat and jugulum. *Female, first winter*: Acquired by complete postjuvenal molt. Similar to adult female in winter, but upper surface averaging lighter, particularly pileum, which is deep russet to dull russet; sides of head and of neck, including superciliary stripe, decidedly paler, particularly superciliary stripe, which is broad, conspicuous, and cream buff to ochraceous tawny; chin decidedly paler, usually more or less dull white or pale buff; remainder of lower surface averaging paler, so far as both gray ground color and edgings of feathers are concerned. Iris burnt umber. *Juvenal*: Acquired by complete postnatal molt. Above chaetura drab to dark hair brown, but feathers edged more or less broadly with auburn to tawny; tail as in first winter female, but more brownish with little or no metallic sheen; wings fuscous, coverts, primaries, and secondaries edged externally with tawny or rather light tawny; sides of head like pileum, but somewhat lighter; superciliary stripe and postocular stripe still paler—dull verona brown to sayal brown; chin pale cinnamon buff to whitish buff; throat, jugulum, and breast dull sayal brown; remainder of lower surface dull mouse gray, washed with sayal brown or dull pale buff. Bill dark brown, but base of mandible decidedly paler; legs and feet dull brown or black.

MEASUREMENTS: *Adult male*: Wing, 111.0–119.9 (average, 115.3) mm.; tail, 81.5–94.0 (86.4); bill (exposed culmen), 18.5–20.1 (19.3); height of bill at base, 7.6–8.1 (7.9); tarsus, 30.5–32.5 (31.8); middle toe without claw, 19.6–21.6 (20.9). *Adult female*: Wing, 102.1–109.0 (105.6); tail, 75.9–85.1 (81.3); bill, 16.8–19.0 (17.8); height of bill, 7.1–8.1 (7.6); tarsus, 28.4–31.5 (29.7); middle toe, 18.5–20.6 (19.3).

RANGE: Alaska and mainland Canada, south to n.e. North Dakota and Maine. Winters from n.w. Minnesota and n.e. Massachusetts to Texas, n. Gulf coast, and n. Florida.

TEXAS: *Winter*: Taken north to Cooke, east to Harrison and Jefferson, south to Calhoun, west to Bexar cos. Two specimens from Brewster Co.: 22 mi. south of Alpine (Mar. 4, 1935, J. Van Tyne); Big Bend Nat. Park (Dec. 10, 1967, R. H. Wauer).

BREWER'S BLACKBIRD, *Euphagus cyanocephalus* (Wagler)

SPECIES ACCOUNT   *See colorplate 27*

Male: iridescent black (duller in winter), appearing

violet on head; pale yellow eye. *Female*: grayish; dark brown eye (year-round). Length, 9¼ in.; wingspan, 15¼; weight, 2½ oz.

RANGE: C. British Columbia to w. Great Lakes region, south to n.w. Baja California, s. Nevada, n.e. Arizona, n. New Mexico, and Iowa. Winters from s.w. British Columbia, Montana, Kansas, and w. Tennessee to n.w. Guatemala, Gulf states, and n.w. Florida.

TEXAS: (See map.) *Breeding*: One definite record: eggs taken, Wilbarger Co., Vernon (May 13, 1928, G. E. Maxon, R. L. More); reported nesting in Davis Mts. (Pansy Espy, fide R. H. Wauer). *Winter*: Late Sept.—often mid-July in western third—to late Apr. (extremes: July 5, June 8). Abundant to fairly common in all parts, but local in heavily wooded eastern portion.

HAUNTS AND HABITS: The Brewer's Blackbird is much less dependent upon wetlands for nesting habitat than are its relatives, the Yellow-headed, Red-winged, and Rusty blackbirds, and the Boat-tailed Grackle, *Cassidix major*. Over much of the arid and agricultural West it is the dominant native blackbird. Although the Brewer's often nests and roosts in trees or bushes, it spends most of its life walking over deserts, cattle pastures, stock pens, and open fields.

Huge flocks may fly in tight formation or stretch, loosely formed, for more than a mile. Flight is stronger and more rapid than that of the Redwing. Massive foraging flocks consume great quantities of grain (two-thirds of the diet) and insects (about one-third). They eat principally oats, corn, wheat, barley, and rye, but also some fruit; beetles, ants, wasps, termites, grasshoppers, crickets, caterpillars, two-winged flies, and bugs, together with some spiders and snails, form the animal portion of the diet. Feeding flocks frequently "roll"

across a plowed or stubble field in the manner described under Red-winged Blackbird.

The Brewer's usual call note is a harsh *tcheck*, but the bird has others—squeaks, trills, whistles, and cacks —which combine to produce a noisy chatter when birds are flocked. The "song" is a wheezy *que-ee* or *ksh-eee*, much like the creak of a rusty hinge.

CHANGES: During the first half of the twentieth century enormous numbers of Brewer's Blackbirds flew southeast to winter in the rice fields of the upper Texas coast. These and other blackbirds that wintered with them were called "ricebirds" by Texas farmers. "Smokebirds" was another folk name because the huge flocks resembled palls of oil smoke, also frequent in the same region.

Since 1950 the flocks have thinned somewhat with decline of rice growing and upsurge of poison and pollution. However, those ranches and livestock feed lots, particularly in the western half of Texas, which are not heavily poisoned have retained impressive numbers of wintering Brewer's Blackbirds.

DETAILED ACCOUNT: FOUR SUBSPECIES

IDAHO BREWER'S BLACKBIRD, *Euphagus cyanocephalus cyanocephalus* (Wagler)

No races recognized by A.O.U. check-list, 1957 (see Appendix A).

DESCRIPTION: *Adult male, nuptial plumage*: Acquired by wear from winter plumage. Top and sides of head, together with chin and throat, metallic dull violet black; remainder of upper and lower parts metallic dusky olive green to dusky yellowish green, tips of feathers rather duller, imparting shadowy barred or scaled effect; tail same, inner margins of feathers dull chaetura black; wings chaetura black, outer margins of quills, together with coverts, like back; lining of wing chaetura black, feathers edged mostly with metallic green of under parts. Bill, legs, feet, and claws black; iris sulphur yellow, straw yellow, lemon yellow, or cream white. *Adult male, winter*: Acquired by complete postnuptial molt. Similar to nuptial adult male, but upper surface duller, feathers edged and tipped, particularly on pileum, hindneck, and back, with dull drab or snuff brown; lower surface and sides of head also duller, posterior lower parts somewhat, but rather obscurely, tipped with dull brown; feathers of sides of head, throat, and jugulum more or less tipped with tilleul buff or light drab. *Adult female, nuptial*: Acquired by wear from winter. Pileum between hair brown and drab; remainder of upper surface somewhat metallic dusky olive green; tail same, but rather more metallic, inner margins of feathers fuscous; wings fuscous, outer webs of primaries and secondaries metallic green like back, but tips of primaries and inner secondaries and tertials margined with fuscous, wing-coverts green like back, narrowly edged on outer webs with fuscous; sides of head like crown, but paler and rather darker; postocular streak and lores somewhat darker; sides of neck similar but a little more deeply colored; chin and throat between smoke gray and tilleul buff or between light drab and vinaceous buff, tip of chin palest; jugulum buffy drab to dull light buffy brown; remainder of lower surface, including lining of wing, chaetura drab to between hair brown and fuscous. Bill black; iris light brown, dark brown, dark hazel, black, exceptionally dull buffy yellow or reddish yellow; legs and feet black or brownish black. *Adult female, winter*: Acquired by complete postnuptial molt. Similar to nuptial adult female, but upper surface lighter, more brownish, and much overlaid by buffy brown and olive brown tips of feathers; sides of head and of neck lighter and more brownish; lower surface lighter, more brownish, and more uniform, plumage more blended, breast and jugulum light buffy brown or dull tawny olive.

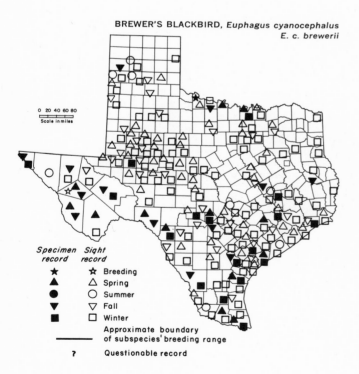

BREWER'S BLACKBIRD, *Euphagus cyanocephalus*
E. c. brewerii

0 20 40 60 80
Scale in miles

Specimen record	Sight record	
★	☆	Breeding
▲	△	Spring
●	○	Summer
▼	▽	Fall
■	□	Winter

Approximate boundary of subspecies' breeding range
? Questionable record

Male, first nuptial: Acquired by wear from first winter. Except for retained juvenal feathers, similar to nuptial adult male, but pileum and upper hindneck, together with throat, more greenish or bluish (less purely or strongly violet). *Male, first winter*: Acquired by partial or complete postjuvenal molt. Similar to adult male in winter, but head less strongly violet (more bluish or greenish); upper surface, particularly pileum, hindneck, and back, much overlaid with drab or light drab edgings and margins of feathers, almost entirely concealing metallic color of pileum; feathers of sides of head and of neck, and parts of back, and of anterior lower surface much more broadly tipped with light drab or drab, in places almost entirely obscuring metallic green portions of feathers. *Female, first nuptial*: Acquired by wear from first winter. Like nuptial adult female except for retained juvenal feathers. *Female, first winter*: Acquired by partial or complete postjuvenal molt. Similar to adult female in winter but somewhat lighter and more brownish on upper surface, particularly on pileum and hindneck, and more brownish, rather lighter on lower surface, particularly on anterior portion. *Male, juvenal*: Acquired by complete postnuptial molt. Pileum light fuscous; remainder of upper surface, including wings, fuscous; tail fuscous black; throat light mouse gray; sides of head similar, but darker, and rather more brownish; jugulum dull light sayal brown; remainder of lower surface brownish deep mouse gray. Bill, legs, and feet dull brown; iris pale yellow. *Female, juvenal*: Acquired by complete postnatal molt. Similar to juvenal male but lighter and more rufescent brown; pileum buffy brown, back and wings olive brown; tail between clove brown and fuscous; chin and throat between light drab and avellaneous; jugulum dull light buffy brown, middle of abdomen dull (rather buff drab), sides, flanks, and crissum rufescent hair brown. *Natal* (this plumage of this race not seen in Texas): Dull pale tilleul buff.

MEASUREMENTS: *Adult male*: Wing, 125.0–136.9 (average, 130.8) mm.; tail, 95.0–104.6 (100.3); bill (exposed culmen), 18.5–21.6 (19.8); tarsus, 31.5–34.5 (32.8); middle toe without claw, 20.6–22.6 (21.4). *Adult female*: Wing, 116.6–125.0 (121.2); tail, 88.4–95.5 (91.9); bill, 16.5–20.6 (19.0); height of bill at base, 8.6–9.4 (9.1); tarsus, 30.5–33.0 (31.8); middle toe, 18.0–21.1 (19.3).

RANGE: C. Alberta and s.e. Wyoming, south to c. Arizona and n. New Mexico. Winters from s.w. Washington and c. Idaho through California, Arizona, and Texas to s. Baja California and n. Guatemala.

TEXAS: *Winter*: Taken north to Oldham (Oct. 26), east to Angelina (Nov. 26), south to Cameron, west to El Paso cos. Common.

NESTING: (This race does not nest in Texas.) *Nest*: On mesas, uplands, and in river valleys; in more open parts of country, even in gardens, ornamental grounds, and other cultivated areas, along irrigation ditches or in similar places; often in colonies; either on ground or in a bush or tree, rarely above 30 ft.; when on ground usually sunk in tuft of grass, and well concealed, often in damp situations or even among reeds; large, bulky cup, composed of sticks, twigs, rootlets, grasses, weed stalks, grass stems, reeds, strips of bark, roots, sometimes moss, these materials usually, but not always, plastered together with mud or with cow or horse droppings; lined with grasses, rootlets, decayed bark, moss, and horse and cow hair. *Eggs*: 4–8, usually 5–6; usually ovate, sometimes short ovate, elliptical ovate, or rarely almost elliptical oval; dull greenish white, bluish white, or grayish white, or even dull greenish gray or olivaceous gray, with blotches, streaks, and spots of seal brown, walnut brown, liver brown, clove brown, rood brown, cameo brown, russet, cinnamon rufous, fawn color, and with shell markings of lilac and lavender, sometimes so numerous and confluent as almost to conceal ground color; average size, 25.9 × 18.5 mm.

DAKOTA BREWER'S BLACKBIRD, *Euphagus cyanocephalus brewerii* (Audubon)

No races recognized by A.O.U. check-list, 1957 (see Appendix A).

DESCRIPTION: *Adult male and female, nuptial plumage*: Like *E. c. cyanocephalus* in size and color of male, though slightly more bluish (less yellowish) green, but female is much darker and more grayish (less rufescent) brown, both above and below. *Natal*: Probably similar to *E. c. cyanocephalus*.

MEASUREMENTS: *Adult male*: Wing, 125.0–133.1 (average, 128.8) mm.; tail, 95.5–103.6 (99.6); bill (exposed culmen), 18.0–20.1 (19.3); tarsus, 31.0–33.5 (32.3); middle toe without claw, 19.6–22.6 (21.4). *Adult female*: Wing, 113.0–121.2 (117.1); tail, 85.6–93.0 (89.7); bill, 17.0–19.6 (17.8); tarsus, 29.4–32.5 (30.7); middle toe, 19.0–20.6 (19.8).

RANGE: S.w. Montana to w. Ontario, south to n. Texas. Winters from s. Montana and n. South Carolina to s.e. New Mexico, Texas, and n.w. Florida.

TEXAS: *Breeding*: Eggs collected at Vernon probably of this subspecies (see species account). *Winter*: Taken north to Cooke, east to Chambers, south to Cameron, west to Midland cos. Common.

NESTING: Similar to that of *E. c. cyanocephalus*.

WESTERN BREWER'S BLACKBIRD, *Euphagus cyanocephalus aliastus* Oberholser

No races recognized by A.O.U. check-list, 1957 (see Appendix A).

DESCRIPTION: *Adult male and female, nuptial plumage*: Similar to *E. c. cyanocephalus*, but male with posterior lower surface more bluish (less yellowish) metallic green; female darker, particularly on lower surface, and usually much less rufescent (more grayish).

MEASUREMENTS: *Adult male*: Wing, 128.0–133.6 (average, 131.3) mm.; tail, 97.1–111.0 (102.4); bill (exposed culmen), 18.0–22.6 (20.3); tarsus, 30.5–36.1 (33.5); middle toe without claw, 19.8–23.1 (21.4). *Adult female*: Wing, 115.1–124.0 (119.4); tail, 87.1–95.0 (91.2); bill, 17.0–19.0 (18.3); tarsus, 29.9–33.0 (31.2); middle toe, 18.5–21.6 (19.8).

RANGE: S. British Columbia, south to Washington, Oregon, Idaho, and Nevada. Winters from s. British Columbia and s.w. Wyoming to w. California, s. Arizona, and Trans-Pecos Texas.

TEXAS: *Winter*: Taken northwest to El Paso, east to Kinney, south to Brewster (May 2) and Presidio (May 1) cos. Rare.

CALIFORNIA BREWER'S BLACKBIRD, *Euphagus cyanocephalus minusculus* Grinnell

No races recognized by A.O.U. check-list, 1957 (see Appendix A).

DESCRIPTION: *Adult male and female, nuptial plumage*: Similar to *E. c. cyanocephalus* but smaller; female darker and less brownish (more grayish below).

MEASUREMENTS: *Adult male*: Wing, 126.5–130.0 (average, 128.3) mm.; tail, 95.5–103.1 (98.8); bill (exposed culmen), 18.5–20.9 (19.8); tarsus, 29.9–33.5 (31.8); middle toe without claw, 20.6–22.9 (21.9). *Adult female*: Wing, 115.1–118.1 (116.3); tail, 87.1–91.4 (88.9); bill, 17.0–18.5 (17.8); tarsus, 29.9–31.0 (30.2); middle toe, 19.8–22.1 (21.4).

RANGE: W. Oregon, south to n. Baja California. Winters from breeding range to s. Baja California, n. Sonora, and Veracruz. Casual in Trans-Pecos Texas.

TEXAS: *Winter*: One specimen: Jeff Davis Co., 6 mi. northeast of Fort Davis (Apr. 30, 1937, J. Van Tyne).

GREAT-TAILED GRACKLE, *Cassidix mexicanus* (Gmelin)

SPECIES ACCOUNT

"Jackdaw" and "crow-blackbird" of colloquial speech. The Boat-tailed Grackle of A.O.U. check-list, 1957, includes both *Cassidix major* and *C. mexicanus*.

A large grackle with long pointed bill. Adults of both sexes have pale yellow eyes (eyes of *C. major* in Texas and Louisiana are dark brown). *Male*: black with strong blue and violet iridescence; long, keel-shaped tail—so heavy it sags downward when bird flies. Distinguished from male *C. major* by flat (not rounded) crown; truly great tail—longer than wing; and comparatively low-pitched voice. *Female*: smaller than male; tail keeled only slightly or not at all; brown with faint gloss confined to upper parts. Grayer brown under parts than in female *C. major*. Length, 18¼ in. (male), 14 (female); wingspan, 23¼ (male), 18¾ (female); weight, 8 oz. (male), 4 (female).

RANGE: S.e. Arizona, New Mexico, Oklahoma, and s. Kansas (arrived 1964), south through Texas, Mexico, and Central America to n.w. South America. First Nevada specimen collected, Apr. 16, 1973. See CHANGES.

TEXAS: (See map.) *Resident*: Breeds, Mar. to early Aug. (eggs, Apr. 1 to July 19) from near sea level to 3,800 ft. Abundant to common (chiefly through open or partly wooded flatlands) from Oklahoma border (Red River) south along eastern edge of Edwards Plateau to mouth of Rio Grande; fairly common very locally in Trans-Pecos. Scarce straggler (nonbreeder) to Panhandle, Edwards Plateau, and most of wooded eastern portion. Now (1972) apparently resident in Henderson and Anderson cos. (fide C. D. Fisher).

HAUNTS AND HABITS: The Great-tailed Grackle inhabits flatlands, both along the coast and inland; it avoids hills, mountains, waterless deserts, and heavily wooded areas. This highly gregarious bird is greatly attracted to towns, cities, and agricultural lands.

In early morning, a flock flies out from its roost in an isolated shade tree or grove, often one surrounded by houses, to forage in farmlands, gardens, pastures, live-

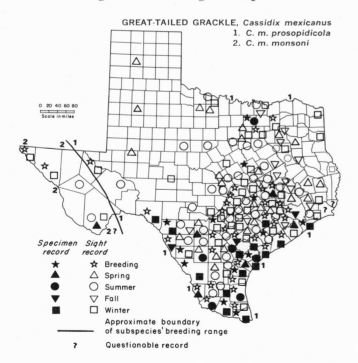

GREAT-TAILED GRACKLE, *Cassidix mexicanus*
1. *C. m. prosopidicola*
2. *C. m. monsoni*

0 20 40 60 80
Scale in miles

Specimen   Sight
record   record

★ ☆ Breeding
▲ △ Spring
● ○ Summer
▼ ▽ Fall
■ □ Winter

——— Approximate boundary of subspecies' breeding range

?   Questionable record

stock feed lots, puddles, and garbage dumps. However, numerous individuals remain in town through the day to feed in parks, yards, and lawns, and on sidewalks and streets. As the sun sinks low in the west, long lines of birds stream back to their roost. On clear afternoons, groups fly one hundred or more feet above tree and house tops, in contrast to morning flights of birds which usually "hedge-hop." *Cassidix mexicanus* is, in theory, strictly diurnal and nonmigratory. However, during fall migration season, the senior editor has seen one old bird dragging his great tail across the face of the full moon.

On sunny days in late winter, adult male grackles begin separating from their flocks to take up breeding territories. Each bird stations himself on a tree, bush, post, or other eminence. Here he puffs out his feathers, shrieks, and, with his yellow eyes glaring, attempts to look fierce to other males. If an intruding male is not intimidated by this ogre, the territory holder is likely to fly toward the interloper and go into a different display. Now he threatens the trespasser by smoothing down his feathers and pointing his bill skyward—as if poised to crash his "sword" down upon the skull of his rival. The intruder usually strikes a similar pose. Often the two grackles will face each other in their "star-gazing" position for minutes at a time without moving a muscle. In the breeding season this threat display is very frequently used on both nesting and feeding plots; on the latter, the threat is usually acted out upon the ground. As a rule, the interloper eventually walks off, or is driven away.

In spring, females leave their flocks and fly into, or near, male territories. Males solicit them with insistent *chee-chee-chee* notes. Often, one will chase a female, but she, unencumbered with an oversized tail, flies faster—*Cassidix mexicanus* is one of the few members of the animal kingdom in which rape is extremely unlikely! When hen grackles have just about finished weaving their basket-shaped nests, they allow the cocks to mate with them. Ordinarily a male takes no part in nesting activities other than standing guard—to some extent—near his section of a nesting colony. Occasionally a male Great-tail will feed young out of the nest, but this is freak behavior, not normal as it is with the male Nicaraguan Grackle, *Cassidix nicaraguensis*. In her colony nest—located in bushes or trees standing in water or on dry land—a female Great-tailed Grackle incubates her eggs for thirteen or fourteen days. Then she broods and feeds her nestlings for twenty to twenty-three days. During spring and early summer she usually tries to raise two families.

In late summer, hen grackles, along with their semi-protectors, begin to molt. In September, numerous Great-tails lose so many of their caudal feathers that they become no-tails. However, they do not molt all their flight feathers at once, as do waterfowl; a land bird must be able to fly away from pouncing cats, dogs, etc., at all times. By the time autumn northers are cold enough to chill, both sexes have grown a sleek new coat of feathers. Adult males and females forage and roost largely in separate flocks until warm days of late winter when increasing day length triggers a new breeding cycle.

Great-tailed Grackles, like rats and people, are omnivorous. They are heavy eaters of corn (25 to 50 percent of the diet in some localities), rice, sorghum, oats, and other field and feedlot grain. Birds also consume grapes, figs, other fruits, berries, chufa tubers, and all sorts of root and leafy vegetables. On garbage dumps they gobble up meat, potato, bread, and other food scraps. Animal food, live or carrion, includes grasshoppers, beetles, caterpillars, army worms, crayfish, crabs, shrimps, lizards, frogs, toads, mice, and shrews. In the lower Rio Grande Valley, a grackle paradise created by man's clearing and agriculture, the Great-tail has become a serious predator on White-winged Dove eggs. The San Antonio Zoo is a good place to witness the universal diet of *Cassidix mexicanus*. Here wild grackles eat food intended for such diverse animals as monkeys, hippopotami, longhorn steers, cassowaries, ducks, cranes, and goldfish. Only the snakes are spared this pilferage—their live mouse diet is given to them in grackle-proof cages.

Male Great-tailed Grackles are extremely noisy at all times of the year—ear-splittingly so in the warmer months as a flock gathers to go to roost. In addition to their *chee-chee-chee*'s, sounded chiefly in the breeding season, they utter a variety of whistles, wheezes, shrieks, rattles, clatters, crashes, stick-breaking noises, *cack*'s, *wheee*'s, *may-ree*'s, etc. Females are notably quiet in comparison but at times utter *cac*'s and *cluck*'s.

CHANGES: In the first dozen years of the twentieth century, the Great-tailed Grackle flourished in, and was apparently confined to, what Texans call the south Texas brush country—the rangeland from San Antonio to the mouth of the Rio Grande—and to the coastal prairie. Then, during World War I (1914–1918), the species began a range expansion within and beyond Texas that still (early 1970's) continues.

First serious northward range extension was noted on June 3, 1915, when Elton Perry, Jr., found four slightly incubated eggs at Austin. Grackle population build-up was moderate for some years thereafter. As late as the mid-1920's, the Great-tail was only a "rare and local summer resident; early March to July," according to George Finlay Simmons (1925, *Birds of the Austin Region*, p. 185). By the 1950's, the average number in the city of Austin at any time of the year was approximately 10,000, according to grackle expert Robert K. Selander. At Waco, one hundred miles north of Austin, the species established itself in about 1938, fide E. C. Fritz and Hal Kirby.

Cassidix mexicanus took another great leap forward during World War II (1939–1945) and the 1950's. In order to learn of grackle advance, the senior editor sent a questionnaire dated October 20, 1957, to members of the Texas Ornithological Society living in the northern half of the state. Some information condensed from replies of these sharp-eyed observers follows:

North central Texas: The species reached Fort Worth on April 26, 1944 (Mrs. Robert H. Bowman). Warren M. Pulich observed that although the species was absent from a list of Fort Worth (Tarrant Co.) birds compiled by G. M. Sutton in 1938 and from a thorough check-list of nearby Dallas County birds published by Jerry Stillwell in 1939, the Great-tail was well established and nesting when he arrived in the Fort Worth area in 1952. C. E. Kiblinger summarized Great-tailed Grackle increase in the Dallas vicinity thus: First bird appeared in 1947; in 1951 there were several pairs; nesting was recorded from 1952 through 1957. In 1956, Bachman Lake had more than 100 individuals; White Rock Lake, at least 25; Trinity River bottoms, over 100; and Mountain Creek, 100 plus. The species was seldom seen around Denton in 1950, but by 1956 birds were coming in flocks of up to 60 individuals, and some were nesting (Kent and Roddy Rylander).

Trans-Pecos: This grackle has been present—and nesting most of the time—in the El Paso area since 1932 or earlier (J. E. Galley, Lena McBee, W. W. Wimberly). By 1950 the bird was well established at numerous places along the Pecos River and in the irrigated fields around Balmorhea in Reeves County (W. L. Ammon, H. L. Williams).

Edwards Plateau: The "jackdaw" had not penetrated this region much as of 1957. It was not present at Brady, McCulloch County (Clarence Snider), Boerne, Kendall County (Mr. and Mrs. D. T. Smith), Kerrville, Kerr County (L. R. Wolfe), Fredericksburg, Gillespie County (Smith), Wimberley, Hays County (Hazel Green), or Blanco, Blanco County (Elizabeth Galligher). Mary Walker wrote that she sometimes saw Great-tails pass over Leander, Williamson County, in spring and fall; however, Georgetown, a lowland grackle haunt just east of the plateau, is situated only about eleven airline miles away. During the 1950's, a few birds followed the Colorado River into the plateau as far as the shores of Lake Travis, western Travis County (F. S. Webster, Jr., et al.).

East Texas: The heavy forests of this region were still repelling the big grackle up to 1957, but on the western fringes, where trees are more widely spaced, invasion was beginning. No *C. mexicanus* had been seen around Marshall, Harrison County (Vera Allen) or Nacogdoches, Nacogdoches County (C. W. Deaton, Howard McCarley, Bill Stephenson, Mary W. Thomson). Presence in Paris, Lamar County, was unconfirmed (Addie E. Beacham). The species was first recorded in nearby Commerce, Hunt County, in 1949 (Mrs. Mike O'Neil). In the town of Van, Van Zandt County, three or four pairs started nesting in the spring of 1956; in pastures near Lake Trinidad, Henderson County, more than 200 grackles were seen in the mid-1950's; the first record for Smith County was a female which appeared near Tyler on May 1, 1956 (O. C. Sheffield).

Panhandle: The Panhandle south to Midland was the last major part of Texas to be infiltrated. As of 1957, the species had not been reported in Lubbock (R. E. Hammond, W. E. McMillan) or Amarillo (Peggy

Acord, J. D. Thompson, Jr.). However, the very next year, 1958, Mrs. Acord saw three of the large grackles in Amarillo; in 1967, she remarked that they were increasing at this northernmost Texas city. In Midland, one was carefully identified on March 9 and 10, 1960 (Ola D. Haynes, Anne LeSassier, Frances Williams).

From the late 1950's through the 1960's, *Cassidix mexicanus* somewhat consolidated its gains in Texas, but the main advance took place north of the Lone Star State. First Oklahoma record was established on April 28, 1953, when a female was noted on a lawn of the Central State Hospital at Norman (G. M. Sutton, et al.). First male appeared on a farm near Alva, Woods County, June 29, 1953 (Paul Nighswonger). First record of breeding occurred in 1958 when a small colony nested successfully near Norman (W. M. Davis). The big "crow-blackbird" has been a permanent resident of Oklahoma since it overwintered in 1963–64.

The Great-tail reached still another milestone when it arrived in Kansas. The first bird was recorded in early April, 1964, at Sedan, Kansas, by J. W. Humphrey (1964, *Audubon Field Notes* 18: 465). Further Kansas sightings were at Wichita, spring and summer, 1968 (J. A. Cox, Kenn Kaufman); and in Woodson County, July 6, 1969 (Cox). By 1971, it was nesting in several locations in Kansas, including a colony of about 30 nests in Barton County (M. D. Schwilling). By the winter of 1972–73, at least one Great-tail had moved into Missouri (1 reported on Springfield Audubon Christmas Bird Count, Dec. 26, 1972).

The species is moving farther into the West also. In 1973, it was reported from as far west as Havasu Refuge, Arizona (May 1, Steve Burr); Blythe, California (Apr. and May, James Snowden); and Lincoln County, Nevada (Apr. 28–May 2, J. and Kay Burk). A first Nevada specimen was taken at Tule Springs Park near Las Vegas on April 16, 1973 (Charles Lawson, et al.). On the southern Great Plains and deserts of the Southwest temperatures above 100° F. can be expected in summer, and near zero readings in winter are not unusual. For a bird of tropical origin, *C. mexicanus* has come a long way into the Temperate Zone.

According to G. M. Sutton (1967, *Oklahoma Birds*, p. 555), it is the Mesquite Great-tailed Grackle, *C. m. prosopidicola*, that is thrusting northward into the Great Plains. The expansion has been hard on small relatives. This race has crowded out the Bronzed Grackle, *Quiscalus aeneus*, as a nester in all of its south and much of its central Texas range (see CHANGES under the latter species). Of further interest is the expansion of the Mexican Great-tailed Grackle, *C. m. mexicanus*, up-mountain from its tropical lowlands during the first quarter of the twentieth century. Apparently, the resulting competition from Mexican Great-tails swarming into the increasingly urbanized Valley of México (elevation, 7,000–8,200 ft.) exterminated the smaller Slender-billed Grackle, *Cassidix palustris*, which was endemic in the marshes of Lerma (8,200 ft.), State of México; the Slenderbill has not certainly been seen alive since 1910.

It is remarkable that a bird adapted to a densely civilized landscape should have evolved in the New World where few cities and towns have histories going back thousands of years. Perhaps even more astonishing is the Great-tail's relatively rapid adjustment from a tropical to a temperate climate. The Great-tailed Grackle is one of the few native American success stories of the twentieth century.

DETAILED ACCOUNT: THREE SUBSPECIES

MEXICAN GREAT-TAILED GRACKLE, *Cassidix mexicanus mexicanus* (Lesson)

Race not in A.O.U. check-list, 1957 (see Appendix A).

DESCRIPTION: *Adult male and female, nuptial plumage*: Similar to *C. m. prosopidicola* (see below), but larger; female with pileum and under parts darker.

MEASUREMENTS: *Adult male*: Wing, 185.0–210.0 (average, 194.0) mm.; tail, 203.0–239.0 (215.3); bill (exposed culmen), 38.5–46.0 (41.3); height of bill at base, 13.0–15.3 (14.5); tarsus, 49.0–52.5 (51.0); middle toe without claw, 35.3–38.3 (36.5). *Adult female*: Wing, 146.0–164.0 (154.8); tail, 143.0–170.0 (156.3); bill, 31.3–36.0 (33.5); bill from nostril, 24.0–28.5 (26.0); height of bill, 10.5–12.3 (11.5); height of bill at nostril, 10.8–11.5 (11.0); tarsus, 41.0–45.0 (43.0); middle toe, 28.5–30.5 (29.0).

RANGE: Nuevo León and s. Tamaulipas, south through Mexico and Central America to Colombia; casual in winter in s. Texas.

TEXAS: *Winter*: One specimen: Cameron Co., near Brownsville (Jan. 4, 1927, G. S. Wing).

MESQUITE GREAT-TAILED GRACKLE, *Cassidix mexicanus prosopidicola* Lowery

DESCRIPTION: *Adult male, nuptial plumage*: Acquired by wear from winter plumage. Upper and lower parts metallic dusky dull violet blue to diamin-azo blue, posteriorly becoming more bluish and finally more greenish, passing on upper tail-coverts and crissum into metallic dull blackish green; wings and tail dull black, with slight greenish or bluish metallic sheen, inner edges of rectrices and of primaries and secondaries fuscous black; lesser wing-coverts like back; median wing-coverts green like crissum; greater coverts duller, like outer edges of wing-quills; under wing-coverts metallic dull blackish green. Bill black; inside of mouth yellow; iris lemon yellow, pale straw color, white, or yellowish white; legs and feet black. *Adult male, winter*: Acquired by complete postnuptial molt. Similar to nuptial adult male. *Adult female, nuptial (dark—normal—phase)*: Acquired by wear from winter. Pileum sepia to dull bister; hind-neck fuscous; remainder of upper surface passing gradually into fuscous black on rump and upper tail-coverts; back and rump, also upper tail-coverts slightly, glossed with metallic dull dusky olive green; wings and tail fuscous to fuscous black, slightly glossed with metallic green; upper wing-coverts same but slightly more metallic; chin and throat dull cream buff to dull cinnamon buff, passing on jugulum, breast, and upper abdomen into saccardo umber to cinnamon brown; crissum and lining of wing clove brown. Bill dull black or brownish black; iris light yellow or yellowish white; legs and feet dull black or brownish black. *Adult female, nuptial (light phase)*: Similar to dark phase, but pileum between saccardo umber and snuff brown; remainder of upper surface slightly paler and more brownish; sides of head and of neck lighter and more buffy; entire lower surface, except abdomen and crissum, very much paler, more buffy (less grayish); chin light warm buff; throat cinnamon buff or pinkish buff; breast tawny olive or clay color; lower breast and upper abdomen dull cinnamon buff; in this phase almost as light as female of *C. major*, but may be distinguished by darker pileum and anterior lower parts. *Adult female, winter*: Acquired by complete postnuptial molt. Similar to nuptial adult female, but feathers of upper parts with more conspicuous edgings of dark brown, back with more pronounced metallic greenish sheen; colors of lower parts more blended, with more pale feather tips on sides and flanks. *Male and female, second winter*: Acquired by complete postnuptial molt. Similar to corresponding sex of adult in winter. *Male, first nuptial*: Acquired by wear from first winter. Similar to nuptial adult male but more brownish, greenish, or bluish above, and decidedly duller, less metallic; lower parts with little or no violet sheen, much duller and more brownish, particularly posteriorly; abdomen fuscous black to fuscous. *Male, first winter*: Acquired by partial or complete postjuvenal molt. Similar to first nuptial male. *Female, first nuptial*: Acquired by wear from first winter. Similar to nuptial adult female. *Female, first winter*: Acquired by partial or complete postjuvenal molt. Similar to adult female in winter, but feathers of upper parts more rufescent, with broader dark brown edgings and tips; sides of head and anterior lower surface more rufescent and ochraceous. *Juvenal*: Acquired by complete postnatal molt. Similar to adult female in winter but more uniformly brownish above, without metallic gloss (olive brown to sepia); wings and tail fuscous to fuscous black, wing-coverts lighter; chin buffy white, remainder of lower surface pale buff to dull cinnamon buff or clay color; crissum fuscous to chaetura drab with dull buffy edgings; jugulum, breast, and abdomen more or less obscurely streaked, mostly narrowly, with fuscous. Bill, iris, legs, and feet dark brown. *Natal*: Drab; or upper parts fuscous, crown mikado brown, and lower surface paler or more grayish.

MEASUREMENTS: *Adult male*: Wing, 172.0–199.9 (average, 184.9) mm.; tail, 190.0–224.1 (204.2); bill (exposed culmen), 36.6–41.4 (38.9); height of bill at base, 12.7–14.5 (13.7); tarsus, 43.9–52.1 (49.3); middle toe without claw, 29.9–36.1 (33.0). *Adult female*: Wing, 140.0–150.1 (144.8); tail, 135.9–151.9 (145.5); bill, 29.9–36.0 (32.0); height of bill, 10.7–12.2 (11.4); tarsus, 36.6–41.9 (39.6); middle toe, 25.9–28.4 (27.2).

RANGE: S. New Mexico, Oklahoma, Kansas (arrived 1964), Texas, and s.w. Louisiana, south to c. Coahuila, c. Nuevo León, and n.e. Tamaulipas.

TEXAS: *Resident*: Altitudinal breeding range, near sea level to 1,000 ft. Collected north to Denton, east to Harris and Galveston, south to Cameron, west to Val Verde cos. Abundant to common.

NESTING: *Nest*: In coastal or interior regions; in marshes, swamps, ponds, or dry land, in cultivated areas, such as ornamental grounds, pastures, and roadsides, also in more open country; in colonies, sometimes of considerable size; in reeds, bushes, or trees, usually 5–15 ft. above ground; large bulky structure, with deep and well-constructed cavity; composed of leaves, grasses, straw, Spanishmoss, weed stems, various dry plants, bits of cloth, and cemented with mud; lined with finer grasses, weed stems, and roots. *Eggs*: 3–5, usually 4; elliptical ovate or elongate ovate to short ovate, sometimes nearly cylindrical ovate; bluish gray, greenish gray, olive gray, purplish gray, pale blue, greenish white, grayish white, light drab, or brownish drab, sometimes pale greenish blue; clouded with brown, spotted, splashed, and otherwise marked, sometimes heavily, and more numerously at smaller end, with umber, other shades of dark brown, black, and smoke gray, sometimes with lavender shell markings; average size, 32.0 × 21.6 mm.

MONSON'S GREAT-TAILED GRACKLE, *Cassidix mexicanus monsoni* Phillips

DESCRIPTION: *Adult male and female, nuptial plumage*: Resembling *C. m. prosopidicola*, but bill somewhat more slender; female darker on head and lower parts. Similar also to *C. m. mexicanus*, but bill more slender, and tarsus somewhat so.

MEASUREMENTS: *Adult male*: Wing, 186.3–192.0 (average, 188.5) mm.; tail, 191.5–225.0; bill from nostril, 31.8–34.8 (33.5); height of bill at nostril, 12.5–13.0 (12.8). *Adult female*: Wing, 147.0–151.7 (148.5); tail, 157.5–165.0 (161.0); bill from nostril, 24.0–26.3 (25.0); height of bill at nostril, 9.5–10.5 (10.0).

RANGE: S.e. Arizona and c. New Mexico, south to Chihuahua and Trans-Pecos Texas.

TEXAS: *Resident*: Altitudinal breeding range, 2,100 to 3,800 ft. Two specimens, both from Brewster Co.: Castolon (May 7, 1935, J. B. Semple); 4 mi. southwest of Marathon (May 29, 1935, G. M. Sutton).

NESTING: Similar to that of *C. m. prosopidicola*.

BOAT-TAILED GRACKLE, *Cassidix major* (Vieillot)

SPECIES ACCOUNT

Regarded as a race of *Cassidix mexicanus* by A.O.U. check-list, 1957 (see Appendix A). *Voice*: high-pitched and squeaky. *Male*: resembles Great-tail, but eye brown (Texas to Alabama); head appears more rounded; tail about equal to wing (instead of longer). *Female*: similar to Great-tail, but eye brown (except in yellow-eyed Atlantic race *torreyi*); rich buff below. Length, 16½ in. (male), 13 (female); wingspan, 22½ (male), 17¾ (female); weight, 7½ oz. (male), 3¾ (female).

RANGE: Atlantic seaboard from New Jersey to Florida (most of peninsula) and along U.S. Gulf to c. Texas coast. Winters in and near breeding range, chiefly south of Chesapeake Bay.

TEXAS: (See map.) *Resident*: Breeds, early Apr. to mid-July (eggs, Apr. 10 to May 8) from near sea level to 50 ft. Common to fairly common in coastal vicinities from Orange, southwest to Rockport. Casual in winter in southern tip.

HAUNTS AND HABITS: The Boat-tailed Grackle, in marked contrast to its relative the Great-tailed Grackle, is highly restricted in Texas. It is typically confined to marshes—fresh, brackish, or salt—mostly within thirty

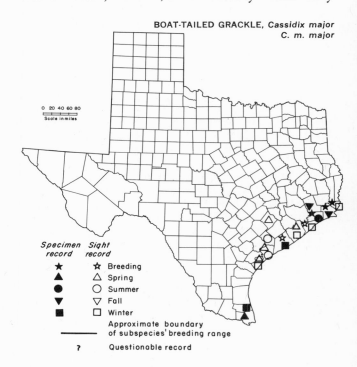

BOAT-TAILED GRACKLE, *Cassidix major*
C. m. major

0 20 40 60 80
Scale in miles

Specimen record	Sight record	
★	☆	Breeding
▲	△	Spring
●	○	Summer
▼	▽	Fall
■	□	Winter

——— Approximate boundary of subspecies' breeding range

? Questionable record

male Boat-tailed Grackle, *Cassidix major,*
in cattail (*Typha*) marsh

miles of the Gulf of Mexico. A visitor to Galveston Island can readily view the differing habitats. The built-up areas and garbage dumps in and near the city of Galveston are inhabited by flocks of Great-tails; remote cattail (*Typha*) ponds, *Spartina* marshes, and wet prairies are frequented by Boat-tails. The Boat-tail's avoidance of civilization is apparently confined to Texas. Certainly in Florida, and in other places where there are no Great-tails, *Cassidix major* commonly lives in areas where houses are thick.

Flight is strong and direct, and usually even; the long tail is shaped like the keel of a boat. Boat-tails breed in loose colonies, and forage and roost in small flocks throughout the year. On the ground they walk slowly and with seeming dignity, often wading for their food. Animal food includes many aquatic species, such as crayfish, crabs, shrimps, snails, and some fish, together with grasshoppers and beetles. Vegetable matter, such as corn, rice, and weed seeds, and a small quantity of fruit also constitute an important portion of the diet.

The Boat-tail's vocalizations include harsh *check*'s and *cluck*'s, with intermittent high-pitched whistles and squeaks; some recall those of the Red-winged Blackbird.

DETAILED ACCOUNT: ONE SUBSPECIES

LOUISIANA BOAT-TAILED GRACKLE, *Cassidix major major* (Vieillot)

DESCRIPTION: Similar to Mesquite Great-tailed Grackle, *Cassidix mexicanus prosopidicola*, but smaller, tail relatively shorter, in adult male tail averaging about equal to wing instead of longer. *Adult male, nuptial plumage*: Similar to adult male of *C. m. prosopidicola*, but metallic violet of anterior lower parts extending much less farther back, usually not over breast, nor even anterior part of sides, which are more or less decidedly green or greenish blue; crissum less metallic green, often dull black, with very little gloss. Bill, legs, and feet black; iris reddish brown or dark brown. *Adult female, nuptial*: Similar to normal phase adult female of *C. m. prosopidicola*, but decidedly lighter, both on upper and lower surfaces; lower parts more buffy or ochraceous (less grayish or brownish). Iris dark brown. *Male, first nuptial*: Similar to first nuptial male of *C. m. prosopidicola*, but tail shorter, metallic sheen of upper and lower parts somewhat more greenish (less bluish). Bill, legs, and feet dull black; iris dark brown. *Female, first winter*: Similar to corresponding plumage in *C. m. prosopidicola*, but rather lighter above, and very much paler, more brightly ochraceous below, except on crissum. *Juvenal*: Similar to juvenal of *C. m. prosopidicola*, but upper parts lighter, more rufescent; lower surface somewhat more ochraceous and much less conspicuously, sometimes not at all, streaked, thus more uniform. *Natal*: Pileum dull cinnamon; posterior upper parts drab.

MEASUREMENTS: *Adult male*: Wing, 167.1–183.9 (average, 172.2) mm.; tail, 161.0–193.0 (172.2); bill (exposed culmen), 37.1–41.1 (39.4); height of bill at base, 11.9–14.0 (13.2); tarsus, 48.0–52.1 (49.3); middle toe without claw, 33.5–36.1 (34.5). *Adult female*: Wing, 129.0–137.9 (134.4); tail, 119.9–135.1 (126.0); bill, 28.9–34.0 (31.8); height of bill, 9.4–11.7 (10.7); tarsus, 39.1–42.9 (40.4); middle toe, 26.4–28.9 (27.7).

RANGE: Central and upper coastal Texas, east along Gulf marshes to s.w. Alabama.

TEXAS: *Resident*: Collected northeast to Jefferson and Liberty, southwest to Matagorda cos. Two specimens outside known breeding range: Willacy Co., El Sauz Ranch (Feb. 9, 1947, I. N. Gabrielson); Cameron Co., Brownsville (Mar., 1853, S. Van Vliet; identified by S. F. Baird).

NESTING: *Nest*: In coastal region; in marshes, in swamps, occasionally on prairies some distance from water; often in colonies; in reeds and rushes of marsh, or tree or bush, 2–40 ft. above ground; large, bulky, but strongly built bowl of sticks, grass, weeds, strips of bark, sedges, roots, Spanishmoss, eelgrass, seaweed, cotton, rags, and feathers, sometimes cemented with mud; lined with finer stems of plants, roots, and fine grasses. *Eggs*: 2–5, usually 4; ovate to elliptical ovate; grayish white, pale blue, pale olive, greenish white, dull bluish white, even brownish drab or pinkish stone color, with blotches, spots, and lines of umber, purplish brown, black, and various shades of gray, colors often blurred and smeared; average size, 31.5 × 22.6 mm.

PURPLE GRACKLE, *Quiscalus quiscula* (Linnaeus)

SPECIES ACCOUNT

This form and the Bronzed Grackle are merged into Common Grackle, *Quiscalus quiscula*, by A.O.U. check-list, 1957 (see Appendix A). A small grackle. *Male*: glossy black, showing glints of purple, blue, green (hybrids with *Q. aeneus* show iridescent bars on back); keeled, wedge-shaped tail. *Female*: somewhat smaller; duller. Length, 12½ in. (male), 11¼ (female); wingspan, 17¾ (male), 16 (female); weight, 4 oz. (male).

RANGE: S.e. New York and Connecticut, south (chiefly east of Appalachian Mts.) to s. Louisiana and s. Florida. Winters within breeding range mainly from New Jersey southward.

TEXAS: *Casual*: One specimen: Hardin Co., Sour Lake (July 15, 1902, N. Hollister). Sighted: Chambers Co., Cove (Oct. 4, 7, 1939, A. K. McKay).

HAUNTS AND HABITS: The Purple Grackle, unlike the Great-tail and Boat-tail, is primarily a woods bird. Its habits and habitat requirements appear to be very similar to those of its extremely close relative, the Bronzed Grackle.

DETAILED ACCOUNT: ONE SUBSPECIES

NORTHERN PURPLE GRACKLE, *Quiscalus quiscula stonei* Chapman

DESCRIPTION: *Adult male, nuptial plumage (purple phase)*: Acquired by wear from winter plumage. Forehead metallic dusky dull violet; crown and occiput metallic dark indian purple or metallic dark perilla purple; hindneck metallic brussels brown; back and scapulars metallic dark perilla purple, each feather with narrow subterminal bar of metallic prussian green, passing into metallic dusky greenish blue toward base and to metallic dark yellow ocher toward tip; lower rump and shorter upper tail-coverts between metallic medal bronze and metallic brussels brown, longest upper tail-coverts like forehead; tail varied with metallic raisin black and metallic dusky greenish blue to metallic dusky dull bluish green, inner edges of feathers, particularly basally, blackish brown, raisin black mostly on outer webs of feathers; wings blackish brown, inner edges of primaries and secondaries fuscous; outer edges of primaries and alula somewhat metallic dull dusky greenish blue or greenish slate black, outer edges of secondaries and tertials metallic dark livid purple to dusky dull violet; wing-coverts metallic violet like crown, lesser coverts with broad metallic terminal green and blue bars, like narrow subterminal bars of back; lores and malar spot velvety black; rest of sides of head, together with chin and upper throat, like crown but duller; sides of neck, together with lower throat, jugulum, and upper breast, like hindneck, passing into metallic indian purple with brownish or bronzy tinge on abdomen and lower tail-coverts; but anal region dull blackish brown with little if any metallic sheen; feathers of lower breast often with more or less solid bars, sometimes similar terminally to those of back, but often much broader; lining of wing clove brown or blackish brown, mixed with dark metallic blue, violet, and bronzy feathers. Bill, legs, and feet black; iris straw yellow, sulphur yellow, or white. *Adult male, nuptial (green phase):* Similar to purple phase, but pileum metallic forest green to metallic dark green; back dusky yellowish green; rump and shorter upper tail-coverts metallic indian purple with bronzy brown tinge; wing-coverts and scapulars metallic dusky greenish blue; sides of head, chin, and throat metallic dusky greenish blue, shot with metallic dark green, most conspicuously on center of throat and of jugulum; breast metallic dusky yellowish green; abdomen metallic dusky violet. *Adult male, nuptial (blue-headed phase):* Like green or purple phase, but top and sides of head, together with chin, throat, and jugulum, metallic dusky greenish blue, shot with metallic dark green. *Adult male, winter:* Acquired by complete postnuptial molt. Like nuptial adult male. *Adult female, nuptial:* Acquired by wear from winter. In general, similar to nuptial adult male, but colors very much duller; pileum metallic hellebore green or metallic dusky greenish blue, mixed with metallic dark green; tail fuscous to fuscous black, outer webs of feathers with more or less metallic green sheen; wing-quills fuscous to light fuscous, outer webs with dull metallic sheen of dark blue or dull dark green; lesser wing-coverts metallic dusky greenish blue mixed with metallic dark livid purple or metallic dusky dull violet; remainder of wing-coverts similar but duller; anterior lower parts dull, somewhat metallic—green like crown or more or less metallic dull blue; posterior lower parts fuscous to clove brown or light clove brown with very slight purplish, bluish, or greenish sheen. *Adult female, winter:* Acquired by complete postnuptial molt. Similar to nuptial adult female. *Male and female, first nuptial:* Acquired by wear from first winter. Like corresponding sex in winter adult, except for retained juvenal feathers. *Male and female, first winter:* Acquired by partial or complete postjuvenal molt. Like corresponding sex in winter adult, except for retained juvenal feathers. *Male, juvenal:* Acquired by complete postnatal molt. Upper surface chaetura black to light fuscous; tail chaetura black to fuscous black, with slight metallic greenish or bluish sheen; wings chaetura drab, fuscous, fuscous black, or dark buffy brown, with faint metallic greenish sheen, particularly on outer webs of primaries and secondaries; sides of head and neck like upper surface; lower surface dark chaetura drab to dark buffy brown, usually not obviously streaked with darker brown, and if so, very obscurely. Bill, legs, and feet dull dark brown; iris dark slate color. *Female, juvenal:* Acquired by complete postnatal molt. Similar to juvenal male, but upper parts lighter and more rufescent (less grayish or blackish) brown, fuscous to light olive brown; lower parts also decidedly lighter and more rufescent brown—light olive brown to buffy brown, breast dull sayal brown, abdomen grayish pale pinkish buff; lower parts more or less conspicuously streaked with darker brown.

MEASUREMENTS: *Adult male:* Wing, 137.7–146.8 (average, 143.8) mm.; tail, 129.5–139.7 (135.6); bill (exposed culmen), 28.4–33.0 (30.2); height of bill at base, 12.4–14.0 (13.2); tarsus, 34.3–38.4 (36.8); middle toe without claw, 25.1–26.7 (25.7). *Adult female:* Wing, 122.2–133.9 (127.8); tail, 101.9–122.7 (112.0); bill, 24.9–28.4 (27.2); height of bill, 11.4–13.5 (12.2); tarsus, 32.8–36.1 (34.3); middle toe, 22.4–25.1 (23.4).

RANGE: S.e. New York, south to e. Tennessee, s. Louisiana, and—exclusive of their coasts—s. Mississippi, s. Alabama, and n.w. Florida. Winter range same as that of species.

TEXAS: *Casual:* One specimen (see species account).

BRONZED GRACKLE, *Quiscalus aeneus* Ridgway

SPECIES ACCOUNT

Regarded as a race (*versicolor*) of Common Grackle, *Quiscalus quiscula*, by A.O.U. check-list, 1957 (see Appendix A). Like Purple Grackle, but has bronzy body, particularly evident on back. Length, 12¼ in. (male), 10¾ (female); wingspan, 17½ (male), 15¾ (female); weight, 4¾ oz. (male).

RANGE: S.w. Mackenzie to s.w. Newfoundland, south (east of Rocky Mts. and chiefly west of Appalachians) to e. Texas, Louisiana, n.w. Alabama, and Massachusetts. Winters (mainly east of Rockies) from Canadian border (casually) to Texas and Georgia.

TEXAS: (See map.) *Breeding:* Early Mar. to early Aug. (eggs, Apr. 12 to June 17) from near sea level to 3,200 ft. Common to fairly common in northeastern half. Formerly bred southwest to San Antonio and Refugio. *Winter:* Mid-Sept. to late Mar. (extremes: Sept. 9, May 1). Abundant to common in eastern quarter; common to uncommon in most of remaining portion east of 98th meridian; fairly common (some years) to rare in western parts, though casual in Trans-Pecos and southern tip.

HAUNTS AND HABITS: In Texas the Bronzed Grackle is mostly a bird of forested regions or partially cutover areas which have been well wooded in the past. Preferred habitat of this species and the two large grackles is illustrated in the vicinity of Houston and Galveston. Galveston Island, originally treeless and now with some shade trees, is occupied largely by Great-tails in the built-up parts and by Boat-tails in the more remote fresh, brackish, and salt marshes. On the mainland, un-

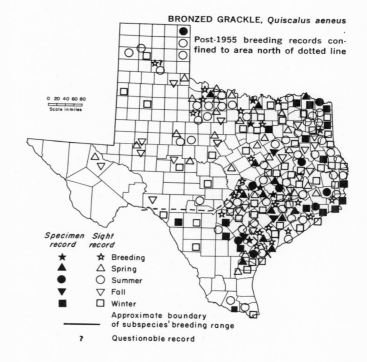

BRONZED GRACKLE, *Quiscalus aeneus*

● Post-1955 breeding records confined to area north of dotted line

0 20 40 60 80
Scale in miles

Specimen record	Sight record	
★	☆	Breeding
▲	△	Spring
●	○	Summer
▼	▽	Fall
■	□	Winter

—— Approximate boundary of subspecies' breeding range

? Questionable record

til recently well supplied with wooded bottomlands, the Bronzed Grackle still dominates where trees are lush and thick. However, the piney woods and Big Thicket regions of deep east Texas constitute the real headquarters of the Bronzed in the state. Here in virtual absence of competition with other grackles, the Bronzed flourishes in woods, towns, pastures, and fields.

The Bronzed, like other grackles, usually occurs in flocks—sometimes of great size. Flight is rather labored but fairly steady and usually at moderate heights. These grackles feed on a great variety of ground-dwelling insects—including beetles and weevils, grasshoppers, crickets, and caterpillars—as well as a smaller quantity of crayfish, snails, earthworms, spiders, and myriapods, and an occasional mouse, snake, fish, salamander, frog, lizard, or tree frog, or the eggs or young of small birds. About two-thirds of the diet is vegetable, however, including large amounts of grain (corn, wheat, oats, rice; some rye and buckwheat), a considerable variety of fruit, some acorns, and weed seeds. The birds spend much time sedately walking around—often with a nodding of the high-held head—or wading in shallow water and digging for food.

Noisy chucking call notes issue from foraging or roosting flocks. The "song" is a combination of squeaks and squawks, simultaneously husky and squeaky. When sounding off, the Bronzed often opens its wings, spreads its tail, and puffs out its plumage, as if vocalizing took great effort.

CHANGES: In Texas the Bronzed Grackle is declining at the southwestern edge of its breeding range. This decline is illustrated by the history of this bird in and near the two largest cities of upper south Texas—San Antonio and Austin. In San Antonio and other parts of Bexar County, it was abundant in winter and a common summer resident from 1886 well into the 1890's (C. W. Beckham, H. P. Attwater). At Pilgrim Lake (Atascosa Co.), just south of the city, there were fifty-three Bronzed Grackles, August 30, 1937 (H. C. Oberholser). The latter year seems to be approximately the last that a summer population flourished in the San Antonio region. There is apparently no record of breeding from the 1940's through the early 1970's.

Within the three-county region surrounding the city of Austin, Travis County, the decline came somewhat later. Near Taylor (extreme eastern Williamson Co.), the Bronzed Grackle was probably still nesting in 1970; however, it was certainly not an abundant summer resident all through this county as A. E. Schutze reported it to be in 1902. In 1890, C. D. Oldright considered the species an abundant resident and nester in rural Travis County and Austin; 1955 saw what may have been the last nesting of the species in this city where an adult was observed feeding a fledgling at the edge of Waller Creek in Eastwoods Park (E. B. Kincaid, Jr.). Last nesting record in San Marcos (Hays Co.) was May 22, 1936 (A. K. Boyles).

From the 1880's through the 1950's, there was a dramatic increase and expansion of the Great-tailed Grackle in south, central, and even north Texas. The big, aggressive Great-tail, competing strongly in what is for it prime habitat, has apparently virtually eliminated the Bronzed Grackle from its marginal habitat.

DETAILED ACCOUNT: NO SUBSPECIES

DESCRIPTION: *Adult male, nuptial plumage (purple phase)*: Acquired by wear from winter plumage. Pileum and hindneck metallic dark indian purple to metallic dark perilla purple; remainder of upper surface metallic olive to metallic medal bronze, longest upper tail-coverts sometimes tinged with metallic violet; outer webs of tail feathers mostly metallic raisin black, inner webs varied with dusky dull bluish green to dusky greenish blue, inner edges of feathers blackish brown; wing-quills blackish brown, outer margins of primaries and secondaries dull metallic raisin black, exposed surfaces of tertials mostly dull metallic olive brown, with more or less purplish sheen, particularly on inner webs; lesser wing-coverts like back, outer webs of median and greater wing-coverts metallic raisin black, slightly tinged with bronzy olive of back; lores and malar spot velvety black; remainder of sides of head and of neck, together with chin, throat, jugulum, and upper breast, like pileum; middle of breast tinged with violet; remainder of lower surface metallic olive to metallic medal bronze; lower tail-coverts dull—somewhat metallic raisin black; lining of wing brownish black with metallic purplish sheen. Bill black; iris canary yellow, straw yellow, sulphur yellow, or primrose yellow, or white; legs, feet, and claws black. *Adult male, nuptial (green phase)*: Similar to purple phase, but head, neck, throat, and jugulum metallic dark yellowish green to metallic dark green; breast and abdomen with more or less evident metallic purplish tinge. *Adult male, nuptial (blue-headed phase)*: Similar to purple phase, but head, neck, throat, and jugulum metallic dusky greenish blue. *Adult male, winter*: Acquired by complete postnuptial molt. Not essentially different from nuptial adult male. *Adult female, nuptial*: Acquired by wear from winter. Similar to nuptial adult male, but colors very much duller; head and neck dark metallic blue or green; lores fuscous black; remainder of upper surface very much duller, less metallic, and more brownish, without any purplish or bluish sheen; tail similar to that of male, but somewhat more brownish; posterior lower surface much paler, duller, and more brownish, with little or no metallic sheen; wings very much duller than in adult male—mostly dark olive brown to clove brown, outer webs of quills and outer edgings of median and greater wing-coverts with more or less purple or bluish metallic sheen. It is very similar to the adult female Northern Purple Grackle, *Q. quiscula stonei*, but somewhat larger in size, and lacking any metallic bluish, greenish, or purplish sheen on back, rump, and posterior lower parts. Bill black; iris straw yellow, pale straw yellow, light naples yellow, or primrose yellow; legs, feet, and claws black. *Adult female, winter*: Acquired by complete postnuptial molt. Like nuptial adult female. *Male and female, first nuptial*: Acquired by wear from first winter. Not essentially different from that of corresponding sex in nuptial adult. *Male and female, first winter*: Acquired by complete postjuvenal molt. Similar to that of corresponding sex in adult winter. *Male, juvenal*: Acquired by complete postnatal molt. Upper parts fuscous black to light fuscous, slightly mottled with darker and with tendency to have paler tips on feathers; wings and tail similar, but tail with slight dull bluish or greenish sheen; sides of head like upper parts; lower surface dull hair brown to between light fuscous and buffy brown, feathers of abdomen with very narrow obscure paler tips, imparting slightly barred appearance, and entire lower surface with very slight indication of darker streaking, instead more or less obscurely mottled or spotted with darker centers of feathers. Bill, legs, and feet dull dark brown; iris dark brown. *Female, juvenal*: Acquired by complete postnatal molt. Similar to juvenal male, but upper surface decidedly lighter (more rufescent brown); lower surface decidedly paler—dull buffy brown to olive brown or to grayish pale pinkish buff, obviously, though not sharply, streaked with fuscous except on

PLATE 31: Blue Grosbeak, *Guiraca caerulea*
adult male (top), immature male (center), adult female (bottom)

chin and crissum. *Natal*: Pale sepia, light hair brown, drab, or between brownish drab and hair brown.

MEASUREMENTS: *Adult male*: Wing, 136.7–153.2 (average, 143.3) mm.; tail, 119.6–136.4 (129.5); bill (exposed culmen), 30.7–33.5 (32.3); height of bill at base, 12.7–14.0 (13.0); tarsus, 35.6–37.8 (36.8); middle toe without claw, 24.1–26.9 (25.4). *Adult female*: Wing, 122.7–133.1 (126.5); tail, 108.0–125.0 (116.6); bill, 28.7–31.2 (29.7); height of bill, 11.2–12.7 (11.9); tarsus, 31.5–34.8 (33.8); middle toe, 22.6–23.9 (23.1).

TEXAS: *Breeding*: Collected north to Lipscomb, east to Bowie and Hardin, south to Calhoun, west to Williamson cos.; prior to 1955, south to Refugio, west to Bexar cos. *Winter*: Taken north to Red River, east to Newton and Orange, south to Bee, west to Kinney cos.; casual (1 specimen) in Hidalgo Co.

NESTING: *Nest*: On uplands and bottomlands, in semiopen country or woodlands; often in large colonies; 8–40 ft. or more above ground, on branch of tree or bush, in hollow limb, stump, or cavity in tree, sometimes under cornices of building, on stringer of railroad bridge, or even in birdhouse, rarely in marsh reeds very close to ground; large, bulky open-topped nest, usually rather strongly constructed; composed of grasses, roots, weed stalks, binding twine, rags, and similar materials, cemented together with mud; lined with fine dry grasses, wool, or horsehair. *Eggs*: 3–8, usually 5; ovate to short ovate; light green, light blue clouded with brown, bluish white, or pale greenish white to pale brown, bluish green, or dull gray; blotched, dotted, lined, and scrawled over entire surface with dark and reddish brown and black, with shell markings of lavender; average size, 28.9 × 20.9 mm.

BROWN-HEADED COWBIRD, *Molothrus ater* (Boddaert)

SPECIES ACCOUNT

A small blackbird with a finchlike bill. *Male*: brown head; iridescent black body. *Female*: brownish gray. Length, 7¼ in.; wingspan, 12¾; weight, 1½ oz.

RANGE: N.e. British Columbia and s. Mackenzie to

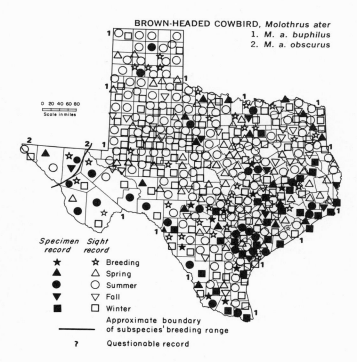

BROWN-HEADED COWBIRD, *Molothrus ater*
1. *M. a. buphilus*
2. *M. a. obscurus*

0 20 40 60 80
Scale in miles

Specimen / Sight
record / record

★ / ☆ Breeding
▲ / △ Spring
● / ○ Summer
▼ / ▽ Fall
■ / □ Winter

——— Approximate boundary of subspecies' breeding range

? Questionable record

s. Nova Scotia, south to n. Baja California, Guerrero, n. Tamaulipas, s. Texas, Mississippi, and n. Florida. Winters from n. United States to s. Mexico and s. Florida.

TEXAS: (See map.) *Resident*: Breeds, mid-Mar. to early Sept. (eggs, Mar. 29 to Aug. 5) from near sea level to 8,000 ft. Abundant—seemingly more so in winter—to common in most parts; uncommon as a breeder some years in southern tip.

HAUNTS AND HABITS: Cowbirds are appropriately named: They very frequently walk about the feet of cattle where they ingest much grain and many flying insects stirred up by the feeding livestock. The Brown-headed species occurs throughout the state in cities, towns, feed lots, fields, pastures, ranches, desert, and general countryside, with or without trees.

Molothrus ater is famed for its reproductive habit of laying its eggs in nests of other species and abandoning them to be hatched and the young raised by the foster parents; the Brown-headed Cowbird parasitizes more than 250 species. Normally, the female cowbird removes one egg with her bill from the host's nest one day before or after she imposes her egg, which will hatch with a day or two less incubation than those of her usual hosts.

In Texas it is only in the south that the Brown-headed has to compete with another nest parasite, the Bronzed Cowbird. In this region the former tends to be more numerous in the cooler, drier parts; the Red-eyed Bronzed predominates most years during the breeding season on the warm, relatively humid lower coastal plain (south of Corpus Christi).

Flight is somewhat swifter and more direct than that of the Red-winged Blackbird and is performed with more continuous wing-beats. Throughout the year—but particularly in autumn and winter—the Brown-headed moves in flocks that are sometimes enormous and often associated with other blackbird species. These mixed flocks sometimes perform incredible aerial evolutions, moving in a given direction, then suddenly reversing course, and in this manner gyrating back and forth for a considerable period. During flock gyrations, individuals generally retain their relative positions. At night cowbirds roost communally in a marsh or tall grass or shade trees of town and country.

While feeding by cows, *Molothrus ater* walks deliberately, often with nodding head and uplifted tail. Half its food consists of weed seeds, including those of barngrass, ragweed, knotweed, sorrel, amaranth, and thistle; where available, seeds of foxtail grass may comprise a large proportion of its vegetable diet. It also takes an insignificant quantity of plant leaves and fruit and a considerable quantity of grain (corn, wheat, oats, buckwheat), much of which is waste. It swarms to coastal rice fields in fall and winter and consumes rice and insects. Animal food, about 25 percent of the diet, is largely insects—particularly grasshoppers, caterpillars, and beetles—with a small portion of snails, spiders, ticks, and myriapods.

The usual call is a *chuck* or a chatter. A distinctive

high whistle followed by two lower notes is uttered in flight. The song, which usually accompanies an interesting courtship display, is bubbly and terminates with a high-pitched phrase: *glug-glug-gleeee*.

CHANGES: Almost everything the white man has done since he came to North America has benefited the Brown-headed Cowbird. His slaughter of the American bison in the second half of the nineteenth century may have lowered the "buffalo bird" population briefly, but quick replacement of bison with cattle started *Molothrus ater* on the upward curve again.

Since the opening up of Texas and spreading of livestock and grain throughout the state, this cowbird has become ubiquitous. Even the increasingly popular twentieth century development of bird feeding favors this brood parasite. For example, feeders by suburban homes in the hills west of Austin are currently (1970's) feeding such a heavy population of Brown-headed Cowbirds that the two great central Texas specialties —the Black-capped Vireo and Golden-cheeked Warbler—are finding it ever more difficult to raise their own young.

DETAILED ACCOUNT: FOUR SUBSPECIES

EASTERN BROWN-HEADED COWBIRD, *Molothrus ater ater* (Boddaert)

DESCRIPTION: *Adult male, nuptial plumage*: Acquired by wear from winter plumage. Pileum and hindneck sepia to between mummy brown and prout brown, but posterior edge of hindneck metallic dark slate violet; remainder of upper surface metallic dusky dull yellowish green to metallic dusky dull green, and in places to metallic dusky dull bluish green; tail chaetura black to fuscous black, outer webs of feathers more or less metallic dusky dull yellowish green; wings chaetura black to fuscous black, inner edges of quills fuscous; lesser and median wing-coverts metallic green like back, as are outer edgings of greater coverts and outer edges of primaries and secondaries and both webs of tertials; when upper parts are somewhat bluish, edgings of wings and tail appear more greenish than upper surface; lores clove brown or deep clove brown; remainder of sides of head and of neck anteriorly, with chin, throat, and jugulum, brown like pileum; rest of lower surface similar to back; lining of wing fuscous black with more or less metallic greenish or bluish sheen. Bill black; iris vandyke brown or burnt umber; legs and feet black. *Adult male, winter*: Acquired by complete postnuptial molt. Not appreciably different from nuptial adult male. *Adult female, nuptial (brown phase)*: Acquired by wear from winter. Pileum dull buffy brown, small centers of feathers darker, thus imparting rather spotted appearance; hindneck similar, with little or no indication of darker centers of feathers; remainder of upper surface dull olive brown, feathers more or less edged with dull buffy brown; tail between fuscous and olive brown, outer edges of feathers narrowly margined with dull buffy brown; wings dull olive brown, quills and coverts more or less edged narrowly with dull buffy brown; sides of head and of neck like hindneck, but lores slightly mixed with grayish or brownish white, region below eye and auriculars slightly and narrowly streaked with buffy white or very pale buff; lower surface between light buffy brown and drab, chin and middle of throat more buffy—dull grayish pinkish buff, with an obscure darker submalar stripe bounding each side of throat; jugulum, breast, sides, flanks, and abdomen narrowly streaked with dull brown, between hair brown and buffy brown; thighs, flanks, and crissum dull buffy brown; lining of wing between hair brown and buffy brown, somewhat mottled with darker brown. Bill blackish brown, but base of mandible paler; iris dark brown; legs and feet blackish brown. *Adult female, nuptial (gray phase)*:

Similar to brown phase but much more grayish throughout—between dark olive and hair brown; throat tilleul buff; jugulum drab; remainder of lower surface hair brown to light hair brown. *Adult female, winter*: Acquired by complete postnuptial molt. Similar to corresponding phase of nuptial adult female, but upper surface darker, somewhat more uniform, and with decidedly dull greenish metallic sheen, particularly on wings; colors of lower surface more blended and uniform, dark streaking less evident—more or less obscured by lighter tips of feathers. *Male and female, first nuptial*: Acquired by wear or partial molt from first winter. Practically like that of corresponding sex in nuptial adult. *Male and female, first winter*: Acquired by complete or partial postjuvenal molt. Like winter adult of corresponding sex, except for feathers retained from juvenal. *Male, juvenal*: Acquired by complete postnatal molt. Somewhat similar to nuptial adult female, but upper parts dark olive brown to light olive brown, all feathers edged or tipped more or less conspicuously with pale dull cartridge buff to dull cream buff, producing more or less scaled appearance; tail between light olive brown and fuscous, very slightly margined on outer webs of feathers with pale brown or dull buff; wings hair brown, outer edges of primaries and secondaries and both webs of tertials narrowly margined with cartridge buff or cream buff, lesser coverts edged and tipped with same; greater coverts edged with dull cream buff and tipped, as are median coverts, with pale cartridge buff; chin and throat dull cartridge buff, slightly streaked with pale brown; lower surface cartridge buff to cream buff, more or less streaked or spotted by olive brown centers of feathers, most heavily on jugulum, flanks, and crissum; lining of wing olive brown, outer portion broadly edged and tipped with cartridge buff. Bill slate black or brownish black, but mandible paler and somewhat lilaceous or tinged with flesh color; iris hazel; legs and feet dark brown or brownish black. *Female, juvenal*: Acquired by complete postnatal molt. Similar to juvenal male, but upper parts and dark markings of lower surface lighter and more rufescent brown. Maxilla brownish olive or blackish slate, but cutting edges olive buff; mandible deep olive buff or dark gull gray to pale gull gray, but cutting edges chamois; iris sudan brown; legs and feet wood brown, buffy brown, or slate black. *Natal* (this plumage of this race not seen in Texas): Olive gray. Maxilla raw umber or drab; mandible raw umber or fawn color; legs and feet pinkish white or raw umber.

MEASUREMENTS: *Adult male*: Wing, 104.9–113.8 (average, 109.2) mm.; tail, 67.3–77.7 (71.7); bill (exposed culmen), 17.3–18.8 (17.5); height of bill at base, 10.2–11.4 (10.7); tarsus, 24.4–26.7 (25.7); middle toe without claw, 17.0–18.0 (17.5). *Adult female*: Wing, 96.5–101.1 (97.6); tail, 64.0–69.1 (65.8); bill, 15.0–16.0 (15.2); height of bill, 9.9–10.7 (10.2); tarsus, 23.6–25.9 (24.6); middle toe, 15.0–16.5 (15.7).

RANGE: E. Minnesota to Nova Scotia, south to w. Missouri, e. Mississippi, and e. North Carolina. Winters from Texas to s. Florida.

TEXAS: *Winter*: Taken northwest to Randall (Aug. 9), east to Newton (Oct. 14), south to Cameron, west to Kinney (Mar. 8) cos. Common.

NESTING: (This race does not breed in Texas.) *Nest*: None; eggs deposited in nests of other birds, ordinarily of species smaller than itself, though occasionally of birds much greater in size. *Eggs*: Probably 4–5 (possibly more) laid by each female, 1 (sometimes more) deposited in a single nest; 7 eggs have been found in nest of a host, but were probably the product of more than one cowbird; elliptical oval, usually short or rounded ovate to elliptical ovate; white, bluish white, or grayish white; with numerous dots, spots, and sometimes blotches, well distributed over entire surface, of chocolate, reddish brown, yellowish brown, and claret brown, with shell markings of lilac, lavender, and pale gray; average size, 21.4 × 16.5 mm.

NEVADA BROWN-HEADED COWBIRD, *Molothrus ater artemisiae* Grinnell

DESCRIPTION: *Adult male and female, nuptial plumage*: Similar to *M. a. ater* but larger, particularly wing and bill, latter also decidedly more slender; female somewhat lighter and averaging more brownish.

MEASUREMENTS: *Adult male*: Wing, 110.0–117.3 (average, 113.5) mm.; tail, 72.2–79.5 (74.7); bill (exposed culmen), 17.5–19.8 (18.3); height of bill at base, 9.7–10.7 (10.2); tarsus, 26.2–28.7 (27.7); middle toe without claw, 17.0–19.0 (18.8). *Adult female*: Wing, 97.1–104.9 (101.9); tail, 65.0–73.4 (68.8); bill, 15.0–17.0 (15.7); height of bill, 9.4–10.4 (9.9); tarsus, 25.9–27.9 (27.2); middle toe, 16.0–18.0 (16.8).

RANGE: S. Mackenzie to c. Manitoba, south to c. California and e. Kansas. Winters from c. California and n.e. Kansas to s. Baja California, c. Mexico, Texas, and s.e. Louisiana.

TEXAS: *Winter*: Taken north to Haskell (Apr. 22), east to Dallas, south to Cameron, west to Culberson (July 8, Apr. 27) cos. Common.

LOUISIANA BROWN-HEADED COWBIRD, *Molothrus ater buphilus* (Oberholser)

Race not in A.O.U. check-list, 1957 (see Appendix A).

DESCRIPTION: *Adult male and female, nuptial plumage*: Similar to *M. a. ater* but much smaller, particularly wing and bill; bill averaging relatively stouter. *Natal*: Probably similar to *M. a. ater*.

MEASUREMENTS: *Adult male*: Wing, 97.1–109.0 (average, 105.1) mm.; tail, 66.5–79.5 (72.2); bill (exposed culmen), 14.5–17.5 (16.3); height of bill at base, 9.9–11.4 (10.7); tarsus, 23.6–29.4 (26.2); middle toe without claw, 15.0–18.0 (16.8). *Adult female*: Wing, 93.0–98.1 (95.8); tail, 63.0–69.1 (65.8); bill, 13.0–15.5 (14.2); height of bill, 8.9–10.4 (9.7); tarsus, 23.6–25.4 (24.4); middle toe, 14.0–16.8 (15.2).

RANGE: W. New Mexico to e. Arkansas, south to e. Trans-Pecos Texas, n.e. Tamaulipas, and s.e. Louisiana. Winters from n.w. Texas and e. Arkansas to Sinaloa, Michoacán, Tamaulipas, and s. Mississippi.

TEXAS: *Resident*: Altitudinal breeding range, near sea level to 7,500 ft. Collected north to Randall, east to Orange, south to Cameron, west to Presidio, Jeff Davis, and Culberson (migrant) cos. Abundant to common.

NESTING: Similar to that of *M. a. ater*, but average egg size, 19.8 × 15.2 mm.

DWARF BROWN-HEADED COWBIRD, *Molothrus ater obscurus* (Gmelin)

DESCRIPTION: *Adult male and female, nuptial plumage*: Similar to *M. a. buphilus*, but wing and tail shorter, and bird otherwise smaller; bill usually much more slender; female lighter and more brownish (less grayish). *Natal*: Probably similar to *M. a. ater*.

MEASUREMENTS: *Adult male*: Wing, 94.7–104.6 (average, 100.3) mm.; tail, 63.8–72.7 (68.3); bill (exposed culmen), 15.2–17.8 (16.5); height of bill at base, 8.6–10.4 (9.1); tarsus, 22.6–26.4 (24.1); middle toe without claw, 15.0–17.0 (16.3). *Adult female*: Wing, 87.6–90.9 (89.7); tail, 59.4–64.5 (63.0); bill, 13.5–14.5 (14.0); height of bill, 8.6–9.1 (8.9); tarsus, 22.6–23.9 (23.4); middle toe, 14.0–15.7 (15.0).

RANGE: S. California to w. Trans-Pecos Texas, south to s. Nayarit and s.w. Tamaulipas. Winters from breeding range to s. Baja California, s.w. Sinaloa, Colima, s.e. Oaxaca, and Isla Cozumel.

TEXAS: *Resident*: Altitudinal breeding range, 2,500 to 8,000 ft. Collected in Hudspeth and Culberson cos. Collected outside breeding range in Jeff Davis and Brewster cos. Locally common.

NESTING: Similar to that of *M. a. ater*, but average egg size, 18.8 × 15.0 mm.

BRONZED COWBIRD, *Tangavius aeneus* (Wagler)

SPECIES ACCOUNT   *See colorplate 28*

Red-eyed Cowbird of many writers. Bulkier than

Brown-headed Cowbird; longer bill; red eye; neck-ruff, especially in male, imparts fat-neck look. *Male*: black, glossed mostly with greenish bronze, some bluish or purplish on wings and tail (Arizona male with strong violet sheen on rump). *Female*: somewhat smaller body; neck-ruff reduced; plumage dull black (mouse gray in Arizona race). Length, 8¾ in.; wingspan, 14¼.

RANGE: C. Arizona and s. Texas, south through Mexico and Central America to w. Panama. Winters chiefly from n.w. Mexico and s. Texas southward.

TEXAS: (See map.) *Breeding*: Mid-Mar. to early Sept. (eggs, Mar. 26 to Aug. 9) from sea level to 2,000 ft. Abundant (most years) to common from Laredo to Beeville and Corpus Christi, south to southern tip; common (some years) to uncommon north to Uvalde, San Antonio, and Rockport; irregularly uncommon to rare northeast to Austin, Lee Co., and Galveston; scarce but apparently increasing in southern Trans-Pecos. Parasitism observed on Edwards Plateau (Tom Green and Schleicher cos.) in 1972 marks considerable northward extension. *Winter*: Late Sept. to late Mar. Locally and erratically common to very rare through south Texas, northeast to Brazos and Galveston cos. Unconfirmed sightings at Fort Davis and Fort Worth.

HAUNTS AND HABITS: One of the most curious springtime sights in southern Texas is the tiny black "helicopter." In residential areas of Brownsville, and other towns in the Rio Grande delta, each lawn is likely to display at least one male Red-eyed Bronzed Cowbird hovering in the air a foot or two over a female. With red eye blazing and neck-ruff puffed out, he flutters over her, often for minutes at a time, as she seemingly ignores him and continues to forage in the short grass. When the male "helicopter" lands near the female, he

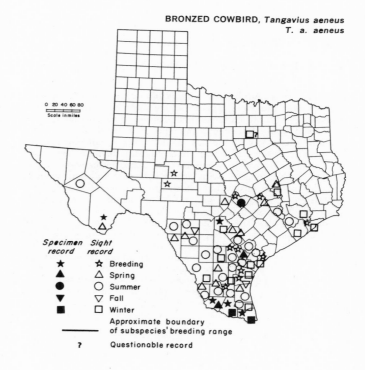

BRONZED COWBIRD, *Tangavius aeneus*
T. a. aeneus

0 20 40 60 80
Scale in miles

Specimen record   Sight record

★ (filled star)   ☆ Breeding
▲ (filled triangle) △ Spring
● (filled circle) ○ Summer
▼ (filled inverted triangle) ▽ Fall
■ (filled square) □ Winter

—— Approximate boundary of subspecies' breeding range

?   Questionable record

puffs up still more. Now his neck and shoulders appear to be transformed into a sinister black cape. The female at this point is overcome—or she is frightened away, leaving the male to deflate his plumage slowly.

Optimum habitat for this cowbird includes mostly open country with occasional trees and patches of tall brush in a fairly humid, hot climate; cows in the landscape are helpful. In winter many individual Bronzed Cowbirds migrate to Mexico, but those that stay gather in flocks and forage in pastures and livestock pens—often in association with other blackbirds. Food consists of weed and grass seeds, oats, ticks, and insects; the bird has been observed picking ticks from cattle. In south Texas, flocks usually roost in shade trees of towns. In the late 1960's, there was a big roost in date palms in a park in Kingsville. This and other winter flocks almost constantly emitted squeaky and creaky sounds, which greatly resembled those made by metal signs swinging in the wind. The usual call note is a harsh, rather guttural *chuck*.

CHANGES: Since the great freeze of 1951, the 98-percent-cleared southern tip of Texas has been planted largely to cotton, vegetables, sorghum, and cattle. Bronzed Cowbirds have increased greatly. By 1960 this nest parasite had contributed heavily to the reduction of species smaller than itself—wrens, vireos, warblers, and the smaller species of orioles. In fact, of this cowbird's favorite Texas hosts—Orchard Oriole, Black-headed Oriole, Hooded Oriole, Bullock's Oriole, Lichtenstein's Oriole, and Cardinal—only the last two species are large and aggressive enough (at least in theory) to raise some of their own young along with those of *T. aeneus*. When favorite victims become scarce, Bronzed Cowbirds lay eggs in the nests of surprising hosts—Mockingbirds, Long-billed Thrashers, even Mourning Doves!

DETAILED ACCOUNT: ONE SUBSPECIES

RED-EYED BRONZED COWBIRD, *Tangavius aeneus aeneus* (Wagler)

DESCRIPTION: *Adult male, nuptial plumage*: Acquired by wear from winter plumage. Upper surface metallic silky dark olive, sometimes with bronzy tinge, but pileum somewhat duller; scapulars and upper tail-coverts metallic dusky dull blue-green to metallic dusky violet blue; tail metallic dusky dull bluish green or metallic dusky dull green, inner edges of feathers sometimes a little dark brownish; wings fuscous black, outer webs of primaries and secondaries, with tips of primaries and both webs of tertials, metallic dusky dull bluish green to metallic dusky yellowish green, greater and primary coverts similar; lesser and median wing-coverts metallic dusky dull bluish green to metallic dusky violet blue; sides of head and of neck, including conspicuous ruffs on neck, like upper surface, but sides of head rather duller; lower surface like upper surface, throat a little less bright; lining of wing and crissum like upper tail-coverts but somewhat duller and more blackish. Bill black; iris scarlet or crimson; legs and feet black or brownish black. *Adult male, winter*: Acquired by complete postnuptial molt. Similar to nuptial adult male but slightly duller. Bill black; iris brownish orange,

orange-brown, or chocolate; legs and feet black. *Adult female, nuptial*: Acquired by wear from winter. Pileum clove brown to blackish clove brown; upper parts similar to pileum but with more or less metallic bluish black, greenish blue, or dull violet sheen; tail metallic dusky olive green, inner margins of feathers clove brown, outer webs edged very narrowly with same color; wings clove brown, but primaries and inner edges of secondaries fuscous, though outer webs of secondaries and inner primaries, together with both webs of tertials, metallic dusky dull olive green to metallic dusky dull bluish green, outer edges of wing-coverts of same color; sides of head and of neck like pileum but usually slightly paler and more brownish; chin and throat fuscous to clove brown; remainder of lower surface blackish clove brown with slight metallic dull greenish or bluish sheen. Iris probably similar to that of adult male in winter. *Adult female, winter*: Acquired by complete postnuptial molt. Like nuptial adult female but rather duller. *Male, second winter*: Acquired by complete postnuptial molt. Like adult male in winter. *Male, first nuptial*: Acquired by partial prenuptial molt. Head and neck all around similar to same parts in adult male, though somewhat duller; remainder of plumage practically identical with that of adult female, but posterior under surface with somewhat brighter metallic violet or bluish sheen. *Male, first winter*: Acquired by complete postjuvenal molt. Similar to adult female in winter but larger, with metallic sheen of upper surface more pronounced. Bill, legs, and feet black. *Female, second winter*: Acquired by complete postnuptial molt. Like adult female in winter. *Female, first nuptial*: Acquired by wear from first winter. Similar to nuptial adult female. *Female, first winter*: Acquired by complete postjuvenal molt. Like adult female in winter. *Male, juvenal*: Acquired by complete postnatal molt. Similar to first winter male, but bill and wing shorter; plumage very much duller and more brownish, upper surface lighter and more brownish—olive brown to fuscous, and without metallic sheen, feathers more or less edged, often obscurely, with lighter brown, imparting somewhat scaled effect; median and greater coverts very narrowly tipped with very pale buff or buffy white; sides of head and of neck and entire lower surface of same color, and differing in same manner from lower parts of first winter male, feathers more or less tipped or edged, sometimes conspicuously, with pale buff or dull pale brown, this posteriorly imparting somewhat scaled effect. Bill dull brown, but mandible paler; iris probably similar to that of adult male in winter; legs and feet dull brown. Similar to nuptial adult female, but lighter and more brownish, both above and below, with paler edgings on feathers and without metallic gloss. *Female, juvenal*: Acquired by complete postnatal molt. Similar to juvenal male but decidedly smaller; upper and lower surfaces much paler and somewhat more grayish—light olive brown to olive brown. Legs and feet lighter brown. *Natal*: Deep mouse gray or between drab gray and tilleul buff.

MEASUREMENTS: *Adult male*: Wing, 111.8–120.1 (average, 116.3) mm.; tail, 75.7–82.3 (79.2); bill (from base), 22.4–23.6 (23.4); height of bill at base, 11.7–13.2 (12.2); tarsus, 29.7–32.0 (30.7); middle toe without claw, 21.4–23.4 (22.9). *Adult female*: Wing, 97.6–106.7 (102.9); tail, 64.0–74.7 (70.6); bill (from base), 19.8–21.4 (20.6); height of bill, 10.4–11.2 (10.9); tarsus, 26.2–29.7 (27.9); middle toe, 19.8–21.9 (20.9).

RANGE: S. Texas, south through e. Mexico to w. Panama.

TEXAS: *Breeding*: Collected north to Bexar (eggs), northeast to Travis (grown young), south to Bee and Cameron, west to Starr and Brewster cos. *Winter*: Taken in Hidalgo and Cameron cos.

NESTING: *Nest*: None; eggs laid in nests of other birds, preferably those living in brush and semiopen to open ranch, farm, and residential areas. *Eggs*: Usually 4 or 5 laid by each bird, ordinarily 1 in a nest, although 8 have been found, possibly the product of more than one female; rounded ovate to ovate; glossy; light bluish green, pale blue, greenish white, or nearly white, ordinarily unmarked; average size, 22.9 × 17.8 mm.

Tanagers: Thraupidae

WESTERN TANAGER, *Piranga ludoviciana* (Wilson)

SPECIES ACCOUNT *See colorplate 29*

Only U.S. tanager with wing-bars (upper yellow, lower white). *Male*: yellow with red or orange face; black back, wings, tail. *Female*: greenish above; wing-bars as in male; yellow below. Length, 7¼ in.; wingspan, 11½; weight, 1¼ oz.

RANGE: W. North America from n.w. British Columbia (perhaps occasionally s. Alaska), south to highest mountains of Baja California and Trans-Pecos Texas. Winters mainly from Mexico to Costa Rica.

TEXAS: (See map.) *Breeding*: Probably late Apr. to mid-Aug. (no egg dates available, but nest being incubated, located June 24, 1960, at 8,000 ft., by F. R. Gehlbach). Uncommon in The Bowl, Guadalupe Mts. Occasionally summers in Davis, Chinati, and Chisos mts., but no nests discovered in these places; only good evidence of breeding: Chisos Mts., Pine Canyon (several young birds barely able to fly, July 24, 1936, T. F. Smith). *Migration*: Early Apr. to mid-May; late Aug. to early Nov. (extremes: Feb. 27, June 20; July 4, Dec. 15). Fairly common west of 100th meridian, though irregular east of Pecos River; increasingly scarce eastward in remainder of state. *Winter*: Late Dec. to late Mar. Rare in southern tip; casual in central portion and along coast; accidental in northern Panhandle (Amarillo, Jan. 1, 1973, Peggy Acord).

HAUNTS AND HABITS: Montane coniferous forests of western North America are the summer home of the Western Tanager, northernmost ranging of the world's 196 species of Thraupidae. Where cool evergreen forests come down to the Pacific, as in British Columbia and Washington, this tanager ranges to sea level, but in Texas it is strictly a mountain bird during the breeding season. In The Bowl, eight thousand feet high in the Guadalupe Mountains, it frequents Douglasfir-pine-oak forest from April to August. In late summer most members of the species migrate to the highlands of Mexico and Central America to winter. Some individuals migrate through, and a few even winter in, lowlands in Texas and elsewhere. They are usually found singly or in pairs.

The Western's flight is strong, swift, and performed with powerful wing-beats. This tanager spends much time in the upper canopy of tall trees, but it also feeds on the ground more than other U.S. tanagers. It forages deliberately and quietly through the trees; sometimes it catches insects on the wing flycatcherlike. Often it perches for some time without changing position. Food consists largely of insects: wasps, ants, termites, stinkbugs, cicadas, beetles, grasshoppers, craneflies, dragonflies, and caterpillars. It also eats some fruit (hawthorn, wild cherries, elderberries, blackberries, mulberries, serviceberries), occasionally proving locally destructive to cultivated cherries.

The call note is a dry *pi-tik* or *pit-i-tik*. The male's song is similar in form to that of the Robin, but hoarser and less sustained. In Texas males sing from April to July.

DETAILED ACCOUNT: TWO SUBSPECIES

PACIFIC WESTERN TANAGER, *Piranga ludoviciana ludoviciana* (Wilson)

No races recognized by A.O.U. check-list, 1957 (see Appendix A).

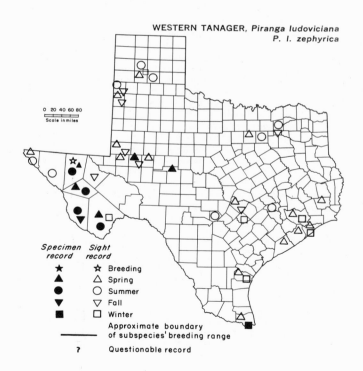

WESTERN TANAGER, *Piranga ludoviciana*
P. l. *zephyrica*

0 20 40 60 80
Scale in miles

Specimen record / Sight record

★ / ☆ Breeding
▲ / △ Spring
● / ○ Summer
▼ / ▽ Fall
■ / □ Winter

—— Approximate boundary of subspecies' breeding range

? Questionable record

DESCRIPTION: *Adult male, nuptial plumage (red-headed phase):* Acquired by partial prenuptial molt. Forehead and crown scarlet red to scarlet, passing into lemon chrome or gamboge yellow on hindneck; back and scapulars black, a few feathers sometimes with dull yellow margins; rump and upper tail-coverts lemon chrome to gamboge yellow; tail dull black, feathers narrowly tipped with mouse gray, most broadly on outermost rectrices; wing-quills chaetura drab to fuscous, inner margins of primaries and secondaries paler, outer webs more blackish, narrowly edged on middle or subterminal portion with yellowish citrine, secondaries very narrowly tipped on outer webs with dull white; tertials chaetura black or fuscous black, broadly tipped and margined on apical portion of outer webs with yellowish white or very pale yellow; lesser wing-coverts black; median wing-coverts lemon yellow; greater wing-coverts dull black, broadly tipped with dull straw yellow; primary coverts dull black, chaetura black, or fuscous black; lores mixed with dull red, pale brown, buff, or yellow; cheeks scarlet or orange, sometimes streaked with lemon yellow; auriculars dull lemon yellow to pale scarlet; sides of neck gamboge yellow or lemon chrome; chin scarlet to scarlet red; remainder of lower surface deep lemon chrome to deep wax yellow, but throat and jugulum more or less stained with scarlet; lining of wing lemon yellow; under wing-coverts more or less streaked or spotted with hair brown or chaetura drab. Maxilla dark sepia tinged with green, but cutting edges and mandible light wax yellow tinged with green; iris grayish brown or black; legs and feet light plumbeous, soles of toes paler. *Adult male, nuptial (orange-headed phase):* Similar to red-headed phase, but pileum, cheeks, and chin orange chrome to orange. *Adult male, winter:* Acquired by complete postnuptial molt. Similar to nuptial adult male, but pileum, sides of head, and chin with much less red or orange, these parts much obscured by chaetura black and olive green tips of feathers; black feathers of back and scapulars much tipped with warbler green or greenish olive; rump, sometimes upper tail-coverts, more or less washed with olive green; anterior lower parts duller, feathers somewhat obscured by olive green tips; sides and flanks somewhat washed with olive green. *Adult female, nuptial (yellow phase):* Acquired by partial prenuptial molt. Forehead and crown brazil red to grenadine red; hindneck yellowish warbler green to light citrine; back and scapulars deep olive to deep greenish olive, somewhat streaked or mottled with olive brown feather centers; rump and upper tail-coverts bright sulphine yellow; tail fuscous to olive brown, margined on outer webs with sulphine yellow and narrowly tipped on inner webs with yellowish or buffy white; wings fuscous to light fuscous, inner margins of wing-quills drab to light brown, outer margins of primaries and secondaries narrowly yellowish warbler green; tertials narrowly tipped on outer webs with yellowish white; lesser wing-coverts tipped and margined with yellowish warbler green; median coverts broadly tipped with wax yellow, forming wing-bar; greater coverts edged on outer webs with dull yellowish citrine and rather broadly tipped with yellowish white, forming second conspicuous wing-bar; rather inconspicuous superciliary stripe brazil red anteriorly, becoming mixed with yellow or entirely wax yellow posteriorly; cheeks strongly tinged with brazil red or entirely dull wax yellow; auriculars yellowish warbler green, as are sides of neck; chin brazil red to grenadine red; remainder of lower surface wax yellow to primuline yellow to gamboge yellow, but sides and flanks light yellowish citrine, which sometimes slightly invades jugulum and breast; lining of wing citrine yellow to strontian yellow. Bill dark sepia with greenish tinge, but base of mandible yellow, rest of mandible and cutting edges of bill light greenish yellow; iris burnt umber; legs and feet plumbeous. *Adult female, nuptial (gray phase):* Similar to yellow phase, but upper surface much more grayish (less yellowish), back and scapulars between hair brown and grayish olive or deep grayish olive, rump more grayish (less yellowish), yellow wing-bar on median coverts paler; lower surface decidedly paler; sides and flanks more grayish or buffy (less olive or yellow). *Adult female, winter (yellow phase):* Acquired by complete postnuptial molt. Similar to nuptial yellow phase, but head, chin, and cheeks with less red; upper surface some-

what duller, pileum obscured by olive edgings of feathers; light edgings of tertials broader, sides of head lighter, duller, less yellowish; yellow of lower surface duller, more washed with olive green. *Adult female, winter (gray phase):* Similar to winter yellow phase, but upper surface more grayish; pileum and rump duller; lower surface paler and more grayish (less brightly yellow). *Male, second winter:* Acquired by complete postnuptial molt. Like adult male in winter. *Male, first nuptial:* Acquired by partial prenuptial molt, which does not involve primaries. Similar to nuptial adult male, but upper surface somewhat duller, yellow of hindneck and rump obscured by olivaceous edgings of feathers, black of back more brownish, feathers more or less edged with olive green or dull yellow; wings and tail much more brownish, primary coverts always—also some or all primaries—olive brown or fuscous instead of black; sides and flanks more grayish or olivaceous. *Male, first winter:* Acquired by partial postjuvenal molt, which does not involve wing-quills or tail. Similar to yellow phase of adult female in winter, but upper surface usually more yellowish (less brownish or grayish); lower parts more brightly yellow (less brownish or buffy)—strontian yellow to dull lemon chrome; sides and flanks more grayish or olive (less buffy). *Female, second winter:* Acquired by complete postnuptial molt. Similar to corresponding phase of adult female in winter. *Female, first nuptial (yellow phase):* Acquired by partial prenuptial molt. Similar to yellow phase of nuptial adult female, but without red on head or chin; upper surface duller, back more grayish (less greenish yellow), rump duller and darker, often more mixed or washed with gray, pileum duller yellowish citrine, more obscured by olivaceous edgings of feathers and thus more uniform; lower surface decidedly paler and duller, less olivaceous (more grayish) on sides and flanks; throat decidedly paler and more buffy, usually paler than breast. *Female, first nuptial (gray phase):* Similar to first nuptial female, yellow phase, but paler above, head and rump decidedly less yellowish, all parts much more grayish; sides of head and lower surface much paler and more grayish, chin and throat buffy white with little or no tinge of yellow; middle of abdomen straw yellow; crissum citrine yellow; remainder of lower surface dull pale cartridge buff, washed with pale yellow; sides and flanks between light drab and light grayish olive. Similar to nuptial adult female, gray phase, but head entirely without yellow, upper surface very much paler, more grayish, particularly on head, rump, and upper tail-coverts; wings and tail lighter; chin without red; entire lower surface lighter, duller, more grayish or buffy (less yellowish). *Female, first winter (yellow phase):* Acquired by complete postnuptial molt. Similar to adult female in winter, yellow phase, but upper surface duller, more uniform, and more brownish, upper tail-coverts and lower rump light brownish olive, citrine, or brownish orange citrine; lower surface duller and more brownish (less clearly yellowish). Similar to first nuptial female, but upper surface duller, more brownish, back more brownish olive (less grayish), upper tail-coverts much more brownish; lower surface duller, more brownish, particularly on jugulum. Similar to first winter male but somewhat smaller; upper parts lighter and duller, more brownish or grayish (less yellowish); wing-bars less clearly yellow, usually duller and more buffy; lower parts lighter, duller, much more brownish—ochraceous or buffy (much less clearly and less brightly yellow), throat usually dull buff or buffy white with little or no yellow. *Female, first winter (gray phase):* Similar to gray phase of adult female in winter, but upper surface much duller, more uniform, head, rump, and upper tail-coverts but slightly yellowish; lower surface much paler, more buffy, often with little yellow, this chiefly on middle of breast and of abdomen and on crissum; chin and upper throat dull pale buff, jugulum drab or between drab and dark olive buff. Similar to gray phase of first nuptial female, but upper surface darker, duller, more brownish, particularly on upper tail-coverts, with less yellow on head; lower surface darker, duller, and more brownish or buffy, with less yellow, there being none on chin. *Juvenal:* Acquired by complete postnatal molt. Pileum dull old gold to brownish orange citrine; back and scapulars light brownish olive to buffy olive; upper tail-coverts brownish orange citrine to brownish old gold; wings and tail similar to first winter female, but wing-bars more buffy—dull naples yellow; sides of head similar to pileum but lighter; lower surface dull buffy or yellowish white, throat, jugulum, breast, sides, and flanks—sometimes abdomen slightly—more or less broadly streaked or spotted with mouse gray; crissum amber yellow. Maxilla dark olive or saccardo umber; mandible dull yellow, light orange, or old gold; iris fuscous black; legs and feet dark gull gray. *Natal* (this plumage of this race not seen in Texas): Pale drab gray.

MEASUREMENTS: *Adult male*: Wing, 89.4–96.0 (average, 92.2) mm.; tail, 65.0–71.1 (67.8); bill (exposed culmen), 14.0–16.0 (15.2); tarsus, 17.0–21.1 (19.3); middle toe without claw, 12.4–15.0 (14.2). *Adult female*: Wing, 87.6–91.9 (89.7); tail, 65.0–71.1 (67.8); bill, 14.2–15.2 (14.7); tarsus, 18.5–20.6 (19.3); middle toe, 13.7–15.0 (14.2).

RANGE: S.w. British Columbia, Washington, and s.e. Idaho, south to n. Baja California and c. Utah. In migration, east to c. Montana, c. Colorado, Trans-Pecos Texas, and c. Coahuila. Winters from c. California and s.e. Tamaulipas to w. Guatemala.

TEXAS: *Migration*: Three specimens: Culberson Co. (The Bowl, May 19, 1938, T. D. Burleigh; 7 mi. north of Pine Springs, Aug. 16, 1940, S. N. Whitehead); Brewster Co., Marathon (May 18, 1901, H. C. Oberholser).

NESTING: (This race does not nest in Texas): *Nest*: On mountains and mesas, in valleys and canyons; in evergreen tree, such as Douglasfir or pine, or in deciduous tree; often saddled on branch, ordinarily 20–60 ft. above ground; a rather frail, open, flat bowl, with only a relatively slight cavity for eggs; composed of twigs, weed stalks, pine needles, strips of bark, grasses, roots, and mosses; lined with rootlets, sometimes grasses or hair, and other soft vegetable substances. *Eggs*: 3–5, usually 4; ovate; light niagara green; dotted rather sparingly, chiefly at larger end, with fuscous, clove brown, reddish brown, umber, dark grayish olive, and with shell markings of lilac, lavender, and drab; average size, 22.9 × 16.5 mm.

ROCKY MOUNTAIN WESTERN TANAGER, Piranga ludoviciana zephyrica Oberholser, new subspecies (see Appendix A)

DESCRIPTION: *Adult male and female, nuptial plumage*: Similar to *P. l. ludoviciana* but larger, male averaging brighter below; female averaging paler both above and below. *Natal*: Probably similar to *P. l. ludoviciana*.

MEASUREMENTS: *Adult male*: Wing, 89.9–98.6 (average, 95.8) mm.; tail, 65.0–73.9 (71.9); bill (exposed culmen), 13.5–16.0 (14.7); tarsus, 18.8–21.1 (19.8); middle toe without claw, 14.0–16.0 (15.2). *Adult female*: Wing, 87.1–93.5 (90.2); tail, 66.0–73.7 (69.3); bill, 13.5–17.0 (14.7); tarsus, 19.0–21.1 (19.8); middle toe, 13.5–15.0 (14.2).

TYPE: Adult male, no. 262925, U.S. National Museum, Biological Surveys collection; Madera Canyon, Santa Rita Mts., Santa Cruz Co., Arizona; Aug. 12, 1918, A. B. Howell, original no., 415.

RANGE: N.w. British Columbia, s. Mackenzie, and c. Saskatchewan, south through Rocky Mts. to s.e. Arizona and n. Trans-Pecos Texas. Winters from s. Baja California and s. Texas to s.e. Tamaulipas, s.e. Oaxaca, and s. Guatemala.

TEXAS: *Breeding*: Collected in Culberson Co. Collected in summer (no nests found) in Jeff Davis, Presidio, and Brewster cos. *Migration*: Collected north to Culberson, east to Tom Green, southwest to Brewster and Presidio cos. Fairly common. *Winter*: Taken in Cameron Co. (5 specimens). Rare.

NESTING: Similar to that of *P. l. ludoviciana*, but average egg size, 24.1 × 16.5 mm.

SCARLET TANAGER, Piranga olivacea (Gmelin)

SPECIES ACCOUNT   *See colorplate 30*

Nuptial male: scarlet; black wings, tail. *Female*: dull

green above; yellow below; dusky wings, tail. *Fall male*: similar to female but retains black wings, tail. Length, 7 in.; wingspan, 11¾; weight, 1¼ oz.

RANGE: S.e. Manitoba to New Brunswick, south to e. Oklahoma and n.w. South Carolina. Winters in n.w. South America from Colombia to c. Peru.

TEXAS: (See map.) *Migration*: Mid-Apr. to early May; mid-Sept. to mid-Oct. (extremes: Feb. 19, June 29; July 17, Oct. 19). Common (some years) to uncommon in spring and early summer east of 99th meridian (97th north of Waco), though often very common on upper coast late Apr. to early May; increasingly scarce westward to Trans-Pecos, where casual. Rare in fall.

HAUNTS AND HABITS: Among tanagers, the Scarlet excels on two counts: It is the only species that undergoes drastic seasonal color change; and it is the champion long-distance migrant. The Scarlet Tanager breeds in mature woodlands and shady suburbs, where it saddles its nest well out on a horizontal limb, often high in a tree. In Texas it is seen mostly in April and May at the time when the male's scarlet and black plumage is at its highest brilliance. In spite of its vivid colors, this species is rather difficult to find. The male habitually keeps himself well hidden in the tops of elm, oak, maple, and other broad-leaved trees, and the female's green and yellow plumage blends with leaves and patches of sunlight. Finally, this tanager's slow and deliberate search for food and its scant vocalizations allow it to pass through Texas mostly unobserved in the course of its long spring journey from northwestern South America to northeastern United States. The Scarlet is even more inconspicuous and quieter in fall; at this season, Texas records of its occurrence are rare indeed. It is generally a solitary bird, rarely found in groups.

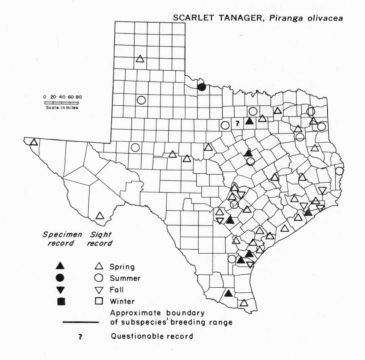

SCARLET TANAGER, *Piranga olivacea*

0 20 40 60 80
Scale in miles

Specimen record   Sight record

▲ △ Spring
● ○ Summer
▼ ▽ Fall
■ □ Winter

—— Approximate boundary of subspecies' breeding range

? Questionable record

In flight, this tanager is swift and graceful. When foraging, it frequently sits almost still for a considerable time and may work on one caterpillar for several minutes. Food consists chiefly of tree-infesting insects, many of them injurious. Moths, butterflies, caterpillars (tent, forest tent, leaf-rollers, cankerworms), beetles (leaf, wood-boring, engraver, cottonwood-leaf, darkling, predaceous ground, click, wireworms, June, leaf-chafers, curculios, nut weevils, billbugs), gall insects, dragonflies, termites, craneflies, ants, wasps, flies, hornets, bees, grasshoppers, locusts, soldier bugs, leaf- and tree-hoppers, spittle insects, cicadas, plant lice, and scale insects have all been identified in stomach contents. Snails, millipedes, spiders and their eggs, as well as harvestmen and earthworms are apparently relished also. The Scarlet eats some fruit, mostly berries, especially in autumn.

The usual call note is an occasional low *chip-burr*. Song consists of four or five short phrases, Robin-like but hoarser. Rarely are snatches of song heard in Texas.

DETAILED ACCOUNT: NO SUBSPECIES

DESCRIPTION: *Adult male, nuptial plumage*: Acquired by partial prenuptial molt. Entire plumage, except wings and tail, scarlet to scarlet red; tail dull black, outer pair of feathers narrowly tipped, chiefly on inner webs, with dull white or grayish white; wings black, inner webs of primaries and secondaries chaetura black or chaetura drab, inner margins of primaries and secondaries, except tips, white or yellowish white; lining of wing white or yellowish white, outer portion black. Maxilla olive, raw umber, brown, dull pea green, olive yellow, greenish black, plumbeous, or hair brown tinged with yellow, its tip black or blackish slate; mandible dull white, olive yellow, dull pea green, yellowish white, or slightly paler than maxilla; tongue white; iris prout brown; legs and feet plumbeous; blackish slate, or black. *Adult male, winter*: Acquired by complete postnuptial molt. Upper surface olive green to warbler green, sometimes lighter and more yellowish on upper tail-coverts; wings and tail black as in nuptial adult male; sides of head and neck similar to upper parts, but rather lighter—dull lemon yellow; ill-defined yellowish supraloral streak; eyelids dull lemon yellow; throat pale lemon yellow to wax yellow, often more or less washed with olive green; jugulum pale sulphine yellow to pyrite yellow; abdomen citrine yellow to strontian yellow; sides and flanks grayish olive or light grayish olive washed with yellow; crissum strontian yellow to light cadmium; lining of wing white or yellowish white, outer under wing-coverts black. *Adult female, nuptial*: Acquired by partial prenuptial molt. Similar to adult male in winter, but upper parts duller, tail hair brown, edged on outer webs of feathers with yellowish warbler green of upper tail-coverts, most of feathers narrowly edged on inner webs with dull white; wings hair brown, inner edges of primaries and secondaries, except tips, dull white or yellowish white, all wing-quills and coverts edged on outer webs, coverts also tipped, with warbler green of upper surface, that on primaries duller and sometimes more grayish; eye-ring strontian yellow, sides of head paler, somewhat more grayish than adult male in winter, with less evident supraloral yellowish streak; lower surface duller and somewhat lighter than adult male in winter, more tinged or washed with olive or citrine; lining of wing yellowish white or very pale yellow, the outer part hair brown, tipped with warbler green. Bill dull light olive, but tip darker, mandible somewhat paler; iris dark brown; legs and feet plumbeous. *Adult female, winter*: Acquired by complete postnuptial molt. Very similar to nuptial adult female, but olive green of upper surface and yellow of lower surface averaging somewhat more buffy. *Male, third winter*: Acquired by complete postnuptial molt. Like adult male in winter. *Male, second nuptial*: Acquired by partial prenuptial molt. Similar to nuptial adult male, but red of upper and lower parts usually lighter and duller, with at least one or two scattered feather patches of saffron yellow, greenish yellow, or olive yellow. *Male, second winter*: Acquired by complete postnuptial molt. Similar to adult male in winter, but upper surface darker and duller; exposed surface of wing-quills and primary coverts more brownish (not so deeply black) and edged on outer webs with olive green; tertials tipped with yellowish or greenish white. *Male, first nuptial*: Acquired by partial prenuptial molt, which does not involve wing-quills and coverts. Similar to second nuptial male, but red with still more admixture and patches of saffron yellow and olive green or olive gray; primaries, secondaries, primary coverts, and alula not black, but like those of nuptial adult female. *Male, first winter (gray-green phase)*: Acquired by partial postjuvenal molt, which does not involve wing-quills or tail. Similar to adult female in winter, but upper surface darker, including wings and tail; lesser, median, and greater wing-coverts, and scapulars black; lower parts usually of a deeper yellow, otherwise somewhat darker. Similar to second winter male, but wing-quills, including secondaries, primary coverts, alula, and tail, more brownish (less blackish), and like those of adult female in winter. *Male, first winter (yellow-green phase)*: Similar to adult female in winter, but much more citrine yellow above and more deeply yellowish below; in these respects differing still more from gray-green phase. *Female, second winter*: Acquired by complete postnuptial molt. Very similar to adult female in winter. *Female, first nuptial*: Acquired by partial prenuptial molt, which does not involve wing-quills or coverts. Similar to nuptial adult female, but upper surface less clearly greenish; wing-quills somewhat more brownish. *Female, first winter*: Acquired by partial postjuvenal molt, not including wing-quills or tail. Similar to adult female in winter, but upper surface averaging more yellowish or brownish (less purely greenish); light edgings of tertials usually broader; eye-ring obscure; lower surface more brownish or buffy, jugulum darker and more tinged with brown or olivaceous; sides and flanks darker, more olivaceous or brownish (less grayish). Similar to first winter male but lighter, more brownish above; wings and tail paler and more brownish, coverts not black; eye-ring obscure; lower parts more ochraceous, particularly on jugulum. Bill dull flesh color, but cutting edges dull green, tip dull light brown; iris dark brown. *Male, juvenal*: Acquired by complete postnatal molt. Upper surface citrine or dull orange citrine, but back darker; wings and tail similar to those of first winter male, but median and greater wing-coverts fuscous (not black), edged with citrine, tips of median and greater coverts olive ocher or colonial buff; upper surface streaked or barred more or less obscurely with olive or buffy olive, this most evident on back and crown; lower surface anteriorly yellowish white or primrose yellow; abdomen primrose yellow to colonial buff; breast and jugulum heavily streaked or spotted, posterior lower parts more lightly, with dark hair brown or chaetura drab. *Female, juvenal*: Acquired by complete postnatal molt. Similar to juvenal male, but wings and tail lighter, more brownish; upper surface somewhat paler.

MEASUREMENTS: *Adult male*: Wing, 91.7–99.3 (average, 95.8) mm.; tail, 65.0–71.7 (68.3); bill (exposed culmen), 14.5–15.7 (15.2); height of bill at base, 8.6–9.7 (9.1); tarsus, 19.8–20.9 (20.1); middle toe without claw, 13.2–15.5 (14.0). *Adult female*: Wing, 87.9–94.5 (92.7); tail, 64.0–70.4 (67.3); bill, 14.2–15.7 (15.0); height of bill, 8.4–9.1 (8.6); tarsus, 17.8–20.9 (19.8); middle toe, 13.0–14.7 (13.7).

TEXAS: *Migration*: Collected northwest to Wilbarger (June 4), east to Galveston, south to Hidalgo, west to Bexar cos.

HEPATIC TANAGER, *Piranga flava* (Vieillot)

SPECIES ACCOUNT

Blackish bill; dark gray cheeks. *Male*: dull red ("liver colored"). *Female*: mostly dusky gray above; gray cheeks; yellow below. Length, 8¼ in.; wingspan, 12¾.

RANGE: N. Arizona, n. New Mexico, and Trans-Pecos Texas, south through Mexico and Central America to c. Argentina. Northern races winter chiefly in Mexico.

TEXAS: (See map.) *Breeding*: Early May to late Aug. (no egg dates available, but fledglings and nest located, Guadalupe Mts.) from 5,000 to 8,000 ft. Fairly common to probably increasingly uncommon in Guadalupe, Davis, and Chisos mts. *Migration*: Late Apr. to mid-May; late Aug. to early Oct. (extremes: Apr. 19, June 3; Aug. 20, Oct. 16). Fairly common at high elevations in Trans-Pecos; scarce in El Paso region. Rare to casual in spring along central coast and in Rio Grande delta. Casual in fall east of Pecos River. Edwards Plateau records need verification.

HAUNTS AND HABITS: The Hepatic Tanager is one of the very few highland South American birds whose breeding range extends north as far as the United States. In this country it occurs in dry pine-oak woods on the small mountain ranges which rise like islands above the deserts of Arizona, New Mexico, and Trans-Pecos Texas. It seems to prefer tall trees, particularly pines. It is normally found singly or in pairs, but family parties or autumn groups may number five to ten individuals.

This shy bird moves with deliberation through foliage, restlessly flying from tree to tree—often across canyons. Little is definitely known of the Hepatic's diet, but it is probably similar to that of other tanagers of its genus. It has been observed to feed on wild grapes and wild cherries.

The Hepatic's call note is a distinctive *chuck*, Hermit Thrush–like. Its breeding-season song, delivered at dawn and occasionally at other times of the day, is very

similar to that of a Black-headed Grosbeak but usually somewhat shorter.

CHANGES: The existence of the Hepatic Tanager as a breeder in Texas seems precarious. For many years, especially since 1950, droughts, insects, and overgrazing have been killing the mature junipers, pines, and oaks within the Trans-Pecos. By 1972, only the Guadalupe Mountains, highest in Texas, still maintained extensive acreage suitable for this species. In the Davis and Chisos mountains to the south—lower and drier—this tanager's habitat looked poor in the 1960's. However, in the Chisos, an adult male was seen carrying food near the Basin lodge, June 10, 1967, and a nest was discovered in the same area, May 12, 1968 (R. H. Wauer).

DETAILED ACCOUNT: ONE SUBSPECIES

NORTHERN HEPATIC TANAGER, *Piranga flava oreophasma* Oberholser

Texas birds are *P. f. dextra* in A.O.U. check-list, 1957 (see Appendix A).

DESCRIPTION: *Adult male, nuptial plumage*: Acquired by wear from winter plumage. Pileum brazil red to light brazil red or dull dark scarlet; back, scapulars, and rump dull ferruginous or between hays russet and kaiser brown; hindneck and upper tail-coverts vinaceous rufous or dark vinaceous rufous, upper parts, except forehead and crown, more or less tipped and edged with rather light mouse gray to hair brown, these edgings broadest on back and rump, where sometimes they hide most of ground color; tail feathers rood brown or bister, margined on outer webs with ferruginous or light vinaceous rufous; wings fuscous or light fuscous, inner edges of quills, except tips of primaries, dull light vinaceous or vinaceous fawn; tips of median wing-coverts, outer edges of greater coverts and of primary coverts, with outer margins of wing-quills, like outer margins of tail feathers; lesser coverts darker; lores fuscous; rictal stripe to below eye dull light smoke gray; remainder of sides of head dull smoke gray, slightly washed with red; sides of neck like hindneck, posteriorly much edged with gray, anteriorly less so; lower surface dull scarlet or between scarlet and dull grenadine red; crissum grenadine pink to bittersweet orange; sides and flanks darker and duller, more or less tinged with light gray; lining of wing flame scarlet or grenadine red, sometimes slightly mottled with hair brown. Bill brownish black or plumbeous black, but mandible plumbeous; iris dark brown; legs and feet bluish gray or dull brown. *Adult male, winter*: Acquired by complete postnuptial molt. Similar to nuptial adult male, but upper surface more extensively gray, feathers with broader edgings, upper surface thus appearing lighter in color; lower surface paler and duller, feathers much edged with pale gray, dull white, or pale buff, except on chin and throat. *Adult female, nuptial*: Acquired by wear from winter. Forehead sulphine yellow to analine yellow; supraloral spot or streak dull cadmium yellow to gamboge yellow; remainder of upper surface light grayish olive to deep grayish olive, upper tail-coverts rather light yellowish olive or olive lake; tail light brownish olive or light olive, outer webs edged with color of upper tail-coverts; wings hair brown or between hair brown and buffy brown, but inner edges of primaries and secondaries, except tips of primaries, very dull pale pinkish buff, and outer margins like color of upper tail-coverts; outer edges of greater coverts dull light yellowish olive; tertials tipped and edged on outer webs with dull light drab or light grayish olive; upper part of lores chaetura drab; lower part of lores dull mouse gray, this extending back under eyes; rest of sides of head and of neck like back, but paler, middle of sides of neck behind head invaded by dull analine yellow washed or overlaid with gray; chin and throat gamboge yellow, apex of chin sometimes whitish or buffy; jugulum and breast analine yellow or between this and sulphur yellow;

HEPATIC TANAGER, *Piranga flava*
P. f. oreophasma

0 20 40 60 80
Scale in miles

Specimen Sight
record record

★ ☆ Breeding
▲ △ Spring
● ○ Summer
▼ ▽ Fall
■ □ Winter

Approximate boundary
—— of subspecies' breeding range

? Questionable record

abdomen grayish wax yellow to amber yellow; crissum wax yellow to lemon chrome; sides and flanks grayish olive to deep olive buff; lining of wing wax yellow to primuline yellow. *Adult female, winter*: Acquired by complete postnuptial molt. Similar to nuptial adult female, but upper surface more uniform, colors more blended; pileum duller, feathers much edged with gray, particularly on crown and occiput; light edgings of wing-quills broader; yellow of lower parts rather lighter but obscured, particularly on jugulum, by mouse gray tips of feathers. *Male, third winter*: Acquired by complete postnuptial molt. Practically identical with adult male in winter. *Male, second nuptial*: Acquired by wear from second winter. Similar to nuptial adult male, but coloration somewhat duller; upper surface with some patches of olive green or olive gray, occasionally wing-quills, wing-coverts, and tail feathers edged with olive green; lower surface with irregular patches of saffron yellow, olive yellow, lemon chrome, light yellowish olive, or isabella color, although these parts are predominantly red. *Male, second winter*: Acquired by complete postnuptial molt. Similar to second nuptial male but duller, more blended in appearance both above and below, particularly on crown, sides, and flanks; pileum and back more edged with gray. *Male, first nuptial*: Acquired by wear from first winter. Similar to nuptial adult female but larger; upper surface darker, more greenish (less grayish); pileum, particularly forehead, usually with spots or tinge of red; outer webs of tail feathers sometimes saffron or even reddish; lower parts darker, richer yellow, more or less spotted or tinged with orange or red, although predominant color is, of course, yellow. *Male, first winter*: Acquired by partial postjuvenal molt. Similar to first nuptial male, but upper surface more blended by grayish edgings of feathers, light tips of wing-quills broader; lower surface duller, yellow more obscured by gray or olive. Similar to adult female in winter but larger, darker above, and more deeply and richly yellow below, usually with more or less indication of red or orange on pileum and at least anterior lower parts. *Female, first nuptial*: Acquired by wear from first winter. Like nuptial adult female. *Female, first winter*: Acquired by partial postjuvenal molt. Very similar to adult female in winter and often indistinguishable, but lower surface usually duller yellow, which is somewhat more obscured by dull gray or olivaceous edgings of feathers. *Male, juvenal*: Acquired by complete postnatal molt. Upper surface isabella color or clay color, back palest; everywhere heavily streaked, on back also somewhat barred, with olive brown or clove brown; wings and tail as in first winter male, but lesser and greater wing-coverts tipped with pale dull yellow or yellowish buff, forming two rather indistinct wing-bars; sides of head like upper parts but rather duller; a more or less obvious supraloral streak of dull yellow; eyelids pale yellow; lower surface amber or straw yellow, but crissum yellow ocher; everywhere heavily streaked, except sometimes on crissum, with clove brown or olive brown. *Female, juvenal*: Acquired by complete postnatal molt. Similar to juvenal male, but upper surface lighter, much less heavily streaked; lower surface also paler, streaks narrower and rather paler. *Natal*: Unknown.

MEASUREMENTS: *Adult male*: Wing, 103.1–105.9 (average, 104.6) mm.; tail, 81.5–86.6 (84.8); bill (exposed culmen), 16.0–17.8 (17.3); tarsus, 21.1–23.1 (22.4); middle toe without claw, 15.0–16.5 (16.0). *Adult female*: Wing, 98.1–101.1 (99.3); tail, 79.5–84.6 (82.8); bill, 16.3–19.0 (17.5); tarsus, 21.6–23.4 (22.4); middle toe, 14.5–16.0 (15.2).

RANGE: W. and n. New Mexico and Trans-Pecos Texas, south to Chihuahua, s.e. Coahuila, and Nuevo León. Winters from Chihuahua to Michoacán and State of México.

TEXAS: *Breeding*: Collected in Culberson, Jeff Davis, and Brewster cos. *Migration*: Collected in Jeff Davis, Brewster, Nueces, and Cameron cos.

NESTING: *Nest*: On mountains and within canyons; in juniper-pinyon-pine-oak forests; on branch of tree, usually horizontal; loosely constructed saucer of rootlets, weeds, and dry plant stems; lined with fine roots and thin plant stems. *Eggs*: 3–4; ovate; bluish green or pale green; spotted and blotched, chiefly about larger end, with purplish brown and dull purple; average size, 23.4 × 16.3 mm.

SUMMER TANAGER, *Piranga rubra* (Linnaeus)

SPECIES ACCOUNT   *See colorplate 30*

Large bill (yellowish in summer). *Male*: rose red. *Female and immature*: olive above (including wings and tail); dull yellow below. Length, 8 in.; wingspan, 12¼; weight, 1–1¼ oz.

RANGE: S.e. California, c. Oklahoma, s.e. Nebraska, Ohio Valley, and Delaware, south to n. Mexico, U.S. Gulf coast, and Florida. Winters chiefly from Mexico through Central America to Bolivia and Guyana.

TEXAS: (See map.) *Breeding*: Late Apr. to mid-July (egg dates, Apr. 30 to June 17) from near sea level to 5,050 ft., possibly to 6,500 ft. Common to fairly common in eastern third and on Edwards Plateau; fairly common (but local) in Trans-Pecos; rare in Panhandle (breeds?) and south Texas brush country. *Migration*: Late Mar. to early May; early Aug. to mid-Oct. (extremes: Feb. 23, June 30; July 25, Dec. 7). Common to fairly common in most parts, though often very common along coast in Apr. and early May; uncommon in northern Panhandle. *Winter*: Late Dec. to late Feb. Rare to casual in coastal vicinities and in central portions.

HAUNTS AND HABITS: The Summer Tanager—formerly called summer redbird to distinguish it from that all-year redbird, the Cardinal—is the most numerous species of its family in Texas. In most of the state it prefers oak, hickory, pecan, or even pine woods. West of the Pecos, however, it occurs in cottonwoods and willows along lowland streams. The pines and oaks of the mountains are inhabited by its relative the Hepatic Tanager. It is not a gregarious species and is usually found singly or in pairs.

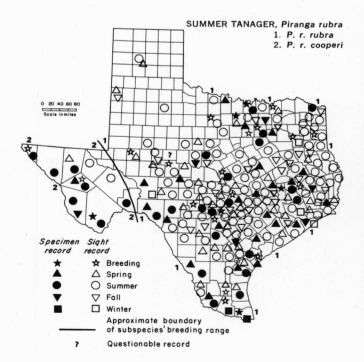

SUMMER TANAGER, *Piranga rubra*
1. *P. r. rubra*
2. *P. r. cooperi*

0 20 40 60 80
Scale in miles

Specimen record / Sight record

★ / ☆ Breeding
▲ / △ Spring
● / ○ Summer
▼ / ▽ Fall
■ / □ Winter

—— Approximate boundary of subspecies' breeding range

? Questionable record

Its flight is strong and swift, performed with moderate though vigorous wing-beats. It is an expert "flycatcher" and often takes insects on the wing. Deliberate, like other tanagers, it moves slowly in the foliage of tall trees but it also descends to lower levels—even the ground—and is less shy than its Texas relatives. Although wild berries and some seeds are taken at times, food consists largely of flying insects: beetles, bumblebees, honeybees, hornets, wasps, gall flies, bugs, dragonflies; also caterpillars and spiders and their eggs.

The Summer's call is a staccato rattle, *pi-tuck* or *pik-i-tuck-i-tuck*. The male's song is a series of Robin-like phrases, more musical than those of the Western or Scarlet and more closely connected than those of a Robin. He sings chiefly from April into July.

CHANGES: Nowadays, the Summer Tanager rarely nests in or near the Rio Grande delta. Most recent indication of breeding appears to be two pairs seen carrying nesting material at Anzalduas tract (Hidalgo Co.), May 2, 1971, by J. C. Arvin; however, Arvin annotated this report by remarking that the species has become very rare as a delta breeder in recent years. Most recent regular summer records come from Texas' southernmost live oak groves, which begin a few miles north of the delta. Range shrinkage of *P. rubra* is so far slight, but it should be watched, since erosion on the southern edge of the breeding range is fairly widespread among North American birds.

DETAILED ACCOUNT: TWO SUBSPECIES

EASTERN SUMMER TANAGER, *Piranga rubra rubra* (Linnaeus)

DESCRIPTION: *Adult male, nuptial plumage*: Acquired by wear from winter plumage. Pileum and upper tail-coverts nopal red, brazil red, or dark brazil red; back, rump, and scapulars nopal red, tips of feathers sometimes tinged with brown, making back prussian red; tail dark nopal red, tips of outer feathers and inner webs of all but middle pair sometimes slightly brownish; wings fuscous to light fuscous; lesser and median wing-coverts, outer webs of greater and primary coverts, and outer margins of wing-quills red like back, tips of greater and median coverts sometimes paler than rest; inner edges of wing-quills drab to dull onion skin pink; lores mixed with buff or mouse gray and red; remainder of sides of head like crown but slightly paler; lower surface scarlet red to scarlet; lining of wing similar but somewhat paler and sometimes mixed with dull white. Bill above brownish olive, but cutting edges and mandible salmon color to wax yellow; iris dark brown; legs and feet lilac gray. *Adult male, winter*: Acquired by complete postnuptial molt. Similar to nuptial adult male, but upper surface usually darker and duller, less purely red, feathers often with very narrow and inconspicuous brownish margins. Bill brownish to dark brown. *Adult female, nuptial (saffron yellow—normal—phase)*: Acquired by wear from winter. Upper surface orange citrine, forehead and upper tail-coverts verging toward sulphine yellow; tail orange citrine, passing into light brownish olive on some of middle feathers, feathers edged on outer webs with color of upper tail-coverts; wings light olive brown, outer edges of coverts and quills orange citrine, inner edges of primaries and secondaries, except tips of primaries, dull colonial buff to cream buff; supraloral spot or streak dull cadmium yellow or orange, washed with citrine; sides of head like forehead but rather paler, lores more or less mixed with buff; chin and throat dull cadmium yellow, this extending to malar region; jugulum and breast saffron yellow, verging toward raw sienna; abdomen like throat but lighter;

lower tail-coverts dull light cadmium; sides and flanks between buckthorn brown and analine yellow; lining of wing dull light cadmium. Maxilla dull, rather light brown, but its cutting edges and mandible dull yellow; iris dark brown; rictus yellow. *Adult female, nuptial (greenish yellow phase)*: Acquired by wear from winter. Similar to saffron yellow phase, but upper surface, including edgings of wings, yellowish warbler green—between warbler green and pyrite yellow; tail citrine to light brownish olive, feathers edged with color of upper tail-coverts; lower surface between wax yellow and primuline yellow; sides and flanks light yellowish olive. *Adult female, nuptial (gray phase)*: Acquired by wear from winter. Similar to greenish yellow phase, but upper surface mouse gray, with wash or mottling of dull yellowish citrine, longer upper tail-coverts entirely of this color, edgings of wing-quills and wing-coverts similar; lower parts light smoke gray, washed with citrine or amber yellow, this most evident on middle of breast and of abdomen; sides darker smoke gray, and crissum wax yellow. *Adult female, nuptial (reddish phase)*: Acquired by wear from winter. Similar to saffron yellow phase, but upper surface, including scapulars, tertials, and some of wing-coverts, more or less spotted or washed with dull red, sometimes with a number of tail feathers entirely of this color; lower surface more or less washed, in places heavily, with dull red. Most specimens are more or less intermediate between saffron yellow and greenish yellow phases. Some individuals in greenish yellow phase resemble very closely in coloration nuptial adult female Scarlet Tanager, but large bill of Summer is distinctive. *Adult female, winter*: Acquired by complete postnuptial molt. Similar to nuptial adult female in corresponding phase and often nearly indistinguishable, but averaging duller and more brownish below. Bill brownish to dark brown. *Male, second nuptial*: Acquired by wear from second winter. Similar to nuptial adult male, but red of upper and lower parts more brownish or yellowish and paler; wings and tail more brownish (less clearly reddish) and often paler. *Male, second winter*: Acquired by complete postnuptial molt. Similar to second nuptial male but darker—differing as does adult male in winter from nuptial adult male. *Male, first nuptial*: Acquired by partial prenuptial molt, which does not include primaries or secondaries. Similar to nuptial adult female in saffron yellow or greenish yellow phases, but larger, upper surface more or less mottled with nopal red or brazil red; wings and tail sometimes slightly tinged with red; lower surface more or less mottled or washed with scarlet to strawberry pink; sometimes these red markings are both above and below, but few and scattered; in other individuals, they form extensive areas, and plumage may even be much like nuptial adult male, except for greenish-edged wings. *Male, first winter*: Acquired by partial postjuvenal molt, which does not involve wing-quills or tail. Similar to first nuptial male, but upper surface duller and darker, often somewhat more brownish, without red, except tinge on tail and sometimes suffusion on outer webs of primaries and secondaries; lower surface darker, duller, more saffron buff or brownish, and without red except as wash on crissum. Similar to adult female in winter but larger, averaging darker, duller, and more brownish above, with some reddish wash on tail; sometimes outer webs of primaries darker; usually more brownish below; crissum more or less washed with reddish or dull orange. *Female, first nuptial*: Acquired by wear from first winter. Like corresponding phase of nuptial adult female. *Female, first winter*: Acquired by partial postjuvenal molt, which does not involve wing-quills or tail. Similar to nuptial adult female in corresponding phase, but upper surface darker, duller, and more brownish; lower surface duller, jugulum more tinged with brown or olivaceous. *Male, juvenal*: Acquired by complete postnatal molt. Pileum and hindneck dull olive buff, conspicuously streaked with olive brown; back and scapulars more olive, tinged with broad dull grayish brown streaks; rump pale buff and upper tail-coverts more fulvescent, both streaked with olive brown; wings and tail similar to those of first winter male; greater coverts grayish olive brown, edged with olivaceous and broadly tipped with light yellowish buff, producing distinct band across wing; sides of head and of neck similar to pileum; lower surface dull white or partly buffy white, streaked everywhere, most broadly on jugulum, breast, and sides, with olive brown or fuscous; crissum orange buff with dull brown shaft streaks. Bill dusky. *Female, juvenal*: Acquired by complete postnatal molt. Similar to juvenal male, but edges of primaries without reddish tinge; tail olivaceous. Bill dusky. *Natal*: Unknown.

MEASUREMENTS: *Adult male*: Wing, 92.5–99.8 (average, 95.5) mm.; tail, 68.6–79.5 (74.2); bill (exposed culmen), 16.8–19.3 (17.5); height of bill at base, 9.1–10.2 (9.7); tarsus, 18.3–19.8 (19.3); middle toe without claw, 12.7–14.7 (14.0). *Adult female*: Wing, 88.6–95.8 (91.7); tail, 66.5–73.7 (70.4); bill, 17.5–18.3 (18.0); height of bill, 9.7–10.7 (10.2); tarsus, 18.5–19.8 (18.8); middle toe, 13.2–14.0 (13.5).

RANGE: S.e. Nebraska, c. Wisconsin, and n. Delaware, south to Tamaulipas (at least formerly), U.S. Gulf states, and s. Florida. Winters from s. Texas (rarely) through Mexico and Central America to c. Peru, w. Bolivia, w. Brazil, and Guyana; casual in w. Cuba.

TEXAS: *Breeding*: Altitudinal range, near sea level to 2,300 ft. Collected north to Clay, east to Bowie and Jefferson, south to Cameron, west to Val Verde and Crockett cos. Common. *Winter*: Taken in Hidalgo (1 specimen) and Cameron (3) cos. Rare.

NESTING: *Nest*: On uplands or slopes, or in stream valleys; usually in open woodlands, sometimes even in towns, along highways, and in groves; in tree or bush, usually on a horizontal or drooping branch and near its extremity, 5–50 ft. above ground; rather thin, frail saucer, so thin that eggs may sometimes be seen from below, but still more or less firmly put together; composed of strips of bark, leaves, cottony weeds, Spanishmoss, catkins, plant stems, grasses, and fragments of other plants; lined with fine grass and a few catkins. *Eggs*: 3–6; rounded ovate to nearly elliptical oval; bright, light emerald green, light bluish green, or light greenish blue; dotted, spotted, and blotched with dark brown, reddish brown, rufous, umber, and brownish purple, with shell markings of lilac, mostly concentrated irregularly about larger end; average size, 23.9 × 16.3 mm.

COOPER'S SUMMER TANAGER, *Piranga rubra cooperi* Ridgway

DESCRIPTION: *Adult male and female, nuptial plumage*: Similar to *P. r. rubra* but much larger, particularly wing, tail, bill, and tarsus; in both sexes decidedly lighter above and below; female also usually much more grayish.

MEASUREMENTS: *Adult male*: Wing, 96.5–105.9 (average, 100.1) mm.; tail, 77.0–85.1 (81.0); bill (exposed culmen), 17.5–21.1 (19.3); height of bill at base, 9.9–11.4 (10.4); tarsus, 19.6–22.6 (21.4); middle toe without claw, 13.0–15.0 (14.0). *Adult female*: Wing, 91.4–102.6 (97.8); tail, 71.7–84.6 (78.2); bill, 17.5–22.1 (19.0); height of bill, 9.7–11.4 (10.4); tarsus, 20.1–22.1 (21.4); middle toe, 12.4–15.0 (13.7).

RANGE: S.e. Nevada and Trans-Pecos Texas, south to s.e. Sonora, n. Durango, and Nuevo León. Winters from s. Baja California and s. Sinaloa to Colima, c. Guerrero, and Morelos.

TEXAS: *Breeding*: Altitudinal range, 1,800 to 5,050 (locally) ft. Collected in El Paso, Hudspeth, Culberson (breeding unconfirmed), Jeff Davis, Presidio, and Brewster cos. Fairly common. *Migration*: One specimen apparently outside normal breeding range: Val Verde Co., mouth of Pecos River (Apr. 25, 1939, T. D. Burleigh). Fairly common in breeding range.

NESTING: Similar to that of *P. r. rubra*, but nest usually placed in cottonwood; average egg size, 23.1 × 17.0 mm.

Finches: Fringillidae

CARDINAL, *Richmondena cardinalis* (Linnaeus)

SPECIES ACCOUNT

Also known as Common Cardinal, Kentucky Cardinal, and redbird. *Male*: only all-red-bodied U.S. bird with conspicuous crest; has black patch at base of heavy, conical red bill. *Female*: yellowish brown with touches of red; has similar crest and bill. *Immature*: similar to female, but bill dusky. Length, 8¾ in.; wingspan, 11¾; weight, 1¼ oz.

RANGE: S.e. South Dakota, east across s. Great Lakes region to New York, south to Gulf coast and s. Florida; also extreme s.e. California to Texas (but absent from c. New Mexico), south through Mexico (mostly in lowlands) to British Honduras. Gradually colonizing Canada from s.e. Manitoba to Nova Scotia. Naturalized in Hawaii, s.w. California (very locally), and Bermuda.

TEXAS: (See map.) *Resident*: Breeds, late Feb. to late Aug. (eggs, Mar. 3 to July 31) from near sea level to 5,000 ft. Very common to fairly common east of 102nd meridian; fairly common, but local, in Trans-Pecos; uncommon to scarce in western Panhandle.

HAUNTS AND HABITS: The Cardinal is an attractive member of the finches, a nearly cosmopolitan family of 425 species, according to the Mayr-Amadon classification. *Richmondena cardinalis* exhibits characteristics unusual in the bird world: Its plumage and song are equally brilliant, and it has so far adapted to changing habitats over wide areas in both temperate and subtropical climates. In the more humid areas of Texas (basically the eastern half), the redbird is a numerous inhabitant of town and country wherever trees, bushes, or tall weeds occur. In the arid western half, however, it is not as generally distributed; here the Cardinal is localized amid streambottom vegetation and in the tallest available native or introduced bushes.

R. cardinalis is an enthusiastic breeder. A pair usually attempts to raise two, sometimes three, broods per season. The male is quick to attack another male which invades his nesting territory; often he will tirelessly fight his own image as reflected in a mirror, automobile hubcap, or even a window pane. As bird banders know, a Cardinal bites hard and holds on like a bulldog.

Though sprightly, the Cardinal is not excessively graceful. Flight is quick, jerky, noisy, and performed with many flirts of the tail. Movement is confined chiefly to short transits between bushes, trees, and the ground, or amid thickets. Cardinals, during winter months, are social and gather in small companies where food is plentiful. Birds, mainly on the ground, forage for an impressive variety of seeds (sunflower, cantaloupe, doveweed, bristlegrass, knotweed, smartweed, ragweed, panicum, many others) and wild fruits (a few including grape, dogweed, mulberry, dewberry, nightshade, pricklypear). Insects include mainly beetles, grasshoppers, caterpillars, and true bugs; spiders, snails, slugs, and mollusks are also eaten. *R. cardinalis*, like many other seed-eating finches, feeds its young largely on insects.

The call note is a sharp emphatic *tchip* or *whit*. Cardinal songs are loud, clear, rich, variable whistles, usually sustained and distinctly phrased: *hew, hew, hew hew hew hew* or *what-cheer, hew hew hew* or *hew, whoit whoit whoit whoit*. The female sings softer and somewhat less frequently than the male. Singing, mostly from mid-January to late August, is usually done from a high wire or atop a tree or tall bush.

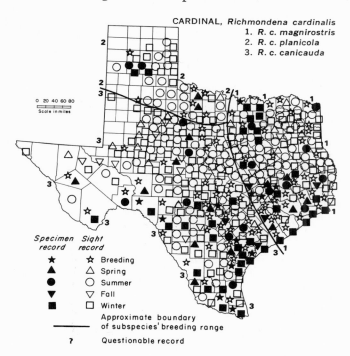

CARDINAL, *Richmondena cardinalis*
1. *R. c. magnirostris*
2. *R. c. planicola*
3. *R. c. canicauda*

0 20 40 60 80
Scale in miles

Specimen record	Sight record	
★	☆	Breeding
▲	△	Spring
●	○	Summer
▼	▽	Fall
■	□	Winter
———	Approximate boundary of subspecies' breeding range	
?	Questionable record	

DETAILED ACCOUNT: THREE SUBSPECIES

LOUISIANA CARDINAL, *Richmondena cardinalis magnirostris* (Bangs)

DESCRIPTION: *Adult male, nuptial plumage*: Acquired by wear from winter plumage. Pileum and sides of head dull scarlet, scarlet red, or nopal red, but tips of feathers somewhat darker and duller; back and scapulars brick red or madder brown, upper tail-coverts lighter; feathers of all these parts with lighter edgings, between mouse gray and hair brown to buffy brown, which slightly veils and dulls the red; tail brick red on inner webs and terminally passing into cameo brown or hays brown, inner margins of feathers, except middle pair, paler; primaries and secondaries between light fuscous and dark hair brown, outer webs, except tips, dragon blood red; inner edges of primaries and secondaries, except tips of primaries, coral red or light coral red; tertials duller like back; exposed surface of wing-coverts brick red; narrow line across forehead, lores, malar region, chin, and upper throat black, forming continuous and conspicuous mask; lower surface of body dull scarlet or scarlet to scarlet red; lining of wing similar but somewhat lighter. Bill scarlet to scarlet vermilion; iris dark reddish brown, chocolate brown, or hazel; legs flesh color, pale flesh color, drab gray, or vinaceous buff; feet drab gray, drab, or prout brown; claws rather dark brown. *Adult male, winter*: Acquired by complete postnuptial molt. Similar to nuptial adult male, but upper parts somewhat lighter, back and rump with broader edgings of mouse gray or buffy brown; red of lower surface rather duller. *Adult female, nuptial (buffy phase)*: Acquired by wear from winter. Upper surface buffy brown to between dark buffy brown and hair brown; thin crest of rather narrow pointed feathers brick red to dragon blood red, feathers somewhat margined and tipped with brown of back; wings and tail similar to those of adult male, but rectrices edged on outer webs with mouse gray to hair brown, these edgings broadest on middle feathers and sometimes practically absent on one or two outermost feathers; both wing-quills and coverts, except for middle portion of primaries and secondaries, edged on outer webs with brown of back; narrow line across forehead, together with lores, malar region, chin, and upper part of throat, mouse gray to dark mouse gray, somewhat mixed with paler gray; remainder of sides of head and of neck like hindneck but somewhat paler; lower throat and jugulum clay color to cinnamon buff; abdomen and middle of breast pinkish buff or pale pinkish buff to buffy white; sides and flanks like jugulum but more or less tinged with gray; crissum pinkish buff to cinnamon buff; lining of wing peach red to light coral red. Bill scarlet, scarlet vermilion, or vermilion; iris chocolate, hazel, or reddish brown; legs ecru drab, drab gray, or clay color; feet drab, drab gray, clay color, or purplish brown. *Adult female, nuptial (reddish phase)*: Similar to buffy phase of nuptial adult female, but breast and jugulum tinged or mottled with peach red or dragon blood red. *Adult female, winter*: Acquired by complete postnuptial molt. Similar to nuptial adult female, but upper parts usually more buffy or ochraceous; gray edgings of tail wider; lower surface more deeply buff and ochraceous. *Male, first nuptial*: Acquired by wear from first winter. Essentially the same as nuptial adult male. *Male, first winter*: Acquired by complete postjuvenal molt. Similar to adult male in winter, but upper surface with broader brown or gray edgings; red of lower surface duller and more veiled by dull buff edgings and tips of feathers, particularly on posterior portion. Bill white with reddish tinge near base, dull brown tinge toward tip; iris chocolate, hazel, or dark red; legs drab gray, drab, or flesh color; feet drab, flesh color, or purplish brown. *Female, first nuptial*: Acquired by wear from first winter. Practically identical with nuptial adult female. *Female, first winter*: Acquired by complete postjuvenal molt. Similar to adult female in winter, but upper surface more brownish; lower surface darker and duller, more extensively brownish, particularly on jugulum, breast, and sides. *Male, juvenal*: Acquired by complete postnatal molt. Similar to adult female, but upper surface duller, usually more brownish or ochraceous, and more or less washed or clouded with dull red; crest much shorter, its red much duller and much tinged with brown or ochraceous, red color sometimes almost obsolete or at least covered by brown or ochraceous feathers; tail without gray edgings; wings duller, edgings more brownish (less grayish); upper surface, except pileum, with more or less obvious shadowy bars of darker brown; sides of head dull ochraceous with often a wash of dull red; lower surface darker, duller, more brownish (less buffy), and obscurely streaked, mottled, or spotted with buffy brown; middle of abdomen pale buff or dull white. Bill dull brown. *Female, juvenal*: Acquired by complete postnatal molt. Similar to juvenal male, but upper surface lighter, sometimes more ochraceous, and without tinge or mottling of red, even crest without red; tail duller, middle pairs of feathers edged with mouse gray to buffy brown; lower surface averaging lighter and brighter and more ochraceous or buff (less brownish), also usually less heavily streaked or spotted. *Natal*: Mouse gray. Bill, legs, and feet pinkish buff.

MEASUREMENTS: *Adult male*: Wing, 90.9–99.1 (average, 93.7) mm.; tail, 96.0–109.5 (102.4); bill (exposed culmen), 16.0–19.0 (17.8); height of bill at base, 14.0–15.0 (14.2); tarsus, 24.9–27.4 (26.4); middle toe without claw, 15.0–17.0 (15.7). *Adult female*: Wing, 85.6–92.5 (89.2); tail, 89.4–99.1 (95.2); bill, 16.0–18.0 (16.8); height of bill, 13.2–14.0 (13.7); tarsus, 23.6–25.9 (24.9); middle toe, 15.2–17.0 (16.3).

RANGE: C. Oklahoma to s. Arkansas, south to s.e. Texas, Louisiana, and s.w. Mississippi.

TEXAS: *Resident*: Altitudinal breeding range, near sea level to 800 ft. Collected north to Cooke, east to Bowie and Jefferson, south to Matagorda, west to McLennan cos. Common.

NESTING: *Nest*: On uplands and bottomlands; in forests and open country, often along streams and in all kinds of cultivated areas, wherever there are thickets, brushy fence rows, or brushy roadsides, sometimes in open fields or pastures; in a bush, vine, or tree, usually 3–10 ft. above ground, or on fence rail, vine-covered stump, or brush heap; large, rather loosely constructed cup, sometimes partly roofed over, but more or less compact; composed of slender twigs, strips of grapevine, juniper, and other bark, weed stalks, grass, leaves of corn and other plants, paper, moss, rootlets, sometimes covered with a gray moss; lined with rootlets, grasses, pine needles, thin twigs, grass stems, clover stems, and sometimes with horsehair. *Eggs*: 3–6, usually 3 or 4; between ovate and oval; white, bluish white, greenish white, brownish white, or grayish white, finely spotted, usually over entire surface, although sometimes more so about larger end, sometimes so thickly as to obscure ground color, with cinnamon brown, umber, reddish brown, and with shell markings of lilac, dull purple, lavender, and various shades of gray; average size, 25.4 × 18.5 mm.

PALO DURO CARDINAL, *Richmondena cardinalis planicola* Stevenson

Race not in A.O.U. check-list, 1957 (see Appendix A).

DESCRIPTION: *Adult male and female, nuptial plumage*: Similar to *R. c. magnirostris*, but bill stouter. Red on lower parts of male brighter. Female with upper surface more grayish and somewhat paler, grayish edgings on tail broader; lower surface much lighter, middle of abdomen more whitish.

MEASUREMENTS: *Adult male*: Wing, 90.9–98.1 (average, 94.2) mm.; tail, 98.1–110.0 (103.9); bill (exposed culmen), 16.5–18.5 (17.5); height of bill at base, 14.2–15.7 (15.2); tarsus, 23.9–26.9 (25.1); middle toe without claw, 15.0–17.0 (15.7). *Adult female*: Wing, 87.9–96.5 (92.7); tail, 97.6–110.0 (104.6); bill, 16.0–18.0 (17.0); height of bill, 13.2–15.0 (14.2); tarsus, 23.6–26.9 (24.6); middle toe, 14.5–16.0 (15.2).

RANGE: S.w. Kansas, w. Oklahoma, and extreme n. Texas.

TEXAS: *Resident*: Altitudinal breeding range, 900 to 3,800 ft. Collected in Randall, Armstrong, Wilbarger, and Baylor cos. Fairly common.

NESTING: Similar to that of *R. c. magnirostris*.

GRAY-TAILED CARDINAL, *Richmondena cardinalis canicauda* (Chapman)

R. c. canicaudus of A.O.U. check-list, 1957 (see Appendix A).

DESCRIPTION: *Adult male and female, nuptial plumage*: Similar to *R. c. planicola*, but wing slightly shorter; bill decidedly longer and much less stout; middle toe longer. Edgings of upper parts in male lighter, more grayish (less olivaceous). Female with gray edgings of tail much broader.

MEASUREMENTS: *Adult male*: Wing, 88.4–96.5 (average, 93.0) mm.; tail, 97.8–109.2 (104.1); bill (exposed culmen), 15.5–18.0 (16.8); height of bill at base, 12.4–14.2 (13.2); tarsus, 23.6–25.9 (24.9); middle toe without claw, 15.2–18.3 (16.8). *Adult female*: Wing, 81.8–93.2 (88.4); tail, 90.9–104.6 (99.3); bill, 14.7–17.0 (15.7); height of bill, 12.4–13.5 (13.0); tarsus, 22.6–26.4 (24.9); middle toe, 15.2–17.8 (16.5).

RANGE: Texas (southwestern two-thirds), south to San Luis Potosí and Hidalgo.

TEXAS: *Resident*: Altitudinal breeding range, near sea level to 5,000 ft. Collected north to Haskell, east to Lee and Calhoun, south to Cameron, west to Jeff Davis cos. One specimen outside resident range: Grayson Co., Hagerman Nat. Wildlife Refuge (Feb. 21, 1947, I. N. Gabrielson). Common.

NESTING: Similar to that of *R. c. magnirostris*, but average egg size, 24.6 × 18.8 mm.

PYRRHULOXIA, *Pyrrhuloxia sinuata* (Bonaparte)

SPECIES ACCOUNT

A desert-frequenting version of the Cardinal with a thin pointed crest; rounded yellow bill. *Male*: gray, sprinkled with red chiefly on crest and under parts. *Female*: mostly grayish brown. *Immature*: similar to female, but bill dusky. Length, 8½ in.; wingspan, 11¾; weight, 1¼ oz.

RANGE: Brushy deserts of Baja California, Arizona, New Mexico, and Texas, south to c. Mexico.

TEXAS: (See map.) *Resident*: Breeds, mid-Mar. to mid-Aug. (eggs, Mar. 28 to Aug. 3) from near sea level to 4,500 ft. Very common to fairly common in arid southwestern half, though rare on Edwards Plateau

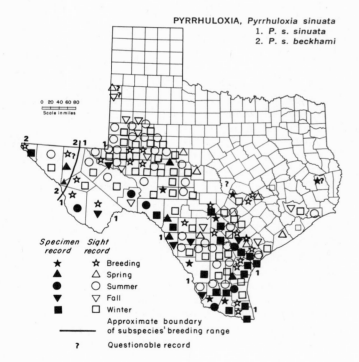

PYRRHULOXIA, *Pyrrhuloxia sinuata*
1. *P. s. sinuata*
2. *P. s. beckhami*

0 20 40 60 80
Scale in miles

Specimen record	Sight record	
★	☆	Breeding
▲	△	Spring
●	○	Summer
▼	▽	Fall
■	□	Winter

——— Approximate boundary of subspecies' breeding range

? Questionable record

east of 100th meridian; casual east to Lee Co.; one doubtful record from Tyler Co. (see detailed account). Very rarely individuals are sighted during nonbreeding season east to Brazos Co. and along coast to Brazoria Co.

HAUNTS AND HABITS: The Pyrrhuloxia, sympatric with the Cardinal through virtually all of the former's Texas range, lives in arid brush country, preferring thorny scrub—an admixture of mesquite, cactus, acacia, and yucca—to the bushes, woods, and streambottom vegetation inhabited by its more eastern relative. In winter, it often wanders from thickets to feed in flocks along road shoulders, fence rows, in weed patches, and borders of fields; these loose aggregations, generally larger than those of the Cardinal, exceptionally contain as many as a thousand individuals.

This thornbrush dweller is basically similar to the Cardinal in its behavior. Movement is largely restricted to brief, noisy fluttering amid bushes and trees. Though well camouflaged in its arid haunts, the Pyrrhuloxia often seems reluctant to show itself when a bird watcher squeaks. Most feeding is done on the ground; however, the present species forages in vegetation perhaps somewhat more than the Cardinal. The Pyrrhuloxia diet includes seeds of bristlegrass, doveweed, sandbur, panicum, sorghum, pigweed, and others; fruits of cactus and nightshade; also such insects as grasshoppers, caterpillars, beetles, stinkbugs, and cicadas.

A sharp metallic *cheek* is the Pyrrhuloxia's call note. Songs include a series of loud metallic *quink*'s and a thin slurred *what-cheer, what-cheer*, etc. Both suggest vocalizations of the Cardinal, but neither is as long nor as full and rich. Males vocalize chiefly from mid-February to mid-August, usually from atop a mesquite or similar thorny shrub, also from a high wire. Females, though apparently capable, rarely sing.

CHANGES: Since the 1880's, mesquite has been pushing northward into the Panhandle; by the 1940's, it was widespread in all but the northernmost tier of counties. The Pyrrhuloxia has followed this invasion as far as the southern Panhandle, so that it now occurs farther north than range maps based solely on old data indicate. However, habitat gains in the north are being more than offset by losses in the south. Between 1933 and 1968, six million acres were cleared in south Texas alone. Brush removal in most parts of the Southwest continues to accelerate. In the early 1970's, even the nearly one-million-acre King Ranch was being bulldozed and root-plowed.

DETAILED ACCOUNT: TWO SUBSPECIES

TEXAS PYRRHULOXIA, *Pyrrhuloxia sinuata sinuata* (Bonaparte)

DESCRIPTION: *Adult male, nuptial plumage*: Acquired by wear from winter plumage. Upper surface between hair brown and drab, but back somewhat darker; forehead carmine to nopal red; a loose crest of narrow pointed feathers carmine, with broad terminal shaft streaks of burnt umber; tail garnet brown to morocco red, tips of feathers burnt umber to clove brown or olive brown, and extreme base of tail light jasper red to coral pink; wings olive brown to dark olive brown, primaries and outer secondaries edged on outer webs, except at tips, with garnet brown to morocco red, the inner secondaries and tips of wing-quills, together with tertials, margined on outer webs with drab or rather brownish drab, inner edges of primaries and secondaries, except tips, coral pink to light coral red to old rose; lores, malar region, and eye-ring carmine or dark carmine; remainder of sides of head and sides of neck between hair brown and drab; chin, middle of throat, of jugulum, and of breast scarlet red to light scarlet red to spectrum red; remainder of lower surface between dull light olive gray and smoke gray; sides and flanks identical or light grayish olive; middle of abdomen and crissum paler and usually more or less tinged with red of anterior under parts; thighs red like breast; lining of wing scarlet red to light scarlet red; inner margins of under surface of basal portion of primaries and secondaries coral red to light jasper red. Bill bright yellow or orange; iris dark brown; legs and feet dull light brown. *Adult male, winter*: Acquired by complete postnuptial molt. Similar to nuptial adult male, but upper surface somewhat darker, red of jugulum, breast, and abdomen more overlaid by pale gray edgings of feathers, this sometimes entirely obscuring red on jugulum. Bill more or less brownish, particularly maxilla. *Adult female, nuptial (gray phase)*: Acquired by wear from winter. Upper surface, wings, and tail like nuptial adult male, but, except for crest, without red on head or face; red of crest, wings, and tail somewhat duller; wings and tail with more extensive brown edgings; upper surface in general more brownish or ochraceous; malar spot, streak under eyes, and sometimes part or all of lores chaetura drab; lower surface dull pinkish buff but sometimes slightly washed with red on middle of breast, abdomen, or middle of throat; jugulum, sides and flanks smoke gray, occasionally with pinkish or reddish wash; thighs streaked with dull scarlet red; lining of wing as in nuptial adult male. *Adult female, nuptial (buff phase)*: Similar to gray phase, but upper surface somewhat more tinged with ochraceous; below tinged with cinnamon buff. *Adult female, winter*: Acquired by complete postnuptial molt. Similar to nuptial adult female, but colors of upper surface more blended, thus more uniform; edges of tertials broader, feathers of crest more obscured by brown margins; lower surface somewhat darker, anterior parts, sides, and flanks more distinctly gray. *Male, first nuptial*: Acquired by wear from first winter. Like nuptial adult male. *Male, first winter*: Acquired by complete postjuvenal molt. Similar to adult male in winter, but upper and lower parts more brownish or ochraceous, particularly on jugulum, sides, and flanks. Bill still more brownish. *Female, first nuptial*: Acquired by wear from first winter. Practically identical with nuptial adult female. *Female, first winter*: Acquired by complete postjuvenal molt. Similar to adult female in winter, but upper surface more brownish and somewhat darker; lower parts also darker and more ochraceous or brownish. *Male, juvenal*: Acquired by complete postnatal molt. Similar to first winter female but larger; upper surface more grayish (less ochraceous or brownish), somewhat darker, the median and greater coverts very narrowly tipped with pale dull buff, forming two rather inconspicuous and narrow wing-bars; forehead, lores, and chin with more or less red; below paler, more grayish (less ochraceous), washed in places with dull red or pink, and obscurely spotted or mottled with hair brown or dark hair brown, middle of abdomen whitish, thighs chiefly red. *Female, juvenal*: Acquired by complete postnatal molt. Similar to juvenal male, but upper surface lighter, more ochraceous or buffy, forehead, malar region, and chin entirely without red; lower surface usually paler and more buffy or ochraceous (less grayish), and without tinge of red; thighs entirely buff, with at most a very slight wash of pink (no red). *Natal*: Pileum drab gray; remainder of upper parts pale drab gray or very pale smoke gray.

MEASUREMENTS: *Adult male*: Wing, 88.4–94.5 (average, 93.0) mm.; tail, 93.5–104.9 (98.8); bill (exposed culmen), 15.2–17.0 (16.0); tarsus, 23.9–25.4 (24.6); middle toe without claw, 16.5–18.5 (17.3). *Adult female*: Wing, 86.1–90.4 (88.4); tail, 83.8–96.5 (92.5); bill, 14.2–16.5 (15.2); tarsus, 23.1–25.4 (24.4); middle toe, 16.0–17.3 (16.5).

RANGE: S. Panhandle of Texas, south through most of s.w. Texas to e. Tamaulipas.

TEXAS: *Resident*: Altitudinal breeding range, near sea level to 4,500 ft. Collected north to Tom Green, east to Travis (eggs) and Aransas, south to Cameron, west to Brewster and Presidio cos. One doubtful record from Tyler Co., Colmesneil (eggs collected, Apr. 18, 1898, E. F. Pope). Common to fairly common locally.

NESTING: *Nest*: On flatlands, mesas, and in valleys; in thickets and brush, sometimes isolated; in thorny bush, mesquite, or other low tree, from 3 to 8 ft. above ground; rather large, compact cup; composed of strips of bark, thin and coarse grasses, and twigs; lined with rootlets, fine grasses, and other vegetable fibers. *Eggs*: 3–4, usually 4; ovate to nearly oval; white; dotted and blotched over entire surface, but more so at larger end, with umber, other shades of dark brown, and shell markings of purplish gray; average size, 23.4 × 18.5 mm.

BECKHAM'S PYRRHULOXIA, *Pyrrhuloxia sinuata beckhami* Ridgway

Race not in A.O.U. check-list, 1957 (see Appendix A).

DESCRIPTION: *Adult male and female, nuptial plumage*: Like *P. s. sinuata* in color; but in size decidedly greater, especially length of wing and tail, although bill is actually as well as relatively smaller.

MEASUREMENTS: *Adult male*: Wing, 94.5–101.1 (average, 97.3) mm.; tail, 100.6–112.0 (107.4); bill (exposed culmen), 14.0–15.5 (15.0); height of bill at base, 13.5–14.0 (13.7); tarsus, 23.9–27.4 (25.4); middle toe without claw, 16.5–18.5 (17.3). *Adult female*: Wing, 88.4–96.0 (93.2); tail, 96.0–105.9 (101.9); bill, 13.5–15.5 (14.7); height of bill, 13.0–14.0 (13.2); tarsus, 23.1–25.9 (24.6); middle toe, 15.5–18.5 (16.8).

RANGE: S. New Mexico and Trans-Pecos Texas, south to s.w. San Luis Potosí.

TEXAS: *Resident*: Altitudinal breeding range, 2,100 to 4,500 ft. Collected in El Paso, Culberson, and Jeff Davis cos. Common to fairly common locally.

NESTING: Similar to that of *P. s. sinuata*.

ROSE-BREASTED GROSBEAK, *Pheucticus ludovicianus* (Linnaeus)

SPECIES ACCOUNT

A medium-sized grosbeak. *Male*: black above with white wing-bars, wing-patches, and rump; white below with a triangular rose red patch on breast. *Female*: streaked brown and dingy white above with buff-striped head; two whitish wing-bars; brownish-streaked buffy breast. Length, 8 in.; wingspan, 12¾; weight, 1½ oz.

RANGE: N.e. British Columbia, southeast across s. Canada to Nova Scotia, south to Kansas and Georgia. Winters from c. Mexico to n. South America; also Cuba (rarely).

TEXAS: (See map.) *Migration*: Late Apr. to mid-May; early Sept. to early Nov. (extremes: Mar. 18, June 26; July 25, Dec. 4). Locally very common (some years; usually on upper and central coasts) to uncommon in spring east of 99th meridian; scarce to very scarce in western half. Uncommon to scarce in fall through east; casual in west. *Winter*: Late Dec. to late Feb. Very scarce in general vicinity of coast. One inland occurrence: San Antonio (2 immatures seen, Jan. 30, 1972, L. K. Patterson, seen again on Jan. 31,

Helene Moore, Wini Smith; 1 seen same place, Feb. 6, 1972, C. R. Bender).

HAUNTS AND HABITS: Woods adjacent to an open area (timber bordering a marsh, stream, or abandoned field, etc.) comprise choice nesting habitat for the Rose-breasted Grosbeak. Here its flimsy cup of twigs, stems, grass, and rootlets is placed usually six to fifteen feet above the ground on a limb of a small tree. During migration through the eastern half of Texas, the Rose-breast inhabits woodlands and woodland edges of various kinds, but is perhaps more frequent in mulberry (spring only), pecan, and oak trees. However, on the coast in spring, like other migrants, it is sometimes forced by wet northers to resort to mesquites, low-growing scrub, and at times even the ground. Foraging is done in treetops as well as bushes near the ground. The Rosebreast's deliberate, rather stiff, teetering mannerisms are suggestive of a parrot's. Wild fruits —mulberry, elderberry, dogwood, dewberry, nightshade, honeysuckle—are especially relished by *P. ludovicianus*. Seeds of ragweed, smartweed, pigweed, and others, plus insects (beetles, caterpillars, ants, bees, wasps, moths, grasshoppers) are also important in its diet.

A very sharp, metallic *ick* or *eek* is the Rose-breasted Grosbeak's call note. The male's mellow, fluent song is a series of rising and falling warbles often interspersed with and usually ending with the *ick* or *eek* notes; the female sometimes sings a softer, shorter version of his vocalization.

DETAILED ACCOUNT: NO SUBSPECIES

DESCRIPTION: *Adult male, nuptial plumage*: Acquired by partial prenuptial molt. Upper surface slightly glossy black, but

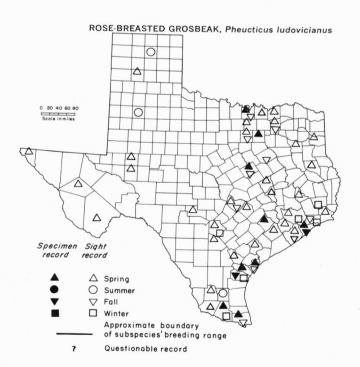

ROSE-BREASTED GROSBEAK, *Pheucticus ludovicianus*

0 20 40 60 80
Scale in miles

Specimen   Sight
record   record

▲   △   Spring
●   ○   Summer
▼   ▽   Fall
■   □   Winter
──── Approximate boundary of subspecies' breeding range
?   Questionable record

middle of back usually with at least indications of white spots, sometimes with several white feathers forming a patch; rump white, spotted or streaked with black; upper tail-coverts broadly tipped with white; tail dull black or brownish black, but outer three feathers with large subterminal white spots on inner webs, sometimes occupying half the length of the feather; wings dull black, primaries and secondaries, except basal portion of outer webs, fuscous black, tertials and inner secondaries with small white terminal spots on outer webs, basal half of primaries, except shafts, white, forming conspicuous wing spot; most of median coverts (except outermost) and inner greater coverts broadly tipped with white, forming conspicuous white areas on wing, these white areas on median coverts tipped, however, with black; sides of head and neck, together with chin and throat, dull black; jugulum dull scarlet red to light spectrum red, this extending backward in a point along middle of breast; remainder of lower surface white, but sides and flanks sparingly spotted with dull black or chaetura drab; outer under wing-coverts dull black; remainder of lining of wing rose doree to light geranium pink. Bill dull yellowish white, dull pinkish white, or grayish white, but usually tip and sometimes culmen slate black or dull dark brown, and maxilla washed with drab gray; iris dark brown; legs and feet plumbeous or olive gray; claws light brown. *Adult male, winter*: Acquired by complete postnuptial molt. Similar to nuptial adult male, but upper surface much clouded by edgings and tips of grayish olive to clay color and sayal brown, this in places often entirely obscuring the black feathers, particularly on hindneck; white of upper tail-coverts and rump much obscured by dull black or light brown bars; white markings of tertials larger; a more or less conspicuous dull white or pale buff superciliary stripe; lores and region under eye buffy white or dull pale buff, often mixed with dull black; remainder of sides of head dull black, washed with buff or dull light brown; sides of neck more or less mixed with black and sayal brown or clay color; throat and occasionally part of chin red like jugulum, but this red everywhere more or less obscured by clay color to tawny olive or pale dull buff or buffy white tips and edgings of feathers; sides and flanks, also occasionally breast and abdomen, more or less washed with buff; sides and flanks often more heavily streaked or spotted with black. *Adult female, nuptial (yellow-winged—normal—phase)*: Acquired by partial prenuptial molt. Pileum fuscous black to chaetura drab, feathers tipped with olive brown or buffy brown, broad median stripe of dull white or buffy white spotted or streaked with fuscous black; remainder of upper surface pale olive buff to light brownish olive (on hindneck and upper back sometimes to dull chamois), everywhere, except on upper tail-coverts, broadly streaked with chaetura black, fuscous, or fuscous black, but on rump with brownish olive; tail olive brown to dull buffy brown; wings light olive brown, outer edgings of quills and coverts somewhat paler, more like back, inner margins of basal portion of primaries and secondaries lighter brown; basal portion of primaries dull white, this showing but slightly beyond tips of primaries; tertials and secondaries tipped on outer webs with buff or brownish white, median coverts broadly, greater coverts more narrowly, tipped on outer webs with dull white or yellowish white, forming two wing-bars; superciliary stripe dull white or yellowish white, connecting with white collar on hindneck; lores dull pale buff or grayish white; broad stripe below eye of identical color; rictal streak and auriculars rather rufescent hair brown or dull black; sides of neck like hindneck; chin and throat dull light buff or dull white; jugulum pale cream buff to antimony yellow; remainder of lower surface buffy white or very light dull buff; sides and flanks light isabella color or dull buff; jugulum, breast, and sides all rather narrowly, also flanks more broadly, streaked with chaetura drab to hair brown, these streaks sometimes almost absent on breast and jugulum; thighs fuscous to hair brown; lining of wing orange buff to light cadmium, outer edge more or less mottled with fuscous. Bill grayish brown or broccoli brown but sometimes lighter, mandible drab; iris dark brown; legs and feet cinereous. *Adult female, nuptial (pink-winged phase)*: Similar to yellow-winged phase, but lining of wing light coral red to apricot orange, which sometimes also tinges middle of throat and jugulum. Occasionally female in color of under wing-coverts is similar to Black-headed Grosbeak, but may usually be distinguished by the slightly more golden or orange tinge of these feathers in the present bird. *Adult female, winter*: Acquired by complete postnuptial molt. Similar to nuptial adult female, but upper surface more brownish and ochraceous, dark feathers of head and back more obscured by lighter edgings; lower surface darker and usually more suffused with ochraceous or buff. *Male, third nuptial*: Acquired by partial prenuptial molt. Like nuptial adult male. *Male, third winter*: Acquired by complete postnuptial molt. Similar to adult male in winter. *Male, second nuptial*: Acquired by partial prenuptial molt. At least some males do not attain fully black plumage until third nuptial. These individuals in second nuptial have wings and tail more brownish than those of nuptial adult male; pileum more brownish with a broad central stripe of buffy white or buff, upper parts with many edgings of buff or clay color; white of lower rump and upper tail-coverts more spotted with blackish or dull light brown; sides of head more mixed with brown or whitish, sometimes with a narrow whitish or buffy superciliary stripe; black of chin and throat invaded by white or buff, or on middle of throat even by red of jugulum; red of jugulum more or less obscured by pale buff or buffy white tips of feathers, more or less marked with roundish spots of fuscous or fuscous black; sides and flanks distinctly tinged with buff. *Male, second winter*: Acquired by complete postnuptial molt. Similar to adult male in winter, but upper surface much more extensively buff, ochraceous tawny, and ochraceous, and white of rump and upper tail-coverts much more strongly suffused with these colors, black of pileum, hindneck, and back often largely concealed by lighter feather edgings; pileum with a broad lighter middle stripe; sides of head much more rufescent brown, superciliary stripe more deeply buff; red of throat and jugulum usually less extensive and paler, also much more obscured by buff, ochraceous buff, or clay colored edgings of feathers; sides, flanks, remainder of lower parts much more strongly tinged with buff or ochraceous; little or no black on chin or throat, this confined at most to a few spots. *Male, first nuptial*: Acquired by partial prenuptial molt. Similar to second nuptial male, but upper surface usually with very much more buff, ochraceous, or sayal brown; crown with usually some indication of a whitish or buffy median stripe; tail entirely or in part brown like that of female; primaries, secondaries, alula, primary coverts, and some of lesser coverts also brown as in nuptial adult female, though sometimes somewhat darker, leaving remainder of lesser coverts, median and greater coverts, and tertials dull black or fuscous black; lower surface usually more buffy or ochraceous, particularly on sides and flanks. *Male, first winter*: Acquired by partial postjuvenal molt which excepts wing-quills and tail. Similar to adult female in winter but averaging larger; upper surface more deeply ochraceous and averaging darker; wings and tail, particularly former, darker, wing-coverts with more or less black; visible white spot on primaries larger, succeeded distally by a blackish spot; sides of head usually somewhat more deeply colored; lower surface darker, more ochraceous, breast, throat, or jugulum, sometimes all, with more or less pink or red; lining of wing pink or light red. Similar to second winter male, but upper surface lighter, with much less of black or dark brown, this on back and scapulars reduced to central feather stripes; rump not white, but brown as in adult female in winter; wings and tail mostly brown instead of black; visible part of white wing speculum on primaries smaller; lower surface more deeply ochraceous or brownish, with less of pink or red on chin, throat, and jugulum, but much more heavily streaked with fuscous or fuscous black. *Female, first nuptial*: Acquired by partial prenuptial molt. Similar to nuptial adult female, but upper surface more ochraceous; lower parts more deeply ochraceous or buffy, and much more heavily streaked with fuscous or fuscous black; very much like adult female in winter but averaging darker above and more deeply ochraceous or buffy below. *Female, first winter*: Acquired by partial postjuvenal molt, which does not involve either wing-quills or tail. Similar to adult female in winter, but

upper surface even more strongly ochraceous, pileum usually more brownish (less blackish), wing-bars more buffy; lower surface more deeply and extensively ochraceous or buffy. Similar to first winter male but averaging smaller; wings and tail of a lighter brown, none of coverts black; visible part of white speculum on primaries very small or absent, and without a distally adjoining blackish area; no red or pink on anterior lower surface or lining of wing. *Male, juvenal*: Acquired by complete postnatal molt. Similar to first winter male, but upper surface darker and duller, pileum clove brown, more or less obscurely barred with fuscous black, and with little or no indication of a light crown stripe; feathers of back streaked with dark brown or fuscous black, more or less barred posteriorly by dull buff tips of feathers; wings and tail similar but without black and with little evident white speculum on primaries; wing-bars cinnamon buff to pinkish buff; upper tail-coverts barred terminally with tawny olive; below white or buffy white, slightly streaked or spotted on jugulum, sides, and flanks with fuscous or fuscous black, sides and flanks sometimes ochraceous or cinnamon buff, sometimes with but a slight wash of this color; lining of wing begonia rose or rose doree. Maxilla drab gray or olive gray, but culmen blackish slate; mandible dull white; commissure straw yellow; iris prout brown; legs and feet plumbeous; claws drab gray. *Female, juvenal*: Acquired by complete postnatal molt. Similar to juvenal male, but upper surface lighter; wings and tail of a lighter brown; lower surface more numerously and heavily spotted or streaked on jugulum, sides, and flanks with fuscous or fuscous black; lining of wing light cadmium to light salmon orange. Bill hair brown or slate gray, but mandible dull pinkish white; iris dark brown; legs and feet plumbeous or olive gray.

MEASUREMENTS: *Adult male*: Wing, 98.1–104.4 (average, 101.3) mm.; tail, 72.7–78.2 (74.7); bill (exposed culmen), 15.0–17.5 (16.8); tarsus, 21.4–23.6 (22.9); middle toe without claw, 15.0–16.0 (15.7). *Adult female*: Wing, 95.2–101.3 (98.8); tail, 69.8–74.7 (72.7); bill, 15.5–17.8 (17.3); tarsus, 21.9–24.1 (22.4); middle toe, 14.2–16.0 (15.2).

TEXAS: *Migration*: Collected north to Cooke, east to Galveston, southwest to Cameron and Hidalgo cos.

BLACK-HEADED GROSBEAK, *Pheucticus melanocephalus* (Swainson)

SPECIES ACCOUNT

Similar in size and shape to Rose-breasted Grosbeak, with which it is lumped by extremists. *Male*: black head, wings, tail, and stripes on back; tawny hindneck, back, rump, under parts (but middle of breast and wing-linings yellow); white wing-bars and wing-patches. *Female*: resembles female Rosebreast, but is browner with finely streaked sides; has pale tawny wash on virtually unstreaked breast. Length, 8¼ in.; wingspan, 12¾; weight, 1¾ oz.

RANGE: Extreme s.w. Canada, south through w. United States and highland Mexico to Oaxaca. Winters chiefly in Mexico.

TEXAS: (See map.) *Breeding*: Early May to late July (eggs, May 21 and June 17) from 3,700 to 8,000 ft. Fairly common to uncommon in mountains of Trans-Pecos. *Migration*: Early Mar. to mid-May; mid-Aug. to mid-Nov. (extremes: late Feb., May 21; Aug. 5, Dec. 12). Common (some years) to fairly common in Trans-Pecos; uncommon (some years) to very scarce east of Pecos River Valley. *Winter*: Late Dec. to late Feb., sometimes into Apr. Scarce; sightings from Trans-

Pecos, Rio Grande delta, central portions, and along coast.

HAUNTS AND HABITS: During its nesting season in Texas, the Black-headed Grosbeak is restricted to mountainous areas of the Trans-Pecos, where it frequents pine, pinyon, juniper, and oak on higher slopes. Sometimes, however, it descends to bushes, willow, and cottonwood along streams in foothills—a habitat more usual for the Blue Grosbeak. Outside the breeding season, it migrates through a wide variety of habitats but usually avoids low desert scrub. Occasionally, where ample food is available, such as at a well-stocked feeder, this grosbeak will remain throughout a winter well north of its regular winter home in Mexico.

The Black-headed Grosbeak is a bird of trees and bushes; infrequently it descends to the ground. If frightened, it flies upward to a higher perch rather than diving into a thicket as would a towhee. Unsuspicious and rather bold, it comes eagerly to feeding trays; it even sips sugar water from hummingbird bottles. On such occasions, it usually dominates smaller birds and vies handily with Scott's, Hooded, and Bullock's orioles. The Black-headed Grosbeak supplements seeds of chickweed, sunflower, dock, pigweed, alfilaria, and others with fruits of wildcherry, sumac, elderberry, dewberry, mulberry, haw, and nightshade. In summer especially, it eats and feeds its nestlings insects (beetles, true bugs, caterpillars, grasshoppers, ants, bees). Other animal matter that it consumes includes spiders, small fish (!), and snails.

Call note is a sharp *spik* or *eek*. Black-headed Grosbeak song, very similar to that of the Rosebreast, is a series of loud, rich, melodious warbles. The male delivers this vocalization from late April to late July,

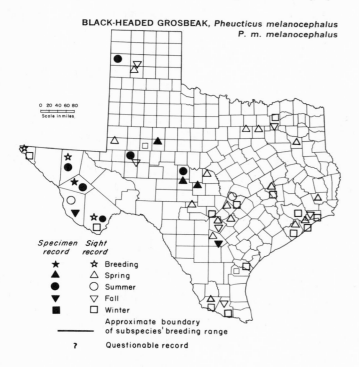

BLACK-HEADED GROSBEAK, *Pheucticus melanocephalus P. m. melanocephalus*

0 20 40 60 80
Scale in miles

Specimen record / Sight record
★ / ☆ Breeding
▲ / △ Spring
● / ○ Summer
▼ / ▽ Fall
■ / □ Winter

——— Approximate boundary of subspecies' breeding range

? Questionable record

usually from a bush or tree, sometimes in flight, at times while on the nest. The female infrequently renders a quiet version of this song generally in the vicinity of the nest.

DETAILED ACCOUNT: ONE SUBSPECIES

ROCKY MOUNTAIN BLACK-HEADED GROSBEAK,
Pheucticus melanocephalus melanocephalus (Swainson)

DESCRIPTION: *Adult male, nuptial plumage*: Acquired by partial prenuptial molt. Top and sides of head, also chin, brownish black, very slightly glossy; a rather broad collar on hindneck between ochraceous tawny and raw sienna to between umber brown and sudan brown; back and scapulars slightly brownish black, more or less streaked with color of hindneck or with ochraceous; rump like hindneck or somewhat lighter; upper tail-coverts dull black, broadly tipped with color of rump or with dull white; tail brownish black, outer two feathers with large terminal squarish white spots on inner webs, next pair or two with more or less mixture of white on terminal portion of inner web, and occasionally remainder of feathers narrowly tipped with dull white; wings brownish black, primaries and secondaries chaetura black on inner webs, basal portion of primaries white, forming large conspicuous wing speculum, in which area, feather shafts are black, some of outer primaries narrowly margined with white on terminal portion of outer webs, tips buff; tertials and secondaries with conspicuous white or light buff tips on outer webs; lesser wing-coverts without light markings; median wing-coverts broadly tipped with white or buffy white, and greater coverts narrowly tipped with same, forming two conspicuous wing-bars; sides of neck and lower surface (except chin, middle of breast and of abdomen) like hindneck; crissum cinnamon buff to pinkish buff; lower abdomen buffy white to light buff; middle of breast and of upper abdomen, together with lining of wing, empire yellow to between lemon chrome and light cadmium; outer under wing-coverts black, posterior outer wing-coverts hair brown or chaetura drab. Maxilla seal brown or slate color; mandible at tip seal brown but greater and basal portion bluish white or cream color; iris broccoli brown; legs and feet slate color, plumbeous, or light plumbeous; claws seal brown. *Adult male, winter*: Acquired by complete postnuptial molt. Similar to nuptial adult male, but black feathers of pileum, back, sides of head and of neck edged more or less with mouse gray, grayish olive, or dull buff; tawny areas of lower surface duller because feathers are narrowly tipped with pale buff. *Adult female, nuptial (dark phase)*: Acquired by partial prenuptial molt. Pileum with two broad lateral stripes of fuscous black, feathers more or less broadly tipped with dull buff on forehead to dull cinnamon brown posteriorly; broad median stripe of ochraceous tawny to cream buff, more or less streaked with fuscous black; hindneck ochraceous buff to ochraceous and streaked with fuscous black; back and scapulars dull light buff to ochraceous, broadly streaked with fuscous black or fuscous; rump clay color to light ochraceous, somewhat streaked or spotted with fuscous; upper tail-coverts dull citrine drab, tipped with buffy white to clay color; tail rather dark hair brown, all but middle pair of feathers with evident tips of brownish white or buffy white on inner webs; wings dark hair brown, inner edges of primaries and secondaries lighter basally, primaries basally yellowish white, this forming large patch which usually shows in closed wing beyond tips of primary coverts; primaries and secondaries margined on middle portion of outer webs with grayish olive, lesser wing-coverts edged exteriorly with grayish olive, outer vanes of greater coverts margined with light brownish olive, median coverts broadly tipped with white or yellowish white, as are also outer webs of greater coverts, tertials, and inner secondaries; broad superciliary stripe dull pale olive buff to deep colonial buff, sometimes ochraceous posteriorly, and continuous with a narrow collar of same color on hindneck; lores dull drab gray to dull tilleul buff; auriculars light brownish olive to chaetura drab; a small postauricular area of fuscous black tipped with dull cinnamon brown; sides of neck and lower parts ochraceous to dark ochraceous buff, but sides and flanks warm buff to dull ochraceous buff, narrowly streaked with fuscous; crissum and abdomen dull ochraceous buff to pale pinkish buff; middle of breast and of upper abdomen tinged with lemon yellow or lemon chrome; sides of throat and of breast with small spots or short narrow streaks of fuscous or fuscous black; lining of wing lemon chrome. Maxilla slate color; mandible bluish white, but gonys sometimes slightly tinged with lilaceous; iris dark hazel; legs and feet light plumbeous. *Adult female, nuptial (light phase)*: Acquired by partial prenuptial molt. Similar to dark phase but very much lighter, particularly below; middle stripe of pileum and light areas of hindneck and back buffy white or very pale buff; anterior lower parts and sides of body dark cinnamon buff to dull light buff. *Adult female, winter*: Acquired by complete postnuptial molt. Similar to nuptial adult female, but upper surface duller and more brownish, dark areas reduced in extent, light edgings thus somewhat broader; lower surface duller because most feathers are edged and tipped with pale buff, for the same reason dark brown streaks on sides and flanks and spots on sides of breast and throat are more or less obscured. *Male, third winter*: Acquired by complete postnuptial molt. Like adult male in winter. *Male, second nuptial*: Acquired by partial prenuptial molt. Similar to nuptial adult male, but upper surface more extensively tawny; pileum nearly always with broad central tawny or ochraceous stripe, at least on posterior portion, which, however, is streaked or spotted with black; wings and tail duller, somewhat more brownish, particularly tips of quills and posterior lower surface which average paler and more buffy, the chin thus less extensively black. *Male, second winter*: Acquired by complete postnuptial molt. Similar to adult male in winter, but upper surface more extensively tawny, pileum usually with broad middle tawny stripe spotted or streaked with black or fuscous black; wings and tail duller and more brownish, posterior lower surface averaging paler and more buffy (less tawny), chin usually with less black. *Male, first nuptial*: Acquired by partial prenuptial molt. Similar to second nuptial male, but upper surface duller and somewhat more brownish; pileum usually with a more extensive broad middle stripe of buff, ochraceous, or tawny; tail usually all or in part brown like that of female; primaries, secondaries, and primary coverts, also sometimes tertials and at least parts of wing-coverts, dark hair brown as in nuptial adult female; posterior lower surface still more extensively buff (less tawny). *Male, first winter*: Acquired by partial postjuvenal molt, which does not involve primaries, secondaries, primary coverts, or tail. Similar to dark phase of adult female in winter, but larger; pileum more blackish (less brownish); remainder of upper surface darker, duller, and rather more spotted (less streaked); median stripe of pileum and superciliary stripe paler, more whitish; wing-bars somewhat more buffy; sides of head more blackish (less brownish); lower surface duller, chin more extensively whitish. Maxilla of a darker brown. *Female, first nuptial*: Acquired by partial prenuptial molt. Very similar to nuptial adult female. *Female, first winter*: Acquired by partial postjuvenal molt, which does not involve primaries, secondaries, primary coverts, or tail. Similar to adult female in winter, but crown more blackish, feathers less broadly tipped and obscured by brown; remainder of upper surface lighter and duller, crown stripe and superciliary stripe dull white or very pale buff; lower surface paler, posterior parts, particularly abdomen, more extensively dull white, and jugulum often with narrow streaks of fuscous; sides of head darker and duller. Similar to first winter male but smaller; rather paler above, pileum and sides of head somewhat more brownish (less blackish); lower surface lighter and usually with more streaking on sides and flanks. *Male, juvenal*: Acquired by complete postnatal molt. Similar to first winter male but lighter, less ochraceous (more grayish) above, and still more distinctly spotted; lower surface paler and more whitish, cinnamon buff on anterior surface and pale cinnamon buff to buffy white posteriorly, with a few fuscous spots or streaks on sides and flanks and sometimes on jugulum. *Female, juvenal*: Acquired by complete postnatal molt. Similar to juvenal male, but pileum and sides of head more brownish (less blackish); upper surface averaging lighter; lower surface usually more streaked on sides

and jugulum. *Natal*: Dull white, slightly buffy white, very pale smoke gray, or very pale vinaceous fawn.

MEASUREMENTS: *Adult male*: Wing, 99.3–109.2 (average, 103.4) mm.; tail, 76.2–86.9 (81.8); bill (exposed culmen), 17.5–20.3 (18.5); height of bill at base, 15.0–17.5 (15.5); tarsus, 22.9–25.1 (24.1); middle toe without claw, 16.3–19.3 (17.8). *Adult female*: Wing, 96.5–104.6 (99.8); tail, 74.2–86.4 (79.2); bill, 18.0–20.3 (19.3); height of bill, 15.0–16.3 (15.7); tarsus, 22.9–25.7 (23.6); middle toe, 17.3–18.5 (17.5).

RANGE: S.e. British Columbia to s.w. Saskatchewan, south through Rocky Mts. to Coahuila and Tamaulipas. Winters mainly from Sonora and Tamaulipas to Guerrero and Puebla.

TEXAS: *Breeding*: Collected in Culberson, Jeff Davis, and Brewster cos. *Migration*: Collected north to Oldham (Aug. 29), southeast to Atascosa, west to Presidio cos.

NESTING: *Nest*: In mountains and valleys, wherever there are open woodlands and thickets, particularly along streams; placed in tree (such as apple, chokecherry, cedar, willow) or in brush; rather loosely built saucer, with a very slight depression for eggs, frequently so thin that contents may be seen from below; composed of a few thin twigs, weeds, grasses, roots, weed stalks, and twigs with green leaves; lined with rootlets and other similar materials. *Eggs*: 2–5, usually 4; ovate to rounded ovate; bluish green, bluish white, greenish white, or pale to light niagara green; spotted and blotched, usually more numerously toward large end, with reddish brown, grayish brown, and with shell markings of pale gray; average size, 26.9 × 17.8 mm.

BLUE GROSBEAK, *Guiraca caerulea* (Linnaeus)

SPECIES ACCOUNT   *See colorplate 31*

Smallest U.S. grosbeak. *Male*: deep violet blue with two tawny wing-bars; large heavy bill. *Female*: an all-brown version of male. Length, 7 in.; wingspan, 11; weight, 1 oz.

RANGE: C. California and c. South Dakota to New Jersey, south through s. United States and Mexico to

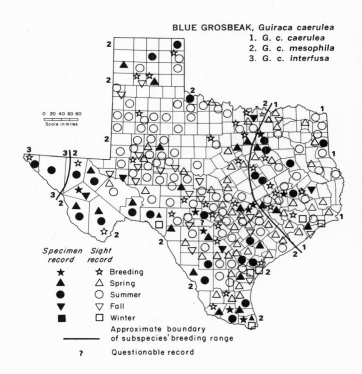

BLUE GROSBEAK, *Guiraca caerulea*
1. G. c. caerulea
2. G. c. mesophila
3. G. c. interfusa

0 20 40 60 80
Scale in miles

Specimen record   Sight record
★   ☆   Breeding
▲   △   Spring
●   ○   Summer
▼   ▽   Fall
■   □   Winter
———— Approximate boundary of subspecies' breeding range
?   Questionable record

Costa Rica. Winters chiefly from Mexico to Panama; also West Indies (rarely).

TEXAS: (See map.) *Breeding*: Late Apr. to mid-Aug. (eggs, May 1 to July 29) from near sea level to 6,000 ft. Common to fairly common in most parts, though rare in heavily wooded eastern portion. *Migration*: Mid-Apr. to mid-May; early Aug. to late Oct. (extremes: Mar. 2, June 2; July 22, Nov. 24). Common to fairly common through most of state; fairly common (locally) to uncommon in deep east Texas. *Winter*: Late Dec. to early Feb. Casual; all sightings from coastal areas or along Rio Grande.

HAUNTS AND HABITS: In Texas, the Blue Grosbeak inhabits semiopen country with scattered trees and bushes; hence, though not numerous, it is widespread as a breeder, avoiding only those parts of the state where trees are either too sparse or too dense. In montane areas of the Trans-Pecos it is restricted to foothills, often occurring in willow, cottonwood, and other streamside vegetation. During migration (particularly in fall) this handsome grosbeak frequents, sometimes in considerable flocks, grass and weed patches.

Interthicket flights of the Blue Grosbeak are swift, low, and undulatory. When disturbed, the bird flies quickly into the nearest bush. Foraging is done regularly on the ground, often in open plowed fields, where the bird hops about diligently but with little grace. When gleaning on branches of trees and shrubs it moves with more ease. Mainstay items in its diet include beetles, bugs, caterpillars, grasshoppers, ants; also seeds of bristlegrass, panicum, wheat, corn, oats, burclover, and dropseedgrass.

Blue Grosbeak notes are a sharp metallic *tink* or *spink* and a harsh *pchick* or *chuk*. The song—long, rapid, mellow warbles—is somewhat Orchard Oriole-like, but lower, more guttural, and lacking clear whistled notes. Males sing from mid-April to August, usually from a high wire or atop a tree or tall bush, occasionally on the wing.

DETAILED ACCOUNT: FOUR SUBSPECIES

EASTERN BLUE GROSBEAK, *Guiraca caerulea caerulea* (Linnaeus)

DESCRIPTION: *Adult male, nuptial plumage (black-backed—normal—phase)*: Acquired by wear from winter plumage. Pileum and rump slightly violet, tinged cadet blue to deep cadet blue; back chaetura black to fuscous black, feathers more or less edged with deep cadet blue; tail fuscous black, feathers narrowly edged on outer webs with blue of upper surface and narrowly tipped with white or brownish white; primaries and secondaries fuscous to light fuscous, inner edges, except tips, drab, outer edges of primaries, except tips, narrowly delft blue to grayish blue (dull medici blue); tertials dull black or fuscous black, broadly edged on terminal portion of outer webs and narrowly tipped with cinnamon buff to dull cinnamon; lesser wing-coverts blue like pileum, median wing-coverts tawny or russet to bay, greater coverts edged narrowly on outer webs with dull dark blue and broadly tipped with tawny to dull ochraceous tawny; primary coverts margined on outer webs with blue; lores and malar spot dull black; sides of head and of neck like pileum; lower surface deep dull violaceous blue, but crissum rather duller, feathers tipped with dull white; lining of wing mouse gray to hair brown, outer edge and axillars blue like

under surface. Bill blackish brown or dark plumbeous, but mandible lighter, somewhat dull vinaceous white, plumbeous blue, or pale plumbeous; iris dark brown or hazel; legs and feet dark brown or dull black. *Adult male, nuptial (blue-backed phase)*: Similar to black-backed phase, but back entirely deep cadet blue with practically no black. *Adult male, winter*: Acquired by complete postnuptial molt. Similar to nuptial adult male, but feathers of pileum, sides of head and of neck, back, and scapulars conspicuously tipped, most broadly on back, with cinnamon rufous to light tawny or ochraceous buff; rump and upper tail-coverts tipped with ochraceous buff or buffy white; tertials broadly tipped and margined on terminal portion with cinnamon rufous to light tawny; feathers of lower surface conspicuously tipped with buff, ochraceous buff, or dull white—the flanks and abdomen most broadly where the tips are dull white or buffy white. *Adult female, nuptial*: Acquired by wear from winter. Pileum and hindneck dull tyrian blue to light orient blue, this color usually more or less mixed or washed with various shades of dark or rufescent brown; back and scapulars between olive brown and light fuscous, feathers edged with dull buffy brown, or back dull sepia edged with sayal brown, and occasionally a tinge of blue; rump deep glaucous gray to deep green-blue gray, but longest upper tail-coverts brown like back; tail fuscous to fuscous black, the outermost two feathers narrowly tipped with dull buff or buffy white, most feathers edged narrowly on outer webs with color of rump; wings, including upper wing-coverts, fuscous or light fuscous, inner edges of primaries and secondaries, except tips, drab to rather light drab, primaries and secondaries edged on outer webs with drab or light drab, tertials broadly margined on outer webs with cinnamon buff to dull cinnamon buff; lesser wing-coverts edged with blue of pileum, more or less mixed with dull cinnamon rufous; median and greater wing-coverts broadly tipped with tawny, russet, or bay, greater coverts more narrowly tipped and edged on outer webs with dull ochraceous tawny, these wing-covert edgings forming two conspicuous wing-bars, of which anterior one is much broader; lores dull buff or light drab; remainder of sides of head and of neck variously mixed with blue of crown, light drab, and dull buffy brown or dull ochraceous; lower surface dull pale buff or pinkish buff to cinnamon buff, but chin and middle of throat paler, sometimes whitish, jugulum, sides, and flanks more or less shaded with rufescent brown or hair brown; throat, jugulum, and sometimes middle of breast more or less extensively blue like crown, but mixed or overlaid with buff or dull pale ochraceous; crissum hair brown, sometimes slightly tinged with blue, feathers broadly tipped with dull pale buff; lining of wing pale ochraceous buff or dull ochraceous buff, more or less mottled with hair brown or mouse gray. Bill dark brown or brownish plumbeous, but mandible dull, somewhat vinaceous, white, or brownish flesh color; iris dark brown or hazel; legs and feet dull rather light brown. *Adult female, winter*: Acquired by complete postnuptial molt. Similar to nuptial adult female but darker, duller, and much more rufescent, pileum and back overlaid with rufescent brown, that on crown between umber brown and dresden brown, back and scapulars somewhat duller; dull blue of rump more washed with brown of back; brown edgings of tertials broader; sides of head more brightly ochraceous or rufescent; lower surface darker, more uniform ochraceous or clay color. *Male, third winter*: Acquired by complete postnuptial molt. Like adult male in winter. *Male, second nuptial*: Acquired by wear from second winter. Similar to nuptial adult male, but outer edges of primaries and primary coverts brown or buff, instead of dull blue, or at most very faintly bluish. *Male, second winter*: Acquired by complete postnuptial molt. Differs from second nuptial male as does adult male in winter from nuptial adult male. *Male, first nuptial*: Acquired by partial prenuptial molt, involving all but some of primaries. Similar to nuptial adult female but larger and darker, blue of upper parts much more extensive and of a dark, deep dull violaceous blue; wings and tail also darker; blue of lower surface more extensive and deeper, bars often dark ochraceous tawny, but lower surface everywhere usually with more gray and more blue (less buff or brown), crissum nearly always more or less tinged with blue.

Similar to nuptial adult male, but back and often parts of pileum brown instead of blue or black, and all blue areas more or less washed with dull or rufescent brown; wings and tail more brownish, primary coverts brown like rest of wings and without blue edgings, outer margins of wing-quills brown or buff, not blue; sides of head and of neck much mixed with brown; lower parts much mixed with brown and gray, throat often whitish. *Male, first winter*: Acquired by partial postjuvenal molt, which does not involve wing-quills or tail. Similar to first nuptial male, but upper surface much overlaid with reddish brown—between mars brown and hazel to buffy brown; wing edgings much broader; lower surface much overlaid with dark ochraceous to light buff. Similar to adult female in winter but larger; upper surface much darker and more uniform—cinnamon brown or rather light cinnamon brown—usually without trace of blue above or below, but rump lighter, more grayish than back; upper tail-coverts more or less obscurely barred with ochraceous; wing-bar formed by tips of greater coverts paler—cinnamon buff; sides of head decidedly darker—rather light cinnamon brown; lower surface darker, jugulum buckthorn brown to light cinnamon brown, remainder of lower surface ochraceous; chin and middle of throat sometimes paler. *Female, second nuptial*: Acquired by wear from second winter. Similar to nuptial adult female, but head, rump, and upper tail-coverts without blue; bend of wing blue; general plumage somewhat more rufescent, particularly upper surface. *Female, second winter*: Acquired by complete postnuptial molt. Similar to first winter male but smaller; wing-bar formed by tips of greater wing-coverts darker—deep ochraceous tawny. Similar to adult female in winter, but upper surface very much darker and of more rufescent brown, without blue on rump or upper tail-coverts, and everywhere more uniform, lesser wing-coverts with very little blue, this mostly overlaid by rufescent brown feathers; lower surface much darker and more deeply rufescent brown. *Female, first nuptial*: Acquired by partial prenuptial molt. Similar to second nuptial female but above darker, more rufescent (less grayish); sides of head and wing-bars more deeply ochraceous tawny; below much darker and more richly colored, more ochraceous or ochraceous tawny, particularly on jugulum. *Female, first winter*: Acquired by partial postjuvenal molt, not including wing-quills or tail. Similar to second winter female, but upper and lower surfaces averaging darker and duller, posterior wing-bar on tips of greater coverts paler and more buffy. *Juvenal*: Acquired by complete postnatal molt. Similar to first winter female, but upper surface duller and rather lighter, back obscurely barred by light ochraceous or buckthorn brown edges of feathers; upper surface between saccardo umber and snuff brown; sides of head duller, less rufescent—like pileum but paler; anterior wing-bar (that on tips of median coverts) paler—dull cinnamon buff, dull ochraceous buff, or clay color; lower surface duller. Bill dull yellowish brown, but darker above; iris dark brown; legs and feet brown. *Natal*: Brownish mouse gray. Bill, legs, and feet dull brownish pink.

MEASUREMENTS: *Adult male*: Wing, 81.5–88.9 (average, 86.4) mm.; tail, 63.0–68.6 (65.3); bill (exposed culmen), 15.0–17.0 (16.0); height of bill at base, 11.9–13.5 (12.7); tarsus, 18.5–21.6 (19.8); middle toe without claw, 15.0–17.0 (15.7). *Adult female*: Wing, 79.5–84.6 (81.5); tail, 58.9–65.0 (61.7); bill, 14.5–16.0 (15.2); height of bill, 10.9–13.0 (12.2); tarsus, 19.0–21.1 (20.3); middle toe, 15.0–16.0 (15.2).

RANGE: S.e. Illinois (casually) to e. Maryland, south to s.e. Texas and w. Florida. Winters chiefly from n.e. Mexico to Panama; also West Indies (rarely).

TEXAS: *Breeding*: Altitudinal range, near sea level to 800 ft. Collected north to Dallas, east to Harrison, south to Walker and Washington, west to McLennan cos. Fairly common to rare. *Migration*: Collected north to Dallas, east to Galveston, south to Nueces, west to Val Verde cos. Fairly common. *Winter*: No specimen but individuals sighted in Harris and Chambers cos. possibly belong to this race.

NESTING: *Nest*: In semiopen country of uplands and bottoms, in cultivated areas, as well as in wilder parts of the country, along roadsides, borders of weed patches, and in thickets; on branch of tree or bush; cup of leaves, weed stalks, rootlets, grass, strips of bark, bits of newspaper, and sometimes pieces of snake skin; lined with small rootlets and in some instances horsehair. *Eggs*: 3–5, usually 3–4; ovate to oval; light blue, bluish white, or light bluish green; normally without markings, but occasionally with spots and dots of chestnut and lilac; average size, 21.6 × 16.3 mm.

TEXAS BLUE GROSBEAK, Guiraca caerulea mesophila
Oberholser, new subspecies (see Appendix A)

DESCRIPTION: *Adult male and female, nuptial plumage*: Similar to *G. c. caerulea* but larger, particularly wing and tail. Male averaging somewhat lighter, less purplish above, particularly on rump; decidedly lighter below; tawny or buff wing-bars wider and lighter, particularly that on greater coverts. Female much lighter, somewhat more grayish both above and below, this paleness including wing-bars.

MEASUREMENTS: *Adult male*: Wing, 85.6–92.5 (average, 88.4) mm.; tail, 63.5–72.9 (67.8); bill (exposed culmen), 15.5–17.0 (16.3); height of bill at base, 11.7–13.7 (12.4); tarsus, 19.6–21.1 (20.3); middle toe without claw, 14.5–17.3 (15.7). *Adult female*: Wing, 79.0–86.1 (84.1); tail, 61.0–68.6 (65.8); bill, 14.0–17.0 (16.0); height of bill, 11.7–13.0 (12.7); tarsus, 19.8–21.1 (20.6); middle toe, 14.5–16.5 (15.2).

TYPE: Adult male, no. 186740, U.S. National Museum, Biological Surveys collection; Lipscomb, Texas; June 27, 1903; A. H. Howell, original no., 110.

RANGE: C. South Dakota, south through c. United States to n.e. Mexico. Winters chiefly from s. Sinaloa to Guatemala.

TEXAS: *Breeding*: Altitudinal range, near sea level to 6,000 ft. Collected north to Lipscomb, east to Cooke, south to Refugio and Cameron, west to Culberson cos. Common. *Migration*: Collected north to Oldham, east to Polk, south to Cameron, west to Presidio cos. Common. *Winter*: No specimen, but individuals sighted in Val Verde, Aransas, San Patricio, and Cameron cos. possibly belong to this race.

NESTING: Similar to that of *G. c. caerulea*, but average egg size, 22.4 × 16.0 mm.

WESTERN BLUE GROSBEAK, Guiraca caerulea interfusa
Dwight and Griscom

DESCRIPTION: *Adult male and female, nuptial plumage*: Similar to *G. c. mesophila* but much larger, especially wing and tail. Male with rump somewhat paler; buffy wing-bars broader and somewhat lighter; lower surface of body paler. Female somewhat paler, more grayish, both above and below.

MEASUREMENTS: *Adult male*: Wing, 87.9–93.5 (average, 90.7) mm.; tail, 67.6–73.9 (70.4); bill (exposed culmen), 15.0–17.8 (16.5); height of bill at base, 11.4–13.0 (12.2); tarsus, 20.1–23.6 (21.4); middle toe without claw, 15.0–16.5 (16.3). *Adult female*: Wing, 80.0–88.4 (84.8); tail, 61.7–69.1 (65.8); bill, 14.5–17.5 (16.0); height of bill, 11.9–13.2 (12.7); tarsus, 19.0–22.6 (20.3); middle toe, 14.5–16.5 (15.7).

RANGE: S.e. Nevada to n. Colorado, south through s.w. United States and n.w. Mexico to Jalisco. Winters mainly from s. Baja California, s. Sonora, and Durango to c. Guatemala.

TEXAS: *Breeding*: Altitudinal range, 3,500 to 4,000 ft. Collected in El Paso and Hudspeth cos. Fairly common.

NESTING: Similar to that of *G. c. caerulea*, but average egg size, 21.9 × 16.5 mm.

MEXICAN BLUE GROSBEAK, Guiraca caerulea eurhyncha
(Coues)

Race not in A.O.U. check-list (see Appendix A).

DESCRIPTION: *Adult male and female, nuptial plumage*: Similar to *G. c. interfusa* but much larger, notably wing, tail, and bill. Blue color of male decidedly darker, the wing-bars darker (chestnut or tawny); female darker above with somewhat darker wing-bars.

MEASUREMENTS: *Adult male*: Wing, 90.4–97.1 (average, 93.5)

mm.; tail, 70.1–78.0 (73.4); bill (exposed culmen), 16.5–18.0 (17.5); height of bill at base, 11.9–13.7 (13.0); tarsus, 21.1–23.1 (21.9); middle toe without claw, 15.0–17.0 (16.0). *Adult female*: Wing, 87.6–91.9 (89.2); tail, 69.1–72.9 (71.4); bill, 17.0–17.8 (17.3); height of bill, 12.4–14.0 (13.5); tarsus, 20.9–23.6 (21.9); middle toe, 15.0–16.3 (15.7).

RANGE: Coahuila to c. Tamaulipas, south to Oaxaca.

TEXAS: *Vagrant*: One specimen: Brewster Co., 35 mi. south of Alpine (July 2, 1901, L. A. Fuertes).

INDIGO BUNTING, *Linaria cyanea* (Linnaeus)

SPECIES ACCOUNT

Passerina cyanea of A.O.U. check-list, 1957 (see Appendix A). A small finch. *Nuptial male*: all blue; suggests dwarf Blue Grosbeak with sparrowlike bill, but lacks wing-bars. *Winter male*: mottled blue and brown. *Female*: brown, but paler below with faint breast streaks. Length, 5½ in.; wingspan, 8½; weight, ½ oz.

RANGE: S.w. South Dakota, east across Great Lakes region to s. Maine, and south to U.S. Gulf coast (irregularly) and n. Florida. Winters chiefly from c. Mexico and West Indies to Panama.

TEXAS: (See map.) *Breeding*: Late Apr. to mid-July (eggs, May 15 to July 7) from near sea level to 2,000 ft. Locally common (some years) to fairly common in northeastern third; uncommon and irregular on eastern Edwards Plateau; nested at Welder Wildlife Refuge, San Patricio Co., 1961. *Migration*: Early Apr. to mid-May; late July to early Nov. (extremes: Feb. 25, June 18; July 14, Dec. 4). Very common (sometimes abundant on coast) to fairly common in spring through eastern half; scarce between Pecos River and 100th meridian; rare west of Pecos River. Less numerous (or less noticed) in fall in all sections. *Winter*: Late Dec. to mid-Feb. Scarce along coast and in Rio Grande delta.

HAUNTS AND HABITS: The Indigo Bunting is an important contributor to one of nature's color shows: Along the Gulf coast, wet northers in April and early May sometimes force down thousands of migrating birds. On these occasions coastal live oaks, mesquites, bushes, and grass patches "drip" with a whole spectrum of birds—red tanagers, orange orioles, yellow warblers, green immature and female Painted Buntings, and blue male Indigo Buntings.

In late spring and early summer the Indigo frequents chiefly deciduous woods (sometimes with an admixture of pines) and their edges. It is particularly attracted to bottomlands. A partially cutover oak-sweetgum area near a creek is almost certain to detain loud-singing Indigos, though the number that remain to nest in Texas (southwestern pole of the breeding range) varies considerably from year to year. Little groups of this bunting drift through the state in late summer and fall, at which time they are especially attracted to giant ragweed (*Ambrosia trifida*). The few that linger into winter are to be looked for in coastal scrub and tall grass patches.

Flight of the Indigo Bunting is quick and jerky, even when the bird flies at a considerable height and for some distance. When perched, it often twitches its tail. Much time is spent in thickets or low branches of trees, sometimes on the ground, in search of seeds (mainly of ragweed, bristlegrass, smartweed, goldenrod, aster) and fruits of blackberry and elderberry. Insects (caterpillars, beetles, moths, grasshoppers, others) are taken also, especially in summer. The male, a bold defender of his territory, is frequently seen on an exposed vantage; the female, however, is much more reclusive and difficult to spy in her thicket retreats.

Call notes of this bunting include a thin emphatic *spit* or *pit*; also a metallic *cheep, cheep*. The male's song—a high, loud, and lively performance—is a distinctly phrased, but variable, *sweet-sweet, swee-swee, here-here, see it-see it*. This is delivered usually from a tall tree or bush or high wire, occasionally in flight; it is heard in Texas from early April to mid-July, rarely in August.

DETAILED ACCOUNT: NO SUBSPECIES

DESCRIPTION: *Adult male, nuptial plumage (green-blue phase)*: Acquired by partial prenuptial molt. Forehead and crown prussian blue, passing into methyl green on back and scapulars, into motmot blue on upper tail-coverts; tail chaetura drab, feathers, except outermost pair, edged narrowly on outer webs with blue, somewhat duller than upper tail-coverts; wings light chaetura drab to dark hair brown, outer webs of primaries and secondaries narrowly margined with dull greenish blue, tertials more broadly with same; inner margins of primaries and secondaries, except at tips, brownish white, shading to drab or light drab on primaries, all wing-coverts, including primary coverts, broadly edged with blue of back, this slightly more violet-tinged on bend of wing; lores dull black; chin and cheeks like forehead but slightly more greenish, shading over auriculars into more greenish blue of sides of neck, which is identical with that of upper parts; throat like chin but somewhat more greenish blue, passing

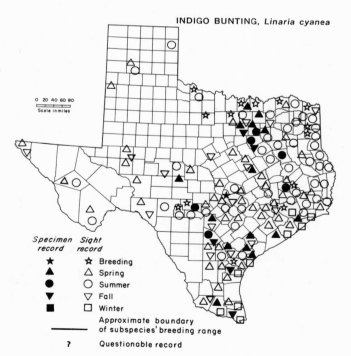

INDIGO BUNTING, *Linaria cyanea*

0 20 40 60 80
Scale in miles

Specimen record | Sight record
★ | ☆ Breeding
▲ | △ Spring
● | ○ Summer
▼ | ▽ Fall
■ | □ Winter

—— Approximate boundary of subspecies' breeding range

? Questionable record

on jugulum and breast into a color between capri blue and chessylite blue; abdomen and crissum more greenish; lining of wing hair brown, edge of wing blue like chin but rather more greenish, remainder of coverts more or less washed with greenish blue of back. Maxilla black or plumbeous black; mandible smoke gray or cinnamon, with narrow brownish black line along gonys, and dull light yellow cutting edges; iris dark brown; legs and feet black, slate black, brownish black, or dull brown; anterior claws dark brown; posterior claw whitish. *Adult male, nuptial (violet blue phase)*: Similar to green-blue phase, but considerably less greenish (more violet blue), pileum dull helvetia blue, back italian blue, breast helvetia blue; most adult males more or less intermediate in color between these two phases. *Adult male, winter*: Acquired by complete postnuptial molt. Upper surface dull cinnamon brown to between mars brown and hazel, but rump and upper tail-coverts methyl green though almost entirely overlaid by brown of upper parts; tail as in nuptial male; wings similar to those of nuptial male, with blue edgings on primary coverts, but remaining coverts edged, median and greater coverts broadly tipped, and tertials broadly edged on outer margins with dull cinnamon or sayal brown; sides of head and of neck similar to upper parts but usually somewhat lighter, although lores dull buff; feathers of most of lower surface with dark gobelin blue or dark bluish gray-green subterminal spots, these, however, mostly hidden by overlying various shades of brown and buff; jugulum buckthorn brown, ochraceous, or dresden brown, but middle of throat and chin sometimes pale buff or buffy white; abdomen pinkish buff to buffy white; edge of wing methyl green to gobelin blue; remainder of wing-lining as in nuptial adult. *Adult female, nuptial (rufous brown phase)*: Acquired by partial prenuptial molt. Upper surface between cinnamon brown and dresden brown; in more or less worn plumage showing darker light olive brown centers of feathers; wings and tail between dark buffy brown and light fuscous; tail, also lesser wing-coverts, with narrow edgings of methyl green; inner margins of primaries and secondaries, except at tips of primaries, dull pinkish buff, light drab, or drab, tertials edged on outer webs and tipped with dull brown—between buffy brown and dull tawny olive; greater and median wing-coverts broadly tipped with dull cinnamon buff or between ochraceous tawny and russet; sides of head like crown but somewhat paler, lores particularly so; sides of neck like hindneck; anterior lower surface dull pale buff, more or less brownish on jugulum, where narrowly streaked or finely spotted with hair brown to drab; sides and flanks dull cinnamon buff to clay color, also similarly streaked; abdomen very pale buff or dull white, crissum somewhat more deeply buff; lining of wing pinkish buff or pale pinkish buff, outer under wing-coverts somewhat mottled with hair brown or mouse gray. Bill blackish brown, but mandible paler, usually with narrow dark brown line along gonys; iris dark brown; legs and feet brown. *Adult female, nuptial (gray-brown phase)*: Acquired by partial prenuptial molt. Similar to rufous brown phase, but upper surface much duller and more grayish—dull buffy brown or between dark buffy brown and fuscous—edgings of wings somewhat less rufescent; sides of head and of neck, also lower surface, less strongly buff. Most individuals more or less intermediate between these two phases. *Adult female, winter*: Acquired by complete postnuptial molt. Similar to nuptial adult female, but upper surface usually somewhat lighter and brighter, more uniform, also decidedly more rufescent; in rufous brown phase usually between ochraceous tawny and cinnamon brown, edgings of tertials also somewhat broader; streaks on lower surface more obscured by lighter edgings of feathers. Maxilla chaetura black; mandible olive gray. *Male, first nuptial*: Acquired by partial prenuptial molt. Similar to nuptial adult male and sometimes almost as brilliantly colored, but primary coverts always brown without blue edgings, some or all of primaries and secondaries dull brown without blue margins, lesser and median wing-coverts and tertials often with more or less extensive brown, cinnamon buff, or clay colored edgings; usually upper surface with more or less admixture, sometimes extensive, of light dull buffy brown to tawny; lower surface often extensively mixed with white, grayish white, or buff, giving

plumage a strongly mottled appearance. *Male, first winter*: Acquired by partial postjuvenal molt. Similar to adult female in winter but larger and averaging darker above; wing-bars averaging darker and more brownish; sides of head darker, duller, and more rufescent; lower surface usually darker, duller, and more brownish, particularly on jugulum. Bill brownish slate, but mandible brownish white; iris dark brown; legs and feet clove brown or slate color. *Female, first nuptial*: Acquired by partial prenuptial molt. Very similar to nuptial adult female. *Female, first winter*: Acquired by partial postjuvenal molt. Similar to adult female in winter, but upper surface averaging duller and darker, including wing-bars; lower surface also averaging darker, more brownish, particularly on sides, flanks, and jugulum. Similar to first winter male but smaller; averaging lighter above, rather more rufescent; below averaging somewhat more ochraceous or buff; some birds are, however, practically indistinguishable except by smaller size. *Juvenal*: Acquired by complete postnatal molt. Much like first winter female but averaging somewhat darker and duller above, where obscurely streaked or mottled with darker brown; lower surface duller, usually more grayish or brownish, and much more conspicuously streaked, except on middle of throat and middle of abdomen, with hair brown or fuscous. Bill drab, but maxilla maize yellow at commissure; iris prout brown; legs and feet dull brown or black; claws lighter. *Natal*: Brownish mouse gray. Bill, legs, and feet pinkish buff.

MEASUREMENTS: *Adult male*: Wing, 65.5–71.4 (average, 67.8) mm.; tail, 48.5–54.3 (51.3); bill (exposed culmen), 10.2–11.2 (10.4); height of bill at base, 7.4–7.9 (7.6); tarsus, 16.3–18.0 (17.3); middle toe without claw, 11.7–13.0 (12.4). *Adult female*: Wing, 62.7–66.8 (63.8); tail, 47.3–54.1 (50.3); bill, 9.7–10.7 (10.2); height of bill, 7.4–7.9 (7.6); tarsus, 16.5–18.0 (17.5); middle toe, 11.7–13.0 (12.4).

TEXAS: *Breeding*: Collected north to Cooke, southeast to Walker, west to Travis (eggs) and Kerr cos. *Migration*: Collected outside breeding range east to Galveston, south to Cameron, west to Menard cos.

NESTING: *Nest*: On uplands and bottoms, along stream valleys, or on slopes, sometimes in pastures; in thickets, vines, in a bush or low tree; usually in upright crotch 4–8 ft. above ground; cup composed of weed stalks, twigs, coarse grass, leaves, sedges, strips of bark, and other plant fibers; lined with finer materials of same sort, also fine grasses, rootlets, and hair. *Eggs*: 3–5, usually 4; ovate to rounded ovate; white with bluish or greenish tinge; unmarked, though sometimes thinly dotted with reddish brown; average size, 19.0 × 14.0 mm.

LAZULI BUNTING, *Linaria amoena* (Say)

SPECIES ACCOUNT

Passerina amoena of A.O.U. check-list, 1957 (see Appendix A). Regarded as conspecific with Indigo Bunting by some authors. Size and shape of Indigo Bunting, with which it sometimes interbreeds where nesting ranges join. *Nuptial male*: cerulean blue head and upper parts; tawny breast-band, sides; white belly, wing-bars. *Winter male*: grayish brown with patches of blue; retains white wing-bars. *Female*: brownish above with two whitish wing-bars; dingy white below with faint tawny wash on breast. Length, 5½ in.; wingspan, 8¾; weight, ½ oz.

RANGE: S.w. Canada, south through w. United States to n.w. Baja California, c. Coahuila (fide M. C. Johnston), and w. Oklahoma; formerly to c. Texas. Winters chiefly from s. Baja California, s. Arizona, and s. Tamaulipas to Guerrero and c. Veracruz.

TEXAS: (See map.) *Breeding*: Early May to early

July (eggs, May 15, 26, 1903, Lacey Ranch, Kerr Co.) at 1,650 ft. Individuals occasionally linger into June in northern Panhandle, Trans-Pecos, and on Edwards Plateau, but there has been no conclusive evidence of nesting since 1903. *Migration:* Mid-Apr. to mid-May; early Aug. to mid-Sept. (extremes: Apr. 13, June 25; Aug. 7, Oct. 24). Uncommon to scarce in spring through most of state; unrecorded in forested areas of deep east Texas. Scarce to rare in fall in western half; apparently only one record during this season from eastern portion: Brazoria Co., Freeport (1 bird in winter plumage with Indigo Buntings, Nov. 15, 1972, T. B. Feltner). *Winter:* Accidental; sight records for McLennan, Bexar, and Hidalgo cos.

HAUNTS AND HABITS: In Texas, as elsewhere, the Lazuli generally occurs in more open habitat than its eastern counterpart, the Indigo Bunting. Where both species sometimes linger from spring into summer, as on the Edwards Plateau, the Indigo prefers lush vegetation of canyons and riverbottoms, while the Lazuli favors dry, brushy, semiopen hillsides. West of the Indigo's breeding range, for example in the Trans-Pecos, the Lazuli frequents willows and streamside thickets as well as brush along dry gulches and ravines. In fall and winter both buntings are to be looked for in weed (especially *Ambrosia trifida*) and grass patches.

The Lazuli in flight and behavior is essentially Indigo-like. In bushes, lower parts of trees, and on the ground, it forages for seeds of needlegrass, canary-grass, bluegrass, filaree, and others; also grasshoppers, caterpillars, beetles, and cicadas. Individuals sometimes alight on heads of grasses and bend the stems to the ground in order to pick out the seeds.

A sharp *tsip* or *quit* is the Lazuli's call note. The

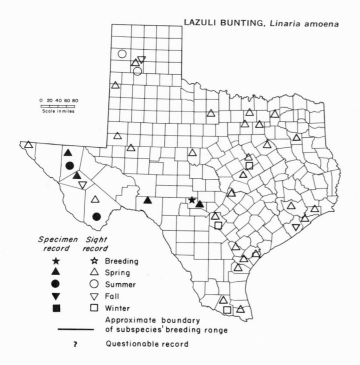

LAZULI BUNTING, *Linaria amoena*

0 20 40 60 80
Scale in miles

	Specimen record	Sight record
Breeding	★	☆
Spring	▲	△
Summer	●	○
Fall	▼	▽
Winter	■	□

——— Approximate boundary of subspecies' breeding range

? Questionable record

song is somewhat like that of the Indigo, but more rapid, less lively, and often with a few scratchy notes intermingled. In Texas, Lazuli males sing from mid-April into June, usually from atop a tall bush or tree, from a high wire, or sometimes in flight.

DETAILED ACCOUNT: NO SUBSPECIES

DESCRIPTION: *Adult male, nuptial plumage:* Acquired by wear from winter plumage. Pileum light cerulean blue, bremen blue, calamine blue to cendre blue; back and scapulars chaetura drab to dark neutral gray, washed and more or less streaked with blue of pileum; rump and most upper tail-coverts blue like pileum, but rather lighter, longer upper tail-coverts like back; tail chaetura black to fuscous black, most feathers, except outermost pair, margined narrowly, middle pair rather broadly, on outer webs, with blue of longer upper tail-coverts, and edged narrowly on terminal portion of inner webs with grayish white; primaries and secondaries chaetura drab, inner margins, except at tips of primaries, dull white on base of secondaries, becoming drab to drab gray on primaries, outer webs of primaries and secondaries narrowly margined with blue of back; tertials chaetura black, edged on outer webs, as are also some of inner secondaries, with dull buff or dull cinnamon buff, which quickly disappears by abrasion; lesser wing-coverts blue like hindneck; median and greater wing-coverts chaetura black, median series broadly tipped with white, greater coverts narrowly margined on outer webs with blue, and tipped on outer webs with white or dull pale buff, white tips on median and greater coverts forming two conspicuous wing-bars, of which the latter is much narrower; primary coverts margined on outer webs with blue of upper surface; lores dull black or fuscous black; sides of head and of neck, with chin and throat all around, blue like pileum; broad band across jugulum and extending onto sides ochraceous tawny to dark ochraceous tawny; remainder of lower surface white; thighs blue like rump, feathers slightly margined with dull white; lining of wing dull white, edge of wing and axillars blue like throat, under wing-coverts slightly mottled with hair brown or mouse gray. Bill black, but mandible plumbeous, light medici blue, or plumbeous white, with brownish black line along gonys; iris prout brown; legs and feet dark sepia or brownish black. *Adult male, winter:* Acquired by complete postnuptial molt. Similar to nuptial adult male, but blue of upper surface more or less obscured by broad cinnamon brown to light cinnamon brown tips of feathers; wing-coverts and tertials broadly tipped with buckthorn brown to clay color; sides of head and of neck, with chin and throat, similarly obscured by brown feather tips; jugulum darker—between buckthorn brown and ochraceous tawny, this color much extended posteriorly more or less over breast, sides, and flanks. *Adult female, nuptial (gray—normal—phase):* Acquired by wear from winter. Pileum, sometimes also throat and sides of neck, dull porcelain blue, more or less overlaid with buffy brown to snuff brown, thus this blue sometimes scarcely evident; hindneck, back, and scapulars light buffy brown to between light buffy brown and drab; centers of feathers darker, imparting more or less obscurely mottled appearance; lower rump and upper tail-coverts porcelain blue to dull gobelin blue, often more or less obscured by buffy brown or drab; tail light clove brown to fuscous, outer edges of feathers narrowly margined with blue of upper tail-coverts, though usually duller and somewhat more greenish; wings fuscous to dark buffy brown, inner margins of primaries and secondaries, except at tips, dull drab or light drab, outer webs edged with greenish blue like tail, but lesser wing-coverts greenish blue like upper tail-coverts, and rather darker, outer greater wing-coverts and primary coverts narrowly margined on outer webs with same blue, lesser and greater wing-coverts tipped with pinkish buff or dull pale pinkish buff, forming two noticeable wing-bars; lores smoke gray to light drab; sides of head between drab and light grayish olive to drab, with sometimes here and there a touch of dull blue, auriculars usually somewhat more deeply buff; sides of neck light grayish olive to dull drab; chin dull cartridge buff to cream buff; jugulum and upper breast dull cinnamon buff to dull clay color; middle of lower breast, with abdomen and crissum, pale dull cartridge buff; sides and flanks similar to jugulum but paler and washed with light grayish olive; lining of wing smoke gray washed with buff, outer portion somewhat darker and more or less washed with greenish blue of lesser wing-coverts. Bill dull black, but cutting edges light plumbeous, mandible pale plumbeous with dark brown line along gonys; iris dark vandyke brown; legs and feet dull sepia. *Adult female, nuptial (brown phase)*: Similar to gray phase, but upper surface rufescent brown—saccardo umber; jugulum darker—ochraceous. *Adult female, winter*: Acquired by complete postnuptial molt. Similar to nuptial adult female, but upper surface and sides of head much more uniform and more rufescent, obscuring blue of head, rump, upper tail-coverts, and bend of wing; light margins of tertials broader; lower surface darker, more deeply ochraceous. *Male and female, second winter*: Acquired by complete postnuptial molt. Similar to corresponding sex of adult in winter. *Male, first nuptial*: Acquired by partial prenuptial molt. Similar to nuptial adult male, but upper surface duller, sometimes otherwise almost like nuptial adult, often with considerable sayal brown on back, mostly in form of tips on feathers; wing-bars often more buffy or ochraceous; wings and tail more brownish, primaries and secondaries wholly or partly of brown of first winter male, and primary coverts wholly olive brown or fuscous without blue edgings; chin and throat with usually some, sometimes considerable, admixture of white or buffy white; jugulum usually somewhat paler and duller; posterior lower parts strongly washed with buff. *Male, first winter*: Acquired by partial postjuvenal molt, not involving wing-quills or tail. Similar to adult male in winter but somewhat larger; wings and tail somewhat darker, with more pronounced bluish edgings on tail, though without blue edgings on primary coverts; jugulum and upper breast of a darker and duller ochraceous. *Female, first nuptial*: Acquired by partial prenuptial molt. Similar to nuptial adult female but averaging duller and darker; head and throat without blue; blue on rump and upper tail-coverts very much duller, of less extent or practically absent, that on bend of wing duller and usually less extensive; wings rather lighter and slightly more rufescent brown; primary coverts entirely brown without blue edgings; outer edges of primaries and secondaries with little or no blue. *Female, first winter*: Acquired by partial postjuvenal molt, which involves neither wing-quills nor tail. Similar to adult female in winter, but upper surface duller; no blue on head, rump, upper tail-coverts, wings, or tail, except occasionally very slight indication on lesser wing-coverts; primary coverts entirely brown; lower surface duller, sometimes obscurely streaked, on jugulum, breast, sides, and flanks with dull dark brown. Similar to first winter male but smaller; upper surface lighter; wings and tail without edgings of blue and with less or no blue on bend of wing; jugulum and breast usually somewhat paler. *Male, juvenal*: Acquired by complete postnatal molt. Similar to first winter male, but above rather lighter with paler brown edgings, imparting more mottled appearance; lower surface dull cream buff to cartridge buff, numerously streaked, except on chin, throat, abdomen, and crissum, with hair brown. *Female, juvenal*: Acquired by complete postnatal molt. Similar to juvenal male, but upper surface, wings, and tail lighter; rump and upper tail-coverts without trace of blue; tail without blue edgings; lower surface paler, less heavily streaked. *Natal*: Pileum rather dull light vinaceous buff; back and rump tilleul buff.

MEASUREMENTS: *Adult male*: Wing, 70.9–76.5 (average, 73.2) mm.; tail, 52.8–57.7 (55.3); bill (exposed culmen), 9.7–10.2 (9.9); height of bill at base, 7.4–7.9 (7.6); tarsus, 16.3–17.8 (17.3); middle toe without claw, 12.2–13.2 (12.7). *Adult female*: Wing, 65.8–71.7 (69.3); tail, 50.8–58.7 (53.3); bill, 9.1–10.2 (9.7); height of bill, 6.9–7.9 (7.4); tarsus, 16.3–17.5 (17.3); middle toe, 12.2–12.7 (12.4).

TEXAS: *Breeding*: Only definite collection record: Kerr Co., Lacey Ranch (nest and eggs collected, May 15 and 26, 1903, H. Lacey). One bird collected in summer, but no evidence of breeding: Brewster Co., n.w. base of Chisos Mts. (June 25, 1901,

L. A. Fuertes). *Migration*: Collected in Culberson (1 specimen, Aug. 15), Jeff Davis (1), Val Verde (1), and Kerr (1) cos.

NESTING: *Nest*: On uplands and lowlands, in thickets and timber along streams, canyons, also more open parts, including cultivated areas, often near water; on stalk of low weed, bush, such as willow or manzanita, or on low limb of tree, 3–4 ft. above ground; rather roughly built, though thick walled, cup; composed of small twigs, shreds of bark, grasses, weeds, stems of flowering plants, leaves, and roots; lined with finer stems from flowering plants, hair, vegetable down, fine grass, cobwebs, and horsehair. *Eggs*: 3–6, usually 4; rounded ovate to elliptical ovate to nearly oval; light bluish green or bluish white; usually plain, but sometimes dotted or spotted with black or blackish brown; average size, 19.0 × 14.0 mm.

VARIED BUNTING, *Linaria versicolor* (Bonaparte)

SPECIES ACCOUNT

Passerina versicolor of A.O.U. check-list, 1957 (see Appendix A). A small dark finch. *Nuptial male*: overall purplish plum (may appear black in some lights); has scarlet patch on back of head; blue crown and rump. *Winter male*: chiefly drab brown. *Female*: uniformly nondescript grayish brown. Length, 5½ in.; wingspan, 8¼; weight, ½ oz.

RANGE: S. Arizona to s.w. Texas, south to Guatemala. Winters chiefly in Mexico and Guatemala.

TEXAS: (See map.) *Breeding*: Mid-Apr. to mid-July (eggs, Apr. 26 to July 7; just-fledged young being fed as late as Sept. 13) from near sea level to 5,300 ft. Fairly common (some years) to scarce from Culberson Co., south along arid drainage of Rio Grande to Cameron Co. *Migration*: Mid-Apr. to mid-May; mid-July to late Aug. (extremes: Apr. 6, June 26; July 10, Sept. 6). Fairly common to scarce in spring along Texas-Mexico

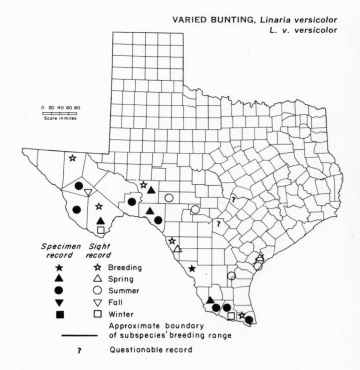

VARIED BUNTING, *Linaria versicolor*
L. v. versicolor

0 20 40 60 80
Scale in miles

Specimen record	Sight record	
★	☆	Breeding
▲	△	Spring
●	○	Summer
▼	▽	Fall
■	□	Winter

—— Approximate boundary of subspecies' breeding range

? Questionable record

border; a few sight records east to Kerrville and Rock-port. Uncommon to scarce in fall within breeding range. *Winter*: Early Dec. to early Mar. Scarce in Rio Grande delta. One sighting in Brewster Co., Basin campground in Big Bend Nat. Park (1 male, Dec. 28, 1968, R. H. Wauer).

HAUNTS AND HABITS: In Texas, the Varied Bunting apparently prefers a combination of low dense thorn brush, at least somewhat hilly terrain, and an arid climate—conditions that are found along the Rio Grande and its tributary rivers, arroyos, and dry washes. In spring migration, however, *L. versicolor* is occasionally found as far east as the sometimes humid central coast.

In its natural haunts, the shadow-dark Varied is well camouflaged. It is a shy and secretive bird and stays closer to cover than does the Indigo. Though little known, its habits are probably similar to those of closely related buntings.

Note of the Varied Bunting is a sharp emphatic *chip*. The song is a thin, crisp, energetic warbling similar to that of the Painted Bunting, but more obviously phrased and less rambling. The male, from atop a bush or yucca stalk, sometimes a high wire, sings from mid-April to July.

DETAILED ACCOUNT: ONE SUBSPECIES

EASTERN VARIED BUNTING, *Linaria versicolor versicolor* (Bonaparte)

DESCRIPTION: *Adult male, nuptial plumage (reddish phase)*: Acquired by wear from winter plumage. Forehead narrowly black; fore part of crown mazarine blue to light amparo blue; occiput nopal red to scarlet red; hindneck light violet overlaid by magenta; center of back madder brown to pompeian red; rump and shorter upper tail-coverts light to pale bluish violet to pale violet; longest upper tail-coverts similar but darker; tail fuscous black, feathers margined on outer webs with deep slate blue; wings fuscous to dark fuscous, inner edges of primaries and secondaries basally paler, outer webs of primaries and secondaries, except at tips, margined with bluish gray-green; lesser wing-coverts dull violet blue; median wing-coverts and scapulars anthracene purple overlying slate violet or dark slate violet; greater wing-coverts margined on outer webs with analine black; lores, malar region, and chin black; sides of head like hindneck; sides of neck deep hyssop violet to dark dull bluish violet; anterior lower parts dahlia carmine to indian lake, throat sometimes the same but sometimes pomegranate purple; lower breast and abdomen dark dull bluish violet to dark hyssop violet; crissum dull dark madder blue; lining of wing slate violet to dusky dull violet. Bill black, blackish brown, or dark plumbeous, but mandible paler; iris dark brown; legs and feet brownish black. *Adult male, nuptial (bluish phase)*: Similar to reddish phase, but above much more bluish, middle of throat dragon blood red or coral red, though sometimes like jugulum; jugulum light perilla purple to naphthalene violet; crissum dark madder blue or deep slate blue. *Adult male, winter*: Acquired by complete postnuptial molt. Similar to nuptial adult male, but upper surface much obscured by feather tips and edgings of saccardo umber to buffy brown, snuff brown, and drab, this sometimes almost obscuring bright colors beneath, these edgings broadest on back and scapulars, least evident on rump and upper tail-coverts; tertials, with greater and median wing-coverts, more or less broadly tipped with identical browns; feathers of lower surface also conspicuously tipped with buffy brown to cinnamon, on abdomen sometimes with buffy white; entire plumage both above and below thus duller and darker. *Adult female, nuptial*: Acquired by wear from winter. Upper surface grayish olive, much washed

or overlaid with buffy brown, crown and rump more or less extensively bluish gray-green; tail chaetura drab to dark hair brown, margined on outer webs of rectrices with bluish gray-green; wings rather dark hair brown, inner webs of primaries and secondaries, except at tips of primaries, dull drab, outer webs of primaries and secondaries narrowly margined with bluish gray-green of rump; lesser wing-coverts slightly tinged with bluish gray-green, all coverts edged with dull buffy brown, median and greater coverts tipped, chiefly on outer webs, with dull buff or buffy brown, forming two conspicuous though narrow wing-bars; sides of head and of neck dull buffy brown to grayish olive; throat smoke gray washed with dull buff, or entirely dull cream buff; jugulum similar but darker; sides and flanks grayish olive, washed with cream buff; middle of breast, with abdomen and crissum, pale dull cartridge buff or dull cream buff, but feathers of crissum with light grayish olive centers; lining of wing dull pale cartridge buff. *Adult female, winter*: Acquired by complete postnuptial molt. Similar to nuptial adult female, but upper surface darker, more rufescent, and, on account of broad brown edgings, colors more blended; lower surface more deeply buff. *Male, second nuptial*: Acquired by wear from second winter. Similar to nuptial adult male, but posterior lower parts very much duller, more brownish, buffy, or grayish, particularly on abdomen and flanks. *Male, second winter*: Acquired by complete postnuptial molt. Similar to adult male in winter, but wing-bars formed by tips of median and greater coverts much more broadly buffy or brown; feathers of upper surface even more broadly tipped with brown, thus covering more completely bright colors of feathers; feathers of lower surface even more broadly tipped with brown and buff, particularly on breast, sides, jugulum, and abdomen; posterior lower surface much duller, more grayish, brownish, or buffy (less blue or violet), differing thus from first nuptial male as does winter adult male from nuptial adult male. *Male, first nuptial*: Acquired by partial prenuptial molt. Similar to nuptial adult female but larger. *Male, first winter*: Acquired by partial postjuvenal molt. Similar to adult female in winter but larger, somewhat less rufescent both above and below. *Female, second winter*: Acquired by complete postnuptial molt. Like adult female in winter. *Female, first nuptial*: Acquired by partial prenuptial molt. Similar to nuptial adult female, but brown of upper surface more buffy (less grayish), with less blue on head, rump, upper tail-coverts, bend of wing, and tail; brown of wings lighter, more rufescent; lower surface averaging more buffy (less grayish). *Female first winter*: Acquired by partial postjuvenal molt. Similar to adult female in winter, but upper surface of a darker, more rufescent brown—light cinnamon brown to between cinnamon brown and saccardo umber; wing-bars decidedly darker; rump, upper tail-coverts, bend of wing, outer edges of primaries and of tail feathers with little or no tinge of bluish green; sides of head and lower surface darker, duller, and more brownish. *Juvenal*: Acquired by complete postnatal molt. Similar to first winter female, but upper surface duller, less rufescent —buffy brown or dull buffy brown to dull wood brown; greater and lesser wing-coverts narrowly tipped with dull vinaceous buff or avellaneous; sides of head paler and less rufescent, more buffy; lower surface paler, less buffy (more grayish); chin and throat dull pale buff, jugulum between wood brown and buffy brown or drab; sides and flanks similar; middle of breast dull pale buff, abdomen grayish or buffy white. *Natal*: Unknown.

MEASUREMENTS: *Adult male*: Wing, 64.5–69.1 (average, 67.1) mm.; tail, 53.1–57.4 (55.6); bill (exposed culmen), 8.9–10.4 (9.7); height of bill at base, 6.9–7.6 (7.1); tarsus, 17.5–19.0 (18.3); middle toe without claw, 11.2–12.4 (11.7). *Adult female*: Wing, 62.0–66.0 (64.3); tail, 49.5–55.1 (53.8); bill, 8.9–9.9 (9.4); height of bill, 7.1–7.6 (7.4); tarsus, 17.5–18.8 (18.3); middle toe, 11.4–11.9 (11.7).

RANGE: S.e. New Mexico (casually) and s.w. Texas, south to Guerrero and Oaxaca. Winters from s. Sonora and extreme s. Texas (rarely) to Guerrero and Oaxaca.

TEXAS: *Breeding*: Collected northwest to Jeff Davis, Presidio, and Brewster, east to Crockett, southeast to Webb (eggs), Starr, and Cameron cos.

NESTING: *Nest*: In more or less open country, on mesas, in canyons, and along watercourses; in thicket or thornbrush; in crotch of bush, tall weed, or low tree, only a few feet above ground; cup composed of grasses, various vegetable fibers, small twigs, cotton, and cast-off snake skins; lined with horsehair, grasses, and similar materials. *Eggs*: 3–4; ovate; dull or pale bluish white or cream white, unspotted; average size, 19.0 × 14.5 mm.

PAINTED BUNTING, *Linaria ciris* (Linnaeus)

SPECIES ACCOUNT   *See frontispiece, vol. 2*

Passerina ciris of A.O.U. check-list, 1957 (see Appendix A). *Male*: the most multicolored Texas bird—violet blue head; yellow-green back; red rump and under parts; retains bright plumage throughout the year. *Female*: only all-green U.S. finch. Length, 5½ in.; wingspan, 8¾; weight, ½ oz.

RANGE: S.e. New Mexico, e. Kansas, and c. Virginia (casually), south through Gulf states to n.e. Mexico and c. Florida. Winters chiefly in Mexico, Central America, s. Florida, and n. West Indies.

TEXAS: (See map.) *Breeding*: Mid-Apr. to late Aug. (eggs, Apr. 27 to Aug. 19) from near sea level to 4,700 ft. Common east of Pecos River with exceptions of northern Panhandle, wooded eastern portion, and extreme southern tip, where uncommon to scarce; fairly common, but local, in Trans-Pecos. *Migration*: Apr. to mid-May; late July to mid-Oct. (extremes: Mar. 6, May 22; June 30, Dec. 7). Very common to fairly common in spring through most parts. Fairly common in fall in all sections. *Winter*: Mid-Dec. to Feb. Rare to casual along coast and in Rio Grande delta; one specimen from Cooke Co. (see detailed account).

HAUNTS AND HABITS: The vivid Painted Bunting is

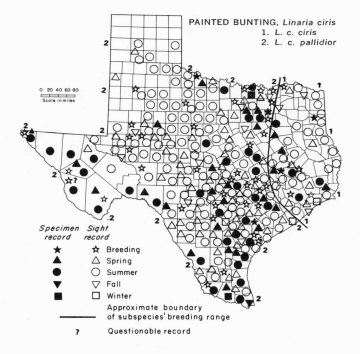

PAINTED BUNTING, *Linaria ciris*
1. *L. c. ciris*
2. *L. c. pallidior*

0 20 40 60 80
Scale in miles

Specimen record / Sight record
★ / ☆ Breeding
▲ / △ Spring
● / ○ Summer
▼ / ▽ Fall
■ / □ Winter

—— Approximate boundary of subspecies' breeding range

? Questionable record

widespread in Texas, inhabiting semiopen country with scattered bushes and trees, tall roadside or streamside brush, and patches of grasses (particularly *Setaria*), weeds, and wild flowers. Where trees are either too sparse—as in the northern Panhandle—or too dense—as in parts of the eastern quarter—the Painted, otherwise the most ubiquitous Texas bunting, becomes an uncommon to scarce item.

The Painted is usually very animated. It is quick and jerky on the wing. Males, pugnacious defenders of territory, are hardly to be described as shy. They usually proclaim boundaries from elevated (3 to 30 ft.), exposed perches atop a tree or bush or on a high wire. Nor is the female, though well camouflaged, particularly elusive. Amid bushes, to moderate height in trees, and at times on the ground, Painted Buntings glean seeds—mainly of bristlegrass, panicum, Johnsongrass, pigweed, and ragweed—as well as grasshoppers, beetles, caterpillars, other insects, spiders, and snails. Captive birds have been raised to healthy adulthood on a diet consisting almost wholly of small grasshoppers (Lovie M. Whitaker).

The sharp *chip* note is similar to that of the Indigo Bunting. Painted Bunting song, a bright simple warble, is heard in Texas mainly from mid-April to mid-July.

DETAILED ACCOUNT: TWO SUBSPECIES

EASTERN PAINTED BUNTING, *Linaria ciris ciris* (Linnaeus)

DESCRIPTION: *Adult male, nuptial plumage*: Acquired by wear from winter plumage. Pileum and hindneck dark diva blue to light bright navy blue; sometimes below the blue a narrow more or less interrupted collar of deep corinthian red or hydrangea red; back and scapulars yellowish green or calliste green to between greenish yellow and javel green; rump and upper tail-coverts dark dragon blood red or dragon blood red to old rose or deep vinaceous; tail dark mouse gray to hair brown, middle pair of feathers (except inner margins) and outer webs of remaining rectrices hays brown to between army brown and buffy brown; wings hair brown to dark hair brown, inner edges of primaries and secondaries, except at tips of primaries, drab, outer webs of tertials and margins of outer webs of primaries and secondaries brownish drab to cameo brown, inner webs of tertials with chaetura drab or chaetura black stripe along inner margins, this sometimes occupying nearly entire web and extending nearly to ends of feathers; lesser wing-coverts dull blue washed with vinaceous brown; median coverts vinaceous brown; greater wing-coverts cress green to spinach green; lores deep grayish olive; narrow eye-ring vermilion; sides of head, of neck, of throat, and of jugulum blue like pileum; chin, middle of throat, and remainder of lower surface scarlet to dark scarlet red, posteriorly becoming peach red; lining of wing light mouse gray to deep mouse gray, washed with dull red, and outer portion sometimes with dull green. Bill dark brown, but mandible plumbeous; iris dark brown or hazel; legs and feet dark plumbeous or dull brown; claws brown. *Adult male, winter*: Acquired by complete postnuptial molt. Similar to nuptial adult male, but upper surface rather duller, particularly pileum and hindneck, the feathers of which are narrowly tipped with buffy brown; lower surface averaging darker and duller. *Adult female, nuptial (yellow-green—normal—phase)*: Upper surface cerro green, but back sometimes yellowish oil green; rump yellowish oil green, parrot green, or peacock green; pileum sometimes duller and slightly more brownish; tail dark hair brown, middle pair of feathers (excepting shaft line) and outer webs of other rectrices (except perhaps outermost pair) green like upper tail-coverts;

wings hair brown, inner edges of primaries and secondaries except at tips, light drab, outer edges of primaries, secondaries, and tertials like upper surface but rather duller, outer edgings of all wing-coverts similar, lesser wing-coverts brighter and slightly more bluish; sides of neck like upper surface; sides of head, with jugulum, between olive yellow and light yellowish olive, lores rather duller; chin and throat olive ocher to greenish colonial buff; abdomen and middle of breast amber yellow to straw yellow; sides and flanks grayish olive; lining of wing grayish olive or mouse gray, washed or tinged on outermost margin with amber yellow or dull green; axillars pale dull amber yellow. *Adult female, nuptial (gray phase)*: Acquired by wear from winter. Similar to yellow-green phase, but green of upper surface much duller, more grayish; lower surface much paler, more grayish, with little or no buff and no tinge of green; throat and jugulum deep tilleul buff washed with light gray; sides and flanks darker, more brownish; abdomen buffy white; crissum very pale buff. *Adult female, winter*: Acquired by complete postnuptial molt. Similar to nuptial adult female, but upper surface darker and duller, somewhat more brownish; lower surface somewhat darker, duller, and more yellowish (less greenish). *Male, third winter*: Acquired by complete postnuptial molt. Like adult male in winter. *Male, second nuptial*: Acquired by wear from second winter. Similar to nuptial adult male, but red of lower surface rather lighter and more or less spotted with yellow or olive green; some of primaries, secondaries, and tertials with green edgings on outer webs. *Male, second winter*: Acquired by complete postnuptial molt. Similar to second nuptial male, but differs as does adult male in winter from nuptial adult male. *Male, first nuptial (yellow-green phase)*: Acquired by wear from first winter. Similar to yellow-green phase of nuptial adult female but larger; upper and lower surfaces averaging brighter and more yellowish, often with scattered blue or red feathers above and scattered red feathers, or reddish tinge, below; bend of wing more extensively blue. *Male, first nuptial (gray-green phase)*: Similar to yellow-green phase of first nuptial male, but green of upper surface much duller, less yellowish (more grayish or bluish); wings and tail more grayish (less yellowish) green; lower surface paler, much less yellowish (more grayish or whitish). Similar to gray phase of nuptial adult female, but more greenish above and more yellowish below. *Male, first winter*: Acquired by complete postjuvenal molt. Similar to first nuptial male but averaging darker, brighter, and somewhat more brownish above; darker, brighter, more deeply yellow below. *Female, first nuptial*: Acquired by wear from first winter. Very similar to nuptial adult female. *Female, first winter*: Acquired by complete postjuvenal molt. Similar to adult female in winter, but upper surface duller, rather more brownish; lower parts duller, more brownish or buffy. *Juvenal*: Acquired by complete postnatal molt. Upper surface light brownish olive, but pileum buffy brown, upper tail-coverts isabella color; tail dark hair brown; wings rather lighter, outer edges of tertials, and secondaries and primaries, except tips, light brownish olive; lesser, median, and greater wing-coverts tipped with dull pinkish buff; sides of head between drab and wood brown; lower surface cartridge buff or light cream buff, obscurely streaked or spotted on sides and jugulum with drab or light drab. *Natal*: Light drab. Maxilla dark umber brown; mandible umber brown.

MEASUREMENTS: *Adult male*: Wing, 67.6–72.9 (average, 69.8) mm.; tail, 54.1–58.2 (55.6); bill (exposed culmen), 8.9–10.9 (10.2); height of bill at base, 6.6–7.6 (7.1); tarsus, 18.0–20.1 (19.3); middle toe without claw, 11.9–13.5 (12.7). *Adult female*: Wing, 64.0–66.0 (65.3); tail, 51.6–55.6 (53.3); bill, 9.4–10.9 (10.2); height of bill, 6.9–7.6 (7.4); tarsus, 18.0–19.0 (18.8); middle toe, 11.9–13.5 (12.7).

RANGE: E. Kansas to c. Virginia (casually), south to s.e. Texas and c. Florida. Winters chiefly in Mexico, Central America, s. Florida, and n. West Indies.

TEXAS: *Breeding*: Altitudinal range, near sea level to 500 ft. Collected north to Harrison (eggs), south to Hardin, west to Harris and Grimes (eggs) cos. Fairly common. *Migration*: Collected north to Wilbarger, east to Jefferson, south to Hidalgo, west to Val Verde cos. Common.

NESTING: *Nest*: On uplands and bottoms, in open low woodlands, brush, thickets, edges of forests, or even in rose plants about ranch houses; on branch or in fork of tree, sapling, bush, or vine, 3–6 ft. above ground, sometimes more than one nest in same tree; compact cup of leaves, twigs, rootlets, fine grasses, strips of bark and weeds, and other plants; lined with fine grass and horsehair. *Eggs*: 3–5, usually 4; ovate to rounded ovate; dull white, pale bluish white, or grayish white; dotted and blotched with umber, reddish brown, brick red, purplish red, and with shell markings of lilac and lavender gray, particularly at larger end; average size, 20.1 × 15.2 mm.

TEXAS PAINTED BUNTING, *Linaria ciris pallidior* (Mearns)

DESCRIPTION: *Adult male and female, nuptial plumage*: Similar to *L. c. ciris*, but wing longer. Male with rump and upper tail-coverts lighter, of more purplish red; red of lower parts paler. Female lighter; green of upper surface more grayish (less yellowish); lower surface more buffy (less yellowish).

MEASUREMENTS: *Adult male*: Wing, 70.6–74.9 (average, 72.4) mm.; tail, 54.1–59.4 (57.2); bill (exposed culmen), 9.9–10.9 (10.7); height of bill at base, 7.1–8.1 (7.4); tarsus, 18.3–20.1 (19.3); middle toe without claw, 11.9–13.5 (12.7). *Adult female*: Wing, 65.5–69.6 (67.3); tail, 51.6–54.1 (53.3); bill, 9.9–10.9 (10.2); height of bill, 7.1–7.9 (7.4); tarsus, 18.8–19.6 (19.3); middle toe, 11.9–13.5 (12.7).

RANGE: S.e. New Mexico to s. Kansas, south to n. Tamaulipas. Winters from c. Sinaloa to extreme s. Texas (probably this race) through Mexico to w. Panama.

TEXAS: *Breeding*: Altitudinal range, near sea level to 4,700 ft. Collected north to Wilbarger (eggs), east to Cooke and Kaufman, south to Nueces and Cameron, west to Brewster and El Paso cos. Common to fairly common. *Migration*: Collected north to Wilbarger, east to Wharton, south to Cameron, west to El Paso cos. Common. *Winter*: One specimen: Cooke Co. (Feb. 7, 1884, G. H. Ragsdale). A winter specimen from Hidalgo Co. (exact date not available) probably belongs to this race.

NESTING: Similar to that of *L. c. ciris*, but average egg size, 18.0 × 14.0 mm.

[ORANGE-BREASTED BUNTING, *Passerina leclancherii* Lafresnaye

Leclancher's Bunting of some authors. Mexican Rainbow Bunting of cage bird fanciers. *Male*: bright yellow-green crown; turquoise blue on sides of head and upper parts (wings and tail tinged with dusky); bright yellow lores, eye-ring, and under parts, breast usually with orange suffusion. *Female*: grayish green on sides of head and above (obscure bluish tinge on wings and tail); yellow lores, eye-ring, and under parts, washed with olive on breast and sides. Length, 5 in.

RANGE: Tropical thornbrush and grass patches on dry Pacific slope of Mexico from Colima to Isthmus of Tehuantepec.

TEXAS: *Hypothetical*: One record: Hidalgo Co., brushy area 3 mi. south of Mission (male netted, Dec. 2, 1972, A. D. McGrew, F. O. Novy; shortly thereafter, turned over alive to Pauline James who caged it for observation). The chances of natural occurrence in the United States of this nonmigratory endemic of lowland southwestern Mexico are poor. In order to reach Texas, it would have to cross at least two mountain systems, both without suitable habitat—the Transverse Volcanic Cordillera and Sierra Madre Oriental. Most individuals would have to cross in addition the Sierra

Madre del Sur. It must be remembered that *Passerina leclancherii* is a popular cage bird and that it is frequently sold in markets throughout Mexico. The Texas individual showed no indication of having been caged; however, escape from captivity is most likely soon after capture before the bird's bright feathers have had time to fade and abrade.]

DICKCISSEL, *Spiza americana* (Gmelin)

Species Account

A sparrow-sized "meadowlark." *Male*: brown-streaked upper parts; rusty shoulder-patch; yellow breast and eye-stripe; black bib (indistinct or absent in winter); whitish belly. *Female*: paler, bibless version of male; streaked very lightly with dark brown on crown and under parts. Length, 6¼ in.; wingspan, 10; weight, 1 oz.

RANGE: E. Montana, east through Great Lakes region to Massachusetts, south to s. Texas, Mississippi Delta, and South Carolina; sporadic east of Mississippi River. Winters chiefly from c. Mexico (rarely) through Central America to n. South America.

TEXAS: (See map.) *Breeding*: Early Apr. to mid-Aug. (eggs, Apr. 16 to July 30) from near sea level to 3,800 ft. Common, though numbers variable, east of 100th meridian; usually rare in remainder of state with exception of northern Panhandle, where fairly common. *Migration*: Late Mar. to mid-May; late July to mid-Oct. (extremes: Mar. 10, June 13; July 10, Nov. 23). Abundant to fairly common in spring east of Pecos River; uncommon to casual west of Pecos River. Fairly common to scarce in fall through most parts. *Winter*: Dec. to Feb. Very scarce along coast; casual inland.

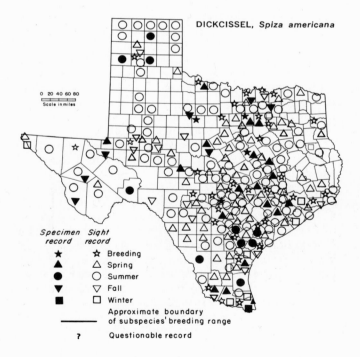

DICKCISSEL, *Spiza americana*

0 20 40 60 80
Scale in miles

Specimen record / Sight record

★ / ☆ Breeding
▲ / △ Spring
● / ○ Summer
▼ / ▽ Fall
■ / □ Winter

——— Approximate boundary of subspecies' breeding range

? Questionable record

HAUNTS AND HABITS: Normally a migrating Dickcissel's first sight of Texas for the year comes in April moonlight or starlight. As it flies inland, Gulf of Mexico breakers give way to sand, sea-oats, saltgrass, and mesquite. By sunrise or shortly thereafter, unless beach lights have distracted it overmuch, *Spiza americana* has usually alighted in habitat similar to that of its summer home. The day after a good Dickcissel flight, oat fields, grass patches, meadows, weeds, bush tops, wires, and roadsides resound as thousands of "dear little chaps" (the name usually bestowed by visiting English folk) recite with body-shaking vigor: *dick, dick, ciss-ciss-ciss!*

In wet years (25 inches of rain or more), many Dickcissels remain in Texas to nest where grasses and forbs, especially Johnson grass, sorghums, and sunflowers, grow rank between widely scattered bushes. Texas breeders usually lay just as many eggs per nest as do females in the Dakotas (fide E. B. Kincaid, Jr.), thus violating the biological rule that says clutch size averages larger in colder climates.

As July slides into August, the tireless chanter of April, May, and June falls largely silent. But the Dickcissel retains the "electric buzz" note—*bzrrt*—by which nocturnal migrants keep in touch. The return to Central and South America is mostly complete by December. Very occasionally though, an Audubon Christmas counter near the Gulf will stumble upon a few Dickcissels in coastal brush or salt marsh; he is, or should be, properly astounded.

During the breeding season and on its spring and fall passage, the Dickcissel sustains itself and its offspring primarily on insects—chiefly grasshoppers, katydids, crickets, locusts, beetles, and ants; also a few spiders. Some seeds of bristlegrass, oats, panicum, Johnson grass, wheat, and corn are also taken. In winter, seeds of weeds and grasses predominate in its diet.

Detailed Account: No Subspecies

DESCRIPTION: *Adult male, nuptial plumage (gray-headed gray phase)*: Acquired by partial prenuptial molt. Pileum and hindneck mouse gray, the former with very narrow shaft lines of darker gray; remainder of upper surface drab, back and scapulars broadly streaked with fuscous black, scapulars tinged with sayal brown, rump narrowly and inconspicuously streaked or spotted with hair brown, and feathers of rump and upper tail-coverts pale tipped; tail olive brown, inner margins of feathers narrowly paler, even whitish, particularly near tips; wing-quills light fuscous, tertials darker, inner margins of primaries and secondaries, except at tips, cartridge buff, outer margins of primaries, secondaries, and tertials drab to buffy drab; inner lesser wing-coverts dull tawny; remainder of lesser coverts, together with median and greater coverts, fuscous, and all but greater coverts tipped with dull light tawny, greater coverts edged on outer webs with drab or buffy drab; lores light drab; superciliary stripe cream color, anteriorly tinged with dull pale yellow; auriculars mouse gray; rather darker narrow postocular streak; malar stripe dull white or grayish white, slightly washed with dull yellow; sides of neck mouse gray; sides of throat dull white; chin and upper throat dull white or yellowish white; triangular patch ("bib") extending from upper throat to middle of jugulum black to fuscous black; rest of jugulum and middle of breast gamboge yellow to empire yellow, this ending posteriorly in a point that extends sometimes to middle of abdomen; sides of breast mouse gray; sides of body and flanks mouse gray, more or less washed with sayal brown; posterior lower parts dull white, slightly tinged with buff or drab; lining of wing gamboge yellow to empire yellow, becoming light drab or dull white on posterior and inner portions. Bill pearl blue, but culmen and tip slate black; iris dark brown; legs and feet drab, brownish slate, or brownish blue; claws brown. *Adult male, nuptial (yellow-headed gray phase)*: Similar to gray-headed gray phase, but forehead and crown yellowish citrine; superciliary stripe anteriorly gamboge yellow, middle part of malar stripe also gamboge yellow. *Adult male, nuptial (gray-headed brown phase)*: Similar to gray-headed gray phase, but upper surface, except pileum and hindneck, much more brownish, back rather dull ochraceous tawny. *Adult male, nuptial (yellow-headed brown—normal—phase)*: Similar to gray-headed brown phase, but forehead and crown buffy citrine to yellowish citrine; superciliary stripe and middle of malar stripe gamboge yellow. *Adult male, winter*: Acquired by complete postnuptial molt. Similar to nuptial adult male, but upper surface darker, duller, more rufescent, and more uniform, pileum and hindneck sometimes almost as brown as back due to overlying brown tips of feathers, black streaks on back not so sharply defined owing to their broad brown edgings; tawny bend of wing darker, feathers more or less narrowly tipped with sayal brown; sides of head more brownish (less grayish), its yellow duller, more buffy; black of throat obscured by buffy white or sayal brown tips of feathers; yellow of throat darker and usually of more orange tint, more or less obscured by light buffy brown tips of feathers; sides and flanks more buffy, between avellaneous and cinnamon buff. *Adult female, nuptial (brown—normal—phase)*: Acquired by partial prenuptial molt. Similar to nuptial adult male, gray-headed brown phase, but upper surface duller and somewhat darker and more uniform, rather grayish light buffy brown, pileum with narrow olive brown streaks or central spots; back and scapulars dull cinnamon buff, broadly streaked with olive brown or dark olive brown; bend of wing cinnamon to dull cinnamon rufous, paler, less extensive, and more broken by fuscous and buffy centers of many feathers (more so than in nuptial adult male); superciliary stripe of duller yellow, posteriorly dull pale buff; sides of head light buffy brown or between light buffy brown and drab; narrow black or fuscous black submalar streak, this sometimes consisting of a chain of spots and connecting with brown spot on throat or with circlet of streaks across throat and jugulum; lower surface dull cartridge buff, but flanks dull cinnamon buff, jugulum, breast, sides, and flanks with narrow fuscous streaks, these sometimes absent, except on sides and flanks; yellow of jugulum and breast less extensive—honey yellow, wax yellow, or primuline yellow; middle of throat with more or less triangular or crescentic spot of light cinnamon brown to mummy brown. *Adult female, nuptial (gray phase)*: Similar to brown phase of nuptial adult female, but much more grayish (less buffy or brownish) on upper surface. Similar to gray-headed gray phase of nuptial adult male, but more brownish above, tawny on lesser wing-coverts paler, superciliary stripe deeper yellow. *Adult female, winter*: Acquired by complete postnuptial molt. Similar to corresponding phase of nuptial adult female, but upper surface averaging darker, more brownish, colors more blended due to brownish tips of feathers on pileum and on back, which latter obscure more or less the broad black streaks of these parts; light edgings of wings broader, tawny bend of wing more obscured by brown tips of feathers; lower parts duller, more brownish or buffy; yellow of jugulum and breast obscured by buff; breast and jugulum more densely streaked; superciliary stripe more buffy or of duller yellow. *Male, first nuptial*: Acquired by partial prenuptial molt. Very much like nuptial adult male. *Male, first winter*: Acquired by partial postjuvenal molt, which does not involve wing-quills or tail. Similar to adult male in winter, but upper parts duller, averaging less rufescent; head duller, more brownish (less grayish or yellowish); superciliary stripe duller, more brownish or buffy; tawny patch on bend of wing with conspicuous buffy or ochraceous edgings; lower surface duller, more brownish or buffy; yellow of jugulum less extensive, more obscured and buffy; throat without black patch, but with narrow dull black submalar streak connecting with circlet of dull black streaks across throat as in adult female; jugulum, sides, and flanks more or less streaked with fuscous or fuscous black. Much like adult female in winter but larger; bend of wing more extensively chestnut and this color darker; jugulum with less yellow and more heavily streaked; sides and flanks more grayish (less rufescent). Maxilla brown; mandible light plumbeous; iris brown; legs and feet light brown. *Female, first nuptial*: Acquired by partial prenuptial molt. Similar to nuptial adult female, but bend of wing with little or no rufous; throat without brown patch. *Female, first winter*: Acquired by partial postjuvenal molt, which does not involve wing-quills or tail. Similar to adult female in winter, but averaging darker and duller above; superciliary stripe dull buff, without yellow; bend of wing with little or no rufous; lower surface averaging darker, duller, more brownish, and with less yellow on breast and jugulum. Similar to first winter male but smaller; tawny wing-patch smaller, paler, and much more broken by fuscous and buffy centers of many of feathers; superciliary stripe paler, more buffy, not distinctly yellow—dull cinnamon buff or pinkish buff; jugulum and breast less extensively yellow. Bill dull brown, but mandible lighter; iris dark brown; legs and feet light brown. *Juvenal*: Acquired by complete postnatal molt. (Not seen, description adapted from Jonathan Dwight, Jr., 1900, *Ann. New York Acad. Sci.*, vol. 13, no. 1.) Upper surface clay color; sides of crown with obscure blackish stripes; back with broad, dull black stripes; tail and wings dull black, tail feathers edged with dull white, secondaries edged externally with cinnamon, tertials and wing-coverts with clay color, and median and greater coverts tipped with same, forming two wing-bars; lores, together with rictal and submalar stripe, fuscous; superciliary stripe ochraceous buff; auriculars sepia; lower surface cream buff, but breast, sides, and crissum clay color. Bill and feet dull brown. *Natal*: Pure white. Bill and feet pale pinkish buff.

MEASUREMENTS: *Adult male*: Wing, 79.0–85.9 (average, 82.6) mm.; tail, 56.4–62.5 (60.2); bill (exposed culmen), 14.7–15.5 (15.2); height of bill at base, 10.2–11.2 (10.7); tarsus, 22.9–24.1 (23.4); middle toe without claw, 16.8–18.0 (17.5). *Adult female*: Wing, 74.7–77.5 (75.7); tail, 50.0–55.6 (52.6); bill, 12.7–14.2 (13.5); height of bill, 9.7–10.7 (10.2); tarsus, 21.9–22.9 (22.4); middle toe, 16.3–17.3 (16.8).

TEXAS: *Breeding*: Collected northwest to Oldham and Hutchinson, east to Cooke, south to Cameron, west to Menard and Shackelford (eggs) cos. *Migration*: Collected north to Wilbarger, east to Ft. Bend, south to Cameron, west to Presidio, Jeff Davis, and Winkler cos. *Winter*: One specimen: Cameron Co., Brownsville (Jan., 1892, F. B. Armstrong).

NESTING: *Nest*: In open country of uplands and bottoms, in clover, grass, or other fields, meadows, and areas of tall grass along streams, on coastal prairies, dry or wet; on ground or on thistle or other weed, tall grass, bush, or tree, up to 20 ft. above ground; a bulky, though compact cup; composed of grasses, roots, leaves, husks of corn, weed stalks, and mosses; lined with fine grass, rootlets, thin stems of weeds, and horsehair. *Eggs*: 3–6, usually 4–5; rounded ovate to nearly elliptical oval; bluish white, pale blue, or bright greenish blue, unmarked; average size, 20.1 × 15.2 mm.

EVENING GROSBEAK, *Hesperiphona vespertina* (Cooper)

SPECIES ACCOUNT

A stocky, short-tailed grosbeak with huge conical bill, pale yellowish green in color. *Male*: yellow with brownish forequarters; yellow forehead and eye-stripe; bold white patch on black wing; all-black tail. *Female*: gray with touches of yellow; black and white wings and tail. Length, 7¾ in.; wingspan, 13¼; weight, 2½ oz.

RANGE: N. British Columbia to New Brunswick, south through w. United States to c. Mexican highlands; in the e. United States, south to n.e. Minnesota, n. Michigan, and n. New York. Northern races winter in vicinity of breeding range, south irregularly to s. California, Texas, and South Carolina.

TEXAS: (See map.) *Winter*: Late Oct. to late Apr. (extremes: Oct. 9, May 13). Scarce and erratic (although may appear in flocks of 50 or more during incursions) west of 100th meridian; very irregular in eastern parts. Not recorded south of 28th parallel. An unprecedented irruption occurred in the winter of 1968–69 with flocks appearing as far south as San Antonio (15 birds, late Jan., C. R. Bender), Austin (150 plus, Mar., Mary H. Moon, et al.), and Cove, Chambers Co. (14, Mar. 7, 18, A. K. McKay); a similar invasion occurred during the winter of 1972–73 when birds were reported as far south as San Antonio and Brazoria Co.

HAUNTS AND HABITS: In its northern and montane summer homes, the Evening Grosbeak nests mostly in conifers. Twenty to sixty feet above the ground, it places its shallow cup of twigs and bark on a branch in a terminal cluster of needles. During its winter irruptions into Texas, *H. vespertina* is not so restricted; in fact, it perches in any species of tree—provided the branches are located near a feeder stocked with sunflower seeds!

Flight of this robust bird is strong and undulating (though the dips are shallow). On the wing, members of a flock often sound shrill *cleer* notes. Evening Grosbeaks are bold birds, especially in winter. When forag-

ing, they hop energetically on the ground, turning over leaves and debris in search of food. In spring, when eating buds in trees and shrubs (chiefly elm, walnut, poplar, maple, hackberry, ash, and various conifers), Evening Grosbeaks work agilely to the ends of branches. In addition to sunflower seeds, they eat seeds of hemp, maple, pine, boxelder, ragweed, and burdock; also fruits of hackberry, juniper, mistletoe, poison-ivy, and sumac. Beetles, caterpillars, ants, bees, wasps, other insects, and a few spiders are eaten, primarily in summer. Usually these grosbeaks go to their night roosts an hour or so before sunset and on dark winter days they often retire in the middle of the afternoon.

A shrill loud *tsee-ip* or *cleer* and a lower pitched trill (at times alternating with the former) are Evening Grosbeak call notes. The song is an uneven warble, which resembles the Purple Finch's but is inferior. It is seldom heard in Texas.

DETAILED ACCOUNT: TWO SUBSPECIES

NOTE: Since the death of Dr. Oberholser, at least nine specimens of the eastern race, *Hesperiphona vespertina vespertina*, have been collected in the state (see L. R. Wolfe, 1970, *Auk* 87: 378; W. M. Pulich, 1971, *Condor* 73: 111). A detailed description of this race written by Oberholser is apparently not available.

WESTERN EVENING GROSBEAK, *Hesperiphona vespertina montana* Ridgway

Not the *H. v. montana* of A.O.U. check-list, 1957 (see Appendix A).

DESCRIPTION: *Adult male, nuptial plumage*: Acquired by wear from winter plumage. Narrow line across forehead next to bill black; remainder of forehead and superciliary stripe gamboge yellow; crown and occiput dull black; hindneck brownish olive or sepia to between mummy brown and prout brown; scapulars analine yellow, but outer edges gamboge yellow, inner portion shading into color of back; back orange citrine to dresden brown or dark dresden brown, shading posteriorly into light orange citrine or gamboge yellow on shorter upper tail-coverts; longer upper tail-coverts and tail black, inner edges of rectrices slightly brownish; wings, including superior coverts, black, inner margins of primaries and outer secondaries fuscous black, secondaries white for more than half their terminal portion, except on outermost; outer webs of inner secondaries also white, their inner webs, with terminal portion of tertials and of inner greater coverts, light drab or white washed with light drab; lores and narrow eye-ring dull black, fuscous black, or brownish black, remainder of sides of head, with chin and throat, like hindneck, chin and throat sometimes rather paler; jugulum and breast orange citrine to dark orange citrine; sides, flanks, and abdomen somewhat more yellowish; crissum lemon chrome to gamboge yellow; axillars and posterior inner under wing-coverts citrine yellow to amber yellow; remainder of wing-lining dull black or fuscous black, feathers edged with dull pale yellow. Bill dull green, dull pale yellowish green, or greenish yellow, but base of mandible flesh color; iris dark brown or black; legs light brown to dull flesh color; feet similar but somewhat darker; claws dark brown. *Adult male, winter*: Acquired by complete postnuptial molt. Similar to nuptial adult male, but hindneck, back, scapulars, tertials, and rump darker, more sooty (less yellowish), tertials also more deeply drab; lower surface darker, duller, less yellowish, particularly on anterior portion. *Adult female, nuptial*: Acquired by wear from winter. Pileum dark hair brown; broad collar on hindneck sulphine yellow, sometimes mixed with light brown of pileum; back between hair brown and drab, almost uniform but sometimes more or less tinged

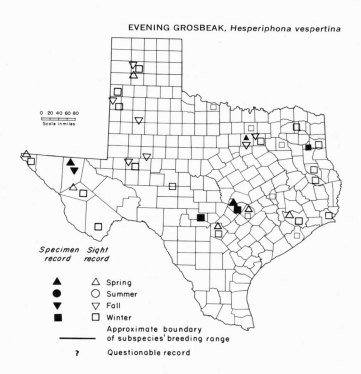

EVENING GROSBEAK, *Hesperiphona vespertina*

0 20 40 60 80
Scale in miles

Specimen record *Sight record*

▲ △ Spring
● ○ Summer
▼ ▽ Fall
■ ☐ Winter

Approximate boundary of subspecies' breeding range

? Questionable record

Plate 32 (top to bottom): male American Goldfinch, *Spinus tristis*; male Lawrence's Goldfinch, *Spinus lawrencei*; male Lesser Goldfinch, *Spinus psaltria* tree in background: boxelder (*Acer negundo*)

Evening Grosbeak, *Hesperiphona vespertina*

with yellow of hindneck, this color when present usually on subterminal portion of feathers and, therefore, much concealed; rump and shorter upper tail-coverts dull deep olive buff; longer upper tail-coverts dull black or brownish black, broadly tipped with oblong or more or less triangular spots of white or buffy white; tail brownish black, inner edges of feathers fuscous black, all rectrices with large squarish terminal white spots on inner webs, these largest on outermost pair and diminishing sometimes almost to vanishing point on middle pair; primaries and secondaries fuscous black, outer webs, except on tips of primaries, dull black, inner margins of inner webs of primaries, except at tips, fuscous, inner webs of secondaries broadly white on inner margins, diminishing in extent outwardly, outer webs of secondaries with broad white tip on innermost, this diminishing to relatively small spot on outermost secondaries, inner secondaries also more or less white near base of outer web, six inner primaries with large white spot on both webs at base, this showing as conspicuous white spot even in closed wing; tertials fuscous, terminal half of outer webs and broad tip on both webs between light drab and mouse gray, sometimes becoming dull white at tips of longest feathers; sides of head light hair brown; sides of neck sulphine yellow, sometimes washed with dull hair brown; narrow submalar stripe fuscous black or fuscous; chin and middle of throat buffy white or dull pale buff; jugulum rather buffy light drab, often washed or tinged with sulphine yellow, this largely concealed; sides and flanks of somewhat paler buffy light drab; breast and abdomen similar, but middle of abdomen lighter; crissum buffy white; lining of wing strontian yellow, outer under wing-coverts fuscous black tipped with yellow. Bill light yellowish green; iris dark brown or hazel; legs and feet light yellowish brown; claws dark brown. *Adult female, winter*: Acquired by complete postnuptial molt. Similar to nuptial adult female, but upper tail-coverts and lower surface usually more buffy and somewhat darker. *Male, second winter*: Acquired by complete postnuptial molt. Like adult male in winter. *Male, first nuptial*: Acquired by wear from first winter. Similar to nuptial adult male, but primaries, secondaries, and primary coverts duller, more brownish, inner margins of inner webs of tertials fuscous, ends of tertials somewhat spotted with fuscous; tips of rectrices on inner webs grayish white or brownish white, these whitish areas, however, not so large as in nuptial adult female and sometimes practically absent. *Male, first winter*: Acquired by partial postjuvenal molt, which does not involve wing-quills, primary coverts, or tail. Similar to adult male in winter, but tail tipped on inner webs of rectrices with grayish or brownish white, this usually very narrow or absent on middle feathers; primaries, secondaries, and primary coverts more brownish; primaries and secondaries with narrow tips of brownish white; inner webs of tertials fuscous on inner margins, basally this occupying whole inner web. Similar to first nuptial male, but upper surface darker, more sooty (less yellowish); lower parts, particularly chin, throat, and jugulum, duller, darker, more greenish (less yellowish). *Female, first nuptial*: Acquired by wear from first winter. Similar to nuptial adult female, but wings and tail usually more brownish. *Female, first winter*: Acquired by partial postjuvenal molt, which does not affect wing-quills, tail, or primary wing-coverts. Similar to adult female in winter, but upper surface more brownish or rufescent (less grayish); lower parts more deeply and richly buff. Bill dull straw yellow, but olive buff toward tip of maxilla, and washed with pinkish buff at base of culmen and on rami of mandible; iris vandyke brown; legs dark ecru drab; toes chocolate; claws seal brown. *Male, juvenal*: Acquired by complete postnatal molt. Much duller, paler, and more uniform than adult male in winter; forehead dull ochraceous tawny; remainder of pileum cinnamon brown; back and scapulars between medal bronze and dresden brown; nape tinged with ochraceous or saffron yellow; shorter upper tail-coverts and rump light isabella color; longest upper tail-coverts fuscous black or dull black, mostly tipped with isabella color; tail fuscous black, middle feathers brownish black, most of feathers with brownish white or grayish white tip on inner web, this often absent on middle feathers; wings brownish black or fuscous black, inner secondaries ter-

minally white on one or both webs, this decreasing on outer feathers, inner edges of primaries at base drab; tertials drab to light drab, inner webs at base and margins of inner webs at tip fuscous to dark fuscous; lesser wing-coverts rather more brownish than wing-quills and obscurely tipped with lighter brown; median coverts with small terminal spots of dull buff; inner greater coverts on outer webs and partly at tips barium yellow; outer webs of outer scapulars of same yellow; lores fuscous; auriculars dresden brown; malar region, throat, and sides of neck saffron yellow, the last somewhat brownish; narrow fuscous black submalar streak; jugulum between ochraceous tawny and buckthorn brown; sides and flanks similar but lighter, shading into pale buff on center of abdomen; crissum buffy white or very pale buff; lining of wing wax yellow to strontian yellow, outer portion fuscous black tipped with yellow. Bill greenish olive, but yellowish green at base; iris dark brown; legs, feet, and claws brown. *Female, juvenal*: Acquired by complete postnatal molt. Similar to juvenal male but upper parts duller, of more grayish (less yellowish) brown; forehead not distinctly paler; tertials and inner secondaries without extensive white areas, except sometimes on inner webs of secondaries; tail feathers with much larger white spots; sides of head more grayish (less saffron tinged or rufescent); lower parts duller, decidedly less yellowish (more grayish or buffy).

MEASUREMENTS: *Adult male*: Wing, 108.0–114.0 (average, 109.7) mm.; tail, 59.9–66.0 (63.2); bill (exposed culmen), 18.0–20.3 (19.3); tarsus, 20.3–22.6 (21.1); middle toe without claw, 17.0–19.6 (17.8). *Adult female*: Wing, 103.6–110.0 (107.2); tail, 58.9–62.5 (60.5); bill, 18.0–19.6 (18.8); tarsus, 20.1–23.1 (21.9); middle toe, 16.0–19.0 (17.8).

RANGE: C. Idaho and n. Wyoming, south to c. Arizona and n. New Mexico. Winters through much of breeding range to s. New Mexico and Texas.

TEXAS: *Winter*: Two specimens: Culberson Co., Guadalupe Mts. (Oct. 9, 1938, and Apr. 28, 1939, T. D. Burleigh).

PURPLE FINCH, *Erythrina purpurea* (Gmelin)

SPECIES ACCOUNT

Carpodacus purpureus of A.O.U. check-list, 1957 (see Appendix A). A chunky finch with large conical bill; well-notched tail. *Male*: purplish red head and rump; rosy breast; brown-striped brownish red back; unstreaked whitish belly. *Female*: brown above; brown-streaked white below; broad white postocular stripe; whitish upper border on brown malar streak. Length, 6¼ in.; wingspan, 10¼; weight, 1 oz.

RANGE: N. British Columbia to Newfoundland, south through Pacific states to n.w. Baja California, and south through n.e. United States to Great Lakes region and West Virginia. Winters from s.w. British Columbia to n. Baja California and s. Arizona; also through e. United States with exception of extreme s. Texas and s. Florida.

TEXAS: (See map.) *Winter*: Early Nov. to early Apr. (extremes: Oct. 10, May 6). Common (some years) to scarce in eastern half with exception of Rio Grande delta, where absent; scarce in northern Panhandle and on western Edwards Plateau; one Trans-Pecos specimen (see detailed account).

HAUNTS AND HABITS: On its northern breeding grounds, the Purple Finch seeks clearings in mainly coniferous forests—openings caused by a swamp, stream, pond, or, nowadays, more than likely by man. High or low on a branch of a tree—usually a conifer—

or sometimes in a deciduous shrub, it saddles its shallow nest of weeds, bark, and rootlets. While in Texas, *E. purpurea* is found in eastern woodlands and streamside thickets. It is not unusual, though irregular, where tall trees grow in canyons along the eastern edge of the Edwards Plateau. However, it consistently avoids plains areas where trees are either scattered or scarce. In winter, small parties, often roving with American Goldfinches and Pine Siskins, visit well-provisioned feeding trays or forage in less inhabited areas.

This finch hops about on the ground as it hunts for food. A bird frequently stops to flick away fallen leaves with its bill. It also works in trees and bushes where it expertly gleans even terminal foliage. Season largely determines the Purple's diet. In the cold season, it eats mainly seeds of cedar elm (fall) and American elm (late winter), ragweed, sweetgum, sycamore, sunflower, hemp, and pine; with spring, it adds buds of elm, peach, pear, maple, and sycamore. Many wild fruits of elderberry, redcedar, dogwood, grape, poison-ivy, and others are taken, especially in late spring and summer. Insects (plant lice, beetles, caterpillars) are apparently eaten only sparingly, at least in its U.S. haunts.

A short metallic *krik* or *kick*, often sounded in flight, is the Purple's call note; it is distinct from that of the House Finch. The rich liquid song does resemble the House Finch's, but is lower pitched, less sustained, and less obviously phrased. It can be heard in Texas mostly in February and March.

DETAILED ACCOUNT: ONE SUBSPECIES

EASTERN PURPLE FINCH, *Erythrina purpurea purpurea* (Gmelin)

DESCRIPTION: *Adult male, nuptial plumage (dark phase)*: Ac-

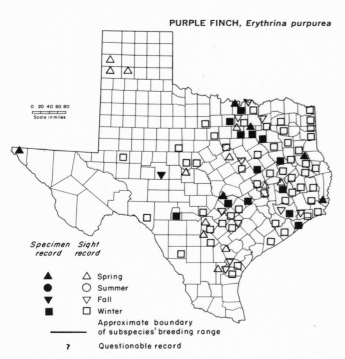

PURPLE FINCH, *Erythrina purpurea*

0 20 40 60 80
Scale in miles

Specimen   Sight
record   record

▲ △ Spring
● ○ Summer
▼ ▽ Fall
■ □ Winter

Approximate boundary
of subspecies' breeding range

?   Questionable record

quired by wear from winter plumage. Darker, more reddish color of adult male in worn nuptial is caused by wearing away of barbules on winter feathers. Pileum carmine to pomegranate purple; hindneck similar but somewhat duller; remainder of upper surface carmine or pompeian red to dragon blood red, everywhere rather obscurely but broadly streaked with clove brown to prout brown; lower rump and upper tail-coverts dull old rose to jasper red; tail dark hair brown or light fuscous, outer webs of feathers narrowly edged with kaiser brown to hazel; wings dark hair brown to light fuscous, inner margins of primaries and secondaries, except at tips, paler, on inner feathers dull drab, outer webs of wing-quills, except at tips of primaries, narrowly margined with brown, between snuff brown and cinnamon brown; wing-coverts edged on outer webs with red of upper surface, greater and median wing-coverts tipped with light vinaceous rufous to dull flesh color, forming two wing-bars; lores dull light buff; remainder of sides of head, with chin, throat, jugulum, breast, and sides of body, eugenia red to rose red, feathers with obscure hair brown crescentic subterminal bars that impart peculiar shadowy scalelike appearance to plumage; middle of abdomen dull white or buffy white; crissum similar but more or less washed with red of under surface; flanks washed with dull buff and red of anterior lower surface, these, with sides of body, more or less streaked with fuscous or olive brown; lining of wing dull pinkish buff to pinkish buff, outer posterior part more or less mottled or spotted with hair brown or fuscous. Bill reddish broccoli brown or dark brown, but mandible paler, somewhat plumbeous; corner of mouth yellow; iris dark brown; legs and feet seal brown. *Adult male, nuptial (light phase)*: Similar to dark phase but much lighter, more pinkish, particularly on lower surface; rump jasper pink, anterior lower parts alizarine pink. *Adult male, winter*: Acquired by complete postnuptial molt. Similar to nuptial male, but red of upper and lower parts very much more pinkish, pileum acajou red, jugulum much lighter; feathers of hindneck and back with conspicuous tips of mouse gray to buffy brown; feathers of anterior lower parts as well as sides of body tipped with pale buff or buffy white, this increasing dullness of reddish pink areas; light edgings of tertials broader. Bill slate color, but basal half of mandible drab gray, a spot at base of maxilla ocher yellow; corner of mouth orange to orange-yellow; iris prout brown; legs, feet, and claws seal brown. *Adult female, nuptial (olive phase)*: Acquired by wear from winter. Upper surface grayish rather dark isabella color, more grayish on pileum, upper tail-coverts sometimes inclining toward sulphine yellow, entire upper surface broadly streaked with brownish olive, on back and pileum also rather obscurely with dull white; wings and tail rather dark hair brown, but outer webs of tail feathers with very narrow olivaceous edging, inner margins of primaries and secondaries, except at tips, buffy drab, tertials and inner secondaries edged on outer webs with dull light brown, lesser wing-coverts tipped with rather rufescent brownish olive; greater and median coverts margined on outer webs with same and tipped with buffy or brownish white, forming two rather well defined wing-bars; superciliary stripe beginning at about middle of eye and extending backward to nape, with lores and cheeks, dull buffy white, sometimes slightly mixed with brownish olive, cheeks also finely streaked; auriculars of darker dull brownish olive; sides of neck dull white, much streaked with brownish olive; lower surface dull white or buffy white, broadly streaked on sides of throat, on jugulum, breast, sides, and flanks with rather light brownish olive; lining of wing pale buff or buffy white, under wing-coverts mottled with hair brown. Bill blackish slate, but mandible slate gray; iris dark brown; legs and feet mouse gray or brown. *Adult female, nuptial (gray phase)*: Acquired by wear from winter. Similar to olive phase but very much more grayish (less olivaceous), upper surface light grayish olive, streaked with dark hair brown; below dull white or buffy white, streaks hair brown. *Adult female, winter*: Acquired by complete postnuptial molt. Similar to nuptial adult female, but colors of upper surface somewhat more blended; streaks on lower surface duller and less sharply defined. *Male, second nuptial*: Acquired by wear from second winter. Similar to nuptial adult male, but upper surface lighter, duller, and decidedly more brownish (less reddish). *Male, second winter*: Acquired by complete postnuptial molt. Similar to adult male in winter, but upper surface lighter, much more brownish, hindneck, back, and scapulars much less extensively red; red of lower surface duller, with more wash of brown or buff from edgings of feathers. *Male, first nuptial*: Acquired by wear from first winter. Practically identical in color with nuptial adult female, but size larger. Bill gray or dull brown above, but paler below; legs and feet light brown. *Male, first winter*: Acquired by complete postjuvenal molt. Similar to nuptial adult female but larger; upper surface more brownish or buffy; light wingbars duller and darker—clay color, dull cinnamon buff, or between ochraceous tawny and yellow ocher or buckthorn brown, or between dresden brown and ochraceous tawny; lower surface more buffy or ochraceous. Bill slate gray or slate black, mandible dull slate gray; iris dark brown; legs and feet blackish brown, drab, or dark drab gray. *Female, second winter*: Acquired by complete postnuptial molt. Like adult female in winter. *Female, first nuptial*: Acquired by wear from first winter. Like first nuptial male but averaging smaller. *Female, first winter*: Acquired by complete postjuvenal molt. Like first winter male but smaller. *Juvenal*: Acquired by complete postnatal molt. Similar to first winter male and female, but upper surface duller, much less conspicuously streaked with olive brown or light olive brown, markings tending more to irregular spots than streaks, except on back; sides of head and of neck similar; lower surface dull white or buffy white, broadly streaked or spotted, but less sharply, with hair brown or light olive brown. Bill, legs, and feet sepia. *Natal*: Slate gray. Bill, legs, and feet pinkish buff.

MEASUREMENTS: *Adult male*: Wing, 79.0–86.4 (average, 83.1) mm.; tail, 54.8–61.0 (58.7); bill (exposed culmen), 10.2–11.7 (11.2); height of bill at base, 8.6–9.4 (8.9); tarsus, 16.0–18.8 (17.8); middle toe without claw, 11.9–13.2 (12.7). *Adult female*: Wing, 76.5–84.6 (80.5); tail, 50.8–57.9 (54.6); bill, 10.2–11.4 (10.7); height of bill, 8.6–9.4 (8.9); tarsus, 17.0–18.8 (18.0); middle toe, 11.9–13.5 (12.7).

RANGE: Great Lakes region from n. North Dakota to c. Quebec, south to s.e. Iowa (casually) and West Virginia. Winters mainly through e. United States (chiefly east of 100th meridian) with exception of extreme s. Texas and s. Florida.

TEXAS: *Winter*: Collected north to Cooke, east to Nacogdoches (Mar. 9) and Orange (Apr. 15), south to Galveston, west to Real and Tom Green (Oct. 20) cos. One Trans-Pecos specimen: El Paso Co., El Paso (Mar. 31, 1888, G. Armstrong).

CASSIN'S FINCH, *Erythrina cassinii* (Baird)

SPECIES ACCOUNT

Carpodacus cassinii of A.O.U. check-list, 1957 (see Appendix A). Also known as Cassin's Purple Finch. A pale version of the Purple Finch, with an even larger conical bill. *Male*: bright red cap contrasting sharply with brown-striped grayish hindneck and back; pale rose wash on breast and rump; virtually unstreaked whitish sides and belly. *Female*: liberally brown-streaked; buffy white postocular stripe; under parts whiter and breast-streaks sharper (less broad) than in female of Purple or House finch. Length, 6½ in.; wingspan, 11.

RANGE: S. interior British Columbia to s.e. Montana, south through higher mountains of w. United States to n. Baja California, s. Nevada, n. Arizona, and n. New Mexico. Winters at lower elevations in vicinity of breeding range, south in highlands to Zacatecas, San Luis Potosí and Veracruz.

TEXAS: (See map.) *Winter*: Fairly common in El Paso region; scarce to rare and irregular in remainder of western third; casual east to Bosque Co. (collected, see detailed account) and Travis Co., Mansfield Dam (2 males seen, Jan. 27, 1963, G. F. Oatman, Jr., J. L. Rowlett, Rose Ann Rowlett). Recorded every month but May and Sept. in Chisos Mts., Big Bend Nat. Park (fide R. H. Wauer).

HAUNTS AND HABITS: The Cassin's Finch is a bird of western mountains, principally between 5,000 and 10,000 feet, becoming especially numerous at the higher altitudes—7,000 feet plus. It is found in yellow and Jeffrey pines and upward to near timberline in open forests of lodgepole pine, alder, red fir, aspen, and hemlock. The nest is a bulky cup of pine twigs, weed stems, and rootlets, occasionally decorated with lichens; it is lined with rootlets, hair, and sometimes shredded bark. This is placed from ten to eighty feet above the ground, usually in terminal needles of a pine branch.

In winter, some birds drop to pinyon pine–juniper foothills, and a few straggle into valleys; others, however, remain at higher elevations. *E. cassinii* is gregarious, except during the three months or so of the nesting season. Foraging is done in treetops or on the ground, apparently rarely in bushes. A flock flits rather fitfully from one feeding place to another in search of various buds, berries (cotoneaster, others), and seeds (especially conifer, also sunflower, etc.); a few insects are taken in summer.

One note is a brief clear *cheep*; a hurried *tee dee yip* is given in flight. The song is a bright lively warble, between the Purple and House finches in speed and pattern. Adult and immature males usually sing from

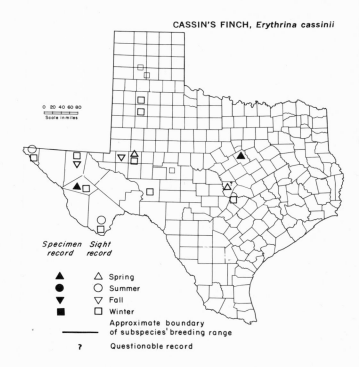

CASSIN'S FINCH, *Erythrina cassinii*

0 20 40 60 80
Scale in miles

Specimen record / Sight record

▲ △ Spring
● ○ Summer
▼ ▽ Fall
■ □ Winter

Approximate boundary of subspecies' breeding range

? Questionable record

a high treetop perch, occasionally in the air. Chief singing months are May, June, and July.

DETAILED ACCOUNT: ONE SUBSPECIES

EASTERN CASSIN'S FINCH, *Erythrina cassinii cassinii* (Baird)

No races recognized by A.O.U. check-list, 1957 (see Appendix A). NOTE: Although the specimens taken in Texas are not identified to race, Oberholser considered *E. c. cassinii* to be the form normally occurring in the state.

DESCRIPTION: *Adult male, nuptial plumage*: Acquired by wear from winter plumage. Pileum rather light carmine; hindneck and back dull drab or dull buffy gray, overlaid or washed with light pompeian red, and broadly and conspicuously streaked with olive brown; rump and upper tail-coverts light jasper red, unstreaked, longest upper tail-coverts light fuscous, more or less washed with red; tail rather light fuscous, feathers with very narrow, sometimes almost absent, pale brownish edgings; wings rather light fuscous, inner margins rather paler, secondaries margined on their outer webs with rather rufescent brown, and tipped with brownish white, tertials margined terminally on outer webs rather broadly with dull buff or pale brown, greater and median coverts tipped with salmon buff, lesser coverts tipped with dull brownish red; sides of head like ground color of upper parts, but ear-coverts mostly deep old rose; chin deep old rose; throat alizarine pink, shading to coral pink on jugulum and upper breast; remainder of lower parts buffy or pinkish white, with slightly indicated dark brown streaks on sides of breast and on flanks; lower tail-coverts with median stripes of chaetura drab; lining of wing between drab and mouse gray, feathers edged with buffy white; edge of wing tinged with dull pink. Bill dark bluish gray or dark slate color, but mandible drab or dull flesh color with a somewhat lilaceous tinge; iris burnt umber; legs and toes sepia or drab. *Adult male, winter*: Acquired by complete postnuptial molt. Similar to nuptial adult male but duller; upper parts, including pileum, obscured by pale brown or buffy tips of feathers, thus producing a more blended appearance, pink areas of lower surface clouded by buff tips of feathers; posterior lower parts more buffy. *Adult female, nuptial (olivaceous phase)*: Acquired by wear from winter. Upper parts grayish olive or light grayish olive, broadly streaked throughout with fuscous, though less conspicuously so on rump and upper tail-coverts; tail light fuscous; wings fuscous, greater and median coverts very narrowly edged with dull buff or pale brown, lesser coverts edged with grayish olive; sides of head and of neck like upper parts, but streaks very narrow; lower parts dull buffy white, conspicuously streaked with chaetura drab, streaks fewest and least conspicuous in middle of chin and throat, and on abdomen, which last is often immaculate; lining of wing buff or brownish white, outer portion spotted with dark. Bill rather brownish drab, but paler and more lilaceous basally and on mandible; iris dark brown; legs and toes light brown. *Adult female, nuptial (gray phase)*: Similar to olivaceous phase but upper parts much less olivaceous (more grayish). *Adult female, winter*: Acquired by complete postnuptial molt. Similar to nuptial adult female, but upper parts more blended, therefore less sharply streaked, due to broader light edgings of feathers of upper surface; streaks below also less sharply defined. *Male, first nuptial (olivaceous and gray phases)*: Acquired by wear from first winter. Similar to adult female but larger. *Male, first winter (olivaceous and gray phases)*: Acquired by postjuvenal molt. Similar to first nuptial male, but upper parts more uniform, blending of colors caused by broader light edges and tips of feathers; streaks on lower parts likewise not so sharply defined. *Female, first nuptial (olivaceous and gray phases)*: Acquired by wear from first winter. Similar to nuptial adult female. *Female, first winter (olivaceous and gray phases)*: Acquired by postjuvenal molt. Similar to adult female in winter. *Juvenal*: Acquired by complete postnatal molt. Similar to first winter female, but upper parts more uniform, less broadly and conspicuously streaked, darker and

sometimes more ochraceous; sides of head and of neck more uniform and less streaked with dark brown; streaks below narrower, paler, and more numerous; plumage more fluffy. Maxilla dusky neutral gray; mandible dark quaker; iris fuscous black; legs and feet dark neutral gray.

MEASUREMENTS: *Adult male*: Wing, 89.2–96.5 (average, 92.2) mm.; tail, 59.7–68.8 (64.0); bill (exposed culmen), 11.7–12.7 (12.4); height of bill at base, 10.2–11.2 (10.4); tarsus, 17.8–20.3 (19.3); middle toe without claw, 14.0–16.5 (15.2). *Adult female*: Wing, 87.1–91.4 (88.9); tail, 58.4–63.2 (61.5); bill, 12.2–12.7 (12.4); height of bill, 10.2–10.7 (10.4); tarsus, 17.8–20.1 (18.8); middle toe, 13.7–15.5 (15.0).

RANGE: Identical with that of species, with exception of Pacific coast mountains from British Columbia to s. California which are occupied by *E. c. vinifer*.

TEXAS: *Winter*: Two specimens: Jeff Davis Co., Sawtooth Mt., 6,300 ft. (Mar. 4, 1967, J. F. Scudday; Sul Ross State University collection, no. 206); Bosque Co., 7 mi. east of Cayote (female, Apr. 8, 1961, W. M. Pulich, Robert Pulich; see *Condor* 73 [1971]: 111).

HOUSE FINCH, *Erythrina mexicana* (Müller)

SPECIES ACCOUNT

Carpodacus mexicanus of A.O.U. check-list, 1957 (see Appendix A). A sparrow-sized finch with short conical bill; tail only slightly notched. *Male*: bright red to reddish orange (occasionally yellow) head, breast, and rump; brown-streaked buffy belly and sides. *Female*: sparrowlike with streaked under parts; lacks reddish washes and noticeable facial markings. Length, 6¼ in.; wingspan, 9¾; weight, ¾ oz.

RANGE: S. British Columbia to w. Nebraska, south through w. United States and arid parts of Mexico to c. Oaxaca. Naturalized in Hawaii and along Atlantic coast from Connecticut to Maryland.

TEXAS: (See map.) *Resident*: Breeds, early Mar. to

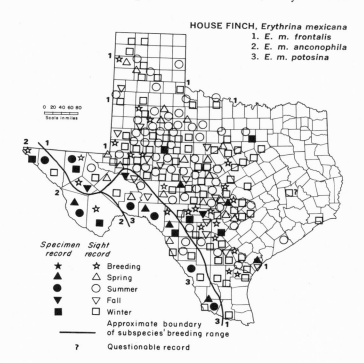

HOUSE FINCH, *Erythrina mexicana*
1. *E. m. frontalis*
2. *E. m. anconophila*
3. *E. m. potosina*

0 20 40 60 80
Scale in miles

Specimen record / Sight record

★ / ☆ Breeding
▲ / △ Spring
● / ○ Summer
▼ / ▽ Fall
■ / □ Winter

——— Approximate boundary of subspecies' breeding range

? Questionable record

early Sept. (eggs, Mar. 18 to Aug. 4) from 400 to 7,000 ft. Common west of 98th meridian with exception of Rio Grande delta, where rare and doubtful as a breeder; irregular east to Fort Worth, Bastrop, and Rockport; recent (1967) nesting discovered in Jim Wells and Nueces cos. Casual (nonbreeders) along upper coast.

HAUNTS AND HABITS: In Texas, the House Finch is widespread in the dry western half. It frequents a variety of habitats from desert thornbrush and juniper-oak hills and canyons to vicinities of houses and cities. Its chief prerequisite for breeding seems to be a combination of low humidity (with an average rainfall of 35 in. or less) and hilly terrain. This gregarious bird often roves in flocks of variable size during the nonbreeding season.

The bounding flight of the House Finch is usually over treetops and buildings. When perching, birds select a high vantage in a tree or on a power line. If frightened, they fly up and away rather than dropping to the ground or flitting into a bush as do many other sparrows. Seeds (chiefly of pigweed, alfilaria, thistle, filaree, knotweed, sunflower, chickweed) are gleaned from the ground; fruits of cactus, elderberry, poison-ivy, apricot, cherry, peach, plum, and fig are generally taken from the tree or bush. House Finches also eat a few caterpillars, plant lice, beetles, ants, and grasshoppers.

The varied notes of *E. mexicana* are somewhat melodious when run together; a few suggest those of the House Sparrow but are considerably more musical. Notes are frequently given in flight. The male's bright, rambling, rippling song is phrased mostly in triplets with great variation; it often closes with a nasal *wheer* or *churr*. He sings virtually year-round from a treetop, high wire, boulder, or building, and in flight; however, he is most persistent from January to late July and from September to early November. The female also sings occasionally.

CHANGES: Since 1930, the House Finch has colonized the eastern Edwards Plateau from west Texas. The species was first recorded in Erath County on February 1, 1938 (C. T. Gill). At Hamilton, pairs were feeding young, September 6 and 7, 1938 (Mrs. L. C. Chesley). Near Austin, in Travis County, several hundred appeared on November 4, 1933, and by June 20, 1934, a nest containing young had been inspected (J. J. Biesele).

Permanent establishment in Texas east of Austin seems doubtful. Although a small group of House Finches was once seen and heard thirty-two miles east of Austin at Bastrop State Park in the mid-1950's (E. B. Kincaid, Jr.), intensive bird observations in the same region during the 1960's by J. L. Rowlett and others failed to reveal a single individual. Hilly terrain and similar vegetation are found at both Austin and Bastrop. Slightly more humid conditions at the latter place may be inhibiting colonization. Average annual rainfall at Bastrop is 36.22 inches; at Austin it is 32.58.

It is perhaps likely that had the Austin birds come directly from the foggy Pacific coast, the species would by now be established in Bastrop and various other "eastern" localities. Following importation and release of "Hollywood finches" near New York City in 1940, the House Finch quickly (within 20 years) established itself along the humid Atlantic coast from Connecticut to Maryland.

DETAILED ACCOUNT: FOUR SUBSPECIES

COMMON HOUSE FINCH, *Erythrina mexicana frontalis* (Say)

DESCRIPTION: *Adult male, nuptial plumage (dark phase)*: Acquired by wear from winter plumage. Forehead, crown, superciliary stripe, and narrow collar on hindneck nopal red; shorter upper tail-coverts similar but brighter, toward scarlet red; remainder of upper surface drab to hair brown, more or less tinged or washed with red of pileum and streaked, sometimes inconspicuously, with light olive brown, these streaks broadest and occupying most of feathers on longest upper tail-coverts; tail dark olive brown, feathers with very narrow buffy white edgings on inner margins and very narrow pale dull buff or whitish edgings on outer webs; wings olive brown, but inner edges of primaries and secondaries, except at tips of primaries, drab to tilleul buff, outer webs of wing-quills and coverts drab to dull hair brown, median and greater coverts narrowly tipped with buffy white or pale dull buff; lores dull pale pinkish buff to smoke gray; auriculars dull wood brown, more or less washed with dull red; sides of neck like upper surface; chin, throat, jugulum, and breast carmine to dull scarlet red; remainder of lower surface tilleul buff to buffy white, streaked, most broadly on sides, flanks, and crissum, with buffy brown to olive brown; lining of wing dull pinkish buff, more or less spotted or mottled with buffy brown or drab. Bill dull brown or plumbeous, but mandible paler and somewhat pinkish; iris dark brown; legs and feet light brown or sepia. *Adult male, nuptial (light phase)*: Similar to dark phase, but red areas both above and below decidedly paler, more yellowish; forehead and crown scarlet; superciliary stripe sometimes mixed with yellow; breast grenadine red. *Adult male, nuptial (yellow phase)*: Similar to light phase, but plumage entirely without red; forehead and crown ochraceous tawny or even more distinctly yellow; anterior lower parts similar but rather lighter. *Adult male, winter (dark phase)*: Acquired by complete postnuptial molt. Similar to dark phase of nuptial adult male, but upper surface duller, more grayish (less brownish), colors more blended by broader light edgings of feathers; crown, superciliary stripe, and rump much duller, more pinkish; forehead anteriorly red or corinthian purple, much obscured by light brown or dull pale buff tips of feathers; rump between eugenia red and pompeian red; light edgings of tertials and wing-coverts much broader; red of anterior lower surface much more pinkish—acajou red, this color much obscured by pale buff or dull white tips of feathers; posterior lower surface much less sharply streaked due to broader light tips of feathers. *Adult male, winter (light phase)*: Acquired by complete postnuptial molt. Similar to adult male in winter, dark phase, but paler, anterior lower parts between old rose and jasper pink. *Adult female, nuptial*: Acquired by wear from winter. Upper surface between dull pinkish buff or tawny olive and light drab, shorter upper tail-coverts inclining to dull tawny olive; entire upper surface streaked with light olive brown, most broadly on back, very little on rump; wings and tail similar to those of nuptial adult male; sides of head like upper surface but paler, with poorly defined light superciliary stripe; lower surface buffy white or tilleul buff, broadly streaked with light olive brown; lining of wing pale buff or buffy white, somewhat mottled on outer portion with light olive brown or hair brown. Bill gray or purplish drab, but mandible somewhat vinaceous at base; iris dark brown; legs and feet dark brown. *Adult female, winter*: Acquired by complete postnuptial molt. Similar to nuptial adult female, but upper surface slightly more buffy, colors more blended by broader edgings of feathers; lower surface somewhat more buffy, streaks less sharply defined, owing to broader light edgings. *Male, first nuptial*: Acquired by wear from first winter. Similar to nuptial adult female but larger; forehead, rump, jugulum, and throat often with more or less red, pink, yellow, or orange. *Male, first winter*: Acquired by complete postjuvenal molt. Similar to first nuptial male, but upper surface duller and more buffy; wing-bars more deeply buff; entire plumage usuallly without red. *Female, first nuptial*: Acquired by wear from first winter. Essentially identical with nuptial adult female. *Female, first winter*: Acquired by complete postjuvenal molt. Similar to adult female in winter, but somewhat more buffy or ochraceous both above and below; wing-bars more deeply buff. Similar to first winter male but smaller. *Juvenal*: Acquired by complete postnatal molt. Similar to first winter male and female, but upper surface usually more thickly and distinctly streaked; streaks of lower surface darker and more sharply defined. *Natal*: Dull cartridge buff to dull cream buff.

MEASUREMENTS: *Adult male*: Wing, 74.9–82.3 (average, 78.0) mm.; tail, 55.1–63.5 (58.9); bill (exposed culmen), 8.9–11.4 (9.9); tarsus, 16.8–18.8 (17.5); middle toe without claw, 12.4–14.7 (13.7). *Adult female*: Wing, 73.9–80.0 (76.2); tail, 53.8–61.0 (56.6); bill, 9.4–10.7 (10.2); tarsus, 16.5–17.8 (17.0); middle toe, 13.7–14.5 (14.0).

RANGE: S.w. Colorado to s.w. Kansas, south to s.e. Arizona and c. Texas; east in winter occasionally to c. Oklahoma and upper Texas Gulf coast.

TEXAS: *Resident*: Altitudinal breeding range, 400 to 5,000 ft. Collected in Culberson, Jeff Davis, Mitchell, Menard, Kerr, and Bexar cos. Taken in winter in Tarrant Co.; in spring in Aransas Co. Common.

NESTING: *Nest*: In open country, on slopes and mesas, in valleys and canyons, also in cultivated areas and in towns; on limb of tree or bush (such as saltbush, sagebush, mountainmahogany, cactus), in various crevices of buildings, side of a haystack tin can on a porch, or even nest of other bird (such as Cliff Swallow or orioles), or bird box; when in an open situation it is a rather shallow though somewhat well built cup-shaped structure; composed of grasses, roots, straw, twigs, dried grass stems, weeds, various other plant fibers, and string; lined with horsehair and soft grass, and sometimes wool. *Eggs*: 3–6, usually 5; rounded ovate; white with a pale bluish green or pale greenish blue tinge; sparingly marked with spots, dots, and lines of dark brown or black, chiefly about large end; not infrequently unspotted; average size, 20.9 × 14.7 mm.

TEXAS HOUSE FINCH, Erythrina mexicana anconophila
Oberholser, new subspecies (see Appendix A)

DESCRIPTION: *Adult male, nuptial plumage*: Similar to *E. m. frontalis*, but upper surface lighter, more brownish (less grayish), and more suffused with red; red of lower parts more extensive.

MEASUREMENTS: *Adult male*: Wing, 74.9–82.0 (average, 78.7) mm.; tail, 56.9–65.0 (61.5); bill (exposed culmen), 9.4–11.9 (10.4); height of bill at base, 8.1–8.9 (8.6); tarsus, 17.5–19.0 (18.3); middle toe without claw, 12.7–14.0 (13.2). *Adult female*: Wing, 70.1–75.9 (74.7); tail, 54.1–61.0 (58.4); bill, 9.4–10.9 (10.2); height of bill at base, 7.6–8.9 (8.4); tarsus, 17.0–18.0 (17.8); middle toe, 11.9–14.0 (12.7).

TYPE: Adult male, no. 139226, U.S. Nat. Museum, Biological Surveys collection; Chinati Mts., Presidio Co., Texas; Apr. 1, 1890; William Lloyd.

RANGE: S.w. New Mexico and s.w. Trans-Pecos Texas, south to c. Chihuahua.

TEXAS: *Resident*: Altitudinal breeding range, 1,800 to 7,000 ft. Collected in El Paso, Hudspeth, Presidio, and Brewster cos.; taken in winter in Real and Kinney cos. Common.

NESTING: Similar to that of *E. m. frontalis*.

FIGGINS' HOUSE FINCH, Erythrina mexicana smithi
(Figgins)

Race not in A.O.U. check-list, 1957 (see Appendix A).

DESCRIPTION: *Adult male and female, nuptial plumage*: Similar to *E. m. frontalis*, but ground color of posterior lower parts darker; streaks on lower parts wider, thus appearing heavier; red portions of plumage darker, especially in worn condition.

MEASUREMENTS: *Adult male*: Wing, 76.7–79.7 (average, 78.0) mm.; tail, 57.4–62.0 (59.9); bill (exposed culmen), 9.4–10.7 (10.2); tarsus, 17.0–18.3 (17.5); middle toe without claw, (13.2).

RANGE: S. Wyoming to w. Nebraska, south to c. Colorado; in winter south to extreme w. Texas (casually).

TEXAS: *Winter*: Two specimens: El Paso Co., El Paso vicinity (Feb. 10, 27, 1892, E. A. Mearns, F. X. Holzner; identified by R. T. Moore).

POTOSI HOUSE FINCH, Erythrina mexicana potosina
(Griscom)

DESCRIPTION: *Adult male and female, nuptial plumage*: Similar to *E. m. frontalis*, but upper parts much darker.

MEASUREMENTS: *Adult male*: Wing, 77.5–85.1 (average, 80.0) mm.; tail, 60.5–71.1 (63.8); bill (exposed culmen), 9.4–10.9 (10.2); height of bill at base, 7.9–8.9 (8.4); tarsus, 17.5–19.6 (18.3); middle toe without claw, 13.0–14.5 (13.7). *Adult female*: Wing, 73.9–80.5 (77.5); tail, 56.4–66.0 (61.0); bill, 9.4–10.9 (10.2); height of bill, 8.1–8.6 (8.4); tarsus, 17.0–18.8 (18.0); middle toe, 13.0–14.5 (13.7).

RANGE: Texas-Coahuila border vicinity, south to c. San Luis Potosí.

TEXAS: *Resident*: Breeding suspected, but no nest, eggs, or bird in breeding condition collected. Collected in all seasons in Crane, Val Verde, Kinney, Webb, and Starr cos. Fairly common.

NESTING: Presumably similar to that of *E. m. frontalis*.

WHITE-COLLARED SEEDEATER, Sporophila morelleti (Bonaparte)

SPECIES ACCOUNT

A.O.U. check-list, 1957, merges *S. morelleti* into *Sporophila torqueola* (see Appendix A). Texas population

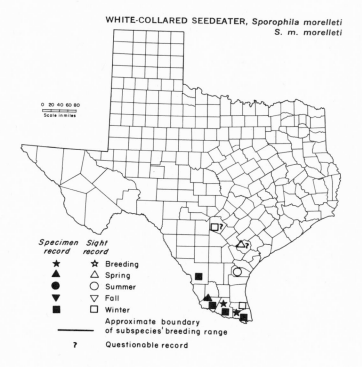

WHITE-COLLARED SEEDEATER, *Sporophila morelleti*
S. m. morelleti

0 20 40 60 80
Scale in miles

Specimen record	Sight record	
★	☆	Breeding
▲	△	Spring
●	○	Summer
▼	▽	Fall
■	□	Winter

——— Approximate boundary of subspecies' breeding range

? Questionable record

long known as Sharpe's Seedeater. A tiny finch with a stubby, "round" bill; brownish olive back; whitish wing-bars; dusky, rounded wings and tail; buffy under parts. Some Texas males show black feathers on crown, sides of head, back, and upper breast. Conspicuous white collars (for which the species was named), clear-cut black upper parts, and complete black breast-bands are restricted to adult males from Veracruz southward. Length, 4½ in.; wingspan, 6½.

RANGE: Rio Grande delta of Texas, south through e. Mexico to Costa Rica (*S. morelleti*); w. and c. Mexico from Sinaloa to Distrito Federal and Oaxaca (*S. torqueola*, in restricted sense). White-collared Seedeaters on Pacific slope of Chiapas, Guatemala, and El Salvador appear to belong to the *morelleti* group.

TEXAS: (See map.) *Resident*: Breeds, early Mar. to mid-Sept. (eggs, Mar. 12 to Sept. 3) from near sea level to 200 ft. Rare, formerly common, in Rio Grande delta; recorded upriver to Laredo and up coast to Corpus Christi. Questionable sightings at San Antonio and Victoria.

HAUNTS AND HABITS: The White-collared Seedeater is the northernmost representative of the seedeaters, which, together with their relatives the grassquits, flourish like mice in the weedy cornfields and cow pastures of the American Tropics.

Within its Texas range, which is subhumid most years, preferred habitats are tall grasses, cattails, sunflowers, or giant ragweed in the vicinity of scattered, low-growing bushes (often huisache or retama). These rank grasses and forbs grow mostly beside the Rio Grande, resacas, irrigation ditches, wet-weather ponds, and edges of orchards and fields.

Seedeaters generally forage industriously in recesses of low bushes and weeds; thus, good views of them are often difficult. Here they glean seeds of grasses (*Paspalum* and other genera) and composites (*Zexmenia*, others); also insects.

The flock note of the Whitecollar is a double clicking *tick-tick*. A disturbed individual sounds a goldfinch-like *che*. Song of the Texas seedeater, somewhat Indigo Bunting–like, is surprisingly loud for such a midget-sized bird. Though variable, it commonly resembles *sweet sweet sweet cheer cheer cheer!* Birds sing from March to late July, occasionally into September, while perched atop a low bush, tall weed, or grass stalk.

CHANGES: During the first half of the twentieth century, 95 percent of the woods and brush in the Rio Grande delta was cleared to make way for cultivated crops, roads, and towns. This clearing lowered populations of practically all subtropical species which reach their "north pole" in this region; the big exception was the tiny seedeater, since grasses and forbs increased on the cleared land. Citrus was the dominant crop until January 29, 1951. Beginning on this day, a bitter norther froze 85 percent of the grapefruit and orange trees.

Since 1951 cotton has replaced citrus as the dominant crop; also cow and cowbird populations have risen steeply. Cotton in south Texas is sprayed—often via airplane—from five to twenty times per season with insecticides (mostly DDT-based), weed killers, and defoliants. Much spray drifts into fieldside vegetation. Anything a seedeater eats or drinks carries a load of poison. Decline of the species in Texas—and the United States—dates from the onset of extremely widespread and heavy cotton spraying, as the following Audubon Christmas Bird Count figures indicate:

Christmas Season	Delta Counts	White-collared Seedeaters
1946	1	36
1947	1	75
1948	1	10
1949	2	107
1950	3	55
1951	1	0
1952	2	1
1953	2	9
1954	2	16
1955	2	16
1956	2	3
1957	2	5
1958	2	3
1959	4	23
1960	4	60
1961	2	7
1962	4	3
1963	4	3
1964	3	12
1965	3	0
1966	4	0
1967	5	0
1968	5	0
1969	5	0
1970	6	0
1971	6	0
1972	6	0

DETAILED ACCOUNT: ONE SUBSPECIES

MORELLET'S WHITE-COLLARED SEEDEATER,
Sporophila morelleti morelleti (Bonaparte)

Sporophila torqueola sharpei of A.O.U. check-list, 1957 (see Appendix A). NOTE: Dr. Oberholser is virtually alone among mid-twentieth-century ornithologists in not recognizing the race *sharpei*. Males of the northeasternmost population, unlike those from Veracruz southward, apparently never attain fully adult plumage. Here seems to be a case of arrested development; this, in itself, is probably sufficient excuse for segregating northern birds subspecifically. A similar case is that of the Green-backed Lesser Goldfinch, *Spinus psaltria hesperophilus*, of the American Pacific coast. Males of this race retain their green backs, a sign of immaturity in Texas birds, throughout their lives.

DESCRIPTION: *Adult male, nuptial plumage* (not seen in Texas): Acquired by partial prenuptial molt. Upper surface slightly glossy black; narrow collar around hindneck, wide band on shorter upper tail-coverts, and tips of feathers on rump white; tail brownish black without markings; wing-quills chaetura drab, slightly paler on inner margins, outer webs, together with wing-coverts, brownish black, but basal portion of inner primaries and secondaries white, this occupying nearly half the feather and showing as conspicuous white spot on primaries, even in closed wing, and on secondaries extending farther toward end of feathers on inner webs than on outer; greater wing-coverts more or less conspicuously tipped with white; lesser wing-coverts with narrow dull white tips; median coverts also narrowly tipped with white; sides of head black, but lores slightly grayish; broad collar on sides of neck joining narrow white collar on hindneck and white on chin and throat; jugulum broadly black; remainder of lower surface white or slightly yellowish white, but sides with obscure blackish or chaetura drab spots; thighs black, feathers tipped with white; axillars white; under wing-coverts dull black or chaetura drab, edged with dull white. Bill bluish black or brownish black; iris dark brown; legs and feet dark brown, brownish black, or dark plumbeous. *Adult male, winter*: Acquired by complete postnuptial molt. Similar to nuptial adult male, but rump and abdomen very slightly washed with buff. *Adult female, nuptial (ochraceous phase)*: Acquired by partial prenuptial molt. Upper surface between light brownish olive and orange citrine; upper tail-coverts between tawny olive and isabella color; tail dull olive brown, feathers edged on outer margins with color of upper surface; wings dark hair brown, inner margins of primaries and secondaries buffy white at base, shading to drab toward ends, but this not reaching tips of feathers; outer vanes of primaries, secondaries, and tertials margined with color of back, as are wing-coverts; median coverts tipped with cinnamon buff and greater coverts tipped with cream buff, forming two fairly well defined wing-bars; sides of head and of neck, together with lower parts, ochraceous, somewhat paler on abdomen and crissum; lining of wing dull cream buff to light cinnamon buff, more or less spotted with drab or dull light hair brown. Bill light brown; iris brown; legs and feet dark brown. *Adult female, nuptial (olivaceous phase)*: Acquired by partial prenuptial molt. Similar to ochraceous phase, but upper surface very much duller, more olivaceous (less rufescent); upper surface grayish light brownish olive; wing-bars cartridge buff to dull cream buff; lower surface paler—chamois to cream buff; sides and flanks darker. *Adult female, summer*: Similar to nuptial adult female but much paler, by reason of wear and fading. *Adult female, winter*: Acquired by complete postnuptial molt. Similar to nuptial adult female, but upper surface darker, usually somewhat more brownish; wing-bars more deeply buff or ochraceous; lower surface somewhat darker and more richly colored. *Male, third winter*: Acquired by complete postnuptial molt. Like adult male in winter. *Male, second nuptial*: Acquired by partial prenuptial molt. Similar to nuptial adult male, but light portions of plumage duller; wing-quills and sometimes primary coverts more brownish; black of upper surface sometimes somewhat mixed with brown or gray; rump and shorter upper tail-coverts light cream buff to deep cinnamon buff, this on rump more or less mixed with dull gray; posterior lower surface decidedly buff—cartridge buff to warm buff or cinnamon buff, this usually deepest on sides, flanks, and crissum. *Male, second winter*: Acquired by complete postnuptial molt. Similar to second nuptial male, but black of upper surface more veiled by broad brown edgings of feathers; rump, upper tail-coverts, and lower parts more deeply buff. *Male, first nuptial*: Acquired by partial prenuptial molt. Similar to second nuptial male, but upper surface much more mixed with buffy brown, this sometimes occupying all of back and scapulars with but a few small spots of black, sometimes almost none, but sometimes black occupies major portion of upper surface, though everywhere, except possibly on pileum, broken by brown; there is thus a very wide range in color of upper surface, and in worn plumage in summer many of brown edgings wear off and any concealed black becomes more visible; lower surface more deeply and extensively buff, this usually invading throat and even chin; black jugular band narrower and much broken by buff or ochraceous. *Male, first winter*: Acquired by complete postjuvenal molt. Similar to first nuptial male, but upper surface, including black of pileum when present, much overlaid with buffy brown or grayish olive; tertials without white, but edged and tipped with drab; lower surface deep buff, dull cinnamon buff to dull ochraceous, decidedly deeper than in first nuptial male. *Female, first nuptial*: Acquired by partial prenuptial molt. Like nuptial adult female. *Female, first winter*: Acquired by complete postjuvenal molt. Like adult female in winter. *Juvenal*: Acquired by complete postnatal molt. Pileum between sayal brown, buckthorn brown, and light cinnamon brown; back sepia to light cinnamon

brown; hindneck, rump, and upper tail-coverts dull ochraceous tawny; wings and tail similar to those of first winter female, but wing-bars darker—deep cinnamon buff; remainder of wing-coverts more brownish or ochraceous; lower surface dull ochraceous buff to light ochraceous buff, without dark streaks or spots. *Natal*: Unknown.

MEASUREMENTS: *Adult male*: Wing, 47.8–53.8 (average, 51.1) mm.; tail, 40.1–47.3 (43.7); bill (exposed culmen), 8.1–9.1 (8.6); height of bill at base, 6.9–8.1 (7.4); tarsus, 14.2–16.5 (15.5); middle toe without claw, 10.4–12.2 (11.2). *Adult female*: Wing, 48.0–51.3 (49.8); tail, 39.6–45.2 (43.2); bill, 8.1–8.9 (8.6); height of bill, 7.4–8.1 (7.6); tarsus, 15.2–16.0 (15.7); middle toe, 10.7–11.4 (11.2).

RANGE: Rio Grande delta of Texas, south through e. Mexico and Caribbean slope of n. Central America to Costa Rica (where subspecies also occupies Pacific slope). The usually recognized race *sharpei* occupies the Rio Grande delta, Nuevo León, Tamaulipas, and n. Veracruz.

TEXAS: *Resident*: Collected in Starr (no evidence of nesting), Hidalgo, and Cameron cos. Three specimens taken in winter in Webb Co. (Dec. 22–24, 1948; University of Oklahoma Museum of Zoology, G. M. Sutton collection).

NESTING: *Nest*: In fields (especially their edges), pastures, or sparse brush; within tall weeds, vines, bush, or low tree, 3–6 ft. above ground; rather loosely woven cup, fastened at rim, and supported beneath by stalks or twigs, but not pensile; composed of dry grass, roots, dry weeds, yucca fibers, and similar materials; lined with fine grass and horsehair. *Eggs*: 2–4; ovate, varying toward elliptical oval; pale greenish blue, light bluish green, or greenish white; with blotches, streaks, and spots over most of egg surface of dark purplish brown, brownish black, and pale rufous, and with shell markings of violet gray and lavender; average size, 16.8 × 12.4 mm.

PINE GROSBEAK, *Pinicola enucleator* (Linnaeus)

SPECIES ACCOUNT

A very large, plump fringillid; has a dark swollen bill (small for a grosbeak); long, blackish wings and tail; two whitish wing-bars. *Male*: rose red with gray belly. *Female*: gray with olive yellow head and rump. Length, 8½ in.; wingspan, 13½.

RANGE: Boreal forests of Northern Hemisphere; in North America, n. Alaska to Newfoundland, south through high mountains of w. United States to c. California and n. New Mexico, and south through New England states to New Hampshire. Nearctic races winter in vicinity of breeding range, south irregularly to s. New Mexico, n.w. Texas (casually), and Virginia.

TEXAS: *Winter*: Casual (extremes: Oct. 10, Mar. 23) north of 30th parallel, although not reported from wooded eastern quarter.

HAUNTS AND HABITS: The Pine Grosbeak is a bird of northern conifer forests. Its nest is a rather flat bowl of moss, twigs, grass, and lichens placed on a branch of a conifer or shrub, usually near (6 to 30 ft.) the ground. The species very rarely appears in Texas, but when it does—probably due to a food shortage to the north—it is likely to be found in budding coniferous or deciduous trees, a weed patch, garden or nursery evergreens, or at a feeding tray.

This stocky finch is slow moving and dawdling. It is exceptionally tame and usually permits very close approach. When foraging, however, it moves skillfully on branches of trees and bushes, sometimes hanging head down on the end of a twig. It also feeds on the ground. Primary foods are buds of spruce, pine, alder, ash, maple, and boxelder; also fruits of sumac, cherry, hawthorn, juniper, and barberry. Seeds include chiefly those of ragweed, burdock, hemp, and sunflower. The Pine Grosbeak also eats caterpillars, grasshoppers, leaf beetles, wasps, flies, and ants; frequently it takes salt. Birds during the winter often bathe in soft snow by whipping it up in a fine mist with their wings, much as if it were water.

Chief notes are various short low whistles; another call, usually given in flight, consists of two or three high whistles suggesting the cry of the Greater Yellowlegs. The clear liquid song resembles that of the Purple Finch but is lower pitched. Pine Grosbeaks very seldom sing in Texas.

DETAILED ACCOUNT: ONE SUBSPECIES

ROCKY MOUNTAIN PINE GROSBEAK, *Pinicola enucleator montana* Ridgway

DESCRIPTION: *Adult male, nuptial plumage*: Acquired by wear from winter plumage. The rosy or pinkish hue of winter plumage becomes bright red by wearing off of feather barbules. Pileum and hindneck scarlet to dull scarlet red, but more or less broken by hair brown centers of feathers, which show as irregular spots; remainder of upper surface hair brown to light hair brown, but upper tail-coverts usually somewhat lighter, middle of back, rump, and upper tail-coverts with more or less red, this on back duller than on pileum, and toward jasper red, on rump and upper tail-coverts jasper red to carnelian red, middle of rump sometimes almost entirely red; tail light chaetura drab, but outermost feathers somewhat lighter, more brownish, outer webs of rectrices very narrowly edged with dull hair brown; wings dark hair brown, but inner margins of primaries and secondaries, except at tips, paler and inclining to drab; narrow outer edges of primaries and secondaries brownish or buffy white, but those on inner secondaries and tertials dull white; lesser wing-coverts tipped with hair brown, some feathers with tinge of dull red; greater and median wing-coverts broadly tipped with buffy white, greater coverts tipped only on outer webs; lores dull drab or dull buff; small spot in front of eye chaetura drab; broad stripe under eye dull buffy gray or dull grayish buff; remainder of sides of head and of neck red like pileum; lower surface between light hair brown and light mouse gray, but chin, throat, jugulum, breast, and sometimes sides of body also more or less extensively dull scarlet red to dull carnelian red, this everywhere more or less interrupted and clouded by underlying brownish gray of feathers; feathers of lower tail-coverts tipped and margined with dull white; lining of wing mouse gray to light hair brown, more or less mottled with darker brown. Bill black or brownish black, but mandible sometimes naples yellow, dull olive, or seal brown at base; iris prout brown; legs and feet brownish black or blackish brown. *Adult male, winter*: Acquired by complete postnuptial molt. Similar to nuptial adult male, but red of upper and lower surfaces duller, much more pinkish—that of upper surface eugenia red to light jasper red or jasper red, of lower parts paler; wings and tail rather darker; white edgings of wing-coverts and tertials broader; feathers of sides tipped with dull white; lower tail-coverts broadly tipped and edged with white, sometimes almost entirely obscuring dark centers. Maxilla blackish brown; mandible dark brown, but tip blackish; iris sepia. *Adult female, nuptial*: Acquired by wear from winter. Pileum, sometimes hindneck, olive ocher or primuline yellow to between analine yellow and raw sienna; remainder of upper surface between hair brown and mouse gray, but rump somewhat lighter, and occasionally with some analine yellow to sulphine yellow; lores, malar region,

and area below eye dull tilleul buff; small triangular spot in front of eye chaetura drab; remainder of sides of head yellow like crown; sides of neck like upper surface; chin dull tilleul buff; wings and tail practically identical to nuptial adult male; lower surface like upper parts but rather lighter, usually without yellow, occasionally with a few dark spots on sides of breast. Bill slate black, but base of mandible dark drab. *Adult female, winter*: Acquired by complete postnuptial molt. Similar to nuptial adult female, but colors of upper surface rather more blended, feathers of back broadly edged with light brownish gray; white edgings of greater and median wing-coverts and of tertials broader. *Male, first nuptial*: Acquired by wear from first winter. Similar to nuptial adult female, but pileum and rump often darker, more reddish—antique brown to vinaceous rufous; wing-bars more brownish, more buffy, or drab. Bill dark olive brown; iris dark brown; legs and feet black. *Male, first winter*: Acquired by partial postjuvenal molt, which does not involve wing-quills or tail. Similar to first nuptial male, but reddish or yellow of head and rump averaging darker and duller. Maxilla blackish brown; mandible dark brown; iris sepia; legs and feet sepia. *Female, first nuptial*: Acquired by wear from first winter. Like nuptial adult female. *Female, first winter*: Acquired by partial postjuvenal molt. Similar to adult female in winter, but pileum duller; back washed with buff, ochraceous, dull brown, or olive yellow; wing-bars and edgings of tertials duller, more buffy or drab; lower surface duller, more washed with buff (less purely gray). Bill blackish brown, but base of mandible lighter; iris sepia; legs and feet very dark brown. *Juvenal*: Acquired by complete postnatal molt. Similar to first winter female, but pileum still duller, more brownish or grayish, although still decidedly yellowish or saffron tinged—antique brown to dull cinnamon; upper tail-coverts more brownish; sides of head more brownish or buffy (less greenish or yellowish); back washed with light brownish olive; lower surface duller than that of first winter female.

MEASUREMENTS: *Adult male*: Wing, 118.1–128.0 (average, 121.2) mm.; tail, 91.9–103.1 (97.8); bill (exposed culmen), 14.0–16.5 (15.5); height of bill at base, 10.9–11.9 (11.7); tarsus, 22.6–24.9 (23.6); middle toe without claw, 15.0–17.5 (16.3). *Adult female*: Wing, 115.6–122.5 (119.1); tail, 90.9–100.1 (96.0); bill, 14.5–16.5 (15.7); height of bill, 9.9–11.9 (11.2); tarsus, 23.1–24.9 (23.6); middle toe, 14.7–17.5 (16.0).

RANGE: S.w. Canada, south through Rocky Mts. to c. Arizona and n. New Mexico. Winters in vicinity of breeding range, south to n.w. Texas (casually).

TEXAS: *Winter*: Two collections: Gray Co., Pampa (adult female found alive, but died two weeks later, preserved?, Dec., 1933, V. E. Moore); Dallas Co., Dallas (adult male found dead, Nov. 24, 1969, Mrs. Phil Huey, preserved as skin, fide W. M. Pulich; identified by R. C. Banks).

[**COMMON REDPOLL,** *Acanthis flammea*
(Linnaeus)

Similar in size and shape to American Goldfinch; brown-streaked above; bright red on forehead; black chin; two white wing-bars; whitish below with brown-streaked sides. Male has touches of pink on breast and rump. Length, 5¼ in.; wingspan, 8½; weight, ½ oz.

RANGE: Circumpolar through arctic and subarctic regions; in North America, w. Alaska and n.w. British Columbia, east across n. Canada to Greenland. Nearctic races winter in southern parts of breeding range, south erratically to c. United States.

TEXAS: *Hypothetical*: Most likely to occur, if at all, in extreme northern portions. No specimen, but a scattering of sightings in northern Panhandle; also reported east to Fannin (winter of 1885–86, H. F. Peters) and

Harris (Apr. 2, 1926, R. A. Selle), south to Aransas (Jan. 3, 1935, Connie Hagar) cos.]

PINE SISKIN, *Spinus pinus* (Wilson)

SPECIES ACCOUNT

A small finch, liberally streaked above and below with brown; has very pointed, conical bill; patches of yellow in wings and in deeply notched tail, the yellow showing best when feathers are spread. Female is dimmer than male. Length, 5 in.; wingspan, 8¾; weight, ½ oz.

RANGE: S. Alaska, southeast through Canada to n.e. United States, and south through w. United States and highland Mexico to Guatemala. Northern races winter from s.e. Alaska and s. Canada through United States to n. Mexico.

TEXAS: (See map.) *Breeding*: Probably May to late July (no egg dates available, but nest located at 8,000 ft. in Guadalupe Mts. by F. R. Gehlbach; another at Madera Park in Davis Mts. by C. R. Bender). Irregular and uncommon in The Bowl, Guadalupe Mts.; rare and irregular in Davis Mts. *Winter*: Late Oct. to mid-May (extremes: Aug. 4, June 9). Very common, occasionally verging on abundant, to scarce in northern two-thirds; fairly common to virtually absent (some years) in southern third.

HAUNTS AND HABITS: In Texas, in summer, the Pine Siskin occurs only in high mountains of the Trans-Pecos, where it inhabits chiefly pine and Douglasfir woods. In winter, however, it may be found from eight thousand feet to sea level—from conifers to lowland deciduous trees, such as mesquite, sycamore, and sweetgum. Its presence is most apparent in late winter

PINE SISKIN, *Spinus pinus*
S. p. vagans

0 20 40 60 80
Scale in miles

Specimen record / Sight record

★ / ☆ Breeding
▲ / △ Spring
● / ○ Summer
▼ / ▽ Fall
■ / □ Winter

——— Approximate boundary of subspecies' breeding range

? Questionable record

and early spring when dozens, often in company with scores of American Goldfinches, devour seeds of the American elm. Very occasionally—as at Austin, Texas, from January to April, 1973—siskins outnumber goldfinches.

Pine Siskin flight is quick and undulatory; birds generally fly over the woodland canopy. Close-knit flocks hasten from tree to tree, alighting usually in the uppermost branches. A standard feeding operation is to work down from top to lower limbs of a tree, then fly up to the top of another and repeat the process. Like a crossbill, the Pine Siskin often clings upside down to a twig. It also forages on the ground where it moves with steps interspersed with a few hops. Like the Purple Finch and its close relative the American Goldfinch, it briskly flicks aside dead leaves with its bill. In addition to seeds of American elm, the Pine Siskin eats those of cedar elm, sweetgum, pine, filaree, alder, maple, sycamore, goldenrod, sunflower, chickweed, Douglasfir, and many others. Animal matter is mainly caterpillars, plant lice, fly larvae, and spiders. It frequently takes salt.

A husky buzzing *wee-zee*, slurring upward, is one note of the Pine Siskin; a sharp *tit-i-tit*, often given in flight, is another; most distinctive is a hoarse, drawnout *shreeee*. The song is a coarse version of the American Goldfinch's; it is often much prolonged. Males, at times in companies, sing from late January to late July while perched near the top of a tree or in flight.

DETAILED ACCOUNT: TWO SUBSPECIES

NORTHERN PINE SISKIN, *Spinus pinus pinus* (Wilson)

DESCRIPTION: *Adult male, nuptial plumage (brown phase)*: Acquired by wear from winter plumage. Pileum between drab and buffy brown; hindneck, back, and scapulars drab; rump and upper tail-coverts tilleul buff; everywhere broadly streaked with fuscous, most broadly on back; upper tail-coverts sometimes slightly tinged with yellow; tail fuscous to chaetura drab, base of feathers lemon yellow, this most extensive on second, third, and fourth pairs from outside, on which it occupies half or more of feather, at least on inner web, and all feathers terminally more or less edged with white or yellowish white on inner webs, and with dull pale yellow on outer webs, except on outermost pair; wings fuscous, outer edges of primaries, except at tips, and middle part of secondaries edged with dull citrine or sulphine yellow; inner edges of primaries and secondaries, except at tips, picric yellow to barium yellow, bases of primaries and secondaries, except outermost primaries, lemon yellow—this showing as spot on closed wing—and also on under surface of wing; tertials edged terminally on outer webs with yellowish or buffy white; lesser wing-coverts edged with color of back; greater and median wing-coverts broadly tipped with pale dull buff; sides of head between wood brown and deep olive buff, sometimes to dull cream buff on cheeks, everywhere finely streaked with light fuscous; sides of neck similar but more thickly or densely streaked fuscous; lower parts dull light cream buff, but middle of abdomen and crissum paler, everywhere streaked, rather narrowly on chin and throat, broadly on remainder of lower surface, except middle of abdomen, with hair brown to fuscous; axillars light yellow; lining of wing hair brown to drab, edged with buffy white, yellowish white, or pale yellow. Maxilla plumbeous, tinged with flesh color or vinaceous, but basal portion and all mandible paler; iris sepia, grayish sepia, or black; legs and feet sepia or brownish black. *Adult male, nuptial (gray phase)*: Similar to brown phase, but more grayish (less buffy or brownish);

upper surface light grayish olive, varying slightly toward drab, broadly streaked with chaetura drab; below grayish white with little buff tinge, streaks chaetura drab or dark hair brown. *Adult male, winter*: Acquired by complete postnuptial molt. Similar to corresponding phase of nuptial adult male, but upper surface more brownish, buffy, or yellowish, less sharply streaked because of broader light edgings of feathers; lower surface more buffy or more deeply buff or yellowish, streaks duller, somewhat obscured by broader buffy edgings of feathers. Maxilla brown or drab, its tip dull black; mandible paler or fawn color, also with blackish tip, iris vandyke brown; legs, feet, and claws seal brown. *Adult female, nuptial*: Acquired by wear from winter. Similar to nuptial adult male, but upper surface averaging lighter and somewhat more buffy or rufescent; yellow of wings and tail less extensive. *Adult female, winter*: Acquired by complete postnuptial molt. Similar to nuptial adult female, but upper surface more buffy or ochraceous and less conspicuously streaked due to broader light feather margins; streaks on lower surface less sharply defined, being more or less obscured by light edgings of feathers. *Male, first nuptial*: Acquired by wear from first winter. Similar to nuptial adult male, but upper parts somewhat more buffy or brownish; wing-bars more deeply buff. *Male, first winter*: Acquired by partial postjuvenal molt, which does not involve wing-quills or tail. Similar to adult male in winter, but upper surface much more deeply and richly buff or rufescent brown, buff of wing-bars much deeper. Bill brownish plumbeous; iris burnt umber; legs and feet dark purplish brown. *Female, first nuptial*: Acquired by wear from first winter. Similar to nuptial adult female, but somewhat more buffy or brownish above; wing-bars more deeply buff. Similar to first nuptial male, but with less yellow in wings or tail; also averaging darker, duller, less yellowish on upper surface. *Female, first winter*: Acquired by partial postjuvenal molt, which does not involve wing-quills or tail. Similar to adult female in winter, but more rufescent brown, and more deeply buff above; wing-bars deeper buff. *Male, juvenal*: Acquired by complete postnatal molt. Similar to first winter male, but upper surface with decidedly more yellowish tinge; more conspicuously dark marked above, these markings more inclining to spots than streaks, conveying more mottled appearance; lower surface somewhat more narrowly streaked or spotted and strongly washed with straw yellow instead of buff. *Female, juvenal*: Acquired by complete postnatal molt. Similar to juvenal male but with less yellow on wings and tail. Maxilla brownish black, but base lighter; mandible dull white, tip brownish black; legs and feet brownish black. *Natal* (this plumage of this race not seen in Texas): Between hair brown and drab. Bill, legs, and feet pinkish buff.

MEASUREMENTS: *Adult male*: Wing, 69.3–76.2 (average, 73.2) mm.; tail, 39.6–46.5 (43.7); bill (exposed culmen), 9.7–11.2 (10.7); height of bill at base, 5.8–7.4 (6.4); tarsus, 12.7–15.0 (14.2); middle toe without claw, 10.7–12.2 (11.2). *Adult female*: Wing, 66.8–75.2 (71.7); tail, 40.6–46.0 (43.2); bill, 9.7–11.7 (10.7); height of bill, 6.4–6.9 (6.6); tarsus, 13.0–15.2 (14.2); middle toe, 10.7–12.4 (11.2).

RANGE: S.e. Alaska to e. Canada, south to c. Kansas, Great Lakes region, and w. North Carolina (casually). Winters erratically in southern parts of breeding range, south to Tamaulipas and U.S. Gulf states.

TEXAS: *Winter*: Taken north to Cooke (Mar. 23), south to Travis and Bexar, west to Kerr and Callahan (Mar. 18) cos. Very common to scarce.

NESTING: (This race does not nest in Texas.) *Nest*: On uplands or bottoms; in forests or more open country; saddled on horizontal branch of pine, cedar, or other tree, 8–30 ft. above ground; well built, though rather thin and flat cup, varying much in size and beauty; composed of dry grasses, rootlets, pine needles, twigs, strips of bark, stems and ends of pine twigs, and outside of weed stalks, lichens, sedges, wool, coarse hair, and plant down; lined with pine needles, moss, thin twigs, plant down, fine rootlets, thin shreds of bark, hair, fur, and feathers. *Eggs*: 3–6, usually 4; rounded ovate to nearly oval; greenish white, pale bluish white, pale greenish blue, or light bluish green; with spots of reddish brown to pale rufous brown, dull

purple, or black, and with lilac gray shell markings; average size, 16.8 × 12.4 mm.

WESTERN PINE SISKIN, *Spinus pinus vagans* Aldrich

Race not in A.O.U. check-list, 1957 (see Appendix A).

DESCRIPTION: *Adult male and female, nuptial plumage*: Similar to *S. p. pinus*, but coloration paler, ground color of upper surface lighter and more buffy (less brownish); blackish streaks on upper and lower parts less heavy. *Natal*: Probably similar to *S. p. pinus*.

MEASUREMENTS: *Adult male*: Wing, 68.1–74.9 (average, 71.7) mm.; tail, 41.9–47.0 (45.0); bill (exposed culmen), 9.1–11.4 (10.2); tarsus, 14.0–15.0 (14.5); middle toe without claw, 9.9–11.9 (10.9). *Adult female*: Wing, 67.6–72.9 (70.1); tail, 40.9–46.0 (43.9); bill, 9.7–10.9 (10.4); tarsus, 14.0–15.0 (14.7); middle toe, 10.4–11.2 (10.7).

RANGE: S. Alaska, south through w. Canada and w. United States to n. Baja California and n. and c. Trans-Pecos Texas. Winters at lower elevations in and near breeding range, east erratically to Maine and south to n. Mexico.

TEXAS: *Breeding*: Two specimens: Culberson Co., Guadalupe Mts., The Bowl (July 11, 1938, G. H. Lowery, Jr.; June 14, 1939, T. D. Burleigh). *Winter*: Taken in Presidio (Nov. 8) and Brewster cos. Fairly common, but erratic.

NESTING: Similar to that of *S. p. pinus*, but restricted to forested mountains.

AMERICAN GOLDFINCH, *Spinus tristis* (Linnaeus)

SPECIES ACCOUNT   *See colorplate 32*

A small plump finch. *Nuptial male*: bright yellow with black cap on forehead; white markings on black wings (in form of wing-bars, edgings on tertials, and spots on primaries) and on notched black tail. *Winter male*: buffy olive yellow with whitish rump; lacks dark cap; usually retains small yellow patch on shoulder. *Female*: similar to winter male, but white-marked

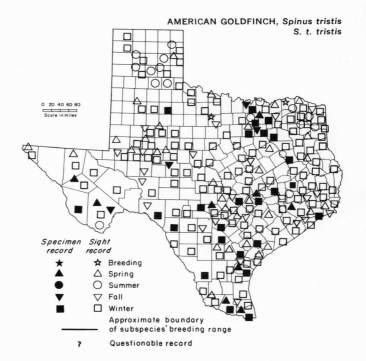

AMERICAN GOLDFINCH, *Spinus tristis*
S. t. tristis

0 20 40 60 80
Scale in miles

Specimen   Sight
record   record

★   ☆   Breeding
▲   △   Spring
●   ○   Summer
▼   ▽   Fall
■   □   Winter

——   Approximate boundary of subspecies' breeding range

?   Questionable record

wings and tail not so black; lacks yellow shoulder-patch. Length, 5 in.; wingspan, 8¾; weight, ½ oz.

RANGE: S. Canada, south to n. Baja California, s. Colorado, Oklahoma, and South Carolina. Winters in vicinity of breeding range, south to c. Mexico, Gulf states, and s. Florida.

TEXAS: (See map.) *Breeding*: July to early Sept. (no egg dates available) from 600 to 2,300 ft. Rare and local in northeastern portions (north of 33rd parallel). Last mention: Lamar Co., Paris ("breeding," June 1–15, 1915, J. Dunseth). *Winter*: Mid-Oct. to late May (extremes: July 31, June 20). Abundant to fairly common in eastern half; fairly common to scarce in western half.

HAUNTS AND HABITS: The American Goldfinch is typically a late nester—summer is well underway and many plants have gone to seed (food for both adults and nestlings), before breeding commences. In summer *Spinus tristis* inhabits chiefly riverbottoms of cottonwood, sycamore, pecan, and willow, or similar wet regions. Less particular in the nonbreeding season, it occurs, often in sizable flocks, from arid open country to humid coastal plains, as well as its favored eastern woodlands and meadows. At this season it especially frequents weedy fields and seed-bearing trees. In late winter and early spring large flocks of American Goldfinches, in company with Pine Siskins, eat seeds of the American elm. Smaller flocks feast on seeds of fall-fruiting cedar elm.

Flight is swift, steeply undulating, and often accompanied, especially in summer, with this goldfinch's distinctive *per-chic-o-ree* call. Almost always in a flock, birds bound over open fields and from tree to tree as they rove in search of food. Seldom is an individual seen alone or far removed from his flock-mates. Seeds of American elm, other elms, thistle, sunflower, sycamore, sweetgum, ragweed, dandelion, cottonwood, gaillardia, mullein, and many others predominate in its diet. A few insects (plant lice, beetles, caterpillars, cicadas, grasshoppers, crickets, and flies) are taken, especially in spring.

The mellow *per-chic-o-ree* call note is diagnostic; birds also sound a variety of finchlike "gossip." Song is rapid, often sustained, and canarylike. It is heard from late March to mid-September, occasionally early October. Males sing, often in groups, from near the top of a tree or bush or in flight.

DETAILED ACCOUNT: TWO SUBSPECIES

EASTERN AMERICAN GOLDFINCH, *Spinus tristis tristis* (Linnaeus)

DESCRIPTION: *Adult male, nuptial plumage*: Acquired by partial prenuptial molt. Forehead and fore part of crown black; upper tail-coverts pale drab gray, becoming white in worn summer condition; remainder of upper surface lemon chrome; tail dull black, but terminal portion of inner webs of all feathers extensively white, this extending in an oblique spot, largest on outer feathers, for almost half the length of feathers, though on middle feathers reduced in width to broad terminal edging, with also sometimes very narrow edging of dull white on outer webs of middle feathers; inner webs of primaries and of secondaries

chaetura black, outer webs, except at tips of primaries, black, as are wing-coverts and tertails, tertials and secondaries rather broadly edged with dull white on outer webs of terminal portion and also tipped with same; greater coverts black, narrowly tipped with white; lesser wing-coverts lemon chrome; median coverts white edged with yellow; sides of head and of neck, with lower surface, lemon chrome; crissum white, grayish white, or white washed with yellow; outer under wing-coverts dull black edged with white or yellowish white, remaining coverts mostly dull white; axillars white washed with yellow. Bill orange-yellow, straw yellow, dull maize yellow, orange ochraceous, or rufous, but tip chaetura black, dark brown, or ecru drab; iris dark sepia or prout brown; legs and feet ecru drab, fawn color, wood brown, pale flesh color, flesh color, light reddish sepia, or chocolate; claws drab. *Adult male, winter (red-brown phase)*: Acquired by complete postnuptial molt. Similar to gray-brown phase of adult female in winter (see below), but larger; base of forehead black, more or less concealed; upper surface more yellowish or rufescent brown; rump usually more yellowish; light wing edgings brighter; wings and tail black; sides of head and lower surface more yellowish; sides and flanks darker, more richly colored; under wing-coverts lemon yellow or lemon chrome. Bill dull flesh color, but base of mandible with tinge of yellow; iris dark brown; legs and feet pale flesh color. *Adult male, winter (gray-brown phase)*: Acquired by complete postnuptial molt. Similar to red-brown phase but more grayish, particularly on upper surface; sides and flanks lighter, more grayish. Bill brownish black, but base and mandible dull yellow or naples yellow; iris vandyke brown; legs and feet ecru drab. *Adult female, nuptial (yellow phase)*: Acquired by partial prenuptial molt. Pileum yellowish warbler green, sometimes a little mottled, spotted, or obscurely streaked by darker, more brownish centers of feathers; hindneck citrine; back between citrine and orange citrine, sometimes darker and more brownish; shorter upper tail-coverts similar but tinged or mixed sometimes considerably with lemon yellow; remaining upper tail-coverts light drab to smoke gray; tail chaetura drab, feathers edged externally narrowly with color of upper tail-coverts, and all feathers with large lengthened dull pale drab gray or dull tilleul buff spot on terminal portions of inner webs, this smallest and least definitely outlined on middle pair; wings chaetura drab to rather dark hair brown, inner margins of primaries and secondaries a little paler basally; terminal portion of outer webs of secondaries margined with dull pale drab gray or dull white; lesser coverts margined with color of back but somewhat duller; median and greater series tipped more or less broadly with dull white or tilleul buff; sides of head like crown but paler and often more yellowish, auriculars usually isabella color; lower surface wax yellow or lemon yellow to between strontian yellow and chalcedony yellow; under wing-coverts hair brown, inner coverts tipped with dull white; axillars dull white washed with yellow or pale drab. Bill yellow, ivory yellow, or dull light yellow, but tip dull brown; iris dark brown; legs and feet dull flesh color, vinaceous, clay color, yellow, or broccoli brown. *Adult female, nuptial (red-brown phase)*: Acquired by partial prenuptial molt. Similar to yellow phase, but upper surface light brownish olive, rump saccardo umber; sides of head more brownish (less yellowish); chin and throat dull olive yellow; jugulum dull light drab; flanks dull vinaceous buff or buffy avellaneous, with little or no tinge of yellow on shorter upper tail-coverts; breast, abdomen, and crissum dull white, buffy white, or very pale buff. *Adult female, nuptial (gray-brown phase)*: Similar to red-brown phase, but upper surface, sides of head, and flanks lighter, much more grayish (less brownish or buffy). *Adult female, winter*: Acquired by complete postnuptial molt. Similar to nuptial adult female, but in all three phases upper surface is duller and darker; in gray-brown phase somewhat more brownish; yellow of rump obscured by brownish or buffy tips of feathers or absent; edgings of primaries, secondaries, tertials, and wing-coverts broader and more buffy or brownish; lower surface duller and more generally brownish or buffy, yellow obscured by dull buffy tips of feathers. Bill clove brown, blackish slate, or dull black, but base of mandible isabella color, flesh color, dull light yellow, or brownish white; iris dark brown; legs and feet broccoli brown, chocolate, or fawn color. *Male and female, second winter*: Acquired by complete postnuptial molt. Normally like corresponding sex in adult winter, but sometimes with more or less olive on lesser wing-coverts. *Male, first nuptial*: Acquired by partial prenuptial molt. Similar to nuptial adult male, but lesser wing-coverts deep olive or citrine drab, instead of yellow; wings and tail somewhat duller, more brownish. *Male, first winter (red-brown phase)*: Acquired by partial postjuvenal molt, which does not involve wing-quills or tail. Similar to red-brown phase of adult male in winter, but upper parts less yellowish; wings somewhat more brownish, their light edgings, including those of wing-coverts, more buffy, sometimes cinnamon buff; lesser wing-coverts olive or dull brown; lower parts duller, of more rufescent brown, particularly on sides and flanks. Bill blackish slate, olive brown, or clove brown, but base of mandible dull yellow or dull white, sometimes with pinkish tinge; iris dark brown; legs and feet chocolate, seal brown, or drab. *Male, first winter (gray-brown phase)*: Similar to gray-brown phase of adult male in winter, but upper surface duller, more brownish (less yellowish), and usually darker, light wing edgings, including wing-bars, more deeply buff; lower parts duller and usually more brownish, particularly on sides and flanks. *Female, first nuptial*: Acquired by partial prenuptial molt. Similar to corresponding phase of nuptial adult female. *Female, first winter*: Acquired by partial postjuvenal molt. In all three phases similar to adult female in winter, but brown of upper parts more rufescent; wings and tail more brownish, light edgings even broader and much more deeply buff; lower parts more deeply and more extensively buff or light rufescent brown; yellow of lower surface deeply veiled by buffy tips of feathers. Similar to first winter male but smaller, more brightly rufescent above, wing-quills and tail dark olive brown to fuscous, instead of dull black; wing-bars and edgings of tertials and secondaries more deeply buff; lesser coverts more brownish or buffy (less yellowish); lower parts of more rufescent brown, particularly on sides and flanks. Maxilla blackish slate or broccoli brown, clove brown at tip; mandible vinaceous cinnamon, but base dull pale yellow; iris dark brown; legs hair brown, broccoli brown, dark flesh color, or dark cinnamon; feet clove brown. *Male, juvenal*: Acquired by complete postnatal molt. Similar to first winter male, but upper surface more rufescent; usually more or less obscurely mottled with darker brown; back sudan brown; shorter upper tail-coverts light buckthorn brown; longer upper tail-coverts mouse gray, washed with identical brown; tips of tail feathers dull drab; wing-bars and edgings of tertials ochraceous tawny; lower parts dull straw yellow to wax yellow, overlaid by ochraceous tawny, this sometimes in form of irregular blotches. Maxilla chaetura drab; mandible quaker drab; legs dull coral pink. *Female, juvenal*: Acquired by complete postnatal molt. Similar to juvenal male but smaller; duller, rather less rufescent above; wings and tail dark olive brown to fuscous, instead of dull black; wing-bars and edgings of tertials usually not quite so deeply buff; below averaging duller. *Natal*: Tilleul buff. Bill, legs, and feet pinkish buff.

MEASUREMENTS: *Adult male*: Wing, 70.9–75.2 (average, 72.7) mm.; tail, 43.2–51.3 (47.0); bill (exposed culmen), 9.7–10.2 (9.9); height of bill at base, 7.4–7.9 (7.6); tarsus, 12.7–14.7 (13.7); middle toe without claw, 10.2–11.2 (10.7). *Adult female*: Wing, 65.8–70.9 (68.8); tail, 39.6–46.8 (43.2); bill, 9.1–10.2 (9.7); height of bill, 7.4–7.9 (7.6); tarsus, 13.0–14.7 (14.0); middle toe, 10.2–11.2 (10.7).

RANGE: S. Manitoba to s. Quebec, south through e. two-thirds of United States to extreme n. Texas (rarely) and South Carolina. Winters in vicinity of breeding range, south to n.e. Mexico and s. Florida.

TEXAS: *Breeding*: No specimen, but a nest noted in Young Co., Eliasville (between 1884 and 1890, H. Y. Benedict) and reports of "breeding" in Lamar Co., Paris (June 1–15, 1915, J. Dunseth) considered to be of this race. *Winter*: Taken north to Dickens and Cooke, east to Chambers, south to Cameron, west to Kinney and Presidio cos. Usually common to fairly common.

NESTING: *Nest*: On uplands and bottoms, slopes, and valleys; in wild and cultivated land, orchards, ornamental grounds, fields, and roadsides; in crotch of tree or bush, evergreen or deciduous, such as willow or maple, or orchard tree, in top of thistle or other plant, occasionally in an abandoned blackbird's nest, 3–40 ft. above ground; beautiful, compact, symmetrical, cup-shaped nest, firmly fastened to twigs against which it rests; composed of grasses, leaves, shreds of bark, moss, thistle down, weeds, soft vegetable wool, shreds of dried grasses, and various other vegetable fibers; lined with thistle down, milkweed silk, hair, fine roots, horsehair, cotton, rags, string, hair, and occasionally feathers. *Eggs*: 3–6, usually 4–5; ovate to rounded ovate; plain bluish white, greenish white, or pale niagara green; unspotted, very rarely dotted with dull black or brown; average size, 16.3 × 13.0 mm.

PALE AMERICAN GOLDFINCH, *Spinus tristis pallidus* Mearns

DESCRIPTION: *Adult male, nuptial plumage*: Similar to *S. t. tristis* but larger, particularly wing and tail; yellow portions of plumage averaging paler; white spots on tail feathers usually larger; white edgings of tertials averaging broader. *Adult female and immature male*: Similar to *S. t. tristis* but decidedly paler, more grayish, light colored markings of wings and tail more extensive.

MEASUREMENTS: *Adult male*: Wing, 71.4–78.2 (average, 75.2) mm.; tail, 43.7–52.3 (50.3); bill (exposed culmen), 10.2–10.7 (10.4); tarsus, 13.7–14.7 (14.2); middle toe without claw, 9.7–11.2 (10.7). *Adult female*: Wing, 68.8–74.2 (72.2); tail, 43.2–51.6 (46.8); bill, 9.7–11.2 (10.2); tarsus, 13.2–14.7 (13.7); middle toe, 10.2–11.2 (10.7).

RANGE: S.e. British Columbia to s.w. Manitoba, south through w. United States, with exception of Pacific slope, to c. Nevada and s. Colorado. Winters in and near breeding range, south to s. Arizona and c. Veracruz.

TEXAS: *Winter*: Taken north to Tarrant, east to Walker, south to Hidalgo, west to Val Verde and Jeff Davis (Mar. 17) cos. Usually fairly common.

LESSER GOLDFINCH, *Spinus psaltria* (Say)

SPECIES ACCOUNT								*See colorplate 32*

Dark-backed Goldfinch, Black-backed Goldfinch, and Arkansas Goldfinch have often been applied to Texas birds. A tiny finch with a sharp conical bill. *Texas male*: glossy black above, including wings and notched tail; bright yellow below; bold white patches in wings and tail. *Immature male*: green-backed like adult male Green-backed Goldfinch, *S. p. hesperophilus*, of California. *Female*: olive above, including rump; greenish yellow below; dark wings with one or two white wing-bars. Length, 4½ in.; wingspan, 8; weight, ½ oz.

RANGE: S.w. Washington, Oregon, and California to n. Colorado, south through s.w. United States, Mexico, and Central America to South America; partially migratory in colder portions of its range. Naturalized in Cuba.

TEXAS: (See map.) *Breeding*: Early Mar. to late July (eggs, Mar. 18 to June 20) from 100 to 7,000 ft. Common to fairly common in rough terrain of Trans-Pecos and Edwards Plateau; uncommon and local in live oak areas of south Texas. Nesting unconfirmed in Panhandle. A few spring and summer records east to Dallas, Montgomery, and Galveston cos. *Winter*: Common to scarce from breeding range south to mouth of Rio Grande.

HAUNTS AND HABITS: The Lesser Goldfinch is one of the few species which nests widely in both western North America and highland Middle America. In Texas this bird occurs in lightly wooded areas where rainfall is very moderate (normally less than 35 in. per year); ordinarily it prefers hilly terrain, but it can extend into trees growing on plains if the average annual humidity is low.

The Guadalupe Valley on the Edwards Plateau supplies optimum habitat. Here this charming "Mexican canary" is, especially in warm months, almost constantly in sight and sound as it undulates from one streamside baldcypress or American sycamore to another. In the town of Kerrville it is a frequent brightener of bird baths, while in summer and fall, flocks of these seed eaters feed in patches of wild sunflowers and giant ragweed growing on vacant lots, in fallow fields, and along the river floodplain. In the hills this goldfinch forages in grass patches, junipers, oaks, and elms, usually at no great distance from water. Apparently, it must drink frequently to help digest the seeds it eats. *Spinus psaltria* supplements its mainly vegetable diet with a few plant lice, caterpillars, flies, beetles, wasps, and bees.

The Lesser's call note is a plaintive *tee-yee* (ascending) *tee-yer* (descending), or often simply *tee-yee* or *whee*; it is frequently given in flight. The male's rapid, jumbled, musical song is similar to the American Goldfinch's, but softer and less run together. From early March to September he sings from a perch near the top of a bush or small tree; frequently in late summer, males will perch together and sing in chorus.

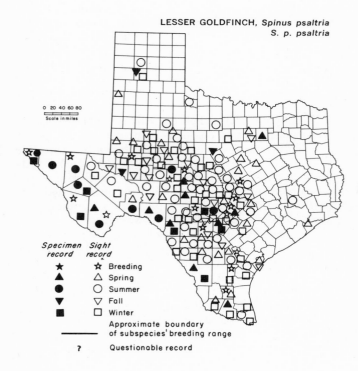

LESSER GOLDFINCH, *Spinus psaltria*
S. p. psaltria

0 20 40 60 80
Scale in miles

Specimen record / Sight record
★ / ☆ Breeding
▲ / △ Spring
● / ○ Summer
▼ / ▽ Fall
■ / □ Winter

——— Approximate boundary of subspecies' breeding range

? Questionable record

DETAILED ACCOUNT: ONE SUBSPECIES

ARKANSAS LESSER GOLDFINCH, *Spinus psaltria psaltria* (Say)

This race was named for the Arkansas River in Colorado.

DESCRIPTION: *Adult male, nuptial plumage*: Acquired by complete prenuptial molt. Upper parts black with faint bluish gloss; feathers of rump with large, mostly concealed, white spots, these sometimes with tinge of light yellow; tail brownish black, middle pair of feathers brownish black to chaetura black, two middle pairs of feathers unmarked, third pair often more or less white basally in form of shaft streak, outermost three pairs of feathers mostly white on inner webs, except for broad truncated tip of black; wing-quills chaetura black to chaetura drab, but inner margins of primaries and secondaries, except at tips of primaries, rather light fuscous, secondaries and inner primaries with very narrow dull white tips, basal portion of primaries, except for two outermost, white, this forming conspicuous white spot in closed wing; terminal portion of outer webs of tertials extensively dull white or white; wing-coverts edged externally with glossy black of upper parts; sides of head and neck black like upper surface, malar region and entire lower surface lemon chrome to gamboge yellow, but crissum lemon yellow; lining of wing chaetura black to chaetura drab, inner portion edged with dull white or yellowish white; axillars chaetura black to chaetura drab, tipped with dull white or yellowish white. Maxilla blackish brown or olive; mandible of lighter brown or yellowish olive; iris dark brown; legs and feet sepia. *Adult male, winter*: Acquired by complete postnuptial molt. Like nuptial adult male. *Adult female, nuptial (dark olive phase)*: Acquired by complete prenuptial molt. Upper parts yellowish olive to dull citrine, but centers of feathers darker—chaetura drab, imparting slightly spotted appearance to pileum; upper tail-coverts broadly chaetura drab, tipped with color of upper surface; tail chaetura drab, outer webs edged with color of upper surface but rather duller, more grayish, outermost two tail feathers with large oblique dull white spot on middle portion of inner webs; wings chaetura drab to fuscous, inner edges somewhat lighter, tertials tipped and broadly edged on terminal portion of outer webs with light drab, inner secondaries terminally margined on outer webs with same color, large white area at base of both webs of primaries, except outermost two or three, showing as a spot even on closed wing, lesser wing-coverts edged with color of back; median coverts tipped narrowly with hair brown; greater coverts broadly tipped with drab; sides of head and of neck dull, rather dark yellowish olive; malar region and lower surface wax yellow to dark wax yellow, but crissum amber yellow, sides and flanks yellowish olive, jugulum and sides of breast sometimes obscurely streaked with this color; lining of wing chaetura drab to light drab, inner portion broadly tipped with dull white or very pale drab, outer part tipped with drab. *Adult female, nuptial (light olive phase)*: Acquired by complete prenuptial molt. Similar to dark olive phase but very much paler both above and below, upper surface light, grayish dull citrine; lower surface dull citrine yellow. *Adult female, nuptial (gray phase)*: Acquired by complete prenuptial molt. Similar to light olive phase, but upper surface very much more grayish, slightly greenish citrine drab; lower surface dull barium yellow, in places more or less washed with smoke gray. *Adult female, winter (light and dark olive phases)*: Acquired by complete postnuptial molt. Similar to nuptial adult female in corresponding phase, but colors of upper parts more blended; edgings of tertials broader; lower surface somewhat duller due to buffy or olivaceous edgings of feathers. *Adult female, winter (gray phase)*: Acquired by complete postnuptial molt. Similar to nuptial adult female in gray phase, but upper surface duller, colors more blended; lower surface duller, more brownish or grayish. *Male, second winter*: Acquired by complete postnuptial molt. Like adult male in winter. *Male, first nuptial*: Acquired by complete prenuptial molt. Similar to nuptial adult male, but upper surface, except on pileum, much mixed with yellowish serpentine green to dull citrine, sometimes this color occupying entire upper surface, except pileum, there being thus great variation in amount of black on upper surface, this usually appearing in spots or more or less extensive patches; yellow of lower surface lighter and somewhat duller. *Male, first winter*: Acquired by complete postjuvenal molt. Similar to first nuptial male, but black feathers of pileum usually with citrine or brownish tips; upper surface likewise duller and more brownish, with but little black and this usually on pileum; wings and tail like those of adult female in winter; tertials edged and tipped with dull pale drab gray or dull yellowish white; wing-bars dull buff; wings without any clear white. *Female, first nuptial*: Acquired by complete prenuptial molt. Like adult female. *Female, first winter*: Acquired by complete postjuvenal molt. Similar to corresponding phase of adult female in winter, but averaging more brownish, and in gray phase somewhat darker; wing-bars more buffy to dull cinnamon buff; yellow of lower parts more brownish or buffy, and in dark phase, to honey yellow or olive ocher; tail nearly always with very little or no white. *Male, juvenal*: Acquired by complete postnatal molt. Similar to first winter female, but wing longer; upper parts rather paler and more inclined to be obscurely mottled; wing-bars more decidedly and brightly buffy—cinnamon buff; and, like female, with little or no white on tail. *Female, juvenal*: Acquired by complete postnatal molt. Similar to juvenal male but smaller; upper surface usually darker, duller, more brownish (less yellowish); lower parts duller, usually more brownish or grayish (less yellowish). *Natal*: Pileum light drab; other upper parts drab gray to pale drab gray or tilleul buff to light vinaceous buff.

MEASUREMENTS: *Adult male*: Wing, 62.0–68.8 (average, 64.5) mm.; tail, 38.4–44.4 (41.1); bill (exposed culmen), 9.1–10.7 (9.9); tarsus, 11.9–13.2 (12.7); middle toe without claw, 9.1–10.7 (9.9). *Adult female*: Wing, 61.0–65.5 (63.5); tail, 38.1–42.9 (39.9); bill, 8.9–10.2 (9.7); tarsus, 12.4–13.2 (12.7); middle toe, 9.7–10.7 (10.2).

RANGE: S. Wyoming (casually) to n.w. Oklahoma, south through w. and c. Texas to c. Guerrero and c. Oaxaca; somewhat migratory in colder parts of its range.

TEXAS: *Breeding*: Collected northwest to El Paso, east to Tom Green, southeast to Hays, west to Brewster cos. *Winter*: Taken north to Randall (Sept. 30), east to Dallas (May 2), south to Hidalgo (May 1) and Webb, west to El Paso cos.

NESTING: *Nest*: On uplands and bottomlands, in semiopen country, wild and cultivated areas; in fork of tree or bush; small, compactly woven, deeply cupped structure; composed of fine grasses, fibers of weeds and other plants; lined with vegetable down and other soft materials, grass, cotton, and horsehair. *Eggs*: 3–5, usually 4; ovate to rounded ovate; very pale greenish blue or greenish white; unspotted; average size, 15.5 × 11.4 mm.

LAWRENCE'S GOLDFINCH, *Spinus lawrencei* (Cassin)

SPECIES ACCOUNT   *See colorplate 32*

A gray goldfinch with bold yellow wing-markings; yellow wash on breast and rump; pink bill. Male has black face. Length, 4¾ in.; wingspan, 8¼; weight, ½ oz.

RANGE: California (mainly west of Sierra Nevada) and n. Baja California. One Arizona nesting (at Parker, 1952). Winters in breeding range and southeast to c. Sonora, Arizona, and occasionally to New Mexico and extreme w. Texas.

TEXAS: *Winter*: Apparently no specimen or photograph, but numerous meticulous sight records in cold season (extremes: Nov. 16, Mar. 20) at irregular intervals between 1934 and 1954 in El Paso Co. by members of El Paso Audubon Society. One unconfirmed

sighting in Hidalgo Co., Bentsen–Rio Grande Valley State Park (1 female, Jan. 1, 1972).

HAUNTS AND HABITS: Lawrence's Goldfinch is probably the prettiest and certainly the most restricted of North American goldfinches. It is, in fact, practically endemic as a breeder within the dry Pacific foothills and valleys of California and northern Baja California. Los Angeles County south to San Diego County was especially favored, but now that this former fair land has been turned into a smog-palled sea of automobiles, freeways, parking lots, houses, and Australian eucalyptus, *Spinus lawrencei* is reduced here. Unlike most other California chaparral birds, it does not adapt readily to lawns and plantings of foreign trees and shrubs. Nowadays the best places to find Lawrence's Goldfinches are the same as those inhabited by the last California Condors—the primitive areas from the Sespe Condor Refuge north to Mount Pinos. Here this goldfinch lives chiefly in stands of foothill chaparral dominated by the bush chamise (*Adenostoma fasciculatum*). Water must also be available since this dryseed eater apparently must drink daily. Salty bits of soil are also swallowed, especially during the nesting season.

The female builds her neatly woven nest cup in various species of trees or dense bushes. Nests may be solitary or in colonies. Territory defense in this gregarious bird seems to be rather weak; the male's song appears to serve the purpose more of cementing the pair-bond than of proclaiming breeding territory. Lawrence's Goldfinch is notably less attracted to a previous nesting locality than are birds in general. If food or water declines, it readily moves to another valley or hillside where conditions are more favorable. Its undulating flight is similar to that of other goldfinches.

In California, Lawrence's avidly eats chamise achenes from midsummer until late winter. Sometimes the bird appears to consume buds and flowers of this shrub also. Seeds of the herb fiddleneck (*Amsinckia intermedia*) are the main food in spring and early summer. In Arizona, *S. lawrencei* feeds with Lesser and American goldfinches on sunflowers and thistles in open fields.

Flight note is a wee bell-like *tink-oo* (F. G. Watson). Sometimes a harsh *kee-yerr* is uttered from a perch. Spring song of the male resembles that of the American Goldfinch but may be weaker (R. T. Peterson). Flocking Lawrence's Goldfinches usually keep up a nearly continuous tinkling of thin clear notes, varied and musical; in autumn, finch-type slurs are interspersed among flock vocalizations (J. M. Lindsdale).

CHANGES: Apparently Lawrence's Goldfinch was unknown in or near Texas until 1934 when the bird was first recorded on an El Paso Audubon Christmas Bird Count. The species was subsequently found on this count in 1943, 1951, and 1953. A Mr. Williams reported that one of these goldfinches was shot at Las Cruces, New Mexico, in approximately 1940. At about this time T. M. Kirksey saw an individual in a yard on Federal Street, El Paso, Texas.

During the cool season of 1947–48, there was a flight of this bird along the Rio Grande from Hatch, New Mexico, to the El Paso region. Ornithologist Allan R. Phillips recorded the species at Hatch on November 8, 1947. Twelve miles north of El Paso, in sight of Anthony, New Mexico, but a few yards inside Texas, a flock of 50 Lawrence's Goldfinches was present on March 8, 1948 (Lena G. McBee and Mary Belle Keefer).

Next incursion into the upper Rio Grande Valley was in the autumn of 1950. At Ascarate Park, within the city limits of El Paso, 4 birds were identified on November 16, and 6 on November 27, 1950 (Keefer); a flock of 43 was flitting about the park on December 3, 1950 (McBee, Keefer). A few individuals reached as far southeast as Fabens, Texas; some lingered at El Paso until March 20, 1951 (Fred Cornelius). In 1953–54, groups of *Spinus lawrencei* wintered again in El Paso. The Audubon Christmas count turned up 7 on December 29, 1953, and this goldfinch was occasionally encountered up to February 18, 1954 (Keefer).

Movements of the Lawrence's Goldfinch are extremely unpredictable. However, it is perhaps significant that peak flight years were in the late 1940's and early 1950's. These years coincide with the time when the smog-concrete octopus in the bird's southern California home was becoming difficult to live with. Also, the terrific drought that gripped the Southwest from 1950 to 1957 may have caused migrating birds to seek oasis along that permanent stream called the Rio Grande in the United States, and the Río Bravo del Norte in Mexico.

DETAILED ACCOUNT: NO SUBSPECIES

DESCRIPTION: *Adult male, nuptial plumage*: Acquired by wear from winter plumage. Following description taken from Ridgway (1901, *Bull. U.S. Nat. Mus.*, no. 50, pt. 1, p. 121): Anterior portion of head all round, including throat and fore part of crown, black; above brownish gray (back sometimes tinged with olive green), changing to yellowish olive green on rump; sides of head and lateral under parts paler brownish gray, becoming white on under tail-coverts and abdomen; outer webs of wing-coverts and remiges partly yellow; inner webs of rectrices (except middle pair) with subterminal white patch; chest and median portion of breast yellow. *Adult male, winter*: Acquired by complete molt from nuptial. Like nuptial adult male, but posterior black feathers of crown tipped with gray; back darker, more brownish—between brownish olive and light brownish olive; yellow of back completely, that of rump and upper tail-coverts partly, obscured by brownish olive. Bill, legs, and feet brownish flesh color; iris brown. *Adult female, nuptial*: Acquired by wear from winter. Similar to nuptial adult male, but black of head and throat replaced by grayish olive; yellow of back absent; wings and tail fuscous, white spots on the latter of less extent, yellow on wings usually duller and lighter; yellow on breast and jugulum duller and less extensive. *Adult female, winter*: Acquired by complete molt from nuptial adult female. Similar to nuptial adult female, but upper surface darker and more brownish; yellow on rump and wings mostly duller, more or less obscured by brown; lower parts duller, yellow of breast somewhat obscured by brown. *Male and female, first winter*: Acquired by partial molt from juvenal. Like corresponding sex of adult in winter. *Male, juvenal*: Acquired by complete molt from natal. Similar to adult female in winter, but upper parts obscurely streaked, instead of being nearly uniform; no yellow on rump; wings above duller, wing-coverts buff to ochraceous, instead of dull yellow; breast, jugulum, and sides obscurely streaked with dull grayish olive on a dull yellowish or grayish white ground, and without any definite yellow area. *Female, juvenal*: Acquired by complete molt from natal. Similar to juvenal male, but upper surface duller, more grayish brown; yellow on wings duller and less extensive; lower surface darker, duller, more brownish (less olive), and more pronouncedly streaked, almost no trace of yellow in the ground color; white tail-spots smaller.

MEASUREMENTS: *Adult male*: Wing, 66.3–70.1 (average, 68.1) mm.; tail, 46.0–50.8 (47.5); bill (exposed culmen), 7.9–8.6 (8.1); tarsus, 12.7–13.2 (13.0); middle toe without claw, 10.2–10.9 (10.4). *Adult female*: Wing, 63.0–67.1 (65.5); tail, 41.9–47.5 (44.7); bill, 7.9–8.9 (8.4); tarsus, 12.7–13.7 (13.0); middle toe, 9.7–10.4 (10.2).

TEXAS: *Winter*: See species account.

RED CROSSBILL, *Loxia curvirostra* Linnaeus

SPECIES ACCOUNT

A chunky finch with crossed mandibles; blackish wings and tail. *Male*: brick red. *Female*: dull olive gray. Length, 6½ in.; wingspan, 11; weight, 1½ oz.

RANGE: Boreal conifer forests of Northern Hemisphere; in Americas, from s. Alaska to Newfoundland, south through w. United States and Mexico to Nicaragua, and through n.e. United States to n. Wisconsin and s.e. New York; isolated populations south in high Appalachian Mts. to w. North Carolina. Northern nearctic races wander erratically through Canada and United States (casually to Gulf coast) in winter.

TEXAS: (See map.) *Breeding*: Scarce and irregular in summer in Guadalupe Mts., nesting at least sporadically: 1 of 3 birds recently collected carried a developed soft egg, 19 × 13 mm., low in oviduct; these speci-

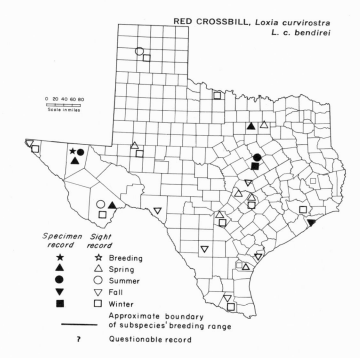

RED CROSSBILL, *Loxia curvirostra*
L. c. bendirei

0 20 40 60 80
Scale in miles

Specimen record	Sight record	
★	☆	Breeding
▲	△	Spring
●	○	Summer
▼	▽	Fall
■	□	Winter

—— Approximate boundary of subspecies' breeding range

? Questionable record

mens (race as yet undetermined) taken at head of Bear Canyon, 8,000 ft. (July 7, 1972, G. A. Newman; original nos., 335, 336, 337). Three specimens collected, but nesting unconfirmed, summer 1938, in The Bowl (see detailed account). Rare and erratic in summer in Chisos Mts. (breeding unconfirmed). *Winter*: Late Nov. to mid-Apr. (extremes: Aug. 13, June 11). Scarce and erratic in Trans-Pecos, Panhandle, and central portions; rare to casual along coast and in Rio Grande delta; apparently only one sight record from wooded eastern quarter: Polk Co., near Livingston (Dec. 16, 1972, J. R. Stewart, fide V. L. Emanuel). During the massive winter irruption of 1972–73, the species was recorded as far south as Hidalgo Co., Santa Ana Nat. Wildlife Refuge (flock of 25, Dec. 13, 1972, W. A. Shifflett).

HAUNTS AND HABITS: The Red Crossbill's crossed mandibles are well adapted to extracting seeds from cones in its great northern forest home. Invasions of this wanderer into Texas, some bird students believe, are triggered by failures of the conifer seed crop to the north. In southern regions it seeks food in pine woods, deciduous trees, weed fields, plant nurseries, gardens, and feeding trays.

Crossbill flight is strong, swift, and mildly undulating. In trees it forages efficiently and deliberately. Using feet as well as bill, it suggests a tiny parrot. In fact, one European form of the Red Crossbill is officially named Parrot Crossbill. Often it hangs head down or temporarily suspends itself with its beak. It is more nervous when feeding on the ground and frequently flies up to low bushes if disturbed. After gorging, the Crossbill sits inactive on a shady limb of a tree. It is ordinarily tame and permits close approach—especially when resting. Sojourning crossbills feed on—in addition to conifer seeds—seeds of ragweed, elm, maple, hemp, sunflower, and evening primrose; buds of various deciduous trees; and a few insects—chiefly caterpillars, ants, beetles, plant lice, and spittlebugs. Upon occasion they take salt, such as that sprinkled on highways to melt snow and ice.

A sharp metallic *kimp kimp* note is frequently given in flight. From a tall conifer, or in flight, the male Red Crossbill sings his melodious finchlike *too-tee too-tee too-tee-tee-tee* from early January to mid-July.

DETAILED ACCOUNT: THREE SUBSPECIES

BENT'S RED CROSSBILL, *Loxia curvirostra benti* Griscom

DESCRIPTION: *Adult male, nuptial plumage*: Acquired by wear from winter plumage. Upper parts light scarlet, scarlet, or brazil red to english red or grenadine red, but rump and shorter upper tail-coverts light brazil red to light scarlet, and longest upper tail-coverts fuscous edged with brazil red; on all upper surface, except shorter upper tail-coverts and rump, fuscous or light fuscous centers of feathers show more or less through red and produce irregularly mottled or spotted appearance; tail fuscous, narrowly margined on outer webs of feathers with dull red, and on inner webs narrowly with drab or dull light drab; wings fuscous, inner margins of primaries and secondaries, except tips of primaries, dull drab, verging to light drab at extreme base, outer

margins of primaries and secondaries with slight wash of reddish, as have also lesser wing-coverts, this sometimes verging to light brownish olive; lores dull drab; sides of head red like upper surface, more or less mottled with pale fuscous or dull hair brown of underlying portions of feathers; lower parts red like upper parts and mottled in same way by underlying dull colors of feathers, which are here dull drab to dull hair brown, palest on chin and middle of abdomen; crissum hair brown, feathers tipped with dull olive drab; lining of wing hair brown, feathers tipped with pale gray or drab and somewhat washed with pale dull red. Bill sepia or blackish brown, but paler on cutting edges and at base of mandible; iris raw umber, dark claret brown, or hazel; legs and feet rather grayish sepia, dark olive drab, or dull dark or blackish brown. *Adult male, winter*: Acquired by complete postnuptial molt. Similar to nuptial adult male, but red of upper and lower parts darker, duller, of more rosy hue; red feathers of throat with obscure pale gray or dull white tips; lighter, brighter red of summer plumage is acquired by wearing off of feather barbules. Bill and legs drab. *Adult female, nuptial*: Acquired by wear from winter. Upper parts hair brown, but feather centers darker, producing spotted effect, and everywhere washed more or less strongly with light yellowish olive; rump and shorter upper tail-coverts dull or bright olive ocher to primuline yellow, only slightly spotted with dark brown centers of feathers; tail dark hair brown to fuscous, very narrowly margined on outer webs of feathers with yellow of rump; wings dark hair brown to fuscous, wing-coverts and quills very narrowly edged with dull citrine; sides of head and of neck light dull hair brown or between drab and hair brown, lores paler and everywhere slightly mottled or streaked with darker brown; lower parts dull smoke gray, feather centers darker and more or less overlaid, chiefly on throat, jugulum, breast, and sides of body, with olive ocher or dull greenish olive ocher; sides and flanks more or less obscurely streaked with dull hair brown; lining of wing drab, edged with paler drab. Maxilla chaetura black, ochraceous black, dark olive slate, or dull black; mandible dark dull gray, cutting edges light gray or drab; iris dull dark brown or reddish brown; legs and feet chaetura drab, light brown, or dull black. *Adult female, winter*: Acquired by complete postnuptial molt. Similar to nuptial adult female, but colors rather brighter both above and below. *Male, second nuptial*: Acquired by wear from second winter. Similar to nuptial adult male, but red of upper and lower parts lighter, more tinged with yellow or orange; above mixed somewhat with light yellowish olive or olive yellow, below spotted or mixed with same colors and also with olive ocher or honey yellow; entire plumage thus presenting much mottled or patched appearance. *Male, second winter*: Acquired by complete postnuptial molt. Similar to second nuptial male, but upper and lower parts duller and colors more blended. *Male, first nuptial*: Acquired by wear from first winter. Similar to second nuptial male, but both upper and lower surfaces duller, with little or almost no red—replaced mostly by yellow to yellowish olive, with often only little of this. *Male, first winter*: Acquired by partial postjuvenal molt, not involving wing-quills or tail. Similar to first nuptial male, but coloration in general rather brighter and colors more blended. *Female, first nuptial*: Acquired by wear from first winter. Similar to nuptial adult female, but upper parts duller, of more grayish brown, much less washed with greenish yellow; yellow of rump duller; lower parts also duller, more grayish, much less washed with greenish yellow, and this color also less bright. *Female, first winter*: Acquired by partial postjuvenal molt, not including wing-quills or tail. Similar to first nuptial female but lighter and brighter, colors somewhat more blended. Similar to adult female in winter but duller, more grayish or brownish, and with much less wash of olive yellow, particularly above, also this color paler. *Juvenal*: Acquired by complete postnatal molt. Upper parts grayish olive to pale olive buff or tilleul buff, broadly streaked everywhere on feather centers with chaetura drab to fuscous; wings and tail chaetura drab to fuscous, drab tips of wing-coverts forming two obscure wing-bars; lower surface and sides of head tilleul buff to olive buff, narrowly streaked on chin, throat, and sides of head and neck, broadly streaked elsewhere, with chaetura drab. *Natal* (this plumage of this race not seen in Texas): Light drab to mouse gray. Bill, legs, and feet olive gray.

MEASUREMENTS: *Adult male*: Wing, 89.9–98.1 (average, 94.0) mm.; tail, 53.6–58.4 (56.1); bill (exposed culmen), 17.0–19.0 (18.0); height of bill at base, 9.9–10.4 (10.2); tarsus, 17.0–19.0 (17.8); middle toe without claw, 12.4–14.0 (13.5). *Adult female*: Wing, 88.4–91.9 (89.2); tail, 50.0–55.9 (53.6); bill, 17.3–18.5 (18.0); height of bill, 9.9–10.4 (10.2); tarsus, 18.0–18.5 (18.3); middle toe, 12.7–13.2 (13.0).

RANGE: S.e. Montana and w. North Dakota, south to c. Colorado. Wanders erratically (chiefly nonbreeders) to s.w. California, s.e. Texas, and n.e. Tennessee.

TEXAS: *Winter*: Taken in McLennan, Galveston (Nov. 21), and Brewster (May 3) cos. Scarce and erratic.

BENDIRE'S RED CROSSBILL, *Loxia curvirostra bendirei*
Ridgway

DESCRIPTION: *Adult male and female, nuptial plumage*: Similar to *L. c. benti*, but wing shorter; upper and lower surfaces darker and duller; male less rosy (more scarlet). *Natal*: Probably similar to *L. c. benti*.

MEASUREMENTS: *Adult male*: Wing, 88.9–95.5 (average, 92.5) mm.; tail, 45.5–56.1 (52.1); bill (exposed culmen), 16.3–19.6 (18.0); height of bill at base, 10.2–11.7 (11.2); tarsus, 16.0–18.3 (17.3); middle toe without claw, 12.7–15.5 (14.0). *Adult female*: Wing, 83.1–93.0 (87.4); tail, 43.2–54.3 (50.3); bill, 16.8–19.0 (17.8); height of bill, 10.2–11.4 (10.9); tarsus, 16.5–17.8 (17.0); middle toe, 13.0–14.7 (14.0).

RANGE: Chiefly from interior s. Yukon, south to s.w. Utah and w. Wyoming. Wanders erratically (mainly nonbreeders) to n. Baja California, w. Texas, and n.e. Iowa.

TEXAS: *Summer*: Three specimens: Culberson Co., Guadalupe Mts. (May 19, 20, 1938, G. H. Lowery, Jr.). (See species account for evidence of breeding in 1972; specimens perhaps of this race.)

NESTING: *Nest*: In mountains; mostly in forests and their margins; in fork or on horizontal branch of coniferous tree, 18 ft. or more above ground, sometimes at a considerable height, and often well concealed; rather flat bowl; composed of evergreen twigs, strips of soft bark, moss, lichens, and green stems of plants, fine grass, and pine needles; lined with rootlets, slender twigs, grasses, moss, horsehair, other hair, and feathers. *Eggs*: 3–4, usually 4; ovate; greenish white, pale bluish white, or bluish green; spotted, blotched, and marbled with cinnamon, chocolate, purplish brown, or purplish black, and with lavender or lilac shell markings; average size, 21.9 × 15.2 mm.

MEXICAN RED CROSSBILL, *Loxia curvirostra stricklandi*
Ridgway

DESCRIPTION: *Adult male and female, nuptial plumage*: Similar to *L. c. benti* but decidedly larger, particularly wing, exposed culmen, and height of bill at base; coloration in both male and female darker.

MEASUREMENTS: *Adult male*: Wing, 96.0–102.9 (average, 100.3) mm.; tail, 54.3–58.4 (56.4); bill (exposed culmen), 19.0–21.1 (19.8); height of bill at base, 12.4–13.5 (13.0); tarsus, 17.5–18.5 (18.0); middle toe without claw, 15.0–16.3 (15.5). *Adult female*: Wing, 93.5–98.6 (96.3); tail, 47.8–54.3 (52.1); bill, 19.3–20.3 (19.6); height of bill, 12.2–12.7 (12.4); tarsus, 17.5–18.3 (17.8); middle toe, 14.0–15.2 (14.7).

RANGE: N. Baja California, s.e. Arizona, and s. New Mexico, south through mainland Mexico to c. Veracruz. Wanders erratically (chiefly nonbreeders) to e. Nevada, n.e. Wyoming, n.e. Kansas, and Texas.

TEXAS: *Vagrant*: One specimen: Tarrant Co., Fort Worth (female, May 17, 1954, W. M. Pulich; U.S. Nat. Museum collection, no. 463051). Six birds—3 males and 3 females—sighted in Brewster Co., Chisos Mts. (June 13, 1901, V. Bailey) were considered to belong to this very large race.

OLIVE SPARROW, *Arremonops rufivirgatus*
(Lawrence)

SPECIES ACCOUNT

Arremonops rufivirgata of A.O.U. check-list, 1957. Texas Sparrow of older books. Resembles the Green-tailed Towhee (see below), but is smaller, duller, and lacks clear-cut white throat-patch. Olive above; gray buff and whitish below; broad brown stripe on each side of crown, a narrower one of same color through eye. Length, 6¼ in.; wingspan, 8½.

RANGE: Sinaloa and s. Texas, south through both coastal slopes to Chiapas and British Honduras; also Pacific side of Costa Rica.

TEXAS: (See map.) *Resident*: Breeds, early Mar. to late Sept. (eggs, Mar. 16 to Sept. 7) from near sea level to 948 ft. Locally fairly common from Del Rio, Sabinal (Uvalde Co.), Atascosa Co., Beeville, and Rockport south to mouth of Rio Grande; recorded in extreme southern Trans-Pecos. Doubtful sight records north to Waco and Austin. Normal distribution coincides almost exactly with Tamaulipan Biotic Province.

HAUNTS AND HABITS: The Olive Sparrow is the last of the Texas-only U.S. birds. This unobtrusive bird has two other distinctions: It is the first in the series of Texas-inhabiting sparrows (1) to have a yellow spot on the edge of the bend of the wing; and (2) to forage by scratching backward with both feet at the same time. Both of these characteristics are frequently encountered—but not always combined in the same species—from the Olive Sparrow to the end of the Texas bird list.

Arremonops rufivirgatus spends its life on and near

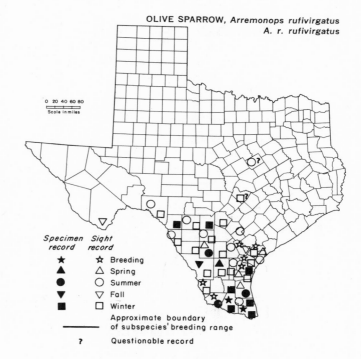

OLIVE SPARROW, *Arremonops rufivirgatus*
A. r. rufivirgatus

0 20 40 60 80
Scale in miles

Specimen record / Sight record
★ ☆ Breeding
▲ △ Spring
● ○ Summer
▼ ▽ Fall
■ □ Winter
——— Approximate boundary of subspecies' breeding range
? Questionable record

the ground in dense thickets. In the Rio Grande delta, optimum habitat is a tangle of thorny shrubs—mesquite, Texas ebony, anacua, huisache, and retama; farther north, modest numbers of this sparrow hide in streamside growths of cane, briars, willow, ash, even live oak. Its habitat in Texas is almost identical with that of the Long-billed Thrasher; however, the sparrow usually sings from a secluded perch closer to the ground.

Its tangled haunts prohibit easy view of the Olive Sparrow. Most flights are short, flitting junkets amid bushes. It feeds here or on the ground, where it noisily scratches in leaf litter as it searches for insects and seeds (only those of wild tomato are recorded for the species).

Call notes include a squeak and an insectlike buzz. The Olive Sparrow's song is a monotonous series of notes: *chip chip chip chip-chip-chip-chipchipchip* which sounds like a small steel ball bouncing to rest on concrete; it is louder and more metallic than the Field Sparrow's similar vocalization. Singing is chiefly from early March to late July.

CHANGES: Since 1933, the twenty million acres that constitute the sole U.S. range of this bird have been subjected to increasingly widespread brush removal, chiefly for the purpose of "improving" livestock rangeland; over six million acres, including 98 percent of its optimum habitat in the Rio Grande delta, had been cleared by 1968. The Olive Sparrow population has been somewhat reduced, but as yet there has been little or no withdrawal from extremities of its range.

Arremonops rufivirgatus is one of the few small songbirds that still (early 1970's) maintains a fairly healthy breeding population in and near the Rio Grande delta. Apparently its extraordinarily well concealed nest is hard for even a cowbird to find. Also, much of its remaining thicket habitat is fairly well removed from drifting poisonous agricultural sprays. However, severe overbrowsing by Spanish goats and cattle has rendered thickets unsuitable for Olive Sparrows on some ranches in Texas and Mexico.

DETAILED ACCOUNT: ONE SUBSPECIES

TEXAS OLIVE SPARROW, *Arremonops rufivirgatus rufivirgatus* (Lawrence)

DESCRIPTION: *Adults, nuptial plumage*: Acquired by wear from winter plumage. Pileum and hindneck with two broad lateral stripes of prout brown to cinnamon brown, with broad central stripe that, with remainder of upper surface, is between olive citrine and saccardo olive, sometimes more or less washed with mouse gray; tail brownish olive to light brownish olive, outer edges of feathers, which occupy most of outer web, light yellowish olive; primaries, secondaries, and tertials fuscous, but inner edges of primaries and secondaries, except at tips, dull vinaceous buff to light drab, outer edges of all wing-quills light yellowish olive, lesser wing-coverts mostly yellowish citrine, remainder of wing-coverts light fuscous edged with light yellowish olive; superciliary stripe light grayish olive anteriorly, verging to light vinaceous buff; lores varying from light drab to clove brown; sides of head buffy drab to rather buffy mouse gray, with narrow postocular streak of prout brown to cinnamon brown, and sometimes short dull buffy streak on upper and lower eye-

lids; sides of neck drab, washed with mouse gray; chin and center of throat dull buffy white or very pale dull brownish white; jugulum between drab and avellaneous or smoke gray, washed with light pinkish buff; breast and abdomen white or buffy white; sides and flanks dull isabella color; crissum dull cinnamon buff or cream buff; edge of bend of wing lemon yellow to lemon chrome; lining of wing and axillars dull drab, outer under wing-coverts and axillars washed with pale yellow; thighs dull light yellowish olive. Bill dull brown, but mandible lighter; iris brown; legs and feet light dull brown. *Adults, winter*: Acquired by complete postnuptial molt. Practically identical to nuptial adults. *First nuptial*: Acquired by wear from first winter. Like nuptial adults. *First winter*: Acquired by partial postjuvenal molt, which does not involve wing-quills or tail. Like adults in winter. *Juvenal*: Acquired by complete postnatal molt. Similar to nuptial adults, but without brown stripes on pileum; upper parts duller, more brownish, buffy, or yellowish green—between deep grayish olive and dark grayish olive; pileum with small, back with larger, obscure spots or short streaks of fuscous or chaetura drab; tail between hair brown and deep grayish olive, edged externally with buffy olive; wings hair brown, outer webs of feathers margined with buffy olive citrine; wing-coverts tipped with isabella color to tawny olive, forming two rather poorly defined wing-bars; sides of head and of neck between grayish olive and drab, but lores between hair brown and deep grayish olive; chin and throat pale olive buff; jugulum and breast deep olive buff with rather large spots or numerous streaks of hair brown or light chaetura drab; abdomen olive buff; sides and flanks tinged with isabella color and, with breast, marked with obscure spots or streaks of hair brown to light fuscous; crissum dull deep olive buff, or somewhat darker, and unmarked; edge of wing dull colonial buff. *Natal*: Drab.

MEASUREMENTS: *Adult male*: Wing, 62.2–67.3 (average, 65.8) mm.; tail, 62.2–69.8 (65.3); bill (exposed culmen), 12.2–14.0 (13.0); height of bill at base, 6.9–7.9 (7.4); tarsus, 23.4–25.1 (23.9); middle toe without claw, 14.7–15.7 (15.2). *Adult female*: Wing, 58.7–62.2 (60.7); tail, 56.6–63.5 (59.7); bill, 11.7–13.2 (12.7); height of bill, 6.4–7.4 (7.1); tarsus, 22.9–24.6 (23.4); middle toe, 14.7–15.7 (15.2).

RANGE: S. Texas and n.e. Mexico (e. Coahuila to s. coastal Tamaulipas).

TEXAS: *Resident*: Collected northwest to Kinney and Medina, east to Nueces, south to Cameron, Hidalgo, and Starr cos.

NESTING: *Nest*: On lowlands along streams or on drier land, in thickets or brush; in low bush or cactus, usually not more than 3 ft. above ground; a rather large, practically domed structure, somewhat bulky, with side entrance; composed of weeds, grass, twigs, straw, bark strips, and leaves; lined with finer grass, straw, and hair. *Eggs*: 2–4; between oval and elliptical oval; white, unmarked; average size, 22.4 × 16.5 mm.

GREEN-TAILED TOWHEE, *Oberholseria chlorura* (Audubon)

SPECIES ACCOUNT

Chlorura chlorura of A.O.U. check-list, 1957 (see Appendix A). A handsome, trim finch with long rounded tail. Greenish above; rusty crown on gray head; conspicuous white throat; gray breast, sides; whitish belly. Length, 7¼ in.; wingspan, 9¾; weight, 1¼ oz.

RANGE: S.e. Washington to s.e. Wyoming, south through interior mountains to California, Nevada, c. Arizona, New Mexico, and w. Texas (very rarely). Winters from s. California, Arizona, New Mexico, and Texas to c. Mexico.

TEXAS: (See map.) *Breeding*: June to Aug. (eggs, July 10, 1936, Chisos Mts.) from 4,600 to 7,000 ft., probably higher. Extremely rare and irregular in high mountains of Trans-Pecos. Only definite report of breeding since 1936: Culberson Co., McKittrick Canyon (adult observed with 1 young unable to fly, Aug. 20, 1969, H. M. Ohlendorf). Recent breeding suspected: Brewster Co., Big Bend Nat. Park, Laguna Meadow (1 male apparently defending territory, May 28, 1971, R. H. Wauer). *Winter*: Oct. to Apr. (extremes: Sept. 4, May 25). Common to fairly common in Trans-Pecos; uncommon to scarce in remainder of state with exception of heavily wooded eastern portion, where casual.

HAUNTS AND HABITS: This species, like its relatives, the Olive Sparrow and Rufous-sided Towhee, is a thicket dweller. In its breeding range in the western United States it frequents bushes in or near timbered areas, chiefly at elevations between 6,000 and 11,000 feet; but in Texas, where this bird is almost entirely a migrant and winter resident, it inhabits brush growing at any elevation.

If alarmed, this shy towhee dives into a bush. When distracting intruders from its nest, it generally runs rapidly along the ground with tail upraised. One observer (A. H. Miller) has remarked of this towhee's resemblance to a chipmunk when retreating in this manner. Low in bushes or on the ground—where it scratches in orthodox Olive Sparrow and towhee fashion—the Greentail searches for seeds of pigweed, filaree, dandelion, and ricegrass; elderberry and other fruits; and insects (beetles, ants, bees, wasps, caterpillars, grasshoppers, crickets, true bugs, and flies).

Notes include a soft thin *mew* and a plaintive, kitten-like *pee-you-wee*; an emphatic *keek* is sounded in alarm. The Green-tailed Towhee's song is a bright

melodious variation of *wheet chur cheeeweee-churrrr*. The male sings from March to late July, usually from an uppermost twig of a bush.

CHANGES: The Green-tailed Towhee, like other North American montane-nesting birds, probably does not regularly breed as low in altitude or in latitude as it did prior to 1900. Increasing aridity and multiplying goats have apparently practically eliminated it as a breeder from Texas. Even on the crests and high canyons of the Guadalupe range, the one area of the state still possibly suitable, Frederick R. Gehlbach, Donald R. Standiford, and other trained ornithological observers found no evidence of its nesting during their investigations in the 1950's and 1960's. The adult and young observed in McKittrick Canyon in 1969 by H. M. Ohlendorf, though encouraging, is hardly conclusive evidence of a changing trend in the species' breeding status.

DETAILED ACCOUNT: TWO SUBSPECIES

EASTERN GREEN-TAILED TOWHEE, *Oberholseria chlorura chlorura* (Audubon)

No races recognized by A.O.U. check-list, 1957 (see Appendix A).

DESCRIPTION: *Adult male, nuptial plumage*: Acquired by partial prenuptial molt and wear from winter plumage. Forehead mouse gray to deep mouse gray; crown and occiput burnt sienna; hindneck, back, and scapulars yellowish olive to buffy olive; rump and upper tail-coverts dull grayish olive; hindneck, back, and scapulars with edgings of dull grayish olive, somewhat obscuring greenish ground color; tail dull citrine to buffy citrine, inner edges of feathers, together with central portion of middle pair and most tips of all rectrices, light olive brown to dark olive brown, outer feathers edged on terminal portion of inner webs and tipped with pale dull buff or buffy white, outer web of outermost pair of feathers olive ocher to olive yellow; wings light fuscous, inner edges of primaries and secondaries, except at tips, drab, outer webs of primaries, except at tips, buffy citrine, outer webs of secondaries dull citrine, outer edges of tertials similar but sometimes more brownish or grayish; lesser wing-coverts between pyrite yellow and warbler green, remainder of coverts edged externally with color of back; supraloral streak dull white or buffy white; sides of head and of throat between mouse gray and neutral gray, lores darker and with a few specks of dull white, auriculars often very narrowly and more or less obscurely streaked with drab or pale drab; malar streak dull grayish white or buffy white; submalar streak deep to dark mouse gray and submalar region with numerous small specks or narrow short streaks of dull white; center of chin and of throat white or dull white; sides of neck yellowish olive like hindneck; jugulum between neutral gray or rather deep neutral gray and light mouse gray; breast and abdomen dull buffy white or dull grayish white; sides and flanks pale gray, tinged with dull cream buff; crissum dull cream buff; thighs between hair brown and mouse gray; lining of wing lemon yellow to lemon chrome including edge of wing-bend, under wing-coverts more or less spotted or mottled with mouse gray. Bill black or plumbeous black, but cutting edges and mandible, except tip, plumbeous; iris cinnamon or dark reddish brown; legs pale brown; feet darker. *Adult male, winter*: Acquired by complete postnuptial molt. Similar to nuptial adult male, but feathers of crown conspicuously tipped with mouse gray; upper tail-coverts tipped with dull buff; upper surface of body more brownish; tertials edged on outer webs and tipped with buffy brown to wood brown; posterior lower surface more brightly buff, gray of jugulum washed with dull buff. *Adult female, nuptial*: Acquired by partial prenuptial molt and wear from winter. Similar to nup-

GREEN-TAILED TOWHEE, *Oberholseria chlorura*
O. c. chlorura

0 20 40 60 80
Scale in miles

Specimen record   *Sight record*

★   ☆ Breeding
▲   △ Spring
●   ○ Summer
▼   ▽ Fall
■   □ Winter

——— Approximate boundary of subspecies' breeding range

?   Questionable record

tial adult male but averaging smaller; burnt sienna area of pileum averaging less in extent and somewhat paler; remainder of upper surface usually rather duller; some specimens, however, are indistinguishable from male. *Adult female, winter*: Acquired by complete postnuptial molt. Differs from nuptial adult female, as does adult male in winter from nuptial adult male. Bill black or slate black, but mandible and cutting edges of maxilla plumbeous white or light plumbeous, base of mandible sometimes white; iris raw sienna or rather purplish rufous; legs and feet sepia to plumbeous. *Male, first nuptial*: Acquired by partial prenuptial molt. Like nuptial adult male, except wing-quills and primary coverts are more brownish. *Male, first winter*: Acquired by partial postjuvenal molt, which does not involve wing-quills, primary coverts, or tail. Similar to adult male in winter, but burnt sienna of crown still more obscured by brown or gray edgings; upper surface averaging more brownish, with outer edges of tertials usually more distinctly or deeply buff or dull tawny. Bill light slate color, cutting edges and base of mandible somewhat pinkish; legs and feet dull brown. *Female, first nuptial*: Acquired by partial prenuptial molt. Similar to nuptial adult female, except for somewhat more brownish wing-quills, primary coverts, and tail. *Female, first winter*: Acquired by partial postjuvenal molt, which does not involve wing-quills, primary coverts, or tail. Similar to adult female in winter, but burnt sienna crown-patch missing or very small; upper surface averaging more brownish, outer edges of tertials usually more deeply buff or dull tawny. *Juvenal (gray-brown phase)*: Acquired by complete postnatal molt. Pileum drab; remainder of upper surface light brownish olive, broadly streaked everywhere, though less conspicuously on upper tail-coverts and rump, with chaetura drab to fuscous; wings and tail like those of first winter male and female, but wing-coverts, except primary coverts, broadly edged with wood brown, tawny olive to dull pinkish buff, these edgings often forming two rather inconspicuous light wing-bars; sides of head and of neck like upper parts but more finely streaked; lower surface dull white or buffy white, everywhere streaked, but least conspicuously on abdomen and throat, with chaetura drab to hair brown, crissum dull light cream buff, unstreaked. *Juvenal (rufous brown phase)*: Acquired by complete postnatal molt. Similar to gray-brown phase, but upper surface dull rufescent sayal brown, streaked with olive brown; lower parts dull pinkish buff with olive brown to fuscous streaks. *Natal*: Drab.

MEASUREMENTS: *Adult male*: Wing, 75.4–83.1 (average, 79.7) mm.; tail, 77.5–87.9 (83.8); bill (exposed culmen), 11.9–13.5 (12.7); tarsus, 23.1–25.9 (24.6); middle toe without claw, 15.0–18.0 (16.5). *Adult female*: Wing, 71.9–79.0 (74.9); tail, 70.6–85.6 (77.2); bill, 11.9–13.2 (12.2); tarsus, 23.1–25.4 (23.6); middle toe, 14.5–17.5 (15.7).

RANGE: S.e. Washington to s.e. Wyoming, south to c. Arizona and Trans-Pecos Texas (very rarely). Winters from Arizona, New Mexico, and Texas to s. Baja California, Jalisco, and Morelos.

TEXAS: *Breeding*: No specimen (see species account). *Winter*: Taken north to Howard, east to Bexar and Nueces, south to Cameron, west to El Paso cos. Fairly common.

NESTING: *Nest*: On slopes and mesas; in brush or thickets; on ground, well concealed by bushes or other vegetation, in scrub oak, or low bush, such as currant, sage, or cactus; cup, sometimes rather bulky, composed of stems and leaves of grass and weeds, strips of bark, twigs, and pine needles; lined with rootlets and sometimes horsehair. *Eggs*: 3–5, usually 4; oval; white, with bluish, greenish, or grayish tinge; finely dotted and spotted with reddish brown and pinkish drab, sometimes so uniformly distributed as almost to hide ground color, or less numerous with markings concentrated about large end; average size, 21.6 × 16.5 mm.

OREGON GREEN-TAILED TOWHEE, *Oberholseria chlorura zapolia* Oberholser

No races recognized by A.O.U. check-list, 1957 (see Appendix A).

DESCRIPTION: *Adults, nuptial plumage*: Similar to *O. c. chlorura*, but upper parts, particularly back, more grayish (less greenish or brownish), and in winter, if brownish above, this color less rufescent (more grayish), and olive green less yellowish; flanks more grayish (less extensively and less brightly buff); anterior lower surface slightly more clearly gray (less buffy) and averaging somewhat darker.

MEASUREMENTS: *Adult male*: Wing, 77.0–81.5 (average, 78.7) mm.; tail, 74.9–86.6 (80.2); bill (exposed culmen), 11.7–13.5 (12.2); tarsus, 23.9–26.9 (24.6); middle toe without claw, 15.0–17.0 (15.7). *Adult female*: Wing, 73.9–78.0 (75.7); tail, 74.4–83.6 (79.5); bill, 10.9–13.0 (11.7); tarsus, 22.1–24.9 (23.6); middle toe, 15.0–16.8 (15.7).

RANGE: C. Oregon, south to s. California and s. Nevada. Winters from c. California, Arizona, New Mexico, and w. Texas to s. Baja California and s. Sonora.

TEXAS: *Winter*: Taken northeast to Dallas (Mar. 15), south to Cameron, west to Webb (Nov. 22) and Culberson (May 1) cos. Scarce.

RUFOUS-SIDED TOWHEE, *Hortulanus erythrophthalmus* (Linnaeus)

SPECIES ACCOUNT

Pipilo erythrophthalmus of A.O.U. check-list, 1957 (see Appendix A). Prior to 1957, eastern birds were called Red-eyed Towhee (except White-eyed Towhee of Florida); various western races were lumped under the name Spotted Towhee. *Male*: black hood and upper parts; rusty sides; white belly; conspicuous white patches in wings and at corners of tail; backs and wings of western races liberally spotted with white. *Eastern female*: brown where male is black. *Western females*: depending on race, a pale version of male, or brown where male is black. Length, 8¼ in.; wingspan, 10¾; weight, 1½ oz.

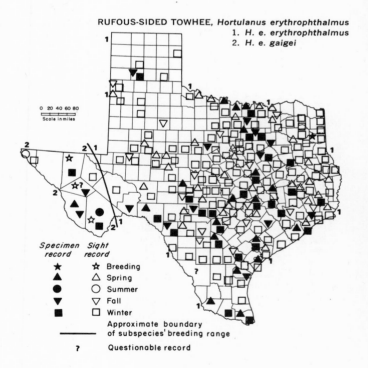

RUFOUS-SIDED TOWHEE, *Hortulanus erythrophthalmus*
1. *H. e. erythrophthalmus*
2. *H. e. gaigei*

0 20 40 60 80
Scale in miles

Specimen   Sight
record   record

★   ☆ Breeding
▲   △ Spring
●   ○ Summer
▼   ▽ Fall
■   □ Winter

——— Approximate boundary of subspecies' breeding range

? Questionable record

RANGE: S. Canada, south through w. United States and highland Mexico to Guatemala, and through e. United States to s.e. Louisiana and peninsular Florida (to Miami area). Migratory races winter from U.S.-Canada border to U.S.-Mexico border and U.S. portion of Gulf of Mexico.

TEXAS: (See map.) *Breeding*: May to early Sept. (no egg dates available, but male gathering food, May 28, 1957; "young, barely able to fly," taken Sept. 10, 1916) from 5,700 to 8,000 ft. Fairly common to rare in high mountains of Trans-Pecos. Eggs of eastern race taken once, 375 ft., northeastern corner of state (see detailed account). *Winter*: Mid-Oct. to late Apr. (extremes: Sept. 10, May 27). Common to fairly common in most parts; rare in extreme south.

HAUNTS AND HABITS: The Rufous-sided is a towhee of semiopen woodlands and forest edges, inhabiting thickets, underbrush, and second growth. It spends most of its life on or near the ground. So much of a bush bird is it that veteran central Texas naturalist Roy Bedichek remarked upon seeing one Rufous-sided perched high in a tree, "There is an *immoral* towhee!"

Ordinarily *H. erythrophthalmus* is noisy, bustling, and hardly to be overlooked, although thicket-hampered glimpses are seldom of a whole bird. At other times, however, it is quiet and elusive. Flight is jerky, labored, and rarely sustained. Sometimes an alarmed individual may freeze or flee on foot rather than fly. On the ground, where it scratches vigorously with both feet, or in the low parts of bushes, the Rufous-sided gleans acorns, ragweed, bristlegrass, and other seeds; also fruits of dewberry, sumac, and dogwood. Animal matter in its diet consists of insects (such as beetles, caterpillars, ants, cockroaches, walking-sticks), spiders, snails, millipedes, and earthworms.

The standard call of the eastern race, *H. e. erythrophthalmus*, is a loud emphatic *chee-wink*, or a simple *wink*; western races utter a nasal *wank*. The former's song is *drink-yur-teeeeee*, the trailing syllable higher pitched and wavering. Western birds sound a buzzy trill frequently introduced by an abrupt note: *chup-zreeeeeeee*. Rufous-sided Towhees sing from mid-April to late July while perched in a bush or small tree.

DETAILED ACCOUNT: FOUR SUBSPECIES

EASTERN RUFOUS-SIDED TOWHEE, *Hortulanus erythrophthalmus erythrophthalmus* (Linnaeus)

DESCRIPTION: *Adult male, nuptial plumage*: Acquired by wear from winter plumage. Upper parts black, slightly brownish; tail brownish black, inner edges of feathers fuscous black, terminal two-thirds of outer web, large terminal area at tip of inner web of outermost feather, and smaller tips on inner webs of next two pairs of feathers white, these spots mostly on inner webs but on second and third pairs from outermost they also extend over to outer web; primaries and secondaries chaetura drab to fuscous, edges of inner webs, except at tips, dull white to very pale buff, outer webs of primaries and secondaries, except at tips, brownish black, basal portion of outer webs of primaries, except outermost, white, forming spot even on closed wing; edging on outer webs of second to fifth or sixth primary white,

which shows as streak or stripe on closed wing; tertials and wing-coverts brownish black, tertials sometimes fuscous black, and always with broad white terminal edgings on outer webs, this white edging sometimes occupying on shortest tertial almost entire length of feather, and almost entire outer web; sides of head and of neck, with chin, throat, and jugulum, black like upper surface, this on middle of jugulum terminating posteriorly in slightly rounded point; sides and flanks dull hazel to between russet and chestnut, often along edge of sides next to breast more or less obscurely streaked or spotted with chaetura black or fuscous; breast and abdomen white; crissum ochraceous tawny; lining of wing white, mottled, particularly on hinder part, with hair brown to chaetura black. Bill black to slate black, but mandible slate color, olive gray, drab, or slate gray; iris red, dark red, chestnut, maroon, or dark hazel; legs and feet drab, dark drab gray, fawn color, or flesh color. *Adult male, winter*: Acquired by complete postnuptial molt. Very similar to nuptial adult male, but edgings of tertials more or less buff, upper tail-coverts tipped with sayal brown, black of upper and lower surfaces somewhat duller; sides and flanks averaging darker. *Adult female, nuptial*: Acquired by wear from winter. Pileum between auburn and argus brown to cinnamon brown; remainder of upper surface cinnamon brown to between snuff brown and saccardo umber, slightly darker centers of feathers imparting rather mottled appearance in many specimens; tail clove brown, middle feathers and narrow edgings of outer webs of other feathers brown like back; white spots on tail similar to those of male but smaller; wings light fuscous, inner edges of primaries and secondaries, except at tips, dull buffy drab, outer webs of primaries and secondaries like upper surface, those of secondaries rather brighter, more rufescent, basal portion of outer webs of primaries white, this showing as white spot even in closed wing, more or less narrow white edging showing on middle portion of webs of second to fourth primary, this sometimes extending in diagonal line to join white basal wing spot, tertials edged more or less broadly on outer webs at tips with white or pale dull buff, innermost tertial with these markings most whitish; wing-coverts edged with color of back; sides of head and of neck like pileum; chin, throat, and jugulum similar to pileum but somewhat lighter; sides and flanks bright russet to dull tawny; crissum dull cinnamon buff; breast and abdomen white; lining of wing pinkish buff to pale pinkish buff, more or less mixed with white, and irregularly spotted, particularly on posterior portion, with hair brown to chaetura drab. Maxilla black; mandible slate gray or dark gull gray; iris dark red; legs drab gray or ecru drab; feet drab gray or light ecru drab; claws light ecru drab. *Adult female, winter*: Acquired by complete postnuptial molt. Similar to nuptial adult female, but upper parts darker, often more rufescent, white markings on tertials buffy or more deeply buff; sides and flanks averaging darker. *Male, first nuptial*: Acquired by wear from first winter. Similar to nuptial adult male, but black areas averaging somewhat duller and more brownish; wings more brownish, particularly primary coverts, which are dark olive brown to fuscous instead of black; white markings of tertials usually with tinge of buff. *Male, first winter*: Acquired by partial postjuvenal molt, which does not involve wing-quills or coverts. Similar to adult male in winter, but feathers of upper surface more or less tipped with dull brown, general appearance thereby more brownish; light edgings of tertials more deeply buff; wing-quills, and particularly primary coverts, more brownish; black of lower parts duller, feathers very narrowly edged with dull brown. Bill blue black; iris raw umber; feet brown. *Female, first nuptial*: Acquired by wear from first winter. Similar to nuptial adult female. *Female, first winter*: Acquired by partial postjuvenal molt, which does not involve wing-quills or coverts. Similar to adult female in winter. *Male, juvenal*: Acquired by complete postnatal molt. Upper parts between russet and cinnamon brown or between cinnamon brown and sudan brown, streaked, sometimes narrowly, on pileum, always broadly on back, with bister to fuscous black; tail fuscous black to brownish black, white markings as in adult; wing-quills fuscous to chaetura drab, broad edgings of terminal portion of tertials dull pinkish buff to amber brown or dull russet; white markings of primaries as in adult; wing-coverts edged with ground color of back, greater series conspicuously tipped with dull cinnamon buff; sides of head similar to upper surface but paler and more finely streaked or spotted; supraloral streak dull buff; lower surface dull cream buff to dull cinnamon buff, sides, flanks, and crissum dull cinnamon buff to clay color; submalar streak and broad streaks on lower throat, jugulum, breast, sides, and flanks olive brown to fuscous black or hair brown. Bill blackish slate or dull black above, but mandible mouse gray, slate gray, dull flesh color, or plumbeous, tinged at base with flesh color; iris light brown to dark red-brown; legs and feet drab or drab gray. *Female, juvenal*: Acquired by complete postnatal molt. Similar to juvenal male, but upper surface lighter, more rufescent, and usually less densely streaked, these streaks usually olive brown to sepia; tail bister to rufescent clove brown; wing-quills rather dark olive brown; lower surface more deeply buff and more brownish, streaks olive brown to warm dresden brown. Maxilla slate color, slate black, or blackish slate; mandible cinereous, dull drab, drab gray, or dull brown; iris pale brown; legs and feet drab, drab gray, flesh color, or dull light pinkish vinaceous. *Natal*: Pale clove brown. Bill, legs, and feet pinkish buff.

MEASUREMENTS: *Adult male*: Wing, 83.8–94.5 (average, 89.2) mm.; tail, 88.1–99.3 (94.2); bill (exposed culmen), 13.5–14.7 (14.0); tarsus, 27.2–29.7 (28.4); middle toe without claw, 18.8–21.4 (19.8); white on inner web of outermost tail feather, 33.0–53.3 (39.6). *Adult female*: Wing, 76.2–83.8 (81.0); tail, 80.5–89.2 (86.4); bill, 13.0–14.7 (13.7); tarsus, 26.2–28.2 (26.7); middle toe, 17.5–19.3 (18.8); white on inner web, 26.7–39.6 (33.0).

RANGE: S. Saskatchewan to s.w. Maine, south to n. Arkansas and n.w. North Carolina. Winters from Nebraska and s. Great Lakes region to s. Texas and s. Florida (casually).

TEXAS: *Breeding* (formerly): No skin, but eggs taken: Harrison Co., Marshall (July 31, 1914, A. D. Martin). *Winter*: Taken north to Cooke (Mar. 14), east to Hardin, south to Cameron, west to Kerr cos. Fairly common.

NESTING: *Nest*: On uplands and bottoms, in semiopen country, wild and cultivated areas; in bushy pastures, damp or dry woodlands, thickets, and similar places; on ground under a bush, high weed, grass, or sapling, or in a bush or low tree as high as 10 ft. above ground; rather loosely built, bulky cup; composed of weed stalks, twigs, grapevine and other bark, grasses, leaves, and roots; lined with fine grasses, weed stems, and rootlets. *Eggs*: 3–5, usually 4; oval or between oval and elliptical oval; white, bluish white, or grayish white; thickly dotted with light reddish brown or sometimes dull pink, brick red, or maroon, with shell markings of lavender gray and lilac; average size, 23.4 × 18.3 mm.

ARCTIC RUFOUS-SIDED TOWHEE, *Hortulanus erythrophthalmus arcticus* (Swainson)

DESCRIPTION: *Adult male, nuptial plumage*: Acquired by wear from winter plumage. Upper surface dull black to brownish black, but back and especially rump more or less mixed with hair brown, occasionally rump mostly of this color, scapulars and sometimes back more or less broadly streaked with white, chiefly on outer webs of feathers; tail fuscous black to brownish black, inner margins of rectrices more brownish, terminal two-thirds of outer web of outermost pair of feathers white, outer three tail feathers with large truncate white spots on tips, these largest on outermost feathers, fourth pair of feathers usually also with similar white spot but still smaller, and most of feathers edged on outer webs with hair brown to mouse gray; wings fuscous to light fuscous, inner edges of primaries and secondaries, except at tips, light drab to drab, basal portion of outer webs of the few outermost primaries white, showing as very small white spot, sometimes in closed wing, but usually concealed by primary coverts, outer edges of primaries and secondaries, except at tips, fuscous black, as are also both webs of tertials, with more or less conspicuous white edging on outer webs of middle portion of outermost primaries, except outermost which appears as narrow white line in closed wing; tertials

edged broadly on terminal portion of outer webs with dull white; wing-coverts dull black or brownish black, greater and median coverts conspicuously tipped with white; sides of head and of neck, with chin, throat, and jugulum, black like upper surface; sides and flanks ochraceous tawny to cinnamon rufous or between ochraceous tawny and tawny; crissum ochraceous buff to light ochraceous buff, breast and abdomen white; lining of wing light buff or buff white, slightly mottled, particularly on posterior part, with mouse gray or hair brown. Bill black, brownish black, blackish slate, slate black, or chaetura black, but mandible often slaty; iris carmine, scarlet, dull vermilion red, morocco red, dull orange, hazel, rufous, or light brownish yellow; legs sorghum brown, cacao brown, dull sepia, chaetura black, chaetura drab, ecru drab, or flesh color; toes and claws darker—rood brown, dark sorghum brown, drab, or flesh color. *Adult male, winter*: Acquired by complete postnuptial molt. Similar to nuptial adult male, but upper parts duller and more brownish, back with often a few fuscous spots and dull brown tips on feathers; white markings on wings and scapulars somewhat washed with buff, these markings less sharply defined, due to obscure edges of feathers; upper tail-coverts more broadly tipped with mouse gray; throat and jugulum duller, more brownish; sides and flanks somewhat darker and more frequently with fuscous spots or short streaks along inner edge of white area of breast. *Adult female, nuptial*: Acquired by wear from winter. Upper surface hair brown to between deep grayish olive and hair brown, but nape slightly more rufescent, scapulars broadly streaked on outer webs with white, and back also with a few white streaks; tail fuscous black, inner margins of feathers and all middle pair of feathers fuscous, outer webs, except of outermost pair, narrowly margined with color of back; white spots on tail similar to those of male but less extensive; wings hair brown or dark hair brown to between hair brown and light fuscous, outer webs of primaries and secondaries, except at tips, fuscous, outer webs of most of outer primaries for a short distance at base white, these together showing as small white spot beyond tips of primary coverts; also narrow white edgings on middle portion of outer webs of several of outermost primaries except outermost; inner edges of primaries and secondaries, except at tips, drab to rather light drab, tertials fuscous with broad white margins on terminal portion of outer webs; upper wing-coverts fuscous black, greater and median series broadly tipped with white, forming two conspicuous wing-bars; sides of head and of neck, chin, throat, and jugulum—ending in a rounded point on middle of jugulum—light fuscous to chaetura black washed with fuscous; sides and flanks cinnamon rufous or verging toward tawny; crissum dull ochraceous tawny to dull cinnamon buff; breast and abdomen white or buffy white; lining of wing pinkish buff to pale dull pinkish buff, edge of wing more whitish, and posterior coverts more or less extensively fuscous or fuscous black. Bill black or slate black, but mandible olive gray or brownish slate, paler at base; iris orange chrome, rufous, or light dull red; legs dark drab, deep flesh color, or dull sepia with slight purplish tinge; toes ecru drab or dull brown. *Adult female, winter*: Acquired by complete postnuptial molt. Similar to nuptial adult female, but upper parts duller, more brownish, light markings on scapulars and tertials mostly buff instead of white; upper tail-coverts more conspicuously tipped with sayal brown; feathers of pileum with broader brown edgings; sides of breast more or less inconspicuously spotted with fuscous. *Male, first nuptial*: Acquired by wear from first winter. Similar to nuptial adult male but everywhere duller and more brownish; rump mostly, sometimes entirely, hair brown with rufescent tinge and with but little black, never entirely or mostly black as in adult male; primaries, secondaries, and tertials lighter, of more rufescent brown, outer edges not dull black, these, together with primary coverts, between light fuscous and buffy brown, primary coverts thus conspicuously brown as compared with dull black of same parts in adult male. *Male, first winter*: Acquired by partial postjuvenal molt. Similar to first nuptial male, but upper parts duller, more brownish, feathers much edged and tipped with sayal brown, buffy brown, olive brown, and snuff brown; light streaks on back, scapulars, and tertials decidedly buffy—pale buff or drab to clay color; rump more edged with dull buffy brown, upper tail-coverts more broadly edged with dull buffy brown or mouse gray; chin, throat, and jugulum more brownish, jugulum sometimes edged with sayal brown or dull cinnamon rufous. Similar to adult male in winter, but all blackish areas lighter and more brownish; feathers of upper surface much more conspicuously tipped and edged with brown; rump lighter, with less black, more extensively brown or gray; primaries, secondaries, and particularly primary coverts lighter and brown instead of black or dull black; throat and jugulum lighter, more brownish, sometimes edged more or less extensively with brown. *Female, first nuptial:* Acquired by wear from first winter. Similar to nuptial adult female, but upper parts and dark anterior lower parts, including wings and tail, averaging lighter and more rufescent brown, primary coverts and outer edgings of secondaries of decidedly lighter, more rufescent brown. *Female, first winter:* Acquired by partial postjuvenal molt. Similar to adult female in winter, but upper surface, throat, and jugulum lighter, of more rufescent brown; light streaks on scapulars, back, and tertials more deeply buff or brownish; primary coverts and outer edges of primaries and secondaries decidedly lighter, of more rufescent brown. *Male, juvenal:* Acquired by complete postnatal molt. Upper surface sayal brown to between snuff brown and buffy brown, broadly and numerously streaked on back, less so on pileum and upper tail-coverts, and more or less spotted on rump, with fuscous to clove brown; scapulars broadly streaked on outer webs with buffy white to dull cinnamon buff; wings and tail like those of first winter male, but outer edges of greater coverts edged with sayal brown, tips of median and greater coverts narrower and rather more deeply buff—cinnamon buff to buffy white; sides of head like pileum but rather duller and less conspicuously streaked; submalar streak buffy white, and below this a broad streak of chaetura drab; middle of throat and remainder of lower surface dull cartridge buff, throat obscurely spotted, jugulum and breast broadly streaked, most densely on jugulum, with fuscous black; sides, flanks, and crissum dull cinnamon buff, sides and flanks obscurely and finely streaked or spotted with fuscous. Bill dull brown, dull plumbeous, or black, but mandible somewhat bluish; iris light brown or red; legs and feet grayish brown or light brown. *Female, juvenal:* Acquired by complete postnatal molt. Similar to juvenal male, but upper surface lighter and rather more rufescent brown —between cinnamon or clay color and sayal brown—and very much less densely streaked—sometimes scarcely at all on pileum, most conspicuously so on back and upper tail-coverts—with light to dark olive brown; wings and tail similar to first winter female, but greater and median wing-coverts tipped with cinnamon buff, and greater coverts edged exteriorly with sayal brown; sides of head more brownish than in juvenal male; streaks of lower parts lighter, less blackish—hair brown to olive brown, posterior lower surface averaging rather more deeply buff, as is also jugulum. Iris brownish yellow. *Natal* (this plumage of this race not seen in Texas): Drab or rather light drab.

MEASUREMENTS: *Adult male:* Wing, 84.8–91.2 (average, 87.6) mm.; tail, 90.7–104.4 (97.3); bill (exposed culmen), 11.7–13.7 (13.0); tarsus, 25.1–28.2 (26.7); middle toe without claw, 17.8–20.3 (19.3); white on inner web of outermost tail feather, 29.2–41.7 (35.3). *Adult female:* Wing, 78.7–90.7 (83.8); tail, 86.9–104.4 (92.5); bill, 12.2–13.7 (12.7); tarsus, 25.1–27.7 (26.7); middle toe, 17.8–20.3 (18.5); white on inner web, 27.7–36.3 (31.8).

RANGE: C. Alberta to s.w. Manitoba, south to n.e. Colorado. Winters from Nebraska to extreme n. Mexico.

TEXAS: *Winter:* Taken north to Randall (Sept. 30), east to Kaufman (Nov. 3), south to Williamson and Cameron (Mar. 3), west to Culberson cos. Fairly common.

NESTING: (This race does not nest in Texas.) *Nest:* On plains and prairies, in thickets along streams or elsewhere; on ground in grass or at base of bush, or placed in low bush; when on the ground, it is sunken in a depression made by the birds, with rim level with surface; a rather bulky cup; composed of strips of bark, small twigs, weed stalks, dry grass, leaves, and some-

times pine needles; lined with yellow straw or fine grass and rootlets. *Eggs:* 3–5, usually 3 or 4; white, greenish white, bluish white, or grayish white, with spots and dots of umber, purplish brown, rood brown, or maroon, and shell markings of lavender and lilac gray, these sometimes most numerous about large end, where forming a cap; average size, 23.9 × 17.5 mm.

SPURRED RUFOUS-SIDED TOWHEE, *Hortulanus erythrophthalmus montanus* (Swarth)

DESCRIPTION: *Adults, male and female, nuptial plumage:* Similar to *H. e. arcticus* but wing and tarsus slightly, tail and hind claw decidedly, longer; colors darker; white on lateral tail feathers less in extent. Male above more solidly black except on rump; white scapular markings usually edged with black in fresh plumage; sides and flanks darker. Female darker above and on chin, throat, and jugulum; white tail spots smaller; upper surface rather less conspicuously streaked. *Juvenal:* Darker than juvenal *arcticus*.

MEASUREMENTS: *Adult male:* Wing, 86.4–92.7 (average, 89.7) mm.; tail, 99.1–111.5 (104.1); bill (exposed culmen), 12.4–14.7 (13.5); tarsus, 26.7–28.4 (27.7); middle toe without claw, 17.8–20.3 (18.8); white on inner web of outermost tail feather, 21.4–35.8 (30.2). *Adult female:* Wing, 83.8–88.4 (85.9); tail, 89.2–105.6 (99.8); bill, 12.4–14.2 (13.2); tarsus, 25.4–27.9 (26.7); middle toe, 16.5–18.5 (18.0); white on inner web, 24.6–31.8 (27.9).

RANGE: N. Idaho, n.w. Montana, and n. Wyoming, south through Rocky Mts. to s.e. California, n.w. Chihuahua, and s.w. New Mexico. Winters from s.e. Nevada and c. Colorado to extreme n. Mexico.

TEXAS: *Winter:* Taken north to Randall, east to Dallas, south to Colorado (Oct. 27) and Victoria, west to Brewster (Apr. 11) and Culberson cos. Fairly common.

CHISOS RUFOUS-SIDED TOWHEE, *Hortulanus erythrophthalmus gaigei* (Van Tyne and Sutton)

DESCRIPTION: *Adults, nuptial plumage:* Similar to *H. e. montanus* but smaller. Male with sides of body paler and on average with less white on back and scapulars. Female with sides also paler, and likewise with less white on mantle; dark throat and upper parts more blackish (less grayish or brownish). *Natal:* Probably similar to *H. e. arcticus*.

MEASUREMENTS: *Adult male:* Wing, 83.1–89.9 (average, 85.9) mm.; tail, 97.1–104.9 (100.8); bill (exposed culmen), 11.2–15.0 (13.2); height of bill at base, 8.1–9.4 (8.6); tarsus, 26.9–29.4 (28.4); middle toe without claw, 16.0–18.5 (17.3); white on inner web of outermost tail feather, 26.9–32.5 (30.2). *Adult female:* Wing, 77.5–84.1 (82.3); tail, 88.9–103.1 (96.8); bill, 12.7–14.0 (13.2); height of bill, 8.6–9.4 (9.1); tarsus, 26.9–28.9 (27.7); middle toe, 16.5–17.8 (17.3); white on inner web, 25.4–30.5 (27.2).

RANGE: S.e. New Mexico, south through mountains of Trans-Pecos Texas to s.w. Tamaulipas.

TEXAS: *Resident:* Altitudinal breeding range, 5,700 to 8,000 ft. Collected in Culberson, Jeff Davis, Presidio, and Brewster cos. Fairly common.

NESTING: Probably similar to *H. e. arcticus*.

BROWN TOWHEE, *Hortulanus fuscus* (Swainson)

SPECIES ACCOUNT

Pipilo fuscus of A.O.U. check-list, 1957 (see Appendix A). Birds from Arizona to w. Texas were formerly known by the more appropriate name of Canyon Towhee. A nondescript towhee (grayish in Texas; brown in California). *Details of Texas birds:* tawny crown; dark brown central breast-spot; necklace of brown streaks (often indistinct) edging pale buffy throat; dark brownish tail; pale rufous crissum. Length, 8½ in.; wingspan, 12; weight, 1½ oz.

RANGE: S.w. Oregon, Arizona, s.e. Colorado, and c. Texas, south through California and deserts of w. and c. Mexico to Oaxaca.

TEXAS: (See map.) *Resident*: Breeds, early Mar. to late Sept. (eggs, Mar. 30 to June 13) from 950 to 6,800 ft. Common in west Texas and on western half of Edwards Plateau, becoming increasingly scarce east on Plateau to Burnet and San Antonio (casual to Austin); scarce and local visitor to northern Panhandle. Sight records from Aransas Co.

HAUNTS AND HABITS: Rough, rocky, semiarid country is terrain suited for the Canyon Brown Towhee; here it dwells on hills, in canyons and gulches, about campgrounds and ranch houses. On the Edwards Plateau, ranch people often call their gray *H. fuscus texanus* "catbird." This is a consequence of misleading bird guides. In most U.S. books, the only gray bird with rusty under its tail is the Catbird; very seldom mentioned is the fact that Brown Towhees in Texas are more gray than brown.

The Canyon Towhee usually perches in a low tree or bush or on a rock. When undisturbed, it may be seen scratching on the ground—executing the typical towhee forward hop and backward kick—as it searches for food: chiefly seeds of panicum, sorrel, chickweed, pigweed, and lupine; fruits of dewberry, elderberry, and poison-oak; also various insects, millipedes, snails, and spiders.

Usual call of *H. fuscus mesoleucus*, also used as an alarm note, is a hoarse *tscheddap, sheddap,* or *tschedd'p*; individuals keep in touch with an occasional *see*. Song is a lively jingle: *chili-chili-chili-chili-chili-*

chili; sometimes this degenerates to a dull series of *chilp*'s. All vocalizations except the duet squeal (used in cementing the pair-bond) are different from those uttered by the truly brown-colored towhee of California (Joe T. Marshall, Jr., R. Roy Johnson). Singing in Texas occurs chiefly from March to early July.

DETAILED ACCOUNT: THREE SUBSPECIES

CANYON BROWN TOWHEE, *Hortulanus fuscus mesoleucus* (Baird)

DESCRIPTION: *Adults, nuptial plumage*: Acquired by wear from winter plumage. Pileum dull tawny to dark ochraceous tawny, but feathers more or less edged with grayish drab; remainder of upper surface between drab and hair brown, but upper tail-coverts obscurely tipped with dull pale buff or buffy white; tail olive brown to dark olive brown, but middle pair of feathers usually somewhat lighter, most feathers, except two middle pairs, tipped with dull cinnamon buff, this sometimes extending as an edging on both outer and inner webs of outermost pair of feathers; wings between buffy brown and hair brown, inner edges of primaries and secondaries somewhat paler, outer edges of wing-quills and exposed surfaces of wing-coverts like upper surface but rather lighter; lores and narrow eye-ring pale pinkish buff to tilleul buff, lores somewhat mixed with light fuscous; region below eye dull pale buff, finely spotted with fuscous and with minute shaft streaks of white; auriculars drab with very narrow shaft streaks of very pale buff or buffy white; sides of neck and of body between smoke gray and light drab; chin and middle of throat cream buff to cinnamon buff; chain of short streaks or more or less triangular elongated spots along sides of throat and across lower throat olive brown to fuscous, sides of throat sometimes washed with light buff; jugulum gray like sides of neck but much paler and more or less washed with buff, conspicuous spot of fuscous in center of upper breast; breast and upper abdomen dull white, grayish white, or buffy white, breast sometimes with obscure slightly darker gray spots; lower abdomen cinnamon buff; flanks and crissum clay color; lining of wing dull light cinnamon buff or pinkish buff, outer portion hair brown, tipped with dull white or buffy white; axillars similar but more or less washed or tinged with gray of sides. Bill brown but lighter below; iris light brown or dull hazel; legs and feet light brown or flesh color. *Adults, winter*: Acquired by complete postnuptial molt. Similar to nuptial adults, but upper surface darker, plumage somewhat more blended; pileum with broader light brown tips, thus more veiling tawny on top of head; upper tail-coverts more broadly tipped with buff or ochraceous; spots and streaks of fuscous on throat and jugulum less sharply defined, owing to more extensive lighter edgings of feathers; gray spots on breast larger and more evident. *First nuptial*: Acquired by wear from first winter. Practically identical with nuptial adults. *First winter*: Acquired by partial postjuvenal molt, which does not involve primary coverts. Similar to adults in winter, but tawny crown more obscured by light brown tips of feathers, sometimes almost entirely so; edges and tips of greater coverts lighter, more distinctly buff. *Juvenal*: Acquired by complete postnatal molt. Similar to first winter, but upper surface more buffy, pileum rather rufescent drab to between sayal brown and snuff brown; upper tail-coverts similar to pileum but somewhat darker; edges of all upper wing-coverts pale pinkish buff to dull cinnamon buff; sides of head slightly more buffy than in first winter; chin and throat pale pinkish buff, this likewise usually tinging jugulum; breast and upper abdomen dull white or very pale buff, jugulum, breast, upper abdomen, and sides streaked with hair brown to deep mouse gray; lower abdomen cinnamon buff; crissum dull clay color. *Natal*: Drab.

MEASUREMENTS: *Adult male*: Wing, 91.2–100.1 (average, 94.5) mm.; tail, 98.6–107.4 (103.6); bill (exposed culmen), 14.5–16.3 (15.5); tarsus, 25.1–26.9 (25.9); middle toe without claw, 17.3–19.6 (18.3). *Adult female*: Wing, 85.9–92.7 (91.2); tail, 96.0–109.5 (101.6); bill, 14.0–15.5 (15.0); height of bill,

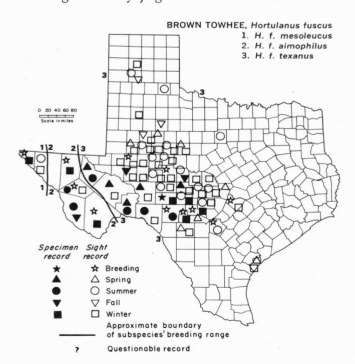

BROWN TOWHEE, *Hortulanus fuscus*
1. *H. f. mesoleucus*
2. *H. f. aimophilus*
3. *H. f. texanus*

0 20 40 60 80
Scale in miles

Specimen   Sight
record   record

★   ☆ Breeding
▲   △ Spring
●   ○ Summer
▼   ▽ Fall
■   □ Winter

——— Approximate boundary
of subspecies' breeding range

?   Questionable record

8.9–9.4 (9.1); tarsus, 22.9–26.4 (25.1); middle toe, 15.5–18.8 (18.0).

RANGE: C. Arizona and n. New Mexico, south to n. Sonora, n.w. Chihuahua, and extreme w. Texas.

TEXAS: *Resident*: Altitudinal breeding range, 3,500 to 5,000 ft. No breeding specimen, but nest with young found in El Paso Co., Fusselman Canyon (July 12, 1923, A. H. McLellan) considered to be of this subspecies. Two winter specimens: El Paso Co., El Paso (Dec. 12, 1889, V. Bailey; Feb. 6, 1892, E. A. Mearns).

NESTING: *Nest*: On slopes and mesas and in valleys; in brush and low open woodlands; in bush or low tree, such as sagebush, pinyon, juniper, cactus, or yucca, 2–8 ft. above ground; rather large, bulky, loosely built cup; composed of grasses, twigs, weeds, bark, and other kinds of vegetable fibers; lined with rootlets, fine grass, and horsehair. *Eggs*: 3–6, usually 3; ovate or verging toward oval; pale blue, greenish blue, pearly gray, or grayish white, spotted, speckled, lined, scrawled, and sometimes blotched with black, purplish brown, blackish brown, and dark purple, with shell markings of slate gray and light purple; average size, 25.9 × 19.3 mm.

PECOS BROWN TOWHEE, Hortulanus fuscus aimophilus
Oberholser, new subspecies (see Appendix A)

DESCRIPTION: *Adults, nuptial plumage*: Similar to *H. f. mesoleucus*, but tail shorter; color of upper parts slightly darker; flanks usually somewhat lighter.

MEASUREMENTS: *Adult male*: Wing, 91.9–101.1 (average, 95.8) mm.; tail, 94.0–105.9 (100.1); bill (exposed culmen), 14.5–16.0 (15.5); height of bill at base, 9.7–10.7 (10.2); tarsus, 24.9–27.4 (26.4); middle toe without claw, 17.0–18.5 (17.5). *Adult female*: Wing, 83.1–91.4 (87.9); tail, 84.1–96.0 (95.8); bill, 14.5–16.0 (15.2); height of bill, 9.4–9.9 (9.7); tarsus, 24.6–26.9 (26.2); middle toe, 16.0–17.3 (16.8).

TYPE: Adult male, no. 135832, U.S. National Museum, Biological Surveys collection; Fort Davis, Texas; Jan. 8, 1890; Vernon Bailey.

RANGE: Trans-Pecos (except extreme western and eastern portions) and adjacent Mexico.

TEXAS: *Resident*: Altitudinal breeding range, 1,800 to 6,800 ft. Collected in Culberson, Jeff Davis, Presidio, and Brewster cos. Common.

NESTING: Similar to that of *H. f. mesoleucus*.

TEXAS BROWN TOWHEE, Hortulanus fuscus texanus
(van Rossem)

DESCRIPTION: *Adults, nuptial plumage*: Similar to *H. f. aimophilus*, but wing and tail shorter; upper parts decidedly darker and more grayish.

MEASUREMENTS: *Adult male*: Wing, 88.9–95.5 (average, 91.7) mm.; tail, 89.9–97.1 (94.2); bill (exposed culmen), 15.5–16.5 (15.7); height of bill at base, 9.4–10.4 (10.2); tarsus, 25.4–27.4 (26.7); middle toe without claw, 16.0–18.8 (17.3). *Adult female*: Wing, 86.1–93.0 (89.7); tail, 90.9–95.5 (92.7); bill, 14.2–16.3 (15.5); height of bill, 9.1–9.9 (9.7); tarsus, 26.4–27.7 (26.9); middle toe, 16.0–17.5 (16.8).

RANGE: E. Trans-Pecos and c. Texas, south to s.e. Coahuila.

TEXAS: *Resident*: Altitudinal breeding range, 950 to 3,600 ft. Collected northwest to Reeves, east to Concho, southeast to Kerr, west to Val Verde cos. Fairly common.

NESTING: Similar to that of *H. f. mesoleucus*.

[ABERT'S TOWHEE, Hortulanus aberti (Baird)

Pipilo aberti of A.O.U. check-list, 1957. A large, uniformly cinnamon brown towhee with a black face. Length, 9 in.; wingspan, 11¼.

RANGE: S.e. Nevada, s.w. Utah, and s.w. New Mexi-

co, south chiefly through Colorado River drainage to n. shores of Gulf of California.

TEXAS: *Hypothetical*: On Apr. 19, 1930, H. S. Peters, U.S. Bureau of Entomology, collected an individual from El Paso Co.; the following day he collected another. Unfortunately neither bird was preserved. This sedentary species is otherwise unreported from Texas.]

LARK BUNTING, *Calamospiza melanocorys* Stejneger

SPECIES ACCOUNT

A chunky, heavy-billed fringillid. *Nuptial male*: black with large white wing-patch. *Winter male*: resembles female, but with black chin. *Female*: blackish-striped grayish brown above; finely blackish-streaked whitish below; wing often shows white patch. Length, 7 in.; wingspan, 11; weight, 1¼ oz.

RANGE: S. Alberta and s.w. Manitoba, south through Great Plains to s.e. New Mexico and n. Texas. Winters from s. California and w. Oklahoma (rarely) to c. Mexico.

TEXAS: (See map.) *Breeding*: May and June (eggs, May 24 to June 8) from 1,100 to 2,500 ft. Rare and irregular in Panhandle area, south casually to northern Trans-Pecos and northern Edwards Plateau. *Migration*: Late Mar. to early May; mid-July (mid-Oct. east of 100th meridian) to late Nov. Abundant to common in western two-thirds; east occasionally to upper coast; casual inland east of 97th meridian. *Winter*: Mid-Oct. to early Apr. Abundant to fairly common in most of western two-thirds with exception of northern Pan-

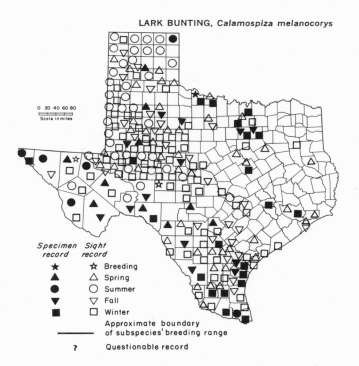

LARK BUNTING, *Calamospiza melanocorys*

0 20 40 60 80
Scale in miles

Specimen record	*Sight record*	
★	☆	Breeding
▲	△	Spring
●	○	Summer
▼	▽	Fall
■	□	Winter
———		Approximate boundary of subspecies' breeding range
?		Questionable record

handle, where scarce; uncommon to rare on Edwards Plateau; casual east of 97th meridian.

HAUNTS AND HABITS: The Lark Bunting breeds on dry short-grass and, to a lesser extent, damp long-grass prairies. In winter, birds inhabit flat, semiarid country where they wander on plains, open fields, and in brushland.

Gregariousness is the chief trait of the species in winter. Flocks, though often large, are not necessarily conspicuous, since they contain variously plumaged— many sparrowlike—individuals. At this season, the birds are generally cautious and easily frightened— neither so bold nor exuberant as during the breeding season. Lark Buntings feed largely on the ground; also at times in low-growing bushes. They consume, especially in winter, a variety of weed, grass, and grain seeds (purslane, sorghum, needlegrass, pigweed, others). In summer, insects (grasshoppers, weevils and other beetles, true bugs, bees, and ants) are primary in their diet.

Call note is a soft *hoo-ee*. The Lark Bunting's song is a varied series of slurs, chugs, and clear piping notes periodically interspersed with trills. The male sings on a bush, fence post, or from the ground. At times, this long rich song is sounded in flight as he ascends rapidly ten to thirty feet in the air, then drifts down slowly, with wings held in a sharp upward dihedral. Twenty or more males often execute their flight songs in the same field. In Texas, vocalizing, though doubtless scant, may be expected from March through late July.

DETAILED ACCOUNT: NO SUBSPECIES

DESCRIPTION: *Adult male, nuptial plumage*: Acquired by partial prenuptial molt. Upper surface chaetura black; tail fuscous black to brownish black, feathers tipped chiefly on inner webs, sometimes rather broadly, with white; primaries fuscous black, outer webs, except tips, together with secondaries and tertials, brownish black, primaries and secondaries scarcely more brownish on inner edges, a few outermost primaries near tips with very narrow white edgings, inner secondaries edged with white for terminal third, innermost tertials broadly tipped with white, innermost secondary and longest tertial narrowly tipped with white and more broadly edged on terminal portion of outer webs with same; lesser wing-coverts black, greater coverts and broad tips of median coverts white, forming large conspicuous white patch on wing; lower surface, including lining of wing, brownish black, lower tail-coverts broadly tipped with white. Maxilla and tip of mandible rather dark brownish plumbeous or slate black; rest of mandible much paler—light plumbeous or pearl gray; iris vandyke brown or hazel; legs seal brown; feet sometimes of darker brown. *Adult male, winter*: Acquired by complete postnuptial molt. Similar to adult female in winter but larger; upper surface less rufescent (more grayish); tail darker, feathers black except middle pair; primaries, secondaries, primary and lesser coverts, and dark parts of other wing-coverts more blackish or black (less brownish), whitish wing-patch less deeply buff, and edges of tertials and scapulars lighter, more grayish (less rufescent); lores, cheeks, chin, and lower parts with more black. *Adult female, nuptial*: Acquired by partial prenuptial molt. Upper surface drab to dull cinnamon buff or dull pinkish buff, scapulars sometimes dull clay color, pileum and back broadly streaked with olive brown; hindneck more narrowly streaked, rump and upper tail-coverts more narrowly and sparsely streaked with olive brown; tail dark clove brown, middle pair of feathers and outer webs of remaining rectrices light olive brown, except outermost pair of feathers which are

edged on outer webs with white, and outer four pairs of feathers with broad, rather squarish tips on inner webs; wing-quills between light fuscous and buffy brown, tertials similar but rather paler, inner edges of primaries and secondaries slightly paler, except at tips, outer webs of primaries edged with color of back, but terminally often whitish or very pale buff, inner secondaries and tertials broadly edged on outer webs with pale pinkish buff to cinnamon, secondaries and tertials more or less broadly tipped with dull white or very pale buff; upper wing-coverts like wing-quills, but lesser coverts darker and broadly tipped with grayish or buffy white, median coverts broadly tipped and greater coverts entirely white, forming large elongated wing-patch; primary coverts and alula brown like wing-quills; superciliary stripe white or buffy white, posteriorly becoming pale pinkish buff to dull pinkish buff, anteriorly more or less mixed with dull brown; lores pale dull pinkish buff, much mixed with light olive brown or light fuscous; eye-ring white or buffy white; malar region streaked or spotted with chaetura black to fuscous black on buffy white or very pale buff ground; auriculars buffy brown, sometimes with more or less inconspicuous buffy white shaft streaks; stripe below auriculars buffy white or pale buff, connecting with broad stripe up on sides of neck back of auriculars; sides of neck like hindneck; lower surface white or buffy white, but chin more or less chaetura black or fuscous black, feathers with white or buffy white tips; sides of throat fuscous black, finely streaked with white or buffy white, middle of chin and throat very finely streaked with fuscous to olive brown; jugulum, breast, sides, and flanks more or less broadly streaked with fuscous to olive brown, these streaks on center of jugulum fading and coalescing into more or less well defined spot; lower tail-coverts fuscous to olive brown, broadly tipped with white or buffy white; lining of wing hair brown, outer edge fuscous black, feathers more or less tipped with dull white or buffy white. Maxilla and tip of mandible dull black; rest of mandible and basal part of cutting edges of maxilla lavender gray; iris vandyke brown; legs fawn color or dull brown; feet and claws seal brown. *Adult female, winter*: Acquired by complete postnuptial molt. Similar to nuptial adult male, but upper parts duller, darker, and less sharply streaked (somewhat more rufescent), colors more blended due to broader brown or dull buff edgings of feathers; wings more deeply buff, ochraceous, or tawny, white wing-patch cinnamon buff, edges of tertials sometimes between cinnamon brown and russet, light edgings of tertials broader; lower surface more distinctly suffused with buff. *Male, third winter*: Acquired by complete postnuptial molt. Like adult male in winter. *Male, second nuptial*: Acquired by partial prenuptial molt. Similar to nuptial adult male, but above decidedly brownish or grayish, less purely black; lesser wing-coverts wholly or in part brown, although primary coverts are black as in adult; occasionally some tail feathers brown instead of black. *Male, second winter*: Acquired by complete postnuptial molt. Similar to adult male in winter, but upper parts of rather lighter, more rufescent (less grayish) brown, lesser wing-coverts more brownish (less blackish); lower surface averaging more buffy, especially on posterior part, usually with less black anteriorly, and black streaks lighter, more brownish, less deeply black. *Male, first nuptial*: Acquired by partial prenuptial molt. Similar to second nuptial male, but primary coverts buffy brown to dark buffy brown, some or many wing-quills and usually some tail feathers olive brown to light olive brown or dark buffy brown. *Male, first winter*: Acquired by partial postjuvenal molt, which does not involve wing-quills or tail. Similar to second winter male, but lesser wing-coverts still lighter, with less dark brown showing, this more concealed by light brown or grayish edgings; wings and tail lighter, more brownish (less blackish); primary coverts, secondaries, inner primaries, and tips of outer primaries brown instead of black, leaving only basal two-thirds of outermost primary black. *Female, first nuptial*: Acquired by partial prenuptial molt. Similar to nuptial adult female, but brown of wing-quills averaging somewhat lighter; dark streaks on lower parts averaging lighter; chin without black, but this part, with middle of throat, white. *Female, first winter*: Acquired by partial postjuvenal molt. Similar to adult female in winter, but upper parts averaging lighter, brown of wings also averaging lighter; lower surface paler, dark streaks more brownish (less blackish); chin and middle of throat without black, being entirely white or buffy white. Similar to first winter male but smaller; upper surface, including wings and tail, averaging lighter, more rufescent; wing-coverts and alula lighter, more brownish (less blackish); basal part of outer primaries all brown like rest, not black as in first winter male; lower surface lighter, more buffy, and without black on chin or center of throat, streaks also lighter, more brownish (less blackish). *Male, juvenal*: Acquired by complete postnatal molt. Pileum sayal brown to buffy drab; hindneck light pinkish buff to cartridge buff; upper back like pileum; middle of back like hindneck; lower back and rump like pileum or toward dull light pinkish buff; upper tail-coverts tawny olive to sayal brown, everywhere conspicuously spotted with olive brown to fuscous and fuscous black, these spots largest on back and rump; wings and tail like first winter male; lower parts in general buffy white or very pale buff, but jugulum, sides, flanks, and crissum cartridge buff to light cream buff, everywhere (except on chin, abdomen, and middle of breast) with spots or short streaks of chaetura drab to chaetura black. *Female, juvenal*: Acquired by complete postnatal molt. Similar to juvenal male, but upper surface, wings, and tail averaging lighter, outer primaries particularly so; tail of more rufescent brown, particularly middle pair of feathers. *Natal*: Mouse gray.

MEASUREMENTS: *Adult male*: Wing, 85.3–91.9 (average, 87.6) mm.; tail, 65.5–71.4 (68.8); bill (exposed culmen), 13.2–14.7 (14.0); height of bill at base, 10.7–12.2 (11.2); tarsus, 22.9–25.7 (24.1); middle toe without claw, 16.8–18.0 (17.3). *Adult female*: Wing, 81.8–85.3 (83.3); tail, 60.5–68.8 (66.0); bill, 12.7–13.2 (13.0); height of bill, 10.2–11.9 (10.7); tarsus, 22.4–25.1 (23.6); middle toe, 16.5–17.8 (17.0).

TEXAS: *Breeding*: Eggs collected: Wilbarger Co., Vernon (June 8, 1935, R. L. More). Two summer specimens within possible breeding range: Lipscomb Co., Lipscomb (June 30, and July 6, 1903, A. H. Howell). *Winter*: Taken north to Randall (May 3), east to Cooke and Harris, south to Cameron, west to El Paso cos.

NESTING: *Nest*: On plains and prairies; on ground, often in a depression, so that top is even with surface, at base of a bush, tuft of grass or cactus, or in grass; rather poorly constructed cup, very similar to that of a Dickcissel; composed of grasses, weed stalks, straw, and fine roots; lined with finer weed stalks, straw, grasses, vegetable down, and hair. *Eggs*: 4–6, usually 5; rounded ovate; light blue, bluish white, pale bluish green, or light greenish blue; unmarked, but rarely with a few reddish brown or light rufous dots; average size, 21.6 × 16.5 mm.

[IPSWICH SPARROW, *Passerculus princeps* Maynard

A large, pale version of the Savannah Sparrow (see below); walks more often than hops, moving head back and forth. Length, 6¼ in.; wingspan, 9¾.

RANGE: Sable Island, Nova Scotia. Winters along Atlantic coast from Nova Scotia to Georgia.

TEXAS: *Hypothetical*: It is extremely improbable that the adult male specimen, allegedly taken at Dallas on Dec. 10, 1884, by Clothier Pierce, was collected in Texas.]

SAVANNAH SPARROW, *Passerculus sandwichensis* (Gmelin)

SPECIES ACCOUNT

A small grassland sparrow with short notched tail.

Liberally brown-streaked above and below with whitish crown-stripe; yellow of lores variable, often extending above eye. Length, 5½ in.; wingspan, 9; weight, ¾ oz.

RANGE: N. Alaska to n. Labrador, south through w. United States and w. Mexico (locally) to Guatemala, and south through e. Canada to s. Iowa and New Jersey. Winters from s. British Columbia, s. Nevada, U.S. Gulf states, and s.w. Maine to El Salvador and West Indies.

TEXAS: (See map.) *Winter*: Late Sept. to mid-May (extremes: Aug. 19, June 1). Abundant to fairly common in most parts; irregular or scarce in northern Panhandle during coldest months.

HAUNTS AND HABITS: An open-country sparrow, the Savannah inhabits grasslands and marshes throughout its extensive range. On the ground in dense vegetation, its nest of grasses and rootlets is well hidden. Wintering birds in Texas frequent prairies, grassy pastures, weed fields, cultivated land, boggy meadows, and borders of ponds, lakes, and coastal marshes; occasionally bushes seem acceptable. Though Savannahs may be numerous in a field, they remain scattered and are not in the strict sense gregarious.

When frightened, the Savannah has several options: It may run mouselike amid grass and weeds; fly low above vegetation briefly, then drop to cover; or flit up to a perch in a small tree or bush. Foraging individuals hop about—sometimes scratching towhee style—in search of weed and grass seeds (namely of panicum, goosegrass, pigweed, woodsorrel, bristlegrass, sedge, sunflower); also insects (beetles, weevils, caterpillars, grasshoppers, moths, crickets), spiders, and snails.

A thin *tsip* is the Savannah's call. The usual song consists of several short staccato notes followed by one

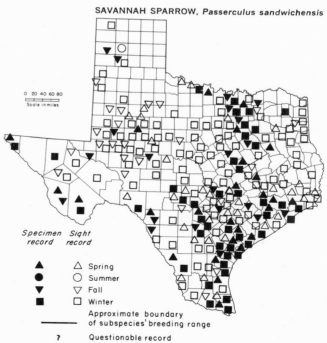

SAVANNAH SPARROW, *Passerculus sandwichensis*

0 20 40 60 80
Scale in miles

Specimen record | Sight record
▲   △ Spring
●   ○ Summer
▼   ▽ Fall
■   □ Winter

—— Approximate boundary of subspecies' breeding range
?   Questionable record

or two insectlike buzzy trills, the trailing buzz lower pitched: *tsip-tsip-tsit tseeeeee-tsaayr.* Delivery is from a low post, weed, stone, or the ground. Song is seldom heard in Texas.

DETAILED ACCOUNT: SEVEN SUBSPECIES

EASTERN SAVANNAH SPARROW, *Passerculus sandwichensis savanna* (Wilson)

DESCRIPTION: *Adult male and female, nuptial plumage*: Similar to *P. s. mediogriseus* (see below), but lighter, more brownish above (less grayish or blackish); dark streaks on lower parts lighter and more brownish (less blackish).

MEASUREMENTS: *Adult male*: Wing, 68.1–73.9 (average, 69.8) mm.; tail, 48.5–54.1 (50.8); bill (exposed culmen), 10.4–11.9 (10.9); height of bill at base, 6.1–7.1 (6.9); tarsus, 19.0–22.6 (21.4); middle toe without claw, 14.0–14.5 (14.2). *Adult female*: Wing, 63.0–68.6 (66.3); tail, 46.0–53.6 (48.2); bill, 10.4–11.4 (10.7); height of bill, 6.1–7.1 (6.9); tarsus, 19.0–22.1 (20.9); middle toe, 13.0–15.5 (14.2).

RANGE: S.e. Quebec and Nova Scotia. Winters from n. Texas and w. North Carolina to s. Florida.

TEXAS: *Winter*: Taken northeast to Collin (Mar. 22), south to Aransas and Cameron, west to Val Verde cos. Rare.

SOUTHEASTERN SAVANNAH SPARROW, *Passerculus sandwichensis mediogriseus* Aldrich

Race not in A.O.U. check-list, 1957 (see Appendix A).

DESCRIPTION: *Adult male, nuptial plumage*: Acquired by partial prenuptial molt. Upper surface dull buffy brown to drab, but on back more or less tinged or mixed with cinnamon, hindneck sometimes washed with dull yellow or buff, pileum always broadly streaked with brownish black to fuscous, particularly on sides, leaving more or less well defined median light stripe, hindneck narrowly streaked with fuscous and sometimes with grayish or buffy white, back broadly streaked with brownish black or fuscous and narrowly with grayish or buffy white, rump and upper tail-coverts less broadly so streaked; tail between olive brown and fuscous, feathers edged narrowly on outer webs, except on outermost pair, with dull light drab, outermost pair of feathers with outer webs and parts or all of inner webs dull light drab; wings between olive brown and light fuscous, but tertials and median and greater coverts fuscous to fuscous black, inner edges of primaries and secondaries light drab to dull drab, except at tips, outer edges of primaries and outer secondaries like upper surface, middle portion of outer two or three primaries with pronounced whitish edging, inner secondaries edged on outer webs with brown, between tawny olive and wood brown, tertials broadly margined on outer webs and tips with same color or russet, shortest tertial also margined with dull buffy white or pale buff; lesser wing-coverts edged with deep olive buff, greater and median coverts with light brown—between tawny olive and wood brown; broad superciliary stripe lemon yellow or wax yellow but posteriorly white; lores mixed with yellowish white and light brownish olive; postocular streak of brownish black; auriculars isabella color, anteriorly shading into color of lores; broad rictal streak and submalar streak dull black to fuscous, enclosing malar streak of buffy white or very pale buff; anterior sides of neck dull white or buffy white, streaked with fuscous or brownish black; posterior sides of neck like upper surface but less conspicuously streaked; lower surface white, sometimes slightly washed with buff on sides and flanks, the jugulum, upper breast, sides, and flanks more or less broadly streaked with dull black to fuscous, these streaks sometimes forming small spot in middle of jugulum; edge of wing primrose yellow to colonial buff to almost white; remainder of wing-lining drab, pale drab, or dull white, slightly washed with buff or yellow. Maxilla and tip of mandible blackish brown, brownish gray, black, seal brown, chocolate, or slate color, rest of mandible

paler—dull white, flesh color, light fawn color, yellow, light pinkish cinnamon, or even lilaceous; iris bay, seal brown, vandyke brown, or black; legs and feet flesh color, clay color, pale fawn color, pinkish gray, sayal brown, pinkish white, or white tinged with straw yellow, but toes sometimes verona brown; claws drab. *Adult male, winter*: Acquired by complete postnuptial molt. Similar to nuptial adult male, but upper surface lighter, colors more blended because of light edgings of feathers—thus, back less conspicuously streaked with blackish and black areas reduced in extent; superciliary stripe duller and paler; greater coverts and edges of tertials more brownish, often inclining to snuff brown; lower surface slightly washed with buff and less sharply streaked, dark markings more or less obscured by broader pale edges of feathers. *Adult female, nuptial*: Acquired by partial prenuptial molt. Similar to nuptial adult male but smaller; yellow of superciliary stripe duller; upper surface and sides of head more tinged with buff, and this sometimes the case on lower surface. *Adult female, winter*: Acquired by complete postnuptial molt. Differs from nuptial adult female as does adult male in winter from nuptial adult male. *Male and female, first nuptial*: Acquired by partial prenuptial molt, which does not involve wing-quills or tail. Similar to corresponding nuptial adult, but upper parts more brownish (less grayish); sides of head more buffy (less grayish); anterior lower parts more tinged with buff. *Male and female, first winter*: Acquired by partial postjuvenal molt, which does not involve wing-quills or tail. Similar to corresponding adult in winter, but upper surface duller, more brownish; hindneck and sides of head often more yellowish; anterior lower surface, sides, and flanks decidedly buffy. Maxilla benzo brown to fuscous; mandible yellow or light cinnamon drab; legs and feet light cinnamon drab; claws cinnamon drab. *Juvenal*: Acquired by complete postnatal molt. Similar to nuptial adult male and female, but upper surface paler, more yellowish or buffy; pale buff or pale gray edgings of hindneck and back more extensive; median and greater coverts broadly tipped with dull pale yellow or dull buff; sides of head more buffy; superciliary stripe duller or whitish; lower surface decidedly more buffy or yellowish, streaks on jugulum, sides, and flanks narrower, more brownish (less blackish).

MEASUREMENTS: *Adult male*: Wing, 66.5–71.7 (average, 69.1) mm.; tail, 45.0–52.6 (49.8); bill (exposed culmen), 9.9–11.9 (11.2); height of bill at base, 6.1–7.6 (6.9); tarsus, 19.0–21.1 (19.6); middle toe without claw, 14.2–15.5 (14.7). *Adult female*: Wing, 63.5–71.7 (66.3); tail, 41.9–51.6 (46.3); bill, 10.4–11.4 (10.9); height of bill, 6.1–7.6 (6.9); tarsus, 19.0–20.1 (19.3); middle toe, 13.0–15.0 (14.2).

RANGE: C. Minnesota to s. Quebec, south to s. Iowa and New Jersey. Winters from c. Oklahoma, s.e. Illinois, s.e. Pennsylvania, and s.w. Maine to Yucatán; also West Indies.

TEXAS: *Winter*: Taken north to Cooke, east to Titus and Chambers, south to Cameron, west to Kimble cos. Common.

LABRADOR SAVANNAH SPARROW, *Passerculus sandwichensis labradorius* Howe

DESCRIPTION: *Adult male and female, nuptial plumage*: Similar to *P. s. savanna,* but much darker above, black areas more extensive; on lower parts blackish streaks darker and heavier. Similar to *P. s. oblitus* (see below) but much more brownish both above and below.

MEASUREMENTS: *Adult male*: Wing, 67.1–73.7 (average, 70.9) mm.; tail, 50.0–55.6 (53.3); bill (exposed culmen), 9.4–10.9 (10.2); tarsus, 20.6–23.1 (21.4); middle toe without claw, 14.0–16.0 (14.7). *Adult female*: Wing, 63.0–68.6 (65.8); tail, 43.9–51.6 (47.3); bill, 9.4–10.9 (10.2); tarsus, 19.6–22.4 (20.9); middle toe, 13.0–15.5 (14.5).

RANGE: N. Quebec and n. Labrador, south to s.e. Quebec and Newfoundland. Winters from Massachusetts and Rhode Island, east of Appalachian Mts. to s.e. Texas and s. Florida; also w. Cuba (casually).

TEXAS: *Winter*: Two specimens: Anderson Co., Palestine

(Mar. 20, 1894, J. A. Loring); Matagorda Co., Matagorda (Jan. 23, 1892, W. Lloyd).

CHURCHILL SAVANNAH SPARROW, *Passerculus sandwichensis oblitus* Peters and Griscom

DESCRIPTION: *Adult male and female, nuptial plumage:* Similar to *P. s. savanna*, but upper parts decidedly darker, dark areas more blackish and of greater extent.

MEASUREMENTS: *Adult male:* Wing, 68.6–72.9 (average, 71.4) mm.; tail, 49.0–55.6 (52.8); bill (exposed culmen), 9.4–10.9 (10.2); tarsus, 19.0–21.6 (20.9); middle toe without claw, 13.0–15.0 (14.0). *Adult female:* Wing, 64.0–67.1 (65.8); tail, 45.5–51.6 (48.3); bill, 9.4–10.7 (9.9); tarsus, 19.0–21.1 (20.3); middle toe, 13.0–15.2 (14.0).

RANGE: N.e. Manitoba to n.w. Quebec, south to n.w. Minnesota and s. Quebec. Winters from e. Oklahoma to s. Texas and s.e. Georgia; also w. Cuba.

TEXAS: *Winter:* Taken north to Denton, east to Galveston, southwest to Cameron cos. Uncommon.

WESTERN SAVANNAH SPARROW, *Passerculus sandwichensis anthinus* Bonaparte

DESCRIPTION: *Adult male and female, nuptial plumage:* Similar to *P. s. nevadensis* (see below), but larger; upper surface, sides, and flanks darker, more rufescent brown; eyebrows usually more deeply yellow.

MEASUREMENTS: *Adult male:* Wing, 68.6–76.2 (average, 72.2) mm.; tail, 48.3–53.8 (51.8); bill (exposed culmen), 10.2–10.9 (10.4); tarsus, 19.0–21.1 (20.3); middle toe without claw, 14.7–16.8 (15.7). *Adult female:* Wing, 65.5–69.1 (66.8); tail, 48.8–50.8 (50.0); bill, 9.9–10.4 (10.2); tarsus, 19.0–20.3 (19.8); middle toe, 14.7–15.2 (15.0).

RANGE: N. Alaska to n. Mackenzie, south to s. Alaska, n. British Columbia and n.w. Saskatchewan. Winters from n. California and n. Texas to c. Mexico.

TEXAS: *Winter:* Taken north to Clay (Apr. 11), east to Dallas (Apr. 10) and Lee, south to Cameron, west to Culberson cos. Scarce.

CHIHUAHUA SAVANNAH SPARROW, *Passerculus sandwichensis rufofuscus* Camras

DESCRIPTION: *Adult male and female, nuptial plumage:* Resembling *P. s. anthinus* but smaller and darker.

MEASUREMENTS: *Adult male:* Wing, 70.1–71.4 (average, 70.9) mm.; tail, 49.8–50.0 (49.8); bill (exposed culmen), 10.7–10.9 (10.7); height of bill at base, 5.8–6.1 (6.0). *Adult female:* Wing, 64.5–65.0 (64.8); tail, 43.7–45.5 (44.7); bill, 9.9–10.9 (10.4); height of bill, 5.8–6.1 (5.8); tarsus, 20.1–20.6 (20.3).

RANGE: C. Arizona and n. New Mexico, south to c. Chihuahua. Winters from s.e. Arizona (probably) and c. Texas to Jalisco.

TEXAS: *Winter:* Two specimens: Navarro Co., Rice (Jan. 11, 1880, J. D. Ogilby); Kinney Co., Fort Clark (Apr. 2, 1898, E. A. Mearns).

NEVADA SAVANNAH SPARROW, *Passerculus sandwichensis nevadensis* Grinnell

DESCRIPTION: *Adult male and female, nuptial plumage:* Similar to *P. s. savanna*, but wing averages slightly longer, tail shorter; bill decidedly more slender; upper parts lighter, more grayish (less brownish); superciliary stripe less deeply yellow.

MEASUREMENTS: *Adult male:* Wing, 67.3–74.9 (average, 70.9) mm.; tail, 47.5–52.6 (49.0); bill (exposed culmen), 9.9–10.7 (10.2); tarsus, 19.8–21.1 (20.6); middle toe without claw, 14.2–15.5 (14.7). *Adult female:* Wing, 66.0–69.3 (67.6); tail, 46.3–50.8 (48.0); bill, 9.7–10.2 (9.9); tarsus, 19.0–20.6 (20.1); middle toe, 13.5–15.0 (14.0).

RANGE: C. British Columbia to c. Manitoba, south to e. Cali-

fornia and n. New Mexico. Winters from n. California, n. Texas, and s. Mississippi through Mexico to Guatemala.

TEXAS: *Winter:* Taken north to Oldham, east to Collin and Galveston (Nov. 6), south to Cameron, west to El Paso cos. Common.

GRASSHOPPER SPARROW, *Ammodramus savannarum* (Gmelin)

SPECIES ACCOUNT

A very small, flat-headed sparrow with unstreaked buffy breast; white belly; narrow stub tail. Chestnut-, black-, and gray-striped above with pale median crown-stripe; yellow lores; whitish eye-line. Length, 5 in.; wingspan, 8¼; weight, ½ oz.

RANGE: U.S.-Canada border, south to s. California, c. Colorado, Texas, and c. Gulf states; also s. Mexico and West Indies, south through Central America to Ecuador. Northern races winter from s. United States through Mexico to El Salvador; also West Indies.

TEXAS: (See map.) *Breeding:* Early Apr. to late July (eggs, Apr. 20 to July 24) from near sea level to 2,800 ft. Fairly common, but very local, in open areas, although absent from Trans-Pecos, most of south Texas brush country, and wooded eastern quarter. *Migration:* Mid-Mar. to mid-May; late July to mid-Nov. (extremes: Feb. 13, June 6; July 23, Dec. 21). Common to fairly common east of Pecos River; uncommon to scarce west of Pecos River. *Winter:* Mid-Oct. to mid-Apr. Fairly common locally on coastal prairies and savannahs; uncommon to rare inland south of 34th parallel; absent from northern and middle Panhandle.

HAUNTS AND HABITS: The present species is appropri-

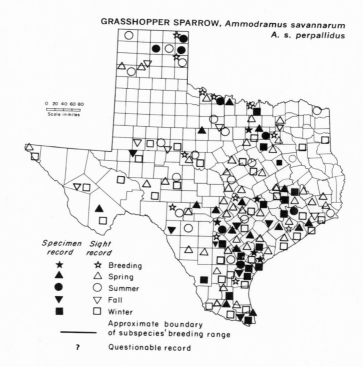

GRASSHOPPER SPARROW, *Ammodramus savannarum*
A. s. perpallidus

0 20 40 60 80
Scale in miles

Specimen record / Sight record

★ / ☆ Breeding
▲ / △ Spring
● / ○ Summer
▼ / ▽ Fall
■ / □ Winter

—— Approximate boundary of subspecies' breeding range

? Questionable record

ately named. It is very insectivorous—with a propensity for grasshoppers—and it sings a grasshopperlike song. Nesting grounds for *A. savannarum* are wet or dry prairies and grassy pastures dotted with bushes and small trees. During migration, dozens of Grasshopper Sparrows may accept the same weed patch; in winter they seek protection of dense grass, bushes, and brush piles.

Rather diffident, the Grasshopper Sparrow usually stays well hidden. When alarmed it retreats on foot; at times, however, it flies. On flickering wings, the bird lists and zigzags barely over the vegetation, then quickly drops back to the ground. Besides grasshoppers, it gleans beetles, weevils, caterpillars, locusts, crickets, moths, spiders, millipedes, and snails; also seeds of bristlegrass, ragweed, panicum, woodsorrel, smartweed, and others, and a few berries.

A weak *tillic* is the call note. The male's "grasshopper" song is a thin, weak, single-pitched *tzick tzick tzurrrrrrrr* (preliminary notes often inaudible); he also utters a more musical jumble: *zeeeee sic-a-zeedle sic-a-zeedle sic-a-zeedle-zeeeee*. From March to late June, he sings persistently, even on moonlit nights, from a grass or weed stalk or fence wire.

DETAILED ACCOUNT: TWO SUBSPECIES

EASTERN GRASSHOPPER SPARROW, *Ammodramus savannarum pratensis* (Vieillot)

DESCRIPTION: *Adults, nuptial plumage*: Acquired by partial prenuptial molt. Pileum chaetura black, feathers very narrowly edged with very pale buff or buffy white, imparting finely streaked appearance, but with a broad central stripe pinkish buff to pale pinkish buff; remainder of upper surface mouse gray to between smoke gray and olive buff, hindneck usually most grayish with irregular spots or very short streaks of olive brown to auburn, back densely spotted with dull black, scapulars spotted with dull black and dull tawny to russet, and lower back and rump with spots or short streaks of dull black or russet, upper tail-coverts broadly streaked centrally with fuscous to fuscous black; tail olive brown, outer and inner webs edged more or less conspicuously with paler brown, between light drab and dull tilleul buff, outermost pair of feathers same color for terminal half; primaries and secondaries between buffy brown and hair brown, inner edges, except at tips, between avellaneous and light drab, primaries edged on outer webs with pale dull buff, secondaries on basal portion of outer webs with sayal brown; terminal portion of tertials, as well as spots on middle portion of outer webs, fuscous or fuscous black; tips of tertials dull buffy brown, a broad linear spot on outer webs near tips dull pale buff; lesser wing-coverts olive yellow to olive ocher; median and greater coverts mouse gray to hair brown, median coverts with subterminal roundish spot of chaetura black to fuscous, greater coverts with elongated wedge-shaped spot of same color on most of feathers, their outer edges smoke gray; elongated supraloral spot or streak dull cadmium yellow to dull orange; sides of head, including superciliary stripe, dull pale pinkish buff, but auriculars dull cinnamon buff; sides of neck like hindneck; chin and throat dull pale pinkish buff; sides of throat, together with jugulum, dull cinnamon buff, jugulum sometimes spotted with dull cinnamon rufous; sides similar to jugulum but duller, with obscure streaks of hazel; flanks similar but more mixed or washed with pale gray; crissum between pinkish buff and cream buff; lining of wing drab; axillars similar but somewhat paler, even dull white, and washed with buff or pale yellow; edge of wing-bend lemon chrome. Bill dull brownish plumbeous or dull rather light brown, but mandible dull flesh color; iris dark brown or light brown; legs and feet light flesh color, sometimes tinged with pale yellow. *Adults, winter*: Acquired by complete postnuptial molt. Similar to nuptial adults, but upper surface darker, colors more blended because of broader light edgings of feathers; back less conspicuously spotted with black, spots elsewhere more obscured; buff of jugulum, of sides, and of flanks darker, often brighter. *First nuptial*: Acquired by partial prenuptial molt. Similar to nuptial adult male and female, but upper surface averaging somewhat more buffy, less grayish; lower surface more extensively buff, whitish areas more distinctly washed with buff. *First winter*: Acquired by complete postjuvenal molt. Similar to adults in winter, but upper surface lighter, averaging more buffy and more extensively chestnut; lower surface still more deeply and extensively buff. *Juvenal*: Acquired by complete postnatal molt. Pileum clove brown to fuscous, sometimes streaked with olive brown, a narrow (in very young bird, scarcely indicated) central stripe of tilleul buff to cartridge buff; hindneck pale dull buff or even buff or grayish white, streaked with brown of pileum; back and rump brown like pileum, but rump lighter, feathers of both tipped and edged with cream buff to light isabella color, producing scaled or irregularly barred effect; primaries and secondaries light fuscous to dark hair brown; outer edges of secondaries sayal brown, except on terminal portion; wing-coverts olive brown to fuscous, but outer webs of greater coverts margined with buffy brown, those of lesser coverts with isabella color, greater and median coverts tipped with dull buff or buffy white; tertials olive brown to fuscous, tips and broad outer edgings buffy white; sides of head buffy wood brown, narrowly streaked and spotted with fuscous, thus producing rather mottled effect; posterior portion of superciliary stripe, together with sides of neck, grayish white or buffy white, narrowly streaked with fuscous, lower surface pale dull naphthalene yellow or buffy white, sides of throat very narrowly, jugulum and upper breast rather broadly, streaked with fuscous; sides and flanks more sparingly streaked with light fuscous. Bill blackish slate, but mandible pale pinkish vinaceous; iris hazel; legs and feet pale flesh color. *Natal* (this plumage of this race not seen in Texas): Light drab. Bill, legs, and feet pinkish buff.

MEASUREMENTS: *Adult male*: Wing, 58.7–62.2 (average, 61.0) mm.; tail, 41.1–45.7 (44.4); bill (exposed culmen), 10.7–12.2 (11.2); tarsus, 19.8–20.9 (20.3); middle toe without claw, 14.7–15.5 (15.0). *Adult female*: Wing, 58.2–62.7 (60.2); tail, 40.1–45.7 (43.7); bill, 10.7–11.7 (11.2); tarsus, 19.3–20.9 (19.8); middle toe, 14.2–15.2 (15.0).

RANGE: Great Lakes region to Maine, south (east of Mississippi Valley) to c. Alabama, c. Carolinas, and e. Virginia. Winters from s.w. Illinois and Maryland (casually) through s.e. United States and e. Mexico to Guatemala; also West Indies.

TEXAS: *Winter*: Taken in Travis (Mar. 27), Atascosa (Nov. 22), and Cameron (Mar. 21) cos. Rare.

NESTING: (This race does not nest in Texas.) *Nest*: On uplands or lowlands; on prairies and plains, in grassy fields, pastures, and even in cultivated areas; usually in dry situations, sunk in ground and well concealed by tufts of grass, weeds, or low bushes; arched over though not bulky; composed of grasses and weeds; lined with finer grasses, rootlets, and hair. *Eggs*: 3–6, usually 4; rounded ovate or ovate; somewhat glossy; white, or slightly tinged with green or brown; spotted and blotched, more or less numerously, chiefly at large end where sometimes forming a wreath, with light reddish or golden brown (pecan brown to burnt umber), and with shell markings of lilac; average size, 18.5 × 14.2 mm.

WESTERN GRASSHOPPER SPARROW, *Ammodramus savannarum perpallidus* (Coues)

DESCRIPTION: *Adults, nuptial plumage*: Similar to *A. s. pratensis*, but wing longer; bill decidedly more slender; upper surface paler, tawny spots lighter and more numerous or extensive, with less accompanying black. *Natal*: Probably similar to *A. s. pratensis*.

MEASUREMENTS: *Adult male*: Wing, 59.4–65.5 (average,

PLATE 33: Bachman's Sparrow, *Aimophila aestivalis*

63.8) mm.; tail, 42.9–47.5 (45.2); bill (exposed culmen), 11.2–11.9 (11.7); tarsus, 18.5–20.1 (19.3); middle toe without claw, 13.5–15.0 (14.2). *Adult female*: Wing, 57.9–64.5 (61.2); tail, 38.6–47.8 (42.7); bill, 11.2–11.9 (11.7); tarsus, 19.0–20.1 (19.3); middle toe, 13.5–15.5 (14.2).

RANGE: Interior U.S.-Canada border, south (chiefly west of Mississippi River) to s. California, c. Colorado, and Texas (local). Winters from c. California, s. Arizona, and Arkansas through Mexico to El Salvador.

TEXAS: *Breeding*: Collected northwest to Lipscomb, east to Cooke, south to Aransas cos. *Winter*: Taken north to Cooke, east to Walker and Galveston (Apr. 7), south to Cameron, west to Webb and Brewster (Apr. 17) cos. Locally fairly common.

NESTING: Similar to that of *A. s. pratensis*, but average egg size, 19.0 × 14.5 mm.

BAIRD'S SPARROW, *Centronyx bairdii* (Audubon)

SPECIES ACCOUNT

Ammodramus bairdii of A.O.U. check-list, 1957 (see Appendix A). A small sparrow with a broad ocher crown-stripe; breast-band of blackish streaks; blackish-streaked buffy above; whitish below. Length, 5½ in.; wingspan, 9¼; weight, ¾ oz.

RANGE: S. prairie provinces of Canada, south to n.w. Montana, Dakotas, and w. Minnesota. Winters from s.e. Arizona and plains areas of Texas to n. Mexico.

TEXAS: (See map.) *Winter*: Mid-Sept. to mid-May (extremes: Sept. 6, May 21). Scarce and local west of 96th meridian; casual on upper coast; apparently absent from wooded eastern quarter.

HAUNTS AND HABITS: In its restricted breeding range, the Baird's Sparrow inhabits short-grass prairies with scattered low bushes and old matted vegetation. *C. bairdii* often goes unnoticed as it moves due south to the wintering grounds. In Texas during cold months it frequents grassland prairies and plains where grass cover is densest. Occasionally it occurs in overgrown fields.

Like other grassland sparrows, the Baird's is reluctant to flush and most often retreats by running on the ground under cover of vegetation. Mainly in fall, winter, and spring, this sparrow eats seeds of sorghum, pigweed, green bristlegrass, lambsquarter, Russian-thistle, ragweed, plantain, bromegrass, and bluestem. In summer, when it becomes more insectivorous, grasshoppers, crickets, moths, leafhoppers, beetles, flies, and caterpillars are added to its diet; also a few spiders.

A rather sharp *chip* is the Baird's call note. The male's clear, musical, somewhat insectlike song is three or four deliberate notes followed by a lower pitched trill: *zip zip zip-zrrrrrr*. It is very seldom heard in Texas.

CHANGES: This sparrow has greatly declined since the 1880's with the wholesale overgrazing and plowing of its habitat. Present-day sight records of the Baird's are mostly based on misidentifications of the Savannah Sparrow, which as its many races indicate, is far more adaptable to changes than is the present species.

DETAILED ACCOUNT: NO SUBSPECIES

DESCRIPTION: *Adults, nuptial plumage*: Acquired by partial prenuptial molt. Pileum ochraceous, laterally streaked broadly with black, these streaks usually more or less uniting to form two broad lateral stripes, leaving immaculate or slightly streaked middle stripe of ochraceous; remainder of upper surface dull grayish buff, hindneck narrowly streaked with dull black, back and scapulars with numerous large spots of olive brown to fuscous black, lower back often with terminal spots of sayal brown, rump streaked with fuscous to fuscous black, upper tail-coverts with broad central streaks of fuscous; tail light olive brown, outermost pair of tail feathers tilleul buff on outer webs and on broad tips of inner webs, outer webs of all other feathers narrowly margined with tilleul buff, central pair of feathers also broadly edged with same on terminal portion of inner webs; primaries and secondaries between buffy brown and light fuscous, but inner edges, except at tips, pinkish buff to dull buffy drab; tertials, with median and greater coverts, olive brown to clove brown; outer webs of primaries narrowly edged with dull buff, outer edges of secondaries and tertials sayal brown, becoming cinnamon buff on innermost secondaries and outer webs of tertials, terminal portions of broad edgings on tertials pale dull buff or buffy white; lesser wing-coverts between wood brown and fawn; median and greater coverts hair brown, terminally in part fuscous, outer edges dull buff like upper surface; superciliary stripe dull light ochraceous buff; malar streak olive; sides of head, including lores, light ochraceous or dull light buff, sometimes with decided wash of light gray; a more or less concealed narrow postocular streak, a rictal streak extending to below auriculars, and a poorly defined submalar streak, often made up of short narrow streaks, all dull black; sides of neck like hindneck and similarly streaked; lower surface dull light buff or buffy white, most deeply buff on jugulum, but sides of throat, jugulum, sides, and flanks conspicuously streaked with fuscous to fuscous black; lining of wing pale pinkish buff, pinkish buff to dull white, outer portion more or less spotted with drab gray. Maxilla and tip of mandible light brown or drab tinged with fawn color; rest of mandible flesh color or dull vinaceous, sometimes with dull brown tip; iris brown; legs flesh color or light cream color; feet and claws darker, somewhat brownish. *Adults, winter*: Acquired by complete postnuptial molt. Similar to nuptial adults, but upper surface darker and more richly colored, light edgings and tips of feathers broader

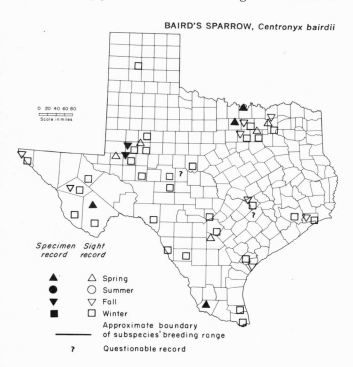

BAIRD'S SPARROW, *Centronyx bairdii*

0 20 40 60 80
Scale in miles

Specimen   Sight
record   record

▲ △ Spring
● ○ Summer
▼ ▽ Fall
■ □ Winter

—— Approximate boundary of subspecies' breeding range

? Questionable record

on back and on tertials; lower surface, particularly jugulum and sides, more deeply buff, dark streaks on lower surface broader and less sharply defined. *First nuptial*: Acquired by partial prenuptial molt. Like nuptial adults. *First winter*: Acquired by partial postjuvenal molt. Similar to adults in winter, but pileum and hindneck of more yellowish or buffy cast, blackish feathers of back at first with very broad white or buffy white tips, giving upper surface decidedly squamate appearance, however, this soon wearing off, but still leaving feathers with decidedly more conspicuous edgings than in winter adults; anterior lower surface, sides, and flanks still more deeply buff and more densely streaked. *Juvenal*: Acquired by complete postnatal molt. Upper surface fuscous to fuscous black, pileum and hindneck numerously streaked with dull cream buff, median stripe barely indicated; feathers of back and scapulars narrowly edged and tipped with dull pale pinkish buff, buffy white to dull snuff brown; rump much mixed with dull or light isabella color; edges of upper tail-coverts dull pinkish buff; tail as in first winter male and female; wings similar to those of first winter male and female, but outer edgings of tertials, particularly on terminal portion of feathers, more whitish; outer edgings of greater coverts duller—tawny olive; lesser wing-coverts dull buff with small fuscous centers; median wing-coverts dark buffy brown, edged and tipped with dull pale buff to cartridge buff; sides of head as in first winter male and female, but duller, paler, less strongly buff; anterior lower parts cartridge buff, but sides of throat, jugulum, sides, and flanks streaked rather narrowly with fuscous to light fuscous, much less broadly than in first winter male and female.

MEASUREMENTS: *Adult male*: Wing, 67.1–72.4 (average, 69.8) mm.; tail, 41.5–54.1 (50.3); bill (exposed culmen), 9.7–11.4 (10.7); height of bill at base, 6.9–7.6 (7.4); tarsus, 20.1–22.6 (21.4); middle toe without claw, 14.5–16.5 (15.7). *Adult female*: Wing, 65.0–71.7 (67.6); tail, 43.7–53.1 (48.8); bill, 9.4–11.4 (10.7); height of bill, 6.6–7.6 (7.1); tarsus, 20.1–22.1 (20.9); middle toe, 14.5–16.8 (15.2).

TEXAS: *Winter*: Taken northeast to Cooke (Mar. 19), south to Starr (Apr. 25), west to Brewster (May 14) cos.

LE CONTE'S SPARROW, *Passerherbulus caudacutus* (Latham)

SPECIES ACCOUNT

A very small sparrow with sharp tail; has bright ocher eye-line; whitish median crown-stripe; pinkish brown nape, finely streaked with chestnut; dark-striped tawny above; buffy breast fading to whitish on belly; dark-brown-streaked on buffy sides. Length, 5 in.; wingspan, 7; weight, ½ oz.

RANGE: S. Mackenzie and Alberta, southeast to w. Great Lakes region. Winters locally from Kansas and South Carolina to n.e. Tamaulipas and s. Florida.

TEXAS: (See map.) *Winter*: Mid-Oct. to late Apr. (extremes: Oct. 4, May 20). Uncommon and local in eastern half; casual in Panhandle and Big Bend of Trans-Pecos.

HAUNTS AND HABITS: The Le Conte's Sparrow nests where it finds thick concentrations of deep grass, reeds, and wet matted vegetation, often among scattered willows. Its clutch of usually four eggs is laid in a neat, fine-grass cup near the ground in a tuft of grass. In Texas, this bird frequents tall prairie grass, damp weedy fields, stands of broomsedge, and cattails; or it may occur on short-grass prairies and in dry overgrown fields.

The bird, though it often retreats on foot, will occasionally flit up to a low perch. Thus, with a little determination, an observer, preferably several, can flush a Le Conte's by shuffling through grassy habitat where scant bushes or small trees offer suitable vantages for the bird. Its flights, like those of its grassland relatives, are brief and zigzag. This sparrow eats seeds of grasses and forbs; flies, leafhoppers, plant lice, stinkbugs, caterpillars, and other insects; also spiders.

The Le Conte's low *tick* note sounds like two small stones clicking together. The short, thin, grasshopperlike song—*tzeek-tzzzzzz tick*—is seldom heard in Texas.

DETAILED ACCOUNT: NO SUBSPECIES

DESCRIPTION: *Adults, nuptial plumage*: Acquired by partial prenuptial molt. Pileum brownish black to fuscous black, obscurely streaked with dull snuff brown, with broad median stripe anteriorly dark cinnamon buff, posteriorly pale pinkish buff; narrow collar on anterior part of hindneck dull cream buff, this, together with remainder of hindneck (which is dull smoke gray to dull pale pinkish buff), narrowly streaked or spotted with russet to tawny and slightly with dull black; remainder of upper surface pale pinkish buff to cinnamon buff, broadly streaked or spotted on back with fuscous black, sometimes these black spots or streaks edged or tipped with russet, tawny, or dull buffy brown; tail clove brown to olive brown, with broad inner and outer edgings of feathers between wood brown and drab to between wood brown and cinnamon buff, often restricting dark brown of tail to narrow shaft streaks; primaries and secondaries between hair brown and buffy brown, outer edges of primaries like those of tail but rather duller, inner edges of primaries and secondaries, except at tips, between avellaneous and pinkish cinnamon or light pinkish cinnamon to dull pale pinkish cinnamon, outer edges of secondaries sayal brown, sometimes verging toward snuff brown; tertials with large terminal central oblong spots of fuscous black and with broad edgings on both inner and outer webs of terminal portion pale buff or buff white, but basal

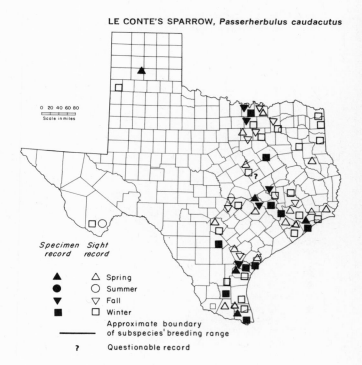

LE CONTE'S SPARROW, *Passerherbulus caudacutus*

0 20 40 60 80
Scale in miles

Specimen   Sight
record   record

▲   △   Spring
●   ○   Summer
▼   ▽   Fall
■   □   Winter

—————— Approximate boundary of subspecies' breeding range

?   Questionable record

portion of tertials with margins of dull sayal brown; wing-coverts sayal brown to dull cinnamon, terminal portion of greater coverts with oblong shaft spot of fuscous black, median coverts with smaller spot of same character; lores pale dull pinkish buff; rest of sides of head bright clay color, with rather broad postocular stripe of fuscous black, and auriculars dull smoke gray; upper sides of neck like hindneck; chin and throat dull pinkish buff; jugulum dull cinnamon buff; sides and flanks dull cinnamon buff, streaked conspicuously with fuscous to fuscous black; crissum dull pinkish buff; lining of wing dull pinkish buff, sometimes whitish, particularly on outer edges. Bill black or plumbeous, but cutting edges and mandible cinereous; iris vandyke brown or dull black; legs dull white or flesh color; toes and claws dark brown or light smoke gray. *Adults, winter*: Acquired by complete postnuptial molt. Similar to nuptial adults, but upper surface duller and darker, blackish areas of pileum more broadly tipped with buff or dull brown, as are also black feathers of back; buff of lower surface darker, jugulum sometimes very narrowly streaked with fuscous. *First nuptial*: Acquired by partial prenuptial molt. Similar to nuptial adults, but upper surface, sides of head, and of neck more deeply buff or ochraceous; superciliary stripe darker, more richly colored; buff of lower surface much darker and richer, jugulum, sides, and flanks dull ochraceous. *First winter*: Acquired by partial postjuvenal molt. Similar to adults in winter, but upper parts and sides of head darker, more deeply ochraceous or buff; below more deeply buff or dull ochraceous. Similar to first nuptial male and female, but pileum and back more broadly edged with buff or brown, upper surface, therefore, duller; ochraceous of lower surface duller; jugulum often narrowly streaked with fuscous. *Juvenal*: Acquired by complete postnatal molt. Similar to adults in winter, but pileum more deeply buff; dark areas more obscured with buff or ochraceous; median stripe warm buff; hindneck ochraceous tawny to clay color or cream buff, narrowly streaked with fuscous; wings rather duller; sides of head ochraceous to dull cream buff; throat dull cream buff; jugulum chamois; remainder of lower surface light cream buff to dull cartridge buff, jugulum, upper breast, sides, and flanks narrowly streaked with fuscous to olive brown. Bill between drab and fawn color.

MEASUREMENTS: *Adult male*: Wing, 49.3–53.8 (average, 51.8) mm.; tail, 46.5–55.9 (49.8); bill (exposed culmen), 8.4–10.2 (9.1); height of bill at base, 5.3–5.8 (5.6); tarsus, 17.8–18.8 (18.3); middle toe without claw, 13.2–15.2 (14.2). *Adult female*: Wing, 49.0–53.3 (51.3); tail, 46.5–53.3 (49.3); bill, 8.4–9.7 (9.1); height of bill, 5.3–5.8 (5.6); tarsus, 17.5–18.8 (18.0); middle toe, 11.7–15.2 (14.2).

TEXAS: *Winter*: Taken northwest to Randall (May 3), east to Cooke and Galveston, south to Cameron, west to Atascosa cos.

HENSLOW'S SPARROW, *Nemospiza henslowii* (Audubon)

SPECIES ACCOUNT

Passerherbulus henslowii of A.O.U. check-list, 1957 (see Appendix A). A very small, flat-headed, top-heavy sparrow with a stout whitish bill. Blackish-striped olive head; rufous wings; blackish-streaked reddish brown back; short, sharp tail; whitish under parts with fine blackish streaks on breast and sides. Length, 5 in.; wingspan, 7; weight, ½ oz.

RANGE: E. South Dakota to New Hampshire, south to e. Kansas, and North Carolina; also s.e. Texas (first nesting, 1973). Winters from e. Texas to South Carolina and Florida.

TEXAS: (See map.) *Breeding*: One definite record: Harris Co., moist grassy prairie in southeast Houston

(singing male first observed, Apr. 8, 1973, Mike Braun; singing birds observed throughout summer; immature bird first seen, July 31, Noel Pettingell; a census of the 180-acre field on Aug. 12 yielded 71 Henslow's Sparrows, 9 immatures and 62 adults, Mike Braun, V. L. Emanuel, T. B. Feltner, D. H. Hardy, Noel Pettingell). One previous summer record: Harris Co., prairie near Deer Park (6 singing males discovered, May 27, 1952, F. G. Watson; several days later, 21 singing males found over area of about 1 square mile; birds continued to sing from perches until at least July 27; further proof of nesting not determined; see *Audubon Field Notes* 6 [1952]: 291). *Winter*: Mid-Oct. to late Apr. (extremes: mid-July, June 27). Rare and local in eastern half.

HAUNTS AND HABITS: A sparrow of damp open meadows, the reclusive Henslow's summers in broomsedge fields and weed patches—the same habitat occupied by more conspicuous species, such as the Marsh Hawk, meadowlark, and Red-winged Blackbird. On the ground, usually at the base of a grass clump, it builds a nest of coarse and fine grasses and weeds. In Texas, it frequents grass stands and weedy places in humid, open or semiopen country. Occasionally it occurs in grassy areas among open pine woods.

During the nonbreeding season, much of the bird's time is spent on the ground from where, if pressed, it reluctantly flushes. Before dropping into the grass, it flies low, jerkily, and with a swiveling motion of its tail. Breeding males, however, are much less reclusive and sing persistently from exposed perches in bushes. The Henslow's eats seeds of grasses, sedges, ragweed, and smartweed, also berries; animal matter in its diet includes insects (chiefly beetles, weevils, true bugs, cat-

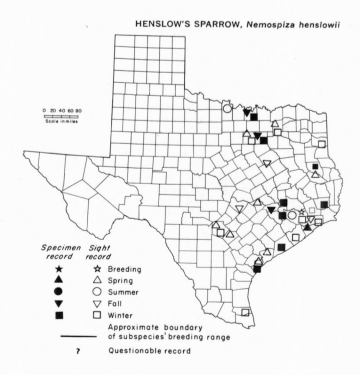

HENSLOW'S SPARROW, *Nemospiza henslowii*

0 20 40 60 80
Scale in miles

Specimen record	Sight record	
★	☆	Breeding
▲	△	Spring
●	○	Summer
▼	▽	Fall
■	□	Winter

——— Approximate boundary of subspecies' breeding range

? Questionable record

erpillars, grasshoppers, crickets), spiders, and small mollusks.

Call note of the Henslow's is a thin *sip* or *tip*. With head thrown back, the male repeats his song: a brief but loud, Dickcissel-like *tsi-lick*; also described as *si-chi-lick*, with the last two notes merging (Mike Braun). The birds which nested in Harris County in 1973 sang vigorously throughout the day and as late as 9:30 P.M.

DETAILED ACCOUNT: ONE SUBSPECIES

WESTERN HENSLOW'S SPARROW, *Nemospiza henslowii henslowii* (Audubon)

DESCRIPTION: *Adults, nuptial plumage*: Acquired by partial prenuptial molt. Pileum chaetura black, narrowly streaked with buffy olive or between buffy olive and light yellowish olive, with broad median stripe of same color; hindneck like median stripe but narrowly streaked with chaetura black; remainder of upper surface sayal brown to buckthorn brown; upper tail-coverts similar or between russet and hazel; back with large spots or streaks of chaetura black to fuscous black, also with spots and edgings of russet to hazel and narrow edgings of pale gray or grayish white, some feathers tipped also with this color, black and russet markings often largely concealing ground color; rump narrowly streaked with fuscous black and upper tail-coverts with shaft streaks of same; tail fuscous, middle feathers broadly edged with hazel on inner webs, outer webs and those of remaining tail feathers between dull drab and buffy brown, tips of outer rectrices of same color; primaries and secondaries dull hair brown, inner edges, except at tips, dull light drab, sometimes rather buff, narrow outer margins of primaries buffy olive; tertials fuscous black, outer edges and those of inner secondaries hazel, tips of tertials dull pale buff; lesser wing-coverts light buffy citrine, mixed somewhat or washed more or less with hazel; median wing-coverts similar but rather paler and with fuscous or fuscous black subterminal shaft spots; outer edges of greater coverts dull hazel verging toward russet and washed with light buffy citrine, feathers with conspicuous oblong subterminal shaft spots of fuscous or fuscous black; superciliary stripe buffy olive like hindneck; narrow supraloral streak wax yellow; lores grayish or buffy drab; region below eye similar; auriculars light, rather buffy isabella color, postocular stripe interrupted close to eye fuscous black; a few irregular spots of fuscous black along posterior edge of auriculars; rictal streak and submalar streak fuscous black, these enclosing malar stripe of dull cinnamon buff to pale buff, which broadens posteriorly and extends upward behind auriculars; sides of neck like hindneck; lower surface white or buffy white; jugulum rather light pinkish buff, narrowly streaked with fuscous, these streaks sometimes obsolescent along median line; sides and flanks tawny olive, streaked with fuscous or fuscous black; crissum dull cinnamon buff; axillars and lining of wing dull yellowish white, with a few spots of smoke gray; edge of wing straw yellow to amber yellow. Bill brown or brownish slate, but mandible flesh color or white; iris vandyke brown; legs and feet light brown, white, light flesh color, or clay color; claws brown. *Adults, winter*: Acquired by complete postnuptial molt. Similar to nuptial adults, but upper parts darker, especially hindneck which, with rump, averages more brownish or rufescent; whitish edges and tips of dark feathers of back broader; lower parts more buffy, this color decidedly deeper on jugulum, sides, and flanks; dark streaks broader and less sharply defined. *First nuptial*: Acquired by partial prenuptial molt. Similar to nuptial adults, but hindneck more brownish; rump more rufescent; sides of head more buffy or ochraceous; lower surface more deeply buff; jugulum cinnamon buff; flanks clay color. *First winter*: Acquired by complete postjuvenal molt. Similar to adults in winter, but upper surface, particularly hindneck, more decidedly brownish; rump more rufescent; lower surface, particularly jugulum, sides, and flanks, more deeply buff to ochraceous. This plumage differs from that of first nuptial male and female as do winter adults

from nuptial adults. *Juvenal*: Acquired by complete postnatal molt. Upper surface tawny olive to rather rufescent sayal brown, head with two broad lateral stripes composed of spots or streaks of fuscous black to dark sepia; hindneck slightly spotted or narrowly streaked with black or sepia; back with broad fuscous black or sepia elongated spots on centers of feathers; rump and upper tail-coverts very narrowly and obscurely streaked with fuscous; tail olive brown, with broad edgings and often obscure, interrupted narrow bars of sayal brown to light cinnamon brown, these mostly on terminal portion of feathers; wings light fuscous, outer edges of secondaries between sayal brown and ochraceous tawny, sometimes those of inner secondaries between russet and ochraceous tawny, edges of wing-coverts tawny olive, tips of median and greater series rather paler; lores dull chamois or antimony yellow; auriculars between sayal brown and clay color, dark markings on sides of head much the same as in adult; sides of neck between sayal brown and saccardo umber; lower surface warm buff to dull cream buff, but jugulum dull dark cinnamon buff to antimony yellow or dull naples yellow. *Natal*: Smoke gray.

MEASUREMENTS: *Adult male*: Wing, 50.8–54.1 (average, 52.6) mm.; tail, 47.8–52.8 (50.0); bill (exposed culmen), 10.2–12.2 (10.9); tarsus, 15.7–18.3 (16.5); middle toe without claw, 12.7–15.2 (14.0). *Adult female*: Wing, 50.8–53.8 (52.6); tail, 47.0–51.1 (49.0); bill, 10.4–11.9 (10.9); tarsus, 15.2–17.3 (16.5); middle toe, 12.7–15.0 (14.0).

RANGE: E. South Dakota to w. New York, south to e. Kansas and w. West Virginia. Winters from e. Texas to s. Alabama and w. Florida.

TEXAS: *Breeding*: The one definite nesting record in Texas cannot be safely assigned to race (see species account). However, *henslowii* would seem to be the more likely breeding subspecies since it (according to the A.O.U. check-list, 1957) nests closer to Texas than does the eastern race, *susurrans*, and is also the race which winters in Texas. *Winter*: Taken north to Cooke, east to Nacogdoches (perhaps this race) and Hardin, southwest to Aransas cos.

NESTING: *Nest*: In open country; in meadows, moist grassy lands, swales, weedy or grassy fields, often near lake or river; usually a deep cup, well concealed on ground in grass; composed of coarse and fine grasses and weeds; lined with finer grasses, soft leaves of reeds and grasses, and a few horse, cow, or other animal hairs. *Eggs*: 4–6, usually 4; ovate; white, greenish white, or grayish white; numerously dotted and blotched with reddish brown and other shades of brown, and with lilac shell markings; average size, 19.0 × 14.5 mm.

SHARP-TAILED SPARROW, *Ammospiza caudacuta* (Gmelin)

SPECIES ACCOUNT

A small sparrow with a sharp tail; has dark gray-brown crown; broad ocher facial stripes bordering triangular gray cheek-patch; dark brown upper parts; buffy breast fading to whitish on belly. In Texas most individuals show white-striped back; unstreaked breast; faintly streaked sides. Length, 5½ in.; wingspan, 7¾.

RANGE: N.e. British Columbia and s. Mackenzie, southeast to s. Manitoba and e. Dakotas; James Bay area; Atlantic coast from lower St. Lawrence Valley and Nova Scotia to North Carolina. Winters chiefly along U.S. coast from New York to s. Texas.

TEXAS: (See map.) *Winter*: Mid-Oct. to late Apr. (extremes: Sept. 25, May 11). Fairly common, but local, along upper and central coasts to Corpus Christi;

casual south to mouth of Rio Grande. A few unconfirmed sightings in the interior.

HAUNTS AND HABITS: Meadowlike marshes, fresh or salt, are breeding haunts for the Sharp-tailed Sparrow. Here, the bird places its loosely woven nest of grasses amid stems of marsh plants several inches above the ground. In Texas, it winters in salt and brackish marshes almost exclusively, occurring both in tidal reeds and in *Spartina* grass on slightly higher ground. Occasionally it ventures into cattails.

Although basically retiring, the Sharptail exhibits moments of inquisitiveness. At times it will flit from cover to a more or less exposed perch in response to a bird watcher's squeak. It runs or walks on floating vegetation as well as on the ground as it searches for food: seeds of cordgrass, wildrice, panicum, lambsquarters, saltbush, clover, others; various insects, sand fleas, snails, spiders, and worms.

A short *chuck* is the Sharp-tailed Sparrow's note. The song, seldom heard in Texas, is a faint gasping hiss preceded by a pair of barely audible *tup*'s.

DETAILED ACCOUNT: THREE SUBSPECIES

SOUTHERN SHARP-TAILED SPARROW, *Ammospiza caudacuta diversa* (Bishop)

DESCRIPTION: *Adults, nuptial plumage*: Similar to *A. c. nelsoni* (see below), but bill larger; plumage lighter throughout; lower parts more heavily and distinctly streaked.

MEASUREMENTS: *Adult male*: Wing, 55.1–59.4 (average, 57.2) mm.; tail, 45.0–50.0 (47.8); bill (exposed culmen), 11.7–13.0 (12.4); tarsus, 20.6–22.6 (21.4); middle toe without claw, 14.5–16.0 (15.2). *Adult female*: Wing, 52.1–56.4 (54.3); tail, 42.9–50.0 (45.7); bill, 11.4–12.7 (12.2); tarsus, 20.1–22.1 (20.9); middle toe, 14.0–16.0 (15.2).

RANGE: Atlantic coast from Delaware to North Carolina. Winters along U.S. coast from Virginia to Texas.

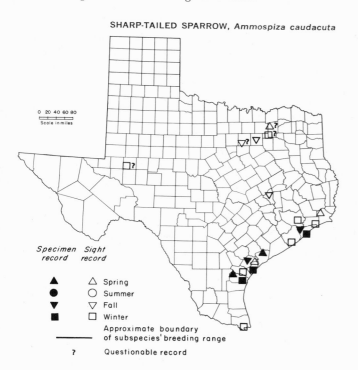

SHARP-TAILED SPARROW, *Ammospiza caudacuta*

0 20 40 60 80
Scale in miles

Specimen record / Sight record

▲ △ Spring
● ○ Summer
▼ ▽ Fall
■ □ Winter

—— Approximate boundary of subspecies' breeding range

? Questionable record

TEXAS: *Winter*: Two specimens: Galveston Co., High Island (Feb. 19, 1907, A. H. Howell); Refugio Co., Tivoli (Oct. 8, 1915, A. P. Smith).

ONTARIO SHARP-TAILED SPARROW, *Ammospiza caudacuta altera* Todd

DESCRIPTION: *Adults, nuptial plumage*: Similar to *A. c. nelsoni* (see below), but wing and tail longer; upper parts lighter and usually more grayish (less brownish); black stripe on side of pileum narrower, gray middle stripe, therefore, broader; upper parts with less black and dark brown, and white streaks there usually duller, more grayish, narrower, and less prominent; sides of head paler; gray of auriculars more strongly contrasted with ochraceous on side of head.

MEASUREMENTS: *Adult male*: Wing, 54.6–61.0 (average, 58.7) mm.; tail, 49.0–52.1 (50.5); bill (exposed culmen), 9.4–11.4 (10.7); tarsus, 21.6–23.1 (22.4); middle toe without claw, 14.0–15.5 (14.7). *Adult female*: Wing, 55.1–58.9 (56.1); tail, 45.5–52.1 (47.8); bill, 9.4–11.7 (10.7); tarsus, 21.9–22.6 (22.4); middle toe, 14.0–15.5 (14.7).

RANGE: Marshes bordering James Bay, Canada. Winters along U.S. coast from South Carolina to Texas.

TEXAS: *Winter*: Two specimens: Galveston Co., 5 mi. west of Galveston (Jan. 15, 1938, W. B. Davis); Aransas Co., Copano Bay (Dec. 2, 1893, H. P. Attwater).

NELSON'S SHARP-TAILED SPARROW, *Ammospiza caudacuta nelsoni* (Allen)

DESCRIPTION: *Adults, nuptial plumage*: Acquired by complete prenuptial molt. Broad central stripe of pileum mouse gray, broad lateral stripes brownish black, obscurely streaked with bister; remainder of upper surface dull sudan brown to dark amber brown on middle of hindneck, passing to tawny olive on upper tail-coverts; back broadly streaked with fuscous black to brownish black, also with dull cinnamon buff and white; rump narrowly streaked with fuscous; outer tail feathers dull buffy brown; middle tail feathers, except for broad fuscous shaft streaks, drab or light hair brown; remainder of tail fuscous to olive brown; primaries and secondaries dark hair brown, inner edges, except at tips of primaries, light drab to drab, narrow outer edges of primaries saccardo olive, outer edges of inner secondaries between cinnamon rufous and buckthorn brown or dull tawny; tertials fuscous black, outer edges like outer edges of inner secondaries, two innermost tertials broadly margined on inner and outer webs terminally with buffy white or pale buff; lesser wing-coverts olive buffy brown or dull sayal brown; median coverts similar with obscure subterminal fuscous black spots; greater coverts between cinnamon rufous and buckthorn brown or dull tawny, with elongated subterminal or terminal shaft spots of fuscous black, these largest on inner feathers; superciliary stripe anteriorly antimony yellow to ochraceous buff, posteriorly ochraceous tawny to bright ochraceous tawny; postocular streak of fuscous black; remainder of sides of head like posterior part of superciliary stripe, but auriculars washed with gray, lores sometimes paler like anterior portion of superciliary stripe, short blackish streak on cheeks and narrow obscure submalar streak fuscous; sides of chin, sides of throat, and jugulum ochraceous buff; middle of chin and of throat buffy white or pinkish buff; jugulum sometimes faintly and narrowly streaked with hair brown; breast and abdomen white; sides and flanks dull ochraceous buff, more or less washed or tinged with gray and streaked with fuscous; crissum dull, rather light cinnamon buff; lining of wing dull white, more or less washed and spotted with smoke gray or pale buff; edge of wing amber yellow to straw yellow. Bill black or slate color, but mandible cinereous or dull plumbeous, with white tip; iris prout brown; legs and feet hair brown, yellowish brown, or flesh color, latter sometimes darker; claws brown. *Adults, winter*: Acquired by complete postnuptial molt. Similar to nuptial adults, but upper surface duller and somewhat darker, black markings of back and pileum more or less obscured by lighter edgings of feathers, light edgings of tertials broader; lower surface duller, jugulum more distinctly streaked with brown. *First nuptial*: Acquired by complete prenuptial molt. Similar to nuptial adults, but upper parts somewhat darker, more rufescent or ochraceous, thus more richly colored, jugulum usually more deeply ochraceous and more densely streaked; sides and flanks more deeply buff or ochraceous. *First winter*: Acquired by partial postjuvenal molt, which does not involve primaries, secondaries, and upper wing-coverts. Similar to adults in winter, but upper surface decidedly darker, more rufescent; jugulum more deeply buff or ochraceous and more distinctly streaked, streaks darker, sometimes fuscous; sides and flanks darker, usually more densely and conspicuously streaked. Similar to first nuptial male and female, but upper surface duller, jugulum rather darker, streaks on jugulum, sides, and flanks usually not so sharply defined, being more obscured by lighter edgings of feathers. *Juvenal*: Acquired by complete postnatal molt. Very similar to juvenal *A. c. caudacuta* (this race not seen in Texas), which on upper parts is cinnamon buff to dull ochraceous buff or dull ochraceous tawny, but hindneck saccardo umber to between dresden brown and cinnamon brown; pileum with two broad lateral stripes of fuscous black mixed with warm olive brown, central buffy stripe more or less finely streaked with fuscous; back broadly streaked with fuscous or fuscous black to warm olive brown, rump and upper tail-coverts much more narrowly and conspicuously streaked with same brown; wings and tail similar to those of first winter male and female; sides of head clay color to dull cinnamon buff; throat dull warm buff; remainder of lower surface dull cinnamon buff, but jugulum, sides, and flanks darker, more or less streaked with fuscous to olive brown.

MEASUREMENTS: *Adult male*: Wing, 53.1–61.0 (average, 55.3) mm.; tail, 45.0–52.6 (47.8); bill (exposed culmen), 10.4–11.4 (10.9); height of bill at base, 5.8–6.6 (6.1); tarsus, 19.0–21.6 (20.6); middle toe without claw, 14.0–15.5 (14.7). *Adult female*: Wing, 51.1–57.4 (54.3); tail, 42.9–49.5 (46.3); bill, 9.9–11.7 (10.9); height of bill, 5.8–6.4 (6.1); tarsus, 19.6–21.6 (20.6); middle toe, 13.5–16.0 (14.7).

RANGE: Freshwater prairie marshes from n.e. British Columbia and s. Mackenzie to s. Manitoba and e. Dakotas. Winters chiefly along U.S. coast from North Carolina to Texas.

TEXAS: *Winter*: Taken northeast to Galveston, southwest to Nueces cos. Locally fairly common.

SEASIDE SPARROW, *Thryospiza maritima* (Wilson)

SPECIES ACCOUNT

Ammospiza maritima of A.O.U. check-list, 1957 (see Appendix A). A large chunky sparrow with long stout bill. Brown- or blackish-streaked dingy gray; yellow loral streak; whitish malar stripe, bordered below by black whisker; whitish chin; short pointed tail. Restricted to coastal salt marshes. Length, 6 in.; wingspan, 8.

RANGE: Atlantic coast from Massachusetts to n. Florida, and Gulf coast from s. Texas to c. peninsular Florida. Winters chiefly south of Chesapeake Bay.

TEXAS: (See map.) *Resident*: Breeds, early Apr. to late July (eggs, Apr. 15 to July 4) at sea level or just above. Common to fairly common along upper coast; uncommon to scarce along central coast. In winter, south casually (extremes: Nov. 4, Mar. 16) to mouth of Rio Grande.

HAUNTS AND HABITS: Aptly named, the Seaside Sparrow rarely occurs out of sound of the sea. This saltwater-marsh dweller inhabits tall rank *Spartina* grass, rushes, and tidal reeds. It generally frequents the wet-test, muddiest parts of the marsh, though sometimes it retreats to relatively dry ground.

Large feet permit the Seaside to walk and run easily on boggy soil. If undisturbed, this sparrow may be seen feeding along the shore mud or investigating washed-up debris; or at times it may be squeaked up from seclusion to a reed-top perch. Insects—leafhoppers, true bugs, flies, grasshoppers, moths, beetles, weevils, midges, and ants—are primary in its diet; it also eats sand fleas, shrimp, small crabs, spiders, and snails. In winter, the bird supplements animal matter with seeds of cordgrass, saltbush, smartweed, bristlegrass, dandelion, clover, wildrice, others.

A low *chack* and a thin squeaky *zeep* are notes of this sparrow. Seaside Sparrow song is notably meager. It is a few preliminary notes followed by a thin buzz and a lower pitched trill: *tut-tut tze-rrrrrrrrrr*. The male sings this song from a grass or reed stalk, occasionally in flight, from April to July.

CHANGES: Since World War II much of this bird's saltmarsh habitat, formerly almost unbroken from Sabine Pass to Corpus Christi, has been developed out of existence. Smog-producing oil refineries, chemical plants, and hordes of automobiles continue to sprout like evil-smelling mushrooms. At present, seaside portions of four national wildlife refuges—Anahuac, Brazoria, San Bernard, and Aransas—offer some sanctuary.

DETAILED ACCOUNT: THREE SUBSPECIES

HOWELL'S SEASIDE SPARROW, *Thryospiza maritima howelli* (Griscom and Nichols)

Race not in A.O.U. check-list, 1957 (see Appendix A).

DESCRIPTION: *Adults, nuptial plumage (brown, black-backed phase)*: Acquired by wear from winter plumage. Pileum brown-

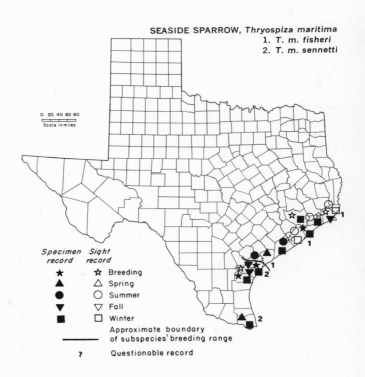

SEASIDE SPARROW, *Thryospiza maritima*
1. *T. m. fisheri*
2. *T. m. sennetti*

0 20 40 60 80
Scale in miles

Specimen record / Sight record
★ / ☆ Breeding
▲ / △ Spring
● / ○ Summer
▼ / ▽ Fall
■ / □ Winter
——— Approximate boundary of subspecies' breeding range
? Questionable record

ish black, streaked with dull russet, with middle stripe of rather dull neutral gray, this also narrowly streaked with brownish black; hindneck dresden brown, narrowly streaked or spotted with fuscous black; remainder of upper surface between deep grayish olive and hair brown, with broad conspicuous streaks of dark clove brown that often practically conceal ground color, and further with streaks of grayish white or light grayish olive; rump rather inconspicuously streaked with fuscous; upper tail-coverts dull dresden brown; tail between clove brown and fuscous, rectrices margined on outer webs with light brownish olive, outermost pair of feathers between hair brown and drab on terminal portion of inner webs, and sometimes obscurely dark-barred; primaries and secondaries between hair brown and fuscous, inner edges, except at tips, drab, narrow outer edges of primaries, except at tips, light brownish olive, outer margins of secondaries dull cinnamon brown; tertials between clove brown and fuscous, margined on outer webs basally with dull cinnamon brown, toward tips with pale buff or buffy white; lesser wing-coverts orange citrine; median coverts similar but rather more brownish, and with large central spots of fuscous; greater coverts between fuscous and clove brown, outer edges dark hazel; supraloral streak lemon chrome; remainder of superciliary stripe deep olive to light citrine drab; lores dull mouse gray; irregular spot of olive brown to clove brown behind and above auriculars; subocular region chaetura drab to deep mouse gray; auriculars similar but partly of lighter gray; behind auriculars an irregular vertical stripe dull cinnamon buff to saccardo umber, this connecting below with cinnamon buff malar stripe which is whitish anteriorly; short rictal stripe and submalar stripe dark neutral gray to chaetura drab; chin and middle of throat dull white; jugulum neutral gray to mouse gray, with broad band of dull cinnamon buff to dull tawny olive, and streaked with chaetura drab or fuscous; breast of somewhat lighter gray than jugulum, obscurely and narrowly streaked with hair brown; middle of abdomen dull white; sides of abdomen gray and streaked like breast; sides and flanks saccardo umber to dull buffy brown, streaked conspicuously with olive brown; crissum dull tawny olive to dull cinnamon buff, with shaft streaks of fuscous; lining of wing dull white to buffy light drab, spotted and streaked with light hair brown to drab; edge of wing lemon yellow. Bill plumbeous, black, or light slate color, but paler below; iris prout brown; legs broccoli brown; toes and claws drab. *Adults, nuptial (gray, black-backed phase)*: Similar to brown, black-backed phase, but upper surface much more grayish, between neutral gray and dark olive gray; pileum with but little admixture of russet; hindneck less distinctly brown; spots and streaks on back fuscous black, verging toward chaetura black. *Adults, nuptial (brown-backed phase)*: Similar to brown, black-backed phase, but upper surface very much lighter, pileum almost or entirely without black streaks, back completely without black, but centers of feathers dark brownish olive. *Adults, winter*: Acquired by complete postnuptial molt. Similar to corresponding phase of nuptial adults, but upper surface duller, colors more blended due to broader light edgings; dark markings of back somewhat obscured; ochraceous or buff of jugulum darker and usually more extensive; sides and flanks more buffy. *First nuptial*: Acquired by wear from first winter. Like nuptial adults. *First winter*: Acquired by complete postjuvenal molt. Similar to adults in winter, but edgings of primary coverts, greater coverts, and tertials lighter and duller; sides of head also lighter and duller, yellow of superciliary stripe duller and lighter. *Juvenal (black phase)*: Acquired by complete postnatal molt. Upper surface light olive brown to between hair brown and light grayish olive, broadly and numerously streaked with fuscous to fuscous black, so much so that sometimes upper surface appears almost solidly black; pileum sometimes entirely black but usually with light median stripe indicated; streaks on hindneck and rump narrowest; wings and tail as in first winter male and female; sides of head dull pinkish buff to dull pale pinkish buff, superciliary stripe faint, supraloral streak pale pinkish buff, sides of head streaked and spotted with chaetura drab; chin and throat dull pale pinkish buff, poorly indicated submalar stripe of fuscous borders malar stripe of dull pinkish buff; jugulum dull pinkish

buff to dull cinnamon buff, numerously streaked with fuscous; lower breast and upper abdomen pale pinkish buff or buffy white; sides and flanks dull pinkish buff, streaked with fuscous; lower abdomen and crissum dull pale buff; edge of wing dull pale pinkish buff; under wing-coverts mottled with hair brown. *Juvenal (brown phase)*: Acquired by complete postnatal molt. Similar to juvenal black phase, but general appearance of upper surface much lighter, more brownish (less blackish), light areas usually more brownish (less grayish)—light cinnamon brown to sayal brown, broadly streaked with warm clove brown, these streaks very much narrower and less numerous than in black phase; edgings of tertials cinnamon brown; greater coverts edged and tipped with light cinnamon; sides of head pinkish buff to dark cinnamon buff; lower surface dull ochraceous to tawny olive; edge of wing cartridge buff.

MEASUREMENTS: *Adult male*: Wing, 58.9–62.0 (average, 60.7) mm.; tail, 50.0–59.4 (54.8); bill (exposed culmen), 14.5–16.0 (15.2); height of bill at base, 6.6–8.1 (7.6); tarsus, 22.1–24.1 (23.4); middle toe without claw, 15.7–17.0 (16.3). *Adult female*: Wing, 55.9–61.5 (58.4); tail, 46.0–55.6 (50.8); bill, 14.0–15.0 (14.7); height of bill, 7.1–7.6 (7.4); tarsus, 22.1–23.4 (22.9); middle toe, 15.0–17.5 (16.0).

RANGE: Gulf coast from s.e. Louisiana to n.w. Florida. Winters west along coast to s.e. Texas.

TEXAS: *Winter*: Taken in Jefferson (1 specimen, Apr. 17) and Galveston (3) cos. Uncommon.

NESTING: (This race does not nest in Texas.) *Nest*: In saltwater marshes along seacoast, coastal bays, and inlets, sometimes in brackish areas; in grass of marshes, a few inches above ground under mat of grass, or concealed by tufts of tall grass or bush, attached to grass a short distance above ground or water, rarely in a low bush; rather well built cup, sometimes domed with entrance in side; composed of dry grass, seaweed, weed stems, and sedges; lined with fine grass and occasionally rootlets. *Eggs*: 3–6, usually 4; oval to elliptical oval; dull white, grayish white, bluish white, or greenish white; thickly dotted, sometimes blotched, with cinnamon brown, umber, reddish brown, and sepia, and with pale gray shell markings, these all heavier at large end; average size, 19.3 × 14.5 mm.

LOUISIANA SEASIDE SPARROW, *Thryospiza maritima fisheri* (Chapman)

DESCRIPTION: *Adults, nuptial plumage*: In corresponding phases similar to *T. m. howelli*, but bill shorter; upper parts, including wings and tail, averaging more extensively black and more deeply rufescent; lower surface darker and more rufescent; jugulum and sides of darker ochraceous—ochraceous tawny or buckthorn brown to dull ochraceous buff; streaks on jugulum, sides, and flanks more blackish. *Juvenal*: Similar to juvenal of *T. m. howelli* but more brownish, buffy, or ochraceous. *Natal*: Smoke gray or mouse gray (R. A. Norris).

MEASUREMENTS: *Adult male*: Wing, 58.4–61.0 (average, 59.4) mm.; tail, 50.8–59.2 (54.6); bill (exposed culmen), 13.7–15.0 (14.2); tarsus, 22.4–24.1 (23.1); middle toe without claw, 16.3–17.5 (16.8). *Adult female*: Wing, 55.9–58.4 (56.9); tail, 49.0–53.6 (51.8); bill, 13.5–14.7 (14.0); tarsus, 21.6–23.6 (22.6); middle toe, 15.7–17.0 (16.5).

RANGE: C. coast of Texas to s.w. Louisiana. Winters along coast from s. Texas to n.w. Florida.

TEXAS: *Resident*: Altitudinal breeding range, at sea level or just above. Collected northeast to Harris and Jefferson, southwest to Refugio cos. Fairly common. *Winter*: Taken outside breeding range in Aransas (Oct. 4) and Nueces cos.

NESTING: Similar to that of *T. m. howelli*.

TEXAS SEASIDE SPARROW, *Thryospiza maritima sennetti* (Allen)

DESCRIPTION: *Adults, nuptial plumage*: In corresponding phases similar to *T. m. howelli*, but bill shorter; upper parts much paler, duller, and usually more grayish (less brownish) with fewer dark streaks—ground color grayish olive to deep grayish olive, streaked with chaetura drab to light brownish olive; lower surface washed with pale buff; jugulum also lighter, less grayish, with streaks much lighter, duller, and less conspicuous (these streaks light grayish olive to mouse gray), and the buff duller and paler—dull cinnamon buff to light dull cream buff. *Adults, winter*: Similar to nuptial adults but brighter, usually lighter, and somewhat more buffy. Individuals show much variation in color, some having heavy blackish markings on pileum, back, and scapulars; others lacking these entirely on back, and having few on pileum; some have broad white streaks on back; others almost none—these gray or olive gray, instead of white; some specimens very grayish above; others very yellowish green; also, sometimes sides of head have almost no blackish markings. All these variations are conspicuous when a number of specimens are compared; in fact, there are four or five color phases, as above indicated, which it does not seem necessary to describe here in detail. *Juvenal*: Resembling same stage of *howelli*, but coloration lighter, less blackish (more olive grayish) above; much less densely streaked, less ochraceous, rather yellowish below; upper surface rather narrowly and somewhat sparingly streaked with dark brown; wings lighter, more grayish (less brownish) than in young of *howelli*; sides of head also paler; lower surface much lighter. *Juvenal (buff phase)*: Upper parts deep buff, heavily streaked with fuscous or fuscous black, most heavily on back and sides of pileum, leaving narrow median stripe of buff on crown; wings and tail fuscous, rectrices and wing-quills edged with dull tawny, wing-coverts with buff and dull ochraceous tawny; sides of head and of neck cinnamon buff, with a fuscous subocular stripe and fuscous sub-auricular and supra-auricular stripes that meet posteriorly; lower parts buffy white; breast and sides cinnamon buff; crissum dull cinnamon buff. *Juvenal (gray phase)*: Like juvenal, buff phase, but color of upper surface pale brownish gray, rectrices margined with pale citrine drab, wing-quills and coverts margined with vinaceous buff and grayish white; lower surface white, with barely perceptible cream-colored wash; thighs avellaneous. There are all grades of intermediates between these phases. *Natal*: Probably similar to *T. m. fisheri*.

MEASUREMENTS: *Adult male*: Wing, 58.4–61.5 (average, 60.2) mm.; tail, 48.8–57.7 (54.6); bill (exposed culmen), 12.7–13.7 (13.2); tarsus, 20.9–22.9 (22.4); middle toe without claw, 15.7–17.3 (16.5). *Adult female*: Wing, 54.6–58.4 (56.1); tail, 50.8–54.6 (52.1); bill, 11.9–13.5 (13.0); tarsus, 21.1–22.9 (22.1); middle toe, 15.5–17.3 (16.5).

RANGE: Coastal Refugio, Aransas, San Patricio, and Nueces cos., Texas. Winters south locally along coast to mouth of Rio Grande.

TEXAS: *Resident*: Altitudinal breeding range, essentially at sea level. Collected northeast to Refugio, southwest to Nueces cos. Uncommon. *Winter*: Taken outside breeding range in Cameron Co.

NESTING: *Nest*: Similar to that of *T. m. howelli*. *Eggs*: Usually 4; oval to elliptical oval; white or greenish white; sprinkled with small dots of reddish brown, mostly at large end.

VESPER SPARROW, *Pooecetes gramineus* (Gmelin)

SPECIES ACCOUNT

A brown-streaked, rather pale sparrow with white outer feathers on notched tail; narrow white eye-ring; chestnut shoulder-patch. Length, 6¼ in.; wingspan, 10½; weight, 1 oz.

RANGE: S. Canada, south to middle United States. Winters from c. California, c. Arizona, s. Illinois, and Connecticut to Guatemala and Gulf states.

TEXAS: (See map.) *Breeding*: One definite record: eggs collected, Tom Green Co., San Angelo (May 13 and 16, 1885, W. Lloyd). *Winter*: Late Oct. to early Apr. (extremes: Aug. 23, May 23). Common to fairly common in most parts with exception of northern Panhandle, where common as a migrant but scarce between late Dec. and early Mar.

HAUNTS AND HABITS: The Vesper is a sparrow of open dry country. In Texas it winters on plains, prairies, and savannahs and in weedy or grassy pastures, fields, and woodland clearings. It commonly occurs near roads, where it stands on the ground or perches on fence wires, in low bushes, and in isolated small trees.

As the Vesper flies, flashes of white on its outer tail feathers make it more conspicuous than other sparrows that frequent roadsides and fence rows. On the ground, this bird forages for seeds of ragweed, bristlegrass, smartweed, pigweed, bluegrass, and others; also insects (beetles, grasshoppers, caterpillars, etc.), spiders, snails, and earthworms. The Vesper takes frequent dust baths, especially in ruts of dusty country lanes.

A sharp *chirp* is the bird's call note. The Vesper acquired fame as a singer in large part because of the popular early-twentieth-century nature writer John Burroughs, who considered the bird's song most impressive toward eventide. G. M. Sutton has also remarked on how striking it sounds on calm evenings. This vocalization is loud, clear, and plaintive; it suggests the buzzing and trilling of the Song Sparrow, but is introduced by two or three low slurred whistles. Birds sing from a low perch, fence wire, or in flight. In early spring, singing may occasionally be heard in Texas.

DETAILED ACCOUNT: FOUR SUBSPECIES

EASTERN VESPER SPARROW, *Pooecetes gramineus gramineus* (Gmelin)

DESCRIPTION: *Adults, nuptial plumage (gray phase)*: Acquired by wear from winter plumage. Upper surface between hair brown and drab, everywhere streaked with fuscous or fuscous

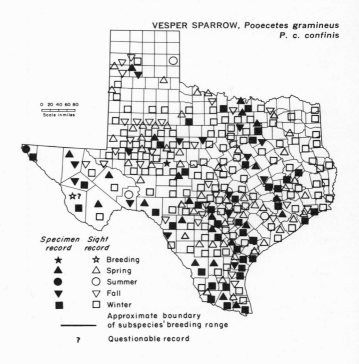

VESPER SPARROW, *Pooecetes gramineus*
P. c. confinis

0 20 40 60 80
Scale in miles

Specimen record / Sight record

★ / ☆ Breeding
▲ / △ Spring
● / ○ Summer
▼ / ▽ Fall
■ / □ Winter

——— Approximate boundary of subspecies' breeding range

? Questionable record

black, these streaks broadest on pileum and back, sometimes almost obsolete on rump; tail fuscous, but outer webs of rectrices narrowly margined with color of upper surface, outermost pair of feathers white on terminal portion for most of length of outer webs and for more than half length of inner web, this latter white area wedge-shaped and extending much farther toward base of feather along shaft than on outer edge of feather, second pair of tail feathers also white on terminal portion of outer web and terminal portion of inner web only along shaft, sometimes inner web with merely a narrow tip of white; wing-quills dark hair brown, but inner edges of primaries and secondaries, except tips of primaries, between drab and avellaneous, outer edges of primaries and secondaries tilleul buff, outer webs of inner secondaries and tertials dull drab or buffy drab; lesser wing-coverts hazel, with some terminal or subterminal spots of fuscous; median coverts fuscous, broadly tipped with dull pinkish buff or buffy white; greater coverts fuscous, broadly edged on outer webs with between drab and light grayish olive, and tipped with very pale buff or buffy white; superciliary stripe grayish or buffy white, somewhat mixed with very fine streaks of fuscous; postocular stripe cinnamon buff, somewhat mixed with fuscous; auriculars dull light buffy drab with some narrow buffy white shaft streaks; postocular bar fuscous, mixed with cinnamon buff or clove brown, this extending forward and below auriculars; behind this a narrow buffy white or dull white stripe running up as far as postocular stripe; back of this, sides of neck are like hindneck and, like it, narrowly streaked with fuscous; lores like auriculars but rather duller; eye-ring dull white; malar region, chin, and throat dull grayish white or slightly buff, but sides of throat with short streaks of fuscous; remainder of lower surface buffy white, but jugulum, sides, and flanks pale pinkish buff, sides and flanks slightly tinged with gray, and jugulum, upper breast, sides, and flanks streaked with fuscous; lining of wing grayish white with a few spots of hair brown or mouse gray on outer portion. Maxilla and tip of mandible slate color, seal brown, brownish slate, chaetura black, or hair brown; rest of mandible flesh color, pale dull vinaceous, ecru drab, pinkish white, or even yellow, and cutting edges of maxilla similar; iris vandyke brown, mummy brown, raw umber, or burnt umber; legs and feet flesh color, pale fawn color, ecru drab, pale vinaceous white, pinkish white, or brownish white, toes usually somewhat darker—pale brown or drab; tips of claws dull black. *Adults, nuptial (brown phase):* Similar to gray phase, but upper surface decidedly more buffy and rufescent, ground color buffy brown to dull buffy brown, streaked with olive brown to fuscous black, dull russet, and dull light cinnamon rufous; sides of head also much more rufescent and buffy, superciliary stripe dull buff; lower surface pale buff, only chin dull buffy white, dark streaks olive brown to cinnamon brown, thus much more rufescent than in gray phase. *Adults, winter:* Acquired by complete postnuptial molt. Similar to corresponding phase of nuptial adults, but upper surface averaging darker, rather more rufescent, and, by reason of broader light edgings of feathers, less sharply streaked; sides of head more rufescent and buffy; lower surface more buffy; dark streaks on jugulum, sides, and flanks broader, duller, and less sharply defined. *First nuptial:* Acquired by wear from first winter. Essentially like nuptial adults, except wings and tail are sometimes duller. *First winter:* Acquired by partial postjuvenal molt, which does not involve wing-quills or tail. Similar to adults in winter. Maxilla seal brown; mandible ecru drab; iris prout brown; legs, feet, and claws ecru drab. *Juvenal:* Acquired by complete postnatal molt. Similar to nuptial adults, but scapulars and tertials with broad central areas of clove brown to fuscous, rather broadly edged on each side with dull pale buff or buffy white, this extending across tips of feathers; central dark streaks much broader than in adults; upper tail-coverts edged with pale buff; lesser wing-coverts not hazel but paler, more brownish; most of posterior lower parts, except middle of abdomen, narrowly streaked with fuscous. *Natal* (this plumage of this race not seen in Texas): Pileum drab to light drab; posterior upper parts light drab to pale drab gray. Bill, legs, and feet pinkish buff.

MEASUREMENTS: *Adult male:* Wing, 76.7–83.8 (average, 81.0) mm.; tail, 58.7–66.0 (61.2); bill (exposed culmen), 10.7–12.2 (11.2); tarsus, 20.3–22.4 (21.4); middle toe without claw, 13.7–15.2 (14.5). *Adult female:* Wing, 72.7–81.3 (77.5); tail, 55.3–62.0 (58.7); bill, 10.2–11.7 (10.7); tarsus, 20.3–21.4 (20.9); middle toe, 13.2–15.2 (14.0).

RANGE: S.e. Saskatchewan to Nova Scotia (excluding s.e. Ontario and Michigan), south to c. Missouri and s.w. North Carolina. Winters chiefly from s. Illinois and Connecticut to n.e. Tamaulipas and Gulf states.

TEXAS: *Winter:* Taken north to Cooke, east to Chambers, south to Cameron, west to Kerr cos. Fairly common.

NESTING: (This race does not nest in Texas.) *Nest:* On uplands and lowlands, generally in open country, on prairies, plains, and other grassy areas and cultivated fields; on ground, usually sunk level with surface, not especially well concealed, but under a small bush, weed, or tuft of grass, or even in a place without concealing vegetation; rather slight cup; composed of dry grass and rootlets; lined with grasses, rootlets, and horsehair. *Eggs:* 3–6, usually 4 or 5; ovate to rounded ovate; dull white, grayish white, brownish white, or greenish white; with spots, dots, irregular lines, and blotches of various shades of light brown, reddish brown, and purplish brown, and with lavender or lilac gray shell markings, all these most numerous about large end; average size, 20.3 × 15.2 mm.

NORTHERN VESPER SPARROW, *Pooecetes gramineus polius* Braund and Aldrich

Race not in A.O.U. check-list, 1957 (see Appendix A).

DESCRIPTION: *Adults, nuptial plumage:* Similar to *P. g. gramineus*, but upper parts decidedly more grayish and somewhat darker; lower surface less buffy.

MEASUREMENTS: *Adult male:* Wing, 77.5–85.6 (average, 82.8) mm.; tail, 58.9–64.5 (62.2); bill (exposed culmen), 11.4–13.0 (12.2); tarsus, 21.1–22.6 (21.9). *Adult female:* Wing, 75.7–79.0 (77.0); tail, 55.9–61.0 (57.7); bill, 10.9–12.4 (11.7); tarsus, 21.6–22.1 (21.9).

RANGE: S.e. Ontario and Michigan. Winters to s. Mississippi.

TEXAS: *Winter:* One specimen: Denton Co., Lake Dallas (Mar. 30, 1941, W. A. Mayer, H. P. Kirby).

WESTERN VESPER SPARROW, *Pooecetes gramineus confinis* Baird

DESCRIPTION: *Adults, nuptial plumage:* Similar to *P. g. gramineus*, but wing and tail somewhat longer; bill more slender; upper surface paler, more grayish (less rufescent) brown; dark streaks of lower surface lighter.

MEASUREMENTS: *Adult male:* Wing, 78.0–86.1 (average, 82.6) mm.; tail, 59.9–64.5 (62.2); bill (exposed culmen), 9.9–11.4 (10.7); tarsus, 20.1–22.1 (21.1); middle toe without claw, 14.0–15.0 (14.7); white on inner web of outermost tail feather, 34.0–61.5 (40.6). *Adult female:* Wing, 75.9–82.6 (79.2); tail, 58.4–64.0 (60.2); bill, 10.9–12.7 (11.7); tarsus, 20.6–23.1 (21.9); middle toe, 13.0–15.5 (14.2); white on inner web, 31.5–45.0 (38.9).

RANGE: S. Mackenzie to s.w. Saskatchewan, south through Rocky Mts. and Great Plains to c. Arizona and w. Nebraska. Winters chiefly from c. California, c. Arizona, and w. Texas through w. Mexico to Guatemala.

TEXAS: *Breeding:* Eggs taken in Tom Green Co. in 1885 considered to be of this subspecies (see species account). *Winter:* Taken north to Randall (Oct. 2), east to Dallas (Mar. 18) and Victoria, south to Cameron, west to El Paso cos. Fairly common.

NESTING: Similar to that of *P. g. gramineus*, but average egg size, 20.6 × 15.2 mm.

GREAT BASIN VESPER SPARROW, *Pooecetes gramineus definitus* Oberholser

Race not in A.O.U. check-list, 1957 (see Appendix A).

DESCRIPTION: *Adults, nuptial plumage:* Similar to *P. g. confinis*, but with white area on inner web of outermost pair of tail feathers much less in linear extent, sometimes absent on inner web of second rectrix from outside, except for very narrow tip or whitish edging; upper surface averaging paler; size slightly greater.

MEASUREMENTS: *Adult male*: Wing, 80.0–86.6 (average, 83.8) mm.; tail, 61.0–68.1 (64.3); bill (exposed culmen), 9.9–10.9 (10.2); tarsus, 20.1–22.1 (21.4); middle toe without claw, 13.5–15.0 (14.2); white on inner web of outermost tail feather, 26.4–42.4 (32.5). *Adult female*: Wing, 75.4–82.0 (78.7); tail, 57.9–65.5 (61.2); bill, 9.9–10.9 (10.4); tarsus, 20.1–22.1 (20.9); middle toe, 13.2–14.5 (14.0); white on inner web, 25.9–39.1 (32.3).

RANGE: S.e. British Columbia and s.w. Alberta, south to interior c. California and n.w. Wyoming. Winters from c. California, s.w. Arizona, and c. Texas to c. Mexico.

TEXAS: *Winter*: Taken north to Randall (Sept. 30), east to Travis and Bee (Mar. 12), south to Brooks, west to Culberson (Apr. 26) cos. Uncommon.

LARK SPARROW, *Chondestes grammacus* (Say)

SPECIES ACCOUNT

A large roadside sparrow with rounded, white-cornered tail; chestnut crown (broken by whitish median stripe) and ear-patch; black and white stripes on side of head—these stripes with the chestnut areas create harlequin facial pattern; unstreaked white breast with central black spot. Length, 6¾ in.; wingspan, 10¾; weight, 1 oz.

RANGE: S. interior British Columbia to s. Great Lakes region, south through United States west of Appalachian Mts. to n. mainland Mexico and w. Gulf states; locally along Atlantic seaboard from Connecticut (casually) to c. North Carolina. Winters from s. United States to El Salvador; also Cuba.

TEXAS: (See map.) *Breeding*: Early Mar. to early Sept. (eggs, Mar. 30 to Aug. 18) from near sea level to 6,300 ft. Very common to fairly common in most parts,

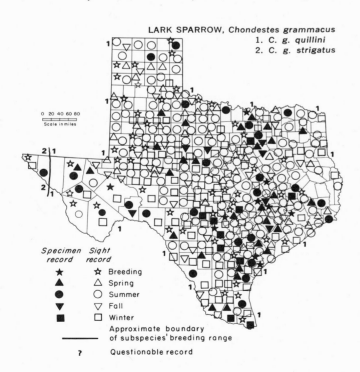

LARK SPARROW, *Chondestes grammacus*
1. *C. g. quillini*
2. *C. g. strigatus*

0 20 40 60 80
Scale in miles

Specimen Sight
record   record

★ ☆ Breeding
▲ △ Spring
● ○ Summer
▼ ▽ Fall
■ □ Winter

——— Approximate boundary of subspecies' breeding range

? Questionable record

though uncommon in woods of eastern quarter and treeless portions of northern Panhandle. *Winter*: Fairly common (very common locally) in southern third; uncommon in northern two-thirds with exception of northern Panhandle, where rare or absent between mid-Oct. and mid-Mar.

HAUNTS AND HABITS: The Lark Sparrow inhabits both flat and rough terrain where scattered trees and bushes occur. Optimum Texas habitat is a mesquite or oak savannah, preferably with scattered patches of weeds, grass, grain, and bare ground. Of lesser importance are sparsely clad foothills of oak and juniper, open grasslands, and grassy clearings in open pine woods. Throughout its haunts the Lark Sparrow, often in small flocks, is commonly seen along roads.

On the ground, it walks or hops; in fact, the Lark Sparrow is one of the few birds which progresses either way when undisturbed. It forages for insects—grasshoppers, beetles, crickets, caterpillars. Seeds of panicum, ragweed, bristlegrass, sunflower, doveweed, bromegrass, Johnsongrass, wheat, corn, sorghum, oats, pigweed, and purslane are also eaten.

A sharp metallic *cheep* is the call note. Lark Sparrow song is a long melodious jumble of rich notes and clear trills interspersed with unmusical purrs and buzzes. This is sung from late February to August as the bird stands on the ground, perches in a bush or tree, or hovers in mid-air.

DETAILED ACCOUNT: THREE SUBSPECIES

EASTERN LARK SPARROW, *Chondestes grammacus grammacus* (Say)

DESCRIPTION: *Adults, nuptial plumage*: Acquired by partial prenuptial molt. Forehead and anterior part of crown black, except for broad central stripe of dull light buff which becomes buffy or grayish drab on crown and light buffy drab to grayish drab on occiput; sides of pileum auburn, sometimes sparingly and narrowly streaked with black; remainder of upper surface between light hair brown and grayish olive or light grayish olive; sides of hindneck narrowly, back and scapulars rather broadly, streaked with fuscous black or fuscous; tail brownish black, middle pair of tail feathers fuscous, all feathers, except middle pair, broadly tipped with white, this tip broadest on outermost pair of feathers and gradually decreasing toward center of tail; primaries and secondaries between light fuscous and hair brown, but inner edges, except at tips, dull avellaneous to drab, outer webs of second, third, and fourth primaries light buff or light cinnamon buff at bases, this showing as small spot beyond tips of primary coverts; remainder of outer webs of primaries narrowly edged with buffy white, outer edges of secondaries dull wood brown, those of fuscous tertials often darker or more buffy or even somewhat more rufescent; lesser wing-coverts like ground color of upper surface; median coverts fuscous, their broad tips dull cream buff to dull buffy white; greater wing-coverts light fuscous, edged on outer webs with dull light drab, tips rather paler; superciliary stripe light cinnamon buff, becoming very pale buff or buffy white anteriorly; lores buffy white with dull black stripe extending from eye to bill; narrow postocular streak dull black, this broadening into series of fuscous black or fuscous spots on posterior part of sides of head; sides of neck beyond this like upper surface; stripe below eye dull white or buffy white, below this an elongated spot of black reaching auriculars but spotted by dull white at base of bill; auriculars auburn; postauricular region narrowly white, this connecting with broad white malar stripe and separated from throat by a broad black submalar stripe which, however, does not reach bill; malar region and lower surface white or dull white, but jugulum tinged or washed with light brownish gray or dull pale buff, and with conspicuous spot in center of breast chaetura black to chaetura drab; sides of breast and of body, with flanks, between grayish olive or light grayish olive and drab; crissum white to very pale dull buff, centers of feathers hair brown to buffy drab; lining of wing buffy drab gray or dull vinaceous buff, more or less mottled or spotted, particularly on outer wing-coverts, with hair brown. Bill dark brown, but mandible much paler, sometimes bluish or lilaceous; iris brown; legs flesh color or very pale brown; feet slightly darker; claws brown. *Adults, winter*: Acquired by complete postnuptial molt. Similar to nuptial adults, but colors of upper surface more blended; feathers of posterior part of lateral auburn stripes on pileum more or less edged with buff or light brown; black streaks of back more obscured by grayish or buffy edgings of feathers, these streaks, therefore, less sharply defined; lighter tips of upper tail-coverts and tertials broader. *First nuptial*: Acquired by partial prenuptial molt. Practically identical with nuptial adults. *First winter*: Acquired by complete postjuvenal molt. Similar to adults in winter, but pileum with less, sometimes very little, auburn, and this duller, its place taken by narrow streaks of dull black, but even when present auburn often much streaked with dull black; auriculars lighter or duller, sometimes fuscous with no auburn; light edges of tertials broader; jugulum, sides, and flanks more or less narrowly streaked with fuscous or chaetura black. *Juvenal*: Acquired by complete postnatal molt. Pileum olive brown to fuscous, feathers narrowly streaked or edged with lighter brown, middle of pileum with broad, more or less interrupted stripe of dull buffy white or very pale buff; remainder of upper surface dull light cream buff or dull pale pinkish buff, broadly streaked on back, less broadly on hindneck, with fuscous or olive brown, rump less broadly streaked with dark buffy brown or light olive brown; tail as in first winter male and female; wings olive brown to light fuscous, but wing-coverts darker, lesser and median series broadly edged with cream buff, greater coverts edged on outer webs with buffy wood brown and tipped rather broadly with dull cream buff; superciliary stripe light cream buff; postocular streak hair brown or fuscous; stripe below eye dull buffy white; auriculars dull cinnamon buff to saccardo umber; remainder of sides of head dull buffy white, much streaked with fuscous or olive brown, but postauricular region dull white, similarly streaked; lower surface dull white, but jugulum slightly washed with buff and together with remaining lower parts, except middle of abdomen, streaked with chaetura drab to chaetura black, these streaks broadest on jugulum, narrowest and least conspicuous on sides and flanks, where they become hair brown. *Natal* (this plumage of this race not seen in Texas): Dull white.

MEASUREMENTS: *Adult male*: Wing, 82.0–93.7 (average, 87.1) mm.; tail, 64.5–78.2 (70.6); bill (exposed culmen), 10.2–12.2 (11.4); tarsus, 19.8–20.3 (20.1); middle toe without claw, 13.2–15.7 (14.7). *Adult female*: Wing, 81.3–85.9 (83.8); tail, 64.5–68.8 (66.5); bill, 11.2–11.7 (11.4); tarsus, 19.8–20.3 (20.3); middle toe, 14.7–15.2 (15.0).

RANGE: E. Dakotas to s. Great Lakes region, south along drainage and valley of Mississippi River to Gulf coast; locally along Atlantic seaboard from Connecticut (casually) to c. North Carolina. Winters from n.e. Texas and Florida to Guerrero and Oaxaca; also Cuba.

TEXAS: *Winter*: Taken north to Denton (Mar. 29) and Collin (Mar. 22), east to Camp (May 16), south to Cameron (Oct. 4), west to Kerr cos. Scarce.

NESTING: (This race does not nest in Texas.) *Nest*: On uplands or bottomlands, in semiopen country; on prairies, in pastures, fields, or even in gardens and yards near dwellings; sometimes on ground, but often in tree or bush 6–30 ft. up; on ground, ordinarily sunk in depression and well concealed by grass or other vegetation; in tree, rather flat, somewhat shallow cup; occasionally nest of another bird made over; composed of grasses, clover, weed stalks, roots, sedges, and horsehair; lined with fine grasses, rootlets, and horsehair. *Eggs*: 3–6; rounded ovate; pure white, bluish white, brownish white, grayish white, or even cream white; with spots, dots, blotches, and crooked and straight fine lines of umber, deep purplish brown, and black, and shell markings of lilac and lavender gray; average size, 20.3 × 15.5 mm.

TEXAS LARK SPARROW, Chondestes grammacus quillini Oberholser, new subspecies (see Appendix A)

DESCRIPTION: *Adults, nuptial plumage*: Similar to *C. g. grammacus*, but tail shorter, wing somewhat so; upper parts much more ochraceous, and brown more rufescent; likewise paler, particularly on hindneck and auburn of head; sides and flanks more buffy (less grayish). Similar to *C. g. strigatus* (see below), but smaller, darker, and more grayish, less ochraceous above, particularly on head and neck. *Natal*: Probably similar to *C. g. grammacus*.

MEASUREMENTS: *Adult male*: Wing, 80.5–88.9 (average, 86.1) mm.; tail, 61.0–71.7 (67.6); bill (exposed culmen), 11.4–13.0 (11.9); tarsus, 19.0–21.1 (20.1); middle toe without claw, 13.5–16.0 (15.0). *Adult female*: Wing, 80.0–83.1 (81.5); tail, 62.0–68.1 (65.0); bill, 11.4–12.4 (11.9); tarsus, 18.5–20.1 (19.6); middle toe, 14.0–15.0 (14.5).

TYPE: Adult female, no. 230377, U.S. National Museum, Biological Surveys collection; Cotulla, Texas; May 10, 1900; Harry C. Oberholser, original no., 132.

RANGE: W. Nebraska to c. Arkansas, south to s. Coahuila and c. Tamaulipas. Winters from e. Trans-Pecos Texas and c. Oklahoma (rarely) to s. Mexico.

TEXAS: *Breeding*: Altitudinal range, near sea level to 6,300 ft. Collected north to Lipscomb, east to Lamar and Jefferson, south to Cameron, west to Brewster and Culberson cos. Common in most parts. *Winter*: Taken north to Dallas, east to Walker, south to Cameron, west to Kerr cos. Fairly common.

NESTING: Similar to that of *C. g. grammacus*, but average egg size, 19.8 × 15.7 mm.

WESTERN LARK SPARROW, Chondestes grammacus strigatus Swainson

DESCRIPTION: *Adults, nuptial plumage*: Similar to *C. g. quillini*, but wing and tail longer; coloration paler, particularly on head and hindneck, as well as more ochraceous (less grayish) on all upper surface. *Natal*: Probably similar to *C. g. grammacus*.

MEASUREMENTS: *Adult male*: Wing, 86.1–92.5 (average, 89.4) mm.; tail, 67.1–74.9 (70.6); bill (exposed culmen), 11.2–13.5 (12.4); tarsus, 19.6–21.9 (20.6); middle toe without claw, 14.5–16.5 (15.0). *Adult female*: Wing, 80.0–87.9 (84.3); tail, 61.7–70.1 (65.8); bill, 11.4–13.0 (12.2); tarsus, 19.0–21.1 (20.1); middle toe, 14.0–16.0 (14.7).

RANGE: S. interior British Columbia to s.w. Manitoba, south through e. Great Basin and Rocky Mt. regions to n.w. Mexico (excluding Sierra Madre region). Winters from s. California and s.w. Texas to c. Mexico.

TEXAS: *Breeding*: Altitudinal range, 3,200 to 5,600 ft. Two specimens: Hudspeth Co., Fort Hancock (June 9, 21, 1893, E. A. Mearns). Nest and eggs found in El Paso Co., Cañutillo (June 5, 1937, A. H. McLellan) thought to be of this subspecies. *Winter*: Taken north to Taylor (Sept. 28), east to Brazos (Sept. 26), south to Cameron, west to Culberson (Apr. 27) cos. Uncommon.

NESTING: *Nest*: On mesas, slopes, and in valleys, often in grassy area or dry brush; placed on ground, concealed by grass or bushes, or in tree, such as live oak, sycamore, mesquite, or in mistletoe on tree, usually not over 20 ft. above ground; rather thickly walled structure, and well cupped when in tree; composed of dry grass, rootlets, weed stalks, bark fibers, twigs, string, and various trash; lined with leaves, rootlets, horsehair, and sometimes cow hair. *Eggs*: 3–6, usually 4 or 5; ovate to rounded ovate; white, bluish white, or brownish white; irregularly lined and speckled, particularly at large end, with black, liver brown, purplish brown, and other shades of dark brown, and with shell markings of lilac and lavender gray; average size, 20.3 × 16.5 mm.

RUFOUS-CROWNED SPARROW, *Aimophila ruficeps* (Cassin)

SPECIES ACCOUNT

A sparrow of rocky areas. Brown-streaked gray above with rufous crown-patch and black whisker mark; unstreaked buffy gray below. Length, 6¼ in.; wingspan, 8¼; weight, ¾ oz.

RANGE: C. California to s.e. Colorado and c. Oklahoma, south to c. Oaxaca and w. Veracruz. Largely withdraws from Colorado in winter.

TEXAS: (See map.) *Resident*: Breeds, mid-Mar. to mid-Aug. (eggs, Apr. 4 to July 25) from 500 to 8,000 ft. Common to fairly common in Trans-Pecos and on Edwards Plateau; north locally to northern Panhandle (no actual breeding records) and Cooke and Grayson cos. Questionable sightings on coastal plain.

HAUNTS AND HABITS: The Rufous-crowned Sparrow lives on or near the ground in rocky, hilly, partly open, semiarid country. In Texas, optimum habitat includes scattered cedars (*Juniperus*), oaks, sumacs, brush piles, grass clumps, weed patches, and heaped boulders. Of these, the boulders seem to be the most important single habitat ingredient. Dry hills, rocky canyons, and Rufous-crowns are frequent from the western outskirts of Austin, Texas, to the Pacific Ocean; all three items are missing from Austin to the Atlantic.

Although wary, *A. ruficeps* is generally not so elusive as the Grasshopper, Henslow's, Sharp-tailed, or similar marsh or grassland sparrows. It is often inquisitive and

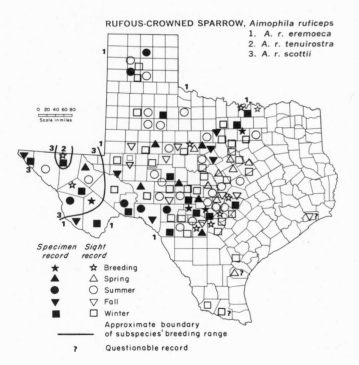

RUFOUS-CROWNED SPARROW, *Aimophila ruficeps*
1. *A. r. eremoeca*
2. *A. r. tenuirostra*
3. *A. r. scottii*

0 20 40 60 80
Scale in miles

Specimen   Sight
record   record
★   ☆ Breeding
▲   △ Spring
●   ○ Summer
▼   ▽ Fall
■   □ Winter

————— Approximate boundary
       of subspecies' breeding range

?   Questionable record

will respond quickly to a bird watcher's squeaks. When foraging, it hops about on the ground. In winter, the mainstays are seeds of knotweed, chickweed, pigweed, filaree, grasses, and dock; during the nesting season, many insects (chiefly grasshoppers, beetles, true bugs, bees, wasps, ants, caterpillars, and crickets) are eaten.

Notes of the Rufous-crowned Sparrow include a nasal *dear dear dear* and various squeaks and mews. The song, delivered from atop a bush or rock, is a rapid *chipity-chipity-chipity* which stutters into a jumble. It is heard in Texas from March to early August.

DETAILED ACCOUNT: THREE SUBSPECIES

ROCK RUFOUS-CROWNED SPARROW, *Aimophila ruficeps eremoeca* (Brown)

DESCRIPTION: *Adults, nuptial plumage (gray phase)*: Acquired by wear from winter plumage. Pileum russet, but extreme forehead mixed with fuscous black, and with inconspicuous middle line of grayish white; remainder of upper surface mouse gray to light hair brown, streaked rather obscurely, though somewhat broadly on back and scapulars, with dark hair brown; tail light olive brown, changing to dull buffy brown on outer feathers; remainder of rectrices edged narrowly on outer webs with buffy brown; wings between hair brown and light fuscous, but inner edges of primaries and secondaries, except at tips, dull wood brown, narrow outer edges of primaries pale dull buff, outer margins of secondaries buffy brown, of tertials gray like back; edges of lesser coverts like back; median coverts narrowly tipped with paler gray; outer margins of greater coverts between mouse gray and light drab, tips slightly paler; superciliary stripe gray like upper surface but rather paler and changing anteriorly to narrowly dull white above eye and lores; lores dull white mixed with mouse gray; eye-ring dull white; narrow postocular streak dull russet or dull tawny; auriculars between light drab and dull mouse gray, anteriorly becoming dull mouse gray, and everywhere very finely streaked with dull white; malar streak pale dull buff or pale grayish buff; submalar streak chaetura black; sides of neck between light mouse gray and light drab; chin and throat grayish white or very pale buff; jugulum like auriculars but paler, rather more buffy; sides of lower breast, sides of abdomen, flanks, and crissum light pinkish buff; middle of abdomen and of lower breast buffy white; lining of wing very pale pinkish buff, outer and posterior parts spotted or mottled with hair brown to light hair brown; edge of wing grayish white. Bill dark brown or dark bluish slate color, but mandible paler; iris brown; legs and feet light yellowish brown or pale flesh color. *Adults, nuptial (rufous phase)*: Similar to gray phase, but lighter and very much more rufescent, particularly on back; pileum tawny, streaks and spots on back and hindneck between russet and cinnamon brown; wings and tail also lighter and more rufescent brown; lower parts slightly more buffy. *Adults, winter*: Acquired by complete postnuptial molt. Similar to corresponding phase of nuptial adults, but upper surface rather lighter, colors more blended, light gray edgings of feathers broader and, therefore, much obscuring dark centers; pileum more edged and tipped with gray, thus obscuring russet color underneath; lower surface more distinctly tinged with buff, particularly on jugulum, sides, and flanks. *First nuptial*: Acquired by wear from first winter. Like nuptial adults. *First winter*: Acquired by partial postjuvenal molt. Similar to adults in winter. *Juvenal (gray phase)*: Acquired by complete postnatal molt. Pileum drab, very finely and obscurely streaked or very finely spotted with brown—between buffy brown and snuff brown; hindneck somewhat paler; remainder of upper surface hair brown, somewhat buffy on upper tail-coverts, sparingly and narrowly streaked with hair brown on back; wings and tail as in nuptial adults, but edges of wing-coverts more buffy; sides of head and neck duller, somewhat more buffy than in adults, also somewhat paler, dark markings lighter, less sharply defined; jugulum and sides of breast streaked with dark hair brown. *Juvenal (rufous phase)*: Acquired by complete postnatal molt. Similar to gray phase of juvenal, but upper surface decidedly more rufescent or buffy— buffy brown—and more or less streaked, sometimes on pileum finely spotted, with olive brown; edges of wing-quills and coverts more rufescent or deeply buff; lower surface more buffy, streaks on jugulum and sides of breast hair brown to fuscous. *Natal*: Light drab.

MEASUREMENTS: *Adult male*: Wing, 63.0–70.1 (average, 66.3) mm.; tail, 65.0–72.4 (68.8); bill (exposed culmen), 11.9–14.0 (12.7); tarsus, 20.1–23.1 (21.1); middle toe without claw, 15.0–17.0 (15.7). *Adult female*: Wing, 58.9–65.0 (62.7); tail, 61.5–71.7 (66.8); bill, 11.4–13.0 (12.2); tarsus, 19.0–21.1 (20.3); middle toe, 14.0–17.0 (15.2).

RANGE: S.e. Colorado and Oklahoma, south to Nuevo León. In winter casually to Puebla and n. Veracruz.

TEXAS: *Resident*: Altitudinal breeding range, 500 to 7,800 ft. Collected north to Mitchell, northeast to Cooke, south to Travis and Medina, west to s.e. Presidio cos.; in the Panhandle, taken (but no evidence of nesting) in Randall and Hutchinson (probably this race) cos. Common locally.

NESTING: *Nest*: On slopes, mesas, or low hills; often on rocky land or along ledges; on ground, under tuft of grass or bush, or protected by rocks, or in low bush, usually not more than 2 ft. above ground; rather well constructed, somewhat deeply cupped, sometimes bulky; made of coarse grass, weed stalks, thin twigs, strips of cedar and other bark, and various kinds of weeds; well lined with strips of bark, fine grass, various plant fibers, and horsehair. *Eggs*: 3–5, usually 4; short ovate or almost oval; white or bluish white, unmarked; average size, 20.3 × 16.0 mm.

GUADALUPE MOUNTAINS RUFOUS-CROWNED SPARROW, *Aimophila ruficeps tenuirostra*
Burleigh and Lowery

Race not in A.O.U. check-list, 1957 (see Appendix A).

DESCRIPTION: *Adults, nuptial plumage*: Similar to *A. r. eremoeca*, but bill shorter and more slender, also wing averaging shorter; upper surface appreciably darker.

MEASUREMENTS: *Adult male*: Wing, 66.0–67.3 (average, 66.8) mm.; tail, 72.4–73.9 (73.4); bill (exposed culmen), 11.4–11.9 (11.7); tarsus, 21.1–22.1 (21.9); middle toe without claw, 13.7–14.5 (14.2). *Adult female*: Wing, 63.0–67.3 (64.3); tail, 64.5–71.7 (67.8); bill, 10.4–13.0 (11.9); tarsus, 21.1–22.1 (21.6); middle toe, 14.0–15.0 (14.2).

RANGE: Guadalupe Mts. of s.e. New Mexico and n. Trans-Pecos Texas.

TEXAS: *Resident*: Altitudinal breeding range, 5,300 to 8,500 ft. Collected in Guadalupe Mts., Culberson Co. Fairly common.

NESTING: Similar to that of *A. r. eremoeca*.

SCOTT'S RUFOUS-CROWNED SPARROW, *Aimophila ruficeps scottii* (Sennett)

DESCRIPTION: *Adults, nuptial plumage*: Similar to *A. r. eremoeca*, but bill slenderer; upper surface much more rufescent (less grayish) brown, back and pileum particularly so, with broader streaks of rufescent brown; lower surface paler, less clearly gray.

MEASUREMENTS: *Adult male*: Wing, 62.5–70.1 (average, 65.5) mm.; tail, 61.0–74.9 (67.8); bill (exposed culmen), 10.9–13.0 (11.7); tarsus, 19.0–22.1 (20.3); middle toe without claw, 14.0–15.5 (14.7). *Adult female*: Wing, 58.9–68.1 (63.2); tail, 58.9–73.9 (66.3); bill, 9.9–13.0 (11.7); tarsus, 19.0–22.1 (20.3); middle toe, 13.5–16.0 (14.7).

RANGE: N.w. and s.e. Arizona to n.e. New Mexico, south to n.e. Sonora and n.w. Chihuahua.

TEXAS: *Resident*: Altitudinal breeding range, 2,600 to 8,000 ft. Collected in El Paso, Reeves, Jeff Davis, n.e. Presidio, and Brewster cos. Fairly common.

NESTING: Similar to that of *A. r. eremoeca*, but average egg size, 20.3 × 15.2 mm.

BACHMAN'S SPARROW, *Aimophila aestivalis* (Lichtenstein)

SPECIES ACCOUNT   *See colorplate 33*

Also known as Pinewoods Sparrow. A dark sparrow with chestnut-streaked grayish back; unstreaked buffy gray under parts; yellow at bend of wing; dark upper mandible. Best identified by habitat and song. Length, 6¼ in.; wingspan, 7¾.

RANGE: N.e. Illinois to s.w. Pennsylvania, south to s.e. Texas and c. Florida. Winters from extreme s.e. Oklahoma, c. Mississippi, n. Georgia, and North Carolina to Gulf coast.

TEXAS: (See map.) *Resident*: Breeds, mid-Apr. to late July (eggs, Apr. 25 to July 5) from near sea level to 750 ft. Uncommon to rare and local in wooded eastern quarter, west to Cooke Co. and south to Harris Co. After breeding season a few individuals may drift south; there are unconfirmed winter sightings on central coast.

HAUNTS AND HABITS: The Bachman's Sparrow, last on the list of birds endemic to the southeastern United States, prefers open, parklike stands of tall pines with grass, wild flowers, scattered oaks, a few bushes, and an occasional fallen branch.

Within its pinewoods haunts, the hermitlike Bachman's is generally difficult to spy. It spends most of the time on the ground, from where it flushes reluctantly. Here, especially in summer, it gleans beetles, grasshoppers, caterpillars, crickets, moths, leafhoppers, ants, and bees, plus a few spiders and snails. It also eats seeds of panicum, paspalum, goldstar (*Hypoxis*), bristlegrass, nutrush, crabgrass, pine, and doveweed, and some berries.

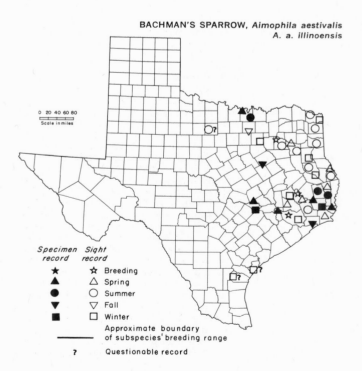

BACHMAN'S SPARROW, *Aimophila aestivalis*
A. a. illinoensis

0 20 40 60 80
Scale in miles

Specimen record	Sight record	
★	☆	Breeding
▲	△	Spring
●	○	Summer
▼	▽	Fall
■	□	Winter

——— Approximate boundary of subspecies' breeding range

?   Questionable record

Call note is a thin hissing *tsissp*. The song, for which the Bachman's is renowned, is a clear, mellifluous whistle followed by a loose warble and/or a somewhat staccato trill on an alternate pitch; occasionally the trill gives way to a few Cardinal-like *chur*'s. From early March to September, individuals sing from a perch, usually a dead branch, ten to twenty feet high in a bush, tree, or brush pile.

CHANGES: The above described habitat existed over thousands of square miles in the Old South when the white man discovered America. Since the 1920's, almost all of these pinewoods have been closely managed for timber production and repeatedly lumbered before the pines have a chance to grow large. Exclusion of fire has, in many places, allowed pines, oaks, and brush to grow so dense that grass is choked out. Bachman's Sparrows have no use for thickets except occasionally in winter. In Georgia and other southern states this species has adapted to tung-oil groves and borders of cultivated fields; these groves and fields are very local in the piney woods of east Texas and so is the Bachman's Sparrow.

DETAILED ACCOUNT: ONE SUBSPECIES

ILLINOIS BACHMAN'S SPARROW, *Aimophila aestivalis illinoensis* (Ridgway)

DESCRIPTION: *Adults, nuptial plumage*: Acquired by partial prenuptial molt. Pileum russet, with more or less well defined, though rather narrow, central stripe of rather light mouse gray, this inclining to buff on forehead; hindneck between hazel and russet; back russet, sometimes with a few short streaks or spots of fuscous black; rump sometimes mostly gray with narrow tawny or hazel streaks or spots; upper parts everywhere conspicuously streaked with rather light mouse gray; tail between olive brown and fuscous or between fuscous and hair brown, tips of outer feathers more or less extensively dull light drab, outer edges of most of feathers hair brown, middle pair of tail feathers broadly so on inner webs; primaries and secondaries dull hair brown, but inner edges, except at tips, drab to light drab, outer webs of primaries narrowly margined with citrine drab, a few of outer feathers with lighter, more grayish or buffy margin where sinuation of quills begins, and outer webs of secondaries and of basal portion of tertials between russet and hazel; tertials olive brown, verging toward fuscous, terminally margined and tipped with very pale dull buff or buffy white; lesser coverts between tawny and hazel, tipped with dull olive yellow or olive ocher; median coverts light fuscous, with a few flecks of dull hazel or russet, sometimes nearly all of this color, and tipped with dull pale buff; greater coverts light fuscous, broadly edged on outer webs with dull cinnamon, this color on innermost coverts becoming russet; broad superciliary stripe grayish buff to dull cream buff; rest of sides of head similar, but more or less washed with gray, and with dull russet postocular streak which broadens posteriorly, dull buffy eye-ring which is more or less interrupted anteriorly, and streak below eye and in front of auriculars fuscous to fuscous black, also auriculars very obscurely streaked with darker buff or brown, dark spot or short stripe below eye and short submalar streak of chaetura drab or chaetura black; sides of neck more grayish and narrowly streaked with russet; chin and throat buffy white; jugulum dull pinkish buff, often more or less washed with pale gray; sides and flanks similar but lighter—cream buff to pinkish buff, crissum deep cartridge buff; abdomen and lower breast buffy white or very pale dull buff; lining of wing buffy or grayish white, sometimes washed with pale yellow and more or less spotted or mottled with drab or light hair brown; edge of wing

lemon chrome to lemon yellow. Bill rather light brown, but mandible paler; iris brown; legs and feet light brown or flesh color. *Adults, winter*: Acquired by complete postnuptial molt. Similar to nuptial adults, but upper surface rather duller, colors more blended, gray and buffy edgings of feathers broader; sides of head and of neck more deeply buff; buff areas of lower parts, particularly jugulum, sides, and flanks, much darker, and throat and abdomen with more distinctly buffy tinge. *First nuptial*: Acquired by partial prenuptial molt. Similar to nuptial adults, but some specimens with small spots or short streaks of fuscous on jugulum. *First winter*: Acquired by complete postjuvenal molt. Similar to adults in winter, but sometimes with a few spots or streaks of fuscous on jugulum. *Juvenal*: Acquired by complete postnatal molt. Upper surface light buffy brown or tawny olive, pileum streaked, remainder of upper surface with spots or short streaks of olive brown to clove brown, these streaks often margined with russet; wings and tail as in adults, but lesser and median wing-coverts and tertials conspicuously edged and tipped with dull cinnamon buff or dull pinkish buff; superciliary stripe not plainly delineated; sides of head dull buff, much narrowly streaked and rather finely spotted with fuscous and olive brown; lower surface white or buffy white, sometimes strongly buff, with cream buff throat and dull cinnamon buff jugulum, sides, and flanks; everywhere, except on middle of abdomen, streaked or spotted with hair brown or chaetura drab, these streaks sometimes broad on jugulum; thighs dull hair brown, feathers broadly edged with buffy white. *Natal*: Light drab.

MEASUREMENTS: *Adult male*: Wing, 58.4–63.5 (average, 61.5) mm.; tail, 59.9–66.0 (62.2); bill (exposed culmen), 11.4–12.7 (12.2); tarsus, 18.3–20.3 (19.3); middle toe without claw, 14.5–15.5 (15.0). *Adult female*: Wing, 58.4–63.0 (60.7); tail, 61.0–65.5 (63.2); bill, 10.9–11.9 (11.4); tarsus, 19.0–22.1 (20.3); middle toe, 14.0–15.2 (14.5).

RANGE: N.e. Illinois to s.w. Ohio, south to s.e. Texas and s.e. Louisiana. Winters in extreme s.e. Oklahoma, e. Texas, Louisiana, and s. Mississippi.

TEXAS: *Resident*: Collected northwest to Cooke (spring, summer), southeast to Jasper and Orange, south to Chambers, west to San Jacinto cos. Taken in winter and spring in Lee Co.

NESTING: *Nest*: On bottomlands or uplands; in open woods or bushy slopes; on ground in a depression, either under fallen branches, or more or less hidden by vegetation; rather loosely constructed cup, domed with entrance at side; large for size of bird, roof projecting over entrance; composed of fine and coarse dry grass; lined with fine grass and grass tops. *Eggs*: 4–5, usually 4; oval; not very glossy; white, unspotted; average size, 19.0 × 15.0 mm.

BOTTERI'S SPARROW, *Aimophila botterii* (Sclater)

SPECIES ACCOUNT

A plain buffy sparrow with longish, rounded, rusty-tinged tail; streaked crown with no median stripe; heavily dark-streaked brownish above; unstreaked pale buffy below. Best identified in field by song. Length, 6¼ in.; wingspan, 8¾; weight, ¾ oz.

RANGE: S.e. Arizona and s. Texas, south to Guerrero, Oaxaca, s. Chiapas, and interior c. Veracruz. Winters in Mexico.

TEXAS: (See map.) *Breeding*: Early Apr. to mid-July (eggs, Apr. 16 to June 16) from near sea level to 40 ft. Fairly common locally from Kenedy Co. (Rudolf and Norias) to mouth of Rio Grande; casual (breeding unconfirmed) north to Corpus Christi. *Winter*: Periodic sightings in Cameron Co. on Audubon Christmas Bird Counts, but species has not been collected between Sept. 23 and Apr. 16.

HAUNTS AND HABITS: The Botteri's Sparrow is last on the list of subtropical birds which extend northward into southeastern Arizona and south Texas. An inhabitant of tall bunchgrass, it lives in Texas mostly within twenty miles of the Gulf of Mexico. Plenty of rank grass, a foot or more tall, growing between widely scattered mesquite and huisache bushes, plus some wild flowers for seeds and an occasional low fence wire for perching, are ingredients of prime habitat.

This largely terrestrial bird is little seen and near impossible to identify; it is ordinarily a male sounding the distinctive song which announces a genuine Botteri's Sparrow. Food recorded for the species includes grasshoppers, beetles, termites, true bugs, locusts, crickets, caterpillars, ants, bees, lacewings, ant lions, and a few spiders; also seeds of panicum, spurge, acalypha, purslane, leafflower, bulrush, and ruellia.

The call note is a sharp *pit* or *tsip*. The male's song is a jumble of notes: assiduous pitting with some tinkling and churring, often accelerating into a brief rattle. From a low perch, often a fence wire, sometimes from the ground, the Botteri's Sparrow sings from mid-March to late July, occasionally to September.

CHANGES: Except for Laguna Atascosa National Wildlife Refuge and the outskirts of the Brownsville airport, this species has been virtually plowed, sprayed, and paved out of existence in Cameron County; it was here, prior to World War II, that most United States specimens of this bird were collected. Fortunately, some excellent habitat remains (as of the early 1970's) for the Botteri's on the southeasternmost portion of the King Ranch, whose 830,000 acres constitute what is probably the world's largest and most heavily guarded private wildlife preserve.

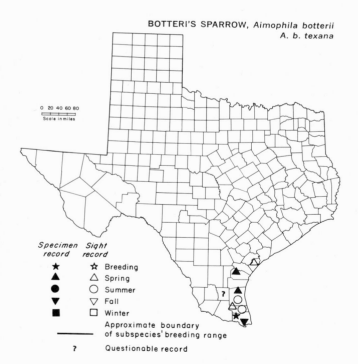

BOTTERI'S SPARROW, *Aimophila botterii*
A. b. texana

0 20 40 60 80
Scale in miles

Specimen Sight
record record

★ ☆ Breeding
▲ △ Spring
● ○ Summer
▼ ▽ Fall
■ □ Winter

——— Approximate boundary
of subspecies' breeding range

? Questionable record

DETAILED ACCOUNT: ONE SUBSPECIES

TEXAS BOTTERI'S SPARROW, *Aimophila botterii texana* Phillips

DESCRIPTION: *Adults, nuptial plumage (tawny phase):* Acquired by partial prenuptial molt. Upper parts russet to near cinnamon brown, pileum usually darker and streaked with clove brown and bister; remainder of upper surface everywhere streaked with grayish olive or light grayish olive; back usually with additional streaks of clove brown; tail dark olive brown, feathers broadly edged on outer webs with buffy brown to sayal brown, outermost pair and middle pair of feathers terminally largely of this color; on middle rectrices dark olive brown is restricted to broad shaft stripe and sometimes these feathers are more or less evidently barred numerously with olive brown; primaries and secondaries between hair brown and fuscous, but inner edges, except at tips, drab; outer margins of primaries between deep olive buff and drab, outer edges of secondaries between sayal brown and mikado brown; tertials dark olive brown, but outer webs basally margined as are secondaries, but somewhat paler, and terminally margined and tipped with same color or pale dull buff; lesser wing-coverts dull russet or hazel, edged and tipped with sulphine yellow or pyrite yellow, centers fuscous or clove brown; median wing-coverts light fuscous to clove brown, tipped with pale dull tawny, sometimes with dull brownish gray; greater wing-coverts fuscous, but outer webs broadly margined with dull tawny to hazel; lores dull drab to smoke gray; superciliary stripe grayish or buffy drab; postocular streak dull russet; remainder of sides of head buffy or grayish drab, ear-coverts very finely and obscurely streaked with paler drab or buff; short, sometimes scarcely indicated, submalar streak of fuscous; sides of neck similar to sides of head, but mixed or streaked with light russet; jugulum, sides, and flanks light warm buff to dull warm buff, but sides and flanks washed with light gray and sometimes with dull buckthorn brown; crissum dull deep warm buff to dull light buff; remainder of lower surface buffy white or very pale buff; lining of wing light drab to light hair brown, more or less mixed or tipped with buffy white; edge of wing lemon yellow to lemon chrome. Bill dark brown or dark olive, but mandible and cutting edges of maxilla plumbeous; iris olive brown or light chocolate; legs, feet, and claws brownish flesh color or pale brown. *Adults, nuptial (gray phase):* Acquired by partial prenuptial molt. Similar to tawny phase, but upper surface very much more grayish; ground color light grayish olive or between drab and mouse gray, streaked more or less broadly on pileum and back, less conspicuously elsewhere, with clove brown, fawn color, and snuff brown; greater wing-coverts dull avellaneous, edges of secondaries sayal brown; wings and tail generally of much more grayish (less rufescent) brown; lower surface paler, less deeply buff; jugulum dull pinkish buff to rather gray pinkish buff. *Adults, winter:* Acquired by complete postnuptial molt. Practically identical with nuptial adults. *First nuptial:* Acquired by partial prenuptial molt. Like corresponding phase of nuptial adults. *First winter:* Acquired by partial postjuvenal molt. Like corresponding phase of adults in winter. *Juvenal:* Acquired by complete postnatal molt. Upper surface dull tilleul buff to cartridge buff or dull clay color, broadly streaked, though usually less so on hindneck and rump, with olive brown to bister; tail olive brown, sometimes verging toward bister, but feathers margined broadly with sayal brown to snuff brown; primaries and secondaries hair brown to light fuscous, but outer edges of secondaries rufescent sayal brown; tertials dark olive brown; wing-coverts olive brown to dark olive brown but margined on outer webs with tawny olive to clay color, tips of median and greater series dull buff; supraloral stripe cream buff to cartridge buff; remainder of sides of head buffy drab, sometimes in part even dull yellow, more or less obscurely streaked and spotted with fuscous; narrow submalar streak fuscous; lower surface dull colonial buff to dull light pinkish buff, abdomen usually most yellowish—colonial buff; jugulum rather broadly, sides and flanks rather more narrowly, streaked with olive brown to fuscous; edge of wing cream buff to colonial buff. Similar to juvenal of Cassin's Sparrow, *A. cassinii*, but upper surface darker, back and pileum much so, and decidedly streaked instead of spotted; lower surface much more deeply buff, center of abdomen inclining to yellow, jugulum more densely streaked with hair brown and fuscous. *Natal:* Crown and nape pale buffy gray; lighter (whitish) on back, wings, and sides of rump (R. R. Graber).

MEASUREMENTS: *Adult male:* Wing, 65.3–69.1 (average, 67.1) mm.; tail, 61.5–67.1 (64.0); bill (exposed culmen), 12.4–12.7 (12.4); tarsus, (21.6); middle toe without claw, (17.3). *Adult female:* Wing, 65.0–69.6 (67.3); tail, 63.5–66.5 (65.3); bill, (13.0); tarsus, (22.4).

RANGE: Coastal grass of s. Texas and n.e. Tamaulipas. Winters (entirely?) south of Texas.

TEXAS: *Breeding:* Collected in Cameron Co. One specimen from apparently breeding population in Kenedy Co., King Ranch, 4 mi. northeast of Rudolf (male, May 30, 1969, B. A. Fall; Texas A&M University collection, no. 8150). Two specimens outside regular breeding range: Nueces Co., Corpus Christi (May 27, 1899, and May 2, 1904, F. B. Armstrong).

NESTING: *Nest:* On lowlands and prairies; in brush or open grassy land; on or near ground, in tall grass or at base of tuft of grass; sometimes under projecting mat of grass; rather roundish and flat; composed of grass and stems of grass; lined with finer grasses and a few fine grass stalks. *Eggs:* 3–5, usually 4; ovate to short ovate; pure white, unmarked; average size, 19.8 × 15.5 mm.

CASSIN'S SPARROW, *Aimophila cassinii*
(Woodhouse)

SPECIES ACCOUNT

A plain, gray-brown sparrow with longish, rounded dark gray tail; finely spotted crown with no median stripe; brown-spotted dull gray above; dingy white below with a few flank streaks. Song is distinctive. Length, 6 in.; wingspan, 8; weight, ½ oz.

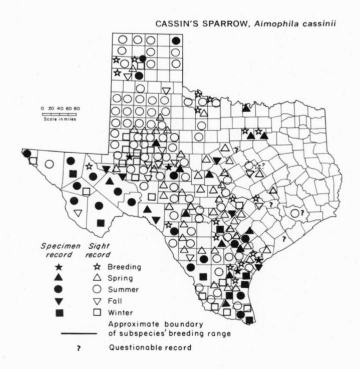

CASSIN'S SPARROW, *Aimophila cassinii*

0 20 40 60 80
Scale in miles

Specimen Sight
record   record
★   ☆   Breeding
▲   △   Spring
●   ○   Summer
▼   ▽   Fall
■   □   Winter

——— Approximate boundary of subspecies' breeding range
?   Questionable record

RANGE: S.e. Colorado and s.w. Kansas, south to s.e. Arizona (summers) and n.e. Mexico. Winters from s.e. Arizona, s. New Mexico, and s.w. Texas to c. Mexico.

TEXAS: (See map.) *Breeding:* Early Mar. to early Aug. (eggs, Mar. 1 to Aug. 1) from near sea level to 5,000 ft. Common to fairly common in western two-thirds. *Winter:* Mid-Oct. to early Mar. Fairly common to uncommon in western and southern portions; very scarce north of 33rd parallel.

HAUNTS AND HABITS: In spring and summer, the Cassin's inhabits short-grass plains, chiefly where scattered low mesquites, cacti, yucca, or oaks occur. In the Texas Panhandle, however, it thrives in lush, open grasslands with occasional low bushes or sunflowers. Along the southern coast, it and its close relative, the Botteri's Sparrow, both live in tall bunchgrass. During fall and winter in desert areas, *A. cassinii* seeks brushy draws and canyons, while in south Texas it skulks in prickly-pear cactus and thick brush that dot the savannahs.

The Cassin's far-carrying flight song is the chief mark of identity. It is in fact one of the few bird vocalizations that can be recognized at 70 m.p.h. W. D. Anderson and other Texas birders, otherwise addicted to closed air-conditioned automobiles, leave their windows open when driving through ranchlands for the purpose of hearing Cassin's Sparrows. Without song, this furtive ground-dwelling bird is difficult to find. In late summer, however, birds of the year are often less wary than their parents and may be observed on conspicuous perches. Grasshoppers, true bugs, ants, bees, wasps, weevils, spiders, and snails are eaten in warm months; seeds of chickweed, plantain, woodsorrel, sedge, panicum, other grasses, and sorghum are largely wintertime food. *A. cassinii* eats flower buds of *Condalia spathulata* in season. Apparently, it seldom drinks water (Frances Williams, Anne LeSassier).

A weak *tsip* is the common call note. The male Cassin's Sparrow sings a clear, sweet, trilled *tseeeeeeeeeeeee* followed by a lower pitched *tay tay*. At close range one or two introductory *ti* notes are audible. This he sounds from atop a bush or—usually when another male arrives in the area—in flight. A proclaimer rises from a bush to about fifteen feet in the air, then sings as he flutters down in an arc to a nearby bush. The song is heard from mid-February to early September, with considerable night singing at the height of the season.

CHANGES: Habitat of this bird has actually increased somewhat since 1933, starting year for a still-continuing U.S. Soil Conservation Service subsidy to ranchers for brush control. By 1968, brush removal had been attempted on much of this species' range in the western two-thirds of Texas. In cases where clearing was followed by a growth of native grasses and a sprouting of young mesquites and low bushes, Cassin's has benefited. However, each year sees more efficient mechanical and chemical means of extirpating all woody vegetation and supplanting native grasses with foreign plants. The future of even the Cassin's Sparrow is clouded.

Detailed Account: No Subspecies

DESCRIPTION: *Adults, nuptial plumage (gray—normal—phase)*: Acquired by partial prenuptial molt. Upper surface between drab gray or pale drab gray and light mouse gray, spotted everywhere, most densely on pileum and back, with olive brown to fuscous and sayal brown to dull snuff brown or cinnamon brown and dull russet; on back cinnamon brown or dull russet spots occupy large part of terminal portion of feathers, with usually much smaller subterminal spots of olive brown or fuscous; on rump and upper tail-coverts there is often terminal spot or tip of sayal brown; tail fuscous, but feathers narrowly edged on outer webs with tilleul buff to pale drab gray, inner margins of central pair of feathers drab to light hair brown, these feathers with obscure, often imperfect, bars, and most of feathers, except middle pair, with paler tips, outermost feathers with dull white tips and subterminal portions of drab or light drab, tips of rest drab; primaries and secondaries dull hair brown, but inner edges drab, outer edges of primaries pale dull buff, very pale on portion of outer webs where sinuation begins, outer webs of secondaries margined with sayal brown to tawny olive; tertials dark olive brown towards hair brown, margined on terminal portions and tips with tilleul buff, very pale buff, or buffy white; lesser wing-coverts yellowish citrine to sulphine yellow, centers darker—fuscous or cinnamon brown; median and greater coverts fuscous, but edged on outer webs and tipped with rather buffy smoke gray; superciliary stripe and lores smoke gray, dull cartridge buff, or pale cream buff; remainder of sides of head dull light cream buff washed with pale gray, but auriculars very finely streaked with buffy white, as is also region below and behind eye; eye-ring dull white or buffy white; sides of neck gray like upper surface but rather paler and streaked rather sparingly with brown of upper surface; postocular streak light cinnamon brown; submalar streak chaetura drab; anterior lower parts pale smoke gray, jugulum darkest and washed with pale cartridge buff, but chin whitish; breast and abdomen buffy white or very pale buff; sides of body like jugulum but darker, rather sparingly streaked with olive brown to buffy brown; flanks and crissum dull cream buff, flanks also streaked with olive brown to buff brown; thighs tinged with olive buff or pale dull primrose yellow; lining of wing light hair brown, feathers tipped with dull tilleul buff, washed sometimes with yellow; edge of wing and sometimes axillars wax yellow to primuline yellow. Bill dark brown above, but cutting edges and mandible pale plumbeous, even dull white at base; iris brown; legs and feet light brown or flesh color; claws rather darker. *Adults, nuptial (rufous phase)*: Acquired by partial prenuptial molt. Similar to gray phase of nuptial adults, but upper surface much more rufescent, due to larger and more numerous brown spots, which are more rufescent—between light cinnamon brown and tawny, this color often predominating on hindneck, back, and scapulars; sides of head more buffy, sometimes much streaked or spotted with dull light cinnamon brown; lower surface also more deeply buff, particularly on jugulum, sides, flanks, and crissum. *Adults, winter*: Acquired by complete postnuptial molt. Similar to nuptial adults, but colors of upper surface rather more blended, by reason of somewhat broader light edgings of feathers; edgings of wings, including wing-coverts and tertials, wider. *First nuptial*: Acquired by partial prenuptial molt. Like nuptial adults, but upper parts somewhat lighter and more streaked; sides of head paler. *First winter*: Acquired by complete postjuvenal molt. Like adults in winter, except occasionally a few small spots or narrow short streaks of hair brown to fuscous on jugulum. *Juvenal*: Acquired by complete postnatal molt. Similar to nuptial adults, but upper surface duller, rather more buffy and more or less distinctly streaked on pileum and hindneck, but back spotted with olive brown or clove brown; rump feathers barred with dull cinnamon buff, formed by tips; median wing-coverts tipped with dull pinkish buff and greater coverts tipped with buffy white, forming two rather obscure wing-bars; lesser coverts with little or no yellow; edge of wing cream buff; sides of head dull buff, much streaked with buffy brown; lower surface cartridge buff to cream buff, jugulum with short streaks or spots, sides and flanks con-

siderably streaked and more broadly so with olive brown to fuscous. *Natal*: Down sparse and very dark. Gape dull orange-yellow (F. Williams, A. LeSassier).

MEASUREMENTS: *Adult male*: Wing, 59.7–67.3 (average, 64.3) mm.; tail, 61.0–71.7 (67.3); bill (exposed culmen), 10.2–11.7 (10.7); height of bill at base, 5.8–7.4 (6.4); tarsus, 18.5–20.9 (19.8); middle toe without claw, 14.0–16.0 (15.0). *Adult female*: Wing, 61.0–64.3 (62.7); tail, 63.5–69.8 (66.3); bill, 10.2–11.7 (10.7); height of bill, 5.8–6.4 (6.1); tarsus, 18.3–20.9 (19.3); middle toe, 14.5–15.2 (15.0).

TEXAS: *Breeding*: Collected north to Potter and Lipscomb, east to Dallas, south to Cameron, west to El Paso cos. *Winter*: Taken northwest to Culberson and Brewster, east to Bexar and Nueces, south to Cameron cos.

NESTING: *Nest*: On slopes and level land of uplands and bottoms; in brush or clearings on dry grass, sometimes stony ground; on ground, at foot of small bush, in tuft of grass, or in low bush, usually not over 1 ft. above ground; when on ground, particularly well concealed; rather loosely constructed but somewhat deeply cupped; composed of stems and leaves of grasses, shreds of bark, and other vegetable fibers; lined with fine grasses and hairs. *Eggs*: 3–5, usually 4; nearly oval, but somewhat elongate; a little glossy; white or white tinged with greenish blue; unspotted; average size, 18.8 × 14.5 mm.

BLACK-THROATED SPARROW, *Amphispiza bilineata* (Cassin)

SPECIES ACCOUNT

Also known as Desert Sparrow. A small, grayish sparrow with jet-black throat; two prominent white face-stripes; blackish bill; unstreaked gray back; plain white belly; rounded, white-edged blackish tail. Length, 5½ in.; wingspan, 8¾; weight, ½ oz.

RANGE: N.e. California to s.w. Wyoming and s.e. Colorado, south to c. Mexico. Winters from s.w. United States to c. Mexico.

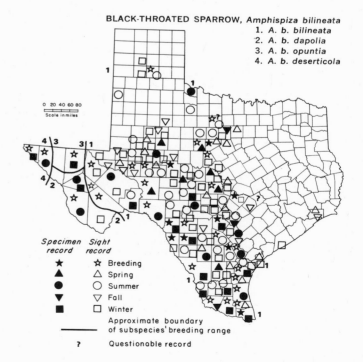

BLACK-THROATED SPARROW, *Amphispiza bilineata*
1. *A. b. bilineata*
2. *A. b. dapolia*
3. *A. b. opuntia*
4. *A. b. deserticola*

0 20 40 60 80
Scale in miles

Specimen record | Sight record
★ | ☆ Breeding
▲ | △ Spring
● | ○ Summer
▼ | ▽ Fall
■ | □ Winter

——— Approximate boundary of subspecies' breeding range

? Questionable record

Black-throated Sparrow, *Amphispiza bilineata*

TEXAS: (See map.) *Resident*: Breeds, early Mar. to early Oct. (eggs, Mar. 10 to Sept. 8) from near sea level to 7,000 ft. Common to fairly common in most western, central, and southern portions, though scarce and local north of 33rd parallel; irregular along eastern fringe of range. During nonbreeding season a very few individuals sometimes wander east along coast.

HAUNTS AND HABITS: A confiding sparrow of arid country, the Black-throated inhabits low brush. In Texas it frequents either flat or rough terrain where cacti, ocotillo, yuccas, thorn bushes, mesquites (sometimes high, even dense), or junipers occur. On the ground or low in bushes, *A. bilineata* gleans seeds of spurge, croton, panicum, and bristlegrass; also small grasshoppers, ants, cottonworms, and other insects.

The bell-like notes of the Black-throated Sparrow are a jumble of tinkling *weet*'s and *wee*'s. The male sings his clear sweet song from atop a low bush or pricklypear. It is two brief *weet*'s followed by a quavering trill on an alternate pitch, and suggests a distant song of the Bewick's Wren. Singing in Texas is from early March to late September.

CHANGES: Increasingly intensive brush clearing on rangelands since the 1930's has reduced this sparrow locally, but its wide range and its acceptance of low and scattered second-growth brush has so far prevented any serious decline. Furthermore, it is common in two large protected areas, Big Bend and Guadalupe Mountains national parks.

DETAILED ACCOUNT: FOUR SUBSPECIES

TEXAS BLACK-THROATED SPARROW, *Amphispiza bilineata bilineata* (Cassin)

DESCRIPTION: *Adults, nuptial plumage (gray phase)*: Acquired by wear from winter plumage. Pileum and sometimes hindneck mouse gray, slightly washed, particularly posteriorly, with dull brown, extreme anterior part of forehead next to bill sometimes dull black; back and scapulars rather rufescent hair brown; upper tail-coverts mouse gray; tail brownish black, but middle pair of feathers fuscous, and all more or less narrowly edged on outer webs with mouse gray, outer web of outermost pair mostly white, nearly or quite to base, inner web with large squarish terminal spot of white, leaving only narrow shaft stripe fuscous, next pair of feathers with narrow tip of white on inner web, sometimes also on outer, the third and fourth pairs sometimes also with white tip on inner web; primaries and secondaries between hair brown and light fuscous; tertials rather darker, but inner edges of primaries and secondaries, except at tips, drab, outer webs of primaries narrowly margined with very pale gray or grayish white, secondaries and tertials and most of wing-coverts margined with drab, this sometimes buffy on outer webs of greater coverts and rather grayish on lesser coverts; superciliary stripe white; auriculars between mouse gray and neutral gray to deep mouse gray; postocular region similar but usually somewhat lighter, sides of neck like hindneck, sometimes rather more grayish; lores brownish black or fuscous black; lower eyelid white; broad malar streak extending to back of head white; chin, throat, and jugulum black, terminating in point on breast; sides mouse gray, sometimes slightly washed with pinkish buff; flanks dull pinkish buff; remainder of lower surface dull white or buffy white; thighs mouse gray, feathers tipped and edged with dull white; lining of wing white, some of posterior coverts light hair brown, outer coverts more or less finely spotted with same. Bill black or plumbeous black, but mandible, except tip, bluish

plumbeous, sometimes rather lilaceous at base; iris dark grayish brown, burnt umber, or hazel; legs and feet black or brownish plumbeous. *Adults, nuptial (brown phase)*: Similar to gray phase, but upper surface much more rufescent; crown and forehead usually more washed with brown and thus less clearly grayish; back and scapulars buffy brown. *Adults, winter*: Acquired by complete postnuptial molt. Similar to corresponding phase of nuptial adults, but colors of upper surface more blended and somewhat darker; pileum more washed or overlaid with brown; edges of tertials and tail broader; sides and flanks a little more buffy. *First nuptial*: Acquired by wear from first winter. Like nuptial adults. *First winter*: Acquired by partial postjuvenal molt, which does not include wing-quills or tail. Practically identical with corresponding phase of adults in winter. *Juvenal*: Acquired by complete postnatal molt. Similar to nuptial adults, but upper surface lighter—drab to grayish drab, back spotted or narrowly streaked with light fuscous to hair brown, rump sometimes also slightly spotted; edges of tertials and secondaries dull pinkish buff to dull cinnamon buff, wing-bars formed by tips of median and greater coverts cinnamon buff to pinkish buff; sides of head mouse gray, but lores mouse gray or drab, without black; malar stripe white; lower surface, including chin and throat, white or buffy white, throat without black but often very finely spotted with mouse gray, as are also sides and flanks; jugulum streaked with mouse gray to hair brown. *Natal*: Pale grayish white.

MEASUREMENTS: *Adult male*: Wing, 61.7–66.0 (average, 63.2) mm.; tail, 58.2–62.7 (59.2); bill (exposed culmen), 9.1–10.9 (10.4); height of bill at base, 6.1–6.6 (6.4); tarsus, 18.0–19.8 (18.8); middle toe without claw, 12.7–14.7 (13.2). *Adult female*: Wing, 60.5–66.0 (62.0); tail, 55.3–62.2 (58.2); bill, 9.4–10.9 (10.2); height of bill, 6.1–6.6 (6.4); tarsus, 17.5–18.5 (18.0); middle toe, 12.4–13.2 (12.7).

RANGE: N.w. Texas, south to n.e. Coahuila, Nuevo León, and Tamaulipas.

TEXAS: *Resident*: Altitudinal breeding range, near sea level to 3,000 ft. Collected north to Palo Pinto, south to Travis and Cameron, west to Pecos cos. Two summer specimens (no evidence of breeding): Hardeman Co., 12 mi. southwest of Quanah (July 2 and 4, 1898, W. A. Mayer). Fairly common

NESTING: *Nest*: On uplands and lowlands; on stony or gravelly slopes, flats, and in valleys and canyons; in more open country, brushy pastures, and scrub, often along streams; in bush, cactus, or low tree, 1–6 ft. above ground, on ground at root of cactus or bush or in tuft of grass; loose cup, constructed of weed stalks, grasses, and strips of bark, occasionally a few twigs; lined with fine grasses, rootlets, bits of cotton, wool, horsehair, cow hair, and sometimes a few feathers. *Eggs*: 3–5, usually 3 or 4; oval; white, greenish white, or bluish white; in rare instances slightly spotted with brown; average size, 17.8 × 13.0 mm.

CHISOS BLACK-THROATED SPARROW, *Amphispiza bilineata dapolia* Oberholser, new subspecies (see Appendix A)

DESCRIPTION: *Adults, nuptial plumage*: Similar to *A. b. bilineata* but larger; upper parts lighter and much more grayish; terminal white spot on outermost pair of tail feathers decidedly smaller. Like *A. b. opuntia* (see below), but somewhat smaller, with upper surface darker and somewhat more grayish.

MEASUREMENTS: *Adult male*: Wing, 61.5–68.1 (average, 65.3) mm.; tail, 58.4–68.6 (62.7); bill (exposed culmen), 10.2–11.4 (10.7); height of bill at base, 6.1–7.1 (6.6); tarsus, 18.0–20.1 (18.8); middle toe without claw, 11.4–12.4 (11.9). *Adult female*: Wing, 60.5–64.0 (62.5); tail, 54.1–62.5 (58.7); bill, 9.9–10.9 (10.7); height of bill, 6.1–6.6 (6.4); tarsus, 18.0–19.6 (18.8); middle toe, 11.9–12.7 (12.2).

TYPE: Adult male, no. 168416, U.S. National Museum, Biological Surveys collection; Pine Canyon, 6,000 ft., Chisos Mts., Brewster Co., Texas; June 8, 1901; Harry C. Oberholser, original no., 324.

RANGE: S. Trans-Pecos Texas and n.w. Coahuila.

TEXAS: *Resident*: Altitudinal breeding range, 1,800 to 5,800 ft. Collected in Jeff Davis, Presidio, and Brewster cos. Two winter specimens from Terrell Co., Sanderson (both taken on Jan. 15, 1930, J. C. Braly). Fairly common.

NESTING: Similar to that of *A. b. bilineata*.

FRIJOLE BLACK-THROATED SPARROW, *Amphispiza bilineata opuntia* Burleigh and Lowery

DESCRIPTION: *Adults, nuptial plumage*: Similar to *A. b. dapolia* but somewhat larger; upper parts lighter.

MEASUREMENTS: *Adult male*: Wing, 64.0–69.1 (average, 67.3) mm.; tail, 60.5–66.5 (63.2); bill (exposed culmen), 9.9–11.4 (10.2); tarsus, 18.0–20.1 (19.0); middle toe without claw, 11.4–13.0 (12.2). *Adult female*: Wing, 62.2–65.5 (63.8); tail, 55.1–63.0 (58.9); bill, 9.4–9.9 (9.7); tarsus, 18.8–19.8 (19.3); middle toe, 11.4–13.0 (12.2).

RANGE: Guadalupe Mts. region of s.e. New Mexico and n. Trans-Pecos Texas. Winters west (casually) to El Paso region.

TEXAS: *Resident*: Altitudinal breeding range, 4,000 to 7,000 ft. Collected in Guadalupe Mts., Culberson Co. Two summer specimens (no evidence of breeding): Jeff Davis Co., 11 mi. west of Valentine (June 8, 21, 1948, H. W. Phillips, W. A. Thornton). One winter specimen from El Paso Co., El Paso (mid-Feb., year and collector unknown). Fairly common.

NESTING: Similar to that of *A. b. bilineata*.

DESERT BLACK-THROATED SPARROW, *Amphispiza bilineata deserticola* Ridgway

DESCRIPTION: *Adults, nuptial plumage*: Similar to *A. b. dapolia* but larger; much more brownish (less grayish) above, particularly on back and scapulars; also decidedly lighter.

MEASUREMENTS: *Adult male*: Wing, 64.0–70.9 (average, 67.3) mm.; tail, 61.0–68.3 (64.3); bill (exposed culmen), 9.7–10.7 (10.2); tarsus, 18.0–19.8 (19.3); middle toe without claw, 12.7–14.0 (13.0). *Adult female*: Wing, 62.2–66.0 (64.3); tail, 58.7–63.2 (60.2); bill, 9.1–10.2 (9.7); tarsus, 17.0–18.8 (18.3); middle toe, 12.4–13.0 (12.7).

RANGE: N.e. California to s.w. Wyoming and s.e. Colorado, south to c. Baja California, n. Sonora, n.w. Chihuahua, and extreme w. Texas. Winters from s.e. California and w. Texas through southern breeding range to c. Sonora.

TEXAS: *Resident*: Altitudinal breeding range, 3,500 to 6,000 ft. Collected in El Paso and Hudspeth cos. Fairly common.

NESTING: Similar to that of *A. b. bilineata*, but average egg size, 18.5 × 14.7 mm.

SAGE SPARROW, *Amphispiza belli* (Cassin)

SPECIES ACCOUNT

Amphispiza nevadensis of older books. A gray-headed sparrow with dusky central breast-spot; white eyeline and eye-ring; blackish whiskers (faint except in Pacific coast birds) bordering white throat; blackish bill; white under parts; fine dusky streaks on back and sides. Bird often flicks and cocks white-edged blackish tail. Length, 6¼ in.; wingspan, 9½.

RANGE: S.e. Washington to n.w. Colorado, south to c. Baja California, n. Arizona, and n.w. New Mexico. Winters in coastal portions of breeding range, and from s. Great Basin and s. Rocky Mt. regions to n. Sonora and w. Texas.

TEXAS: (See map.) *Winter*: Mid-Nov. to mid-Mar. (extremes: Oct. 23, Apr. 1). Uncommon to scarce in western fourth; fairly common some years in northern Trans-Pecos.

HAUNTS AND HABITS: Throughout its breeding range,

the Sage Sparrow lives in, and on the ground near, sagebrush (*Artemisia*) and similar gray or green desert scrub. Its nest of twigs, dry grasses, weed stalks, and hemp is placed well within a bush on a limb a few inches above the ground, infrequently in a depression in the earth. The few Sages that winter in Texas inhabit brushy gulches, hills overgrown with gray-leaved ceniza (*Leucophyllum*) and arid plains sparsely dotted with creosotebush, saltbush, low mesquites, or a few weeds and grass.

The Sage Sparrow generally goes little noticed, except when males—stationed atop desert shrubs—sing in spring and summer. If alarmed, it may flit briefly to the top of a bush but quickly drops and flies low amid thickets or, more than likely, descends to the ground and flees on foot. When running, it often cocks its tail in a wrenlike manner. The Sage Sparrow hops and runs on the ground or works in low branches as it forages for seeds of eriogonum, filaree, and others; it also eats beetles, ants, bees, wasps, grasshoppers, and true bugs.

A thin, juncolike chitter is its note. The simple plaintive song is a high *tsit-tsoo-tseee-tsay* (third syllable accented), but the Sage Sparrow seldom sings in Texas.

DETAILED ACCOUNT: TWO SUBSPECIES

NEVADA SAGE SPARROW, *Amphispiza belli nevadensis* (Ridgway)

DESCRIPTION: *Adults, nuptial plumage*: Acquired by wear from winter plumage. Pileum and hindneck mouse gray with obscure narrow darker streaks; remainder of upper surface between buffy brown and light drab, streaked on back and scapulars with fuscous to light fuscous; middle pair of tail feathers olive brown, remainder between olive brown and fuscous, outer webs of outermost pair white or buffy white, inner webs tipped with

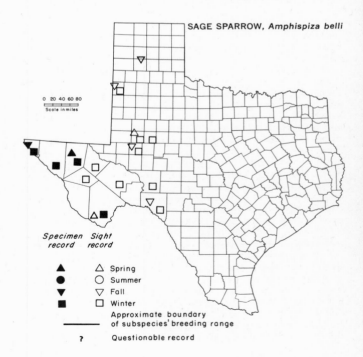

SAGE SPARROW, *Amphispiza belli*

0 20 40 60 80
Scale in miles

Specimen record	Sight record	
▲	△	Spring
●	○	Summer
▼	▽	Fall
■	□	Winter

———— Approximate boundary of subspecies' breeding range

? Questionable record

white and margined terminally with white, remaining rectrices narrowly edged with color of rump, second pair of feathers narrowly tipped with buffy white, this sometimes, however, only narrow edging on terminal portion of feather of outer web; wings between hair brown and buffy brown; tertials olive brown, inner edges of primaries and secondaries, except at tips, dull vinaceous buff to dull avellaneous, outer webs of primaries margined narrowly with tilleul buff, those of secondaries and tertials more broadly with buffy wood brown, and secondaries narrowly tipped with pale buff or buffy white, tertials tipped with dull buff; lesser wing-coverts buffy avellaneous or between sayal brown and cinnamon, sometimes washed with dark olive buff, median and greater coverts hair brown with broad middle stripes of fuscous and tipped with pale dull pinkish buff or buffy avellaneous, sometimes on median and inner greater coverts inclining to cinnamon, and forming two wing-bars; lores dark mouse gray; eye-ring dull white or buffy white; broad streak above lores white; auriculars mouse gray to light fuscous; sides of neck like hindneck; lower parts white or buffy white, row of streaks on side of throat and jugulum ("whiskers"), not quite reaching to bill, deep mouse gray to fuscous; lower parts white or buffy white, but sides and flanks pale pinkish buff, streaked with fuscous; conspicuous spot in center of breast deep mouse gray to dark mouse gray; crissum sometimes washed with buff; lining of wing pale cinnamon buff, outer posterior coverts and spots on other feathers light hair brown; edge of wing straw yellow to massicot yellow. Bill plumbeous black or slate color, but cutting edges paler, mandible pale light bluish plumbeous, sometimes with lilaceous tinge; iris bister, hazel, or reddish vandyke brown; legs dark reddish brown or sepia or brown with plumbeous tinge; toes and claws darker, sometimes black. *Adults, winter*: Acquired by complete postnuptial molt. Similar to nuptial adults, but upper surface rather lighter; crown more washed with brown or dull buff, colors of remaining upper parts more blended, streaks, therefore, more obscured by light edges of feathers; outer margins of tertials, secondaries, and wing-coverts broader; lower surface more buffy, streaks less sharply defined. *First nuptial*: Acquired by wear from first winter. Like nuptial adults. *First winter*: Acquired by partial postjuvenal molt, which does not involve wing-quills or tail. Similar to adults in winter, but pileum much more overlaid with buffy brown; remainder of upper surface more deeply brown or buff; sides, flanks, and jugulum more deeply buff. *Juvenal*: Acquired by complete postnatal molt. Upper surface dull tilleul buff to dull vinaceous buff, pileum duller and more grayish, streaked everywhere, most broadly on back and scapulars, with hair brown to fuscous, wings and tail as in first winter; lores dull mouse gray; rest of sides of head dull grayish drab, more or less streaked everywhere with mouse gray, and rather poorly indicated dull white or buffy white superciliary stripe which is much finely streaked with mouse gray; lower surface white or buffy white, jugulum cartridge buff or slightly washed with buff; lower parts, except chin, abdomen, and crissum, streaked with hair brown to chaetura drab, crissum dull light cream buff, very obscurely spotted or streaked with pale gray.

MEASUREMENTS: *Adult male*: Wing, 74.9–80.5 (average, 77.7) mm.; tail, 68.1–73.4 (70.4); bill (exposed culmen), 9.7–10.9 (10.2); tarsus, 20.6–22.6 (21.6); middle toe without claw, 11.9–14.0 (13.2). *Adult female*: Wing, 70.1–77.5 (73.7); tail, 63.5–72.9 (68.8); bill, 9.4–10.9 (10.2); tarsus, 20.1–22.1 (20.9); middle toe, 11.9–13.5 (13.2).

RANGE: C. Oregon to s.w. Wyoming and n.w. Colorado, south to n.e. California, n. Arizona, and n.w. New Mexico. Winters from c. California, c. Nevada, and c. New Mexico to n. Baja California and w. Texas.

TEXAS: *Winter*: Taken in El Paso (2 specimens), Hudspeth (1), Culberson (2, Mar. 6), and Brewster (1, probably this race) cos. Scarce.

IDAHO SAGE SPARROW, *Amphispiza belli campicola* Oberholser

Race not in A.O.U. check-list, 1957 (see Appendix A).

DESCRIPTION: *Adults, nuptial plumage*: Similar to *A. b. nevadensis* but somewhat larger; upper parts darker, more grayish (less ochraceous or buffy); flanks also more grayish (less buffy).

MEASUREMENTS: *Adult male*: Wing, 76.5–82.0 (average, 79.2) mm.; tail, 69.6–77.0 (72.7); bill (exposed culmen), 9.4–11.4 (10.7); tarsus, 20.1–23.1 (21.9); middle toe without claw, 12.4–14.0 (13.5). *Adult female*: Wing, 70.6–78.0 (73.4); tail, 68.1–73.9 (70.1); bill, 9.1–10.4 (9.9); tarsus, 19.8–20.6 (20.3); middle toe, 12.4–14.0 (13.2).

RANGE: S.e. Washington (east of Cascades) and c. Idaho, south to s.e. Oregon and s. Idaho. Winters from n. Oregon (casually) and n.w. Utah to s.e. California and w. Texas.

TEXAS: *Winter*: Taken in El Paso (2 specimens) and Culberson (2) cos. Scarce.

WHITE-WINGED JUNCO, *Junco aikeni* Ridgway

SPECIES ACCOUNT

Resembles Slate-colored Junco (see below), but is larger and paler. Often has two distinct white wing-bars; wing feathers sometimes edged with white; and more white on outer tail feathers—first three and part of fourth on each side. Female and immature are brown-tinged, especially on back. Length, 6¾ in.

RANGE: Black Hills and outlying rough terrain of s.e. Montana, w. South Dakota, n.e. Wyoming, and n.w. Nebraska. One Colorado nesting (at Boulder, 1905); nested in Oklahoma (Cimarron Co., 1910). Winters from breeding area to Colorado, n. New Mexico, and w. Oklahoma. Casual in n. Arizona; accidental, perhaps casual, in Texas Panhandle.

TEXAS: *Winter*: One specimen: Briscoe Co., Quitaque (immature male, Dec. 19, 1968, J. S. Weske; U.S. Nat. Museum collection, no. 531924).

HAUNTS AND HABITS: The White-winged Junco has long been cited as the only bird species endemic as a nester to the Black Hills—that isolated outpost of the Rocky Mountains located chiefly in southwestern South Dakota. This distinction probably is nearing its end, however. Nowadays (early 1970's), the radical lumpers seem on the point of prevailing. These taxonomists would merge all brown-eyed juncos, including the White-winged, into the Dark-eyed Junco, *Junco hyemalis*. Then, their only other junco would be the Yellow-eyed Junco, *J. phaeonotus* (currently called Mexican Junco). The fact that a Yellow-eyed Junco spends most of its youth with brown eyes doesn't seem to bother these theorists much—perhaps they could solve the problem that might be involved by classifying young birds in the dark-eyed species and old ones in the yellow-eyed species!

The White-winged, largest and palest of the juncos, inhabits mountain forests of pine or spruce; also aspens and groves of other deciduous trees in canyons and gulches. Nests are built on the ground under a log, exposed root, or rock; sometimes a discarded tin can is used. In winter, flocks frequent pine woods and various bushes along streams and roads.

Flight is fairly rapid but ordinarily of short duration; typically a flock flushes from the ground to the nearest tree or thicket. In spring and early summer a male often flits up to a high branch to sing. Breeding adults eat and feed to their offspring small insects, such as grasshoppers. Winter birds, in flocks with their own species or other juncos, glean weed and grass seeds from bare ground and snow.

Members of a White-winged Junco group communicate by a high, single-noted musical squeak. A *chip* is also sounded. The male's territorial song, apparently confined to spring and early summer, is a trill which resembles that of the Chipping Sparrow, but is somewhat more musical and variable.

DETAILED ACCOUNT: NO SUBSPECIES

Following description and measurements are taken from Ridgway, 1901, *Bull. U.S. Nat. Mus.*, no. 50, pt. 1, p. 277.

DESCRIPTION: Winter birds, especially young, are more or less tinged with light grayish brown, especially on back. In some adult males, tertials are edged with white. *Adult male*: Head, neck, chest, sides, flanks, and upper parts plain slate gray, darker (slate color) on head; middle and greater wing-coverts usually tipped with white, forming two distinct bars; three outermost tail feathers wholly white, the third sometimes with a little dusky, the fourth with more or less white. *Adult female*: Similar to adult male but rather paler gray; upper parts (especially back) tinged more or less with light grayish brown, wing-bars usually less distinct, frequently obsolete, and third tail feather more often with a little dusky.

MEASUREMENTS: *Adult male*: Wing, 81.53–92.96 (average, 88.65) mm.; tail, 75.18–78.74 (76.45); bill (exposed culmen), 11.68–12.95 (12.19); height of bill at base, 7.62–8.38 (8.13); tarsus, 20.83–21.84 (21.34); middle toe, 13.72–14.99 (14.48). *Adult female*: Wing, 81.03–84.33 (82.55); tail, 71.12–76.20 (73.66); bill, 11.43–12.45 (11.94); tarsus, 19.81–21.08 (20.57); middle toe, 13.21–14.99 (13.97).

TEXAS: *Winter*: One specimen (see species account).

SLATE-COLORED JUNCO, *Junco hyemalis* (Linnaeus)

SPECIES ACCOUNT

A dark, sparrow-sized bird with pale pink bill; white outer tail feathers. Uniformly slate gray upper parts, forequarters, and sides contrast sharply with white belly. Length, 6¼ in.; wingspan, 9¾; weight, ¾ oz.

RANGE: Alaska, Canada, n. Great Lakes region, and New England, south in Appalachian Mts. to n. Georgia. Winters from s. Canada to n. Mexico, Gulf states, and n. Florida.

TEXAS: (See map.) *Winter*: Mid-Oct. to early Apr. (extremes: Sept. 14, May 5). Common, locally abundant, in wooded eastern quarter and central portions; irregularly fairly common south to San Antonio and Galveston; uncommon in Panhandle, eastern Trans-Pecos, western Edwards Plateau, and most of south Texas brush country; casual in western Trans-Pecos and Rio Grande delta.

HAUNTS AND HABITS: Breeding to tree-limit, the Slate-colored Junco is a bird of boreal conifer forests and brushy clearings during spring and summer. The deep bulky nest of grass, bark, moss, and straw is placed in a depression in the ground or secluded in a crevice of a bank, about upturned tree roots, or in a tuft of grass.

Wintering birds in Texas frequent woodlands and their edges, scrubby canyons, streamside undergrowth, and tall brush.

Like other juncos, the Slate-colored spends most of its life on the ground, often feeding in sizable flocks. It forages in soil, leaf litter, and snow. It scratches—a hop forward, then a kick backward—with both feet simultaneously. Food includes various seeds, namely of bristlegrass, ragweed, dropseedgrass, pigweed, goosefoot, sunflower, purslane, knotweed, crabgrass, panicum, chickweed, woodsorrel, dock, paspalum, and sedge. Insects—caterpillars, beetles, ants, wasps, true bugs, grasshoppers, others—are eaten as well, especially in summer; also spiders and snails.

Slate-colored Junco notes are sharp *tsic*'s, often given rapidly in a series, and various soft twitterings. The song is a loose, simple, single-pitched trill which suggests the Chipping Sparrow's, but is higher and sweeter. On the breeding grounds, the male often vocalizes from a high perch—fifty to seventy-five feet above the ground—in a tall tree. He seldom sings in Texas.

DETAILED ACCOUNT: ONE SUBSPECIES

EASTERN SLATE-COLORED JUNCO, *Junco hyemalis hyemalis* (Linnaeus)

DESCRIPTION: *Adult male, nuptial plumage*: Acquired by wear from winter plumage. Pileum and hindneck deep or dark mouse gray to fuscous black or chaetura black, more or less sharply defined from mouse gray to deep mouse gray of remainder of upper surface, which, however, sometimes deepens to fuscous black, at least in form of obscure spots on back; tail between dark mouse gray and chaetura black, but sometimes all but middle pair of feathers hair brown, outer two feathers white or almost so, third pair with basal portion of outer webs and long broad shaft stripe on terminal portion of inner webs white, several pairs of middle feathers with outer webs narrowly margined

SLATE-COLORED JUNCO, *Junco hyemalis*

0 20 40 60 80
Scale in miles

Specimen record *Sight record*

▲ △ Spring
● ○ Summer
▼ ▽ Fall
■ □ Winter

——— Approximate boundary of subspecies' breeding range

? Questionable record

with hair brown or mouse gray; wings fuscous to between hair brown and fuscous, outer edges of primaries, secondaries, tertials, and greater coverts mouse gray to deep mouse gray, inner edges of primaries and secondaries, except tips, light drab to drab, tips of lesser and greater coverts deep mouse gray; sides of head and of neck, with chin, throat, and jugulum, dark mouse gray to deep mouse gray; sides and flanks deep mouse gray to mouse gray; remainder of lower surface white; lining of wing white, outer edge and posterior portion mostly mouse gray. Bill flesh color, pinkish vinaceous, pale vinaceous fawn, light vinaceous fawn, or pale congo pink, but tip clove brown, dull black, or olive brown, tip of mandible sometimes heliotrope purple; iris vandyke brown, burnt umber, sepia, bister, or black; legs olive brown, wood brown, hair brown, buffy brown, clove brown, natal brown, army brown, broccoli brown, pale pinkish vinaceous with brownish tinge, ecru drab, pale flesh color, pale drab, clay color, or pale clay color; feet light flesh color, drab, bone brown, olive brown, clove brown, or seal brown. *Adult male, winter*: Acquired by complete postnuptial molt. Similar to nuptial adult male, but upper surface very slightly, sometimes not at all, tinged with brownish, this due to narrow brown edgings of feathers; tertials also sometimes slightly more brownish (less purely gray); colors above more blended, with less evident contrast between pileum and back; lighter gray edgings of tertials broader; feathers of pileum and back with lighter tips, this difference sometimes evident also on jugulum. Bill flesh color, vinaceous or pinkish vinaceous, but tip dull brown, cutting edges and base of mandible sometimes whitish. *Adult female, nuptial*: Acquired by wear from winter. Similar to nuptial adult male but smaller; upper surface and throat lighter, duller, somewhat more brownish, particularly back; pileum between deep mouse gray and hair brown; back hair brown or between hair brown and mouse gray; wings and tail fuscous; jugulum between mouse gray and deep mouse gray; sides and flanks between drab and hair brown or between hair brown and mouse gray. Bill vinaceous, pinkish vinaceous, or white with vinaceous tinge, but tip narrowly dull brown or bluish plumbeous; iris dark brown; legs broccoli brown, drab, hair brown, drab gray, or flesh color; feet seal brown, clove brown, hair brown, or broccoli brown. *Adult female, winter*: Acquired by complete postnuptial molt. Similar to nuptial adult female, but upper surface darker; colors more blended; back usually of more rufescent brown, light edgings of tertials broader. *Male, second nuptial*: Acquired by wear from second winter. Practically identical with nuptial adult male. *Male, second winter*: Acquired by complete postnuptial molt. Similar to adult male in winter, but back, lower hindneck, and secondaries with evident brown edgings, gray area on sides and flanks less extensive. *Male, first nuptial*: Acquired by wear from first winter. Similar to nuptial adult male, but upper surface averaging lighter; pileum less extensively blackish, upper surface, therefore, usually more uniform and somewhat more brownish (less purely grayish), due to edgings and tips of feathers; this most evident on hindneck, back, and edges of tertials, but often also on wing-quills and superior coverts; throat and jugulum averaging lighter and somewhat more brownish (less purely grayish). *Male, first winter*: Acquired by partial postjuvenal molt, which does not involve wing-quills or tail. Similar to adult male in winter, but upper surface and outer edgings of tertials usually much more brownish, back and scapulars sometimes between snuff brown and sayal brown, but usually darker and duller than this; pileum less extensively blackish and thus more like back; throat and jugulum usually paler, with brownish, buffy, or dull whitish tips, sometimes these tips practically obscuring underlying gray; sides and flanks more buffy or washed with brown. *Female, first nuptial*: Acquired by wear from first winter. Similar to nuptial adult female, but upper surface decidedly more brownish (less grayish), back usually buffy brown; throat and jugulum averaging lighter, more brownish, with more conspicuous edgings of pale brown or dull buff; sides and flanks more buffy or brownish (less grayish). *Female, first winter*: Acquired by partial postjuvenal molt, not including wing-quills or tail. Similar to adult female in winter, but upper surface duller and more uniformly brown, sometimes becoming

on back even light bister; outer edgings of tertials broader and more brownish (less grayish); throat and jugulum usually paler, also much more brownish or buffy, gray often much obscured by pale buff, dull light brown, or dull white edgings of feathers; sides and flanks more brownish or buffy (less grayish). Similar to first nuptial female, but upper parts more brownish (less grayish) and more uniform, pileum often almost as brown as back, on account of extensive brown edgings of feathers; colors above more blended; edgings of tertials broader and often more brownish; throat and jugulum more veiled with pale brown, dull buff, or dull light gray. Similar to first winter male but smaller; upper surface lighter, decidedly more brownish (less grayish) and usually more uniform, with less difference between pileum and back; throat and jugulum paler, duller, more brownish, with usually much more extensive dull buff or pale brown feather edgings. Bill dark gull gray, but tip black; legs ecru drab; toes and claws seal brown. *Male, juvenal*: Acquired by complete postnatal molt. Upper surface drab to buffy brown, pileum and hindneck numerously streaked or spotted, and remainder of upper surface streaked, most broadly on back, with fuscous to fuscous black; tail dark fuscous, outer margins of middle pairs of feathers buffy brown; wings fuscous, margins of tertials and greater coverts dull snuff brown to sayal brown; sides of head like upper surface but duller, everywhere streaked but less conspicuously with fuscous; throat and jugulum pale pinkish buff, dull cartridge buff, or buffy white, jugulum often washed with dull pale gray, throat sometimes very pale dull gray or dull white, both broadly streaked with fuscous, chaetura drab, or hair brown; breast and abdomen dull white or buffy white; sides of body buffy drab; flanks and crissum cinnamon buff to pinkish buff or pale pinkish buff; chin, breast, sides, and flanks narrowly streaked with fuscous. Bill pale vinaceous or slate gray, but tip dull brown, mandible somewhat lighter; iris dark brown or reddish brown; legs clay color or broccoli brown; feet drab, flesh color, or seal brown. *Female, juvenal*: Acquired by complete postnatal molt. Similar to juvenal male, but tone of upper surface generally lighter and usually more rufescent brownish or buffy (less grayish); dark streaks of lower surface averaging lighter, more yellowish (less grayish) brown, and usually narrower; breast and abdomen much more buffy or yellowish. Bill slate gray, but mandible dull pinkish vinaceous; iris dark brown; legs and feet drab.

MEASUREMENTS: *Adult male*: Wing, 76.7–82.3 (average, 79.2) mm.; tail, 63.2–71.4 (66.8); bill (exposed culmen), 10.2–11.7 (10.7); height of bill at base, 6.4–6.9 (6.6); tarsus, 20.3–21.9 (21.4); middle toe without claw, 13.7–15.0 (14.5). *Adult female*: Wing, 70.9–78.2 (74.7); tail, 62.2–67.3 (64.3); bill, 9.7–11.7 (10.7); height of bill, 6.4–6.9 (6.6); tarsus, 20.3–21.9 (21.4); middle toe, 13.5–15.0 (14.2).

RANGE: N.w. Alaska to Labrador, south to n.w. British Columbia and Connecticut. Winters chiefly east of Rocky Mts., from s. Canada to n. Mexico, Gulf states, and n. Florida.

TEXAS: *Winter*: Taken north to Randall, east to Nacogdoches and Hardin, south to Bee and Webb, west to Presidio (Oct. 4) and El Paso (Mar. 7) cos.

OREGON JUNCO, *Junco oreganus* (Townsend)

SPECIES ACCOUNT

A rusty-backed junco with black hood (duller and paler in female); white belly; pinkish brown sides. Length, 5 in.; wingspan, 9½; weight, ¾ oz.

RANGE: S.e. Alaska to s.w. Alberta, south to n. Baja California and s. Idaho. Winters from extreme s.e. Alaska and s. British Columbia throughout w. United States to n.w. Mexico and c. Texas.

TEXAS: (See map.) *Winter*: Mid-Oct. to late Mar. (extremes: Sept. 2, Apr. 11). Fairly common to scarce in western two-thirds, north of 29th parallel, though common some years in western Trans-Pecos; very scarce in eastern third, except in wooded eastern quarter, where apparently absent.

HAUNTS AND HABITS: Conifer forests and their bushy edges are chief summer haunts of the Oregon Junco. Here the bird constructs a loose nest of weed stems, grasses, and moss, placing it in a hollow in the ground, about tree roots, in a woodpile, or in a tuft of grass. In winter, *J. oreganus* inhabits hills, mountains, and canyons overgrown with trees and bushes—juniper, pinyon, pine, oak, sumac—and a mixture of grasses and forbs. An observer in the Guadalupe, Davis, or Chisos mountains may find this species with other wintering Texas juncos in one large flock.

In behavior it is like the other juncos. Most time is spent on the ground scratching for seeds, berries, insects, and a few spiders. A startled flock will fly up into a tree or bush, individuals spreading their tails and uttering light twittering notes.

Oregon vocalizations are similar to the Slate-colored Junco's. Likewise, singing males are seldom heard in Texas.

DETAILED ACCOUNT: THREE SUBSPECIES

SHUFELDT'S OREGON JUNCO, *Junco oreganus shufeldti* Coale

DESCRIPTION: *Adult male, nuptial plumage*: Acquired by wear from winter plumage. Pileum and hindneck brownish black; back and scapulars buffy brown to sepia or snuff brown; upper tail-coverts deep mouse gray; rump similar but somewhat paler; tail fuscous black, outer webs of middle pairs of feathers edged with mouse gray, outermost two feathers practically all white, third feather from outside with long broad terminal shaft stripe mostly on inner web, and extending often half length of feather,

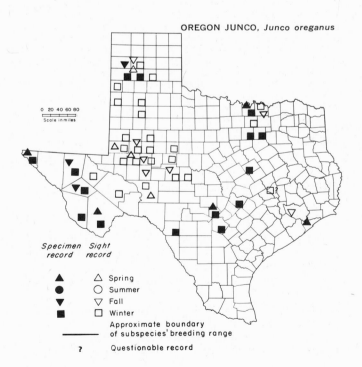

OREGON JUNCO, *Junco oreganus*

0 20 40 60 80
Scale in miles

Specimen   Sight
record   record

▲   △   Spring
●   ○   Summer
▼   ▽   Fall
■   □   Winter

——————   Approximate boundary
              of subspecies' breeding range

?   Questionable record

occasionally more, and sometimes broadened to include most of inner web, as well as most of outer web; wing-quills between hair brown and fuscous, inner webs of primaries and secondaries, except tips, dull grayish drab to dull drab gray, outer webs of primaries narrowly margined with dull smoke gray, outer webs of secondaries edged with dull hair brown; tertials fuscous, outer webs between drab and buffy brown; wing-coverts like primaries, but lesser coverts dull mouse gray, greater coverts margined on outer webs with between mouse gray and drab, inner greater coverts edged with brown of outer webs of tertials; sides of head and of neck, with chin, throat, and jugulum, between dark mouse gray and fuscous black; sides of body light pinkish cinnamon to avellaneous; flanks either similar and washed with pale gray or all drab; remainder of lower surface white or buffy white; lining of wing white, outer portion hair brown edged with white. Bill flesh color, pinkish white, pink, or lilaceous white, but tip light dull brown or blackish brown; iris madder brown, vandyke brown, dark red, or claret brown; legs light sepia, flesh color, brownish flesh color, drab, or pale reddish brown; feet and claws dark brown, dull umber brown, or sepia. *Adult male, winter*: Acquired by complete postnuptial molt. Similar to nuptial adult male, but feathers of pileum more or less tipped with mouse gray and with color of back; back darker and rather duller; light edgings of tertials broader; upper tail-coverts distinctly tipped with pale gray or dull buff; jugulum averaging somewhat lighter and more slaty (less blackish), feathers more or less tipped with mouse gray or dull pale buff; sides and flanks darker, more pinkish. Bill rose pink or flesh color, but tip black; iris claret brown; legs flesh color or hair brown; toes drab. *Adult female, nuptial*: Acquired by wear from winter. Similar to nuptial adult male but paler and duller; wings and tail also lighter and more rufescent (less grayish) brown; pileum brownish deep mouse gray to chaetura drab; back and scapulars buffy brown to between snuff brown and saccardo umber; throat and jugulum between mouse gray and deep mouse gray or between mouse gray and chaetura drab; sides and flanks light pinkish cinnamon or between light pinkish cinnamon and pinkish buff, thus more buffy, less pinkish than in male. Bill pale flesh color, pinkish or lilaceous white, but tip dull brown; iris burnt sienna or dark brown; legs brownish white, light brown, or brownish flesh color; feet similar or dark sepia. *Adult female, winter*: Acquired by complete postnuptial molt. Similar to nuptial adult female, but upper surface duller, colors somewhat more blended, pileum much obscured by brown or dull gray edges of feathers; light edgings of tertials wider; upper tail-coverts tipped with pale gray or dull buff; gray of throat and jugulum much veiled by brown or mouse gray tips of feathers; sides and flanks more pinkish. *Male, first nuptial*: Acquired by wear from first winter. Similar to nuptial adult male, but pileum, sides of head, throat, and jugulum duller, lighter, more brownish or slaty, these differences usually most evident on throat and jugulum. *Male, first winter*: Acquired by partial postjuvenal molt. Similar to adult male in winter, but pileum, throat, and jugulum lighter, more slaty or brownish, feathers of pileum much more broadly tipped with mouse gray and brown of back; jugulum and throat even more obscured by mouse gray, pale gray, or dull pale buff tips of feathers. *Female, first nuptial*: Acquired by wear from first winter. Similar to nuptial adult female, but pileum lighter and more brownish, also much more overlaid with brown of back; back averaging more rufescent; throat and jugulum more brownish and often paler, feathers with light gray or buffy tips. *Female, first winter*: Acquired by partial postjuvenal molt. Similar to adult female in winter, but upper parts duller, that of back usually more rufescent, pileum usually lighter, less blackish, and much more overlaid with brown of back, upper surface thus more uniform; throat and jugulum duller, usually lighter, more brownish, and more overlaid with light brown, light gray, or dull buffy tips of feathers. *Male, juvenal*: Acquired by complete postnatal molt. Upper surface buffy brown to snuff brown, pileum and rump duller and less rufescent, everywhere narrowly streaked with fuscous to fuscous black; tail like that of male in first winter; primaries and secondaries between hair brown and fuscous; tertials fuscous, outer edges snuff brown, as are those of inner secondaries; lesser wing-coverts drab, washed with rufescent brown; median coverts similar, with shaft stripes of fuscous and terminal spots of tilleul buff or dull pale buff; greater coverts light fuscous, outer webs margined with buffy brown, and with small terminal spots of tilleul buff, these forming narrow, rather inconspicuous wing-bar; sides of head like crown but more or less finely streaked and spotted with fuscous, these markings sometimes absent; lower surface light cream buff or cartridge buff, but throat between drab gray and dull smoke gray, often washed with pale buff; lower throat, jugulum, breast, sides, and flanks more or less broadly streaked with chaetura drab to hair brown. Bill dark quaker drab; iris gray; legs flesh color. *Female, juvenal*: Acquired by complete postnatal molt. Similar to juvenal male, but upper surface averaging duller, lighter, and less rufescent; lower surface paler, jugulum usually less deeply buff and less densely streaked with fuscous. Bill quaker drab; legs flesh color.

MEASUREMENTS: *Adult male*: Wing, 76.5–81.8 (average, 79.7) mm.; tail, 66.8–72.2 (69.3); bill (exposed culmen), 10.7–11.7 (10.9); tarsus, 20.3–21.9 (20.9); middle toe without claw, 13.5–14.5 (14.0). *Adult female*: Wing, 71.7–78.2 (74.7); tail, 58.2–68.8 (64.5); bill, 10.2–10.7 (10.4); tarsus, 20.3–21.4 (20.9); middle toe, 12.7–14.5 (14.0).

RANGE: Pacific slope of s.w. British Columbia, south through w. Washington and w. Oregon to lat. 43° N. Winters at lower elevations throughout breeding range, south to s. California, also, sparsely southeast to c. Chihuahua and w. Texas.

TEXAS: *Winter*: Taken in El Paso, Culberson, Jeff Davis, and Brewster (Mar. 4) cos. Rare.

COUES' OREGON JUNCO, Junco oreganus eumesus
Oberholser, new subspecies (see Appendix A)

DESCRIPTION: *Adults, nuptial plumage*: Similar to *J. o. shufeldti*, but upper parts, particularly back and scapulars, decidedly more grayish (less rufescent).

MEASUREMENTS: *Adult male*: Wing, 74.9–82.0 (average, 79.2) mm.; tail, 65.5–72.9 (69.3); bill (exposed culmen), 9.4–10.9 (10.2); tarsus, 20.1–22.1 (21.4); middle toe without claw, 13.0–14.0 (13.7). *Adult female*: Wing, 71.9–77.5 (74.2); tail, 63.0–69.1 (65.8); bill, 9.9–10.4 (10.2); tarsus, 19.6–21.4 (20.9); middle toe, 11.9–14.0 (12.7).

TYPE: Adult male, no. 269406, U.S. National Museum, Biological Surveys collection; ridge on east fork of Touchet River, 3,500 ft., Blue Mts., 21 mi. southeast of Dayton, Washington; June 16, 1919; W. P. Taylor, original no., 474.

RANGE: S.e. British Columbia and s.w. Alberta, south through e. Washington to n.e. Oregon. Winters from e. Washington (probably) and s. South Dakota to s.e. Arizona and upper Texas coast.

TEXAS: *Winter*: Taken north to Oldham (Nov. 19), southeast to Galveston (Mar. 21), west to Bexar, Presidio, and Culberson cos. Fairly common to scarce.

MONTANA OREGON JUNCO, Junco oreganus montanus
Ridgway

DESCRIPTION: *Adults, nuptial plumage*: Similar to *J. o. shufeldti*, but male with head, neck, and jugulum slate gray or slate color, not black or dull black; back duller, less rufescent (more grayish); cinnamon of sides and flanks more vinaceous (less pinkish); female with head, neck, and jugulum lighter than in female *shufeldti*. Similar to the Pink-sided Junco, *J. mearnsi*, but wing and tail shorter; head, neck, and jugulum of darker gray, back of a more rufescent (less grayish) brown; sides and flanks less extensively pinkish, this color also more cinnamomeous.

MEASUREMENTS: *Adult male*: Wing, 73.4–80.5 (average, 77.7) mm.; tail, 64.5–70.6 (68.6); bill (exposed culmen), 9.9–10.9 (10.7); tarsus, 20.6–23.4 (21.9); middle toe without claw, 13.0–14.0 (13.5). *Adult female*: Wing, 68.6–75.9 (73.2); tail, 62.0–68.1 (65.3); bill, 9.9–10.9 (10.2); tarsus, 19.6–22.1 (20.9); middle toe, 11.9–13.5 (13.0).

RANGE: S.w. Alberta, w. Montana, and Idaho. Winters from e. Washington and Idaho to n.w. Mexico, c. Texas, and n.e. Oklahoma.

TEXAS: *Winter*: Taken north to Randall, east to Cooke and McLennan, south to Kinney, west to El Paso cos. Scarce.

PINK-SIDED JUNCO, *Junco mearnsi* Ridgway

SPECIES ACCOUNT

Considered a race of the Oregon Junco, *J. oreganus*, by A.O.U. check-list, 1957 (see Appendix A). A brown-backed junco with gray hood; bright pinkish brown sides. Length, 6¼ in.; wingspan, 9¾; weight, ¾ oz.

RANGE: S.e. Alberta and s.w. Saskatchewan, south through c. Montana to n. Utah and s.w. Wyoming. Winters from s.e. Idaho and n.w. Nebraska to n.w. mainland Mexico and c. Texas.

TEXAS: (See map.) *Winter*: Early Nov. to late Apr. (extremes: Oct. 17, May 21). Common to uncommon in western two-thirds, but rare to absent in south Texas brush country; scarce in eastern third.

HAUNTS AND HABITS: In its behavior and choice of haunts, *J. mearnsi* differs little from the Oregon Junco. During many winters in Texas, at least since 1950, the Pink-sided has been the most numerous form in mixed junco flocks which roam mountains and canyons in the Trans-Pecos and western Panhandle.

Vocalizations are similar to those of the Slate-colored Junco.

DETAILED ACCOUNT: NO SUBSPECIES

DESCRIPTION: *Adult male, nuptial plumage*: Acquired by wear from winter plumage. Pileum between deep neutral gray and deep mouse gray; back and scapulars between drab and buffy

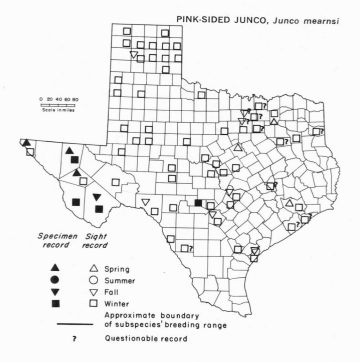

PINK-SIDED JUNCO, *Junco mearnsi*

0 20 40 60 80
Scale in miles

Specimen record   Sight record

▲   △ Spring
●   ○ Summer
▼   ▽ Fall
■   □ Winter

——   Approximate boundary of subspecies' breeding range

?   Questionable record

brown; upper tail-coverts and rump mouse gray; tail dark hair brown, outer two feathers mostly white, third pair of feathers with broad wedge-shaped white terminal shaft stripe on inner web, occupying about half length of feather, sometimes more, sometimes also involving most of terminal portion of outer web, middle pairs of feathers narrowly margined on outer webs with deep mouse gray; primaries and secondaries dark hair brown, outer webs of primaries narrowly margined with light mouse gray to grayish white, secondaries edged narrowly on outer webs with hair brown; tertials fuscous, margined outwardly with drab or rufescent drab; wing-coverts dark hair brown, lesser and median series broadly tipped and edged with mouse gray, outer margins of greater coverts and tips drab to light drab, innermost greater coverts sometimes edged with brown like scapulars; lores deep mouse gray to dark mouse gray; sides of head and of neck like pileum but lighter; chin, throat, and jugulum still paler; sides and flanks fawn color to bright or light fawn color; lining of wing grayish or brownish white, outer portion deep mouse gray or mouse gray tipped with grayish or brownish white. Bill pinkish white or flesh color, but tip dull dark brown; iris similar to that of *J. oreganus shufeldti*; legs light brown; feet similar but darker. *Adult male, winter*: Acquired by complete postnuptial molt. Similar to nuptial adult male but darker above; pileum duller, more brownish due to narrow brown edgings of feathers; back and scapulars duller, usually somewhat more rufescent; upper tail-coverts tipped with light brown, dull buff, or dull pale buff; light brown edgings of outer webs of tertials broader, chin, throat, and jugulum darker and duller, more brownish or buffy, with more and broader light buff or pale gray tips; fawn color of sides and flanks more pinkish. *Adult female, nuptial*: Acquired by wear from winter. Similar to nuptial adult male but smaller; upper surface paler, particularly pileum and hindneck which are more brownish (less purely grayish); wings and tail lighter and more brownish (less grayish); tail usually with less white, particularly third rectrices from outside; chin, throat, and jugulum paler, less purely gray (somewhat more brownish or buffy); sides and flanks somewhat less pinkish (more cinnamomeous). *Adult female, winter*: Acquired by complete postnuptial molt. Similar to nuptial adult female, but upper surface darker, back somewhat more rufescent—and pileum more or less overlaid with brown of back; light outer edges of tertials broader; chin, throat, and jugulum duller, rather lighter, more overlaid with buff or with color of sides; sides and flanks more pinkish. Similar to adult male in winter but smaller; upper parts paler, head also less purely gray (more overlaid with brown); tips of upper tail-coverts lighter; wings and tail more brownish, third tail feathers from outside with less white on inner web; chin, throat, and jugulum less clearly gray (more brownish or buffy); sides and flanks somewhat less pinkish. *Male, first nuptial*: Acquired by wear from first winter. Very similar to nuptial adult male, but pileum and hindneck duller, more brownish (less purely gray), though not quite so much as in adult female; outer edges of tertials usually more brownish or buffy; chin, throat, and jugulum lighter, more brownish or buffy (less purely gray). *Male, first winter*: Acquired by partial postjuvenal molt. Resembling adult male in winter, but upper surface lighter, particularly pileum, the latter less purely gray (more brownish or buffy), by reason of broad light brown or dull buff tips of feathers; chin, throat, and jugulum paler, less purely gray (more buffy or brownish). *Female, first nuptial*: Acquired by wear from first winter. Similar to nuptial adult male, but head nearly always less purely gray (more brownish); wings and tail averaging slightly lighter and more brownish; throat paler, less purely gray (more washed, tinged, or overlaid on tips of feathers with dull buff or color of sides). *Female, first winter*: Acquired by partial postjuvenal molt. Similar to adult female in winter, but upper surface averaging darker and duller, pileum more overlaid with brown, so that upper surface is thus more uniform; chin, throat, and jugulum less purely gray, duller and more overlaid with buff, light brown, or fawn color of sides and flanks. *Male, juvenal*: Acquired by complete postnatal molt. Upper surface light hair brown to near buffy brown, pileum a little more grayish, everywhere above streaked, most broadly on

back, with chaetura drab, chaetura black, or fuscous; wings and tail as in first winter male, but lesser coverts brown like back; greater coverts margined on outer webs with drab to buffy brown and tipped with dull pale buff or buffy white; sides of head similar to pileum but usually somewhat more buffy and more finely streaked with fuscous, sometimes these streaks few and obscure; jugulum dull pale gray, buffy white, or even dull pinkish buff or dull cartridge buff; chin and throat pale dull buff or dull pale gray, often washed with buff; crissum light pinkish buff; lower breast and abdomen dull white or buffy white, occasionally very pale buff; sides and flanks tinged with dull buff; throat and upper breast rather narrowly, jugulum, sides, and flanks more broadly, streaked with hair brown, chaetura drab, or sometimes fuscous. *Female, juvenal*: Acquired by complete postnatal molt. Similar to juvenal male, but upper surface lighter and decidedly more rufescent (less grayish); wings and tail similarly different but not so strikingly; lower surface lighter and more buffy, dark streaks narrower and of more rufescent brown, usually fuscous.

MEASUREMENTS: *Adult male*: Wing, 79.7–85.3 (average, 82.3) mm.; tail, 67.3–73.2 (69.8); bill (exposed culmen), 10.2–10.7 (10.4); tarsus, 18.8–21.9 (20.3); middle toe without claw, 12.2–15.0 (14.0). *Adult female*: Wing, 73.7–85.9 (78.5); tail, 65.8–73.7 (67.3); bill, 10.2–11.2 (10.7); tarsus, 18.5–21.4 (20.3); middle toe, 13.2–14.5 (13.7).

TEXAS: *Winter*: Taken west to El Paso (Mar. 1) and Presidio, east to Kerr cos.

GRAY-HEADED JUNCO, *Junco caniceps*
(Woodhouse)

SPECIES ACCOUNT

A rufous-backed junco with gray hood, sides, wings, and rump; entirely pale pinkish bill; dark brown eyes. Length, 6¼ in.; wingspan, 9¾; weight, ¾ oz.

RANGE: S. Idaho and s. Wyoming, south to e. California (White Mts.), Nevada, c. Colorado, extreme n.

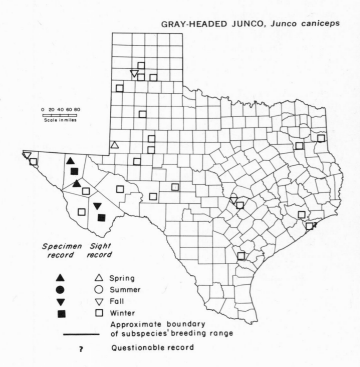

GRAY-HEADED JUNCO, *Junco caniceps*

0 20 40 60 80
Scale in miles

Specimen record / Sight record

▲ △ Spring
● ○ Summer
▼ ▽ Fall
■ □ Winter

——— Approximate boundary of subspecies' breeding range

? Questionable record

Arizona, and extreme n. New Mexico. Winters from n. Utah and w. Nebraska to n.w. mainland Mexico and w. Texas.

TEXAS: (See map.) *Winter*: Late Oct. to late Apr. (extremes: Oct. 1, May 27). Fairly common to uncommon in western third; scarce and irregular to virtually absent east of 100th meridian.

HAUNTS AND HABITS: Breeding as well as winter homes of *J. caniceps* are similar to haunts of the other widespread western mountain junco, *J. oreganus*.

In habits, the Gray-headed doesn't deviate from the junco norm. It is a ground feeder which forages for seeds of pigweed, other forbs and grasses; also caterpillars, caddis flies, and other insects.

Vocalizations resemble those of the Slate-colored Junco.

DETAILED ACCOUNT: NO SUBSPECIES

DESCRIPTION: *Adult male, nuptial plumage*: Acquired by wear from winter plumage. Most of upper surface, including scapulars, between deep neutral gray and deep mouse gray, rump slightly paler; but back mostly occupied by large roughly triangular area of light reddish brown, this between cinnamon rufous and tawny; tail between hair brown and mouse gray or dark mouse gray, middle pairs of feathers edged on outer webs narrowly with mouse gray, outer two feathers mostly white, third outer feather with long terminal area of white, occupying usually more than half the feather, and involving middle portion along shaft, chiefly on inner web; wings dark hair brown, inner edges of primaries and secondaries, except at tips, drab, becoming whitish basally on secondaries; outer webs narrowly margined with light mouse gray, becoming darker on inner secondaries and inclining to drab on outer webs of tertials, which color on tertials occupies most of outer webs; edgings of lesser wing-coverts gray like pileum, of median and greater coverts between light mouse gray and drab; lores dark mouse gray to blackish mouse gray; remainder of sides of head and of neck, with chin, throat, jugulum, and sometimes upper breast, between neutral gray and mouse gray; sides and flanks between smoke gray and light mouse gray; lower breast, abdomen, and crissum white or buffy white; lining of wing like jugulum or grayish white, usually more or less streaked and spotted with mouse gray to deep mouse gray, mostly so on outer part. Bill flesh color, purplish white, or pinkish white, but tip of maxilla sometimes dark brown; iris claret brown, hazel, or vandyke brown; legs flesh color, vinaceous buff, or light yellowish brown; feet deep brownish drab or brown tinged with flesh color; claws dark drab. *Adult male, winter*: Acquired by complete postnuptial molt. Similar to nuptial adult male, but tawny of back darker, feathers conspicuously tipped with sayal brown, tawny olive, or mouse gray; upper tail-coverts tipped with dull buff or light gray; light edgings of tertials broader; chin, throat, and jugulum averaging lighter and more purely gray, feathers more tipped with lighter gray, this sometimes giving an obscurely shadowy barred appearance, particularly on jugulum. *Adult female, nuptial*: Acquired by wear from winter. Similar to nuptial adult male but smaller; head and neck above and below lighter, more brownish (less clearly gray), this particularly apparent on anterior lower surface, where gray of jugulum is less trenchantly defined from white of breast. *Adult female, winter*: Acquired by complete postnuptial molt. Similar to nuptial adult female, but tawny of back averaging darker, feathers conspicuously tipped with tawny olive or sayal brown, these edgings sometimes largely obscuring ground color; pileum often considerably veiled by brown or tawny tips of feathers; upper tail-coverts tipped with light gray or dull pale buff; light edgings of tertials broader; anterior lower surface usually darker and more clearly gray. Similar to adult male in winter but smaller; upper surface lighter, pileum duller, more

brownish (less clearly gray); wings and tail of somewhat more rufescent (less grayish) brown; anterior lower surface averaging lighter and duller, somewhat more buffy or brownish (less purely gray). *Male, first nuptial*: Acquired by wear from winter. Similar to nuptial adult male, but outer edgings of tertials more rufescent (less clearly gray), head, neck, and particularly anterior lower surface averaging somewhat lighter, less purely grayish (more tinged with brown or buff). *Male, first winter*: Acquired by partial postjuvenal molt. Similar to adult male in winter, but much veiled on occiput with tawny olive and on remainder of pileum, particularly on forehead, with tawny or hazel; thus entire aspect of pileum and hindneck is much duller and more brownish; outer edges of tertials and secondaries of more rufescent (less grayish) brown—buffy brown to snuff brown; throat duller, more buffy (less purely gray), and often lighter. *Female, first nuptial*: Acquired by wear from first winter. Similar to nuptial adult female, but tertials usually of somewhat more rufescent (less grayish) brown, head, throat, and jugulum paler, more brownish or buffy (less purely gray), flanks usually more tinged with dull buff or pale brown. *Female, first winter*: Acquired by partial postjuvenal molt. Similar to adult female in winter, but pileum much duller, often lighter, much more overlaid with dull brown, buff, or hazel edges of feathers; outer edges of tertials and secondaries more decidedly rufescent brown (less grayish); throat and jugulum duller, more washed with brownish or buffy, and often lighter; flanks more strongly tinged with light brown or buff (less grayish). *Juvenal*: Acquired by complete postnatal molt. Pileum and hindneck mouse gray to drab, numerously streaked with fuscous to fuscous black; back russet or dull tawny to between sayal brown and snuff brown, more or less streaked with fuscous black; rump and upper tail-coverts similar to pileum but often somewhat washed with sayal brown and narrowly streaked with fuscous or fuscous black; wings and tail as in first winter female; lesser wing-coverts edged with dull buffy drab, outer webs of greater coverts with light buffy brown, and both median and greater coverts with small terminal spots of buffy white or dull very pale buff; sides of head like pileum but somewhat more buffy, more narrowly and less conspicuously streaked, or very finely spotted with fuscous; lores fuscous or fuscous black, though often mixed with gray; anterior lower surface dull buff, smoke gray, or dull tilleul buff, jugulum sometimes pale cartridge buff; remainder of lower surface buffy white, flanks sometimes dull pale buff, sides sometimes also tinged with same; throat, jugulum, and breast thickly streaked and spotted with hair brown to chaetura black and fuscous; sides and flanks also similarly streaked, though usually less thickly.

MEASUREMENTS: *Adult male*: Wing, 81.5–86.9 (average, 84.8) mm.; tail, 68.8–74.7 (72.2); bill (exposed culmen), 10.7–11.7 (11.2); height of bill at base, 6.9–7.4 (7.1); tarsus, 19.8–21.9 (20.9); middle toe without claw, 13.7–15.2 (14.2). *Adult female*: Wing, 74.7–83.8 (78.7); tail, 63.0–71.4 (66.8); bill, 10.2–11.7 (10.7); height of bill, 6.9–7.4 (7.1); tarsus, 19.3–21.4 (20.9); middle toe, 13.2–15.2 (14.2).

TEXAS: *Winter*: Taken in Culberson, Jeff Davis, and Brewster cos.

RED-BACKED JUNCO, *Junco dorsalis* (Henry)

SPECIES ACCOUNT

Considered a race of the Gray-headed Junco, *J. caniceps*, by A.O.U. check-list, 1957 (see Appendix A); formerly regarded as a race of the Mexican Junco, *J. phaeonotus*, which it resembles in plumage but not in eye color. A rufous-backed junco with gray hood, sides (pale), wings, and rump; dark brown eyes; blackish upper mandible. The dark upper bill is unique among regular Texas juncos; beaks of other forms are pale pink. Length, 6½ in.; wingspan, 10; weight, ¾ oz.

RANGE: N. Arizona (south rim of Grand Canyon) and c. New Mexico, south to c. Arizona and n. Trans-Pecos Texas. Winters in and near breeding range, south to s.e. Arizona, n.w. Chihuahua (San Diego), and s. Trans-Pecos Texas.

TEXAS: (See map.) *Breeding*: Mid-Apr. to mid-Aug. (egg dates not available, but young in nest to Aug. 5) from 7,000 to 8,700 ft. Common to fairly common in Guadalupe Mts. *Winter*: Mid-Nov. to late Mar. (extremes: Nov. 12, Apr. 3). Fairly common in northern Trans-Pecos; uncommon in Davis Mts.; scarce in Chisos Mts.; casual east of Pecos River.

HAUNTS AND HABITS: The Red-backed Junco is the least migratory of Texas juncos and the only one which nests within the state. It summers in montane pine-Douglasfir forests, but in winter some individuals move down-mountain and south a few miles, although they seldom get below the pinyon-oak belt.

It forages, like other juncos, mainly on the ground for seeds (of ladies-thumb, sunflower, various grasses) and insects (mostly beetles, caterpillars, and grasshoppers).

Notes are *tsic*'s and various other twitters. Song resembles the Slate-colored's, but is lighter. In the Guadalupes, Red-backed Juncos sing from prominent perches in conifers or fallen trees from April to July.

DETAILED ACCOUNT: NO SUBSPECIES

DESCRIPTION: *Adult male, nuptial plumage*: Acquired by wear from winter plumage. Upper surface, including scapulars, between deep neutral gray and mouse gray, except large triangular area on back terminating in point posteriorly which is tawny to light tawny; tail between deep mouse gray and dark hair brown, middle pairs of feathers narrowly edged on outer webs with mouse gray, and central pair tipped on inner webs with hair

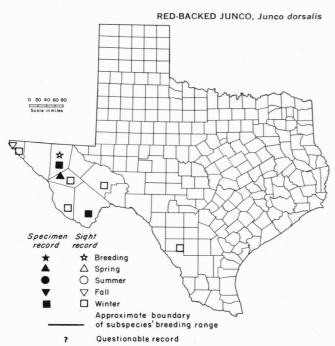

RED-BACKED JUNCO, *Junco dorsalis*

0 20 40 60 80
Scale in miles

*Specimen   Sight
record   record*

★ ☆ Breeding
▲ △ Spring
● ○ Summer
▼ ▽ Fall
■ □ Winter

━━━ Approximate boundary
     of subspecies' breeding range

?   Questionable record

brown; outer two pairs of feathers mostly white, third pair with broad white tip and long terminal stripe along shaft on inner web white, this sometimes extending for half length of feather, shaft of feather white in this space as are also shafts of outer two feathers; primaries and secondaries dark hair brown, inner edges, except tips, drab gray to dull pale drab, basally dull white; outer webs of primaries narrowly margined with dull light mouse gray, outer edges of inner secondaries drab or mouse gray; tertials largely fuscous, outer webs of shortest feathers margined and those of remaining tertials barred with drab to between drab and mouse gray; lesser and median wing-coverts gray like upper surface, greater coverts hair brown, broadly margined on outer webs with dull light mouse gray; lores dull black to fuscous black; rest of sides of head like crown but slightly washed with dull buff; chin, throat, and jugulum, with sides and flanks, light smoke gray, slightly buffy, particularly on flanks; remainder of lower surface dull white; lining of wing mostly dull white or grayish white, outer coverts more or less spotted with neutral gray to deep mouse gray, rest of coverts with a few streaks of same color. Maxilla brownish black; mandible flesh color or lilaceous white; iris dark hazel; legs light yellowish brown; feet darker. *Adult male, winter*: Acquired by complete postnuptial molt. Similar to nuptial adult male, but tawny area of back darker and duller, usually russet, feathers conspicuously edged with sayal brown to dull cinnamon; upper tail-coverts tipped with dull light gray or even grayish white; anterior lower surface averaging darker. *Adult female, nuptial*: Acquired by wear from winter. Similar to nuptial adult male but averaging smaller; upper surface, including back, wings, and tail, lighter; pileum more brownish (less purely gray); wings and tail of more rufescent (less grayish) brown. *Adult female, winter*: Acquired by complete postnuptial molt. Similar to nuptial adult female, but upper surface darker; head usually somewhat tinged with brown, from brownish tips of feathers; feathers of tawny area of back conspicuously tipped with tawny olive or sayal brown; upper tail-coverts tipped with pale gray or grayish white or pale dull buff; light edges of tertials somewhat broader, these feathers often narrowly tipped with dull white. *Male, first nuptial*: Acquired by wear from first winter. Very similar to nuptial adult male but often somewhat duller. *Male, first winter*: Acquired by partial postjuvenal molt. Similar to adult male in winter, but outer edgings of tertials more brownish (less grayish); pileum, hindneck, and rump averaging more brownish (less purely gray). *Female, first nuptial*: Acquired by wear from first winter. Similar to nuptial adult female but often somewhat duller. *Female, first winter*: Acquired by partial postjuvenal molt. Similar to adult female in winter, but outer edgings of tertials more brownish (less grayish); pileum, hindneck, and rump also averaging more brownish (less purely gray). *Juvenal*: Acquired by complete postnatal molt. Pileum grayish drab to buffy brown or between light drab and avellaneous, numerously streaked with fuscous to olive brown; back and scapulars tawny or dull tawny, shading to sayal brown anteriorly, and more or less streaked with olive brown to fuscous posteriorly; rump and upper tail-coverts similar to pileum, but often washed with sayal brown, and obscurely and narrowly streaked with fuscous or olive brown; wings and tail like those of first winter; lesser coverts broadly margined with light dull buffy brown, median coverts with small dull white or buffy white terminal spots, outer webs of greater coverts broadly margined with light buffy brown, becoming more rufescent on innermost feathers, and all of feathers with terminal spot of dull white or buffy white on outer webs, sometimes also on inner webs, forming an evident narrow wing-bar, as do also tips of median coverts; sides of head like pileum but usually not so broadly or conspicuously streaked, instead mostly spotted with light fuscous; auriculars often tinged with dull buff; lower surface dull grayish white, washed with pale pinkish buff, particularly on jugulum, sides, and flanks, and streaked on throat, jugulum, sides of breast and of body, and on flanks with hair brown to chaetura drab; crissum dull light pinkish buff. *Natal*: Light drab to hair brown.

MEASUREMENTS: *Adult male*: Wing, 81.8–86.9 (average, 84.8) mm.; tail, 72.7–77.0 (75.2); bill (exposed culmen), 11.2–12.7

(11.9); height of bill at base, 7.4–8.4 (7.9); tarsus, 19.8–22.4 (21.4); middle toe without claw, 14.2–15.2 (15.0). *Adult female*: Wing, 76.2–81.5 (79.2); tail, 68.3–74.2 (70.4); bill, 11.2–12.2 (11.7); height of bill, 7.4–7.9 (7.6); tarsus, 20.9–21.4 (21.1); middle toe, 13.0–14.5 (13.7).

TEXAS: *Breeding*: Collected in Guadalupe Mts., Culberson Co. *Winter*: Taken in Culberson, Jeff Davis (Apr. 3), and Brewster cos.

NESTING: *Nest*: Chiefly in mountains, but sometimes on high mesas; in forests, usually in more open parts, and on slopes with scattered brush or trees of pine or other evergreen, or oaks or other deciduous trees; usually on ground, either at base of bush, tuft of grass, or clump of weeds, usually well concealed; cup, at times rather loosely constructed; composed of stalks of various plants, grasses, roots, and occasionally feathers; lined with similar but finer materials. *Eggs*: 3–4, usually 4; ovate to rounded ovate; white, bluish white, or greenish white; rather sparingly dotted with dark brown, and with shell markings of lilac, mostly at larger end, and even in form of wreath; or occasionally entirely unmarked; average size, 19.3 × 14.7 mm.

[MEXICAN JUNCO, *Junco phaeonotus* Wagler

Northernmost race formerly known as Arizona Junco. Resembles Red-backed Junco, but adults have rich yellow eyes. Instead of hopping like other U.S. juncos, it shuffles; song is varied, sweet, and thin (not a simple mechanical trill). Length, 6¼ in.

RANGE: Sierras from n. Sonora, s.e. Arizona, s.w. New Mexico, n. Chihuahua, and n. Coahuila, south to Guerrero, Oaxaca, and w. Veracruz.

TEXAS: *Hypothetical*: One explicit sighting: Brewster Co., Big Bend Nat. Park (Jan. 2, 1972, T. B. Feltner). One undated sighting from the park, along the Window Trail (fide Nat. Park Service Files). This is a common breeding bird in the Fronteriza (Sierra del Carmen) Mts. of Coahuila, 50 mi. southeast of Big Bend; postnuptial visitors should be watched for (R. H. Wauer).]

TREE SPARROW, *Spizella arborea* (Wilson)

Species Account

Also known as American Tree Sparrow. The largest rusty-capped U.S. sparrow with white wing-bars. Dusky-streaked brownish back; grayish forequarters; rusty postocular stripe; black central breast-spot; whitish belly; bill black above, yellow below; dark brown legs. Length, 6¼ in.; wingspan, 9¼; weight, ¾ oz.

RANGE: N. Alaska and n. Canada. Winters from U.S.-Canada border to n. California, c. Arizona, n. Texas, and North Carolina.

TEXAS: (See map.) *Winter*: Mid-Nov. to late Feb. (extremes: Sept. 29, Apr. 20). Common (some years) to scarce in northern third; scarce to casual south of 32nd parallel; accidental in Rio Grande delta.

HAUNTS AND HABITS: Despite the arboreal implications of its name, the Tree Sparrow finds prime breeding haunts not in forests or woods but just south of tundra where stunted alders, willows, and birches form thickets four to five feet high. The sturdy grass-moss-lichen-bark nest is nestled amid dense tangles in a tussock of grass or depression in earth. Most Tree Sparrows migrate on the average of 1,500 to 2,000 miles to U.S. winter grounds; studies show females generally winter farther south than do males. In the northern portion of Texas, *Spizella arborea* spends cold months in weedy fields, thickets at woodland edges, fence rows lined with tumbleweed (*Salsola kali*), brushy shelter belts, and on plains with only occasional bushes. Casually this northerner occurs in southern parts of the state, where it has been found in weed patches and heaped brush.

When not hurried, Tree Sparrow flight is rather graceful and undulating; otherwise it is quick and jerky. Birds flushed from the ground rise usually three to twelve feet to perches in the nearest tree or bush. Feeding Tree Sparrows mainly scratch on the ground for seeds—at least 90 percent of their winter diet—of bristlegrass, crabgrass, panicum, pigweed, ragweed, others. A few insects are picked from leaves and branches of thickets; in spring, birds will pluck low-growing buds and catkins from dwarf willows and birches. Tree Sparrows in winter feed in loose flocks; observations show that one forager seldom encroaches within six inches of its neighbor.

Tree Sparrow notes are a thin *tseep* and a twittering musical *teel-whit*. One version of the slight, sweet song is *seet-seet, seetiter-sweet-sweet*. It is most likely to be heard in Texas during February and March.

DETAILED ACCOUNT: Two Subspecies

EASTERN TREE SPARROW, *Spizella arborea arborea* (Wilson)

DESCRIPTION: Similar to *S. a. ochracea* (see below), but wing

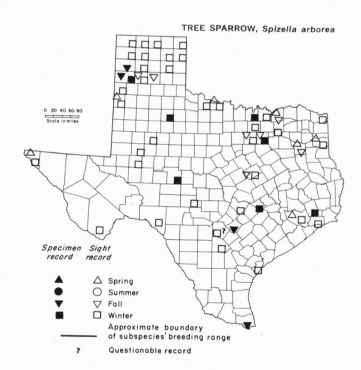

TREE SPARROW, *Spizella arborea*

and tail shorter; colors of upper parts darker and richer; edgings of feathers less whitish and dark streaks broader; light margins of tail feathers less whitish.

MEASUREMENTS: *Adult male*: Wing, 72.9–82.0 (average, 77.5) mm.; tail, 65.8–73.2 (69.6); bill (exposed culmen), 9.7–10.2 (9.9); tarsus, 20.3–21.6 (20.9); middle toe without claw, 13.2–15.0 (14.0). *Adult female*: Wing, 72.9–78.7 (75.2); tail, 66.0–68.6 (67.6); bill, 8.6–9.9 (9.1); tarsus, 20.1–21.4 (20.9); middle toe, 13.2–14.2 (13.7).

RANGE: N. Canada east of Rocky Mts. Winters from Great Lakes region and Nova Scotia to s.e. Texas (casually).

TEXAS: *Winter*: One record (specimen?): Liberty Co., Hardin (bird killed, Dec. 25, 1929, had previously been banded at Berlin, Massachusetts).

WESTERN TREE SPARROW, *Spizella arborea ochracea* Brewster

DESCRIPTION: *Adults, nuptial plumage*: Acquired by wear from winter plumage. Pileum tawny or verging toward cinnamon rufous; hindneck between light neutral gray and mouse gray, more or less washed with tawny; remainder of upper surface between light grayish olive and avellaneous, back broadly streaked with fuscous to fuscous black, also streaked with tawny, particularly on scapulars, and with pale dull pinkish buff to pinkish buff, sometimes also with buffy white, and scapulars sometimes streaked with cinnamon; tail dark hair brown, narrowly edged on outer webs of feathers and terminally on inner webs with buffy white or very pale dull buff, this edging broadest on outermost pair of feathers; primaries and secondaries dark hair brown, inner edges, except at tips, dull light vinaceous buff, palest basally; narrow outer edges of primaries dull buffy white, broader outer edges of secondaries light buffy brown to sayal brown, those of tertials cinnamon to cinnamon buff, except terminal portion which is very pale buff or buffy white; remaining portions of tertials fuscous, except for often a narrow cinnamon edging on inner web; lesser wing-coverts between mouse gray and drab; median wing-coverts fuscous, broadly tipped with white or buffy white, forming a bar; greater coverts fuscous, broadly edged on outer webs with hazel, this often changing to sayal brown on outer feathers, and tipped with white or buffy white, forming a second bar; sides of head and of neck gray like hindneck but rather paler; broad superciliary stripe light gray, becoming somewhat buffy or dull white over lores; postocular stripe auburn; lores dull light buff or dull cinnamon, often mixed with mouse gray; lower eyelid dull buff or buffy white; sometimes an auburn or light auburn spot in front of eye; a short, sometimes interrupted malar stripe or spot of auburn to fuscous; chin, throat, and jugulum very pale gray washed with buff; a conspicuous spot on upper breast and lower jugulum hair brown to fuscous black; remainder of lower surface buffy white or very pale buff, but sides and flanks tinged with dull pale pinkish buff; lining of wing buffy white; axillars sometimes pale buff, outer and posterior portion sometimes mottled or finely spotted with light drab to mouse gray; axillars buffy white or pale buff. Bill black, slate black, or blackish slate, but basal half or two-thirds of mandible deep chrome, chrome yellow, gamboge yellow, orange buff, or wax yellow, extreme base of culmen often light yellow; iris red-brown, hazel, vandyke brown, or dark sepia; legs fawn color, broccoli brown, chaetura drab, dark drab, prout brown, seal brown, or hair brown; feet and claws dark drab, sepia, clove brown, or seal brown. *Adults, winter*: Acquired by complete postnuptial molt. Similar to nuptial adults, but colors of upper surface much more buffy or ochraceous; pileum much obscured by feather edgings of mouse gray, light dull brown, and dull buff; streaks on back narrower and much less sharply defined owing to broader buff or ochraceous edgings of feathers; light edges of tertials broader; buffy or grayish tips of upper tail-coverts wider; sides of head and lower parts more buffy, brown spot on lower jugulum often veiled by pale edgings of feathers. *First nuptial*: Acquired by wear from first winter. Similar to nuptial adults, but upper parts more ochraceous, brownish,

or buffy (less grayish), and averaging darker and duller; lower surface averaging more buffy. *First winter*: Acquired by partial postjuvenal molt, which does not involve wing-quills or tail. Similar to adults in winter, but upper surface darker, duller, more deeply ochraceous or buffy; pileum more edged with light brown or buff, sometimes some of feathers with dark shafts; gray of hindneck more obscured with brown, ochraceous, or buff; sides of head and lower surface, on the average, decidedly more buffy or ochraceous; brown spot on jugulum even more obscured, sometimes almost invisible. *Juvenal*: Acquired by complete postnatal molt. Crown buffy brown; hindneck, as well as forehead, similar but paler than crown; back dull pinkish buff; rump between avellaneous and deep olive buff; pileum narrowly streaked with fuscous black, fuscous, or hair brown, and a little with tawny; hindneck more narrowly and obscurely streaked with fuscous or fuscous black; rump and upper tail-coverts also streaked or sometimes obscurely barred with fuscous or hair brown; back and scapulars densely streaked with fuscous black and tawny, latter color particularly on scapulars; wings and tail as in first winter female; lower surface dull buffy white, washed anteriorly with light gray and tinged with dull pale pinkish buff to pinkish buff, particularly on throat and jugulum; throat, jugulum, breast, sides, and flanks conspicuously streaked with hair brown to chaetura black.

MEASUREMENTS: *Adult male*: Wing, 72.7–82.0 (average, 77.5) mm.; tail, 65.8–73.2 (69.8); bill (exposed culmen), 9.7–10.2 (9.9); height of bill at base, 6.9–7.4 (7.1); tarsus, 20.3–21.9 (20.9); middle toe without claw, 13.2–15.0 (14.0). *Adult female*: Wing, 72.7–78.7 (75.2); tail, 66.0–68.8 (67.8); bill, 8.6–9.7 (9.1); height of bill, 6.4–6.9 (6.6); tarsus, 20.3–21.4 (20.9); middle toe, 13.2–14.2 (13.7).

RANGE: N. Alaska and extreme n.w. Canada. Winters from s. British Columbia and n.w. Iowa to n.e. California, c. Arizona, and c. Texas.

TEXAS: *Winter*: Taken northwest to Deaf Smith (Nov. 25) and Oldham (Nov. 26), east to Cooke and Dallas, south to Lee and Guadalupe, west to Tom Green cos. One specimen from Cameron Co., Port Isabel (Oct. 28, 1908, A. P. Smith). Common to scarce.

CHIPPING SPARROW, *Spizella passerina* (Bechstein)

SPECIES ACCOUNT   *See colorplate 34*

A small, rusty-capped sparrow with black postocular line; conspicuous white eyebrow-stripe; black-streaked brown back; two white wing-bars; gray rump and breast; black bill; pinkish or light grayish brown legs. Length, 5½ in.; wingspan, 8¾; weight, ½ oz.

RANGE: Canada, south through e. United States to Gulf states and n. Florida, and south through w. United States and highland Mexico to Nicaragua. Northern races winter chiefly from s. United States to Oaxaca.

TEXAS: (See map.) *Breeding*: Late Mar. to early Aug. (eggs, Apr. 14 to May 29) from 200 to 8,000 ft. Fairly common (most years) on eastern half of Edwards Plateau; locally fairly common to scarce in Trans-Pecos, north central portion, and in wooded eastern quarter. *Winter*: Late Sept. to late Apr. (extremes: July 31, May 18). Common to fairly common over most of state with exceptions of northern Panhandle and south Texas brush country, where uncommon to scarce.

HAUNTS AND HABITS: In Canada and the northeastern United States, the Chipping Sparrow nests in trees and bushes growing at almost any elevation in either suburb or country. In Texas it is more selective; here it is confined mostly to parklike woodlands in hills or mountains. Pecan orchards and open oak or elm woods are preferred on the Edwards Plateau. In the Trans-Pecos the Chippy is a bird of the montane pine-oak zone. Even in winter it usually remains in or near trees, especially oaks. It thus leaves plains and mesquite brushlands mainly to its close relative the Clay-colored Sparrow; Trans-Pecos desert scrub goes mostly to the Claycolor and to an additional relative the Brewer's Sparrow.

Chippies feed mostly on the ground. They hop about lightly, scratching and pecking in search of grass and weed seeds—chiefly of crabgrass, bristlegrass, filaree, and pigweed. During the breeding season, they become quite insectivorous; one study showed a June diet to be comprised of 93 percent insects. Grasshoppers, caterpillars, beetles, leafhoppers, true bugs, ants, and wasps are eaten; also spiders. In winter, they usually forage in scattered groups, at which time flockmates occasionally bicker and indulge in brief skirmishes.

Chip's or *tsip*'s are common notes of *S. passerina*. The song is a simple, chipping, monotone trill. This is delivered from a tree, although usually not at the top, chiefly from mid-March to mid-July.

DETAILED ACCOUNT: FOUR SUBSPECIES

EASTERN CHIPPING SPARROW, *Spizella passerina passerina* (Bechstein)

DESCRIPTION: *Adult male, nuptial plumage*: Acquired by partial prenuptial molt. Forehead fuscous black, with a narrow grayish white median line; crown and occiput hazel to tawny, occiput sometimes narrowly streaked with fuscous black; hindneck mouse gray to rather light mouse gray, with a few streaks of fuscous black; back and scapulars dull cinnamon buff to dull

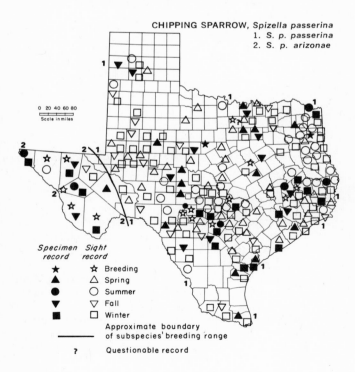

CHIPPING SPARROW, *Spizella passerina*
1. *S. p. passerina*
2. *S. p. arizonae*

0 20 40 60 80
Scale in miles

Specimen / Sight record

★ / ☆ Breeding
▲ / △ Spring
● / ○ Summer
▼ / ▽ Fall
■ / □ Winter

——— Approximate boundary of subspecies' breeding range

? Questionable record

light buffy brown, broadly streaked with fuscous black or fuscous and with light tawny to cinnamon rufous; rump and upper tail-coverts mouse gray, sparingly spotted or streaked with hair brown; tail dark hair brown, very narrowly margined on outer webs with lighter brown, outer feather rather paler than the rest, and most feathers with narrow pale grayish margins on terminal portion of inner web, this broadest on outermost pair; primaries and secondaries rather dark hair brown, inner webs, except at tips, avellaneous; narrow outer edges of primaries pale dull buff, buffy or grayish white, outer webs of secondaries margined more broadly with light buffy brown to sayal brown; broad outer margins of tertials similar but paler at tips of feathers; rest of tertials, together with median and greater wing-coverts, fuscous; median wing-coverts margined subterminally with dull pinkish buff to buffy white and tipped with dull white, buffy white, or pale buff, broad outer margins of greater coverts between olive buff and avellaneous with white or dull buffy white tips; lesser wing-coverts dull grayish olive; broad superciliary stripe grayish white; postocular stripe brownish black; lores dark mouse gray to deep mouse gray; broad stripe under eye grayish white or very pale dull gray; auriculars and remainder of sides of head rather light mouse gray; sides of neck mouse gray; lower parts grayish white, but often more strongly tinged with pale gray on breast and jugulum, and sides of body and flanks smoke gray; lining of wing grayish white or very pale gray, outer portion spotted or mottled with mouse gray, edge of wing white or light gray. Bill slate black, blackish slate, slate, slate gray, brownish slate, or dark brown, but base of mandible often pale flesh color or slate gray, this sometimes involving most of its length; iris vandyke brown; legs and feet flesh color, light dull flesh color, drab, light drab, drab gray, or clay color, but feet sometimes pale cinnamon or seal brown. *Adult male, winter*: Acquired by complete postnuptial molt. Similar to nuptial adult male, but upper surface somewhat darker and duller, pileum much veiled by feather tips of mouse gray and narrow streaks of fuscous black, back and scapulars more blended, blackish streaks less sharply defined; outer edging of tertials broader. *Adult female, nuptial*: Acquired by partial prenuptial molt. Similar to nuptial adult male but smaller; tawny area of pileum of less extent and usually more streaked with black, buff, and gray, this sometimes forming a light median stripe; sides of head more buffy (usually not so clearly gray). Bill mostly black; feet pale brown. *Adult female, winter*: Acquired by complete postnuptial molt. Similar to nuptial adult female, but pileum more streaked or mixed with gray, fuscous black, or dull buff; back and scapulars with colors more blended, dark streaks less sharply defined; outer light edgings of tertials broader. *Male, first nuptial*: Acquired by partial prenuptial molt. Similar to nuptial adult male, but upper surface darker, back and scapulars particularly so, and these parts more rufescent or deeply ochraceous; tawny of crown somewhat mixed with black and gray. *Male, first winter*: Acquired by partial postjuvenal molt, which does not involve wing-quills or tail. Similar to adult male in winter, but upper surface much more rufescent or deeply ochraceous, particularly hindneck, back, scapulars, and wings, and also including edgings of wings; pileum much tipped with tawny olive or dull clay color and somewhat more streaked with dull black, these markings often largely obscuring tawny of pileum; sides of head very much more buffy or ochraceous, including superciliary stripe which is not gray, but dull buff; lower surface much more buffy and tawny olive, particularly on jugulum, sides, and flanks. Bill black, dark brown, or reddish brown, but mandible dark flesh color with dark brown tip; iris brown; legs and feet dark flesh color or reddish brown. *Female, first nuptial*: Acquired by partial prenuptial molt. Similar to nuptial adult female, but back and scapulars darker, light areas decidedly more deeply ochraceous. *Female, first winter*: Acquired by partial postjuvenal molt, which does not involve wing-quills or tail. Similar to adult female in winter, but upper parts, including light wing edgings, more rufescent or buffy; back between snuff brown and sayal brown, pileum more streaked with fuscous black, buff, and tawny olive; sides of head, particularly superciliary stripe, more buffy (less grayish); lower surface much more buffy, especially on jugulum, sides, and flanks, throat sometimes with obscure hair brown streaks or spots. Similar to first winter male but smaller, upper surface averaging lighter, pileum duller, its tawny area much more obscured by streaks of dull buff and fuscous black. Bill black or reddish brown, but mandible, except tip, pinkish vinaceous, and basal part of cutting edges vinaceous; iris brown; legs and feet pinkish white or reddish brown; claws drab. *Juvenal*: Acquired by complete postnatal molt. Upper surface dull cinnamon to sayal brown, tawny olive, or dull ochraceous tawny, hindneck often rather more grayish, rump also paler, and upper tail-coverts similar, sometimes dull cinnamon buff or dull pinkish buff; wings and tail as in first winter, but lesser coverts more brownish or buffy; superciliary stripe dull buffy white or dull pale buff; lores mouse gray to deep mouse gray, sometimes much mixed with dull buff; auriculars drab to buffy drab; lower parts grayish or buffy white, but jugulum, sides, and flanks sometimes rather strongly tinged with buff, throat sometimes with fine streaks or spots of mouse gray, jugulum, breast, sides, and flanks more or less broadly streaked with hair brown to chaetura drab. Bill blackish slate or brownish slate, but mandible somewhat paler, sometimes flesh color; iris dark brown; legs and feet clay color, light flesh color, or mouse gray. *Natal*: Mouse gray. Bill, legs, and feet pinkish buff.

MEASUREMENTS: *Adult male*: Wing, 67.3–71.4 (average, 69.3) mm.; tail, 53.3–59.7 (56.6); bill (exposed culmen), 8.6–9.7 (9.1); tarsus, 15.7–16.8 (16.3); middle toe without claw, 10.9–12.4 (11.7). *Adult female*: Wing, 63.2–71.4 (67.3); tail, 51.3–59.7 (54.8); bill, 8.6–9.7 (9.1); tarsus, 15.5–16.8 (16.3); middle toe, 10.2–12.4 (11.7).

RANGE: E. Canada, south through e. United States (east of 100th meridian) to c. Texas and n.w. Florida. Winters chiefly south of 36th parallel in s.e. United States, also casually in n.e. Mexico.

TEXAS: *Breeding*: Altitudinal range, 200 to 2,000 ft. Collected north to Bowie, south to Jasper, west to Bexar, Kerr, and Eastland (eggs) cos. Fairly common. *Winter*: Taken north to Cooke (Nov. 20), east to Bowie and Hardin, south to Cameron, west to Tom Green (Sept. 28) cos. Fairly common.

NESTING: *Nest*: On uplands and lowlands; in Texas, usually in hilly or rolling terrain with scattered trees; ordinarily in bush or tree, evergreen or deciduous, 1–25 ft. above ground, but occasionally on ground; a compact cup; composed of fine grasses, weed stems, roots, sometimes small twigs, and other vegetable fibers; lined with rootlets, fine grasses, fibers from milkweed, thistle, or other plants, horsehair, and other long hair. *Eggs*: 3–5, usually 3 or 4; ovate; bluish green or greenish blue; rather sparsely spotted and scrawled, sometimes in a wreath about large end, with cinnamon brown, umber, pinkish brown, other shades of reddish and blackish brown, and with shell markings of lilac gray, lilac, and lavender; average size, 17.0 × 13.2 mm.

WESTERN CHIPPING SPARROW, *Spizella passerina arizonae* Coues

DESCRIPTION: *Adult male and female, nuptial plumage*: Similar to S. *p. passerina*, but wing, tail, tarsus, and middle toe longer; upper parts, including pileum, lighter and ground color both paler and less rufescent (more grayish); sides of head lighter; postocular streak narrower. *Juvenal*: Similar to juvenal of S. *p. passerina*, but lighter and more buffy above; both black streaks on upper surface and dark streaks on jugulum narrower. *Natal*: Mouse gray.

MEASUREMENTS: *Adult male*: Wing, 69.6–73.4 (average, 71.7) mm.; tail, 57.9–66.0 (61.7); bill (exposed culmen), 8.9–9.9 (9.4); tarsus, 16.5–18.0 (17.3); middle toe without claw, 10.9–12.4 (12.2). *Adult female*: Wing, 66.0–71.9 (68.8); tail, 57.4–62.0 (59.7); bill, 8.9–9.9 (9.4); tarsus, 16.0–18.0 (17.3); middle toe, 11.4–13.0 (12.2).

RANGE: N. Arizona to n.w. Oklahoma, south to n.e. Sinaloa, n. Chihuahua, and Trans-Pecos Texas. Winters from c. Arizona and c. Texas through Mexican uplands to Guerrero and Oaxaca.

TEXAS: *Breeding*: Altitudinal range, 1,900 to 8,000 ft. Collected in Culberson, Jeff Davis, Presidio, and Brewster cos.;

taken in summer (July 31, 1940) in El Paso Co. Fairly common. *Winter*: Taken north to Oldham (Oct. 15) and Randall (Sept. 24), east to Falls (Apr. 23), south to Cameron (Apr. 22), west to El Paso cos. Fairly common.

NESTING: Similar to that of S. *p. passerina*, but average egg size, 17.8 × 13.0 mm.

CANADIAN CHIPPING SPARROW, *Spizella passerina boreophila* Oberholser

DESCRIPTION: *Adult male and female, nuptial plumage*: Similar to S. *p. passerina* but larger; upper surface, excepting pileum, lighter and more grayish. Similar to S. *p. arizonae*, but darker above, pileum particularly so; sides of head and hindneck more clearly gray (less brownish), also somewhat darker; postocular streak wider.

MEASUREMENTS: *Adult male*: Wing, 70.1–73.9 (average, 71.7) mm.; tail, 59.4–65.0 (62.2); bill (exposed culmen), 8.9–9.9 (9.1); tarsus, 17.0–18.0 (17.3); middle toe without claw, 11.4–13.0 (12.2). *Adult female*: Wing, 65.0–69.6 (67.8); tail, 56.9–61.0 (58.7); bill, 8.9–9.9 (9.4); tarsus, 16.0–17.5 (16.8); middle toe, 11.4–12.7 (12.2).

RANGE: E. Alaska to n.e. Manitoba (casually), south to n. Utah, n. Colorado, and w. Nebraska. Winters from s. California and c. Texas to Michoacán and Puebla.

TEXAS: *Winter*: Taken north to Callahan (Oct. 3), east to Nueces (Mar. 30), south to Cameron (Apr. 22), west to Jeff Davis (Apr. 6) and Culberson (Oct. 5) cos. Uncommon.

CALIFORNIA CHIPPING SPARROW, *Spizella passerina stridula* Grinnell

Race not in A.O.U. check-list, 1957 (see Appendix A).

DESCRIPTION: *Adult male and female, nuptial plumage*: Similar to S. *p. arizonae*, but wing and tail shorter, light areas of upper surface somewhat darker and duller; hindneck and rump of darker gray; back duller; lower parts less whitish (more grayish).

MEASUREMENTS: *Adult male*: Wing, 68.6–72.4 (average, 70.4) mm.; tail, 58.4–65.0 (61.0); bill (exposed culmen), 8.6–9.9 (9.1); tarsus, 16.5–18.0 (17.3); middle toe without claw, 10.9–12.4 (11.7). *Adult female*: Wing, 65.0–69.6 (67.3); tail, 55.6–61.5 (58.4); bill, 8.6–9.9 (9.1); tarsus, 16.0–18.0 (17.3); middle toe, 11.4–12.4 (11.7).

RANGE: Washington and n.w. Montana, south through Pacific states and c. Nevada to n. Baja California. Winters from c. California and s.e. Nevada to extreme n.w. Mexico and coastal Texas.

TEXAS: *Winter*: Three specimens: Brazoria Co., Velasco (Mar. 11, 1892, W. Lloyd); Aransas Co., Rockport (Mar. 15, 1892, H. P. Attwater); Nueces Co., Corpus Christi (Apr. 17, 1900, V. Bailey).

CLAY-COLORED SPARROW, *Spizella pallida* (Swainson)

SPECIES ACCOUNT

A small pale sparrow with brown ear-patch, outlined top and bottom with black; brown- and black-streaked crown with buffy white median stripe; whitish eyebrow and malar stripe; black-streaked grayish brown upper parts; two white wing-bars; *brownish* rump (not gray as in Chipping); whitish under parts. Length, 5¼ in.; wingspan, 7¾; weight, ½ oz.

RANGE: N.e. British Columbia, s. Mackenzie, and w. Ontario, south through Great Plains to c. Montana, s.e. Colorado, s. Nebraska, and c. Michigan. Winters

PLATE 34: Chipping Sparrow, *Spizella passerina*

from s. Baja California, n. Sonora, and s. Texas to Chiapas and Guatemala (casually).

TEXAS: (See map.) *Migration*: Late Mar. to mid-May; mid-Sept. to early Nov. (extremes: Mar. 1, May 31; Aug. 18, Nov. 18). Abundant (some years) to fairly common in western two-thirds; uncommon to rare in remainder of state. *Winter*: Mid-Oct. to early Apr. Fairly common (some years) to uncommon in south Texas brush country, especially along Rio Grande south of Laredo; uncommon to scarce in southern Trans-Pecos and extreme southern Panhandle; scarce to casual in northern Trans-Pecos and east of 97th meridian.

HAUNTS AND HABITS: The Clay-colored Sparrow is a bird of the Great Plains. Its nest—a rather loose cup of grass, fine twigs, and rootlets—is placed on the ground in a clump of dead grass at the base of a wild rose, snowberry, willow, or similar bush, or on a low branch of a small shrub or tree. In Texas in spring, this species occurs, often in considerable flocks, primarily in sub-humid country. At this season, it frequents patches of brush, weedy fence rows, and grassy pastures dotted with bushes. Sometimes on the northward journey, small groups pause briefly in tall shade trees. In fall and winter, however, the Claycolor lives almost exclusively in open brushland.

Migrant flocks, from several to as many as fifty individuals, have been seen by day coursing low over prairies. *Spizella pallida* feeds on the ground or low in bushes and if startled usually flushes into a low tree. The diet is mainly seeds of bristlegrass, thistle, pigweed, panicum, and crabgrass. Beetles, grasshoppers, caterpillars, a few moths and spiders are also eaten.

A weak *tsip* is the standard note of this sparrow. The male's monotonous song is a slow, low-pitched, insect-like *bzzz, bzzz, bzzz* or *zzzz, zzzz, zzzz, zzzz*. On the nesting grounds, this is usually delivered from a low tree or shrub; it is also frequently sung during spring migration.

DETAILED ACCOUNT: NO SUBSPECIES

DESCRIPTION: *Adults, nuptial plumage*: Acquired by partial prenuptial molt. Sides of pileum buffy brown to sayal brown, streaked with fuscous black to brownish black; median stripe of pileum dull pinkish buff to dull pale pinkish buff; hindneck rather light mouse gray, streaked less conspicuously with fuscous black, in continuation of streaks on sides of pileum; back and scapulars sayal brown to grayish cream buff, broadly streaked with fuscous black; rump dull grayish olive, upper tail-coverts slightly more buffy with obscure shaft streaks of hair brown; tail between hair brown and buffy brown, outer pair of feathers sometimes inclining to drab, terminal half of inner webs of feathers usually margined with light drab gray, outer webs of rectrices very narrowly margined with dull pale buff, this soon disappearing by abrasion; primaries and secondaries dark hair brown to between hair brown and buffy brown, inner edges, except at tips, dull pale pinkish buff, narrow outer margins of primaries dull pale buff, broader outer margins of secondaries tawny olive; lesser wing-coverts hair brown, very broadly tipped and edged with buffy brown; tertials, median and greater coverts olive brown or between olive brown and fuscous, but outer edgings of tertials rather broadly cinnamon buff, terminally pale buff or buffy white, median coverts broadly tipped with pale buff or buffy white, greater coverts margined on outer webs with dull deep olive buff and tipped with pale buff or buffy white, tips of these coverts and of median series forming two rather distinct wing-bars; broad superciliary stripe dull buffy white or cartridge buff; lores dull pinkish buff; auriculars light tawny olive; postocular stripe of buffy brown or sayal brown with narrow streaks of fuscous black; anterior part of sides of neck like hindneck, unstreaked; posterior part of sides of neck buff like back; submalar streak fuscous to chaetura drab, inclosing a white, anteriorly buff, malar stripe; sides and flanks dull pale buff, more or less washed with pale gray; remainder of lower surface dull white or usually buffy white; lining of wing buffy white, sometimes slightly spotted on outer under wing-coverts with dull light drab. Mandible light reddish brown, ecru drab, flesh color, or yellow, but tip drab, and maxilla brownish black, its tip dull dark brown; iris vandyke brown; legs and feet light brown, pinkish buff, or brownish flesh color; claws drab. *Adults, winter*: Acquired by complete postnuptial molt. Similar to nuptial adults, but upper surface duller, colors more blended, less contrasted, thus more uniform, and also more extensively and deeply buff or ochraceous, black streaks of pileum and back much narrower and less sharply defined, these markings more or less obscured by broader light feather edgings; lower surface more buffy, particularly on jugulum, sides, and flanks. *First nuptial*: Acquired by partial prenuptial molt. Similar to nuptial adults, but upper parts duller, more deeply buff or ochraceous, colors not quite so contrasted; nape and pileum averaging less purely gray (more buffy); jugulum more decidedly tinged with buff, usually forming rather evident band. *First winter*: Acquired by partial postjuvenal molt, not involving wing-quills. Similar to adults in winter, but upper surface darker, more richly buff or ochraceous, gray of nape still more obscured; jugulum almost always more deeply buff, this color forming distinct band. *Juvenal*: Acquired by complete postnatal molt. Upper surface dull grayish light clay color or grayish cinnamon buff, head usually more grayish, streaked narrowly on pileum with olive brown or fuscous, slightly so also on rump, and rather broadly with fuscous black or fuscous on back and scapulars; wings and tail as in first winter, but lesser wing-coverts lighter and more buffy; wing-bars more yellowish; superciliary stripe barely indicated, but pale dull buff or buffy white, more or less mixed with gray or brown; sides of head dull pale buffy gray; jugulum washed with light buff; crissum dark cartridge buff; throat slightly,

CLAY-COLORED SPARROW, *Spizella pallida*

0 20 40 60 80
Scale in miles

?

Specimen Sight
record record

▲ △ Spring
● ○ Summer
▼ ▽ Fall
■ □ Winter

——— Approximate boundary
of subspecies' breeding range

? Questionable record

breast, sides, and flanks rather conspicuously, streaked with fuscous to chaetura black.

MEASUREMENTS: *Adult male*: Wing, 59.2–63.2 (average, 61.2) mm.; tail, 55.3–62.0 (58.2); bill (exposed culmen), 8.6–9.7 (9.1); height of bill at base, 5.3–5.8 (5.6); tarsus, 17.5–18.0 (17.8); middle toe without claw, 12.2–13.2 (12.4). *Adult female*: Wing, 57.7–63.8 (60.5); tail, 52.8–61.0 (57.2); bill, 8.6–9.7 (9.1); height of bill, 5.3–5.8 (5.6); tarsus, 16.8–18.0 (17.5); middle toe, 11.7–12.7 (12.2).

TEXAS: *Migration*: Collected north to Oldham and Potter, east to Cooke and Fort Bend, south to Cameron, west to El Paso cos. *Winter*: Taken northeast to Dallas, south to Cameron, west to Webb cos.

BREWER'S SPARROW, *Spizella breweri* Cassin

SPECIES ACCOUNT

A small, pale nondescript sparrow with finely black-streaked brownish crown (shows no median stripe); gray-brown eyebrow and malar stripe; black-streaked brownish back; two whitish wing-bars; plain dull white under parts. Length, 5½ in.; wingspan, 7¾; weight, ½ oz.

RANGE: S.w. Yukon, southeast to s.w. North Dakota, thence south to s. California, n. New Mexico, Oklahoma Panhandle, and Texas Panhandle (casually). Winters from s. California and s.w. Texas to c. Mexico.

TEXAS: (See map.) *Breeding*: Early May to late June (eggs, May 21 to June 12, 1876, C. A. H. McCauley) from about 3,000 to 4,000 ft. Very irregular and local in northern Panhandle. No nesting evidence in 20th century, but reported nesting in 1950's from adjacent areas of New Mexico and Oklahoma. *Migration*: Mid-Mar. to mid-May; mid-Sept. to early Nov. (extremes: Mar. 5, May 22; Sept. 5, Nov. 18). Common (some

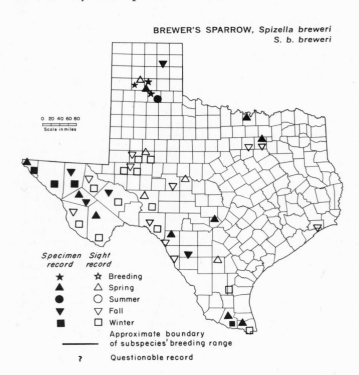

BREWER'S SPARROW, *Spizella breweri*
S. b. breweri

0 20 40 60 80
Scale in miles

Specimen Sight
record   record
★   ☆ Breeding
▲   △ Spring
●   ○ Summer
▼   ▽ Fall
■   □ Winter
━━━━ Approximate boundary
      of subspecies' breeding range
?   Questionable record

years) to uncommon west of Pecos River; fairly common to scarce in southern Panhandle and Midland vicinity; increasingly scarce east of 101st meridian to Dallas, upper coast, and Rio Grande delta. *Winter*: Mid-Oct. to early Apr. Fairly common to uncommon west of Pecos River; uncommon to scarce in southern Panhandle, Midland vicinity, and Del Rio region; casual south of 29th parallel.

HAUNTS AND HABITS: This species inhabits low trees and bushes of the West. The Common Brewer's Sparrow lives mostly in sagebrush (*Artemisia*) and similar vegetation made small and sparse by aridity; the Timberline Brewer's frequents cold-dwarfed plants. In Trans-Pecos Texas, this bird finds congenial migration and winter habitat within desert scrub. East of the Pecos Valley, where bushes are taller and closer together, most sightings of Brewer's Sparrows are based on immature Clay-colored Sparrows.

In summer, when insects—weevils, grasshoppers, ants, caterpillars, others—form a large portion of the diet, Brewer's Sparrows work low leaves and branches of bushes. With fall and winter, plant matter becomes the major source of sustenance; at this time they forage on the ground for seeds, mainly of pigweed, grama grass, and purslane. Flushed birds usually scatter afoot amid thickets. If they do take wing, they retreat in zigzag flight, often moving a considerable distance before dropping into a shrub. In autumn and winter, they assemble in flocks and associate freely with other sparrows, such as Black-throated, Chipping, Clay-colored, and White-crowned. Summer individuals are generally wary and reclusive; however, particularly prior to the peak of the breeding season, groups of males will gather at dawn and dusk to sing their buzzy song in chorus.

Spizella breweri song is a long varied musical series of rapid buzzy trills given on different pitches. It is suggestive of a weak Canary song. Delivery, usually from mid-March to July, is from a bush or fence wire. Note is a thin *tseet*.

DETAILED ACCOUNT: TWO SUBSPECIES

COMMON BREWER'S SPARROW, *Spizella breweri breweri* Cassin

DESCRIPTION: *Adults, nuptial plumage*: Acquired by partial prenuptial molt. Upper surface light buffy brown to buffy smoke gray—hindneck sometimes lighter and slightly more grayish—and conspicuously streaked, most broadly so on back and scapulars, with fuscous to fuscous black, but only slightly and obscurely streaked with hair brown on rump; tail between hair brown and buffy brown, feathers narrowly margined on outer webs with tilleul buff, narrowly on terminal portion of inner webs with same; primaries and secondaries also between hair brown and buffy brown, inner margins light drab to vinaceous buff, outer webs of primaries tilleul buff, and rather broader outer margins of secondaries light buffy brown; tertials fuscous, but broad outer margins wood brown to warm sayal brown, paler terminally; wing-coverts light fuscous or between hair brown and fuscous, lesser coverts broadly margined with color of back, median series broadly, greater coverts more narrowly, tipped with dull pale pinkish buff, outer margins of greater coverts light grayish olive to light buffy brown; broad superciliary stripe very pale dull pinkish buff to dull buffy white; auriculars dull buffy drab; postocular streak fuscous; eye-ring buffy white or grayish white; rather broad rictal stripe, extending backward under auriculars, and narrow submalar streak chaetura drab or fuscous to hair brown, enclosing a malar stripe of dull pale buff or buffy white; ground color of sides of neck similar to that of hindneck but not so conspicuously streaked, sometimes almost plain; sides and flanks between smoke gray and vinaceous buff; lower surface dull white but slightly washed with pale gray or very pale buff; lining of wing dull white or buffy white, posterior portion slightly mottled with smoke gray, and on outer part spotted with mouse gray. Bill dark brown, dull black, or deep plumbeous, but mandible and cutting edges of maxilla light lilaceous brown, light flesh color, dull lilaceous, or even yellow; iris hazel, raw umber, or black; legs and feet light brown or dull flesh color. *Adults, winter*: Acquired by complete postnuptial molt. Similar to nuptial adults, but colors more blended, upper surface thus duller and more uniform, its streaks narrower and less sharply defined due to more extensive light edgings of feathers; light edgings of tertials broader; lower surface more buffy. *First nuptial*: Acquired by partial prenuptial molt. Similar to nuptial adults, but upper surface duller, somewhat darker, and more decidedly buffy (less grayish); lower surface averaging slightly more buffy. *First winter*: Acquired by partial postjuvenal molt, which does not involve wing-quills or tail. Similar to adults in winter, but upper surface more buffy (less grayish); lower surface averaging slightly more buffy. *Juvenal*: Acquired by complete postnatal molt. Similar to nuptial adults, but upper surface rather more buffy, pileum more finely streaked, though mostly spotted, with fuscous; rump more buffy and spotted with fuscous; edgings of wings and tail more deeply buff; superciliary stripe not so clearly defined; lower surface rather more buffy, particularly jugulum, sides, and flanks, which are streaked or spotted with hair brown to light chaetura drab; crissum very pale dull buff. *Natal*: Light drab, buffy white, or pale tilleul buff.

MEASUREMENTS: *Adult male*: Wing, 60.5–64.5 (average, 61.7) mm.; tail, 58.4–67.1 (61.0); bill (exposed culmen), 8.1–8.6 (8.4); tarsus, 16.8–18.0 (17.3); middle toe without claw, 11.4–13.0 (12.2). *Adult female*: Wing, 57.4–59.9 (59.2); tail, 57.4–59.9 (58.7); bill, 8.1–8.6 (8.4); tarsus, 16.3–17.5 (17.3); middle toe, 11.4–13.0 (12.2).

RANGE: S. interior British Columbia to s.w. Saskatchewan and s.w. North Dakota, south (east of Cascades) to s. California, n. New Mexico, Oklahoma Panhandle, and Texas Panhandle (at least formerly). Winters from s. California and s.w. Texas through n. deserts and Central Plateau of Mexico to Jalisco and Guanajuato.

TEXAS: *Breeding*: Birds and eggs collected in 1876 in Randall, Armstrong, and Briscoe cos. by C. A. H. McCauley (see species account). *Migration*: Collected northeast to Cooke and Dallas, south to Cameron, west to El Paso cos. Irregularly fairly common. *Winter*: Taken northwest to El Paso and Culberson, southeast to Hidalgo cos. Irregularly fairly common.

NESTING: *Nest*: On uplands and lowlands; on plains, prairies, brushy slopes, and in canyons, usually in open country, such as desert scrub, and areas with scattered low trees; in bush, such as juniper or sage, usually but a few feet above ground; rather compactly made and often very well concealed; a cup of dry grasses, rootlets, shreds of sage or other bark, fine twigs, weed stalks and leaves; lined with rootlets, hair of horse, cow, and other animals, also rabbit and other fur. *Eggs*: 2–5, usually 4 or 5; ovate to rounded ovate; bluish white, light bluish green, or light greenish blue; with spots and lines of light or dark yellowish brown, reddish brown, and black, sometimes confluent in a wreath about large end; average size, 16.8 × 11.9 mm.

TIMBERLINE BREWER'S SPARROW, *Spizella breweri taverneri* Swarth and Brooks

DESCRIPTION: *Adults, nuptial plumage*: Similar to S. *b. breweri*, but wing and tail longer; bill more slender; upper surface darker, dark streaks on pileum and back broader; flanks darker;

throat and jugulum more washed with gray (less buffy). Bill darker, maxilla dark brown, tip dull black, mandible flesh color, tip also dull black; tarsus brownish flesh color; feet darker—pale drab.

MEASUREMENTS: *Adult male*: Wing, 61.5–66.3 (average, 64.3) mm.; tail, 62.5–68.1 (65.3); bill (exposed culmen), 7.1–8.6 (7.9); tarsus, 17.0–18.0 (17.3); middle toe without claw, 11.4–13.0 (12.2). *Adult female*: Wing, 59.9–62.0 (60.7); tail, 56.9–62.0 (59.4); bill, 8.1–8.6 (8.4); tarsus, 17.0–18.0 (17.8); middle toe, 11.4–12.7 (12.2).

RANGE: S.w. Yukon, south to s.e. British Columbia and s.w. Alberta. Winters presumably south to Arizona, New Mexico, and Trans-Pecos Texas.

TEXAS: *Winter*: Two specimens: Culberson Co., Van Horn (Mar. 6, 1939, W. A. Mayer); Brewster-Jeff Davis county line, 10 mi. northwest of Alpine (Mar. 9, 1935, J. Van Tyne).

FIELD SPARROW, *Spizella pusilla* (Wilson)

SPECIES ACCOUNT

A small, pink-billed sparrow with rusty cap; grayish face; narrow buffy eye-ring; lacks distinct facial stripes. Blackish-streaked reddish brown above; two white wing-bars; clear buffy white below; pinkish legs. Length, 5½ in.; wingspan, 8¼; weight, ½ oz.

RANGE: E. Montana across Great Lakes region to s. Maine, thence south through e. United States and portions of Great Plains to c. Texas, Louisiana, and s. Georgia. Winters chiefly from Missouri, Ohio, and Massachusetts through s.e. United States to Trans-Pecos Texas, n.e. Mexico, Gulf coast, and c. Florida.

TEXAS: (See map.) *Breeding*: Late Mar. to late July (eggs, Apr. 6 to July 10) from 300 to 2,300 ft. Common to fairly common on eastern half of Edwards Plateau; uncommon and local (apparently increasingly so) along Oklahoma border (east of 100th meridian)

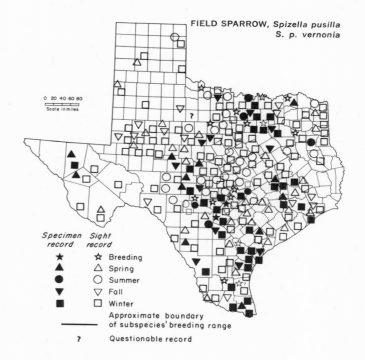

FIELD SPARROW, *Spizella pusilla*
S. p. vernonia

0 20 40 60 80
Scale in miles

Specimen   Sight
record   record

★   ☆ Breeding
▲   △ Spring
●   ○ Summer
▼   ▽ Fall
■   □ Winter

——— Approximate boundary of subspecies' breeding range

?   Questionable record

south to Stephens Co., Dallas, Tyler, and Nacogdoches; has nested recently in Bee Co. (1970, 1971), Brooks Co. (1964, 1969), and possibly Kenedy Co. (1972). *Winter*: Mid-Oct. to mid-Apr. (extremes: Aug. 16, May 18). Usually abundant within breeding range; common to fairly common in most other sections east of Pecos Valley, but uncommon to scarce in northern Panhandle and south Texas brush country; fairly common (some years) to rare in eastern two-thirds of Trans-Pecos; no record for El Paso region.

HAUNTS AND HABITS: The Field Sparrow could very well be named the Old Field Sparrow. Old fields abandoned long enough to have scattered bushes are favored haunts throughout its eastern U.S. range. So are lightly brushed and wooded areas with grass, wild flowers, or other forbs between the bushes and trees. Partially cleared places within juniper-oak growth of the Edwards Plateau usually hold substantial populations of Field Sparrows in both summer and winter; in favorable winters, flocks here can be large (but usually not compact) and numerous.

On the ground, the Field Sparrow hops about seed-searching, taking mainly those of bristlegrass, panicum, dropseed, crabgrass, pigweed, amaranth, knotweed, chickweed, vervain, gromwell, and purslane. Insects (chiefly beetles, grasshoppers, and caterpillars), also a few spiders and earthworms, form a chief portion of the summer diet.

A thin querulous *tseee* is the call of this sparrow. From late February into the hot days of August, the male Field Sparrow sings his sweet plaintive song from atop a bush or small tree. His notes are slow deliberate whistles that accelerate into a trill. The sound has often been likened to a tiny ball bouncing to rest on a hard surface.

DETAILED ACCOUNT: FOUR SUBSPECIES

EASTERN FIELD SPARROW, *Spizella pusilla pusilla* (Wilson)

DESCRIPTION: *Adult male, nuptial plumage*: Acquired by wear from winter plumage. Pileum dark hazel to dull russet, with a more or less well defined median stripe of grayish olive or light grayish olive; hindneck light mouse gray, sometimes washed with russet and sometimes entirely russet on median portion; back and scapulars brighter than crown—russet to dark cinnamon rufous, but broadly streaked with fuscous black or fuscous and with dull pale buff; rump and upper tail-coverts between grayish olive and light buffy brown; tail hair brown to dark hair brown, very narrow inner edges of most of feathers drab, outer webs very narrowly margined, particularly toward base, with mouse gray; primaries and secondaries dark hair brown, inner edges drab to avellaneous; narrow outer margins of primaries drab to buffy drab, those of secondaries between sayal brown and snuff brown; tertials fuscous, outer edges cinnamon, becoming paler, even pale buff, terminally; lesser wing-coverts mouse gray, washed with buff; median coverts fuscous, more or less broadly tipped with white or buffy white; greater coverts fuscous, with broad edgings of drab on outer webs, also rather broad tips of buffy white or dull pale buff on outer webs and of sayal brown on inner webs; sides of head, including superciliary stripe and eye-ring, light mouse gray to dull smoke gray; short broad stripe behind and above auriculars like pileum; auriculars often more or less washed with buff or dull cinnamon; an often poorly defined malar streak pale dull gray or dull cinnamon;

jugulum, sides, flanks, and sometimes crissum dull pinkish buff; remainder of lower surface dull white, buffy white, or grayish white; lining of wing buffy white, outer portion somewhat spotted with mouse gray. Bill vinaceous cinnamon, pinkish vinaceous, reddish brown, or reddish pink, but tip of maxilla darker; iris vandyke brown or reddish brown; legs and feet clay color, yellowish ecru drab, reddish brown, buff pink, or reddish pink; toes usually darker; claws brown or slate black. *Adult male, winter*: Acquired by complete postnuptial molt. Similar to nuptial adult male, but colors of upper surface more blended, thus duller and more uniform, as well as averaging somewhat darker; median crown-stripe broader, more buffy (less grayish); nape more veiled with buff or reddish brown, streaks on back and scapulars less sharply defined by reason of broader light edgings of feathers; light outer edgings of tertials also wider; sides of head more buffy (less grayish); lower surface more conspicuously and extensively buff, particularly jugulum, sides, and flanks. *Adult female, nuptial*: Acquired by wear from winter. Similar to nuptial adult male but smaller; upper parts lighter, duller, more grayish (less rufous), sometimes conspicuously so. *Adult female, winter*: Acquired by complete postnuptial molt. Similar to nuptial adult female, but upper surface duller, more blended, gray or buff edgings of feathers broader and, therefore, black streaks more obscured. *Male and female, first nuptial*: Acquired by wear from first winter. Very similar to nuptial adult male and female, respectively. *Male and female, first winter*: Acquired by partial postjuvenal molt, which does not involve wing-quills or most of tail. Similar to adult male and female in winter, respectively, but upper surface darker, more rufescent, and more deeply ochraceous; lower surface somewhat more deeply buff. Bill vinaceous rufous, but maxilla somewhat darker; iris vandyke brown; legs and feet hazel; claws drab. *Male, juvenal*: Acquired by complete postnatal molt. Pileum between dull sayal brown and snuff brown, very slightly and obscurely streaked or spotted with darker brown; back and scapulars broadly streaked with fuscous, russet, and dull cinnamon buff; rump dull rufescent drab; wings and tail as in first winter, but lesser coverts less grayish (more dull brownish), or edged with dull pale buff; sides of head dull buff or rufescent drab; chin, throat, and jugulum dull light cream buff; lower breast and abdomen dull light cartridge buff to buffy white; sides and flanks more buffy, sometimes like anterior lower parts; jugulum, sides, flanks, and sometimes breast streaked with hair brown to fuscous. Bill reddish brown, reddish pink, or slate gray, but mandible lighter, sometimes yellowish along gonys; iris dark brown; legs and feet flesh color, reddish pink, or clay color. *Female, juvenal*: Acquired by complete postnatal molt. Similar to juvenal male, but averaging paler above. *Natal* (this plumage of this race not seen in Texas): Mouse gray.

MEASUREMENTS: *Adult male*: Wing, 62.0–66.0 (average, 63.8) mm.; tail, 60.5–69.6 (64.3); bill (exposed culmen), 8.6–9.9 (9.4); height of bill at base, 6.1–6.6 (6.4); tarsus, 17.5–19.6 (18.3); middle toe without claw, 11.9–13.0 (12.2). *Adult female*: Wing, 58.7–63.5 (60.5); tail, 57.4–64.0 (60.2); bill, 8.6–9.4 (9.1); height of bill, 5.8–6.6 (6.4); tarsus, 17.0–18.5 (17.8); middle toe, 11.4–12.4 (11.9).

RANGE: E. Minnesota across Great Lakes region to s. Maine, thence south through e. United States (east of 100th meridian) to e. Kansas, e. Arkansas, e. Louisiana, and n. Florida (casually). Winters chiefly from Missouri, Ohio, and Massachusetts to s. Texas, Gulf coast, and s.w. Florida.

TEXAS: *Winter*: Taken in Tom Green (Oct. 31), Menard (May 6), Bexar, Nueces (Mar. 9), and Cameron cos. Scarce.

NESTING: (This race does not nest in Texas.) *Nest*: On hill slopes, in valleys, and lowlands; usually in more open parts of country, such as brushy pastures, edges of woodland, open brushy woods, and various kinds of cultivated areas, such as orchards, fields, fence rows, gardens, ornamental grounds, and even about country dwellings; on ground or in a low bush 2–10 ft. above ground, in briar or weed patch, under bush or tuft of grass, sometimes well concealed; loose, bulky cup; composed of weed stalks, leaves, rootlets, and sedges; lined with fine grasses, shreds of bark, thin threadlike stems of plants, and horse or cow hair. *Eggs*: 3–5, usually 4; ovate to rounded ovate; buffy white, greenish white, bluish white, or pale greenish blue; speckled and spotted with various shades of yellowish and reddish brown, dull brick red, ferruginous, and grayish purple, and with shell markings of lilac and lilac gray, sometimes these markings so dense as to obscure ground color, at least at large end; average size, 17.3 × 13.2 mm.

TEXAS FIELD SPARROW, Spizella pusilla vernonia
Oberholser, new subspecies (see Appendix A)

DESCRIPTION: *Adult male and female, nuptial plumage*: Similar to *S. p. pusilla*, but upper surface duller, lighter, and more grayish, particularly on back and pileum, where russet and cinnamon rufous areas are less extensive. Similar to *S. p. arenacea* (see below), but wing and tail shorter; upper surface darker, much more tawny or russet (less grayish), pileum with much more russet, and black streaks on back broader; lower surface darker, jugulum more buffy (less grayish). *Natal*: Probably similar to *S. p. pusilla*.

MEASUREMENTS: *Adult male*: Wing, 62.0–66.0 (average, 64.3) mm.; tail, 61.5–67.1 (64.8); bill (exposed culmen), 7.9–9.7 (9.1); tarsus, 16.5–20.1 (18.3); middle toe without claw, 10.4–11.9 (11.4). *Adult female*: Wing, 58.9–63.0 (61.2); tail, 59.9–65.0 (62.2); bill, 7.6–9.7 (8.9); tarsus, 16.0–19.0 (18.0); middle toe, 10.9–13.2 (12.2).

TYPE: Adult male, no. 184188, U.S. National Museum, Biological Surveys collection; Japonica, Kerr Co., Texas; July 8, 1902; Merritt Cary, original no., 33.

RANGE: C. Kansas and s.w. Missouri, south through Oklahoma and w. Arkansas to n. and c. Texas. Winters from n.e. Oklahoma and n.w. Arkansas to w. Nuevo León, n.e. Tamaulipas, Gulf coast, and n.e. Florida.

TEXAS: *Breeding*: Collected northeast to Lamar, southwest to Travis, Bexar (eggs), and Kerr cos. *Winter*: Taken north to Cooke, east to Galveston, south to Cameron, west to Dimmit (Mar. 6) and Concho cos. Fairly common.

NESTING: Similar to *S. p. pusilla*, but average egg size, 17.3 × 12.7 mm.

NEBRASKA FIELD SPARROW, Spizella pusilla perissura
Oberholser, new subspecies (see Appendix A)

DESCRIPTION: *Adult male and female, nuptial plumage*: Similar to *S. p. pusilla*, but wings and tail longer, particularly the latter; upper surface much paler, more grayish (less rufous or russet); pileum with often very little russet; black streaks on back narrower; lower surface paler, jugulum averaging more grayish (less buffy). Similar to *S. p. vernonia*, but wing and tail longer; upper surface and sides of head more grayish (less rufescent), also lighter, pileum with much less russet, and black streaks on back narrower; lower surface paler, jugulum usually more grayish. These differences are not so great, except in size, as those distinguishing the present race from *S. p. pusilla*.

MEASUREMENTS: *Adult male*: Wing, 64.0–71.7 (average, 68.3) mm.; tail, 67.6–74.7 (70.1); bill (exposed culmen), 8.6–9.9 (9.1); tarsus, 18.3–20.6 (19.3); middle toe without claw, 11.4–13.7 (12.2). *Adult female*: Wing, 59.9–64.0 (62.5); tail, 62.0–64.5 (63.2); bill, 8.6–9.4 (8.9); tarsus, 18.0–19.6 (18.8); middle toe, 10.9–12.4 (11.7).

TYPE: Adult male, no. 113894, U.S. National Museum, Biological Surveys collection; Valentine, Nebraska; June 21, 1888; Vernon Bailey, original no., 2.

RANGE: S.e. South Dakota and Nebraska. Winters from c. Oklahoma through w. Texas to w. Nuevo León and n. Tamaulipas.

TEXAS: *Winter*: Taken north to Dallas (Mar. 15), east to Brazos (Mar. 12), south to Cameron, west to Culberson (May 1) cos. Fairly common.

WESTERN FIELD SPARROW, Spizella pusilla arenacea
Chadbourne

DESCRIPTION: *Adult male and female, nuptial plumage*: Simi-

lar to *S. p. perissura*, but still paler above and below; more grayish above, nearly lacking rufous edgings on back and with much less and decidedly paler russet on head.

MEASUREMENTS: *Adult male*: Wing, 65.5–70.1 (average, 67.3) mm.; tail, 67.6–74.7 (70.1); bill (exposed culmen), 8.6–9.9 (9.1); tarsus, 18.5–20.1 (19.3); middle toe without claw, 11.9–14.0 (12.7). *Adult female*: Wing, 62.0–65.0 (63.2); tail, 61.0–68.6 (65.0); bill, 8.6–9.4 (9.1); tarsus, 17.5–19.0 (18.3); middle toe, 11.4–12.4 (11.9).

RANGE: E. Montana, North Dakota, and South Dakota. Winters from s.e. South Dakota (casually) to s. Texas and c. Louisiana.

TEXAS: *Winter*: Taken north to Tom Green (May 11), east to Blanco and Aransas, south to Brooks, west to Jeff Davis (Mar. 29) and Culberson cos. Uncommon.

BLACK-CHINNED SPARROW, Spizella atrogularis (Cabanis)

SPECIES ACCOUNT

A small, pink-billed, juncolike sparrow with gray head, neck, and under parts; black-streaked brown back; two buffy wing-bars; blackish tail showing no white. *Male*: has black face and chin. Length, 5½ in.; wingspan, 8; weight, ½ oz.

RANGE: C. California, s. Nevada, s.w. Utah, c. Arizona, s. New Mexico, and Trans-Pecos Texas, south to n. Baja California, and through arid mountains of mainland Mexico to Guerrero and Oaxaca. Northern races winter from s. California, s. Arizona, and w. Texas southward.

TEXAS: (See map.) *Breeding*: Probably Mar. to late July (no egg dates available, but nest recently located in Guadalupe Mts., Culberson Co., by F. R. Gehlbach) from 5,500 to 8,000 ft. Common (seldom) to scarce in

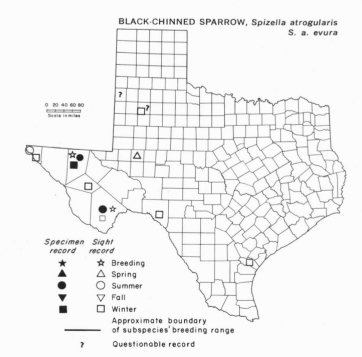

BLACK-CHINNED SPARROW, *Spizella atrogularis*
S. a. evura

0 20 40 60 80
Scale in miles

Specimen record	Sight record	
★	☆	Breeding
▲	△	Spring
●	○	Summer
▼	▽	Fall
■	▢	Winter

——— Approximate boundary of subspecies' breeding range

? Questionable record

942

The Bird Life of Texas

mountains of Trans-Pecos. *Winter*: Aug. to late Mar., once to May 8. Very irregular in mountains of Trans-Pecos—common (some years) to uncommon in Davis Mts., common (seldom) to scarce in Chisos Mts., uncommon to scarce in Guadalupe and Franklin mts.; scarce to casual in Del Rio region. Accidental at Midland (May 8, 1972, Kate Raney, et al.) and on central coast (Welder Wildlife Refuge, Aug. 3, 1966, B. A. Fall, Stephen Nesbitt). Questionable sighting at Lubbock.

HAUNTS AND HABITS: The Black-chinned Sparrow is a *Spizella* of brushy mountain slopes. The high (over 5,000 ft.), arid ranges of the Trans-Pecos provide suitable Texas habitat throughout the year. Occasionally, wintering birds will accept scrubby desert foothills and bushy canyons at lower elevations.

The austerity of its rugged haunts and its generally shy manner combine to make the Black-chinned Sparrow less than easy to observe. When approached, it flees quickly to cover of thick brush. Low in shrubs and on the ground, it forages for grass and weed seeds and some insects, though its exact preferences are apparently little known. In order to drink or bathe, the Blackchin must range far to find widely spaced watering places at canyon streams and seeps.

A sharp *chit* and a faint *tsip* are the usual call notes. In spring and early summer (early April to mid-July), a male proclaims territory from atop a low bush with his plaintive, high-pitched song. Similar to the Field Sparrow's, it begins with several thin clear *sweet*'s and quickens into a slightly descending, somewhat rough trill.

DETAILED ACCOUNT: ONE SUBSPECIES

ARIZONA BLACK-CHINNED SPARROW, *Spizella atrogularis evura* Coues

DESCRIPTION: *Adult male, nuptial plumage*: Acquired by partial prenuptial molt. Forehead deep mouse gray or dark mouse gray but sometimes mouse gray like remainder of pileum and hindneck; back dull sayal brown, scapulars mostly cinnamon rufous, conspicuously streaked with fuscous or fuscous black; rump mouse gray washed with buffy brown; tail rather light fuscous, narrowly edged on outer webs and largely on inner webs, at least terminally, with very pale pinkish buff; primaries and secondaries light fuscous, inner edges, except at tips, between light drab and vinaceous buff, outer edges of primaries very narrowly dull smoke gray, and broader outer edges of secondaries sayal brown; greater and median coverts and tertials fuscous, outer webs of the last dull or light pinkish buff; lesser wing-coverts brownish mouse gray, median coverts broadly tipped on outer webs, as are also greater coverts, with pinkish buff, forming two rather evident wing-bars; outer edges of greater coverts sayal brown; lores brownish black to rather deep mouse gray; rest of sides of head and of neck rather light mouse gray; chin and throat dark mouse gray; remainder of lower surface between neutral gray and smoke gray, except abdomen, center of lower breast, and crissum grayish or buffy white; under tail-coverts with broad median streaks of rather light mouse gray to smoke gray; lining of wing between smoke gray and drab gray, sometimes dull white, outermost coverts with darker spots. Maxilla bay or vinaceous cinnamon; mandible buff pink or vinaceous cinnamon, but tip somewhat darker; iris auburn; legs verona brown; toes and claws fuscous black. *Adult male, winter*: Acquired by complete postnuptial molt. Similar to nuptial adult male, but pileum more or less overlaid with brown on tips of feathers; colors of back and scapulars more or less blended, black streaks less sharply defined by reason of broader light edgings of feathers; light edgings of tertials and wing-coverts broader; chin and upper throat with less dark mouse gray, this usually confined to chin; lower surface distinctly washed with buff. *Adult female, nuptial*: Acquired by partial prenuptial molt. Similar to nuptial adult male but smaller; pileum and hindneck lighter and somewhat more brownish (less purely grayish); back averaging paler; wings and tail somewhat lighter; lower surface lighter and more buffy, chin and throat lighter and less extensively dark gray, usually deep mouse gray. *Adult female, winter*: Acquired by complete postnuptial molt. Similar to nuptial adult female, but colors of upper parts more blended; pileum more overlaid with brown or buff, dark streaks of back somewhat obscured by light edgings of feathers and, therefore, less sharply defined; light edgings of tertials broader; chin without deep mouse gray of nuptial, thus like remainder of anterior lower parts. Similar to adult male in winter but smaller, upper surface somewhat paler and without dark mouse gray on chin. *Male, first nuptial*: Acquired by partial prenuptial molt. Similar to nuptial adult male, but pileum decidedly more brownish (less clearly grayish); rump slightly so; lower surface more washed with buff, dark gray of chin and upper throat more brownish and less in extent. *Male, first winter*: Acquired by partial postjuvenal molt. Similar to adult male in winter, but upper surface lighter; pileum still more overlaid with brown or buff; chin pale gray, washed with buff, but with no dark gray; throat with sometimes a few small spots of gray; sides of head lighter. *Female, first nuptial*: Acquired by partial prenuptial molt. Similar to nuptial adult female, but pileum darker, more brownish (less clearly grayish); sides of head somewhat more buffy, as is usually lower surface; dark gray of chin lighter, of much less extent, or absent. *Female, first winter*: Acquired by partial postjuvenal molt. Similar to adult female in winter, but upper surface decidedly lighter; pileum duller and even more brownish (less grayish); sides of head lighter; lower parts averaging also somewhat more buffy. *Male, juvenal*: Acquired by complete postnatal molt. Similar to first nuptial female, but pileum and hindneck lighter and less brownish—fuscous or fuscous black; back duller, paler, more grayish, and with broader black streaks; wing-coverts more deeply buff—cinnamon buff to sayal brown or cinnamon; sides of head less buffy; lower parts duller, rather darker, and usually less buffy, and on both anterior and posterior portions very obscurely and lightly streaked with darker gray; chin with no indication of dark gray but concolor with rest of anterior lower surface; abdomen white. *Female, juvenal*: Acquired by complete postnatal molt. Similar to juvenal male but upper surface darker, more brownish or rufescent on both pileum and back, pileum decidedly more brownish, back darker and more deeply ochraceous or rufescent; wings more rufescent; jugulum more strongly tinged with buff. *Natal*: Drab or buffy drab.

MEASUREMENTS: *Adult male*: Wing, 64.0–67.6 (average, 65.8) mm.; tail, 68.1–73.9 (71.1); bill (exposed culmen), 9.4–10.4 (9.9); height of bill at base, 6.6–7.1 (6.9); tarsus, 20.6–21.1 (20.9); middle toe without claw, 13.0–13.5 (13.2). *Adult female*: Wing, 60.5–64.0 (62.2); tail, 65.0–70.6 (68.6); bill, 8.6–9.4 (9.1); height of bill, 5.6–6.6 (6.1); tarsus, 19.0–21.6 (19.8); middle toe, 11.4–13.0 (12.2).

RANGE: C. California (chiefly eastern slope of s. Sierra Nevada), s. Nevada, s.w. Utah, c. Arizona, s. New Mexico, and Trans-Pecos Texas, south to n.e. Sonora. Winters from s. Arizona, n. Sonora, and w. Texas southward.

TEXAS: *Breeding*: Collected in Culberson and Brewster cos. *Winter*: One specimen: Culberson Co., McKittrick Canyon (Jan. 3, 1939, G. H. Lowery, Jr.).

NESTING: *Nest*: On desert mountains; on slopes or in canyons; preferably in brush but also in more open parts of meadows; ordinarily in low bush, often well concealed; a rather compact cup; composed of grasses, weed stems, and similar materials; lined with fine grasses and horsehair. *Eggs*: 3–5, ovate to rounded ovate; light greenish blue or bluish green; unspotted or rarely very sparingly marked with dark brown and brownish black; average size, 17.3 × 12.7 mm.

HARRIS' SPARROW, *Zonotrichia querula* (Nuttall)

Species Account

Very large (often cited as largest American sparrow). Has pink bill; striking black crown, face, and bib; grayish cheeks; black-striped brownish back; two white wing-bars; whitish breast, abdomen; brown-streaked buffy sides. In winter, most individuals show much buff about their heads and reduced areas of black. Length, 7½ in.; wingspan, 10¾; weight, 1½ oz.

RANGE: N. Canada—from Mackenzie Valley to Hudson Bay, south to n.e. Saskatchewan and n. Manitoba. Winters normally from s.e. Nebraska, Kansas, and w. Missouri through Oklahoma and n.w. Arkansas to c. Texas.

TEXAS: (See map.) *Winter*: Early Nov. to mid-Apr. (extremes: Sept. 3, May 9). Very common to common in central portions (between 96th and 99th meridians) from Oklahoma border to Austin, irregularly to San Antonio, increasingly less numerous west, east, and south of this central strip; rare, often absent, in Panhandle, south Texas brush country, and along eastern boundary of state; casual west of Pecos River; accidental in Rio Grande delta (Laguna Atascosa Nat. Wildlife Refuge, Jan. 2, 1955, E. B. Kincaid, Jr.).

HAUNTS AND HABITS: The Harris' Sparrow is very much an edge-of-the-woods bird. In Canada it nests on the ground where cold-stunted spruces give way to open tundra. The nest of grass, moss, and weed stems is usually sunk in the earth at the base of a tree or shrub or in a mossy hummock surrounded by water. In its migration and wintering on the Great Plains, it frequents areas where streams, hedgerows, and shelter belts carry some eastern-style trees and bushes westward into open prairie country. Thus, in the cold months in central Texas, almost any patch of brush or grove of scrubby trees at the edge of a weedy pasture, field, or creek is likely to contain Harris' Sparrows.

On the breeding ground, this sparrow is extremely elusive; wintering birds are generally less wary. When frightened, they ordinarily fly up from the ground and perch rather high in a tree. Largely terrestrial feeders, Harris' Sparrows rustle noisily as they scratch towhee fashion for seeds of ragweed, smartweed, knotweed, pigweed, bristlegrass; also wild fruits, pyracantha, others. Some animal matter (up to 40 percent in summer; about 8 percent in winter) is eaten: insects—leafhoppers, grasshoppers, and beetles; also spiders and snails.

Harris' Sparrow call notes include a loud *cheenk* and a *chip!* The winter song, which resembles a White-throated Sparrow's, is a series of high, clear, quavering minor notes intermingled with husky chuckling sounds. Summer song, plaintive and flutelike, is one to five quavering notes, equally pitched, followed after a pause with several clear notes, higher or lower in pitch. During the nesting season, the males sound as if they were singing in chorus.

Detailed Account: No Subspecies

DESCRIPTION: *Adult male, nuptial plumage*: Acquired by partial prenuptial molt. Pileum black, this sometimes extending over anterior part of median portion of hindneck; hindneck between mouse gray and neutral gray, median portion often clove brown to bister, or at least streaked with this color; remainder of upper surface between grayish olive and drab, back somewhat more rufescent or buffy and broadly streaked, as are also scapulars, with fuscous to fuscous black and with grayish buff or buffy white; upper tail-coverts tipped with dull grayish white; tail dark hair brown to between hair brown and buffy brown, but feathers narrowly margined on outer webs with color of rump, except outermost pair, which is edged with dull buffy white or brownish white, also most of feathers very narrowly margined for at least terminal half on inner webs and often more broadly tipped on both webs with white or buffy white; primaries and secondaries dark hair brown, but inner edges of secondaries and of primaries, except at tips of primaries, dull vinaceous buff to dull drab, outer edges of primaries narrowly margined with color of rump, outer edges of inner secondaries similar but somewhat more rufescent; tertials between fuscous and olive brown, outer edges more rufescent brown, between snuff brown and wood brown and cinnamon buff, tertials also tipped on both webs with pale pinkish buff or tilleul buff; greater and median coverts between fuscous and olive brown, outer edges of greater coverts of same grayish olive as rump, but often much lighter and more buffy, the innermost of these feathers buffy or rufescent brown like tertials; both median and greater coverts broadly tipped with white or buffy white, forming two conspicuous wing-bars; lesser coverts between hair brown and fuscous, broadly edged and tipped with grayish olive; lores, malar region, a rather large postauricular spot, chin, throat, and middle of jugulum black, but black of jugulum often more or less mixed with white; remainder of sides of head and of anterior part of neck between smoke gray and drab gray, the broad postocular stripe which extends to hindneck somewhat lighter, and auriculars often decidedly washed with buff; sides of jugulum, sometimes sides of

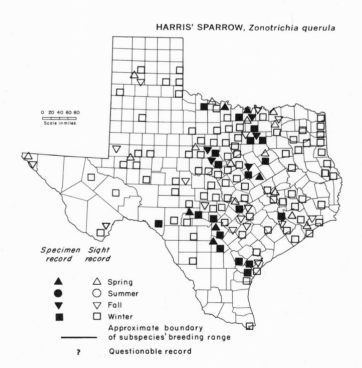

HARRIS' SPARROW, *Zonotrichia querula*

0 20 40 60 80
Scale in miles

Specimen record / Sight record

▲ △ Spring
● ○ Summer
▼ ▽ Fall
■ □ Winter

——— Approximate boundary of subspecies' breeding range

?   Questionable record

throat, together with breast and abdomen, white, but abdomen sometimes washed with buff; sides and flanks between drab or light hair brown and buffy brown, washed with pinkish buff or cinnamon buff, sides broadly and conspicuously, flanks obscurely, streaked with fuscous to hair brown, sometimes sides of breast streaked with auburn to bay; crissum dull light cream buff; lining of wing dull vinaceous buff, more or less mottled or spotted on outer side with drab to light hair brown. Bill pale cinnamon, rather dull yellowish red, reddish brown, or coral red; iris burnt umber; legs light, rather reddish flesh color, or light cinnamon; toes fawn color; claws dark brown or dull black. *Adult male, winter*: Acquired by complete postnuptial molt. Similar to nuptial adult male, but upper surface decidedly more buffy, brownish, and ochraceous (less grayish); hindneck lighter and more rufescent—between cinnamon brown and russet; feathers of pileum much tipped with dull white or dull buff; blackish or dark brown streaks of back duller and more brownish, less sharply defined, being more obscured by lighter edgings of feathers; outer light edgings of tertials broader; wing-bars somewhat broader and more buffy; sides of head and of anterior part of neck cinnamon buff to dull light tawny olive; lores sometimes mixed with grayish white, pale gray, or dull buff; sides and flanks rather more buffy. Bill light reddish brown, but tip usually rather dark brown, and base of mandible paler —or bill dull flesh color, paler below; iris dark brown; legs wood brown; feet prout brown. *Adult female, nuptial*: Acquired by partial prenuptial molt. Similar to nuptial adult male but smaller; black of head duller, somewhat more brownish, that of pileum usually less extended posteriorly; lores, malar region, chin, and throat not so intensively black (more brownish or grayish). *Adult female, winter*: Acquired by complete postnuptial molt. Similar to nuptial adult female, but upper surface much more deeply buff, ochraceous, or brown, feathers of pileum much tipped with dull buff or dull white, dark brown or blackish streaks of back less sharply defined, being more obscured by light edgings of feathers; light edgings of tertials broader; lores much mixed with dull buff or buffy white; sides of head dull cinnamon buff or dull tawny olive, instead of gray. Similar to adult male in winter but smaller; black of pileum more brownish, less extensive posteriorly, duller and more obscured by whitish or buffy tips of feathers; lores less blackish. *Male, second nuptial*: Acquired by partial prenuptial molt. Practically identical with nuptial adult male. *Male, second winter*: Acquired by complete postnuptial molt. Similar to adult male in winter, but differing chiefly in having throat partly white, separating black of chin from that of jugulum, instead of solidly black as in adult. *Male, first nuptial*: Acquired by partial prenuptial molt. Similar to nuptial adult male, but black of pileum somewhat more brownish and usually less extensive posteriorly; sides of head decidedly more buffy (less purely gray). *Male, first winter*: Acquired by partial postjuvenal molt, which does not affect wing-quills or tail. Similar to adult male in winter, but black of pileum less extensive, duller, more brownish, and largely replaced or obscured by buffy white, dull buff, or dull brown (like hindneck) tips and edgings of feathers; chin and throat white, buffy white, or dull buff; black of jugulum much reduced in extent and replaced by fuscous, fuscous black, or blackish mouse gray; lores dull cinnamon buff, often mixed with dull gray. Bill dull reddish brown or blackish brown, but cutting edges and corners of mouth dull yellow; iris dark brown. *Female, first nuptial*: Acquired by partial prenuptial molt. Similar to nuptial adult female, but sides of head, particularly auriculars, much more decidedly buff (less purely grayish); thus, very much like first nuptial male but smaller and black of chin and lores less purely black (more brownish or mixed with dull gray). *Female, first winter*: Acquired by partial postjuvenal molt, not involving wing-quills or tail. Similar to adult female in winter, but pileum more brownish (less blackish), this still more obscured by broader and more numerous edgings and tips of dull buff and brown; lores dull cinnamon buff or cinnamon buff mixed with mouse gray; chin and throat dull pale buff or buffy white; black markings of jugulum duller, lighter, and more brownish, replaced by fuscous, fuscous black, or blackish mouse gray. Similar to first winter male but smaller, dark area of pileum not so extended posteriorly, likewise more brownish and more obscured by light edgings of feathers; general tone of upper surface averaging lighter and less heavily streaked. Bill reddish yellow; iris and feet brown. *Juvenal*: Acquired by complete postnatal molt. Pileum fuscous black to chaetura black or brownish black, more or less streaked or spotted with buffy white, cartridge buff, or dull light cream buff, but occiput bister to dark bister, somewhat mixed with fuscous black; hindneck between olive brown and bister but much streaked or spotted with chamois, dull cream buff, or buffy white, these markings imparting slight collared effect; back sayal brown, tawny olive, fuscous, or fuscous black, much spotted and streaked with dull light cream buff, dull light cinnamon buff, or dull light buff; rump dull tawny olive to saccardo umber, streaked or spotted with chaetura drab, or between drab and wood brown, narrowly streaked with fuscous and fuscous black; scapulars and lesser wing-coverts dull snuff brown with large central spots of fuscous; median coverts tipped with dull pale buff; greater coverts tipped with dull pinkish buff; remainder of wings similar to corresponding parts of first winter female; auriculars sayal brown to dull cinnamon buff, more or less spotted or narrowly streaked or mottled with fuscous or light fuscous; remainder of sides of head dull cream buff to light cream buff, somewhat spotted or streaked with fuscous to buffy brown; lower surface cartridge buff, cream buff, or pale pinkish buff, but chin and throat usually tinged with pale gray; crissum light pinkish buff; sides and flanks also pinkish buff; jugulum, sides, flanks, and sometimes breast and throat streaked with hair brown to chaetura black, these streaks densest on jugulum and sides.

MEASUREMENTS: *Adult male*: Wing, 87.4–91.2 (average, 89.2) mm.; tail, 79.7–85.9 (83.8); bill (exposed culmen), 12.7–13.2 (13.0); height of bill at base, 8.6–9.7 (9.1); tarsus, 23.4–24.6 (24.1); middle toe without claw, 16.0–17.8 (17.3). *Adult female*: Wing, 80.0–85.3 (82.8); tail, 77.2–80.2 (79.0); bill, 12.2–12.7 (12.4); height of bill, 8.6–9.7 (9.1); tarsus, 23.4–24.1 (23.9); middle toe, 16.0–17.3 (16.5).

TEXAS: *Winter*: Taken north to Wilbarger and Cooke, east to Waller, south to San Patricio, west to Val Verde cos. An adult bird was captured, photographed, banded, then released in Brewster Co., Panther Junction (early Dec., 1968, R. H. Wauer).

WHITE-CROWNED SPARROW, *Zonotrichia leucophrys* (Forster)

SPECIES ACCOUNT

A large, pinkish-billed sparrow with bold black and white stripes on top half of head. Brown-streaked gray above; two white wing-bars; clear gray breast. Length, 7 in.; wingspan, 10; weight, 1 oz.

RANGE: S.e. British Columbia and s.w. Alberta to s.e. Mackenzie and n. Manitoba, east across n. Canada to Quebec and Labrador, and south through w. United States to c. California, c. Nevada, n. Arizona, and n. New Mexico. Winters from s.w. British Columbia, n. Utah, n. Colorado, Kansas, and w. North Carolina to c. Mexico, U.S. Gulf coast, and Florida (rarely); also Cuba.

TEXAS: (See map.) *Winter*: Late Oct. to early May (extremes: Sept. 15, June 6). Very common, verging on abundant, to fairly common in western three-quarters; common (some years) to rare in eastern quarter.

HAUNTS AND HABITS: In their boreal and high mountain summer homes, White-crowned Sparrows choose

White-crowned Sparrow, *Zonotrichia leucophrys*

open scrubby forests containing dwarf firs, spruces, alpine flowers, and sedges—cold- and snow-adapted plants. The nest is usually built on the ground under a bush or tree with low-hanging branches; it is a sturdy cup of grass, bark, lichens, and moss, lined with fine root fibers. Wintering Whitecrowns occur widely in Texas, but are most numerous in low altitude, flat, semiarid brushlands where plants are adapted to heat and dryness. The birds seem partial to areas where mesquite dominates. Individuals and groups often take shelter in wood and brush piles, and thickets.

Whitecrowns, like their close relatives, feed generally on the ground where they scratch vigorously for seeds of ragweed, pigweed, sunflower, amaranth, goosefoot, knotweed, panicum, and many others. In winter, they often enter cow lots to feed on waste grain. Especially in summer, insects (ants, parasitic wasps, caterpillars, beetles, grasshoppers, true bugs), also spiders and snails are eaten. Occasionally a bird will leap a foot or so into the air to seize a passing gnat or fly. Though skittish on the breeding grounds, White-crowned Sparrows are rather quiet and deliberate in winter. They are reluctant to flush but, if pressed, they either fly up to a tree perch or dive into a thicket.

A sharp *chip* or *pink* and a raspy *tsit* or *tseet* are call notes. The White-crowned Sparrow sings its song nearly all year—longer than most other U.S. songbirds; group singing from perches in a bush or small tree is normal on warm winter days. This vocalization varies from a basic theme: one to three clear plaintive whistles on steady pitch followed by a buzzy trilled whistle of three notes.

WHITE-CROWNED SPARROW, *Zonotrichia leucophrys*

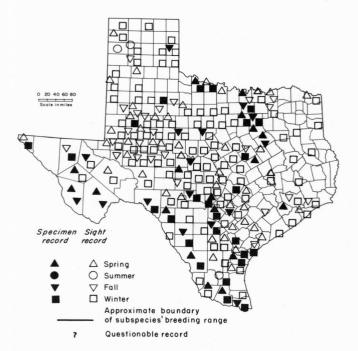

Specimen record | Sight record

▲ △ Spring
● ○ Summer
▼ ▽ Fall
■ □ Winter
——— Approximate boundary of subspecies' breeding range
? Questionable record

DETAILED ACCOUNT: THREE SUBSPECIES

EASTERN WHITE-CROWNED SPARROW, *Zonotrichia leucophrys leucophrys* (Forster)

DESCRIPTION: *Adult male, nuptial plumage*: Acquired by partial prenuptial molt. Pileum black, with a broad middle white stripe not extending through black forehead; hindneck between mouse gray and neutral gray; back mouse gray, broadly streaked with olive brown; rump between grayish olive and buffy brown; upper tail-coverts light brownish olive; tail olive brown, outermost feather lighter, terminally buffy brown, remainder of feathers narrowly edged on outer webs with color of rump; primaries and secondaries light fuscous, inner webs, except at tips of primaries, margined with drab, very narrow outer edgings of primaries like rump, those of secondaries similar but slightly more rufescent; tertials fuscous, broadly margined basally on outer webs with russet, this changing to buffy white on terminal portion of outer webs; lesser wing-coverts between mouse gray and deep grayish olive; median coverts dark hair brown or light chaetura drab, and greater coverts fuscous, rather broadly margined on outer webs with color of rump, but inner feathers with russet, both median and greater coverts broadly tipped with white or buffy white, forming two conspicuous wing-bars; upper and posterior parts of lores black; lower part of lores pale gray sometimes tinged with buff; superciliary stripe white, beginning above anterior corner of eye and extending to nape where it often joins white crown stripe; broad postocular stripe black; supraloral stripe black, this connecting eye with black forehead; remainder of sides of head between light neutral gray and mouse gray; sides of neck similar but rather darker; chin and upper throat dull white or grayish white; jugulum and upper breast smoke gray; flanks between drab and buffy brown; sides of body somewhat tinged with same color; lower tail-coverts dull cream buff, with central streaks of dull buffy brown; lower breast and abdomen grayish white or buffy white; lining of wing smoke gray to light hair brown edged with dull white or grayish white and sometimes washed with buff; edge of wing white or buffy white. Bill reddish brown, dark reddish brown, orange-brown, or flesh color, but sometimes lighter or yellow below, culmen and tip sometimes of darker brown or dull black; iris dark brown; legs and feet light reddish brown, flesh color, or dark reddish brown; claws dark brown. *Adult male, winter*: Acquired by complete postnuptial molt. Similar to nuptial adult male, but upper tail-coverts somewhat more definitely light-tipped; upper surface averaging darker and more brownish (less grayish). *Adult female, nuptial*: Acquired by partial prenuptial molt. Very similar to nuptial adult male but smaller; usually with median crown stripe averaging narrower, posteriorly more grayish, hind part of superciliary stripe also light gray. *Adult female, winter*: Acquired by complete postnuptial molt. Differs from nuptial adult female as does adult male in winter from nuptial adult male. *Male and female, first nuptial*: Acquired by partial prenuptial molt. Similar to nuptial adult male and female, but back, rump, and scapulars much more brownish—rather olivaceous buffy brown; tail and wings more rufescent; lower surface more washed with buff; flanks also more buffy or brownish. *Male and female, first winter*: Acquired by partial postjuvenal molt, which does not involve wing-quills or tail. Like first nuptial male and female, but with no black or white on pileum, this part dark chestnut; broad middle stripe between sayal brown and saccardo umber, this color suffusing hindneck; remainder of upper surface decidedly more buffy; sides of head more or less buffy; superciliary stripe dull pale buff; auriculars between wood brown and cinnamon or between sayal brown and buffy brown. *Juvenal*: Acquired by complete postnatal molt. Pileum fuscous to fuscous black, more or less streaked or spotted with cartridge buff to buffy white, also buffy white bases of feathers in central stripe more or less showing through overlying dark brown feathers, whitish streaks forming rather poorly indicated collar on hindneck; remainder of upper surface dull chamois to dull cartridge buff, with latter color chiefly anteriorly, and broadly streaked on back and scapulars, more narrowly and rather obscurely on rump, with fuscous black; upper tail-coverts between saccardo umber and snuff brown to between cinnamon brown and russet, somewhat streaked with fuscous black; tail as in first winter female; wings also similar but darker; edges of tertials dark russet, wing-bars narrower and more buffy, less whitish; posterior part of superciliary stripe buffy white; upper and posterior part of lores light fuscous, anterior and lower portion dull buffy drab, cartridge buffy, or light cream buff, sometimes mixed with light fuscous; auriculars dull wood brown to dull cinnamon buff, much spotted or narrowly streaked with light fuscous, remainder of sides of head buffy white or dull pale buff, more or less spotted or narrowly streaked with fuscous or light fuscous; sides of neck similar; lower surface dull cream white or pale dull cartridge buff, but sides and flanks dull light pinkish buff; throat, jugulum, sides, and flanks broadly streaked with chaetura drab, chaetura black, dark hair brown, and with fuscous on flanks, breast also sometimes narrowly streaked.

MEASUREMENTS: *Adult male*: Wing, 74.9–80.0 (average, 78.7) mm.; tail, 67.6–77.0 (72.2); bill (exposed culmen), 9.9–11.7 (10.7); tarsus, 22.1–23.9 (23.1); middle toe without claw, 15.5–17.0 (16.3). *Adult female*: Wing, 71.9–78.5 (75.9); tail, 65.5–71.9 (70.1); bill, 10.4–10.9 (10.7); tarsus, 22.1–23.6 (22.9); middle toe, 15.5–16.5 (16.3).

RANGE: S.e. British Columbia and s.w. Alberta to s.e. Mackenzie and n. Manitoba, thence to e. Quebec, and south through Rocky Mts. to n. Arizona and n. New Mexico. Winters from s. California, n. Utah, n. Colorado, Kansas, Ohio Valley, and w. North Carolina to c. Mexico, U.S. Gulf coast, and Florida (rarely); also Cuba.

TEXAS: *Winter*: Taken north to Wheeler (Nov. 13), east to Navarro (Oct. 26), south to Cameron, west to El Paso cos. Common.

IDAHO WHITE-CROWNED SPARROW, *Zonotrichia leucophrys aphaea* Oberholser, new subspecies (see Appendix A)

DESCRIPTION: *Adult male and female, nuptial plumage*: Similar to *Z. l. leucophrys*, but tail a little longer; upper surface lighter, much more brownish (less grayish), particularly on rump, nape, and back; lower surface more washed with buff.

MEASUREMENTS: *Adult male*: Wing, 74.4–81.5 (average, 78.2) mm.; tail, 69.6–78.0 (73.9); bill (exposed culmen), 10.7–11.2 (10.9); tarsus, 22.1–23.9 (23.4); middle toe without claw, 15.0–17.0 (16.3). *Adult female*: Wing, 72.4–77.0 (74.7); tail, 68.6–73.4 (69.8); bill, 10.7–11.9 (11.2); tarsus, 22.1–23.9 (22.9); middle toe, 15.0–17.0 (16.3).

TYPE: Adult male, no. 34893, Cleveland Museum of Natural History; Caribou Mt., Bonneville Co., Idaho; July 4, 1930; P. E. Trapier, original no., 4763.

RANGE: Idaho and n.w. Wyoming. Winters from n.w. Arizona and w. Texas to s. Arizona and n.e. Mexico.

TEXAS: *Winter*: Taken north to Cooke (May 1), east to Fort Bend (Apr. 19), south to Cameron, west to Culberson cos. Fairly common.

OREGON WHITE-CROWNED SPARROW, *Zonotrichia leucophrys oriantha* Oberholser

DESCRIPTION: *Adult male and female, nuptial plumage*: Similar to *Z. l. leucophrys*, but upper parts paler, more brownish (less grayish), particularly nape, back, and rump; lower parts paler, more buffy. Similar to *Z. l. aphaea*, but upper surface paler, decidedly more brownish, particularly nape, back, and rump; lower parts more buffy.

MEASUREMENTS: *Adult male*: Wing, 77.0–82.0 (average, 79.2) mm.; tail, 71.7–77.5 (73.7); bill (exposed culmen), 10.4–11.4 (10.9); tarsus, 23.6–24.4 (23.9); middle toe without claw, 16.0–17.5 (16.3). *Adult female*: Wing, 71.7–77.0 (74.2); tail,

67.1–72.9 (70.4); bill, 10.7–11.7 (11.2); tarsus, 22.1–23.9 (22.9); middle toe, 15.0–17.0 (16.0).

RANGE: S.e. Oregon, south through e. California and n. Nevada to c. California (east of Sierra Nevada) and s.w. Nevada. Winters from s. California, s. Arizona, and c. Texas to s. Baja California, s. Sonora, n. Chihuahua, and extreme s. Texas.

TEXAS: *Winter*: Taken in Bexar, Nueces, Cameron, and Webb (Nov. 16) cos. Scarce.

GAMBEL'S SPARROW, *Zonotrichia gambelii* (Nuttall)

SPECIES ACCOUNT

Zonotrichia leucophrys gambelii of A.O.U. checklist, 1957 (see Appendix A). Very similar to the White-crowned Sparrow, but white eye-stripe starts at bill instead of eye; bill usually yellow, rather than pinkish. Length, 6½ in.; wingspan, 9½; weight, 1 oz.

RANGE: Alaska, n.w. Mackenzie, n. Saskatchewan, and n.e. Manitoba, south to s. British Columbia, s.w. Montana, n.w. Wyoming, c. Alberta, and n.w. Ontario. Winters from s. British Columbia, s. Idaho, c. Wyoming, and n.e. Kansas to s. Baja California, Nayarit, San Luis Potosí, and n. Tamaulipas.

TEXAS: (See map.) *Winter*: Mid-Oct. to late Apr. (extremes: Sept. 6, May 31). Fairly common in western three-quarters; scarce to rare in eastern quarter.

HAUNTS AND HABITS: The Gambel's Sparrow, considered by most ornithologists to be a race of the White-crowned Sparrow, varies little, if at all, from its relative in habits and choice of haunts. Song is likewise similar to that of *Z. leucophrys*, but is said to be slower and more wheezy.

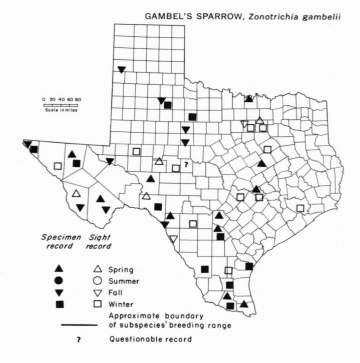

GAMBEL'S SPARROW, *Zonotrichia gambelii*

0 20 40 60 80
Scale in miles

Specimen record	Sight record	
▲	△	Spring
●	○	Summer
▼	▽	Fall
■	□	Winter

——— Approximate boundary of subspecies' breeding range

? Questionable record

DETAILED ACCOUNT: NO SUBSPECIES

DESCRIPTION: *Adult male, nuptial plumage*: Acquired by partial prenuptial molt. Similar to nuptial adult male of *Z. l. leucophrys*, but lores without black; white or grayish white superciliary stripe extending uninterruptedly to bill; upper surface darker, back somewhat more densely streaked. Maxilla yellow, saffron yellow, or burnt umber, but tip black or dark brown; tip of mandible dark brown, rest of mandible ocher yellow or wax yellow, somewhat paler basally; iris burnt umber, vandyke brown, or reddish hazel; legs tawny olive or light reddish brown; toes similar but darker; claws black or dark brown. *Adult female, nuptial*: Acquired by partial prenuptial molt. Much like nuptial adult male, but differs as does female of *Z. l. leucophrys* from male of that species. *Adult male and female, winter*: Acquired by complete postnuptial molt. Differs from corresponding sex in nuptial adult in more evident light tips of upper tail-coverts and in more brownish (less purely grayish) tone of upper surface. *Male and female, first nuptial*: Acquired by partial prenuptial molt. Similar to corresponding sex in nuptial adult but more brownish (less grayish) above; usually more buffy below. *Male and female, first winter*: Acquired by partial postjuvenal molt, which does not involve wing-quills or tail. Similar to first winter *Z. l. leucophrys*, but light gray or buffy superciliary stripe not interrupted on lores by brown of forehead; upper parts averaging slightly paler. *Juvenal*: Acquired by complete postnatal molt. Similar to juvenal of *Z. l. leucophrys*, but lores entirely drab or buff (not all fuscous), with only a little wash or admixture of this color; superciliary stripe more plainly defined and not cut off from base of bill by extension of dark brown of sides of forehead; upper surface more deeply buff or brown—dull tawny olive to light dull buffy brown, rump and upper tail-coverts sometimes varying to between cinnamon brown and ochraceous tawny; lower surface averaging more buffy. Bill brownish slate color, but mandible paler at base; iris dark brown; feet clay color.

MEASUREMENTS: *Adult male*: Wing, 76.5–83.3 (average, 79.0) mm.; tail, 65.8–74.2 (70.9); bill (exposed culmen), 9.7–11.2 (10.7); height of bill at base, 6.9–7.4 (7.1); tarsus, 21.4–23.9 (22.9); middle toe without claw, 15.5–17.0 (16.3). *Adult female*: Wing, 73.7–82.8 (75.9); tail, 67.3–74.2 (69.8); bill, 9.7–10.7 (10.4); height of bill, 6.9–7.4 (7.1); tarsus, 21.9–22.4 (22.1); middle toe, 15.0–16.0 (15.5).

TEXAS: *Winter*: Taken north to Deaf Smith (Oct. 8), east to Cooke (May 16) and Lee (May 6), south to Cameron, west to El Paso cos.

GOLDEN-CROWNED SPARROW, *Zonotrichia atricapilla* (Gmelin)

SPECIES ACCOUNT

A large, dusky-billed sparrow with dull yellow crown bordered broadly in black (head markings poorly developed in many individuals); grayish olive back, streaked with dark brown; two white wing-bars; gray to brownish gray on sides of head and neck, and sides of body; buffy white belly. Length, 7 in.; wingspan, 10; weight, 1 oz.

RANGE: N.w. Alaska, southeast to extreme n. Washington, s.e. British Columbia, and s.w. Alberta. Winters from s. British Columbia along Pacific coast to n. Baja California; rarely to s. Baja California and n. Sonora, and east to Utah, Colorado, and New Mexico; casual in Texas.

TEXAS: *Winter*: Seven reports, including two specimens: Brewster Co., Big Bend Nat. Park, near Castolon (1 immature banded, Dec. 9, 1971, R. H. Wauer; same individual seen, Dec. 28, Wauer; unbanded immature observed, Jan. 3, 1972, T. B. Feltner); Potter Co., Amarillo (Jan. 17, 1954, J. and B. Bailey; Jan. 2, 1955, Audubon Christmas Bird Count); Orange Co. (2 specimens, Mar. 15, and Apr. 4, 1887, F. B. Armstrong); Cameron Co., near Harlingen (Sept. 5, 1943, L. I. Davis).

HAUNTS AND HABITS: The Golden-crowned Sparrow nests in high northern Pacific coast mountains from near timberline, where grow stunted alders and willows, to brushy canyons of spruce forests. The nest of sticks and moss, lined with grass, is built either on the ground or low in a tree or shrub. In winter this bird of subarctic climes sometimes ranges almost to the Tropic of Cancer in Baja California. In this season, it is usually found skulking in dense thickets, often in association with the White-crowned and Gambel's sparrows.

Most time is spent on the ground where the bird progresses by hopping; if startled the Goldencrown generally flies up quickly to cover in bushes. When standing, a bird holds its head well elevated, giving it a very perky posture. The Goldencrown forages mainly by scratching amid leaves and debris on the ground. Winter food is predominantly—almost 100 percent—vegetable matter, including an extraordinary quantity of flowers (ranunculus, stock, pansies, chrysanthemums), also weed seeds, eucalyptus seeds, newly planted lawn grass, and various leafy vegetables from truck gardens. Diet on the breeding grounds presumably contains more insects, such as wasps, bees, caterpillars, and beetles.

Call notes of the Golden-crowned Sparrow include a hard, loud *chink* and a sharp *tizeet*. The usual three-note song, plaintive and flutelike, resembles the phrase "Three blind mice" or "Oh, dear me."

DETAILED ACCOUNT: NO SUBSPECIES

DESCRIPTION: *Adult male, nuptial plumage (gray phase)*: Acquired by partial prenuptial molt. Forehead and sides of crown black, slightly brownish; center of fore part of crown dull lemon chrome to dull empire yellow, posterior part of middle crown pale mouse gray; hindneck between pale neutral gray and pale mouse gray, slightly washed with brownish and with a few streaks of sepia or bister; remainder of upper surface between grayish olive and drab, mixed with a little dull russet on back, streaked broadly on back and scapulars with olive brown to dark olive brown, and also slightly with dull cartridge buff to between dull cartridge buff and drab gray; rump and upper tail-coverts with a bare indication of obscure darker streaks; tail olive brown to light buffy brown on outer pair of rectrices, feathers narrowly edged on outer webs with color of rump; primaries and secondaries dark hair brown, very narrowly margined on outer webs with grayish olive, inner edges, except on terminal portion, drab; tertials fuscous, broad outer edges rufescent sayal brown, terminally becoming buffy white; lesser wing-coverts grayish olive, somewhat brownish (between grayish olive and buffy brown); median and greater coverts fuscous, median coverts broadly tipped with white or buffy white, forming wing-bar, greater coverts margined on outer webs with brownish gray (between light grayish olive and light drab), and tipped on outer webs with buffy white, constituting another wing-bar; very narrow eye-ring white; sides of head and neck, including poorly defined superciliary stripe, between light neutral gray and light mouse gray, sometimes with slight buffy wash, becoming on hind part of sides of neck more buffy or brownish, sometimes almost like hindneck but lighter; anterior lower parts similar to sides of head but paler; lower throat and jugulum usually decidedly more washed with buff than chin and upper throat, thus similar to sides of neck but lighter; sides of body and flanks light gray washed with buff and obscurely streaked with drab; crissum dull pinkish buff, with broad shaft streaks of hair brown to drab; lower breast and abdomen buffy white; thighs drab; lining of wing like sides but paler and with slight wash of yellow, and more or less spotted with hair brown to drab; axillars paler, decidedly washed with yellow; edge of wing ivory yellow to yellowish white. Bill dark brown or blackish brown above, but paler on cutting edges and on mandible, the latter dull gray at base, with a greenish or yellowish tinge; iris olive brown; legs and feet flesh color or light reddish brown. *Adult male, nuptial (brown phase)*: Similar to gray phase, but hindneck, back, and posterior upper parts darker, much more brownish or rufescent, and near saccardo umber, with much snuff brown or dull russet on back; tail between bister and olive brown; lower surface much more buffy, particularly on jugulum; sides and flanks much more ochraceous—between tawny olive and isabella color—and likewise darker; edge of wing colonial buff. *Adult male, winter*: Acquired by complete postnuptial molt. Similar to nuptial adult male, but upper surface rather lighter, colors somewhat more blended due to broader light edgings of feathers, thus dark streaks are somewhat less sharply defined; pileum much duller, black areas decidedly brownish and, together with yellow and gray central areas, much duller and much overlaid by brown on tips of feathers; tips of upper tail-coverts mouse gray to light mouse gray, much more evident than in nuptial; sides of head and of neck much more buffy (less grayish); lower surface more buffy or brownish (less grayish); sides and flanks more rufescent. *Adult female, nuptial*: Acquired by partial prenuptial molt. Similar to nuptial adult male but smaller; yellow area of central part of crown paler and duller, gray of occiput duller, more brownish, often more or less streaked with dull black or dark brown; sides of head less purely gray (more brownish or buffy). *Adult female, winter*: Acquired by complete postnuptial molt. Similar to nuptial adult female, but upper surface decidedly more brownish, also duller and more uniform, dark streaks of back less sharply defined and narrower due to broader light edgings of feathers; yellow of crown duller and much overlaid by brown, gray of occiput concealed by brown or dull buff and narrowly streaked with olive brown or fuscous; black of pileum replaced by streaks of fuscous, fuscous black, olive brown, clove brown, or snuff brown; lower surface more buffy, flanks more rufescent. Similar to adult male in winter but smaller; yellow of crown much duller and more overlaid by brown; gray of occiput mostly replaced by brown or buff, black of pileum by brown or blackish brown streaks. *Male, first nuptial*: Acquired by partial prenuptial molt. Similar to nuptial adult female but larger. *Male, first winter*: Acquired by partial postjuvenal molt, which does not involve wing-quills or tail. Similar to adult male in winter, but yellow of crown duller, more overlaid with brown, and usually less in extent; gray of occiput replaced by dull light brown like back, and by dark brown streaks; sides of pileum much more brownish (less blackish); lower surface duller, somewhat darker, and more brownish or buffy. *Female, first nuptial*: Acquired by partial prenuptial molt. Similar to nuptial adult female. *Female, first winter*: Acquired by partial postjuvenal molt. Similar to adult female in winter, but averaging more brownish, both above and below; yellow of crown duller and of less extent, sometimes absent. *Juvenal (ochraceous phase)*: Acquired by complete postnatal molt. Upper surface ochraceous or light ochraceous to buckthorn brown, sometimes becoming cream buff on pileum; pileum without distinct yellow, but its central portion narrowly streaked with fuscous or fuscous black, lateral portion with very narrow obscure streaks of dark brown or with none; center of forehead with small yellowish buffy spot; back and scapulars broadly streaked with fuscous black or fuscous, rump very narrowly and obscurely streaked with fuscous; wings and tail as in first winter female; sides of head dark olive buff, with narrow

and irregular streaks or small obscure spots of fuscous; chin dull pale buff; rest of lower surface dull chamois, but middle of breast and abdomen between chamois and deep colonial buff, and crissum dull chamois; sides and flanks similar but much tinged with brown; throat and jugulum streaked with fuscous to fuscous black, as are also sides and flanks. *Juvenal (brown phase)*: Acquired by complete postnatal molt. Similar to juvenal in ochraceous phase, but pileum cartridge buff, laterally much more streaked with chaetura black or fuscous black, sides being almost solidly of this color, with slight sayal brown edgings, center of crown also much more broadly streaked with fuscous black, whole appearance of crown much more definitely striped than in ochraceous phase; remainder of upper surface duller, less distinctly ochraceous—tawny olive to dark tawny olive to warm buff, streaks darker, more blackish and broader; wings and tail somewhat darker, of a more grayish brown; sides of head dull cartridge buff or paler, often with numerous streaks or blotches of fuscous black or fuscous, particularly on cheeks and auriculars; lower surface much paler than in ochraceous phase—dull cartridge buff—abdomen and crissum dull cream buff; streaks on jugulum, sides, and flanks broader, more blackish (usually fuscous black or chaetura black), and more conspicuous.

MEASUREMENTS: *Adult male*: Wing, 75.9–83.3 (average, 79.5) mm.; tail, 73.2–83.3 (76.2); bill (exposed culmen), 11.2–13.2 (12.2); height of bill at base, 7.9–8.4 (8.1); tarsus, 23.4–25.7 (24.1); middle toe without claw, 17.0–18.3 (17.8). *Adult female*: Wing, 73.7–80.5 (78.2); tail, 68.8–82.8 (75.9); bill, 11.2–12.7 (11.7); height of bill, 7.6–8.1 (7.9); tarsus, 23.4–24.6 (24.1); middle toe, 15.7–17.5 (17.0).

TEXAS: *Winter*: Two specimens (see species account).

WHITE-THROATED SPARROW, *Zonotrichia pensylvanica* (Linnaeus)

SPECIES ACCOUNT

Zonotrichia albicollis of A.O.U. check-list, 1957 (see Appendix A). A large, blackish-billed sparrow with

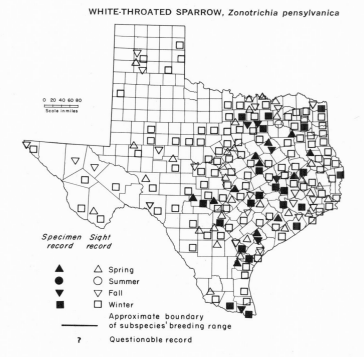

WHITE-THROATED SPARROW, *Zonotrichia pensylvanica*

0 20 40 60 80
Scale in miles

Specimen record / Sight record

▲ △ Spring
● ○ Summer
▼ ▽ Fall
■ □ Winter

——— Approximate boundary of subspecies' breeding range

? Questionable record

white throat; yellow loral spot; bold black and white stripes on top half of head; black-streaked brown upper parts; two white wing-bars; clear gray breast. Length, 6¾ in.; wingspan, 9¼; weight, 1 oz.

RANGE: S. Yukon to Newfoundland, south to c. British Columbia, n. North Dakota, c. Great Lakes region, n. West Virginia, and Connecticut. Winters from n. California, s. Arizona, and Connecticut to U.S.-Mexico border and Gulf states.

TEXAS: (See map.) *Winter*: Early Oct. to late Apr. (extremes: Sept. 26, May 26). Very common, verging on abundant, to fairly common in eastern third; common to uncommon in remainder of state east of 100th meridian, though scarce some years in south Texas brush country; uncommon to rare west of 100th meridian.

HAUNTS AND HABITS: In both summer and winter, the White-throated is a sparrow of bushy forest or woodland edges. On the breeding grounds, it nests in semi-open tracts of conifers or mixed woods where it finds ample low shrubs, saplings, and tangly thickets, wet or dry. The nest, built by the female, is well concealed on the ground amid vines or briars and/or under a canopy of grass or ferns. It is made of coarse grass and wood chips and lined with finer grasses and rootlets. Usually nearby is a stump, log, or similar large object suitable as a lookout for the bird as it flies to and from the nest. In Texas in winter, the Whitethroat is generally easily squeaked up by bird watchers in abandoned bushy fields, creek valleys, and fence rows skirting woodlands.

On the wing, this rather plump sparrow is quick and jerky; with strong wing-beats and pumping movements of the tail it flits through thickets. Most foraging is done on the ground in understory. Towheelike, it rattles noisily in leaves, scratching with both feet at once and often digging in the earth with its bill. Here it finds seeds, especially of ragweed and smartweed. *Zonotrichia pensylvanica* and its close relatives eat more fruit (blackberry, elderberry, blueberry, wild cherry, wild strawberry, others) than do most other sparrows. Animal matter, taken chiefly in spring and summer, includes ants, wasps, beetles, caterpillars, grasshoppers, crickets, spiders, millipedes, and snails.

A loud sharp *jink* and a slurred *tseet* are the common notes of the White-throated Sparrow. Its clear, plaintive, quavering *O Sam Peabody, Peabody, Peabody* song, usually issuing from a thicket, is frequently heard during Texas winters, especially as February is turning into March.

DETAILED ACCOUNT: NO SUBSPECIES

DESCRIPTION: *Adult male, nuptial plumage (dark phase)*: Acquired by partial prenuptial molt. Pileum and anterior part of hindneck brownish black with broad median stripe of white or grayish white; remainder of hindneck, back, and scapulars chestnut, broadly streaked with brownish black, dull ochraceous buff, and cinnamon; rump and upper tail-coverts grayish olive with brownish tinge; tail dull sepia, feathers narrowly margined on outer webs with snuff brown; primaries and secondaries light fuscous, outer webs of primaries very narrowly margined with grayish olive, outer webs of secondaries dull russet, narrow inner edges of both primaries and secondaries wood brown to dull avellaneous, excepting terminal portion of primaries; lesser wing-coverts grayish olive to citrine drab, washed with dull chestnut; tertials, median and greater wing-coverts fuscous, tertials broadly margined on outer webs with tawny to between tawny and chestnut, tips paler and more buffy or even buffy white, median coverts margined on outer webs with same and rather broadly tipped with white or buffy white, outer greater coverts broadly margined on external webs with sayal brown, inner greater coverts like outer webs of tertials and of greater coverts, conspicuously tipped on outer webs with white or buffy white; broad supraloral stripe or elongated spot lemon yellow to lemon chrome; lores dark gray to mouse gray; broad superciliary stripe, continuous with yellow supraloral stripe, white; broad postocular stripe brownish black; rictal streak blackish mouse gray; remainder of sides of head deep mouse gray; chin and throat white; jugulum and sides of breast mouse gray, slightly washed with buff on sides of breast, and with an obscure narrowly barred effect on lower jugulum and sides of breast; sides and flanks light grayish olive washed with buff; crissum cartridge buff, abdomen and middle of breast white; axillars and lining of wing dull colonial buff, outer under wing-coverts more or less spotted with mouse gray to hair brown, edge of wing citron yellow to strontian yellow. Bill above blackish slate, slate black, slate color, slate gray, brownish black, or brownish slate, but mandible bluish white, dark gull gray, or plumbeous, its base dull light yellow or white with flesh-colored tinge, dull pinkish white, or even flesh color; iris burnt umber, vandyke brown, or hazel; legs and feet light brown, clay color, ecru drab, flesh color, or rather reddish brown; claws ecru drab or dark brown. *Adult male, nuptial (light phase)*: Similar to dark phase but paler, including wings, tail, and particularly gray of jugulum and breast; back with much less chestnut, its place taken by buff, grayish olive, dull tawny, and light russet; dark streaks on back and scapulars fuscous black, many of light streaks cartridge buff; most specimens are variously intermediate between light and dark phases, with colors variously combined. *Adult male, winter*: Acquired by complete postnuptial molt. Similar to nuptial adult male of corresponding phase, but black of pileum more brownish, obscure spots of jugulum and breast somewhat more numerous and evident; sides and flanks somewhat more buffy. *Adult female, nuptial*: Acquired by partial prenuptial molt. Similar to nuptial adult male but smaller; very similar in color but black lateral stripes of crown somewhat mixed with russet or other dark rufescent browns; posterior end of superciliary stripe, together with median crown-stripe, tinged with buff or gray; yellow supraloral stripe duller; white throat-patch usually smaller, sometimes finely spotted, at least laterally and posteriorly, with mouse gray; a better defined submalar streak of mouse gray; gray of jugulum and breast duller, often more buffy; usually sides of breast obscurely and narrowly streaked with brown or gray. Bill slate gray, but basal two-thirds of mandible plumbeous, fading to slightly dull yellow at base; iris dark brown; feet clay color. *Adult female, winter*: Acquired by complete postnuptial molt. Similar to nuptial adult female, but pileum averaging laterally more brownish (less blackish); medially more buffy (less whitish); jugulum, sides, and flanks more buffy; jugulum and breast more streaked or spotted with dark gray or brown. *Male, first nuptial*: Acquired by partial prenuptial molt. Similar to nuptial adult male, but pileum more brownish (less purely blackish) and more mixed with chestnut or russet; middle of crown and superciliary stripe much tinged with buff; jugulum and breast paler, less purely gray (more buffy); center of breast usually with small dark gray spot; yellow of supraloral stripe duller; white throat less well defined. Similar to nuptial adult female but larger, sides of head averaging somewhat less brownish; jugulum and breast less streaked; sides and flanks averaging less buffy (more grayish). *Male, first winter*: Acquired by partial postjuvenal molt, which does not include wing-quills or tail. Similar to adult male in winter, but crown still more brownish (less blackish); back and scapulars averaging more rufescent and darker; yellow supraloral stripe duller; sides of head and lower surface less purely gray (more buffy or brownish); sides and flanks more buffy; jugulum, sides, and flanks more spotted and streaked with dark gray and fuscous. Similar to adult female in winter but larger, somewhat darker above and averaging more rufescent; lower surface somewhat more buffy and with much dark streaking. Bill brownish slate, but mandible dull white with pinkish tinge at base; iris dark brown; feet pale flesh color. *Female, first nuptial*: Acquired by partial prenuptial molt. Similar to nuptial adult female, but lateral stripes of pileum more brownish (less blackish); jugulum and breast lighter, more buffy (less grayish); throat less purely white, but more tinged with buff or gray; yellow supraloral stripe smaller and duller. *Female, first winter*: Acquired by partial postjuvenal molt, which does not involve wing-quills or tail. Similar to adult female in winter, but median stripe more deeply buff; yellow supraloral stripe smaller and duller; jugulum, sides, and flanks more conspicuously streaked or spotted with dark gray or fuscous. Similar to first nuptial female, but upper parts averaging darker; lower parts more buffy and more streaked with dark brown. Maxilla brownish slate or dark reddish brown; mandible olive gray or dull blue but yellow or dull white at base and tip; iris prout brown; legs and feet light brown or fawn color. *Juvenal (dark phase)*: Acquired by complete postnatal molt. Pileum dark olive brown, slightly mixed or streaked with bister or sepia, its broad central stripe dull light pinkish buff; back and scapulars chestnut to auburn, broadly streaked with fuscous to brownish black, more narrowly with dull cream buff; wings and tail similar to those of first winter female; superciliary stripe pale dull pinkish buff, with no yellow on supraloral region; sides of head mixed with pale dull buff and fuscous to light fuscous, with a rather well defined postocular streak of fuscous; lower surface dull cartridge buff; chin and throat dull grayish white or buffy white; sides and flanks tipped with gray; entire lower surface, except center of chin and throat, broadly streaked with chaetura black to hair brown. *Juvenal (light phase)*: Acquired by complete postnatal molt. Similar to dark phase juvenal, but upper surface much paler, pileum sepia; remainder of upper surface hazel to dark russet, streaked broadly with fuscous to fuscous black, rather more narrowly with dull warm buff; superciliary stripe light dull buff; dark streaks and spots on sides of head drab to buffy brown; streaks on lower surface fuscous to light fuscous, much narrower and less numerous than in dark phase, and more inclined to be absent on lower breast and abdomen.

MEASUREMENTS: *Adult male*: Wing, 72.2–77.2 (average, 74.7) mm.; tail, 71.4–76.2 (73.2); bill (exposed culmen), 10.7–12.2 (11.2); height of bill at base, 7.9–8.4 (8.1); tarsus, 22.9–24.6 (23.9); middle toe without claw, 16.3–17.3 (16.8). *Adult female*: Wing, 69.8–73.2 (71.4); tail, 68.3–73.7 (69.8); bill, 11.2–11.7 (11.4); height of bill, 7.4–7.9 (7.6); tarsus, 22.4–23.9 (23.4); middle toe, 15.2–16.5 (16.0).

TEXAS: *Winter*: Taken north to Cooke (1888), east to Bowie and Newton, south to Cameron, west to Kerr cos.

FOX SPARROW, *Passerella iliaca* (Merrem)

SPECIES ACCOUNT

A very large, plump sparrow. Rusty, brown, or gray above (some races with whitish wing-bars); rusty tail; whitish breast, heavily streaked with dark brown. Length, 7 in.; wingspan, 10¾; weight, 1½ oz.

RANGE: Wooded portions of Alaska and Canada (Yukon to Newfoundland), south to n.w. Washington and mountains of s. California and c. Colorado. Winters along Pacific coast from s. British Columbia to n. Baja California, and in interior from s. Utah, Great Lakes region, and s. New Brunswick to s. Arizona, Texas, and n. Florida.

TEXAS: (See map.) *Winter*: Late Oct. to mid-Apr. (extremes: Sept. 20, May 6). Common (some years) to fairly common in eastern third, though uncommon along coast; fairly common to uncommon in remainder of state east of 100th meridian with exception of south Texas brush country where scarce; increasingly rare west of 100th meridian.

HAUNTS AND HABITS: The widespread breeding haunts of the Fox Sparrow share one essential condition: a good supply of dense shrubs for cover. Southwestern birds often find protection in mountain misery (*Ceanothus*); north and eastward, moist coniferous and alder-willow thickets provide shelter. The sturdy nest is hidden on the ground under a bush or secured on a low crotch of a tree. It is built of grass, moss, roots, and leaves, and lined with feathers and fur. From cold-country woody vegetation, the Fox Sparrow migrates southeast and south to winter as far as the southern United States. During its stay in Texas, *P. iliaca* prefers wooded bottomlands along rivers and creeks. It seems especially numerous in and near yaupon (*Ilex vomitoria*) thickets.

This large and robust sparrow bursts from bush to bush with quick jerky movements; the tail is often fanned as the bird flies. Like the Whitethroat, the Fox Sparrow forages towhee style. On the ground, it scratches vigorously in leaf litter for ragweed, smartweed, and other seeds, and plucks berries—Virginia creeper, *Smilax*, blackberry, grape, and others. Occasionally, the bird flies up into trees—hackberry, elm, ash, etc.—to feed or sing a few notes.

The Fox's song, one of the finest among sparrows, is

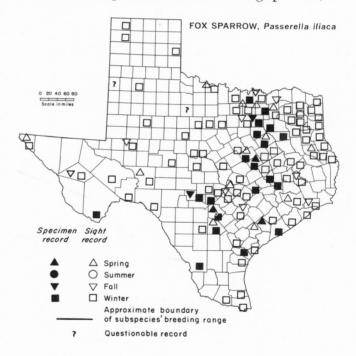

FOX SPARROW, *Passerella iliaca*

0 20 40 60 80
Scale in miles

	Specimen record	Sight record
▲	△	Spring
●	○	Summer
▼	▽	Fall
■	□	Winter

——— Approximate boundary of subspecies' breeding range

? Questionable record

a collection of short, clear, flutelike notes and sliding whistles; though variable, it usually ascends in pitch at first, then falls off at the end. In Texas, song is most likely in March. A sharp *smack* or *tchek* and a thin, drawn-out *stssp* are the usual call notes.

DETAILED ACCOUNT: THREE SUBSPECIES

EASTERN FOX SPARROW, *Passerella iliaca iliaca* (Merrem)

DESCRIPTION: *Adults, nuptial plumage:* Acquired by wear from winter plumage. Upper surface largely bright russet or chestnut, becoming burnt sienna or tawny on upper tail-coverts, but feathers edged, most broadly on upper back and rump, with light brownish olive, and on back slightly with isabella color; upper tail-coverts narrowly tipped with isabella color; tail prout brown, outer webs of feathers mostly russet, except outermost pair; wing-quills light fuscous, primaries paler and rather more buffy terminally and on tips, outer webs rather broadly margined with dull tawny, inner edges of primaries and secondaries, except at terminal portions, avellaneous to dull wood brown; tertials light fuscous, their outer webs margined with dull tawny, becoming light russet terminally; all exposed surface of lesser, median, and greater wing-coverts dull tawny to light russet, median and greater series narrowly tipped with dull very pale buff or buffy white, forming two wing-bars; primary coverts fuscous, very narrowly margined on outer webs with dull russet; lores between olive buff and cream buff, sometimes with small olive brown spot in front of eye; narrow interrupted dull pale buff eye-ring; remainder of sides of head russet, slightly mixed on auriculars with isabella color and with a few very fine streaks of dull pale buff; broad malar stripe of dull white or buffy white mixed with spots of fuscous, extending to a rather irregular transverse spot on side of neck, the rest of which is russet mixed somewhat with grayish olive and isabella color; lower surface white or buffy white, but chin and upper throat with a very few flecks of russet, throat and jugulum with blotches and more or less irregularly triangular spots of russet, breast with triangular spots of russet to fuscous, sides and flanks with broad streaks mostly of fuscous; lower tail-coverts with broad shaft streaks of dull russet; thighs dull russet, feathers narrowly tipped with dull buff; lining of wing hair brown to drab, coverts mostly tipped with white or grayish white. Bill blackish slate, slate color, brownish black, or dull brown, but terminal half of mandible slate gray or dull white with tinge of blue or flesh color, its base and basal cutting edges of maxilla dull yellow, maize yellow, buff yellow, or chrome yellow; tongue white; iris vandyke brown or hazel; legs and feet drab, drab gray, yellowish brown, ecru drab, pale ecru drab, or flesh color; claws dark brown or ecru drab. *Adults, winter:* Acquired by complete postnuptial molt. Similar to nuptial adults, but light tips of upper tail-coverts broader. *First nuptial:* Acquired by wear from first winter. Similar to nuptial adults, but primary coverts more brownish; wing-bars formed by light tips of median and greater coverts duller, narrower, less whitish (more buffy or brownish), sometimes practically absent. *First winter:* Acquired by partial postjuvenal molt, which does not involve wing-quills or tail. Similar to first nuptial male and female, but upper tail-coverts with tips broader and lighter. *Juvenal:* Acquired by complete postnatal molt. Similar to gray phase of nuptial adults, but upper surface darker and duller, more sooty above, gray areas more brownish; pileum between cinnamon brown and russet, not so distinctly spotted, almost plain, but with narrow terminal margins of cinnamon brown, and, in reddish phase, almost uniform dark prout brown; back more uniform—auburn to dark mars brown or between russet and hazel, rather sparsely spotted and obscurely and narrowly streaked with cinnamon brown, with a little admixture of russet, chiefly on edges of feathers; rufous areas darker and more sooty than in nuptial adults; rump and upper tail-coverts russet; wings and tail similar to those of nuptial adults, but wings duller, and bars formed by tips of median and greater coverts darker, less whitish; sides of head darker and duller, without gray superciliary stripe, but with dull buff streaks; lower surface dull white or buffy white, but chin, throat, and jugulum often dull pale buff; crissum darker, of dull pinkish buff; throat and jugulum broadly streaked or blotched with mars brown, chestnut brown, hair brown, russet, clove brown, fuscous, or fuscous black, more narrowly streaked with same colors on breast, abdomen, sides, and flanks; crissum spotted with dark cinnamon.

MEASUREMENTS: *Adult male:* Wing, 85.1–92.7 (average, 89.2) mm.; tail, 66.3–78.7 (73.4); bill (exposed culmen), 10.9–13.0 (11.7); tarsus, 24.6–26.4 (25.4); middle toe without claw, 16.0–17.5 (16.8). *Adult female:* Wing, 83.8–88.9 (85.9); tail, 66.8–76.2 (70.1); bill, 10.7–12.2 (11.7); tarsus, 23.1–25.4 (24.9); middle toe, 15.5–17.5 (16.3).

RANGE: N.e. Ontario to n. Labrador, south to s.e. Quebec and s. Newfoundland. Winters from Great Lakes region and s. New Brunswick to c. Texas (rarely) and n. Florida.

TEXAS: *Winter:* Taken in Cooke, Dallas, Kendall, and Bexar cos. Rare.

ALASKA FOX SPARROW, *Passerella iliaca zaboria* Oberholser

DESCRIPTION: *Adults, nuptial plumage:* Resembling *P. i. iliaca*, but upper parts, including wings and tail, averaging darker and much more grayish or sooty (less rufescent), reddish brown spots usually smaller, less numerous, and decidedly duller; markings on under surface duller, less rufescent (darker, more blackish).

MEASUREMENTS: *Adult male:* Wing, 87.1–91.7 (average, 88.6) mm.; tail, 71.1–77.2 (74.2); bill (exposed culmen), 10.9–13.0 (11.7); height of bill at base, 7.9–8.9 (8.4); tarsus, 24.1–25.4 (24.6); middle toe without claw, 15.0–17.0 (15.7). *Adult female:* Wing, 81.0–86.6 (83.1); tail, 67.1–71.1 (69.3); bill, 10.9–11.9 (11.4); height of bill, 7.6–8.6 (8.4); tarsus, 23.4–25.9 (24.6); middle toe, 14.0–16.0 (14.7).

RANGE: N. Alaska to n. Manitoba, south to s.w. Alaska, n.e. Alberta, and s. Manitoba. Winters along Pacific coast (rarely) from c. California to s. California, and in interior from s.w. Great Lakes region to s.e. Arizona (rarely), s. Texas, and n. Florida.

TEXAS: *Winter:* Taken north to Cooke, east to Henderson, Grimes, and Matagorda, south to Webb, west to Brewster cos. Fairly common.

[SLATE-COLORED FOX SPARROW, *Passerella iliaca schistacea* Baird

DESCRIPTION: *Adults, nuptial plumage:* Similar to *P. i. iliaca* but decidedly smaller, excepting tail, which is much longer; upper surface dark hair brown, with no reddish brown spots or streaks; wings and tail darker and duller; markings below are color of upper parts, instead of russet, tawny, or mars brown, as in *iliaca.*

MEASUREMENTS: *Adult male:* Wing, 75.9–85.1 (average, 80.2) mm.; tail, 75.9–84.6 (80.5); bill (exposed culmen), 10.4–12.4 (11.2); height of bill at base, 8.4–8.9 (8.6); tarsus, 22.6–24.9 (23.9); middle toe without claw, 14.0–15.5 (14.7). *Adult female:* Wing, 74.4–80.5 (78.2); tail, 74.4–81.0 (77.7); bill, 9.9–11.9 (10.9); height of bill, 7.9–8.9 (8.4); tarsus, 23.1–24.9 (23.6); middle toe, 13.7–16.0 (14.7).

RANGE: N.w. Oregon to w. Montana, south to n. Nevada and c. Colorado. Winters from n. interior California, c. Arizona and c. New Mexico (casually) to n. Baja California, s. Arizona, and probably extreme w. Texas.

TEXAS: *Hypothetical:* No specimen, but several sightings in El Paso Co., in and near El Paso, are considered to be of this race (Dec. 8, 1937, C. T. Gill; Dec. 11, 1937, and Feb. 26, 1939, I. M. Epstein; Mar. 16, 1939, Lena McBee; Jan. 28, 1940, T. M. Kirksey).]

LINCOLN'S SPARROW, *Melospiza lincolnii* (Audubon)

SPECIES ACCOUNT

A medium-sized sparrow with rounded tail; has broad buff breast-band, finely streaked with black; thin whitish eye-ring on largely gray face; light gray median stripe on rusty brown crown; black-streaked grayish brown back; whitish belly. Length, 5½ in.; wingspan, 8; weight, ¾ oz.

RANGE: N.w. Alaska to c. Labrador, south in mountains to s. California, c. Arizona, and n. New Mexico, and through s.e. Canada to n. Great Lakes region and Nova Scotia. Winters from n. California, n. Arizona, Oklahoma, c. Missouri, U.S. Gulf coast, and c. Florida (uncommon) through Mexico to Guatemala.

TEXAS: (See map.) *Breeding?*: One unconfirmed report: Dallas Co., Mt. Creek Lake (adult feeding 4 fledglings, May 3, 1964, Hazel Nichols, Dick Asher). On basis of information, impossible to make racial determination. *Winter*: Mid-Oct. to early May (extremes: Sept. 15, June 3). Very common to fairly common in most parts, though less numerous in northern Panhandle during coldest months; uncommon in El Paso region.

HAUNTS AND HABITS: The Lincoln's Sparrow breeds in shrublands—generally swampy or moist—where low bushes, four to eight feet high, are interspersed with short tufts of grass or sedge. The nest, a grass and sedge cup, is very well secluded in a tussock of grass. Eastern visitors to Texas often are surprised to find the Lincoln's Sparrow more numerous in most localities than is the Song Sparrow. The reason for its greater abundance in a basically dry state appears to be that

LINCOLN'S SPARROW, *Melospiza lincolnii*

Specimen Sight
record   record

▲ △ Spring
● ○ Summer
▼ ▽ Fall
■ □ Winter
── Approximate boundary of subspecies' breeding range
? Questionable record

0 20 40 60 80
Scale in miles

in winter *M. lincolnii* is less tied to the vicinity of water. In addition to bushes and brush piles, it frequents patches of tall forbs—especially giant ragweed (*Ambrosia trifida*) and frostweed (*Verbesina virginica*)—particularly if these are located near bushes.

Well described a skulker, the Lincoln's Sparrow feeds and hides on the ground. Even territory-declaring males as a rule sing from within tall grass or a low bush. An alarmed individual often disappears on foot through understory; if it does take wing, it flits swiftly and low to the ground and soon vanishes into a thicket. Seeds of bristlegrass, pellitory, and panicum are chief fare; in spring and summer, beetles, ants, bugs, grasshoppers, spiders, and millipedes are eaten also.

A faint *tsick* or lower pitched *tschuck* are the Lincoln's call notes. The sweet gurgling song, more like a House Wren's than a sparrow's, is infrequently heard in Texas.

DETAILED ACCOUNT: THREE SUBSPECIES

EASTERN LINCOLN'S SPARROW, *Melospiza lincolnii lincolnii* (Audubon)

DESCRIPTION: *Adults, nuptial plumage (gray phase)*: Acquired by wear from winter plumage. Pileum between sayal brown and snuff brown, with broad median stripe between neutral gray and light mouse gray, entire pileum conspicuously streaked with brownish black; remainder of upper surface light grayish olive to dull grayish olive, but upper tail-coverts buffy brown, back very broadly streaked with brownish black, hindneck very narrowly streaked with fuscous black or fuscous, rump and upper tail-coverts more broadly streaked with same; tail olive brown, middle pair of feathers and outermost pair rather light olive brown, all rectrices edged on outer webs with buffy brown; primaries and secondaries between hair brown and fuscous, primaries narrowly margined on outer webs with light grayish olive, secondaries margined on outer webs more broadly with brown—between sayal brown and hazel, inner margins of primaries and secondaries, except at tips, drab to rather light drab; terminal portion of tertials fuscous to fuscous black, margined basally on outer webs broadly with brown—between hazel and sayal brown, terminally with light dull buff; lesser wing-coverts buffy brown to sayal brown; median and greater coverts fuscous to fuscous black, median coverts tipped with pale dull buff, greater series margined broadly on outer webs with light grayish olive, innermost with a little dull hazel; lores smoke gray; superciliary stripe between neutral gray and mouse gray, its supraloral portion dull pale buff; auriculars and submalar region buffy drab; postocular streak of sayal brown or snuff brown, finely streaked with brownish black; rictal streak of fuscous or fuscous black, sometimes slightly mixed with sayal brown; malar stripe warm buff; sometimes a rather well defined, though usually interrupted, submalar streak of fuscous or fuscous black; chin and throat grayish white or buffy white, throat slightly streaked with fuscous; jugulum warm buff, conspicuously streaked with fuscous or fuscous black; sides of neck mouse gray, slightly streaked with fuscous; breast and abdomen white or buffy white; sides and flanks light gray, washed with pale dull buff and streaked with fuscous; crissum pale buff, with central streaks of fuscous; lining of wing pale dull buff or buffy white, somewhat spotted or blotched particularly on posterior and outer portions with mouse gray to dull light drab; edge of wing yellowish white. Bill dull blackish slate or dark brown, but cutting edges and mandible dull pale yellowish olive, light olive gray, or grayish olive, becoming bluish or maize yellow at base; inside of mouth light yellow; iris vandyke brown, bister, or black; legs light yellowish brown, light cinnamon, light drab, or reddish flesh color; toes similar, light drab or pale cinnamon; claws light drab or even dull black. *Adults, nup-*

tial (brownish olive phase): Similar to gray phase, but upper surface light brownish olive; superciliary stripe not so purely gray (more buffy). *Adults, nuptial (brown phase)*: Similar to brownish olive phase but darker, general tone of upper parts more brownish—between saccardo umber and sayal brown or snuff brown. *Adults, nuptial (rufescent phase)*: Similar to brown phase, but above rather lighter, of more rufescent brown, back rufescent sayal brown. *Adults, winter*: Acquired by complete postnuptial molt. Similar to nuptial adults of corresponding phase but duller above, more brownish or buffy, colors more blended and less sharply streaked because of broader light edgings of feathers; buff of jugulum and flanks deeper, their dark brown streaks less sharply defined. *First nuptial*: Acquired by wear from first winter. Practically identical with nuptial adults. *First winter*: Acquired by partial postjuvenal molt, which does not involve wing-quills or tail. Similar to corresponding phase of adults in winter, but upper surface darker and duller (more sooty); lower surface averaging somewhat darker, more richly colored. *Juvenal*: Acquired by complete postnatal molt. Pileum streaked with snuff brown to fuscous black, often with a middle stripe of dull light cream buff, more or less mixed with fuscous black streaks; remainder of upper surface dull cream buff to ochraceous to light cinnamon brown, more streaked, most broadly on back and scapulars, with fuscous to fuscous black; wings and tail as in first winter, but wing-bars of lighter and paler buff; superciliary stripe dull pale buff mixed with fine streaks of fuscous; auriculars tawny olive to saccardo umber; lores like superciliary stripe or dull drab hair brown; postocular streak and irregular stripe below or across auriculars fuscous; sides of neck similar to sides of head but streaked with fuscous; throat grayish white or buffy white; jugulum, flanks, and crissum warm buff; breast and abdomen buffy white; sides of chin, throat, jugulum, upper breast, sides of body, and flanks conspicuously streaked with hair brown to chaetura black or fuscous black, these streaks less conspicuous on upper breast. Similar to juvenal Song Sparrow, *M. melodia*, but bill more slender; upper surface of body darker, more densely streaked; postocular streak not reddish brown; upper surface more rufescent or tawny olive; middle of throat considerably streaked; jugulum more deeply buff. Similar to juvenal Swamp Sparrow, *M. georgiana*, but upper surface lighter, less densely streaked, particularly on pileum, where median stripe is less well defined; lower parts lighter, less deeply and extensively buff, especially jugulum, sides, and flanks. *Natal* (unrecorded in Texas): Drab. Bill, legs, and feet pinkish buff.

MEASUREMENTS: *Adult male*: Wing, 57.4–66.0 (average, 62.7) mm.; tail, 52.6–60.5 (56.4); bill (exposed culmen), 10.7–11.7 (11.2); tarsus, 19.8–21.1 (20.6); middle toe without claw, 13.7–16.5 (15.0). *Adult female*: Wing, 58.4–60.7 (59.7); tail, 50.3–56.4 (53.3); bill, 10.2–11.2 (10.7); tarsus, 18.8–20.9 (20.1); middle toe, 13.5–15.0 (14.2).

RANGE: N.w. Alaska to c. Labrador, south to s. interior British Columbia, n. Great Lakes region, and Nova Scotia. Winters from n. California, n. Arizona, Oklahoma, c. Missouri, U.S. Gulf coast, and c. Florida (uncommonly) through Mexico to Guatemala and El Salvador.

TEXAS: *Winter*: Taken north to Potter (Sept. 27), east to Brazoria, south to Cameron, west to Presidio (Nov. 8), Jeff Davis (Mar. 21), and Culberson (Apr. 30) cos. Common.

MONTANE LINCOLN'S SPARROW, *Melospiza lincolnii alticola* (Miller and McCabe)

DESCRIPTION: *Adults, nuptial plumage*: Similar to *M. l. lincolnii*, but larger; upper surface usually distinctly darker.

MEASUREMENTS: *Adult male*: Wing, 63.5–68.6 (average, 65.8) mm.; tail, 56.9–63.5 (59.7); bill (exposed culmen), 9.9–11.7 (10.9); height of bill at base, 5.6–6.6 (6.4); tarsus, 19.8–22.6 (21.9); middle toe without claw, 13.5–15.0 (14.7). *Adult female*: Wing, 59.9–65.0 (62.2); tail, 54.1–62.0 (57.4); bill, 9.7–11.4 (10.7); height of bill, 5.8–6.4 (6.1); tarsus, 20.1–22.1 (21.4); middle toe, 14.0–15.0 (14.2).

RANGE: Mountain meadows from n. Washington to n. Wyoming, south to s. California, n. Arizona, and n. New Mexico.

Winters from n.w. California, n. Arizona, Chihuahua, and Texas through Mexico to Guatemala and El Salvador.

TEXAS: *Winter*: Taken north to Denton (Apr. 14), east to Dallas (Apr. 17) and Ellis (Mar. 15), south to Cameron, west to Presidio (Sept. 28) and Jeff Davis (Sept. 24) cos. Uncommon.

NORTHWESTERN LINCOLN'S SPARROW, *Melospiza lincolnii gracilis* (Kittlitz)

DESCRIPTION: *Adults, nuptial plumage*: Similar to *M. l. lincolnii* but smaller; upper parts darker and more heavily streaked; breast, jugulum, and sides of body also more broadly streaked.

MEASUREMENTS: *Adult male*: Wing, 57.5–60.5 (average, 59.1) mm.; tail, 50.5–54.0 (52.9); bill (exposed culmen), 9.0–10.0 (9.6); tarsus, 19.5–22.0 (20.4); middle toe without claw, 11.0–14.0 (13.1). *Adult female*: Wing, 55.5–58.0 (56.7); tail, 49.0–56.5 (52.5); bill, 8.5–9.5 (9.2); tarsus, 19.0–20.5 (19.5); middle toe, 13.0–14.0 (13.8).

RANGE: Coastal district of s.e. Alaska and c. British Columbia. Winters chiefly in c. California; rarely south to Baja California, c. Sonora, s. Texas, and w. Guatemala.

TEXAS: *Winter*: One specimen: San Patricio Co., Welder Wildlife Refuge (Mar. 11, 1956, C. Cottam).

SWAMP SPARROW, *Melospiza georgiana* (Latham)

SPECIES ACCOUNT

A medium-sized, mostly rusty sparrow with rounded tail; has black forehead; chestnut cap; whitish throat; unstreaked gray breast. Immature resembles Lincoln's Sparrow but lacks gray on side of head; breast-streaks blurry (instead of sharp). Length, 5¾ in.; wingspan, 7¾; weight, ½ oz.

RANGE: Mackenzie to Newfoundland, south to c. Alberta, e. Nebraska, Ohio Valley, and Delaware. Winters from Nebraska, Iowa, s. Great Lakes basin, and

SWAMP SPARROW, *Melospiza georgiana*

0 20 40 60 80
Scale in miles

Specimen   Sight
record   record

▲ △ Spring
● ○ Summer
▼ ▽ Fall
■ □ Winter

——— Approximate boundary of subspecies' breeding range

? Questionable record

Massachusetts to n.e. Mexico (rarely), Gulf states, and s. Florida; rarely west to California.

TEXAS: (See map.) *Winter*: Mid-Oct. to early May (extremes: Oct. 1, May 23). Locally common (some years) to fairly common in eastern third, though often very common along upper coast; fairly common to uncommon in remainder of state east of 100th meridian; fairly common (some years) to rare west of 100th meridian with exceptions of northern and middle Panhandle and El Paso region, where apparently absent.

HAUNTS AND HABITS: The Swamp Sparrow is aptly named; even better would be Swamp-edge Sparrow. It nests in freshwater marshes, swamps, and bogs that are grown with cattails, bulrushes, willows, alders, and/or buttonbushes. Close to the ground amid stalks of plants, the cupped nest is built of grass, usually on a sturdy foundation of coarse vegetation. In Texas in winter, *M. georgiana* feeds and skulks in similar wetland situations, especially in growths of *Aster spinosus* and *Baccharis*. On both the breeding and winter grounds, it may sometimes be found in salt marshes, but usually prefers the vicinity of fresh water.

Through marshy recesses, the Swamp Sparrow climbs from stem to stem with mouselike agility. Seldom does it take wing; if it does so, it flies only briefly and rarely more than a few feet over vegetation. When foraging, it often wades sandpiperlike in shallow water where it finds insects and seeds. The Swamp Sparrow, a highly insectivorous *Melospiza*, eats beetles, ants, caterpillars, grasshoppers, and crickets, which in spring and summer often comprise 85 percent or more of its diet. It also eats a few seeds, chiefly of sedges, smartweed, panicum, and vervain.

Metallic *chink* or *chip* notes announce a hidden Swamp Sparrow. The male's frequent song is a rapid trill of short *weet*'s; another richer vocalization is a double upslurred *peet-peet peet-peet*. In spring he usually sings loud and long from a regular vantage atop an alder, willow, or cattail. In winter he may infrequently sound off, usually from a low perch.

DETAILED ACCOUNT: TWO SUBSPECIES

EASTERN SWAMP SPARROW, *Meplospiza georgiana georgiana* (Latham)

DESCRIPTION: *Adult male, nuptial plumage*: Acquired by partial prenuptial molt. Forehead black to fuscous black, varying in extent; narrow median stripe between light neutral gray and mouse gray; remainder of pileum chestnut to burnt sienna; hindneck between mouse gray and deep olive gray, sparingly streaked with fuscous black or chaetura black; back, scapulars, and rump dresden brown, back and scapulars broadly streaked with fuscous black, cartridge buff, buffy white, and between cinnamon brown and russet; rump much less streaked with fuscous black, sometimes almost immaculate; upper tail-coverts dull hazel with shaft stripes of fuscous black; tail between dark olive brown and fuscous or fuscous black, outer feathers lightest, broadly edged on middle tail feathers, narrowly on outer webs of remaining rectrices, with sayal brown or between hazel and light cinnamon brown; primaries and secondaries hair brown, verging toward fuscous—primaries margined on outer webs with cinnamon brown, except at tips, outer margins of secondaries between cinnamon brown and russet, inner margins of primaries and secondaries, except at tips, avellaneous on basal portion but

drab toward tips; long terminal portion of tertials black or fuscous black, outer webs of these feathers, together with outer webs of innermost secondaries, margined with russet, except at tips, where edged with white; base of inner webs of tertials hair brown; lesser wing-coverts dull mouse gray or dresden brown, washed with hazel, often, however, only on tips; subterminal portion of median coverts fuscous, sometimes restrictedly fuscous black, and tipped with hazel; terminal portion of greater coverts fuscous black, outer webs broadly margined with hazel; lores dull mouse gray, sometimes decidedly tinged with dull buff; superciliary stripe mouse gray, sometimes washed with buff; postocular stripe fuscous black mixed with dark chestnut; rest of sides of head similar to superciliary stripe and more or less narrowly and obscurely streaked or finely spotted with dark mouse gray to fuscous, auriculars usually decidedly more brownish than surrounding area, and with very fine paler shaft streaks; narrow more or less irregular malar streak and submalar streak, made up often of chain of spots, dark mouse gray or fuscous, enclosing pale gray or dull buff stripe; chin and throat dull white, grayish white, or dull buff; jugulum smoke gray to mouse gray, often decidedly washed with buff and often showing obscurely streaked appearance; flanks and sides of body tawny olive, streaked rather obscurely with olive brown to fuscous; crissum dull warm buff to buffy white with shaft streaks of fuscous; middle of breast and abdomen buffy white or grayish white; thighs sepia; edge of wing white; lining of wing grayish or buffy white, outer under wing-coverts spotted or blotched with hair brown. Maxilla black or dark brown; cutting edges lighter; mandible olive gray or light brown; iris prout brown; legs flesh color, ecru drab, or light brown; feet flesh color or seal brown. *Adult male, winter*: Acquired by complete postnuptial molt. Similar to nuptial adult male, but chestnut pileum much streaked with black, gray, or buff, often with a poorly defined median stripe of gray or dull buff; hindneck less purely gray (more brownish) or often more streaked with dull black or fuscous; back and scapulars less sharply and less broadly streaked, due to broad light edgings of feathers; edgings of tertials somewhat broader; lower surface averaging more buffy; sides and flanks darker. *Adult female, nuptial*: Acquired by partial prenuptial molt. Similar to nuptial adult male but smaller; chestnut area of pileum smaller, often streaked with black or fuscous. Maxilla black; mandible lighter, base and cutting edges of bill very pale gray or dull white; legs, feet, and claws light fawn color. *Adult female, winter*: Acquired by complete postnuptial molt. Similar to nuptial adult female, but pileum densely streaked with black and mouse gray, and with distinct middle stripe of gray, buff, or light brown; entire upper surface duller and more uniform, contrasting colors much obscured by dull edgings of feathers, and fuscous black streaks on back less sharply defined; light edgings of tertials somewhat broader; lower surface averaging more buffy. *Male and female, second winter*: Acquired by complete postnuptial molt. Like corresponding sex of adult in winter. *Male, first nuptial*: Acquired by partial prenuptial molt. Similar to nuptial adult male, but chestnut area of pileum less extensive and much streaked with black and mouse gray, usually with narrow mouse gray median stripe. Similar to nuptial adult female, but larger; upper surface slightly less rufous; pileum more densely streaked. *Male, first winter*: Acquired by partial postjuvenal molt, which does not involve wing-quills or tail. Similar to adult male in winter, but upper surface duller and more uniform; hindneck with usually less gray; pileum darker and duller, chestnut area less extensive, duller, and much more streaked with dull black, often thus reduced to chestnut streaks, middle gray or buff stripe broader and more conspicuous. Bill dull brown, but base of mandible dull yellow; legs and feet brown. *Female, first nuptial*: Acquired by partial prenuptial molt. Similar to nuptial adult female, but pileum much more streaked with dull black and gray, thus without a clear chestnut patch; upper surface averaging rather duller and darker. *Female, first winter*: Acquired by partial postjuvenal molt. Similar to adult female in winter, but upper surface darker, duller, and less rufous, particularly on pileum, which often has no chestnut area, back more broadly streaked. Similar to first winter male but smaller; upper surface darker, duller, averaging less rufescent, pileum darker and with less chestnut, often with almost none, and more densely streaked with black. Maxilla dark reddish brown; mandible yellow, but tip brown; legs and feet brown. *Juvenal (light phase)*: Acquired by complete postnatal molt. Upper surface tawny olive to dull clay color, pileum dull isabella color, everywhere much streaked with fuscous or fuscous black, these streaks sometimes well distributed over crown, sometimes so concentrated laterally that crown appears to have two broad dark brown lateral stripes, with narrower and lighter middle stripe; hindneck, rump, and upper tail-coverts much more narrowly streaked, hindneck sometimes with numerous narrow cartridge buff streaks, mostly on lateral portion; back very broadly streaked with fuscous black; wings and tail like first winter female, but lesser wing-coverts less uniform due to sayal brown edgings on these fuscous feathers, and median and greater coverts tipped with dull buff; sides of head dull grayish buff; superciliary stripe practically absent or only slightly indicated, being finely streaked with fuscous; conspicuous postocular stripe fuscous; most of sides of head more or less narrowly streaked with fuscous; throat buffy white or very dull pale buff; jugulum warm buff to buffy white; sides of body, flanks, and crissum light buff, the throat, jugulum, sides, and flanks numerously streaked with chaetura drab to fuscous and hair brown; abdomen and lower breast buffy white to very pale buff. Inside of mouth yellow. *Juvenal (dark phase)*: Acquired by complete postnatal molt. Similar to juvenal light phase, but very much darker both above and below; pileum and back much more densely streaked with fuscous black; upper surface light cinnamon brown or dark ochraceous; jugulum rather light buckthorn brown.

MEASUREMENTS: *Adult male*: Wing, 59.9–64.5 (average, 61.7) mm.; tail, 58.9–64.5 (60.7); bill (exposed culmen), 9.7–11.4 (10.4); tarsus, 21.1–22.1 (21.9); middle toe without claw, 14.7–16.0 (15.5). *Adult female*: Wing, 56.4–62.5 (59.2); tail, 51.1–61.0 (55.6); bill, 9.1–10.9 (10.4); tarsus, 19.6–22.1 (21.1); middle toe, 14.5–16.5 (15.2).

RANGE: S.e. Ontario, Michigan, and s.w. Quebec, south to c. Indiana, s.e. New York, and e. Nova Scotia. Winters from s. Michigan (casually) and n.e. Massachusetts to c. Texas, U.S. Gulf coast, and c. Florida.

TEXAS: *Winter*: Taken in Galveston (Nov. 1), Calhoun (Mar. 25), Aransas, and Val Verde cos. Rare.

WESTERN SWAMP SPARROW, *Melospiza georgiana ericrypta* Oberholser

DESCRIPTION: *Adult male and female, nuptial plumage*: Similar to *M. g. georgiana*, but tail much shorter; upper parts lighter, less rufescent, and brighter, light edgings of back and scapulars more whitish.

MEASUREMENTS: *Adult male*: Wing, 57.9–63.5 (average, 61.2) mm.; tail, 54.6–60.5 (57.4); bill (exposed culmen), 9.4–10.4 (10.2); tarsus, 20.6–22.6 (21.4); middle toe without claw, 14.0–16.0 (15.2). *Adult female*: Wing, 55.6–59.7 (56.6); tail, 50.3–58.9 (53.8); bill, 9.9–10.4 (10.2); tarsus, 20.1–21.1 (20.6); middle toe, 14.5–15.5 (15.0).

RANGE: S.w. Mackenzie (casually), c. Ontario, and Newfoundland, south to s.w. Alberta, s.w. South Dakota, c. Illinois, and c. Wisconsin. Winters from e. Nebraska, n.e. Illinois, and New York to s. Texas, Gulf coast, and s.w. Florida; rarely south to Jalisco and Tamaulipas.

TEXAS: *Winter*: Taken north to Dallas, east to Jefferson, south to Cameron, west to Brewster (Oct. 24) and Jeff Davis (Mar. 30) cos. Fairly common.

SONG SPARROW, *Melospiza melodia* (Wilson)

SPECIES ACCOUNT

A plump sparrow with longish, rounded tail. Generally grayish brown above, variably streaked with

blackish; whitish below; most subspecies show heavy blackish breast streaks and large blackish central breast-spot. Length, 6¼ in.; wingspan, 8½; weight, ¾ oz. (large Alaskan races not included).

RANGE: Aleutian Islands to Newfoundland and Nova Scotia, south to s. Baja California, n. Sonora, Mexican highlands locally to Michoacán, Valley of México, and Puebla, n. New Mexico, n. Arkansas, and n. Georgia. Migratory races winter, in part, south to n. Mexico, s. Texas, U.S. Gulf coast, and s. Florida.

TEXAS: (See map.) *Winter*: Early Oct. to late Apr. (extremes: July 15, May 26). Common to fairly common in most parts, though locally very common (some years) in eastern half; increasingly uncommon south of 29th parallel.

HAUNTS AND HABITS: In body size and in bill shape, the Song Sparrow is the most plastic North American passerine. Thus, the Giant Song Sparrow, *Melospiza melodia maxima*, of the western Aleutian Islands is a very large (length, 7¼ in.) sparrow with a long, pick-axlike bill adapted to catching crustaceans and mollusks on beaches; races that occur in Texas are much smaller with short conical bills adapted to husking and cracking seeds.

In southern Canada and adjacent northern United States, the Song Sparrow tends to be generally distributed both in town and country. First nests of the breeding season—a female commonly rears three broods a year—are usually constructed on the ground under a bush or tuft of grass; later they may be placed two to four, sometimes as high as twelve, feet up in thick shrubs, conifers, or amid marsh vegetation. In Texas, except of course during migration, *M. melodia* appears more restricted; cattails, tall grass or weed

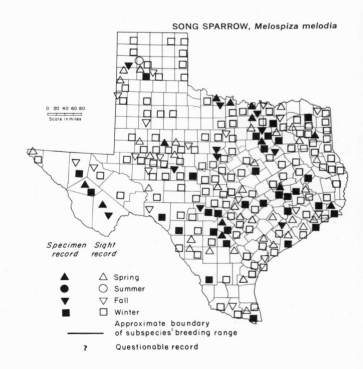

SONG SPARROW, *Melospiza melodia*

0 20 40 60 80
Scale in miles

Specimen   Sight
record   record

▲ △ Spring
● ○ Summer
▼ ▽ Fall
■ □ Winter

——— Approximate boundary of subspecies' breeding range

? Questionable record

patches, and bushes growing near streams or lakes constitute usual cold-weather habitat. Texas birds are almost—but not quite—as tied to the vicinity of water as are Swamp Sparrows.

Flights through thickets on quick jerky wing-beats are short and seldom prolonged. When frightened, like the Lincoln's and Swamp sparrows, it slinks away through understory or works down into shrubbery. On the ground in search of food—mostly seeds of smartweed, bristlegrass, ragweed, and panicum—it scratches with both feet simultaneously. Especially in warm months, it gleans beetles, grasshoppers, crickets, caterpillars, and ants, often working twenty to thirty feet up into foliage to find these insects.

A light hissing *tseet* or *sst* and a nasal *tchuk* are Song Sparrow call notes. In spring and summer, the male well earns his name. The song, though extremely variable, is often three or four whistled *cheet*'s followed by a rapid trill, then a series of widely pitched notes. At dawn in early spring, he may repeat this song six to eight times per minute. It becomes lower, slower, and less frequent as summer wanes. Song Sparrows seldom sing on their southern wintering grounds. In fact, in Texas, most so-called "Song Sparrow" songs actually come from the Bewick's Wren.

DETAILED ACCOUNT: EIGHT SUBSPECIES

EASTERN SONG SPARROW, *Melospiza melodia melodia* (Wilson)

DESCRIPTION: Similar to *M. m. callima* (see below), but bill somewhat smaller; upper parts decidedly darker and more rufescent (less grayish).

MEASUREMENTS: *Adult male*: Wing, 64.5–71.1 (average, 66.5) mm.; tail, 62.5–72.9 (67.6); bill (exposed culmen), 10.4–11.9 (11.7); tarsus, 22.6–23.9 (23.1); middle toe without claw, 14.0–15.5 (14.7). *Adult female*: Wing, 59.4–66.5 (64.3); tail, 63.0–68.1 (65.5); bill, 11.4–11.9 (11.7); tarsus, 21.6–23.6 (22.6); middle toe, 14.5–15.0 (14.7).

RANGE: S.e. Ontario, s. Quebec, and s.w. Newfoundland, south to s. New York, n.w. New Jersey, s. New Brunswick, and Nova Scotia. Winters from s.e. Ontario to s.e. Texas, s. Mississippi, and s.w. South Carolina.

TEXAS: *Winter*: Taken in Kerr (2 specimens), Galveston (1), and Matagorda (1) cos. Rare.

MASSACHUSETTS SONG SPARROW, **Melospiza melodia callima** Oberholser, new subspecies (see Appendix A)

DESCRIPTION: *Adults, nuptial plumage*: Acquired by wear from winter plumage. Pileum dull hazel to russet, with more or less well defined median stripe of smoke gray though somewhat mixed with russet, also streaked on pileum, particularly laterally, with fuscous black; remainder of upper surface rather light grayish olive, hindneck rather narrowly and irregularly streaked with dull russet, back broadly streaked with fuscous black and russet and a little with grayish white; upper tail-coverts rather narrowly streaked or spotted with dull hazel, longest upper tail-coverts hazel edged with light grayish olive; tail dark olive brown, broad edges of middle feathers on both webs and outer webs of remaining feathers buffy brown to sayal brown, entire outer pair of feathers also of this color or sometimes light buffy brown; primaries and secondaries light fuscous, outer webs of primaries margined with sayal brown, outer webs of secondaries more broadly margined with light cinnamon brown, inner edges of primaries and secondaries, except on terminal portion, tilleul buff to dull wood brown; basal part of tertials light fuscous;

terminal portion of tertials fuscous to fuscous black, these feathers broadly edged on outer webs with light cinnamon brown, terminally becoming buffy white or dull buffy gray; lesser wing-coverts dull hazel, edged with dull gray; median coverts fuscous, tipped with brownish or buffy white; greater coverts terminally fuscous black, outer feathers broadly edged on outer webs with sayal brown, inner feathers with rufescent sayal brown to dull hazel; superciliary stripe smoke gray flecked with grayish white; lores between dull light grayish olive and mouse gray, sometimes washed with dull buff; sides of head similar but more washed with buff, and with broad cinnamon brown postocular stripe; rictal stripe cinnamon brown to russet; submalar stripe chaetura black or brownish black, broadening posteriorly and enclosing malar stripe of light buff or white; sides of neck like hindneck; lower surface dull white or buffy white, but flanks and crissum dull buffy white to light cream buff; lower throat and jugulum broadly streaked with fuscous black to brownish black, these streaks often margined with russet and coalescing in center of lower jugulum into usually more or less conspicuous irregular spot, also sides and flanks broadly streaked with fuscous and dull russet; thighs between cinnamon brown and russet; feathers more or less edged with dull pale buff; lining of wing dull white or washed with buff, much blotched with hair brown, particularly on posterior portion. Bill slate black, blackish slate, dark brown, or brownish slate, but cutting edges at base, also mandible, except tip, dull white with slight tinge of flesh color, wholly flesh color, pale brown, or cinereous with base tinged with flesh color; iris prout brown; legs clay color, flesh color, or dull fawn color; feet olive, flesh color, dull fawn color, light cinnamon, clay color, or clay color with drab tinge; claws somewhat darker. *Adults, winter*: Acquired by complete postnuptial molt. Similar to nuptial adults, but upper surface darker, more rufescent, including wing edgings, colors also more blended, somewhat more uniform, dark streaks less sharply defined because more hidden by light edgings of feathers; sides of head and lower surface more buffy; streaks on lower parts broader, less sharply defined and more brownish (less blackish). *First nuptial*: Acquired by wear from first winter. Similar to nuptial adults, but wing edgings duller, particularly lesser coverts, lighter, less rufescent brown, instead of hazel. *First winter*: Acquired by nearly complete postjuvenal molt. Like adults in winter, but upper parts sometimes with slightly more yellowish or buffy tone; lesser wing-coverts and wing edgings duller and lighter, particularly lesser wing-coverts, less rufescent sayal brown or snuff brown, instead of dull hazel. Similar to first nuptial, but differing as does winter adult from nuptial adult. *Juvenal*: Acquired by complete postnatal molt. Similar to nuptial adults, but upper surface lighter, duller, and more buffy, likewise more uniform, and usually less streaked with fuscous black, pileum very finely streaked, duller, more uniform, and with little or no indication of median stripe; upper surface with little or no chestnut or russet; wing edgings lighter and duller, lesser wing-coverts fuscous or light fuscous, broadly tipped and edged with sayal brown or dull buff; sides of head duller, more buffy (less grayish); superciliary stripe often poorly defined, sometimes practically absent; lower surface much more buffy, particularly jugulum, sides, and flanks; fuscous streaks on jugulum decidedly narrower and somewhat longer; fuscous streaks on sides and flanks much narrower and less conspicuous. Bill slate gray, blackish slate, brownish slate, slate black, or clove brown, but cutting edges and mandible dull light brown, dull white, drab gray, dull flesh color, or slate gray, basal portion pale drab gray or tinged with flesh color or dull white; inside of mouth pale dull pink or dull pale gray; iris dark brown; legs clay color, pale brown, light ecru drab, or pale flesh color; feet flesh color, pale brown, wood brown, drab, or clay color.

TYPE: Adult male, no. 310402, U.S. National Museum; West Point, New York; Apr. 15, 1900; Wirt Robinson, original no., 1352.

MEASUREMENTS: *Adult male*: Wing, 64.3–69.6 (average, 66.3) mm.; tail, 63.0–71.7 (67.1); bill (exposed culmen), 11.9–12.4 (12.2); tarsus, 21.9–23.6 (22.9); middle toe without claw, 14.0–15.5 (14.7). *Adult female*: Wing, 61.0–69.1 (65.8); tail, 63.0–

71.1 (66.5); bill, 11.2–12.4 (11.7); tarsus, 21.6–23.1 (22.6); middle toe, 14.0–15.0 (14.5).

RANGE: S.e. New York and n. Massachusetts, south to n.e. New Jersey and e. Massachusetts. Winters from e. Ohio and e. Massachusetts to c. Texas, Gulf states, and n. Florida.

TEXAS: *Winter*: Taken in Tom Green (Nov. 30), Navarro (Oct. 27), Bexar, and Kinney cos. Rare.

ALLEGHENY SONG SPARROW, *Melospiza melodia euphonia* Wetmore

DESCRIPTION: *Adults, nuptial plumage*: Similar to *M. m. beata* (see below), but bill averaging larger; upper parts, particularly ground color of back, rump, and upper tail-coverts, darker, more rufescent (less grayish); black spots and streaks on back less heavy.

MEASUREMENTS: *Adult male*: Wing, 64.5–69.1 (average, 66.5) mm.; tail, 67.1–72.9 (68.6); bill (exposed culmen), 10.9–12.7 (12.2); tarsus, 22.1–23.1 (22.6); middle toe without claw, 14.0–14.7 (14.2). *Adult female*: Wing, 61.0–64.0 (62.5); tail, 61.0–69.6 (64.5); bill, 9.9–11.9 (11.4); tarsus, 21.6–23.9 (22.4); middle toe, 14.5–15.5 (14.5).

RANGE: N. and e. West Virginia, south to n.w. Georgia and n.w. South Carolina. Winters from n. West Virginia and s. Maryland to n.e. Oklahoma, Gulf states, and n. Florida; casually to e. Texas.

TEXAS: *Winter*: One specimen: Trinity Co., about 1 mi. east of Trinity (Dec. 31, 1936, P. D. Goodrum).

OHIO SONG SPARROW, Melospiza melodia melanchra
Oberholser, new subspecies

DESCRIPTION: *Adults, nuptial plumage*: Similar to *M. m. euphonia*, but upper parts decidedly darker, duller, and more sooty, averaging also somewhat less rufescent. Similar to *M. m. beata* (see below), but wings and tail longer; upper parts much darker, duller, and more sooty; black spots on back averaging smaller.

MEASUREMENTS: *Adult male*: Wing, 65.0–70.1 (average, 68.1) mm.; tail, 65.5–71.7 (68.8); bill (exposed culmen), 10.9–12.4 (11.9); tarsus, 21.6–23.6 (22.6); middle toe without claw, 14.5–15.5 (15.0). *Adult female*: Wing, 61.0–67.1 (64.0); tail, 58.9–71.1 (65.0); bill, 10.9–12.4 (11.7); tarsus, 21.1–23.1 (22.1); middle toe, 13.7–15.5 (14.5).

TYPE: Adult male, no. 29986, Cleveland Museum of Natural History; Bay Point, 3 mi. north of Sandusky, Ottawa Co., Ohio; June 30, 1931; John Dittrick, J. W. Aldrich, original no., 1286.

RANGE: S.e. Ontario and w. New York, south to s.e. Kentucky and w. Pennsylvania. Winters from s. Michigan, s.e. New York, and e. Delaware to e. Texas, Gulf states, and w. North Carolina.

TEXAS: *Winter*: Taken in Titus (1 specimen), Kaufman (1), Ellis (1), and Liberty (1) cos. Rare.

MISSISSIPPI SONG SPARROW, *Melospiza melodia beata*
Bangs

Race not in A.O.U. check-list, 1957 (see Appendix A).

DESCRIPTION: *Adults, nuptial plumage*: Similar to *M. m. melodia*, but upper surface lighter, decidedly more grayish (less rufescent), blackish streaks broader; sides of head averaging lighter, more buffy, but superciliary stripe only slightly buffy, if at all; lower surface more purely white with less buffy wash, dark brown or blackish streaks averaging narrower and less rufescent.

MEASUREMENTS: *Adult male*: Wing, 64.5–68.1 (average, 66.5) mm.; tail, 66.0–70.6 (67.6); bill (exposed culmen), 10.9–12.4 (11.7); height of bill at base, 7.6–8.1 (7.9); tarsus, 21.6–23.1 (22.4); middle toe without claw, 13.5–15.0 (14.5). *Adult female*: Wing, 63.0–65.5 (64.8); tail, 62.0–71.7 (66.5); bill, 10.4–12.4 (11.4); height of bill, 7.1–8.6 (7.9); tarsus, 21.6–23.6 (22.6); middle toe, 13.0–15.5 (14.5).

RANGE: S.e. Manitoba and n.e. Ontario, south to e. Nebraska, s. Missouri, s.w. Kentucky, and e. Michigan. Winters from c.

Minnesota and s.e. Ontario to s.e. Texas, Gulf states, and e. Florida, and along Atlantic coast to Delaware.

TEXAS: *Winter*: Taken north to Cooke (Mar. 21), east to Jefferson (Mar. 18), south to Matagorda and Atascosa, west to Kerr cos. Common.

DAKOTA SONG SPARROW, *Melospiza melodia juddi*
Bishop

DESCRIPTION: *Adults, nuptial plumage (gray—normal—phase)*: Similar to *M. m. melodia* but larger with stouter bill; upper surface lighter, more grayish, back more heavily streaked and with less rufescent brown, gray paler and less clouded; superciliary stripe lighter, more creamy or buffy white (less purely grayish); sides of head and neck lighter, brighter, more whitish or buffy (less grayish); white of lower surface less buffy, blackish streaks narrower. *Adults, nuptial (rufous phase)*: Much more like *M. m. melodia*, but differs from gray phase of present subspecies in darker, more rufescent upper surface; more rufescent brown (less blackish) streaks on lower parts. Similar in both phases to *M. m. beata* but larger with heavier bill; upper surface lighter, light streaks and general tone paler and more grayish; superciliary stripe more creamy or buffy white (less clearly grayish); dark streaks on anterior lower surface averaging somewhat narrower. *Juvenal*: Acquired by complete postnatal molt. Similar to juvenal of *M. m. melodia*, but upper surface lighter, brighter, more grayish (less buffy or brownish); lower surface lighter, brighter, and less deeply buff.

MEASUREMENTS: *Adult male*: Wing, 66.0–71.9 (average, 68.6) mm.; tail, 66.0–73.9 (70.6); bill (exposed culmen), 10.7–12.4 (11.7); tarsus, 21.6–23.1 (22.4); middle toe without claw, 14.0–15.0 (14.5). *Adult female*: Wing, 63.0–69.1 (66.0); tail, 61.0–71.1 (66.0); bill, 10.4–11.9 (11.2); tarsus, 20.6–23.1 (22.1); middle toe, 14.2–15.5 (14.7).

RANGE: S. Mackenzie, e. Saskatchewan, and s.w. Manitoba, south to c. Alberta, e. Montana, and e. South Dakota. Winters from n. Montana and s. Minnesota to s.e. Arizona, s. Texas, and s.w. Louisiana.

TEXAS: *Winter*: Taken north to Randall, east to Gregg (Mar. 27), south to Webb, west to Culberson cos. Fairly common.

MOUNTAIN SONG SPARROW, *Melospiza melodia montana*
Henshaw

DESCRIPTION: *Adults, nuptial plumage*: Similar to *M. m. fallax* (see below), but wing and tail longer; upper parts averaging somewhat brighter.

MEASUREMENTS: *Adult male*: Wing, 69.1–73.4 (average, 70.6) mm.; tail, 70.1–75.4 (72.4); bill (exposed culmen), 10.7–11.9 (11.2); tarsus, 20.6–24.1 (23.1); middle toe without claw, 13.5–15.5 (15.0). *Adult female*: Wing, 63.5–70.6 (66.0); tail, 66.8–72.9 (69.1); bill, 9.7–11.9 (10.9); tarsus, 21.9–23.6 (22.9); middle toe, 14.0–15.0 (14.2).

RANGE: W. Idaho and c. Montana, south to s. Wyoming, c. Colorado, and n. New Mexico. Winters from c. Idaho and s. Montana to n. Sonora, c. Chihuahua, and s. Texas.

TEXAS: *Winter*: Taken north to Oldham (Oct. 27), east to Cooke (Mar. 14), south to Cameron, west to Brewster (Oct. 26) cos. Fairly common.

UTAH SONG SPARROW, *Melospiza melodia fallax* (Baird)

DESCRIPTION: *Adults, nuptial plumage*: Similar to *M. m. montana* but smaller and averaging somewhat duller on upper parts. Resembling *M. m. melodia*, but bill decidedly more slender; upper parts lighter, more grayish; back less streaked with dark brown or black; below with less dark streaking; sides of head paler. Similar to *M. m. juddi*, but wing and tail somewhat longer; bill much more slender; upper parts lighter and much less streaked with dull black; lower surface also less heavily streaked.

MEASUREMENTS: *Adult male*: Wing, 65.0–71.1 (average, 67.8) mm.; tail, 67.1–72.9 (69.8); bill (exposed culmen), 10.4–

12.4 (11.4); tarsus, 21.6–24.4 (23.1); middle toe without claw, 14.5–15.5 (15.0). *Adult female*: Wing, 63.5–69.1 (65.8); tail, 64.5–70.4 (66.8); bill, 9.9–11.9 (11.2); tarsus, 22.1–23.1 (22.9); middle toe, 14.0–15.0 (14.5).

RANGE: E. Oregon and n. Utah, south to s.e. Nevada and e. Arizona. Winters from c. California, w. Nevada, and s.e. Oregon to c. Sonora, c. Chihuahua, Trans-Pecos Texas, and n. Tamaulipas.

TEXAS: *Winter*: Two specimens, both from Jeff Davis Co.: Limpia Canyon (Dec. 24, 1885, W. Lloyd); 1 mi. north of Fort Davis (Apr. 15, 1937, J. Van Tyne).

McCOWN'S LONGSPUR, *Rhynchophanes mccownii* (Lawrence)

SPECIES ACCOUNT

A sparrowlike bird of open country; told in all plumages by inverted black T on white tail. *Female and winter male*: nondescript, buff with brown streaks. *Nuptial male*: in early spring, gradually acquires black crown and patch on jugulum; whitish face and under parts. Length, 6 in.; wingspan, 11; weight, 1 oz.

RANGE: S. Alberta to s.w. Manitoba, south on Great Plains to n.e. Colorado. Winters from c. Arizona, e. Colorado, w. Kansas, and s.e. Oklahoma to n. Sonora, n. Durango, and c. Texas.

TEXAS: (See map.) *Winter*: Late Oct. to early Apr. (extremes: Sept. 3, Apr. 30). Irregularly fairly common to uncommon and declining in western two-thirds, though usually absent in Trans-Pecos and south of 30th parallel. Formerly (prior to 1900) very common in northern half of state; it then ranged fairly regularly south to Brownsville, Cameron Co.

HAUNTS AND HABITS: Two longspurs, McCown's and

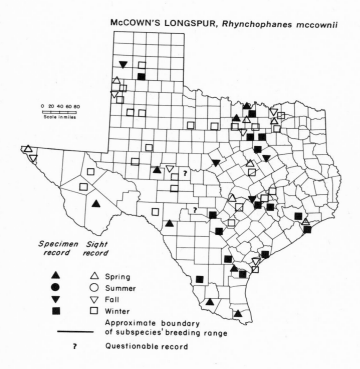

McCOWN'S LONGSPUR, *Rhynchophanes mccownii*

0 20 40 60 80
Scale in miles

Specimen   Sight
record   record

▲   △   Spring
●   ○   Summer
▼   ▽   Fall
■   □   Winter

Approximate boundary of subspecies' breeding range

?   Questionable record

Chestnut-collared, continue to occupy the old range of the North American Great Plains bison. Although habitats of the two birds overlap somewhat, McCown's tends to feed and nest on semiarid ground where grass is very short and/or sparse. Each spring on remnants of these sage-buffalograss-pricklypear plains, males declare territory with delightful flight songs. A proclaimer rises fifteen or twenty feet in the air, then randomly drifts down on stiff, spread wings while twittering his song. Usually the nest of grass is hollowed in the ground near where the male regularly launches into his flights.

The McCown's preference for bare or nearly bare ground continues throughout the year; thus, dry lake beds, plowed fields, and plains where grass or stubble is less than two inches high are situations where it winters in Texas. During cold months, birds live in flocks, at times in association with Horned Larks, sparrows, and other longspur species.

Longspur flight is strong, swift, and undulating. When flushed, members of a party rise quickly and confusedly; they fly a short distance, then drop to the ground and resume their previous occupation. When feeding, individuals walk or run, but occasionally hop over clods. Birds forage for grass and weed seeds (chiefly of such plants as knotweed, sunflower, goosefoot, and needlegrass), as well as some grain. Grasshoppers, beetles, and other insects are additional summertime food; a few berries are taken in winter.

Call note of the McCown's Longspur is a low dry rattle. The rapid, loud, warbling flight song (described by one listener as *see, see, see me, see me, hear me, hear me, see*) is not to be expected off the Great Plains nesting grounds.

CHANGES: McCown's Longspur has declined throughout its Texas range. In the northern half of the state its apparent last season of abundance was the winter of 1939–40; during this period the latest specimens reported to Oberholser were taken—two in a field eight miles north of Dallas on January 8, 1940, by W. A. Mayer and H. P. Kirby.

In the southern half of Texas, the species has been decreasing since about 1900. In fact it was last reported as common within this lower half during 1890—January 30 to February 7 in Val Verde County near Del Rio, as noted by Vernon Bailey. Last specimen localities in south Texas were: Kinney Co., Fort Clark (Mar. 28, 1893, E. A. Mearns); Bexar Co., San Antonio (Dec., 1890, H. P. Attwater); Galveston Co. (shot, Feb. 28, 1877, G. B. Sennett); Calhoun Co., Port Lavaca (Feb. 15, 19, 1894, J. G. Parker, Jr.); Bee Co., Beeville (Feb. 15, 1895, F. A. Lockhart); Nueces Co., Corpus Christi (Feb. 13, and Mar. 10, 1899, F. B. Armstrong); Cameron Co., near Brownsville (Mar. 9, 1898, Armstrong); and Starr Co., near Rio Grande City (Apr. 10, 1880, M. A. Frazar).

This gradual disappearance is doubtless correlated with shrinkage of the breeding range to the north of Texas; by mid-twentieth century, only portions of Montana retained sizable breeding populations. Overgrazing, too rigid control of prairie fires (which paradoxically tend to preserve grass turf), too much plowing and building, and too rampant use of pesticides are suspected causes of decline on McCown's nesting and wintering grounds.

DETAILED ACCOUNT: NO SUBSPECIES

DESCRIPTION: *Adult male, nuptial plumage*: Acquired by partial prenuptial molt. Forehead and anterior crown black, but posterior portion of crown usually with small spots of pale dull gray or grayish white; occiput and hindneck forming rather well defined collar of smoke gray, washed with pale cartridge buff; back and scapulars similar to hindneck, but rather darker, or dull grayish buff, rather broadly streaked with fuscous to fuscous black; rump between light mouse gray and light smoke gray, washed with dull buff, and rather obscurely streaked with deep mouse gray; tail mostly white, but middle pair of feathers fuscous to fuscous black, margined on outer webs and on terminal portion of inner webs with light brown; remainder of feathers with some fuscous or hair brown at their bases and, excepting outer pair, with broad tips of fuscous or fuscous black, these truncate on inner webs and extending farther toward base of feather on outer webs, this long outer dark area being longest on second pair of feathers from middle, and giving the general effect of square tip on tail; primaries and secondaries rather light drab, terminal portion of primaries fuscous to light fuscous, secondaries tipped with tilleul buff and some of inner primaries narrowly tipped with pale dull buff to buffy white, narrowly margined on outer webs with same, as are also secondaries, though edgings of the latter are rather more deeply buff, and inner edges of primaries and secondaries, except tips of primaries, rather broadly dull white or buffy white, this basally sometimes occupying all of inner webs; tertials olive brown, broadly edged on outer webs with dull buff; anterior lesser wing-coverts between smoke gray and pale mouse gray, centers of these feathers dark smoke gray, posterior series of lesser wing-coverts and median coverts forming tawny to near hazel wing-patch, this often tipped with buff; greater coverts fuscous to chaetura drab, broadly margined on outer webs and tipped with smoke gray to between pinkish buff and avellaneous; lores, sides of forehead, superciliary stripe, and broad stripe from bill to auriculars below eye grayish white or buffy white; broad postocular stripe deep mouse gray; auriculars dull buffy white to between smoke gray and light mouse gray, this sometimes mixed with dull gray; remainder of sides of neck like hindneck; broad malar stripe black; chin and throat white or buffy white, gradually merging into sides of neck, which are like auriculars or between neutral gray and mouse gray; broad crescent on jugulum black, sides of jugulum and breast deep mouse gray, feathers tipped with white, grayish white, or very pale gray; sides of body and flanks neutral gray to deep mouse gray, often broadly tipped with dull white; remainder of posterior lower parts white or buffy white; thighs mouse gray; lining of wing white with a few light gray or hair brown flecks on outer portion. Bill black, dark plumbeous, or slate color, but base of mandible somewhat lighter; iris vandyke brown or black; legs light seal brown; toes and claws, including the long hind "spurs," clove brown. *Adult male, winter*: Acquired by complete postnuptial molt. In general appearance very different from nuptial adult male; black of pileum is practically hidden by buffy brown and dull pinkish buff edges and tips of feathers; upper surface is dull pinkish buff to clay color on back and paler on hindneck; back, rump, and upper tail-coverts much streaked with dark olive brown, but these streaks on upper parts not so sharply defined as in nuptial; upper tail-coverts, tail, tertials, and wing-coverts broadly tipped with dull pinkish buff, including tawny patch on lesser and median wing-coverts, which is also darker; sides of head dull cinnamon buff to dull pinkish buff, obscuring almost entirely black or dark markings; lower surface decidedly more buffy, black of jugulum and breast wholly or partly veiled by buff, sometimes entire lower surface pale buff. Bill dull yellow or reddish flesh color, but

tip, sometimes also maxilla, dull brown; legs and feet slate color, somewhat paler than in nuptial. *Adult female, nuptial (ochraceous phase)*: Acquired by partial prenuptial molt. Pileum dull cinnamon buff, but narrowly and numerously streaked and somewhat finely spotted with fuscous to olive brown, on forehead almost concealing ground color; remainder of upper surface dull light cinnamon buff, but rump slightly more grayish, back and upper tail-coverts broadly, rump sparingly, streaked with fuscous to olive brown; tail with middle rectrices fuscous black to olive brown, tips paler, the remaining feathers white, broadly tipped with same color, pattern being very similar to that of male, outer pair of tail feathers without dark brown tip and with only a slight subterminal streak of buffy brown on outer web; primaries and secondaries between drab and buffy brown, terminal portions of primaries and subterminal portion of outer webs of secondaries olive brown, tips of secondaries dull pale buff, outer margins of primaries dull pale buff or buffy white; those of secondaries broader and dull pale buff; inner margins of primaries and secondaries, except on terminal portion of primaries, white or buffy white, this occupying large part of inner web on secondaries; tertials olive brown, tips buffy brown; lesser wing-coverts fuscous, broadly edged with dull cinnamon buff; median wing-coverts dark ochraceous tawny to hazel, tipped with dull cinnamon buff; greater coverts fuscous, margined on outer webs with dull light cinnamon buff; sides of head dull pinkish buff, slightly mixed with fuscous but without distinct markings; chin and throat dull pale buff; jugulum and breast mouse gray to deep mouse gray, washed with buff and much mixed with dull white, except in much worn condition; remainder of lower surface buffy white, but sides and flanks strongly tinged with buff; thighs dull buffy drab or hair brown, washed with buff; lining of wing white. Bill reddish brown or light brown, but tip dark brown and mandible yellow; iris black; legs and feet light brown or flesh color. *Adult female, nuptial (gray phase)*: Similar to ochraceous phase, but upper surface much more grayish throughout, and lower surface less buffy; pileum dull pale pinkish buff or dull pale cartridge buff; back paler and very much less deeply buff, as are also wings; rump and hindneck distinctly gray. *Adult female, winter (ochraceous phase)*: Acquired by complete postnuptial molt. Similar to female nuptial ochraceous phase but much more uniformly deep ochraceous above, plumage much more blended, dark brown streaks less sharply defined, ground color deep cinnamon buff to sayal brown; light wing edgings broader and more deeply buff—light pinkish buff to light cinnamon buff, but median wing-coverts dull cinnamon; sides of head more uniformly deep buff, dull light cinnamon buff to dull pinkish buff; lower surface much more deeply and extensively buff, jugulum dull clay color to dull cinnamon buff, almost entirely covering gray of jugulum and breast. Similar to adult male in winter but smaller; lacks solidly black area on pileum or jugulum; lesser wing-coverts not gray, but dull light brown or buff; median wing-coverts between cinnamon and dull orange cinnamon; jugulum and flanks more deeply buff or clay color. Bill reddish yellow, but tip black; iris black; legs and feet brown. *Adult female, winter (gray phase)*: Acquired by complete postnuptial molt. Differs from grayish phase of nuptial adult female as does female ochraceous phase in winter from same phase in nuptial; very much lighter, more grayish everywhere than ochraceous phase of female in winter; upper surface dull pinkish buff, as is jugulum. *Male, second nuptial*: Acquired by partial prenuptial molt. Similar to nuptial adult male, but upper surface, including wings, more buffy; black jugular crescent decidedly narrower and bases of feathers on breast of lighter gray; black of pileum slightly more brownish; lesser wing-coverts sometimes more buffy or brownish, longer series often with less tawny, thus reducing size of tawny wing-patch. *Male, second winter*: Acquired by complete postnuptial molt. Similar to adult male in winter, but upper surface averaging more richly buff, including wings; black jugular crescent narrower; bases of breast feathers paler; lesser wing-coverts more often washed with buff; tawny wing-patch often somewhat smaller. *Male, first nuptial*: Acquired by partial prenuptial molt. Similar to second nuptial male, but pileum duller, more brownish and this black area less extensive and more often tipped with dull buff or dull gray; tawny wing-patch smaller and usually paler; lesser wing-coverts dull buff or buffy brown; black jugular crescent averaging narrower. *Male, first winter*: Acquired by partial postjuvenal molt. Similar to second winter male, but black areas of pileum smaller, more brownish, and more obscured by dull buff edgings of feathers; tawny wing-patch smaller, usually lighter, lesser wing-coverts much edged with dull buff or buffy brown; black areas of jugulum narrower. *Female, first nuptial*: Acquired by partial prenuptial molt. Similar to nuptial adult female, but upper surface more buffy or ochraceous (less grayish); median wing-coverts lighter, less distinctly and less extensively rufous; lower surface lighter, more whitish, or buffy; gray of jugulum and breast largely replaced by white or buff. *Female, first winter*: Acquired by partial postjuvenal molt. Similar to adult female in winter, but median wing-coverts less extensively and less deeply tawny, mostly light dull cinnamon rufous, mixed with brown; lower parts more deeply buff, particularly jugulum. *Male, juvenal*: Acquired by complete postnatal molt. Upper surface cartridge buff to cinnamon buff; most buffy on scapulars and lower tail-coverts, most grayish on pileum and hindneck, but everywhere more or less spotted with dark olive brown to fuscous black, and feathers narrowly tipped with dull white or buffy white, producing slightly scaled effect in addition to spotted appearance; upper tail-coverts broadly streaked with dark olive brown; wings and tail like those of first winter male, but greater wing-coverts mouse gray to dark hair brown, edged and tipped with dull light cream buff to cinnamon buff; lesser and median wing-coverts dark gray to hair brown on exposed portions, and tipped with cartridge buff to light dull cream buff or dull cream buff; sides of head dull cream buff to cinnamon buff, more or less streaked irregularly, but not broadly, with hair brown to fuscous; chin and throat white, throat slightly spotted with hair brown; jugulum dark cinnamon buff to dull cream buff, streaked and spotted with hair brown to fuscous to chaetura black; remainder of lower surface white or buffy white, but sides and flanks obscurely streaked or spotted with hair brown to fuscous. *Female, juvenal*: Acquired by complete postnatal molt. Similar to juvenal male, but dark areas of tail of a lighter brown; inner edges of secondaries more buffy, less purely white.

MEASUREMENTS: *Adult male*: Wing, 88.6–93.7 (average, 91.2) mm.; tail, 48.3–55.9 (53.8); bill (exposed culmen), 11.2–13.0 (11.7); tarsus, 19.3–20.9 (19.8); middle toe without claw, 12.7–13.7 (13.2). *Adult female*: Wing, 80.0–86.9 (84.3); tail, 45.7–50.3 (48.3); bill, 10.7–11.7 (11.2); tarsus, 18.0–19.8 (19.0); middle toe, 12.2–13.7 (12.7).

TEXAS: Taken north to Oldham (Oct. 15), east to Cooke and Galveston, south to Cameron (Mar. 9), west to Webb and Brewster (Apr. 12) cos.

LAPLAND LONGSPUR, *Calcarius lapponicus* (Linnaeus)

SPECIES ACCOUNT

Lapland Bunting of Old World authors. In all plumages shows mostly blackish tail with only partly white outer feathers. *Winter male*: buffy-streaked brownish above with dull rusty nape and blackish smudge on jugulum; whitish below. *Nuptial male*: in early spring, begins to acquire black cap, face, and throat; bright rusty nape-patch; a few black streaks on sides. *Female*: in all seasons, resembles winter male but is duller with reduced areas of black; brownish nape. Length, 6¼ in.; wingspan, 11; weight, 1 oz.

RANGE: Circumpolar in Arctic. Winters in North America, from U.S.-Canadian border to California, Texas, and Virginia; in Old World, from England, n.

Europe, and c. Siberia to s. Europe, s. Russia, China, and Japan.

TEXAS: (See map.) *Winter*: Mid-Nov. to late Feb. (extremes: Oct. 18, Mar. 12). Locally fairly common to scarce in northern Panhandle and northeastern portion (north of 32nd parallel, east of 98th meridian); increasingly scarce south to Austin, San Antonio, and Houston.

HAUNTS AND HABITS: On arctic tundra of Alaska, Canada, Greenland, Lapland, and Siberia, the Lapland Longspur is, in many years, the most abundant breeding land bird. At Cape Thompson, Alaska, in a study area of excellent Lapland habitat—*Eriophorum* tussock tundra and *Carex* meadow—as many as fifty-nine to sixty-five pairs were recorded per one hundred acres. The typical nest, depressed in the side of a small moss or sedge hummock or in a tussock of grass or sedge, is made of thick, coarse grass, sometimes interwoven with moss.

That such a far northerner ever winters as far south as Texas is remarkable. At this season, *C. lapponicus* should be looked for in plowed fields, low and frost-sered stubble, young wheat or oats only a few inches high, or about well-mowed airports. It is gregarious and often joins flocks of Horned Larks, sparrows, and other longspurs.

In flight and behavior, the Lapland is similar to its longspur relatives. Much time is spent on the ground where it walks about, often at a hurried pace, looking for seeds of grasses and weeds, mainly of bristlegrass, crabgrass, pigweed, panicum, goosefoot, purslane, and amaranth. Crowberry and other wild fruits are sometimes consumed. From one-tenth to almost half its diet may be comprised of animal matter; in summer, wee-

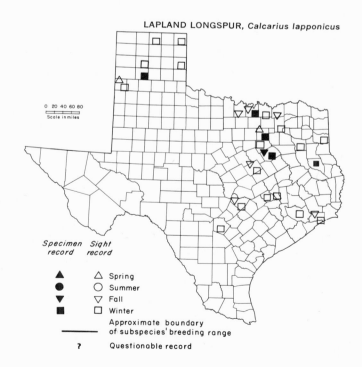

LAPLAND LONGSPUR, *Calcarius lapponicus*

0 20 40 60 80
Scale in miles

Specimen record — Sight record

▲ △ Spring
● ○ Summer
▼ ▽ Fall
■ □ Winter

——— Approximate boundary of subspecies' breeding range

? Questionable record

vils, ground and leaf beetles, and grasshoppers are standard food.

Notes of the Lapland Longspur include a soft musical *teeu* or *ee-yu* and a rattling call, usually given in flight, rendered as *ticky-tick-tew* or *dikerick, dikerick, psu 'o, psu 'o*. The male's springtime flight song is delivered as he wind-hovers or in a drifting parachute descent similar to that of the McCown's. This vocalization is a rapid, tinkling jumble suggestive of the Bobolink's song though less powerful; it is not heard in the bird's winter haunts.

DETAILED ACCOUNT: TWO SUBSPECIES

COMMON LAPLAND LONGSPUR, *Calcarius lapponicus lapponicus* (Linnaeus)

DESCRIPTION: *Adult male, nuptial plumage*: Acquired by partial prenuptial molt. Pileum black; hindneck dull chestnut to bright tawny; back and scapulars fuscous black, conspicuously streaked with russet and cinnamon buff to cartridge buff, or even buffy white; rump dull light tawny olive to dull light cinnamon buff or sayal brown, streaked with fuscous to fuscous black; upper tail-coverts light buff to dull cartridge buff, with broad central streaks of dark olive brown to fuscous; tail between dark clove brown and fuscous black, outermost pair of feathers fuscous at base and along most of outer webs (except basally and at tip) and white on broad terminal portion on inner web, this extending narrowly along shaft for about half the length of feather; next pair also with terminal shaft streak of white, sometimes dull buff, broadening toward end of feather, and sometimes extending around end of feather to inner edge as narrow tip or margin; all other tail feathers edged on outer webs and terminally on inner webs very narrowly with dull pale buff; primaries and secondaries hair brown, inner edges drab to dull pale pinkish buff, tips and outer webs of basal part of primaries fuscous with very narrow dull pale buff edging on outer webs, outer edges of inner secondaries light sayal brown and broader than light edgings of primaries; tertials fuscous to fuscous black, broadly margined on outer webs with dull russet; lesser wing-coverts dark hair brown, edged with dull light grayish drab; median coverts between hair brown and fuscous, broadly tipped with dull pale buff; greater coverts fuscous, broadly margined on outer webs with sayal brown to between sayal brown and avellaneous, and tipped with dull pale buff or buffy white; primary coverts dark hair brown, tipped and edged with dull pale buff or buffy white; broad light cream buff to cinnamon buff stripe beginning above eye, extending back to chestnut of hindneck and downward at right angles to chestnut, broadening on side of throat, where it becomes whitish; sides of neck behind this whitish stripe fuscous black broadly streaked with buffy white or dull buff, like upper back; lores and remaining portion of sides of head, chin, throat, and poorly defined crescent on jugulum black; remainder of lower surface buffy white, but sides of jugulum, sides of body, and flanks streaked with brownish black to chaetura black; lining of wing white, spotted on outer portion with hair brown. Bill citron yellow, maize yellow, or lemon yellow, but tip brown or dull black; iris prout brown; legs and feet vandyke brown, brownish slate, or brownish black. *Adult male, winter*: Acquired by complete postnuptial molt. Similar to nuptial adult male, but black of top and sides of head and chestnut of nape mostly hidden by feather edgings of cream buff, cinnamon buff, dull tawny olive, dull cinnamon, and dull clay color; black areas of back, scapulars, and rump much hidden by broader buff or cinnamomeous edgings of feathers, which form streaks on these areas; buff or tawny edges of tertials broader; black of lores replaced by dull buff, stripe behind and above eye dull ochraceous; chin grayish, buffy white, or pale dull buff instead of black; black of jugulum much veiled by light dull buff; lower part of jugulum, upper breast, and sides of body light warm buff to warm buff. Bill dull

yellow or reddish yellow, tipped with dark brown; legs and feet dark brown or brownish black. *Adult female, nuptial (dark—normal—phase)*: Acquired by partial prenuptial molt. Pileum fuscous black, somewhat dulled or obscured by rufescent brown, buff, or dull white edgings of feathers; sometimes rather well defined central stripe of buffy white, ochraceous buff, or warm buff; collar on hindneck burnt sienna, slightly veiled by ochraceous buff, with narrow streaks or small spots of fuscous, these sometimes almost obsolete (sometimes in summer, tips of feathers on pileum and hindneck wear off until pileum is nearly plain fuscous black and hindneck plain hazel); remainder of upper surface dull ochraceous buff, dull light tawny olive, or dull cinnamon buff, broadly streaked with fuscous, fuscous black, to cinnamon brown, these streaks most conspicuous on back and scapulars; tail between olive brown and fuscous, feathers narrowly edged on outer webs and on terminal portion of inner webs, most broadly on middle pair of feathers, with dull cartridge buff, outermost pair of tail feathers chiefly buffy white on outer webs, except at extreme base, and also on terminal portion of inner webs, extending in wedge-shaped spot along shaft to center of feather; narrow oblong spot of drab along shaft near or at tip; second pair of rectrices with oblong white or buffy white terminal spot on inner web and a narrow buffy white terminal margin on outer web; primaries and secondaries hair brown, tips fuscous, inner edges between dull cinnamon buff and avellaneous, outer edges of primaries narrowly dull pale buff, and broader outer edges of secondaries drab to sayal brown; tertials fuscous, broad outer margins tawny; lesser wing-coverts dark hair brown to fuscous, with lighter edgings of between drab or grayish olive; median coverts fuscous, broadly tipped with light cinnamon buff; greater coverts light fuscous, broadly edged on terminal portion of outer webs with dull hazel to dull cinnamon rufous; lores dull light cream buff; sides of head dull chamois to dull dark cinnamon buff; auriculars sometimes slightly gray; postocular stripe, broadening posteriorly, fuscous black to brownish black; broad rictal stripe of same color, but more or less flecked or narrowly streaked with dull buffy white or dull pale buff; postauricular region buffy white or pale buff; posterior to this, sides of neck are burnt sienna, and posterior to this, ochraceous streaked with fuscous; chin and throat dull buffy white or very dull pale buff, throat streaked with black; jugulum with more or less obscured crescent of brownish black to fuscous black, sometimes reduced to streaks; remainder of lower parts dull white, buffy white, or very pale buff, but sides and flanks broadly streaked with fuscous to fuscous black; lining of wing dull white or buffy white, somewhat spotted, particularly on outer coverts, with light hair brown. Bill dull yellow, reddish yellow, or brownish yellow, but tip dark brown; iris dark brown; legs and feet dark brown or brownish black. *Adult female, nuptial (light phase)*: Acquired by partial prenuptial molt. Similar to dark phase but much paler and less rufescent or ochraceous on light areas of upper surface, these areas dull pale pinkish buff to dull pinkish buff, dull light cream buff, or even buffy avellaneous; upper wing-coverts, secondaries, and tertials likewise paler, less rufescent—buffy wood brown or buffy avellaneous without any tawny or hazel. *Adult female, winter*: Acquired by complete postnuptial molt. Similar to nuptial adult female, but upper surface much duller and more uniform, dull black or dark brown areas, together with burnt sienna of nape, very much more obscured by buffy and brownish edgings and, therefore, whole aspect of upper surface is paler; also blackish markings on upper surface less sharply defined; lower parts somewhat more buffy; jugulum with less black, this usually more brownish and still more obscured by dull buff or dull white margins of feathers, sometimes these black areas practically hidden. Similar to adult male in winter but smaller, upper surface decidedly lighter and less rufescent, pileum more brownish (less blackish), rufous collar on hindneck paler, narrower, and even more hidden by buff tips of feathers; sides of head paler; lower surface generally somewhat more buffy; throat and jugulum with very much less of dark color and this dark brown instead of black. *Male and female, second winter*: Acquired by complete postnuptial molt. Like corresponding sex of adult in winter. *Male, first nuptial*: Acquired by partial prenuptial molt. Similar to nuptial adult male, but black of pileum more mixed with buff and brown; black of chin, throat, and jugulum less extensive and more or less mixed with white or pale buff feathers. *Male, first winter*: Acquired by partial postjuvenal molt, which does not involve wing-quills or tail. Similar to adult male in winter, but above averaging darker and duller; lower surface averaging more buffy throughout; black of throat and jugulum less extensive and usually still more obscured by buff or dull white tips of feathers. *Female, first nuptial*: Acquired by partial prenuptial molt. Similar to nuptial adult female, but pileum more brownish (less blackish); hindneck paler rufous; dark markings on sides of head, throat, and jugulum duller and more brownish, those on throat and jugulum much less extensive and more hidden by buffy tips of feathers; entire lower surface more buffy. *Female, first winter*: Acquired by partial postjuvenal molt. Similar to adult female in winter, but upper surface darker, more brownish and ochraceous (less blackish and buffy); cinnamon rufous of hindneck duller; lower parts more buffy. Similar to first winter male but smaller; upper surface averaging lighter, cinnamon rufous of hindneck much paler, duller, and less extensive; sides of head lighter; lower surface averaging slightly more deeply buff, dark areas of throat and jugulum less extensive, less blackish (more brownish), and mostly in form of dark brown streaks or spots rather than solid area. *Male, juvenal (ochraceous phase)*: Acquired by complete postnatal molt. Hindneck cream buff, streaked with fuscous; remainder of upper surface between ochraceous tawny and antique brown or dull clay color, everywhere conspicuously streaked with fuscous black, these streaks broadest on back and narrowest on pileum; wings and tail similar to those of male in first winter, but lesser and median wing-coverts tipped with pale buff; auriculars ochraceous, more or less streaked with fuscous; cheeks dull buff, somewhat mixed with fuscous; lower parts cartridge buff to cream buff, but jugulum ochraceous streaked with fuscous; sides and flanks also streaked with fuscous. *Male, juvenal (buff phase)*: Acquired by complete postnatal molt. Similar to juvenal ochraceous phase, but upper surface lighter, more buffy (less deeply ochraceous), and somewhat more densely streaked with black; ground color mostly cartridge buff to light cream buff, pileum similarly streaked with clay color, jugulum clay color or dull chamois densely streaked with fuscous. Bill dark brownish gray with yellow spot along middle of cutting edge of maxilla; iris dark brown; legs and feet brownish flesh color or brownish gray, posterior part of tarsus and soles of toes more or less yellowish. *Female, juvenal*: Acquired by complete postnatal molt. Similar to juvenal male, but upper surface averaging lighter, less densely streaked with blackish, outer margins of greater wing-coverts and tertials duller and lighter. Bill light brownish gray, but tip dark brown; iris dark brown; legs and feet blackish brown.

MEASUREMENTS: *Adult male*: Wing, 90.2–100.8 (average, 96.0) mm.; tail, 59.7–66.8 (63.0); bill (exposed culmen), 10.2–12.2 (11.2); height of bill at base, 6.4–7.4 (6.9); tarsus, 20.9–22.9 (21.9); middle toe without claw, 13.2–15.0 (14.0). *Adult female*: Wing, 87.9–92.2 (90.2); tail, 58.2–64.8 (61.0); bill, 10.2–11.2 (10.7); height of bill, 6.4–7.4 (6.9); tarsus, 20.9–22.4 (21.9); middle toe, 13.0–14.0 (13.5).

RANGE: Melville Island, e. Baffin Island, and Greenland to n. Scandinavia, n. Russia, and n. Siberia (excluding n.e. portion), south to c. Mackenzie, n.e. Manitoba, n. Quebec, and e. Labrador. Winters from s. Manitoba, n. Michigan, s.w. Quebec, Nova Scotia, England, n. Europe, and c. Siberia to c. Colorado, n.e. Texas, Virginia, s. Europe, s. Russia, s. Siberia, and c. China.

TEXAS: *Winter*: Taken in Cooke, Dallas, Ellis, and Navarro cos. Two specimens recently taken in Nacogdoches Co. perhaps of this race (skins in Stephen F. Austin State University collection). Irregular and uncommon.

ALASKAN LAPLAND LONGSPUR, *Calcarius lapponicus alascensis* Ridgway

DESCRIPTION: *Adult male and female, nuptial plumage*: Simi-

lar to *C. l. lapponicus*, but upper surface decidedly lighter, including rufous hindneck, which ranges from hazel to tawny; wing edgings paler, particularly those of tertials and greater coverts; black streaks on upper surface narrower (edgings wider). *Adult male and female, winter*: Paler than *C. l. lapponicus*. *Juvenal*: Similar to juvenal of *C. l. lapponicus* but much paler, particularly hindneck, sides of head, and jugulum.

MEASUREMENTS: *Adult male*: Wing, 91.2–99.8 (average, 95.8) mm.; tail, 58.2–68.3 (63.8); bill (exposed culmen), 10.2–12.4 (11.7); height of bill at base, 6.9–7.4 (7.1); tarsus, 20.9–22.9 (21.9); middle toe without claw, 13.0–15.7 (14.5). *Adult female*: Wing, 86.4–93.2 (89.2); tail, 55.9–63.0 (58.2); bill, 10.2–11.7 (10.7); height of bill, 5.8–7.4 (6.4); tarsus, 20.3–22.4 (21.4); middle toe, 13.0–15.2 (13.7).

RANGE: N.e. Siberia, n. Alaska, n. Yukon, and n.w. Mackenzie, south to islands in Bering Sea and s.w. Alaska. Winters from s. British Columbia, s.w. Saskatchewan, and c. North Dakota to n.e. California, w. Nevada, c. Colorado, and n.w. Texas (rarely).

TEXAS: *Winter*: One specimen: Randall Co., 10 mi. east of Canyon (Feb. 9, 1936, J. O. Stevenson).

SMITH'S LONGSPUR, *Calcarius pictus* (Swainson)

SPECIES ACCOUNT

In all plumages shows white outer feathers on blackish tail. *Female and winter male*: sparrowlike; buffier below than other longspurs; male usually shows white shoulder-patch. *Nuptial male*: in early spring, starts to attain striking head pattern (black crown and white side of head with black lines forming triangle); deep buff under parts. Length, 6½ in.; wingspan, 11¼; weight, 1 oz.

RANGE: N. Alaska, southeast to Hudson Bay. Winters from Kansas, c. Iowa, and Illinois to n.e. Texas, n.w. Louisiana, c. Arkansas, n.w. Mississippi, and s.w. Tennessee.

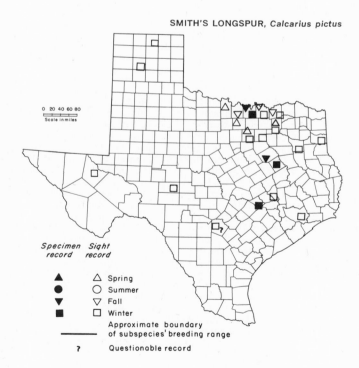

SMITH'S LONGSPUR, *Calcarius pictus*

Specimen record	Sight record	
▲	△	Spring
●	○	Summer
▼	▽	Fall
■	□	Winter
——		Approximate boundary of subspecies' breeding range
?		Questionable record

0 20 40 60 80
Scale in miles

TEXAS: (See map.) *Winter*: Mid-Nov. to early Apr. (extremes: Nov. 10, Apr. 27). Scarce, although apparently regular, in northeastern section; irregular in northern Panhandle; casual southwest to Lake Balmorhea (Reeves Co.) and Edwards Plateau, southeast to Houston.

HAUNTS AND HABITS: The Smith's Longspur shares New World tundra with the more abundant and widely distributed Lapland Longspur. On their mutual range, *C. pictus* is said to inhabit somewhat higher, drier areas, such as the summits of ridges. Like other longspurs, it nests on the ground; a natural depression or cavity scratched out by the bird holds the grass nest, lined with fine grass, caribou hair, down, and feathers.

During winter on the southeastern Great Plains, this longspur inhabits chiefly airports and ground near ponds where grass has been closely grazed by livestock. In the buffy winter dress, foraging Smith's Longspurs are well camouflaged in these sere, short-grass situations. Usually, their low clicking notes first announce them. When flushed, in typical longspur fashion, they burst from the ground, fly briefly and erratically, then land again. In and near airports, Smith's Longspurs often live in, and eat seeds of, three-awn grass (*Aristida*). Seeds of dropseedgrass, bristlegrass, panicum, clover, and other forbs and grasses are consumed also. This diet is supplemented, particularly in summer, with a few beetles (especially ground beetles), caterpillars, and spiders.

In flight or on the ground, Smith's Longspurs chipper rapid ticks and clicks which suggest the winding of a cheap watch. The male's spring song, usually given from the ground, combines this ticking with melodious warbles and concludes with an energetic *wee-chew*.

DETAILED ACCOUNT: TWO SUBSPECIES

EASTERN SMITH'S LONGSPUR, *Calcarius pictus pictus* (Swainson)

No races recognized by A.O.U. check-list, 1957 (see Appendix A).

DESCRIPTION: *Adult male, nuptial plumage*: Acquired by partial prenuptial molt. Pileum brownish black; collar on hindneck clay color to buff; remainder of upper surface sayal brown to dull tawny olive to dull pale pinkish buff—except upper tail-coverts which are between tawny olive and clay color—with centers of feathers fuscous black to brownish black, thus giving upper surface a decidedly streaked appearance, these blackish areas most evident on back and scapulars; tail fuscous black, but middle pair of feathers fuscous, and all rectrices narrowly margined on outer webs with pale dull buff or brownish white, though these edgings widest on middle pair of feathers; outer three pairs of tail feathers partly white, outermost pair wholly so except for narrow wedge-shaped marking at base of inner web and dark drab oblong shaft marking at tip; second pair with white tip, except for narrow dark drab terminal shaft marking, the white extending in wedge-shaped area along shaft for more than half the length of feather, outer webs entirely white; third pair with outer web practically all white and often with white streak near tip of feather along shaft on inner web; primaries and secondaries dark hair brown, tips fuscous, outer webs of primaries narrowly margined with buffy white, secondaries more broadly edged with sayal brown, feathers also tipped with brownish white; tertials fuscous, outer webs margined with sayal brown; lesser and median wing-coverts black, except for large white patch on inner lesser coverts, and broad white tips on longest lesser coverts and on median coverts; greater coverts fuscous, outer webs between dull pinkish buff and dull vinaceous buff, tips dull white; superciliary stripe extending from bill to hindneck white; lores and remainder of sides of head black, with conspicuous spot on auriculars, submalar line bordering the black, and a spot behind and below auriculars all white or buffy white; sides of neck clay color, continuous with nuchal collar; chin and upper throat cinnamon buff; remainder of lower surface clay color, but flanks obscurely streaked with fuscous; lower tail-coverts light cinnamon buff; lining of wing and axillars white, outer coverts spotted with hair brown to dark hair brown. Maxilla and tip of mandible dark brown or black; base of mandible orange or dull light reddish yellow; iris hazel or dark brown; legs and feet yellowish brown, light brown, or flesh color; claws dark brown. *Adult male, winter*: Acquired by complete postnuptial molt. Upper surface tawny olive, clay color, cinnamon buff, pale pinkish buff, and ochraceous, everywhere streaked with olive brown, clove brown, or fuscous black, these streaks narrowest and least obvious on hindneck, broadest and most conspicuous on back; tail like that of nuptial adult male, but light edges of middle feathers broader; wings similar to those of nuptial adult male, including lesser coverts, but tips of median coverts slightly buff, and remainder of light edgings of wing broader—light saccardo umber, tawny olive, sayal brown, and toward snuff brown, with a little tawny; sides of head dull light pinkish buff to dull cinnamon buff, but auriculars encircled with streaks of fuscous to olive brown; sides of neck dull clay color, more or less obscurely streaked with fuscous; lower surface rather light yellowish clay color, series of short streaks on sides of throat fuscous, middle of throat slightly, jugulum obscurely, streaked with fuscous, olive brown, tawny olive, or sayal brown, sides and flanks also rather more densely streaked with same; thighs buffy white; lining of wing white with slight spotting of dark hair brown on outer portion. *Adult female, nuptial*: Acquired by partial prenuptial molt. Median stripe of pileum pale pinkish buff or dull cream buff, remainder of upper surface sayal brown to light grayish olive on rump, or between light grayish olive and pinkish buff, upper tail-coverts more buffy and everywhere streaked, most narrowly on pileum, with fuscous black or fuscous; tail between clove brown and fuscous black, middle pair of feathers fuscous, all narrowly edged on outer webs with dull pale buff, two outer feathers partly white, outermost wholly so, except for narrow wedge-shaped fuscous area at base of inner web and dark drab shaft streak on terminal portion; second pair of rectrices with outer web white, except for narrow terminal shaft streak of dark drab, inner web with long wedge-shaped terminal white spot which is broadest at tip and extends narrowly along shaft for about half the length of feather; primaries and secondaries dark hair brown, tips fuscous, outer webs light fuscous, primaries margined on outer webs with tilleul buff, secondaries with sayal brown, tips of secondaries tilleul buff, inner edges of primaries and secondaries tilleul buff to dull vinaceous buff; tertials fuscous, shading to hair brown at base, and edged on outer webs with sayal brown; lesser wing-coverts dark hair brown, very narrowly edged and tipped with smoke gray or tilleul buff, large pure white patch on inner longest lesser wing-coverts; median coverts fuscous, broadly tipped with tilleul buff; greater coverts fuscous, broadly edged with buffy drab on outer webs and tipped with dull light buff or tilleul buff; broad superciliary stripe light cartridge buff; postocular stripe fuscous; auriculars dull buffy brown; postauricular stripe light dull cream buff; a fuscous submalar stripe, curving upward posteriorly; lores dull cream buff; malar stripe of dull buffy white, anteriorly usually dull pale buff; submalar stripe made up of spots or short streaks of fuscous; sides of neck like hindneck but anteriorly with vertical band of dull cinnamon buff to dull pinkish buff, cutting off posterior end of dark brown postocular stripe and subauricular stripe; lower surface dull cinnamon buff, but crissum dull pinkish buff; chin and upper throat sometimes decidedly paler, even dull white, upper jugulum and sides of jugulum very obscurely streaked with olive brown or buffy brown; sides of breast and of body, together with flanks, streaked with olive brown to fuscous; thighs dull buffy brown but dull cinnamon buff anteriorly; lining of wing buffy white, outer portion slightly spotted with hair brown to dark hair brown. Maxilla black or plumbeous brown, sometimes bluish black at tip; tip of mandible bluish black; rest of mandible brownish white or ecru drab; iris hazel; legs and feet pale brown or fawn color. *Adult female, winter*: Acquired by complete postnuptial molt. Similar to nuptial adult female, but upper surface more buffy or ochraceous and more blended, less clearly streaked, edgings of feathers broader and more obscuring dark brown or blackish centers; edgings of tertials also broader, as well as other wing edgings; lower surface darker; chin and throat dull cinnamon buff like rest of lower surface; jugulum more distinctly streaked with dull cinnamon to fuscous; lining of wing dull cinnamon buff to buffy white. *Male, third winter*: Acquired by complete postnuptial molt. Like adult male in winter. *Male, second nuptial*: Acquired by partial prenuptial molt. Similar to nuptial adult male, but dark areas of back more brownish (less blackish); upper surface with more of light brown, buff, or dull white edgings; lesser wing-coverts decidedly more brownish, less intensely black, white area on lesser coverts smaller; median coverts tipped with dull buff instead of white. *Male, second winter*: Acquired by complete postnuptial molt. Similar to adult male in winter, but lesser wing-coverts duller, more brownish; median coverts more brownish and tipped with dull buff instead of white; also lesser coverts with less white. *Male, first nuptial*: Acquired by partial prenuptial molt. Similar to second nuptial male, but upper surface usually more extensively edged with buff or dull white, especially on pileum; lesser wing-coverts hair brown, much edged with dull light tawny olive to light grayish olive; median coverts lighter, more brownish— hair brown to fuscous; white area on lesser coverts distinctly smaller; differs in these respects still more markedly from nuptial adult. *Male, first winter*: Acquired by partial postjuvenal molt. Similar to second winter male, but lesser and median wing-coverts still lighter, more brownish—hair brown to fuscous—and much more broadly edged and tipped with dull light brown or dull buff, with still less white on lesser wing-coverts. *Female, third winter*: Acquired by complete postnuptial molt. Like adult female in winter. *Female, second nuptial*: Acquired by partial prenuptial molt. Similar to nuptial adult female, but coloration duller, particularly on head and lower parts; jugulum rather more distinctly streaked; pattern of coloration on sides of head not so brightly defined; superciliary stripe dull cream buff; lesser and median wing-coverts more brownish; white patch on inner lesser wing-coverts smaller and more mixed with dark brown or dull black. *Female, second winter*: Acquired by complete postnuptial molt. Differs from second nuptial female as adult female in winter differs from nuptial adult female; also from adult female in winter as second nuptial female differs from nuptial adult female. *Female, first nuptial*: Acquired by partial prenuptial molt. Similar to second nuptial female, but lesser wing-coverts less blackish (lighter, more brownish, and more broadly edged with buff or gray), with little or no white, this mostly as edgings of lesser coverts, seldom forming distinct patch but if so, very small. *Female, first winter*: Acquired by partial postjuvenal molt. Similar to first nuptial female, but upper surface darker and more ochraceous or buffy, plumage more blended, with less dark brown or blackish visible on back, this obscured by light edgings of feathers, and upper surface thus appearing less sharply streaked; lower surface averaging rather darker, and dark brown streaks less sharply defined, being more or less obscured by light margins of feathers. Bill dull dark brown, but most of mandible decidedly paler; iris dark brown; legs light brown; toes somewhat darker brown. *Male, juvenal*: Acquired by complete postnatal molt. Pileum confusedly streaked with fuscous black, russet, and clay color, occiput with some streaks of dull white, with little or no indication of median light stripe; hindneck light clay color, rather narrowly streaked with fuscous; back, scapulars, and rump fuscous black, with conspicuous feather tips and edgings of clay color to russet and grayish white or buffy white; most of edgings of rump light clay color; upper

tail-coverts between ochraceous tawny and russet, with broad shaft streaks of fuscous black; wings and tail similar to those of first winter male, but rectrices, except outer pairs, conspicuously edged with color of upper tail-coverts; sides of head as in first winter, but rather more buffy; chin and crissum cinnamon buff; remainder of lower surface clay color to dull cinnamon buff, but throat, jugulum, upper breast, and, to a lesser extent, sides of body conspicuously streaked with fuscous to fuscous black.

MEASUREMENTS: *Adult male*: Wing, 86.4–96.3 (average, 91.7) mm.; tail, 59.2–68.8 (63.2); bill (exposed culmen), 10.2–11.2 (10.7); height of bill at base, 5.8–6.4 (6.1); tarsus, 19.8–20.3 (20.1); middle toe without claw, 14.0–15.2 (14.7). *Adult female*: Wing, 86.4–89.7 (87.6); tail, 55.3–58.7 (57.7); bill, 10.2–11.2 (10.7); height of bill, 5.8–6.4 (6.1); tarsus, 20.3–20.9 (20.6); middle toe, 13.7–15.2 (14.5).

RANGE: C. Alaska, n. Yukon, and n. Mackenzie, south to c. Mackenzie and n.e. Manitoba. Winters from c. Kansas and c. Missouri to n.e. Texas and n.w. Arkansas.

TEXAS: *Winter*: Taken in Cooke and Lee cos. One specimen (not identified to race) from Freestone Co. (Feb., 1973, C. D. Fisher).

NORTHWESTERN SMITH'S LONGSPUR, *Calcarius pictus roweorum* Kemsies

No races recognized by A.O.U. check-list, 1957 (see Appendix A).

DESCRIPTION: *Adult male and female, nuptial plumage*: Similar to *C. p. pictus*, but cervical collar and entire lower surface of adult male more deeply colored, particularly cervical collar and throat; female darker above and below than corresponding female.

MEASUREMENTS: *Adult male*: Wing, 89.0–96.0 (average, 92.3) mm.; tail, 60.5–67.0 (64.6); bill (exposed culmen), (10.5); tarsus, (20.3). *Adult female*: Wing, 84.0–90.0 (87.7); tail, 56.0–63.0 (58.6); bill, (10.4); tarsus, (20.1).

RANGE: N. central Alaska. Winters from Kansas and Iowa to n.e. Texas and n.w. Louisiana.

TEXAS: *Winter*: Two specimens: Cooke Co., Gainesville (Feb. 28, 1879, G. H. Ragsdale); Navarro Co., Rice (Nov. 26, 1880, J. D. Ogilby).

CHESTNUT-COLLARED LONGSPUR, *Calcarius ornatus* (Townsend)

SPECIES ACCOUNT

Blackish triangle on white tail is diagnostic. *Female and winter male*: sparrowlike. *Nuptial male*: in early spring, starts to acquire black cap and under parts; white on face and throat; black outline on rear portion of auriculars; chestnut collar on nape. Length, 6 in.; wingspan, 10¾; weight, ¾ oz.

RANGE: S. Alberta to s. Manitoba, southeast to n.e. Colorado and s.w. Minnesota; formerly to w. Kansas. Winters chiefly from n. Arizona and w. Nebraska to n.w. mainland Mexico, Texas, and n. Louisiana; casually to c. Mexico.

TEXAS: (See map.) *Winter*: Late Oct. to mid-Apr. (extremes: Sept. 27, Apr. 30). Locally fairly common to uncommon in northwestern two-thirds; scarce to casual east of 96th meridian and south of 30th parallel. Formerly fairly common south to Brownsville, Cameron Co.

HAUNTS AND HABITS: Until some hardy birder certifies a Snow Bunting in a Panhandle blizzard, the Chestnut-collared Longspur remains the last and presumably the most modern species on the systematic list of Texas birds. This handsome longspur normally nests on uncultivated prairies where grass bunches are less than eight inches high. In contrast to the other Great Plains longspur, the McCown's, the present species tends to be found in grassy areas which are a bit thicker, taller, and damper. The nest of dry grasses, built by the female, is cupped in the earth amid a clump of grass; the rim is usually flush with the ground.

In winter in the Southwest, the Chestnut-collared stays on the ground in dense flocks. It thus behaves like other longspurs, except, even during cold months, it sometimes selects grass slightly denser and a few inches taller than that preferred by its relatives. Seeds of dropseedgrass, sunflower, needlegrass, three-awn, pigweed, and other weeds and grasses are eaten, together with some grain (particularly wheat in spring). It sometimes eats insects—beetles, grasshoppers, and crickets especially—and a few spiders.

The standard call note of the Chestnut-collared is a short finchlike *ji jiv* or *zhi zhiv*; this bird lacks the usual longspur rattle. Unlike the McCown's and Lapland which sing regularly from the air in spring, *C. ornatus* frequently uses weed stalks, rocks, and fence posts for territorial singing perches. This song, which resembles that of a wee Western Meadowlark, is almost never heard on the wintering grounds.

CHANGES: Much of the Chestnut-collared Longspur's breeding range has been rendered unsuitable by man's farming, spraying, building, and transportation activities. Today, it and the other comparatively southern-nesting longspur, the McCown's, do not winter as far south as they used to, thus indicating there is a reduced population. Both species are nowadays very sel-

dom seen in the southern half of Texas. In contrast, the two arctic-breeding longspurs, Lapland and Smith's, appear to be still (early 1970's) as numerous as ever on their Great Plains wintering grounds. Recent and future atomic testing and oil drilling and spilling, however, are very likely to damage the arctic bird sanctuary. Man's ratlike breeding and ferocious "development" of the planet threaten all wildlife everywhere.

DETAILED ACCOUNT: NO SUBSPECIES

DESCRIPTION: *Adult male, nuptial plumage (buff-throated phase)*: Acquired by partial prenuptial molt. Pileum black, usually with some white in middle of occiput, and sometimes with small patches or flecks of white along median line of crown; broad collar on hindneck chestnut to hazel; back dull cream buff to dull light cream buff, much streaked and spotted with fuscous to fuscous black, upper back and scapulars less so, in very worn plumage back sometimes appears nearly solidly black because lighter color on edgings of feathers has worn off; rump deep olive buff, streaked with hair brown to chaetura drab; upper tail-coverts similar to back; tail fuscous to fuscous black, middle pair of feathers edged on outer webs with drab to buffy brown, basal portion of inner webs mostly white, outer four rectrices largely white, outermost two with only narrow terminal shaft line of dark drab, third pair broadly tipped on both webs with fuscous, more extensively on outer webs, fourth pair with still broader tips of fuscous, fifth pair of rectrices with basal two-thirds of inner webs white and only basal half of outer webs white, rest fuscous or fuscous black; primaries and secondaries hair brown, rather darker on outer webs, but tips of primaries fuscous, of secondaries narrowly dull brownish white, primaries narrowly edged on outer margins with buffy white to between buffy drab gray and smoke gray, becoming more brownish on outer margins of secondaries where these edgings are broader, inner edges of primaries and secondaries dull white to buffy white except on terminal portions of primaries and outer secondaries; tertials fuscous, margined on outer webs and at tips with buffy drab; lesser wing-coverts brownish black, longest posterior row and conspicuous patch on inner longest lesser coverts white; median coverts fuscous, tipped with dull cream buff or somewhat paler buff, greater coverts rather light fuscous, very broadly margined on outer webs with dull cream buff; broad superciliary stripe extending to hindneck white or buffy white; postocular stripe and subauricular stripe black, both extending to chestnut nape, but latter extending only as far forward as middle of hind part of auriculars, but sometimes passing behind auriculars; postauricular stripe dull white or buffy white; auriculars, cheeks, chin, and throat light ochraceous tawny to warm buff, posterior part of throat usually dull white or buffy white; lores dull buff—lighter than cheeks; jugulum, breast, and upper abdomen black, last more or less mixed with dull white or buffy white; lower abdomen and crissum white; sides buffy white or very pale buff; lining of wing white; thighs hair brown, feathers edged and tipped with buffy white. Tip of bill and culmen dark brown or slate black; remainder of bill lilac gray or dull yellow sometimes with bluish tinge; iris vandyke brown; legs dull flesh color, light brown, or vandyke brown; feet and claws vandyke brown; claws black. *Adult male, nuptial (white-throated phase)*: Similar to buff-throated phase, but throat wholly white or pale buffy white. *Adult male, nuptial (tawny-breasted phase)*: Similar to buff-throated and white-throated phases, but black of under surface, particularly breast and jugulum, with more or less extensive spots or patches of tawny. *Adult male, winter*: Acquired by complete postnuptial molt. Similar to nuptial adult male of corresponding phase, but black and dark brown areas of upper surface much overlaid with dull pale pinkish buff, dull pinkish buff, dull cinnamon buff, sayal brown, and tawny olive, these light colors as edgings and tips of feathers, so that entire aspect of bird is much lighter;

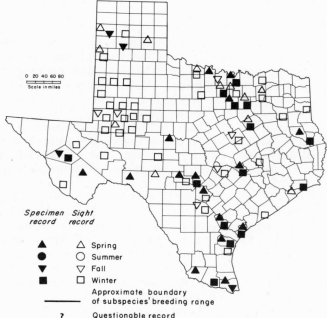

CHESTNUT-COLLARED LONGSPUR, *Calcarius ornatus*

0 20 40 60 80
Scale in miles

Specimen   Sight
record   record

▲   △   Spring
●   ○   Summer
▼   ▽   Fall
■   □   Winter

            Approximate boundary
——————   of subspecies' breeding range

?   Questionable record

black lesser wing-coverts slightly edged with white or dull pale buff; black areas of lower surface much overlaid with cartridge buff to chamois or with buffy white. Bill brownish plumbeous but paler at base of mandible. *Adult female, nuptial (dark ochraceous phase)*: Acquired by partial prenuptial molt. Pileum olive brown to fuscous black, usually much streaked with dull light buff to tawny olive or sayal brown, sometimes worn nuptial plumage in summer appearing almost uniform dull dark brown; hindneck cinnamon rufous, more or less streaked or spotted with fuscous and buff; back olive brown to dark clove brown, much streaked with tawny olive, sayal brown, to between tawny olive and dark olive buff, and somewhat with dull light buff; scapulars between snuff brown and sayal brown, with fuscous or fuscous black shaft streaks; ground color of remainder of upper surface similar to light streakings of back, rump duller, but upper tail-coverts more buffy, all streaked with fuscous; tail between dark olive brown and fuscous, outer five pairs of tail feathers largely white, as in male, terminal shaft streaks on outer two feathers olive brown; primaries and secondaries drab, but outer webs rather darker, particularly those of secondaries, inner edges of primaries and secondaries and tips of secondaries pale pinkish buff to buffy white, outer webs of primaries very narrowly margined with buffy white or very pale dull buff, tips of primaries, together with tertials, blackish brown to fuscous, tertials and secondaries broadly edged on outer webs with dull buff of rump and upper tail-coverts; lesser wing-coverts deep fuscous black, more or less edged with buffy drab; median coverts fuscous, tipped with cinnamon buff; greater coverts light fuscous to hair brown, broadly margined on outer webs with dull light buffy brown; superciliary stripe dull cartridge buff to buffy white; lores and rest of sides of head dull cream buff, but rather poorly defined postocular streak fuscous, overlaid by streaks of buff, cheeks somewhat streaked or spotted with fuscous, submalar streak fuscous, and auriculars more or less narrowly streaked or spotted with fuscous and light fuscous; chin and throat dull cream buff; jugulum and breast olive brown to clove brown, feathers much edged with buffy drab to between tawny olive and cinnamon; sides and flanks dull pinkish buff; upper abdomen dull brownish buff passing into buffy white on crissum; lining of wing buffy white, outer and posterior parts somewhat spotted with drab gray. Bill dull brown, but base of mandible and cutting edges of maxilla lighter, sometimes dull pink; iris dark brown; legs dull flesh color or pale brown; feet darker. *Adult female, nuptial (light ochraceous phase)*: Similar to nuptial adult female in dark ochraceous phase, but upper and lower surfaces much paler; light areas more buffy. *Adult female, nuptial (gray phase)*: Similar to nuptial adult female in light and dark ochraceous phases but much more grayish throughout, pileum fuscous (even when worn); buff streaks on upper surface more grayish; rump light grayish olive, with only rather slight buff tinge; ground color of back fuscous; dark areas of lower surface less brownish (more blackish)—fuscous black to brownish black; throat usually more whitish, less deeply buff, and remainder of lower surface more grayish (less distinctly buff); these differences from other phases evident even in worn plumage. *Adult female, nuptial (tawny-breasted phase)*: Similar to other phases of nuptial adult female, but breast and jugulum sometimes with considerable admixture of tawny. *Adult female, winter*: Acquired by complete postnuptial molt. Colors similar to those of nuptial adult female in corresponding phase, but lighter; buff edgings on upper surface cover practically all but central feather streaks of fuscous black to olive brown and also cover all cinnamon rufous or tawny of hindneck; light wing edgings also broader, so that whole aspect of bird on upper surface is decidedly paler; lower surface much more uniform, black and dark brown areas almost or quite hidden by dull buff edges of feathers. Similar to adult male in winter but smaller; pileum less blackish; hindneck with less rufous or chestnut; postauricular spot dark brown or blackish, and smaller, duller, and often less evident; lesser and median wing-coverts dark brown (not black) and broadly edged with buffy drab, dull buff, or dull buffy wood brown; lower surface with much less black and this duller, more brownish, and usually more hidden by buff edges

of feathers. *Male, third nuptial*: Similar to adult male in winter but smaller, cinnamon rufous on hindneck lighter and less extensive; lesser wing-coverts lighter, less blackish; lower parts with less black and this usually more brownish. *Male, third winter*: Acquired by complete postnuptial molt. Identical to adult male in winter. *Male, second nuptial*: Acquired by partial prenuptial molt. Similar to nuptial adult male in corresponding phase, but lesser wing-coverts more brownish, usually fuscous to fuscous black, sometimes brownish black, and in some individuals somewhat edged and tipped with buffy brown or dull buff, and usually with not so much white on posterior portion; median coverts between olive brown and fuscous or fuscous to dark fuscous; upper surface averaging more deeply buff, pileum usually more brownish and with more buff and white admixture; black of lower surface more brownish. *Male, second winter*: Acquired by complete postnuptial molt. Similar to adult male in winter, but median wing-coverts fuscous to olive brown (not black); greater coverts more brownish—fuscous black to fuscous, sometimes brownish black; lesser coverts usually with somewhat less white. *Male, first nuptial*: Acquired by partial prenuptial molt. Similar to corresponding phase of second nuptial male, but lesser and median coverts olive brown to fuscous, much edged and tipped with dull buff of upper parts, sometimes this color obscuring ground color; lesser wing-coverts with little or no white. *Male, first winter*: Acquired by partial postjuvenal molt, which does not involve wing-quills or tail. Similar to second winter male in corresponding phase, but lesser wing-coverts still more brownish, much edged and tipped with dull buff; median coverts averaging still lighter brown (less blackish); lesser wing-coverts with usually less white; black of lower surface usually more brownish. *Female, third winter*: Acquired by complete postnuptial molt. Like adult female in winter. *Female, second nuptial*: Acquired by partial prenuptial molt. Similar to nuptial adult female in all phases, but hindneck less extensively cinnamon rufous and this color lighter; lesser wing-coverts with less white; lower surface with less dark brown or dull black, the dark areas averaging lighter, more brownish (less blackish). *Female, second winter*: Acquired by complete postnuptial molt. Similar to adult female in winter in corresponding phase, but hindneck with less cinnamon rufous; lesser wing-coverts with less white, also more brownish and lighter; lower surface with dark brown areas less extensive and not so blackish. *Female, first nuptial*: Acquired by partial prenuptial molt. Similar to second nuptial female in corresponding phase, but usually with very little or no cinnamon rufous on hindneck; little or no white on lesser wing-coverts, which, with median coverts, are lighter brown; blackish brown areas of jugulum, breast, and upper abdomen reduced to narrow streaks of olive brown or fuscous, and even these are often absent. *Female, first winter*: Acquired by complete postnuptial molt. Similar to second winter female, but with little or no cinnamon rufous on hindneck; little or no white on lesser coverts; very little or no dark brown or blackish brown below, this in form of streaks or small spots which are practically hidden by buff edgings of feathers. *Juvenal*: Acquired by complete postnatal molt. Upper surface fuscous to fuscous black, pileum narrowly streaked or spotted with cartridge buff, dull cream buff, or sayal brown, occiput somewhat streaked with grayish white, hindneck mostly dull cream buff, with narrow fuscous streaks and small spots, back with streaks of cartridge buff, light cartridge buff, cream buff, chamois, honey yellow, and sayal brown, and with scalelike edgings of dull white or grayish white; upper tail-coverts sayal brown with broad shaft streaks of fuscous; wings and tail as in first winter female, but edgings of lesser wing-coverts paler buff; median and greater coverts broadly tipped with pale buff or buffy white; superciliary stripe dull grayish white or buffy white, anteriorly sometimes dull pale buff, and throughout with very narrow streaks or small spots of fuscous; lores dull cinnamon buff or pinkish buff; auriculars fuscous to dark olive brown, streaked with dull buff or dull pinkish buff; chin pinkish buff; remainder of lower surface dull pinkish buff to light dull cinnamon buff, throat lightly spotted or streaked, jugulum, breast, sides, and flanks rather densely streaked with olive brown, fuscous, or fuscous black, these streaks densest on jugulum. Bill and feet paler than in nuptial adult female; maxilla slate gray; mandible of a paler gray; legs, feet, and claws pinkish ecru drab.

MEASUREMENTS: *Adult male*: Wing, 81.3–90.2 (average, 85.3) mm.; tail, 51.3–60.7 (55.9); bill (exposed culmen), 9.7–11.2 (10.4); height of bill at base, 5.8–6.4 (6.1); tarsus, 18.8–20.9 (19.8); middle toe without claw, 12.2–14.0 (13.2). *Adult female*: Wing, 76.2–84.1 (80.2); tail, 48.3–57.2 (52.3); bill, 9.7–10.7 (10.2); height of bill, 5.8–6.4 (6.1); tarsus, 19.3–21.4 (19.8); middle toe, 12.4–13.7 (13.5).

TEXAS: *Winter*: Taken north to Oldham (Oct. 17), east to Cooke, San Augustine, and Chambers, south to Cameron (last, 1908), west to Brewster (Mar. 13) and Jeff Davis cos.

APPENDIX A: Nomenclature

COMMON LOON, *Gavia immer*

The validity of the Lesser Common Loon, *G. i. elasson*, has been questioned by some authors, but measurements, if taken by the same method, will serve to distinguish the two forms, at least by average characters. This smaller race was originally described by L. B. Bishop[1] from Carpenter Lake, Rolette Co., North Dakota.

[1] *Auk* 38 (July 5, 1921): 367.

RED-NECKED GREBE, *Pedetaithya grisegena*

The generic name *Colymbus* Linnaeus[1] has been used, at least by American ornithologists, for the grebes, although some writers have continued to contend that this name should be applied in a generic sense to the loons, or abandoned altogether! The first author to designate for this genus a type that was originally included by Linnaeus was Gray[2] who fixed *Colymbus arcticus* Linnaeus, a loon, as the type, but he specifically indicated that the genus *Colymbus*, for which he was thus designating the type, was of Linnaeus 1735, nec 1766. This designation thus is invalid since *Colymbus* Linnaeus of 1735 is not citable in nomenclature, being anterior to the 10th edition of *Systema Naturae*. The first valid designation of a type for *Colymbus* Linnaeus of 1758 was in 1884 by Baird, Brewer, and Ridgway,[3] and the species selected was *Colymbus cristatus* Linnaeus, a grebe. This designation was definite, even though arrived at by elimination, and, as it is otherwise valid, should be accepted. By this arrangement the generic name *Podiceps* Latham becomes a synonym of *Colymbus*, as the same species is the type of both. Furthermore, by use of the genus name *Colymbus* for the grebe genus *Podiceps*, the family designation becomes Colymbidae instead of Podicepitidae.

Colymbus proves to be a monotypic genus from which the Red-necked Grebe differs generically as follows: nostrils less basal, the distance from tip of culmen to anterior end of nostril not more than 1.25 times distance from latter point to rictus, instead of about 1.5 times; wing less than 4.6 times length of exposed culmen, instead of more; length of exposed culmen decidedly less than 4 times height of bill at base, and decidedly less than 5 times its width at base, instead of not less; gonys about .4 length of exposed culmen, instead of about .63; neck shorter, not nearly as long as body, instead of almost as long; no lateral or gular ruff just behind head, instead of conspicuous ruff all around neck.

This group comprises only a single species, *Colymbus grisegena* Boddaert, with its subspecies, the Holboell's Red-necked Grebe of North America. The proper generic name for this grebe is *Pedetaithya* Kaup[4] of which the type by monotypy is *Podiceps subcristatus*, which is the same as *Colymbus grisegena* (Boddaert). The species should, therefore, be known as *Pedetaithya grisegena*.

The earliest technical name of the Holboell's Red-necked Grebe is *Podiceps rubricollis major* Temminck and Schlegel,[5] since birds of this species from northeastern Asia are identical with those from North America. While this bird remained in the genus *Colymbus* its subspecific name *Colymbus grisegena major* was preoccupied by *Colymbus major* Boddaert[6] which is *Aechmophorus major* (Boddaert). When, however, the Holboell's Red-necked Grebe is referred to another genus, the subspecific name *major* becomes available and has priority over *Podiceps holböllii* Reinhardt,[7] since it was not originally described in *Colymbus* and would become untenable only if transferred to that genus. The name of the present race under this arrangement now becomes *Pedetaithya grisegena major* (Temminck and Schlegel).

[1] *Syst. Nat.* 10th ed., vol. 1 (Jan. 1, 1758), p. 135.
[2] *Cat. Genera and Subgenera Birds British Mus.* (1855), p. 125.
[3] *Water Birds North Amer.*, vol. 2 (1884), p. 425.
[4] *Skizz. Entwickel.-Gesch. Natürl. Syst. Eur. Thierwelt* (1829 [after April]), p. 44.
[5] *Fauna Japonica* (1842), p. 22, pl. 78-B (Japan).
[6] *Tabl. Planch. Enlum. d'Hist. Nat.* (1783), p. 24.
[7] *Videnskab, Meddelelser Naturh. Før. Kjøvenhaven* for 1853, nos. 3–4 (1854), p. 76 (Nenortalik Julianehaab Dist. Greenland).

HORNED GREBE, *Dytes auritus*

This is another species which is structurally different from both the Old World Great Crested Grebe, *Colymbus cristatus* (= *Podiceps cristatus*), and *Pedetaithya grisegena*, and thus deserves generic separation. It is similar to *Colymbus* (= *Podiceps* Latham), but the exposed culmen is decidedly shorter than the head, and only 3 times breadth of bill at base, instead of 5; exposed culmen about 3 times height of bill at base, instead of more than 4; distance from anterior end of nostril to tip of culmen not more than the distance from the former point to rictus, instead of much greater—1.5 times; wing 5.5 times exposed culmen, instead of 3; height of bill at base 1.1 times its width at base, instead of 1.33; tarsus about twice length of exposed culmen, instead of 1.2 times; crest only lateral, not also occipital. The name to be applied to this group is *Dytes* Kaup,[1] of which the type by subsequent designation (Gray, 1842) is *Dytes cornutus* Gmelin, which is a race of *Colymbus auritus* Linnaeus. The Horned Grebe, now known as *Dytes auritus*, is the only species to be referred to this genus.

[1] *Skizz. Entwickel.-Gesch. Natürl. Syst. Eur. Thierwelt* (1829 [after April]), p. 41.

EARED GREBE, *Proctopus caspicus*

This is another generically distinct grebe. It differs from *Dytes auritus* as follows: distance from tip of culmen to anterior end of nostril much more (1.17 times) than distance from latter point to rictus, instead of less; exposed culmen only 3 times its height at base, instead of at least 3.75; height of bill at base about 1.07 times its width at base, instead of decidedly less than its width at base. The name to be applied to this genus is *Proctopus* Kaup,[1] of which the type by monotypy is *Podiceps auritus* Latham, which equals *Podiceps nigricollis* Brehm and *Podiceps caspicus* (Hablizl).

[1] *Skizz. Entwickel.-Gesch. Natürl. Syst. Eur. Thierwelt* (1829 [after April]), p. 49.

LEAST GREBE, *Limnodytes dominicus*

Limnodytes Oberholser, new genus. Similar to *Dytes* Kaup, but distance from anterior end of nostril to tip of culmen decidedly greater than distance from anterior end of nostril to rictus, instead of less or nearly equal; height of bill at base 1.3 times its width at same point, instead of about equal; head without crest; wing about 3.75 times length of exposed culmen, instead of 5.5; tarsus decidedly shorter than middle toe without claw, instead of equal. Type: *Colymbus dominicus* Linnaeus.

The Least Grebe, which has commonly been considered generically the same as most of the other grebes, proves to differ very interestingly in structural characters from all the others, and to constitute a monotypic genus. It is most closely allied to members of *Tachybaptus* Reichenbach (type, *Colymbus ruficollis* Pallas), but differs as follows: distance from tip of culmen to anterior end of nostril is more than distance from latter point to rictus, instead of less or equal; feathering on culmen reaches not quite as far forward as that on sides of maxilla; tarsus only 1.3 to 1.4 times exposed culmen, instead of 1.8 or more; wing 2.9 times tarsus, instead of 2.5 to 2.6; wing less than 4 times exposed culmen, instead of more.

The North American race, therefore, stands as *Limnodytes dominicus brachypterus*.

WHITE PELICAN, *Cyrtopelicanus erythrorhynchos*

The American White Pelican differs structurally from the typical White Pelican of Europe, *Pelecanus onocrotalus*, which is the type of genus *Pelecanus*, almost as much as does the Brown Pelican, and likewise should be generically separated from the typical species. Characters that separate *Pelecanus erythrorhynchos* Gmelin from *Pelecanus onocrotalus* may be outlined as follows: lower base of mandible feathered instead of bare; bare area around eye rather narrow instead of very wide; supraloral region feathered instead of bare; supraloral region on sides of forehead not swollen; outline of feathers on base of culmen broad with a median and blunt point, instead of being sharply and acutely pointed; culmen possessing a semicircular bony crest during breeding season, a character unique among the pelicans. From *Leptopelicanus occidentalis* the White Pelican differs generically in its feathered base of the lower mandible; wider bare area around eye; bluntly and singly pointed anterior outline of feathers on base of culmen; conspicuous terminal constriction of culminicorn; basal phalanges of middle toe scutellate instead of reticulate; tarsus longer than middle toe without claw; twenty-four tail feathers; and presence of a bony crest on maxilla during breeding season. The name for this genus is *Cyrtopelicanus* Reichenbach,[1] of which the type is by original designation, *Pelecanus trachyrhynchus* Latham, which is *Pelecanus erythrorhynchos* Gmelin.

[1] *Avium Syst. Nat.* (1852 [1853]), p. 7.

BROWN PELICAN, *Leptopelicanus occidentalis*

All pelicans are currently included in a single genus. There are, however, excellent structural characters separating the Brown Pelican from the European bird, *Pelecanus onocrotalus* Linnaeus, which should be recognized generically. *Pelecanus occidentalis* Linnaeus differs from *Pelecanus*, of which *P. onocrotalus* is the type, in the following characters: supraloral region feathered; bare area around eye very narrow; anterior configuration of feathering on base of culmen V-shaped with two sharply pointed projections; supraloral region on sides of forehead not swollen; culminicorn not constricted terminally; naked part of pouch extending halfway down side of neck; tarsus shorter than middle toe without claw, and about equal to length of two basal phalanges; basal phalanx of middle toe reticulate instead of scutellate; twenty-two tail feathers. The generic name to be applied to the Brown Pelican is, of course, *Leptopelicanus* Reichenbach,[1] of which the type by original description is *Pelecanus fuscus* Gmelin, which is the same as *Pelecanus occidentalis* Linnaeus.

[1] *Avium Syst. Nat.* (1852 [1853]), p. 7.

BLUE-FACED BOOBY, *Parasula dactylatra*

This species is very different structurally from the typical members of the genus *Sula* (type, *Pelecanus piscator* Linnaeus), with which it is commonly associated and it should, therefore, be separated as a distinct generic group. It differs from *Sula* in its very short tail—much less than half length of wing (instead of decidedly more), much less strongly wedge-shaped (the central pair of feathers projecting but little beyond the next pair), and with all sixteen rectrices broadly, less sharply pointed; stouter bill, in length only 2½ times its height at base, instead of 3; long wing tip, the wing only 3¾ times length of wing tip, instead of 6 or more, and 1½ times length of middle toe, instead of about equal to this; and rather long tarsus, which is ⅗ length of exposed culmen (about half in *Sula*), and longer than basal two phalanges of middle toe, instead of not longer. The name for this group is *Parasula* Mathews,[1] the type of which is by original designation *Sula dactylatra bedouti* Mathews.

[1] *Austral Avian Record*, vol. 2, nos. 2 & 3 (Oct. 23, 1913), p. 55.

BROWN BOOBY, *Sula leucogastra*

The specific name of this species, *Pelecanus leucogaster* Boddaert, becomes *leucogastra* when combined with the generic name *Sula*, which is of feminine gender, since *leucogaster* is an adjective, not a noun.

RED-FOOTED BOOBY, *Sula piscator*

Some authors, including Mathews[1] and Peters,[2] have rejected the name *Pelecanus piscator* Linnaeus as unidentifiable. It is true, of course, that in the original description of this species, Linnaeus confused four species and, therefore, the description as a whole is not applicable to any one of them.[3] Most of the description, however, clearly applies to the Red-footed Booby, and the name has been used by many subsequent authors for this species, including Baird, Brewer, and Ridgway.[4] There is no doubt that Linnaeus' description refers to a booby; and his name is based on his diagnosis, which is drawn from five different authors: Catesby, Ray, Sloane, Browne, and Osbeck, all of which he cites as references. Catesby's description is apparently of *Sula leucogastra*; Ray's bird is *Sula piscator* as currently recognized; Sloane describes *Sula leucogastra*; Browne, the same species; and Osbeck describes the male of *Sula cyanops* and the female of *Sula piscator*.[5] Were application of name dependent entirely on references, *Sula leucogastra* would have the preference, but Linnaeus' original description must, of course, be taken into consideration, and this, as above indicated, mostly applies to the bird now known as *Sula piscator*. As in similar complicated cases in which the original diagnosis is drawn from the characters of more than one species, the name should be fixed on that species to which the original description most applies, if this is determinable; else the action of the first reviser should hold. Otherwise, we should have to reject a great many names of similar origin that are now in current use. Since *piscator* has been clearly applied to this species by several authors and with evident intent, there would seem to be no valid reason for not continuing the name *Sula piscator* for this species.

The name of the North American bird should be a trinomial, since there is a recognizable race in Australia and the Indian Ocean called *S. p. rubripes* Gould, and another in the Galápagos Islands called *S. p. websteri* Rothschild. The North American bird would, therefore, stand as *S. p. piscator*.

[1] *Birds Australia*, vol. 4, pt. 3 (June 23, 1915), p. 212–216.
[2] *Check-List Birds World* 1 (Oct. 6, 1931): 84fn.
[3] Linnaeus, *Syst. Nat.* 10th ed., vol. 1 (Jan. 1, 1758), p. 134.
[4] *Water Birds North Amer.*, vol. 2 (1884), p. 182.
[5] Catesby, *Nat. Hist. Carolina, Florida, and Bahama Is.*, vol. 1 (1731), p. 87, also pl. 87; Ray, *Syn. Meth. Avium et Piscium* (1713), p. 191; Sloane, *Voyage Madera, Barbados, . . . and Jamaica*, vol. 2 (1725), p. 322, pl. 271, fig. 2; Browne, *Nat. Hist. Jamaica* (1789), p. 481; Osbeck, *Voyage China*, Eng. ed. (1772), p. 128.

OLIVACEOUS CORMORANT, *Phalacrocorax brasilianus*

The technical name of this cormorant in current use is *Phalacrocorax olivaceus*, but this now apparently needs to be changed. The specific term *olivaceus* is antedated by *Phalacrocorax brasilianus* (Gmelin),[1] which is based on a bird from Brazil described by Piso,[2] now identified by Hellmayr and Conover[3] as the present species.

[1] *Syst. Nat.*, vol. 1, pt. 2 (1789), p. 564.
[2] *Ind. Utrinsque Re. Nat. Med.* (1658), p. 83.
[3] *Zool. Series Field Mus. Nat. Hist.*, vol. 13, pt. 1, no. 2 (Aug. 18, 1948), pp. 141–145, 141fn.

ANHINGA, *Anhinga anhinga*

The subspecific name of the Florida Anhinga should be spelled *leucogastra*, since *leucogaster* is an adjective, not a noun, and should agree in gender with the generic name.

Taxonomic investigation of the Anhinga indicates there are at least three races, and that the nominate race, *A. a. anhinga* (Linnaeus) is confined to South America and Panama. The bird from n.w. Mexico to El Salvador differs from the South American race in its much smaller general size and in having the tips of the tail feathers paler and more grayish (less buffy); it has been named *A. a. minima* by A. J. van Rossem[1] from Acaponeta, Nayarit, Mexico. It apparently occurs occasionally in Texas.

[1] *Annals and Mag. Nat. Hist.*, 11th ser. 4 (Oct., 1939): 439.

SNOWY EGRET, *Leucophoyx thula*

Snowy Egrets from the e. United States differ very considerably from birds from s. South America in their decidedly longer bills and tarsi, but scarcely longer wings, and represent a recognizable race. Males from Chile range in wing length from 235 to 264 (average, 249) mm.; bill (exposed culmen), 66.5 to 78.5 (73.4); and length of tarsus, 75 to 86.5 (81.7). Male specimens from the e. United States range in wing length from 237 to 263

(250.1); bill, 76.5 to 86.5 (80.8); and in length of tarsus, 95 to 109.5 (100). Similar differences are shown by females. Resident birds from Argentina, Peru, Brazil, Guyana, French Guiana, and Trinidad are apparently the same as those from Chile; but birds from Venezuela and c. Ecuador, also probably Colombia, as well as Central America, are larger and nearer—if indeed not identical—to birds from the e. United States. Wanderers of the northern race, both in and outside the breeding season, range also to n.e. and s.e. Brazil.

The oldest name for the species is *Ardea thula* Molina,[1] based on the bird from Chile, which is therefore available for the bird ranging over most of South America. The name for the northeastern race is apparently *Ardea candidissima* Gmelin,[2] based on the bird from n. Colombia. This, without much doubt, is the same as the northern bird, since in migration it occurs south to e. Ecuador and Brazil. It is probably safe to use this name in this sense, for even in case it should develop that the breeding bird of Colombia is the same as the bird from Chile, the northern bird certainly occurs there in winter or in migration. The present writer, therefore, definitely fixes the name *Ardea candidissima* Gmelin on the larger northeastern form that breeds in Florida and other parts of the s.e. United States; type locality, Carthagena, n. Colombia. Thus, the name of this race would become *L. t. candidissima* (Gmelin). In case *Ardea candidissima* of Gmelin should be found unavailable, another name that is applicable to this race is *Ardea carolinensis* Ord,[3] the type locality of which is "Sommer's Beach, Cape May, New Jersey," —a name formerly used for the present site of Ocean City, New Jersey.

The race of the Snowy Egret occurring in the U.S. Great Basin, now named *L. t. arileuca*, has sometimes been referred to the Brewster's Snowy Egret, *L. t. brewsteri*, of Baja California, and sometimes to the eastern bird now distinguished as *L. t. candidissima*; however, as shown in the detailed account, it is not properly referable to either.

[1] *Saggio Stor. Nat. Chile* (1782), p. 235.
[2] *Syst. Nat.*, vol. 1, pt. 2 (1789 [before Apr. 20]), p. 633 ("prope Carthagenam Americae").
[3] See Wilson, *Amer. Ornith.*, vol. 7 (1824 [1825]), p. 125, pl. 62, fig. 4.

AMERICAN BITTERN, *Botaurus lentiginosus*

The use of a trinomial for the Eastern American Bittern becomes necessary because of the separation of the bird from the Pacific coast as an additional subspecies, *B. l. peeti*. This latter race, some time ago described, seems recognizably distinct. It was named by Pierce Brodkorb[1] from birds taken from Black Point Cutoff, Sonoma Co., California.

[1] *Occas. Papers Mus. Zool. Univ. Michigan*, no. 333 (May 26, 1936), p. 2.

WHITE-FACED IBIS, *Plegadis mexicana*

The technical name for this ibis now apparently should be *Plegadis mexicana* (Gmelin),[1] as shown by Hellmayr and Conover,[2] since this antedates *Plegadis chihi* (Vieillot) presently used for the species.

[1] *Syst. Nat.*, vol. 1, pt. 2 (Apr., 1789), p. 652 ("Novae Hispaniae" = Mexico).
[2] *Zool. Series Field Mus. Nat. Hist.*, vol. 13, pt. 1, no. 1 (Apr. 20, 1942), p. 301.

CANADA GOOSE, *Branta canadensis*

There is available for the Interior Canada Goose a name

much older than *B. c. interior* Todd which, up to the present, has been used for this bird. This is *B. c. major* (Rae),[1] proposed for the bird from the region about Moose Factory, Ontario. Comparing it to birds from west of Hudson Bay to the Mackenzie River, Rae diagnosed it by the "ruddy brown colour of the plumage on the breast, by the extreme loudness and sonorousness of the call, and by the so much greater size." This goose, therefore, should be known as *B. c. major* (Rae).

Delacour[2] has recently separated the bird from the Aleutian Islands from the birds of the Alaska mainland and called the latter *B. c. taverneri*, whereby this becomes the name of the Lesser Canada Goose. The race was originally included as a winter resident in Texas on the basis of mention of this state in the winter range of Delacour's original description.

[1] *Canadian Rec. Sci.* 3 (July, 1888): 127 ("Ruperts River, about 100 miles to the East of Moose").
[2] *Amer. Mus. Novitates*, no. 1537 (Nov. 12, 1951), p. 7 ("Colusa, California").

RICHARDSON'S GOOSE, *Branta hutchinsii*

While the Eastern Richardson's Goose, *B. h. hutchinsii*, is considered a subspecies of the Canada Goose, data presented by P. A. Taverner[1] indicate that the small pale Canada Goose of n.e. North America is a distinct species. Its relatively short, narrow bill, more like that of a brant than of the Canada Goose, its very small size, its different nesting habits, characteristic voice, and the fact that its breeding range is partly coincident with that of *B. canadensis major*, *B. c. parvipes*, and *B. c. taverneri* all apparently point to its specific distinctness. Compared to *B. c. taverneri*, its bill is smaller, usually not over 35 mm. in length, and relatively high at the base, with length of culmen usually about 1.62 times (instead of 1.9) its height at base; furthermore, the width of bill at base of posterior end of nail is less than its height at base, whereas in the forms of *B. canadensis* this dimension is greater than, or at least equal to, the height at base.

Also, J. W. Aldrich[2] is probably right in considering that *B. h. hutchinsii* is but subspecifically related to *Branta minima*, which is also specifically different from *B. canadensis*.

[1] *Annual Report Nat. Mus. Canada* for 1929 [1931], pp. 37–40.
[2] *Wilson Bull.* 58 (June [Aug. 5], 1946): 95.

BLACK BRANT, *Branta nigricans*

It has been shown by Delacour and Zimmer[1] that the Black Brants of the Pacific area are subspecifically different from those of the Atlantic coast. For the former, the available name is *Branta nigricans orientalis* Tougarinov.[2] The eastern race is probably extinct.

[1] *Auk* 69 (Jan. 2, 1952): 82–84.
[2] *Faune de l'URSS Aves* (Acad. Sci. URSS, Moscow), vol. 1, no. 4 (1941), p. 180.

ROSS' GOOSE, *Exanthemops rossii*

This species is commonly called *Chen rossii*, although in some publications it is placed in a separate subgenus. *C. hyperborea* (Pallas) and *C. caerulescens* (Linnaeus), the other two species which comprise the present genus, are strictly congeneric. The Ross' Goose, however, differs so greatly in structural characters from these two that it deserves not only subgeneric but generic distinction, because these characters do not overlap by either individual variation or by intervention of intermediate species. *Chen rossii* differs from the typical genus *Chen* as follows: bill

relatively, as well as actually, shorter than head; commissure not widely gaping; anterior outline of feathering on sides of base of maxilla nearly straight, instead of triangular or strongly convex; wing 8¾, instead of 7, times length of exposed culmen; and, in adult, base of maxilla much wrinkled and warty, instead of always smooth; also, tarsus 1¾, instead of 1⅓, times exposed culmen.

Separation of *C. rossii* has usually been made chiefly on the wrinkled and warty appearance of the adult's bill. One reason for lack of recognition as a distinct genus has been that in some specimens this warty appearance is not visible; it should be noted, however, that this smooth condition is due to immaturity, and that all *rossii* adults have the warts. This never occurs in the two other species, except perhaps as an abnormality. Furthermore, the other characters mentioned are amply sufficient to warrant generic separation. The name to be applied to it as a monotypic genus is *Exanthemops* Elliott,[1] the type of which by original designation is *Anser rossii* Cassin.

[1] *New and Unfigured Birds North America*, vol. 2, pt. 9 (1868), pl. 44 and text.

FULVOUS TREE DUCK, *Dendrocygna bicolor*

The currently recognized race of this species from Mexico and the United States, *D. b. helva*,[1] apparently now cannot be maintained. Herbert Friedmann[2] in his review of the tree ducks considered this subspecies valid; however, after further investigation, he has verbally informed the writer that he cannot separate it from the nominate form. Following this opinion, the name of the North American bird, therefore, becomes a binomial, *Dendrocygna bicolor* (Vieillot).

[1] Wetmore and Peters, *Proc. Biol. Soc. Washington* 35 (Mar. 20, 1922): 42.
[2] *Condor* 49 (Aug. 8, 1947): 191–194.

MALLARD, *Anas platyrhyncha*

The specific name of this bird was originally written *Anas platyrhynchos* by Linnaeus,[1] and in much current literature this spelling has been perpetuated. The specific name *platyrhynchos* is a Latinized Greek adjective of masculine gender—not a noun as used by Linnaeus—so that when combined with a genus of feminine gender, as in this case with *Anas*, it should be spelled *platyrhyncha*.

The American Mallard has heretofore been considered identical with that of Europe and Asia, but since the Greenland bird, *A. p. conboschas*, is an easily recognizable race, it seems reasonable that the American bird should be different from the European form, and such now proves to be the case. A comparison of series of birds from Europe and Asia with a series from North America reveals birds from the latter to be larger, particularly the wings. Furthermore, upper parts of North American males—especially backs, scapulars, and wings—are lighter (more grayish, less brownish). Females, however, are not so different in color (North American birds are only somewhat more grayish above); thus, the best character for identification of females is the smaller size of the Old World bird. Following measurements of the European Mallard may be compared with those given for the American bird: *Adult male*: Wing, 257.0–274.1 (average, 265.4) mm.; tail, 81.0–90.9 (85.9); bill (exposed culmen), 48.5–59.9 (55.6); height of bill at base, 18.0–23.1 (21.1); tarsus, 42.9–46.5 (45.2); middle toe without claw, 50.0–55.1 (52.8). *Adult female*: Wing, 248.9–265.9 (258.5); tail, 81.0–90.9 (85.9); bill, 48.0–54.1 (51.1); height of bill, 18.0–20.1 (19.0); tarsus, 41.4–45.0 (43.7); middle toe, 47.0–51.6 (49.5).

From *A. p. conboschas*, the North American subspecies is easily distinguished by its lighter, somewhat more brownish upper parts, particularly the scapulars; paler posterior lower parts; more finely vermiculated sides of body; and lack of black spots on breast and jugulum.

This American race was, a number of years ago, separated and named *A. p. americana*,[2] for which information the writer is indebted to Herbert Friedmann. This name, however, is preoccupied by *A. americana* Gmelin,[3] which is *Mareca americana* (Gmelin), and is therefore not available for the American race of the Mallard. It is instead to be called *A. p. neoborea*.

[1] *Syst. Nat.* 10th ed., vol. 1 (Jan. 1, 1758), p. 125.
[2] Stechow, *Münchener Medizinische Wochenschrift*, vol. 70, pt. 1, no. 16 (Apr. 20, 1923), p. 517 ("Manitoba, Kanada").
[3] *Syst. Nat.*, vol. 1, pt. 2 (Apr., 1789), p. 526.

GADWALL, *Chaulelasmus streperus*

This species seems to be generically different from the Mallard, which is the type of the genus *Anas* Linnaeus. The former differs structurally as follows: culmen shorter than middle toe without claw, also shorter than head; feathering on side of maxilla reaching farther forward than that of side of mandible; and lamellae of bill much more prominent. The available generic name for the Gadwall is *Chaulelasmus* Bonaparte.

PINTAIL, *Dafila acuta*

Some authors include this species in the genus *Anas* along with the Mallard. It seems, however, to have sufficient characters of its own to separate it generically. It differs from *Anas* in having tail nearly as long as wing, instead of not half as long, graduated for more than ⅓ its total length, with middle feathers very long and pointed; and bill shorter than head. The generic name for the Pintail is, of course, *Dafila* Stephens.

GREEN-WINGED TEAL, *Nettion carolinense*

This duck differs generically from the Mallard, genus *Anas*, in the following respects: head somewhat crested; bill very narrow, its nail only ⅕, instead of ⅓, width of bill at tip; feathers on side of culmen reach farther forward than feathers on base of mandible below. The generic name to be used for this species is, of course, *Nettion* Kaup.

BLUE-WINGED TEAL, *Querquedula discors*

The present species and its ally, the Cinnamon Teal, differ generically from *Anas* in the following characters: bill decidedly narrower at base than terminally, with convex sides, not nearly parallel; nail of bill more sharply hooked and semicircular; feathers on side of culmen extending farther forward than those on base of mandible. Consequently, they should be referred to *Querquedula* Stephens, which seems to be a recognizable genus, notwithstanding many attempts to throw it into the wastebasket *Anas*.

CINNAMON TEAL, *Querquedula cyanoptera*

See Blue-winged Teal.

REDHEAD, *Nyroca americana*

The Redhead is generically separable from the Canvasback, *Aristonetta valisineria*, as explained under that species; it is likewise generically different from the scaups, *Aythya*. *Nyroca* Fleming,[1] of which the type by tautonomy is *Anas nyroca* Guldenstädt, seems to be the proper generic name for the Redhead, since it belongs to the same group as the Old World Ferruginous White-eyed Pochard, *Nyroca nyroca*, which is the type of *Nyroca*.

[1] *Philos. Zool.* 2 (1882): 260.

RING-NECKED DUCK, *Perissonetta collaris*

Although this species is commonly associated with the scaups, *Aythya*, it is much more closely related to the Redhead, *Nyroca americana*, but differs in several important structural particulars. In fact, it is rather closer in some characters to the Canvasback, *Aristonetta valisineria*. From *Nyroca* it differs in having length of exposed culmen equal to length of inner toe with claw, instead of decidedly shorter; feathering on sides of maxilla extending forward as far as feathering at base of culmen; anterior outline of feathering at base of culmen broadly convex; and length of wing only about 4 times length of exposed culmen. It and the Canvasback are the only species among its near allies, most of which are commonly included in *Nyroca*, that have length of exposed culmen about equal to length of inner toe with claw, and on this character alone are easily separable. However, the Ring-necked differs in a number of other characters from the Canvasback, notably in having base of culmen not deeply concave; anterior outline of feathering at base of culmen not acutely pointed, but broadly convex; bill less flattened anteriorly, shorter, stouter, and decidedly wider near end than at base; tip of maxilla strongly hooked; and nail of bill rather wide and subtriangular, instead of narrow with parallel sides.

The Ring-necked Duck, therefore, should be separated generically from the other species, with no others apparently in the same group. For this bird, the generic name *Perissonetta* Oberholser[1] is available (type by original designation, *Anas collaris* Donovan).

[1] *Proc. Indiana Acad. Sci.* for 1920 [Oct. 1, 1921], p. 110.

CANVASBACK, *Aristonetta valisineria*

By reason of very different structural characters, the Canvasback is well worthy of generic separation from other nominal members of the genus *Nyroca*. It differs from the typical species, the Ferruginous White-eyed Pochard, *Nyroca nyroca*, as follows: length of exposed culmen about equal to length of inner toe with claw, instead of decidedly shorter; base of culmen deeply concave; tip of maxilla little or not at all hooked; nail of bill narrower and straplike; length of exposed culmen about 3 times greatest width of bill; and no occipital crest. The only generic name applicable is *Aristonetta* Baird,[1] the type of which by original designation and monotypy is *Anas valisineria* Wilson. It is the only species of the genus.

[1] *Report Explor. and Surv. R. R. Pacific* 9 (1858): 793.

COMMON GOLDENEYE, *Glaucionetta clangula*

Some authors have questioned the generic separation of the Common Goldeneye from the Bufflehead, *Bucephala albeola*, but the latter differs in important generic characters from *Glaucionetta*, as has been well shown by Leonhard Stejneger[1] and Allan Brooks.[2] *Glaucionetta* is here restored to use for the Common Goldeneye, leaving *Bucephala* the monotypic genus of the Bufflehead. The Bufflehead stands apart in having nostrils in basal half of bill, instead of beyond middle; nostril narrow and its tubercle visible from outside; lamellae of bill not visible below cutting edges; and outer toe without claw decidedly longer than middle claw, instead of equal as in *Glaucionetta*; tip of inner toe reaching only to second joint of middle toe; tail long, more than twice length of tarsus and reaching beyond folded wings by nearly twice length of culmen. These characters are amply sufficient to render desirable the generic separation.

[1] *Bull. U.S. Nat. Mus.*, no. 29 (Dec. 16, 1885), p. 164.
[2] *Auk* 62 (Oct. 19, 1945): 519.

BARROW'S GOLDENEYE, *Clanganas islandica*

Clanganas Oberholser, new genus. Similar to *Glaucionetta* Stejneger (type, *Anas clangula* Linnaeus), but skull with frontal bone abruptly truncated at base of bill, producing a vertical depression that interrupts the even contour of the culmen to top of the head as in *Glaucionetta*; trachea without conspicuous bulbous enlargement that exists in the Common Goldeneye; bill smaller, relatively higher, the culmen depressed medially, and the nail large (occupying all tip of bill), and with lateral outlines very convex, and much less nearly parallel than in *Glaucionetta*. Type: *Anas islandica* Gmelin, the only species.

Structural characters separating Barrow's from the Common are so outstanding and actual, as well as relative, that there seems to be no reason for including the two species in the same genus.

SURF SCOTER, *Pelionetta perspicillata*

Many authors place this species in the same genus as the White-winged Scoter, *Melanitta deglandi*. Examination of structural characters, however, indicates it is fully entitled to separation from that species. Characters distinguishing the Surf from the White-winged are as follows: culmen at base gradually—instead of abruptly—elevated, the bare elevated portion of culmen at base very narrow; swollen base of maxilla unfeathered; width of bill at posterior end of nail much less than width at base; length of nail much greater than its width; nail of mandible narrower; symphysis of mandible narrower, acute; feathering on forehead advancing much farther anteriorly than feathers on side of bill, the latter falling short by almost the length of exposed culmen; exterior nares rather small and ovate, instead of very large and almost round; wing not over 3 times length of tail, usually less. By reason of these excellent generic characters the Surf Scoter should be recognized generically; there is available the generic name *Pelionetta* Kaup,[1] the type of which by monotypy is *Anas perspicillata* Linnaeus.

[1] *Skizz. Entwickel.-Gesch. Natürl. Syst. Eur. Thierwelt* (1829), p. 107.

AMERICAN SCOTER, *Oidemia americana*

Although certain authors treat this duck as a subspecies of the Common Scoter, *Oidemia nigra*, of Europe and Asia, it seems to be trenchantly different in some of its characters to be considered a distinct species. It differs in the following respects: knob at base of bill in adult male is very much less abruptly elevated, giving culmen, when viewed from the side, a gradually sloping outline, whereas in *O. nigra* the basal knob is level on top or even slightly ascending anteriorly; bill, when viewed from above, is very much wider, being greatly bulged laterally, instead of very narrow with almost parallel sides; anterior outline of feathering on side of maxilla is concave, instead of convex; and base of maxilla is yellow, instead of black. In none of these characters is there any evidence of intergradation when adult males are compared.

MASKED DUCK, *Nomonyx dominicus*

Some authors unite the genus *Nomonyx* with *Oxyura*, but they do so, it seems, without full consideration of the characters sep-

arating these two groups. Many trenchant structural differences appear to warrant their treatment as distinct genera. *Nomonyx* is distinguished from *Oxyura* as follows: tail much more than half wing length; outer toe with claw shorter than middle toe without claw; exposed culmen not longer than two basal phalanges of middle toe; feathering on sides of maxilla not reaching as far forward as that on culmen; greatest width of bill not greater than its height at base, nor more than half length of exposed culmen; width of base of bill on forehead much more than half greatest width of bill; height of bill at base much more than half length of exposed culmen; culmen little—instead of much—concave, and broad—instead of narrow—between nostrils; nail of maxilla, when viewed from above, very broad and triangular, instead of narrow and linear; and palatine bones of skull almost meeting each other at their posterior ends where they articulate with the pterygoids, instead of being widely separated at this point.

BLACK VULTURE, *Coragyps atratus*

Notwithstanding doubt expressed by some authors, there seem to be two recognizable races of the Black Vulture. Pierce Brodkorb has discussed this problem and arrived at the conclusion that ranges of the North American and temperate South American birds, *C. a. atratus*, are separated by a smaller tropical race ranging from Mexico to Brazil. To this supposed tropical race he assigned the name *C. a. brasiliensis* (Bonaparte).[1] The recognition of a South American race, *C. a. foetens*,[2] has been questioned by Friedmann,[3] in whose measurements there are included birds from all South America. If, however, the birds of extreme s. South America be considered apart, it is evident that they are decidedly smaller than birds from farther north, and apparently are representative of a different subspecies. By this arrangement, *foetens* would be confined chiefly to Paraguay, Uruguay, Chile, and Argentina. The North American bird would continue to be called *atratus*, with *brasiliensis* (Bonaparte) a synonym.

[1] Brodkorb, *Papers Michigan Acad. Sci., Arts, and Letters*, vol. 29 for 1943 [1944], pp. 115–121.
[2] *Cathartes foetens* Lichtenstein, *Verz. ausgest. Säug. und Vög.* (1818), p. 30 (Paraguay).
[3] *Proc. Biol. Soc. Washington* 46 (Oct. 26, 1933): 188.

GOSHAWK, *Accipiter gentilis*

Many papers have been written concerning the validity of the Western Goshawk. One by Taverner[1] resulted in his considering *A. g. striatulus* identical with *A. g. atricapillus*; but recognizing the distinctness of a western North American race, he described *Astur atricapillus laingi* as a new subspecies from the Queen Charlotte Islands, British Columbia. However, examination of material on which his form was based, reveals that birds from the Queen Charlotte Islands are no more different from birds from the e. United States than are the breeding birds from s.e. Alaska, w. Washington, w. Oregon, south as far as c. California; thus, the range of the Pacific coast race, whatever its name, must be extended from that given by Taverner to include all the coastal country between s.e. Alaska and c. California. Specimens which undoubtedly represent localities of breeding have been examined from Sitka, Alaska; Fort Simpson and Queen Charlotte Islands, British Columbia; Fort Steilacoom, Washington; Douglas Co., Oregon; and Mt. Shasta and Big Trees, California. Moreover, a reexamination of the type of *A. g. striatulus* from Fort Steilacoom, Washington—and evidently a breeding bird—shows, when compared with a series of eastern birds and with the western birds above indicated, that it is nearer the Pacific coast race than to typical *atricapillus*, although apparently a little intermediate. For this reason it is evident that the Pacific coast race, which has commonly been called *striatulus*, should continue to be called this. The southern race described by van Rossem as *A. g. apache*,[2] from Paradise, Cochise Co., Arizona, is too dark to be referred to other than the Pacific coast race. Birds from Idaho, Utah, w. Colorado, and New Mexico are decidedly intermediate, but somewhat nearer the western subspecies.

While the Western Goshawk is not very strongly characterized subspecifically, it is recognizable on the basis of darker color of upper parts in the adult, and of darker upper and lower parts in the immature.

[1] *Condor* 42 (May 15, 1940): 157–160.
[2] *Proc. Biol. Soc. Washington* 51 (May 19, 1938): 99.

ZONE-TAILED HAWK, *Buteo albonotatus*

The technical name of this hawk becomes a trinomial because of a South American subspecies, *B. a. abbreviatus* Cabanis.

BROAD-WINGED HAWK, *Craxirex platypterus*

The genus *Buteo* includes about twenty-eight distinct species well scattered over much of the world. More or less closely allied to it, and sometimes considered distinct, and sometimes wholly or in part merged with it, are the genera *Tachytriorchus* Kaup (type, *Buteo albicaudatus* Vieillot); *Asturina* Vieillot (type, *Falco nitidus* Latham); *Rupornis* Kaup (type, *Falco magnirostris* Gmelin); *Coryornis* Ridgway (type, *Rupornis ridgwayi* Cory); and *Percnohierax* Ridgway (type, *Falco leucorrhous* Quoy and Gaimard).

In order to determine satisfactorily the proper generic names for our North American forms of *Buteo*, the writer has carefully studied the structural characters of all species in these groups, with the single exception of *Buteo auguralis*.

The bird called *Buteo leucorrhous*, which was the type of Ridgway's genus *Percnohierax*, does not, so far as is determinable, differ in any important structural respect from other allied species of *Buteo*. This generic name, therefore, should be synonymized with *Buteo*. The same is true of *Coryornis* Ridgway, which was thought to be a monotypic group comprising only *Rupornis ridgwayi* Cory. None of the characters assigned in the original description hold when several specimens are examined and compared with all species in the typical genus *Buteo*.

Furthermore, much to the writer's surprise, and notwithstanding a remarkably different pattern of coloration, there seem to be no structural characters whatever to distinguish any of the forms of *Asturina* Vieillot from the type and congeneric species in *Buteo*. Unless mere difference in color pattern is to be considered a sufficient basis for generic separation, which does not seem desirable, *Asturina* should be merged with *Buteo*, the type of which by tautonymy is *Falco buteo* Linnaeus, and which becomes the generic name for the species having four emarginate primaries. The species now considered are those of the current *Buteo* and those of *Asturina*, *Coryornis*, and *Percnohierax*.

When carefully examined, one perfectly good character divides these species into two groups, apparently with no intermediates. (There are other minor modifications, particularly of relative length of primaries, but none seems sufficient to make possible a constant further division into even subgeneric groups, because there is so much overlapping and interdigitating.) This character consists in the emargination of the inner webs of the primaries. In a group comprising most of the species, four primaries are emarginate; also, in many cases an additional primary is sinuate. In the other group, only three primaries are emarginate and one sinuate. The species of the latter group are *Polyborus galapagoensis* Gould, *Falco leucorrhous* Quoy and Gaimard, *Falco vulpinus* Gloger, *Buteo brachyurus* Vieillot, *Buteo swainsoni* Bonaparte, and *Sparvius platypterus* Vieillot. These hawks form a group that is readily separable from the remaining species of *Buteo*; the earliest name applicable to these six species is *Craxirex* Gould,[1] the type of which is by monotypy *Polyborus galapagoensis* Gould.

The genus *Buteo* Lacépède,[2] the type of which by tautonymy is *Falco buteo* Linnaeus, includes the species having four emarginate primaries, with one single exception. This is *Buteo albicaudatus* Vieillot, which is so different that it is readily separable generically from all other species here considered. Its generic name is *Tachytriorchis* Kaup (see White-tailed Hawk).

[1] *Zool. Voyage Beagle, Birds* (Jan., 1839), p. 22.
[2] *Tableau Oiseaux* (1799), p. 4.

SWAINSON'S HAWK, *Craxirex swainsoni*

As explained under the Broad-winged Hawk, this species is one of the hawks formerly included in *Buteo* which belongs in the genus *Craxirex*.

WHITE-TAILED HAWK, *Tachytriorchis albicaudatus*

The bird now called *Buteo albicaudatus* is structurally so different from other birds of *Buteo* that it belongs in a separate genus. It differs from *Buteo* (as defined under the Broad-winged Hawk) in its relatively long tarsus, which is about ½ as long as the tail, at least not much less, whereas in *Buteo* it is much less, usually about ⅓; relatively long wings, which are decidedly more than twice or about twice length of tail (never decidedly less than twice), and when folded do not materially fall short of tip of tail, instead of decidedly so; secondaries very short— when wing is folded their tips fall short of tips of primaries by about ¾ length of tail, whereas in *Buteo* they fall short by very much less, often less than half, at most not more than ⅔; tarsus about 2⅔ length of exposed culmen, including cere, instead of 2⅓ or less; and wing about 4½ length of tarsus, instead of 5½ times or more. The only generic name applicable to this species is *Tachytriorchis* Kaup,[1] the type of which by monotypy is *Falco pterocles* Temminck (=*Buteo albicaudatus* Vieillot).

[1] *Classif. Säug. und Vögel* (1884), p. 123.

BALD EAGLE, *Haliaeetus leucocephalus*

Investigations of the status of the northern and southern races of the Bald Eagle have shown that the range of the Northern Bald Eagle extends much farther south than has heretofore been supposed, and includes at least the northern half of the United States, in places even more. This change in the conception of the range of the two subspecies has considerable bearing on the names to be used for each. It is found that the name for the northern bird must be taken from Audubon's description of his "Bird of Washington." This he named *Falco washingtoniensis* in the folio edition of *Birds of America* (Aug.–Sept., 1827, pl. 11) from a bird taken by him near Henderson, Kentucky. This is a large bird, certainly a Bald Eagle, differing very little, if at all, from the large birds found in Alaska and other of the most northern parts of North America (even if Audubon did give measurements rather too large). Therefore, without reasonable doubt, it is of the same subspecies. If so, the name should be used for the northern bird now called *H. l. alascanus* Townsend. This has been indicated by James L. Peters,[1] and Herbert Friedmann.[2]

Shortly after the appearance of this name *Falco washingtoniensis*, Audubon[3] published an article on the "Bird of Washington," in which he called it *Falco washingtoniana*. Furthermore, it now develops that there must have been two issues, or editions, of plate 11 of the folio edition of *Birds of America*. In most copies of this work, plate 11 is labeled *Falco washingtonii*, horizontally at the bottom of the plate under the figure. However, in the copy in the Museum of Comparative Zoology, Cambridge, Massachusetts, which Peters consulted, and in at least two other copies now examined, the plate is labeled *Falco washingtoniensis*; this, with the vernacular name, is placed on the left foreground somewhat oblique to the figure and edge of the paper. In the article in which Audubon calls the bird *Falco washingtoniana*, figure 53, which represents the "Bird of Washington," is evidently taken from the edition of plate 11 in which the bird is given as *Falco washingtoniensis*, since it bears the inscription on the base of the mount "The Bird of Washington" much as in that issue, although the figure is reversed in position. It is known that the first ten plates of Audubon's *Birds of America* were engraved by Lizars and that the plates subsequent to number ten were engraved by R. Havell. From existence of two different sets of plates it is probable that the first issue of plate 11 by Lizars,[4] which is after the style of the first ten—with the name of the bird on the rock at the left side of the plate, was subsequently replaced by Havell to agree with the new style that the subsequent plates followed; that is, with the scientific name at the base of the plate and centered on the page. Thus, those plates in which the name of this bird appears as *Falco washingtonii* are of the latter style, as are also the subsequent plates of the work. Apparently but few copies of what may be regarded as the first edition of this plate were distributed, since most copies of the folio edition contain the plate labeled *Falco washingtonii*. The circumstances mentioned above would seem to indicate that Peters is correct in using this subspecific name *washingtoniensis*, instead of *washingtonii*, because of the fact that this edition of plate 11 by Lizars was the earlier one. At any rate, with present knowledge, authors can do no better than accept *H. l. washingtoniensis* (Audubon) on the basis of facts detailed.

It has been contended that Outram Bangs[5] was the first reviser and therefore settled the name of the North American Bald Eagle when he separated this northern race and applied to it the name *H. l. washingtoni* (Audubon). An author to be a real first reviser must, in making a selection, consider all the names available, else his decision can scarcely be conclusive.

In this case, however, there is no evidence that Bangs even knew of the name *washingtoniensis*. He, therefore, can hardly be considered the first reviser. The same principle applies, of course, to the action by Baird[6] who first proposed separation of the two races of the Bald Eagle, but made no mention of the name *washingtoniensis*. If any first reviser is to be used in this case he certainly should be Peters, not Bangs.

[1] *Check-List Birds World* 1 (Oct. 6, 1931): 258.
[2] *Bull. U.S. Nat. Mus.*, no. 50, pt. 11 (Sept. 29, 1950), pp. 494, 495fn.
[3] *Loudon's Mag. Nat. Hist.* 1 (July, 1828): 115–120, and fig. 53.
[4] Authoritative texts on Audubon's plates state that Lizars did only the first ten plates and no more. Apparently, Oberholser is in error here; however, his opinion has been left intact. —EDITOR
[5] *Auk* 15 (Apr., 1898): 174.
[6] *Rep. Explor. and Surv. R. R. Pacific* 9 (1858): 42.

CARACARA, *Caracara plancus*

North American birds of this species have commonly been considered subspecifically identical and have been treated as a race of *Caracara cheriway*—a species ranging only to n. South America. However, Hellmayr and Conover[1] seem to have shown conclusively that *C. cheriway* intergrades with, and thus cannot be specifically separated from, *C. plancus* (Miller), whose range extends to Tierra del Fuego. This being the case, the North American birds become a subspecies of *C. plancus*.

The Caracara inhabiting n.w. Mexico has been described as a new race, *Polyborus cheriway ammophilus*.[2] While the birds from n.e. Mexico and from Texas are intermediate between the bird inhabiting Florida, *C. p. audubonii* (Cassin), and the bird from n.w. Mexico, they still seem probably better referred to this Mexican race, as was done by van Rossem; thus, the name of the Texas bird would be *C. p. ammophilus*.

[1] *Zool. Series Field Mus. Nat. Hist.*, vol. 13, pt. 1, no. 4 (Aug. 19, 1949), pp. 283–284.
[2] van Rossem, *Annals and Mag. Nat. Hist.* 11th ser. 4 (Oct., 1939): 441 ("Tesia, Sonora, Mexico").

PRAIRIE FALCON, *Planofalco mexicanus*

In order to determine the proper generic name to be applied to this species it has been necessary to redetermine the proper type of the genus *Falco* Linnaeus. This has been commonly regarded as *Falco subbuteo* Linnaeus. The true type, however, now proves to be *Falco rusticolus* Linnaeus, on the basis of information in John Gould's *Birds of Europe*, where he wrote, "The Jerfalcon may be considered the type of the true Falcons."[1] The bird he calls the "Jerfalcon" is his *Falco islandicus*, as evidenced by the distribution he gives—n. Europe and occasionally Orkney and Shetland islands. Thus, it is equal to *Falco rusticolus* of Linnaeus. His plate represents a very dark bird, and a bird nearly white, thus showing two color phases of this species. That he regards his "Jerfalcon" as the European bird is further evident from the fact that he compares it with the Iceland Falcon, thus indicating he regarded the latter as a different bird. There seems to be no reason to doubt that Gould regarded the Gyrfalcon, *Falco rusticolor* Linnaeus, as the type of the genus *Falco*. If, however, a more definite statement is desired, it is to be found in an article by Shirley Palmer,[2] in which the author definitely fixes the type of *Falco* as the *Falco islandicus* of Gould, which is *Falco rusticolus*. Under these circumstances the genus called *Hierofalco* Cuvier,[3] including the Gyrfalcon, becomes a synonym of the genus *Falco* Linnaeus, and the latter becomes the proper generic name for the Gyrfalcon. Furthermore, the group including *Falco subbuteo* Linnaeus and a number of other Old World forms will need another generic designation. This is available in *Hypotriorchis* Boie,[4] of which the type by monotypy is *Falco subbuteo* Linnaeus, which therefore, now should be called *Hypotriorchis subbuteo* (Linnaeus).

The Prairie Falcon which is commonly included in *Falco*, and therefore considered congeneric with the Gyrfalcon, is generically distinct. As there seemed to be no name available for it, the writer has proposed *Planofalco*, from *planum*, a plain (or prairie), and *falco*, a hawk.[5] It differs from *Rhynchodon* Nitzsch (type, *Falco peregrinus* Tunstall) as follows: two primaries emarginate on inner web; two primaries sinuate on outer web; first (outermost) primary shorter than third; primary coverts not longer than shortest secondary; tarsus feathered for only about half its length; and its scales in front small. From *Falco* Linnaeus (type, *Falco islandicus* Gould=*Falco rusticolus* Linnaeus),[6] it may be distinguished by the following characters: claw of inner toe not reaching to base of claw of middle toe; outer toe without claw decidedly longer than inner toe without claw; tarsus feathered in front for only about half its length; and cere larger, occupying about ¼ of culmen. From *Gennaia* Kaup (type, *Falco biarmicus* Temminck), with which it is apparently most closely allied, *Planofalco* differs in having the first (outermost) and second primaries—instead of only the first primary—emarginate on inner web; the first primary much shorter than the third, instead of about equal; tarsus feathered for about half its length in front; middle toe without claw equal to tarsus, not decidedly shorter; hallux without claw not longer than basal joint of middle toe, instead of decidedly longer; claw of hallux long, equal to hallux itself, not shorter.

A further examination of plumages of this species has revealed the existence of a hitherto unrecognized subspecies inhabiting the n.w. United States and s.w. British Columbia. The species was originally described by Schlegel[7] from Mexico, and the type locality was subsequently determined as Monterrey, Nuevo León, Mexico. Since, in all probability, the majority of the birds that winter or migrate through the region of this type locality belong to the eastern and southern race, it would seem logical to consider this the nominate form and to apply to it Schlegel's name *Falco mexicanus*; its name by this procedure would be *Planofalco mexicanus mexicanus* Schlegel. The name to be used for the northwestern subspecies is apparently *Falco polyagrus* Cassin,[8] since this is based evidently on a specimen from California belonging to this form. If this is correct, the name of this race will be *Planofalco mexicanus polyagrus* (Cassin).

[1] *Birds Europe*, vol. 1 (1835), text to pl. 19.
[2] *Analyst* 4 (1836): 271.
[3] *Règne Animal* 1 (1817 [Dec. 7, 1816]): 312 (type by monotypy, *Falco candicans* Gmelin).
[4] *Isis (von Oken)* 19 ([Oct.] 1826): column "976" [= 970].
[5] Oberholser, *American Midland Nat.* 9 (Nov. 25, 1925): 601 fn.
[6] *Syst. Nat.* 10th ed., vol. 1 (Jan. 1, 1758), p. 88.
[7] *Falco mexicanus* Schlegel, *Abh. Geb. Zool.*, no. 3 (1850), p. 15.
[8] *Illust. Birds Calif., Texas, . . . Russian Amer.*, pt. 3 (Jan., 1854), p. 88, pl. 16, left fig.

PEREGRINE FALCON, *Rhynchodon peregrinus*

The group to which the Peregrine Falcon belongs is undoubtedly entitled to independent generic rank. Its proper name is *Rhynchodon* Nitzsch,[1] the type of which is *Falco peregrinus* Tunstall, by subsequent designation of the A.O.U. Nomenclature Committee.[2] *Rhynchodon* differs from *Aesalon* (type, *Falco aesalon* Tunstall=*Falco regulus* Pallas) as follows: only one primary —instead of two—emarginate on inner web; only one primary —instead of two—sinuate on outer web; first (outermost) primary longer than fourth, and also longer than third; primary coverts longer than shortest secondary; bill large; cere occupying about ¼ culmen; and tarsus stout, its entire front and inner face without transverse scutellae.

[1] *Observ. Avium Art. Carot. Com.* (1829), p. 20.
[2] *Check-List North Amer. Birds* (1886), p. 194.

APLOMADO FALCON, *Rhynchofalco femoralis*

The present species, *Falco fusco-coerulescens* Vieillot (=*Falco femoralis* Temminck), the type by original designation of the genus *Rhynchofalco* Ridgway,[1] is generically distinct from other members of *Falco* as at present constituted. It differs from *Tinnunculus* Vieillot as follows: bill relatively large; tarsus decidedly longer than middle toe with claw; claw of inner toe reaching

to base of claw of middle toe; and outer toe without claw decidedly longer than inner toe without claw.

[1] *Proc. Boston Soc. Nat. Hist.* 16 (1873): 46.

PIGEON HAWK, *Aesalon columbarius*

The generic name *Tinnunculus* Vieillot[1] has been found to apply to the group of small hawks including the Sparrow Hawk, *Tinnunculus sparverius*, and the Kestrel, *Tinnunculus tinnunculus*, the latter of which is the type by tautonymy.[2] Therefore, the proper generic name for the Pigeon Hawk proves to be *Aesalon* Kaup,[3] of which *Falco aesalon* Tunstall (=*Falco regulus* Pallas) is the type. The last-mentioned species and its close allies form a group of generic rank, which is distinguishable from *Rhynchofalco*, its apparently nearest generic relative, as follows: most of basal joint of middle toe without transverse scutellae on upper side; bill relatively smaller; and cere relatively more restricted, occupying only about ⅕ of culmen, instead of ¼.

[1] *Hist. Nat. Oiseaux Amér. Sept.*, vol. 1 (1807 [Jan., 1808]), p. 39, pl. 11.
[2] Friedmann, *Bull. U.S. Nat. Mus.*, no. 50, pt. 11 (Sept. 29, 1950), p. 616fn.
[3] *Skizz. Entwickel.-Gesch. Natürl. Syst. Eur. Thierwelt* (1829), pp. 40, 190.

SPARROW HAWK, *Tinnunculus sparverius*

The super-specific group *Tinnunculus*, to which the Sparrow Hawk belongs, is without doubt of generic rank.[1] It differs from *Hypotriorchis* Boie,[2] of which *Falco subbuteo* Linnaeus is by monotypy the type, in the following respects: two primaries sinuate on outer webs; two primaries emarginate on inner webs; first (outermost) primary not longer than fourth, and shorter than third; primary coverts not longer than shortest secondary; tarsus decidedly longer than middle toe with claw, its lower end in front with transverse scutellae; basal joint of middle toe with transverse scutellae on all of upper side; claw of inner toe reaching to base of claw of middle toe; outer toe without claw not decidedly longer than inner toe without claw, but about equal. The proper generic name for this species is *Tinnunculus* Vieillot as shown under the Pigeon Hawk, since this term antedates all other generic names applicable to the Sparrow Hawk.

[1] Vieillot, *Hist. Nat. Oiseaux Amér. Sept.*, vol. 1 (1807 [Jan., 1808]), p. 39, pl. 11 (type by tautonymy, *Falco tinnunculus* Linnaeus).
[2] *Isis (von Oken)* 19 ([Oct.] 1826), column "976" [= 970].

GREATER PRAIRIE CHICKEN, *Tympanuchus cupido*

The subspecific designation of the Greater Prairie Chicken, ever since it was separated from the Heath Hen, *T. c. cupido*, has been more or less a subject of controversy. William Brewster,[1] who named the northern bird *Cupidonia pinnata*, makes no mention of the *Cupidonia americana* of Reichenbach.[2] It, therefore, remained for Robert Ridgway[3] to call attention to this name and to substitute it for *Cupidonia pinnata* Brewster as the proper name. For this reason, the bird has in the past been known as *T. c. americanus* (Reichenbach). However, a few authors, notably Outram Bangs,[4] have advocated the use of Brewster's name in the combination *T. c. pinnatus*. This proposal is based on the opinion that Reichenbach's *Cupidonia americana*, as Bangs says, "as far as human knowledge can ever go applies only to the eastern bird [*cupido*]." Other writers consider Reichenbach's name unidentifiable subspecifically.

The *Cupidonia americana* of Reichenbach was based primarily, if not exclusively, on figures 1896, 1897, and 1898 of his

Icones Avium, and the references he cites as synonyms have no real bearing on the application of the name, since his *Avium Systema Naturalis* was in reality the text as well as index to his *Icones*, for no technical names appear in the latter.

The identification of Reichenbach's bird depends entirely on the figures in *Icones*. As has been several times stated by recent authors, the largest of these three figures is evidently a copy of the figure in Alexander Wilson's *American Ornithology*, but the two others were apparently drawn from specimens. It is rather hard to understand why there has been any difficulty in determining the subspecific identity of these figures. The largest one, copied from Wilson, is readily seen to be the northern race from the character of the neck-tufts, which are composed of numerous (about 10) broad, bluntly pointed feathers—instead of the few, narrower, more or less sharply tipped feathers characterizing the Heath Hen. Also barring of the lower surface is that of the northern race, which is less heavy with broader light interspaces than in the Heath Hen. Careful examination of the two smaller figures discloses, even without a magnifying glass, that they also represent the northern subspecies. So far as the present writer can see, Reichenbach's name *Cupidonia americana* is not a synonym of *Tympanuchus cupido* (Linnaeus), but should stand for the Northern Greater Prairie Chicken in the combination *T. c. americanus* (Reichenbach).

[1] *Auk* 2 (Jan., 1885): 82.
[2] *Avium Syst. Nat.* (1852 [1853]), p. xxix.
[3] *Auk* 3 (Jan., 1886): 132–133.
[4] *Bull. Mus. Comp. Zool.* 70 (Mar., 1930): 155–156.

BOBWHITE, *Colinus virginianus*

In a revision of the U.S. forms of the Bobwhite, J. W. Aldrich[1] has separated the population of the Mississippi Valley southwest to e. Texas as an additional subspecies. Texas birds heretofore called *C. v. virginianus* should now be known as *C. v. mexicanus* (Linnaeus).[2]

[1] *Auk* 63 (Oct. 26, 1946): 494–503.
[2] *Tetrao mexicanus* Linnaeus, *Syst. Nat.* 12th ed., vol. 1 (1766 [after May 24]), p. 277 ("Mexico, Ludovicia"; type locality, Louisiana, ex Brisson).

WHOOPING CRANE, *Limnogeranus americanus*

This bird is, as contended by Sharpe, generically distinct from the rest of the species commonly in the genus *Grus*. It differs in having the malar region essentially bare—although sparsely covered with stiff hairlike feathers—and extending in a long point down the sides of the neck; whereas in *Grus* (type, *Grus grus* Linnaeus), all these parts are completely feathered. The Whooping Crane is further distinguished generically in having a long double fold of the trachea which occupies the entire interior of the sternum and reaches to the posterior end, instead of the short convolution as in *Grus canadensis* that fills only the anterior half, or less, of the keel of the sternum. The proper generic name for the Whooping Crane is *Limnogeranus* Sharpe,[1] of which the monotypic type is by original designation *Ardea americana* (Linnaeus). Thus, this bird would be called *Limnogeranus americanus* (Linnaeus).

[1] *Bull. Brit. Ornith. Club* 1 (Mar. 28, 1893): 37.

JAÇANA, *Asarcia spinosa*

Although now called *Jacana spinosa*, this bird seems generically distinct from the other species commonly referred to the genus *Jacana* Brisson, the type of which by tautonymy is *Parra jacana* Linnaeus. The Central American bird differs structurally

as follows: hind toe decidedly longer than exposed culmen, not including frontal lappet; frontal lappet shorter and relatively broader, usually wider than long, and trifid; malar wattles lacking. In the typical species of *Jacana* the hind toe is about the same length as exposed culmen; frontal lobe is longer in proportion to its width, usually longer than wide, and only bifid on its posterior edge; and a long malar wattle pendant extends from base of each side of maxilla. The generic name for the Central American Jaçana is *Asarcia* Sharpe[1] (type by monotypy, *Parra variabilis* = *Fulica spinosa* Linnaeus).

[1] *Cat. Birds Brit. Mus.* 24 (1896 [after July 10]): ix, 86.

SNOWY PLOVER, *Leucopolius alexandrinus*

While this species is generally referred to the genus *Charadrius*, it seems without doubt to be generically distinct from the typical forms of that group, the type of which is *Charadrius hiaticula* Linnaeus. The Snowy Plover differs from typical *Charadrius* in longer and slenderer bill, the exposed culmen 3 to 3½ times height of bill at base, instead of 2¼ to 2¾; legs relatively longer and more slender, the exposed culmen equal to or longer than middle toe without claw, in *Charadrius* shorter; length of dertrum nearly twice height of bill at base, instead of only 1⅓ times. Also in osteological characters, among others, it is set off by having free lachrymals with conspicuously outwardly projecting processes, and with no foramen for the nasal duct; in these respects, as in others, it resembles *Squatarola*, while *Charadrius* osteologically resembles *Pluvialis*, as shown by P. R. Lowe.[1] It is thus apparent that the birds most closely allied to *Charadrius alexandrinus* represent a well-defined generic group, for which the name *Leucopolius* Bonaparte[2] (type by tautonymy, *Charadrius marginatus* Vieillot) has been provided. In this same genus the following and other extralimital species should be included: *Leucopolius marginatus* (Vieillot) and *Leucopolius peroni* (Bonaparte).

Notwithstanding the statement by Conover[3] that Snowy Plovers from Texas, Louisiana, and Alabama are like those from the Pacific coast of North America, the present writer is able to distinguish the breeding birds of the Texas coast as well as those of the Panhandle as decidedly nearer the West Indian race *L. a. tenuirostris*.

[1] *Ibis*, 11th ser., 4 (July 1, 1922): 475–490.
[2] *Comptes Rendus Acad. Sci.* 43 (Sept. 1, 1856): 417.
[3] *Condor* 47 (Sept. 29, 1945): 211.

SEMIPALMATED PLOVER, *Aegialeus semipalmatus*

Although currently included in the genus *Charadrius* Linnaeus (type, *Charadrius hiaticula* Linnaeus), the present plover is structurally distinct from all other members of this group. It has relatively much larger feet, the exposed culmen being equal to only the basal two phalanges of the middle toe; in fact, the feet are actually as large as those of the Old World Ringed Plover, *Charadrius hiaticula*, which is a much larger bird. The Semipalmated Plover also has a web between base of inner and middle toes, extending forward to about half length of basal phalanx of middle toe, and the web between outer and middle toes is as long as the whole of the basal phalanx of the middle toe. In *Charadrius hiaticula* there is no web at all between inner and middle toes, and the web between middle and outer toes is only half length of the basal phalanx of the middle toe. Since the web between the toes is properly used as a generic character in *Ereunetes*, it is likewise of value in the present species, and this, coupled with the relatively much larger feet, clearly entitles this species to generic separation from the other members of *Charadrius*. Furthermore, it is the only species exhibiting these characters. *Aegialeus* Reichenbach[1] (type by monotypy, *Charadrius semipalmatus* Bonaparte) should be its generic name. P. R. Lowe[2] also has placed this species in a separate monotypic genus on purely anatomic grounds.

In view of the above evidence, it seems rather remarkable that several authors, including James L. Peters,[3] have considered *Aegialeus semipalmatus* a subspecies of *Charadrius hiaticula*. It is true that in general appearance the birds look very much alike, but the external structural characters given above, to say nothing of the important osteological differences, will easily serve to separate them. Aside from this, the Semipalmated Plover, as compared with *Charadrius hiaticula*, is of decidedly smaller size, and has the pectoral band narrower. Also, both species are reported to breed on Baffin Island. Further evidence, if any were needed, of the specific distinctness of this species is afforded by the breadth of the white stripe on the outer web along the shaft on the middle portion of the inner primaries. In the Semipalmated Plover this stripe or lengthened patch is very much narrower and more inconspicuous than in the Ringed Plover. In none of the considerable number of specimens of each species examined is there any indication of intergradation of this character.

[1] *Syst. Avium* (1852 [1853]), p. 18.
[2] *Ibis*, 13th ser., 1 (Oct. 20, 1931): 722.
[3] *Check-List Birds World* 2 (June 15, 1934): 247.

MOUNTAIN PLOVER, *Podasocys montanus*

Since the present writer[1] proposed to merge *Podasocys* Coues, the type and only species of which is *Podasocys montanus* (Townsend), with *Eupoda* on the basis of lack of external generic characters, P. R. Lowe[2] published a careful study of the osteology of these plovers. In it he clearly shows that there is enough difference in internal structure between *P. montanus* and *E. asiatica*, the type of *Eupoda*, to warrant their separation into even different subfamilies. Important osteological characters separating *Podasocys* generically from *Eupoda asiatica* include the lachrymals, which are not free but merged into the supraorbital rim; supraorbital grooves which are narrower, approximately parallel, and do not meet in the middle line of the frontal region (thus the sides of the frontal region give a much more turgid appearance to the skull); and the presence of nasal foramen. In these characters *Podasocys* is much like *Vanellus* and *Oxyechus*. Surely such important internal differences should warrant at least generic recognition.

External differences distinguishing *Podasocys montanus* from *Eupoda asiatica* which the writer considered insufficient for generic separation are the somewhat longer tarsus, more extensive bare portion of tibia, and relatively longer middle pair of rectrices. The species *Eupoda vereda* (Gould) which has commonly been considered generically identical with *Eupoda asiatica*, is in structural characters very close to *Podasocys montanus*, and should probably be placed in the same genus with it. The Mountain Plover should, by virtue of the characters given above, be called *Podasocys montanus*.

[1] Oberholser, *Trans. Wisconsin Acad. Sci., Arts, and Letters* 19, pt. 1 (Dec. 30, 1918): 516.
[2] *Ibis*, 11th ser., 4 (July 1, 1922): 480–490.

KILLDEER, *Oxyechus vociferus*

The Killdeer is structurally so different from the genus *Charadrius* that it should be separated generically as *Oxyechus* Reichenbach. These characters are long tail, much more than half length of wing, and much more strongly graduated; and

long wing, the longest primary exceeding longest secondary by more than half total length of (folded) wing.

BLACK-BELLIED PLOVER, *Squatarola squatarola*

The American Black-bellied Plover has been subspecifically separated by Thayer and Bangs as *S. s. cynosurae*[1] from birds taken at Baillie Island, District of Franklin, Canada. James L. Peters[2] has, however, shown that in size—which is the only character of importance in this group—there is practically no difference between birds from North America and those from Europe. The writer also has measured a considerable series of these birds and has reached the same conclusions. Therefore, there seems to be no valid basis on which to maintain the separation of *S. s. cynosurae* from *S. s. squatarola* of Europe and w. Siberia.

However, birds from the Bering Sea coast of Alaska and from n.e. Siberia are decidedly larger than both European and other North American birds. Wing measurements of this larger form are as follows: adult male, 189–213 (average, 195.8) mm.; adult female, 190–200 (195.7). Birds from n.w. Alaska are somewhat intermediate between the large birds from n.e. Siberia and the smaller birds from the remaining arctic region of North America, but apparently are nearer the Asiatic race. This larger form migrates a considerable distance south along the Pacific coast of North America as well as down the coast of e. Asia. From the considerable number of specimens available at present, it seems that the east Asian and northwestern Alaska birds are a recognizable race. Gregory M. Mathews[3] used the name *Charadrius hypomelus* Pallas[4] for this bird, but Peters has —it seems to the writer—conclusively shown that this name is unavailable, as are also all the other names proposed by Pallas for this species. Apparently, the proper name is *Squatarola helvetica australis* Reichenbach,[5] based on Gould's *Birds of Australia* (vol. 4, pl. 8) and Reichenbach's *Vögel Neuholland* (p. 334, no. 549). By recognition of *S. s. australis* the name of the American Black-bellied Plover needs to be a trinomial, *S. s. squatarola*.

[1] *Proc. New England Zool. Club* 5 (Apr. 9, 1914): 23.
[2] *Condor* 36 (Jan. 15, 1934): 27–28.
[3] *Birds Australia*, vol. 3, pt. 1 (Aug. 18, 1913), pp. 69–72.
[4] *Reise Versch. Prov. Russ. Reichs* 3 (1776): 699.
[5] *Novitiae Synopsin Avium*, no. 5 (1851), p. 3.

AMERICAN WOODCOCK, *Rubicola minor*

The generic name in use for many years has been *Philohela* Gray. This name, however, is antedated by *Rubicola* Richardson,[1] the type of which by monotypy is *Scolopax minor* Gmelin. *Rubicola* was replaced with *Philohela* by the A.O.U. Committee on Nomenclature on the grounds that *Rubicola*, though an earlier name and valid, was introduced apparently by mistake.[2] There is no reason, so far as the writer is aware, for rejecting a valid name that is introduced by mistake, if in other respects it fulfills the requirements. There is, therefore, apparently no conclusive reason for the rejection of *Rubicola* as a generic name for the American Woodcock.

[1] See Wilson, *Amer. Ornith.*, Jameson ed., vol. 3 (1831), p. 98.
[2] *Auk* 40 (July 10, 1923): 516.

HUDSONIAN CURLEW, *Phaeopus hudsonicus*

Although some authors have merged *Phaeopus* into *Numenius*, the former seems to have sufficient trenchant characters to warrant its separation. It differs from *Numenius* in having exposed culmen shorter than combined length of tarsus and middle toe without claw; length of tarsus less than twice that of middle toe without claw; and tail longer than tarsus and middle toe without claw combined.

Some authors further consider the Hudsonian Curlew a subspecies of the Whimbrel, *Phaeopus phaeopus*, instead of a distinct species. In the former bird, the rump and upper tail-coverts are dark brown, edged and otherwise marked with buff, and the axillars and wing-linings are buff barred with brown; whereas in the Whimbrel the rump and upper tail-coverts are white, the latter with some markings of dark brown, and the axillars and wing-linings white barred with dark brown. While *Phaeopus phaeopus variegatus*, a subspecies of the Old World bird, has the rump spotted or barred with dark brown or blackish, *Phaeopus hudsonicus* always has a brown, instead of white, rump and upper tail-coverts barred with darker brown, also axillars and inner webs of wing-quills barred with cinnamon, instead of white. In comparing fully adult birds, the present writer is unable to find any specimens that bridge the differences between these two curlews, nor any that cannot be unequivocally identified by even casual examination. Therefore, it seems better to treat both as specifically distinct.

ESKIMO CURLEW, *Phaeopus borealis*

Some authors separated this species generically from those grouped in *Phaeopus* Cuvier (type, *Scolopax phaeopus* Linnaeus), and it has been referred by Ridgway to the genus *Mesoscolopax* Sharpe (type by original designation, *Numenius minutus* Gould). While it is true that the Eskimo Curlew differs in some structural respects from the other members of *Phaeopus*, it is in none of these characters entirely trenchantly separable; therefore, it should be called *Phaeopus borealis* (Forster). The genus *Mesoscolopax* Sharpe, however, is readily separable from *Phaeopus*, if confined entirely to the single species which is its type. The distinctly scutellate posterior face of the tarsus is a conspicuous and easily appreciated character separating *Mesoscolopax* from *Phaeopus*.

SPOTTED SANDPIPER, *Actitis macularia*

A new subspecies, originally discovered by T. D. Burleigh[1] from Lewiston, Nez Perce Co., Idaho and described by him as *A. m. rava*, appears to be an easily recognizable form. It necessitates the use of a trinomial for the nominate form, *A. m. macularia*.

[1] *Auk* 77 (Apr. 30, 1960): 210.

GREATER YELLOWLEGS, *Glottis melanoleuca*

There has been much difference of opinion regarding the genus or genera of the two North American yellowlegs. Sharpe,[1] who placed both birds in *Totanus*, has been followed by most authors. Mathews[2] placed the Greater Yellowlegs, *Scolopax melanoleucus* Gmelin, along with the Greenshank, *Glottis nebularia*, in the genus *Glottis* Koch; and *Totanus flavipes*, together with the Marsh Sandpiper, *Iliornis stagnatilis*, in the genus *Iliornis* Kaup. Ridgway,[3] however, considered both *Totanus melanoleucus* and *Totanus flavipes* congeneric and made for them a new genus *Neoglottis*. A careful examination of all the species that have at one time or another been referred to *Totanus* shows that none of these arrangements—even as affecting only the two North American species—is entirely satisfactory. It is evident, however, that all should not be included in one genus, as there are good structural differences characterizing the six species involved.

Totanus was proposed by Bechstein,[4] its type by tautonymy,

Scolopax totanus Linnaeus. The essential characters of *Totanus* are as follows: nasal groove of maxilla not less than half, sometimes more than half, length of exposed culmen; symphysis of rami always anterior to middle of mandible; tarsus decidedly less than twice length of middle toe without claw; exposed culmen ⅔ to ⅞ length of tarsus; wing at least 3 times length of tarsus; bill 5½ to 7½ times its height at base, and 1½ times length of middle toe without claw, or less; bare portion of tibia about half length of tarsus.

The writer has been unable to find any trenchant generic character to separate the Lesser Yellowlegs, *Totanus flavipes*, from the Redshank, *Totanus totanus*. The only appreciable difference is in the more slender, rather shorter bill of the former, but these differences are so slight that they do not afford good reason for separating the two.

Iliornis Kaup,[5] of which *Totanus stagnatalis* Bechstein is the monotypic type, differs from *Totanus* in having nasal groove of maxilla less than half length of culmen; symphysis of rami of mandible at about middle of bill; tarsus 2 or more times middle toe without claw; wing less than 3 times length of tarsus, usually 2½ times or less; bill very slender, its length 8 or more times its height at base; and bare portion of tibia about ⅔ length of tarsus.

The Spotted Redshank, *Scolopax erythropus* Pallas (= *Totanus fuscus*) stands likewise as a monotypic group; it differs decidedly from both *Totanus* and *Iliornis* in having a much shorter nasal groove, this equal to, not more than, ⅓ length of culmen; exposed culmen longer than tarsus; and bill nearly twice length of middle toe. As this group has no generic name, the writer proposes *Totanornis*, with *Scolopax erythropus* Pallas as the type.

This leaves but two species, one of which is the Greater Yellowlegs, *Scolopax melanoleucus* Gmelin, and the other, the Greenshank, *Scolopax nebularius* Gunnerus, the type by tautonymy of the genus *Glottis* Koch.[6] This genus differs from *Totanus* in having nasal groove decidedly less than half length of exposed culmen—a character which is as fully pronounced in the skeleton as on the external bill; symphysis of rami at about middle of bill; tarsus about 9/10 or more of exposed culmen; and bill decidedly more than 1½, usually 1⅔ to 1¾, times middle toe without claw. The only constant structural difference the writer is able to discover between *Totanus melanoleucus* and *Glottis nebularia* is the somewhat recurved bill of the latter, and this seems hardly pronounced enough to justify generic separation, though perhaps the subgeneric designation *Neoglottis* Ridgway for the former would be convenient. There are, however, excellent characters for the generic separation of *Totanus melanoleucus* from *Totanus flavipes*, as above indicated. It is but fair to state that Mathews indicated the proper reference of *Totanus melanoleucus* to *Glottis*, although he referred *Totanus flavipes* to *Iliornis*. By the arrangement here proposed, the name of the Lesser Yellowlegs would be *Totanus flavipes*, and that of the Greater Yellowlegs, *Glottis melanoleuca*, as *Glottis* is of feminine gender.

The species here involved should, in conformity with above details, stand as follows: *Glottis nebularia* (Gunnerus), *Glottis melanoleuca* (Gmelin), *Iliornis stagnatilis* (Bechstein), *Totanus totanus* (Linnaeus), *Totanus flavipes* (Gmelin), and *Totanornis erythropus* (Pallas).

[1] *Cat. Birds Brit. Mus.* 24 (1896): 426–436.
[2] *Birds Australia*, vol. 3, pt. 2 (May 2, 1913), pp. 197–199.
[3] *Bull. U.S. Nat. Mus.*, no. 50, pt. 8 (June 26, 1919), pp. 329–342.
[4] *Ornith. Taschenb. Deutschl.* 2 (1803): 282.
[5] *Skizz. Entwickel.-Gesch. Natürl. Syst. Eur. Thierwelt* (1829 [after Apr.]), p. 54.

[6] *Syst. Baier. Zool.* (1816), pp. xlii, 304.

PURPLE SANDPIPER, *Arquatella maritima*

The Purple Sandpiper differs structurally from the genus *Erolia* (type, *Erolia variegata* Vieillot), in having the bill stouter, straight, not decurved terminally; tarsus less than ⅕ as long as wing, and shorter than middle toe with claw. The generic name available is *Arquatella* Baird (type, *Tringa maritima* Brunnich).

PECTORAL SANDPIPER, *Pisobia melanota*

The present species—together with its close allies the White-rumped, Baird's, and Least sandpipers—differs structurally from *Erolia* Vieillot in having exposed culmen not longer than tarsus, and bill straight, not decurved anteriorly. The generic name to be applied to these species is *Pisobia* Billberg, type *Tringa minuta* Leisler.

The current spelling of the specific name of this species as *melanotos* is another case in which the specific name has been treated as a noun, although it should be considered an adjective, and therefore, agree in gender with the generic name. This would require the specific name to be spelled *melanota*. Apparently this was not done in the original description,[1] but now when the name is used in combination with the feminine genus *Pisobia*, the name should stand as *Pisobia melanota*.

[1] *Tringa melanotos* Vieillot, *Nouv. Dict. d'Hist. Nat.*, new ed. 34 (1819): 462.

WHITE-RUMPED SANDPIPER, *Pisobia fuscicollis*

See Pectoral Sandpiper.

BAIRD'S SANDPIPER, *Pisobia bairdii*

See Pectoral Sandpiper.

LEAST SANDPIPER, *Pisobia minutilla*

See Pectoral Sandpiper.

DUNLIN, *Pelidna alpina*

This sandpiper differs from the genus *Erolia* Vieillot in the following respects: tarsus and bill relatively shorter, the latter much less decurved terminally; and lateral membranes of anterior toes much narrower. The generic name to be applied is *Pelidna* Cuvier.

DOWITCHER, *Limnodromus griseus*

Some authors treat the Long-billed Dowitcher as a full species, *Limnodromus scolopaceus*, but there are so many intermediate individuals between this and the other races that it is difficult to maintain this view. In fact, the most recently described form, *L. g. caurinus* Pitelka,[1] is intermediate, both in characters and geography, between *L. g. hendersoni* and *L. g. scolopaceus*.

[1] *Univ. California Pub. Zool.* 50 (Mar. 31, 1950): 43.

MARBLED GODWIT, *Vetola fedoa*

The use of the generic name *Vetola* for this species is fully explained under the Hudsonian Godwit.

HUDSONIAN GODWIT, *Vetola haemastica*

G. M. Mathews[1] was apparently the first to call attention to the striking generic differences among the godwits, which for a long time have been grouped in the genus *Limosa*. He showed that *Limosa* Brisson is a monotypic group confined to its type species, *Scolopax limosa* Linnaeus, and in this he has been followed by Ridgway and some other authors.

Since this view has not been adopted by American writers, it seems well to call attention again to the important differences on which this separation was based. Mathews transferred all other species commonly associated in *Limosa* to a genus he called *Vetola*, and designated as its type *Scolopax lapponica* Linnaeus. This group differs from *Limosa* very astonishingly in the short, nonpectinate, stout, strongly decurved claw of the middle toe, which is about ¼ length of middle toe without claw. This remarkably different structure of the claw of the middle toe—which in *Limosa* is long, slender, straight, or even upcurved, ⅓ length of middle toe without claw, and strongly pectinate on its inner edge—is a character that is sometimes used as a diagnostic mark of higher groups than genera. A further difference is the bill which is decidedly upcurved at the tip, the culmen much flattened for its terminal ⅓ or more, instead of being flattened only near the tip. These characters clearly seem to warrant recognition of *Vetola* as a genus for all the godwits except *Limosa limosa*. The other characters given by Mathews and Ridgway, which do not seem to be constant, may have been the basis for rejecting this generic group, while the really diagnostic characters were overlooked.

[1] *Birds Australia*, vol. 3, pt. 2 (May 2, 1913), pp. 184–191.

RED PHALAROPE, *Phalaropus fulicaria*

The proper spelling of the specific name of this bird should be *fulicaria*—not *fulicarius*—even when coupled with a masculine generic term, since Linnaeus[1] in his original description of the species spelled the specific name with a capital letter, thus indicating he intended to regard *fulicaria* as a noun.

A trinomial is necessary for this bird because of an apparently recognizable race from Spitzbergen, *Phalaropus fulicarius jourdaini*,[2] which differs in paler edgings of the upper surface. Supposedly it also breeds in Iceland and e. Greenland.

[1] *Tringa Fulicaria* Linnaeus, *Syst. Nat.* 10th ed., vol. 1 (Jan. 1, 1758), p. 148.
[2] Iredale, *Bull. Brit. Ornith. Club* 42 (Oct. 29, 1921): 8 ("Liefde Bay, N. W. Spitzbergen").

POMARINE JAEGER, *Coprotheres pomarinus*

This species is commonly referred to the genus *Stercorarius* Brisson, but Robert Ridgway was apparently right in segregating it as a distinct genus under the name *Coprotheres* Reichenbach,[1] of which it is the monotypic type. This genus is similar to *Stercorarius*, which includes *S. parasiticus* and *S. longicaudus*, but the middle tail feathers are broad and rounded and terminally twisted—instead of narrow, sharply pointed, and flat; lachrymal bones of the skull have the outer process narrow and pointed terminally, instead of broad and rounded; and notches in posterior end of sternum are much broader (less linear).

The use of a trinomial becomes necessary because birds from n.e. Asia and w. North America seem to differ sufficiently from birds from e. North America, n. Europe, and w. Siberia to warrant subspecific separation. *Coprotheres pomarinus camtschaticus* (Salvin) may be distinguished as follows:

Catarracta parasita var. *camtschatica* Salvin, *Cat. Birds Brit. Mus.*, vol. 25 (1896), p. 323 (no locality, but based on *Avis camtschatica major* of Pallas, which is the bird from Kamchatka).

DESCRIPTION: Similar to *C. p. pomarinus*, but wing averaging somewhat longer; upper parts, in both light and dark phases, darker, particularly on pileum.

MEASUREMENTS: *Adult male*: Wing, 342.0–370.0 (average, 354.3) mm.; tail, 192.0–251.0 (223.3); bill (exposed culmen), 37.5–42.5 (39.2); height of bill at base, 14.5–16.0 (15.1); tarsus, 53.5–56.5 (54.4); middle toe without claw, 41.0–45.5 (42.9). *Adult female*: Wing, 340.0–366.0 (354.7); tail, 173.0–235.0 (189.9); bill, 37.0–41.0 (38.6); height of bill, 14.0–16.0 (15.1); tarsus, 53.0–56.0 (54.4); middle toe, 41.5–47.0 (43.5).

RANGE: Arctic regions of e. Siberia and w. North America (east to Hudson Bay). Winters south to s.e. Australia and New Zealand. Casual in Arizona.

While difference in measurements between this race and the typical form of n. Europe is not large, it is accompanied by a difference in coloration as indicated above. There is some difficulty in determining the proper name to be applied to this additional race. The species was first described by Temminck as *Lestris pomarinus*,[2] and the locality that he gives is "Les Régions du Cercle Arctique; Côtes Maritimes de Holland et de France," from which the type locality has been restricted to the arctic regions of Europe.[3] Therefore, this seems clearly the proper name for the European bird. Of this, *Lestris spaeriuros* Brehm, *L. sphaeriuros* Brehm, *L. striatus* Eyton, and *L. pomatorhinus* Sclater are all synonyms.[4] The specific or subspecific name *camtschatica* has frequently been credited to Pallas,[5] but that he did not intend it as either a specific or subspecific name is readily ascertainable by reference to the original, where he says merely "*Avis camtschatica major*, gallinam fere aequans," and follows this with a further description. Thus, it is evident that Pallas merely wished to call attention to the fact that the Kamchatkan bird was different in certain respects from the European one. Salvin[6] was apparently the first author to give this name nomenclatural standing; he cites Pallas' *Zoographia Rosso-Asiatica* (1811), p. 312, as the basis of the name, by which action it becomes the valid name for this race. *Coprotheres pomarinus nutcheri* Mathews[7] and *Stercorarius nigricapillus* Bergmann[8] are both synonyms, therefore, of *Coprotheres pomarinus camtschatica*. It is interesting to note that if Pallas in 1811 had given this bird a technical name, instead of merely comparing the Kamchatkan bird with that of Europe, it would have been the earliest name for any form of the species.

[1] *Avium Syst. Nat.* (1850), pl. 5.
[2] *Manuel Ornith.* (1815), p. 514.
[3] *Check-list North Amer. Birds* 5th ed. (1957), p. 212.
[4] Brehm, *Isis (von Oken)* 23 ([Oct.] 1830): column 993; Brehm, *Vog. Deutschlands* (1831), p. 718; Eyton, *Cat. Brit. Birds* (1836), p. 5; Sclater, *Ibis*, 1st ser., 4 (July, 1862): 297.
[5] *Zoog. Rosso-Asiatica* 2 (1811): 312.
[6] *Cat. Birds Brit. Mus.* 25 (1896): 323.
[7] *Austral Avian Record* 3 (July 21, 1917): 72 ("Broken Bay, New South Wales").
[8] *Fauna och Flora* 18 (Oct., 1923): 232 ("Kamtchatkas sydostkust").

LAUGHING GULL, *Larus atricilla*

Careful examination of specimens from the West Indies, South America, and North America shows that the latter are considerably larger, particularly in measurements of wing, tail, and tarsus, and apparently represent another subspecies. The following measurements of adult males from the West Indies when compared with measurements of the North American race show these differences: Wing, 288.0–321.0 (average, 305.0) mm.; tail, 116.0–123.0 (119.9); bill (exposed culmen), 37.0–42.0 (39.8); tarsus, 40.0–46.0 (43.1).

Distribution of the typical (nominate) form, *L. a. atricilla*, reaches north to the Bahamas, east to Lesser Antilles, south to islands in s. Caribbean, and west to Yucatán; in winter it ranges south to Oaxaca, Guatemala, Peru, Guyana, Surinam, and n.

Brazil. The North America bird is found occasionally in the Bahamas and West Indies, even in late spring and summer; this is not surprising, however, in view of the species' habit of wandering far from breeding areas during summer and passing that season regularly in areas where it is not known to breed.

When G. K. Noble[1] proposed to recognize the North American bird as a separate subspecies, he very conservatively made use of the name *Atricilla megalopterus* Bruch.[2] This name was based on specimens in the Mainz collection of Rheinischen Naturforschenden Geschellschaft at Mainz, Germany. Bruch says, "Dieser Vogel hat Lange Jahre in unsrer Sammlung, sowie auch in meiner früheren Aufstellung als *L. serranus* figurirt."[3] In a previous article under [*Chroicocephalus*] *serranus* Tschudi, he cites only a single specimen from Peru, which is evidently his type.[4] A number of years ago, inquiry of Professor Doctor Schmidtgen, then director of Naturhistorisches Museum der Stadt Mainz, at Mainz, Germany, revealed that there was then no specimen of *Larus atricilla* either under this name or *Atricilla megalopterus*, from any part of South America, so apparently Bruch's type of *Atricilla megalopterus* has disappeared. It is rather safe to say, however, that it would prove to be an example of the southern bird. Since South American birds are the same as those from the West Indies, it follows that *Atricilla megalopterus* Bruch is a synonym of *Larus atricilla* Linnaeus,[5] which is based on the bird of the Bahamas as described by Catesby,[6] and which applies to the southern race, thus leaving the North American bird to be provided with a name.

The name *Larus atricapillus* Abbot[7] cited in the synonymy of *Larus atricilla* by Ridgway was not only a nomen nudum, but was of somewhat doubtful application to this species, until thus synonymized by Ridgway.[8]

There is, however, a name available for the North American bird in *Xema wilsonii* of Boie,[9] which is a new name for *Larus ridibundus* of Wilson[10] on which it is wholly based. Wilson's locality is "the coast of New Jersey . . . Fishing Creek, Delaware Bay." Fishing Creek may be designated as the type locality of *Xema wilsonii* Boie. The North American Laughing Gull should take the name *L. a. wilsonii* (Boie).

[1] *Bull. Mus. Comp. Zool.* 60 (Aug., 1916): 367–368.
[2] A[*tricilla*] *megalopterus* "Bonaparte," Bruch, *Journ. f. Ornith.* 3 (July, 1855): 287 ("Peru und der Mexicanische Meerbusen").
[3] Ibid.
[4] *Journ. f. Ornith.* 1 (Mar., 1853): 106.
[5] *Syst. Nat.* 10th ed., vol. 1 (Jan. 1, 1758), p. 136.
[6] *Larus major* Catesby, *Nat. Hist. Carolina, Florida, and Bahama Is.*, vol. 1 (1731), p. 89, pl. 89.
[7] *Proc. Boston Soc. Nat. Hist.* 1 (1842): 61.
[8] *Bull. U.S. Nat. Mus.*, no. 50, pt. 8 (June 26, 1919), p. 641.
[9] *Isis (von Oken)* 21, nos. 3 & 4 ([Apr.] 1828): column 358 (in text of footnote).
[10] *Amer. Ornith.*, vol. 9 (1814), p. 89, pl. 74, fig. 4.

BONAPARTE'S GULL, *Microlarus philadelphia*

Microlarus Oberholser, new genus. Similar to genus *Larus* Linnaeus, but bill much more slender, its height at base about ¼ length of exposed culmen, instead of ⅓; nostrils linear oval, instead of guttate; and length of exposed culmen 2½ times length of gonys, instead of 3 to 3½ times. Type: *Sterna philadelphia* Ord.

From *Hydrocoloeus* (see Little Gull), in which the Bonaparte's was placed by Dwight,[1] this species differs in having tarsus longer than middle toe with claw, in which it agrees with *Larus*.

[1] *Bull. Amer. Mus. Nat. Hist.* 52 (Dec. 31, 1925): 260–314.

LITTLE GULL, *Hydrocoloeus minutus*

Hydrocoloeus is a recognizable group if restricted to the type species, *Larus minutus* Linnaeus; it differs from *Larus* in having tarsus not longer than middle toe with claw; bill much more slender, its height at base about ¼ length of exposed culmen, instead of about ⅓; nostrils linear oval, instead of guttate; and length of exposed culmen only 2½ to 2¾ times length of gonys, instead of 3 to 3½.

FORSTER'S TERN, *Sterna forsteri*

As has already been shown, the Forster's Tern living in summer along the coasts of the e. United States and Gulf of Mexico to s. Texas represents a subspecies distinct from birds inhabiting interior North America. It has been named *S. f. litoricola*.[1] It differs from the inland race in its decidedly smaller size, and the lighter gray of the upper surface, particularly on the mantle. Measurements are given under each of these races. While the difference in color is very evident on comparison of series, this is not as good a character as the smaller size of *litoricola*, which, although somewhat variable, will distinguish practically all adults.

The original description of the Forster's Tern, *Sterna forsteri* Nuttall,[2] was based on the bird described by Richardson[3] from the Saskatchewan River in Saskatchewan, Canada. Thus, this name applies to the interior race. A tern obtained by Audubon on the Mississippi River near New Orleans, Louisiana, was named by him *Sterna havelli*.[4] The type as figured in the *Birds of America* is evidently an adult in winter plumage, and the measurements that he gives, together with the dark coloration, indicate clearly that this is an example of true *S. f. forsteri* from the interior; this name, therefore, becomes a synonym of that bird.

[1] Oberholser, *Bull. Louisiana Dept. Conservation*, no. 28 (June 30, 1938), p. 290 ("Smith Island, Northampton County, Virginia").
[2] *Manual Ornith. U.S. and Canada, Water Birds* (1834), p. 274fn.
[3] *Fauna Bor.-Amer.* 2 (1831 [Feb., 1832]): 413.
[4] *Birds America*, folio ed., vol. 4 (1838), pl. 409, fig. 1; *Ornith. Biog.* 5 (1839 [after May 1]): 122 ("broad eddies, opposite New Orleans").

LEAST TERN, *Sternula albifrons*

Though often placed in the genus *Sterna*, along with the Common Tern and its allies, the Least Tern is structurally and trenchantly different from the other American species of the typical *Sterna*. So it, along with the Little Tern, *Sterna minuta*, as already shown by Ridgway,[1] should be referred to *Sternula* Boie,[2] of which the type by monotypy is *Sterna minuta* (= *Sterna albifrons* Pallas).

Sternula differs from *Sterna* in having tail not more than ½ length of wing, whereas it is decidedly more in *Sterna*; gonys much longer than bare portion of the mandibular rami, instead of little, if any, longer; and middle toe with claw not longer than gonys, whereas it is decidedly longer in *Sterna*. By reason of these suggested changes in generic and specific names, the designation of our Least Tern would be *Sternula albifrons*.

Since the generic name *Sternula* is of feminine gender, the subspecific name of the Interior Least Tern, which is an adjective, should agree in ending, and thus be spelled *athalassa*.

[1] *Bull. U.S. Nat. Mus.*, no. 50, pt. 8 (June 26, 1919), p. 520.
[2] *Isis (von Oken)* 15 ([May] 1822): column 563.

CASPIAN TERN, *Hydroprogne caspia*

In the past, American birds belonging to this species have been regarded as representing a subspecies distinct from the Old World bird, which is typical *Hydroprogne caspia*; currently, the A.O.U. check-list, 1957, recognizes no races. In this connection the writer has investigated the status of the American bird, and concurs that it, as compared with those of Europe and Asia, does not seem to differ in either size or color with sufficient constancy to make the American bird recognizable as even a poor subspecies. However, the Australian bird has a larger bill, and is recognizable as a subspecies, *H. c. strenua* (Gould). This makes necessary a trinomial, *H. c. caspia*, for the American bird.

BAND-TAILED PIGEON, *Chloroenas fasciata*

See Red-billed Pigeon.

RED-BILLED PIGEON, *Chloroenas flavirostris*

This species has commonly been referred to the genus *Columba* Linnaeus, but it differs in several important structural characters from both groups in the genus to which the type has been assigned by different authors. The type of *Columba* (Linnaeus)[1] was subsequently designated by Vigors[2] in 1825 as *Columba oenas* Linnaeus. In the same year, Selby[3] designated *Columba palumbus* Linnaeus. Since, at present, there seems to be no way to determine which of these two designations was first published, the present writer now selects that of Selby, since his occurs on an earlier page; comparisons for the separation of the American groups are based on this arrangement. This is explained in more detail under the Rock Dove.

Taking *Columba palumbus* as typical of *Columba*, the Red-billed Pigeon of America, *Columba flavirostris* Wagler, differs in having the tarsus shorter than middle toe without claw; exposed portion of secondaries longer than exposed part of greater coverts; and two outermost primaries not distinctly sinuate on their inner webs. These characters seem to be constant in the species referred to this group, and in the writer's opinion are sufficiently characteristic to justify the separation of this species generically from *Columba* as has already been proposed by Ridgway.[4]

The name for this group is *Chloroenas* Reichenbach,[5] of which the type is *Columba monilis* Vigors, which is a race of *Columba fasciata* Say. Under this arrangement, the name of the Red-billed Pigeon will be *Chloroenas flavirostris* (Wagler). The only other North American bird included in the genus is the Band-tailed Pigeon, which will be *Chloroenas fasciata*.

[1] *Syst. Nat.* 10th ed., vol. 1 (Jan. 1, 1758), p. 162.
[2] *Trans. Linn. Soc. London*, vol. 14, pt. 3 (1825): 481.
[3] *Illust. British Ornith.* 1 (1825): xxx.
[4] *Bull. U.S. Nat. Mus.*, no. 50, pt. 7 (May 5, 1916), pp. 280–288.
[5] *Avium Syst. Nat.* (1852 [1853]), p. xxv.

ROCK DOVE, *Lithoenas domestica*

Leonhard Stejneger[1] many years ago called attention to the fact that the Rock Dove, commonly known as *Columba livia* Gmelin, should take the name *C. domestica* Gmelin.[2] The present writer is inclined to agree with this opinion, since both description and references given in this case are certainly pertinent. Gmelin gives *C. domestica* as species no. 2 of his genus *Columba*, with a description and a number of references, of which Linnaeus' *Fauna Suecica* (1761 edition) is the first. This, in turn, is based on the Swedish bird with references to Willughby[3] and Ray.[4] Both these authors call the bird *Columba domestica seu vulgaris*, "common pigeon or dove," and speak of it impliedly as the common wild pigeon that is also domesticated. Furthermore, Albin, also cited by Gmelin, treats and describes this bird in the same way and calls it "the common dove, house, or wild pigeon."[5] The type locality of *C. domestica* Gmelin should, therefore, be Sweden, and if present designation is necessary it is herewith made.

There seems no reason not to use the domestic bird as a basis for a scientific name, since canon 9 of the A.O.U. Code of Nomenclature, as well as current practice, justifies this. Otherwise, we should have to discard such names as *Meleagris gallopavo* Linnaeus, *Streptopelia risoria* (Linnaeus), and *Phasianus torquatus* Gmelin. Another point in favor of *C. domestica* is that *C. livia*, which is commonly credited to Gmelin, is given by him as [*Columba*] *domestica β livia*, and is based on Brisson, Ray, Willughby, Buffon, and Albin, whose descriptions are essentially the same as those under Linnaeus' *C. domestica*. As already stated, *C. domestica* is species no. 2 of Gmelin's *Columba*, under which *livia* is a side heading evidently indicating a variety, since it—like eighteen others which follow—is designated by a Greek letter to indicate its relationship to *C. domestica*. To reject *domestica*, the regular specific name in this case, in favor of the variety *livia*, with essentially the same basis, does not seem reasonable.

If Linnaeus' varietal names are to be used in nomenclature, as they have been in *Columba livia* and *Phasianus torquatus*, then there is no reason for rejecting *Columba oenas b. domestica* of Linnaeus[6] for this bird. This is based on the *C. domestica* of Willughby and Ray, which are two of the references cited under Gmelin's *C. domestica*. Linnaeus gives Europe as the locality for his *C. domestica*, and since Willughby's detailed description is the chief basis of Linnaeus' name, the type locality of *C. domestica* Linnaeus is hereby designated as England. Thus in either case, the name *C. livia* must give place to *C. domestica* whether Linnaeus or Gmelin be cited as author. There seems to be just as much reason in this particular case, as in others that affect names in common use, for employing names that Linnaeus used as side headings, with what is evidently intended as a varietal letter, but which names are placed on the side in the same column as the regular specific names on the left hand side of the page. If this view is adopted, Linnaeus becomes the authority for *C. domestica*.

Authors have had considerable difficulty in determining the type of *Columba* Linnaeus. It has often been given as *Columba livia*, but there are other prior designations. As already stated under the Red-billed Pigeon, Selby in 1825 designated the type as *Columba palumbus*; in the same year, Vigors designated *Columba oenas*. There seems to be no certain means of determining at the present time which of these designations has absolute priority; however, under the circumstances, it seems desirable to select one of the two. Also it seems best to fall back on the first subsequent reviser of the group who designated the type, which again appears to have been done by two authors simultaneously —Selby[7] and Gray.[8] In this case, however, both give *Columba palumbus* as the type. Either or both of these may be regarded as the first reviser, and until it is possible to determine the exact dates of the publications by Vigors and Selby, it seems desirable to regard *C. palumbus* as the type of *Columba* Linnaeus. This leaves *C. livia* (=*domestica*) free from entanglements as the type of *Columba* Linnaeus, and if it is generically separable should bear the name *Lithoenas* Reichenbach,[9] the type of which is *C. livia* (=*domestica*).

The Rock Dove, *Columba domestica* of Linnaeus and Gmelin, differs structurally from both *C. palumbus* and *C. oenas* as fol-

lows: first primary not shorter than third—instead of much shorter—and much greater than the fourth—instead of equal or a little longer; no primaries sinuate on the inner web, instead of two; only two (the second and third) instead of three or four primaries sinuate on outer webs. From these characters it is apparent that *C. domestica* differs sufficiently from the type, *C. palumbus* and from other species of *Columba* to warrant segregation as a separate group. It would by this arrangement be called *Lithoenas domestica*.

[1] *Proc. U.S. Nat. Mus.* 10 (Nov. 3, 1887): 424.
[2] *Syst. Nat.*, vol. 1, pt. 2 (Apr. 20, 1789), p. 769.
[3] *Ornithologia* (1676), p. 130, t. "32" [= 33].
[4] *Syn. Meth. Avium et Piscium*, p. "51" [= 59], no. 1.
[5] *Nat. Hist. Birds*, vol. 3 (1738), p. 39, pl. 42.
[6] *Syst. Nat.* 10th ed., vol. 1 (Jan. 1, 1758), p. 162.
[7] *List Genera and Subgenera Birds* (1840), p. 39.
[8] *List Genera Birds* (1840), p. 58.
[9] *Avium Syst. Nat.* (1852 [1853]), p. xxv.

PASSENGER PIGEON, *Ectopistes canadensis*

The change of name from *E. migratorius* to *E. canadensis* has already been published, but it seems well again to call attention to this change.[1] The name commonly used for this bird is taken from *Columba migratoria* Linnaeus,[2] but in the same work on a previous page[3] he describes *Columba canadensis*, which he based on the *Turtur canadensis* of Brisson.[4] Examination of Brisson shows conclusively that his detailed description is that of the female Passenger Pigeon, as he particularly mentions the rufescent tail spots. Since both *Columba canadensis* Linnaeus and *Columba migratoria* Linnaeus are equally pertinent, and since it is the practice, at least of American ornithologists, to use names that have anteriority, there is no reason for not accepting this prior name *Columba canadensis* and calling the Passenger Pigeon *Ectopistes canadensis* (Linnaeus).

[1] Oberholser, *Science*, n.s. 48 (Nov. 1, 1918): 445.
[2] *Syst. Nat.* 12th ed., vol. 1 (1766 [after May 24]), p. 285.
[3] Ibid., p. 284.
[4] *Ornith.* 1 (1760): 118.

WHITE-WINGED DOVE, *Melopelia asiatica*

In rearranging the classification of the North American pigeons, James L. Peters[1] unites the genus *Melopelia* Bonaparte (type, *Columba asiatica* Linnaeus) with *Zenaida* Bonaparte (type, *Columba zenaida* Bonaparte) because he fails to find characters to separate these groups. Careful examination and comparison of the species of each group reveals, however, that *Melopelia* differs from *Zenaida* as follows: lores and space about eye unfeathered, instead of feathered; feathering on culmen not reaching beyond (if to) posterior end of nasal operculum, and not to posterior end of nasal opening, instead of reaching on culmen beyond posterior end of operculum and close up to posterior end of nasal opening; feathers on side of base of culmen fall far short of posterior end of nasal operculum, instead of reaching close up to operculum; exposed culmen almost as long as tarsus, about 75 percent, instead of only about 55 percent; wing less than 8 times length of culmen, instead of more than 10; second and third primaries counting from outermost strongly sinuated on subterminal portion of their outer webs, instead of not sinuated. In view of these characters, which, so far as the writer has been able to determine, do not overlap, it seems desirable to continue the recognition of *Melopelia* for the White-winged Dove.

[1] *Condor* 36 (Sept. 15, 1934): 213–215.

ROADRUNNER, *Geococcyx californianus*

Roadrunners inhabiting most of Texas differ from the typical form from California and Arizona in the characters indicated, and seem sufficiently distinct to warrant subspecific separation. Birds from Trans-Pecos Texas are nearer the typical form and apparently should be so referred; birds from the Texas Panhandle and Oklahoma are likewise large and, though somewhat intermediate, apparently should be called *G. c. californianus*. Birds from the greater part of Texas are referable to *G. c. dromicus*.

SCOPS OWL, *Otus scops*

In the *Distributional Check-List of the Birds of Mexico*, Friedmann, Griscom, and Moore[1] consider this little owl a subspecies of the Old World *Otus scops* (Linnaeus). In this they seem correct, since there is no observable difference of specific rank between the American Flammulated Scops Owl and the various races of *Otus scops*. In fact, some of the races are astonishingly similar even subspecifically! The name of our Scops Owl therefore becomes *O. s. flammeolus*.

[1] *Pacific Coast Avifauna*, no. 29 (June 30, 1950), p. 138.

PYGMY OWL, *Glaucidium gnoma*

The opinion that *G. g. pinicola* is only a color phase of *G. g. californicum* has already been published.[1] A further examination of a large series of birds of this species from North America and Mexico, however, shows that the Rocky Mt. race is separable from *californicum* when birds in comparable phases are compared. The former is much more grayish above, even in the slightly brownish phase.

[1] Bishop, *Proc. Biol. Soc. Washington* 44 (July 15, 1931): 97–98.

ELF OWL, *Micropallas whitneyi*

By application of the so-called "one letter rule," James L. Peters[1] rejects the generic name *Micropallas* Coues, which was proposed to replace *Micrathene* Coues, because it was supposed to be preoccupied by *Micrathena* Sundevall. Peters regards *Micrathena* Sundevall (1833) and *Micrathene* Coues (1866) as two different tenable generic terms, and, therefore, uses *Micrathene* as the generic name of the Elf Owl. The difference in the terminal letter of these two words seems in this case not sufficient reason for regarding them as separable, since they result merely from a difference in transliteration. According to the principles adopted in the present work, they would be considered identical, and consequently the latter would be preoccupied by the former. As a result of the application of such a rule, the name *Micropallas* Coues would continue as the proper name of the Elf Owls.

[1] *Check-List Birds World* 4 (June 5, 1940): 135.

CHUCK-WILL'S-WIDOW, *Antrostomus carolinensis*

This bird, although returned to the Old World genus *Caprimulgus*, certainly is not at home in such company. Its conspicuously different pterylosis, long lateral filaments of the rictal bristles (a unique character in the family), and more rounded tail, to say nothing of its important cranial characters, render desirable that it be kept in a distinct genus. In fact, the peculiar form of the palatines, which are relatively narrow, roughly club-shaped, and widely separated posteriorly, is sufficient to separate *Antrostomus* at a glance.

WHIP-POOR-WILL, *Setochalcis vocifera*

Although frequently associated in the same genus with the Chuck-will's-widow, the present species is rather strongly differentiated structurally from that bird, and should, along with the other species of the genus, be separated from the type of *Antrostomus*, which is *Antrostomus carolinensis*. With respect to external structure, the Whip-poor-will differs from *A. carolinensis*, in having no lateral filaments on the rictal bristles, the presence of which in *A. carolinensis* is unique in this section of the goatsucker family. In the Whip-poor-will the second primary counting from the outermost is longest, the third but little shorter, the first considerably shorter than the third and about equal to the fourth; in *A. carolinensis* the second primary is longest, but the third is decidedly shorter, and the first still a little shorter but very much longer than the fourth. Three primaries are sinuate on their outer webs, instead of two; and the wing is relatively shorter, the secondaries twelve or thirteen, instead of fourteen. As has already been pointed out by H. L. Clark,[1] the pterylosis is also different enough to separate the two groups generically without other characters. The palatines are conspicuously different, their inner edges parallel and fused at their inner posterior angles, thus forming a continuous truncate hinder margin; whereas in *Antrostomus* the palatines are broadly club-shaped and widely flaring, even along their inner edges, so that their terminal portions are far separated.

The Whip-poor-will also differs very much from the Old World genus *Caprimulgus* Linnaeus in external and particularly osteological characters and, by no means, is to be referred to that group. The numerous osteological differences between these two genera are fully detailed in the writer's revision.[2] Since *A. carolinensis* differs generally from all the other American species of the group, and these, in turn, depart markedly from the Old World genus *Caprimulgus*, to which they have been frequently referred, the proper course seems to be to consider them as constituting different generic groups; the name *Setochalcis* has already been given to the Whip-poor-will, which should, therefore, be called *Setochalcis vocifera* (Wilson).[3]

[1] *Auk* 18 (Apr., 1901): 168–171.
[2] Oberholser, *Bull. U.S. Nat. Mus.*, no. 86 (Apr. 6, 1914), p. 9 et seq.
[3] Ibid., p. 11.

POOR-WILL, *Phalaenoptilus nuttallii*

The Frosted Poor-will from e. Kansas to c. Texas differs from the typical Poor-will of the n. Rocky Mts., *P. n. nuttallii*, in its decidedly smaller size; much lighter, more silvery grayish (less brownish) upper surface—particularly in the light phase; and in the paler, more grayish (less brownish) lower parts. They evidently represent a well-characterized subspecies. This bird was originally described by William Brewster[1] as *P. n. nitidus* from specimens collected on the Nueces River in Texas.

For many years past, this bird has been considered a synonym of the typical *nuttallii*, since the species is well known to possess two very distinct color phases. But careful comparison of a good series of specimens from c. Texas and the n. Rocky Mts. shows that, without doubt, the Texas bird is subspecifically separable and should bear the name originally given by Brewster, the type of which the writer has examined in the present connection. Comparisons of size may easily be made by reference to the measurements given under both these forms. Birds from

Trans-Pecos Texas are larger, darker, and belong undoubtedly to the typical race as already indicated. *P. n. nitidus* differs also from *nyctophilus* described from Oregon[2] in its smaller size; lighter, more silvery grayish upper surface; and in narrower white tips of outer rectrices, particularly in the female.

[1] *Auk* 4 (Apr., 1887): 147.
[2] Oberholser, *Scient. Publ. Cleveland Mus. Nat. Hist.* 4 (Sept. 19, 1932): 2.

COMMON NIGHTHAWK, *Chordeiles minor*

Examination of a series of the birds commonly referred to the Howell's Nighthawk, *C. m. howelli*, reveals that apparently two races are involved. When this bird was first described, only a rather small series of specimens was available, particularly from the region whence came the type; but it is now seen that birds from n.w. Texas, extreme n.w. Oklahoma, and n. New Mexico are much more buffy or ochraceous than are birds from Colorado and Wyoming; in fact, they are somewhat intermediate between Wyoming birds and *C. m. henryi* of s. Arizona. Measurements of both races are given in the detailed account of the species. In the original description of *howelli*[1] the type locality is given as Lipscomb, Texas, and birds from this region are practically typical of the more buffy or ochraceous race, so that the name *howelli* will apply to this buffy race, leaving the more grayish (less buffy and ochraceous) bird from Wyoming and Colorado to be named *C. m. divisus*.

[1] *Chordeiles virginianus howelli* Oberholser, *Bull. U.S. Nat. Mus.*, no. 86 (Apr. 6, 1914), p. 57.

BROAD-TAILED HUMMINGBIRD, *Platurornis platycercus*

An examination of the structural characters of the Broad-tailed Hummingbird, heretofore called *Selasphorus platycercus*, reveals that this bird is structurally very different from other birds of the same genus. The name chosen for this new genus is *Platurornis*. The Broad-tailed Hummingbird is the type and only species.

In order to determine the generic affinity of *Platurornis platycercus* it has been necessary to examine all other species currently referred to *Selasphorus*; this has revealed that it is divisible into three groups by structural characters that seem of obvious generic value. The type of *Selasphorus* is *Trochilus rufus* Gmelin, and it appears to be strictly congeneric with the Allen's Hummingbird, *Selasphorus alleni*, and *Selasphorus scintilla* of Costa Rica. This group is characterized by very narrow, sharply pointed, and incurved first (outermost) primary, but without sinuation on either web; rather narrow, pointed second primary; much rounded tail with very narrow, sharply pointed feathers; and gorget much lengthened on either side.

The remaining species, namely *Selasphorus flammula* Salvin, *S. torridus* Salvin, *S. ardens* Salvin, and *S. simoni* Carriker, seem to be structurally different from typical *Selasphorus* and from *Platurornis*, so apparently should constitute a genus by themselves, which is fully as well characterized as *Selasphorus*, as now restricted, is from other genera. This group differs from *Selasphorus* in its broad, though pointed, outermost primary; very broad second primary, which is obtusely pointed or rounded at tip; very broad tail feathers, which are rounded or obtusely pointed at tip; relatively much shorter bill, the wing being from 3⅓ to 3¾ times—instead of 2⅔ to 3¹⁄₁₀—length of bill; and tail also 2⅓ to more than 2½ times length of bill, instead of 1½ to 2⅕.

From *Platurornis* the present group differs in relative length of bill, wing, and tail as from *Selasphorus*, and additionally, in

its broad first (outermost) primary, which is neither emarginate nor sinuate at the tip, the tip not attenuated, and incurved—instead of curved—outwardly at the tip; second primary regularly rounded or obtusely pointed at tip, without peculiar curved incision at tip so characteristic of *Platurornis*; tail much rounded; and gorget much lengthened laterally. This genus may be called *Selasornis*. Its type is *Selasphorus flammula* Salvin. The species mentioned above would consequently stand as follows: *Selasornis flammula* (Salvin), *Selasornis torridus* (Salvin), *Selasornis ardens* (Salvin), and *Selasornis simoni* (Carriker).

CALLIOPE HUMMINGBIRD, *Stellula calliope*

By reason of an additional subspecies,[1] the technical name of this hummingbird becomes *S. c. calliope*.

[1] *Stellula calliope lowei* Griscom, *Bull. Mus. Comp. Zool.* 75 (Jan., 1934): 380 ("Taxco, Guerrero").

BLUE-THROATED HUMMINGBIRD, *Lampornis clemenciae*

Birds of this species inhabiting the Chisos Mts. of Texas have been referred to either the typical bird from Mexico, *L. c. clemenciae*, or to the Arizona race, *L. c. bessophilus*; however, they combine the characters of these two forms to such an extent that it seems best to recognize birds from this area as a distinct subspecies, to be called *L. c. phasmorus*. Birds from Santa Catarina in c. western Nuevo León verge somewhat towards *clemenciae*, but are decidedly nearer the Chisos Mts. race. Therefore, *phasmorus* would have a limited range along the n.e. edge of the Mexican tableland.

COPPERY-TAILED TROGON, *Trogon ambiguus*

This species is generally considered a subspecies of *Trogon elegans*. This treatment appears to have developed from the seeming intergradation evident when comparing female and immature birds, or those in transition plumage. Fully adult males of *Trogon ambiguus ambiguus* are entirely distinct in lacking the regular narrow black barring of the three outer tail feathers, which is so conspicuous and characteristic a feature of *T. elegans*, and which is very different from the mottled appearance of the same feathers in *T. ambiguus*. Examination of a large number of specimens shows no indication of intergradation in this respect. Even in the female of *T. elegans* the outer tail feathers are more numerously and regularly barred with black than are the same feathers in the adult female of *T. ambiguus*. Thus, it would seem to be more representative of the true relationships of these two birds to consider *T. ambiguus* a distinct species.

Van Rossem has described the bird from n.w. Mexico as *Trogon elegans canescens*,[1] but the bird from e. Mexico, which race has occurred in extreme s. Texas, is the "typical," or nominate form, *T. a. ambiguus*.

[1] *Bull. Mus. Comp. Zool.* 77 (Dec., 1934): 441 (San Javier, Sonora, Mexico).

PILEATED WOODPECKER, *Hylatomus pileatus*

The Old World genus *Dryocopus* Boie, of which the type is *Picus martius* Linnaeus, and from which some authors have considered the Pileated Woodpecker not separable, seems, however, to be sufficiently different. It has a subfalcate outermost primary and entirely lacks the crest which is such a conspicuous characteristic of the Pileated Woodpecker. The generic name of the Pileated, under present procedure will become *Hylatomus* Baird[1] (type by original designation, *Picus pileatus* Linnaeus), since this is now not considered preoccupied by *Hylotoma* Latreille (1802), proposed for a genus of insects.

[1] *Rep. Explor. and Surv. R. R. Pacific* 9 (1858 [after Oct. 20]): 107.

ACORN WOODPECKER, *Balanosphyra formicivora*

The genus *Balanosphyra* Ridgway[1] (type by monotypy, *Picus formicivorus* Swainson), is generally considered inseparable from *Melanerpes*. However, reexamination of these groups indicates that the former is recognizable by the following characters as distinguished from *Melanerpes*: first (outermost) primary much narrower, more acuminate, and shorter, only ¼ length of second primary, instead of about ⅓ or more; nostrils more broadly (less lengthened) oval, and almost completely, instead of only lightly and partly, covered by the greater development of the nasal plumes, which form dense bristly tufts; and the breast feathers of normal character, instead of decomposed and more or less hairlike.

The race of Acorn Woodpeckers from Nuevo León, Mexico, shows the greatest differentiation from the typical (nominate) subspecies, *B. f. formicivora*, of c. and s. Mexico, in greater length of exposed culmen and short middle toe. Birds from the Chisos Mts. and from Kerr Co., Texas, are even smaller so far as length of wing and tail are concerned, with also a somewhat shorter tarsus, and they are a little intermediate between *formicivora* and the Arizona race, *aculeata*, which is the bird of the Davis and Guadalupe mts. in Trans-Pecos Texas. Altogether, however, these c. Texas birds are decidedly referable to the race from n.e. Mexico here described. Examples from s. Tamaulipas are intermediate in size between the present race and the Mexican *formicivora*, but are nearer *phasma*. The measurements of typical *formicivora* given by Ridgway[2] are too small, since he included specimens belonging to *phasma*. Following are measurements of the Mexican race, *formicivora*, for comparison with the measurements of the more northern *phasma*: *Adult male*: Wing, 135.8–151.1 (average, 142.0) mm.; tail, 68.6–83.1 (78.0); bill (exposed culmen), 23.1–28.4 (25.9); tarsus, 20.1–22.6 (21.6); middle toe without claw, 15.5–19.0 (17.5). *Adult female*: Wing, 132.1–148.1 (140.5); tail, 66.5–82.0 (77.5); bill, 22.1–27.9 (24.6); tarsus, 19.6–23.1 (21.4); middle toe, 15.0–19.0 (17.0). So far as the black areas on the breast are concerned there does not seem to be any constant difference between *phasma* and *formicivora*.

A statement by van Rossem[3] that *aculeata* is not separable from the Mexican *formicivora* was based on the color characters on which its distinctness was supposed largely to rest. A reexamination in the present connection seems to show that in this respect van Rossem is correct, although there is a tendency in *aculeata* toward a more solid black area on breast and jugulum. However, in a large series this appears very inconstant and cannot be relied on as a character to separate *aculeata* from the Mexican race. There is, nevertheless, a size difference. Measurements of a large number of specimens show, when compared to *formicivora*, that the Arizona bird, in average dimensions is smaller with respect to wing, tail, bill, and middle toe. This difference, though not great, probably constitutes a sufficient reason for keeping the Mearn's Acorn Woodpecker as a separate subspecies.

[1] *Proc. Biol. Soc. Washington* 24 (Feb. 24, 1911): 34.
[2] *Bull. U.S. Nat. Mus.*, no. 50, pt. 6 (Apr. 8, 1914), pp. 102–103.
[3] *Bull. Mus. Comp. Zool.* 77 (Dec., 1934): 444.

YELLOW-BELLIED SAPSUCKER, *Sphyrapicus varius*

A northern race, *S. v. atrothorax* (Lesson) has been separated from the southern bird that breeds in the Allegheny Mts. of the e. United States.[1] This northern form is far more numerous in Texas, as would be expected from its geographic range. The typical race occupies a relatively restricted region in the mountains from Ohio and Pennsylvania to n.w. Georgia. The birds from Ohio and Pennsylvania are intermediate between the northern and southern races, but apparently average somewhat nearer the southern bird.

The Yellow-bellied Sapsucker was first described by Linnaeus,[2] who based his description on *Picus varius carolinus* of Brisson[3] and on *Picus varius minor ventre luteo* of Catesby.[4]

Brisson's name is based on Klein's *Picus varius minor ventre luteo*, which is, in turn, based on Catesby. Thus, the entire synonymy resolves itself into the South Carolina bird as the basis for the name. So far as one is able to judge from the measurements and weights given by these authors, and by the fact that the southern bird is of common occurrence in South Carolina, it is obvious that the southern race has better claim to the name *Picus varius* Linnaeus. Furthermore, the A.O.U. check-list, 1957, gives South Carolina as the type locality. For this reason the present writer assigns *Picus varius* Linnaeus to the southern race, and further restricts the type locality to the vicinity of Charleston in s.e. South Carolina.

The name to be applied to the northern bird seems to be *Picus atrothorax* of Lesson,[5] described without locality. Some years later, Pucheran[6] stated that the specimen from Newfoundland in the Paris Museum was probably the type. At the present writer's request, Jacques Berlioz, then in charge of the bird collection in the Museum National d'Histoire Naturelle, at Paris, France, looked up this specimen and found that it had been sent in 1928 with some other birds from North America to another museum in France. He fortunately was able to recover this bird, and it is now in the Paris Museum. Although it appears that the original description by Lesson evidently was based in part on two specimens, both of these birds—one from Newfoundland and one from Philadelphia, Pennsylvania—are examples of the northern race. Since Pucheran and Berlioz regarded the former specimen as the type, and since the present writer has already designated this as the type, we hereby confirm this designation and consider this specimen as the type, and the type locality Newfoundland. The name of the northern bird, therefore, should continue to be *S. v. atrothorax* (Lesson).

[1] Oberholser, *Bull. Louisiana Dept. Conservation*, no. 28 (June 30, 1938), p. 372.
[2] [*Picus*] *varius* Linnaeus, *Syst. Nat.* 12th ed., vol. 1 (1766 [after May 24]), p. 176.
[3] *Ornith.* 4 (1760): 62.
[4] *Nat. Hist. Carolina, Florida, and Bahama Is.*, vol. 1 (1731), p. 21, pl. 21, fig. (1) ("in American Septentrionali").
[5] *Traité d'Ornith.* (1831), p. 229.
[6] *Revue et Mag. Zool.*, no. 1 (Jan., 1855), pp. 21–23.

HAIRY WOODPECKER, *Dryobates villosus*

Van Rossem[1] has made use of the generic name *Dendrocopos* Koch[2] in place of *Dryobates* Boie. This, though unexplained, is evidently because he considers *Dendrocopos* Koch not to be preoccupied by *Dendrocopus* Vieillot,[3] since these two names are not spelled exactly alike. They differ, however, only in the terminal syllable and this difference of a single letter is due merely to transliteration from the Greek. Such a difference in present codes of nomenclature is not considered sufficient for the recognition of both names as valid.

In this case the later name *Dendrocopos* Koch is preoccupied by *Dendrocopus* Vieillot; the former should be replaced by *Dryobates* Boie, as is reflected in current usage.

[1] *Occas. Papers. Mus. Zool. Louisiana State Univ.*, no. 21 (Oct. 25, 1945), pp. 137–141.
[2] *Syst. Baier. Zool.* 1 (1816 [before July]): 72.
[3] *Analyse* (Apr. 14, 1816), pp. 45, 69.

DOWNY WOODPECKER, *Dryobates pubescens*

See Hairy Woodpecker.

LADDER-BACKED WOODPECKER, *Dryobates scalaris*

See Hairy Woodpecker.

RED-COCKADED WOODPECKER, *Phrenopicus borealis*

As has already been shown by Ridgway,[1] the present species exhibits sufficient structural characters to warrant its generic separation from other species commonly referred to *Dryobates*; these characters seem to be not only readily appreciated but also constant. This bird differs from the species of *Dryobates* in its relatively much longer and more pointed wing; longer wing tip, the longest primaries exceeding the outer secondaries by ⅓ or more of length of wing; much smaller first (outermost) primary, this being not more than ¼ as long as second (outermost) primary; relatively much shorter bill; and relatively longer tarsus, this being as long as outer hind toe with claw or longer, instead of shorter. The generic name to be employed for this species, which is the only one of its group, is *Phrenopicus* Bonaparte,[2] the type of which by subsequent designation of Gray in 1855 is *Picus borealis* Vieillot.

[1] *Bull. U.S. Nat. Mus.*, no. 50, pt. 4 (Apr. 8, 1914), pp. 11, 268.
[2] *Ateneo Italiano* 2 (1854): 123.

EASTERN KINGBIRD, *Tyrannus tyrannus*

The western form of the Eastern Kingbird described as *T. t. hespericola*[1] was based on a type collected at the mouth of Twenty-Mile Creek in Warner Valley, 9 mi. south of Adel, Oregon; birds as far east as c. Montana, North Dakota, and New Mexico are referable to this race. Size and other differences between the eastern and western forms may be appreciated by comparing each in the detailed account of the species.

[1] Oberholser, *Scient. Publ. Cleveland Mus. Nat. Hist.* 4 (Sept. 19, 1932): 3.

SAY'S PHOEBE, *Sayornis sayus*

The grammatical gender of *Sayornis* has been a matter of considerable uncertainty among ornithologists. As originally proposed it was combined with specific names which gave no indication of the gender intended by its author, Bonaparte. The name is a compound of the name of the zoologist Thomas Say and the Greek word *ornis*, which is of common gender. As applied to a bird, *ornis* is a proper noun in that it is the name of an actual organism. Hence, its gender, according to the rule for classical compounds, is determined by its own gender, which in this case happens to be impossible. The fact that it is combined with a masculine noun, Say, would determine the gender of this combination to be masculine. Furthermore, Spencer F. Baird, the first author to make use of the name in combination with a specific name indicative of gender, was exercising his first reviser prerogative by using *Sayornis* as masculine. *Sayornis*, therefore, should be treated as a masculine noun, not feminine as has been done by some authors.

TRAILL'S FLYCATCHER, *Empidonax traillii*

The Plains race of this flycatcher, *E. t. campestris*, described by J. W. Aldrich[1] from Oakes, North Dakota, is a dividing of the population heretofore included in *E. t. traillii*. It is an easily recognizable subspecies, in all but the young plumage, almost if not quite as pale above as *extimus*. From this form, however, it differs in being more greenish (less brownish or grayish) on the upper surface, and having the outermost primary appreciably longer than the sixth (counting from outermost).

The Little Traill's Flycatcher, *E. t. extimus*, is in part *traillii* of most authors. For explanation of the change see the present writer's revision of this species.[2] The present race was originally described by Allan R. Phillips,[3] from the lower San Pedro River in Arizona.

The Mountain Traill's Flycatcher, *E. t. adastus*, was originally described from specimens taken in c. southern Oregon.[4] It is the bird of the n.w. United States east of the range of *brewsteri* and north of the range of *extimus*.

[1] *Wilson Bull.* 63 (Sept., 1951): 195.
[2] *Ohio Journ Sci.* 18 (Jan. [Feb. 8], 1918): 88–90.
[3] *Auk* 65 (Oct. 22, 1948): 512.
[4] Oberholser, *Scient. Publ. Cleveland Mus. Nat. Hist.* 4 (Sept. 19, 1932): 3 ("Hart Mountain, northern end of Warner Valley, 20 miles northeast of Adel, Oregon").

DUSKY FLYCATCHER, *Empidonax oberholseri*

Birds from the Warner Valley and Warner Mts. in c. southern Oregon and from e. Oregon are intermediate between the new subspecies, *E. o. spodius*, and *oberholseri*, but are nearer the new form. This Idaho race has much the same relation to the typical race as has *E. traillii adastus* to *E. traillii brewsteri*, occupying in summer very much the same relative area.

GRAY FLYCATCHER, *Empidonax obscurus*

The name *Empidonax obscurus* (Swainson) has been applied both to *E. oberholseri* and *E. wrightii* (as these species are listed in the A.O.U. check-list, 1957). It was originally described by Swainson as *Tyrannula obscura* as follows:

10. Muscicapa querulae ? Vieil. Ois. de l'Am. pl. 39. Above olive gray, beneath yellowish-white; wings short, brown, with two whitish bands; tail brown, even, the outer feather with a pale yellow margin.
Mexico. Rather larger than the last [*Tyrannula affinis*]. Total length, 5¼ [in.]; bill, nearly ⁷⁄₁₀; wings, 2½; tail, 2½; tarsi, ⁶⁄₁₀.[1]

The increase in our knowledge of the Mexican forms of *Empidonax*, and careful comparisons with all the known forms of this genus, point to the identification of Swainson's *Tyrannula obscura* as the bird now known as *Empidonax wrightii*. Both the color and structural characters, as well as the measurements given by Swainson in his original description, agree very well with the Gray Flycatcher, and these points cannot fail to impress the reader of the probability that Swainson had *E. wrightii* in hand. The type of the original description of *Tyrannula obscura* is so far as is known lost; nevertheless, the name still seems applicable. Thence, the Gray Flycatcher would be known as *E. obscurus* (Swainson).

[1] *Philosophical Mag.*, n.s. 1 (May, 1827): 367.

COUES' FLYCATCHER, *Syrichta pertinax*

The proper generic name for this species, instead of *Contopus*, is *Syrichta* Gray[1] (type, *Tyrannula ardosiaca* Lafresnaye). *Con-*

topus differs from *Syrichta* in having longest primaries exceeding length of secondaries by more than combined length of tarsus, middle toe, and middle claw—instead of being shorter; first (outermost) primary much longer than fifth, and nearly equal to fourth; second—instead of third or fourth—primary longest; and fourth decidedly shorter than third.

[1] *Handlist Genera, Species Birds* 1 (1869 [after May 10]): 362.

OLIVE-SIDED FLYCATCHER, *Nuttallornis borealis*

Although there is considerable individual variation in both western and eastern birds of this species, it would appear that the average measurements based on a considerable series of both show sufficient difference to warrant the recognition of two subspecies. These differences of measurements can be compared in the detailed account of the species. The present writer[1] some time ago called attention to the applicability of the name *Tyrannus borealis* Swainson,[2] based on a specimen from Cumberland House (= Carlton House), Saskatchewan, Canada. Since the bird from Saskatchewan is within the range of the western race—formerly called *N. b. majorinus* Bangs and Penard[3]—this subspecies has clear title to the name *N. b. borealis*. It now becomes necessary to provide another name for the Eastern Olive-sided Flycatcher—formerly known as *N. b. borealis*. The earliest available name is *Muscicapa cooperi* Nuttall,[4] and the proper name for this bird is, therefore, *N. b. cooperi* (Nuttall).

[1] *Scient. Publ. Cleveland Mus. Nat. Hist.* 1 (Dec. 31, 1930): 114–115.
[2] *Fauna Boreali-Amer.* 2 (1831 [Feb., 1832]): 141, pl. 35.
[3] *Proc. Biol. Soc. Washington* 34 (June 30, 1921): 190.
[4] *Man. Ornith. U.S. and Canada* 1 (1832): 282 (Sweet Auburn [= Mt. Auburn], near Boston, Mass.).

BEARDLESS FLYCATCHER, *Camptostoma imberbis*

The technical name of this species as commonly written is based on the assumption that the generic designation *Camptostoma* is of neuter gender. The Greek word *stoma* which forms the terminal element is, of course, neuter; however, it is not a proper but a common, or descriptive (appellative), noun. Therefore, according to etymological rule, as the terminal part of a generic name, it cannot determine the whole name as of neuter gender; such a generic term must become either masculine or feminine. Since *Camptostoma* has an ending of regular Latin feminine form, it seems better to consider it as feminine, particularly as no author has treated it other than as neuter. The Beardless Flycatcher would thus be called *Camptostoma imberbis*.

This case involves the same principle as does the generic name *Toxostoma*, which is discussed under the Brown Thrasher. Furthermore, it might be worthwhile to mention that *Antrostomus*, which terminally is compounded from the same Greek word, *stoma*, with a Latin masculine ending is used always as a masculine noun.

HORNED LARK, *Eremophila alpestris*

The Chihuahua race of the Horned Lark, *E. a. aphrasta*, is the breeding bird inhabiting the region from extreme s.e. Arizona and the s.w. corner of New Mexico, south to Chihuahua, Coahuila, and Durango. It may be readily distinguished from *adusta*, with which it is frequently confused, in much less reddish back and more pinkish (less cinnamomeous) hindneck and bend of wing, and from *leucolaema* and *occidentalis* as indicated in the detailed account. Since it is nearly resident, its occurrence in Trans-Pecos Texas is probably explainable only as a postnuptial wanderer. This race was originally described by the writer[1] from

specimens taken from Casas Grandes, Chihuahua, Mexico. Birds from s.e. Arizona and s.w. New Mexico are somewhat paler than typical birds from Chihuahua, but are much nearer this race than to any other.

[1] Oberholser, *Proc. U.S. Nat. Mus.* 24 (June 9, 1902): 860.

TREE SWALLOW, *Iridoprocne bicolor*

Tree Swallows from California seem to differ sufficiently—chiefly in their smaller size—from those of other parts of North America to be subspecifically separable. The Tree Swallow was originally described as *Hirundo bicolor* by Vieillot[1] and its type locality fixed as New York.[2] Most of the other synonyms refer to the same bird, but there is an available name for the California race in *Hirundo bicolor* var. *vespertina* Cooper,[3] its type locality now determined as Haywood, California. This name is available for the California bird, even though the original diagnosis "larger and bluer than the eastern tree swallow" is erroneous. Using this name, the California Tree Swallow will become *I. b. vespertina* (Cooper). The decidedly smaller size of the California bird is evident by the following measurements: *Adult male*: Wing, 107.5–114.5 (average, 109.7) mm.; tail, 50.5–54.0 (52.5); bill (exposed culmen), 5.8–6.5 (6.0); tarsus, 11.0–12.3 (11.6); middle toe without claw, 10.3–12.0 (11.1). *Adult female*: Wing, 107.5–115.0 (110.5); tail, 51.0–56.3 (53.1); bill, 5.5–6.3 (5.9); tarsus, 11.3–12.0 (11.6); middle toe, 10.5–12.0 (11.3). The distribution of *vespertina* is from n. to s. California; it winters south to Sinaloa (Mazatlán).

Separation of this subspecies, of course, renders necessary the use of the trinomial *I. b. bicolor* for the Eastern Tree Swallow. Tree Swallows from Oregon and Washington, though slightly smaller than the eastern birds, are much nearer *bicolor* than *vespertina*.

[1] *Hist. Nat. Oiseaux Amér. Sept.*, vol. 1 (1807 [1808]), p. 61, pl. 31 ("Centre des États-Unis").
[2] *Check-list North Amer. Birds* 4th ed. (Oct. 1, 1931), p. 216.
[3] *Amer. Nat.* 10 (Feb., 1876): 91.

BANK SWALLOW, *Riparia riparia*

As already shown by the writer,[1] the Bank Swallows from North America are subspecifically different from the birds inhabiting Europe, on which the original description of *R. r. riparia* is based.[2] All the other names applied to this species refer to the European bird, except *Hirundo riparia americana*,[3] which is based on the bird from the upper Missouri River, but which is preoccupied by *Hirundo americana* Gmelin. Leonhard Stejneger was, therefore, entirely correct in bestowing on the American bird the name *Clivicola riparia maximiliani*;[4] his type is a specimen, no. 83253, U.S. National Museum, from Ipswich, Massachusetts. (This specimen was incorrectly given as no. 8325 in the writer's notice of the species above cited.)

Since the distinctness of the American race has been questioned,[5] another examination of the matter has been made with an increased series of nearly two hundred specimens, representing breeding birds of England, Germany, Switzerland, Algeria, Libya, Russia, Austria, Hungary, and various parts of North America, as well as a considerable number of migrants from various parts of Africa. A large number of specimens from both continents have been measured, and careful comparisons have been remade with breeding birds from Europe and e. North America.

When breeding birds of similar plumage and season are compared, there is no difficulty in separating a good series of the American bird from an adequate series of the European bird. That there are occasionally specimens that are close in coloration does not in the least affect nor invalidate the average characters, these particularly obvious in coloration of upper surface —which in *maximiliani* is a darker and more sooty (less rufescent) brown. Furthermore, the difference in size, especially in wing and tail, is very appreciable, the American bird averaging decidedly smaller. The wing of *maximiliani* normally ranges in the male from 95.5 to 103.5 mm., rarely as high as 106 mm.; the European bird varies from 100 to 112.5 mm. Thus, in length of wing the American bird is almost always below 100 mm., and the European bird almost never. The length of tail is likewise significantly less in the American bird. Following are measurements of breeding European birds for comparison with *maximiliani*: *Adult male*: Wing, 100.0–112.5 (average, 105.9) mm.; tail, 50.0–58.5 (53.5); bill (exposed culmen), 5.5–6.8 (5.9); tarsus, 10.5–11.5 (10.8); middle toe without claw, 8.5–9.5 (8.9). *Adult female*: Wing, 101.0–109.5 (104.2); tail, 48.5–55.0 (51.8); bill, 4.9–7.0 (5.8); tarsus, 10.0–11.5 (11.0); middle toe, 9.0–10.0 (9.5).

The measurements given in the detailed account for *maximiliani* are only for birds from e. North America. Birds from Idaho and Alaska average slightly larger—the maximum wing measurement of Idaho birds being 106.5 mm. Males from Alaska and Idaho compare in averages as follows: *Alaska*: Wing, 101.5 mm.; tail, 49.4; bill (exposed culmen), 6.0; tarsus, 11.0; middle toe without claw, 9.4. *Idaho*: Wing, 101.8; tail, 50.1; bill, 6.0; tarsus, 11.3; middle toe, 9.6.

From these measurements it is evident that the European bird, particularly when compared with birds from e. North America, is to the extent of about 7 percent larger, whether males or females be considered. Even if larger birds from Alaska and Idaho be included, the European race would still average about 5 percent larger.

It is of note that Ernst Hartert,[6] in discussing this subject, apparently without adequate series of American birds for comparison, remarked that Ridgway gave 111.0 mm. as the maximum wing measurement of North American birds. This, however, is not exactly the case, because Ridgway's measurements of *Riparia riparia* include both European and American birds, since he made no distinction between the two. Also, his own measurement sheets show that the bird with the 111.0-mm. wing was from Europe! In light of the above, it seems reasonable to consider *maximiliani* distinct from the European race. The other races in Africa and Asia have no important bearing on the status of the North American bird.

[1] Oberholser, *Bull. Louisiana Dept. Conservation*, no. 28 (June 30, 1938), p. 407.
[2] [*Hirundo*] *riparia* Linnaeus, *Syst. Nat.* 10th ed., vol. 1 (Jan. 1, 1758), p. 192 ("In Europae Collibus" [type locality, Sweden]).
[3] *Hir*[*undo*] *riparia americana* "Lin." Wied, *Journ f. Ornith.* 6 (Mar., 1858): 101.
[4] *Bull. U.S. Nat. Mus.*, no. 29 (Dec. 16, 1885), p. 378fn.
[5] *Proc. U.S. Nat. Mus.* 86 (Jan. 31, 1939): 202–203.
[6] *Vögel Paläarkt. Fauna*, vol. 1, pt. 6 (June, 1910), p. 811.

ROUGH-WINGED SWALLOW, *Stelgidopteryx ruficollis*

A western race of this species, *S. r. aphractus*, was described by the writer[1] from specimens taken at Twenty-Mile Creek in Warner Valley, 9 mi. south of Adel, Oregon. Characters given in the detailed account will serve to separate it from the eastern race, *serripennis*; the larger size is the best available character for the identification of individual specimens. In comparison of plumage it is important to use specimens in comparable condition of season and wear. Freshly molted autumn birds are exceedingly dark, and gradually—at times rather rapidly—become

lighter; thus, no safe comparison of color is possible unless care is taken to have birds in proper plumage. Occasionally, large birds occur in the e. United States during migration, which seem to represent wandering individuals of the western race.

[1] *Scient. Publ. Cleveland Mus. Nat. Hist.* 4 (Sept. 19, 1932): 5.

BARN SWALLOW, *Hirundo rustica*

The spelling of the subspecific name of the Barn Swallow is one that has caused considerable controversy. Boddaert, who first described this bird,[1] wrote the name *Hirundo erythrogaster*, but as already shown, words like *erythrogaster* are properly considered adjectives, this particular word meaning red-bellied—not a noun meaning red belly. As an adjective it is properly declinable as of the third declension, which would give *erythrogaster* as the nominative singular masculine, and *erythrogastris* as the nominative singular feminine. There is, however, usage for the declension of such adjectives as of the first declension, in which case the nominative singular masculine would be *erythrogaster* and the nominative singular feminine *erythrogastra*. The present writer[2] has on a previous occasion made use of the third declension ending *erythrogastris* for the subspecific name, but since the form *erythrogastra* for the feminine is permissible and has been used by a number of previous authors, it seems better to revert to this form rather than to attempt to change to the other, even though it is more in accordance with classical usage. For further elucidation of this subject and this particular case, see Walter Faxon's comments in "The Name *erythrogaster*."[3]

[1] *Tabl. Planch. Enlum.* (1783), p. 45.
[2] *Bull. U.S. Nat. Mus.*, no. 98 (June 30, 1917), p. 31.
[3] *Auk* 36 (Apr., 1919): 294–295.

CLIFF SWALLOW, *Petrochelidon pyrrhonota*

Study of the forms of this species has shown that the conglomeration of birds included under the so-called Northern Cliff Swallow, to which several names have been applied, requires elucidation. Birds from the c. northern United States—from Wisconsin to Illinois and Indiana—differ decidedly from birds breeding in the n.e. United States in paler forehead. In Vieillot's original account of *Hirundo pyrrhonota*, the description, "a le front d'un brun roussâtre," plus the length, 5.25 in., indicates clearly that this refers to the northeasternmost race, that is, the bird breeding in New York and the New England states. To this race, the name *P. p. pyrrhonota* is now restricted; of this, the *Hirundo opifex* Clinton[1] is a synonym.

The next name to be considered is *Hirundo albifrons* Rafinesque,[2] which, without much doubt, applies to the bird breeding in Indiana and Illinois, as the original description and locality indicated. This name is herewith adopted as the earliest name for the Northern Cliff Swallow; the designation for this subspecies, therefore, should be *P. p. albifrons*. *Hirundo republicana* of Audubon[3] applies to the same race and is a synonym of Rafinesque's name.

The Cliff Swallow inhabiting the c. United States from the Great Plains to New Mexico differs from *albifrons* in its paler rump; paler brownish gray of the hindneck; slightly lighter, more whitish forehead; and in its more grayish (less buffy or ochraceous) lower parts, the breast and jugulum particularly lighter. While this bird occupies an intermediate area, its range is sufficiently extensive to make desirable its recognition as a distinct subspecies. The name to be applied to it is *Hirundo lunifrons* Say,[4] which was described from a bird taken on the

Arkansas River, 30 mi. east of the mouth of the Royal Gorge, near a place called "Swallows," a station on the Denver and Rio Grande Western Railroad in Colorado. The name for the Great Plains Cliff Swallow will, therefore, be *P. p. lunifrons*.

The original description of the Oregon Cliff Swallow, *P. p. aprophata*, was based on specimens from the Warner Valley in c. southern Oregon.[5]

[1] *Ann. Lyc. Nat. Hist. New York* 1 (Dec., 1824): 161 ("Winchell's Tavern, 5 miles south of White-Hall, near Lake Champlain [N. Y.]").

[2] *Kentucky Gazette* (Feb. 14, 1822), p. 3, col. 4 ("Newport, Ky.").

[3] *Ann. Lyc. Nat. Hist. New York* 1 (Dec., 1824): 164 ("Henderson, 120 miles below the falls of the Ohio").

[4] See Long, *Expedition Pittsburgh to Rocky Mts.*, vol. 2 (1823), p. 47.

[5] *Scient. Publ. Cleveland Mus. Nat. Hist.* 4 (Sept. 19, 1932): 6.

STELLER'S JAY, *Cyanocitta stelleri*

The Arizona Steller's Jay, *C. s. browni*, which replaces *diademata* in s.w. North America, was described by Allan R. Phillips.[1]

[1] *Condor* 52 (Dec. 6, 1950): 253.

SCRUB JAY, *Aphelocoma coerulescens*

The technical subspecific name of the Woodhouse's Scrub Jay is often written *woodhouseii*. The original spelling, however, is *woodhousii*,[1] although written *woodhouseii* on pages 584 and 585 of the same volume. However, since the spelling *woodhousii* stands first in the book it becomes the proper one. A parallel case is the generic name *Pooecetes* Baird in the same work, in which the anterior spelling is now in current use.

A new subspecies, the Pecos Scrub Jay, *A. c. mesolega*, differs from *woodhousii* in its decidedly shorter bill; somewhat shorter wing, tail, and middle toe; its lighter, less bluish back; jugulum with less blue; paler bluish, sometimes white, under tail-coverts; paler, more whitish (less grayish) breast and abdomen; streaks on throat and jugulum more whitish (less grayish). While this bird is intermediate in range and, to some extent, in characters between *texana* and *woodhousii*, it seems sufficiently different from either to warrant its recognition by name.

[1] Baird, Cassin, and Lawrence, *Rep. Explor. and Surv. R. R. Pacific*, vol. 8 (1858 [after Oct. 20]), p. xliii.

GREEN JAY, *Xanthoura yncas*

The genus *Xanthoura*, which some ornithologists merge with *Cyanocorax*, is structurally easily separable from the latter group by the following characters: wing much shorter than tail, instead of equal or much longer; first (outermost) primary relatively shorter; graduation of tail much greater, 39 percent of tail instead of 17 percent; tarsus much shorter, 1.6 times, instead of 2 times, length of exposed culmen; and feathers of forehead less stiff and less thickly bushy.

Birds from Texas are separable from *X. y. luxuosa* from Veracruz and comprise *glaucescens*, which is a race recognizable by the following characters: upper surface averaging lighter, more bluish; lower parts somewhat more bluish (less greenish or yellowish); and blue malar area, particularly posterior portion where it reaches the eye, almost always paler. This last distinction has apparently hitherto been overlooked.

PINYON JAY, *Gymnorhinus cyanocephalus*

That there are three races of the Pinyon Jay in the United

States has been pointed out by Pierce Brodkorb.[1] The species was first described by Wied[2] as *Gymnorhinus cyanocephalus* from a specimen taken on the Marias River in n.w. Montana; to the race from Montana the name, therefore, applies. Birds from New Mexico and Arizona, however, differ from those in Montana by reason of somewhat longer bill; lighter (not deeper as stated by Brodkorb) color of upper parts, particularly pileum; also lighter (not darker) under parts. For purposes of comparison, measurements of *G. c. cyanocephalus* follow: *Adult male*: Wing, 146.3–158.0 (average, 150.4) mm.; tail, 103.0–117.5 111.0); bill (exposed culmen), 31.0–37.0 (33.8); tarsus, 37.0–41.5 (38.9); middle toe without claw, 19.0–22.5 (20.6). *Adult female*: Wing, 136.0–153.0 (145.1); tail, 98.5–112.5 (104.4); bill, 27.8–37.0 (31.4); tarsus, 34.5–40.5 (36.9); middle toe, 18.5–22.0 (20.2).

[1] *Occas. Papers Mus. Zool. Univ. Michigan*, no. 332 (May 26, 1936), pp. 1–3.

[2] *Reise Innere Nord-Amer.* 2 (1841): 22.

CAROLINA CHICKADEE, *Parus carolinensis*

The Carolina Chickadee found from e. Oklahoma to s.w. Kentucky, south to e. Texas and c. Alabama is generally considered as a part of *P. c. carolinensis*. The writer, however, has described this bird as *Penthestes carolinensis guilloti*[1] from a type specimen collected at Belair in s.e. Louisiana. Since the generic name *Penthestes* has been changed to *Parus*, the Louisiana Carolina Chickadee will be *Parus carolinensis guilloti* (Oberholser).

[1] Oberholser, *Bull. Louisiana Dept. Conservation*, no. 28 (June 30, 1938), p. 425.

TUFTED TITMOUSE, *Baeolophus bicolor*

The generic name *Baeolophus* Cabanis[1] (of which the type is *Parus bicolor* Linnaeus), commonly used for this and allied species, has been merged by some authors with *Parus* Linnaeus. However, it and its allies, the Black-crested and Plain, seem to be a sufficiently well differentiated generic group, differing from *Parus* in the much stouter bill (height at base is more than half length of exposed culmen); and in possession of a well-developed crest.

A comparison of the Tufted Titmouse of Texas and Louisiana with the one of the middle Atlantic and c. northern United States indicates differences which seem to warrant subspecific separation. The southern bird is somewhat smaller, paler, more purely grayish on the upper surface, particularly in winter plumage. These distinctions seem readily recognizable when unworn specimens are compared. It ranges north to n. Florida, Georgia, n. Alabama, n. Louisiana, and n. Texas; birds from the remainder of the species' range belong to the typical race, *B. b. bicolor*. Comparison of Florida birds indicates that such are all referable to the southern subspecies.

The Tufted Titmouse was originally described by Linnaeus.[2] His description was based on Catesby and Brisson, both of whom refer to the bird from s.e. South Carolina. This proves to be the same as the northern bird, to which *B. b. bicolor* is properly applied. To the southern race the name *Parus bicolor floridanus*, proposed by Bangs[3] for the birds from Florida, seems to be available. This race, therefore, should be known as *B. b. floridanus* (Bangs).

[1] *Mus. Heineanum*, pt. 1 (1851 [after Oct. 23]), p. 91.

[2] *Syst. Nat.* 12th ed., vol. 1 (1766 [after May 24]), p. 340 ("America Septentrionale" [=South Carolina]).

[3] *Auk* 15 (Apr., 1898): 181 ("Clearwater, Hillsboro County, Florida").

BLACK-CRESTED TITMOUSE, *Baeolophus atricristatus*

See Tufted Titmouse.

PLAIN TITMOUSE, *Baeolophus inornatus*

Charles W. Richmond long ago called attention to the fact that a prior *Parus griseus* preoccupied the name of our Gray Plain Titmouse so long as the species was referred to the genus *Parus*, and, therefore, he renamed this race *Parus inornatus ridgwayi*.[1] However, the genus *Baeolophus* seems to be a valid generic group (see Tufted Titmouse); and so long as this titmouse remains in *Baeolophus* it can continue in possession of the name *Baeolophus inornatus griseus*.

[1] *Proc. Biol. Soc. Washington* 15 (Apr. 25, 1902): 155.

LEAD-COLORED BUSHTIT, *Psaltriparus plumbeus*

Some authors and the A.O.U. check-list, 1957, consider the Lead-colored Bushtit a subspecies of the Common Bushtit, *P. minimus*. A reexamination of a considerable number of specimens representing the forms of these two species leads to the conclusion that there seems to be no sufficient evidence to warrant their being regarded as subspecies.

There is at least one additional recognizable race of the Lead-colored Bushtit, *P. plumbeus cecaumenorum*;[1] and there are several Pacific coast races of *P. minimus*. At the points where the ranges of the Common and Lead-colored approach each other most closely, there is no indication of intergradation between the clear gray head of *P. plumbeus* and the distinctly brown head of *P. minimus*; nor is there sufficient evidence from individual variation in any of the forms of *P. minimus* to bridge over the gap in coloration between these two species. It seems, therefore, the more logical view to consider these two as distinct species, and under these circumstances, the race of Lead-colored Bushtit of Texas should stand as *P. plumbeus plumbeus*.

[1] Thayer and Bangs, *Proc. Biol. Soc. Washington* 19 (Feb. 26, 1906): 20.

WHITE-BREASTED NUTHATCH, *Sitta carolinensis*

The Chisos race of the White-breasted Nuthatch, *S. c. oberholseri*, was named by Herbert W. Brandt[1] from the Chisos Mts. in the Big Bend region of Trans-Pecos Texas. Although it has been synonymized with *mexicana* Nelson and Palmer, it is by no means to be considered the same as that form. In fact, it is even smaller than that bird, as well as very much smaller than *nelsoni* of the Rocky Mts. region. It is so much paler below than the Mexican race, also brighter (less brownish, buffy, or grayish), that it is readily separable on these differences alone. It is, furthermore, rather darker above.

[1] *Auk* 55 (Apr. 20, 1938): 269.

RED-BREASTED NUTHATCH, *Sitta canadensis*

By reason of the description of a new race of this species,[1] the nominate race needs to be a trinomial, *S. c. canadensis*.

[1] *Sitta canadensis clariterga* Burleigh, *Auk* 77 (Apr. 30, 1960): 212 (Clearwater Co., Idaho).

BROWN CREEPER, *Certhia familiaris*

Birds breeding in the Guadalupe Mts. of Texas and s. New Mexico seem to constitute a recognizable subspecies, here named *C. f. iletica*. In characters this race shows a slight tendency toward the breeding bird of s. Arizona, *albescens*, but it is nearer

the Rocky Mts. race, described by Robert Ridgway as *montana*.[1] It seems, however, to be sufficiently different from that subspecies and to represent a local race rather circumscribed in geographical distribution in the breeding season, although it wanders southward and southeastward during autumn and winter. The type of Ridgway's *montana*, which is still in the U.S. National Museum, was not specifically mentioned in the original description, but the specimen now bears on its label this name, accompanied by the statement, in Ridgway's handwriting, that it is the type. It is a typical winter specimen of the Rocky Mts. form that breeds from Colorado northward, and was collected by Henry W. Henshaw on Mt. Graham, Arizona, on Sept. 23, 1874. This leaves no doubt that the name *montana* should apply to the bird from the Rocky Mts., and that the bird from the Guadalupe Mts. has hitherto remained unnamed.

[1] *Proc. U.S. Nat. Mus.* 5 (July 21, 1882): 114 ("Rocky Mountain bird"). ("Middle province of North America, north to Kadiak [*sic*], Alaska, breeding south to New Mexico and Arizona.")

HOUSE WREN, *Troglodytes domesticus*

The change of name of this species from *Troglodytes aedon* Vieillot to *Troglodytes domesticus* (Wilson) made by the writer perhaps should be more fully explained.[1] Vieillot's name, *Troglodytes aedon*[2] seems to be antedated by *Sylvia domestica* Wilson.[3] The date of the first volume of Wilson's *American Ornithology* was 1808, though it appeared after Sept. 1. The date on the title pages of both volumes of Vieillot's *Histoire Naturelle des Oiseaux d'Amérique Septentrionale* is 1807, but there is reason to believe that these title pages were published when the first part of the first volume appeared. This work, it is now known, was published in monthly parts of six plates each with accompanying text, and it is well established that the first part appeared in Dec., 1807. Thus, only the first six plates of the first volume appeared in 1807. These facts are obtainable from the *Journal Typographique* of Dec. 28, 1807, pp. 331–332, where it says that one *livraison* is to be published regularly on the first of each month. There were to have been four or more volumes of this work, but it was abandoned after the concluding parts of volume two appeared, possibly on account of the beginning of the publication of Wilson's *American Ornithology*. Quoting further from the same issue of the *Journal Typographique*, we have this information regarding the manner of publication: "Vieillot—Hist. Nat. Oiseaux d'Amér. Sept. Cet ouvrage sera publié par souscription et par Livraison composées chacune de six planches et du Texte. Il paroîtra régulièrement une Livraison la premier de chaque mois à commencer du 1er Décembre, 1807, et il ne sera rien payé d'avance."

Furthermore, a year later in the same magazine of Nov. 21, 1808, the same information is repeated, that is, that each part consists of six plates and of corresponding text, and that these parts will appear regularly, an issue on the first of each month; and on this occasion the second issue—that is *livraison deuxième* —is reviewed. It is barely possible that *deuxieme* is a typographical error for *douzième*, since the date would be about right for the twelfth *livraison*, but whether it was the second or the twelfth, and even assuming it was the twelfth, this means that, at most, only plates one through seventy-two appeared up to Nov., 1808.

Since *Troglodytes aedon* occurs in the second volume and is plate 107, it would be a part of the eighteenth *livraison* and, therefore, could not in the regular course of publication have appeared earlier than at least May, 1809. Thus, it would be inconceivable that the eighteenth issue could have appeared at any time in 1808; since it is well established that Wilson's first volume came out in 1808, it is as certain—as such things can well be—that *Sylvia domestica* Wilson antedates *Troglodytes aedon* Vieillot. There is no evidence to suppose that the regularity of the appearance of the parts of Vieillot's *Oiseaux d'Amérique Septentrionale* was in any way interrupted until publication ceased; therefore, there seems to be no good reason for refusing to accept the priority of Wilson's name. In fact, the appearance of parts of works such as Vieillot's is far more likely to be delayed than shortened to the extent that all eighteen parts would have come out in 1808. Under these circumstances, the House Wren would be called *Troglodytes domesticus.*

[1] Oberholser, *Ohio Journ. Sci.* 34 (Mar. 25, 1934): 87–88.
[2] *Hist. Nat. Oiseaux Amér. Sept.*, vol. 2 ("1807" [May, 1809]), p. 52, pl. 107.
[3] *Amer. Ornith.*, vol. 1 (1808 [after Sept. 1]), p. 5, pl. 8, fig. 3.

WINTER WREN, *Nannus troglodytes*

The genus *Nannus* Billberg, although sometimes merged with *Troglodytes* Vieillot, is nevertheless possessed of characters so important that unless it is kept as a separate generic group there is no reason for not combining many other allied genera now currently recognized as distinct. *Nannus* differs from *Troglodytes* as follows: bill decidedly more slender; culmen almost straight, instead of much decurved toward tip; maxilla with no subterminal notch on cutting edge; nostril slitlike, instead of oval or pear-shaped; tail much abbreviated, shorter than combined length of tarsus, middle toe, and middle claw (instead of much longer), also very little, if any, more than ⅔ length of wing (instead of much more, sometimes even more than ¾); and middle toe without claw less than ⅔ length of tarsus (instead of more).

The Newfoundland Winter Wren, *N. t. aquilonaris*, is an apparently recognizable subspecies described from Tompkins, Newfoundland, by T. D. Burleigh and H. S. Peters.[1]

The Idaho Winter Wren, *N. t. salebrosus*, was named by T. D. Burleigh[2] from specimens he collected in Idaho (Dismal Lake, Shoshone Co.). It is one of the most distinct forms of the species.

[1] *Proc. Biol. Soc. Washington* 61 (June 16, 1948): 116.
[2] Ibid., 72 (Apr. 22, 1959): 16.

BEWICK'S WREN, *Thryomanes bewickii*

The Colorado Bewick's Wren, *T. b. niceae*, was described by G. M. Sutton[1] from specimens taken at Kenton, Cimarron Co., in extreme n.w. Oklahoma. In order to determine the relationship of it with birds from n.w. Texas, it has been necessary to examine a considerable amount of material from Colorado, Wyoming, Utah, and New Mexico, as well as Texas. Comparison of this material indicates that color characters given by the original describer apparently do not hold, and the bird from this plains area is indistinguishable in the color of upper parts from the gray phase of *eremophilus* of Arizona and Trans-Pecos Texas. There is, however, a good average character—though this is not wholly constant—in extent of the broad light gray tips on the outer tail feathers. In *niceae* only two outer tail feathers have these broad pale gray tips, the rest of the tail feathers having only very narrow grayish tips, if any. In *eremophilus*, however, these broad tips are often on three or four of the outer feathers of the tail. Birds from Colorado and s.w. Wyoming are apparently the same as those from n.w. Oklahoma, although occasionally a specimen is found with broad gray tips on three of the outer tail feathers. Birds from s.w. Utah and s. Nevada are so predominantly like birds from Arizona—although occasionally

specimens like *niceae* are found—that they should probably be referred to *eremophilus*. As Sutton has indicated, the bird seems to be migratory in at least its Oklahoma range, and it has been traced as far as s. Texas.

[1] *Auk* 51 (Apr. 4, 1934): 217.

CAROLINA WREN, *Thryothorus ludovicianus*

Further study of the Carolina Wrens by W. Earl Godfrey has revealed that not only are the Ohio birds referable to *T. l. ludovicianus* instead of to *carolinianus*, but also that breeding birds from w. Indiana to Missouri, Kansas, Oklahoma, and c. Texas represent a new race, which Godfrey has named *alamoensis*.[1] Specimens from Fort Clark, Texas, verge toward *oberholseri*, but are nearer the Bexar Carolina Wren.

The Southwestern Carolina Wren, *oberholseri*, has a limited distribution in s.w. central Texas. It was originally described by G. H. Lowery, Jr.,[2] and its type locality given as Del Rio, Texas.

[1] *Auk* 63 (Oct. 25, 1946): 565.
[2] *Auk* 57 (Jan. 4, 1940): 101.

CACTUS WREN, *Campylorhynchus brunneicapillus*

Careful comparisons of adequate material from Arizona and Texas show that the birds from these two regions are subspecifically separable, as long ago pointed out by Edgar A. Mearns. The original description of the Northern Cactus Wren, *C. b. couesi*,[1] was based on the bird from Laredo, Texas, and therefore is applicable to the eastern race. Mearns later characterized the Arizona Cactus Wren as *Heleodytes b. anthonyi*,[2] a name which is now applicable to this race. Birds from the e. Trans-Pecos Texas verge somewhat toward *couesi*, but are large and heavily spotted below, as well as more heavily black-barred on the tail, and are somewhat more rufescent above than the latter race. They should surely be considered as belonging to the Arizona subspecies, *C. b. anthonyi*.

[1] Sharpe, *Cat. Birds Brit. Mus.* 6 (1881 [Jan., 1882]): 196.
[2] *Auk* 19 (Apr., 1902): 143 ("Adonde Siding, Southern Pacific Railroad, Arizona").

LONG-BILLED MARSH WREN, *Telmatodytes palustris*

Discovery that the breeding Long-billed Marsh Wren of Ohio is decidedly different from birds breeding both east and west of that state, and that it is a dark sooty race, forms an interesting parallel with the House Wrens inhabiting the same area. That it is not the result of a soot-stained bird is perfectly evident from the condition of the specimens taken during the breeding season in Ohio marshes, for they are in perfectly clear plumage, the white and light areas not at all stained by any extraneous matter. *T. p. canniphonus* apparently has a relatively limited distribution, for almost all birds breeding north and east of Ohio belong to other races. It occurs, however, in extreme s.e. Ontario and s.e. Michigan.

The Prairie Long-billed Marsh Wren, *T. p. cryphius*, has commonly passed under the name of *T. p. iliacus* Ridgway, though sometimes united with *T. p. dissaëptus*, from which, however, it differs in longer wing and middle toe, and on the average, somewhat shorter bill; much paler, more ochraceous (less sooty or rufescent) flanks and upper surface. In the breeding season it occupies the upper Mississippi Valley, chiefly from Indiana and Michigan to North Dakota and Kansas. When considered separate from *palustris* and *dissaëptus*, this race has been called *T. p. iliacus* Ridgway. This separation of the Mississippi Valley bird from that breeding on the Massachusetts coast has already been made by the writer.[1] However, an examination of the type of Ridgway's *iliacus* (a specimen from Wheatland, Knox Co., Indiana) shows it to be not the breeding bird of that general region, but a transient from the far north, since it is an example of the bird described as *laingi* by Harper[2] from the Athabaska Delta in Alberta. Unfortunately, this latter name will become a synonym of *iliacus* Ridgway; and the bird to which the name *iliacus* has been commonly applied, that is, the breeding bird at present under discussion, needs a new name, which has been provided in *T. p. cryphius.*

[1] Oberholser, *Bull. Louisiana Dept. Conservation*, no. 28 (June 30, 1938), p. 448.
[2] *Occas. Papers Boston Soc. Nat. Hist.* 5 (Dec. 10, 1926): 221.

CANYON WREN, *Catherpes mexicanus*

Further accumulation of material from Texas and other parts of the w. United States has thrown additional light on the relationships of the Canyon Wrens, particularly those inhabiting Texas. The White-throated Canyon Wren, *C. m. albifrons* (Giraud),[1] which was described by Giraud from specimens supposedly taken in Texas, has been recorded by the writer as occurring in the region about the mouth of the Pecos River in Texas. The type of Giraud's bird, which is now in the U.S. National Museum, is juvenal and has a broken bill. Without doubt, it did not come from Texas, but from n.e. Mexico, for it agrees with specimens from that region. A reexamination of this type and comparison with birds from the mouth of the Pecos River shows that they clearly do not belong to the same subspecies, and therefore, *albifrons* should be excluded from the A.O.U. check-list of North American birds, as well as from Texas. (This is another indication that nearly all the birds described by Giraud in this now famous publication did not come from Texas, but from Mexico.)

Birds from the mouth of the Pecos River are identical with birds from Trans-Pecos, s., and c. Texas. Therefore, the proper name for Canyon Wrens in all of Texas, excepting the n.w. part, becomes *C. m. polioptilus*, originally described by the writer[2] from Brewster Co., Texas.

[1] *Certhia albifrons* Giraud, *Sixteen Species North Amer. Birds* (1841), p. [33], pl. [8].
[2] *Auk* 20 (Apr., 1903): 197 (Deer Mt. [=Plateau Mt.], Chisos Mts.).

CATBIRD, *Lucar carolinense*

The International Code of Zoological Nomenclature sanctions the use of generic names from binomial authors, and also from authors called binary, which latter term means that these authors use generic names in the proper modern generic sense, but that their specific names are polynomial and, therefore, not tenable under the rules. Thus, while specific names of such authors are invalid, their generic names can be used as though their specific names were binomial. Up to the present time, few, if any, generic names of birds from binary authors have been current in literature, except the names from the famous *Ornithologia* of Brisson, 1760, which is so outstanding in its character that these names have been employed more or less by common consent, even before the principle of binary authors was recognized in codes of nomenclature.

In addition to Brisson, however, there are some other authors whose generic names conform to the requirements of the International Code, and these authors, therefore, can qualify as binary authors. One of these whose names have been in this respect generally overlooked is William Bartram, whose *Travels in North and South Carolina, Georgia, East and West Florida*, published in 1791, has become famous. Bartram's specific names are either nomina nuda or polynomial, so that these are in no sense usable. Some of them can be cited from later authors, such as Zimmerman or Mayer, but not from Bartram's own publications. His generic names, however, have been lost sight of except by Charles W. Richmond, who cited most of those that are tenable in one of his lists of generic names.[1] One of these generic names is *Lucar* Bartram, of which the type is by monotypy *Muscicapa carolinensis* Linnaeus.[2] This, where first used on p. 290 bis [*sic*] of the *Travels* is included in the list of birds observed as "Lucar lividus, apice nigra; the cat bird, or chicken bird." There is a further description on pp. 299–301, and Catesby's name of the same bird ("muscicapa vertice nigro") is cited on p. 299. These citations, of course, validate the name, so *Lucar* becomes the proper name for our Catbird, and should replace *Dumetella* S. D. W.

This generic name *Lucar* is used also by Zimmerman[3] and by Harper.[4] Since the noun *Lucar* is of neuter gender, the name of our Catbird will become *Lucar carolinense* (Linnaeus);[5] and because of additional subspecies, the Northeastern Catbird becomes *L. c. carolinense.*

The Catbird, which has for long been considered indivisible into subspecies, now proves to comprise three races. J. W. Aldrich described the western form as *Dumetella carolinensis ruficrissa*,[6] which seems to be a valid subspecies.

The Southeastern Catbird, *L. c. meridianus*, was originally described by T. D. Burleigh,[7] and is a recognizable form.

[1] *Proc. U.S. Nat. Mus.* 53 (Aug. 16, 1917): 565–636.
[2] *Travels North and South Carolina, Georgia, East and West Florida* (1791), p. 290; 2nd ed. (1792), p. 288.
[3] *Mag. Merkw. neuen Reisebeschreibungen* 10 (1793): 284.
[4] *Proc. Rochester Acad. Sci.* 8 (Sept. 10, 1942): [215]–216.
[5] See Mathews, *Auk* 31 (Jan., 1914): 88–91.
[6] *Proc. Biol. Soc. Washington* 59 (Oct. 25, 1946): 132 ("Colville Lake, Sprague, Washington").
[7] *Oriole* 24 (Sept.–Dec., 1959): 30 ("Athens, Clarke County, Georgia").

BROWN THRASHER, *Toxostoma rufa*

Determination of the gender of compound generic names affects the generic name *Toxostoma* as used for the present species. Since *Toxostoma* is a feminine noun, the specific and subspecific names must agree therewith. Therefore, we should write *T. rufa* instead of *T. rufum.*

LONG-BILLED THRASHER, *Toxostoma longirostris*

Attention has been called to the fact (see Brown Thrasher) that *Toxostoma* is of feminine gender; therefore, the present species should be written *T. longirostris* instead of *T. longirostre.*

CURVE-BILLED THRASHER, *Toxostoma curvirostris*

The reason for spelling the specific name of this species *curvirostris* instead of *curvirostre* is explained under the Brown Thrasher.

CRISSAL THRASHER, *Toxostoma dorsalis*

As explained under the Brown Thrasher, the feminine gender of *Toxostoma* requires that this species should be called *dorsalis* instead of *dorsale.*

ROBIN, *Turdus migratorius*

Robins breeding in c. and n. California and in Oregon are sub-specifically separable not only from the Western Robin, *T. m. propinquus*, but also from the other races allied to that form. It differs from *propinquus* and from the eastern race, *migratorius*, as already indicated. From *caurinus*, of the Pacific Coast north of Oregon, it may be separated by its much paler color, both above and below. It resembles *phillipsi*, of e. Mexico, but its bill is smaller; upper and lower parts average paler; and there is little or no white on tip of the tail. There seems to be no available name for this California race, since the type of *propinquus* Ridgway is a typical example of the breeding bird of the Rocky Mts. region. (This specimen, a male, is now no. 38372 of the U.S. National Museum collection, and was collected at Laramie Peak, Wyoming, in May, 1864, by R. T. Hitz. It is marked "type" in Robert Ridgway's handwriting.) Hence, the California Robin is here named *T. m. aleucus*.

WOOD THRUSH, *Hylocichla mustelina*

Wood Thrushes breeding in Texas and s.e. United States differ from birds from the n. United States in smaller size, chiefly of wing and tail; and in duller, more olivaceous (less rufescent) upper parts. Following are measurements of the Northern Wood Thrush, *H. m. mustelina*, for comparison with the southern race: *Adult male*: Wing, 105.5–111.5 (average, 108.5) mm.; tail, 71.5–78.0 (73.6); bill (exposed culmen), 15.2–17.5 (16.4); tarsus, 30.5–33.5 (32.0); middle toe without claw, 16.8–19.8 (18.1). *Adult female*: Wing, 104.0–109.0 (106.1); tail, 68.0–72.5 (69.6); bill, 15.0–17.0 (16.1); tarsus, 29.0–32.8 (31.5); middle toe, 17.0–19.0 (18.0).

The original description of the Wood Thrush, *Turdus mustelinus*, by Gmelin[1] was based on the Tawny Thrush of Pennant[2] and of Latham;[3] the specimen that Pennant used was from the Museum of Mrs. Blackburn in England, who obtained her New York birds from Hempstead, Long Island, New York. The type locality, therefore, of the Northern Wood Thrush is Hempstead, Long Island, New York. *Turdus melodus* of Wilson[4] is a synonym of *Turdus mustelinus*.

There seems to be, however, an available name for the small southern race in *Turdus densus* of Bonaparte,[5] which was described as from "Tabasco, Mexique," with the diagnosis "Simillimus t. mustelino, sed valde minor," from a specimen that he found in the museum at Brussels, Belgium. This diagnosis seems to be almost perfect for the small Wood Thrush of the s. United States, and is now adopted as its name. This bird, therefore, will be called *Hylocichla mustelina densa* (Bonaparte).

By segregation of the southern birds as a subspecies, the geographic distribution of the Northern Wood Thrush will be restricted to the following limits: Breeds from c. South Dakota, c. Minnesota, c. Wisconsin, n. Michigan, s.e. Ontario, s.w. Quebec, n. New York, n. Vermont, c. New Hampshire, and s.e. Maine, south to Kansas, Missouri, c. Illinois, c. Indiana, and w. North Carolina. Winters from Puebla to Guatemala, Honduras, Costa Rica, and Nicaragua; casually in c. Ohio and Florida. Of casual occurrence in Bahamas, Cuba, Jamaica; West Indian birds have not been examined, but probably are of this race.

[1] *Syst. Nat.*, vol. 1, pt. 2 (1789 [before Apr. 20]), p. 817 ("In Noveboraco").
[2] *Arctic Zool.* 2 (1785): 337 ("Province of New York; Bl[ackburn] Museum").
[3] *General Synop. Birds*, vol. 2, pt. 1 (1783), p. 28 (no locality; based evidently on Tawny Thrush of Pennant).
[4] *Amer. Ornith.*, vol. 1 (1808), p. 29, pl. 2, fig. 1 ("Pennsylvania").

[5] *Comptes Rendus Acad. Sci.* 38, no. 1 [after Jan. 2, 1854] [published Jan. 7, 1854]: 2fn.

HERMIT THRUSH, *Hylocichla guttata*

The Vancouver Hermit Thrush, *H. g. vaccinia*, was first described by R. A. Cumming[1] from specimens taken at 4,000 ft. on Mt. Seymour, Vancouver District, British Columbia. Although during the breeding season it occupies a relatively small area in s.w. British Columbia and n.w. Washington, it seems to be a recognizable race by reason of its very dark sooty coloration, as compared with the typical Alaska race, *guttata*. It is darker than either *guttata* or *oromela*, although geographically lying between them. Material is not at present available to show northern limits of distribution of this race, although doubtless it extends for some distance northward along the coast of British Columbia, but probably not east of the Selkirk Mts. Birds from Glacier Bay, Hoonah Sound, and Ketchikan, Alaska, are definitely *guttata*.

The Cascade Hermit Thrush, *H. g. oromela*, was described by the writer[2] from specimens taken in c. southern Oregon in the region of the Cascade Mts. It was subsequently redescribed by L. B. Bishop as *H. g. dwighti*,[3] the type of which came from 5,500 ft. at Lion Creek, Priest Lake, Idaho; there seems to be no essential difference between breeding birds of the Cascades and those of n. Idaho, although s. Idaho is occupied by another race. The present race is somewhat like the Big Tree Thrush, *H. g. sequoiensis*, whose range it practically joins on the south, but *oromela* is smaller, and has more grayish upper parts. Likewise, it somewhat resembles *sleveni* but is larger and more grayish, as well as somewhat darker. Birds from c. northern California are somewhat intermediate between this race and *sequoiensis*, but are nearer the present race. Like the other races, the Cascade Hermit Thrush has two distinct color phases—a rufescent and a gray phase—but the rufescent is not nearly so reddish as is the same phase in *guttata*.

The Yukon Hermit Thrush, *H. g. euboria*, was originally described from specimens taken in Yukon.[4] It is similar to *sequoiensis* but somewhat darker; in general size about the same, that is, excepting the wing and bill which are very small, actually as well as relatively. It resembles *polionota* but is smaller, the bill decidedly so; also much darker and somewhat more rufescent (less grayish) above. Birds of this species obtained during the breeding season in Yukon have been referred by Robert Ridgway and other authors to *sequoiensis*, but they differ definitely from that race as explained in the detailed account. By separation of birds from Yukon and n. British Columbia as a distinct subspecies, the distribution of *sequoiensis* is made much more logical, since between Yukon and the range of *sequoiensis* there intervenes the range of *oromela*. A specimen from Stewart Lake, British Columbia, although it has a larger bill, is relatively dark and rufous, and is too large for *guttata*, since its wing measurement is 96.5 mm. It is also too large and too rufescent above to be referable to *oromela*, so unless the birds of this region are separated as still another race they probably should be referred to *euboria*.

[1] *Murrelet* 14 (Sept. [published ca. Nov. 1], 1933): 79.
[2] Oberholser, *Scient. Publ. Cleveland Mus. Nat. Hist.* 4 (Sept. 19, 1932): 8.
[3] *Proc. Biol. Soc. Washington* 46 (Oct. 26, 1933): 201.
[4] Oberholser, *Proc. Biol. Soc. Washington* 69 (Sept. 12, 1956): 69.

GOLDEN-CROWNED KINGLET, *Orchilus satrapa*

By transfer of the generic name *Regulus* to the Ruby-crowned

Kinglet to displace *Corthylio* (see A.O.U. check-list, 1931), the Goldencrown was left without a generic name, since *Regulus* Cuvier, 1800, which has been in use for this species, is invalidated by *Regulus* Bartram, 1791—this being an example of using generic terms of binary authors (see Catbird). The earliest available generic name for the Golden-crowned Kinglet is *Orchilus* Morris,[1] the type of which by designation herewith is *Orchilus cristatus* Wood (which is the same as *Motacilla regulus* Linnaeus).

Since there seems to be doubt in the minds of some ornithologists regarding the distinctness of *Orchilus* from *Regulus* it might be well to give the generic characters separating the two. In *Orchilus* the nostril is oblong or rounded, and but little opercular; there is only one large feather covering each nostril; pad on sole of hind toe is abruptly narrowed behind and broadest near hind portion, while reticulations on its surface are large and relatively few. In *Regulus*, however, the nostril is linear and strongly opercular; nasal plumes covering nostrils are several and small; also pad on sole of hind toe (hallux) is gradually pointed behind, broadest in middle, with reticulations on its surface small and numerous. These very important structural differences fully justify the separation of *Regulus* and *Orchilus*; in fact, these differences seem to be even supergeneric.

[1] Neville Wood's *Naturalist* 2 (June, 1837): 124.

WATER PIPIT, *Anthus spinoletta*

All North American birds of this species have been called *A. s. rubescens* (Tunstall), until W. E. Clyde Todd described two additional subspecies from w. North America.[1] In order to determine the proper names to be used for the different forms to be found in Texas it has been necessary to canvass the matter again, with the result that it appears desirable to recognize two subspecies additional to the three already recognized as breeding in North America.

The earliest name applicable to any North American form of this species is *Alauda rubescens* Tunstall,[2] based on the Red Lark of Pennant's "British Zoology, Vol. II, page 239." This bird, very deeply cinnamon colored on the lower surface and very considerably spotted with dark brown, agrees perfectly with breeding birds of Labrador, n. Ungava, and Newfoundland, to which the name *A. s. rubescens* is applicable. This bird migrates southward through the e. United States.

However, birds from the Hudson Bay region are subspecifically different, being on the upper surface more purely grayish (less rufescent); on lower parts much less deeply buff (seldom, if ever, cinnamomeous) with jugulum rather more heavily streaked or spotted. The earliest name available for this race is *Alauda ludoviciana* Gmelin,[3] based on La Farlouzanne of Buffon[4] from Louisiana, and on the Louisiana Lark of Latham,[5] the description of which excellently characterized the Hudson Bay bird. The Hudson Bay race should bear the name *A. s. ludovicianus*.

The breeding bird of s.w. Alaska, *A. s. geophilus*, although included by W. E. Clyde Todd in his range of *A. s. pacificus*, appears to be a recognizable form.[6] Thereby, *A. s. pacificus* now should be restricted in the breeding season to s.e. Alaska, s.w. Canada, and n.w. United States.

[1] *Proc. Biol. Soc. Washington* 48 (May 3, 1935): 63–64.
[2] *Ornith. Britannica* (1771), p. 2.
[3] *Syst. Nat.*, vol. 1, pt. 2 (1789 [before Apr. 20]), p. 793.
[4] *Hist. Nat. Oiseaux* 5 (1778): 38.
[5] *General Synop. Birds*, vol. 2, pt. 1 (1782), p. 376.
[6] Oberholser, *Journ. Washington Acad. Sci.* 36 (Nov. 15, 1946): 388 ("False Pass, Unimak Island, Alaska").

BOHEMIAN WAXWING, *Bombycilla garrulus*

American birds of this species were many years ago separated from the European race as *B. g. pallidiceps* by Anton Reichenow;[1] his type came from the Shesly River in n. British Columbia. It differs from the European race in its decidedly more grayish (less cinnamomeous) color of both upper and lower parts, and is a well-marked, easily distinguishable subspecies.

It now develops, however, that there is an earlier name for this bird in *Ampelis carlinensis* Miller,[2] whose plate represents clearly the American race of *Bombycilla garrulus*. Since the locality and grayish color of the bird show on the plate, this undoubtedly is the proper name for the American bird now called *B. g. pallidiceps*. In Shaw's *Cimelia Physica*, 1796, p. 18, pl. 8, which is practically a second edition of Miller's *Icones Animalium*, the plate is also of the North American bird, and is named *Ampelis carolinensis*; but the text is headed *Ampelis garrula* and most of the comment relates to *Ampelis cedrorum*, the localities given being "Carolina, New York, North America, and South America." Thus, although Shaw confused the two birds, his action does not at all invalidate the applicability of the name *Ampelis carolinensis* as dating from Miller's *Icones Animalium*. Even though called *Ampelis carolinensis* by Miller, this bird does not occur in either of the Carolinas; hence, the implication of this name must be disregarded in fixing the type locality, which was given by Miller as America septentrionali. For future use the type locality is herewith definitely designated as Quebec City, Province of Quebec, Canada. The name of the North American Bohemian Waxwing should, therefore, be *B. g. carolinensis* (Miller).

[1] *Ornith. Monatsber.* 16 (Dec., 1908): 191.
[2] *Icones Animalium*, p. 2 (1776), text of pl. 8 ("America septentrionali").

CEDAR WAXWING, *Bombycilla cedrorum*

The Idaho Cedar Waxwing, *B. c. larifuga*, is a readily recognizable subspecies described by T. D. Burleigh.

LOGGERHEAD SHRIKE, *Lanius ludovicianus*

The Nevada Loggerhead Shrike, *L. l. nevadensis*, may be distinguished from the Sonoran race, *sonoriensis*, by its shorter wing; decidedly shorter tail; shorter white tip on outermost tail feather (about 5 percent); smaller white spot on primaries; upper parts somewhat darker; lower parts with more gray on sides —thus lower surface as a whole appearing darker. This subspecies does not breed in Texas. It may be of more frequent occurrence in the state during migration and winter than is indicated by the few specimen records. This race was described by A. H. Miller[1] from a type taken at Lone Pine Creek, 4,500 ft., Inyo Co., California.

[1] *Condor* 32 (May 15, 1930): 156.

YELLOW-THROATED VIREO, *Lanivireo flavifrons*

Use of the generic name *Lanivireo* for this species is explained under the Warbling Vireo.

A trinomial becomes necessary for the typical form of this vireo by recognition of an additional subspecies. Birds breeding in the s.e. United States differ from those of the n.e. United States in smaller size; and more golden or orange-yellow of anterior lower parts. Average measurements of males of the southern race are: Wing, 72.9 mm.; tail, 48.3; bill (exposed culmen), 11.4; tarsus, 19.0; middle toe without claw, 10.4.

Detailed measurements of the northern race are as follows:

Adult male: Wing, 73.0–79.0 (average, 76.3) mm.; tail, 47.5–52.0 (49.2); bill (exposed culmen), 11.0–13.5 (11.8); tarsus, 19.0–21.0 (19.8); middle toe without claw, 10.5–12.0 (11.3). *Adult female*: Wing, 72.5–79.5 (76.2); tail, 46.0–51.5 (49.9); bill, 11.5–12.0 (11.7); tarsus, 19.0–20.5 (19.7); middle toe, 10.5–11.5 (11.0). The breeding range of this northern race extends from c. eastern Saskatchewan, s. Manitoba, s.e. Ontario, s.w. Quebec, and Maine, south to Kansas, Missouri, Illinois, Kentucky, n. Tennessee, n.w. South Carolina, and s.w. North Carolina. In winter it ranges south to Yucatán, Nicaragua, Costa Rica, and Panama.

Birds from n. Texas and Oklahoma are somewhat intermediate between the northern and southern races, but are nearer the bird from s. Texas and Louisiana. Specimens from n.w. South Carolina, however, are nearer the northern race.

The Yellow-throated Vireo was first described by Vieillot as *Vireo flavifrons* from "Louisiane."[1] Both the larger and smaller races occur in Louisiana, but the smaller, more brightly colored bird is the more common; thus, it is more likely to have been the bird Vieillot described, even though there is no certain way to determine this from the original description which gave no measurements. The present writer, therefore, designates as the type of *Vireo flavifrons* Vieillot the breeding bird of New Orleans, Louisiana, and *L. f. flavifrons* will be the name of the more southern, smaller race.

For the northern bird there is available the name *Muscicapa sylvicola* Wilson,[2] which is described without locality, though with a citation of "Peale's Museum No. 6827"; it appears that, without much doubt, this refers to the bird from e. Pennsylvania. The type locality of *Muscicapa sylvicola* Wilson is hereby designated as Philadelphia, Pennsylvania. The bird described by Gmelin as *Muscicapa ochroleuca*,[3] although sometimes cited in the synonymy of this species, is not a Yellow-throated Vireo. The northern race would thus be called *L. f. sylvicola* (Wilson).

[1] *Hist. Nat. Oiseaux Amér. Sept.*, vol. 1 ("1807" [=1808]), p. 85, pl. 54.
[2] *Amer. Ornith.*, vol. 1 (1808 [after Sept. 1]), p. 117, pl. 8, fig. 3.
[3] *Syst. Nat.*, vol. 2, pt. 2 (1789 [not later than Apr. 20]), p. 946.

SOLITARY VIREO, *Solivireo solitarius*

Solivireo Oberholser, new genus. Similar to the genus *Lanivireo* Vieillot, but first (outermost) primary less than ⅓ length of second; second primary (counting from outermost) very much shorter than fifth. Type: *Muscicapa solitaria* Wilson.

The bird now known as the Plumbeous Solitary Vireo, *S. s. plumbeus*, is a composite of two races, one of which inhabits Arizona; the other, Trans-Pecos Texas. The bird breeding in the Guadalupe Mts. of Texas differs from the breeding bird of Arizona in having a smaller bill; and more grayish (less olivaceous) upper surface, sides, and flanks. Type of *S. s. plumbeus* is a spring bird from Fort Whipple, Arizona, taken by Elliott Coues on May 17, 1865, and now in the U.S. National Museum; it was on this bird alone that Coues based the name *Vireo plumbeus*.[1] This specimen is fairly well preserved, and, although its bill is damaged, enough remains to show that the bird belongs to the small-billed race of Trans-Pecos Texas; furthermore, its upper surface and flanks show the pale grayish, only very slightly olivaceous, characteristic of the same race. There seems no doubt that this bird, although taken in Arizona, is but a spring migrant of the eastern race, as might well be the case, since breeding birds from all of New Mexico are the same, although breeding birds from Colorado, Arizona, and Wyoming are different and belong to the race here called *S. s. jacksoni*. The sub-

species described by van Rossem as *Vireo solitarius pinicolus*[2] from Mound Valley, Chihuahua, is apparently not the same as the breeding bird from Arizona, being much darker on the lower parts with a greater extension of olivaceous and gray on the sides and flanks.

[1] *Proc. Acad. Nat. Sci. Philadelphia* 18 (1866, sig. 1–7, Jan.–Mar. [June 11]): 74 (Fort Whipple, Arizona).
[2] *Bull. Mus. Comp. Zool.* 67 (Dec., 1934): 467.

YELLOW-GREEN VIREO, *Vireosylva flavoviridis*

The use of the generic name *Vireosylva* instead of Vireo is explained under the Warbling Vireo.

RED-EYED VIREO, *Vireosylva virescens*

The technical name of the Red-eyed Vireo was for many years *Vireosylva olivacea*, but *Vireo* is currently in general use for this species. The change from this back again to *Vireosylva* Bonaparte is explained under the Warbling Vireo.

Also, the specific name of this bird apparently must be changed, as Bangs and Penard have already shown.[1] The name *Muscicapa olivacea* was first proposed by Linnaeus,[2] whose diagnosis is so general that it covered at least two or three species. It is based on the Olive-colored Flycatcher of Edwards[3] from Jamaica, a specimen of which he had in hand at the time; on *Muscicapa oculis rubris* Catesby,[4] from Carolina; and on *Muscicapa Jamaicensis* of Brisson,[5] from Carolina and Jamaica.

The bird described by Edwards is not the Red-eyed Vireo, but the Jamaican Black-whiskered Vireo, *Vireosylva calidris calidris* (Linnaeus) (= *Vireo altiloquus*). Catesby's bird is the Red-eyed Vireo; Brisson's is a mixture of the Jamaican Black-whiskered and the Red-eyed, but largely the former. Thus, we have a name which has to be determined by the references that Linnaeus gives, and these seem to be preponderantly the Jamaican Black-whiskered Vireo. Spencer F. Baird discusses this matter, but while tentatively using *Vireosylva olivacea* for the Red-eyed Vireo, is doubtful concerning the applicability of this name, as is indicated by his remark, "I am not quite satisfied, however, that either of these names [*olivacea* for the Red-eyed Vireo, and *Mimus polyglottos* for the Mockingbird] should be retained."[6] Bangs and Penard[7] definitely assign *Muscicapa olivacea* Linnaeus to the synonymy of *Vireosylva calidris*,[8] and use *Vireo virescens* Vieillot[9] for the Red-eyed Vireo. C. E. Hellmayr[10] rejects both *Muscicapa olivacea* Linnaeus and *Motacilla calidris* Linnaeus, using *Vireo virescens* Vieillot for the former.

In view of the fact that the original basis of the Linnaean name *Muscicapa olivacea* is about two-thirds Jamaican Black-whiskered Vireo and one-third Red-eyed Vireo, it would seem more logical to consider this name, which is based on two perfectly identifiable species, as applying better to the former. Cases of this kind must be decided either on the preponderance of evidence in the original description or on the verdict of the first reviser who discusses the matter and weighs all the evidence. If the present case is to be decided by the latter method it seems that Baird was really not the first reviser, since he did not discuss all the bases of Linnaeus' name and made no actual decision; nor, as a matter of fact, did Bangs and Penard, although they were more definite than Baird in their statement regarding final disposition of the name. Hellmayr, however, discussed all the points at issue, but erred in rejecting *Muscicapa olivacea* Linnaeus entirely, which must be referred to one of the two species on which it is based. Since, however, both Hellmayr and Bangs and Penard came to the same conclusion regarding the inapplicability of *Muscicapa olivacea* Linnaeus to the Red-eyed Vireo, and since whether or not it be considered a synonym of *Vireosylva calidris* will not alter its inapplicability to the Red-eyed Vireo, it seems now better to follow their dictum; so if any further statement is necessary to settle the matter, the present writer definitely assigns the name *Muscicapa olivacea* Linnaeus to the bird known as *Vireosylva calidris calidris*, and by this arrangement another name is necessary for the Red-eyed Vireo. This will not alter the status of the name *Vireosylva calidris*, since the latter is of earlier date.

The earliest name for the Red-eyed Vireo is *Vireo virescens* Vieillot,[11] for which he gave in the original description no locality except inferentially from the title of his work, *L'Amérique Septentrionale*. Vieillot later states the type locality as New Jersey, citing at the same time pl. 53 of his *Histoire Naturelle des Oiseaux L'Amérique Septentrionale*.[12] Bangs and Penard, however, designate Pennsylvania as the type locality.[13] Under the circumstances, it seems better to accept Vieillot's designation as this was earlier and as he was the original describer; hence, the type locality would be New Jersey. By the arrangement discussed above, the name of the Red-eyed Vireo would become *Vireosylva virescens* (Vieillot).

The Northwestern Red-eyed Vireo, *V. v. caniviridris*, is a new subspecies originally described by T. D. Burleigh[14] from specimens collected by him at Moscow, Idaho. It is a readily recognizable race, necessitating a trinomial for the nominate form—*V. v. virescens*.

[1] Bangs and Penard, *Bull. Mus. Comp. Zool.* 67 (June, 1925): 205.
[2] *Syst. Nat.* 12th ed., vol. 1 (1776 [after May 24]), p. 327 ("American septentrionali").
[3] *Gleanings Nat. Hist.* (1758), p. 93, pl. 253.
[4] *Nat. Hist. Carolina, Florida, and Bahama Is.*, vol. 1 (1731), p. 54, pl. 54.
[5] *Ornith.* 2 (1760): 410.
[6] *Review Amer. Birds* 1 (May, 1866): 335.
[7] Loc. cit.
[8] [*Motacilla*] *calidris* Linnaeus, *Syst. Nat.* 10th ed., vol. 1 (Jan. 1, 1758), p. 184.
[9] Vieillot, *Hist. Nat. Oiseaux Amér. Sept.*, vol. 1 ("1807" [1808]), p. 84, pl. 53.
[10] *Zool. Ser. Field Mus. Nat. Hist.* 13, pt. 8 (Sept. 16, 1935): 130, note 3.
[11] Loc. cit.
[12] *Nouv. Dict. d'Hist. Nat.*, new ed. 36 (1819): 104.
[13] Loc. cit.
[14] *Auk* 77 (Apr. 30, 1960): 214.

PHILADELPHIA VIREO, *Vireosylva philadelphica*

The use of *Vireosylva* Bonaparte is discussed under the Warbling Vireo.

WARBLING VIREO, *Melodivireo gilvus*

Melodivireo Oberholser, new genus. Similar to *Lanivireo* Vieillot, but first primary (counting from outermost) less than ⅓ length of second; and second primary (counting from outermost) very much shorter than fifth, instead of longer, or at most only very slightly shorter; and height of bill less than half its length from nostril to tip. Type: *Muscicapa gilva* Vieillot.

The change in name of *Vireo gilvus*—or *Vireosylva gilva*—to *Melodivireo gilvus* is made necessary by the generic separation of it from *Vireosylva* as fully explained below. Most authors have used *Vireo* Vieillot for all vireos, including the Yellow-throated Vireo, *Lanivireo flavifrons*, and the Yellow-green Vireo, *Vireosylva flavoviridis*. The significance of the generic groups *Lanivireo* Baird and *Vireosylva* Bonaparte has been obscured by the inclusion of species in both genera which are not congeneric

with the types of these groups. Heretofore, generic divisions of the North American vireos have included in the same group some species with an evident first (outermost) primary, and some without, which, of course, is unsatisfactory. A logical division would segregate those which have no visible first primary from those that possess an evident one. The former will fall naturally into two groups, the remainder into three. By this arrangement there will be five genera of vireos in North America, instead of one—all of which are capable of trenchant definition. For the sake of comparison, the characters and included species of the North American groups are given herewith:

Vireo Vieillot: This genus, type *Muscicapa noveboracensis* Gmelin (= *Vireo griseus noveboracensis*), has evident first (outermost) primary more—usually much more—than ⅓ length of second; second primary less in length than seventh or at most but equal to it; wing-tip decidedly less than length of commissure plus rictus; and height of bill less than half length of bill from nostril to tip, or at most barely equal. This group includes all small species commonly associated in *Vireo* that are not included in the lists of species given under the following groups.

Melodivireo Oberholser: This group, of which the type is *Muscicapa gilva* Vieillot, resembles *Vireo*, but has length of first evident (outermost) primary less, instead of more, than ⅓ length of the second; second primary not longer than sixth; wing-tip longer than length of commissure taken together with that of rictus. Species to be referred to this group are *Melodivireo gilvus* (Vieillot), *Melodivireo leucophrys* (Lafresnaye), and *Melodivireo amauronotus* (Salvin and Godman).

Solivireo Oberholser: This new genus, of which the type is *Muscicapa solitaria* Wilson, differs from *Melodivireo* in having a very stout bill, its height at base decidedly more than half length of bill from nostril to tip. While on paper this character may seem a slight distinction, the appearance of the bird's bill is remarkably and trenchantly different. In other characters it is similar to *Melodivireo*. It differs from *Vireo* as from *Melodivireo*, and additionally in having the first evident primary less, instead of more, than ⅓ length of second; second primary decidedly longer than seventh; and wing-tip longer than length of commissure taken together with rictus. Species belonging to this group are only *Solivireo solitarius* (Wilson) and *Solivireo propinquus* (Baird).

Lanivireo Baird: This genus, type *Vireo flavifrons* Vieillot, when recognized, usually has been extended to include *Vireo solitarius* (Wilson), but the inclusion of that species completely obscures the real generic characters of the group. If restricted as a monotypic group to *Vireo flavifrons* Vieillot, it can be defined trenchantly as follows: Similar to *Solivireo*, but with no evident first primary; second primary decidedly longer than sixth. Similar to *Melodivireo*, but without evident first primary; second primary decidedly longer than sixth; and height of bill at base more than half length of bill from nostril. From *Vireo* it differs in having no evident first primary; second primary much longer than seventh, even longer than sixth; wing-tip longer than length of commissure and rictus taken together; and height of bill at base greater than length of bill from nostril.

Vireosylva Bonaparte: This genus, type *Muscicapa olivacea* Linnaeus (= *Motacilla calidris* Linnaeus), by elimination of *Vireo gilvus* and *Vireo amauronotus*, becomes definable as follows: similar to *Lanivireo*, but bill long and slender, its height at base very much less than half length of bill from nostril. Similar to *Solivireo*, but without evident first primary; height of bill at base decidedly less than half length of bill from nostril to tip. Similar to *Melodivireo*, but without an evident first primary. Similar to *Vireo*, but without an evident first primary. The species belonging to this group are *Vireosylva philadelphica* (Cassin), *Vireosylva virescens* (Vieillot), *Vireosylva chivi* (Vieillot),

Vireosylva flavoridis (Cassin), *Vireosylva calidris* (Linnaeus), *Vireosylva caymanensis* (Cory), *Vireosylva magister* (Lawrence), and *Vireosylva gracilirostris* (Sharpe).

WORM-EATING WARBLER, *Vermivora americ*

In the rediscovered article by Linnaeus discussed by W. L. McAtee[1] in a private publication, and later by J. L. Peters,[2] the Worm-eating Warbler is called *Vermivora Americ*.[3] Thus, both generic and specific current names of this species are antedated by the terms used by Linnaeus. Hence, *Vermivora americ* Linnaeus will have to replace *Helmitheros vermivorus* (Gmelin).

[1] *A Linnaean Paper Needing Further Attention* (Mar., 1949), p. [1].
[2] *Auk* 67 (July, 1950): 375–377.
[3] A Cat. of Birds, Beasts, Fishes, Insects, Plants, etc., p. 13, pl. 305 (Pennsylvania, near Philadelphia). In: Edwards' *Natural History*, 7 vols. (1776).

GOLDEN-WINGED WARBLER, *Helminthophila chrysoptera*

The generic term *Vermivora* Linnaeus,[1] 1776, preoccupies *Vermivora* Swainson, 1827, now used for the group of warblers closely allied to the present species (see Worm-eating Warbler). Therefore, the name of this genus will revert to *Helminthophila* Ridgway, formerly in use.[2] Although no type was mentioned in the original introduction of *Helminthophila*, it was proposed as a substitute for *Helminthophaga* Cabanis, of which the type by original designation is *Motacilla chrysoptera* Linnaeus; the type, therefore, remains the same. This change of generic name makes it necessary to call the species of this group as follows: Golden-winged Warbler, *Helminthophila chrysoptera* (Linnaeus); Bachman's Warbler, *Helminthophila bachmanii* (Audubon); Blue-winged Warbler, *Helminthophila pinus* (Linnaeus); Tennessee Warbler, *Helminthophila peregrina*; Orange-crowned Warbler, *Helminthophila celata*; Nashville Warbler, *Helminthophila ruficapilla*; Colima Warbler, *Helminthophila crissalis*; and Lucy's Warbler, *Helminthophila luciae*.

[1] A Cat. of Birds, Beasts, Fishes, Insects, Plants, etc., p. 13, pl. 305 (type by monotypy, *Vermivora americ* Linnaeus). In: Edwards' *Natural History*, 7 vols. (1776).
[2] *Bull. Nuttall Ornith. Club* 7 (Jan., 1882): 53 (type, *Motacilla chrysoptera* Linnaeus).

BLUE-WINGED WARBLER, *Helminthophila pinus*

See Golden-winged Warbler.

TENNESSEE WARBLER, *Helminthophila peregrina*

See Golden-winged Warbler.

ORANGE-CROWNED WARBLER, *Helminthophila celata*

See Golden-winged Warbler.

NASHVILLE WARBLER, *Helminthophila ruficapilla*

See Golden-winged Warbler for explanation of the use of the generic name *Helminthophila* Ridgway in place of *Vermivora*.
A. J. van Rossem has renamed the Calaveras Nashville Warbler *Vermivora ruficapilla ridgwayi*,[1] because he considers the genus *Oreothlypis* Ridgway—proposed for two Middle American species, *Oreothlypis gutturalis* and *O. superciliosa*—not separable from *Vermivora* Swainson (= *Helminthophila* Ridgway). By this action *Oreothlypis gutturalis* (Cabanis) would be brought into the genus *Vermivora*, and as this name antedates

Vermivora ruficapilla gutturalis (Ridgway) another name would be necessary for the latter.
Since, however, *Oreothlypis* is retained by the present writer (see Virginia's Warbler), *Oreothlypis gutturalis* would be in another genus and would no longer preoccupy the subspecific name of the Calaveras Nashville Warbler; therefore, Ridgway's subspecific name *gutturalis* is perfectly tenable, as it was not a homonym when originally proposed.

[1] *Proc. Biol. Soc. Washington* 42 (June 25, 1929): 179.

COLIMA WARBLER, *Helminthophila crissalis*

See Golden-winged Warbler.

LUCY'S WARBLER, *Helminthophila luciae*

See Golden-winged Warbler.

VIRGINIA'S WARBLER, *Oreothlypis virginiae*

Many years ago Robert Ridgway proposed a genus *Oreothlypis*,[1] designated as its type *Compsothlypis gutturalis* Cabanis, and included in this genus also *Conirostrum superciliosum* Hartlaub. These are two small warblers allied to *Vermivora*[2] and *Parula*, which are found in Mexico and Central America. This genus was originally proposed because the two included species were found by Ridgway not to belong to *Parula* (= *Compsothlypis*), in which they had been placed by authors of that day. Later, however, Ridgway recognized that the two species of *Oreothlypis* had much closer affinities with *Vermivora* than with *Parula*.[3] Subsequently A. J. van Rossem[4] considered that *Oreothlypis* was actually inseparable and proposed to unite these two genera, following Miller and Griscom.[5]
A careful study of the structural characters of all the species of *Vermivora* and the two species of *Oreothlypis* reveals that none of the characters Ridgway gives are valid.[6] However, further study reveals that there is a good structural character separating these two groups. In the species of *Vermivora* only three of the outer primaries (second, third, and fourth counting from outermost) have the terminal portion of outer webs sinuate (more or less cut out); in *Oreothlypis* there are four (second, third, fourth, and fifth) with such sinuation. This is a good character used, for instance, to diagnose the genus *Arceuthornis* from *Turdus*. Thus, *Oreothlypis* can be regarded as a valid genus.
One adjustment needs to be made. Since the Virginia's Warbler agrees with *O. gutturalis* and *O. superciliosa* in having four primaries sinuate on the outer webs, it should be transferred to *Oreothlypis*.

[1] *Auk* 1 (Apr., 1884): 169.
[2] When revising the Virginia's Warbler, Oberholser evidently failed to note that the *Vermivora* group he here compared with *Oreothlypis* is that same group he considered properly to be *Helminthophila*; hence, in this account *Vermivora* apparently is synonymous with *Helminthophila*. See Golden-winged Warbler. —EDITOR
[3] *Bull. U.S. Nat. Mus.*, no. 50, pt. 2 (Oct. 16, 1902), p. 475.
[4] *Proc. Biol. Soc. Washington* 42 (June 25, 1929): 179.
[5] *Amer. Mus. Novitates*, no. 183 (July 18, 1925), p. 8.
[6] *Bull. U.S. Nat. Mus.*, no. 50, pt. 2 (Oct. 16, 1902), p. 475.

PARULA WARBLER, *Parula americana*

The Southern Parula Warbler is a small bird with a relatively large bill; anterior lower parts dull, with little chestnut or blackish in the band on the throat or jugulum, even in the adult male; and orange or tawny of breast not so deep or so extended as in

the other races. It is the bird of the s.e. United States and occurs only casually in Texas. The name of this race is *P. a. americana* since Linnaeus' original description[1] was based wholly on
Catesby's description and figure,[2] the type locality of which is
Carolina, further restricted to South Carolina,[3] and now again
restricted by the present writer to s.e. South Carolina. *Motacilla
eques* of Boddaert[4] refers also to the bird from South Carolina.

The Western Parula differs sufficiently from both the southern
race, *americana*, and the northern, *pusilla*, to warrant its separation as a distinct subspecies. It is still smaller than *americana*,
particularly in so far as the bill is concerned; anterior lower parts
are more richly colored, the blackish throat-band being decidedly
broader as in *pusilla*; and cinnamon rufous on the jugulum deeper and more extended. From *pusilla* it differs in being decidedly
smaller, excepting the bill; upper parts somewhat paler; and anterior lower parts less richly colored and usually with less black.
It inhabits the lower Mississippi Valley, and is the breeding bird
of Texas. Differences in measurements are evident from the
figures given under all three races. This subspecies was originally described by Robert Ridgway as *Compsothlypis americana
ramalinae*.[5] His type, no. 152380 in the U.S. National Museum,
was a breeding adult male collected on Gallagher's Ranch, northwest of San Antonio, Texas, June 10, 1890, by H. P. Attwater.
It bears on the label in Robert Ridgway's handwriting: "type of
Compsothlypis americana ramalinae Ridgway." Unfortunately
there is an earlier name for this same bird in *Motacilla ludoviciana* Gmelin.[6] This name was based on *Ficedula ludoviciana* of
Brisson,[7] which is an excellent description of the Western Parula
Warbler; on Le Figuier à gorge jaune Buffon;[8] on the Louisiane
Warbler of Pennant;[9] and on the Louisiane Warbler of Latham.[10] An examination of these descriptions shows clearly
that the bird they had in mind was the Parula Warbler inhabiting chiefly Louisiana. Since the race that is most frequent there
—almost to the exclusion of the others—is the Western Parula
Warbler, described by Ridgway as *Compsothlypis americana
ramalinae*, it follows that *Motacilla ludoviciana* of Gmelin is
based on this bird. Of this there seems to be no doubt; thus, it
becomes necessary to use this name instead of Ridgway's. Since
it is based almost entirely on the bird from Louisiana, and probably on specimens obtained not far from New Orleans, it seems
wise to restrict the type locality to New Orleans, Louisiana,
which is hereby done.

The Northern Parula Warbler, *P. a. pusilla*, is a perfectly good
race along with *ludoviciana*, notwithstanding Parkes' attempted
suppression.[11]

[1] [*Parus*] *americanus* Linnaeus, *Syst. Nat.* 10th ed., vol. 1
(Jan. 1, 1758), p. 190 ("America Septentrionali").
[2] *Nat. Hist. Carolina, Florida, and Bahama Is.*, vol. 1 (1731),
p. 64, pl. 64.
[3] *Check-list North Amer. Birds* 4th ed. (Oct. 1, 1931), p. 284.
[4] *Tabl. Planch. Enlum* (1783 [after Dec. 1]), p. 46.
[5] *Bull. U.S. Nat. Mus.*, no. 50, pt. 2 (Oct. 16, 1902), pp. 479,
486.
[6] *Syst. Nat.*, vol. 1, pt. 2 (1789 [before Apr. 20]), p. 983
("Louisiana et insula S. Dominici").
[7] *Ornith.* 3 (1760): 500, pl. 26, fig. 4 ("Louisiane & à S.
Domingue").
[8] *Hist. Nat. Oiseaux*, Montbeillard quarto ed. 5 (1778): 288.
[9] *Arctic Zool.* 2 (1785): 407 ("Louisiana and St. Domingo")
(based on accounts of Brisson and Buffon, above cited).
[10] *General Synop. Birds*, vol. 2, pt. 2 (1783), p. 480 ("Louisiana and St. Domingo") (based on Brisson, Buffon, and Pennant's *Arctic Zool.*, above cited).
[11] *Ann. Carnegie Mus.* 33 (1854): 165–166.

YELLOW WARBLER, *Dendroica petechia*

It now seems necessary to change the names of two races of
this species—the Newfoundland Yellow Warbler, currently *D. p.
amnicola*, and the Eastern Yellow Warbler, currently *D. p. aestiva*. Gmelin first described the Yellow Warbler as *Motacilla
aestiva*,[1] and gives as references *Ficedula canadensis* of Brisson;[2]
Le Figuier Tachete of Buffon;[3] Figuier de la Caroline of D'Aubenton;[4] Olive Warbler of Pennant;[5] Yellow-poll Warbler of
Latham;[6] and Yellow-poll Warbler of Pennant.[7] With the possible exception of Latham's Yellow-poll Warbler and the Yellow-
poll Warbler of Pennant, all these references are, without much
doubt, to the Newfoundland Yellow Warbler instead of to the
Yellow Warbler of the United States. With this preponderance
of evidence it seems necessary to transfer the name *aestiva* to the
bird now called *amnicola*, unfortunate as this transfer appears.

Another name, therefore, is necessary for the Yellow Warbler
of the eastern United States. The earliest one available is *Sylvia
flava* Vieillot,[8] based on a supposed female (which evidently was
an immature male), but is without doubt the Eastern Yellow
Warbler. As it is desirable to have a definite type locality for
this bird, New York City is hereby designated as such, since this
is a locality where Vieillot might readily have obtained the
specimen on which he based his description. The *Sylvia carolinensis* of Latham[9] is founded chiefly on D'Aubenton's *Planches
Enlum.*, fig. 1, and on the Olive Warbler of Pennant's *Arctic
Zoology*; so the bird is apparently a young female of the Canadian bird. Therefore, Vieillot's name, *Sylvia flava*, seems to have
a clear title, and the Eastern Yellow Warbler should stand as
D. p. flava.

[1] *Syst. Nat.*, vol. 1, pt. 2 (1789 [before Apr. 20]), p. 996
("Gujana, Aestate in Canada").
[2] *Ornith.* 3 (1760): 492, pl. 26, fig. 3 ("Canada").
[3] *Hist. Nat. Oiseaux* 5 (1778: 285 ("Canada").
[4] *Planches Enlum.*, no. 58, fig. 1.
[5] *Arctic Zool.* 2 (1785): 409.
[6] *General Synop. Birds*, vol. 2, pt. 2 (1783), p. 515.
[7] *Arctic Zool.* 2 (1785): 402.
[8] *Hist. Nat. Oiseaux Amér. Sept.*, vol. 2 ("1807" [1809]), p.
31, pl. 89 ("États-Unis").
[9] *Index Ornith.* 2 (1790): 551 ("Fretum hudsonis").

MAGNOLIA WARBLER, *Dendroica lutea*

Because of an overlooked paper by Linnaeus, *Dendroica magnolia* (Wilson) apparently must now acquire a new specific
designation. This was first brought to light by W. L. McAtee[1] in
a privately published sheet; subsequently, J. L. Peters[2] called
attention to the fact. In this work by Linnaeus[3] the Magnolia
Warbler appears as *Muscicapa lutea*; therefore, the bird should
stand as *Dendroica lutea* (Linnaeus).

[1] *A Linnaean Paper Needing Further Attention* (Mar., 1949),
p. [1].
[2] *Auk* 67 (July, 1950): 377.
[3] A Cat. of Birds, Beasts, Fishes, Insects, Plants, etc., p. 11, pl.
255 (Pennsylvania, near Philadelphia). In: Edwards' *Natural
History*, 7 vols. (1776).

BLACK-THROATED GRAY WARBLER, *Dendroica nigrescens*

This species is very much like the Audubon's Warbler, *D. auduboni*, in that birds from the Pacific coast are subspecifically
different from those of the Rocky Mts. region. The original description of the present species by John Kirk Townsend[1] was
based on the Pacific coast bird, now in the U.S. National Museum, collected near Fort William (present-day Portland), Oregon. This specimen belongs to the coast race to which the name
D. n. nigrescens is applicable.

It follows that another name is necessary for the Rocky Mts.
bird. This is found in *Sylvia halseii* Giraud,[2] as already pointed

out by the present writer.[3] The type locality is no more definite than as indicated on the title page of the publication, but since it probably did not come from Texas, the present writer has designated c. Mexico as the type locality of *Sylvia halseii* Giraud.[4]

[1] *Journ. Acad. Nat. Sci. Philadelphia* 1st ser., vol. 7, pt. 2 (Nov. 21, 1837), p. 191 (no locality).
[2] *Description of Sixteen New Species of North Amer. Birds* (1841), p. [13], pl. [iii] (no locality given, but birds described in this publication are stated on title page to have come from Texas).
[3] Oberholser, *Scient. Publ. Cleveland Mus. Nat. Hist.* 1 (Dec. 31, 1930): 101–102.
[4] *Ibid.*, p. 102.

YELLOW-THROATED WARBLER, *Dendroica dominica*

Yellow-throated Warblers of Indiana and Ohio differ from those from Louisiana and Texas, although they are commonly referred to the same race—*D. d. albilora*. The Indiana bird is distinguishable from *dominica* by its entirely white eyebrow; smaller bill; more golden or orange-yellow throat; and shorter white area on inner web of outermost tail feather. Breeding birds from Tennessee and Kentucky are somewhat intermediate between *dominica* and *axantha*, but seem to be nearer the latter, although they sometimes have a yellowish tinge on the anterior portion of the superciliary stripe. Breeding birds from n. Georgia and n. Alabama are nearer *dominica*. The original description of the Sycamore Yellow-throated Warbler, *D. d. albilora*,[1] was based on a migrant specimen from British Honduras, which has been examined and found to belong to the large-billed race breeding in Texas, to which, therefore, this name is to be restricted, leaving the bird from Indiana with a subspecific name accordingly provided in *axantha*.

[1] *Dendroica Dominica* var. *albilora* Ridgway (Baird ms.), *Amer. Naturalist* 7 (Oct., 1873): 605 ("Belize, Honduras").

BLACKPOLL WARBLER, *Dendroica breviunguis*

The present species has long been known as *Dendroica striata*, but it appears that this specific name is preoccupied as already shown by C. E. Hellmayr.[1] This bird was originally described by Forster as *Muscicapa striata*.[2] This name is rendered invalid for use by *Motacilla striata* Pallas[3] (the Spotted Flycatcher of the Old World) so long as this is considered—as it is now—to belong to the genus *Muscicapa*.

This change of name has been challenged[4] on the ground that the A.O.U. Code of Zoological Nomenclature differs from the International Code of Zoological Nomenclature in treatment of "secondary synonyms," and that if the A.O.U. Code be followed, this name would not be preoccupied, because the two names are not now both employed in the same genus. That this is not the intent of either code is shown by the following quotations. The International Code reads: "Art. 35.—A specific name is to be rejected as a homonym when it has been previously used for some other species or subspecies of the same genus."
The A.O.U. Code says: "Canon XXX.—A specific or subspecific name is to be changed when it has been previously used for some other species of the same genus, or has been used in combination with the same generic name in the description of a new species or in the renaming of an old one."
It will thus be seen that the A.O.U. Code is even more explicit than the International. Furthermore, the present writer was one of the framers of the revised edition of the A.O.U. Code, published in July, 1908, and he is certain that there was no intention of ruling out such synonyms as are here discussed,

and that from the explicit wording of the code it is difficult to see how such interpretation can be read into it.
Under these circumstances it appears that Hellmayr was entirely right in substituting the name *Dendroica breviunguis* (Spix) for *Dendroica striata* (Forster).
A western race of this species has been described by T. D. Burleigh and H. S. Peters as *Dendroica striata lurida*.[5] It differs from the form occupying e. North America in having upper parts in the male darker but with narrower black streaks; in the female and autumn plumage of the male, the same areas duller, more brownish or olive (less yellowish) green, and with less distinct dark brown or black streaks. It is the race that occurs in Texas. The specific name *breviunguis* Spix,[6] in so far as it is determinable from the original description and poorly colored plate, is better assigned to the eastern race, particularly since the western bird has so recently been described by Burleigh and Peters. To make this allocation definite, the name *Anthus breviunguis* Spix is hereby restricted to the eastern race that breeds in Newfoundland, and the western subspecies should thus be called *D. b. lurida*.

[1] *Zool. Series Field Mus. Nat. Hist.*, vol. 13, pt. 8 (Sept. 16, 1935), p. 403.
[2] *Philosophical Trans. London*, vol. 62, article 29 (1772 [read June 18 and 25]), p. 406, 408 ("ad Sinum hudsonis").
[3] Vroeg, *Cat. Raisonné D'Oiseaux, Quadrupèdes, et D'Insectes; Adumbratiunculae* (Oct. 6, 1764), p. 3.
[4] *Proc. U.S. Nat. Mus.*, vol. 86, no. 3050 (Jan. 31, 1939), pp. 225–226.
[5] *Proc. Biol. Soc. Washington* 61 (June 16, 1948): 119 ("Nushagak, Alaska").
[6] *Av. Spec. Nov. Brasil* 1 (1824): 75, pl. 76 ("provincia Parae [Brazil]").

OVENBIRD, *Seiurus aurocapillus*

The Southeastern Ovenbird, *S. a. canivirens*, is a recognizable subspecies originally described by T. D. Burleigh and A. J. Duvall[1] from Margret, Fannin Co., Georgia.

[1] *Wilson Bull.* 64 (Mar., 1952): 39.

KENTUCKY WARBLER, *Oporornis formosus*

A trinomial is necessary for this species since it is divisible into two races, one of which inhabits the n.e. United States, the other the s.e. portion. The Kentucky Warbler was originally described by Alexander Wilson as *Sylvia formosa*.[1] His statement regarding its habitat reads, "moist woods along the Tennessee and Cumberland Rivers," without much doubt in Kentucky. The type locality, therefore, may be considered as the Tennessee River in s.w. Kentucky. Hence, Wilson's name applies to the southern race, herewith called *S. f. formosus*. Birds from still farther north in Wabash Co., Illinois, belong to the same race as birds from the southern states.
As there are apparently no synonyms for the species, the northeastern race is without a name. It, therefore, may be called **O. f. umbraticus**. This new subspecies is similar to *formosus*, but larger; upper parts somewhat lighter, more yellowish (less grayish) olive green; and yellow of lower parts decidedly lighter and less orange-hued.
MEASUREMENTS: *Adult male*: Wing, 68.0–72.5 (average, 69.8) mm.; tail, 48.0–54.0 (50.8); bill (exposed culmen), 11.0–12.5 (11.8); tarsus, 22.0–23.0 (22.4); middle toe without claw, 12.0–14.5 (12.9). *Adult female*: Wing, 64.5–70.5 (66.8); tail, 45.5–51.0 (48.5); bill, 10.5–12.0 (11.5); tarsus, 21.5–23.0 (22.1); middle toe, 12.0–13.5 (12.8).
TYPE: Adult male, no. 137220, U.S. National Museum, Bio-

logical Surveys collection; near mouth of Four-mile Run, 1½ mi. down Ohio River from Vanport, Beaver Co., Pennsylvania; June 19, 1893; W. E. C. Todd; original no., 213.

RANGE: N.e. Iowa, s. Michigan, and Connecticut, south to n. Missouri, s. Ohio, and Virginia. Winters from Oaxaca and Campeche to Guatemala and Nicaragua.

[1] *Amer. Ornith.*, vol. 3 (1811 [after Feb. 12]), p. 85, pl. 25, fig. 3.

MacGILLIVRAY'S WARBLER, *Oporornis tolmiei*

Two races of this species have been described by A. R. Phillips.[1] The Intermediate MacGillivray's Warbler, *O. t. intermedius*, he originally named *O. t. intermedia* from Okanagan (Landing), British Columbia. Although intermediate in both diagnostic characters and geographic distribution between *tolmiei* and *monticola*, it is nevertheless a recognizable form. From the latter it may be separated by its brighter coloration above and below; and shorter wings and tail, the tail relatively as well as actually. The subspecific name should be written *intermedius*, instead of *intermedia*, as originally proposed, because *Oporornis* is of masculine gender, with which the subspecific name should agree.

A northeastern race was christened from a specimen taken at Emigrant Gulch, 6,500 ft., 3 mi. southeast of Chico, Park Co., Montana.[2] In a way it is intermediate between *intermedia* and *monticola*, but actually it combines the relatively short tail of the former with coloration of the latter. Its distribution, however, lies northeast of that of both of these birds.

[1] *Auk* 64 (Apr. 14, 1947): 299.
[2] Ibid., p. 298.

YELLOWTHROAT, *Geothlypis trichas*

ATHENS YELLOWTHROAT, *G. t. trichas*: This race was described by T. D. Burleigh[1] as *Geothlypis trichas typhicola* from Athens, Georgia. However, a thorough investigation of all races of *Geothlypis trichas* shows clearly that this name must be changed in favor of *G. t. trichas* (Linnaeus). This involved the reexamination of the basis of the name *Turdus trichas* Linnaeus,[2] described from "America septentrionali." Most authors have restricted this name to the breeding bird of Maryland, and the type locality has been cited commonly as Maryland. That this is incorrect was long ago pointed out by Frank M. Chapman,[3] but his careful analysis has been entirely overlooked. The original description of Linnaeus was based on the Maryland Yellowthroat of Edwards,[4] on *Ficedula Marilandica* of Brisson,[5] and *Avis marylandica gutture luteo* of Petiver.[6]

The first and most important source of information cited by Linnaeus is George Edwards, who, according to his own statement, drew his figure and made his description from a bird captured in Carolina. Of it he said, "This bird was the property of Mr. Elliot, merchant in Broad Street, London, who received it with others preserved in spirits from Carolina in North America . . ." Edwards also cites Petiver's *Gazophylacium*, and gives Petiver's bird as from Maryland, although he somewhat doubtfully considers it the same as his own. Edwards also mentions another specimen and drawing sent by Bartram from Philadelphia. Brisson's name was based on the bird from "Caroline à Mariland and en Pensilvanie," and he further stated, "Le sommet de la tête est d'un brun-rougeâtre." Petiver, who is quoted also by Edwards, stated in his description of the bird which he called the Maryland Yellowthroat, "This the Reverend Mr. H. Jones sent me from Maryland."

It is evident that Edwards was the main source of informa-

tion from which Linnaeus drew his description. For this reason, Carolina should be taken as the type locality. Brisson also mentioned Carolina first in his description. Furthermore, the figure given by Edwards is an excellent representation of the bird breeding in most of South Carolina, and occurring in the southeastern corner, where undoubtedly the bird was obtained, as Edwards said. The reddish brown top of the head, which Brisson (who likewise included Carolina in the range of his bird) also mentioned, is characteristic of the breeding bird of most of South Carolina. It is probable that Linnaeus' *Turdus trichas* was fixed on the Maryland bird because of the citation from Petiver. But the type locality should be e. South Carolina, as herewith designated; also that the name *Turdus trichas* should apply to the bird breeding in most of that area, in spite of the fact that Edwards, while he described the bird from Carolina, as his text and figures both show, called it Maryland Yellowthroat.

FLORIDA YELLOWTHROAT, *G. t. restricta*: This race was originally described by Frank M. Chapman[7] as *Geothlypis trichas ignota* from specimens taken at Tarpon Springs, Florida; this name has since been used for this subspecies, despite Chapman's own statement that it should be called *G. t. trichas*.[8] This was before the bird from South Carolina was separated from that of Florida. In order to determine the proper name for the Florida race the present writer sent to England a typical specimen of this form together with typical examples of all other races from eastern North America for direct comparison with the type of C. J. Maynard's *Geothlypis restricta*,[9] which was described from the Bahamas. Comparisons with the type were made by Dr. N. B. Kinnear, at that time curator of birds in the British Museum in London. He found this type specimen to best agree with a typical example of *G. t. ignota*, rather than with any other eastern subspecies that might occur in the Bahamas. Of the type he replied, "Of your specimens, No. 342068 is the nearest to the type of *G. restricta*. On the under parts your specimen differs in having the flanks and sides of the body more buffy brown; on the upper parts your specimen is olive green, while in the type it is more yellowish green. In your specimen the band on the fore part of crown is very slightly more greyish white, and the pileum more brown in colour. This type is not in a very good condition, and there are feathers missing on the head and throat." Following are the particulars of the type specimen: male, Nassau, Bahamas, Feb. 2, 1884; collector's no., 2135, British Museum Register no. 1906.12.7.3409. Measurements of the type as given by Dr. Kinnear are: wing, 59 mm.; tail, 52.5; bill (exposed culmen), tip broken; tarsus, 19. It thus seems necessary to use the name *G. t. restricta* Maynard for the subspecies breeding in Florida and along the Gulf of Mexico coast west to Louisiana.

ARKANSAS YELLOWTHROAT, *G. t. roscoe*: The Yellowthroat breeding in e. Texas has commonly been referred to the Maryland Yellowthroat, *G. t. marilandica* (= *G. t. trichas* of A.O.U., 1957). However, accumulation of additional material from e. Texas, Louisiana, and Arkansas, shows that this bird is subspecifically separable from the bird from Maryland, differing as indicated in the detailed account of the species.

The original description of *Sylvia roscoe* Audubon[10] was based on an immature male taken in s. Mississippi near the Mississippi River. Careful comparisons of immature males of all eastern forms of this species with the original plate of Audubon's bird show clearly that *Sylvia roscoe* is neither the Florida Yellowthroat nor the Athens Yellowthroat; but it does correspond very well in size and coloration with the bird breeding in n. and w. Louisiana, which occurs with apparent regularity as a migrant in s. Mississippi and as a breeder in n. Mississippi. Audubon's plate represents a bird that is very dark olive green above without gray on the forehead; with yellow on the jugulum not extended over the breast; and with sides and flanks moderately dark. Its measurements, so far as it is possible to determine them from the plate and description, are: wing, 50 mm.; bill (exposed culmen), 10; tarsus, 19. It is obviously a male in first autumn plumage. It seems, therefore, proper to make use of this name for the Texas-Arkansas race, which should, therefore, be known as *G. t. roscoe* (Audubon). Breeding birds from Strong, in c. Kansas, are somewhat intermediate between *G. t. roscoe* and the breeding bird of Minnesota but are nearer the present race.

MARYLAND YELLOWTHROAT, *G. t. marilandica*: By separation of the Yellowthroats from Arkansas, Louisiana, and e. Texas as a distinct subspecies, the range of the Maryland Yellowthroat becomes much restricted (see Arkansas Yellowthroat).

Birds from Preston Co., c. northern West Virginia, are certainly to be referred to this race. Those from Huntington and Somerset cos., c. southern Pennsylvania, are intermediate between this race and the one in Ohio, but are rather smaller and darker above, and not so yellow below, for which reasons they are nearer to *marilandica*.

This subspecies has commonly been called *G. t. trichas*, but this name must be transferred to the bird breeding in South Carolina (see Athens Yellowthroat); hence, another name becomes necessary for the present bird. This is found in *Sylvia marilandica* Wilson.[11] The locality given by Wilson for this bird is "United States, from Maine to Florida, and also Louisiana, . . . particularly numerous in . . . Maryland, Pennsylvania, and New Jersey." Most of Wilson's account relates to s.e. Pennsylvania, so that the type locality may be now designated as Philadelphia. Thus, the present race should be called *G. t. marilandica* (Wilson).

NORTHERN YELLOWTHROAT, *G. t. brachidactyla*: This race for a long time has been used to include all northern Yellowthroats east of the Rocky Mts. That several races instead of one occur in this region became evident when specimens from different parts of the range were compared. In order to work out satisfactorily the present subspecies it became necessary to fix the name *G. t. brachidactyla*. Swainson[12] described this bird originally as *Trichas brachidactylus*; the only locality given is "northern province of the United States." In order to settle this matter as far as possible, a typical specimen of the Massachusetts race was included with representatives of other races sent to Dr. N. B. Kinnear of the British Museum for comparison with the type of Swainson's *Trichas brachidactylus*. Kinnear replied, "Swainson's *brachidactylus* is similar to No. 342068 [= *G. t. ignota*] above, but rather lighter on the back, the head less brown and the grey band restricted and similar to No. 167936 [= *G. t. brachidactyla*]. Measurements: wing, 57 mm.; tail, 50; culmen, [not given]; tarsus, 19.5. Below it is similar to *restricta*, but the yellow comes very slightly lower down and is of rather a paler tinge."

A. J. van Rossem, who also has examined this type, supplied the writer with the following notes:

"Old tag as follows:

Trichas brachydactylus	
Even-toed Yellowthroat	
Ward	No. Am^a.

"There is also a female inscribed as *brachydactylus*—the only other yellowthroat so marked in the Swainson birds at Cambridge. However, as Swainson described only the male (Anim. in Menag., pp. 295–296) the above is a holotype.

"Skin in good condition, save that the skin of the throat is broken. Not so yellow as the average *brachydactyla*, but the larger measurements are proper for this form."

Thus, there is little doubt that *G. t. brachidactyla* should be applied to the breeding bird of Massachusetts. Since there is no locality more definitely given by Swainson than "North America" it seems desirable to designate the type locality of *Trichas brachidactylus* Swainson; if comparisons and measurements made by Dr. Kinnear and A. J. van Rossem are indicative, it is safe to designate this as Cambridge, Massachusetts. None of the other names applied to eastern Yellowthroats seem applicable to this race; therefore, it apparently has clear title to *G. t. brachidactyla* (Swainson). Birds breeding in the vicinity of New York City, those on Long Island, and in n. New Jersey are somewhat intermediate between *marilandica* and *brachidactyla*, but nearer the latter.

NOVA SCOTIA YELLOWTHROAT, *G. t. novascoticola*: This race was described by the writer[13] from 4 mi. south of Wolfville, Nova Scotia.

QUEBEC YELLOWTHROAT, *G. t. quebecicola*: This race was described by the writer[14] from Balena, Newfoundland.

OHIO YELLOWTHROAT, *G. t. ohionicola*: This race was described by the writer[15] from Tinker's Creek, 3¼ mi. southeast of Twinsburg, on the Portage-Summit co. line, Ohio.

MINNESOTA YELLOWTHROAT, *G. t. minnesoticola*: Specimens belonging to this race have sometimes been referred to *brachidactyla*, sometimes to *occidentalis*. None of the names applied to eastern or western Yellowthroats appears to be applicable to this subspecies. It was described by the writer[16] from St. Paul, Minnesota.

ALBERTA YELLOWTHROAT, *G. t. alberticola*: This race was described by the writer[17] from the main branch of the Athabaska River, 9 mi. above its mouth in the Athabaska Delta, n.e. Alberta.

YUKON YELLOWTHROAT, *G. t. yukonicola*: This Yellowthroat was described by W. Earl Godfrey[18] from Jarvis River at Alaska Highway, Yukon Territory. It is the most grayish and the northernmost of all races of the species.

COLORADO YELLOWTHROAT, *G. t. coloradonicola*: This race was described by the writer[19] from Las Vegas, New Mexico. Breeding males from Medora and Glen Ullin, s.w. North Dakota, and from Custer Co., n.e. South Dakota, are not so yellow on the upper parts, but without much doubt belong to this race. Similar are some males from the vicinity of Denver, but they even more definitely belong to *coloradonicola*.

UTAH YELLOWTHROAT, *G. t. utahicola*: This race was described by the writer[20] from Fairfield, Utah. Birds from Logan, c. northern Utah, appear to verge somewhat toward the Idaho race but are nearer to *utahicola*.

IDAHO YELLOWTHROAT, *G. t. idahonicola*: This race was described by the writer[21] from 4 mi. south of Parma, Canyon Co., Idaho. Breeding birds from Wellsville, Cache Co., c. northern Utah, are intermediate to a certain extent with *utahicola*, but are nearer the present race.

ARIZONA YELLOWTHROAT, *G. t. arizonicola*: This race was described by the writer[22] from Fort Verde, Arizona.

OREGON YELLOWTHROAT, *G. t. oregonicola*: Along with a considerable number of other birds, Yellowthroats in the Warner Valley region of Oregon seem to differentiate into a different subspecies, here named *G. t. oregonicola*. This race was described by the writer[23] from 6 mi. south of Adel, Warner Valley, c. southern Oregon.

WESTERN YELLOWTHROAT, *G. t. occidentalis*: This race was originally described by William Brewster[24] from a specimen taken on the Truckee River in w. Nevada. By reason of confusion of characters and lack of definite subspecific definition of this race, there has been much lack of uniformity in identification and in ranges assigned to the different races in the western United States. Accumulation of additional material from the Great Basin and other critical areas now seems to show that the true Western Yellowthroat is confined to a rather limited breeding area, mostly, if not entirely, in w. Nevada, although during winter it ranges from s. California to s. Texas and n. Mexico.

[1] *Proc. Biol. Soc. Washington* 47 (Feb. 9, 1934): 21.
[2] *Syst. Nat.* 12th ed., vol. 1 (1766 [after May 24]), p. 293.
[3] *Auk* 24 (Jan., 1907): 30–33.
[4] *Gleanings Nat. Hist.*, vol. 1 (1758), p. 56, pl. 237, fig. 2.
[5] *Ornith.* 3 (1760): 506.
[6] *Gazophylacium Naturae et Artis* (1702), pl. 6, fig. 1.
[7] *Auk* 7 (Jan., 1890): 11.
[8] *Auk* 14 (Jan., 1907): 30–33.
[9] *American Exchange and Mart*, vol. 3, no. 3 (Jan. 15, 1887), p. 33, col. 2.
[10] *Birds America*, folio ed., vol. 1 (1827), pl. 24.
[11] *Amer. Ornith.*, vol. 1 (1808), p. 88, pl. 6, fig. 1.
[12] *Animals in Menageries* (1838 [after Dec., 1837]), p. 295.
[13] *Descriptions of New Races of* Geothlypis trichas (*Linnaeus*) (Jan. 20, 1948), p. 1. [Published privately by Dr. Oberholser, Cleveland, Ohio; article on file in U.S. Fish and Wildlife Service, Washington, D.C.—EDITOR]
[14] Ibid., p. 1.
[15] Ibid., p. 2.
[16] Ibid., p. 2.
[17] Ibid., p. 2.
[18] *Canadian Field Nat.* 64 (May–June, 1950 [July 27]): 104.
[19] *Descriptions of New Races . . . (Linnaeus)* (Jan. 20, 1948), p. 3.
[20] Ibid., p. 3.
[21] Ibid., p. 3.
[22] Ibid., p. 4.
[23] Ibid., p. 3.
[24] *Bull. Nuttall Ornith. Club* 8 (July, 1883): 159.

YELLOW-BREASTED CHAT, *Icteria virens*

The Yellow-breasted Chat inhabiting c. and s. Texas has been sometimes identified as *I. v. virens*, sometimes as *longicauda*, but a good series of specimens from both regions shows that it is a recognizable subspecies. So far as the writer has been able to determine, none of the synonyms applied to the species are based on this bird; thus, *I. v. danotia* is provided for this new race.

The Long-tailed Yellow-breasted Chat is rather wide ranging. As compared to *auricollis* it agrees in size, but differs in its lighter, more greenish (less grayish) upper surface; and darker, decidedly more buffy (less grayish) sides and flanks. It differs still more from *danotia* in its larger size, more greenish (less grayish) upper parts, and more buffy (less whitish or grayish) sides, flanks, and crissum. The proper name for this race is *I. v. longicauda* (Lawrence), as currently applied, the type of which came from Stockton, California. The possibility of separating this subspecies was originally suggested by van Rossem.[1]

[1] *Wilson Bull.* 51 (Sept., 1939): 156.

HOUSE SPARROW, *Passer domesticus*

It is of considerable interest to note that this introduced bird in approximately fifty years varied in the arid west sufficiently to render appreciable difference between western and eastern birds. This has been noted as a result of the introduction of a number of other species of birds, and in this particular case it seems worthwhile to signalize the difference by a subspecific name; hence, the western or pale race of the House Sparrow is herewith called *P. d. plecticus*. In determining this the writer examined approximately three hundred specimens, including a large series from the Great Basin and other parts of the arid w. United States, these representing both summer and winter plumages. Birds from c. and w. Texas are somewhat intermediate, but are decidedly nearer the western race. As is often the case, the plain-colored female shows more difference than does the male.

WESTERN MEADOWLARK, *Sturnella ludoviciana*

Ever since its discovery by Audubon, the Western Meadowlark has been called *Sturnella neglecta*; Audubon[1] originally described the species from a specimen which he obtained on the Missouri River near Old Fort Union, North Dakota.

There is, however, a forgotten name introduced by Linnaeus —*Sturnus ludovicianus*[2]—which needs consideration in this connection. This name was based wholly on the *Sturnus ludovicianus* of Brisson,[3] who gives as the locality for his bird "Ludovicia," or "La Louisiane." Brisson gives a detailed description of plumage, together with a plate, both of which are evidently drawn from a specimen. Both description and plate are excellent of the Western Meadowlark. The plate, in particular, perfectly represents that species, even though it is printed in black and white. His text says (italics added): "Les *joues*, la gorge, la partie inférieure du col, la poitrine et le ventre sont d'un beau *jaune*." The text explicitly mentions, and the plate clearly shows, the distinct and separated bars on wing and tail feathers. Thus, there is no doubt that Brisson's bird is the Western Meadowlark, now called *Sturnella neglecta*. Since Linnaeus' name, *Sturnus ludovicianus*, was based entirely on Brisson's bird, is long anterior to *Sturnella neglecta*, and does not seem to be preoccupied, it should be used for the Western Meadowlark.

The type locality of *Sturnus ludovicianus* Linnaeus is Louisiana. At the time of publication of the works of both Brisson and Linnaeus, the term Louisiana, of course, included a vast area in interior North America, where the Western Meadowlark could easily have been obtained. This bird is rare even today within the present state of Louisiana, but it may have been more common in days gone by, and it may even be more common today in Louisiana than records indicate. Thus, there is no inherent geographic improbability in assigning Louisiana as the type locality of *Sturnus ludovicianus*.

[1] *Birds America*, octavo ed., vol. 7 (1844), p. 339, pl. 489.
[2] *Syst. Nat.*, 12th ed., vol. 1 (1766 [after May 24]), p. 290 ("America").
[3] *Ornith.* 2 (1760): 449, pl. 41, fig. 1.

RED-WINGED BLACKBIRD, *Agelaius phoeniceus*

Breeding birds of Colorado have been considered as belonging to the Thick-billed Red-winged Blackbird, *A. p. fortis*, but recent investigations show it to represent an additional subspecies, here called *A. p. stereus*; though similar to *fortis*, it has a shorter bill; and the female is darker above (in coloring approaching *arctolegus*), the lower parts darker with dark brown streaks broader, the white spaces narrower, and posteriorly with little light streaking; throat paler, more whitish (averaging less buffy or pinkish). Breeding birds from North Dakota and e. and c. Montana are representatives of this race. They formerly were referred to *arctolegus*, as intermediates between the latter and *fortis*.

While it may seem that there are enough races of the Red-winged Blackbird, systematic investigation of the status of the birds in the Rocky Mts. and Great Basin shows that birds from Idaho are more or less different from any of the other segregated races, and in order to clarify these differences, it seems desirable to furnish them with a name. The Idaho race, here described as *A. p. zastereus*, is similar to *stereus*, but differs in having a shorter tail; and a longer, decidedly more slender bill; in the female, the throat is usually pinkish (instead of buffy or whitish), the upper parts in winter are rather darker and duller, and the lower parts are decidedly darker (usually more extensively blackish). Other differences may be found by comparing descriptions, measurements, and ranges in the detailed account.

The breeding Red-winged Blackbird of Utah was described by L. B. Bishop as *A. p. utahensis*,[1] but in the breeding season it has a much more extended distribution than that given by the original describer. It differs from *zastereus* in slightly shorter tail; shorter and relatively stouter bill; and in the female, in lighter, more brownish upper surface, and decidedly lighter lower surface (the dark streaks narrower, with the chin and throat mostly buffy, instead of pinkish). From *fortis* it differs in its more slender bill; shorter tail of the male; and in the female with lower parts averaging darker, the dark streaks more blackish (less brownish), and abdomen darker, usually more extensively blackish. It is similar to *nevadensis*[2] but smaller, with somewhat longer wing and tail; decidedly shorter, relatively somewhat stouter bill; and shorter middle toe; female lighter both above and below, posteriorly below much less extensively blackish. It differs from *sonoriensis* Ridgway in decidedly shorter, much stouter bill, and decidedly shorter middle toe; in the female by reason of its much darker, more blackish (less buffy or ochraceous) upper surface, particularly in winter plumage, and darker lower parts, with the dark streaks broader, much more blackish (less brownish), and more numerous on chin and throat. Birds from n.e. Utah and Fort Bridger in s.w. Wyoming are decidedly to be referred to this Utah race. Birds from extreme s.e. Idaho (that is, from Montpelier, Fish Haven, Preston, and Malad City) are not typical, being intermediate between the present race and *zastereus*, but they are apparently nearer to *utahensis*. Males from St. George in extreme s.w. Utah have longer, more slender bills than birds from farther north, and in this they somewhat approach *sonoriensis*, but are nevertheless nearer to *utahensis*. Breeding birds from most of Arizona, however (as for instance from Phoenix and Camp Verde, east to Marsh Lake and Springerville, south to Pima, Hereford, and Safford) as well as birds from El Paso Co., Texas, are almost typical *utahensis*, notwithstanding the proximity to s.w. Arizona, where *sonoriensis* occurs.

Birds from New Mexico and n.e. Arizona seem to be sufficiently different from other races of the Red-winged Blackbird to make desirable their separation as a distinct race. This bird, now called *A. p. heterus*, differs from *utahensis* in shorter and relatively stouter bill; also the female has lower parts lighter, with dark streaks more brownish (less blackish) and lighter, and abdomen usually less extensively blackish. Birds from extreme n.e. Arizona belong to this race, although birds from farther south and farther west are *utahensis*. This New Mexican race was formerly referred to *neutralis*, but by restriction of that race to s.w. California, and the interposition of *nevadensis* and *utahensis*, it becomes necessary to recognize it as a distinct form, since it is not properly referable to any of the adjoining races.

[1] *Trans. San Diego Soc. Nat. Hist.* 9 (Nov. 21, 1938): 2 ("Saltair, Salt Lake City, Utah").
[2] Grinnell, *Proc. Biol. Soc. Washington* 17 (May 11, 1914): 107 ("Quinn River Crossing, Humboldt County, Nevada").

ORCHARD ORIOLE, *Icterus spurius*

A small western race of the Orchard Oriole was, for quite some time, considered separable from the bird of the e. United States. Robert Ridgway,[1] however, in revising the species came to the conclusion that no races were recognizable. He noted the size difference in birds in Texas that were from the Mississippi Valley as compared with birds from the e. United States, but

evidently was misled by a few large birds from Mexico—apparently migrants or unusual specimens—since birds from the Mississippi River westward, including Mexico, are as a whole decidedly smaller than eastern birds. There is also a color difference in females, the western bird being lighter above, more grayish or brownish (less olive greenish), and somewhat paler below. Mexican birds, however, seem to average somewhat larger than birds from Texas, though practically all these large birds may be migrants from the north.

When this western form was recognized it was usually called *I. s. affinis*, a name proposed by George N. Lawrence[2] for the Texas bird. The type, from Brownsville, Texas, is now in the American Museum of Natural History, where it has been examined and found to be an example of the small western race.

The Orchard Oriole was first described by Linnaeus as *Oriolus spurius*,[3] who based his description on *Icterus minor* of Catesby[4] and *Icterus minor spurius* of Brisson.[5] Both Catesby and Brisson described the eastern race; South Carolina has already been designated as the type locality,[6] which designation the present writer now further restricts to s.e. South Carolina. The *Oriolus varius* of Gmelin,[7] without much doubt, also refers to the eastern bird.

Much more interesting, however, is *Oriolus capensis* Gmelin,[8] the locality for which is given as "Caput bonae spei et in Louisiana." This name is based on *Xanthornus capitis Bonae Spei* of Brisson;[9] Carouge du Cap de Bonne Espérance of D'Aubenton;[10] *Carouge olive de la Louisiane* of Buffon;[11] Olive Oriole of Pennant;[12] and Olive Oriole of Latham.[13]

Although D'Aubenton's plate is poor, and the locality erroneous, this bird of Gmelin's is undoubtedly the Orchard Oriole. Buffon[14] discovered and corrected the mistaken locality and stated that it came from Louisiana, besides reporting from the same locality another specimen with the throat black, evidently an immature male Orchard Oriole.

A number of years later, Vieillot[15] also noted that *Oriolus capensis* is the female of his *Pendulinus nigricollis*, which is, of course, the Orchard Oriole, and a renaming of *Oriolus spurius* Linnaeus.

The descriptions of Brisson and Buffon are good of the female Orchard Oriole, but the statement by various authors that the throat verges toward orange, together with the poor plate of D'Aubenton's, have obscured the true identity of this bird. This is simply their way of indicating the decidedly pale ochraceous tinge that is not infrequently observed on the throat and jugulum of the male and female in the Orchard Oriole in first autumn plumage. The breeding Orchard Oriole of Louisiana is the small western race here again revived, and on account of this, named *I. s. capensis* (Gmelin). It is thus the same application as *affinis*, subsequently proposed by Lawrence, and should be used for this subspecies instead on that name. All other designations—and there have been several based on this species—apply clearly to the eastern race.

By recognition of *capensis*, the Eastern Orchard Oriole becomes a trinomial, *I. s. spurius*.

[1] *Bull. U.S. Nat. Mus.*, no. 50, pt. 2 (Oct. 16, 1902), p. 276.
[2] *Ann. Lyc. Nat. Hist. New York* 5 (May, 1851): 113 ("Rio Grande in Texas").
[3] *Syst. Nat.* 12th ed., vol. 1 (1766 [after May 24]), p. 162 ("America Septentrionali").
[4] *Nat. Hist. Carolina, Florida, and Bahama Is.*, vol. 1 (1731), p. 49, pl. 49.
[5] *Ornith.* 2 (1760): 111, pl. 10, fig. 3 ("Virginia & Canada").
[6] *Check-List North Amer. Birds* 4th ed. (Oct. 1, 1931), p. 306.
[7] *Syst. Nat.*, vol. 1, pt. 1 (1788 [before July 25]), p. 390 ("Cayenna").
[8] Ibid., p. 392.

[9] *Ornith.* 2 (1760): 128 ("in Capite Bonae Spei").
[10] *Planches Enlum.*, no. 607, fig. 2.
[11] *Hist. Nat. Oiseaux* 3 (1775): 251 ("Louisiane").
[12] *Arctic Zool.* 2 (1785): 260 (description translated from Buffon's *Hist. Nat. Oiseaux*, which with D'Aubenton's *Planches Enlum.*, are cited as references).
[13] *General Synop. Birds*, vol. 1, "Pt. 2" [=1] (1781), p. 444 ("Cape of Good Hope"; cites Gmelin, Brisson, Buffon, D'Aubenton, and Pennant, and describes additional specimen "from the same place as having the forehead, cheeks, and all beneath yellow").
[14] *Hist. Nat. Oiseaux* 3 (1775): 251.
[15] *Nouv. Dict. D'Hist.*, new ed. 5 (1816), p. 321.

BULLOCK'S ORIOLE, *Icterus bullockii*

Breeding birds in most of Texas seem racially different from those found farther to the west in the Rocky Mts. This species was originally described by Swainson as *Xanthornus bullockii* from Tamascaltepec, State of México.[1] In order to determine the proper subspecific application of this name, the type was examined by F. R. Parrington of Cambridge, England, and Herbert Friedmann of the U.S. National Museum. It is an adult male in a fairly good state of preservation, measuring as follows: wing, 105 mm.; tail, 83.5; bill (exposed culmen), 19.5; height of bill at base, 8.5; tarsus, 24.5; middle toe without claw, 18.8. It is an example of the race breeding in the Rocky Mts. from Montana to Trans-Pecos Texas, to which, therefore, the name *I. b. bullockii* is applicable. Since *Psarocolius auricollis* Wied[2] from Fort Pierre, South Dakota, is a synonym of *bullockii*, the bird from the more eastern parts of Texas is left without a name. *I. b. eleutherus* is herewith provided for the Texas Bullock's Oriole.

[1] *Philosophical Mag.*, n.s. 1 (June, 1827): 436.
[2] *Reise Nord. Amer.* 1 (1839): 367.

LICHTENSTEIN'S ORIOLE, *Andriopsar gularis*

Structurally this species is rather surprisingly different from other members of the genus *Icterus*, as at present constituted. It diverges from the typical members of that group as follows: palate with a projection 2 mm. broad on the posterior median portion, which is truncate in front or even with a tooth or notch on its anterior lower angle where it is about 1.2–1.5 mm. deep; bill relatively stout (height of culmen at base equal to ca. ½ length of exposed culmen) and culmen practically straight; tarsus slightly longer than culmen; middle toe and claw equal to tarsus or slightly greater. These characters are fully sufficient to warrant generic separation of this particular species from other forms of *Icterus*, as already shown by Alexander Wetmore.[1] This species should, therefore, be called *Andriopsar gularis* (Wagler), and the subspecies occurring in Texas would become *Andriopsar gularis tamaulipensis* (Ridgway).

[1] *Auk* 36 (Apr., 1919): 194–196.

BREWER'S BLACKBIRD, *Euphagus cyanocephalus*

Since three additional races are recognized in the present work, a trinomial is necessary for the Brewer's Blackbird now confined chiefly to the U.S. Rocky Mts. The original description of the Brewer's Blackbird by Wagler[1] was based on a bird from Mexico without more definite locality; it remained for A. J. van Rossem[2] to discover that it was collected at Tamascaltepec, Mexico. This name is apparently applicable to the Idaho Brewer's Blackbird, henceforth to be called *E. c. cyanocephalus*.

The Dakota Brewer's Blackbird, *E. c. brewerii*, is very readily recognizable in the female as distinguished from *cyanocephalus*; however, males are very similar, though slightly more bluish (less yellowish) in shade of the green. It has a name in *Quiscalus brewerii*, which Audubon[3] described from a specimen he obtained at Fort Union, North Dakota. The *Scolecophagus mexicanus* of Swainson[4] described from Mexico, is apparently the same as the bird from Colorado, Arizona, and e. Idaho, which is thus regarded as the typical (nominate) race, *E. c. cyanocephalus*.

Males of the Western Brewer's Blackbird, *E. c. aliastus*, are the same size as males of *cyanocephalus*, but color differences of posterior lower parts are distinctive. Specimens of this race in juvenal plumage are even more different from comparable birds of the typical race than are the adults, as they are much darker both above and below, and decidedly less rufescent. From *brewerii*, the male of this subspecies differs in decidedly more bluish (less yellowish) green of the posterior lower surface; in the female, by more brownish (less sooty) coloration, particularly below. This bird of the Great Basin, from British Columbia to Nevada, was described by the writer[5] from specimens taken at Twenty-Mile Creek, in the Warner Valley, 9 mi. south of Adel, Oregon. Since the several races of this species occur over much of the same territory during the nonbreeding season, it is necessary to make comparison only with breeding birds. The most easily recognized characters are usually in the females.

The California Brewer's Blackbird, *E. c. minusculus*, differs from *aliastus* in much smaller size; in the male, by less bluish, somewhat more yellowish green lower surface; and in the female by more brownish and somewhat paler lower parts. It was originally described by Joseph Grinnell[6] from specimens taken at Palo Alto, Santa Clara Co., California. One reason for lack of general recognition of this subspecies is probably because transients or winter birds of other races, instead of only breeding individuals, have been used in comparisons.

[1] *Ps[arocolius] cyanocephalus* Wagler, *Isis (von Oken)* 22 ([July] 1829): col. 758.
[2] *Trans. San Diego Soc. Nat. Hist.* 7 (May 31, 1934): 354.
[3] *Birds America*, octavo ed., vol. 7 (1844), p. 345, pls. 92, 400.
[4] *Animals in Menageries* (1838 [Dec., 1837]), p. 302.
[5] Oberholser, *Scient. Publ. Cleveland Mus. Nat. Hist.* 4 (Sept. 19, 1932): 9.
[6] *Condor* 22 (Aug. 10, 1920): 153.

GREAT-TAILED GRACKLE, *Cassidix mexicanus*

C. m. mexicanus is new to the fauna of Texas, as a matter of fact, to that of the United States. It was first described by Gmelin[1] as *Corvus mexicanus*, which name was long used by mistake for the Mexican Crow, now known as *Corvus imparatus* Peters.

[1] *Syst. Nat.*, vol. 1, pt. 1 (1788 [after Mar. 16]), p. 375 (Mexico).

BOAT-TAILED GRACKLE, *Cassidix major*

That the Boat-tailed Grackle is specifically distinct from the Great-tailed Grackle has been shown by Selander and Giller.[1]

[1] *Condor* 63 (Jan. 19, 1961): 29–86.

PURPLE GRACKLE, *Quiscalus quiscula*

See Bronzed Grackle.

BRONZED GRACKLE, *Quiscalus aeneus*

Additional evidence presented by Frank M. Chapman,[1] regarding the relationships of the Purple Grackle, *Quiscalus quiscula*, to the bird known as the Bronzed Grackle, *Quiscalus aeneus*, appears sufficient to justify regarding the latter as a distinct species instead of a subspecies of *Q. quiscula*. The fact that so-called and apparent intermediates between the two are of such character as to indicate hybridization—rather than the ordinary process of subspecific intergradation—seems to warrant this conclusion. It is, therefore, proper to use a binomial as its technical name; accordingly, the name of the bird would be *Q. aeneus* instead of *Q. q. aeneus*.

The name *versicolor*, instead of *aeneus*, is used for this form on the grounds that the supposed type of *Q. versicolor*, now in the Muséum d'Histoire Naturelle, Paris, France, is an example of the Bronzed Grackle.

Chapman[2] has subsequently held that the original description on which *Q. versicolor* Vieillot is based does not agree sufficiently with *Q. aeneus*, but is an excellent description of *Q. quiscula*. The present writer has also expressed the opinion that *Q. versicolor* Vieillot is a synonym of *Q. quiscula*.[3]

In the original account of *Q. versicolor*, Vieillot[4] gives a good description of the bird's plumage, the most pertinent parts of which are as follows: "*. . . il offre à l'oeil les couleurs du prisme dans tout leur éclat; les reflets les plus riches et les plus éclatants, bleus, pourpres, violets, dorés, verts, se jouent sur un noir velouté.*"

As will be recalled, *Q. quiscula* has brilliantly iridescent plumage throughout; *Q. aeneus* has only the head so colored, while the body sharply contrasts with the head and—though shiny bronze—is dull in comparison to *Q. quiscula*. Vieillot, evidently describing the entire plumage, emphasizes the brilliance and conspicuousness of the iridescent reflections. He was altogether too good an ornithologist to have overlooked the conspicuous difference between head and body colors, had he been describing the Bronzed Grackle.

It is true, as Wetmore[5] contends, that in a highly plumaged adult Bronzed Grackle, closely examined under bright light, some metallic reflections can be detected on the body; but in comparison to the conspicuous iridescence of the whole plumage of the Purple Grackle, these inconspicuous, microscopic prismatic reflections are negligible. Indeed, they could hardly, even by stretch of imagination, be described in Vieillot's words as "*les reflets les plus riches et les plus éclatants*"! Thus, it is difficult to understand how his description could properly apply to the Bronzed Grackle.

Since it appears that the description of *Q. versicolor* given by Vieillot does not agree with characters exhibited by the so-called type, it is evident that this specimen has been in some way mislabeled. To cover such cases as this, Chapman should have noted canon 41 of the A.O.U. Code of Nomenclature which states: ". . . but in no case is a type specimen to be accepted as the basis of a specific or subspecific name when it radically disagrees with, or is contradictory to the characters given in the diagnosis or description based upon it, nor when the name is a nomen nudum." This is good sense and good nomenclature.

In view of the doubtful authenticity of the type, it seems much better to continue the name *Quiscalus aeneus* for the Bronzed Grackle.

[1] *Auk* 52 (Jan. 8, 1935): 21–29.
[2] *Auk* 56 (June 30, 1939): 364–365.
[3] *Auk* 36 (Oct., 1919): 551.
[4] *Nouv. Dict. d'Hist. Nat.*, new ed. 28 (1819): 488 (North America).
[5] *Auk* 56 (Oct. 4, 1939): 505–506.

BROWN-HEADED COWBIRD, *Molothrus ater*

The Louisiana Brown-headed Cowbird, *M. a. buphilus*, was originally described by the writer[1] from a specimen taken at Marsh Island, c. southern Louisiana. It possesses characters capable of definition and seems subspecifically distinct, although it occupies an intermediate area and is somewhat intermediate in characters between *ater* and *obscurus*. It has, however, a relatively stouter bill than either. Furthermore, the female is darker and much less brownish (more grayish) below than the female of *obscurus*.

None of the names applied to *Molothrus ater* from e. North America are applicable to this race, nor are any of the other names from more western localities.

Birds from Dewitt, c. eastern Arkansas, are not typical of *buphilus*, but are apparently nearer to this than to *ater*. Hitherto, this bird—occupying much of c. and s. Texas—has been called *obscurus*, but the latter is herewith restricted to w. Trans-Pecos Texas.

[1] Oberholser, *Bull. Louisiana Dept. Conservation*, no. 28 (June 30, 1938), p. 611.

WESTERN TANAGER, *Piranga ludoviciana*

This species was first described by Alexander Wilson,[1] and the locality that he gives is "Remote regions of Louisiana . . . plains or prairies of the Missouri." The specimen he used for his description was brought back by the Lewis and Clark Expedition, the locality being the mouth of Lolo Creek Fork of Clearwater River, w. Idaho. Birds from this area are very similar to those found on the Pacific coast of n.w. United States; therefore, birds from the latter region are to be considered as belonging to the nominate race, which will bear the name *P. l. ludoviciana*, since an additional subspecies inhabiting the Rocky Mts. has now been described.

The bird described by Vieillot as *Pirange erythropis*[2] is based on pl. 20, fig. 1 in Wilson's *American Ornithology*, and, therefore, is a strict synonym of *Tanagra ludoviciana* Wilson. *Tanagra columbianus* of Jardine[3] was really a new name for *Tanagra ludoviciana* Bonaparte and *Piranga erythropis* Vieillot, that is to say *Tanagra ludoviciana* Wilson, and, in fact, is based on Wilson's description, specimen, and figure, and stated to have come from "Remote regions of Louisiana." Thus, it is merely a renaming of Wilson's bird, and, of course, of identical application. Since there are no other synonyms of this species, the more eastern race inhabiting the Rocky Mts. region is the one hitherto unnamed. It should now be called *P. l. zephrica*.

Birds from Idaho (particularly the w. part), Nevada, and e. Oregon are intermediate between this Rocky Mts. race and *ludoviciana*, but are nearer the latter to which also belong breeding birds from California.

[1] *Tanagra ludoviciana* Wilson, *Amer. Ornith.* 3 (1811 [after Feb. 12]): 27, pl. 10, fig. 1 (female).
[2] *Nouv. Dict. d'Hist. Nat.*, new ed. 28 (1819): 291.
[3] Wilson, *Amer. Ornith.*, Jardine ed., vol. 1 (1832), p. 317, pl. 19, fig. "2" [= 1] (female).

HEPATIC TANAGER, *Piranga flava*

A northern race of this species, named *P. f. oreophasma*, was originally described by the writer[1] from Pine Canyon at 6,000 ft. in the Chisos Mts. of Trans-Pecos Texas. It is a recognizable form differing from *hepatica* in larger size and relatively smaller bill; in the male, in darker upper (back more reddish) and lower parts; in the female, in rather darker coloration and on the average somewhat more grayish (less greenish) back. This race is by no means to be united with *dextra*, since it is so much larger —a character alone sufficient for its separation. Furthermore, the male is lighter both above and below; the female, lighter and less greenish above.

[1] *Auk* 36 (Jan., 1919): 74.

CARDINAL, *Richmondena cardinalis*

The Palo Duro Cardinal, *R. c. planicola*, differs from *canicauda* in its longer bill; shorter middle toe; darker and more olivaceous (less grayish) edgings on feathers of upper surface of male; and darker, more grayish (less brownish) upper parts of female. It was described by J. O. Stevenson.[1] His type is an adult female collected by T. F. Smith in Palo Duro Canyon, Elkins Ranch, 2 mi. north of Palo Duro State Park, Randall Co., Texas, Dec. 26, 1936.

[1] *Proc. Biol. Soc. Washington* 53 (Feb. 16, 1940): 16.

PYRRHULOXIA, *Pyrrhuloxia sinuata*

The Pyrrhuloxia from extreme w. Trans-Pecos Texas, principally the El Paso region, differs from the bird from the lower Rio Grande, *P. s. sinuata*, in decidedly larger size, particularly that of wing and tail, although in color it is practically identical. This larger bird ranges south to the city of San Luis Potosí, Mexico, and probably at least to w. Zacatecas.

It has already been shown that the type specimen of the species is the same as the bird found in the lower Rio Grande area, the only question being the exact locality from where it came—which seems not to be positively determinable. Van Rossem[1] thinks it came from Zacatecas, as indicated by Bonaparte, but if it came from this Mexican state it must have been obtained in the extreme eastern part, since birds from the remainder of that state and from w. San Luis Potosí are the same as the large birds found about El Paso. Be that as it may, there seems no doubt that the type of *Pyrrhuloxia sinuata* identifies with the lower Rio Grande bird, and the large birds from San Luis Potosí and Ahualulco in w. San Luis Potosí with those of the El Paso region. The name for this large bird is *P. s. beckhami*.[2] It was based on a type taken at El Paso, Texas, which the writer has examined.

[1] *Trans. San Diego Soc. Nat. Hist.* 7 (May 31, 1934): 356.
[2] *Auk* 4 (Oct., 1887): 347.

BLUE GROSBEAK, *Guiraca caerulea*

The Blue Grosbeak inhabiting c. Texas, herewith called *G. c. mesophila*, seems sufficiently different from the race from Arizona, *interfusa*,[1] to warrant subspecific separation. It differs from the typical eastern bird, *caerulea*, as indicated in the detailed account; however, in this, as in the other races, there is much individual variation in width and color of chestnut or buffy bars on the wing.

The Mexican Blue Grosbeak, *G. c. eurhyncha*, was originally described by Elliott Coues[2] to include the forms of this species from the s.w. United States. His type, a specimen apparently from c. Mexico, is marked with no more definite locality than the word "Mexico," but it agrees with the birds breeding in Veracruz, State of México, and Guanajuato. It seems desirable to provide a definite locality for the type specimen, which we, therefore, designate as the Valley of México. It is a very large bird of dark colors, similar to *caerulea*, but it is so much larger that it could not readily be mistaken for any other form occurring in the United States.

[1] Dwight and Griscom, *Amer. Mus. Novitates*, no. 257 (Mar. 14, 1927), p. 4.

[2] *G[oniaphea] coerulea* var. *eurhyncha* Coues, *Amer. Naturalist* 8 (Sept., 1874): 563 ("Mexico").

INDIGO BUNTING, *Linaria cyanea*

The generic name *Linaria* is another one of those originated by Bartram;[1] for an explanation of the use of his generic names see the Catbird. *Linaria* was based on "*Linaria ciris* [= *Emberiza ciris* Linnaeus]; the painted finch or nonpareil"; and *Linaria cyanea* (= *Tanagra cyanea* Linnaeus). Type of the genus, by subsequent designation of C. W. Richmond,[2] is *Tanagra cyanea* Linnaeus, which is the common Indigo Bunting of the e. United States. This bird, therefore, should be called *Linaria cyanea* (Linnaeus). Furthermore, *Linaria* should apply to those species closely allied to the Indigo Bunting—that is, the Lazuli, Varied, and Painted buntings.

Linaria is not citable from Edwards, since he does not use it in his edition of Catesby's work in a binary generic sense;[3] furthermore, it occurs in a reprint of Catesby's pre-Linnaean work. It is, however, used by Zimmerman,[4] although this name is subsequent to the binary name *Linaria* of Bartram.

[1] *Travels North and South Carolina, Georgia, East and West Florida* (1791), pp. 291, 299; 2nd ed. (1792), pp. 289, 297.
[2] *Proc. U.S. Nat. Mus.* 53 (Aug. 16, 1917): 599.
[3] Catesby, *Nat. Hist. Carolina, Florida, and Bahama Is.*, vol. 2 (1771), p. 45.
[4] *Mag. Merkw. Neuen Reisebeschreibungen* 10 (1793): 286.

LAZULI BUNTING, *Linaria amoena*

See Indigo Bunting.

VARIED BUNTING, *Linaria versicolor*

See Indigo Bunting.

PAINTED BUNTING, *Linaria ciris*

See Indigo Bunting.

EVENING GROSBEAK, *Hesperiphona vespertina*

The name *H. v. montana* Ridgway[1] was used for many years as the name for all western forms of the Evening Grosbeak, and the type was supposed to have come from Cantonment Burgwyn, near Taos, n. New Mexico, where collected by W. W. Anderson. When Joseph Grinnell[2] reviewed the species and described additional subspecies, he argued that because designation of type was not published in the original description of *montana* Ridgway and because the description seemed to apply better to the Mexican race commonly known as *mexicana*, the specimen in Baird, Brewer, and Ridgway's *History of North American Birds* (vol. 1, 1874, pl. 17, fig. 4) from Mirador, Veracruz, should be considered the type of *montana*. Consequently he transferred *montana* to the Mexican race, formerly known as *mexicana* (Chapman).[3]

However, in the U.S. National Museum collection there is an adult male of this species, no. 11960, from Cantonment Burgwyn, near Taos, New Mexico, collected June 3, 1859. The back of the label is marked in Robert Ridgway's handwriting, "type of supposed var. *montana*, R. R." On the face of the label there is added, also in his handwriting, "var. *montana*, Ridgw." Notwithstanding that the original description mentions no type

—only the locality "southern Rocky Mountains of the United States, and mountains of Mexico"—and that pl. 22, fig. 4 pictures "*Hesperiphona vespertina* var. *montana* Mex., 35150," there should seemingly be no doubt regarding the true type of *montana*. In the past, it has been common practice to describe birds without mentioning a type, although the actual type might be labeled and in the collection from which the writer drew up his description. Such designation and marking of types has been commonly accepted as valid.

If there were any further doubt that citation of the type was not published, it may be noted that E. A. Mearns[4] designated in print in 1890 this very specimen from Cantonment Burgwyn as the type. Under the circumstances, it seems justifiable to consider publication of a figure of a specimen, without other comment, as designation of the type. Thus, the specimen from Cantonment Burgwyn, New Mexico, should be accepted as the true type of *H. v. montana* Ridgway.

With this in view it will be necessary to revert to *H. v. montana* Ridgway for the bird Grinnell described as *H. v. warreni*.[5]

H. v. montana is subspecifically distinct from both *brooksi* and *mexicana*. The upper and lower parts are decidedly paler than in *brooksi*, this particularly obvious in the female, and especially the top of the head. Compared to *mexicana*, which occurs in s. Arizona, it may be distinguished by its larger size; heavier, less slender bill; the male with broader yellow forehead-band and somewhat more greenish (less golden) yellow body coloration; and the female with lighter, much more brownish (less grayish or olivaceous) tone of plumage, particularly below.

[1] Baird, Brewer, and Ridgway, *Hist. North Amer. Birds, Land Birds*, vol. 1 (Mar. 2, 1874), p. 449, pl. 22, fig. 4.
[2] *Condor* 19 (Jan. 15, 1917): 17–22.
[3] *Coccothraustes vespertinus mexicanus* Chapman, *Auk* 14 (July, 1897): 311 ("Las Vegas, Vera Cruz, Mexico").
[4] *Auk* 7 (July, 1890): 247.
[5] *Condor* 19 (Jan. 15, 1917): 21 ("Bear Creek, near Colorado Springs, Colorado").

PURPLE FINCH, *Erythrina purpurea*

The generic name *Carpodacus* Kaup[1] has been used for the Purple Finch and the other birds of this genus because *Erythrina* Brehm[2] has been considered preoccupied by *Erythrinus* Lacépède.[3] *Erythrina* Brehm has for its type, by monotypy, *Fringilla rosea* Pallas, since the only other species mentioned is *Erythrina rubrifrons*, here a nomen nudum. If names differing in grammatical endings be considered different, this name *Erythrina* Brehm should supplant *Carpodacus* Kaup. The Purple Finch, therefore, will be called *Erythrina purpurea*.

[1] *Skizz. Entwickel.-Gesch. Natürl. Syst. Eur. Thierwelt* (1829 [after Apr.]), p. 161 (type, *Fringilla rosea* Pallas, by subsequent designation of Gray, 1842).
[2] *Isis (von Oken)* 21 ([Dec.] 1828): column 1276.
[3] *Hist. Nat. Poiss.* 22 (1803): 347.

CASSIN'S FINCH, *Erythrina cassinii*

See Purple Finch for explanation of change of generic name from *Carpodacus* to *Erythrina*.

On account of the separation of a western subspecies, *E. c. vinifer* (Duvall), the Texas race will stand as *E. c. cassinii*.

HOUSE FINCH, *Erythrina mexicana*

By alteration of the generic name *Carpodacus* to *Erythrina*, as explained under the Purple Finch, the name of the House Finch becomes *Erythrina mexicana*.

House Finches inhabiting most of Trans-Pecos Texas, except-

ing the region along the Pecos River and in the neighborhood of the Guadalupe Mts., have been considered by R. T. Moore[1] as intermediate between the Common House Finch, *E. m. frontalis*, and the race from n.e. Mexico, *E. m. potosina*. These birds occupy a definite area, are readily separable by the characters described in the detailed account, and apparently represent a recognizable race, which is to be called *E. m. anconophila*. It differs from *potosina* in its decidedly lighter, more reddish (less grayish) upper parts; and in somewhat more extensively red lower surface.

Figgins' House Finch, *E. m. smithi*, described from n. central Colorado,[2] seems recognizably different from *frontalis*, described from the Arkansas River in Colorado, only a relatively short distance to the south.

[1] *Condor* 41 (Sept. 15, 1939): 189.
[2] *Carpodacus mexicanus smithi* Figgins, *Proc. Colorado Mus. Nat. Hist.* 9 (Apr. 22, 1930): 2 (near Aurora, Arapahoe Co., Colorado).

WHITE-COLLARED SEEDEATER, *Sporophila morelleti*

The intergradation supposed by some authors to exist between *S. morelleti* and *S. torqueola* is apparently due entirely to immature specimens, which comprise most of the representatives of these species in museum collections. Fully adult males of both these species show no approach at all. Such an "intergradation" is, of course, not indicative of subspecific relationship, and, therefore, *S. morelleti* should apparently best be considered a distinct species.

Birds of the present species that occur in Texas have commonly passed under the name *S. m. sharpei* Lawrence. This race is supposed to differ from the typical (nominate) Mexican bird in having black upper parts much mixed with white or buff, and a narrow or broken jugulum band. Careful study of a large series of skins from all parts of the species' range shows that the adult plumage—that is, the bird with solidly black upper parts, broad jugular band of black, and white instead of buff on other parts of the plumage—is relatively rare, and that various immature plumages make up a large part of male specimens found in collections. Differences that are supposed to distinguish *S. m. sharpei* from *S. m. morelleti* are exactly those that characterize males in immature plumage. While it is true that no specimens in the fully adult black and white plumage seem to have been taken in Texas, Robert Ridgway[1] is undoubtedly correct in his statement that birds occurring in Texas, so far as have been collected or observed, are merely immature representatives of *S. m. morelleti*. On this account, the characters distinguishing them from Mexican birds are certainly not satisfactory; therefore, the Texas birds should be called *S. m. moreletti*.

[1] *Bull. U.S. Nat. Mus.*, no. 50, pt. 1 (Oct. 24, 1901), pp. 575–576.

PINE SISKIN, *Spinus pinus*

The Western Pine Siskin was described by J. W. Aldrich from w. North America as *S. p. vagans*.[1] It appears to be a good form, although it wanders over most of the United States.

[1] *Proc. Biol. Soc. Washington* 59 (Oct. 25, 1946): 133 (Edna, Idaho).

GREEN-TAILED TOWHEE, *Oberholseria*[1] *chlorura*

The generic name *Chlorura* Sclater, currently in use for this species, is without much doubt preoccupied by *Chlorura* Reichenbach. The former generic term was proposed by P. L. Sclater in his *Catalogue of American Birds*, for the *Fringilla chlorura* of Audubon; his catalog did not appear until May, 1862. The *Chlorura* of Reichenbach, however, was published during early 1862, probably in March or April, on p. 33 of the first part of Reichenbach's *Singvögel* (the second part of which, comprising pp. 45–70, appeared on July 1, 1862, or soon thereafter). Thus, the generic designation on *Chlorura* Sclater should not be used for the Green-tailed Towhee. Incidentally, the generic name *Reichenowia*,[2] substituted for *Chlorura* Reichenbach because it was supposed to be preoccupied by *Chlorura* Sclater, should be retired in favor of *Chlorura* Reichenbach, now that the latter seems not to be invalidated.

The Oregon Green-tailed Towhee, *O. c. zapolia*, was described by the writer,[3] from a type obtained at Hart Mt., at the northern end of Warner Valley, 20 mi. northeast of Adel, Oregon.

[1] Although Oberholser clearly designated *Oberholseria* as the genus to be used for the Green-tailed Towhee, nowhere in his nomenclatural discussion of the species does he explain his reasoning for using this genus. He does, however, discuss his opinions on *Chlorura* Sclater vs. *Chlorura* Reichenbach; these are herewith given.—EDITOR
[2] Poche, *Ornith. Monatsberichte*, vol. 12, no. 2 (Feb., 1904), p. 26.
[3] *Scient. Publ. Cleveland Mus. Nat. Hist.* 4 (Sept. 19, 1932): 10.

RUFOUS-SIDED TOWHEE, *Hortulanus erythrophthalmus*

The generic name *Pipilo*, which is currently employed for the towhees of North America, was originally described by Vieillot;[1] its type is *Fringilla erythrophthalmus* Linnaeus. An earlier name by the same author is *Hortulanus*.[2] This name is based on figures of the bills of three species: *H. nigricollis*, *H. erythrophthalmus*, and *H. albicollis*. Several authors have discussed this name, and at least one, Witmer Stone, has proposed to adopt it for the towhees of North America. In this the present writer considers him fully justified. The type of this genus was fixed by Stone[3] as *Hortulanus erythrophthalmus* Vieillot (= *Fringilla erythrophthalma* Linnaeus). The figure of the bill given by Vieillot, which is accompanied by no other identification than the name *H. erythrophthalmus*, is, however, readily identifiable by comparison with the bill of the bird now known as *Pipilo erythrophthalmus*. Thus, there seems no alternative but to use the generic name *Hortulanus* Vieillot in place of *Pipilo* Vieillot.

[1] *Analyse Nouv. Ornith. Élémentaire* (1816), p. 32.
[2] *Hist. Nat. Oiseaux Amér. Sept.*, vol. 1 ([Dec.] 1807), pp. 3 and 4, pl. 1.
[3] *Auk* 24 (Apr. 10, 1907): 193.

BROWN TOWHEE, *Hortulanus fuscus*

The change of generic name of this species is made necessary by the use of *Hortulanus*, instead of *Pipilo*, as explained under the Rufous-sided Towhee.

The Pecos Brown Towhee differs from *H. f. texanus* (van Rossem) in larger size, particularly wing and tail; upper parts, including pileum, paler; flanks and sides lighter; buff throat darker. Birds from c. southern and s.w. New Mexico, as well as from the El Paso region, belong under *H. f. mesoleucus*. Birds from the Chisos Mts. are intermediate in coloration between the present race and *texanus*, which is somewhat darker than typical birds from the Davis Mts., but they are large and are probably better included in the present race. Since *mesoleucus* (Baird) applies to the Arizona bird, as already explained, the present race has hitherto had no subspecific designation. It is herewith called *H. f. aimophilus*.

SAVANNAH SPARROW, *Passerculus sandwichensis*

Investigations by J. W. Aldrich have shown that there are at least two races of Savannah Sparrow which have hitherto been combined under the eastern race, *P. s. savanna*. Comparison shows that the bird from Nova Scotia differs from the breeding bird of the n.e. United States in its lighter, more rufescent coloration. An examination of Wilson's original description and plate of this bird[1] shows clearly that he referred to the breeding bird of Nova Scotia, not to the one from n.e. United States; therefore, when division of this race is carried out, the name *savanna* should be restricted to the breeding birds of Nova Scotia and the Magdalen Islands, Quebec. Birds from the n.e. United States have been named by Aldrich *P. s. mediogriseus*.[2]

Breeding birds from New England are somewhat lighter and more buffy or rufescent than birds from Ohio, whence the new form has been described, and it may be subsequently advisable to recognize them as an additional race, but at present they are included with *mediogriseus*. This gives it a breeding range extending from New England and s.e. Canada west to the c. northern United States and the adjacent area of Canada. Farther northward it gradually merges into *oblitus*.

[1] *Fringilla Savanna* Wilson, *Amer. Ornith.* 3 (1811 [after Feb. 12]): 55, pl. 22, fig. 3 ("Savannah [Georgia]").
[2] *Ohio Journ. Science* 40 (Jan. 30, 1940): 4 (Andover, Ashtabula Co., Ohio).

BAIRD'S SPARROW, *Centronyx bairdii*

The present species, although commonly included in *Ammodramus* Swainson (type, *Ammodramus bimaculatus* Swainson), is structurally very distinct from the Grasshopper Sparrow, *Ammodramus savannarum*, and should be treated as a monotypic genus. From *Ammodramus* Swainson it may be distinguished as follows: nostril elongated (lengthened and pear-shaped, with pointed end in front), situated in lower anterior part of nasal fossa and strongly operculate (in *Ammodramus*, nostril is more rounded or triangular and situated in the middle or upper part of nasal fossa, and not operculate); four (second, third, fourth, and fifth) outer primaries sinuate on outer webs (instead of three); three outer primaries (first, second, and third) sinuate on inner webs (instead of two); fifth primary counting from outermost not decidedly longer than fourth (instead of abruptly shorter than fourth); hind toe longer than outer toe (instead of shorter), its claw longer than the distance from the anterior end of nostril to tip of maxilla (instead of shorter); and claw of hind toe (hallux) at least equal to length of hind toe, or longer (in *Ammodramus* decidedly shorter). From *Passerculus* it differs, among other characters, in having hind toe decidedly longer than outer toe; wing relatively shorter, exceeding length of tail by very little more than length of tarsus; and rectrices narrower, less acuminate. From other allied genera, such as *Ammospiza*, *Thryospiza*, *Passerherbulus*, and *Nemospiza*, it differs sufficiently not to need comparison in the present connection.[1]

The generic name for this group is *Centronyx* Baird,[2] of which the type is *Emberiza bairdii* Audubon.

[1] See Ridgway, *Bull. U.S. Nat. Mus.*, no. 50, pt. 1 (Oct. 24, 1901), pp. 34–35.
[2] *Report Explor. and Surv. R. R. Pacific* 9 (1858): 440.

HENSLOW'S SPARROW, *Nemospiza henslowii*

In structural characters this species is very different from the LeConte's Sparrow, with which it is commonly associated in the genus *Passerherbulus*. Its very short, stout bill, compared to the rather slender bill of the LeConte's, separates it at a glance. It differs from *Passerherbulus* (type, *Emberiza leconteii* Audubon) as follows: tail decidedly shorter than wing, instead of about equal or slightly longer; first primary (counting from outermost) shorter than fifth, instead of longer; bill short and very stout; wing only 4.5 times exposed culmen, instead of 5–5.5 times; length of exposed culmen 1.5–1.75 times height of bill at base, instead of about 2; height of bill at base about equal to length of gonys, instead of decidedly less. There seems to be no reason for not recognizing the Henslow's Sparrow as a monotypic genus. This was pointed out by the writer[1] many years ago when he proposed for this species the generic name *Nemospiza*.

[1] *Ohio Journ. Science* 17 (June 2, 1917): 335.

SEASIDE SPARROW, *Thryospiza maritima*

The various races of the Seaside Sparrow making up the species *Fringilla maritima* Wilson, together with the Dusky Seaside Sparrow, *Ammodramus maritimus* var. *nigrescens* Ridgway, currently included in *Ammospiza* Oberholser, are very distinct in structural characters from the other birds commonly associated in the same generic group. Therefore, they should be segregated generically. This group differs from *Ammospiza* as follows: tail longer, about .9 length of wing; first primary (counting from outermost) shorter than seventh, usually about equal to eighth, instead of longer than sixth; bill much lengthened and less stout; length of exposed culmen 2.25–2.5 times height of bill at base, instead of only about 2; and exposed culmen about equal to middle toe without claw, instead of very much less. The writer[1] many years ago called attention to these differences in segregating this generic group, and in providing it with the generic name *Thryospiza* (type, *Fringilla maritima* Wilson).

Ludlow Griscom[2] has attempted to prove invalid one of his own subspecies, *T. m. howelli*. He contends that all its characters are based on individual variation; therefore, there is no racial difference between birds of this species inhabiting s. Alabama, *howelli*, and those native to coastal Louisiana, *fisheri*.

The Seaside Sparrow group is a difficult one, partly because nearly all the races have two well-marked color phases, which intergrade completely with each other and with the phases of other subspecies. The result is a somewhat bewildering aggregation of plumages. In attempting to sort these into subspecific order, it is necessary to make comparisons with individuals in corresponding phases. Even so, there frequently occur specimens that are difficult, or nearly impossible, to place subspecifically with certainty. However, this condition is present in all complex specific groups, particularly in those whose individual variation is wide.

In the case of *howelli* and *fisheri*, a comparison of a large series of each indicates, to the present writer at least, that there is a discernible average difference in breeding specimens that warrants their being considered distinct subspecies. The most appreciable characters separating *howelli* from *fisheri* are its lighter, more grayish (less buffy or ochraceous), and less heavily black-streaked or spotted upper parts; usually paler buff jugulum; and especially, the larger bill. From *sennetti* it is also told by its larger bill, as well as by its darker, more blackish (less olivaceous) coloration.

[1] *Ohio Journ. Science* 17 (June 2, 1917): 332.
[2] *Occas. Papers Mus. Zool. Univ. Louisiana*, no. 19 (Dec. 10, 1944), pp. 319–321, 327.

VESPER SPARROW, *Pooecetes gramineus*

The Northern Vesper Sparrow, *P. g. polius*, was first discovered by F. W. Braund and J. W. Aldrich[1] in n. Michigan. It is an interesting race of relatively limited geographic distribution, which has been detected in Texas.

Specimens of the Great Basin Vesper Sparrow, *P. g. definitus*, are usually readily separable from *confinis*, by the much smaller amount of white in the tail, both on outermost feathers and on inner margin of second tail feather from outside. *P. g. confinis* nearly always has a readily observable white spot; however, in *definitus* there is usually no white except sometimes as a very narrow tip or whitish edging. The original description of *confinis*[2] was based on a type specimen from Loup Fork of the Platte River in c. Nebraska; it is an example of the race inhabiting the Great Plains and the Rocky Mts. Birds from Idaho are intermediate between the Great Basin and Great Plains races, but are slightly nearer *confinis*. *P. g. definitus* was described by the writer[3] from specimens obtained at Twenty-Mile Creek, Warner Valley, 9 mi. south of Adel, Oregon.

[1] *Oologist* 58 (Sept. [late Oct.], 1941): 104 (4 mi. north of Newberry, Luce Co., Michigan).
[2] Baird, Cassin, and Lawrence, *Report Explor. and Surv. R. R. Pacific* 9 (1858): 448.
[3] *Scient. Publ. Cleveland Mus. Nat. Hist.* 4 (Sept. 19, 1932): 11.

LARK SPARROW, *Chondestes grammacus*

The Texas Lark Sparrow, *C. g. quillini*—specimens of which have usually been identified as *strigatus*—is sufficiently different from birds breeding west of Texas to indicate its subspecific distinctness. It is the only breeding race in e. Texas to the exclusion of typical *C. g. grammacus*, and also in the remainder of the state, except in extreme w. Trans-Pecos. Birds from e. Trans-Pecos are intermediate between *quillini* and *strigatus*, but apparently are nearer the former.

RUFOUS-CROWNED SPARROW, *Aimophila ruficeps*

The Guadalupe Mts. race of this species was described by T. D. Burleigh and G. H. Lowery, Jr., as *A. r. tenuirostra*.[1] It is most closely allied to *eremoeca* of c. Texas, but differs as indicated in the detailed account. It is also different from *scottii* in its more slender bill, and decidedly darker and much less rufescent upper surface.

This new race apparently has a very limited distribution, being confined chiefly to s. New Mexico and n. Culberson Co., Texas. Birds from the Davis Mts., a short distance south of the Guadalupes, are to be referred to *scottii*, from which this race differs in color in the same manner as does *eremoeca*.

[1] *Occas. Papers Mus. Zool. Louisiana State Univ.*, no. 6 (Nov. 10, 1939), p. 67 (McKittrick Canyon, 5,500 ft., Guadalupe Mts., Culberson Co., Texas).

BLACK-THROATED SPARROW, *Amphispiza bilineata*

A new race from the Chisos Mts., *A. b. dapolia*, appears to be different from all surrounding races in Trans-Pecos Texas and c. northern Mexico. From *grisea* Nelson[1] it may be distinguished by its smaller size; paler and still more grayish upper parts. From *opuntia*,[2] it differs in smaller size and darker color. Birds from the Del Carmen Mts., n. Coahuila, belong also to *dapolia*.

[1] *Proc. Biol. Soc. Washington* 12 (Mar. 24, 1898): 61 ("Tula, Hidalgo, Mexico").
[2] Burleigh and Lowery, *Occas. Papers Mus. Zool. Louisiana State Univ.*, no. 6 (Nov. 10, 1939), p. 68 (10 mi. east of Frijole, Guadalupe Mts., Culberson Co., Texas).

SAGE SPARROW, *Amphispiza belli*

The Idaho Sage Sparrow, *A. b. campicola*, inhabits the n. Great Basin. Birds from c. northern Oregon are somewhat smaller than those from s. Idaho, but are of the same color, and should apparently be referred to this subspecies. Specimens examined from Warner Valley, c. southern Oregon, and from Nevada belong to *nevadensis*. Examples from c. western Nevada are smaller; also more grayish, and darker above than *nevadensis*, and verge so much toward *canescens*, of s.e. California, that they probably should be referred to that race.

The original description of the Sage Sparrow was based on the bird from the West Humboldt Mts., Nevada.[1] The type from this region, now in the U.S. National Museum, has been examined and proves to be an example of the light, sandy-colored southern race, so that name will apply to the Nevada race, leaving the large, dark-colored northern bird without any subspecific designation; this lack the present writer[2] has supplied in *A. b. campicola*.

[1] *Poospiza bellii* var. *nevadensis* Ridgway, *Bull. Essex Inst.* 5 (Nov., 1873): 191.
[2] *Journ. Washington Acad. Sci.* 36 (Nov. 15, 1946): 388 (6 mi. south of Hamer, Jefferson Co., Idaho).

OREGON JUNCO, *Junco oreganus*

Coues' Oregon Junco, *J. o. eumesus*, is the lighter, more grayish (less rufescent) race that some authors, following Jonathan Dwight, have called *J. o. couesi*. It was originally described by Dwight,[1] and his type was a specimen taken at Okanagan, c. southern British Columbia. That he intended to name the more grayish bird—as contrasted with the rufescent race, *shufeldti*—is evident from his statements, but unfortunately he chose a type specimen representing an example of *shufeldti*, although intermediate between that and the race he intended to describe. Therefore, *couesi* must be regarded as a synonym of *shufeldti*, and the grayish bird needs another name, which is herewith provided.

While the range of *eumesus* occupies e. Oregon, e. Washington, w. Alberta, and e. British Columbia, and is interposed between the ranges of *shufeldti* and *montanus*, it seems sufficiently different from either to have a name of its own. The type of the bird described by Elliott Coues as *Junco hyemalis connectens*,[2] which came from Colorado City, Colorado, has been carefully examined and compared in the present connection, and seems without doubt to be an immature specimen, evidently in first autumn plumage, of the Eastern Slate-colored Junco, *J. h. hyemalis*; frequently individuals in this plumage show as much brownish or pinkish tinge on the sides and flanks as does this specimen. This same conclusion has been held by many previous authors, including Dwight; therefore, this name is not applicable to the race that Dwight intended when he named *J. o. couesi*.

There is much individual variation in *shufeldti*, amounting to a grayish and a rufescent phase, even on the coast where this race is most nearly typical. At Port Angeles, Washington, a bird much like *thurberi* occurs with one that is very hard to distinguish from the grayish brown race here described as *J. o. eumesus*. In the Maury Mts., w. central Oregon, there occur occasional adult males in summer which are as grayish as birds from e. Oregon, but nearly all are of the rufescent *shufeldti* type. These grayish birds are evidently those to which Dwight[3] applied the name *Junco transmontanus*, considering them hybrids between *J. o. oreganus* and *J. h. hyemalis*. Instead, they are merely individual variants of *J. o. shufeldti*, to which the writer restricts the name *transmontanus*, incidentally proposed by Dwight, to avoid future nomenclatural confusion. Birds from c. Oregon east

of the Cascades, as a group, seem intermediate between *shufeldti* and *eumesus*, but are decidedly nearer the former.

Characters further distinguishing *eumesus* are as follows: similar to *shufeldti*, but male with head and throat not so intensely black, instead duller, more grayish or slaty; upper parts decidedly duller, more grayish (much less rufescent) brown; female has more grayish (less blackish) head, and more grayish (less rufescent) brown back. Compared with *montanus*, the male has darker pileum and throat—much more blackish (less grayish); the female has darker slate throat, and usually somewhat more rufescent (less clearly grayish) back.

[1] Dwight, *Bull. Amer. Mus. Nat. Hist.*, vol. 38, article 9 (June 1, 1918), p. 291.
[2] *J[unco] h[iemalis] connectens* Coues, *Key to North Amer. Birds*, 2nd ed. (1884), p. 378.
[3] Loc. cit., p. 295.

PINK-SIDED JUNCO, *Junco mearnsi*

Some authors treat *J. mearnsi* as a subspecies of *J. oreganus*, ostensibly on account of the former's intergradation with *J. o. montanus*. However, ranges of *J. o. montanus* and *J. mearnsi* overlap over a considerable area in Idaho and in parts of w. Montana; these two juncos and intermediates in these areas occur in the breeding season in such a manner as to indicate hybridism much more strongly than subspecific intergradation. These and several other juncos are known to hybridize rather frequently; thus, in this case it seems more in accord with facts to consider the Pink-sided Junco a distinct species.

GRAY-HEADED JUNCO, *Junco caniceps*

Since the supposed intergradation of this junco with *J. dorsalis* is better explained by hybridism, its technical name should not be a trinomial.

RED-BACKED JUNCO, *Junco dorsalis*

This species is currently regarded as a race of *J. caniceps* or *J. phaeonotus*, or of both. The range of *J. dorsalis*, though complementary to these other forms, shows no locality at which "real intermediates" are to be found. In localities nearest the range of both *J. caniceps* and *J. phaeonotus palliatus*, the Red-backed Junco is just as different from them as elsewhere. It is readily distinguished from *J. caniceps* by its longer tail; much larger bill, the maxilla of which is blackish (instead of pale like the maxilla in *J. caniceps*); and much paler anterior lower parts, with much less sharply defined line of demarcation between jugulum and breast (i.e., the slightly darker gray of the anterior parts merges almost imperceptibly into whitish of posterior portion). The character of the maxilla is entirely constant in adult birds; while there is some variation in the sharpness of demarcation between jugulum and breast in *J. caniceps* this is due largely to condition of plumage. In these characters there are but few intermediate breeding individuals, and these only in n.w. New Mexico where the ranges of these juncos overlap. These intermediates, furthermore, have much more the character of hybrids than of geographic subspecific intergrades, since typical examples of these two species occur in the same breeding localities.

So far as *J. p. palliatus* is concerned, *J. dorsalis* has a decidedly longer wing and tail, and decidedly larger bill, with a flesh-colored or whitish, instead of yellow, mandible; brown, instead of bright yellow, iris; and rufous of the upper surface confined to the back, whereas in *J. p. palliatus* the scapulars, tertials, and wing-coverts are also rufous. In the restriction of rufous and color of mandible and of eye there have been no actual intermediates so far as it has been possible to determine. From these facts it seems much better to consider *J. dorsalis* as a distinct species.

CHIPPING SPARROW, *Spizella passerina*

The California Chipping Sparrow, *S. p. stridula*, originally described by Joseph Grinnell,[1] occupies most of the U.S. Pacific coast. Birds inhabiting s. Oregon and Washington, though rather light and somewhat larger—thus verging toward *arizonae*—are likewise nearer *stridula*, as are birds from n.w. Montana (St. Mary's Lake), and Nevada.

[1] *Condor* 29 (Jan. 15, 1927): 81 (Pasadena, Los Angeles Co., California).

FIELD SPARROW, *Spizella pusilla*

The breeding Field Sparrows of Texas differ from the Eastern Field Sparrow, *S. p. pusilla*, in the characters already presented, although they have hitherto been grouped with this race. Breeding birds from most of Kansas, w. Arkansas, and Oklahoma belong also to this present race, although those from Kansas and Arkansas are somewhat intermediate between it and typical *pusilla*. It is interesting to note that C. W. Richmond[1] long ago called attention to the paler coloration of the Texas bird. Since no name seems available for this Texas race, the writer dedicates it to Vernon Bailey; henceforth it is to be called *S. p. vernonia*.

The Nebraska Field Sparrow, *S. p. perissura*, is most closely allied to *arenacea* from North Dakota, but is less pale and more rufescent (less grayish), the rufous edgings broader and decidedly darker, particularly on the head.

[1] *Auk* 14 (Oct., 1897): 347.

WHITE-CROWNED SPARROW, *Zonotrichia leucophrys*

Geographic distribution of a new race from Idaho, *Z. l. aphaea*, is isolated from both *leucophrys* and *oriantha* by low country unsuitable for this species in the breeding season. It differs from *oriantha* in decidedly darker and more grayish upper and lower parts, particularly hindneck, back, rump, breast, and flanks. Immature birds in the brown-headed plumage have relative characters similar to those of adults. A good series of this subspecies from Idaho has been available for comparison with the other races.

GAMBEL'S SPARROW, *Zonotrichia gambelii*

This bird is commonly considered a race of the White-crowned Sparrow, *Z. leucophrys*. Study of a very large number of skins indicates that intermediates are few and far between and that many of these are apparent intermediates due to the preparation of the specimen. Furthermore, *Z. leucophrys* breeds over considerable areas on the same ground with *Z. gambelii*, notably in the mountains between e. British Columbia and w. Alberta, and along Hudson Bay from Churchill to the York Factory region and Fort Severn, also probably over areas between these localities. In view of these facts it seems logical to consider the two distinct species. It is obvious also that species as closely allied as these and living on the same ground might occasionally hybridize, and this would account for the supposed intermediates that are sometimes found.

WHITE-THROATED SPARROW, *Zonotrichia pensylvanica*

The very appropriate specific name of this sparrow, *albicollis*, must now apparently be changed. As both McAtee and Peters have shown, there is an earlier designation by Linnaeus in an overlooked article, already discussed under the Magnolia Warbler. This is *Passer pensylvanica* Linnaeus;[1] as a consequence, the technical name will become *Zonotrichia pensylvanica* (Linnaeus).

[1] A Cat. Birds, Beasts, Fishes, Insects, Plants, etc., p. 13, pl. 304 (Pennsylvania, near Philadelphia). In: Edwards' *Natural History*, 7 vols. (1776).

SONG SPARROW, *Melospiza melodia*

A Massachusetts subspecies, *M. m. callima*—although commonly considered the same as the typical eastern race, *melodia*—is decidedly different as indicated in the detailed account.

The Song Sparrow of the upper Mississippi Valley is a recognizable race which differs from *euphonia* as indicated in the detailed account. It is separable from *juddi* by its smaller size; more slender bill; darker upper surface, with usually smaller blackish spots; and more grayish (less creamy or buffy white) superciliary stripe. It is apparently most typical in Wisconsin, although it breeds also in Minnesota and much of Michigan. Specimens from s. Michigan (Washtenaw, Jackson, and Livingston cos.) verge slightly toward the dark bird inhabiting Ohio, *melanchra*, but are decidedly nearer *beata*. Birds from Fort Snelling and Elk River, Minnesota, incline a little toward *juddi*, but are smaller, darker, and have mostly less conspicuous black spots on the upper surface. They are thus decidedly nearer *beata*. Specimens from Lake Abitibi, c. eastern Ontario, verge toward *melodia*, but are nearer *beata*. Likewise, breeding birds from the s.w. part of s.e. Ontario (i.e., from Strathroy, Lambton Co.) and from Lac Seul and Kapuskasing, c. Ontario, are to be referred to the present race. The original description of *beata*[1] was based on a specimen obtained at Enterprise, Florida, thus a winter bird. It is an adult male, no. 44704 in Museum of Comparative Zoology collection, taken Apr. 17, 1859. Careful comparison with breeding birds from Wisconsin shows that it is identical, differing from the breeding bird of North Dakota, *juddi*, in the proper characters that distinguish these two races. This specimen has been carefully compared at least three times by the present writer with the same result; while it is rather large for the birds which breed in Wisconsin it is otherwise clearly identical with them.

[1] Bangs, *Proc. New England Zool. Club* 4 (June 5, 1912): 85.

SMITH'S LONGSPUR, *Calcarius pictus*

The Northwestern Smith's Longspur, *C. p. roweorum*, was described by Emerson Kemsies[1] from a specimen collected by Tom Brown at Anaktuvik, Alaska, June 4, 1949.

[1] *Canadian Field Notes* 75 (July–Sept. [Aug. 15], 1961): 148.

APPENDIX B: Glossary of Colors

Since Robert Ridgway's books may be unavailable to many who use the present work, and since many colors bear names that give no clue to their character, the following brief description of the more important colors is provided. Those marked with an asterisk (°) are not illustrated in Ridgway's *Color Standards and Color Nomenclature* but occur in his *Nomenclature of Colors for Naturalists*. Those marked with a dagger (†) do not occur in either but are added because of their importance.

Acajou red: Dark dull red; similar to brick red but more purplish.

Alice blue: Grayish blue; lighter and rather more greenish than tyrian blue.

Alizarine pink: Light old rose.

Amber brown: Dark yellowish brown; rather more reddish than sudan brown.

Amber yellow: Rather dull, somewhat buffy yellow; a little lighter than wax yellow.

American green: Dull, moderately dark, somewhat bluish green; darker, less grayish, and slightly more bluish than sage green.

Amethyst violet: Pure, bright, slightly reddish violet.

Amparo blue: Rather light blue with a slight purplish tinge.

Analine black: Very dark purplish black.

Analine yellow: Very dull, rather dark yellow; much darker and duller than light cadmium.

Andover green: Rather dark, very dull, grayish green; rather more yellowish than sage green.

Anthracene purple: Dark, very dull purple.

Antimony yellow: Rather light yellow ocher.

Antique brown: Dark yellowish brown; much darker than raw sienna; more yellowish than sudan brown.

Antique green: Dark green; somewhat more bluish than cossack green.

Apple green: Light, rather dull, slightly yellowish green.

Apricot buff: Rather light tint of apricot orange; darker than salmon buff but of same hue.

Apricot orange: Dull, slightly brownish orange.

Apricot yellow: Pure, rather orange yellow; somewhat paler than light cadmium.

Argus brown: Yellowish brown; darker than amber brown.

Army brown: Dark fawn color.

Aster purple: Dark rhodamine purple.

Auburn: Dark reddish brown; similar to chestnut but slightly less reddish (more yellowish).

Avellaneous: Decidedly pinkish light drab; similar to wood brown but lighter.

Azure blue:° Clear blue; somewhat lighter than spectrum blue and slightly more greenish.

Barium yellow: Light yellow; similar to straw yellow but somewhat less buffy (more clearly yellow).

Baryta yellow: Light, clear buffy yellow; slightly more buffy than martius yellow.

Bay: Dark reddish brown; somewhat less yellowish than chestnut.

Begonia rose: Pure, deep reddish pink; much lighter than spectrum red and derived from this color by addition of white.

Benzo brown: Rather light fuscous.

Berlin blue: Very dark, slightly greenish blue.

Beryl green: Moderately light, decidedly bluish green.

Bice green: Rather light forest green.

Biscay green: Dark, slightly yellowish apple green.

Bister: Dull, dark yellowish brown.

Bittersweet orange: Pure, rather reddish orange; somewhat lighter than flame scarlet but of same hue.

Bittersweet pink: Moderately light, pure pink, with a decided salmon tinge.

Blackish brown: Very dark, dull brown; very slightly more purplish than fuscous black; barely lighter than black.

Blackish mouse gray: Very dark mouse gray; almost black.

Blackish red-purple: Very deep reddish purple.

Blackish slate: Deep slate color.

Blanc blue: Dark dull blue; very slightly greenish.

Blue violet: Pure, moderately dark bluish violet.

Bluish black: Black with a bluish tinge.

Bluish glaucous: Very light grayish, somewhat greenish blue-green; more greenish than pale glaucous blue.

Bluish gray-green: Moderately light, dull, slightly bluish green.

Bluish violet: Pure, brilliant, slightly bluish violet of moderate darkness.

Bone brown: Dark, dull, very slightly vinaceous brown; produced from fawn color by addition of 87 percent black.

Bordeaux: Dark purplish red.

Bottle green: Very dark, slightly bluish green.

Brazil red: Dark dull scarlet.

Bremen blue: Moderately light greenish blue; more bluish than beryl green.

Brick red: Dark, dull, slightly orange red.

Broccoli brown:° Very slightly vinaceous hair brown.

Brownish black:† Black with very slight brownish tinge.

Brownish drab: Moderately light drab with a decided vinaceous tinge.

Brownish olive: Dark olive with a decided brownish tinge.

Brownish slate:† Slate color tinged with brown.

Brussels brown: Dark yellowish brown; slightly more yellowish than argus brown.

Buckthorn brown: Rather dark, dull yellowish brown; yellow ocher with addition of black.

Buff:° Light, decidedly yellowish orange; about halfway between pale yellow and pale orange.

Buff pink: Light onionskin pink.

Buff yellow: Buffy yellow; somewhat deeper than maize yellow.

Buffy brown: Very dull brown; similar to hair brown but decidedly more buffy; similar to army brown but decidedly less vinaceous.

Buffy citrine: Dull, rather light, decidedly yellowish olive; darker and somewhat more greenish than old gold.

Buffy olive: Light olive with a slightly more buffy appearance.

Burn blue: Very light columbia blue.

Burnt carmine:° Dull carmine; rather brighter than acajou red.

Burnt sienna: Rather light chestnut.

Burnt umber: Very dark, dull, somewhat vinaceous brown.

Cacao brown: Rather light walnut brown.

Cadet blue: Rather bright, moderately light grayish blue.

Cadet gray: Very dull, rather light blue-gray.

Cadmium orange: Brilliant deep orange.

Cadmium yellow: Rather light, yellowish orange.

Calamine blue: Light, somewhat greenish blue.

Calla green: Dark yellowish green; somewhat darker and more yellowish than light green.

Calliste green: Rather dark, dull yellowish green.

Cameo brown: Dark, dull vinaceous brown; rather more reddish than walnut brown.

Canary yellow:° Rather dull yellow; slightly more buff than lemon yellow.

Capri blue: Rather dark, greenish blue; darker than bremen blue.

Capucine buff: Light orange buff.

Capucine orange: Light cadmium orange.

Capucine yellow: Rather light orange.

Carmine: Deep, rather dull rich red; somewhat darker than spectrum red.

Carnelian red: Dull orange-red; slightly more reddish than rufous.

Cartridge buff: Very light, somewhat yellowish buff.

Cedar green: Rather dark, somewhat yellowish green; less yellowish than spinach green but decidedly more yellowish than cossack green.

Cendre blue: Rather light greenish blue; darker than calamine blue.

Cerro green: Dark yellowish green; darker than light green; somewhat less yellowish than calla green.

Cerulean blue: Bright, pure, slightly greenish blue.

Chaetura black: Very dark, slightly olivaceous brown; almost black.

Chaetura drab: Light chaetura black; similar to fuscous but slightly more olivaceous (less vinaceous).

Chalcedony yellow: Rather light greenish yellow.

Chamois: Dull, rather light yellowish buff; darker than cream buff; lighter than honey yellow.

Chessylite blue: Dark, dull greenish blue; more greenish than blanc blue.

Chestnut: Dark reddish brown; rather lighter and more yellowish than bay.

Chestnut brown: Dark hazel.

China blue: Light chessylite blue.

Chinese orange:° Rather dark, somewhat more yellowish orange chrome.

Chocolate: Very dark, decidedly vinaceous brown; similar to burnt umber but somewhat more vinaceous.

Chrome yellow:° Bright, rather orange yellow; between light cadmium and lemon chrome.

Chromium green: Rather dark, decidedly dull yellowish green.

Chrysolite green: Grayish, dull, rather light, decidedly yellowish green.

Cinereous: Light plumbeous.

Cinnamon: Dull, rather light yellowish brown; more vinaceous than clay color.

Cinnamon brown: Dark, rather dull yellowish brown.

Cinnamon buff: Light clay color; more yellowish (less vinaceous) than cinnamon.

Cinnamon drab: Drab with a vinaceous tinge.

Cinnamon rufous: Rather dark, dull yellowish rufous; rather lighter and more pinkish than tawny; apricot orange dulled with black.

Citrine: Dark, dull greenish yellow; less orange-tinged than orange citrine; sulphine yellow with addition of black; lighter and more orange-tinged than olive green.

Citrine drab: Rather light, decidedly grayish citrine.

Citron yellow: Rather light, slightly greenish yellow; dark barium yellow.

Claret brown: Very dark reddish brown; slightly more orange than maroon.

Clay color: Dull, buffy, grayish yellow ocher; similar to cinnamon but more yellowish.

Clear green-blue gray: Bluish gray with greenish tinge; of same hue as green-blue slate but much lighter.

Clove brown: Very dark, dull brown; slightly tinged with vinaceous.

Cobalt blue:° Bright blue with very slight tinge of green, and slightly dull; otherwise similar to spectrum blue.

Colonial buff: Rather light yellowish buff; more yellowish than cream buff; more buffy than primrose yellow.

Columbia blue: Rather light grayish blue; less greenish than alice blue.

Coral pink: Rather dull, slightly orange-tinged pink; a diluted coral red.

Coral red: Dull, moderately light orange-red; slightly more reddish than carnelian red.

Corinthian red: Dull vinaceous red; much duller than jasper red.

Cossack green: Very dark, slightly yellowish green.

Court gray: Very light, dull greenish gray.

Cream buff: Rather yellowish buff; darker than cartridge buff.

Cream color: Very light, dull buffy yellow or yellowish buff.

Cream white:† White with a creamy tinge.

Cress green: Dark, dull, rather yellowish green.

Crimson:° Rather dark carmine.

Dahlia carmine: Dark, dull reddish purple.

Danube green: Very dark, decidedly dull green; very slightly bluish.

Dark citrine: Dark, somewhat greenish (less yellowish) citrine; decidedly more orange-tinged than olive green.

Dark dull yellow-green: Very dark, dull yellowish green; darker and less yellowish than cress green; more yellowish than danube green.

Dark grayish brown: Dark dull brown; similar to fuscous but slightly more purplish; of similar hue as vinaceous drab but much darker.

Dark greenish olive: Dark yellowish olive.

Dark gull gray: Dark shade of gull gray; darker than deep gull gray; of same hue as slate gray but lighter.

Dark mouse gray: Mouse gray darkened by mixture of black, producing a very dark shade of dull gray.

Dark neutral gray: Neutral gray darkened with 70 percent black.

Dark olive buff: Similar to citrine drab but decidedly lighter and more olive yellowish.

Dark quaker drab: Dark shade of quaker drab.

Dark vinaceous drab: Similar to vinaceous drab but darker.

Dawn gray: Light, rather olivaceous gray.

Deep blue violet: Rather dark blue violet.

Deep brownish drab: Darker shade of brownish drab.

Deep chrome: Pure, rather light cadmium yellow.

Deep colonial buff: Dark colonial buff; similar to chamois but more yellowish.

Deep grayish olive: Dull olivaceous gray; about as dark as hair brown but with much more of an olive tinge.

Deep green-blue gray: Rather light, very dull bluish gray with a slight greenish tinge.

Deep gull gray: Rather dark gull gray.

Deep mouse gray: Rather dark mouse gray.

Deep neutral gray: Rather dark neutral gray.

Deep olive: A shade of citrine drab; rather lighter, more grayish (less greenish) than olive.

Deep olive gray: Moderately light, dull, somewhat greenish gray.

Deep plumbeous: Rather dark plumbeous.

Deep slate blue: Dark, dull grayish blue; much more bluish than slate color.

Delft blue: Rather dark, dull grayish blue with a very slight greenish tinge; slightly more greenish than slate blue; lighter than deep slate blue.

Diamin-azo blue: Very dark, dull violet blue.

Diva blue: Rather dark, somewhat dull violet blue.

Drab: Very dull, moderately light, somewhat vinaceous grayish brown.

Drab gray: Very light, rather grayish drab.

Dragon's blood red: Rather dark coral red; somewhat lighter and brighter than brick red.

Dresden brown: Dark yellowish brown; less reddish and duller than cinnamon brown; a dark buckthorn brown.

Dull citrine: Light olive citrine.

Dull violet black: Dull black with decided violet tinge.

Dusky blue: Very dark, dull blue; very slightly purplish.

Dusky dull bluish green: Very dark, dull bluish green; between dusky dull green and dark delft blue—more bluish than the former, more greenish than the latter.

Dusky dull green: Very dark, dull, slightly bluish green; less so than dusky dull bluish green.

Dusky dull violet: Very dark, dull, slightly bluish violet.

Dusky dull violet blue: Very dark, dull blue violet or violet blue; somewhat more violet-tinged than diamin-azo blue.

Dusky greenish blue: Dark, rather dull blue; less greenish than dark chessylite blue, but more greenish than dark cadet blue.

Dusky neutral gray: Very dark shade of neutral gray.

Dusky olive green: Very dark, dull green; darker and somewhat less yellowish than olive green.

Dusky slate violet: Very dark, dull violet, almost blackish.

Dusky violet: Very dark, somewhat dull violet.

Dusky yellowish green: Very dark, dull, somewhat yellowish green.

Dutch blue: Moderately light bluish gray; somewhat more violet-hued than cadet gray.

Ecru drab: Somewhat vinaceous drab gray.

Ecru olive: Light, somewhat yellowish olive.

Emerald green: Bright, rather light pure green.

Empire yellow: Rather light lemon chrome; also similar to lemon yellow but slightly more tinged with orange.

English red: Dark, rather dull orange-red; darker than grenadine red.

Eosine pink: Rather deep, purely reddish pink; lighter than begonia rose.

Eugenia red: Rather dark old rose; similar to jasper red but more purplish.

Eupatorium purple: Moderately light, but dull, pinkish purple.

Fawn color: Moderately light vinaceous brown; still more vinaceous than wood brown.

Ferruginous: Rather dark, dull, slightly reddish orange-brown; darker and duller than rufous; lighter, more pinkish than hazel.

Flame scarlet: Bright orange scarlet; somewhat more orange than even grenadine red.

Flax flower blue: Rather light, slightly purplish blue.

Flesh color: Rather buffy pink.

Flesh ocher: Light rufous.

Flesh pink: Light, rather yellowish pink; a very light tint of coral red.

Fluorite green: Grayish, otherwise pure, green, moderately light; darker and very slightly more yellowish than malachite green.

Forest green: Dark, dull, slightly yellowish green.

French blue:° Near smalt blue but slightly lighter and somewhat less purplish.

French gray: Light cinereous.

French green: Moderately dark, decidedly dull green.

Fuscous: Dark, dull, very slightly vinaceous brown; warmer and darker than hair brown; slightly less olivaceous than chaetura drab.

Fuscous black: Blackish fuscous.

Gallstone yellow:° Dull, slightly orange yellow; between primuline yellow and old gold—darker than the former, lighter than the latter.

Gamboge yellow:° Bright yellow; slightly more orange than lemon chrome and very slightly duller.

Garnet brown: Rich dark red; somewhat lighter than maroon; darker than nopal red.

Gentian blue: Rather dark, grayish purple-blue.

Geranium pink: Rich pure pink with a very slight orange tinge, differing in this respect from eosine pink; lighter than rose doree; darker than la france pink.

Geranium red:° Rather light scarlet red.

Glaucous: Very light, dull, slightly bluish green.

Glaucous blue: Rather light, dull, grayish, somewhat greenish blue; similar to alice blue but decidedly more greenish.

Glaucous gray: Pale, greenish blue-gray.

Glaucous green: Rather light grayish green.

Gobelin blue: Moderately light, dull greenish blue.

Grass green: Dark, somewhat yellowish green.

Grayish olive: Medium gray with a dull, decidedly olivaceous tinge.

Green-blue gray:† Any light tone of green-blue slate; several tones of this color are named respectively "dark green-blue gray," "deep green-blue gray," "clear green-blue gray," and "pale green-blue gray."

Green-blue slate: Decidedly greenish blue, somewhat light slate color.

Greenish slate black: Very dark, dull, somewhat bluish green; almost black.

Green-yellow: Pure, rather light greenish yellow.

Grenadine: Rather light grenadine red.

Grenadine orange:† Same as grenadine.

Grenadine pink: Pure, rather dark pink; somewhat tinged with orange but less so than bittersweet pink.

Grenadine red: Bright orange-red; somewhat less orange than flame scarlet but in effect scarlet with a decided orange tinge.

Gull gray: Rather light bluish gray; much lighter than slate gray but of the same hue.

Hair brown: Dull, decidedly grayish brown; formed by mixture of drab with 45 percent black; decidedly lighter but of same hue as chaetura drab.

Hays brown: Dark, dull, somewhat vinaceous brown.

Hays maroon: Very dark acajou red.

Hays russet: Dark, orange-red brown; a shade of vinaceous rufous.

Hazel: Dark cinnamon rufous.

Heliotrope gray: Dull lavender gray.

Heliotrope purple: * Rather light, dull vinaceous purple.

Heliotrope slate: Dark violet gray; like deep mouse gray but much more purplish.

Hellebore green: Dark, dull, somewhat yellowish green; rather less yellowish than roman green.

Helvetia blue: Dark blue, very slightly tinged with violet.

Hermosa pink: Light eosine pink.

Hessian brown: Dark brick red.

Honey yellow: Dull buffy yellow; similar to clay color but decidedly more yellow; a shade of chamois.

Hyacinth violet: Somewhat dark amethyst violet.

Hydrangea red: Dull, grayish vinaceous red; slightly more purplish and slightly darker than corinthian red.

Hyssop violet: Dull grayish violet.

Indian lake: Rather dark, dull violet red; much more violet-tinged than hydrangea red.

Indian purple: Very dark, dull violet red.

Indian red: Dark, dull, slightly orange vinaceous; slightly darker than corinthian red.

Indian yellow: * Dull, rather less orange cadmium yellow.

Indigo blue: Very dark, decidedly dull, somewhat greenish blue.

Indulin blue: Very dark, dull, slightly violet blue.

Isabella color: Rather light, dull brownish olivaceous; between honey yellow and light brownish olive.

Italian blue: Pure, rather dark greenish blue.

Ivory yellow: Very light yellowish buff; lighter than colonial buff; slightly more yellowish than cartridge buff.

Jade green: Dark, dull yellowish green.

Jasper pink: Rather dull, grayish geranium pink.

Jasper red: Decidedly dull scarlet red; rather less orange than coral red.

Javel green: Dull, rather dark greenish yellow; lighter and more yellowish than oil green.

Juvence blue: Dark, dull greenish blue; decidedly more greenish than chessylite blue; a dark capri blue.

Kaiser brown: Dark, dull reddish brown; more reddish and rather darker than hazel and ferruginous.

Killarney green: Dull, rather dark green; neither bluish nor yellowish.

King blue: Rather light grayish blue, with a very slight greenish tinge.

Kronberg green: Dark, grayish yellow-green; somewhat more yellowish than jade green.

La france pink: Light geranium pink.

Lake red: * Slightly dull rose red.

Lavender: Very light dull violet.

Lavender gray: Very light, dull grayish blue, with a slight violaceous tinge.

Lemon chrome: Pure rich yellow, slightly tinged with orange.

Lemon yellow: Pure rich spectrum yellow.

Lettuce green: Rather dark, somewhat yellowish green; a rather light spinach green.

Lichen green: Very light, slightly bluish green.

Light brownish olive: Dark isabella color; lighter than brownish olive.

Light buff: Pale buff; i.e., yellow ocher very much diluted and neither yellowish- nor orange-tinted.

Light cadmium: Pure, rather orange yellow; between cadmium yellow and lemon chrome.

Light cinnamon drab: Of same tone as cinnamon drab but somewhat paler.

Light drab: Drab with addition of white.

Light glaucous blue: Light grayish blue; more greenish and lighter than alice blue.

Light grayish olive: Light dull gray with an olivaceous tinge; lighter and more grayish (less yellowish olivaceous) than grayish olive.

Light gull gray: Light tint of gull gray.

Light jasper red: Rather orange, moderately light red; somewhat lighter than jasper red.

Light mouse gray: Decidedly light mouse gray, with a slightly more olivaceous tinge.

Light neutral gray: Neutral gray, somewhat lightened by about 10 percent white.

Light ochraceous buff: Rather light buff, a little dull and somewhat tinged with orange or salmon color; a tint of ochraceous buff.

Light pompeian red: † Dull orange-red; between pompeian red and jasper red.

Light vinaceous fawn: Light tint of vinaceous fawn, which is somewhat more pinkish.

Light yellowish olive: Moderately light olivaceous color, strongly tinged with yellow, more so than is ecru olive; decidedly lighter than yellowish olive.

Lilac: Light, rather dull reddish violet; decidedly less bluish and rather brighter than lavender.

Lilac gray: Very light tint of violet gray.

Liver brown: Dull, very dark, rather reddish brown; a very dark vinaceous rufous.

Livid purple: Rather dark, somewhat reddish violet.

Lumiere green: Light, somewhat yellowish green; light apple green.

Lyons blue: Rather dark rich blue; somewhat more purplish than ultramarine blue.

Madder blue: Very dull, somewhat violet blue.

Madder brown: Dark brownish red; somewhat more reddish (less orange) than brick red.

Magenta: Rather dark, dull violet red.

Mahogany red: Dark shade of grenadine red; i.e., a rather light bay.

Maize yellow: Light buffy yellow; somewhat more buffy than baryta yellow.

Malachite green: Grayish light green, without tinge of blue or yellow.

Marguerite yellow: Light primrose yellow.

Marine blue: Very dark, rich, rather greenish blue; slightly more greenish than berlin blue.

Maroon: Very dark, rich red; scarlet red with addition of much black.

Maroon purple: * Somewhat less purplish (more reddish) than indian lake.

Mars brown: Very dark, dull orange-brown; much darker than russet; slightly less yellowish than prout brown.

Mars orange: Dark, dull flame scarlet; more reddish than orange rufous; lighter than burnt sienna—between this color and flame scarlet.

Mars yellow: Dark dull orange; pure orange with addition of 45 percent black.

Martius yellow: Very light lemon yellow.

Massicot yellow: Light straw yellow.

Mathews blue: Rather dull blue, slightly tinged with greenish.

Mazarine blue: Light pure blue, tinged with neither green nor violet.

Medal bronze: Very dark, though rather bright, orange-hued olive; dark orange citrine.

Medici blue: Moderately light, slightly greenish blue-gray; much darker and somewhat more bluish than glaucous gray.

Methyl blue: Bright, pure, rich blue; slightly greenish.

Methyl green: Rather dull bluish green.

Mikado brown: Dull orange-brown; decidedly darker and more orange (less yellowish) than cinnamon.

Mikado orange: Rather light cadmium orange.

Mineral red: Dark, dull vinaceous red; a dark hydrangea red.

Morocco red: Dark, rich, slightly brownish red; darker than brazil red; lighter than claret brown, and between these two colors.

Motmot blue: Rather dull greenish blue; more greenish than mathews blue; much more bluish than methyl green; lighter than capri blue.

Mouse gray: Dull, rather brownish gray; rather lighter and less brownish than hair brown.

Mulberry purple: Dark hyacinth violet.

Mummy brown: Very dark, rather dull brown; slightly more yellowish, less orange or reddish than prout brown; darker than dresden brown.

Mustard yellow: Rather dull yellow; more tinged with orange than amber yellow; darker and much more tinged with orange than straw yellow.

Myrtle green: Very dark, decidedly bluish green.

Naphthalene violet: Dark, decidedly dull, somewhat reddish violet; darker and less reddish than livid purple.

Naphthalene yellow: Very light, rather dull yellow, tinged with neither buff nor green.

Naples yellow: Light mustard yellow; darker than cream color; darker and decidedly more buffy than massicot yellow.

Natal brown: Dark, decidedly dull, rather vinaceous brown; a darker shade of army brown.

Navy blue: Very dark violet blue.

Neutral gray: Dull gray, very slightly tinged with brownish; lighter and much less bluish than slate gray; decidedly more purely gray, as well as slightly more bluish and less vinaceous, than mouse gray.

Niagara green: Rather light, decidedly bluish green; of same hue as terre verte but much lighter.

Nickel green: Dark, dull, somewhat bluish green.

Nile blue: Tint of beryl green; a rather light greenish blue; more greenish than bremen blue; sometimes called nile green.

Nopal red: Dark scarlet red; lighter than garnet brown; somewhat less orange than brazil red.

Ocher yellow:° Yellowish yellow ocher.

Ochraceous:° Rather dull, deep yellowish buff; between ochraceous tawny and yellow ocher; lighter, more orange-tinted than buckthorn brown.

Ochraceous buff: Deep buff; decidedly more tinged with orange than antimony yellow, to which it is otherwise similar.

Ochraceous orange: Decidedly dull orange.

Ochraceous rufous:° Between apricot orange and zinc orange but somewhat darker.

Ochraceous tawny: Dark ochraceous orange; decidedly lighter and more yellowish than cinnamon brown and more orange; less yellowish than buckthorn brown.

Oil green: Dark yellowish green; much darker than javel green.

Old gold: Dull, rather light golden olive; much more orange than olive lake; lighter, more yellowish than buffy citrine; primuline yellow with addition of 45 percent black.

Old rose: Decidedly dull begonia rose, the addition of gray imparting a somewhat violaceous appearance; much deeper than alizarine pink; lighter than eugenia red; similar to light jasper red but less orange (more purely red).

Olivaceous black: Very dark grayish olive; nearly black.

Olive: Very dark, dull, somewhat brownish green.

Olive black: Same as olivaceous black.

Olive brown: Dark, very dull brown; much less vinaceous than natal brown but with little olivaceous tinge; in tone between buffy brown and clove brown.

Olive buff: Light, decidedly olivaceous buff.

Olive citrine: Dull yellowish olive; of more greenish (less grayish) tone and somewhat lighter than olive.

Olive gray: Rather light gray with a decidedly olivaceous tinge; somewhat less brownish or yellowish than grayish olive; i.e., more clearly gray.

Olive green: Pure, dark yellowish olive, not dull.

Olive lake: Much lighter, more yellowish tone of dull citrine; wax yellow darkened and dulled by black.

Olive ocher: Similar to honey yellow but decidedly more greenish; lighter and much more yellowish than ecru olive.

Olive yellow: Dull, rather light olivaceous yellow; much more greenish than olive ocher; lighter, much more clearly greenish yellow than light yellowish olive.

Olympic blue: Rather dull, medium light, slightly greenish blue; slightly less greenish than mathews blue.

Onionskin pink: Rather light, very dull buffy or orangish pink; similar to vinaceous cinnamon but more pinkish (less buffy).

Orange: Rich, pure reddish yellow.

Orange buff: Pure light tint of orange.

Orange chrome: Rich, pure, deep reddish orange.

Orange cinnamon: Cinnamon with a decidedly orange tone.

Orange citrine: Citrine with a strongly orange tinge: darker than analine yellow; lighter than medal bronze.

Orange ochraceous:° Dark, somewhat more orange cadmium yellow.

Orange rufous: Rather dark tone of orange chrome; i.e., orange chrome mixed with 45 percent black; less reddish-tinged than mars orange.

Orange vermilion:° Bright red; between scarlet and scarlet red.

Orient blue: Grayish, medium light, somewhat greenish blue.

Orient pink: Light, pure salmon pink; lighter than bittersweet pink; made from flame scarlet with addition of 45 percent white.

Orpiment orange:° Dark, slightly dull orange chrome.

Ox-blood red: Dark rich carmine; somewhat more purely red than garnet brown.

Pale congo pink: Very light grayish pink; lighter and somewhat more pinkish than vinaceous pink.

Pale drab gray: Light grayish drab gray; slightly more vinaceous than pale smoke gray.

Pale fluorite green: Very light tint of fluorite green.

Pale glaucous blue: Very light glaucous blue.

Pale gull gray: Very light tint of gull gray.

Pale medici blue: Very light tint of medici blue.

Pale mouse gray: Light tone of mouse gray; lighter and decidedly more vinaceous than olive gray.

Pale pinkish buff: Light pinkish buff.

Pale russian blue: Lighter tint of russian blue.

Pale smoke gray: Light, more purely grayish (less olivaceous) smoke gray; rather less vinaceous than pallid mouse gray.

Pale vinaceous fawn: Lighter and somewhat more grayish than light vinaceous fawn.

Pale viridine yellow: Very light tint of viridine yellow.

Pallid mouse gray: Very pale mouse gray.

Pallid neutral gray: Very light tone of neutral gray; even lighter than pale neutral gray.

Paris blue: Pure, dark, slightly greenish blue; somewhat lighter than berlin blue.

Parrot green: Dark yellowish green; decidedly darker than calliste green.

Pea green: Very grayish, rather light green; lighter tone of sage green.

Peach blossom pink:° Rather light eosine pink; between latter and hermosa pink.

Peach red: Pure, light pinkish scarlet.

Peacock blue: Bright, rather dark green-blue; darker than italian blue.

Peacock green: Rather dark, dull emerald green; lighter and less yellowish than grass green.

Pearl blue: Very light grayish, slightly violet blue.

Pearl gray: Very light, slightly greenish gray; much less purplish than french gray.

Pecan brown: Dull orange-brown; slightly less yellowish than mikado brown.

Perilla purple: Dark, grayish violet purple; darker and more reddish than livid purple.

Picric yellow: Pure light yellow; slightly lighter than lemon yellow.

Pinard yellow: Light, pure, rather buffy yellow; lighter than empire yellow; decidedly more buffy than picric yellow.

Pinkish buff: Rather light, dull buff, with a slight pinkish tinge; decidedly more pinkish than cream buff.

Pinkish cinnamon: Light cinnamon, decidedly more pinkish than cinnamon buff.

Pinkish vinaceous: Dull, rather orange-tinted vinaceous; i.e., dull, light, slightly orange pink; strawberry pink with addition of 58 percent neutral gray.

Plumbago blue: Light grayish, slightly lavender blue.

Plumbeous: Rather light bluish gray.

Plumbeous black: Black with a slight tinge of plumbeous.

Pomegranate purple: Pure, rather dark rose red.

Pompeian red: Dark, dull, slightly orange red; darker than jasper red; lighter than madder brown.

Poppy red:° Pure, slightly orange red; rather darker, slightly duller, and somewhat more orange than scarlet red.

Porcelain blue: Moderately dark, grayish green-blue; decidedly more greenish than orient blue; more bluish than terre verte.

Primrose yellow: Rather dull light yellow; darker than marguerite yellow; without orange buff tinge of colonial buff, instead a clear yellow.

Primuline yellow: Rather dull, somewhat orange yellow; darker than mustard yellow; light cadmium dulled with gray.

Prout brown: Very dark, yellow-orange brown; rather dull and darker than cinnamon brown; slightly more orange or reddish than mummy brown.

Prussian blue: Very dark, rich, pure blue; several shades darker than spectrum blue.

Prussian green: Dark, rather dull bluish green.

Prussian red: Dark, dull, somewhat vinaceous brown; more vinaceous than cameo brown.

Puritan gray: Very light dull, slightly greenish blue-gray.

Purple (true): Bright, pure reddish violet; in hue halfway between spectrum violet and rose red.

Purple drab: Dark, decidedly purplish gray; much more purplish than brownish drab or vinaceous drab.

Purplish vinaceous: Rather dark vinaceous, with more tinge of gray.

Pyrite yellow: Rather bright, light yellowish citrine; composed of lemon yellow with 45 percent black.

Quaker drab: Dull reddish gray; similar to mouse gray but more reddish or purplish.

Raisin black: Very dark, dull grayish red violet; almost black.

Raw sienna: Light, very yellowish brown; more yellowish (less orange) than mars yellow; similar to antique brown but lighter, more yellowish; cadmium yellow with 45 percent black.

Raw umber: Very dark orange-yellow brown; less orange than brussels brown; like antique brown but darker and less yellowish.

Reed yellow: Rather dark primrose yellow.

Rhodamine purple: Pure, bright, somewhat reddish purple.

Roman green: Dull grayish olive green, with less orange tone than olive citrine.

Rood blue: Pure, dark, rich blue; lighter than prussian blue.

Rood brown: Dull, dark orange-brown; darker than pecan brown and lighter than vandyke brown; similar to walnut brown but slightly more yellowish (less reddish).

Rose color: Pure, rather light tint of rose red; i.e., rose red with addition of 10 percent white.

Rose doree: Rather light tint of scarlet red; i.e., scarlet red with addition of 10 percent white; similar to begonia rose but slightly less purely red; of same hue as geranium pink but darker.

Rose pink: Very light, pure tint of rose color.

Rose purple: Light tint of magenta, composed of magenta with addition of 23 percent white; similar to lilac but more reddish.

Rose red: Pure, slightly violet spectrum red.

Rosolane purple: Dull reddish purple; somewhat more reddish than magenta; tyrian rose with 32 percent neutral gray.

Royal purple: Pure, rather dark spectrum violet.

Rufescent:† Inclining to a rufous or reddish hue.

Rufous: Very dull, grayish flame scarlet; rather more reddish (less orange) than apricot orange.

Russet: Dark, rather dull tawny; decidedly more reddish than cinnamon brown; lighter and more reddish than mars brown.

Russet vinaceous: Moderately dark purplish brown; similar to fawn color but somewhat more reddish.

Russian blue: Light, very grayish blue; of same hue as delft blue but much lighter.

Saccardo olive: Rather light orange olive; dark buffy citrine; somewhat more orange (less greenish) than olive citrine.

Saccardo umber: Dark yellowish brown; lighter than sepia.

Saffron yellow:° Rich, pure orange-yellow; between light cadmium and cadmium yellow.

Sage green: Very grayish medium green; somewhat darker than pea green.

Salmon buff: Rather dull orange buff; much lighter than apricot orange but of same hue; lighter and decidedly more pinkish than ochraceous buff.

Salmon color: Dull pale rufous; more yellowish than flesh color; more pinkish than salmon buff.

Salmon orange: Pure, rather light orange chrome.

Sanford brown: Dark orange rufous; similar to burnt sienna but somewhat less reddish; lighter and rather more orange than auburn.

Saturn red:° Rather light orange chrome.

Sayal brown: Dull yellowish brown; darker than cinnamon; more yellowish than mikado brown; less yellowish than tawny olive.

Scarlet: Pure, bright, somewhat orange red; more orange than scarlet red, less so than grenadine red.

Scarlet red: Bright, pure, rich red; slightly more orange than spectrum red.

Scarlet vermilion:° Dull, rather reddish scarlet.

Seal brown: Very dark vinaceous brown; similar to clove brown but not so grayish (more purplish).

Seashell pink: Very pale salmon pink; a light tint of salmon buff.

Sepia: Very dark yellowish brown; darker than saccardo umber; more yellowish (less orange or reddish) than bister.

Serpentine green: Light greenish olive; darker and more greenish than yellowish citrine; lighter than roman green; more greenish than dull citrine.

Sevres blue:° Rather dark, slightly less greenish cerulean blue.

Shrimp pink: Pure, light strawberry pink; more salmon or orange-tinged than pink.

Sky blue: Light, rather grayish blue.

Sky gray: Very light grayish blue; a light tint of alice blue.

Slate black: Black with a tinge of slate color.

Slate blue: Rather dark, very grayish blue; rather darker and less violet-tinged than madder blue; more purely greenish blue than delft blue.

Slate color: Dark bluish gray.

Slate gray: Rather light slate color.

Slate purple: Very dull, grayish, rather dark purple.

Slate violet: Very grayish, rather reddish violet; somewhat lighter and more bluish than slate purple.

Smalt blue: Rich, rather dark, slightly violet blue.

Smoke gray: Light, very slightly olivaceous gray.

Snuff brown: Dark, dull yellowish orange-brown; darker and somewhat more vinaceous than sayal brown; lighter than bister; more vinaceous than saccardo umber.

Solferino:° Rather dark, slightly dull rhodamine purple; similar to magenta but brighter, less grayish.

Sorghum brown: Purplish brown; a rather dark shade of russet vinaceous.

Spectrum blue: Rich, moderately dark pure blue of the spectrum, tinged with neither green nor violet.

Spectrum red: Pure, bright, moderately dark red of the spectrum, tinged with neither orange nor violet.

Spectrum violet: Pure, bright, moderately dark violet of the spectrum, tinged with neither blue nor red.

Spinach green: Rather bright, dark yellowish green; darker, more yellowish than parrot green; less yellowish, more purely green than cerro green.

Spinel red: Very dull, grayish rose red.

Stone green: Dull grayish, somewhat bluish green; slightly more bluish than american green.

Storm gray: Moderately light olivaceous gray; slightly more purplish than olive gray.

Straw yellow (straw color): Rather dull, slightly buffy light yellow; darker than massicot yellow; lighter than amber yellow; more yellowish (less buffy) than naples yellow.

Strawberry pink: Rather deep salmon pink; slightly lighter than peach red; much darker than shrimp pink; more salmon-tinged than geranium pink, but less so than grenadine pink.

Strontian yellow: Dull lemon yellow.

Sudan brown: Dark yellowish brown; between mars yellow and brussels brown; more yellowish (less orange) than amber brown; somewhat more orange (less yellowish) than antique brown; darker, less yellowish than raw sienna.

Sulphine yellow: Light yellowish citrine; less orange than analine yellow but more orange than pyrite yellow; lemon chrome with a mixture of 45 percent black.

Sulphur yellow: Very light greenish yellow; lighter and more greenish than picric yellow.

Tawny: Dull reddish brown; more yellowish (less orange) than cinnamon rufous; darker and more brownish (less orange) than hazel; lighter than russet; very much darker, duller, and more brownish than rufous.

Tawny ochraceous:° Rather dark, slightly more orange ochraceous orange.

Tawny olive: Rather dark clay color.

Terre verte (green): Grayish, somewhat dark bluish green.

Testaceous: Rather light vinaceous brown; lighter and more pinkish than pecan brown.

Tilleul buff: Very light vinaceous buff; a grayish, pale, pinkish buff.

Turquoise blue:° Rather greenish blue; more purplish than bremen blue.

Turquoise green: Pure, light bluish green; decidedly more greenish than calamine blue.

Turtle green: Grayish, rather light yellow-green; decidedly more yellowish than malachite green.

Tyrian blue: Very grayish, very slightly greenish blue; more purely blue (less greenish) than orient blue.

Tyrian rose: Pure, bright, rather purplish rose red.

Ultramarine blue: Bright, rich, pure blue; slightly darker than spectrum blue.

Vanderpoel blue: Grayish, very slightly greenish blue; similar to olympic blue but rather darker and slightly duller.

Vandyke brown: Very dark orange-brown; more vinaceous than bister, but less so than burnt umber; similar to rood brown but darker.

Venetian pink: Dull, rather grayish light pink; lighter than alizarine pink; decidedly more salmon-tinged than rose pink.

Verditer blue:° Dull, rather light greenish blue; between motmot blue and glaucous blue.

Vermilion:° Rather dull scarlet red.

Verona brown: Dull, moderately light, rather orange-tinted brown; of same tone as sayal brown but more orange.

Vinaceous: Dull, rather light, decidedly purplish pink.

Vinaceous brown: Rather dark, somewhat purplish brown; much lighter than seal brown.

Vinaceous buff: Very dull, light buffy vinaceous; much darker than tilleul buff; a lighter shade of avellaneous.

Vinaceous cinnamon: Rather light cinnamon with a strong vinaceous tinge; decidedly lighter than orange cinnamon; more pinkish than pinkish cinnamon, but less so than onionskin pink.

Vinaceous drab: Drab with a decided vinaceous tinge.

Vinaceous fawn: Light fawn color.

Vinaceous gray: Light, grayish purple vinaceous; similar to heliotrope gray but more pinkish.

Vinaceous pink: Dull brownish, very slightly purplish pink; lighter and less yellowish in tone than onionskin pink.

Vinaceous purple: Dull, grayish, rather dark violet red; rather darker shade of eupatorium purple.

Vinaceous rufous: Dull orange-red brown; more orange than dragon's blood red; more reddish than ferruginous.

Vinaceous tawny: Dark onionskin pink.

Violet:° Rather dark amethyst violet.

Violet gray: Moderately dark purplish gray.

Viridian green: Rather dark clear green; slightly darker than vivid green.

Viridine green: Light, somewhat yellowish green; less yellowish and lighter than yellow-green.

Viridine yellow: Light, bright, pure yellowish green; of same hue as apple green but decidedly brighter.

Vivid green: Pure bright green; decidedly darker than emerald green.

Walnut brown: Light burnt umber; somewhat more vinaceous than rood brown, but less so than cameo brown.

Warbler green: Rather light, yellowish olive green.

Warm buff: Dull, pale orange-yellow; lighter than antimony yellow; more orange-tinged than naples yellow.

Warm sepia: More reddish sepia, even more so than bister.

Wax yellow: Decidedly dull lemon chrome; less orange-tinged than primuline yellow but slightly more so than strontian yellow.

Windsor blue: Decidedly grayish blue; moderately light with no tinge of green or violet.

Wine purple:° Rather dark, slightly more purplish spinel red.

Wood brown: Moderately light vinaceous brown; less vinaceous than fawn color; much darker than avellaneous; lighter, more pinkish than buffy brown.

Xanthine orange: Dark, very dull cadmium orange; i.e., cadmium orange shaded with black.

Yale blue: Moderately light, somewhat grayish blue; of same hue as olympic blue but lighter.

Yellow-green: Rather bright yellowish green; much more yellowish than emerald green; lighter and brighter than calliste green.

Yellowish citrine: Light, yellowish serpentine green; more greenish than olive lake; similar to pyrite yellow but duller and more greenish; strontian yellow with addition of 45 percent black.

Yellowish glaucous: Pale, very dull grayish green; like glaucous but somewhat more yellowish.

Yellowish oil green: Rather light, somewhat yellowish olive green.

Yellowish olive: Rather light olive with a decidedly yellowish tinge; thus, decidedly more greenish than buffy olive; darker, more greenish than ecru olive.

Yellow ocher: Dull grayish orange-yellow; darker than antimony yellow; more buffy than primuline yellow; cadmium yellow with addition of 32 percent neutral gray.

Zinc orange: Similar to ochraceous orange but slightly less yellowish.

APPENDIX C: Birds Mistakenly Attributed to Texas

The birds in the following list have been reported in print as having occurred within Texas, but these species or subspecies either (1) are not substantiated by an accurately labeled specimen, photograph, or even a careful sight record of a wild bird; or (2) are no longer recognized taxonomically.

No attempt is made here or elsewhere in this book to list the numerous unestablished foreign game and other birds that man has brought to Texas. Naturalized species, those which have bred enthusiastically in the wild for at least ten years, are fully treated in the main text. As of 1970, there were only four: Ring-necked Pheasant (possibly several races), Rock Dove, European Starling, and House Sparrow.

Since Dr. Oberholser last worked on the present appendix, occurrence of the Arctic Loon has been authenticated by a specimen; however, the skin proves to be racially unidentifiable. Thus, the species is treated in the main text, but the Atlantic race has been retained in this list. Details are given in the EDITOR's NOTE under *Gavia arctica arctica* below.

Six species (Costa's Hummingbird, Buff-bellied Flycatcher, Plain-tailed Brown Jay, Bridled Titmouse, Olive Warbler, and Red-faced Warbler) now have enough sight records to be considered hypothetical and are therefore included in the main text. In this list, Oberholser treated four of these six (Buff-bellied Flycatcher, Plain-tailed Brown Jay, Bridled Titmouse, and Olive Warbler) on the subspecies level. Although definite designation of the subspecies of these hypotheticals cannot be made, it is likely that in all four cases the races which have possibly occurred in Texas are not those which Oberholser discussed in this appendix; hence, the races entered below still remain highly untenable.

The other two species (Costa's Hummingbird, Red-faced Warbler) have no recognized races. However, they have been retained in this list because the original records on which their occurrence was based still appear erroneous, although their occurrence in Texas is now considered very possible.

Three species (Yellow-billed Loon, Mexican Chickadee, Blue Bunting) have been added to Oberholser's list of untenable Texas birds. These are entered below in proper phylogenetic order and each concludes with the notation EDITOR. Also, special problems with Burroughs' Turkey Vulture, Thick-billed Parrot, and Mexican Olive Warbler are explained in the EDITOR's NOTE under each of these birds.

Symbols: * Other race(s) of species with valid occurrence records within the state; thus, species is treated in the main text.
      ** Bird is treated on a species level as a hypothetical in the main text.
      † Bird is now generally recognized as a hybrid.
      ‡ Race is generally recognized as no longer tenable.

YELLOW-BILLED LOON, *Gavia adamsii* (Gray)

White-billed Diver of British books.

Loons having some of the characteristics of this species are occasionally seen at Balmorhea Lake, Reeves Co. (see *American Birds* 25: 419) and also from Texas City dike, Galveston Co. The one supposed Texas specimen of *G. adamsii*, taken at Balmorhea Lake, Jan. 3, 1971, by J. C. Henderson, was later identified by R. C. Banks at the U.S. National Museum as an aberrant individual of *G. immer*. This skin is no. 8570 in the Texas A&M University collection (see K. A. Arnold, J. C. Henderson, 1973, *Auk* 90: 421). The chief field mark of the Yellow-billed Loon is its massive, upturned pale yellow or white bill. However, some Common Loons have upturned whitish bills and young Yellow-billed Loons have rather straight, moderate-sized beaks. *G. adamsii*, largest of its family, seldom leaves the Arctic, even in the winter. Only once has the species been certified within one thousand miles of Texas. This was a specimen taken in Adams Co., Colorado, Nov. 7, 1922, by F. S. Smith.—EDITOR

ATLANTIC ARCTIC LOON, *Gavia arctica arctica* (Linnaeus)

Atlantic Black-throated Diver of British authors.

This loon was said by Audubon (1838, *Ornith. Biog.*, vol. 4, p. 345) to have been seen along the Texas coast, probably near Galveston, in April, 1837.

EDITOR's NOTE: The one specimen of the species taken in the state, at Balmorhea Lake, Reeves Co., Jan. 3, 1971, by J. C. Henderson, cannot be identified subspecifically (see K. A. Arnold, J. C. Henderson, 1973, *Auk* 90: 421). However, Oberholser was of the opinion that sightings of the species in Texas were most likely of the Pacific Arctic Loon, *G. a. pacifica*. Thus, the species is now authenticated in the state and is given full treatment in the main text; however, the race *G. a. arctica* is still considered untenable.

FLORIDA DOUBLE-CRESTED CORMORANT,
Phalacrocorax auritus floridanus (Audubon)*

This race was recorded from Texas by William Lloyd (1887, *Auk* 4: 184) from a single bird taken in the autumn of 1880 near San Angelo, and it has been otherwise accredited to the state. Since in the present connection the writer has examined no specimen that is not referable to the Northern Double-crested Cormorant, *P. a. auritus*, and since the normal distribution of *P. a. floridanus* is confined to Florida and the s.e. United States, possibly west to s.e. Louisiana, its retention in the list of Texas birds should await further investigation. Since it differs only in somewhat smaller size, it is not separable in the field from *P. a. auritus*, and even examination of specimens demands care in order to ascertain proper identification.

WÜRDEMANN'S HERON, *Ardea würdemannii* Baird†

This bird was originally described by S. F. Baird (1858, *Rep. Explor. and Surv. R. R. Pac.,* vol. 9, p. 669) from specimens collected by Gustavus Würdemann in s. Florida. It is evidently a hybrid between Ward's Great Blue Heron, *Ardea herodia wardi,* and the Florida Great White Heron, *Ardea occidentalis occidentalis.*

There is a single record of this bird in Texas, an adult seen and carefully studied by Connie Hagar and Guy Emerson near Fulton, Aransas Co., Oct. 9, 1943.

GREATER SNOW GOOSE, *Chen hyperborea atlantica* Kennard*

This form has been reported from Corpus Christi, Refugio Co., San Antonio, and other places in s. Texas. However, all records are unsatisfactory; either they belong clearly to the Lesser Snow Goose, *C. h. hyperborea,* or are so doubtful in character that they are not with safety acceptable. In view of present knowledge of the distribution of *C. h. atlantica,* its appearance in Texas at any season is exceedingly doubtful.

COMMON BLACK DUCK, *Anas rubripes tristis* Brewster‡

Black Ducks answering to the characters ascribed to the Common Black Duck have been taken in Texas. It has been shown, however, that the separation of this supposed subspecies was based on characters now accounted for by differences due to age and individual variation.

BURROUGHS' TURKEY VULTURE, *Cathartes burrovianus* Cassin

This bird has been reported as seen near Brownsville (Dresser, 1865, *Ibis,* ser. 2, vol. 1, no. 3, p. 322), but this probably must be considered as applying to the Mexican Turkey Vulture, since *Cathartes burrovianus* is considered by some authors as a synonym of *Cathartes aura aura,* which is the breeding form at Brownsville.

EDITOR'S NOTE: Many authors currently (1973) apply the name *Cathartes burrovianus* to the Lesser Yellow-headed, or Savanna, Vulture, which ranges locally from s.e. Mexico to n. Argentina.

CALIFORNIA RED-SHOULDERED HAWK, *Buteo lineatus elegans* Cassin*

Richly colored examples of both the Texas Red-shouldered Hawk, *B. l. texanus,* and the Florida race, *B. l. alleni,* are responsible for several Texas records of this California race.

HARPY EAGLE, *Harpya harpyja* (Linnaeus)

This species has been accredited to Texas, as well as to North America, solely on the basis of one seen, but not obtained, by Dr. Felix L. Oswald (1878, *Amer. Nat.* 12: 151) in the jungle along the delta of the Rio Grande. Owing to the circumstances attending this record and to the fact that the bird was not collected, it seems without much doubt to have been a mistake.

DESERT SPARROW HAWK, *Tinnunculus sparverius phaloena* (Lesson)‡

Although for many years considered a bird of Texas, this form must be removed from the state list. It has been found to be inseparable from the Northern Sparrow Hawk, *T. s. sparverius.*

EASTERN RUFFED GROUSE, *Bonasa umbellus umbellus* (Linnaeus)

Audubon (1842, *Birds Amer.,* vol. 5, p. 80) is the authority for the statement that this species occurs in Texas; also, the editor of *Forest and Stream* (1878, vol. 10, p. 256) reported it as having been seen in November, about 1877, near Cedar Lake on the Staked Plains. However, both of these records are undoubtedly erroneous.

MEXICAN SCALED QUAIL, *Callipepla squamata squamata* (Vigors)*

Since restriction of the nominate Scaled Quail to c. Mexico (Bangs, 1914, *Proc. New England Zool. Club,* vol. 4, pp. 99–100), all Texas records of this species belong under either the Arizona Scaled Quail, *C. s. pallida,* or the Chestnut-bellied Scaled Quail, *C. s. castanogastris.*

CARIBBEAN CLAPPER RAIL, *Rallus longirostris caribaeus* Ridgway*

The only Texas records of this race are two specimens recorded by G. B. Sennett (1888, *Auk* 5: 319). One of these was obtained by Mr. Sennett himself at Galveston, Feb. 28, 1877; the other, by J. M. Priour at Corpus Christi, May 19, 1877. Careful examination shows that both belong to the Louisiana Clapper Rail, *R. l. saturatus.*

COMMON WESTERN GULL, *Larus occidentalis occidentalis* Audubon

John Cassin (1855, *Proc. Acad. Nat. Sci. Phila.,* vol. 6, p. lxiv) has recorded a specimen and four eggs of this species as taken by A. L. Herrmann in Texas. This, without much doubt, is a mistake of some kind, since *L. occidentalis* would occur within the boundaries of Texas, if at all, as a mere straggler.

EASTERN CAROLINA PARAKEET, *Conuropsis carolinensis carolinensis* (Linnaeus)*

The eastern form of the Carolina Parakeet did not occur in Texas; all parakeet records refer undoubtedly to the western race, *C. c. ludovicianus.*

THICK-BILLED PARROT, *Rhynchopsitta pachyrhyncha* (Swainson)

A specimen of the Thick-billed Parrot supposed to have been collected on the Rio Grande in Texas by J. W. Audubon was sent to the Academy of Natural Sciences of Philadelphia, as recorded by Sclater (1858, *Proc. Zool. Soc. Lond.,* vol. for 1857, p. 230) and then by S. F. Baird (1858, *Rep. Expl. and Surv. R. R. Pac.,* vol. 9, p. 66). There is much doubt, however, regarding the exact locality from which this specimen came; more than likely it was of Mexican origin.

EDITOR'S NOTE: Since the 1930's, the Thick-billed Parrot has declined catastrophically; nowadays (1970's) the Red-crowned Parrot, *Amazona viridigenalis,* is the only parrot that seems to have even the remotest chance of occurring naturally in Texas.

SOUTHERN FERRUGINOUS OWL, *Glaucidium brasilianum phaloenoides* (Daudin)*

This race, formerly accredited to Texas, is now restricted to South America; all Texas records applying to it should be referred to the Northern Ferruginous Owl, *G. b. cactorum.*

COSTA'S HUMMINGBIRD, *Calypte costae* (Bourcier)**

A specimen of this species was mistakenly recorded by J. Van Tyne (June 18, 1933, *San Antonio Express*) as collected in Wade (Pine) Canyon, in the Chisos Mountains. However, the specimen proved ultimately to be a Lucifer Hummingbird, *Calothorax lucifer.*

COMMON HELOISE'S HUMMINGBIRD, *Atthis heloisa heloisa* (Lesson and Delattre)

Bumblebee Hummingbird of some authors.

This hummingbird was recorded from Texas by J. G. Cooper (1870, *Ornith. California*, vol. 1, p. 363) from a specimen taken at El Paso in 1853 by J. H. Clark. However, this later proved to be an example of the Calliope Hummingbird, *Stellula calliope*.

HYBRID FLICKER, *Colaptes ayresii* (Audubon)†

The Hybrid Flicker is now known to be merely a cross between the Yellow-shafted Flicker, *Colaptes auratus*, and the Red-shafted Flicker, *C. cafer*. Therefore, it is not entitled to a place in the list of accredited Texas birds. Various records of this hybrid will be found on the *C. auratus* × *C. cafer* map in the main text.

BAIRD'S LADDER-BACKED WOODPECKER, *Dryobates scalaris bairdi* (Malherbe)*

Dendrocopos scalaris giraudi of Dist. check-list of Mexico, pt. 2, 1957.

Since the true Baird's Ladder-backed Woodpecker is now known to occur only in Mexico, all Texas references to this bird must be placed under either the Texas Ladder-backed Woodpecker, *D. s. symplectus*, or the Cactus Ladder-backed Woodpecker, *D. s. cactophilus*, according to locality.

LAWRENCE'S OLIVACEOUS FLYCATCHER, *Myiarchus tuberculifer lawrenceii* (Giraud)*

Dusky-capped Flycatcher of some recent authors.

This is one of the birds described by J. P. Giraud, Jr. (1841, *Sixteen Species North Amer. Birds*, p. 9) as from Texas; however, without doubt, it is improperly accredited to the state.

GIRAUD'S VERMILION-CROWNED FLYCATCHER, *Myiozetetes texensis texensis* Giraud

Myiozetetes similis texensis of Dist. check-list of Mexico, pt. 2, 1957; also known as Social Flycatcher.

This is another bird without much doubt improperly accredited to Texas on the basis of the type specimen which Giraud (ibid., pl. 1) claimed came originally from Texas.

FULVOUS BUFF-BREASTED FLYCATCHER, *Empidonax fulvifrons fulvifrons* Giraud**

This race was accredited to Texas by Giraud (ibid., pl. 2), but there is no subsequent record of its occurrence even near Texas; the original specimen undoubtedly came from some part of Mexico. Furthermore, the type is unlike any of the better known races of the species.

WESTERN PURPLE MARTIN, *Progne subis hesperia* Brewster*

The western form of the Purple Martin has been accredited to Fort Davis, Texas (Miller, 1906, *Bull. Amer. Mus. Nat. Hist.*, vol. 22, p. 178). The birds of this region, however, all belong to the eastern race, *P. s. subis*, and there is no certain record of *P. s. hesperia* from Texas.

BLUE-EARED SCRUB JAY, *Aphelocoma coerulescens cyanotis* (Ridgway)*

All Texas records of *A. c. cyanotis*, of Mexico, prove to belong under *A. c. texana*.

SOUTHERN PLAIN-TAILED BROWN JAY, *Psilorhinus morio morio* (Wagler)**

This race is accredited to the Rio Grande delta of Texas by

S. F. Baird (1858, *Rep. Expl. and Surv. R. R. Pac.*, vol. 9, p. XLIII), but apparently without either specimen or definite record.

EASTERN BLACK-CAPPED CHICKADEE, *Parus atricapillus atricapillus* (Linnaeus)*

All Texas records of the Black-capped Chickadee belong under *P. a. septentrionalis*.

MEXICAN CHICKADEE, *Parus sclateri* Kleinschmidt

Also known as Gray-sided Chickadee and Sclater's Chickadee.

From time to time, books on U.S. birds include the Davis Mountains of Texas in the range of *P. sclateri*; the latest is R. H. Pough's *Audubon Western Bird Guide*, 1957, page 195. The Mexican Chickadee is a sedentary bird of fir-pine-oak forests growing at high altitudes. The Davis Mountains group constitutes an island in a sea of semiarid, largely treeless terrain. This mountain clump supports a sparse pine-oak woods that is already occupied to capacity by four members of the Paridae—Mountain Chickadee, Black-crested Titmouse, Lead-colored (Common) Bushtit, and Black-eared Bushtit; in bygone days, apparently a few individuals of the Plain Titmouse sometimes drifted in from the Guadalupe Mountains to the north. In addition, the Verdin inhabits brush at the base of the mountains, and the nearby Edwards Plateau supplies habitat for the Carolina Chickadee. In short, all tit niches in and approaching the Davis Mountains are filled; there is no room for *Parus sclateri*. Furthermore, generations of bird watchers in these popular mountains have failed to come up with even one verified sighting. Probably some collector of long ago got his Mexican specimens mixed with some he had taken in the Davis Mountains.—EDITOR

TEXAS TUFTED TITMOUSE, *Baeolophus bicolor texensis* (Sennett)†

This bird was first described under the name of *Parus bicolor texensis* from Bee Co., Texas, by G. B. Sennett (1887, *Auk* 4: 29) as a supposed subspecies of the Tufted Titmouse.

That this bird, the Chestnut-fronted Titmouse (see below), and the two parent species—*Baeolophus bicolor* and *Baeolophus atricristatus*—all occur in the same locality and, further, that the present bird and the Chestnut-fronted form an unbroken series of intermediates between the two distinct species show conclusively that they are hybrids of the two species. Records of hybrid tits will be found on the *B. bicolor* × *B. atricristatus* map in the main text.

CHESTNUT-FRONTED BLACK-CRESTED TITMOUSE, *Baeolophus atricristatus castaneifrons* (Sennett)†

This bird was first described by G. B. Sennett (ibid., p. 28) from specimens taken in Bee Co., Texas. Like the Texas Tufted Titmouse, it is a hybrid between *Baeolophus bicolor* and *Baeolophus atricristatus*. It occurs only in that region of Texas where the two species live together. Records of hybrid tits will be found on the *B. bicolor* × *B. atricristatus* map in the main text.

PLATEAU BRIDLED TITMOUSE, *Baeolophus wollweberi annexus* (Cassin)**

Parus wollweberi wollweberi of Dist. check-list of Mexico, pt. 2, 1957.

This bird was described by Cassin (1850, *Proc. Acad. Nat. Sci. Phila.*, p. 103) from a specimen collected by J. W. Audubon supposedly on the Rio Grande in Texas. There is, however, much doubt regarding the real source of the type and it undoubtedly came from some part of Mexico. At any rate, the record is too uncertain to give the species a clear title to a place on the Texas list.

The type of *B. w. annexus* has been shown by van Rossem

(1947, *Fieldiana, Zool.* 31: 88) to be identical with *B. w. wollweberi*; and the northern race of the species was therefore described by him as *Parus wollweberi phillipsi* (ibid., p. 89; type locality, "Yank Spring, Sycamore Cañon, Pajaritos Mountains, Santa Cruz County, Arizona"), which subspecies properly belongs on the North American list.

SHORT-WINGED HYLOPHILUS, *Hylophilus decurtatus* (Bonaparte)

Gray-headed Greenlet, Gray-headed Hylophilus, and Lesser Greenlet of various authors.

This species was recorded from Texas by Giraud (1852, *Ann. Lyc. Nat. Hist. New York* 5: 40); however, it is without much doubt a mistake, although it was based on a specimen.

BAHAMA HONEYCREEPER, *Coereba bahamensis* (Reichenbach)

Often merged into *Coereba flaveola*.

This species was accredited to Texas by H. W. Henshaw (1875, *Rep. Sec. of War*, vol. 2, pt. 2, p. 1077), but evidently through inadvertence, since its occurrence in this state must be considered highly improbable.

BREWSTER'S WARBLER, *Helminthophila leucobronchialis* (Brewster)†

This form included in genus *Vermivora* by A.O.U. check-list, 1957, and by most authors.

This bird was originally described by William Brewster (1874, *Amer. Sportsman* 5 [3]: 33) from a specimen taken at Newtonville, Massachusetts. For some years it was supposed to be a distinct species but is now regarded as a hybrid between the Golden-winged Warbler, *Helminthophila chrysoptera*, and the Blue-winged Warbler, *H. pinus*. Texas sightings of this form and of the Lawrence's Warbler, another hybrid form of the same parent species, are discussed in the HAUNTS AND HABITS of the Blue-winged Warbler in the main text.

LUTESCENT ORANGE-CROWNED WARBLER, *Helminthophila celata lutescens* (Ridgway)°

Placed in genus *Vermivora* by A.O.U. check-list, 1957, and by most authors.

Although a number of individuals of this race have been reported from Texas, there is no authentic instance of its occurrence in the state; all previous records refer undoubtedly to the Rocky Mountain form, *H. c. orestera*.

MEXICAN OLIVE WARBLER, *Peucedramus olivaceus olivaceus* (Giraud)°°

The type of this subspecies was supposed by Giraud (1841, *Sixteen Species North Amer. Birds*, p. 31) to have been taken in Texas. There is, however, no evidence to show that this race has ever occurred in the state.

EDITOR'S NOTE: This species is entered in the main text under the name currently (1973) used for the species—*Peucedramus taeniatus*.

EASTERN BELL'S WARBLER, *Basileuterus belli belli* (Giraud)

Golden-browed Warbler of some authors.

The type of this bird described by Giraud (ibid., p. 17) was supposed to have been taken in Texas, but so much doubt has been thrown on Giraud's Texas records that unless otherwise corroborated they should at present be held in abeyance.

RED-FACED WARBLER, *Cardellina rubrifrons* (Giraud)°°

The type specimen of *Cardellina rubrifrons* was reported by

Giraud (ibid., p. 29) to have been taken in Texas. Subsequent investigation, however, has proved that this record is mistaken.

RED WARBLER, *Ergaticus ruber* (Swainson)

The Red Warbler is another species which Giraud (ibid., p. 19) redescribed from a reputed Texas specimen. However, the species' occurrence in Texas is exceedingly questionable.

MEXICAN RED-BELLIED REDSTART, *Myioborus miniatus miniatus* (Swainson)

Slate-throated Redstart of many authors.

This is another species redescribed by Giraud (ibid., p. 15) and accredited by him to Texas. From the distribution of the species, it must be considered as of very doubtful occurrence within the limits of the state.

FLORIDA PURPLE GRACKLE, *Quiscalus quiscula quiscula* (Linnaeus)°

The Florida Purple Grackle has been several times reported from the coastal region of s.e. Texas, but no definite record of its occurrence here has rewarded investigations.

BLUE-HEADED EUPHONIA, *Tanagra elegantissima* (Bonaparte)

Tanagra musica elegantissima of Dist. check-list of Mexico, pt. 2, 1957; Blue-hooded Euphonia and Musical Euphonia of various authors.

This species was reported from Texas by Giraud (1841, *Sixteen Species North Amer. Birds*, p. 23), but the specimen on which this record was based was undoubtedly obtained in Mexico.

BLUE BUNTING, *Cyanocompsa parellina* (Bonaparte)

J. A. Lane (1971, rev. 1972, *A Birder's Guide to the Rio Grande Valley of Texas*, p. 50) reports one sight record of Blue Bunting from Santa Ana National Wildlife Refuge. However, no substantiating details accompanied this first U.S. report of this tropical Mexican species.—EDITOR

ARIZONA LESSER GOLDFINCH, *Spinus psaltria arizonae* (Coues)‡

All Texas references to *S. p. arizonae* belong to the Arkansas Lesser Goldfinch, *S. p. psaltria*, since the former is simply an immature plumage stage of the latter.

MEXICAN LESSER GOLDFINCH, *Spinus psaltria mexicanus* (Swainson)‡

All Texas records of *S. p. mexicanus* belong under *S. p. psaltria*, since the former is not subspecifically separable from the nominate race of the species.

EASTERN HENSLOW'S SPARROW, *Nemospiza henslowii susurrans* (Brewster)°

Placed in genus *Passerherbulus* by A.O.U. check-list, 1957.

So far as it is possible to determine, all Texas records of this species prove to belong under the Western Henslow's Sparrow, *N. h. henslowii*.

ATLANTIC SHARP-TAILED SPARROW, *Ammospiza caudacuta caudacuta* (Gmelin)°

As yet, this race has no authentic Texas record, although it possibly occurs as an occasional winter or autumn visitor in coastal marshes. H. Nehrling (1882, *Bull. Nuttall Ornith. Club* 7 [1]: 12) recorded it from Galveston Bay and the Gulf coast of Galveston Co., but later stated that this observation should be credited to the Nelson's Sharp-tailed Sparrow, *A. c. nelsoni*. Individuals taken at Decatur, Texas, on Jan. 28 and 29, 1890, by John A. Donald, were recorded by L. Jones (1892, *Wilson Quarterly* 4: 29) as *A. c. caudacuta* but they undoubtedly should be referred to *A. c. nelsoni*.

RIDGWAY'S JUNCO, *Junco annectens* Baird †

A specimen of this junco was taken in the Chisos Mountains, Jan. 10, 1914, by F. B. Armstrong. Ridgway has, however, shown that *Junco annectens* is a hybrid between the Gray-headed Junco, *Junco caniceps*, and the Pink-sided Junco, *Junco mearnsi*, and as such has no standing as a species.

WORTHEN'S SPARROW, *Spizella wortheni* Ridgway

This species was recorded from San Angelo, Texas, by W. W. Cooke (1885, *Ornithologist & Oologist* 10: 127) from a specimen collected by William Lloyd. However, this proved on more careful examination to be an example of the Western Field Sparrow, *Spizella pusilla arenacea*.

BIBLIOGRAPHY OF TEXAS ORNITHOLOGY,
A Selected List, 1555–1973

Abbott, C. E. 1929. Birds in western Texas. *Wilson Bull.* 41: 44–45.

Abert, J. W. 1846. *Journal of Lieutenant J. W. Abert, from Bent's Fort to St. Louis, in 1845.* Sen. Doc., 29th Cong., 1st sess., 8, no. 438. [Many references to Texas birds.]

Acord, Peggy (Mrs. I. D.), J. H. Bailey, and Betty Bailey. 1955. *Field Checklist of the Birds of the Panhandle of Texas.* Canyon: West Texas College Press and Texas Panhandle Audubon Society.

Adams, H. H. 1906. The Passenger Pigeon. *Amer. Field* 66: 572.

Aiken, C. H. III. 1961. Observation of White-necked Raven on Galveston Island, Texas. *Wilson Bull.* 73: 384.

Alderman, J. A. 1956. Adventures with Red-tailed Hawks. *Texas Game and Fish* 14: 6–7, 24.

———. 1959a. Before the battle. *Texas Game and Fish* 17: 14–15. [Cooper's Hawks at nest.]

———. 1959b. Ghost birds of Texas. *Texas Game and Fish* 17: 20–21.

———. 1960. The golden monarch. *Texas Game and Fish* 18: 4–5, 28. [Golden Eagle.]

Aldrich, J. W. 1946. The U.S. races of the Bobwhite. *Auk* 63: 493–508.

———. 1968. In memoriam: Harry Church Oberholser. *Auk* 85: 24–29.

Aldrich, J. W., and K. P. Baer. 1970. Status and speciation in the Mexican Duck (*Anas diazi*). *Wilson Bull.* 82: 63–72.

Allaire, P. N. 1972. Field Sparrow uses abandoned nest for August brood. *Auk* 89: 886.

Allan, P. F. 1947. Notes on the Mississippi Kite in Hemphill County, Texas. *Condor* 49: 88–89.

———. 1949. Black-chinned Hummingbird in Tarrant County, Texas. *Condor* 51: 271–272.

———. 1950. Scissor-tailed Flycatcher, *Muscivora forficata*, feeding at night. *Auk* 67: 517.

Allan, P. F., and P. R. Sime. 1943a. Distribution and abundance of the Mississippi Kite in the Texas Panhandle. *Condor* 45: 110–112.

———. 1943b. A hawk census on Texas Panhandle highways. *Wilson Bull.* 55: 29–39.

Allen, Arthur A. 1944. Report of the A.O.U. Committee on Bird Protection for 1943; Part B, Present status of certain endangered species. *Auk* 61: 630–635.

———. 1951. *Stalking Birds with Color Camera.* Washington, D. C.: National Geographic Society. [Color photographs of many wild Texas species published in book form for first time.]

Allen, Arthur A., and Peter Paul Kellogg. 1937. Recent observation on the Ivory-billed Woodpecker. *Auk* 54: 164–184.

Allen, F. H. 1940. Conservation notes. *Auk* 57: 292. [Status of White Ibis and Roseate Spoonbill in Texas.]

Allen, J. A. 1877. Occurrence of the Western Nonpareil and Berlandier's Wren at Fort Brown, Texas. *Bull. Nutt. Ornith. Club.* 2: 109–110. [First U.S. records of Varied Bunting and Lomita Carolina Wren.]

———. 1878. Rufous-headed Sparrow (*Peucaea ruficeps*) in Texas. *Bull. Nutt. Ornith. Club* 3: 188–189.

———. 1880. On recent additions to the ornithological fauna of North America. *Bull. Nutt. Ornith Club* 5: 85–92. [Many Texas records.]

———. 1888a. Descriptions of two new subspecies of the Seaside Sparrow (*Ammodramus maritimus*). *Auk* 5: 284–287.

———. 1888b. Further notes on Seaside Sparrows. *Auk* 5: 426.

———. 1891. Capture of *Geothlypis poliocephala palpebralis* in Cameron County, Texas. *Auk* 8: 316.

———. 1899. Republication of descriptions of new species and subspecies of North American birds. *Auk* 16: 338–350.

———. 1900. The Little Black Rail. *Auk* 17: 1–8.

———. 1901. Republication of descriptions of new species and subspecies of North American birds, no. 2. *Auk* 18: 172–179. [Original description of Northern Least Grebe reproduced.]

———. 1907a. The *Baeolophus bicolor–atricristatus* group. *Bull. Amer. Mus. Nat. Hist.* 23: 467–481. [Texas study of Tufted–Black-crested titmouse complex.]

———. 1907b. The Rio Grande Seedeater, its status and technical history. *Auk* 24: 26–30.

Allen, Robert Porter. 1935a. Notes on some bird colonies on the Gulf coast. *Auk* 52: 198–200.

———. 1935b. Notes on the Roseate Spoonbill on the Gulf coast. *Auk* 52: 77–78. [Accurate census on Texas coast.]

———. 1942. *The Roseate Spoonbill.* Research Report no. 2. New York: National Audubon Society.

———. 1950. The Whooping Crane and its environment. *Audubon Mag.* 52: 92–95.

————. 1952a. Bird colonies along the Texas coast. *Audubon Mag.* 54: 254–259, 270.

————. 1952b. *The Whooping Crane.* Research Report no. 3. New York: Nat. Audubon Soc.

————. 1954. Additional data on the food of the Whooping Crane. *Auk* 71: 198.

————. 1956. The Whooping Crane. *Texas Game and Fish* 14: 16–17, 30.

————. 1960. Do we want to save the Whooping Crane? *Texas Game and Fish* 18: 16–19.

————. 1961. The Whooping Crane's world. In: *Discovery*, J. K. Terres, ed., pp. 156–163. New York: J. B. Lippincott.

American Birds. 1971–. Vol. 25–. See *Audubon Field Notes.*

American Ornithologists' Union. 1935. *Abridged Check-list of North American Birds.* Washington D. C.: American Ornithologists' Union.

————. 1957. *Check-list of North American Birds.* 5th ed. Baltimore: Port City Press.

Anderson, D. W. 1971. Thickness of 1967–69 Whooping Crane egg shells compared to that of pre-1910 specimens. *Auk* 88: 433–434.

Anonymous. 1909. A disappearing bird. *Forest and Stream* 73: 1012. [Texas record of Eskimo Curlew.]

Anonymous. 1970. White-winged Doves . . . international research. *Texas Agricultural Progress* 16, no. 2. College Station: Texas Agric. Exper. Sta., Texas A&M Univ.

Anonymous. 1972. High Island: Haven for Birds. *Horizons*, vol. for Sept., pp. 1–6. Amoco Production Co.

Arnold, Jack. 1952. Whitewing dilemma. *Texas Game and Fish* 10: 4–7.

Arnold, K. A. 1968. Olivaceous Flycatcher in the Davis Mountains of Texas. *Bull. Texas Ornith. Soc.* 2: 28.

————. 1969. Ornithology at Texas A&M. *Bull. Texas Ornith. Soc.* 3: 30–31.

Arnold, K. A., and D. W. Coon. 1972. Modifications of the cannon net for use with cowbird studies. *J. Wildl. Mgmt.* 36: 153–155.

Arnold, K. A., and J. C. Henderson. 1973. First specimen of Arctic Loon from Texas. *Auk* 90: 420–421.

Arthur, Stanley C. 1931. *The Birds of Louisiana.* Bull. Louisiana Dept. Conserv., no. 20.

Attwater, H. P. 1887. Nesting habits of Texas birds. *Ornithologist and Oologist* 12: 103–105, 123–125. [Bexar Co.]

————. 1892a. List of birds observed in the vicinity of San Antonio, Bexar County, Texas. *Auk* 9: 229–238, 337–345.

————. 1892b. Warblers destroyed by a "norther." *Auk* 9: 303.

Audubon, John James. 1838–1839. *Ornithological Biography, or an Account of the Habits of the Birds of the United States of America.* [Many Texas records.]

————. 1839. *A Synopsis of the Birds of North America.*

————. 1840–1844. *The Birds of America, from Drawings Made in the United States and Their Territories.* 7 vols.

Audubon Field Notes. 1947–1970. Vols. 1–24. New York: Nat. Audubon Soc. [Seasonal reports, Christmas counts, and censuses concerning Texas constitute an important source of data for the present book. From 1936 to 1940, seasonal reports by L. Irby Davis were published as "The Season; Lower Rio Grande Valley," in *Bird-Lore*, vols. 38–42. In 1940, *Bird-Lore* began a section called "The Changing Seasons," edited by Ludlow Griscom, to which Texas seasonal reports and Christmas counts were contributed through a regional editor. In 1941, *Bird-Lore* was superseded by *Audubon Magazine* (vol. 43), but "The Changing Seasons" remained unchanged through 1946 (vol. 48). In 1947, *Audubon Field Notes* superseded sect. 2 of *Audubon Magazine* to publish seasonal reports and censuses as follows: Fall Migration (no. 1), Christmas Bird Count (2), Winter Season and Winter Bird Population Study (3), Spring Migration (4), Nesting Season (5), and Breeding Bird Census (6). In the four seasonal issues, Texas is featured or included in the following regional reports: Texas Coastal, 1947–1948 (vols. 1–2); Central Southern, 1949–1958 (vols. 3–12); Southern Great Plains, 1949–1970 (vols. 3–24); South Texas, 1949–1970 (vols. 3–24); and Southwest, 1948–1970 (vols. 2–24). In 1971, *American Birds* incorporated *Audubon Field Notes*; the same regional columns continue with vol. 25.]

Audubon Magazine. 1941–1946. Vols. 43–48. See *Audubon Field Notes.*

Baerg, W. J. 1931. *Birds of Arkansas.* Bull. Univ. Arkansas, Col. Agric., Agric. Exper. Sta., no. 258.

Bailey, Florence Merriam. 1902a. *Handbook of Birds of the Western United States.* Boston and New York: Houghton Mifflin.

————. 1902b. The Scissor-tailed Flycatcher in Texas. *Condor* 4: 30–31.

————. 1903. The Harris' Hawk on his nesting ground. *Condor* 5: 66–68.

————. 1916. Meeting spring halfway. *Condor* 18: 151–155, 183–190, 214–219.

————. 1928. *Birds of New Mexico.* Santa Fe: New Mexico Dept. Game and Fish.

Bailey, Vernon. 1903. The White-necked Raven. *Condor* 5: 87–89. [Habits in Texas.]

————. 1905a. *Biological Survey of Texas.* North Amer. Fauna, no. 25.

————. 1905b. Scraps from an owl table. *Condor* 7: 97. [Diet of Western Great Horned Owl in Texas.]

Baird, S. F. 1852. *Exploration and Survey of the Valley of the Great Salt Lake of Utah, by Howard Stansbury.* Appendix C, Zoology: Birds, pp. 314–335. [Résumé of recent additions to North American avifauna, including many from Texas.]

————. 1859. *United States and Mexican Boundary Survey.* Vol. 2, pt. 2, Birds of the Boundary, pp. 1–34. [Records specimens of many Texas birds.]

————. 1864–1873. *Review of American Birds, in the Museum of the Smithsonian Institution.* Smiths.

Misc. Coll., vol. 12, art. 1 (no. 181), pt. 1. [Many Texas specimens.]

Baird, S. F., T. M. Brewer, and Robert Ridgway. 1874. *A History of North American Birds. Land Birds.* 3 vols. [Includes original Texas records.]

———. 1884. *The Water Birds of North America.* 2 vols. [Numerous Texas records, some previously unpublished.]

Baird, Spencer F., John Cassin, and G. N. Lawrence. 1858. *Reports of Explorations and Surveys . . . for a Railroad from the Mississippi River to the Pacific Ocean.* Vol. 9. [An important work with many original Texas records, chiefly from specimens collected on various expeditions.]

Baird, S. F., and Robert Ridgway. 1873. On some new forms of American birds. *Bull. Essex Inst.* 5: 197–201. [Original description of Lesser Prairie Chicken from Texas specimens.]

Baker, J. H. 1950. Bird sanctuaries of the Texas coast. *Texas J. Sci.* 2: 146–148.

Baker, J. K. 1962a. Associations of Cave Swallows with Cliff and Barn swallows. *Condor* 64: 326.

———. 1962b. The manner and efficiency of raptor depredations on bats. *Condor* 64: 500–504. [Two Texas caves.]

Baldwin, S. P. 1885. Eggs of the Caracara Eagle. *Ornithologist and Oologist* 10: 30.

Baldwin, W. P. 1956. Natural waterfowl foods. *Texas Game and Fish* 14: 6–7, 28.

Bangs, Outram. 1899. A new Barred Owl from Corpus Christi, Texas. *Proc. New England Zool. Club* 1: 31–32. [Original description of Texas Barred Owl.]

———. 1908. A new name for the Texan Barred Owl. *Auk* 25: 316.

———. 1913. An unnamed race of the Carolina Paroquet. *Proc. New England Zool. Club* 4: 93–94.

———. 1925. The history and characters of *Vermivora crissalis* (Salvin and Godman). *Auk* 42: 251–253. [Colima Warbler.]

Banko, W. E. 1956. The Trumpeter Swan. *Texas Game and Fish* 14: 13, 25.

Banks, R. C., Mary H. Clench, and J. C. Barlow. 1973. Bird collections in the United States and Canada. *Auk* 90: 136–170. [See Texas, 164–165.]

Barlow, J. C. 1967. Nesting of the Black-capped Vireo in the Chisos Mountains, Texas. *Condor* 69: 605–608.

Barlow, J. C., and R. R. Johnson. 1967. Current status of the Elf Owl in the southwestern United States. *Southwestern Nat.* 12: 331–332.

Baumgartner, A. M. 1939. Distribution of the American Tree Sparrow. *Wilson Bull.* 51: 137–149. [Texas record.]

Beal, F. E. L. 1900. Food of the Bobolink, blackbirds, and grackles. *Bull. Div. Biol. Survey, U.S. Dept. Agric.*, no. 13. [From Texas specimens.]

Beasom, S. L. 1968. Some observations of social hierarchy in the Wild Turkey. *Wilson Bull.* 80: 489–490.

Beckham, C. W. 1888a. Observations on the birds of southwestern Texas. *Proc. U.S. Nat. Mus.* 10: 633–688, 689–696.

———. 1888b. Occurrence of the Florida Blue Jay (*Cyanocitta cristata florincola*) in southwestern Texas. *Auk* 5: 112.

Bedichek, Roy. 1947. *Adventures with a Texas Naturalist.* Garden City, N.Y.: Doubleday & Co. [Reprinted in 1961; Austin: Univ. Texas Press.]

———. 1950. *Karankaway Country.* Garden City, N.Y.: Doubleday & Co.

Beezley, Clarence. 1970. Double eagle. *Texas Parks & Wildlife* 28(9): 20–22.

Bell, M. W., and D. A. Klebenow. 1973. Hurricane impact on Bobwhite cover. *Southwestern Nat.* 17: 433–435.

Bendire, C. E. 1887. Eggs of the Mississippi Kite. *Ornithologist and Oologist* 12: 12.

———. 1888a. Notes on a collection of birds' nests and eggs from southern Arizona territory. *Proc. U.S. Nat. Mus.* 10: 551–558. [Cites previous Texas record of Northern Aplomado Falcon.]

———. 1888b. Notes on the habits, nests, and eggs of the genus *Glaucidium* Boie. *Auk* 5: 366–372.

———. 1888c. Notes on the nest and eggs of *Peucaea aestivalis bachmani* Aud., Bachman's Sparrow. *Auk* 5: 351–356.

———. 1892. *Life Histories of North American Birds, with Special Reference to Their Breeding Habits and Eggs. Part I.* Smiths. Contrib. to Knowledge, vol. 28.

———. 1894. *Tympanuchus americanus attwateri* Bendire; Attwater's or Southern Prairie Hen. *Auk* 11: 130–132.

———. 1895. *Life Histories of North American Birds, with Special Reference to Their Breeding Habits and Eggs. Part II.* Smiths. Contrib. to Knowledge, vol. 32.

B[enedict], H. Y. 1888. Nidification of *Ictinia Mississippiensis. Oologist* 5: 74.

Benners, G. B. 1887. A collecting trip in Texas. *Ornithologist and Oologist* 12: 48–52, 65–69, 81–84.

———. 1889. Nesting of the Swallow-tailed Kite in Texas. *Ornithologist and Oologist* 14: 83–85.

Bent, Arthur Cleveland. 1919. Life histories of North American diving birds. *U.S. Nat. Mus. Bull.*, no. 107.

———. 1921. Life histories of North American gulls and terns. *U.S. Nat. Mus. Bull.*, no. 113.

———. 1922. Life histories of North American petrels and pelicans, and their allies. *U.S. Nat. Mus. Bull.*, no. 121.

———. 1923. Life histories of North American wildfowl. Pt. 1. *U.S. Nat. Mus. Bull.*, no. 126.

———. 1924. Birds observed in southeastern Texas in May, 1923. *Wilson Bull.* 36: 1–20.

———. 1925. Life histories of North American wildfowl. Pt. 2. *U.S. Nat. Mus. Bull.*, no. 130.

———. 1926. Life histories of North American marsh birds. *U.S. Nat. Mus. Bull.*, no. 135.

———. 1927. Life histories of North American shore birds. Pt. 1. *U.S. Nat. Mus. Bull.*, no. 142.

———. 1929. Life histories of North American shore birds. Pt. 2. *U.S. Nat. Mus. Bull.*, no. 146.

————. 1932. Life histories of North American gallinaceous birds. *U.S. Nat. Mus. Bull.*, no. 162.

————. 1937. Life histories of North American birds of prey. Pt. 1. *U.S. Nat. Mus. Bull.*, no. 167.

————. 1938. Life histories of North American birds of prey. Pt. 2. *U.S. Nat. Mus. Bull.*, no. 170.

————. 1939. Life histories of North American woodpeckers. *U.S. Nat. Mus. Bull.*, no. 174.

————. 1940. Life histories of North American cuckoos, goatsuckers, hummingbirds, and their allies. *U.S. Nat. Mus. Bull.*, no. 176.

————. 1942. Life histories of North American flycatchers, larks, swallows, and their allies. *U.S. Nat. Mus. Bull.*, no. 179.

————. 1946. Life histories of North American jays, crows, and titmice. *U.S. Nat. Mus. Bull.*, no. 191.

————. 1948. Life histories of North American nuthatches, wrens, thrashers, and their allies. *U.S. Nat. Mus. Bull.*, no. 195.

————. 1949. Life histories of North American thrushes, kinglets, and their allies. *U.S. Nat. Mus. Bull.*, no. 196.

————. 1950. Life histories of North American wagtails, shrikes, vireos, and their allies. *U.S. Nat. Mus. Bull.*, no. 197.

————. 1953. Life histories of North American wood warblers. *U.S. Nat. Mus. Bull.*, no. 203.

————. 1958. Life histories of North American blackbirds, orioles, tanagers, and their allies. *U.S. Nat. Mus. Bull.*, no. 211.

Bent, Arthur Cleveland; O. L. Austin, Jr., comp. 1968. Life histories of North American cardinals, towhees, finches, sparrows, and allies. 3 pts. *U.S. Nat. Mus. Bull.*, no. 237. [Although original printings of the bulletins have long since been exhausted, Dover Publications (New York) has reprinted the entire series in paperback, using the original plates and pagination.]

Bird-Lore. 1936–1940. Vols. 38–42. See *Audubon Field Notes*.

Bishop, L. B. 1910. *Petrochelidon fulva pallida* in Texas. *Auk* 27: 459–460. [Coahuila Cave Swallow.]

————. 1912. An apparently unrecognized race of the Red-shouldered Hawk. *Auk* 29: 232–233. [Original description of Texas Red-shouldered Hawk.]

Blacklock, G. W. 1972. The 1972 Cooperative Census of Fish-eating Birds, Texas Upper Coast. Sinton, Texas: Welder Wildlife Foundation.

Blair, W. Frank. 1950. The biotic provinces of Texas. *Texas J. Sci.* 2: 93–117.

Blake, Emmet R. 1949. The nest of the Colima Warbler in Texas. *Wilson Bull.* 61: 65–67.

————. 1953. *Birds of Mexico*. Chicago and London: Univ. Chicago Press.

Blake, S. F. 1957. The function of the concealed throat-patch in the White-necked Raven. *Auk* 74: 95–96.

Blankinship, D. R. 1963. Cha-cha-lac! *Texas Game and Fish* 21: 16–17. [Successful transplants.]

————. 1966. The relationship of White-winged Dove production to control of Great-tailed Grackles in the Lower Rio Grande Valley of Texas. *Trans. N. Amer. Wildl. and Nat. Res. Conf.* 31: 45–58.

Boeker, E. L., and E. G. Bolen. 1972. Winter Golden Eagle populations in the Southwest. *J. Wildl. Mgmt.* 36: 477–484.

Boeker, E. L., and T. D. Ray. 1971. Golden Eagle population studies in the Southwest. *Condor* 73: 463–467.

Bolen, E. G. The Ecology of the Black-bellied Tree Duck in southern Texas. Ph.D. thesis, Utah State Univ., Logan. Unpublished.

————. 1962. Nesting of the Black-bellied Tree Duck in south Texas. *Audubon Field Notes* 16: 482–485.

————. 1964a. Tracer on tree ducks. *Texas Game and Fish* 22: 21, 28.

————. 1964b. Weights and linear measurements of Black-bellied Tree Ducks. *Texas J. Sci.* 16: 257–260.

————. 1967. Nesting boxes for Black-bellied Tree Ducks. *J. Wildl. Mgmt.* 31: 794–797.

————. 1969. The Welder Wildlife Foundation. *Bull. Texas Ornith. Soc.* 3: 26–28.

————. 1971. Some views on exotic waterfowl. *Wilson Bull.* 83: 430–434. [Texas examples.]

Bolen, E. G., and J. J. Beecham. 1970. Notes on the foods of juvenile Black-bellied Tree Ducks. *Wilson Bull.* 82: 325–326.

Bolen, E. G., and B. W. Cain. 1968. Mixed Wood Duck–Tree Duck clutch in Texas. *Condor* 70: 389–390.

Bolen, E. G., and Clarence Cottam. 1967. Wood Duck (*Aix sponsa*) nesting record from southern Texas. *Southwestern Nat.* 12: 198–199.

Bolen, E. G., and B. J. Forsyth. 1967. Foods of the Black-bellied Tree Duck in south Texas. *Wilson Bull.* 79: 43–49.

Bolen, E. G., Burruss McDaniel, and Clarence Cottam. 1964. Natural history of the Black-bellied Tree Duck (*Dendrocygna autumnalis*) in southern Texas. *Southwestern Nat.* 9: 78–88.

Bond, James. 1971. *Birds of the West Indies*. 2nd ed. Boston: Houghton Mifflin.

Bond, Mary W. 1965. Did a Barbados hunter shoot the last Eskimo Curlew? *Audubon Mag.* 67: 314–316.

Borell, A. E. 1938. New bird records for Brewster County, Texas. *Condor* 40: 181–182.

Boyd, W. W. 1922. Wild game. *Annual Report, Texas Game, Fish, and Oyster Comm., for Year Ending Aug. 31, 1922*, pp. 3–5. [Status of Lesser Prairie Chicken in Panhandle.]

Brandt, Herbert W. 1936. Mexican Turkey Vulture (*Cathartes aura aura*) at Brownsville, Texas. *Auk* 53: 325.

————. 1938a. *Texas Bird Adventures*. Cleveland: Bird Research Foundation. [Chisos Mts. and Northern Plains.]

————. 1938b. Two new birds from the Chisos Mountains, Texas. *Auk* 55: 269–270. [Original descriptions of Chisos White-breasted Nuthatch and Chisos Hutton's Vireo.]

Bray, O. E., W. C. Royall, Jr., J. L. Guarino, and J. W. De Grazio. 1973. Migration and seasonal distribution of Common Grackles banded in North and South Dakota. *Bird-Banding* 44: 1–12. [Many Texas records.]

Brazos Ornithological Society. 1967. *A Checklist of the Birds of Brazos Co., Texas.*

Brewer, T. M. 1878. Two more birds new to the fauna of North America. *Bull. Nutt. Ornith. Club* 3: 152. [Yellow-green Vireo and Rio Grande Eastern Meadowlark.]

———. 1879. The cow-blackbird of Texas and Arizona (*Molothrus obscurus*). *Bull. Nutt. Ornith. Club* 4: 123.

———. 1880. Catalogue of the humming-birds (*Trochilidae*) in the Museum of the Boston Society of Natural History. *Proc. Boston Soc. Nat. Hist.* 20: 335–354. [Rivoli's Hummingbird from Texas.]

Brewster, William. 1879*a*. Notes upon the distribution, habits, and nesting of the Black-capped Vireo (*Vireo atricapillus*). *Bull. Nutt. Ornith. Club* 4: 99–103.

———. 1879*b*. On the habits and nesting of certain rare birds in Texas. *Bull. Nutt. Ornith. Club* 4: 75–80.

———. 1882. On Kennicott's Owl and some of its allies, with a description of a proposed new race. *Bull. Nutt. Ornith. Club* 7: 27–33.

———. 1885. Swainson's Warbler. *Auk* 2: 65–80.

———. 1886. Additions to the avi-fauna of Texas. *Auk* 3: 139.

———. 1887. Three new forms of North American birds. *Auk* 4: 145–149. [Original description of Frosted Poor-will, from Texas.]

———. 1888. On three apparently new subspecies of Mexican birds. *Auk* 5: 136–139. [Texas specimen of Sonora Yellow Warbler.]

Brodkorb, W. P. 1933. Remarks on the genus *Limnodromus* Wied. *Proc. Biol. Soc. Washington* 46: 123–128. [Texas specimens.]

———. 1935. A new flycatcher from Texas. *Occas. Papers Mus. Zool. Univ. Mich.*, no. 306, pp. 1–3. [Original description of Chisos Western Flycatcher.]

———. 1936. Geographical variation in the Piñon Jay. *Occas. Papers Mus. Zool. Univ. Mich.*, no. 332, pp. 1–2. [Texas specimens.]

———. 1972. Neogene fossil jays from the Great Plains. *Condor* 74: 347–349.

Broley, Myrtle J. 1952. Our disappearing birds. *Texas Game and Fish* 10: 12–14.

Brooks, Allan C. 1933. Some notes on the birds of Brownsville, Texas. *Auk* 50: 59–63.

Brooks, D. L., and R. W. Strandtmann. 1960. The nasal mites (*Acarina*) of some west Texas flycatchers (Tyrannidae). *J. Parasitology* 46: 418–432.

Brown, Mrs. B. C., and Mrs. F. F. Davidson, eds. 1966. *A Check List of the Birds of McLennan Co., Texas.* Waco Ornithological Society. Waco: Strecker Museum, Baylor Univ.

Brown, Charles. 1973. A second brood attempt by the Purple Martin. *Auk* 90: 442.

Brown, J. W. 1895. Swallow-tailed Kite. *Nidologist* 2: 68–69.

Brown, Leslie, and Dean Amadon. 1968. *Eagles, Hawks and Falcons of the World.* 2 vols. New York: McGraw-Hill.

Brown, N. C. 1882*a*. Description of a new race of *Peucaea ruficeps* from Texas. *Bull. Nutt. Ornith. Club* 7: 26.

———. 1882*b*. A reconnaissance in southwestern Texas. *Bull. Nutt. Ornith. Club* 7: 33–42. [Annotated species list from Kendall Co.]

———. 1882*c*. Supplementary notes on two Texas birds. *Bull. Nutt. Ornith. Club* 7: 127.

———. 1884. A second season in Texas. *Auk* 1: 120–124. [Kendall Co.]

Buckley, S. B. 1880. Owls. *Forest and Stream* 15: 106. [Sight record of Snowy Owl at Austin.]

Buechner, H. K. 1946. The birds of Kerr County, Texas. *Trans. Kansas Acad. Sci.* 49: 357–364.

———. 1950. An evaluation of restocking with pen-reared bobwhite. *J. Wildl. Mgmt.* 14: 363–377.

Buller, R. J. 1955. Ross's Goose in Texas. *Auk* 72: 298–299.

Burleigh, T. D. 1939. Alta Mira Oriole in Texas—an addition to the A.O.U. "Check-list." *Auk* 56: 87–88.

Burleigh, T. D., and G. H. Lowery, Jr. 1939. Description of two new birds from western Texas. *Occas. Papers Mus. Zool. Louisiana State Univ.*, no. 6, pp. 67–68. [Guadalupe Mountains Rufous-crowned Sparrow and Frijole Black-throated Sparrow.]

———. 1940. Birds of the Guadalupe Mountain region of western Texas. *Occas. Papers Mus. Zool. Louisiana State Univ.*, no. 8, pp. 85–151.

Burnham, Gladys L. 1972. Some helminth parasites of the Sandhill Crane in west Texas. *Southwestern Nat.* 17: 200–201.

Burrows, D. B. 1918. The Audubon Oriole. *Oologist* 35: 128–131.

Butcher, H. B. 1868. List of birds collected at Laredo, Texas, in 1866 and 1867. *Proc. Acad. Nat. Sci. Philadelphia* 20: 148–150.

Cabeza de Vaca, Alvar Núñez. 1555. *La Relación y commentarios.* [First mention of birds from Texas.]

Cahn, A. R. 1921. Summer birds in the vicinity of Lake Caddo, Harrison County, Texas. *Wilson Bull.* 33: 165–176.

———. 1922. Notes on the summer avifauna of Bird Island, Texas, and vicinity. *Condor* 24: 169–180.

———. 1923. Corrections as to the summer avifauna of Bird Island, Texas. *Condor* 25: 182–184.

Cain, B. W. 1970. Growth and plumage development of the Black-bellied Tree Duck, *Dendrocygna autumnalis* (Linnaeus). Texas A&I Univ. Studies 3:25–48.

———. 1972. Cold hardiness and the development of homeothermy in young Black-bellied Tree Ducks. *Wilson Bull* 84: 483–485.

Cameron, Angus, and Peter Parnall. 1971. *The Night-*

watchers. New York: Four Winds Press. [Includes owl lore from Texas.]

Carleton, Geoffrey. 1935. Notes from the Brownsville, Texas, region. *Auk* 52: 99.

Carpenter, Curtis. 1960. Chinaberry ceremony. *Texas Game and Fish* 18: 20–21.

Carroll, J. J. 1900. Notes on the birds of Refugio County, Texas. *Auk* 17: 337–348.

———. 1927. Down Bird Island way. *Wilson Bull.* 34: 195–207.

———. 1930a. Breeding of the American White Pelican on the Texas coast. *Condor* 32: 202–204.

———. 1930b. More about the White Pelican on the Texas coast. *Condor* 32: 304.

———. 1932. A change in distribution of the Fulvous Tree Duck (*Dendrocygna bicolor helva*) in Texas. *Auk* 49: 343–344.

———. 1935. Southern Robin (*Turdus migratorius achrusterus*) in Houston, Texas. *Auk* 52: 90–91.

Carroll, J. M. 1909. "Bird Island." *Oologist* 26: 105–106.

Carroll, T. D. 1954a. The Golden Eagle. *Texas Game and Fish* 12: 7, 28.

———. 1954b. The Osprey. *Texas Game and Fish* 12: 10.

———. 1955. Audubon's Caracara. *Texas Game and Fish* 13: 10, 30.

———. 1956. The Bald Eagle. *Texas Game and Fish* 14: 13, 24.

Cartwright, P. W., T. M. Shortt, and R. D. Harris. Baird's Sparrow. *Contrib. Royal Ontario Mus. Zool.* 2: 153–197. [Texas records.]

Cassin, John. 1852. Descriptions of new species of birds. *Proc. Acad. Nat. Sci. Philadelphia* 5: 103–106. [Original descriptions of Black-crested Titmouse and Black-throated Sparrow, from Texas.]

———. 1853. Synopsis of the species of Falconidae which inhabit America north of Mexico; with descriptions of new species. *Proc. Acad. Nat. Sci. Philadelphia* 6: 450–453. [Texas records of Mexican Caracara and Harris' Hawk.]

———. 1853–1855. *Illustrations of the Birds of California, Texas, Oregon, British and Russian America.*

———. 1862. Donations to Museum. *Proc. Acad. Nat. Sci. Philadelphia* 13: 535–539. [Mearns' Harlequin Quail and Harlan's Hawk from Texas.]

———. 1868. Donations to Museum. *Proc. Acad. Nat. Sci. Philadelphia* 19: 246–251. [Apparent specimen of *Jabiru mycteria* from near Austin.]

Casto, Stanley. 1972. Conservation of birds in Texas (1844–1916). *Bull. Texas Ornith. Soc.* 5(1): 2–4.

Central Flyway Council. 1962. *Texas Waterfowl Identification Guide.* [Distributed by Texas Parks and Wildlife Dept., Austin.]

Chadbourne, A. P. 1886. On a new race of the Field Sparrow from Texas. *Auk* 3: 248–249.

Chandler, A. C. 1951. Trematodes from the Man-o-war Bird, *Fregata magnificens rothschildi*, on the Texas coast, with the description of a new species, *Schwartzitrema seamsteri*. *Texas J. Sci.* 3: 186–189.

Chapman, B. R., and S. D. Casto. 1972. Additional vertebrate prey of the Loggerhead Shrike. *Wilson Bull.* 84: 496–497.

Chapman, Frank M. 1888. List of additions to the North American avifauna and eliminations and changes in nomenclature, proposed since the publication of the A.O.U. Check-List. *Auk* 5: 393–402.

———. 1891. On the birds observed near Corpus Christi, Texas, during parts of March and April, 1891. *Bull. Amer. Mus. Nat. Hist.* 3: 315–328.

———. 1907. *The Warblers of North America.* New York.

———. 1930. Notes on the plumage of North American birds. Ivory-billed Woodpecker. *Bird-Lore* 32: 265–267. [Texas record.]

———. 1932. *Handbook of Birds of Eastern North America.* 2d rev. ed. New York and London: D. Appleton–Century Co.

C[hilds], J. L. 1909. The Ruff in Texas. *Warbler* (ser. 2) 5: 31.

Clift, John. 1963. Net gain. *Texas Game and Fish* 21: 4–5. [Goose survey to establish species flight pattern.]

Coale, H. K. 1912. *Ixobrychus exilis* in Texas. *Auk* 29: 100. [Least Bittern at Fort Crockett.]

Coffey, B. B., Jr. 1943. Post-juvenal migration of herons. *Bird-Banding* 14: 34–39.

Committee on Rare and Endangered Wildlife Species. 1966. *Rare and Endangered Fish and Wildlife of the United States.* Resource Publ. no. 34. Bureau of Sports Fisheries and Wildlife.

Compton, L. V. 1934. Fossil bird remains from the Pliocene and Pleistocene of Texas. *Condor* 36: 40–41.

Cooch, Graham. 1960. Ecological aspects of the Blue Goose complex. *Auk* 77: 72–89.

Cook, R. L. 1969. Turkeys—their history and management. *Texas Parks & Wildlife* 27(1): 18–22.

Cook, R. S., D. O. Trainer, and W. C. Glazener. 1966. *Haemoproteus* in Wild Turkeys from the coastal bend of Texas. *J. Protozoology* 13: 588–590.

Cooke, M. T. 1923. *Report on Bird Censuses in the United States, 1916–1920.* Bull. U.S. Dept. Agric., no. 1165.

———. 1937. Some returns of banded birds. *Bird-Banding* 8: 144–155. [Many Texas records.]

Cooke, W. W. 1885a. A new bird for Texas. *Ornithologist and Oologist* 10: 127. [Specimen of supposed Worthen's Sparrow.]

———. 1885b. A re-discovery for Texas. *Ornithologist and Oologist* 10: 172–173. [Arkansas Lesser Goldfinch.]

———. 1888. *Report on Bird Migration in the Mississippi Valley in the Years 1884 and 1885.* Bull. Div. Economic Ornith. and Mammalogy, U.S. Dept. Agric., no. 2. [Hundreds of Texas records.]

———. 1904. *Distribution and Migration of North American Warblers.* Bull. Div. Biol. Survey, U.S. Dept. Agric., no. 18. [Many new Texas records.]

———. 1905. The winter ranges of the warblers (Mniotiltidae). *Auk* 22: 296–299. [Many Texas records.]

————. 1914. *Distribution and Migration of North American Rails and Their Allies.* Bull. U.S. Dept. Agric., no. 128.

Coon, D. W., R. F. Gotie, and K. A. Arnold. 1971. Winter nesting attempts by Great-tailed Grackles. *Wilson Bull.* 83: 440. [At College Station.]

Corpus Christi Outdoor Club. 1967. *A Checklist of the Birds of Nueces Co., Texas.* 2d ed. Corpus Christi: Corpus Christi Chamber of Commerce and Corpus Christi Caller-Times.

Cory, C. B.; C. E. Hellmayr; B. Conover. 1918–1949. Catalogue of birds of the Americas and the adjacent islands. *Field Mus. Nat. Hist. Zool. Series* 13, pts. 1–11. [Many Texas specimens.]

Cottam, Clarence. 1961. Wildlife wonders of Texas. In: *Discovery*, J. K. Terres, ed., pp. 3–14. New York: J. B. Lippincott.

Cottam, Clarence, and W. C. Glazener. 1950. The why of migratory waterfowl regulations. *Texas Game and Fish* 9: 4–7, 31.

————. 1959a. Marine and coastal resources: Late nesting of water birds in South Texas. *Trans. North American Wildl. Conf.* 24: 382–395.

————. 1959b. Offbeat nesting. *Texas Game and Fish* 17: 12–15, 28.

Cottam, Clarence, and J. B. Trefethen, eds. 1968. *Whitewings—Life History, Status, and Management of the White-winged Dove.* Princeton: D. Van Nostrand Co.

Coues, Elliott. 1873. Notice of a rare bird. *Amer. Nat.* 7: 748–749. [Texas specimen of Le Conte's Sparrow.]

————. 1877. *Leptotila albifrons*, a pigeon new to the United States fauna. *Bull. Nutt. Ornith. Club* 2(3): 82–83. [Northern White-fronted Dove, from Texas.]

————. 1879a. Note on the Black-capped Greenlet, *Vireo atricapillus* of Woodhouse. *Bull. Nutt. Ornith. Club* 4: 193–194.

————. 1879b. *Texas ornithology. Amer. Nat.* 13: 516–519.

————. 1888. New forms of North American *Chordeiles. Auk* 5: 37. [Original descriptions of Sennett's and Florida Lesser Nighthawks, from Texas.]

Court, E. J. 1908. Treganza Blue Heron. *Auk* 25: 291–296. [Specimen from Fort Clark.]

Cowles, R. B., and W. R. Dawson. 1951. A cooling mechanism of the Texas Nighthawk. *Condor* 53: 19–22.

Cox, Jim. 1971. Avian architecture. *Texas Parks & Wildlife* 29(6): 6–11.

Craven, Earl. 1946. The status of the Whooping Crane on the Aransas Refuge, Texas. *Condor* 48: 37–39.

Crosby, G. T. 1972. Spread of the Cattle Egret in the Western Hemisphere. *Bird-Banding* 43: 205–212. [Only slight reference to Texas.]

Cross, F. C. 1950. Shrike attacked by Barn Swallows. *Wilson Bull.* 62: 38–39.

Cruickshank, A. D. 1949. Two birds new for the Rio Grande Valley. *Wilson Bull.* 61: 111–112.

————. 1950. Records from Brewster County, Texas. *Wilson Bull.* 62: 217–219.

Cruickshank, Helen. 1968. *A Paradise of Birds: When Spring Comes to Texas.* New York: Dodd, Mead and Co.

Culley, D. D., Jr., and H. G. Applegate. 1967. Pesticides at Presidio. IV. Reptiles, birds, and mammals. *Texas J. Sci.* 19: 301–310.

Dalquest, W. W. 1956. White-winged Scoter in Texas. *Condor* 58: 165.

————. 1958. Pomarine Jaeger from the interior of Texas. *Condor* 60: 258.

Dalquest, W. W., and L. D. Lewis. 1955. Whistling Swan and Snowy Owl in Texas. *Condor* 57: 243.

Davie, Oliver. 1886. *Egg Check List and Key to the Nests and Eggs of North American Birds.* 2d ed. Columbus, Ohio. [Species list for Texas.]

————. 1898. *Nests and Eggs of North American Birds.* 5th ed.

Davis, D. E. 1960. The spread of the Cattle Egret in the United States. *Auk* 77: 421–424.

[Davis, E. C.] 1886a. [Eagle's nest in Caddo Lake.] *Sunny South Oologist* 1: 20.

————. 1886b. [Laughing Gull at Gainesville.] *Sunny South Oologist* 1: 30.

————. 1886c. [Parrots at Brownwood, Texas.] *Sunny South Oologist* 1: 5.

————. 1887a. The Carolina Parrot in northern Texas. *Ornithologist and Oologist* 12: 62.

————. 1887b. Nesting of the Barred Owl in Texas. *Ornithologist and Oologist* 12: 75–76.

————. 1887c. Nesting of the Red-bellied Hawk in Cooke Co. *Ornithologist and Oologist* 12: 110–111.

Davis, L. Irby. 1934. Distribution of **Black-throat**ed Green Warblers and Wilson's Warblers wintering in Cameron Co., Texas, during the season of 1933–1934. *Wilson Bull.* 46: 223–227.

————. 1935. Wintering warblers in Cameron County, Texas, during the season 1934–1935. *Wilson Bull.* 47: 272–274.

————. 1945a. Brasher's Warbler in Texas. *Auk* 62: 146.

————. 1945b. Rose-throated Becard nesting in Cameron County, Texas. *Auk* 62: 316–317.

————. 1945c. Yellow-green Vireo nesting in Cameron County, Texas. *Auk* 62: 146.

————. 1951a. Birds new for the Rio Grande delta area. *Wilson Bull.* 63: 333.

————. 1951b. Fishing efficiency of the Black Skimmer. *Condor* 53: 254.

————. 1955. *Check-list of Birds of the Rio Grande Delta Region of Texas.* Occas. Papers Texas Ornith. Soc., no. 1.

————. 1958. Acoustic evidence of relationship in North American crows. *Wilson Bull.* 70: 157–167.

————. 1961. Songs of North American *Myiarchus. Texas J. Sci.* 13: 327–344.

————. 1962. Acoustic evidence of relationship in *Caprimulgus. Texas J. Sci.* 14: 72–106.

————. 1964a. Biological acoustics and the use of the

sound spectrograph. *Southwestern Nat.* 9: 118–145. [Texas examples.]

———. 1964b. Voice structure in *Spizella*. *Southwestern Nat.* 9: 255–296.

———. 1965. Acoustic evidence of relationship in *Ortalis* (Cracidae). *Southwestern Nat.* 10: 288–301.

———. 1966. *Birds of the Rio Grande Delta Region.* [An annotated check-list published by the author.]

———. 1972a. *Birds of Northeastern Mexico.* Houston: publ. by Mabel Deshayes. [An annotated check-list which includes Rio Grande delta of Texas.]

———. 1972b. *A Field Guide to the Birds of Mexico and Central America.* Austin: Univ. Texas Press.

Davis, L. Irby, and F. S. Webster, Jr. 1970. An intergeneric hybrid flycatcher (*Tyrannus* × *Muscivora*). *Condor* 72: 37–42.

Davis, R. B. 1970. Survival of hatchery raised bobwhite quail. *Texas Parks and Wildlife Dept. Technical Ser.*, no. 4. Austin: Texas Parks and Wildlife Dept.

Davis, W. B. 1938. Baird's Sandpiper in Texas. *Auk* 55: 671.

———. 1940a. Birds of Brazos County, Texas. *Condor* 42: 81–85.

———. 1940b. Mammals compose more than 92 percent of food of the Barn Owl in Texas. *Bull. Texas Game, Fish, and Oyster Comm.* 3: 6.

———. 1961. Woodcock nesting in Brazos County, Texas. *Auk* 78: 272–273.

Davis, W. H. 1941. Birds of Trinity County, Texas. *Oologist* 58: 128–130.

Davis, Walter R. II, and K. A. Arnold. Food habits of the Great-tailed Grackle in Brazos County, Texas. *Condor* 74: 439–446.

Dawson, W. R., J. W. Hudson, and R. W. Hill. 1972. Temperature regulation in newly hatched Laughing Gulls (*Larus atricilla*). *Condor* 74: 177–184.

Deane, Ruthven. 1879. *Vireo atricapillus* in Texas. *Bull. Nutt. Ornith. Club* 4: 58–59.

Delacour, Jean, 1954, 1956, 1959. *The Waterfowl of the World.* 3 vols. London: Country Life Ltd.

DeLaubenfels, M. W. 1924. Summer birds of Brownsville, Texas. *Wilson Bull.* 36: 161–175.

———. 1925. Unusual notes of Texas Nighthawk. *Condor* 27: 210.

———. 1954. A second flock of Whooping Cranes. *Wilson Bull.* 66: 149.

Dennis, J. V. 1954. Meteorological analysis of occurrence of grounded migrants at Smith Point, Texas, April 17–May 17, 1951. *Wilson Bull.* 66: 102–111.

———. 1964. Woodpecker damage to utility poles: with special reference to the role of territory and resonance. *Bird-Banding* 35: 225–253.

———. 1967. Damage by Golden-fronted and Ladder-backed Woodpeckers to fence posts and utility poles in South Texas. *Wilson Bull.* 79: 75–88.

deSchauensee, R. M. 1941. Rare and extinct birds in the collections of the Academy of Natural Sciences of Philadelphia. *Proc. Acad. Nat. Sci. Philadelphia* 93: 281–327.

Dickerman, R. W. 1964. A specimen of Fuertes' Oriole, *Icterus fuertesi*, from Texas. *Auk* 81: 433.

Dickerman, R. W., and A. R. Phillips. 1966. A new subspecies of the Boat-tailed Grackle from Mexico. *Wilson Bull.* 78: 129–131.

Dickerman, R. W., and D. W. Warren. 1962. A new Orchard Oriole from Mexico. *Condor* 64: 311–314. [Discusses south Texas population.]

Dillon, O. W. 1961. Notes on nesting of the Caracara. *Wilson Bull.* 73: 387.

Dixon, K. L. 1952. Scrub Jay in Bexar County, Texas. *Condor* 54: 208.

———. 1955. An ecological analysis of the inter-breeding of the crested titmice in Texas. *Univ. California Publ. Zool.* 54: 125–206.

———. 1957. (Review of) Check-list of the birds of Texas. *Wilson Bull.* 69: 119–120.

———. 1959. Ecological and distributional relations of desert scrub birds of western Texas. *Condor* 61: 397–409.

———. 1960. A courtship display of Scott's Oriole. *Auk* 77: 348–349.

———. 1961. Habitat distribution and niche relationships in North American species of *Parus*. In: *Vertebrate Speciation*, W. Frank Blair, ed. Austin: Univ. Texas Press.

———. 1963. Some aspects of social organization in the Carolina Chickadee. *Proc. 13th International Ornith. Congr., Ithaca*, pp. 240–258.

Dixon, K. L., and O. C. Wallmo. 1956. Some new bird records from Brewster County, Texas. *Condor* 58: 166.

Dobie, J. Frank. 1939. The Roadrunner in Fact and Folklore. In: *In the Shadow of History.* Publ. 15. Texas Folklore Soc. Austin. Reprinted in *Newsletter Texas Ornith. Soc.* 9 (May 1, 1956): 1–14.

———. 1941. Bob More: Man and Bird Man. *Southwest Review* 27 (1). Dallas.

———. 1954. Islands of birds on the Texas coast. *Audubon Mag.* 56: 225.

Donald, J. A., and R. L. More. 1894. A list of the birds of Wise County, Texas. *Naturalist* 1: 33–34, 45–46, 56–57, 101–104.

Douglas, W. O. 1967. *Farewell to Texas: a Vanishing Wilderness.* New York: McGraw-Hill.

Dresser, H. E. 1865–1866. Notes on the birds of southern Texas. *Ibis* (ser. 2) 1: 312–330, 466–495; 2: 23–46.

Driscoll, A. R. 1955. The Bald Eagle. *Texas Game and Fish* 13: 11, 23.

Dumont, P. A. 1933. Old specimen of the Blue-faced Booby from Texas. *Auk* 50: 92.

———. 1934. On the specimens of *Fregata magnificens* in the University of Iowa Museum. *Wilson Bull.* 46: 120–122. [Twenty-one from Texas.]

Dunks, Jim. 1969. Whitewings vs. grackles. *Texas Parks & Wildlife* 27(7): 2–5.

Dusi, J. L. 1967. Migration in the Little Blue Heron. *Wilson Bull.* 79: 223–235.

Dwight, Jonathan, Jr. 1896. The Sharp-tailed Sparrow

(*Ammodramus caudacutus*) and its geographical races. *Auk* 13: 271–278.

———. 1925. *The Gulls of the World: Their Plumages, Moults, Variations, Relationships, and Distribution.* Bull. Amer. Mus. Nat. Hist., vol. 52, art. 3.

Eanes, R. H. 1940. Bird banding on the Gulf coast. *Oologist* 57: 122–131. [Bird Island.]

Easterla, D. A. 1972. Specimens of Black-throated Blue Warbler and Yellow-green Vireo from west Texas. *Condor* 74: 489.

Easterla, D. A., and R. H. Wauer. 1972. Bronzed Cowbird in west Texas and two bill abnormalities. *Southwestern Nat.* 17: 293–295.

[Editor.] 1876. [Notes on hummingbirds.] *Forest and Stream* 7: 99. [Mentions Rieffer's Hummingbird from Texas.]

Editor. 1881. Notes [Wild pigeons]. *Amer. Field* 16: 298. [Passenger Pigeon roost near Austin.]

Editor. 1935. The Ivory-billed Woodpecker. *News from the Bird-Banders* 10: 1–5. [Record of two birds in Texas.]

Edwards, Ernest P. 1972. *A Field Guide to the Birds of Mexico.* Sweet Briar, Va.: Ernest P. Edwards.

Eifrig, C. W. G. 1929–1930. Texan bird habitats. *Auk* 46: 70–78; 47: 512–522.

———. 1930. Season changes in a bird habitat in Texas. *Wilson Bull.* 42: 239–240.

Eisenmann, Eugene. 1952. Olivaceous Cormorant. *Wilson Bull.* 64: 195–196.

———. 1955. The Species of Middle American Birds. *Trans. Linnaean Soc.* Vol. 7.

Eisenmann, Eugene, and J. I. Richardson. 1968. Yellow-green Vireo collected in Texas. *Wilson Bull.* 80: 235.

Elliot, D. G. 1888. The Jacanidae. *Auk* 5: 288–305. [Cites previous Texas record.]

El Paso Bird Study Club. 1944. *Check-list of Birds of El Paso, Texas, and Surrounding Territory.*

Emanuel, V. L. 1961. Another probable record of an Eskimo Curlew on Galveston Island, Texas. *Auk* 78: 259–260.

———. 1962. Texans rediscover the nearly extinct Eskimo Curlew. *Audubon Mag.* 64: 162–165.

Emlen, J. T. 1972. Size and structure of a wintering avian community in southern Texas. *Ecology* 53: 317–329.

Engeling, G. A. 1950*a.* King and Clapper Rail. *Texas Game and Fish* 13: 2–3.

———. 1950*b.* The Nesting Habits of the Mottled Duck in Wharton, Fort Bend, and Brazoria Counties, Texas, with Notes on Molting and Movements. Thesis submitted to Graduate School, Texas A&M Univ., College Station. Unpublished.

———. 1951. Mottled Duck movements in Texas. *Texas Game and Fish* 9: 2–5.

Espy, Pansy E., comp. 1968. Checklist of birds of the Davis Mountains. *Phalarope* 8(11): 3–7.

Fall, Bruce A. 1973. Noteworthy Bird Records from South Texas (Kenedy County). *Southwestern Nat.* 18: 244–247.

Feduccia, Alan. 1972. The Pleistocene avifauna of Klein Cave, Kerr County, Texas. *Southwestern Nat.* 17: 295–296.

Ferguson, E. H., Jr. 1955. The White-winged Dove. *Texas Game and Fish* 13: 10–14.

Ferrell, H. W. 1955. Redheads of Laguna Madre. *Texas Game and Fish* 14: 7, 31.

Fisher, A. K. 1894. Occurrence of *Aphelocoma cyanotis* in western Texas. *Auk* 11: 327.

———. 1895. The Masked Duck (*Nomonyx dominicus*) in the Lower Rio Grande Valley, Texas. *Auk* 12: 297.

Fisher, H. I. 1955. Major arteries near the heart in the Whooping Crane. *Condor* 57: 286–289.

Fisher, H. I., and D. C. Goodman. 1955. *The Myology of the Whooping Crane.* Illinois Biological Monographs, vol. 24, no. 2. Urbana: Univ. Illinois Press.

Fitch, F. W. 1947. The roosting tree of the Scissor-tailed Flycatcher. *Auk* 64: 616.

———. 1948. Extension of the breeding range of the Inca Dove. *Auk* 65: 455–456.

———. 1950. Life history and ecology of the Scissor-tailed Flycatcher, *Muscivora forficata*. *Auk* 67: 147–168.

Fitzpatrick, A. L. 1928. King Rail, *Rallus elegans*. *Oologist* 45: 142–143. [Nest in McLennan Co.]

Fleetwood, R. J. 1973. Jaçana breeding in Brazoria County, Texas. *Auk* 90: 422–423.

Fleetwood, R. J., and E. G. Bolen. 1965. Compound clutch of the Chachalaca. *Condor* 67: 84–85.

Fleetwood, R. J., and J. L. Hamilton. 1967. Occurrence and nesting of the Hook-billed Kite (*Chondrohierax uncinatus*) in Texas. *Auk* 84: 598–601.

Fleetwood, R. J., and C. E. Hudson, Jr. 1965. Probable Green Violet-eared Hummingbird, *Colibri thalassinus*, in Cameron County, Texas. *Southwestern Nat.* 10: 312.

Flickinger, E. L., and Kirke A. King. 1972. Some effects of aldrin-treated rice on Gulf coast wildlife. *J. Wildl. Mgmt.* 36: 706–727.

Forbush, E. H. 1925–1929. *Birds of Massachusetts and Other New England States.* 3 pts. [Color plates by L. A. Fuertes and Allan Brooks; contains records of birds from Texas.]

Ford, E. R. 1938. Notes from the Lower Rio Grande Valley. *Auk* 55: 132–134.

Forsyth, B. J. 1967. Migratory pathways in the Gulf of Mexico region. *Bull. Texas Ornith. Soc.* 1(3 & 4): 9, 16–19.

Forsyth, B. J., and Douglas James. 1971. Springtime movements of transient nocturnally migrating landbirds in the Gulf coastal bend region of Texas. *Condor* 73: 193–207.

Fox, R. P. 1954. Plumages and territorial behavior of the Lucifer Hummingbird in the Chisos Mountains, Texas. *Auk* 71: 465–466.

———. 1956. Large Swainson's Hawk (*Buteo swainsoni*) flight in South Texas. *Auk* 73: 281–282.

Freemyer, Howard, and Sue Freemyer. 1970. Proximal

nesting of Harris' Hawk and Great Horned Owl. *Auk* 87: 170.

Friedmann, Herbert. 1925. Notes on the birds observed in the Lower Rio Grande Valley of Texas during May, 1924. *Auk* 42: 537–554.

———. 1929. *The Cowbirds.* Springfield, Ill.: Charles C. Thomas. [Behavior studies of Red-eyed Cowbird done in south Texas.]

———. 1933. Further notes on the birds parasitized by the Red-eyed Cowbird. *Condor* 35: 189–191.

———. 1943. Critical notes on the avian genus *Lophortyx. J. Washington Acad. Sci.* 33: 369–371. [Original description of Texas Gambel's Quail.]

———. 1941–1950. Birds of North and Middle America. Pts. 9–11. *U.S. Nat. Mus. Bull.,* no. 50. [Continues series started by Robert Ridgway.]

———. 1947. Geographic variations in the Black-bellied, Fulvous, and White-faced tree ducks. *Condor* 49: 189–195.

Friedmann, Herbert, Ludlow Griscom, and R. T. Moore. 1950. *Distributional Check-List of the Birds of Mexico, Pt. 1.* Pacific Coast Avifauna, no. 29. Berkeley: Cooper Ornithological Club.

Friedmann, Herbert, et al., and Alden H. Miller. 1957. *Distributional Check-List of the Birds of Mexico, Pt. 2.* Pacific Coast Avifauna, no. 33. Berkeley: Cooper Ornithological Society.

Fritz, E. C. 1958. Golden-cheeked Warblers in Dallas County, Texas. *Field and Lab* 26: 85.

Fuertes, Louis Agassiz. 1903. With the Mearns' Quail in southwestern Texas. *Condor* 5: 113–116. [Two drawings and photographs.]

Galley, J. E. 1951. Clark's Nutcracker in the Chisos Mountains, Texas. *Wilson Bull.* 63: 115.

Gates, C. E., and W. B. Smith. 1972. Estimation of Density of Mourning Doves from Aural Information. *Biometrics,* no. 28, pp. 345–359.

Geiselbrecht, Velma (Mrs. A. H.). 1962. *Field Checklist, Birds of Bee County, Texas.* Beeville: Beeville and Bee County Chamber of Commerce.

Giraud, J. P., Jr. 1841. *A Description of Sixteen New Species of North American Birds, Described in the Annals of the New York Lyceum of Natural History, Collected in Texas, 1838.*

Glass, B. P. 1946. Notes on bird mortality during nocturnal thunderstorms near College Station, Texas. *Condor* 48: 95–96.

Glazener, W. C. 1946. Food habits of wild geese on the Gulf coast of Texas. *J. Wildl. Mgmt.* 10: 322–329.

———. 1967. Management of the Rio Grande Turkey. In: *The Wild Turkey and Its Management,* O. H. Hewitt, ed., pp. 453–492. Washington, D.C.: The Wildl. Soc.

———. 1952. Quail with one wing. *Texas Game and Fish* 10: 8–10.

———. 1963. Wild Turkey restoration progress in Texas. *Texas Game and Fish* 21(1): 8–10, 27.

———. 1964a. Note on the feeding habits of the Caracara in South Texas. *Condor* 66: 162.

———. 1964b. The Texas drop-net Turkey trap. *J. Wildl. Mgmt.* 28: 280–287.

Glazener, W. C., R. S. Cook, and D. O. Trainer. 1967. A serologic study of diseases in the Rio Grande Turkey. *J. Wildl. Mgmt.* 31: 34–39.

Glazener, W. C., and Clarence Cottam. 1958. Exotics. *Texas Game and Fish* 16: 4–7.

Goering, D. K., and R. Cherry. 1971. Nesting mortality in a Texas heronry. *Wilson Bull.* 83: 303–305. [Refugio County.]

Goldman, Luther C. 1965. The Valley. In: *Bird Watcher's America,* O. S. Pettingell, Jr., ed., pp. 337–344. New York: McGraw-Hill.

Goldman, Luther C., and Frank Watson. 1952–1954. South Texas region. *Audubon Field Notes* 6(1)–8(1).

Goode, G. B. 1893. List of accessions. *Report U.S. Nat. Mus. for the Year Ending June 30, 1890.* Sect. 5, pp. 719–765. [Many Texas specimens.]

———. 1896. List of accessions. *Report U.S. Nat. Mus. for the Year Ending June 30, 1894.* Appendix 6, pp. 108–166.

———. 1897. List of accessions. *Report U.S. Nat. Mus. for the Year Ending June 30, 1895.* Appendix 2, pp. 105–162.

———. 1898. List of accessions. *Report U.S. Nat. Mus. for the Year Ending June 30, 1896.* Appendix 2, pp. 109–164.

Goodrum, P. D. 1941. Statewide Wildlife Survey, Game Management and Demonstration Project in Texas. U.S. Fish and Wildlife Service. *Pittman-Robertson Quart.* 1(4): 335–338.

Goss, N. S. 1888. How far west has *Anas obscura* been found? *Auk* 5: 444. [Mottled Duck breeding at Corpus Christi.]

———. 1889. The Anhinga (*Anhinga anhinga* Linn.). *Trans. Kansas Acad. Sci.* 11: 58–59. [Nesting in Texas.]

Gould, F. W. 1969. *Texas Plants, A Checklist and Ecological Summary,* rev. ed. College Station: Texas A&M Univ. Agric. Exper. Sta.

Gould, P. J. 1961. Territorial relationships between Cardinals and Pyrrhuloxias. *Condor* 63: 246–256.

Graber, Jean W. 1961. Distribution, habitat requirements, and life history of the Black-capped Vireo (*Vireo atricapilla*). *Ecol. Monographs* 31: 313–336.

Graham, Ramon. 1915. Birds that nest in Tarrant Co., Texas, and notes. *Oologist* 32: 191.

———. 1916a. Nesting dates of Texas birds. *Oologist* 33: 81–82.

———. 1916b. Vulture conditions in north Texas. *Oologist* 33: 187–188.

———. 1918. Ducks and other water birds of Lake Worth, Texas. *Oologist* 35: 29–30.

———. 1919a. Bird notes from Lake Worth, Tarrant Co., Texas. *Oologist* 36: 97.

———. 1919b. Fall migration. *Oologist* 36: 69.

———. 1919c. Notes from Camp Graham. *Oologist* 36: 89–90.

————. 1919*d*. Tarrant County, Texas breeders. *Oologist* 36: 187–188.

————. 1920. Texas migration notes. *Oologist* 37: 34.

————. 1922. Glossy Ibis observed and killed near Fort Worth, Texas. *Oologist* 39: 110.

Graham, Ramon, and Jake Zeitlin. 1921. List of breeding birds of Tarrant County, Texas. *Oologist* 38: 93.

Grant, Karen A., and V. Grant. 1968. *Hummingbirds and Their Flowers*. New York and London: Columbia Univ. Press.

Green, E. K. 1890. Notes from Travis Co., Texas. *Oologist* 7: 218–219.

Greenway, J. C., Jr. 1958. *Extinct and Vanishing Birds of the World*. Special Publ. no. 13. New York: Amer. Committee for International Wild Life Protection.

Grimes, S. A. 1953. Black-throated Oriole (*Icterus gularis*) nesting in Texas. *Auk* 70: 207.

Grinnell, Joseph. 1931. The type locality of the Verdin. *Condor* 33: 163–168.

Griscom, Ludlow. 1920. Notes on the winter birds of San Antonio, Texas. *Auk* 37: 49–55.

————. 1937. A monographic study of the Red Crossbill. *Proc. Boston Soc. Nat. Hist.* 41: 77–209. [Texas records.]

————. 1948. Notes on Texas Seaside Sparrows. *Wilson Bull.* 60: 103–108.

Griscom, Ludlow, and M. S. Crosby. 1925–1926. Birds of the Brownsville region, southern Texas. *Auk* 42: 432–440, 519–537; 43: 18–36.

Griscom, Ludlow, and Alexander Sprunt, Jr., eds. 1957. *The Warblers of North America*. New York: Devin-Adair.

Grossman, Mary Louise, and John Hamlet. 1964. *Birds of Prey of the World*. New York: Clarkson N. Potter, Inc.

Grosvenor, Gilbert, ed.; illustrated by Louis Agassiz Fuertes. 1927. *The Book of Birds*. Washington, D.C.: National Geographic Society.

Grosvenor, Gilbert, and Alexander Wetmore, eds.; illustrated by Allan Brooks. 1932–1937. *The Book of Birds*. 2 vols. Washington, D.C.: National Geographic Society.

Gunter, A. Y. (Pete). 1971. *The Big Thicket, A Challenge for Conservation*. Austin, Tex.: Jenkins Publ. Co. [Contains list of "representative" Big Thicket birds, including Bachman's Warbler.]

Gunter, Gordon. 1945. A record of the Gannet from the Texas coast. *Auk* 62: 311–312.

————. 1951. Destruction of fishes and other organisms on the South Texas coast by the cold wave of January 28 to February 3, 1951. *Ecology* 32: 731–736.

————. 1956*a*. Duck blinds as nesting sites for Great Blue Herons on the South Texas coast. *Auk* 73: 131.

————. 1956*b*. On the reluctance of gulls to fly under objects. *Auk* 73: 131–132.

————. 1958. Feeding behavior of Brown and White pelicans on the Gulf coast of the United States. *Proc. Louisiana Acad. Sci.* 21: 34–39.

"H., B. C." 1881. Texas game notes. *Forest and Stream* 17: 311. [Passenger Pigeon at Hearne.]

Hagar, Connie N. (Mrs. Jack). 1932. Double and triple nests of the Red-winged Blackbird. *Wilson Bull.* 44: 184.

————. 1936. The winter in Texas. *Nature Notes* [Peoria, Ill.] 1: 58–59.

————. 1938. Birds in Texas. *Nature Notes* [Peoria, Ill.] 5: 177.

————. 1939. Spring comes to Texas. *Nature Notes* [Peoria, Ill.] 6: 66.

————. 1940. A Gulf coast station. *Inland Bird Banding News* 12: 11. [Aransas Bay.]

————. 1944. Flamingo on the Texas coast. *Auk* 61: 301–302.

————. 1945. Harlequin Duck on the Texas coast. *Auk* 62: 639–640.

Hagar, Connie N., and F. M. Packard. 1952; rev. 1956. *Checklist of the Birds of the Central Coast of Texas*. Rockport: publ. by authors.

Hahn, H. C., Jr. 1951. *Economic Value of Game in the Edwards Plateau Region of Texas*. Federal Aid Rept. Ser. 8. Austin: Texas Game, Fish and Oyster Comm. (Texas Parks and Wildlife Dept.).

Hall, C. E., J. E. Hildebrand, R. T. Binhammer, and Octavia Hall. 1959. The birds of Galveston Island. *Texas J. Sci.* 11: 93–109.

Hamilton, T. H. 1962. The habitats of the avifauna of the mesquite plains of Texas. *Amer. Midl. Nat.* 67: 85–105.

Hamlin, Steve. 1952. Sages of Silsbee. *Texas Game and Fish* 10: 14–15. [East Texas birdlife.]

Hammerstram, F. N. 1947. Status of the Whooping Crane. *Wilson Bull.* 54: 127–128.

Hancock, J. L. 1887. Notes and observations on the ornithology of Corpus Christi and vicinity, Texas. *Bull. Ridgway Ornith. Club*, no. 2, pp. 11–23.

Hannan, H. H., Bernard Callender, and J. D. Woodham. 1964. Some observations and behavior patterns of Prairie Chickens (*Tympanuchus cupido attwateri*) in Galveston County, Texas. *Southwestern Nat.* 9: 305–306.

Harper, Francis. 1930. A historical sketch of Botteri's Sparrow. *Auk* 47: 177–185. [In Texas.]

Hartlaub, Gustav. 1852. Descriptions de quelques nouvelles espèces d'oiseaux. *Revue et Magasin de Zoologie*, ser. 2, vol. 4, no. 1, pp. 3–7. [Original description of American White-fronted Goose, partly from Texas specimens.]

Hartshorne, Charles. 1973. *Born to Sing*. Bloomington: Indiana Univ. Press. [World survey of bird song; includes many examples from Texas.]

Hasbrouck, E. M. 1887. Forms of bird life in central Texas. *Scientific Amer.* 57: 264–265.

————. 1889. Summer birds of Eastland County, Texas. *Auk* 6: 236–241.

————. 1891*a*. The Carolina Paroquet (*Conurus carolinensis*). *Auk* 8: 369–379.

————. 1891*b*. The present status of the Ivory-billed Woodpecker (*Campephilus principalis*). *Auk* 8: 174–186.

————. 1893. The geographical distribution of the genus *Megascops* in North America. *Auk* 10: 250–264. [Many Texas records.]

Hatch, D. E. 1970. Energy conserving and heat dissipating mechanism of the Turkey Vulture. *Auk* 87: 111–124.

Haucke, Harry H. 1971. Predation by a White-tailed Hawk and a Harris' Hawk on a Wild Turkey poult. *Condor* 73: 475.

Haucke, Harry H., and W. H. Kiel, Jr. 1973. Jabiru in south Texas. *Auk* 90: 675–676.

"HAW." 1900. Where are the wild pigeons? *Amer. Field* 53: 254.

Hayse, A. F., and Pauline James. 1964. *Trichomonas gallinae* isolated from the White-fronted Dove (*Leptotila verreauxi*). *J. Parasitology* 50: 89.

Heard Natural Science Museum and Wildlife Sanctuary. 1967. A List of the Vertebrate Animals Observed or Collected on the Heard Wildlife Sanctuary from October, 1965, through December, 1967. Mimeographed.

Heermann, A. L. 1853. *Catalogue of the Oological Collections in the Academy of Natural Sciences of Philadelphia.* [Eastern Brown Pelican from Texas.]

Heiser, J. M., Jr. 1919. Bird-nesting in Texas. *Bird-Lore* 21: 110–111.

———. 1945a. Eskimo Curlew in Texas. *Auk* 62: 635.

———. 1945b. The Phainopepla near San Antonio, Texas. *Auk* 62: 146–147.

———. 1945c. Swallow-tailed Kite in Texas. *Auk* 62: 636.

Hellmayr, C. E. Catalogue of the Birds of the Americas . . . [See Cory, C. B., et al.]

Henderson, J. C. 1960. A Texas record of the Black Brant. *Auk* 77: 227.

Henninger, W. F., and Lynds Jones. 1909. The falcons of North America. *Wilson Bull.* 21: 77–94. [Original Texas records.]

Henze, F. C. 1968. Ducks by the dozens. *Texas Parks & Wildlife* 26(11): 2–5. [Black-bellied Tree Ducks.]

Higgins, H. C. 1891. Eggs of Sharpe's Seed-eater. *Oologist* 8: 202.

Hildebrand, E. M. 1949. Hummingbird captured by praying mantis. *Auk* 66: 286.

Hildebrand, H. H., and G. W. Blacklock. 1967. A Cooperative Census of Large Fish-eating Birds along the Texas Coast from Pass Cavallo to Penescal Point. Sinton, Texas: Welder Wildlife Foundation.

———. 1968. The 1968 Cooperative Census of Fish-eating Birds along the Texas Coast from the Sabine River to the Rio Grande. Sinton, Texas: Welder Wildlife Foundation.

———. 1969. The 1969 Cooperative Census of Fish-eating Birds . . . to the Rio Grande. Sinton, Texas: Welder Wildlife Foundation.

Hobson, M. D., and J. A. Neikirk. 1970. Re-establishing the Mexican Pheasant. *Texas Parks & Wildlife* 28(7): 3–5. [Chachalaca.]

Holt, E. G. 1928. The status of the Great White Heron and Würdemann's Heron. *Scient. Publ. Cleveland Mus. Nat. Hist.* 1: 1–35. [Texas record.]

———. 1933. A record colony of Yellow-crowned Night Herons. *Auk* 50: 350–351. [At Eagle, Texas.]

Hough, E. 1902–1904. Game birds of North America. *Texas Field and Sportsman* 1: 407–418, 475–490, 687–692; 2: 1–8, 105–110, 161–164, 213–223; 3: 57–60. [Distribution of subspecies.]

Hough, F. B. 1864. *Observations upon Periodical Phenomena in Plants and Animals from 1851–1859.* Executive Doc. no. 55, House of Representatives, 36th Cong., 1st sess. Results of Meteorological Observations, vol. 2, pt. 1, pp. 183–206. [Migration dates from Union Hill, Austin, and Williamson Co.]

Houser, John. 1967. Aerial counting. *Texas Parks & Wildlife* 25(1): 8–11. [Duck and goose census.]

Howell, A. H. 1911. *Birds of Arkansas.* Bull. Biol. Survey, U. S. Dept. Agric., no. 38.

———. 1932. *Florida Bird Life.* New York: Coward-McCann and Florida Dept. Game and Freshwater Fish.

Hubbard, J. P. 1972. King Rail and Flammulated Owl at El Paso, Texas. *Condor* 74: 481.

Hunsaker, Don II. 1959. Stomach contents of the American Egret, *Casmerodius albus*, in Travis County, Texas. *Texas J. Sci.* 11: 454.

Hyde, A. S. 1939. *The Life History of Henslow's Sparrow,* Passerherbulus henslowi (*Audubon*). Misc. Publ. Mus. Zool., Univ. Mich., no. 41. [Texas records.]

Ingersoll, Ernest. 1879. Breeding habits of the Hooded Oriole. *Oologist* [Willard's] 4: 49–50.

Jackson, A. S. 1947. A Bobwhite Quail irruption in northwest Texas lower plains terminated by predation. *Twelfth N. Amer. Wildl. Conf.*

———. 1951. *The Bobwhite Quail in Relation to Land Management in the Western Cross Timbers.* Federal Aid Rept. Ser. 7. Austin: Texas Game, Fish and Oyster Comm. (Texas Parks and Wildlife Dept.).

———. 1962. A pattern of population oscillations of the Bobwhite Quail in the lower plains grazing ranges of northwest Texas. *Proc. Southeastern Game and Fish Commissioners Conf.* 16: 120–126.

———. 1964. A study of the introduction, release, and survival of certain European and Asiatic game birds. *Trans. 29th Amer. Wildl. and Nat. Res. Conf.* Washington, D.C.: Wildl. Mgmt. Inst.

———. (1967). *A Handbook for Bobwhite Quail Management in the West Texas Rolling Plains.* Bull. no. 48. Austin: Texas Parks and Wildlife Dept.

Jackson, A. S., and Richard DeArment. 1963. The Lesser Prairie Chicken in the Texas Panhandle. *J. Wildl. Mgmt.* 27: 733–737.

James, Edwin. 1822–1823. *Account of an Expedition from Pittsburgh to the Rocky Mountains, Performed in the Years 1819 and 1820, by Order of the Hon. J. C. Calhoun, Secretary of War, under the Command of Major Stephen H. Long.* 2 vols. [Early records along Canadian River.]

James, Pauline. 1956. Destruction of warblers on Padre Island, Texas, in May, 1951. *Wilson Bull.* 68: 224–227.

————. 1960. Clay-colored Robin in Texas. *Auk* 77: 475–476.

————. 1963*a*. Fork-tailed Flycatcher (*Muscivora tyrannus tyrannus*) taken in Texas. *Auk* 80: 85.

————. 1963*b*. Freeze loss in the Least Grebe (*Podiceps dominicus*) in lower Rio Grande Delta of Texas. *Southwestern Nat.* 8: 45–46.

————. 1968. Border birding: the Valley. *Bull. Texas Ornith. Soc.* 2: 36–37.

James, Pauline, and A. F. Hayse. 1962. Sparrow Hawk preys on Mexican Free-tailed Bat at Falcon Reservoir. *J. Mammalogy* 44: 574.

————. 1963. Elf Owl rediscovered in lower Rio Grande Delta of Texas. *Wilson Bull.* 75: 179–182.

Johnsgard, P. A. 1973. *Grouse and Quails of North America*. Lincoln: Univ. of Nebraska Press.

Johnsgard, P. A., and Dirk Hagemeyer. 1969. The Masked Duck in the United States. *Auk* 86: 691–695.

Johnson, R. R., and J. E. Johnson. 1968. A Swallow-tailed Kite in Trans-Pecos Texas. *Wilson Bull.* 80: 102–103.

Johnston, C. S., and D. E. Savage. 1955. A survey of various late Cenozoic vertebrate faunas of the Panhandle of Texas. Part I. Introduction, description of localities, preliminary faunal lists. *Univ. Calif. Publ. Geol. Sci.* 31: 27–50.

Johnston, R. F. 1959. The Green Jay (*Cyanocorax yncas*) in Kenedy County, Texas. *Texas J. Sci.* 11: 320.

————. 1964. Remarks on the behavior of the Ground Dove. *Condor* 66: 65. [San Patricio Co.]

Jokerst, B. J. 1969. *Palo Duro Canyon: A Nature Guide*. Canyon: publ. by author.

Jones, C. G. 1945*a*. Rare birds of the Rio Grande. *Texas Game and Fish* 3: 17. [Black-bellied Tree Ducks.]

————. 1945*b*. Rare birds of the Rio Grande: the Groove-billed Ani. *Texas Game and Fish* 4: 15.

————. 1945*c*. Rare birds of the Rio Grande: the Red-billed Pigeon. *Texas Game and Fish* 3: 28.

————. 1945*d*. 225,000 Whitewings killed. *Texas Game and Fish* 3: 17.

Jurries, R. W., and Jim Dodd. 1973. The Attwater can be helped. *Texas Parks & Wildlife* 31(5): 13–14.

Keefer, Mary Belle. 1957. Varied Thrush in Texas. *Wilson Bull.* 69: 114.

Keith, A. R. 1968. A summary of the extralimital records of the Varied Thrush, 1848 to 1966. *Bird-Banding* 39: 245–276.

Kelley, Claude. 1935. Birds of Dallas County. *Amer. Midland Nat.* 16: 936–948.

Kellogg, W. H. 1941. Sex ratio of Turkeys in Robertson County. *Quart. Progress Report, Texas Game, Fish, and Oyster Comm.*, pp. 26–27.

Kells, W. L. 1893. The White-faced Glossy Ibis. *Ornithologist and Oologist* 18: 139. [Status in Texas.]

Kent, J. T. 1972. An ecological and statistical survey of the birds and plants of Hensel Park, Brazos County, Texas. *Bull. Texas Ornith. Soc.* 5(1): 10–13.

Kiel, W. H., Jr. 1970. *A Release of Hand-reared Mallards in South Texas*. MP-968. College Station: Texas A&M Univ., Texas Agric. Exper. Sta.

Kincaid, E. B., Jr. 1956. Ringed Kingfisher at Austin, Texas. *Wilson Bull.* 68: 324–325.

————. 1957*a*. Pájaro de siete colores. *Texas Game and Fish* 15(5): 4. [Painted Bunting.]

————. 1957*b*. All dressed up to sing. *Texas Game and Fish* 15(9): 4. [Cardinal.]

————. 1958*a*. They've made Texas home. *Texas Game and Fish* 16(2): 10–11, 24. [Great-tailed Grackle.]

————. 1958*b*. Nestful of splendor. *Texas Game and Fish* 16(4): 12–13, 28. [Bullock's Oriole.]

————. 1958*c*. Architects in adobe. *Texas Game and Fish* 16(5): 4–5, 28. [Cliff Swallow.]

————. 1959*a*. Flamboyant forester. *Texas Game and Fish* 17(3): 4. [Pileated Woodpecker.]

————. 1959*b*. The scarlet tyrant. *Texas Game and Fish* 17(6): 4–5, 30. [Vermilion Flycatcher.]

————. 1960. Black-capped Vireo. *Texas Game and Fish* 18(4): 4–5.

————. 1965. Golden-cheeks of the Edwards Plateau. In: *Bird Watcher's America*, O. S. Pettingell, Jr., ed., pp. 415–421. New York: McGraw-Hill.

————, comp. 1967. "Preliminary Checklist, Birds of Wichita County, Texas." Mimeographed.

Kincaid, E. B., Jr., and Richard Prasil. 1956. Cave Swallow colony in New Mexico. *Condor* 58: 452. [Discovery of northernmost breeding Cave Swallows just north of Texas–New Mexico boundary.]

Kirby, H. P., O. M. Buchanan, Jr., and F. W. Miller. 1960. Occurrence and breeding of the Golden-cheeked Warbler in Dallas County, Texas. *Condor* 62: 66.

Kirn, A. J., and R. W. Quillin. 1927. *Birds of Bexar County, Texas*. San Antonio: Witte Memorial Museum.

Koelz, W. N. 1954. Ornithological studies, pt. II. A new subspecies of Red-bellied Woodpecker from Texas. *Contrib. Inst. Regional Exploration*, vol. 1, p. 32.

Kofahl, H. J. 1903. The first occurrence of the kingbird in Austin, during the breeding season. *Condor* 5: 81.

Kok, O. B. 1971. Experiences in banding Boat-tailed Grackles. *Bird-Banding* 42: 106–109.

————. 1972. Breeding success and territorial behavior of male Boat-tailed Grackles. *Auk* 89: 528–540.

Kortwright, F. H. 1942. *The Ducks, Geese and Swans of North America*. Harrisburg, Pa.: Stackpole Co.

Kumlien, Ludovic. 1877. Ornithological notes from Texas. *Field and Forest* 2(8): 127–132. [Waller Co.]

Lacey, Howard. 1903. Notes on the Texas Jay. *Condor* 5: 151–153.

————. 1911. The birds of Kerrville, Texas, and vicinity. *Auk* 28: 200–219.

————. 1912. Additions to birds of Kerrville, Texas. *Auk* 29: 254.

Lamont, Thair, and W. Reichel. 1970. Organochlorine pesticide residues in Whooping Cranes and Everglade Kite. *Auk* 87: 158–159.

Land, Hugh C. 1970. *Birds of Guatemala*. Wynnewood, Pa.: Livingston.

Lane, J. A. 1971. *A Birder's Guide to the Rio Grande Valley of Texas*. Sacramento: L&P Photography.

————. 1973. *A Birder's Guide to the Texas Coast*. Denver: L&P Photography.

Lanyon, W. E. 1962. Specific limits and distribution of meadowlarks of the desert grassland. *Auk* 79: 183–207.

LaVal, R. K. 1969. Records of birds from McKittrick Canyon. *Bull. Texas Ornith. Soc.* 3: 24.

Law, J. E. 1928. *Toxostoma curvirostris*, pt. I. Description of a new subspecies from the Lower Rio Grande. *Condor* 30: 151–152. [Original description of Brownsville Curve-billed Thrasher.]

Lawrence, C. N. 1852a. Additions to North American ornithology, nos. 1 and 2. *Ann. Lyc. Nat. Hist. New York* 5: 117–119, 123–124. [Eastern Green Kingfisher, Black-tailed Gnatcatcher, and White-collared Seedeater from Texas.]

————. 1852b. Descriptions of new species of birds of the genera *Conirostrum* D'Orb. et Lafr., *Embernagra* Less., and *Xanthornus* Briss., together with a list of other species not heretofore noticed as being found within the limits of the United States. *Ann. Lyc. Nat. Hist. New York* 5: 112–117. [Original description of Olive Sparrow, together with first U.S. records of a number of neotropical species, from specimens collected in Texas by Capt. J. P. McCown.]

————. 1852c. Descriptions of new species of birds of the genera *Toxostoma* Wagler, *Tyrannula* Swainson, and *Plectrophanes* Meyer. *Ann. Lyc. Nat. Hist. New York* 5: 121–123. [Original descriptions of Ash-throated Flycatcher and McCown's Longspur, both from Texas specimens.]

————. 1853a. Descriptions of new species of birds of the genera *Ortyx* Stephens, *Sterna* Linn., and *Icteria* Vieillot. *Ann. Lyc. Nat. Hist. New York* 6: 1–4. [Original description of Texas Bobwhite.]

————. 1853b. Ornithological notes no. 2. *Ann. Lyc. Nat. Hist. New York* 6: 7–14. [Habits and distribution of many Texas birds, from field notes of Capt. J. P. McCown.]

————. 1856. Descriptions of new species of birds of the genera *Chordeiles* Swainson, and *Polioptila* Sclater. *Ann. Lyc. Nat. Hist. New York* 6: 165–169. [Original descriptions of Texas Lesser Nighthawk and Black-tailed Gnatcatcher from Texas specimens.]

————. 1869. List of a collection of birds from northern Yucatán. *Ann. Lyc. Nat. Hist. New York* 9: 198–210. [Texas specimens of Chachalaca.]

————. 1889. A new name for the species of *Sporophila* from Texas, generally known as *S. morelleti*. *Auk* 6: 53–54.

Lawrence, R. B. 1922. Old Squaw (*Clangula hyemalis*) in Texas. *Auk* 39: 250.

————. 1925. Notes on Texas ducks; hybrid Mallard. *Auk* 42: 263.

————. 1926. Golden Eagle at Houston, Texas. *Auk* 43: 369.

————. 1927. Masked Duck (*Nomonyx dominicus*) in Texas. *Auk* 44: 415.

Lay, D. W. 1938a. How valuable are woodland clearings to birdlife? *Wilson Bull.* 50: 245–256. [Walker Co.]

————. 1938b. Some observations in determining the value of cutover pine woodland for Bobwhites. *Progress Report Div. Wildlife Research, Texas Agric. Exper. Sta.*, no. 520, pp. 1–3.

————. 1940. Bobwhite populations as affected by woodland management in eastern Texas. *Texas Agric. Exper. Sta. Bull.*, no. 592.

————. 1952. *Bobwhite Quail in Relation to Land Management in Pine Woodland Type*. Federal Aid Rept. Ser. 10. Austin: Texas Game and Fish Comm. (Texas Parks and Wildlife Dept.).

————. 1965. *Quail Management Handbook for East Texas*. Rev. ed. Bull. no. 34. Austin: Texas Parks and Wildlife Dept.

————. 1969. Destined for oblivion. *Texas Parks & Wildlife* 27(2): 12–15. [Red-cockaded Woodpecker.]

Lay, D. W., and D. N. Russell. 1970. Notes on the Red-cockaded Woodpecker in Texas. *Auk* 87: 781–786.

Leazar, R. F. 1926. 1926 Texas notes. *Oologist* 43: 110. [From Moulton.]

Lehmann, V. W. 1937. The Texas Prairie Chicken. *Activities Report, Texas Cooperative Wildlife Service*, pp. 9–10. [Census in Colorado Co.]

————. 1939. The Heath Hen of the South. *Bull. Texas Game, Fish and Oyster Comm.*, no .16, pp. 1–11.

————. 1940. Drums of the dying: the story of the Attwater Prairie Chicken. *Bull. Texas Game, Fish, and Oyster Comm.*, no. 3, pp. 3, 8. [Texas population: ca. 8,000.]

————. 1941a. *Attwater's Prairie Chicken, Its Life History and Management*. North Amer. Fauna, no. 57.

————. 1941b. Bobwhite Quail: life history and management in south Texas. *Quart. Progress Report, Texas Game, Fish, and Oyster Comm.*, pp. 15–17.

————. 1946. Bobwhite Quail reproduction in southwestern Texas. *J. Wildl. Mgmt.* 10: 111–123.

————. 1952. Vitamin A—vital element for Bobwhites. *Texas Game and Fish* 10: 14–15.

————. 1956. The Prairie Chicken—where next? *Texas Game and Fish* 14: 6–7, 26.

Lehmann, V. W., and J. B. Davis. 1941a. Bobwhite Quail breeding success in south Texas. *Quart. Progress Report, Texas Game, Fish, and Oyster Comm.*, pp. 19–21.

————. 1941b. Composition of fall coveys of Bobwhites. *Quart. Progress Report, Texas Game, Fish, and Oyster Comm.*, p. 21.

Lehmann, V. W., and R. G. Mauermann. 1963. Status of Attwater's Prairie Chicken. *J. Wildl. Mgmt.* 27: 712–725.

Lehmann, V. W., and Herbert Ward. 1941. Some plants

valuable to quail in southwestern Texas. *J. Wildl. Mgmt.* 5: 131–135.

Lemon, R. E. 1968. Coordinated singing by Black-crested Titmice. *Can. J. Zool.* 46: 1163–1167.

Lemon, R. E., and Andrew Hertzog. 1969. The vocal behavior of Cardinals and Pyrrhuloxias in Texas. *Condor* 71: 1–15.

LeSassier, Anne L., and Frances C. Williams. 1959. Notes on a late nesting of Harris' Hawks near Midland, Texas. *Wilson Bull.* 71: 386–387.

Lieftinck, J. E. 1968. Report of an Eskimo Curlew from Texas coast. *Bull. Texas Ornith. Soc.* 2: 28.

Lies, M. F., and W. H. Behle. 1966. Status of the White Pelican in the U.S. and Canada through 1964. *Condor* 68: 279–292.

Ligda, M. C. H. 1958. Radar observations of blackbird flights. *Texas J. Sci.* 10: 255–265. [Texarkana.]

Ligon, J. Stokley. 1946. *History and Management of the Merriam's Wild Turkey.* Albuquerque: Univ. New Mexico Press.

——. 1961. *New Mexico Birds and Where to Find Them.* Albuquerque: Univ. New Mexico Press and New Mexico Dept. Game and Fish.

Lincoln, F. C. 1924. *Returns from Banded Birds, 1920–1923.* Bull. U.S. Dept. Agric., no. 1268. [Many from Texas.]

Lindsey, A. A. 1946. The nesting of the New Mexican Duck. *Auk* 63: 483–492.

Litsey, J. B., Jr. 1918. An eastern record for the Townsend Solitaire. *Condor* 20: 44.

Littlefield, C. D. 1970. A Marsh Hawk Roost in Texas. *Condor* 72: 245.

——. 1973. Swainson's Hawks preying on fall armyworms. *Southwestern Nat.* 17: 433.

L[loyd], W. 1884. Black-capped Vireo. *Ornithologist and Oologist* 9: 104.

Lloyd, William. 1887a. Birds of Tom Green and Concho counties, Texas. *Auk* 4: 181–193, 289–299.

——. 1887b. Some new birds for Texas. *Ornithologist and Oologist* 12: 59–60.

Locke, L. N., and Pauline James. 1962. Trichomonad canker in the Inca Dove, *Scardafella inca* (Lesson). *J. Parasitology* 48: 497.

Loetscher, F. W., Jr. 1956. Masked Duck and Jaçana at Brownsville, Texas. *Auk* 73: 291.

Long, W. R. 1968. Border eagle. *Texas Parks & Wildlife* 26(11): 20–22. [Caracara.]

Long, W. R., and Norrell Wallace. 1963. Texotics. *Texas Game and Fish* 21: 8–10. [Exotic Texas game birds.]

Lowery, G. H., Jr. 1938. A new grackle of the *Cassidix mexicanus* group. *Occas. Papers Mus. Zool. Louisiana State Univ.*, no. 1, pp. 1–11. [Original description of Mesquite Great-tailed Grackle.]

——. 1940. Geographical variation in the Carolina Wren. *Auk* 57: 95–104. [Original description of Southwestern Carolina Wren, from Texas.]

——. 1945. Trans-gulf spring migration of birds and the coastal hiatus. *Wilson Bull.* 62: 92–121.

——. 1946. Evidence of trans-Gulf migration. *Auk* 63: 175–211.

——. 1949. Central southern region. *Audubon Field Notes* 3(1)–3(5).

——. 1960. *Louisiana Birds.* 2d ed. Baton Rouge: Louisiana State Univ. Press.

Lowery, G. H., Jr., and R. J. Newman. 1950–1954. Central southern region. *Audubon Field Notes* 4(1)–8(3).

——. 1954. The birds of the Gulf of Mexico. In: *Gulf of Mexico, its Origin, Waters, and Marine Life,* Fishery Bull. 89, U.S. Fish and Wildlife Service.

——. 1966. A continental view of bird migration on four nights in October. *Auk* 83: 547–586.

Lunk, W. A. 1952. Notes on variation in the Carolina Chickadee. *Wilson Bull.* 64: 7–21. [Texas specimens.]

Lynch, Brother Daniel. 1973. Seasonal and Habitat Distribution of Birds in Two Austin, Texas, Locations. 13 pp. Austin: St. Edward's University. Mimeographed.

Lynch, J. J., and J. R. Singleton. 1964. Winter appraisals of annual productivity in geese and other water birds. *15th Annual Rept., Wildfowl Trust.*

Mabbott, D. C. 1920. *Food Habits of Seven Species of American Shoal Water Ducks.* Bull. U.S. Dept. Agric., no. 862.

MacArthur, R. H. 1959. On the breeding distribution pattern of North American migrant birds. *Auk* 76: 318–325.

MacInnes, C. D., and E. B. Chamberlain. 1963. The first record of the Double-striped Thick-knee in the United States. *Auk* 80: 79. [Kleberg Co.]

MacInnes, C. D., and F. G. Cooch. 1963. Additional eastern records of Ross' Goose (*Chen rossii*). *Auk* 80: 77–79.

Mack, B. A., comp. 1967. *Field Check-list of the Birds of Tarrant County, Texas.* Fort Worth: Fort Worth Audubon Society.

Magee, M. J. 1930. Evening Grosbeak, Robin, and Purple Finch recoveries. *Bull. Northeastern Bird-banding Assoc.* 1: 145. [First state record for Eastern Evening Grosbeak. Apparently, Oberholser overlooked or discounted this record since in his account of the species he does not treat the eastern race.]

Marsh, O. C. 1877. Notice of some new vertebrate fossils. *Amer. Jour. Sci. and Arts* (ser. 3) 14: 249–256. [Original description of *Graculavus lentus* from Texas.]

Marshall, J. T., Jr. 1957. *Birds of Pine-Oak Woodland in Southern Arizona and Adjacent Mexico.* Pacific Coast Avifauna, no. 32. Berkeley: Cooper Ornithological Society.

——. 1967. *Parallel Variation in North and Middle American Screech Owls.* Monographs of the Western Foundation of Vertebrate Zoology, no. 1. Los Angeles.

Martin, A. C., H. S. Zim, and A. L. Nelson. 1951. *American Wildlife and Plants: A Guide to Wildlife Food Habits.* New York: McGraw-Hill.

Martin, A. D. 1917. The nesting of the Louisiana Water Thrush in Harrison County, Texas. *Oologist* 34: 103–104.

———. 1918. The Bobolink. *Oologist* 35: 158. [Supposed nesting in Harrison Co.]

———. 1919. The Broad-winged Hawk. *Oologist* 36: 44–45. [Nesting in Harrison Co.]

Martin, R. F. 1971. The Canyon Wren (*Catherpes mexicanus*) raiding food storage of a trypoxylid wasp. *Auk* 88: 677.

———. Syntopic culvert nesting in central Texas Cave and Barn Swallows (*Petrochelidon fulva, Hirundo rustica*). [Discusses recent (1973) culvert-nesting Cave Swallows in s.w. Texas; forthcoming article in *Auk*.]

Maslowski, Karl, and Ralph Dury. 1931. Catalogue of the Charles Dury Collection of North American birds. *Proc. Junior Soc. Nat. Sciences* 2: 67–107. [Many Texas specimens.]

Mason, R. F., Jr. 1961. Recent White-tailed Kite record in Texas. *Auk* 78: 442.

Maxon, George E. 1919a. Military oologing in Texas. *Oologist* 33: 172–173.

———. 1916b. A soldier ornithologist. *Oologist* 33: 205–206.

———. 1920. Long-eared Owls. *Oologist* 37: 4–5. [At Fort Worth.]

Maxwell, T. C. 1967a. Gannet (*Morus bassanus*) found on Texas coast. *Bull. Texas Ornith. Soc.* 1(2): 10.

———. 1967b. Unusual feeding behavior of Louisiana Heron (*Hydranassa tricolor*). *Bull. Texas Ornith. Soc.* 1(2): 10.

———. ca. 1969. *Checklist of the Birds of Tom Green and Schleicher Counties, Texas.* San Angelo: publ. by author.

May, John Bichard. 1935. *The Hawks of North America.* New York: National Association of Audubon Societies.

McAtee, W. L. 1908. *Food Habits of the Grosbeaks.* Bull. Biol. Survey, U.S. Dept. Agric., no. 32.

McBee, Lena G. 1969. Mississippi Kites fledge three. *Auk* 86: 139.

McBee, Lena G., and Mary Belle Keefer. 1952. *Field Check-list of Birds, Region of El Paso, Texas.*

McCabe, R. A. 1954. Hybridization between the Bobwhite and Scaled Quail. *Auk* 71: 293–297.

McCall, G. A. 1847. Description of a supposed new species of *Columba*, inhabiting Mexico, with some account of the habits of the *Geococcyx viaticus* Wagler. *Proc. Acad. Nat. Sci. Philadelphia* 3: 233–235. [Distribution and habits of the Roadrunner in Texas.]

———. 1852. Some remarks on the habits, etc., of birds met with in western Texas, between San Antonio and the Rio Grande, and in New Mexico; with descriptions of several species believed to have been hitherto undescribed. *Proc. Acad. Nat. Sci. Philadelphia* 5: 213–224.

McCauley, C. A. H. 1877. Notes on the ornithology of the region about the source of the Red River of Texas, from observations made during the explorations conducted by Lieut. E. H. Ruffner, Corps of Engineers, U.S.A. *Bull. U.S. Geol. and Geog. Surv. Terr.* 3(3): 655–695.

McCune, R. A. 1970. Prairie Chicken moving days. *Texas Parks & Wildlife* 28(7): 12–15.

McDaniel, Burruss. 1962. A new species of *Chauliacia oudemans* from Texas (Analgesoidea; Pterolichidae). *Acarologia* 4: 250–256.

———. 1963. The genus *Sphaerogastra trouossart* with description of a new species from Texas (Analgesoidea; Dormglyphidae). *Acarologia* 5: 279–283.

———. 1967. New distribution record and description of *Splegognathopsis benti* Fain from the Black-bellied Plover in Texas. *Proc. Tex. Acad. Sci.* 19: 94–98.

McDaniel, Burruss, Edwin Bogusch, and Shirley McDaniel. 1963. A unique behavior pattern and observations of Roseate Spoonbills (*Ajaja ajaja*) in Kleberg County, Texas. *Texas J. Sci.* 15: 354–356.

McDaniel, Burruss, Clarence Cottam, and E. G. Bolen. 1962. A contribution to the study of the Black-bellied Tree Duck in South Texas. *Texas J. Sci.* 14: 431.

McDaniel, Burruss, and Shirley McDaniel. 1963a. Feeding of Least Terns over land. *Auk* 80: 544.

———. 1963b. Migration pattern of the Scissor-tailed Flycatcher (*Muscivora forficata*) in South Texas. *Texas J. Sci.* 16: 438–439.

McDaniel, Burruss, and I. Patterson. 1966. Nematode infestation of a White Pelican found along the Gulf coast of Texas. *Southwestern Nat.* 11: 312.

McDaniel, Burruss, and M. A. Price. 1963. A new species of *Pteronyssus* from woodpeckers in Texas (Analgesoidea; Pterolichidae). *Ann. Entomology Soc. Amer.* 56: 789–792.

———. 1966. A new species of *Microlichus* (*bubulcus*) from the Cattle Egret (*Bubulcus ibis*) in Texas (Acarina; Epidermoptidae). *J. Kansas Entomology Soc.* 39: 237–241.

McDaniel, Burruss, D. Tuff, and E. G. Bolen. 1966. External parasites of the Black-bellied Tree Duck and other dendrocygnids. *Wilson Bull.* 78: 462–468.

McGahan, J. 1968. Ecology of the Golden Eagle. *Auk* 85: 1–12.

McGrew, A. D. 1971. Nesting of the Ringed Kingfisher in the United States. *Auk* 88: 665–666.

McKay, A. K. 1946. Sage Thrasher in southeastern Texas. *Auk* 63: 255.

McKey, D. B., and C. A. Fischer, Jr. 1972. Notes on food habits of White-tailed Kite (*Elanus leucurus*) in Jackson County, Texas. *Bull. Texas Ornith. Soc.* 5(1): 10.

McKinley, Daniel. 1964. History of the Carolina Parakeet in its southwestern range. *Wilson Bull.* 76: 68–93.

McLaughlin, Lt. V. P., Jr. 1948. Birds in an army camp. *Auk* 65: 180–188.

McMahan, C. A. 1968. Biomass and salinity tolerance of shoalgrass and manateegrass in Lower Laguna Madre, Texas. *J. Wildl. Mgmt.* 32: 501–506.

McMahan, C. A., and R. L. Fritz. 1967. Mortality to ducks from trotlines in Lower Laguna Madre, Texas. *J. Wildl. Mgmt.* 31: 783–787.

Meanley, Brooke, and Ann G. Meanley. 1958*a*. Nesting habitat of the Black-bellied Tree Duck in Texas. *Wilson Bull.* 70: 94–95.

———. 1958*b*. Precopulatory display in Fulvous and Black-bellied Tree Ducks. *Auk* 75: 96.

Mearns, E. A. 1902*a*. An addition to the avifauna of the United States. *Auk* 19: 87. [Rio Grande White-eyed Vireo.]

———. 1902*b*. Description of a hybrid between the Barn and Cliff swallows. *Auk* 19: 73–74.

———. 1902*c*. Two subspecies which should be added to the Check-List of North American Birds. *Auk* 19: 70–72. [Western Mockingbird from Texas.]

———. 1911. Description of a new subspecies of the Painted Bunting from the interior of Texas. *Proc. Biol. Soc. Washington* 24: 217–218.

Meitzen, T. C. 1963. Additions to the known breeding ranges of several species in South Texas. *Auk* 80: 368–369.

———. 1967. Nesting of the Varied Bunting in south Texas. *Bull. Texas Ornith. Soc.* 1(3 & 4): 12.

———. 1968. Nesting of Western Kingbird (*Tyrannus verticalis*) in Refugio, Texas. *Bull. Texas Ornith. Soc.* 2: 28.

———. 1969. Nesting of terns along the Texas coast. *Bull. Texas Ornith. Soc.* 3: 24.

Merriam, C. H. 1888. What birds indicate proximity to water, and at what distance? *Auk* 5: 119.

Merrill, J. C. 1877*a*. A humming-bird new to the fauna of the United States. *Bull. Nutt. Ornith. Club* 2: 26. [Buff-bellied Hummingbird at Fort Brown.]

———. 1877*b*. Notes on *Molothrus aeneus* Wagl. *Bull. Nutt. Ornith. Club* 2: 85–87. [Habits of Red-eyed Cowbird in Texas.]

———. 1878*a*. Notes on the ornithology of southern Texas, being a list of birds observed in the vicinity of Fort Brown, Texas, from February, 1876, to June, 1878. *Proc. U.S. Nat. Mus.* 1: 113–173.

———. 1878*b*. The occurrence of *Myiarchus crinitus* var. *erythrocercus* Sclat., at Fort Brown, Texas. *Bull. Nutt. Ornith. Club* 3: 99–100.

———. 1881. Wild pigeons in Texas. *Forest and Stream* 16: 130. [Wood Co.]

Merritt, Arthur, Jr. 1933. Texas notes. *Oologist* 50: 55.

———. 1937. Nesting notes from Nueces County, Texas. *Oologist* 54: 95–96.

———. 1940*a*. 1939 nesting notes from Nueces County, Texas. *Oologist* 57: 45–46.

———. 1940*b*. Nesting notes from Nueces County, Texas. *Oologist* 57: 141–142.

Michael, E. D. 1967. Behavorial interactions of birds and white-tailed deer. *Condor* 69: 431–432. [Welder Wildlife Refuge.]

———. 1970*a*. Wing flashing in a Brown Thrasher and Catbird. *Wilson Bull.* 82: 330–331.

———. 1970*b*. The Evening Grosbeak in eastern Texas. *Bird-Banding* 41: 40.

Michael, E. D. 1967. Behavioral interactions of birds effects of hardwood removal and prescribed burning on bird populations. *Southwestern Nat.* 15: 359–370.

Michael, E. D., and Wan-tsih H. Chao. 1973. Migration and roosting of Chimney Swifts in East Texas. *Auk* 90: 100–105.

Miller, A. H. 1954. Nomenclature of the Black-throated Sparrows of Chihuahua and western Texas. *Condor* 56: 364–365.

Miller, A. H., and R. I. Bowman. 1956*a*. Fossil birds of the late Pliocene of Cita Canyon, Texas. *Wilson Bull.* 68: 38–46.

———. 1956*b*. A fossil magpie from the Pleistocene of Texas. *Condor* 58: 164–165.

Miller, F. W. 1939. A new bird for the Texas list. *Condor* 41: 218. [Allegheny Winter Wren near Dallas.]

———. 1952. Blue Jay, *Cyanocitta cristata*, "anting" with burning cigarette. *Auk* 69: 87–88.

———. 1954. Ross' Goose in Texas. *Condor* 56: 312.

———. 1955. Black Skimmer in north-central Texas. *Condor* 57: 240.

———. 1959. The Barrow Goldeneye in Texas. *Condor* 61: 434.

Miller, J. W. 1894*a*. Nesting of the Brown-headed Nuthatch in Texas. *Naturalist* 1: 36–38.

———. 1894*b*. Notes on Wood Duck, Water Turkey, and Swallow-tailed Kite. *Naturalist* 1: 32–33.

———. 1895. Nesting of the Least Bittern and Texas Grackle. *Oregon Nat.* 2: 25.

Miller, W. D. 1906. Occurrence of *Progne chalybea* in Texas. *Auk* 23: 226–227. [First Texas specimens of Gray-breasted Martin.]

———. 1912. A revision of the classification of the kingfishers. *Bull. Amer. Mus. Nat. Hist.* 31: 239–311.

Miner, Edna W. 1946. *Bird Check-list of Southeast Texas.* Houston: Outdoor Nature Club.

Mitchell, G. C. 1941. Life history and management of the Rio Grande Turkey in South Texas. *Quart. Progress Report, Texas Game, Fish, and Oyster Comm.*, pp. 27–28.

Mitchell, R. W. 1961. New avian host records for some mesostigmated nasal mites. *Southwestern Nat.* 6: 103–105.

Moffat, E. E. 1915. Breeding birds of Harrison Co., Texas. *Oologist* 32: 141.

Moldenhauer, R. R., and K. B. Bryan. 1970. An interesting recovery of a banded Evening Grosbeak during the 1968–69 winter incursion into East Texas. *Bird-Banding* 41: 39.

Mollhagen, Tony. 1971. A Gray Hawk in the Davis Mountains of Texas. *Bull. Texas Ornith. Soc.* 4: 10.

Monson, Gale. 1948–1964, 1972. Southwest region. *Audubon Field Notes* 2(4)–18(1), 26(1)–26(5).

Montgomery, T. H., Jr. 1905. Summer resident birds of Brewster County, Texas. *Auk* 22: 12–15.

———. 1907. The English Sparrow in Texas. *Auk* 24: 341.

Moore, R. T. 1942. New records of the Colima Warbler from Mexico. *Auk* 59: 31.

More, R. L. 1927. Mississippi Kite in Texas. *Oologist* 44: 24.

More, R. L., and J. K. Strecker. 1929. *The Summer Birds of Wilbarger County, Texas*. Contr. Baylor Univ. Mus., no. 20.

Mulaik, Stanley. 1935. An early nesting date for the Great Horned Owl. *Auk* 52: 187. [Edinburg.]

Murphy, Robert. 1968. *Wild Sanctuaries*. New York: E. P. Dutton. [Photographs and data on national wildlife refuges in Texas and elsewhere.]

Murray, L. T., and Z. E. Murray. 1934. Notes on the food habits of the Golden Eagle. *Auk* 51: 371.

Nehrling, Henry. 1880. Ornithologische Beobachtungen aus Texas, 1. *Monatsschrift des Deutschen Vereins zum Schütze der Vogelwelt* 5: 122–139. [Lee and Fayette cos.]

———. 1881. Ornithologische Beobachtungen aus Texas, 2. *Monatsschrift des Deutschen Vereins zum Schütze der Vogelwelt* 6: 111–123.

———. 1882a. List of birds observed at Houston, Harris Co., Texas, and vicinity, and in the counties Montgomery, Galveston, and Fort Bend. *Bull. Nutt. Ornith. Club* 7: 6–13, 166–175, 222–225.

———. 1882b. Ornithologische Beobachtungen aus Texas, 3, 4, 5. *Monatsschrift des Deutschen Vereins zum Schütze der Vogelwelt* 7: 72–78, 96–104, 127–134.

———. 1885. Der Würmsanger, *Helmintherus vermivorus* Bonap., Worm-eating Warbler. *Zoologische Garten* 26: 214–215.

———. 1886. Die Vögel von Texas. *Zoologische Garten* 27: 216–225, 244–251, 303–312. [Southeastern Texas.]

———. 1893. *Our Native Birds of Song and Beauty*. Vol. 1.

———. 1894–1896. *Our Native Birds of Song and Beauty*. Vol. 2. [Many notes on Texas birds, chiefly in Lee Co.]

Nelson, R. C. 1971. An additional nesting record of the Lucifer Hummingbird in the United States. *Southwestern Nat.* 15: 135–136.

Newman, G. A. 1971. Guadalupe. *Bull. Texas Ornith. Soc.* 4: 2–5.

———. Recent Bird Records from the Guadalupe Mountains, in Texas. *Southwestern Nat.*, in press. [Work covers 1969–1972.]

Newman, R. J. 1954–1958. Central southern region. *Audubon Field Notes* 12(5).

Nice, Margaret M. 1931. *The Birds of Oklahoma*. Publ. Univ. Okla. Biol. Survey, 3 (no. 1).

Nice, Margaret M., and Leonard Blaine. 1924. *The Birds of Oklahoma*. Bull. Univ. Okla., n.s., no. 20, Univ. Studies no. 286.

Nichols, Hazel B., comp. 1965. *Dallas County Aububon Society, Bird Checklist*. Dallas: Dallas Museum of Natural History.

Norris, J. P. 1886a. The eggs of the Swallow-tailed Kite. *Ornithologist and Oologist* 11: 12.

———. 1886b. The eggs of the White-tailed Hawk. *Ornithologist and Oologist* 11: 11.

———. 1886c. Eggs of the White-tailed Hawk. *Ornithologist and Oologist* 11: 103.

———. 1886d. Two species of raptores using the same nest. *Ornithologist and Oologist* 11: 12. [Western Horned Owl and Eastern Red-tailed Hawk, in Lee Co.]

———. 1887a. Eggs of *Dendroeca chrysoparia*. *Ornithologist and Oologist* 12: 202.

———. 1887b. Eggs of kites. *Ornithologist and Oologist* 12: 176. [Swallow-tailed and Mississippi.]

———. 1888a. Eggs of the Texan Kingfisher. *Ornithologist and Oologist* 13: 64. [Comal Co.]

———. 1888b. The Florida Red-shouldered Hawk in Texas. *Ornithologist and Oologist* 13: 102–103.

———. 1889. A series of eggs of the Golden-cheeked Warbler. *Ornithologist and Oologist* 14: 68–69.

Norton, A. H. W. 1896a. Albinos at San Antonio, Texas. *Bull. Wilson Ornith. Chapter*, no. 7, p. 7.

———. 1896b. Audubon's Caracara. *Bull. Wilson Ornith. Chapter*, no. 7, pp. 1–3.

Nyc, F. F., Jr. 1939. Nesting observations outside of [*sic*] Washington County, Texas—Brenham, pt. 3. *Oologist* 56: 86–88.

Oberholser, Harry Church. 1897a. Critical remarks on *Cistothorus palustris* (Wils.) and its western allies. *Auk* 14: 186–196. [Original description of Western Long-billed Marsh Wren, from Texas.]

———. 1897b. Description of a new subspecies of *Dendroica. Auk* 14: 76–79. [Alaska Yellow Warbler specimen.]

———. 1898a. Description of a new *Amazilia. Auk* 15: 32–36. [Original description of Northern Buff-bellied Hummingbird, from Texas.]

———. 1898b. *Amazilia cerviniventris chalconota*—a correction. *Auk* 15: 188. [Error in type locality.]

———. 1899. The Flammulated Screech Owls, *Megascops flammeolus* (Kaup), and *Megascops flammeolus idahoensis* Merriam. *Ornis* 10: 23–38. [Texas specimen of Flammulated Owl.]

———. 1902. Some notes from western Texas. *Auk* 19: 300–301.

———. 1903a. A new Cliff Swallow from Texas. *Proc. Biol. Soc. Washington* 16: 15–16.

———. 1903b. Description of a new vireo. *Proc. Biol. Soc. Washington* 16: 17–18. [Texas Bell's Vireo.]

———. 1903c. Description of a new *Telmatodytes. Proc. Biol. Soc. Washington* 16: 149–150. [Louisiana Long-billed Marsh Wren.]

———. 1903d. A review of the genus *Catherpes. Auk* 20: 196–198. [Original description of Texas Canyon Wren.]

———. 1905. The forms of *Vermivora celata* (Say). *Auk* 22: 242–247.

———. 1917a. Notes on North American birds, II. *Auk* 34: 321–329.

———. 1917b. Second annual list of proposed changes in the A.O.U. Check-List of North American Birds. *Auk* 34: 198–205.

———. 1917c. The status of *Aphelocoma cyanotis* and its allies. *Condor* 19: 94–95.

————. 1918*a*. The migration of North American birds, 2d ser., 7; magpies. *Bird-Lore* 20: 252–255. [Black-billed Magpie in Texas.]

————. 1918*b*. Notes on North American birds, IV. *Auk* 35: 62–65.

————. 1918*c*. The subspecies of *Larus hyperboreus* Gunnerus. *Auk* 35: 467–474. [Texas records of Glaucous Gull.]

————. 1919*a*. An albino Black-chinned Hummingbird. *Condor* 21: 122.

————. 1919*b*. Description of a new Red-winged Blackbird from Texas. *Wilson Bull.* 31: 20–23.

————. 1924*a*. The migration of North American birds, 2d ser., 25; Broad-billed, Rivoli's, and Blue-throated hummingbirds. *Bird-Lore* 26: 247–248. [Texas records.]

————. 1924*b*. The migration of North American birds, 2d ser., 26; Broad-tailed, Rufous, and Allen's hummingbirds. *Bird-Lore* 26: 398–399.

————. 1925. The relation of vegetation to bird life in Texas. *Amer. Midland Nat.* 9: 564–594, 595–661.

————. 1930. The migration of North American birds, 2d ser., 43; Ivory-billed Woodpecker. *Bird-Lore* 32: 265. [Texas records.]

————. 1931. The migration of North American birds, 2d ser., 45; the Coppery-tailed Trogon. *Bird-Lore* 33: 118. [Texas records.]

————. 1932. The migration of North American birds, 2d ser., 51; the Elf Owl. *Bird-Lore* 34: 387. [Distribution in Texas.]

————. 1938. *The Bird Life of Louisiana.* Bull. Louisiana Dept. Conserv., no. 28.

————. 1945. The astounding bird life of Texas. *Southwest Review* 30: 377–381.

————. 1946. Three new North American birds. *J. Washington Acad. Sciences* 36: 388–389. [Alaska Fox Sparrow in Texas.]

————. 1948. *Descriptions of New Races of* Geothlypis trichas *(Linnaeus).* 4 pp. Cleveland, Ohio: publ. by author. [On file in U.S. Fish and Wildlife Service, Washington, D.C.]

Ogilby, J. D. 1882. A catalogue of birds obtained in Navarro County, Texas. *Sci. Proc. Royal Dublin Society* 3: 169–249.

Ohlendorf, H. M. 1971. Arthropod diet of a Western Horned Owl. *Southwestern Nat.* 16: 124–125.

Ohlendorf, H. M., and R. F. Patton. 1971. Nesting record of Mexican Duck (*Anas diazi*) in Texas. *Wilson Bull.* 83: 97.

Ohlendorf, H. M., and Veryl Board. 1972. Nesting records for two species of birds in Trans-Pecos Texas. *Southwestern Nat.* 17: 99–100.

Oldright, C. D. 1887. [Crossbills in Texas.] *Ornithologist and Oologist* 12: 39.

————. 1893. The wrens of Travis County, Texas. *Science* 22: 15–16.

[Oldright, C. D.] "Elanoides." 1890. A list of the birds of McLennan Co., Texas. *Ornithologist and Oologist* 15: 57–59.

Oliver, S. W. 1954. A Whooping Crane named Bill. *Texas Game and Fish* 12: 4–6, 28.

O'Neil, E. J. 1947. Waterfowl grounded at Muleshoe National Wildlife Refuge, Texas. *Auk* 64: 457.

O'Neil, Mrs. Mike. 1957. A Check List of the Birds of the Commerce Area, Hunt County, Texas. Dittoed.

O'Reilly, R. A. 1944. Observations on some water birds at Rockport, Texas. *Jack-pine Warbler* 22: 135–137.

————. 1946. Northern water birds summering on the Gulf coast of Texas. *Wilson Bull.* 58: 216–217.

Oring, Lewis W. 1964. Notes on the birds of Webb County, Texas. *Auk* 81: 440.

Ornithology Group, Houston Outdoor Nature Club. 1952–. *Spoonbill.* Houston: publ. by Ornithology Group, Outdoor Nature Club. [This more or less monthly newsletter largely replaced *The Gulf Coast Migrant.* The first issue (vol. 1, no. 1) appeared in July, 1952; although somewhat sporadic, it was still being published as of Aug., 1973, when vol. 22, no. 4 appeared. With regard to Texas avifauna, the most significant portion of the newsletter is the "Clearing House," which reports sight records of birds on the upper Gulf coast; it first appeared in vol. 2, no. 1 (July, 1953).]

————. 1962. *Checklist of the Birds of the Upper Texas Coast.* Compiled by S. G. Williams. Houston.

————. 1966. *Field Checklist, Birds of the Upper Texas Coast.* 4th ed. Compiled by C. H. Aiken III, et al. Houston.

————. *Field Checklist, Birds of the Upper Texas Coast.* 5th ed. Compiled by T. B. Feltner and Noel Pettingell. Houston. [In press, Dec., 1973.]

Orton, R. B. 1969. *Climate of Texas.* Climatography of the United States, no. 60–41, U.S. Dept. of Commerce, Environmental Data Service.

Otteni, L. C., E. G. Bolen, and Clarence Cottam. 1972. Predator-prey relationships and reproduction of the Barn Owl in southern Texas. *Wilson Bull.* 84: 434–448.

"Ovum." 1877. Bird eggs and nests. *Oologist* [Willard's] 2: 86–87. [Yellow-headed Blackbird egg from Texas.]

Owen, B. L. 1958. Records of nasal mites of the Mourning Dove. *Texas J. Sci.* 10: 447.

Packard, F. M. 1946. California Gull on the coast of Texas. *Auk* 63: 545–546.

————. 1947. Notes on the occurrence of birds in the Gulf of Mexico. *Auk* 64: 130–131.

Palmer, F. A. 1959. New light on an old secret (bird migration). *Texas Game and Fish* 17: 10–11.

Palmer, R. S., ed. 1962. *Handbook of North American Birds, vol. I, Loons through Flamingos.* New Haven and London: Yale Univ. Press.

Palmisano, A. W., Jr., and S. A. Gauthreaux, Jr. 1966. First specimen of the Long-tailed Jaeger from the northern Gulf coast. *Auk* 83: 673.

Pangburn, Clifford. 1945*a*. Extraordinary fatality to a Blue-winged Teal. *Auk* 62: 142.

————. 1945*b*. The Woodcock at San Antonio, Texas. *Auk* 62: 142.

Pangburn, Clifford, and J. M. Heiser. 1945. The Phaino-pepla near San Antonio, Texas. *Auk* 62: 146–147.

Parker, H. G. 1887. Notes on the eggs of the thrushes and thrashers. *Ornithologist and Oologist* 12: 69–73.

Parkes, K. C. 1948. Reddish Egret in central Texas. *Auk* 65: 308.

———. 1950. Further notes on the birds of Camp Barkley, Texas. *Condor* 52: 91–93.

———. 1959. Systematic notes on North American birds. Pt. 3. The northeastern races of the Long-billed Marsh Wren (*Telmatodytes palustris*). *Annals of Carnegie Mus.* 35: 275–281.

Parks, H. B., V. L. Cory, et al. 1936. *The Fauna and Flora of the Big Thicket Area*. Biol. Survey East Texas Big Thicket Area.

———. 1938. *The Fauna and Flora of the Big Thicket Area; Birds of the Big Thicket*. 2d ed. Biol. Survey East Texas Big Thicket Area.

Parmalee, P. W. 1952. Ecto- and endoparasites of the Bobwhite: their numbers, species and possible importance in the health and vigor of quail. *Trans. 17th North American Wildl. Conf.* 174–187.

———. 1953a. *Bruellia illustris* (Kellogg) and other ectoparasites from quail in Texas. *J. Parasitology* 39: 222–223.

———. 1953b. Food and cover relationships of the Bobwhite Quail in east-central Texas. *Ecology* 34: 758–770.

———. 1953c. Hunting pressure and its effect on Bob-white Quail population in east-central Texas. *J. Wildl. Mgmt.* 17: 341–345.

———. 1954a. Food of the Great Horned Owl and Barn Owl in east Texas. *Auk* 71: 469–470.

———. 1954b. The vultures: their movements, economic status and control in Texas. *Auk* 71: 443–453.

———. 1955a. Notes on the winter foods of Bobwhites in north-central Texas. *Texas J. Sci.* 7: 189–195.

———. 1955b. Some factors affecting nesting success of the Bobwhite Quail in east-central Texas. *Amer. Midland Nat.* 53: 45–55.

———. 1967. Results of banding studies of the Black Vulture in eastern North America. *Condor* 69: 146–155.

Parsons, J. K., and B. D. Davis. 1971. The effects on quail, migratory birds and non-game birds from application of malathion and other insecticides. *Texas Parks and Wildlife Dept. Technical Ser.*, no. 8.

Pearsall, Joan. 1967. The eleventh hour, pt. 2. *Texas Parks & Wildlife* 25(2): 25–28.

Pearson, T. G. 1918. A Reddish Egret colony in Texas. *Bird-Lore* 20: 384–386.

———. 1920. Exploring for new bird colonies. *Bird-Lore* 22: 255–262, 321–327. [Texas coast.]

———. 1921. Notes on the bird-life of southeastern Texas. *Auk* 38: 513–523.

———. 1922. Whooping Cranes (*Grus americana*) in Texas. *Auk* 39: 412.

———. 1924. *Herons of the United States*. Bull. Nat. Assoc. Audubon Soc., no. 5.

Peet, M. M. 1948. MacGillivray's Warbler in Cameron County, Texas. *Wilson Bull.* 60: 243.

Pemberton, J. R. 1922a. A large tern colony in Texas. *Condor* 24: 37–42.

———. 1922b. The Reddish Egrets of Cameron County, Texas. *Condor* 24: 1–12.

Pemberton, J. R., and A. J. B. Kirn. 1923. Fish Crow in Texas. *Condor* 25: 65–66.

Peters, H. S. 1931. Abert's Towhee, a new bird for Texas. *Auk* 48: 274–275.

Peters, J. L. 1931. An account of the Yellow-green Vireo (*Vireosylva flavoviridis* Cassin). *Auk* 48: 575–587. [Texas records.]

Peterson, Roger Tory. 1947. *A Field Guide to the Birds.* 2d rev. ed. Boston: Houghton Mifflin and National Audubon Society.

———. 1960. *A Field Guide to the Birds of Texas.* Boston: Houghton Mifflin for Texas Game and Fish Commission.

———. 1961. *A Field Guide to Western Birds.* 2d rev. ed. Boston: Houghton Mifflin. [First regional bird book to include both Texas and Hawaii.]

———. 1963. *A Field Guide to the Birds of Texas and Adjacent States.* Boston: Houghton Mifflin. [Only very slight revision of 1960 Texas book.]

Peterson, Roger Tory, and Edward L. Chalif. 1973. *A Field Guide to Mexican Birds.* Boston: Houghton Mifflin Co.

Peterson, Roger Tory, and James Fisher. 1955. *Wild America*, Chapters 16, 17. Boston: Houghton Mifflin.

Peterson, Roger Tory, et al. *A Field Guide to Bird Songs of Eastern and Central North America.* Peterson Field Guide Series. Boston: Houghton Mifflin Co. [Phonograph recordings to accompany *A Field Guide to the Birds.*]

———. *A Field Guide to Western Bird Songs.* Peterson Field Guide Series. Boston: Houghton Mifflin Co. [Phonograph recordings to accompany *A Field Guide to Western Birds*, 2d ed.; covers w. North America and Hawaiian Islands.]

Petrides, G. A., and W. B. Davis. 1951. Notes on the birds of Brazos County, Texas. *Condor* 53: 153.

Pettingell, Noel. 1967. Eskimo Curlew: valid records since 1945. *Bull. Texas Ornith. Soc.* 1(3 & 4): 14, 21.

Pettingill, O. S., Jr. 1946. King Rail impaled on barbed wire. *Auk* 63: 591.

———. 1953. *A Guide to Bird Finding West of the Mississippi.* New York: Oxford Univ. Press.

———. 1956. Spotting the birds of Texas. *Texas Game and Fish* 14: 18–19.

———. 1960. Bird finding with Sewall Pettingill. *Audubon Mag.* 62: 34–35.

———. 1962. Southwest Texas will offer rich birding at convention time. *Audubon Mag.* 64: 158–161.

Pettus, David. 1955. The call of the Chuck-will's-widow. *Texas J. Sci.* 7: 344–345.

Phillips, A. R. 1942. Notes on the migrations of the Elf and Flammulated Owls. *Wilson Bull.* 54: 132–137. [Flammulated in Presidio Co.]

———. 1943. Critical notes on two southwestern sparrows. *Auk* 60: 242–248. [Texas Botteri's Sparrow.]

―――. 1950a. The Great-tailed Grackles of the Southwest. *Condor* 52: 78–81.

―――. 1950b. The pale races of the Steller Jay. *Condor* 52: 252–254.

―――. 1951. Complexities of migration: a review. *Wilson Bull.* 63: 129–134.

―――. 1957. Las peculiaridades del Sastrecito (*Psaltriparus*, Familia Paridae) y su incubación. *Anales Inst. Biol. Mex.* 29: 355–360.

―――. 1961. Emigraciones y distribución de aves terrestres en México. *Rev. Soc. Mex. Hist. Nat.*

―――. 1962a. Notas sistemáticas sobre aves mexicanas. I. *Anales Inst. Biol. Mex.*

―――. 1962b. Notas sobre la Chuparrosa *Thalurania* y ciertos plumajes de otras aves mexicanas. *Anales Inst. Biol. Mex.*

Phillips, A. R., M. A. Howe, and W. E. Lanyon. 1966. Identification of the flycatchers of eastern North America, with special emphasis on the genus *Empidonax. Bird-Banding* 37: 153–171.

Phillips, A. R., Joe Marshall, and Gale Monson. 1964. *The Birds of Arizona.* Tucson: Univ. Arizona Press.

Phillips, H. W., and W. A. Thornton. 1949. The summer resident birds of the Sierra Vieja range of southwestern Texas. *Texas J. Sci.* 1: 101–131.

Pickwell, Gayle, and Emily Smith. 1938. The Texas Nighthawk in its summer home. *Condor* 40: 193–215.

Pitelka, Frank A. 1938. Notes on birds observed in Lower Texas, June 7–17, 1937. *Audubon Annual Bull.*, no. 28, pp. 7–16.

Popper, D. M. 1951. Notes on the birds of Mount Locke, Texas. *Condor* 53: 51–54.

Pough, R. H. 1949. *Audubon Land Bird Guide.* Garden City, N.Y.: Doubleday & Co.

―――. 1951. *Audubon Water Bird Guide: Water, Game and Large Land Birds.* Garden City, N.Y.: Doubleday & Co.

―――. 1957. *Audubon Western Bird Guide: Land, Water, and Game Birds.* Garden City, N.Y.: Doubleday & Co.

Prevett, J. P., and C. D. MacInnes. 1972. The number of Ross' Geese in central North America. *Condor* 74: 431–438.

Pulich, W. M., Sr. 1954. A record of the Mexican Crossbill (*Loxia curvirostra stricklandi*) from Fort Worth, Texas. *Auk* 72: 299.

―――. 1961a. Birds of Tarrant County. Fort Worth: Allen & Co.

―――. 1961b. A record of the Yellow Rail from Dallas County, Texas. *Auk* 78: 639–640.

―――. 1962. In quest of the Golden-cheeked Warbler—some preliminary findings. *Tex. Ornith. Soc. Newsletter* 10 (5): 5–11.

―――. 1963a. Bird of the cedar brakes. *Texas Game and Fish* 21: 4–5.

―――. 1963b. Some recent records of the Varied Bunting (*Passerina versicolor*) for Texas. *Condor* 65: 334–335.

―――. 1965. The Golden-cheeked Warbler of Texas (*Dendroica chrysoparia*). *Audubon Field Notes* 19: 545–548.

―――. 1966. A specimen of the Little Gull, *Larus minutus*, from Dallas County, Texas. *Auk* 83: 482.

―――. 1968a. 1967 breeding bird survey. *Bull. Texas Ornith. Soc.* 2: 6.

―――. 1968b. The occurrence of the crested hummingbird, *Orthorhynchus cristatus exilis*, in the United States. *Auk* 85: 322. [Galveston Island.]

―――. 1969a. Unusual feeding behavior of three species of birds. *Wilson Bull.* 81: 472.

―――. 1969b. Golden-cheeked Warbler: threatened bird of the cedar brakes. *Nat. Parks Mag.* 43 (258).

―――. 1971. Some fringillid records for Texas. *Condor* 73: 111.

―――. 1973. Golden-cheeked Warbler. *Texas Parks & Wildlife* 31(5): 6–9.

Pulich, W. M., Sr., and W. M. Pulich, Jr. 1963. The nesting of the Lucifer Hummingbird in the United States. *Auk* 80: 370–371.

―――. 1973. First Brown Booby specimen from Texas. *Auk* 90: 683–684.

Purdie, H. A. 1879. The Golden-cheeked Warbler and Black-chinned Humming-bird in Texas. *Bull. Nutt. Ornith. Club* 4: 60.

Purrington, R. D., comp. 1966. *Checklist of the Birds of Brazos County, Texas.* Brazos Ornithological Society.

Quillin, R. W. 1935. New bird records from Texas. *Auk* 52: 324–325. [First state records of Whitney Elf Owl and Broad-billed Hummingbird.]

Quillin, R. W., and Ridley Holleman. 1916. The San Domingo Grebe in Bexar County, Texas. *Condor* 18: 221–222.

―――. 1918. The breeding birds of Bexar County, Texas. *Condor* 20: 37–44.

Rachford, J. H. 1886. Notes from Texas. *Hoosier Nat.* 1: 90. [Effects of freeze in s.e. Texas.]

―――. 1888–1889. The birds of southeast Texas. *Geological and Scientific Bull.* 1: 21–22, 30, 39.

―――. 1889a. The birds of southeast Texas. *Ornithologists' and Oologists' Semi-Annual* 1: 42–44.

―――. 1889b. Nesting of the Purple Gallinule, *Ionornis martinica. Ornithologists' and Oologists' Semi-Annual* 1: 16.

Rachford, R. E. 1886. Eggs of the Roseate Spoonbill. *Ornithologist and Oologist* 11: 101.

Rachford, R. E., and son. 1886a. [Buzzard's eggs taken at Grigsby's Bluff.] *Sunny South Oologist* 1: 39.

―――. 1886b. [Eggs of Turkey Buzzard.] *Hoosier Nat.* 1: 153.

Ragsdale, G. H. 1876. Texas ornithology. *Forest and Stream* 6: 370.

―――. 1877. Capture of *Buteo harlani* (Aud.) in Texas. *Forest and Stream* 9: 24.

―――. 1879a. Lewis' Woodpecker in middle Texas. *Science News* 1: 208.

―――. 1879b. Olive-backed Thrush (*Turdus swainsoni*) in Texas. *Bull. Nutt. Ornith. Club* 4: 116.

―――. 1879c. Song of Cassin's Finch. *Science News* 1: 134–135. [Habits in Texas.]

————. 1880. Additional notes concerning the Black-capped Vireo in Texas. *Bull. Nutt. Ornith. Club* 5: 239.

————. 1881a. *Larus glaucus* in Texas. *Bull. Nutt. Ornith. Club* 6: 187. [Clay Co.]

————. 1881b. Notes on *Trynigites rufescens* in Texas. *Bull. Nutt. Ornith. Club* 6: 61–62. [Buff-breasted Sandpiper.]

————. 1881c. On the range of *Lophophanes atrocristatus* in Texas. *Bull. Nutt. Ornith. Club* 6: 114. [Black-crested Titmouse.]

————. 1884. Nest of the Swallow-tailed Kite. *Ornithologist and Oologist* 9: 90. [Cooke Co.]

————. 1885. Lewis' Woodpecker in Texas. *Ornithologist and Oologist* 10: 79.

————. 1886. Two additions to the Texas avifauna. *Auk* 3: 281. [Florida Barred Owl and Western Veery.]

————. 1887. Change of winter habitat in the Grass Finch [Vesper Sparrow]. *Auk* 4: 259–260.

————. 1889. The American Woodcock as a Texas bird: *Philohela minor. Geological and Scientific Bull.* 1: 41.

————. 1891. The breeding range of the Sparrow Hawk (*Falco sparverius*) in Texas. *Auk* 8: 312–313.

————. 1892. Distribution of the species of *Peucaea* [*Aimophila*] in Cooke County, Texas. *Auk* 9: 73.

————. 1894. Temperature and nest-building. *Auk* 11: 260–261.

Raitt, Ralph. 1967. Relationships between black-eared and plain-eared forms of bushtits. (*Psaltriparus*). *Auk* 84: 503–528.

Ramsey, J. J. 1968. Roseate Spoonbill chick attacked by ants. *Auk* 85: 325.

————. 1969. Unusual Snowy Egret nest. *Bull. Texas Ornith. Soc.* 3: 24.

————. 1971. The status of the Cattle Egret in Texas. *Bull. Texas Ornith. Soc.* 4: 6–7.

Rand, A. L., and M. A. Taylor. 1949. Variation in *Dumetella carolinensis. Auk* 66: 25–28. [Catbird.]

Rathbun, Richard. 1903. List of accessions. *Report U.S. Nat. Mus. for the Year Ending June 30, 1901.* Appendix 2, pp. 95–136. [Golden-cheeked Warbler.]

Raun, G. G. 1960. Barn Owl pellets and small mammal populations near Mathis, Texas, in 1956 and 1959. *Southwestern Nat.* 5: 194–200.

Reddell, J. R. 1967. A checklist of the cave fauna of Texas. III. Vertebrata. *Tex. J. Sci.* 19: 184–226.

Reed, C. A. 1904. *North American Birds' Eggs.* New York.

————. 1905. Golden-cheeked Warbler. *Amer. Ornithology* 5: 64–65.

Reeves, H. M. 1959. First Common Scoter collected in Texas. *Auk* 76: 94.

Reid, Bessie M. 1926. Some random bird observations from Texas. *Wilson Bull.* 38: 237–240.

Reid, D. H. 1970. Blue darter. *Texas Parks & Wildlife* 28(3): 20–22.

Reilly, Edgar M., Jr. 1968. *The Audubon Illustrated Handbook of American Birds.* New York: McGraw-Hill.

Rhoads, S. N. 1892. The birds of southeastern Texas and southern Arizona observed during May, June, and July, 1891. *Proc. Acad. Nat. Sci. Philadelphia* 43: 98–120, 121–126.

[Richards, Ruth.] 1939. *Bird Migration Memorandum no. 4, Spring Migration, 1938.* U.S. Biol. Survey. [Much Texas information.]

————. 1940. *Bird Migration Memorandum no. 6, Bird Migration Study, 1889–1938.* U.S. Fish and Wildlife Service. [Many Texas dates.]

————. 1941. *Bird Migration Memorandum no. 7, Spring Migration, 1939 and 1940.* U.S. Fish and Wildlife Service. [Many Texas dates.]

Ridgway, Robert. 1871. A new classification of the North American Falconidae, with descriptions of three new species. *Proc. Acad. Nat. Sci. Philadelphia* 22: 138–150. [Original description of Richardson's Pigeon Hawk, from Texas.]

————. 1873. On some new forms of American birds. *Amer. Nat.* 7: 602–619. [Habits of the Texas Canyon Wren.]

————. 1876. Studies of the American Falconidae. *Bull. U.S. Geol. and Geog. Surv. Terr.* 2(2): 91–182. [Texas specimen of Swallow-tailed Kite.]

————. 1879. On a new species of *Peucaea* [*Aimophila*] from southern Illinois and central Texas. *Bull. Nutt. Ornith. Club* 4: 218–222.

————. 1880a. Catalogue of Trochilidae in the collection of the United States National Museum. *Proc. U.S. Nat. Mus.* 3: 308–320. [Texas specimens of Rufous and Buff-bellied hummingbirds.]

————. 1880b. Description of an unusual (?) plumage of *Buteo harlani. Bull. Nutt. Ornith. Club* 5: 58–59.

————. 1880c. Note on *Peucaea illinoensis. Bull. Nutt. Ornith. Club* 5: 52. [Texas specimens of Illinois Bachman's Sparrow.]

————. 1881a. Nomenclature of North American birds chiefly contained in the United States National Museum. *Bull. U.S. Nat. Mus.* 21: 1–94. [Many Texas references in Appendix.]

————. 1881b. On *Amazilia yucatanensis* (Cabot) and *A. cerviniventris* Gould. *Proc. U.S. Nat. Mus.* 4: 25–26. [Specimens of Buff-bellied Hummingbird.]

————. 1881c. Swainson's Warbler (*Helonaea swainsoni*) in Texas. *Bull. Nutt. Ornith. Club* 6: 54–55.

————. 1884a. Descriptions of some new North American birds. *Proc. Biol. Soc. Washington* 2: 89–95. [Mexican Crested and Olivaceous flycatchers from Texas.]

————. 1884b. Remarks on the type specimens of *Muscicapa fulvifrons* Giraud, and *Mitrephorus pallescens* Coues. *Proc. Biol. Soc. Washington* 2: 108–110. [Buff-breasted Flycatcher, supposedly from Texas.]

————. 1885a. On *Buteo harlani* (Aud.) and *B. cooperi* Cass. *Auk* 2: 165–166.

————. 1885b. On *Peucaea mexicana* (Lawr.), a sparrow new to the United States. *Proc. U.S. Nat. Mus.* 8: 98–99. [Botteri's Sparrow.]

———. 1887. Description of two new races of *Pyrrhuloxia sinuata* Bonap. *Auk* 4: 347.

———. 1888*a*. Description of a new *Psaltriparus* from southern Arizona. *Proc. U.S. Nat. Mus.* 10: 697. [Texas specimens of Black-eared Bushtit.]

———. 1888*b*. Descriptions of some new species and subspecies of birds from Middle America. *Proc. U.S. Nat. Mus.* 10: 505–510.

———. 1891. Note on the alleged occurrence of *Trochilus heloisa* (Less. and De Latt.) within North American limits. *Auk* 8: 115. [Bumblebee Hummingbird.]

———. 1894. Description of a new *Geothlypis* from Brownsville, Texas. *Proc. U.S. Nat. Mus.* 16: 691–692.

———. 1896. *A Manual of North American Birds.* 2d ed. Philadelphia.

———. 1900. New species, etc., of American Birds, V, Corvidae (concluded). *Auk* 17: 27–29. [Original description of Rio Grande Green Jay, from Texas.]

———. 1902. Descriptions of three new birds of the families Mniotiltidae and Corvidae. *Auk* 19: 69–70. [Original description of Texas Scrub Jay.]

———. 1901–1919. The birds of North and Middle America. Pts. 1–8. *U.S. Nat. Mus. Bull.,* no. 50.

Ridgway, Robert, and Herbert Friedmann. 1941–1950. The birds of North and Middle America. Pts. 9–11. *U.S. Nat. Mus. Bull.,* no. 50.

Ripley, S. D. 1949. Texas habitat of the Botteri Sparrow and Gulf coast records of wintering sparrows. *Wilson Bull.* 61: 112–113.

Robbins, C. S., Bertel Bruun, and H. S. Zim. 1966. *A Guide to Field Identification, Birds of North America.* New York: Golden Press.

Rogers, C. H. 1939. A new swift from the United States. *Auk* 56: 465–468. [Idaho White-throated Swift, Texas specimens.]

Rohwer, S. A. 1972. A multivariate assessment of interbreeding between the meadowlarks, *Sturnella. Systematic Zoology* 21: 313–338.

Rollo, J. D., and E. G. Bolen. 1969. Ecological relationships of Blue- and Green-winged Teal on the High Plains of Texas in early fall. *Southwestern Nat.* 14: 171–188.

Ross, P. V. 1970. Notes on the ecology of the Burrowing Owl, *Speotyto cunicularia,* on the Texas High Plains. *Texas J. Sci.* 21: 479–480.

Ross, R. D. 1965. Big Bend National Park. In: *The Bird Watcher's America,* O. S. Pettingill, Jr., ed., pp. 325–333. New York: McGraw-Hill.

[Rowe, N.] 1900. [Eggs of the Bald Eagle.] *Condor* 2: 29.

Royall, W. C., Jr., and E. R. Ferguson. 1962. Controlling bird and mammal damage in direct seeding loblolly pine in East Texas. *J. Forestry* 60: 37–39.

Russell, D. N. 1971. Food habits of the Starling in eastern Texas. *Condor* 73: 369–372.

Rutland, Don. 1938. *Preliminary Check List, Birds of East Texas.* East Texas Ornithology Club, Junior Acad. Sci.

Ryder, R. A. 1967. Distribution, migration and mortality of the White-faced Ibis (*Plegadis chihi*) in North America. *Bird-banding* 38: 257–277.

Rylander, M. K., ed. 1971. Recent articles about Texas birds. *Bull. Texas Ornith. Soc.* 4: 12–13.

Rylander, M. K. 1972. Winter dormitory of the Roadrunner, *Geococcyx californicus,* in West Texas. *Auk* 89: 896.

Rylander, M. K., and E. G. Bolen. 1970. Ecological and anatomical adaptations of North American tree ducks. *Auk* 87: 72–90.

Rylander, M. K., and Barbara White. 1968. A bibliography of Texas birds. *Bull. Texas Ornith. Soc.* 2(4): 42–51.

Rylander, R. A. 1959. *A Checklist of the Birds of Denton County, Texas.* Denton: publ. by author.

Salvin, Osbert, and F. D. Godman. 1879–1904. *Biología Centrali-Americana, Aves.* 3 vols. [Many Texas records and specimens.]

San Antonio Audubon Society. 1960. *Check List of Bexar County Birds.* San Antonio: SAAS, Witte Museum.

Saunders, G. B. 1953. Starling wintering in central and western Texas. *Auk* 50: 440.

Savary, W. B. 1936. Nests found on a portion of the Nueces River Flats, Texas. *Oologist* 53: 62–66, 77.

Schobee, Barry. 1928. Birds of the Davis Mountains. *West Texas Hist. and Sci. Soc. Publ.* 2: 72–73.

———. 1929. More birds of the Davis Mountains. *West Texas Hist. and Sci. Soc. Publ.* 3: 56–57.

Schorger, A. W. 1955. *The Passenger Pigeon: Its Natural History and Extinction.* Madison: Univ. Wisconsin Press.

———. 1957. The beard of the Wild Turkey. *Auk* 74: 441–446.

———. 1960. The crushing of *Carya* nuts in the gizzard of the Turkey. *Auk* 77: 337–340.

———. 1966. *The Wild Turkey: Its History and Domestication.* Norman: Univ. Oklahoma Press.

Schreiber, R. W., and R. W. Risebrough. 1972. Studies of the Brown Pelican. *Wilson Bull.* 84: 119–135.

Schroeder, M. H., and C. A. Ely. 1972. Recoveries of Mourning Doves banded as nestlings in West-Central Kansas. *Bird-Banding* 43: 257–260. [One reference to Texas.]

Schutze, A. E. 1902. *The Summer Birds of Central Texas.*

———. 1903. A few notes from Texas. *Condor* 5: 81.

———. 1904*a*. The destruction of bird life by light towers. *Condor* 6: 172–173. [Austin.]

———. 1904*b*. The Inca Dove in central Texas. *Condor* 6: 172.

———. 1904*c*. Nesting habits of the Caracara. *Condor* 6: 106–108. [Caldwell Co.]

———. 1904*d*. The Texas Kingfisher at New Braunfels, Texas. *Condor* 6: 172.

Schweer, R. A. 1894. Another prolific flicker. *Oologist* 11: 55. [Laid 40 eggs in 40 days at Denton!]

Sclater, P. L. 1856. Note on some birds from the Island of Ascension. *Proc. Zool. Soc. London*, Aug. 15, pp. 144–145. [Sooty Tern in Texas.]

———. 1858. On a collection of birds received by M. Salle from southern Mexico. *Proc. Zool. Soc. London*, 1857, pp. 226–230. [Mentions supposed capture of a Thick-billed Parrot by Audubon in Texas.]

———. 1865. Note on two rare species of the American genus *Dendroeca*. *Ibis* (ser. 2) 1: 87–89. [First Texas record of Golden-cheeked Warbler.]

———. 1879. Note on the American crows of the subgenus *Xanthura*. *Ibis* (ser. 4) 3: 87–89. [Rio Grande Green Jay from Texas.]

Selander, R. K. 1958. Age determination and molt in the Boat-tailed Grackle. *Condor* 60: 355–376.

———. 1960a. Failure of estrogen and prolactin treatment to induce brood patch formation in Brown-headed Cowbirds. *Condor* 62: 65.

———. 1960b. Sex ratio of nestlings and clutch size in the Boat-tailed Grackle. *Condor* 62: 34–44.

———. 1961. Supplemental data on the sex ratio in nestling Boat-tailed Grackles. *Condor* 63: 504.

———. 1964. Speciation in wrens of the genus *Campylorhynchus*. *Univ. of California Publ. in Zool.*, vol. 74. Berkeley and Los Angeles: Univ. California Press.

———. 1970. Parental feeding in a male Great-tailed Grackle. *Condor* 72: 238.

Selander, R. K., and J. K. Baker. 1957. The Cave Swallow in Texas. *Condor* 59: 345–363.

Selander, R. K., and D. R. Giller. 1959. Interspecific relations of woodpeckers in Texas. *Wilson Bull.* 71: 107–124.

———. 1961. Analysis of sympatry of Great-tailed and Boat-tailed Grackles. *Condor* 63: 29–83.

———. 1963. Species limits in the woodpecker genus *Centurus* (Aves). *Bull. Amer. Mus. Nat. Hist.* 124: 217–273.

Selander, R. K., and R. J. Hauser. 1965. Gonadal and behavioral cycles in the Great-tailed Grackle. *Condor* 67: 157–182. [Texas specimens.]

Selander, R. K., and D. K. Hunter. 1960. On the functions of wing-flashing in Mockingbirds. *Wilson Bull.* 72: 341–345. [At Austin.]

Selander, R. K., and R. F. Johnston. 1967. Evolution in the House Sparrow. *Condor* 69: 217–258.

Selander, R. K., and Linda L. Kuich. 1963. Hormonal control and development of the incubation patch in icterids, with notes on behavior of cowbirds. *Condor* 65: 73–90. [Texas specimens.]

Selander, R. K., and C. J. LaRue, Jr. 1961. Interspecific preening invitation display of parasitic cowbirds. *Auk* 78: 473–504.

Selander, R. K., and F. S. Webster, Jr. 1963. Distribution of the Bronzed Cowbird in Texas. *Condor* 65: 245–246.

Selander, R. K., and S. Y. Yang. 1966. Behavioral responses of Brown-headed Cowbirds to nests and eggs. *Auk* 83: 207–232.

Selander, R. K., S. Y. Yang, and G. Cantu. 1969. Extension of zone of sympatry of *Quiscalus mexicanus* and *Q. major*. *Condor* 71: 435–436.

Selle, R. A. 1918. The Scarlet Ibis in Texas. *Condor* 20: 78–82.

Sennett, G. B. 1878a. Later notes on Texas birds, I. *Science News* 1: 57–59.

———. 1878b. Notes on the ornithology of the lower Rio Grande of Texas, from observations made during the season of 1877. *Bull. U.S. Geol. and Geog. Surv. Terr.* 4(1): 1–66.

———. 1879a. The Curve-billed Thrush (*Harporhynchus curvirostris*), its nest and eggs. *Oologist* [Willard's] 4: 74–75.

———. 1879b. Further notes on the ornithology of the lower Rio Grande of Texas, from observations made during the spring of 1878. *Bull. U.S. Geol. and Geog. Surv. Terr.* 5(3): 371–440.

———. 1879c. Later notes on Texas birds. *Science News* 1: 106–107, 120–121, 132–134, 151–153.

———. 1884. Nest and eggs of Couch's Tyrant Flycatcher (*T. melancholicus couchi*). *Auk* 1: 93. [First egg record for U.S., from Lomita Ranch.]

———. 1886a. Destruction of the eggs of birds for food. *Science* 7: 199–201.

———. 1886b. Ipswich Sparrow in Texas. *Auk* 3: 135.

———. 1887. Descriptions of two new subspecies of titmice from Texas. *Auk* 4: 28–30.

———. 1888a. Descriptions of a new species and two new subspecies of birds from Texas. *Auk* 5: 43–46. [Lloyd's Black-eared Bushtit, Merrill's Pauraque, and Plumbeous Carolina Chickadee.]

———. 1888b. Notes on the *Peucaea ruficeps* group, with description of a new subspecies. *Auk* 5: 40–42. [Rufous-crowned Sparrow.]

———. 1888c. Unexpected occurrence of certain shore birds in Texas in midsummer and in breeding plumage. *Auk* 5: 110.

———. 1889a. The Clapper Rails of the United States and West Indies compared with *Rallus longirostris* of South America. *Auk* 6: 161–166.

———. 1889b. *Micropallas whitneyi*, Elf Owl, taken in Texas. *Auk* 6: 276. [Specimen taken in Hidalgo Co.]

———. 1889c. A new species of duck from Texas. *Auk* 6: 263–265.

———. 1890. A new wren from the Lower Rio Grande, Texas, with notes on Berlandier's Wren of northeastern Mexico. *Auk* 7: 57–60.

———. 1892. Description of a new turkey. *Auk* 9: 167–169. [Rio Grande Wild Turkey.]

Sewell, Ed. 1926. Some of the birds commonly found near Dallas. *Bull. Texas Mus. Nat. Hist.* 1: 11–42.

Sharpe, R. B., et al. 1874–1898. *Catalogue of the Birds in the British Museum.* 27 vols. [Many Texas specimens.]

Sheffield, O. C. 1956. Prairie Warbler breeding in Texas. *Wilson Bull.* 68: 76–77.

Shields, R. H., and E. L. Benham. 1968. Migratory behavior of Whooping Cranes. *Auk* 85: 318.

Shoman, J. J. 1955. Our vanished and vanishing wildlife. *Texas Game and Fish* 13: 2–4, 22.

Short, H. L., and D. E. Craigie. 1958. Pied-billed Grebes mistake highway for water. *Auk* 75: 473–474.

Shufeldt, R. W. 1896. The eggs of *Cyrtonyx. Nidologist* 4: 2–3. [Texas breeding of Mearns' Quail.]

Sibley, G. G., and L. L. Short, Jr. 1964. Hybridization in the orioles of the Great Plains. *Condor* 66: 130–151.

Siegler, H. R. 1938. Some color and color pattern difference between the Eastern and the Texas Bobwhite and their hybrid offspring. *Progress Report, Texas Agric. Exper. Sta.*, no. 560.

Simmons, G. F. 1913. Notes on the Red-cockaded Woodpecker from Texas. *Oologist* 30: 298–299.

———. 1914a. Notes on the Louisiana Clapper Rail (*Rallus crepitans saturatus*) in Texas. *Auk* 31: 363–384.

———. 1914b. Spring migration at Houston, Texas. *Wilson Bull.* 26: 128–140.

———. 1915a. On the nesting of certain birds in Texas. *Auk* 32: 317–331.

———. 1915b. With *Rallus* in the Texas marsh. *Condor* 17: 3–8.

———. 1925. *Birds of the Austin Region.* Austin: Univ. Texas Press.

Singleton, J. R. 1949. Coastal drainage problems in relation to waterfowl. *Texas J. Sci.* 1: 25–28.

———. 1951. Production and utilization of waterfowl food plants on the East Texas Gulf Coast. *J. Wildl. Mgmt.* 15: 46–56.

———. 1953. *Texas Coastal Waterfowl Survey.* Federal Aid Rept. Ser. 11. Austin: Texas Game and Fish Comm. (Texas Parks and Wildlife Dept.).

———. 1955. Review of the 1954 waterfowl season. *Texas Game and Fish* 13: 7–9, 29.

———. 1965. *Waterfowl Habitat Management in Texas.* Bull. no. 47. Austin: Texas Parks and Wildlife Dept.

———. 1968. Texas' mistaken Mallards. *Texas Parks & Wildlife* 26(2): 8–11. [Mottled Ducks.]

Singley, J. A. 1885. Jottings from the note-book of a collector in Texas. *Young Oologist* 1: 122–123. [Various nests in Lee Co.]

———. 1886a. Breeding of the Florida Barred Owl in Texas. *Ornithologist and Oologist* 11: 140–141.

———. 1886b. Early finds. *Sunny South Oologist* 1: 9. [Eggs of a number of species from Giddings.]

———. 1886c. Nesting of the Mississippi Kite in Texas. *Ornithologist and Oologist* 11: 170–172.

———. 1886d. Nesting of the Swallow-tailed Kite. *Ornithologist and Oologist* 11: 154–155.

———. 1887a. Nesting of the Red-bellied Hawk. *Ornithologist and Oologist* 12: 38–39.

———. 1887b. Observations on eggs collected in Lee County, Texas, etc. *Ornithologist and Oologist* 12: 163–165.

———. 1888. Notes on some birds of Texas. *Bay State Oologist* 1: 1–3, 9–11, 25–26, 42–43, 48–49. [Chiefly from Lee Co.]

———. 1893. *Texas Birds.* Fourth Annual Report Geological Survey of Texas for 1892, pp. 345–375.

Skutch, Alexander F. 1954. *Life Histories of Central American Birds, vol. 1.* Pacific Coast Avifauna, no. 31. Berkeley: Cooper Ornithological Society.

———. 1960. *Life Histories of Central American Birds, vol. 2.* Pacific Coast Avifauna, no. 34. Berkeley: Cooper Ornithological Society.

———. 1967. *Life Histories of Central American Highland Birds.* Publ. Nutt. Ornith. Soc., no. 7. Raymond A. Paynter, Jr., ed. Cambridge, Mass.: Nuttall Ornithological Society.

———. 1969. *Life Histories of Central American Birds, vol. 3.* Pacific Coast Avifauna, no. 35. Berkeley: Cooper Ornithological Society.

Smith, A. P. 1908. The Blackburnian Warbler noted at Ft. Brown, Texas, December 21, 1907. *Condor* 10: 92.

———. 1909a. The Derby Flycatcher (*Pitangus derbianus*) a permanent resident within our boundaries. *Condor* 11: 103.

———. 1909b. The Swamp Sparrow on the Lower Rio Grande. *Condor* 11: 101.

———. 1910. Miscellaneous bird notes from the Lower Rio Grande. *Condor* 12: 93–103.

———. 1911. Birds of Brownsville, Texas. *Oologist* 28: 130–132.

———. 1912a. Recent records from the Valley of the Lower Rio Grande. *Auk* 29: 254–255.

———. 1912b. Status of the Picidae in the Lower Rio Grande Valley. *Auk* 29: 241.

———. 1912c. Strange actions of a Red-eyed Cowbird. *Auk* 29: 244. [Brownsville.]

———. 1913. Notes and records from Brooks County, Texas. *Condor* 15: 182–183.

———. 1916a. Additions to the avifauna of Kerr Co., Texas. *Auk* 33: 187–193.

———. 1916b. Winter notes from southern Texas. *Condor* 18: 129.

———. 1917. Some birds of the Davis Mountains, Texas. *Condor* 19: 161–165.

———. 1918. Some Texas bird notes. *Condor* 20: 212.

Smith, Ned. 1958. Introducing—hawks of Texas. *Texas Game and Fish* 16: 12–15.

Smith, P. W., Jr. 1904. Nesting habits of the Rock Wren. *Condor* 6: 109–110. [San Antonio.]

Smith, Mrs. W. A., Mrs. R. H. Bowman, Mrs. George Adams, and W. L. McCart. 1941. *The Birds of Tarrant County, Texas.* Contributions to the Natural History of Central North Texas, bull. no. 1, pt. 4.

Snider, Patricia R. 1964–1971. Southwest region. *Audubon Field Notes* 18(3)–25(5).

Snyder, D. E. 1957. A recent Colima Warbler's nest. *Auk* 74: 97–98.

Sooter, C. A. 1945. Starlings wintering in south Texas. *Condor* 47: 219.

———. 1947. Flight speeds of some south Texas birds. *Wilson Bull.* 59: 174–175.

Sosebee, J. B., Jr. 1971. Notes on the activity levels of

Burrowing Owls in Texas. *Bull. Texas Ornith. Soc.* 4: 10.

Soutiere, E. C., H. S. Myrick, and E. G. Bolen. 1972. Chronology and behavior of American Widgeon wintering in Texas. *J. Wildl. Mgmt.* 36: 752–758. [At Muleshoe and Buffalo Lake national wildlife refuges.]

Speirs, J. M. 1953. Winter distribution of Robins east of the Rocky Mountains. *Wilson Bull.* 65: 175–183.

Spence, Alma W. 1952. Wings over Langley Island. *Texas Game and Fish* 10: 22–23, 30.

Spofford, W. R. 1965. The Golden Eagle in the Trans-Pecos and Edwards Plateau of Texas. Audubon Conserv. Rept. No. 1. New York: National Audubon Society.

Spoonbill. [See Ornithology Group, Houston Outdoor Nature Club.]

Springs, A. J., Jr. 1952. *Relation of Bobwhite Quail to Mesquite Grassland Type.* Federal Aid Rept. Ser. 9. Austin: Texas Game and Fish Comm. (Texas Parks and Wildlife Dept.).

Sprunt, Alexander, Jr. 1935. Increase of the Roseate Spoonbill on the coast of Texas. *Auk* 52: 443.

————. 1950a. The Colima Warbler of the Big Bend. *Audubon Mag.* 52: 84–91.

————. 1950b. Hawk predation at the bat caves of Texas. *Texas J. Sci.*, pp. 462–470.

————. 1951a. Aerial feeding of the Duck Hawk (*Falco p. anatum*). *Auk* 68: 372–373.

————. 1951b. Golden-cheek of the cedar brakes. *Audubon Mag.* 53: 12–16.

————. 1951c. Golden-cheek of the cedar brakes. *Texas Game and Fish* 9: 26–27, 32.

————. 1951d. Second occurrence of the Black-chinned Sparrow (*Spizella atrogularis*) in Texas. *Texas J. Sci.* 3: 141.

————. 1951e. Second occurrence of the Black-throated Gray Warbler (*Dendroica nigrescens*) in Texas. *Texas J. Sci.* 3: 141.

————. 1954. *Florida Bird Life.* New York: Coward-McCann and National Audubon Society. [Based on and supplementary to A. H. Howell's *Florida Bird Life*, published in 1932.]

Stager, K. E. 1941. A group of bat-eating Duck Hawks. *Condor* 43: 137–139. [Medina Co.]

Stallcup, W. B. 1951. Status of the Wood Thrush in Dallas County, Texas. *Field and Lab* 22: 81.

Stenger, J. 1958. Food habits and available food of Ovenbirds in relation to territory size. *Auk* 75: 335–346.

Stephenson, J. D., and Glen Smart. 1972. Egg measurements for three endangered species. *Auk* 89: 191–192. [Includes 9 Whooping Crane eggs from San Antonio Zoo.]

Stevenson, H. M. 1957. The relative magnitude of the trans-Gulf and circum-Gulf spring migration. *Wilson Bull.* 69: 39–77.

Stevenson, J. O. 1932. Bird notes from the upper Rio Grande Valley. *Condor* 34: 101.

————. 1940. Two new birds from northwestern Tex-

as. *Proc. Biol. Soc. Washington* 53: 15–17. [Canyon Black-crested Titmouse and Paloduro Cardinal.]

————. 1942a. Birds of the central Panhandle of Texas. *Condor* 44: 108–115.

————. 1942b. Whooping Crane in Texas in summer. *Condor* 44: 40–41.

————. 1946a. Behavior and food habits of the Sennett's White-tailed Hawk in Texas. *Wilson Bull.* 58: 198–205.

————. 1946b. The migration of the Anhinga in Texas. *Wilson Bull.* 58: 184–185.

————. 1953. Bird notes from the Texas coast. *Wilson Bull.* 65: 42–43.

Stevenson, J. O., and R. E. Griffith. 1946. Winter life of the Whooping Crane. *Condor* 48: 160–178.

Stevenson, J. O., and T. F. Smith. 1938. Additions to the Brewster County, Texas, bird list. *Condor* 40: 184.

Stewart, P. A. 1952. Dispersal, breeding behavior, and longevity of banded Barn Owls in North America. *Auk* 69: 227–245.

Stillwell, J. E. 1934. *Birds of the Dallas Region.* Preliminary Check List.

————. 1939. *Check List of Birds of Dallas County.* 3d ed. Dallas Ornithological Society.

Stillwell, J. E., and Norma Stillwell. 1954. Notes on the call of a Ferruginous Pigmy Owl. *Wilson Bull.* 66: 152.

Stokes, Ted. 1968. *Birds of the Atlantic Ocean.* New York: Macmillan Co.

Stone, C. P., D. F. Mott, J. F. Besser, and J. W. De Grazio. 1972. Bird damage to corn in the United States in 1970. *Wilson Bull.* 84: 101–105. [Includes Texas.]

Stone, Witmer. 1894. Capture of *Ceryle torquata* (Linn.) at Laredo, Texas; a species new to the United States. *Auk* 11: 177. [Ringed Kingfisher.]

————. 1895. Additions to the Museum; birds. *Proc. Acad. Nat. Sci. Philadelphia*, 1894, p. 486.

————. 1897. Proper name for the Western Horned Owl of North America. *Amer. Nat.* 31: 236–237. [Original description based on Texas specimen.]

————. 1899. A study of the type specimens of birds in the collection of the Academy of Natural Sciences of Philadelphia, with a brief history of the collection. *Proc. Acad. Nat. Sci. Philadelphia*, 1899, pp. 5–62.

————. 1901. Report of the Committee on the Protection of North American Birds for the year 1900. *Auk* 18: 68–76. [Many Texas references.]

Storer, R. W. 1961. A hybrid between the Painted and Varied buntings. *Wilson Bull.* 73: 209.

Stout, Gardner, ed., Peter Matthiessen, and R. S. Palmer. 1967. *Shorebirds of North America.* New York: Viking Press.

Strandtmann, R. W. 1956. A case of infertility in a pair of Golden Eagles (*Aquila chrysaëtos*, Aves). *Southwestern Nat.* 1: 89.

————. 1962. Notes on nest building and mating in the Golden Eagle (Garza County, Texas). *Southwestern Nat.* 7: 267–268.

Strandtmann, R. W., Burrus McDaniel, and M. A. Price. 1963. New host and distribution records for *Pellyonyssus passeri* Clark and Yunker (Acarina; Dermanyssidae). *J. Parasitology* 49: 58.

Strecker, J. K., Jr. 1896. The Florida Red-shouldered Hawk. *Nidologist* 3: 116–117.

———. 1897. Notes on the *Ardea herodias* in Texas. *Nidologist* 4: 108–109.

———. 1910. *Notes on the Fauna of a Portion of the Canyon Region of Northwestern Texas.* Bull. Baylor Univ., vol. 13, nos. 4–5.

———. 1912. *The Birds of Texas; an Annotated Check-List.* Bull. Baylor Univ., vol. 15, no. 1.

———. 1927. *Notes on the Ornithology of McLennan County, Texas.* Spec. Bull. Baylor Univ. Mus., no. 1.

———. 1930. *Field Notes on Western Texas Birds, pt. 1.* Contr. Baylor Univ. Mus., no. 22.

Street, P. B. 1948. The Edward Harris collection of birds. *Wilson Bull.* 60: 167–184. [Many Texas specimens.]

Stringham, Emerson. ca. 1950. Kerrville, Texas, and its birds. Kerrville: publ. by author.

Sutton, George M. 1935. An expedition to the Big Bend Country. *The Cardinal* 4: 1–7.

———. 1936. *Birds in the Wilderness.* New York: Macmillan. [Lively memories of Turkey Vultures, Roadrunners, and Elf Owls in Texas, and of Louis Agassiz Fuertes near Ithaca, New York.]

———. 1938. The breeding birds of Tarrant County, Texas. *Ann. Carnegie Mus.* 27: 171–206.

———. 1947. Eye color in the Green Jay. *Condor* 49: 196–198.

———. 1948. Comments on *Icterus cuculatus cuculatus* Swainson in the U.S. *Condor* 50: 257–258. [Cites Texas specimens of subspecies.]

———. 1949. The Rose-throated Becard, *Platypsaris aglaiae*, in the lower Rio Grande Valley of Texas. *Auk* 66: 365–366.

———. 1951*a*. Dispersal of mistletoe by birds. *Wilson Bull.* 63: 235–237.

———. 1951*b*. Subspecific status of the Green Jays of northeastern Mexico and southern Texas. *Condor* 53: 124–128.

———. 1951*c*. *Mexican Birds: First Impressions.* Norman: Univ. Oklahoma Press. [Experiences with birds near the Texas border.]

———. 1960. Flammulated Owl in Lubbock County, Texas. *Southwestern Nat.* 5: 173–174.

———. 1963. Interbreeding in the wild of the Bobwhite (*Colinus virginianus*) and Scaled Quail (*Callipepla squamata*) in Stonewall County, northwestern Texas. *Southwestern Nat.* 8: 108–111.

———. 1967. *Oklahoma Birds.* Norman: Univ. Oklahoma Press.

Sutton, George M., and Josselyn Van Tyne. 1935. A new Red-tailed Hawk from Texas. *Occas. Papers Mus. Zool. Univ. Mich.*, no. 321, pp. 1–6.

Swank, W. G. 1950. Dove wings yield important information. *Texas Game and Fish* 8: 5, 21.

———. 1955. Nesting and production of doves in Texas. *Ecology* 36: 495–505.

Swann, H. K. 1924–1926. *A Monograph of the Birds of Prey (Order Accipitres).* 2 vols. London.

Swenk, M. H. 1916. The Eskimo Curlew and its disappearance. *Annual Report Smiths. Inst. for Year Ending June 30, 1915*, pp. 325–340.

Swenk, M. H., and O. A. Stevens. 1929. Harris' Sparrow and the study of it by trapping. *Wilson Bull.* 41: 129–177.

Tanner, J. T. 1942. *The Ivory-billed Woodpecker.* Research Report no. 1. New York: National Audubon Society.

———. 1956. The Ivory-billed Woodpecker. *Texas Game and Fish* 14: 15, 30.

Tanzer, E. C. 1969. A spring sighting of an aggregate of Fulvous Tree Ducks. *Bull. Texas Ornith. Soc.* 3: 23.

Tarter, D. G. 1940. *Check-List of East Texas Birds.* 2d ed. East Texas Ornith. Club Training School, East Texas State Teachers' College.

Taylor, Gaddis. 1962. *Field Check-list, Birds of Harrison County, Texas.* Marshall: publ. by the author.

Taylor, R. J., and E. D. Michael. 1971. Predation on an island heronry in eastern Texas. *Wilson Bull.* 83: 172–177.

Taylor, W. P. 1937*a*. Prairie Chicken census. *The Survey, Bur. Biol. Survey, U.S. Dept. Agric.*, vol. 18, p. 120.

———. 1937*b*. Present status and needs of vanishing species in Texas. *Activities Report, Texas Cooperative Wildlife Service*, pp. 25–26.

———. 1944. Food habits of Short-eared and Barred Owls in Texas. *Texas Game and Fish* 2: 24.

———. 1946*a*. Scissor-tailed Flycatcher and Redtailed Hawk nest in same tree. *Condor* 48: 94.

———. 1946*b*. Swainson's Hawks working on grasshoppers again. *Condor* 48: 95. [Sutton Co.]

———. 1951. The Lucifer Hummingbird in the United States. *Condor* 53: 202–203.

Taylor, W. S. 1916. *The Mourning Dove.* Bull. Univ. Texas Dept. Extension, no. 57.

Teale, Edwin Way. 1965*a*. Wondrous birds and a wondrous lady. *Audubon Mag.* 67: 222–228. [Connie Hagar at Rockport.]

———. 1965*b*. *Wandering Through Winter.* New York: Dodd, Mead and Co. [Includes observations on birds and birders of south Texas.]

Telfair, Ray C. II. The African Cattle Egret (*Ardeola ibis ibis*) in Texas: Population Dynamics and Ecological Impacts. Portion of Ph.D. thesis to be submitted to Texas A&M Univ., College Station. Unpublished. [Based on two-year study (1972–1973) in heronries in c. and e. Texas and on coastal prairie and coastal islands.]

Texas Game, Fish, and Oyster Commission. 1929. *Review of Texas Wild Life and Conservation; Protective Efforts from 1879 to the Present Time, and Operations of the Fiscal Year Ending Aug. 31, 1929.*

Annual Report, Texas Game, Fish, and Oyster Comm.

———. 1932. Game distribution. *Annual Report, Texas Game, Fish, and Oyster Comm., for 1931–1932*, pp. 5–8. [Population data.]

———. 1945*a*. *Principal Game Birds and Mammals of Texas*. Austin: Von Boeckmann–Jones Co.

———. 1945*b*. Index of federal aid division reports. June 1, 1938–June 30, 1945. Erma Baker, comp. [Indexes all reports on birds for period stated.]

Texas Ornithological Society. 1953–. *Newsletter of the Texas Ornithological Society*. [Informal newsletter appearing more or less monthly since Letter No. 1, issued Mar. 9, 1953; deals mainly with bird observations throughout the state and activities of the T.O.S.; place of publication and, to a certain extent, content subject to editorship.]

———. 1967–. *Bulletin of the Texas Ornithological Society*. [Official publication of T.O.S., usually appearing quarterly; generally handles more scientific articles on Texas avifauna (i.e., ecology, behavior, distribution, etc.) than the *Newsletter*; one important section is "Recent Literature," which cites current articles on bird life in Texas; place of publication subject to editorship.]

Texas Parks and Wildlife Dept. 1967. *Birds of Falcon State Recreation Park*. Austin: Research Planning Division, Texas Parks and Wildlife Dept.

———. 1969. *Birds of Bentsen–Rio Grande Valley State Park*. Rev. ed. Austin: Parks Services Planning Div., Texas Parks and Wildlife Dept.

———. 1970. *Pedernales Falls State Park Birds—A Preliminary Checklist*. Austin: Parks Services Planning Div., Texas Parks and Wildlife Dept.

———. *Pittman-Robertson Research Projects*. Unpublished progress reports: W-1-R Statewide Wildlife Survey, Game Management and Demonstration Project; W-2-D Quail Restoration and Management; W-4-D Deer and Turkey Restoration; W-9-D Statewide Quail Restoration Project; W-10-D Deer and Turkey Restoration Project; W-11-D Lesser Prairie Chicken Restoration and Investigation Project; W-12-D Attwater's Prairie Chicken Restoration Project; W-13-D Northeast Texas Waterfowl Development Project; W-17-R Investigation of the Rio Grande Turkey in Lower South Texas; W-21-R Relation of Bobwhite Quail to Mesquite Grassland Type; W-22-R Wild Turkey in the Live Oak–Spanish Oak Erosion Area of the Edwards Plateau Region; W-29-R Coastal Waterfowl Survey; W-30-R Survey, Status of the White-winged Dove in Texas; W-32-R Survey, Economic Value of Wild Game in the Edwards Plateau Region of Texas; W-33-R Wild Turkeys in the Central Mineral Region of Texas; W-37-R Survey, Wild Turkey in the Live Oak–Shinnery Oak Divide Type of the Edwards Plateau of Texas; W-38-R The Relation of Surface Water to the Disturbance and Abundance of Scaled Quail; W-44-R Survey of Wild Turkey Transplanting in Texas; W-49-D Cross Timbers Bobwhite Quail; W-51-D East Texas

Quail Habitat Development; W-64-R Mourning Dove Trapping and Baiting; W-70-R A Study of the Introduction, Release and Survival of Certain European and Asiatic Game Birds; W-72-M Cross Timbers Bobwhite Quail Maintenance; W-75-D High Plains Scaled Quail Development; W-85-R Survival of Pen-raised Bobwhite Quail in Texas; W-88-R Dynamics of Bobwhite Quail in the West Texas Rolling Plains; W-95-R Statewide Mourning Dove Research; W-100-R Attwater's Prairie Chicken; W-103-R Special Wildlife Investigations (endangered species). Austin: Texas Parks and Wildlife Dept.

Tharp, B. C. 1952. *Texas Range Grasses*. Austin: Univ. Texas Press.

Thayer, J. E. 1914. The Coahuila Cliff Swallow (*Petrochelidon fulva pallida*) in Texas. *Auk* 31: 401–402.

———. 1915. Two species of Cliff Swallows nesting in Kerr County, Texas. *Auk* 32: 102–103.

Thomas, J. W. 1957. Anting performed by Scaled Quail. *Wilson Bull.* 69: 280.

———. 1964. Diagnosed diseases and parasitism in Rio Grande Wild Turkey. *Wilson Bull.* 76: 292.

Thomas, J. W., and R. G. Marburger. 1964. Colored leg markers for Wild Turkeys. *J. Wildl. Mgmt.* 28: 552–555.

Thomas, J. W., Calvin van Hoozer, and R. G. Marburger. 1964*a*. Notes on color aberrances in the Rio Grande Wild Turkey. *Wilson Bull.* 76: 381–382.

———. 1964*b*. Wild Turkey behavior affected by the presence of Golden Eagles. *Wilson Bull.* 76: 384–385.

———. 1965. Wintering concentrations and seasonal shifts in range in the Rio Grande Turkey. *J. Wildl. Mgmt.* 30: 34–39.

Thompson, B. H. 1932. *History and Present Status of the Breeding Colonies of the White Pelican (Pelecanus erythrorhynchos) in the United States*. Occas. Paper, Wildlife Div., Nat. Park Serv., U.S. Dept. Interior, no. 1.

Thompson, F. D. 1950*a*. Adventures of two naturalists. *Texas Game and Fish* 8: 10–11. [Roy Bedichek and Dr. T. P. Harrison, Jr.]

———. 1950*b*. Bird festival at Rockport. *Texas Game and Fish* 8: 6–9.

———. 1950*c*. Bird hunting with binoculars. *Texas Game and Fish* 8: 12–13.

Thompson, Max. 1958. Record of the Knot in Texas. *Wilson Bull.* 70: 197.

Thompson, W. L. 1952. Summer birds of the Canadian "breaks" in Hutchinson County, Texas. *Texas J. Sci.* 4: 220–229.

———. 1953. The ecological distribution of the birds of the Black Gap Area, Brewster County, Texas. *Texas J. Sci.* 5: 158–177.

Thorton, W. A. 1951. Ecological distribution of the birds of the Stockton Plateau in northern Terrell County, Texas. *Texas J. Sci.* 3: 413–430.

Todd, W. E. C. 1913. A revision of the genus *Chaemepelia*. *Ann. Carnegie Mus.* 8: 507–603. [Lists Texas specimens of Ground Dove.]

———. 1942. List of the hummingbirds in the collection of the Carnegie Museum. *Ann. Carnegie Mus.* 29: 271–370. [Important Texas specimens.]

Tomlinson, R. E., S. H. Levy, and J. J. Levy. 1973. New distributional records of breeding Mexican Ducks. *Condor* 75: 120–121.

Townsend, John K. 1839. *Ornithology of the United States.* Vol. 1. [Mexican Caracara in Texas.]

Trautman, M. B. 1964. A specimen of the Roadside Hawk, *Buteo magnirostris griseocauda*, from Texas. *Auk* 81: 435.

Travis Audubon Society. 1972. *Field Check-list, Birds of Austin, Texas, and Vicinity.* 4th ed. Austin: Parks and Recreation Dept.

Tucker, W. J. 1927. Prairie Chickens. *Annual Report, Texas Game, Fish, and Oyster Comm.*, p. 5.

Tutor, B. M. 1962. Nesting studies of the Boat-tailed Grackle. *Auk* 79: 77–84.

Tyler Audubon Society. 1962. *Field Check-list, Birds of Smith County, Texas.* Tyler.

Uhler, F. M., and L. N. Locke. 1970. A note on the stomach contents of two Whooping Cranes. *Condor* 72: 246.

U.S. Fish and Wildlife Service. 1954; rev. 1957. *Birds of Hagerman and Tishomingo National Wildlife Refuges.* Refuge Leaflet 121. [National wildlife refuge bird check-lists are continually being revised. The Bibliography by no means gives a complete listing of all editions for each refuge; instead it cites those referred to most frequently in the present work.]

———. 1954; rev. 1969. *Birds of the Laguna Atascosa Wildlife Refuge.* Refuge Leaflet 125-R-4.

———. 1964a. *Birds of Buffalo Lake National Wildlife Refuge.* Refuge Leaflet 209.

———. 1964b. *Birds of Muleshoe National Wildlife Refuge.* Refuge Leaflet 171-R-2.

———. 1966. *Birds of the Aransas National Wildlife Refuge.* Refuge Leaflet 126-R-3.

———. 1967; rev. 1972. *Birds of the Santa Ana National Wildlife Refuge.* Refuge Leaflet 124-R-6.

———. 1969a. *Birds of the Anahuac National Wildlife Refuge.* Refuge Leaflet 223-R.

———. 1969b. *Birds of the Brazoria National Wildlife Refuge.* Refuge Leaflet 238.

———. 1969c. *Birds of Hagerman National Wildlife Refuge.* Refuge Leaflet 121-R-3.

Uzzell, P. B. 1950. Whitewings; coming back? *Texas Game and Fish* 8: 4–5, 34.

van Rossem, A. J. 1937. The Ferruginous Pygmy Owl of northwestern Mexico and Arizona. *Proc. Biol. Soc. Washington* 50: 27–28. [Texas records.]

———. 1940. Notes on some North American birds of the genera *Myiodynastes, Pitangus,* and *Myiochanes. Trans. San Diego Nat. Hist.* 9: 79–86. [Original description of Texas Kiskadee Flycatcher, from Brownsville.]

———. 1945. Cock roost of the Texas Nighthawk. *Condor* 47: 170.

van Rossem, A. J., and Marquess Hachisuka. 1938. A race of the Green Kingfisher from northwestern Mexico. *Condor* 40: 227–228. [Original description

of Western Green Kingfisher, with record of Texas specimens.]

Van Tries, B. J. 1971. What worth Whoopers? *Texas Parks & Wildlife* 29(3): 2–5.

Van Tyne, Josselyn. 1929. Notes on some birds of the Chisos Mountains of Texas. *Auk* 46: 204–206.

———. 1933a. *Some Birds of the Rio Grande Delta of Texas.* Occas. Paper, Univ. Mich. Mus. Zool., no. 255.

———. 1933b. The 1932 Chisos Mountains Expedition. *Rept. Director Univ. Mich. Mus. Zool., 1931–32:* 19–21.

———. 1936a. *The Discovery of the nest of the Colima Warbler* (Vermivora crissalis). Misc. Publ. Mus. Zool. Univ. Mich., no. 33, pp. 5–11.

———. 1936b. *Spizella breweri taverneri* in Texas. *Auk* 53: 92.

———. 1953. Geographic variation in the Blue-throated Hummingbird (*Lampornis clemenciae*). *Auk* 70: 208–209.

———. 1954. The Black-crested Titmouse of Trans-Pecos Texas. *Auk* 71: 201–202.

Van Tyne, Josselyn, and A. J. Berger. 1959. *Fundamentals of Ornithology.* New York: John Wiley & Sons, Inc.

Van Tyne, Josselyn, and George M. Sutton. 1937. *The Birds of Brewster County, Texas.* Misc. Publ. Mus. Zool. Univ. Mich., no. 37.

Vessels, Jay. 1953. Whooping Cranes make progress. *Texas Game and Fish* 12: 6.

———. 1958. Hard won haven. *Texas Game and Fish* 16: 9. [Whooping Cranes.]

Voous, K. H. 1960. *Atlas of European Birds.* Amsterdam: Thomas Nelson and Sons.

Walker, E. A. 1948. Rio Grande Turkey in the Edwards Plateau of Texas, 1946–1948. Final Report, Texas 22-R, 30 pp. Austin: Texas Game, Fish and Oyster Comm. (Texas Parks and Wildlife Dept.). Unpublished.

———. 1951a. Land use and Wild Turkeys. *Texas Game and Fish* 9: 12–16.

———. 1951b. Wild Turkey studies in the Divide Area of the Edwards Plateau. *Texas Game, Fish, and Oyster Comm. Federal Aid Report Ser.*, no. 6.

———. 1954. Distribution and management of the Wild Turkey in Texas. *Texas Game and Fish* 12: 12–14.

Walkinshaw, L. H. 1965. Attentiveness of cranes at their nests. *Auk* 82: 465–476.

Wallace, Norrell. 1963. Plight of the Prairie Chicken. *Texas Game and Fish* 21: 12–13.

Wallmo, O. C. 1957. *Ecology of Scaled Quail in West Texas.* Austin: Texas Game and Fish Comm.

Wallmo, O. C., and P. B. Uzzell. 1958. Ecological and social problems in quail management in West Texas. *Trans. 23rd N. Amer. Wildl. Conf.* Washington, D.C.: Wildl. Mgmt. Inst.

Warner, D. W. 1952. The Green Kingfisher. *Wilson Bull.* 64: 131–132.

Watson, Frank. 1955. South Texas region. *Audubon Field Notes* 9(1)–9(5).

Wauer, R. H. 1967a. Colima Warbler census in Big Bend's Chisos Mountains. *National Parks Mag.* 41: 8–10.

——. 1967b. Further evidence of Bushtit lumping in Texas. *Bull. Texas Ornith. Soc.* 1(5 & 6): 1.

——. 1967c. First Thick-billed Kingbird record for Texas. *Southwestern Nat.* 12: 485–486.

——. 1967d. Report on the Colima Warbler census. Mimeographed.

——. 1968. The Groove-billed Ani in Texas. *Southwestern Nat.* 13: 452.

——. 1969a. *Check-List of Birds, Big Bend National Park.* Big Bend Natural History Association, Inc.

——. 1969b. Hummingbirds of Big Bend. *Bull. Texas Ornith. Soc.* 3: 18.

——. 1969c. Winter bird records from the Chisos Mountains and vicinity. *Southwestern Nat.* 14: 252–254.

——. 1970a. The occurrence of the Black-vented Oriole, *Icterus wagleri*, in the United States. *Auk* 87: 811–812.

——. 1970b. A second Swallow-tailed Kite record for Trans-Pecos Texas. *Wilson Bull.* 82: 462.

——. 1970c. Upland Plover at Big Bend National Park. *Southwestern Nat.* 14: 361–362.

——. 1971. Ecological distribution of birds of the Chisos Mountains, Texas. *Southwestern Nat.* 16: 1–29.

——. 1973a. *Birds of the Big Bend National Park and Vicinity.* Austin: Univ. Texas Press.

——. 1973b. Status of certain parulids in west Texas. *Southwestern Nat.* 18: 105–110.

Wauer, R. H., and D. G. Davis. 1972. Cave Swallows in Big Bend National Park, Texas. *Condor* 74: 482.

Wauer, R. H., and M. K. Rylander. 1968. Anna's Hummingbird in west Texas. *Auk* 85: 501.

Wauer, R. H., and J. F. Scudday. 1972. Occurrence and status of certain Charadriiformes in the Texas Big Bend Country. *Southwestern Nat.* 17: 210–211.

Webster, F. S., Jr. 1956–. South Texas region. *Audubon Field Notes* 10(1)–.

——. 1962. The Black-capped Vireo in central Texas (*Vireo atricapilla*). *Audubon Field Notes* 16: 414–417.

Webster, J. D. 1948. Bird notes from southeastern Texas. *Wilson Bull.* 60: 245.

Weigel, R. D. 1967. Fossil birds from Miller's Cave, Llano Co., Texas. *Texas J. Sci.* 19: 107–109.

Weldenthal, J. R. 1965. Structure in primary song of the Mockingbird. *Auk* 82: 161–189.

Weller, M. W. 1964. Distribution and migration of the Redhead. *J. Wildl. Mgmt.* 28: 64–103. [78% of existing Redhead population winters on lower Laguna Madre.]

——. 1965. Chronology of pair formation in some nearctic *Aythya* (Anatidae). *Auk* 82: 227–235.

Wells, C. S. 1887. White crane. *Forest and Stream* 29: 487.

Welty, Joel Carl. 1963. *The Life of Birds.* New York: Alfred A. Knopf.

Wentworth, I. H. 1896. Audubon's Caracara. *Oologist* 13: 21–24.

Weston, Francis, and E. A. Williams. 1965. Recent records of the Eskimo Curlew. *Auk* 82: 493–496.

Weston, Fred. 1952. Current Wild Turkey status. *Texas Game and Fish* 10 (3): 25–26.

Wetmore, Alexander. 1948. The Golden-fronted Woodpeckers of Texas and northern Mexico. *Wilson Bull.* 60: 185–186.

Wetmore, Alexander, and Herbert Friedmann. 1933. The California Condor in Texas. *Auk* 35: 37–38.

Wetmore, Alexander, et al. 1964. *Song and Garden Birds of North America.* Washington: National Geographic Society.

——. 1965. *Water, Prey and Game Birds of North America.* Washington: National Geographic Society.

Wheeler, H. E. 1924. *The Birds of Arkansas.* Bureau Mines, Manufactures & Agriculture.

Whitaker, Lovie M. 1943. Notes on roosting habits of the Verdin. *Wilson Bull.* 55.

——. 1952. Notes on birds of the Big Bend Country of Texas. [Paper presented at the 1952 A.O.U. Meeting in Baton Rouge, La.]

——. 1957. Comments on wing-flashing and its occurrence in Mimidae with uniformly colored wings. *Wilson Bull.* 69: 361–363.

Wiley, R. W., and E. G. Bolen. 1971. Eagle-livestock relationships: livestock carcass and wound characteristics. *Southwestern Nat.* 16: 151–169.

Wilke, L. A. 1959. Island retreat. *Texas Game and Fish* 17: 24–25. [Copano Bay.]

Williams, Frances C. 1958. Interspecific defense of roost site by a Loggerhead Shrike. *Wilson Bull.* 70: 95.

——. 1965–. Southern Great Plains region. *Audubon Field Notes* 19(5)–.

——, comp. 1972. *Field Check List, Birds of Midland County, Texas.* 6th ed. Midland Naturalists, Inc.

Williams, G. G. 1936–1947. *The Gulf Coast Migrant,* nos. 1–55. Houston.

——. 1938. Notes on water birds of the upper Texas coast. *Auk* 55: 62–70.

——. 1945. Do birds cross the Gulf of Mexico in spring? *Auk* 62: 98–111.

——. 1947–1948. Texas coastal region. *Audubon Field Notes* 1(1)–2(5).

——. 1948. Curlew Sandpiper on Galveston Island. *Auk* 65: 140–141.

——. 1949–1951. South Texas region. *Audubon Field Notes* 3(1)–5(4).

——. 1950a. Weather and spring migration. *Auk* 67: 52–65.

——. 1950b. The nature and causes of the coastal hiatus. *Wilson Bull.* 62: 175–182.

——. 1951a. Rat snake overpowers Red-shouldered Hawk, *Buteo lineatus. Auk* 68: 372.

——. 1951b. Letter to the editor (on the genus *Icterus*). *Wilson Bull.* 63: 52–54.

————. 1952*a*. Birds of the Gulf of Mexico. *Auk* 69: 428–432.

————. 1952*b*. The origins and dispersal of oceanic birds. *Texas J. Sci.* 4: 139–155.

————. 1954*a*. A captive Gannet. *Auk* 71: 320–321.

————. 1954*b*. The Scissor-tailed Flycatcher. *Texas Game and Fish* 12: 7, 24.

————. 1955. Wilson Phalaropes as commensals. *Condor* 55: 158.

————. 1956. Altitudinal record for Chimney Swifts. *Wilson Bull.* 68: 71–72.

————. 1959. Probable Eskimo Curlew on Galveston Island, Texas. *Auk* 76: 539–541.

————. 1960. Geological factors in the distribution of American birds. Evolutionary aspects of migration. *Lida Scott Brown Lectures in Ornith.*, pp. 1–85. Los Angeles: Univ. California Press.

Williams, L. E., Jr. 1965. Jaegers in the Gulf of Mexico. *Auk* 82: 19–25.

Winckler, Suzanne. 1968. Brown Pelican epitaph. *Texas Parks & Wildlife* 26(12): 24–28.

Witherby, H. F., ed., et al. 1938–1941. *The Handbook of British Birds.* 5 vols. London: H. F. & G. Witherby Ltd.

Wolf, L. L. 1961. Specimen of the Yellow-green Vireo from Texas. *Auk* 78: 258–259.

Wolfe, L. R. 1956. *Check-list of the Birds of Texas.* Lancaster, Pennsylvania: Intelligencer Printing Co.

————. 1965. *Check List of Birds of Kerr County, Texas.* Kerrville: publ. by author.

————. 1967*a*. Common Raven in Hill Country of Edwards Plateau. *Bull. Texas Ornith. Soc.* 1(3 & 4): 4, 8.

————. 1967*b*. The Mississippi Kite in Texas. *Bull. Texas Ornith. Soc.* 1(5 & 6): 2–3, 12, 13.

————. 1968. Recent breeding of Common Raven in west-central Texas. *Condor* 70: 280–281.

————. 1970. The eastern race of the Evening Grosbeak in south-central Texas. *Auk* 87: 378.

Wood, James. 1922. Winter observations in Texas. *Oologist* 39: 20.

Woodhouse, S. W. 1852. Descriptions of new species of birds of the genera *Vireo* Vieill., and *Zonotrichia* Swains. *Proc. Acad. Nat. Sci. Philadelphia* 6: 60–61. [Original descriptions of Black-capped Vireo and Cassin's Sparrow, both from Texas.]

————. 1853. Description of a new snow finch of the genus *Struthus*, Boie. *Proc. Acad. Nat. Sci. Philadelphia* 6: 202–203. [Gray-headed Junco from west Texas.]

————. 1854. *Report of an Expedition Down the Zuñi and Colorado Rivers, by Captain L. Sitgreaves.* Report on the Natural History, pp. 33–40; Zoology, pp. 43–105. [Numerous Texas records.]

Worth, C. B. 1930. Notes from Brownsville, Texas. *Auk* 47: 98.

Wotton, Michael, and D. B. Marshall. 1965. Compound clutch of the Chachalaca. *Condor* 67: 84–85.

Wright, A. H. 1915. Early records of the Wild Turkey, V. *Auk* 32: 348–366. [References to early Texas records.]

Yocum, C. F. 1964. Notes on the birds of Webb County, Texas. *Auk* 81: 440–442.

Zusi, R. L. 1958. Laughing Gull takes fish from Black Skimmer. *Condor* 60: 67–68.

————. 1959. Fishing rates in the Black Skimmer. *Condor* 61: 298.

INDEX OF SPECIES

Entries enclosed in brackets are treated as hypothetical in the main text.

PHYLOGENETIC LIST OF NEW SPECIES & SUBSPECIES